*M*ake American history come to life for your students!

The *EXPLORING AMERICAN HISTORY program comes complete with:*

- Student Edition
- Annotated Teacher's Edition
- Student Workbook
- Annotated Teacher's Edition of Workbook
- Teacher's Resource Book

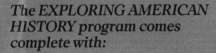

Annotated Teacher's Edition

EXPLORING AMERICAN HISTORY

John R. O'Connor

2 3 4 5 6 7 8 9 10 97 96 95
ISBN: 835-90637-X

GLOBE BOOK COMPANY
A Division of Simon & Schuster
Paramus, New Jersey

Discover EXPLORING AMERICAN HISTORY and see why it's America's best—for readability, comprehensiveness, and skills coverage.

- *Every page invites student involvement and active learning for improved comprehension.*
- *Unit and Chapter Reviews provide thorough, effective coverage of comprehension, Social Studies, and critical thinking skills.*
- *Special features throughout the text add interest and depth to the study of history.*

- *The comprehensive Annotated Teacher's Edition helps you to help your students succeed.*
- *A Workbook and an extensive Teacher's Resource Book provide everything you need to reinforce, motivate, evaluate, and enrich learning.*

The Teacher's Resource Book includes:

- **Vocabulary Reinforcement and Comprehension**
- **Chapter and Unit Tests**
- **Enrichment Readings, including Primary Sources**
- **Map Overhead Transparencies and Activity Sheets**
- **Outline Maps of the United States and Its Regions**
- **Writing Workshop**
- **Annotated Teacher's Edition of the Workbook**
- **Answer Key for the Teacher's Resource Book**

*S*tudent involvement means active learning.

Unit Objectives prepare students for understanding the scope of the material presented in the Unit.

Chapter titles give students a quick outline of the times, places, and events they'll study.

Engaging art at the start of every Unit motivates students and stimulates their curiosity about that period in American history.

Pages from Student Edition. Actual size: 8 × 10″.

Unit Critical Thinking Skills and History Study Skills help students master the content by showing them the skills they will learn and apply.

Unit Time Lines show key events and dates from the Unit.

EXPLORING AMERICAN HISTORY captures your students' interest, focuses their attention, and draws them into each Unit and Chapter. The exciting design, colorful visuals, engaging introductions and narratives, and fascinating Special Features keep them involved and interested. EXPLORING AMERICAN HISTORY has an in-text skills package that's second to none. And because it's from Globe, your students will be able to read and understand the events that have shaped America's growth.

Points of View gives students a personalized introduction to the Unit by presenting two opposing viewpoints on the same issue. Students experience the excitement and controversy of history as it happened.

Introductory text provides information about these key issues and developments that shaped our nation's past.

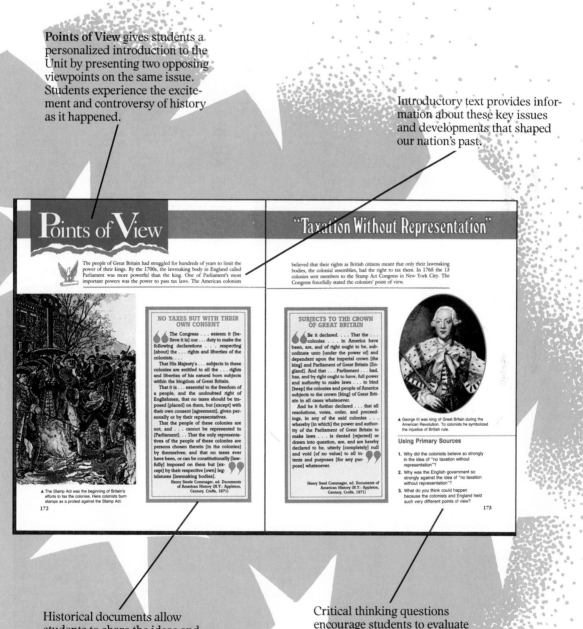

Historical documents allow students to share the ideas and feelings of people who lived in this period of American history.

Critical thinking questions encourage students to evaluate opposing viewpoints and become involved in the historical process.

Readability, controlled chapter length, and section headings improve comprehension.

Chapter Objectives direct students' reading and provide a purpose for reading the Chapter.

Six-page Chapters and numbered paragraphs create manageable learning blocks that maintain interest and facilitate study.

Chapter Introductions help students relate history to their own experience.

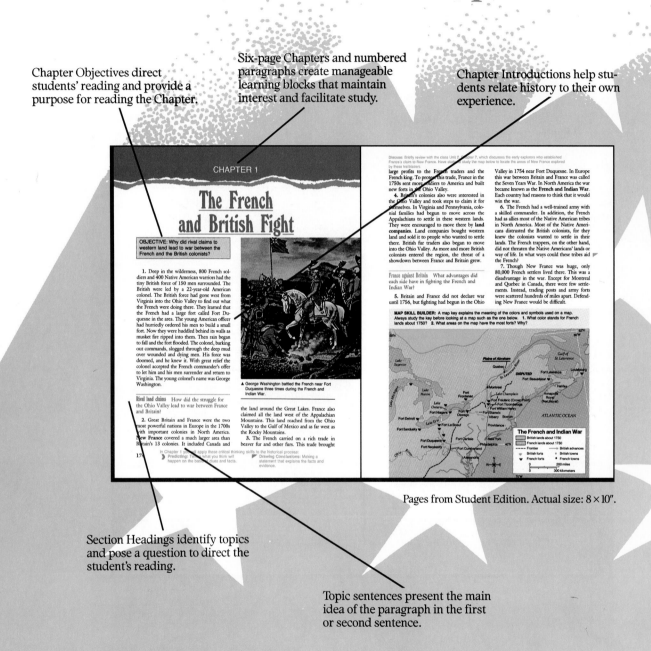

Pages from Student Edition. Actual size: 8 × 10″.

Section Headings identify topics and pose a question to direct the student's reading.

Topic sentences present the main idea of the paragraph in the first or second sentence.

An informal narrative style makes reading about American history interesting, appealing, and accessible to all students. A chronological approach provides comprehensive coverage of all periods in our nation's history. Your students will learn about political and economic history as well as the historical contributions of many different groups of people in American society.

Captions add meaning to the many colorful visuals and connect them to the content of the Chapter and Unit.

8. Great Britain had more colonists, some Native American support, and a powerful navy. Great Britain's colonists greatly outnumbered the French. The 13 colonies had a population of more than 1 million people who would fight to defend their families and their colonies. Although most groups of Native Americans supported the French, the powerful Iroquois nation supported the British. In addition, Britain's large navy controlled the Atlantic. In this way, Britain was able to prevent France from sending more troops to America.

9. The British colonies were not united as they went into the war. The 13 colonies had often quarreled with one another about their boundaries and their claims to western land. Each colony was concerned with its own problems and took little interest in the other colonies. How would this lack of unity be a disadvantage in a war with the French?

People in History

10. Benjamin Franklin Even before war was declared, Benjamin Franklin suggested a plan to help the 13 colonies unite. For years, colonists had enjoyed reading Franklin's *Poor Richard's Almanac*. This book each year gave useful information on farming and the weather. It also was full of clever sayings, like "Early to bed and early to rise makes a man healthy, wealthy, and wise." In addition, Franklin was known for his inventions and scientific experiments. He was the first person to prove that lightning is a form of electricity. A self-taught man, Franklin was one of the outstanding leaders in the colonies.

11. In 1754, Franklin proposed the **Albany Plan of Union** to join the colonies under one government. The idea for this joint government was borrowed from the Iroquois nation. The government would command the **militia** (mih-LISH-uh) in each colony. The militia was a volunteer army that helped defend the colonies. The government also would collect taxes from the colonies to pay for the militia.

176

Spotlight on Sources

12. This is how Franklin explained the purpose of the Albany Plan of Union:

"... A union of the colonies is certainly necessary to us all. A voluntary [freely chosen] union entered into by the colonies themselves, I think, would be preferable to [better than] one imposed [required] by Parliament. Were there a general council formed by all the colonies, everything relating to the defense of the colonies might properly be put under its management [control]."

The Papers of Benjamin Franklin, Leonard Labaree, ed.

13. The colonies turned down the Albany Plan. Franklin hoped the Albany Plan would strengthen the colonies to fight the coming war. However, the colonial assemblies were not willing to give up their power. Each colony insisted on keeping its right to tax itself and control its own affairs. As a result, the British colonies would not join together to fight the French.

Fighting the War What were the major battles of the French and Indian War?

14. The French were successful in the first battles of the French and Indian War in the Ohio Valley. In July 1755, a British army commanded by General Edward Braddock headed for Fort Duquesne. Braddock's army included a force of 500 colonial soldiers led by George Washington. General Braddock had just arrived from Britain. He did not know how wars were fought on the American frontier. Braddock ignored Washington's warning that the French troops and their Native American allies would attack from behind trees and bushes. Braddock insisted on marching his soldiers in their bright red uniforms into open fields. He expected the British soldiers to then stand in rows and shoot at the enemy. As Washington had warned, the French and their allies made a surprise attack. General Braddock was killed, and most of his army was destroyed.

Washington then took command and ordered what was left of the British army to retreat. After this defeat and for another two years, France seemed to be winning the war.

15. In 1757, a new leader named William Pitt took charge of Britain's government and helped turn around the war. Pitt chose able new generals and increased the size of the army. He promised that Britain would pay the colonies for their costs of fighting the war. Pitt's efforts turned the war in Britain's favor. During 1758 and 1759, the British armies won several important victories. First, Fort Duquesne finally was captured. Soon after, General James Wolfe captured Louisbourg, France's main outpost in northeastern Canada.

16. The deciding battle of the war took place at Quebec, the capital of New France. There, in September 1759, Wolfe's army faced the larger French forces led by General Louis de Mont-

▼ By climbing this steep bluff near Quebec, Wolfe's troops surprised the French. The battle that followed lasted less than 15 minutes.

calm (mahnt-KAHM). After sneaking up a cliff at night, the British army launched a surprise attack and overwhelmed the French. Both Wolfe and Montcalm were killed in this battle. The capture of Quebec meant that Britain had won the war. However, the fighting lasted another year, until Montreal fell to the British. In 1763, France and Britain signed the peace treaty that formally ended the French and Indian War.

Results of the War What lands did Britain gain, and how did the war affect the American colonists?

17. Britain's victory in the war gained it a huge new empire in North America. France was forced to give up nearly all of its territory in America. Britain now ruled Canada and all the land east of the Mississippi River except New Orleans. This land included Florida, which Britain got from France's ally Spain. New Orleans and the large territory of Louisiana west of the Mississippi were given to Spain. What problems do you think Britain might have in ruling its great new empire?

18. The British colonists gained from the war in several important ways. They had learned new ways of fighting and winning battles. More important, the colonists were no longer surrounded by French and Spanish colonies. The western lands were open to settlement. British colonists could now look forward to moving into the Ohio Valley.

Outlook

22. The 13 colonies had not been able to unite to fight against the French. They had depended on Great Britain to provide the armies and weapons needed to win the French and Indian War. As a result of the war, Britain's empire in North America now doubled in size. How do you think the colonists felt when the war ended? Do you think Britain might now decide to change the way it ruled the 13 colonies?

177

Key History Words, defined in the text, appear in boldface for easy recognition.

Outlook concludes each Chapter with a Summary that helps students see the historical relevance of what they've read by relating it to today's world.

A closer look at history keeps interest and involvement high.

Linking Geography and History shows how geography and location have had a major part in the development of events in American history.

The President's Corner offers portraits of some of America's most influential leaders and reviews the events and main achievements of their administrations.

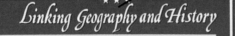

Linking Geography and History

The Geography of the Revolutionary War Every army must have a strategy. Strategy means deciding what places and routeways hold the key to winning a war and taking control of them.

British war strategy centered on winning control of the port cities of New York and Philadelphia. This, it was hoped, would lead to control of the middle states.

Control of the Hudson River was another goal of both armies. The British sought control to break communications and supply routes between New England and the South. In 1777, a British army under General John Burgoyne moved south from Canada into the upper valley of the Hudson. Another British army was supposed to move north from New York to meet Burgoyne. However, the army in New York went to Philadelphia instead. The Americans won the crucial Battle of Saratoga and kept control of the Hudson.

Although the British held New York and Philadelphia for part of the war, the Americans

kept control of the coastal plain between those two cities. General George Washington, in a daring raid, won the battle of Trenton in 1776 and went on to capture Princeton in 1777.

The Revolutionary War spilled over from the 13 states to lands west of the Appalachians. Successful campaigns by George Rogers Clark won the Ohio and Mississippi valleys for the new nation. Spanish troops also helped Americans after Spain declared war on Britain in 1779. Bernardo de Gálvez, governor of Spanish Louisiana, attacked and pinned down British forces in Baton Rouge and Natchez (1779), Mobile (1780), and Pensacola (1781).

Use the map below to answer these questions.

1. What battles were fought in and around New York City?

2. How would the United States have benefited if its Quebec campaign had been successful?

The Revolutionary War

People in History introduces important thinkers and leaders who have influenced America's history.

People in History

16. **Alexander Hamilton** Born on a British island in the Caribbean, Hamilton (1757–1804) was attending college in New York when the American Revolution began. As a teenager, he left school to fight in the war. Hamilton soon became an officer in the American army, where he served as an aide to General Washington. He later worked hard for ratification of the Constitution. What newspaper essays in favor of the Constitution did he help write?

17. As secretary of the treasury, Hamilton proved to be a wizard at money matters. He came up with an unpopular but successful program for settling the nation's debts. He called for the establishment of a national bank that would issue or make paper money. Hamilton argued that a national bank would help the government to collect taxes, control trade, and support the nation's defense.

18. Jefferson and Hamilton held different views about the powers of the national government. Hamilton, a strong supporter of the Constitution, wanted an even more powerful central government for America than the Constitution formed. Jefferson, on the other hand, wanted the average American to have a greater voice in government. Jefferson also strongly opposed Hamilton's plan for a national bank. He felt that the government should save, rather than spend, the people's money.

19. The disagreement between Hamilton and Jefferson spilled over into Congress and helped create America's first political parties. The Federalists, Hamilton's supporters, held the majority in Congress and approved the national bank. The Federalists were mostly wealthy merchants, manufacturers, and lawyers from the East and some plantation owners from the South. The Anti-Federalists, Jefferson's supporters, were in the minority, but were growing in number. Jefferson's party was called the Democratic-Republican Party. Democratic-Republicans were found chiefly in the farming areas of the North and South and in the urban ▶ or city areas of New York. Why do you think

Ask: How can a 200-year-old Constitution still meet people's needs in this modern era?

THE PRESIDENTS' CORNER

During **George Washington's** presidency from 1789 to 1797, the new federal government took shape. America's first national bank was formed. Congress taxed whiskey and other products made in the United States. The taxes supplied the money to run the new government. In 1794, the farmers of Pennsylvania refused to pay the tax on whiskey. Washington sent federal troops to crush the Whiskey Rebellion. Washington's victory showed that the government could enforce federal laws in the states. Washington strongly believed that the United States must stay out of European wars. His 1793 neutrality proclamation forbade American ships from carrying supplies to warring nations. In his Farewell Address, Washington urged the nation to be strong in religion, education, and in promoting peace.

these particular groups supported the parties they did?

Outlook

20. When George Washington was President, the United States was a small nation of 13 states with limited sources of money. America then had little military strength and offered few services to its citizens. Over the next two centuries, the United States grew from 13 to 50 states. It became a world power of huge military strength costing about 13 trillion dollars to support each year. The United States government today offers its citizens many services, including low-income housing, health care, and support for education. The federal government affects people's lives from their first days in school to their old age. Yet it is still basically the same government that was formed when the Constitution went into effect in 1789.

241

Pages from Student Edition. Actual size: 8 × 10".

Special Features in every Chapter offer appealing, close-up looks at people, places, events, and ideas that have affected the course of America's history. Students learn how the past has shaped the nation they live in today.

America's People enriches students' appreciation of their cultural heritage and the achievements of the many groups of people who have played a key role in America's past and present.

Spotlight on Sources gives students an opportunity to read passages from important original historical documents.

America's People

AFRICANS

"We stood in arms, firing on the revolted slaves, of whom we kill'd some and wounded many," wrote John Barbot, captain of a slave ship in 1701. "[M]any of the most mutinous leapt overboard," he added, "and drowned themselves in the ocean. . . ." Barbot stood to make a profit on the sale of every man, woman, and child he carried safely to America. But for the people, stolen from their homelands in Africa, what lay ahead?

At least 11 million Africans were brought to the Americas during the years of the slave trade. Most of them were captured in wars and slave raids ordered by African rulers. Some African rulers tried to stop the slave trade. Others wanted European-made goods, especially guns, in return for slaves. Where did the slaves come from? Some were

captured as they farmed the land or herded cattle along the coast of West Africa. Others were rounded up from inland villages and forced to march to the coast. There slave captains loaded their valuable human cargo. The nightmare voyage across the Atlantic Ocean was known as the Middle Passage. Chained in pairs at their ankles and wrists, the Africans were packed in airless spaces below decks. They could not stand or move about.

Europeans needed cheap labor especially for the rich farmlands of the New World. In Africans, they found strong people who were skilled at farming and used to hard work. Thousands of Africans worked as slaves on the plantations of the South. In the North the slave population was smaller, and more free blacks could be found. Free or slave, African Americans also became skilled craft workers. Without African labor, the colonies of the New World probably would not have been as economically successful as they were.

In addition to its economic growth, African Americans contributed to the cultural and scientific growth of America. Slaves such as Phillis Wheatley, Juniper Hammon, and Gustavus Vasa wrote poetry and non-fiction. African Americans saved and shared African folk tales and music among themselves. Often they were heard singing as they worked in the fields. Other African Americans became scientists and inventors. A free African named Benjamin Banneker was a scientist and inventor. Banneker carved a clock that kept time for more than 50 years. He also helped plan the city of Washington, D.C.

Barbot quotation is cited in Vincent Harding, There is a River: The Black Struggle for Freedom in America.

▼ In slave ships like the one shown here, Europeans brought about 11 million Africans to North America, the Caribbean islands, and Brazil from the 1500s to the 1800s.

Now answer the following questions:

1. What was the main difference in the way Africans came to America and the way other people did?

2. Which African contribution to American culture do you think is most important? Explain your answer.

large profits to the French traders and the French king. To protect this trade, France in the 1750s sent more soldiers to America and built new forts in the Ohio Valley.

4. Britain's colonies also were interested in the Ohio Valley and took steps to claim it for themselves. In Virginia and Pennsylvania, colonial families had begun to move across the Appalachians to settle in these western lands. They were encouraged to move there by **land companies**. Land companies bought western land and sold it to people who wanted to settle there. British fur traders also began to move into the Ohio Valley. As more and more British colonists entered the region, the threat of a showdown between France and Britain grew.

France against Britain What advantages did each side have in fighting the French and Indian War?

5. Britain and France did not declare war until 1756, but fighting had begun in the Ohio

Valley in 1754 near Fort Duquesne. In Europe this war between Britain and France was called the Seven Years War. In North America the war became known as the **French and Indian War**. Each country had reasons to think that it would win the war.

6. The French had a well-trained army with a skilled commander. In addition, the French had as allies most of the Native American tribes in North America. Most of the Native Americans distrusted the British colonists. They knew the colonists wanted to settle in their lands. The French trappers, on the other hand, did not threaten the Native Americans' lands or way of life. In what ways could these tribes aid ▶ the French?

7. Though New France was huge, only 80,000 French settlers lived there. This was a disadvantage in the war. Except for Montreal and Quebec in Canada, there were few settlements. Instead, trading posts and army forts were scattered hundreds of miles apart. Defending New France would be difficult.

8. Great Britain had more colonists, some Native American support, and a powerful navy. Great Britain's colonists greatly outnumbered the French. The 13 colonies had a population of more than 1 million people who would fight to defend their families and their colonies. Although most groups of Native Americans supported the French, the powerful Iroquois nation supported the British. In addition, Britain's large navy controlled the Atlantic. In this way, Britain was able to prevent France from sending more troops to America.

9. The British colonies were not united as they went into the war. The 13 colonies had often quarreled with one another about their boundaries and their claims to western land. Each colony was concerned with its own problems and took little interest in the other colo-
▶ nies. How would this lack of unity be a disadvantage in a war with the French?

People in History

10. **Benjamin Franklin** Even before war was declared, Benjamin Franklin suggested a plan to help the 13 colonies unite. For years, colonists had enjoyed reading Franklin's *Poor Richard's Almanac*. This book each year gave useful information on farming and the weather. It also was full of clever sayings, like "Early to bed and early to rise makes a man healthy, wealthy, and wise." In addition, Franklin was known for his inventions and scientific experiments. He was the first person to prove that lightning is a form of electricity. A self-taught man, Franklin was one of the outstanding leaders in the colonies.

11. In 1754, at Albany, New York, Franklin proposed the Albany Plan of Union to join the

Spotlight on Sources

12. This is how Franklin explained the purpose of the Albany Plan of Union:

". . . A union of the colonies is certainly necessary to us all. A voluntary [freely chosen] union entered into by the colonies themselves, I think, would be preferable to [better than] one imposed [required] by Parliament. Were there a general council formed by all the colonies, everything relating to the defense of the colonies might properly be put under its management [control]."

The Papers of Benjamin Franklin,
Leonard Labaree, ed.

13. The colonies turned down the Albany Plan. Franklin hoped the Albany Plan would strengthen the colonies to fight the coming war. However, the colonial assemblies were not willing to give up their power. Each colony insisted on keeping its right to tax itself and control its own affairs. As a result, the British colonies would not join together to fight the French.

Fighting the War What were the major battles of the French and Indian War?

14. The French were successful in the first battles of the French and Indian War in the Ohio Valley. In July 1755, a British army commanded by General Edward Braddock headed for Fort Duquesne. Braddock's army included a force of 500 colonial soldiers led by George Washington. General Braddock had just arrived from Britain. He did not know how wars were fought on the American frontier. Braddock ignored Washington's warning that the French troops and their Native American allies would attack from behind trees and bushes. Braddock insisted on marching his soldiers in their bright red uniforms into open fields. He expected the British soldiers to then stand in rows and shoot at the enemy. As Washington had warned, the French and their allies made a surprise attack. General Braddock was killed, and most of his army was destroyed.

Map Skill Builders emphasize the importance of maps to the study of American history and encourage students to use historical maps while reinforcing their map skills.

MAP SKILL BUILDER: A map key explains the meaning of the colors and symbols used on a map. Always study the key before looking at a map such as the one below. 1. What color stands for French lands about 1750? 2. What areas on the map have the most forts? Why?

The French and Indian War

- British lands about 1750
- French lands about 1750
- Frontier
- British advances
- British forts
- British towns
- French forts
- French towns

0   200 miles
0   300 kilometers

Extensive review ensures comprehension and skills development.

Study Hints give students important tips on improving study skills.

The **Vocabulary Review** goes over every Key History Word.

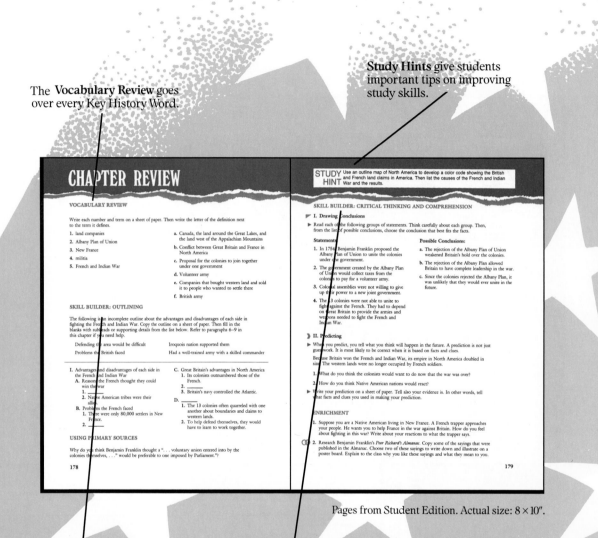

CHAPTER REVIEW

VOCABULARY REVIEW

Write each number and term on a sheet of paper. Then write the letter of the definition next to the term it defines.

1. land companies
2. Albany Plan of Union
3. New France
4. militia
5. French and Indian War

a. Canada, the land around the Great Lakes, and the land west of the Appalachian Mountains
b. Conflict between Great Britain and France in North America
c. Proposal for the colonies to join together under one government
d. Volunteer army
e. Companies that bought western land and sold it to people who wanted to settle there
f. British army

SKILL BUILDER: OUTLINING

The following is an incomplete outline about the advantages and disadvantages of each side in fighting the French and Indian War. Copy the outline on a sheet of paper. Then fill in the blanks with subheads or supporting details from the list below. Refer to paragraphs 6–9 in this chapter if you need help.

Defending the area would be difficult   Iroquois nation supported them

Problems the British faced   Had a well-trained army with a skilled commander

I. Advantages and disadvantages of each side in the French and Indian War
   A. Reasons the French thought they could win the war
      1. _____
      2. Native American tribes were their allies
   B. Problems the French faced
      1. There were only 80,000 settlers in New France
      2. _____

C. Great Britain's advantages in North America
   1. Its colonists outnumbered those of the French.
   2. _____
   3. Britain's navy controlled the Atlantic.
D. _____
   1. The 13 colonies often quarreled with one another about boundaries and claims to western lands.
   2. To help defend themselves, they would have to learn to work together.

USING PRIMARY SOURCES

Why do you think Benjamin Franklin thought a ". . . voluntary union entered into by the colonies themselves, . . ." would be preferable to one imposed by Parliament"?

178

STUDY HINT Use an outline map of North America to develop a color code showing the British and French land claims in America. Then list the causes of the French and Indian War and the results.

SKILL BUILDER: CRITICAL THINKING AND COMPREHENSION

▶ **I. Drawing Conclusions**

▶ Read each of the following groups of statements. Think carefully about each group. Then, from the list of possible conclusions, choose the conclusion that best fits the facts.

Statements

1. In 1754 Benjamin Franklin proposed the Albany Plan of Union to unite the colonies under one government.
2. The government created by the Albany Plan of Union would collect taxes from the colonies to pay for a volunteer army.
3. Colonial assemblies were not willing to give up their power to a new joint government.
4. The 13 colonies were not able to unite to fight against the French. They had to depend on Great Britain to provide the armies and weapons needed to fight the French and Indian War.

Possible Conclusions:

a. The rejection of the Albany Plan of Union weakened Britain's hold over the colonies.
b. The rejection of the Albany Plan allowed Britain to have complete leadership in the war.
c. Since the colonies rejected the Albany Plan, it was unlikely that they would ever unite in the future.

▶ **II. Predicting**

▶ When you predict, you tell what you think will happen in the future. A prediction is not just guesswork. It is most likely to be correct when it is based on facts and clues.

Because Britain won the French and Indian War, its empire in North America doubled in size. The western lands were no longer occupied by French soldiers.

1. What do you think the colonists would want to do now that the war was over?
2. How do you think Native American nations would react?

▶ Write your prediction on a sheet of paper. Tell also your evidence is. In other words, tell what facts and clues you used in making your prediction.

ENRICHMENT

1. Suppose you are a Native American living in New France. A French trapper approaches your people. He wants you to help France in the war against Britain. How do you feel about fighting in this war? Write about your reactions to what the trapper says.

2. Research Benjamin Franklin's *Poor Richard's Almanac*. Copy some of the sayings that were published in the Almanac. Choose two of these sayings to write down and illustrate on a poster board. Explain to the class why you like these sayings and what they mean to you.

179

Skill Builders improve students' abilities to read and use maps, time lines, and diagrams.

A second section of **Skill Builders** introduce, apply, and reinforce critical thinking and comprehension skills. Symbols explain the kind of critical thinking skills being applied.

Pages from Student Edition. Actual size: 8 × 10″.

EXPLORING AMERICAN HISTORY provides the most frequent and complete system of review in any American history text today. Two-page Chapter Reviews reinforce comprehension with skills practice and application, and two-page Unit Reviews summarize the Unit's content. The wide variety of activities available in the review pages let you tailor review and testing to your students' needs and abilities.

Unit Reviews establish continuity by helping students see the relationship between Chapter content and Unit objectives.

Critical Thinking And Comprehension Skill Builders ask students to apply these skills to Unit concepts.

UNIT REVIEW

SUMMARY

In the 1750s, conflicts in the valley of the Ohio River led to the French and Indian War between Great Britain and France. When the war ended in 1763, France had been driven from North America.

In the years following the war, strong disagreements arose between Great Britain and its American colonies. The main issue was taxes. The British government believed that it had the right to tax the colonies. Colonists believed that only their own colonial assemblies could tax them. The colonies protests against the British taxes led to increasing unity of the colonies. Sometimes the protests also led to violence, as in the Boston Massacre of 1770 and the Boston Tea Party of 1773.

The Continental Congress, with delegates from every colony, met in 1774 and again in 1775. When fighting broke out in 1775 at Lexington and Concord, the Congress appointed George Washington as head of the colonial army. A year later, on July 4, 1776, Congress declared that the colonies were now free and independent.

The new country had to fight a war to win its independence. The British forces had many advantages over the small and poorly equipped Continental Army. However, the Continental Army stayed together, thanks mainly to the leadership of George Washington. With French aid, the Americans finally were victorious.

The last important battle of the American Revolution took place at Yorktown, Virginia, in 1781. Two years later, the Treaty of Paris set the boundaries of the United States. Now the new nation would be faced with the task of forming a government on which all the colonies would agree. The new nation also would have to choose a leader to run the new government. What laws do you think would be important to the new nation?

SKILL BUILDER: READING A MAP

North America in 1783

United States
British
Dutch
French
Russian
Spanish
Unexplored
Disputed

1,000 miles
1,600 kilometers

1. What territory was to the north of the United States?

2. Which European country controlled this territory?

3. What river formed the western boundary of the United States?

4. What European country controlled the territory to the west of this boundary?

5. What country controlled New Orleans? Why was control of this city important?

6. To what country did Florida belong in 1783?

SKILL BUILDER: CRITICAL THINKING AND COMPREHENSION

I. Predicting

At the end of the Revolutionary War, Great Britain remained in control of Canada. The United States and Canada shared a long border, stretching from the Atlantic coast through the Great Lakes to the source of the Mississippi River. Predict how this border will affect relations between Great Britain and the United States. Will relations along the border be peaceful and friendly, or hostile and unfriendly? Write a paragraph that states your prediction and gives your reasons for it.

II. Point of View

1. Select one of the major events described in Unit 5. Write a paragraph describing the event from the point of view of an American. The American may be either taking part in the event or standing on the sidelines watching it.

2. Write a second paragraph describing the same event from a British point of view.

ENRICHMENT

1. Choose an event discussed in the unit. Read about the details of this event in your library. Then write a newspaper article telling about the event. Begin the article with a paragraph that includes the five Ws of newspaper articles: who, what, when, where, why. When your article is finished, write a headline for it. OPTIONAL: Draw an illustration for the article.

2. Suppose that it is June 1776. You are a member of the Second Continental Congress. The Congress is trying to decide whether it is a good idea to declare independence from Great Britain. Prepare a speech that you will give at the next meeting of the Congress. Your speech should argue for one of these points of view and against the other two:
   a. The colonies should declare independence, and the sooner the better.
   b. Independence is the goal that the colonies should work toward. However, declaring it now would be dangerous.
   c. Independence would probably create more problems than it solves. The colonies should instead try to work out their problems with Great Britain.

221

Map Skill Builders give a geographically oriented overview of the Unit.

Enrichment activities challenge students' ability to bring together information from the Chapters and use it in new ways, sometimes using outside sources.

An unmatched level of teaching and management support.

Convenient on-page annotations provide background information, additional teaching suggestions, and questions on the Chapter.

Background: Fort Duquesne was especially important to the French military strategy of defending New France, since it comprised a key link in a series of frontier forts connecting the Ohio River region with Lake Erie. After the occupation of Fort Duquesne by the British, they renamed it Fort Pitt, in honor of the British prime minister.

8. Great Britain had more colonists, some Native American support, and a powerful navy. Great Britain's colonists greatly outnumbered the French. The 13 colonies had a population of more than 1 million people who would fight to defend their families and their colonies. Although most groups of Native Americans supported the French, the powerful Iroquois nation supported the British. In addition, Britain's large navy controlled the Atlantic. In this way, Britain was able to prevent France from sending more troops to America.

9. The British colonies were not united as they went into the war. The 13 colonies had often quarreled with one another about their boundaries and their claims to western land. Each colony was concerned with its own problems and took little interest in the other colonies. How would this lack of unity be a disadvantage in a war with the French?

People in History

10. **Benjamin Franklin** Even before war was declared, Benjamin Franklin suggested a plan to help the 13 colonies unite. For years, colonists had enjoyed reading Franklin's *Poor Richard's Almanac*. This book each year gave useful information on farming and the weather. It also was full of clever sayings, like "Early to bed and early to rise makes a man healthy, wealthy, and wise." In addition, Franklin was known for his inventions and scientific experiments. He was the first person to prove that lightning is a form of electricity. A self-taught man, Franklin was one of the outstanding leaders in the colonies.

11. In 1754, at Albany, New York, Franklin proposed the **Albany Plan of Union** to join the colonies under one government. The idea for this joint government was borrowed from the Iroquois nation. The government would command the **militia** (mih-LISH-uh) in each colony. The militia was a volunteer army that helped defend the colonies. The government also would collect taxes from the colonies to pay for the militia.

Background: Franklin based his Albany Plan partly on the organization of the six Iroquois nations. The Iroquois Confederation, or league, included the Seneca, Mohawk, Onondaga, Oneida, Cayuga, and Tuscarora. The close cooperation of their chiefs in keeping peace among these tribes and working together in their own defense also probably later influenced the framers of the Constitution.

176

Spotlight on Sources

12. This is how Franklin explained the purpose of the Albany Plan of Union:

". . . A union of the colonies is certainly necessary to us all. A voluntary [freely chosen] union entered into by the colonies themselves, I think, would be preferable to [better than] one imposed [required] by Parliament. Were there a general council formed by all the colonies, everything relating to the defense of the colonies might properly be put under its management [control]."

The Papers of Benjamin Franklin,
Leonard Labaree, ed.

13. The colonies turned down the Albany Plan. Franklin hoped the Albany Plan would strengthen the colonies to fight the coming war. However, the colonial assemblies were not willing to give up their power. Each colony insisted on keeping its right to tax itself and control its own affairs. As a result, the British colonies would not join together to fight the French.

Fighting the War What were the major battles of the French and Indian War?

14. The French were successful in the first battles of the French and Indian War in the Ohio Valley. In July 1755, a British army commanded by General Edward Braddock headed for Fort Duquesne. Braddock's army included a force of 500 colonial soldiers led by George Washington. General Braddock had just arrived from Britain. He did not know how wars were fought on the American frontier. Braddock ignored Washington's warning that the French troops and their Native American allies would attack from behind trees and bushes. Braddock insisted on marching his soldiers in their bright red uniforms into open fields. He expected the British soldiers to then stand in rows and shoot at the enemy. As Washington had warned, the French and their allies made a surprise attack. General Braddock was killed, and most of his army was destroyed.

Discuss: Ask the class to think about the name of the conflict, the French and Indian War. Why isn't it called the French and Native American War? Suggest that historians name events in terms of name designations of their own period. Why might it be difficult to rename events?

Washington then took command and ordered what was left of the British army to retreat. After this defeat and for another two years, France seemed to be winning the war.

15. In 1757, a new leader named William Pitt took charge of Britain's government and helped turn around the war. Pitt chose able new generals and increased the size of the army. He promised that Britain would pay the colonies for their costs of fighting the war. Pitt's efforts turned the war in Britain's favor. During 1758 and 1759, the British armies won several important victories. First, Fort Duquesne finally was captured. Soon after, General James Wolfe captured Louisbourg, France's main outpost in northeastern Canada.

16. The deciding battle of the war took place at Quebec, the capital of New France. There, in September 1759, Wolfe's army faced the larger French forces led by General Louis de Mont-

▼ By climbing this steep bluff near Quebec, Wolfe's troops surprised the French. The battle that followed lasted less than 15 minutes.

calm (mahnt-KAHM). After sneaking up a cliff at night, the British army launched a surprise attack and overwhelmed the French. Both Wolfe and Montcalm were killed in this battle. The capture of Quebec meant that Britain had won the war. However, the fighting lasted another year, until Montreal fell to the British. In 1763, France and Britain signed the peace treaty that formally ended the French and Indian War.

Results of the War What lands did Britain gain, and how did the war affect the American colonists?

17. Britain's victory in the war gained it a huge new empire in North America. France was forced to give up nearly all of its territory in America. Britain now ruled Canada and all the land east of the Mississippi River except New Orleans. This land included Florida, which Britain got from France's ally Spain. New Orleans and the large territory of Louisiana west of the Mississippi were given to Spain. What problems do you think Britain might have in ruling its great new empire?

18. The British colonists gained from the war in several important ways. They had learned new ways of fighting and winning battles. More important, the colonists were no longer surrounded by French and Spanish colonies. The western lands were open to settlement. British colonists could now look forward to moving into the Ohio Valley.

Outlook

22. The 13 colonies had not been able to unite to fight against the French. They had depended on Great Britain to provide the armies and weapons needed to win the French and Indian War. As a result of the war, Britain's empire in North America now doubled in size. How do you think the colonists felt when the war ended? Do you think Britain might now decide to change the way it ruled the 13 colonies?

177

The comprehensive Annotated Teacher's Edition provides maximum flexibility to suit your teaching style and your students' abilities. You'll find helpful annotated teaching suggestions plus complete lesson plans with clearly stated teaching objectives and an Answer Key.

Each Chapter has a step-by-step lesson plan that provides an overview followed by teaching objectives, lesson development and motivation, suggestions for building Social Studies skills, enrichment activities, and references to ancillary materials.

Lesson plans help you prepare students for the content and objectives of each Unit. You'll find a Unit overview, objectives, suggestions for motivation and lesson development, cooperative teaching strategies, writing activities, and a guide to the Unit Review and Tests.

UNIT 5

America Wins Independence

Unit Overview The French and Indian War resulted in France's loss of almost all of its empire in the New World. After the war, Britain took steps to strengthen its vast land holdings in America. New taxes were imposed on the colonists in order to raise much needed funds for the crown. As a result, relations between Great Britain and the American colonies began to deteriorate. Further attempts by Britain to impose taxes on the colonists led to the Boston Massacre of 1770. For the next five years Britain and the colonies moved closer to war. The fighting began at Lexington in 1775 and led to the Declaration of Independence a year later. After the American victory at Saratoga in 1777, France joined the war. The last major battle of the war was the French and American victory at Yorktown in October 1781.

Unit Objectives

1. To learn about the French and Indian War and its effects on Britain's empire in North America.
2. To identify the events that led to the Revolutionary War.
3. To identify the important historical figures in the Revolutionary War.
4. To learn about the major conflicts of the war.
5. To explain how the war changed American life.

Unit Introduction

1. Motivation: Elicit any information that students already have about the Revolutionary War. Point to the map of North America in 1750 in Chapter 5 of Unit 4. Have students identify the original 13 colonies. Then point to the map of North America in 1783. Show students how the United States increased in size as a result of the war.

Ask: What would our lives be like today if the United States had lost the war to Great Britain? Explain that students will learn more about the causes of the war and its effect on the lives of Americans as they read this Unit.

2. Visual: The visual is John Trumbull's painting *The Battle of Bunker Hill.* Tell students that Trumbull took pains to be historically accurate.

Ask: From this painting, what can you tell about how wars were fought in the 1700s?

3. Time Line: Have students read the events on the unit time line and identify those they are already familiar with.

Ask: In general, what was happening in the colonies from the end of the French and Indian War until the meeting of the First Continental Congress in 1774? How long did the Revolutionary War last? When was the Declaration of Independence signed? When did France enter the war?

4. Historical Points of View: Have students read the introductory paragraph on pages 172–173.

Ask: What was the crucial difference between the British and colonial view of Britain's right to tax the colonies? Have them read the statement by the Stamp Act Congress of 1765, which explains the colonists' point of view.

Ask: How did the colonists compare their rights with those of natural born British citizens?

Have students read the second selection, which is from a British law of 1766.

Ask: How did the British Parliament feel about the rights of the American colonies to be govern themselves? Have students read and answer the questions under "Using Primary Sources."

Unit Activities

1. Cooperative Learning: Have students work together to create a colonial newspaper that reports on the events discussed in Unit 5. Some students can write news accounts of important events in each chapter. Others can write editorials that comment on these events, or they can draw political cartoons that provide another kind of commentary. Display the newspapers on the bulletin board.

2. Research: Have students do additional research on one of the important historical figures discussed in Unit 5. Possibilities include George Washington, Thomas Jefferson, Benjamin Franklin, Samuel Adams, Thomas Paine, or the Marquis de Lafayette. Then have them write a series of four or five diary entries by that person in which he or she comments on the events of the period.

Support Materials

Assignments can include:

1. Unit Review, pp. 220–221
2. Unit Vocabulary and Comprehension Masters V40–V41
3. Unit 5 Test, pp. UT9–UT10
4. Writing Workshop, pp. W13–W16

T53

Unit 5

CHAPTER 1 The French and British Fight

Overview Both Great Britain and France laid claim to the Ohio River valley. Although war was not declared until 1756, fighting began in 1754 near Fort Duquesne. This was the start of the French and Indian War in North America; in Europe, the conflict was called the Seven Years' War. Although the French were outnumbered by the British colonists, they had the Native Americans as their allies. As a result of Britain's victory in the war, France gave up almost all of its territory in America.

Objectives

1. To identify the causes of the French and Indian War.
2. To understand the advantages and disadvantages of both sides in fighting the war.
3. To learn about the major battles of the war.
4. To explain the results of the war.
5. To explain the Albany Plan of Union.

Developing the Chapter

1. Motivation: Begin by referring students to the map of the French and Indian War in their textbooks. Point out that as a result of this war, Britain ruled Canada and all the land east of the Mississippi River except New Orleans, but including Florida. Compare this new area on the map to the land along the eastern seaboard that was the site of Britain's original thirteen colonies.

Ask: What does this conflict show you about the way in which our country grew to its present size? What would have happened if Britain had lost the war with France and had not gained all this territory? What would the United States be like if some of the country were still governed by France?

2. Introduction

a. Write the chapter vocabulary words on the chalkboard. Have students write each word and its glossary definition in their vocabulary notebooks. Ask volunteers to use each word in an original sentence. Write students' sentences on the chalkboard without the vocabulary word. Have other students in the class complete each sentence with the correct vocabulary word.

Great Britain of such vital importance to the future of the British colonies?

c. Have students read the chapter.

3. Review and Recall: After the students have read the chapter:

a. Have them reread and answer the Objective question.
b. Have them reread and answer each section question.
c. Have them turn to the map of the French and Indian War on page 175. Ask them to identify which side was victorious in each of the major battles. Then have them provide two additional facts about each conflict highlighted on the map.
d. Have students make a chart listing the advantages of each side in the conflict.
e. Ask students to identify the results of the war for Britain, France, and the British colonies. List their answers on the chalkboard.
f. Ask students to summarize the Albany Plan of Union.
   Ask: What is the significance of this Plan for the future of the thirteen colonies?

4. Building Social Studies Skills: Remind students of the differences between a primary and secondary source. Have students identify the primary source in this chapter (Benjamin Franklin's letter). Ask them to list the primary and secondary sources they would use in preparing a report on the French and Indian War.

5. Extension

a. Have students write diary entries written from the point of view of a colonial soldier, a French soldier, or a Native American after a major battle of the French and Indian War.
b. Have students write an editorial for a colonial newspaper commenting on the British victory in the French and Indian War and predicting the future course of colonial-British relations.

Support Materials

Assignments can include:

1. Chapter Review, pp. 178–179
2. Vocabulary and Comprehension Master V42
3. Test 5-1, p. CT25
4. Enrichment Master E25

SKILL BUILDER: USING A TIME LINE

1. 492 years 2. 38 years 3. 4 years 4. 1 year 5. 21 years

SKILL BUILDER: CRITICAL THINKING AND COMPREHENSION

I. Generalizing

1. c 2. c 3. c

II. Summarizing

1. Summaries should mention Cortés's greed at hearing of golden cities, his knowledge of the disunity of the Aztec Empire, and his ability to use slaves and other unhappy conquered peoples for his own ends. 2. Montezuma expected Cortés to come because of an old Aztec belief. He agrees to give Cortés all he owns because he wants to obey his people's rightful king. 3. Summaries should mention the role of De Soto helping to subdue the Incas in Peru, and to describe how Pizarro tricked Atahualpa and took him hostage. 4. Dona Mariña had learned the Aztec language and quickly learned Spanish. She taught Cortés about Aztec life and became his interpreter.

USING PRIMARY SOURCES

The letter to the Spanish king should assure him that the Aztecs await his authority and are ready to give him everything they own.

ENRICHMENT

1. The two Native American leaders should have quite similar stories to relate about their impression of the Spaniards and the way they were taken captive, the way their warriors failed to merely elect new leadership and carry on the resistance, and the way their empires fell when confronted by the Spaniards' superior weaponry. 2. Students' maps should use three colors or kinds of lines to distinguish the three voyages.

UNIT 2 CHAPTER 5

VOCABULARY REVIEW

1. b. 2. a 3. d 4. c

SKILL BUILDER: INTERPRETING A MAP

1. Coronado
2. De Vaca and Coronado
3. Narváez was lost at sea. De Vaca led a small group back to Mexico City.
4. Ponce De León and Narváez

SKILL BUILDER: CRITICAL THINKING AND COMPREHENSION

I. Generalizing

1. b. 2. b

II. Summarizing

1. Fray Marcos lied about the richness of the Seven Cities of Cíbola. His only truth was that the houses are made of stone. 2. Estevanico was a black slave from Morocco who served as guide to Cabeza de Vaca and to Mendoza through northern Mexico and southern Arizona. Native Americans from one of the Seven Cities executed him as a spy. 3. Cabeza and his companions pretended to be medicine men and thus walked safely from village to village across Texas to Mexico.

USING PRIMARY SOURCES

Coronado expected to find seven cities built with gold brick and decorated in turquoises. He found stone houses five stories high in seven little villages.

T134

ENRICHMENT

1. Students' drawings should resemble a Pueblo complex, with adobe apartments reached by ladders from the roof below, up to five stories high. 2. The two explorers should describe the bayous, plains, and deserts of the United States from the Mississippi River to Arizona, mention the societies of Native Americans growing corn and fishing or hunting there, and exaggerate the wealth of these people. 3. Students' reports should feature only the geography and climate of Spanish America.

UNIT 2 CHAPTER 6

VOCABULARY REVIEW

Students should have used each of the following words correctly according to their Glossary definitions: 1. encomienda 2. rebellion 3. missions 4. emigrate 5. census 6. missionaries 7. convert

SKILL BUILDER: READING A MAP

1. *Santa Elena*
2. What is the town farthest south in Florida? *Tegesta*
3. *Mississippi River*
4. *Central Camino Real*
5. *Mexico City*

SKILL BUILDER: CRITICAL THINKING AND COMPREHENSION

I. Generalizing

1. Settlers' demand for land for livestock, new silver mines, and water drew them north. 2. The Spanish moved in and settled permanently in a fort at St. Augustine to supply their troops fighting the French. 3. The purpose of the missions was to convert Native Americans to Christianity and teach them European ways of life.

II. Summarizing

1. Spain wasn't interested in holding the Florida lands until it appeared that the French might claim them, so the Spanish built a settlement there even though there were no mineral riches to exploit. 2. At the missions, the Native Americans converted to Christianity, received protection from warring neighbors, learned farming and crafts skills. Las Casas and others tried to improve working conditions for the Native Americans.

USING PRIMARY SOURCES

Father Kino believed that converting Native Americans would pacify them and enable Spain to conquer new territory (and peoples) more easily, thus spreading Spanish and Christian influence.

ENRICHMENT

1. Reports should mention the foods that helped Europeans reduce starvation and increase population: potatoes and corn. Indigo became a valuable cash crop, as did chocolate. For many decades, Europeans did not eat tomatoes, thinking them poisonous. 2. Persons and events chosen from the chapter will vary. 3. Settlements will vary, ranging from towns like Santa Fe to missions.

UNIT 2 CHAPTER 7

VOCABULARY REVIEW

1. tributary 2. pelts 3. Louisiana 4. portaged 5. Jesuit

Check students' responses quickly and accurately with the easy-to-use Answer Key.

*A*n unmatched program of learning resources.

NAME _____ DATE _____

☆☆☆ UNIT 2 TEST
Europeans Explore and Colonize the Americas

I. CLASSIFYING INFORMATION. Each phrase describes an event that related to the European settlement and exploration of the New World. On the blank space at the left write the letter that indicates which country each description relates to.

A. Spain B. France C. England D. Portugal E. Vikings

____ 1. Discovery of Brazil

____ 2. Establish a colony at Hispaniola

____ 3. Hired John Cabot to find a northwest passage

____ 4. Discovery of St. Lawrence River

____ 5. Established settlements at Vinland on Eastern tip of New Foundland

____ 6. Traveled completely around the globe

____ 7. Denied Spain's claims to land in the New World

____ 8. Claimed Louisiana

____ 9. Gained empires in Mexico and South America

____ 10. Settled Florida and Southwest

____ 11. Established colony at Jamestown

____ 12. Explored Great Lakes region

II. TRUE OR FALSE. In each of the following sentences the underlined word makes the sentence true or false. If the statement is true, write T in the blank. If the statement is false, write the word or words that would make it true in the blank to the left.

_____ 1. Early *Viking* explorers reached Greenland and the coast of North America.

_____ 2. Christopher Columbus tried to find a sea route to Asia by sailing *east*.

_____ 3. Pizarro conquered the *Aztec* empire of Peru for Spain.

_____ 4. Spanish explorers searched for the cities of Gold in lands *north of Mexico*.

_____ 5. La Salle's exploration of the Mississippi region gained *no new lands* for France.

EXPLORING AMERICAN HISTORY ■ TEACHER'S RESOURCE BOOK ■ © 1991 Globe Book Co. **UT1**

NAME _____ DATE _____

UNIT 2 ☆ CHAPTER 1 TEST   The Earliest Exploration

I. MULTIPLE CHOICE. Choose the answer that best completes each of the following sentences. Write the letter in the space at the left.

____ 1. The Vikings explored to the west of Scandinavia because
a. they waned a sea route to Asia.
b. they wanted to conquer other countries.
c. they sought fertile land to settle and farm.
d. their country had been attacked by warriors.

____ 2. Because Genoa and Venice had a trade monopoly with the Muslims and Mongols,
a. these cities eventually went to war.
b. only merchants from these cities could trade directly with eastern nations.
c. both cities suffered economically.
d. other European cities also established trade with the East.

____ 3. Because of the Crusades
a. contact between the East and Europe developed more quickly.

b. trade between Europe and the East ended.
c. Muslim soldiers attacked European cities.
d. the Holy Land was recaptured.

____ 4. After the Turks took control of all caravan routes,
a. they conquered Constantinople.
b. trade between the East and Europe increased.
c. Europeans sought new land route to Asia.
d. they limited the number of caravans to the East.

____ 5. Because of Bartholemeu Dias' expedition along the coast of Africa from Portugal,
a. a direct sea rout to Asia was discovered.
b. the New World was discovered.
c. the spice trade ended.
d. Prince Henry conquered Venice and Genoa.

II. SEQUENCING. Read the following events. Number the events from 1 to 5 in the order in which they happened. Write the numbers in the space at the left.

____ 1. Eric the Red and his followers settled Greenland.

____ 2. Constantinople was conquered.

____ 3. Marco Polo began his travels.

____ 4. Vikings settled in Iceland.

____ 5. Vikings established settlements in North America.

III. ESSAY. Write the answer to the essay statement in paragraph form. Use the back of the paper.

What events led Europeans to search for the direct sea route to the East?

EXPLORING AMERICAN HISTORY ■ TEACHER'S RESOURCE BOOK ■ © 1991 Globe Book Co. **CT1**

(partial) ch answers

1680

umbus landed

wrence?

2. What is your opinion of the way the Europeans treated the Native Americans? Give reasons to support your answer.

UT2   EXPLORING AMERICAN HISTORY ■ TEACHER'S RESOURCE BOOK ■ © 1991 Globe Book Co.

A complete evaluation package includes **Chapter Tests** and **Unit Tests** on Blackline Masters. Tests are adaptable to students' needs and abilities. Answers to tests, and all Teacher's Resource Book activities, are found in the **Answer Key** provided.

Full-color **Overhead Transparencies** of maps from the text provide detailed maps for students and a teaching aid for teachers.

Accompanying **Blackline Masters** let students work along with the Overheads to reinforce skills and content.

UNIT 1

Native American Cultures and Lifestyles About 1500 A.D.

Farming
Maize (corn)
Tobacco
Cotton
Hunting
Bison (buffalo)

Hudson Bay

SUBARCTIC

NORTHWEST COAST

PACIFIC OCEAN

EXPLORING AMERICAN HISTORY ■ TEACHER'S RESOURCE BOOK ■ © 1991 Globe Book Co.

NAME _____ DATE _____

UNIT 2 / Chapter 3
Map Transparency 3 Activity Sheet

EARLY VOYAGES OF DISCOVERY

Use Map Transparency 3 or the map on page 58 of *Exploring American History* to answer the questions below.

A. MULTIPLE CHOICE. Write the letter for the best answer to these questions in the space to the left.

____ 1. The first European explorer to reach the southern tip of Africa was
a. Da Gama
b. Columbus
c. Dias
d. Cabral

____ 2. The first European explorer to find an all-water route to India was
a. Da Gama
b. Columbus
c. Dias
d. Cabral

____ 3. The first European to reach the southern tip of South America was
a. Verrazano
b. Cabot
c. Magellan
d. Cartier

____ 4. North America was first visited by Europeans in
a. the 15th century
b. the 16th century
c. the 17th century
d. the 18th century

____ 5. The first European trip around the world was in
a. the 15th century
b. the 16th century
c. the 17th century
d. the 18th century

____ 6. Australia was not visited by Europeans until
a. the 15th century
b. the 16th century
c. the 17th century
d. the 18th century

B. COMPLETION. Complete the following sentences as accurately as possible.

7. Before 1499 Europeans could reach India by traveling eastward through _____

8. The place where Magellan died and Cano continued his voyage was _____

C. TRUE OR FALSE. Decide if these statements are true or false. Write T in the space to the left if the statement is true and F if the statement is false. If the statement is false, rewrite it to make it true on the lines below.

____ 9. Columbus made four voyages to the Americas.

____ 10. Columbus' last voyage to the Americas was in 1492.

EXPLORING AMERICAN HISTORY ■ TEACHER'S RESOURCE BOOK ■ © 1991 Globe Book Co. **A3**

With the students' Workbook and Teacher's Resource Book you'll have everything you need to reinforce, motivate, enrich, and evaluate learning. Use the Workbooks to reinforce and extend reading and comprehension skills, thinking skills, history skills, and visual interpretation skills. The Teacher's Resource Book includes over 500 teaching aids all conveniently organized in an easy-to-use binder.

Activity Worksheets on Blackline Masters reinforce vocabulary; important people, places, and events; and comprehension of content.

Writing Process Worksheets apply the steps of the writing process to American history topics.

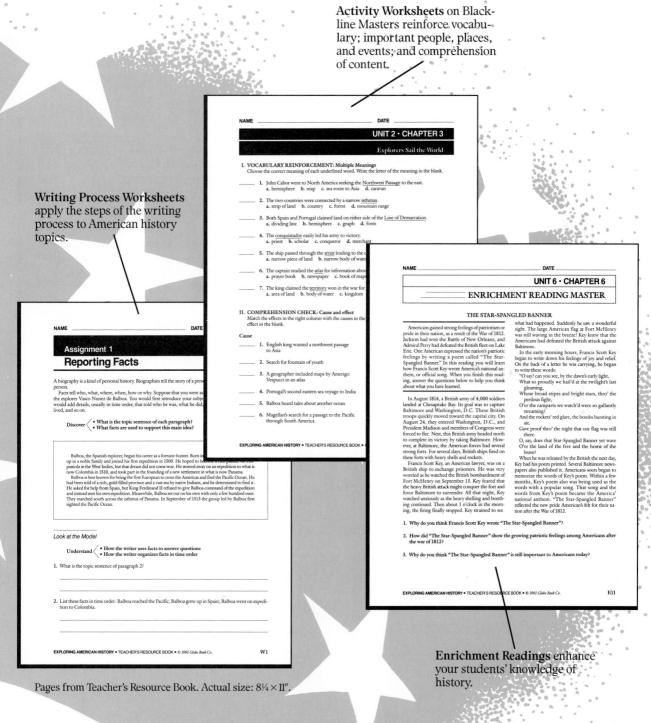

Enrichment Readings enhance your students' knowledge of history.

Pages from Teacher's Resource Book. Actual size: 8¼ × 11″.

CONTENTS

EXPLORING AMERICAN HISTORY *Annotated Teacher's Edition*

TEACHING SUGGESTIONS

Toward Educating the "At-Risk" Child

By Dr. Gwendolyn C. Cooke
Principal, William H. Lemmel Middle School, Baltimore, Maryland

A growing number of our young people, particularly in urban schools, may suffer learning problems because of their home or community environment. These students in recent years have come to be classified as "at-risk" students as young people who are often:

    a. From impoverished backgrounds

    b. Members of minority groups

    c. From households where English is often a second language

    d. Lacking in family and community support

More specifically, many of these students have not mastered basic skills consistent with their age group. They may have:

    a. failed to meet the school's standard for promotion and may have been retained for one or more years.

    b. been a school dropout or have had unexcused absences of 20 or more days during a calendar year.

    c. suffered or are suffering health, social, or family problems that are impairing their ability to succeed in school.

These problems may include, but are not limited to, evidence of physical abuse, alcohol or drug abuse, pregnancy or parenthood, delinquent behavior or attempted suicide.

These students, in most cases, are not uneducable, rather they are often uneducated. In many cases they are just as intelligent as the achieving student. Responsibility for their growth may be debated, but we as educators influence these children during the school day. Consequently we play a major role in their development. We may have to adjust our teaching methods to reach these students. Otherwise, we may actually contribute to the problem.

A school system's failure to serve at-risk students may result from several factors. Low expectations for student performance, inadequate resources and uneven quality of teaching staff contribute to the at-risk student problem. Other factors may include absence of close home-school connections and the inadequacy of school programs. But teachers of at-risk students can and should try to address some of these problems.

HOW YOU CAN HELP

Teachers can address the factor of low expectations for student performance by making the classroom an inviting center for learning.

In such an environment, the display of student work is critical. Students assume a sense of responsibility for classrooms where their products are displayed. They challenge peers who attempt to vandalize or tamper with posted items. Other ways of encouraging a more creative atmosphere may include:

    a. consistently referring to students by name when issuing directions or instructions.

    b. using nonverbal means of positive reinforcement such as smiling or nodding your head in response to correct student behavior and academic performance.

    c. establishing firm ground rules regarding acceptable and nonacceptable behavior.

Concomitant with disciplinary expectations is the choice of instructional strategies. In his research, Thomas Knight (1984) observed that the average high school student has an attention span of 12 to 15 minutes. Teachers can address this challenge by using two or three different approaches to learning within a class period. For example, ask students what kinds of activities interest them. Such activities could include role playing, simulations, or game formats modeled after television shows. Teachers could divide the students into smaller groups for cooperative learning or intensive instructions.

Students' responses to your "invitation for involvement" will vary. Some students will eagerly offer suggested activity choices. A few will refuse to participate. Several will challenge your authority to place this responsibility on them since your are "being paid to teach them." Others will rebel against the "new" structure. But teachers should be prepared for student opposition at this point. According to Purkey's research (1982) students who have not received many invitations from teachers or administrators to participate in shaping the learning environment have a difficult time recognizing and reacting to such invitations. Adult acknowledgement that students may have preferences for learning information may be alien to some students. They may compound this difficulty by acting as if they do not want to be invited to participate. School faculty and staff are often misled by this and may conclude that some students don't want to learn.

HOMEWORK HELPS

Close home-school connections can be established by the teacher requiring parents to sign homework every night that home assignments are given. Regular telephone calls to report "good news" help establish a rapport with the parent. Oftentimes, the only news a parent gets from his or her student's school is bad news. Invitations should be sent to parents when you have open house to display students' work. Another strategy may be a home visit, which is reasonable if you want to reach the at-risk student. Empathy may evolve from such a visit. Knowing what sort of home and community situations your students face may help you understand that student's behavior in your classroom. You may grow to know your student better, which will help when applying disciplinary actions or establishing parameters for assignments.

FILLING THE RESOURCE GAP

Inadequate resources may often exist in urban schools. But there are ways to compensate for a lack of resources. For example, why not invite guest speakers, achieving parents, social workers, or businesses patronized by teachers and students to adopt a class or team? Of course, you may not get a Eugene Lang, the businessman who promised a college education to a class of graduating sixth graders several years ago! But the adoption could take many forms. It could include simply having professionals come in and talk about what they do, while giving hands-on demonstrations. Business people could furnish supplies unique to their business, such as computers, which will help the educational process. Resources become less of a problem when you use this approach. Moreover, your sponsor can help make sure your existing resources are supplemented.

CHECK YOURSELF

Teachers must take time out to evaluate their effectiveness. You may do this with a peer or administrator. If you have set specific goals, make sure you have established target dates along with no more than four activities for each goal. Don't expect dramatic results in less than three months. Be surprised and grateful if the fruits of extra effort get dramatic results that quickly!

Working with at-risk students has its rewards. These students express their appreciation in many important ways: by sharing important items, by offering assistance, by giving gifts, and by demonstrating that they know you are accessible and that you care. Your contribution to them gives them an opportunity to become viable members of society. When at-risk students give back in these ways, you will know that you have begun helping them to become achieving, responsible adults.

For additional information on teaching the at-risk student, the following articles are suggested:

Council of State School Officers, *Assuring School Success for Students at Risk*, Annual Meeting paper, November 16, 1987, Asheville, North Carolina.

Jane Knight, *A Positive Atmosphere in the Classroom*, a paper presented in Frederick County, Maryland, February 24, 1984.

William Purkey "The Most Inviting Place in Town," *Inviting School Success*, Wadsworth Publishing Company, Belmont, California, 1978.

EXPLORING AMERICAN HISTORY
Scope and Sequence Chart for Critical Thinking Skills

Unit/Chapter	Title	Main Idea	Classifying	Summarizing	Generalizing	Sequencing	Cause & Effect	Comparing & Contrasting	Drawing Conclusions	Predicting	Fact Versus Opinion	Point of View	Making Judgments
1/1	The First People of the Americas	I											
1/2	Native Americans of the North and the Pacific Regions Coast	R											
1/3	Native Americans of the Mid-Continent	R											
1/4	Native Americans of the Eastern Woodlands	A	I										
1/5	Native Americans of Latin America	A	R										
2/1	The Earliest Explorations		A	I									
2/2	Columbus Sails West		A	R									
2/3	Explorers Sail the World		A	A									
2/4	Spain Conquers an Empire			A	I								
2/5	Spanish Explorers Move North			A	R								
2/6	Spanish Settlers Move North			A	A								
2/7	The French Explore North America				A	I							
2/8	England Founds a Colony				A	R							
3/1	Europeans Settle in New England				A	A							
3/2	Champions of Religious Freedom					A	I						
3/3	Europeans Settle in the Middle Colonies			A	A	A	R						
3/4	Europeans Settle in the Southern Colonies					A	A						
4/1	Farming in the Colonies						A	I					
4/2	Colonial Trade and Shipping						A	R					
4/3	Religion and Education in the Colonies						A	A					
4/4	Government in the Colonies							A	I				
4/5	Life in New France							A	R				
4/6	Life in Colonial Spain							A	A				
4/7	Colonial Life on the Frontier								A	I			
5/1	The French and English Fight								A	R			
5/2	Britain Tightens Its Grip								A			I	
5/3	The Colonists Resist Taxation without Representation									A	I		
5/4	Give Me Liberty or Give Me Death									A	R		
5/5	Independence Is Declared									A	A		
5/6	The Nation Wins Its Independence										A	R	
5/7	The Revolutionary War Changes American Life										A	R	

I = Introduction **R = Reinforcement** **A = Application**

EXPLORING AMERICAN HISTORY
Scope and Sequence Chart for Critical Thinking Skills

Unit/Chapter	Title	Main Idea	Classifying	Summarizing	Generalizing	Sequencing	Cause & Effect	Comparing & Contrasting	Drawing Conclusions	Predicting	Fact Versus Opinion	Point of View	Making Judgments
6/1	The New Nation Stumbles										A	A	
6/2	Making the Constitution											A	I
6/3	A Federal Government Is Formed											A	R
6/4	Settling Western Lands to the Mississippi											A	A
6/5	Adding the Louisiana Territory	A	A										
6/6	America vs. Britain: The War of 1812	A	A										
6/7	A New Nationalism Takes Shape		A	A									
6/8	The Influence of the West			A	A								
7/1	Pioneer Trails to the West				A	A							
7/2	The Mormons Settle Utah's Salt Basin					A		A					
7/3	The Spanish Settle California						A	A					
7/4	The War Between the United States and Mexico							A	A				
7/5	California Becomes a State							A	A				
7/6	Settlers Move into the Great Plains								A	A			
7/7	The Decline of Native Americans on the Great Plains								A	A			
8/1	Slavery in the Colonies and the Young Nation		A										A
8/2	Southern Planters, Farmers, & African American Slaves										A	A	A
8/3	African Slaves Resist Slavery					A		A		A			
8/4	Factories Grow in the Northeast					A		A					
8/5	Slavery Causes Bitter Feelings						A	A					
8/6	The North and South Grow Further Apart									A		A	
9/1	The Civil War Begins									A		A	
9/2	The Early Years of the Civil War											A	A
9/3	The North Wins the Civil War				A	A			A			A	
9/4	Reconstruction	A					A		A				
9/5	From Slavery to Segregation	A					A		A				
10/1	The Growth of Industry to 1860		A				A		A				
10/2	An Industrial Nation		A								A	A	
10/3	The Rise of Big Business					A		A			A		
10/4	Immigrants Bring New Ways of Life to America	A					A		A				
10/5	The Growth of Cities		A				A		A				

I = Introduction   R = Reinforcement   A = Application

EXPLORING AMERICAN HISTORY
Scope and Sequence Chart for Critical Thinking Skills

Unit/Chapter	Title	Main Idea	Classifying	Summarizing	Generalizing	Sequencing	Cause & Effect	Comparing & Contrasting	Drawing Conclusions	Predicting	Fact Versus Opinion	Point of View	Making Judgments
11/1	Unions Help Workers				A		A				A		
11/2	Farmers Face Hard Times		A			A						A	
11/3	Women Fight for Equal Rights			A					A				A
11/4	Americans Improve Their Lives				A		A			A			
11/5	The Progressive Movement		A				A	A					
12/1	The Spanish-American War			A			A					A	
12/2	Relations with Latin America				A		A						A
12/3	Opening the Pacific		A				A				A		
12/4	World War I					A	A						A
12/5	America Goes to War		A				A	A					
13/1	America in the 1920s				A		A						A
13/2	The Great Depression and the New Deal		A							A			
13/3	World War II Begins	A					A			A			
13/4	The United States Fights in World War II			A			A	A					
13/5	The World at Peace				A							A	A
14/1	America in the Postwar World				A		A					A	
14/2	The Cold War Begins			A			A			A			
14/3	United States Involvement in Asian Conflicts								A			A	A
14/4	The United States and the Middle East					A	A			A			
14/5	America Works for Peace							A	A			A	
15/1	Equal Rights for African Americans							A	A		A		
15/2	Equal Opportunities for American Women							A	A	A			
15/3	Opportunities for All Americans								A		A		A
15/4	A Changing America								A		A		A
15/5	A Nation of Cities									A	A		A
15/6	New Leaders				A					A			A
15/7	Dealing with Other Nations	A		A					A				
15/8	Science and Technology Transform America				A						A	A	
15/9	Challenges of a Changing World									A		A	A

I = Introduction   R = Reinforcement   A = Application

EXPLORING AMERICAN HISTORY SOCIAL STUDIES SKILLS LIST

Unit 1

Chapter 1 Previewing
    2 Making a Chart
    3 Interpreting a Photograph
    4 Reading a Map
    5 Using Context Clues

Unit 2

Chapter 1 Using a Chart
    2 Using an Encyclopedia
    3 Using Primary Sources
    4 Using Primary Sources
    5 Interpreting a Map
    6 Reading a Map
    7 Making a Chart
    8 Reading a Time Line

Unit 3

Chapter 1 Making a Time Line
    2 Making a Time Line
    3 Interpreting a Graph
    4 Reading a Map

Unit 4

Chapter 1 Reading a Map
    2 Completing a Table
    3 Interpreting a Time Line
    4 Making a Chart
    5 Making an Outline
    6 Reading a Map
    7 Studying for a Test

Unit 5

Chapter 1 Outlining
    2 Reading a Map
    3 Completing a Table
    4 Reading a Bar Graph
    5 Reading a Pie Graph
    6 Making a Time Line
    7 Making an Outline

Unit 6

Chapter 1 Completing a Chart
    2 Interpreting a Cartoon
    3 Interpreting a Chart
    4 Reading a Map
    5 Interpreting a Map
    6 Using a Table
    7 Reading a Time Line
    8 Making a Time Line

Unit 7

Chapter 1 Making a Chart
    2 Reading a Map
    3 Interpreting a Picture
    4 Drawing a Time Line
    5 Reading a Map
    6 Comparing Pictures
    7 Making a Time Line

Unit 8

Chapter 1 Using an Encyclopedia
    2 Reading a Map
    3 Reading a Map
    4 Interpreting a Drawing
    5 Using a Time Line
    6 Making a Time Line

Unit 9

Chapter 1 Making a Time Line
    2 Reading a Map
    3 Reading a Map
    4 Giving an Oral Report
    5 Reading a Map

Unit 10

Chapter 1 Reading a Graph
    2 Interpreting a Photograph
    3 Making a Time Line
    4 Reading a Map
    5 Using a Time Line

Unit 11

Chapter 1 Interpreting a Cartoon
    2 Completing a Table
    3 Reading a Time Line
    4 Making a Time Line
    5 Completing a Table

Unit 12

Chapter 1 Reading a Map
    2 Making an Outline
    3 Interpreting a Time Line
    4 Reading a Map
    5 Using a Time Line

A KEY TO SYMBOLS USED IN EXPLORING AMERICAN HISTORY

Recognizing Main Idea: Identifying the most important idea in a paragraph.

Classifying: Organizing facts into categories based on what they have in common.

Summarizing: Giving the main idea of a group of paragraphs in a brief form.

Generalizing: Making a statement that links several facts.

Sequencing: Putting a series of events in the correct time order.

Recognizing Cause and Effect: Matching the action or event that makes something happen to what happens as a result.

Comparing and Contrasting: Recognizing similarities and differences.

Drawing Conclusions: Making a statement that explains the facts and evidence.

Predicting: Guessing what will happen on the basis of clues and facts.

Identifying Fact Versus Opinion: Specifying whether information can be proven or whether it expresses feelings or beliefs.

Understanding Points of View: Recognizing why people have different attitudes about the same thing.

Making Judgments: Stating a personal opinion based on historical facts.

Cooperative Learning: Activities noted with this symbol can be used as cooperative learning activities.

Historical Method: This symbol identifies some of the tools that historians use to research and analyze historical events.

UNIT 1

The Early People of the Americas

Unit Overview About 30,000 years ago the first people to settle in America came from Asia over a land bridge that connected North America and Asia on the present site of the Bering Strait. These Paleo-Indians are the ancestors of the Native Americans. As time went on, these early people migrated across North and South America. They settled along the Northwest Pacific Coast and California, the Great Plains, the Southwest, and in the Eastern Woodlands. Other groups migrated farther south and developed the Mayan, the Aztec, and the Incan cultures of Central and South America. All the Native Americans developed life-styles that varied according to the land and the climate of the regions where they settled.

Unit Objectives

1. To identify the first settlers of the Americas.
2. To describe the civilization of the Native Americans of the North and the Northwest Pacific Coast.
3. To describe the civilization of the Native Americans of the Great Plains.
4. To describe the Native Americans who settled in the Eastern Woodlands.
5. To describe the Native Americans of Central and South America.

Unit Introduction

1. Motivation: Ask students to identify the people who came to your state when the country was being settled. Point out that the first people to settle the Americas actually arrived much earlier—during the Ice Age about 30,000 years ago. Explain that these settlers were the ancestors of the Native Americans who established cultures throughout North and South America.
Ask: Do you know which Native American group used to live in the area where we live today?
  Explain that they will learn more about these people as they read this unit.
2. Visual: Direct students' attention to the unit opening painting of the landscape on pages 2 and 3. Remind students that this peaceful, untouched scene was typical of the land where Native Americans lived before the coming of the Europeans.
3. Time Line: Have the class read the events on the unit time line (pages 2 and 3). Ask students if they are familiar with any of the events shown, and have them share their knowledge with the class. Encourage students to refer to the unit time line as they study the unit.

4. Points of View: Have students read the first introductory paragraph in this section.
Ask: What was one important difference between the views of Native Americans and of Europeans about how to use the land? What do you think accounted for this difference?
  Have students read the second introductory paragraph.
Ask: What will the first selection describe? The second selection?
  Have students read the first selection.
Ask: What was the relationship between the Native Americans and the natural world? What does this writer say will happen when people lack respect for living things? Do you agree or disagree with his sentiments? Explain your answer.
  Have students read the second selection.
Ask: Why were the Native Americans forced off their land? What did the non-Native Americans do to the land? How would you have answered the argument that the Native Americans had stood in the way of developing the land and so had to be removed?

Unit Activities

1. Cooperative Learning: Have students work in small groups to construct an illustrated time line that highlights major events from the arrival of the first people in the Americas to the rise of the various Native American cultures.
2. Mapmaking: On an outline map of North and South America, have students locate and write the names of the different Native American groups that they read about in this unit. Ask students to include also the occupations of these people (hunters, farmers, etc.) and the kinds of crops and animals they depended on.
3. Creative Writing: Have students write a legend that might have been created by a member of one of the Native American groups discussed in this unit to describe a significant historical event or a natural occurrence.

Support Materials

Assignments can include:
1. Unit Review, pp. 36–37
2. Unit Vocabulary and Comprehension Masters V6–V7
3. Unit 1 Test, pp. UT1–UT2

UNIT 1

CHAPTER 1   The First People of the Americas

Overview   The first settlers of the Americas came here over a land bridge across what is now the Bering Strait that connects Siberia in Asia with Alaska in North America. These people were following the herds of animals that were their primary source of food. These so-called Paleo-Indians crossed into North America about 30,000 years ago and eventually moved southward and eastward across the continent. They reached the southern tip of South America by 8,000 B.C. Some of these early people discovered farming in about 5,000 B.C. and changed from nomads to villagers.

Objectives

1. To describe how and when the first settlers arrived in North America.
2. To explain how these early people spread throughout North and South America.
3. To describe what life was like for the earliest settlers of the Americas.

Developing the Chapter

1. Motivation: Turn to the map on page 7 of the students' textbook. Explain that the first settlers of North America crossed a land bridge over the Bering Strait about 30,000 years ago.
Ask: Why do you think these early settlers crossed this land bridge during this period? Where would these people have first lived? How would they have lived? What kind of tools did they use? How did they dress?

Point out that students will learn the answers to these and other questions about the first settlers of the Americas as they read this chapter.

2. Introduction
a. Have students locate the new chapter vocabulary words in the text. Ask them to write each word and its glossary definition in their vocabulary notebook. Then have them make up an original sentence for each word.
b. Ask students to read the chapter title and the Objective question.
c. Have students preview the chapter visuals. Ask students what they can deduce about the early Americans from these visuals.
d. Have students read the chapter.

3. Review and Recall: After the students have read the chapter:

a. Have them answer the Objective question.
b. Have them answer the section questions.
c. Divide the class into pairs. Have each pair of students quiz each other on the content of the chapter.
d. Write the following chart heading on the chalkboard: *The First People of the Americas.* Then write the following heading on the left-hand side of the chart in list form: *Who Were They? Where Did They Come From? When Did They Arrive? Where Did They Settle? How Did They Live?* Have students complete the chart with appropriate information from the chapter.

4. Building Social Studies Skills: Use the map on page 7 of the students' textbook to review map-reading skills with the class. Point out the key, the scale, the direction indicator (compass rose), and lines of longitude and latitude. Have students locate important locations on the map and trace the paths followed by early Native Americans. Ask them to estimate the length of each path and to describe the directions of these paths.

5. Extension
a. Have students prepare written reports on either the plant or the animal life that flourished in the Americas at the time of the early migrations. Students should use encyclopedias as initial research sources.
b. Have students draw pictures that illustrate typical scenes from the lives of America's first inhabitants. Encourage them to do additional research so that their pictures will be accurate.
c. Ask students to imagine themselves as archaeologists in the year A.D. 2,500. They have been examining an archaeological site that was discovered on the location of their school. Have students write reports in which these archaeologists explain what their findings reveal about the culture that created them.

Support Materials

Assignments can include:
1. Chapter Review, pp. 16–17
2. Vocabulary and Comprehension Master V1
3. Test 1-1, p. CT1
4. Map Transparency Activity Sheet A1
5. Enrichment Master E1

CHAPTER 2 Native Americans of the North and the Pacific Coast Regions

Overview   The lives of the Native Americans of the North and the Pacific regions were influenced by the environments in which they lived. The Inuit, or Eskimo, lived in a harsh land with few natural resources. The tribes of the Pacific coastal region, however, led lives that were closely connected with the water, and they depended on hunting and fishing for their food. More than one hundred different tribes lived in what is now the state of California. These Native Americans enjoyed a peaceful existence in the mild climate and had a plentiful food supply.

Objectives

1. To describe how the lives of the Inuit were influenced by their environment.
2. To describe the society that was formed by the tribes of the Pacific Northwest.
3. To identify the way of life that developed among the Native American tribes in California.
4. To describe the culture and the society of the early Hawaiians.

Developing the Chapter

1. Motivation: Ask students to imagine that they live in a society without books, magazines, or newspapers. How would they pass on information about their history from one generation to the next? Then direct students' attention to the picture of the totem pole on page 15 of their textbook. If possible, bring in a book with pictures of other totem poles and show it to the class.

Ask: What do you think the carved images on the totem pole represent? Explain that these carved images stood for people, spirits, or animals that had helped a particular clan in the past.

Ask: How would these totem poles help a clan to remember and tell about its history?

2. Introduction

a. Write the chapter vocabulary words on the chalkboard. Have students write each word and its glossary definition in their vocabulary notebook. Ask students to write synonyms for each of the words. Call on a volunteer to write on the chalkboard an original sentence using one of the synonyms and to underline the synonym. Have another student identify the vocabulary word the synonym stands for.

b. Have students read the chapter title and the Objective question.

c. Have students preview the chapter visuals.
Ask: What clues about the life of these Native Americans of the North and the Pacific regions do these visuals give you?

d. Have students read the chapter.

3. Review and Recall: After the students have read the chapter:

a. Have them answer the Objective question.

b. Have them answer the section questions.

c. Divide the class into teams to play "Who Am I?" based on the Native American tribes discussed in the chapter. A student pretends to be a member of a particular tribe and must answer yes-or-no questions posed by the other team until the team guesses the name of the tribe. The team that guesses the most correct answers wins.

4. Building Social Studies Skills: Remind students that encyclopedias are reference books that have articles about a wide variety of topics. These entries are listed alphabetically. The index volume explains where all the entries about a particular topic can be found. Ask students to use their class or school encyclopedias to find the volume number and page reference of articles about the following topics: Inuit, totem poles, igloos, Chinook, Polynesians.

5. Extension

a. Have students draw or make clay models of totem poles that might have been carved by the Native American tribes discussed in this chapter. Suggest that students do additional research on totem poles before beginning this project. Display students' models and drawings in the classroom.

b. Ask students to choose one of the Native American tribes discussed in this chapter and write a research report on that tribe's culture and customs, including the ceremonies that formed such an important part of these peoples' lives.

Support Materials

Assignments can include:

1. Chapter Review, pp. 16–17
2. Vocabulary and Comprehension Master V2
3. Test 1-2, p. CT2
4. Enrichment Master E2

UNIT 1

CHAPTER 3   Native Americans of the Mid-Continent

Overview   The Native American tribes of the Great Plains region represented two very different lifestyles. Farming tribes lived on the eastern side of the Great Plains and lived in one place, while the buffalo-hunting tribes, who are called the Plains Indians, were nomads. They relied on the buffalo for food and to satisfy their needs for clothing and tools. Three other farming cultures developed in the what is now the American Southwest after 300 B.C.: the Mogollon, the Hohokam, and the Anasazi. Descendents of the Anasazi became known as the Pueblo Indians.

Objectives

1. To explain the two different ways of living that developed among the Native American tribes of the Great Plains.
2. To identify the three important cultures that developed in the American Southwest.
3. To describe the culture and lifestyle of the Pueblos.

Developing the Chapter

1. Motivation: Read students a selection from a book of Indian myths, such as *At the Center of the World* by Betty Baker (Macmillan, 1973). These tales are an excellent introduction to the value structures of the Indian tribes. What can you learn about how these Native Americans viewed nature from these legends? Explain that students will learn more about the Native Americans who lived in the Great Plains region as they read this chapter.

2. Introduction
a. Write the chapter vocabulary words on the chalkboard. Have students write each word and its glossary definition in their vocabulary notebooks. Ask volunteers to use each vocabulary word in a sentence.
b. Have students read the chapter title and the Objective question.
c. Have students preview the chapter visuals. **Ask:** What can you learn about the life of the Native Americans of the Great Plains from these illustrations?
d. Have students read the chapter.

3. Review and Recall: After the students have read the chapter:
a. Have them answer the Objective question.
b. Have them answer the section questions.
c. Divide the class into teams to play "Who Am I?" based on the Native American tribes discussed in this chapter. (This game has been described in the teachers notes to Chapter 2.)
d. Have students make up a crossword puzzle using words and ideas from the chapter. After they have written all the clues, they might try to solve each other's puzzles.
e. Write the following chart headings on the chalkboard: *Mandan, Blackfoot, Mogollon, Hohokam, Anasazi, Hopi, Pueblo*. On the left side of the chart, write the following in list form: *Where They Lived, Farmers or Hunters, Crops, Type of Shelter, Culture*. Call on volunteers to complete the chart with information from the text.*

4. Building Social Studies Skills: Review with students the importance of making up a bibliography of sources to use in research reports. Each book should be listed on a separate file card with the following information: title, author, publisher, date of publication. The bibliography card should include a topical title. Have students use the subject catalogue in the school library to find books on the following topics: buffalo, Great Plains Indians, Cheyenne, Pueblos, Native American legends.

5. Extension
a. Have students write short stories that reflect the culture of one of the Native American tribes discussed in this chapter. Point out that historical fiction must be historically accurate, and suggest that students do additional research on the Native American culture they are writing about.
b. Have students prepare maps on which they show the distribution of the various Native American groups described in this chapter. These maps should also indicate the crops grown by the different groups, the animals they hunted, and the kinds of shelters they lived in. Students should include map legends that explain the symbols used on their maps.

Support Materials

Assignments can include:

1. Chapter Review, pp. 22–23
2. Workbook, pp. 6–7
3. Vocabulary and Comprehension Master V3
4. Test 1-3, p. CT3
5. Enrichment Master E3

*As an answer key for this exercise, you may want to use a chart prepared by a student.

UNIT 1

CHAPTER 4 Native Americans of the Eastern Woodlands

Overview   Native Americans of the Northeast and the Southeast Woodlands created highly developed cultures that were tied to the land. The two large groups of the Northeast Woodlands tribes were the Iroquois and the Algonquin. The tribes of the Southeast Woodlands included the Creek, the Natchez, and the Seminole. The Native Americans of the Eastern Woodland region were both farmers and hunters and led a settled village life. Both the Iroquois and the Creek formed larger groups to maintain peace among the various tribes.

Objectives

1. To describe the cultures of the Iroquois and the Algonquin.
2. To explain the ways of living that developed among the Southeast Woodlands tribes.
3. To describe the Iroquois League.
4. To explain how the Native Americans of the Eastern Woodlands developed life-styles that were suited to the land and the climate.

Developing the Chapter

1. Motivation: Read to students the speech on page 26 of their textbooks. When you have finished, explain that according to Iroquois legend this is the speech that was made by a Native American leader, Hiawatha.

Ask: What do you think the leader was asking his people to do? Why does he think creating a union was so important? When do you think this speech was given?

Then explain that the Iroquois League, which was a union of various Iroquois tribes, was formed around A.D. 1450. Explain that students will learn more about the Iroquois and other Native Americans of the Eastern Woodlands as they read this chapter.

2. Introduction
a. Write the chapter vocabulary words on the chalkboard. Have students write each word and its glossary definition in their vocabulary notebook. Ask volunteers to use each vocabulary word in a sentence.
b. Have students read the chapter title and the Objective question.
c. Have students preview the chapter visuals.

Ask: What can you deduce about the life of the Eastern Woodlands tribes from these pictures?
d. Have students read the chapter.

3. Review and Recall: After the students have read the chapter:
a. Have them ask each other questions about each of the chapter sections.
b. Have them answer the Objective question.
c. Have them answer the section questions.
d. Write the following names, events, and terms on file cards: *Iroquois, Algonquian, "the three sisters," wigwams, longhouse, Iroquois League, Hiawatha, Creek, Natchez, miko, the Great Sun.* Divide the class into two teams. Have a member of each team choose a file card and identify the name, the event, or the term correctly. Each correct answer is worth five points. The team that earns the most points is the winner.
e. Write the following headings on the chalkboard: *Northeast Woodlands, Southeast Woodlands.* On the left side of the chart, write the following in list form: *Group or tribe, Occupation, Location, Religion, Social Organization.* Have students complete the chart with information from the chapter.

4. Building Social Studies Skills: Review with students the importance of taking clear, concise notes on their reading. These notes should be taken on file cards. Each card should have a heading, and the notes should be written in list form in phrases rather than in complete sentences. Have students take notes on Sections 2 through 6 of the chapter.

5. Extension
a. Have students do additional research on one of the Native American tribes discussed in this chapter. Then ask them to write a first-person narrative in which they describe a typical day in the life of a member of the tribe.
b. Have students read selections from a book of myths or legends about the Eastern Woodlands people. Then ask them to make up a myth or a legend that might have been used by a Native American from this region to explain a natural event.

Support Materials

Assignments can include:
1. Chapter Review, pp. 28–29
2. Vocabulary and Comprehension Master V4
3. Test 1-4, p. CT4
4. Enrichment Master E4

CHAPTER 5 Native Americans of Latin America

Overview The three great civilizations of Latin America were the Maya, the Aztec, and the Inca. The Maya, who settled the Yucatán peninsula, built a civilization that was strongly influenced by their religion and their religious leaders. The Aztec were a warlike people of central Mexico who exacted tribute from the people they conquered. The Inca, with an empire in the Andes Mountains, ruled almost all of the west coast of South America at the height of their power. All three cultures made great advances in science, agriculture, and building and engineering.

Objectives

1. To describe the features of Mayan culture.
2. To describe the Aztec empire and how it functioned.
3. To describe the Inca empire and its achievements.
4. To compare and contrast the Mayan, the Aztec, and the Incan cultures.

Developing the Chapter

1. Motivation: Direct students' attention to the picture of Machu Picchu in their textbook on page 33. Then explain that Machu Picchu is located high in the Andes Mountains of South America. (Point to this area on a map.) This city was part of the great Inca empire of Peru that flourished 500 years ago. For centuries people had heard about this famous city; however, all that was known about it came from tales and legends. Finally, in 1911 an American, Hiram Bingham, discovered this lost city.

Ask: How do you think a great city could become ''lost''? What do you think had happened to it? Explain that students will learn more about the Native American cultures of Latin America as they read this chapter.

2. Introduction

a. Write the chapter vocabulary words on the chalkboard. Have students write each word and its glossary definition in their vocabulary notebooks. Then have them make up word-search puzzles with all the vocabulary words in the unit. The words can be hidden horizontally, vertically, or diagonally. Ask students to find and circle the words in each other's puzzles.

b. Have students read the chapter title and the Objective question.

c. Have students preview the chapter visuals.
    Ask: Based on these pictures, what can you conclude about the life of the Mayan, the Aztec, and the Incan civilizations?

d. Have students read the chapter.

3. Review and Recall: After the students have read the chapter:

a. Have them answer the Objective question.

b. Have them answer the section questions.

c. Have them make a time line of the major events described in the chapter.

d. Have different students identify themselves as a Maya, an Aztec, or an Inca by describing three characteristics of their culture. The other students in the class have to identify which Latin American civilization is being described.

e. Have students make up one-sentence identifications of the following: John Lloyd Stephens, Tikal, Tenochtitlán, Montezuma, Andes Mountains, Cuzco, Garcilaso de la Vega.

4. Building Social Studies Skills: Review with students the distinction between a fact and an opinion. Tell students that a fact is a true statement that can be proven. An opinion is what a person or a group of people think or believe; it cannot be proven to be true. Have students reread the first section of the chapter and identify an example of a fact and an opinion.

5. Extension

a. Have students investigate the art of the Maya or the Aztec and bring to class pictures of the art. Students should be prepared to explain the aspect of Mayan or Aztec life that the art reveals.

b. Ask students to do additional research in encyclopedias about the capital cities of the Mayan, the Aztec, and the Incan empires. Then have them draw diagrams or make models or dioramas of the cities as they existed when the empires flourished.

Support Materials

Assignments can include:

1. Chapter Review, pp. 34–35
2. Workbook, pp. 8–11
3. Vocabulary and Comprehension Master V5
4. Test 1-5, p. CT5
5. Enrichment Master E5

UNIT 2

Europeans Explore the Americas

Unit Overview Although the Vikings were the first explorers to reach the North American coast, they did not establish permanent settlements there. The real age of exploration began almost 500 years later when Christopher Columbus discovered the New World in his quest for a western water route to Asia. Soon France, England, and Spain were sending explorers in search of land and riches. The Spanish established empires in Mexico and South America as well as much of the southern and western United States. French colonies were established farther north, in the Great Lakes region. The English colony at Jamestown was founded in 1607. This period of settlement and colonization was marked by conflicts between the Europeans and various Native American groups.

Unit Objectives

1. To identify the factors that led to the discovery of the New World.
2. To understand the contributions made by English, French, and Spanish explorers.
3. To trace these explorations on maps.
4. To learn what life was like in the Spanish, French, and English settlements.
5. To identify the conflicts between the European settlers and the Native Americans who lived in North and South America.

Unit Introduction

1. **Motivation:** Direct students' attention to the picture of the sea monster on page 40. Ask them to infer the meaning of this strange creature. (It represents the map-makers' vision of the dangers of the deep.) Explain that early explorers had to overcome their fear of the unknown before they could set out on long and dangerous voyages of exploration. Although the monsters were imaginary, the dangers of the deep were very real. Have students talk about what characteristics these early navigators must have had. Ask them to speculate on what would have happened if these explorers had not set out on these early voyages.

2. **Visual:** Explain to the class that the unit opener painting is one artist's version of what the coming of the Spanish to the New World was like.

Ask: Based on information in this painting, what advantages might the Native Americans have had in defending their lands against the Spaniards? (they knew the territory; their numbers were large). What advantages did the Spaniards have? (horses, armor, better weapons)

3. **Time Line:** Have the class read the events on the unit time line (pp. 38–39) and ask if they are familiar with any event or name included there. Encourage students to share prior knowledge with the class. Point out that they will learn about the unfamiliar names and events as they read the unit.

Ask: How can you generalize about the events that are included on this time line? How might you account for the lack of exploration between 1000 and 1492?

4. **Historical Points of View:** Have students read the first point of view, written by the Italian map maker Toscanelli. When they have finished, ask them to summarize his ideas about the possibility of finding a western sea route to Asia. Do they think that Columbus would have agreed with this? Have them explain their answers. Next, have students read the passage by Columbus. Ask students to identify parts of Columbus's letter that are facts and those that are opinions. Ask the students to answer the questions on page 41.

Unit Activities

1. **Cooperative Learning:** Have students work together to create a class newspaper that will feature news articles, cartoons, and editorials about events pertaining to the exploration and settlement of North and South America. As students read each chapter, ask them to select a particular historical episode to report on. Their news accounts should be written from the point of view of a reporter of the period. Have the class make up a name for the newspaper they have created.

2. **Creative Writing:** Have students select one of the historical figures from the period covered in Unit 2, such as Marco Polo, Columbus, Sir Walter Raleigh, Queen Elizabeth, Magellan, Cortés; or Pizzaro. Ask them to write a series of three or four diary entries by that person in which he or she discusses the historical events of the period.

Support Materials

Assignments can include

1. Unit Review, pp. 90–91
2. Unit Vocabulary and Comprehension Masters, V16–17
3. Unit 2 test, pp. UT3–UT4

UNIT 2

CHAPTER 1   The Earliest Explorations

Overview   The first European explorers to reach the shores of North America were the Vikings, under the command of Leif Ericsson in the year 1000. Soon afterward, other European countries began a profitable trade with the Muslim and Mongol empires of the East. These economic ties prompted Portuguese explorers, with the support of Prince Henry the Navigator, to seek a direct sea route to the East.

Objectives

1. To identify the early European explorers.
2. To understand the importance of trade between Europe and the East.
3. To understand why a sea route between Europe and the East became necessary.
4. To evaluate the importance of Prince Henry the Navigator in helping to discover sea routes to Asia.

Developing the Chapter

1. Motivation: Bring in news articles about recent exploration of space. Discuss with the class the extensive preparations that were made by NASA, including the crews' training, the maintenance of equipment, and the kind of supplies that were necessary.

Ask: What did the men and women on board know about their mission before setting out?

Invite students to imagine how explorers of the past felt as they set out with primitive equipment and little knowledge of the earth's geography. Have them speculate on the reasons for these voyages of exploration. Have volunteers compare these expeditions to present day space explorations.

2. Introduction

a. Write the chapter vocabulary words on the chalkboard. Have students write each word and its glossary definition in their vocabulary notebooks. Ask volunteers to use each vocabulary word in a sentence.

b. Have students study the picture of the Viking ship on page 42. Then ask them to read the chapter title and the objective. Have them speculate on why the Vikings explored new lands.

c. Have students read the chapter.

3. Review and Recall: After the students have read the chapter:

a. Have them answer the Objective question.

b. Have them reread each section question and then answer it.

c. Divide students into pairs. Have each student make up sentences for the vocabulary words, leaving a blank for each one. Then ask them to exchange papers and complete each other's sentences with the correct words.

d. Have students list the important people mentioned in this chapter and write at least one important contribution under each name.

e. Have students identify the effect that each of the following had on the early explorations described in this chapter: Crusades; Prince Henry the Navigator; spice trade with the East; compass; astrolabe; caravel.

4. Building Social Studies Skills: Use the map on page 44 to review map reading skills with the students, including the key, compass rose, and legend. Have students use the map to trace the trade routes used during this period. From this map, what can they determine about the importance of finding a direct sea route to the East? (It was necessary to find a more direct route to avoid travel through lands controlled by the Turks).

5. Extension

a. Have students write a speech in which one of the explorers discussed in this chapter addresses his crew before the start of a long voyage of exploration. In the speech the leader must deal with the fears of his crew about the uncertainties of the trip. Call on volunteers to read their speeches aloud.

b. Have students write three diary entries from the point of view of a sailor on one of the voyages described in Chapter 1. The entries should reflect the writer's feelings about the trip, in addition to describing discoveries made by the ship's crew. Have students do additional research, if necessary, in encyclopedias.

Support Materials

Assignments can include:

1. Chapter Review, pp. 46–47
2. Workbook, pp. 12–13
3. Vocabulary and Comprehension Master V8
4. Test 2–1, p. CT6
5. Enrichment Master E6

UNIT 2

CHAPTER 2 Columbus Sails West

Overview   Christopher Columbus wanted to find a western, rather than an eastern, water route to Asia. After the Portuguese king refused to finance his proposed venture, he turned to the king and queen of Spain for help. In April of 1492 they agreed to help him, and he set out on his first transatlantic voyage in August of that same year. During each of his four trips, Columbus discovered land in the Western Hemisphere and facilitated the Spanish conquest of the Americas.

Objectives

1. To learn about Columbus's voyages.
2. To understand the results of Columbus's explorations.
3. To use a map to identify the lands that Columbus discovered and claimed for Spain.

Developing the Chapter

1. Motivation: Bring in a picture of one of Columbus's ships and display it in the classroom. If a picture is not available, call attention to the chapter opener picture of Columbus's crew sighting land. Explain that the largest of the three ships that Columbus used was only 85 feet long, about the size of a small house. Ask students to compare the size of Columbus's ships to the ships that make the transatlantic journey today. Ask if students would be willing to sail across the Atlantic in such a small ship. Encourage the class to speculate on the kinds of supplies that Columbus would have taken.

2. Introduction

a. Write sentences on the chalkboard using each vocabulary word from the chapter. Have students try to determine the words' meanings from context clues.

b. Have students read the chapter title and the Objective question. Ask them to speculate why Columbus's voyages were so important.

c. Have students turn to the map on page 50. Explain that the arrows indicate the direction of the winds blowing across the Atlantic. Trace the arrows across the Atlantic Ocean, from Europe to the Atlantic coast of the United States. Have students identify the direction of the winds (west to east). Ask why this would make it difficult for ships sailing from Europe to reach this area of the Atlantic shoreline.

d. Have students read the chapter.

3. Review and Recall: After the students have read the chapter:

a. Have them make up questions about each section to ask one another.

b. Have them reread and answer the Objective question and each subhead question.

c. Make a chart with each of Columbus's four voyages as a heading. To complete the chart, have students identify the lands that he discovered on each voyage. They should refer to the map on page 50 to complete this chart.

d. Call on students to make generalizations about the importance of Columbus's voyages.

e. Have students make a time line on which they include the major events from the chapter.

4. Building Social Studies Skills: Explain to students that using a scale of distance is an important social studies skill that will enable them to better understand the distances between places they are learning about on maps. Guide students through using the scale of distance on the map on page 50 of this chapter. Then, ask them to determine the approximate distance between Spain and the part of the New World that Columbus explored.

5. Extension

a. Divide the class into teams of students. Have each team role-play an interview between Christopher Columbus and a twentieth-century news reporter. The reporter should question Columbus about his voyages and about his original intention in crossing the Atlantic. Have students reverse roles so each will have a chance to play both parts. The various teams should present their interviews for the class.

b. Bring in examples of political cartoons to class from your local newspaper and discuss them with the class. Then have students draw their own political cartoons that comment on Columbus's voyages. They should draw these from the viewpoint of a Spaniard of the 1490s.

Support Materials

Assignment can include:

1. Chapter Review, pp. 52–53
2. Workbook, p. 14
3. Vocabulary and Comprehension Master V9
4. Test 2–2, p. CT7
5. Enrichment Master E7

UNIT 2

CHAPTER 3 Explorers Sail the World

Overview The search for a sea route to Asia led to the exploration of America by other Europeans. John Cabot made two voyages to the new world for England; Giovanni da Verrazano and Jacques Cartier sailed to North America for France. During the same period, the early 1500s, Balboa and Ponce de León explored Caribbean lands for Spain. Finally, Columbus's goal of reaching the Indies by sailing west was realized by the Portuguese sea captain Ferdinand Magellan.

Objectives

1. To understand the continued interest Europeans had in finding a sea route to Asia.
2. To identify the contributions of French, English, Spanish, and Portuguese explorers of this period.
3. To use maps to identify bodies of water and to trace routes of exploration.

Developing the Chapter

1. Motivation: Explain that early explorers set sail for a variety of reasons. For example, in some folk tales there was a reference to the fountain of youth, which was supposed to possess the power of restoring youth to whoever drank its waters. The Spanish explorer Ponce de León went looking for it, believing it to be located in a land called Bimini. His search brought him to the North America mainland on Easter Sunday, 1513. Upon landing, he named the region Florida. Have students identify another discovery that they just read about that was also an accident (the discovery of the New World when explorers were really searching for a western route to Asia).

2. Introduction

a. Write the chapter vocabulary words on the chalkboard. Have students write each word and its glossary definition in their vocabulary notebooks. Then have them write synonyms for each of the vocabulary words.

b. Have students read the chapter title and Objective question.
   Ask: What would have happened if Europeans had not decided to sail west in search of a sea route to the East? Would America still have been discovered? If so, under what circumstances?

c. Have students study the chapter visuals. Ask them to list the European countries that became actively involved in the exploration of the New World. Have students read the chapter.

3. Review and Recall: After the students have read the chapter:

a. Have them reread and answer the Objective question.

b. Have them reread and answer each subhead question.

c. Have students locate on the chapter map on page 58 the lands discovered by each of the explorers mentioned in this chapter.

d. Have students make up a crossword puzzle using words and ideas from the chapter. After they have written all the Down and Across clues, they might try to solve each other's puzzles.

4. Building Social Studies Skills: Explain the importance of a time line in establishing an overview of a particular historical period. Have students make a time line for the key events in this chapter. When they are finished, have them make up questions based on the information in the time line.

5. Extension

a. Have students select one of the voyages of discovery discussed in this chapter. Ask them to write a news account of the event. Their articles should include headlines, the facts about the expeditions, some human interest details, and interviews with either the captain or one of his sailors. Remind them to answer the following questions in their first or "lead" paragraph: who? what? when? where? how?

b. Ask students to imagine that they are among the first colonists to settle in Hispaniola. Have each student write a first-person narrative told from the point of view of a colonist in which they describe the steps needed to establish a settlement on this newly discovered land. Their narratives should include a list of supplies they would have brought with them to the New World from Spain and preparations they had to make in order to survive in the new colony.

Support Materials

Assignments can include:

1. Chapter Review, pp. 58–59
2. Workbook, p. 15
3. Vocabulary and Comprehension Master V10
4. Test 2–3, p. CT8
5. Map Transparency Activity Sheet A3
6. Writing Workshop W1–W4
7. Enrichment Master E8

UNIT 2

CHAPTER 4   Spain Conquers an Empire

Overview   In the 1500s, Spanish conquistadors gained an empire in Mexico and South America. In 1519, Cortés set up a base at Vera Cruz. After building alliances with the non-Aztec people who lived in the area, he marched to the capital of the Aztec empire. By 1521, the conquest of Mexico was over. About ten years later, the explorer Pizarro led an expedition from Panama to Peru. He conquered the Inca leader and declared himself to be the ruler of the country. In less than fifty years two of the world's greatest empires were destroyed.

Objectives

1. To learn how Cortés conquered the Aztec empire of Mexico.
2. To learn how Pizarro conquered the Inca empire of Peru.
3. To identify the effect the Spanish conquerers had on empires in Mexico and South America.
4. To understand the benefits of these conquests for Spain.

Developing the Chapter

1. Motivation: Ask students to imagine themselves the leaders of an expedition of fewer than 600 soldiers. The year is 1519. They have just landed in a new land that extends from the Gulf of Mexico to the Pacific Ocean. (Point to the area on a wall map.) Over three million people live in the area. It would take too long to ask for more troops from Europe. Your goal is to conquer this large empire for your homeland. How would you go about it? Write students' answers on the chalkboard. Explain that they will find out how a Spanish conquistador accomplished this amazing conquest as they read Chapter 4. Remind them to compare the steps he took to conquer the Aztecs with their suggestions on the chalkboard.

2. Introduction

a. Write the chapter vocabulary words on the chalkboard. Have students write each word and its glossary definition in their vocabulary notebooks. Ask students to write the part of speech of each word and to use each word in an original sentence. Which word can be used as both a noun and a verb? (massacre)
b. Have the students read the chapter title and Objective question. Have them try to answer the Objective question.

c. Have students preview the pictures in the chapter. Based on the painting of Cortés's invasion on page 63, why were the Native Americans no match for the Spanish soldiers?
d. Have students read the chapter.

3. Review and Recall: After the students have read the chapter:

a. Have them reread each section, make up two or three questions based on its content, and quiz each other.
b. Have students reread and answer both the Objective question and each subhead question.
c. Have students make a chart that lists the achievements of both Cortés and Pizarro in gaining empires in Mexico and South America.
d. Have students compare the results of the Spanish conquistadors' achievements in Mexico and South America for Spain and for the Native Americans in both areas.

4. Building Social Studies Skills: Remind students that taking clear, concise reading notes can be a valuable study aid. Have them take notes on sections 10, 11, and 12. Each section's note should be written on a separate notecard. Key facts from each section should be summarized and listed. Students may make up questions based on their notecards and quiz one another.

5. Extension

a. Have students reread section 6 about Doña Marina. Then divide the class into small groups. Have each group role-play a meeting between Cortés and the Native American chiefs, with Doña Marina acting as his interpreter. Call on different groups to present their role-play to the class.
b. Have students write first-person accounts of one of the conquests described in this chapter. Ask them to write two versions of the event. One should be written from the point of view of one of the Spanish conquistadors; the second should be written from the point of view of either an Aztec or Inca. Call on volunteers to read their narratives aloud to the class.

Support Materials

Assignments can include:

1. Chapter Review, pp. 64–65
2. Vocabulary and Comprehension Master V11
3. Workbook, p. 16
4. Test 2–4, p. CT9
5. Enrichment Master E9

UNIT 2

CHAPTER 5   Spanish Settlers Move North

Overview   After conquering Mexico and Peru, Spanish explorers went north in search of the Seven Cities of Cíbola. Although they never found the mythical cities, their expeditions greatly increased the size of the Spanish Empire in the New World. De Soto, Coronado, and others discovered huge tracts of land in the southern and southwestern portion of North America. Still other Spanish explorers searched for a sea passage, the Strait of Anian, that was said to link the Atlantic and Pacific Oceans.

Objectives

1. To learn why the Spanish conquistadors continued to explore areas north of Mexico.
2. To understand how these explorations increased the Spanish Empire in the New World.
3. To identify the contributions of the various Spanish explorations of this period.

Developing the Chapter

1. Motivation: Write the word "alchemist" on the chalkboard and ask if students can define it. Point out that since the Middle Ages, people called alchemists have claimed that they could change other metals into gold. Elicit facts students might know about people's fascination with gold, including references to the "gold rush" of the Old West and Alaska. Point out that this same gold fever was responsible for Spanish exploration of much of what is now the southern and southwestern United States. Locate this area on a wall map.

2. Introduction
a. Have students locate the new chapter vocabulary words in the text. Ask them to write each word and its glossary definition in their vocabulary notebooks. Then have them work in pairs to quiz each other on the definitions.
b. Have students reread and answer the Objective question and each subhead question.
c. Have students read the chapter.

3. Review and Recall: After the students have read the chapter:
a. Divide the class into teams to play "Who Am I?" based on people discussed in the chapter. The person pretending to be the historical figure must answer yes or no to questions posed by the other team until the team identifies the figure. The team that identifies the most wins.

b. Have students state one fact and one opinion based on each of the sections in the chapter.
c. Have students identify various places on the Chapter Review map in their textbooks. Suggestions include: the Mississippi River, the Rio Grande, the Isthmus of Panama, and San Diego Bay. Then have students describe the journey of each of the Spanish explorers in terms of the cardinal points of the compass rose.

4. Building Social Studies Skills: Remind students of the importance of making a chart in order to organize information. Have them make a chart that indicates the achievements of each of the explorers mentioned in this chapter. Help students make up appropriate headings for their charts that include the explorer's name, dates of exploration, the areas explored, the reason for the journey, and the results of the trip.

5. Extension
a. Remind students that many of the Spanish explorers they learned about in this chapter encountered Native Americans on land they explored for Spain in North America. Ask students to research and write reports about the lives of the Plains and Pueblo Indians. The reports should include information about their cultures and how they reacted to the Spaniards.
b. Point out that many words in American English were borrowed from Spanish. Have students choose a word with early Spanish origins and write a word history. These histories should include any changes in meaning that have occurred over the years. Students can use vocabulary building books as reference guides. (Possible words: adobe, flotilla, guerrilla, lasso, mosquito, mustang, padre, plaza, tornado)

Support Materials

Assignments can include:
1. Chapter Review, pp. 70–71
2. Vocabulary and Comprehension Master V12
3. Test 2–5, CT10
4. Map Transparency Activity Sheet A4
5. Enrichment Master E10

UNIT 2

CHAPTER 6   Spanish Settlers Move North

Overview   Throughout the 1500s and 1600s, Spaniards established settlements in Florida and throughout the southwest portion of North America. The Native Americans who lived on these lands were forced to work for the Spanish settlers under harsh conditions. Many of them died. These Native Americans made up nearly 95 percent of the population in New Spain.

Objectives

1. To learn why Spaniards emigrated to New Spain.
2. To understand the scope of the Spanish settlements in New Spain.
3. To describe the effect of the Spanish settlement on the lives of the Native Americans.

Developing the Chapter

1. Motivation: Read the introductory paragraph of Chapter 6 to the students. Point out that Santa Fe was one of the earliest Spanish settlements in the Southwest, founded at the beginning of the 1600s. Ask students to speculate on what life might have been like in early Santa Fe.
Ask: What risks and hardships might these early settlers have faced?

2. Introduction

a. Have students locate the new vocabulary words in the text. Ask them to write each word and its glossary definition in their vocabulary notebooks. Then divide the class into pairs. Ask one student to make up a riddle for each word. The other student must correctly identify the word. Reverse roles so that each student has a chance to make up word riddles.

b. Have students study the pictures in the chapter. Ask them what the buildings seem to have in common. Then ask them to look at the map in the Chapter Review and note the distance between settlements. Help students connect the fortresslike architecture of many of the buildings with the need for protection.

c. Have students read the Objective question aloud and try to answer it.

d. Have students read the chapter.

3. Review and Recall: After the students have read the chapter:

a. Have them reread and answer the Objective question.

b. Have them reread and answer the subhead questions.

c. Have students work in pairs. Each student should make up at least two factual questions about each of the sections in the chapter. The other student should answer them.

d. Draw two lists on the board, with the headings ''Cause'' and ''Effect.'' Call on volunteers to identify either the cause or the effect of a particular event that is described in each of the sections. List their answers on the chalkboard. Then have other students identify the accompanying cause or effect.

4. Building Social Studies Skills: Explain to students that topical outlines are useful for organizing information. Explain that these outlines can make information easier to understand and to remember. Ask students to complete the following topical outline by adding subtopics with appropriate information.

  I. Spain Settles Florida
    A. Where the Spanish lived
    B. Relations with the French
  II. Spain Settles the Southwest
    A. Early Spanish Settlements
    B. The Role of the Missionaries
    C. Relations with Native Americans

5. Extension

a. Have students write letters from Spanish settlers in New Spain to friends or relatives in their homeland. The letters should voice their feelings about life in their new country and whether it lived up their expectations.

b. Have students draw maps that show the Spanish settlements in Florida and the Southwest that were discussed in this chapter. Their maps should also indicate the Native Americans who had claim to the land before the Spanish arrived.

c. Have students role-play a discussion between a Spanish missionary and a Spanish settler who disagree about the treatment of Native Americans forced to work in Spanish mines and factories of the period.

Support Materials

Assignments can include:

1. Chapter Review, pp. 76–77
2. Vocabulary and Comprehension Master V13
3. Test 2–6, p. CT11
4. Enrichment Master E11

UNIT 2

CHAPTER 7 The French Explore North America

Overview In the 1600s, France gained a vast empire in North America. Jacques Cartier claimed the lands between New England and the Gulf of St. Lawrence for the French king. Champlain set up trading posts and explored the Great Lakes, and La Salle's exploration of the Mississippi region gained Louisiana for France. France's empire in North America was dependent on a profitable fur trade.

Objectives

1. To understand the reasons why the French explored and settled lands in the New World.
2. To identify the major French explorers and their accomplishments.
3. To understand the problems of establishing settlements in New France.
4. To trace the routes of French explorers in North America.

Developing the Chapter

1. Motivation: Read the selection from Champlain's *The Voyages* on page 79 of this chapter aloud to the students. Explain that in this passage the French explorer describes how he made the Hurons his trading partners. Ask students to comment on Champlain's actions in dealing with the Native Americans. Ask them to predict the course of French relations with the Native Americans in the lands they explored.

2. Introduction

a. Write the chapter vocabulary words on the chalkboard. Have students write each word and its glossary definition in their vocabulary notebooks. Then, ask them to use the words in original sentences.

b. Have students read the chapter title and Objective question. Ask them to predict how French explorers might have gained a French empire in North America.

c. Have students preview the pictures and map in Chapter 7. Ask them to generalize about what was happening in North America during this period, based on the content of these visuals.

d. Have students read the chapter.

3. Review and Recall: After the students have read the chapter:

a. Have them ask each other questions about each section.

b. Have them reread and answer the Objective question.

c. Have them reread and answer each subhead question.

d. Have students make up a crossword puzzle using words and ideas from the chapter. After they have written all the Down and Across clues, they might try to solve each other's puzzles.

e. Have students play "Who Am I?" as a way of identifying important figures described in this chapter. Call on a volunteer to give five clues that will enable other students in the class to identify the person. Continue the game until all figures are identified.

4. Building Social Studies Skills: Have students look closely at the map on page 80. Use the map to review map-reading skills, pointing out the map key, scale, and compass rose. Using the map, have students identify the routes taken by early French explorers. Help them understand how these explorers could have used inland waterways to explore the interior of North America.

5. Extension

a. Ask students to role-play a meeting between prospective French immigrants to New France and a French explorer who is trying to interest them in moving to a French settlement in the New World. Ask students to keep in mind the kinds of questions these men and women would be most likely to ask.

b. Have students write diary entries for one of the explorers discussed in Chapter 7. Entries should include descriptions of the discoveries made during the journey as well as his reactions to what he saw. Encourage students to research additional facts in their class encyclopedias.

Support Materials

Assignments can include:

1. Chapter Review, pp. 82–83
2. Vocabulary and Comprehension Master V14
3. Test 2–7, p. CT12
4. Map Transparency Activity Sheet A5
5. Enrichment Master E12

UNIT 2

CHAPTER 8 England Founds a Colony

Overview   As the Spanish empire began to weaken, England, under the leadership of Queen Elizabeth I, rose to power. English exploration of the New World started in the 1580s with Sir Walter Raleigh's expedition to the east coast of North America. The settlement at Jamestown, Virginia was founded in 1607. Only with the planting of tobacco in 1610 did the first English colony become profitable.

Objectives

1. To understand how the English were able to usurp Spain's power as a world leader.

2. To learn about the first English settlement in the New World.

3. To understand the economic importance of tobacco as a cash crop in Jamestown.

Developing the Chapter

1. Motivation: Write the word "Croatona" on the chalkboard and explain that it is the name of a friendly tribe of Native Americans that lived in North Carolina. Explain that in 1585 a colony was first established on Roanoke Island, which is located off the coast of North Carolina. It did not last. However, in 1587, one hundred more colonists arrived to try to revitalize the settlement. English ships left for supplies and did not return until 1591. They found the settlement completely deserted; "Croatoan" was carved on the bark of a tree. The English settlers were never found, and to this day, historians are not sure what happened to them. Ask students to speculate on the fate of these colonists and why no trace of them was discovered.

2. Introduction

a. Write the vocabulary words on the chalkboard. Have students look up the meaning of each words in the glossaries and write it in their vocabulary notebook. Then, have students make up word search puzzles with all of the vocabulary words in the unit. The words can be hidden horizontally, diagonally, or vertically. Ask students to exchange papers and circle the words in each other's puzzle.

b. Have students read the chapter title and study the visuals. Have students speculate on what our lives would be like today if these early English settlements had not been established.

c. Have students read the chapter.

3. Review and Recall: After the students have read the chapter:

a. Have them reread the Objective question and answer it.

b. Have them reread the subhead question and answer it.

c. Have students identify an important event or concept in each section and explain what caused it to happen and what effect it brought about.

d. Have students look at the time line, page 88.

Ask: What important changes took place in North America between the founding of St. Augustine and exploration of the Mississippi River?

4. Building Social Studies Skills: Explain to students that compiling a bibliography is an important first step in writing a research report. Have students use the card catalog in their libraries to find at least six books that could be used in a report on the Jamestown settlement. Help them determine the subject heading to look under. Ask them to write down the author's name, the book title, its publisher, place of publication, and publication date on a separate file card.

5. Extension

a. Have students write original stories that could be examples of historical fiction. Their stories should be based on one of the incidents described in this chapter. Encourage them to do further research to find out more information about the episode they intend to write about.

b. Have students draw maps of the early Jamestown settlement in which they identify the key structures. Their maps should include legends, compass roses, and titles. Suggest that they use their class encyclopedias as initial research sources for information about the Jamestown colony.

c. Have students write research reports about the Native Americans who lived near the Jamestown colony. They should include information about the Native Americans' way of life as well as their relationship with the English settlers.

Support Materials

Assignments can include:

1. Chapter Review, pp. 88–89

2. Workbook, p. 17

3. Vocabulary and Comprehension Master V15

4. Test 2–8, p. CT13

5. Enrichment Master E13

UNIT 3

Colonies in the Americas Prosper and Grow

Unit Overview   By the middle of the eighteenth century, the English had completed their colonization of the New World, and the last of the original thirteen colonies had been established. These settlements were founded to provide havens for the victims of religious persecution as well as economic security for the immigrants. However, relations with the Native Americans worsened. With the establishment of the plantation system in the Southern colonies, Africans were brought into North America as slaves.

Unit Objectives

1. To understand the underlying causes for the English settlement of North America.
2. To identify similarities and differences between the colonies.
3. To understand how the English achieved colonial dominance in North America.
4. To learn how economic changes resulted in the slave system in the South.

Unit Introduction

1. **Motivation:** Begin by discussing the difficulties that immigrants to the New World faced in making a successful trans-Atlantic crossing in the 17th century. Use a picture of the landing of the Pilgrims at Plymouth Rock, or bring in pictures of the sailing vessels these early colonists would have used.
Ask: What preparations do you think these people would have made for their long journey? What are some of the problems that they would have encountered in crossing and upon arrival? When you consider these difficulties, why do you think the settlers wanted to come to North America?

Write students' answers on the chalkboard. Refer back to their predictions as they read.
2. **Visual:** Ask the students to compare the paintings on pages 92 and 93.
Ask: What is the feeling or tone that each painting creates for you? In which situation would you prefer to find yourself? Why? What do the paintings tell you about the people of the Massachusetts Bay Colony and Pennsylvania?
3. **Time Line:** Have the class read the events on the unit time line (pages 92 and 93). Ask students if they are familiar with any of the events shown, and have them share their knowledge with the class.

Ask: Which colonies were founded during the period covered on the time line? When was the first colony established (1607)? How many years elapsed between the founding of Jamestown and the founding of Georgia (126 years)?
4. **Historical Points of View:** Have students read the introductory paragraph.
Ask: What were the different views of religious freedom in the English colonies in the 1600s?

Have students read the first selection.
Ask: What was the penalty for having anything to do with a religious heretic, according to these early Connecticut laws? What do you think people who lived in this colony and who wanted to practice a different religion eventually had to do?

Next, have students read the second selection.
Ask: How did William Penn's views on religious toleration differ from those expressed in the selection you just read? In which colony would you have chosen to live and why?

Unit Activities

1. **Cooperative Learning:** Have students work in small groups to construct an illustrated time line that highlights major events in the founding of the 13 original colonies. Encourage students to use pictures cut out from old magazines or drawn by students to illustrate the time line.
2. **Research:** Have students research and write reports on the educational system that existed in these first thirteen colonies during the period covered by this unit. Encourage them to include information about the kinds of educational materials, rules, procedures, and equipment used.
3. **Creative Writing:** Have students write a series of diary entries that would have been written by a seventeenth-century colonist as he or she traveled along the Atlantic coast, visiting the different English colonies. The entries should reflect his or her views of the different life-styles in the colonies.
4. **Illustrating:** Have student make up diagrams that reflect how they would have planned an ''ideal'' colony. These plans should include houses and other key structures, such as schools and meeting places.

Support Materials

Assignments can include:
1. Unit 3 Review, pp. 120–121
2. Unit Vocabulary and Comprehension Masters, pp. V22–V23
3. Unit 3 Test, pp. UT5–UT6

UNIT 3

CHAPTER 1   Europeans Settle in New England

Overview   In the seventeenth century, the Pilgrims and the Puritans emigrated to the New World from England seeking religious freedom and economic security. The Pilgrims established a colony at Plymouth Harbor in 1620. Their plan of government was known as the Mayflower Compact. The Great Migration of Puritans from England to the New World began in 1630. Both the Puritans and the Pilgrims were intolerant of other religions.

Objectives

1. To understand why the Puritans and the Pilgrims came to the New World.
2. To understand the hardships faced by the first Pilgrim settlers.
3. To compare and contrast the Pilgrim and the Puritan colonies.
4. To learn about religious intolerance that existed in the Puritan and the Pilgrim colonies.

Developing the Chapter

1. Motivation: Ask students to imagine that they just arrived in a new land and are about to establish a settlement there. They decide to draw up a plan of government for the new colony. This plan will include a list of basic rights that will protect the citizens. Discuss some of the basic laws that students would include in the plan. Write students' answers on the chalkboard. Explain that in this chapter, students will learn about the form of government that was established in one of the original thirteen colonies in the United States.
Ask: Which of the laws just discussed do you think might have been included in this early colonial government?

2. Introduction
a. Write the chapter vocabulary words on the chalkboard. Have students write each word and its glossary definition in their vocabulary notebook. Ask volunteers to use each word in an original sentence.
b. Have students read the chapter title and the Objective question.
c. Have students preview the chapter visuals.
   Ask: What can you learn about life in the colonies from these pictures?
d. Have students read the chapter.

3. Review and Recall: After the students have read the chapter:
a. Have them reread and answer the Objective question.
b. Have them reread and answer each section question.
c. Write the following chart headings on the chalkboard: *Puritans* and *Pilgrims*. On the left-hand side of the chalkboard, write the following headings in list form: *Reasons for Leaving Britain; Where Settled; When Settled; Leaders; Religion; Form of Government; Religious Beliefs*. Ask students to complete the chart with information from the chapter.

4. Building Social Studies Skills: Direct students to the map on page 104. Briefly review map-reading skills, including the use of the direction indicator (compass rose), the scale, the legend, and the longitude and latitude markings. Then have students identify important locations on the map, such as Plymouth, Massachusetts Bay Colony, Salem, Boston, and neighboring colonies.

5. Extension
a. Have students write from the point of view of a Puritan or a Pilgrim settler diary entries that reflect the colonist's feelings about living in the New World. Call on volunteers to read aloud their diary entries to the rest of the class.
b. Have students do additional research about the Plymouth or the Massachusetts Colony in their school encyclopedias. Ask them to draw a diagram or make a diorama of one of the colonies that indicates the main buildings in each settlement.
c. Have groups of students prepare dramatizations in which Squanto helps the Pilgrim settlers by teaching them about their new environment. Call on different groups to present their dramatizations to the rest of the class.

Support Materials

Assignments can include:
1. Chapter Review, pp. 100–101
2. Vocabulary and Comprehension Master V18
3. Test 3-1, p. CT14
4. Enrichment Master E14

CHAPTER 2 Champions of Religious Freedom

Overview By 1700 the Massachusetts Bay, the Rhode Island, the Connecticut, and the New Hampshire colonies had been organized. These colonies were established by religious dissenters who sought the freedom to practice their beliefs and by those who wanted richer farm lands and less government. During this period, the conflict between the Native Americans and the settlers escalated.

Objectives

1. To learn about the founding of other New England colonies in the seventeenth century.
2. To identify the beliefs of such dissenters as Roger Williams and Anne Hutchinson.
3. To learn about the government of these colonies.
4. To identify the causes of conflict between the Native Americans and the settlers.

Developing the Chapter

1. Motivation: Point out that the title of this chapter is "Champions of Religious Freedom." **Ask:** When you think of the word *champion*, what do you usually associate it with? Who are some of the best-known champions in the area of politics or civil rights? Can you think of someone whom you consider to be a champion of religious freedom? Why do you think Americans have long considered religious freedom to be one of their most basic rights?

Explain that by reading this chapter, students will learn exactly who were these champions of religious freedom in the New England colonies.

2. Introduction

a. Write the chapter vocabulary words on the chalkboard. Have students write each word and its glossary definition in their vocabulary notebook. Have students work in pairs. Ask each student to make up an original sentence for each vocabulary word, leaving a blank space for the word. Have the students in each pair exchange papers and complete each other's sentence with the appropriate word.

b. Have students read the chapter title and the Objective question.

c. Have student discuss the chapter visuals.

d. Have students read the chapter.

3. Review and Recall: After the students have read the chapter:

a. Have them ask each other questions about each section in the chapter.

b. Have them reread the Objective question and answer it.

c. Call on volunteers to identify the main idea in each section.

d. Divide the class into teams to play "Who Am I?" based on the historical figures mentioned in this chapter. The students who pretend to be the historical figures must answer yes-or-no questions posed by the other team until the team guesses the identify of the figure.

e. Write the following headings on the chalkboard: *Rhode Island; Connecticut; New Hampshire; Maine.* On the left-hand side of the chart in list form, write the following: *Date Founded; Name of Founder; Why Founded; Result.* Have students complete the chart with appropriate information from the chapter.

4. Building Social Studies Skills: Remind students that a fact is something that can be proven to be true; an opinion cannot be proven because it tells what a person thinks or believes. Ask volunteers to identify one fact from Sections 3, 4, and 6. Then have students make up opinions based on the material in these sections.

5. Extension

a. Divide students into small groups. Have each group prepare an interview between a 20th-century television reporter and one of the historical figures discussed in this chapter. Call on different groups to present their dramatizations to the class.

b. Have students write first-person narratives about one of the conflicts between the Native Americans and the settlers described in this chapter. The narratives can be written from the point of view of either a Native American or a settler.

Support Materials

Assignments can include:

1. Chapter Review, pp. 106–107
2. Workbook, p. 18
3. Vocabulary and Comprehension Master V19
4. Test 3-2, p. CT15
5. Enrichment Master E15

UNIT 3

CHAPTER 3 Europeans Settle in the Middle Colonies

Overview By 1664 the English Middle colonies of New York, New Jersey, Pennsylvania, and Delaware had been established. Although the original Dutch and Swedish control there did not last, the religious toleration in their colonies attracted settlers from other European countries. The Quakers started a colony in Pennsylvania that was open to all religious groups.

Objectives

1. To learn about early Swedish and Dutch settlements in the New World.
2. To learn how New York and New Jersey developed as English colonies.
3. To understand how and why the Quakers settled Pennsylvania.
4. To understand the difference between the society of the Middle colonies and that of the Southern colonies.

Developing the Chapter

1. Motivation: Ask students to imagine that they belong to a religious group that seems dangerous to the government. The time is 1682. They decide to follow a leader to the New World to begin a settlement there. The land for their settlement had originally belonged to a group of Native Americans. Have students think about their own feelings concerning religious toleration and fairness in dealing with the Native Americans.

Ask: Would you require your colony to practice religious freedom? How would you do that? Would you make peace with the Native Americans who live there? How?

Tell students to think about these problems as they read about the settlement of the Middle colonies.

2. Introduction

a. Write the chapter vocabulary words on the chalkboard. Have students write each word and its glossary definition in their vocabulary notebook. Call on volunteers to describe each vocabulary word in a series of phrases or words. Have other students identify the word described.
b. Have student read the chapter title and the Objective question.
c. Have students preview the chapter visuals. Ask the class to list five facts they learned from the illustrations.

3. Review and Recall: After the students have read the chapter:

a. Have them reread the Objection question and answer it.
b. Point to various illustrations in the chapter. Have students explain how the visuals pertain to the chapter.
c. Have students identify the main idea in each section.
d. Write the following chart headings on the chalkboard: *New York; New Jersey; Pennsylvania; Delaware*. On the left-hand side of the chart in list form, write the following: *When Founded; Founder; Nationality; Location; Ideas about Religion*. Have students complete the chart with appropriate information.

4. Building Social Studies Skills: Remind students of the usefulness of a time line as a graphic aid for understanding historical events. Review how a time line should look and how it is constructed. Then work with students to create a time line of important events discussed in this chapter. For extra credit, encourage students to illustrate the time line.

5. Extension

a. Have students write letters to relatives in England from 17th-century Quaker settlers living in Pennsylvania. In the letters, students should express their feelings about their new land and about their leader, William Penn. Encourage students to do additional research about William Penn and the founding of Pennsylvania in their school encyclopedias.
b. Have students role-play interviews between a television journalist and each of the following: an indentured servant who lives in New York; a Quaker settler in Pennsylvania; William Penn; Hannah Penn; a Native American from the Delaware tribe in Pennsylvania. In the interview, the journalist should ask the individual questions about his or her life during this period. Have different groups present their vignettes to the class. Discuss the presentations after all have finished.

Support Materials

Assignments can include:

1. Chapter Review, pp. 112–113
2. Workbook, p. 12
3. Vocabulary and Comprehension Master V20
4. Test 3-3, p. CT16
5. Enrichment Master E16

UNIT 3

CHAPTER 4   Europeans Settle in the Southern Colonies

Overview   By 1773, the last of Great Britain's thirteen colonies in the New World had been established. Maryland was founded as a religious haven for Catholics. Carolina, which later split, was settled in 1670. Georgia gave English debtors a new start. Throughout this period, the status of Africans changed from that of indentured servants in the Northern colonies to slaves in the South.

Objectives

1. To understand why the colony of Maryland was settled.
2. To learn about the establishment of Carolina.
3. To learn how Georgia differed from other colonies.
4. To understand how the status of Africans changed.

Developing the Chapter

1. Motivation: Review some of the reasons why colonists came to the New World in the 17th century. Write students' answers on the chalkboard. Remind students that emigrants from other countries are still coming to the United States.
Ask: Where are these people coming from (South and Central America, the Soviet Union, Southeast Asia, Eastern European countries)? Why do you think these people are coming to the United States? How would you compare their reasons with those of the early settlers who established the original 13 colonies? Can you think of any reasons why you would choose to leave your homeland and move to another country?

Explain that students will learn about the last of the original 13 colonies in this chapter.

2. Introduction
a. Write the chapter vocabulary words on the chalkboard. Have students write each word and its glossary definition in their vocabulary notebook. Conduct a vocabulary bee.
b. Have students read the chapter title and the Objective question.
c. Have students preview the chapter visuals.
   Ask: What do these illustrations tell you about life in the Southern colonies?

3. Review and Recall: After the students have read the chapter:
a. Have them reread each subhead question.
b. Have them reread and answer the Objective question.
c. Have them make up a time line of the major events in the chapter.
d. Have them make up a crossword puzzle using words and ideas from the chapter. After they have written all the Down and Across clues, they might try to solve each other's puzzles.
e. Write the following headings on the chalkboard: *Maryland; Carolina; Georgia*. On the left-hand side of the chart, write the following in list form: *When Founded; Name of Founder; Reason for Settlement; Slavery*. Have students complete the chart with appropriate information from the chapter.

4. Building Social Studies Skills: Remind students that outlines are a useful way of organizing information. Briefly review the use of main headings, headings, and subheadings. Then point out that topical outlines, which do not use complete sentences, are often easier to write. Ask students to reread Sections 2, 4, 6, and 7 and to complete outlines of the paragraphs, using the following as a starter:
I. Establishing the Last Southern Colonies
   A. Maryland
      1. Founded by George Calvert
         a.
         b.
      2. Religious beliefs

5. Extension
a. Have students write speeches that would have been delivered either by Margaret Brent, who demanded the right to vote in the Maryland Assembly, or by a members of the assembly who denied her request. Call on volunteers to present their speeches.
b. Have students make up posters that are designed to attract settlers to one of the colonies. Ask them to include both text and illustrations that would appeal to potential colonists. Display the posters in the classroom.

Support Materials

Assignments can include:

1. Chapter Review, pp. 116–117
2. Workbook, p. 23
3. Vocabulary and Comprehension Master V21
4. Test 3-4, p. CT17
5. Map Transparency Activity Sheet A6
6. Enrichment Master E17

UNIT 4

Life in Colonial America

Unit Overview   Most of the settlers who came to the English colonies in the seventeenth and eighteenth centuries were farmers. The farming methods and the types of crops differed in New England, the Middle Colonies, and the South. Similarly, the exports from each of these three areas also varied. Religion, however, was a dominant force in all of the early colonies. The colonial governments also varied; however, in each colony there was a governor and an assembly of elected representatives. Some settlers moved west in the 18th century, pushing across the Appalachian barrier and bringing the settlers into conflict with Native Americans living on the western lands. While the English colonies continued to grow along the Atlantic coast, France and Spain also solidified their overseas empires in North America.

Unit Objectives

1. To explain how colonists in the thirteen British colonies lived.
2. To describe farming, shipping, and trade during the colonial period.
3. To compare and contrast religion, education, and government of the thirteen colonies.
4. To describe life in New France.
5. To describe life in New Spain.
6. To explain about frontier life and how it differed from life in the coastal colonies.

Unit Introduction

1. Motivation: Ask students to imagine themselves going back in time to America in the 17th and 18th centuries. Based on what they have already learned about the discovery and settlement of the New World, discuss where in North America would they like to live. Ask them to explain the reasons for their answers.
Ask: Would you have liked to live in New France, in New Spain, or in one of the English colonies? What do you think life was like in North America in the area you selected?
2. Visual: Direct students' attention to the unit visual on pages 122–123 of the textbook.
Ask: What does this illustration tell you about the country during this period?
   Point out that as students read the unit, they will see if their predictions are correct.
3. Time Line: Have the class study the time line on page 122–123 and read the events that are listed. Ask students if they are familiar with any of the events shown, and have them share their knowledge with the class.
Ask: What do these events indicate about the settlement and the growth of the country during this period?
   Encourage students to refer to the unit time line as they read the unit to help them put events in perspective.
4. Historical Points of View: Have students read the introduction to the two selections included in this feature. Review the meaning of toleration.
Ask: What do you think of people who want to practice their own religion freely but don't want other people to have the same freedom?
   Have students read the first selection. Explain that a heretic is a person who maintains religious beliefs that are contrary to the established church.
Ask: Who were the heretics referred to in this selection? Then have students read the second selection.
Ask: What is the "freedom of consciences" that William Penn refers to? During this period, would you have preferred Connecticut or Pennsylvania as a place to live? Why?
   Have students answer the question at the end of this feature.

Unit Activities

1. Cooperative Learning: Have students work in small groups to make up an illustrated time line that includes the major events described in this unit. Ask them to add dates to the time line as they read each chapter.
2. Research: Have students do library research on education in North America during the seventeenth and eighteenth centuries. They should prepare reports on education in either the English colonies, the frontier region, New France, or New Spain. Their reports should include reference to the kinds of educational materials available to children during this period.

Support Materials

Assignments can include:
1. Unit Review, pp. 168–169
2. Unit 4 Test UT4, pp. UT7–UT8
3. Map Transparency Activity Sheet A9

UNIT 4

CHAPTER 1   Farming in the Colonies

Overview   Farming methods and agricultural economies differed in the New England, the Middle, and the Southern colonies. In New England, with its short growing season, subsistence farmers grew enough for their own needs. Because of fertile soil and favorable climate, farms in the Middle colonies were larger, and the crops produced there were more varied. Large plantations dominated the fertile lowlands of the South, while subsistence farming developed in the Piedmont region.

Objectives

1. To understand the geographical differences between New England, the Middle colonies, and the South.
2. To describe the ways in which farming differed in the New England, the Middle, and the Southern colonies.
3. To explain how geographical differences resulted in differences in life-styles in the three regions.

Developing the Chapter

1. Motivation: Discuss how the kind of land in your area affects the way your students live.
Ask: How does the land influence the economy of the community, including jobs that are available? How does it affect the kind of homes you live in, your means of transportation, and your choice of recreational activities?

Have students imagine what their lives would be like if they lived in an environment that was radically different from their current one.

2. Introduction
a. Write the chapter vocabulary words on the chalkboard. Have students write each word and its glossary definition in their vocabulary notebook. Call on different students to make up a series of clues that will enable the other students to identify the vocabulary word in question. The clues can be synonyms, antonyms, or descriptions.
b. Have students read the chapter title and the Objective question. Elicit any information they might have about the differences between farming methods in the New England, the Middle, and the Southern colonies.
c. Have students preview the chapter visuals. What can students infer about colonial farming from the maps and illustrations?

d. Have students read the chapter.
3. Review and Recall: After the students have read the chapter:
a. Have them reread and answer the Objective question.
b. Have them reread and answer each subhead question.
c. Have students identify three similarities and three differences between farming in the New England, the Middle, and the Southern colonies.
d. Have students reread each section of the chapter and identify a cause and an effect described in each.
e. Divide students into teams. Have one student in a team describe three characteristics of farming in the New England, the Middle, or the Southern colonies. The other students should then identify the colonies being described. Have students reverse roles.

4. Building Social Studies Skills: Practice map skills using the maps on pages 127 and 130. Review the use of a compass rose, a map scale, and a legend. Have students identify crops that are grown in New England, the Middle colonies, and the Southern colonies. Then have them review the major geographical features of each section and relate these to their economic differences.

5. Extension
a. Have each student write a first-person narrative from the point of view of a farmer in the New England, the Middle, or the Southern colonies. In these narratives, students should describe what their lives are like and how they feel about living in that area of the country. Encourage students to do additional research in encyclopedias. Before they begin to write, review the use of the first-person pronoun.
b. Have students research and write reports about life on a farm in one of the colonies in the eighteenth century. Suggest that they use encyclopedias as sources.

Support Materials
Assignments can include:
1. Chapter Review, pp. 130–131
2. Vocabulary and Comprehension Master V24
3. Test 4-1, p. CT8
4. Map Transparency Activity Sheet A7–A8
5. Enrichment Master E18

UNIT 4

CHAPTER 2 Colonial Trade and Shipping

Overview   England strictly controlled the colonists' trading and shipping in the period before the Revolutionary War. The major colonial exports included forest products, whale oil, dried fish, farm goods from the Middle and the Southern colonies, and furs. Tobacco grown in the South proved to be one of the most profitable colonial exports. The colonists participated in the triangular trade with goods exchanged at three points: New England, the West Indies, and Africa. Eleven million Africans were brought to the Americas as part of this triangular trade route.

Objectives

1. To explain why Great Britain strictly managed the economic life of the colonies.
2. To list the products exported by the New England, the Middle, and the Southern colonies.
3. To explain the products and the routes that made up the triangular trade.
4. To outline the steps involved in the African slave trade.
5. To describe the influence of Africans on colonial life.

Developing the Chapter

1. Motivation: Read a passage from Alex Haley's *Roots* or other source about either the middle passage from Africa to the Americas or about the life of African slaves in the colonies before the Revolution. Encourage students to comment on the selection. In the process, elicit whatever information they might have about the slave trade of this period. Reinforce their knowledge by pointing to the map of the triangular trade route on page 135 of their textbook.

2. Introduction

a. Write the chapter vocabulary words on the chalkboard. Have students write each word and its glossary definition in their vocabulary notebook. Then have pairs of students write original sentences, leaving a blank for the vocabulary word. Have the student pairs exchange papers with another pair and complete each other's sentences with the correct words.

b. Have students read the chapter title and the Objective questions. Then have them preview the chapter visuals. Ask them what they think life in the colonies was like during this period.

c. Have students read the chapter.

3. Review and Recall: After the students have read the chapter:

a. Have students reread and answer the Objective question.

b. Have students reread and answer each subhead question.

c. Have students reread each section and make up questions to ask each other based on the content.

d. Have students identify the products and the routes that made up the triangular trade.

4. Building Social Studies Skills: Explain to students that using a scale of distance is an important map skill that enables them to understand the distances between locations. Help students to use the distance scale on the map on page 135 to calculate the distances between key points on the colonial trade routes.

5. Extension

a. Have students read a book of African folktales from their school library and write a report on it. Call on volunteers to read aloud their reports.

b. Have students imagine themselves as European merchants visiting the American colonies during the years before the Revolutionary War. Ask them to write letters to friends or relatives in which they describe an imaginary trip from New England to Virginia. Their letters should comment on the economic life of the different sections of the country.

c. Stage a class debate between an eighteenth-century Pennsylvania Quaker who doesn't believe in slavery and a Virginia plantation owner who owns large numbers of African slaves. Ask other students in the class to be prepared with five questions each to ask the debaters.

Support Materials

Assignments can include:

1. Chapter Review, pp. 136–137
2. Workbook, pp. 28–29
3. Vocabulary and Comprehension Master V25
4. Test 4-2, p. CT19
5. Enrichment Master E19

UNIT 4

CHAPTER 3 Religion and Education in the Colonies

Overview The lives of most colonists were strongly influenced by religion. Because children had to learn to read the Bible, schools were started in the colonies. The Puritans dominated New England. In the Middle colonies, the settlers represented many religious faiths. This ethnic diversity slowed the development of schools in this part of the country. In the South, education was controlled by the Anglican Church. The Great Awakening of the 1730s and 1740s weakened the power of the established churches.

Objectives

1. To explain the importance of religion and education in the lives of the colonists.
2. To compare and contrast religion and education of the New England, the Middle, and the Southern colonists.
3. To describe the effect of the Great Awakening on the lives of the colonists.
4. To explain how religious tolerance developed in the colonies.

Developing the Chapter

1. Motivation: Read students the following quotation from Jonathan Edwards, in which Edwards characterizes humanity:

A little wretched, despicable creature; a worm, a mere nothing, and less than nothing; a vile insect that has risen up in contempt against the majesty of Heaven and earth.

Ask students to tell you how this quotation makes them feel. Point out that the colonists who listened to Edwards preach in the 18th century were greatly moved by his sermons. Have students imagine themselves attending one of Edwards' services two hundred years ago.

Ask: Why do you think Edwards had such an effect on his followers?

2. Introduction

a. Write the chapter vocabulary words on the chalkboard. Have students write each word and its glossary definition in their vocabulary notebook. Then write sentences on the chalkboard using each vocabulary word in the chapter. Have students try to determine the words' meanings from context clues.

b. Have students read the chapter title and the Ob-

jective question. Then have them preview the chapter visuals.

Ask: How do you think religion influenced the lives of the colonists?

c. Have students read the chapter.

3. Review and Recall: After students have read the chapter:

a. Divide the class into teams. Each team represents either New England, the Middle colonies, or the South. Each team provides clues about its region. Collect the clues, and read them to the class. The students identify the section being described.

b. Have students reread the Objective question and answer it.

c. Have students reread each section question and answer it.

d. Have students make up a crossword puzzle using words from the chapter. After the Down and Across clues have been written, students solve each other's puzzles.

4. Building Social Studies Skills: Help students to make up headings for a chart that shows the religious and educational characteristics of the three areas. At the top, write the headings *New England, Middle Colonies,* and *Southern Colonies.* Along the left side, write the labels *Religion, Education, and Daily Life.* Help students fill in the chart with information from the text.

5. Extension

a. Have students write diary entries from the point of view of a student in a colonial school in either New England, the Middle colonies, or the Southern colonies during the eighteenth century. Students should describe a typical school day. Have students to do additional research in encyclopedias.

b. Have students write the first two pages of an historical novel that takes place in colonial America during the period covered in this chapter. Ask them to base their fictional excerpt on an incident or a concept described in this chapter.

Support Materials

Assignments can include:

1. Chapter Review, pp. 148–149
2. Vocabulary and Comprehension Master V26
3. Test 4-3, p. CT20
4. Enrichment Master E20

UNIT 4

CHAPTER 4 Government in the Colonies

Overview   There were three kinds of colonial government by the middle of the eighteenth century: royal, proprietary, and self-governing. In all of the colonies, the governor was the executive who enforced and carried out the law. The English Bill of Rights of 1689 formed the foundation of colonial liberties. However, discontent in Virginia led to Bacon's Rebellion in 1676.

Objectives

1. To describe the three kinds of government that existed in the colonies.
2. To identify the rights of the colonists.
3. To explain how laws were passed in the colonies.
4. To explain the reasons for discontent in the late 1600s.

Developing the Chapter

1. Motivation: Read students a selection from the Magna Carta. (This document is reprinted in most encyclopedias.) Ask students what rights are granted to citizens under this charter.

Ask: Do we enjoy these same rights in the United States today?

Point out that this document, which was signed by the English king, King John, in 1215 forms the basis of English law. Because American colonists were still British citizens until they declared their independence from Great Britain, they believed in these laws too. Explain that the Magna Carta guaranteed the principle that the king's power must be limited by law.

Ask: Why was this concept so important that it became the basis of the laws by which the American colonists lived?

2. Introduction

a. Write the chapter vocabulary words on the chalkboard. Have students write each word and its glossary definition in their vocabulary notebook. Ask students to work in pairs. Have each student in a pair make up sentences using the vocabulary words. In some sentences the words will be used correctly; in some sentences they will be used incorrectly. Have students exchange papers and correct each other's sentences.

b. Have students read the chapter title and the Objective question.

Ask: How do you think the British colonies were governed? What rights do you think the colonist

had? Write students' answers on the chalkboard in list form. Compare their answers to the information found in the text as the class reads the chapter.

c. Have students read the chapter.

3. Review and Recall: After the students have read the chapter:

a. Have students answer the chapter Objective question.

b. Have students answer each section question.

c. Have students reread each section and make up questions about its content to ask one another.

d. Have students play the game "Who Am I?" by providing clues to the identity of historical figures described in the chapter. The other students identify the person being described.

4. Building Social Studies Skills: Remind students that outlines are useful for organizing information about a particular topic. The main ideas become the headings in the outline; the supporting details, which provide additional information about the main ideas, are the subheadings in the outline. Work with them to complete the following outline:

Colonial Government

  I. Types of colonial government
 II. Responsibilities of a colonial governor
III. Colonial legislature

5. Extension

a. Have students write editorials for colonial newspapers of the late seventeenth century in which they either support or reject Bacon's Rebellion and the principles it represented. Alternatively, students could write news accounts of the rebellion for colonial newspapers of the period. Call on students to read aloud to the rest of the class their editorials or news accounts. Discuss the differences between an editorial and a newspaper article in terms of content and point of view.

b. Ask students to draw up lists of ten basic rights that they think should be guaranteed to members of a new colony or a settlement. Call volunteers to read aloud their lists. Are any rights found on all of the lists?

Support Materials

Assignments can include:

1. Chapter Review, pp. 148–149
2. Workbook, p. 24
3. Vocabulary and Comprehension Master V27
4. Test 4-4, p. CT21
5. Enrichment Master E21

UNIT 4

CHAPTER 5   Life in New France

Overview   New France was an important outpost for the French king because of its lucrative fur trade. He encouraged settlement of the colony, and during the middle of the 17th century he took greater direct control of the North American empire. Catholic priests and nuns took an important role in building New France, influencing both religious and political development. The cold climate proved to be an impediment to settlement, and to attract farmers the French government divided land along the St. Lawrence River into large tracts of land for development.

Objectives

1. To describe what life in New France was like.
2. To explain how New France was governed.
3. To explain the role of the Catholic Church in New France.
4. To describe the main groups of settlers in New France.

Developing the Chapter

1. Motivation: Point to the map of New France in the student textbook. Discuss the geographical location of the French empire in North America. Have students speculate on the climate and its effect on the lives of the settlers. Ask students to imagine themselves about to emigrate to this new land. What would probably attract them to the country? How would it be different from the land they left behind? How would they prepare for their journey?

2. Introduction

a. Write the chapter vocabulary words on the chalkboard. Have students write each word and its glossary definition in their vocabulary notebook. Have students write original sentences, leaving a blank for the vocabulary word. Ask them to exchange papers with a partner and to fill in each other's sentences with the correct vocabulary word.

b. Have students read the chapter title and the Objective question.

c. Have students preview the chapter visuals. Ask them to identify an important historical figure who will be discussed in the chapter.

d. Have student read the chapter.

3. Review and Recall: After the students have read the chapter:

a. Have students reread the chapter Objective question and answer it.

b. Have students reread the section questions and answer them.

c. Have students make up riddles with which to quiz each other about key terms, events, and people discussed in the chapter. One student will provide up to five clues that will enable the other student to make a correct identification. Students then reverse roles and continue the game.

d. Have students make up a time line for the events discussed in this chapter.

4. Building Social Studies Skills: Have students turn to the map of New France on page 151 and review the use of the map legend, the compass rose, the title, and the scale. Ask them to identify key locations in New France and, using the map scale, estimate the distance between them. Have them plot the most direct routes between these locations.

5. Extension

a. Have students create posters that would attract settlers to New France. Posters should include both text and illustration. Brainstorm with the students about the kind of verbal and visual appeals that would be most persuasive. When students have finished their assignment, display the posters.

b. Have students pretend to be settlers in New France. Ask them to write letters to friends or relatives in France in which they tell about their new home.

c. Have students research the Native Americans who lived in the area claimed by France in North America. Ask them to write reports describing the culture of these tribes and telling how they reacted to the French.

Support Materials

Assignments can include:

1. Chapter Review, pp. 154–155
2. Vocabulary and Enrichment Master V28
3. Test 4-5, p. CT22
4. Enrichment Master E22

UNIT 4

CHAPTER 6 Life in New Spain

Overview   The mining of gold and silver was a major source of income in New Spain. In addition, farming and ranching were important economic activities. As towns and cities were established, many Spaniards became skilled craftsworkers, producing silver and leather goods. The empire was ruled by a Spanish viceroy, or governor, who was appointed by the Spanish king. The Catholic Church played a major role in colonial life. The empire relied on forced labor done by Native Americans. However, New Spain was a cultural mixture of both Spanish and Native American traditions.

Objectives

1. To understand the economic objectives of New Spain.
2. To describe the life and the culture of New Spain.
3. To explain the government of New Spain.
4. To understand the relationship between the Spaniards and the Native Americans in New Spain.

Developing the Chapter

1. Motivation: Obtain and display pictures that show people diving in search of sunken treasure in the Caribbean. In addition, show pictures of the gold and silver jewelry recovered by such expeditions. Elicit any information that students already have about these treasure hunts.
Ask: How do you think the jewelry and coins got there? What can you deduce about the people who created them? What does this treasure tell us about the settlement of the New World in the seventeenth and eighteenth centuries?

2. Introduction
a. Write the chapter vocabulary words on the chalkboard. Have students write each word and its glossary definition in their vocabulary notebook. Call on students to give three clues that define one of the vocabulary words. Another student in the class must identify the vocabulary word being described.
b. Have students read the chapter title and the Objective question and review the chapter visuals. Ask them to imagine what life in New Spain was like.
c. Have students preview the map on page 000 and identify the geographical areas on the map.

d. Have students read the chapter.
3. Review and Recall: After students have read the chapter:
a. Have students reread and answer the Objective question.
b. Have students reread and answer each subhead question.
c. Divide the class into teams to play "Who Am I?" based on the people who lived in New Spain during this period and who were described or mentioned by name in the chapter. The person pretending to be a citizen of New Spain must answer yes-or-no questions posed by the other team until the team guesses the identity of the figure. The team with the most correct guesses wins.
d. Have students reread the section and ask each other questions based on the content.

4. Building Social Studies Skills: Have students reread one or more sections of the chapter and take notes on their reading. These notes should be written on file cards that include the subject heading, the book title, and the page reference. The notes should be written in an abbreviated form, with just the key facts and ideas noted. Have students who have read the same chapter section read aloud their note cards.

5. Extension
a. Have students write first-person narratives from the point of view of one of the following: a Native American worker in New Spain, a Spanish viceroy, a friar living in a mission in New Spain, a peninsulare, a criollo, or a mestizo. In their narratives, students should describe their lives and their feelings about living in the Spanish empire in the New World.
b. Have students make a map of a typical settlement in New Spain, including the mission buildings and other key structures. They should do additional research in encyclopedias, if necessary.

Support Materials

Assignments can include:
1. Chapter Review, pp. 160–161
2. Workbook, p. 25
3. Vocabulary and Comprehension Master V29
4. Test 4-6, p. CT23
5. Enrichment Master E23

UNIT 4

CHAPTER 7   Life on the Frontier

Overview   The frontier area of the country included all of the land west of the colonial settlements. Colonists moved west, lured there by the prospect of wilderness adventure and more land to farm and to settle. The Piedmont region was settled by the 1700s. Both the Great Wagon Road and the Wilderness Road were used by settlers to push back the frontier. In this area of the country, there was a spirit of social equality that contrasted with the more rigid social barriers of the established colonies.

Objectives

1. To describe the reasons why colonists moved west.
2. To explain how the early pioneers traveled west.
3. To explain the problems faced by frontier settlers.
4. To describe the conflicts between the Native Americans and settlers.
5. To describe the democratic spirit that characterized life on the frontier.

Developing the Chapter

1. Motivation: Encourage students to speculate on the lives of early frontier settlers.

Ask: Why do you think settlers moved west? What kind of people do you think they were? How did they react to their frontier experience?

2. Introduction

a. Write the chapter vocabulary words on the chalkboard. Have students write each word and its glossary definition in their vocabulary notebook. Then have students make up crossword puzzles with all the vocabulary words in the unit. The word clues must be given horizontally and vertically. Have students exchange papers and solve each others' puzzles.

b. Have students read the Objective question.

c. Have students read each section question.

d. Have students study the map of the Appalachian barrier on page 164 of their textbook. Ask them to locate the Cumberland Gap and to determine why so many settlers used this route to travel west.

e. Have students read the chapter.

3. Review and Recall: After the students have read the chapter:

a. Have them reread and answer the Objective question.

b. Have them reread and answer each section question.

c. Have them reread each section and the feature *Linking Geography and History.* Ask students to make up factual questions to ask each other based on these sections and the special feature.

d. Ask students to make a chart on which they list the reasons why settlers traveled west, how they traveled west, and the problems they faced in the west.

4. Building Social Studies Skills: Have students turn to the map of the Appalachian barrier on page 164 of their textbook. Using the map scale, have them determine the distance from a variety of cities across the Appalachians, using one of the westward routes favored by settlers.

5. Extension

a. Have students make dioramas of frontier cabins of the eighteenth century, in which they include cardboard cutouts of furniture and utensils. They should do additional research on frontier life during this period.

b. Have students write a series of diary entries from the point of view of a colonist traveling westward across the Appalachians in the middle of the eighteenth century. The entries should reflect the settlers' feelings about the journey and about the problems they encounter.

c. Have students role-play a confrontation between a Native American and a frontier settler that demonstrates their differing opinion about the ownership of the land that the colonists were settling. Call on volunteers to present their dramatization to the rest of the class.

Support Materials

Assignment can include:

1. Chapter Review, pp. 166–167
2. Workbook, p. 26–27
3. Vocabulary and Comprehension Master V30
4. Test 4-7, p. CT24
5. Enrichment Master E24

UNIT 5

America Wins Independence

Unit Overview The French and Indian War resulted in France's loss of almost all of its empire in the New World. After the war, Britain took steps to strengthen its vast land holdings in America. New taxes were imposed on the colonists in order to raise much needed funds for the crown. As a result, relations between Great Britain and the American colonies began to deteriorate. Further attempts by Britain to impose taxes on the colonists led to the Boston Massacre of 1770. For the next five years Britain and the colonies moved closer to war. The fighting began at Lexington in 1775 and led to the Declaration of Independence a year later. After the American victory at Saratoga in 1777, France joined the war. The last major battle of the war was the French and American victory at Yorktown in October 1781.

Unit Objectives

1. To learn about the French and Indian War and its effects on Britain's empire in North America.
2. To identify the events that led to the Revolutionary War.
3. To identify the important historical figures in the Revolutionary War.
4. To learn about the major conflicts of the war.
5. To explain how the war changed American life.

Unit Introduction

1. **Motivation:** Elicit any information that students already have about the Revolutionary War. Point to the map of North America in 1750 in Chapter 5 of Unit 4. Have students identify the original 13 colonies. Then point to the map of North America in 1783. Show students how the United States increased in size as a result of the war.

Ask: What would our lives be like today if the United States had lost the war to Great Britain? Explain that students will learn more about the causes of the war and its effect on the lives of Americans as they read this Unit.

2. **Visual:** The visual is John Trumbull's painting *The Battle of Bunker Hill*. Tell students that Trumbull took pains to be historically accurate.

Ask: From this painting, what can you tell about how wars were fought in the 1700s?

3. **Time Line:** Have students read the events on the unit time line and identify those they are already familiar with.

Ask: In general, what was happening in the colonies from the end of the French and Indian War until the meeting of the First Continental Congress in 1774? How long did the Revolutionary War last? When was the Declaration of Independence signed? When did France enter the war?

4. **Historical Points of View:** Have students read the introductory paragraph on pages 172–173.

Ask: What was the crucial difference between the British and colonial view of Britain's right to tax the colonies? Have them read the statement by the Stamp Act Congress of 1765, which explains the colonists' point of view.

Ask: How did the colonists compare their rights with those of natural born British citizens?

Have students read the second selection, which is from a British law of 1766.

Ask: How did the British Parliament feel about the rights of the American colonies to be govern themselves? Have students read and answer the questions under "Using Primary Sources."

Unit Activities

1. **Cooperative Learning:** Have students work together to create a colonial newspaper that reports on the events discussed in Unit 5. Some students can write news accounts of important events in each chapter. Others can write editorials that comment on these events, or they can draw political cartoons that provide another kind of commentary. Display the newspapers on the bulletin board.

2. **Research:** Have students do additional research on one of the important historical figures discussed in Unit 5. Possibilities include George Washington, Thomas Jefferson, Benjamin Franklin, Samuel Adams, Thomas Paine, or the Marquis de Lafayette. Then have them write a series of four or five diary entries by that person in which he or she comments on the events of the period.

Support Materials

Assignments can include:

1. Unit Review, pp. 220–221
2. Unit Vocabulary and Comprehension Masters V40–V41
3. Unit 5 Test, pp. UT9–UT10
4. Writing Workshop, pp. W13–W16

Unit 5

CHAPTER 1 The French and British Fight

Overview Both Great Britain and France laid claim to the Ohio River valley. Although war was not declared until 1756, fighting began in 1754 near Fort Duquesne. This was the start of the French and Indian War in North America; in Europe, the conflict was called the Seven Years' War. Although the French were outnumbered by the British colonists, they had the Native Americans as their allies. As a result of Britain's victory in the war, France gave up almost all of its territory in America.

Objectives

1. To identify the causes of the French and Indian War.
2. To understand the advantages and disadvantages of both sides in fighting the war.
3. To learn about the major battles of the war.
4. To explain the results of the war.
5. To explain the Albany Plan of Union.

Developing the Chapter

1. Motivation: Begin by referring students to the map of the French and Indian War in their textbooks. Point out that as a result of this war, Britain ruled Canada and all the land east of the Mississippi River except New Orleans, but including Florida. Compare this new area on the map to the land along the eastern seaboard that was the site of Britain's original thirteen colonies.

Ask: What does this conflict show you about the way in which our country grew to its present size? What would have happened if Britain had lost the war with France and had not gained all this territory? What would the United States be like if some of the country were still governed by France?

2. Introduction

a. Write the chapter vocabulary words on the chalkboard. Have students write each word and its glossary definition in their vocabulary notebooks. Ask volunteers to use each word in an original sentence. Write students' sentences on the chalkboard without the vocabulary word. Have other students in the class complete each sentence with the correct vocabulary word.

b. Have students read the chapter title and the Objective question. Then have them review the chapter visuals and the map on page 170.

Ask: Why was this conflict between France and Great Britain of such vital importance to the future of the British colonies?

c. Have students read the chapter.

3. Review and Recall: After the students have read the chapter:

a. Have them reread and answer the Objective question.

b. Have them reread and answer each section question.

c. Have them turn to the map of the French and Indian War on page 175. Ask them to identify which side was victorious in each of the major battles. Then have them provide two additional facts about each conflict highlighted on the map.

d. Have students make a chart listing the advantages of each side in the conflict.

e. Ask students to identify the results of the war for Britain, France, and the British colonies. List their answers on the chalkboard.

f. Ask students to summarize the Albany Plan of Union.

Ask: What is the significance of this Plan for the future of the thirteen colonies?

4. Building Social Studies Skills: Remind students of the differences between a primary and secondary source. Have students identify the primary source in this chapter (Benjamin Franklin's letter). Ask them to list the primary and secondary sources they would use in preparing a report on the French and Indian War.

5. Extension

a. Have students write diary entries written from the point of view of a colonial soldier, a French soldier, or a Native American after a major battle of the French and Indian War.

b. Have students write an editorial for a colonial newspaper commenting on the British victory in the French and Indian War and predicting the future course of colonial-British relations.

Support Materials

Assignments can include:

1. Chapter Review, pp. 178–179
2. Vocabulary and Comprehension Master V42
3. Test 5-1, p. CT25
4. Enrichment Master E25

CHAPTER 2 Britain Tightens Its Grip

Overview   After the French and Indian War, Great Britain imposed stricter trade and governmental sanctions on its American colonies. As a result of Pontiac's Rebellion, the Proclamation of 1763 forbade colonists to settle in lands west of the Appalachians. In order to pay off its huge war debt and to provide money for governing the colonies, Great Britain began enforcing the Navigation Acts and imposed new and more restrictive taxes. The Quartering Act was passed in 1763. As a result of these measures, Britain's relations with its American colonies became strained.

Objectives

1. To understand the measures taken by Great Britain to increase its control over its American colonies after the French and Indian War.
2. To learn about the Proclamation of 1763, the Navigation Acts, the Sugar Act of 1764, and the Quartering Act of 1765.
3. To explain how the colonists felt about England's more restrictive trade and governmental policies.

Developing the Chapter

1. Motivation: Read students the excerpt from the Proclamation of 1763 on page 181 of the chapter. Explain that this was a proclamation by King George III of Great Britain that closed lands west of the Appalachians to American colonists. Ask students to imagine themselves living in America during this period.

Ask: How would you feel about this proclamation if you were a Native American? How would you feel about this proclamation if you were an American colonist? How would this new land make you feel about Great Britain? Why do you think Great Britain issued this proclamation?

2. Introduction

a. Write the chapter vocabulary words on the chalkboard. Have students write each word and its glossary definition in their vocabulary notebooks. Then write a phrase defining each on the chalkboard. Have students match each word with the phrase that defines it. Then ask them to use each word in a sentence.

b. Have students read the chapter titles and the Objective question.

Ask: Why do you think that Great Britain wanted to govern its American colonies more strictly?

c. Have students preview the chapter visuals.

Ask: What do you think life in American during this period was like? How is the country changing? Why would it be difficult for Great Britain to govern so vast an empire at such a great distance?

d. Have students read the chapter.

3. Review and Recall: After the students have read the chapter:

a. Have them reread the Objective question and answer it.

b. Have them reread each section question and answer it.

c. Have them make up questions based on the content of each section and quiz one another.

d. Have students make up a chart of the restrictive laws that were passed by Great Britain after the French and Indian War. The headings should include the name of the law, the date when it was passed, and its provisions.

4. Building Social Studies Skills: Use the map on page 184 of this chapter to review map reading skills with the students. Point out the map legend, the scale of distance, the compass rose, and longitude and latitude markings. Then ask students to identify key cities and geographical boundaries. Have them determine the distance between cities.

5. Extension

a. Ask students to draw political cartoons about one of the events described in this chapter. Their cartoons can be illustrations for either a British or a colonial newspaper of the period. Display the cartoons in class, and discuss the differences in point of view expressed by each.

b. Have students role-play an interview between a twentieth-century reporter and an American colonist immediately after one of the restrictive economic or governmental measures was passed by Great Britain. Call on different groups of students to present their dramatizations for the rest of the class.

Support Materials

Assignments can include:

1. Chapter Review, pp. 184–185
2. Vocabulary and Comprehension Master V34
3. Test 5-2, p. CT26
4. Map Transparency Activity Sheet A10
5. Enrichment Master E26

Unit 5

CHAPTER 3   The Colonists Resist

Overview   Relations between Great Britain and the American colonies continued to deteriorate. The British government passed a series of laws that led to protests by the colonists, who opposed both the Stamp Act of 1765 and the Townshend Acts of 1767. Both laws imposed taxes on goods and products produced in the colonies and imported from abroad. Colonists strongly objected to paying taxes without being allowed to vote for members of Parliament. They refused to pay the taxes and boycotted British goods. Antagonism between the two sides led to the Boston Massacre of 1770.

Objectives

1. To identify the various tax laws passed by the British government.
2. To understand why the colonists opposed these laws and what forms these protests took.
3. To identify the differences between the colonies' and Britain's attitudes toward government.
4. To learn how the colonists began to unite during this period.
5. To learn about the Boston Massacre.

Developing the Chapter

1. Motivation: Elicit as much information as possible about the student's knowledge of what taxes are and how the money derived from taxes is used by the state and national governments.

Ask: What would happen to our country if people refused to pay taxes? Do you think the citizens of a country should have the right to refuse to obey a regulation imposed by their government? What are some ways by which citizens can show their dissatisfaction with what the government is doing? What happened when the American colonists became dissatisfied with the way they were being governed by Great Britain?

2. Introduction

a. Have students locate the new chapter vocabulary words in the text. Ask them to write each word and its glossary definition in their vocabulary notebooks. Call on students to volunteer a synonym for each word. Write the synonyms on the chalkboard. Ask other students to identify the original vocabulary words.

b. Have students read the chapter title and the Objective question. Elicit any information students have about how the colonists resisted the new tax laws.

c. Have students preview the chapter visuals. Ask them to imagine what life in the colonies during this period was like.

d. Have students read the chapter.

3. Review and Recall: After the students have read the chapter:

a. Have them reread and answer the Objective question.

b. Have them reread and answer each section question.

c. Have students work in teams. One student will summarize the main points of a particular British law that was discussed in this chapter. The other student will identify the law and give the date when it was passed.

d. Have them list the ways in which the passage of the restrictive measures affected the colonists. Write their answers on the chalkboard.

e. Have students list the ways the colonists began to unite during this period.

4. Building Social Studies Skills: Remind students of the value of making up a time line to organize the major events of a particular period in chronological order. Help students make up a time line from 1765 to 1773 that includes the important events discussed in this chapter.

Ask: What can you conclude about the kinds of events that were taking place in the American colonies during this period?

5. Extension

a. Have students write speeches that might have been made by Samuel Adams to stir up the colonists' anger against the British for their repressive measures. Call on students to read their speeches aloud to the class.

b. Have students role-play a confrontation between a colonial governor, appointed by the king, and a member of the Sons of Liberty or the Daughters of Liberty. Call on different groups to present their dramatizations.

Support Materials

Assignments can include:

1. Chapter Review, pp. 190–191
2. Vocabulary and Comprehension Master V35
3. Test 5-3, p. CT27
4. Enrichment Master E27

Unit 5

CHAPTER 4 Liberty or Death

Overview Between 1773 and 1775 the British government imposed new taxes and laws that pushed both sides close to war. In response to the Tea Act of 1773, Americans staged the Boston Tea Party. As punishment, the British government passed the Intolerable Acts of 1774, restricting the colonists' rights and freedoms. The First Continental Congress was convened in September 1774 and produced a Declaration of Rights. On April 19, 1775, the Revolutionary War began with fighting at Lexington.

Objectives

1. To learn about the Boston Tea Party and its aftermath.
2. To identify the series of repressive measures taken by the British government.
3. To learn how the colonists united to oppose the British.
4. To learn about the First Continental Congress.
5. To understand what took place at the Battle of Lexington.

Developing the Chapter

1. Motivation: Read students the full text of Patrick Henry's speech to the Virginia assembly in March, 1775, when he declared, ''Give me liberty or give me death!'' Ask students to listen to his words and imagine themselves as colonists of the period.
Ask: How would you have reacted to his words? Considering what was happening in the colonies during this period, what do you think these words would incite the colonists to do? What would you have done in their place?
2. Introduction
a. Write the chapter vocabulary words on the chalkboard. Have students write each word and its glossary definition in their vocabulary notebooks. Write sentences on the chalkboard, using each vocabulary word from the chapter. (You might want to use the sentences in the Chapter Review as a guide.) Have students try to determine the words' meanings from context clues.
b. Have students read the chapter title and the Objective question. Call on volunteers to suggest answers to the Objective question.
c. Have students preview the chapter visuals.

Ask: What do you think was happening in the American colonies during this period?
d. Have students read the chapter.

3. Review and Recall: After the students have read the chapter:
a. Have them ask each other questions about the chapter's content.
b. Have them reread and answer the Objective question.
c. Have them reread and answer each section question.
d. Make a chart of the taxes and other laws passed by the British that forced the Americans to unite. The heading should include the following information: Name, Date Passed, Major Provisions, and Reaction of Colonists. Call on different students to complete the chart.

4. Building Social Studies Skills: Review with students the importance of a bibliography of books and articles that can be useful in writing research reports. Ask each student to choose an event discussed in this chapter that could be the topic for a research report. Have students find at least six books in their school library to include in a bibliography. Help them use the subject index of the card catalogue. Ask them to write the author, title, publisher, and date of publication on each book's file card.

5. Extension
a. Have students stage a mock news program in which key historical figures mentioned in this chapter meet twentieth-century reporters to discuss the events that took place between the passage of the Tea Act and the Battle of Lexington. The other students in the class should be members of the studio audience and can ask the panel members questions.
b. Have students write first-person accounts of one of the events described in this chapter from the point of view of an American colonist of the period who witnessed the event.

Support Materials

Assignments can include:
1. Chapter Review, pp. 196–197
2. Workbook, p. 30
3. Vocabulary and Comprehension Master V36
4. Test 5-4, p. CT28
5. Enrichment Master E28

CHAPTER 5   Independence Is Declared

Overview   The members of the Continental Congress, meeting in Philadelphia in May 1775, made preparations for war while trying to maintain peace with Great Britain. At the Battle of Bunker Hill, British troops fought the colonial militia. Hessians were hired by George III to aid the war effort. Americans were urged to fight for their independence by Thomas Paine in *Common Sense*. Six months later, on July 4, 1776, the Second Continental Congress adopted the Declaration of Independence. The ideals set forth in this document have been the basis of democratic freedoms in this country ever since.

Objectives

1. To understand what was accomplished by the Second Continental Congress.
2. To learn how Thomas Paine's *Common Sense* affected the American colonists.
3. To understand the principles of the Declaration of Independence.
4. To identify the underlying causes of the Revolutionary War.
5. To understand how Americans felt about themselves and Great Britain during this period.

Developing the Chapter

1. Motivation: Read students selections from the Declaration of Independence. (Note: This document is reprinted on pages 204–207.) Discuss the selection with the class. Have students identify the most important points in the selection that you read.

Ask: How are we still affected by the principles set forth in this document? How do you think the British king would have reacted to this document? What risks faced the signers of the Declaration? What would have happened to them if the United States had lost the war? What would our lives be like today without this document?

2. Introduction

a. Write the chapter vocabulary words on the chalkboard. Have students write each word and its glossary definition in their vocabulary notebooks. Ask volunteers to use each vocabulary word in an original sentence.

b. Have students read the chapter title and the Objective question.
   Ask: Why do you think the Americans finally

declared their independence from Great Britain?

c. Have students preview the visuals.
   Ask: What are some of the important events that took place during the period covered in this chapter?

d. Have students read the chapter.

3. Review and Recall: After the students have read the chapter:

a. Have them reread the Objective question and answer it.
b. Have them reread each section question and answer it.
c. Have them sum up the achievements of the Second Continental Congress.
d. Have them identify the influence of Thomas Paine's *Common Sense* on the colonists.
e. Have them list key freedoms set forth in the Declaration of Independence.

4. Building Social Studies Skills: Have students take notes on this chapter. Their notes should include the most important points of each section in list form. These should be written in phrases, rather than complete sentences, in order to save time and space. Ask students to write their notes on file cards. Call on volunteers to read their notecards aloud to the class. Compare notecards that were written by different students about the same section of the text.

5. Extension

a. Have students imagine themselves to be American colonists during the period covered by this chapter. They have just read the Declaration of Independence. How do they feel about this document and about the events that led up to it? Have students write diary entries in which these imaginary colonists express their thoughts about recent events.

b. Have students research and write reports about one of the key historical figures discussed in this chapter. Suggest they do additional research in encyclopedias, biographies, and autobiographies.

Support Materials

Assignments can include:

1. Chapter Review, pp. 202–203
2. Workbook, p. 31
3. Vocabulary and Comprehension Master V37
4. Test 5-5, p. CT29
5. Enrichment Master E29

CHAPTER 6   The American Revolution

Overview   The Revolutionary War lasted from 1775 until 1781. Both the British and the Americans had advantages and serious problems in fighting the war. The turning point of the war was the Battle of Saratoga in 1777. The American victory brought France into the war as an American ally. After Saratoga, most of the major battles were fought in the South. The last important battle was at Yorktown in October 1781.

Objectives

1. To identify the advantages and disadvantages faced by the American and British armies in the Revolutionary War.
2. To learn about the major battles and campaigns of the war.
3. To learn about major figures who played a prominent role in the war.
4. To understand the important part played by the French in helping the Americans win the war.

Developing the Chapter

1. Motivation: Ask students what they know about the Revolutionary War. As they respond, write their answers on the chalkboard.

Ask: What do you think it was like to be an American colonist during the Revolutionary War? What are some of the ways in which the colonists' lives were changed by the war?

2. Introduction

a. Write the chapter's vocabulary words on the chalkboard. Have students write each word and its glossary definition in their vocabulary notebooks. Ask students to write a synonym for each word. Have volunteers identify the vocabulary words for the synonyms.

b. Have students read the chapter title and Objective question. Then have them preview the chapter visuals and map on page 210. Ask students to identify some key figures who participated in the Revolutionary War. What conclusions can students reach about the major battles of the war based on the map on page 210? Direct their attention to the picture of Washington reviewing the troops at Valley Forge.

Ask: What conditions did the American soldiers face at Valley Forge? How do you think they reacted to these conditions?

c. Have students read the chapter.

3. Review and Recall: After the students have read the chapter:

a. Have them reread and answer the Objective question.

b. Have them reread and answer each section question.

c. Make a chart of the major battles of the Revolutionary War on the chalkboard. The heading at the top of the chart should include the following items: Battle, Date, Participants, Place, Result, and Effect on the War Effort. Have students complete the chart.

d. On the chalkboard write four columns: American Advantages, American Disadvantages, British Advantages, and British Disadvantages. Have students complete each column with information about the British and colonial forces during the Revolutionary War.

4. Building Social Studies Skills: Review basic map reading skills with the students by asking them questions about the map of the Revolutionary War on page 210 of the chapter. Have them identify the location of the major battles. Using the map legend, ask students what factual information they can find out about each battle.

5. Extension

a. Ask students to imagine themselves as George Washington addressing his troops during the severe winter of 1777–1778 at Valley Forge. Have students write speeches in which Washington exhorts his soldiers not to give up. Call on volunteers to read their speeches aloud.

b. Have students select one of the major battles of the Revolutionary War and make a map illustrating this particular military campaign. Explain that a military map uses symbols to represent both sides in the conflict and arrows to indicate the direction of the assault. The symbols are explained on the map legend. Students should do additional research on the battle.

Support Materials

Assignments can include:

1. Chapter Review, pp. 212–213
2. Workbook, pp. 32–34
3. Vocabulary and Comprension Master V38
4. Test 5-6, p. CT30
5. Map Transparency Activity Sheet A11
6. Enrichment Master E30

UNIT 5

CHAPTER 7   The Revolutionary War Changes American Life

Overview   All Americans were affected by the Revolutionary War in one way or another. Women helped the war effort by taking over men's jobs or traveling to army camps with their husbands. Many African Americans served in the American Army and fought in the major battles of the Revolution. The war divided Patriots, who supported the colonial cause, and Loyalists, who remained loyal to George III. Many Loyalists lost their homes and lands as a result of their political beliefs. The Treaty of Paris benefited the colonists economically, politically, and geographically.

Objectives

1. To understand the contributions of women and African Americans to the war effort.
2. To learn how the Revolution divided Loyalist and Patriot.
3. To identify the key provisions of the Treaty of Paris.
4. To identify key figures in the Revolutionary War.
5. To understand how the boundaries of the United States changed as a result of the war.

Developing the Chapter

1. Motivation: Point out to students that not everyone in the thirteen states supported the cause of independence during the Revolutionary War. There were many people, called Loyalists, who stayed loyal to Great Britain and its king.

Ask: What reasons might an American have for loyalty to Great Britain? If you were an American who supported the Revolution, what would you think should be done about the Loyalists? If you were a Loyalist, what would you try to do?

2. Introduction

a. Write the chapter vocabulary words on the chalkboard. Have students write each word and its glossary definition in their vocabulary notebooks. Then have students make up word-search puzzles with all of the vocabulary words in the unit. The words can be hidden horizontally, vertically, or diagonally. Ask students to exchange papers and circle the words in each other's word-search puzzle.

b. Have students read the chapter title and Objective question. Ask them to speculate on the ways in which the American Revolution changed American life.

c. Direct students' attention to the map on page 220 of their textbooks. Have them study the boundaries of the United States after the Revolutionary War.

Ask: How do the boundaries of the United States in this map of 1783 compare with America of 1763 in the map on page 184 of Chapter 2?

d. Have students read the chapter.

3. Review and Recall: After the students have read the chapter:

a. Have them reread and answer the Objective question.

b. Have them reread and answer each section question.

c. Have students play "Who Am I?" based on the historical figures discussed in this chapter. The student pretending to be the Revolutionary figure must answer yes-or-no questions posed by the other team until the team guesses the identity of the student.

4. Building Social Studies Skills: Remind students of the usefulness of charts to organize information. Help students prepare a chart that shows what Americans gained from the peace settlement with Britain. The headings at the top of the chart should read: Political Results, Economic Results, and Geographical Results. Help students complete the chart with the appropriate information.

5. Extension

a. Have students pretend to be Loyalists who are about to leave the United States for Canada after the Revolutionary War. Have them write letters to their cousins in England in which they express their feelings about the war and give their reasons for supporting Britain.

b. Have students write editorials for eighteenth-century colonial newspapers about the terms of the Treaty of Paris and the effect of this settlement on the United States.

Support Materials

Assignments can include:

1. Chapter Review, pp. 218–219
2. Workbook, p. 35
3. Vocabulary and Comprehension Master V39
4. Test 5-7, p. CT31
5. Enrichment Master E31

UNIT 6

A New Government, a New Nation

Unit Overview   After the Revolutionary War, the Articles of Confederation became the basis for the United States government. But the new government lacked real power, especially the power to raise money through taxes. However, the United States Constitution, which was adopted in 1789, created a federal government strong and flexible enough to meet the challenges of a growing nation. President Thomas Jefferson bought the Louisiana Territory from France in 1803 and financed the Lewis and Clark and the Pike expeditions to explore the new lands. In 1812, the United States found itself again at war with Great Britain. The dispute was resolved by the Treaty of Ghent. President Andrew Jackson expanded the concept of democracy by extending to white men who were not property owners the right to vote. During his term in office, political conventions began to be used to determine party candidates for national elections. Jackson supported the Removal Act, which was passed in 1830 and forced thousands of Native Americans from their homelands.

Unit Objectives

1. To learn why the Articles of Confederation left the central government too weak to function effectively.
2. To understand how the Constitution created a federal government that was strong enough to protect the states and ensure personal freedoms.
3. To understand how each President, from Washington to Jackson, made changes in the government.
4. To understand how early presidential actions such as the Louisiana Purchase affected the country.

Unit Introduction

1. Motivation: Explain to the students that in this unit they will learn about some important compromises. Ask students to define the word *compromise*. Give students five situations that call for compromise, and ask them to quickly write a compromise for each situation. Call on volunteers to share their compromises with the class.

2. Visual: Ask students to look at the unit opening painting by Howard Chandler Christie. Explain that this is a reproduction of a mural in the United States Capitol building.

Ask: Why was the signing of the Constitution a very important event in the history of the United States? What moment does this picture show? (It shows the vote on whether or not to adopt the Constitution.) Ask students to identify as many participants as they can. (George Washington is standing behind the desk; Benjamin Franklin is seated in the chair in the foreground; James Madison is seated to the right of Franklin.)

Explain that in Unit 6 they will read about events that led to the writing of the Constitution and will learn how the United States government functioned in the early years of the Union.

3. Time Line: Have students read the events shown on the unit time line, pages 222–223. Ask them whether they are familiar with any of the events shown, and have them share their knowledge with the class. Encourage students as they study the unit to refer to the unit time line to help them put events in perspective.

4. Historical Viewpoints: Ask students to read the two excerpts on pages 224–225.

Ask: Why did Jonathan Smith object to having a weak central government? What is the "tyranny of many" to which he refers? Why was Jonathan Smith afraid that Americans would never have another chance to change their form of government? How did Patrick Henry see the government under the Articles of Confederation? Why was Patrick Henry against a stronger central government?

Unit Activities

1. Cooperative Learning: Have students work in small groups. Each group should create a news poster for an event on the time line. Encourage students to use pictures cut from magazines or drawn by themselves to illustrate their posters.

2. Research: Have students do additional research on one of the important historical figures discussed in Unit 6. Possibilities might include George Washington, Thomas Jefferson, Patrick Henry, Tecumseh, or Andrew Jackson. Each student should create a display entitled *How I Helped Change America* featuring the contributions of the historical figure.

Support Materials

Assignments can include:
1. Unit 6 Review, pp. 304–305
2. Unit Vocabulary and Comprehension Masters V50–V51
3. Unit 6 Test, pp. UT11–UT12
4. Map Transparency Activity Sheet A13

T61

UNIT 6

CHAPTER 1 The New Nation Stumbles

Overview   In 1777 the Second Continental Congress proposed a plan of government for the new nation. It called for just one branch of government: the Congress. Congress was given the power to make war, negotiate treaties, and coin money but was denied the power to tax individuals or states. It therefore could not raise money for armed forces or settle debts from the Revolutionary War. Because Congress was not empowered to raise money to fund an army, the nation could not defend itself. Pirates seized United States ships on the Mediterranean Sea and Great Britain violated the Treaty of Paris by maintaining forts in the American Northwest. In Massachusetts, taxes increased and landowners accrued debts. Soon farmers owed creditors money. The courts' move to seize these farmers' property led to Shays's Rebellion, an attempt by the farmers to seize an arsenal as a form of protest.

Objectives

1. To identify the plan of government that the United States adopted after the Revolution.
2. To describe the new government's weaknesses in dealing with domestic and foreign problems.
3. To list the effects of Shays's Rebellion on the new nation.

Developing the Chapter

1. Motivation: Show the students pictures of different demonstrations and rebellions such as peace marches and civil-rights marches during the 1960s and the actions of the Chinese students in Tienamen Square in the 1980s, as well as illustrations of Shays's Rebellion in the 1700s. Tell the students that the people who are pictured are expressing discontent with their government. Ask them to tell the changes that can be forged from demonstrations, civil disobedience, and rebellion. List some of the changes that did occur because of the civil-rights demonstrations, for example. Ask them to evaluate the changes and to speculate on why some protests cause beneficial changes while others lead to more oppression.

2. Introduction

a. Write the chapter vocabulary words on the chalkboard. Have students write each word and its glossary definition in their vocabulary notebook. Ask each student, in turn, to use a vocabulary word in a sentence.

b. Have students read the chapter title and the Objective question. Have students read the chapter.

3. Review and Recall: After the students have read the chapter:

a. Have them ask each other questions about the chapter content.

b. Have them reread each subhead question and answer it.

c. Have them work in small groups or in pairs. Assign the following topics: (1) the role of the Second Continental Congress in forming a new government, (2) the role of European nations in forming a stronger government, (3) the role of Shays's Rebellion in strengthening the new government, and (4) the role of popular opinion in strengthening the new government.

d. Have students look at the chart on page 230. **Ask:** Why did the federation government fail to build a strong nation?

4. Building Social Studies Skills: Explain to students that making a chart is an important skill that helps them both to organize and understand new information or concepts. Guide students in reading the chart on page 230. Then assign Skill Builder: Completing a Chart, page 230 of the chapter text.

5. Extension

a. Divide the students into six groups and have each group write six questions for a game category. Topics for the game might include problems that arose because there were no taxes, the components of the new government, and people in history. Have each group ask the other groups questions. Assign two points for a correct answer and one point for an assisted correct answer.

b. Have students research different types of governments, such as parliamentary government, monarchy, democratic monarchies, and Communist party systems. Encourage the students to create a chart that describes the branches of each government and the powers held by each branch.

Support Materials

Assignments can include:

1. Chapter Review, pp. 230–231
2. Vocabulary and Comprehension Master V42
3. Test 6-1, p. CT32
4. Enrichment Master E32

UNIT 6

CHAPTER 2   Making the Constitution

Overview   The Constitutional Convention met in Philadelphia in 1787 to decide on a new plan of government. The Virginia Plan, sponsored by James Madison, proposed that states that have larger populations have a greater number of votes in the legislative branch. New Jersey, a small state, wanted all states to have equal say. Connecticut's Great Compromise resulted, wherein each state elected two senators but was represented in the House of Representatives according to its population. It was agreed that three-fifths of the slave population would be counted in the vote. The plan became law upon ratification by nine of the thirteen states.

Objectives

1. To list the problems in writing a new plan of government.
2. To identify the delegates to the Constitutional Convention.
3. To recognize the issues key to this convention and how conflicts among the states were resolved.
4. To understand the importance of the Constitution to Americans today.

Developing the Chapter

1. Motivation: Ask students to recall what was discussed in the last chapter about the need for a new government. Ask them if they agree that the government under the Articles of Confederation needed changing and, if so, why. Explain that this chapter will show them how the problems of having a weak central government were resolved by the Constitution. Tell them that by reading this chapter, they will learn about the government that is still in operation in the United States today.

2. Introduction

a. Write the chapter vocabulary words on the chalkboard. Have students write each word and its glossary definition in their vocabulary notebook. Ask each student, in turn, to use a vocabulary word in a sentence.
b. Have students read the chapter title and the Objective question.
c. Tell students that there are some people in the world who think that the United States Constitution is the most perfect document in the world. Point out that it has worked for more

than two hundred years. In that time span, the United States government has only once faced a major attempt at revolution. Ask students why they think the American people have, for the most part, been content with the way their country is governed. Direct students' attention to paragraphs 6 and 7. Tell them to memorize what is in those paragraphs, as it is the basis for our entire government.
d. Have students read the chapter.

3. Review and Recall: Ask students to name the three branches of the government and to tell what each does. Then ask about our election system. Use as an example two mock states—one having 10,000 people, the other having 100,000 people. **Ask:** How many votes will there be in a presidential election from each state? How many senators will each state have? How many representatives will each have, assuming that there is one representative for every 10,000 people?

4. Building Social Studies Skills: Show students the map of the Eastern United States on page 674 of their book. Ask them to locate the place where the Constitutional Convention took place. Then ask them to see how far Philadelphia is from New York. Indicate that in the late 1700s, most business took place in New York. Have small groups decide which city would probably become the nation's capital.

5. Extension: Divide the class into two "states" of equal numbers of people. Tell them you are going to create a scenario to help them to understand the election system in the new government. Give them a choice of two "candidates" to vote for, whom you have described as follows: one thinks children should not have to go to school after age 12; the other says that the age should be 16. Give one state one vote for each student, and the other state one vote for every three students. After the votes are cast, ask students to compare the fairness of the voting system assigned to each state. Indicate that this three-fifths vote is what the Constitution decided to use to count the slave population in the state representation.

Support Materials

Assignments can include:
1. Chapter Review, pp. 236–237
2. Vocabulary and Comprehension Master V43
3. Test 6-2, p. CT33
4. Enrichment Master E33

UNIT 6

CHAPTER 3   A Federal Government Is Formed

Overview   The Constitution provides for three separate branches of government: the legislative, the executive, and the judicial. The legislative branch has the power to make laws, coin money, set taxes, raise an army or a navy, and declare war. The executive branch has the power to enforce laws, make treaties, command the armed forces, and nominate federal judges. The judicial branch interprets the laws. The separation of powers keeps any one branch from becoming too strong. Its system of checks and balances keeps governmental power balanced. It gives each branch of government the power to serve as a check on the other branches. An amendment can be added to the Constitution only if approved by two-thirds of Congress and three-fourths of the states. Washington was the first President. His cabinet included Thomas Jefferson, Alexander Hamilton, Edmund Randolph, and Henry Knox.

Objectives

1. To identify the branches of government and their powers.
2. To state how separation of power and a system of checks and balances keeps any one branch from becoming too strong.
3. To state the freedoms guaranteed by the Bill of Rights.
4. To describe how the United States became stronger under Washington's presidency.

Developing the Chapter

1. Motivation: Show students the picture of George Washington on his horse.
Ask: Would you vote for this man for President? Write the name *George Washington* on the chalkboard and under it write the words *For* and *Against*. Have each student quickly write one reason they would vote for or against Washington. Then tell the students that by reading the chapter they will find out why he won the election by a landslide and took office in 1789.
2. Introduction
a. Write the chapter vocabulary words on the chalkboard. Have students write each word and its glossary definition in their vocabulary notebook. Ask each student, in turn, to use a vocabulary word in a sentence.

b. Have students read the chapter title and the Objective question.
c. Have students read the chapter.
3. Review and Recall: After the students have read the chapter:
a. Have them ask each other questions about the chapter content.
b. Have them reread each subhead question and answer it.
c. Have them look at the chart on page 242.
Ask: What plan of government did the authors of the Constitution give the United States?
4. Building Social Studies Skills: Explain to students that writing and using a chart is an important skill that helps them to understand the steps in a process that they are learning about. Guide students in using the chart, *How a Bill Becomes a Law,* on page 242. Then assign Skill Builder: Interpreting a Chart, page 242 of the chapter text.
5. Extension
a. Have students form two groups: the legislative branch and the judicial branch. You will act as the executive branch. Ask student legislators to revise one classroom rule. Encourage reasonable discussion and debate. Have the student judiciary branch read the school rules and decide whether the new classroom rule violates school rules, which will serve as an example of the function of federal law. You as executive can vote the new rule into law or veto it.
b. Write the names of your state's congressional representatives and senators on the chalkboard. Have students write letters to the members of Congress that either ask for information or express their views on political issues. Some information that may be of interest to students is how their people in Congress voted on bills concerning education, the driving age, the age of legal consent, and women's rights. Students may wish to express opinions on the war on drugs, the legal age for alcohol consumption, or the cut in federally funded programs to help the underprivileged.

Support Materials

Assignments can include:
1. Chapter Review, pp 242–243
2. Workbook, p. 36
3. Vocabulary and Comprehension Master V44
4. Test 6-3, p. CT34
5. Enrichment Master E34

UNIT 6

CHAPTER 4   Settling Western Lands to the Mississippi

Overview   To raise money, the government decided to sell to settlers the northwestern land it had won from Britain. The Northwest Ordinance of 1787 provided the rules for operation of this territory. It also guaranteed rights to white males, made provisions for territorial government and education, and prohibited slavery there. The Northwest Territory was divided into townships, defined by the ordinance as sections of land that measured six miles square. Businesses such as the Connecticut Land Company bought up much of the land for resale and a quick profit. Most federal treaties that allowed Native Americans to stay on their own land were ignored by settlers, and many Native Americans were forced from their homelands. Tecumseh, a great Native American leader, protested this unfair treatment of his people and encouraged them not to sign any treaty that gave away land.

Objectives

1. To describe how Americans settled the Northwest Territory.

2. To list the steps the government took to encourage people to move west.

3. To list some of the ways Native Americans were mistreated by settlers and the government.

4. To state why farmers and other settlers wanted to settle in the Northwest Territory.

5. To state how new roads and waterways helped the nation to grow.

Developing the Chapter

1. Motivation: Show students a map of the United States before and after the acquisition of the Northwest Territory. Ask students how they would divide the land if they had to sell it.

2. Introduction

a. Write the chapter vocabulary words on the chalkboard. Have students write each word and its glossary definition in their vocabulary notebook. Ask each student, in turn, to use a vocabulary word in a sentence.

b. Have students read the chapter title and the Objective question. Have students read the chapter.

3. Review and Recall: After the students have read the chapter:

a. Have them ask each other questions about the chapter content.

b. Have them reread each subhead question and answer it.

c. Have students work in small groups or in pairs. Assign the following topics to the groups: (1) the role of the government in settling the Northwest Territory, (2) the role of the settlers in settling the Northwest Territory, (3) the role of the Native Americans in settling the Northwest Territory, and (4) the role of the cavalry in settling the Northwest Territory.

d. Have students look at the map on page 278. **Ask:** How did Americans settle the land between the Appalachians and the Mississippi?

4. Building Social Studies Skills: Explain to students that reading a map is an important skill that helps them to understand the geography of the places about which they are learning. Guide students in reading the map on page 276. Ask for volunteers to explain how to use the scale of miles and the compass rose. Review with the class the specific purpose of this map: to show how the townships were divided in the Northwest Territory.

5. Extension

a. Tell students to imagine that they have moved to a township in the Northwest Territory. Because their township has recently grown to 5,000 people, they can make their own laws. Divide the class into small groups, and have group members work together to create a simple map of their township and a list of laws pertaining to the township.
Ask: How will you elect or appoint a sheriff, a mayor, or members of the town council? Will you allow the sale of liquor or guns in your township? Will commerce stop on religious holidays?

b. Have students do library research on Native American leaders to create a poster-board display that shows an important event from each leader's life. Encourage students to create a visually appealing display with a few well-written captions that explain each scene.

Support Materials

Assignments can include:

1. Chapter Review, pp. 278–279

2. Workbook, p. 37

3. Vocabulary and Comprehension Master V45

4. Test 6-4, p. CT35

5. Enrichment Master E35

UNIT 6

CHAPTER 5   Adding the Louisiana Territory

Overview   In the late 1700s, the Mississippi became important as a commercial waterway. After Spain transferred the Louisiana Territory to France in 1800, negotiations began with France to buy New Orleans and the surrounding territory. However, Napoleon offered to sell all of Louisiana, and in 1803 Jefferson's offer of $15 million was accepted. The purchase doubled the size of the United States. The Lewis and Clark expedition and the Pike expedition explored the Louisiana Purchase territory and the lands that bordered the Louisiana Purchase.

Objectives

1. To describe the background circumstances that led to the purchase of Louisiana.
2. To explain why the United States wanted to acquire New Orleans.
3. To identify the Louisiana Territory.
4. To describe the accomplishments of the Lewis and Clark and the Pike expeditions.

Developing the Chapter

1. Motivation: Bring to class some pictures of exotic animals that students may not recognize. Use issues of *National Geographic, Omni,* or the World Wildlife Foundation magazine as sources. Have the students imagine that they are explorers in unknown regions and have been asked to write descriptions of all unfamiliar species. Place students in small ''exploring parties.'' Give them one animal and have them write a description. Have each group read its description to the class. Have the rest of the class identify the animal. Ask the students about the difficulty of writing accurate descriptions. Discuss why a national leader would want explorers to keep such records and why these reports are valuable. Explain that explorers in the early nineteenth century did just this as they explored newly acquired territory for the United States. They will learn about these explorers in this chapter.

2. Introduction

a. Write the chapter vocabulary words on the chalkboard. Have students write each word and its glossary definition in their vocabulary notebook.

b. Have students read the chapter title and the Objective question.

Ask: Can you predict how the United States was to obtain the vast land between the Mississippi and the Rocky Mountains?

Write their predictions on the chalkboard. Refer to them as students read the chapter.

c. Have students preview the chapter visuals. Based on these visuals, have students identify key events of the period.

d. Have students read the chapter.

3. Review and Recall: After the students have read the chapter:

a. Have them answer the Objective question.

b. Have them answer each section question.

c. Have them ask each other factual questions based on the content of each section.

d. Have them identify a fact from each section. Then have other students volunteer opinions based on this fact.

4. Building Social Studies Skills: Remind students of the importance of using a time line to organize information about important events. Using a time line helps students to keep these events in perspective when they review material for tests. Have students make a time line of the key events of the period. When they have finished, ask them questions based on this study aid. For extra credit, have students illustrate their time lines.

5. Extension

a. Divide the class into groups of four. Then tell students that they have been asked to explore the West. Each group of four explorers has been given a canoe and a list of twenty items. Because they must carry the canoe long distances, each group must choose only fifteen items from the list. Tell the groups to discuss each item on their list and to number their choices. Then have groups share their lists.

b. Have students write facts such as ''I sold thousands of miles of land west of the Mississippi.'' Collect their statements, read them aloud, and have students identify each historical figure.

Support Materials

Assignments can include:

1. Chapter Review, pp. 284–285
2. Vocabulary and Comprehension Master V46
3. Test 6-5, p. CT36
4. Map Transparency Activity Sheet A12
5. Enrichment Master E36
6. Workbook, p. 40

UNIT 6

CHAPTER 6   The War of 1812

Overview   War with the British occurred after they issued the Orders of Council and the Embargo Act. The Orders of Council forbade United States ships to enter French ports and the Embargo Act prohibited United States ships from trading with foreign nations. After repeated attacks on its ships, the United States declared war on Britain. The battle at Lake Erie was an American victory, and the battle at Tippecanoe was a British victory. Six months after the British invaded Washington, D.C., in 1814, the Treaty of Ghent was signed to end the war.

Objectives

1. To show how the war between France and England finally involved the United States.
2. To list the reasons for the War of 1812.
3. To describe United States and British campaigns.
4. To describe the events that led to peace.

Developing the Chapter

1. Motivation: Write the lyrics to "The Star-Spangled Banner" on the chalkboard. You also may wish to play the anthem for the students. Tell them that the lyrics describe the battle at Fort McHenry in 1814. Help them to translate the lyrics into very simple English.

Ask students to tell you what these phrases mean: what so proudly we hailed; at the twilight's last gleaming; o'er the ramparts; so gallantly streaming; rockets. Encourage them to understand that the words relate a United States victory over tremendous odds.

2. Introduction

a. Tell students that there will be two groups discussed in the chapter: hawks and doves. Tell them to watch how each group behaves as they read the chapter.

Ask: With which position do you agree? Discuss why students have chosen their positions. Have the class develop definitions of *hawk* and *dove*. Record the definitions on a transparency for later use. You might give students small pictures of hawks and doves to identify their position. Students might wear replicas of doves and hawks on a piece of paper pinned to their shirts during the cooperative activities to represent their leanings.

b. Write the chapter vocabulary words on the chalkboard. Have students write each word and its glossary definition in their vocabulary notebook. Ask volunteers to use each vocabulary word in a sentence.

c. Have students read the chapter title and the Objective question.

d. Have students read the chapter.

3. Review and Recall: After the students have read the chapter:

a. Have them ask each other questions about the chapter's content.

b. Have them reread each subhead question and answer it.

c. Have them reread and answer the Objective question.

d. Have them write concentration cards using words and ideas from the chapter. After they have written all the clues, have them form two teams and play the concentration game.

4. Building Social Studies Skills: Remind students of the importance of using a time line to organize, in chronological order, information about important events. Remind students that by studying a time line, they may discover cause-and-effect relationships. Have students make a time line in three sections—*Events Leading to War, Events of War, Events Leading to Peace*.

5. Extension

a. Divide the class into two groups: hawks and doves. Have students reread the chapter and do library research to determine which political figures and actions each group supported. Have groups present the findings and the arguments for their positions to the class.

b. Have students write a report on impressment. You may wish to tell the students that impressment was used throughout history to create armies. Encourage the students to research the medieval *kern*, a man impressed to fight for a feudal lord.

Support Materials

Assignment can include:

1. Chapter Review, pp. 290–291
2. Workbook, pp. 38–39
3. Vocabulary and Comprehension Master V47
4. Test 6-6, p. CT37
5. Enrichment Master E37

UNIT 6

CHAPTER 7   A New Nationalism

Overview   The United States was a stronger, more nationalistic nation after the War of 1812. The Era of Good Feelings brought a period of political tranquility. The nation's economy improved after the War of 1812 because of increased manufacturing and the American System. Because of aggressive military action by Andrew Jackson, the United States was able to buy Florida from Spain, an action legalized by the Adams-Onis Treaty. In 1820 President Monroe and Secretary of State John Quincy Adams proclaimed that the United States would stay out of European affairs and would defend new Latin American nations against invasion. Monroe announced this policy, known as the Monroe Doctrine, in an address to Congress. In 1801, John Marshall, one of the most influential men ever to serve on the Supreme Court, was appointed Chief Justice. Under Marshall, the court insured itself the right in *Marbury v. Madison* to review congressional acts.

Objectives

1. To explain why Americans took new pride in their country after the War of 1812.
2. To describe how Florida was added to the United States.
3. To identify the warning President Monroe issued to imperialist nations in 1823.
4. To explain the importance of Chief Justice John Marshall.

Developing the Chapter

1. Motivation: Write *Era of Good Feelings* on the chalkboard or on an overhead transparency. Ask the students what they think that it means. Record all responses.

Ask: What had happened to make Americans feel good? (Americans had once again defeated the British, so they felt proud and powerful. Encourage responses that define *nationalism*.) Continue with: What do you think Americans might do politically during a period of good feelings? What might they do about the economy? What might they do about territory? How might they feel toward European involvement in North and South America? Have them add or revise their definitions of *Era of Good Feelings* based on the discussion. If the class has discussed elements of nationalism, point out that they have identified an important element of the period.

Explain that as they study Chapter 7, they will learn more about this period.

2. Introduction

a. Have students locate the new vocabulary words in the text. Ask them to write each word and its glossary definition in their vocabulary notebook. Then have them make up an original sentence for each word.

b. Have the students read the chapter title and the Objective question.

c. Have the students read the chapter.

3. Review and Recall: After the students have read the chapter:

a. Have them reread and answer each heading question.

b. Have them reread and answer the Objective question.

c. Ask them why they think the Monroe Doctrine is important.

Ask: Can you see an example of its use in modern times? (Nicaragua, Cuba, Grenada, Panama)

4. Building Social Studies Skills: Remind students that time lines are helpful tools for keeping events in chronological order. Have them make a time line of the events in this chapter. Let them illustrate it for extra credit.

5. Enrichment

a. Assign students to six debate teams of four members each. Have each team research one side in the following issues: (1) the Monroe Doctrine, (2) *Marbury v. Madison,* and (3) the "claiming" of Florida. Have each team present its side of the issue in a debate. Have the teams which are not participating act as judges.

b. Have students research the life style of the Native Americans of Florida whose lands Andrew Jackson claimed. Students might include these topics: housing, food, way of life, and religion. Have them present their findings on paper.

Support Materials

Assignments can include:

1. Chapter Review, pp. 296–297
2. Vocabulary and Comprehension Master V48
3. Test 6-7, p. CT38
4. Enrichment Master E38

UNIT 6

CHAPTER 8   The Influence of the West

Overview   President Andrew Jackson, who made the donkey the symbol of the Democratic party, made many changes during his terms in office. ''Jacksonian Democracy'' gave more people a greater voice in government. White men who did not own property were given the vote. He started the ''spoils system'' of rewards and began the system of nominating conventions wherein states' delegates chose the presidential candidates. In 1830 he encouraged Congress to pass the Removal Act, which removed Southern Native Americans from their homes, and in 1832 he vetoed a bill that would have kept the national bank in existence.

Objectives

1. To describe the influence of frontier democracy and Jacksonian democracy on the United States government.
2. To explain how democracy grew during Jackson's presidency.
3. To describe the way Jackson treated Native Americans.

Developing the Chapter

1. Motivation: Explain to students that there is to be a class vote on issues that are important to the class—homework, tardy policy, and class rules. Tell them that only those students who meet the requirements for class citizenship will be allowed to vote. Then explain the requirements for citizenship. Choose requirements that relate to property such as owning a gold or silver pen, wearing a blue shirt, or bringing a three-ring notebook to class. Allow the class to vent their feelings about the fairness of this situation. Discuss what should be done about it and why. Explain that this situation is similar to the voting situation when Jackson came into office because only white, male property owners could vote. Tell them that in this chapter they will learn more about Jackson's democratic changes.

2. Introduction

a. List the chapter vocabulary words on the chalkboard. Have students write each word in an original sentence in their vocabulary notebook. Have them look up the glossary definition of any word whose meaning they do not know.

b. Have students look at the visuals and read the captions. Also have them read the heads and the subheads. Then have them describe the type of person they believe would have been a Jackson supporter and the type who would have opposed him. Have them give reasons for their choices.

c. Have students read the Objective question. Have them propose possible answers. Save the answers until students have read the chapter.

d. Have students read the chapter.

3. Review and Recall

a. Have students answer the Objective questions and the questions in the subheads. Have them compare their answers to the ones they wrote during the introduction.

b. Have students give a two- to three-sentence definition of these terms: *frontier democracy, spoils-system caucus, nominating convention, Removal Act, national bank,* and *''trail of tears.''*

c. Have students write Objective questions with one- or two-word answers. Tell the students you will use these questions in a Jeopardy-type game. Collect the questions, and divide the questions into categories. You might use the chapter sections for classification. Call on volunteers to play the game. Use extra credit points or privileges as prizes. Play several rounds so most students have the opportunity to play.

4. Building Social Studies Skills: Explain to students that summarizing is a skill that can help them to understand chapter content. Divide the class into small groups. Assign each group one section of the chapter to summarize. Share the summaries with the class.

5. Enrichment

a. Have the students imagine that they are friends of Jackson and that they want a position in government. Have them write a letter to the President applying for a job. Remind them to list their qualifications and reasons for wanting the job. Review proper business letter form with the class before they write a final draft.

b. Have students find out how to write with the Cherokee alphabet. Have the students prepare posters that demonstrate the Cherokee alphabet.

Support Materials

Assignments may include:

1. Chapter Review, pp. 302–303
2. Workbook, p. 41
3. Vocabulary and Comprehension Master V49
4. Test 6-8, p. CT39
5. Enrichment Master E39

UNIT 7

Americans Move Westward

Unit Overview From the mid-1700s to the late 1800s, Americans spread west to settle the land from Ohio to California. First came the mountain men, who combed the West for furs. Then came settlers who followed the Santa Fe and Oregon trails to the Southwest and Northwest. Mormons settled in the Great Salt Lake Basin of Utah, where they could follow their religion freely. In California, Spanish priests and administrators established a string of missions, where Native Americans worked and were converted to Christianity. In Texas, Americans settled and fought Mexico for their independence. The Mexican War brought the United States a huge territory in the Southwest. The California Gold Rush brought thousands to that region, and in 1850 California gained American statehood. On the Great Plains, Native Americans fought unsuccessfully to maintain their way of life against a growing tide of miners, ranchers, and farmers.

Unit Objectives

1. To identify the events and situations that caused settlers to move to the West.
2. To describe the role religion played in the settlement of California and Utah.
3. To list the causes of the War with Mexico and its consequences.
4. To describe the settlement of the Great Plains by miners, ranchers, and farmers, and its effect on Native Americans.

Unit Introduction

1. Motivation: Have students recall any Western films they may have seen on televison or in the movies. Ask what was the main theme of most of them. Elicit the fact that often it was the "good guys" against the "bad guys" and that usually the good guys were white settlers and the bad guys were Native Americans. Explain that in such movies the fact that the Native Americans were defending their lands against the encroachment of whites is usually not shown. Tell the students that the settlement of the West as it affected both whites and Native Americans is the theme of this unit.

2. Visual: Direct students' attention to the unit-opening picture on page 307. Explain that this is how thousands of settlers traveled to the West in the 1800s. Discuss such questions as why people traveled in wagon trains, how long their journey took, and what living conditions on the journey were like.

3. Time Line: Direct students to the time line on pages 306 and 307. Remind them that some topics in Unit 6 took place in the period of this time line. These include the growth of nationalism and what was then the West in President Andrew Jackson's administration.

4. Points of View: Ask students to read the Points of View on pages 308 and 309. Have students discuss the differences in point of view between Marsh's letter and the statements of the Native Americans. Remind students that they will encounter these differences many times in the course of studying the unit.

Unit Activities

1. Cooperative Learning: Have students work in small groups to create an illustrated time line of events on the unit time line. Encourage them to use pictures cut out from old magazines or drawn by students.

2. Research: Have students do research on the geography of the region of the United States west of the Mississippi that is covered in this unit. They should include the mountains, rivers, and plains; the climate; and the vegetation and animal life of the region in about 1750.

3. Creative Writing: In the unit, the students will meet people who do many kinds of work, such as hunters, miners, ranchers, farmers, cowboys, missionaries, and railroad builders. Have the students choose one of these occupations and write about the skills and training required, what its advantages and disadvantages might be, and why people might have pursued it.

Support Materials

Assignments can include:
1. Unit Review, pp. 352–353
2. Unit Vocabulary and Comprehension Masters V59–V60
3. Unit 7 Test, pp. UT13–UT14

UNIT 7

CHAPTER 1 Trails to the West

Overview   The mountain men who went into the West before the 1840s did so to bring back the furs that were in demand in the East and Europe. The first settlers began coming in the 1840s. Between then and the 1860s, large numbers of settlers headed west on the Santa Fe Trail. This trail started in Independence, Missouri, and ended in Santa Fe, New Mexico. From there the Old Spanish Trail went farther west to California. The Oregon Trail also left Independence, but went west and then north to the fertile Willamette Valley, in what is now the state of Oregon. People went west to make a new start in life, to escape the overcrowding of cities, and, like Narcissa and Marcus Whitman, to do missionary work among the Native Americans.

Objectives

1. To identify the ways the mountain men helped explore the West.
2. To identify the motives of settlers for going west.
3. To recognize the importance of the Santa Fe and Oregon Trails.
4. To describe the Whitmans' encounter with Native Americans.

Developing the Chapter

1. **Motivation:** Tell the students to imagine they live in a city in 1838. As the head of a family, they are considering going to the Willamette Valley in a train of covered wagons to find cheap and fertile farmland. Tell them that they will live in covered wagons for the six months that it may take to reach Oregon. Tell the students about the dangers of the journey. Ask them whether, considering the limited living space and the dangers, they would have made the journey.

2. **Introduction**
a. Write the vocabulary words on the board. Ask students to look at the words "depression" and "missionary" and find a word within each that gives a clue to the meaning. They should find "depress" in depression, and "mission" in missionary. Discuss the meaning of each.
b. Have students read the chapter title, and tell them they will be finding out about three trails that settlers to the West used in the 1840s to the 1860s. Have students look at the map of the

trails on page 312 and decide which one they would have taken.
c. Have students read the chapter.

3. **Review and Recall:** After students have read the chapter:
a. Have students reread each subhead question and answer it.
b. Have them reread and answer the Objective question.
c. Ask students to discuss their choices of trails made in the Introduction. Ask whether, after reading the chapter, they would now make the same choices, and have them defend their answers.
d. Have students carefully examine the picture on page 313.
   Ask: What does this picture about the Oregon settlers add to what you read about them in the chapter?

4. **Building Social Studies Skills**
a. Have students use the classroom map or use the map on page 312 to locate the city of origin for each trail and its destination.
b. Have students compare the mountain men's experience with that of Native Americans and that of the people on wagon trains with that of Native Americans. Have them explain why they were so different.

5. **Extension**
a. Ask students to write a list of the things they would have taken on a trip west in a covered wagon, taking into account the small traveling space available. Have students compare their lists and discuss why they included what they did and what they left out.
b. Have students write a script for a radio commercial on one of these topics: the Willamette Valley for a real estate owner, a school for mountain men, or a covered wagon manufacturer.

Support Materials

Assignments can include:

1. Chapter Review, pp. 314–315
2. Vocabulary and Comprehension Master V52
3. Test 7-1, p. CT40
4. Map Transparency Activity Sheet A14
5. Enrichment Master E40

CHAPTER 2 Utah Is Settled

Overview Joseph Smith founded Mormonism in 1823, after he believed an angel told him to translate inscriptions from an ancient plate into what became the Book of Mormon. Mormons were loyal to their religion, shared their wealth, and practiced polygamy. To escape persecution, they fled from Ohio to Missouri and then to Illinois, where Smith was killed. Brigham Young then led the Church to the Great Salt Lake Basin, where the Mormons settled and, by mastering the art of desert farming, prospered. Because of their belief in polygamy, their application to become a state of the United States was not accepted until 1896, after they agreed to give up polygamy.

Objectives

1. To identify the steps that preceded the Mormons' move to Illinois.
2. To explain the reasons for the Mormons' move from Illinois to the West.
3. To describe the Mormons' settlement and activities in Utah.

Developing the Chapter

1. Motivation: Tell the students to imagine they are at the Great Salt Lake after fleeing persecution in Illinois. They've planted grain when thousands of crickets swarm in and start eating the grain. Suddenly seagulls fly in and start eating the crickets. Ask the students how they think the pioneers felt when this happened. Tell them that this is a true story about the Mormons they will be reading about.

2. Introduction

a. Direct students to each paragraph where the vocabulary words are used in the chapter. Ask them to record the meanings as given in the text. Ask volunteers to use each vocabulary word in a sentence.

b. Have students read the chapter title and Objective question.

c. Have students read the chapter.

3. Review and Recall: Have the students answer the questions below in "The Question Game." A correct answer receives 10 points. A student answering incorrectly loses the turn. Students who miss a question must answer the question in writing. The highest score wins.

a. Who was Joseph Smith? [founder of Mormon religion]

b. Who succeeded Smith as the Mormon leader? [Brigham Young]

c. Why did the Mormons move from Ohio to Missouri? to Illinois? to the West? [to escape persecution]

d. What was the Great Salt Lake Basin like when the Mormons settled there? [dry, treeless, covered with salt, sand, and hot sulfur springs]

e. What was the "miracle" that occurred there? [the seagulls ate the crickets that were eating the crop]

f. Why was there a delay in Congress's accepting Utah's application for statehood? [reluctance of the Mormons to give up the practice of polygamy]

4. Building Social Studies Skills: Have students use the library to find out about the growth of the Mormon population. Tell them to make a graph with the dates 1840, 1880, 1920, 1960, and 1990, showing the number of Mormons.

5. Extension

a. Organize students in groups of four. Ask each group to prepare a report on the Mormons' experience with non-Mormons as an example of prejudice. Ask them to compare the prejudice the Mormons experienced with that of others they have read about. Ask them what the Mormons believed and whether that caused people to be prejudiced against them. Have them categorize the elements of prejudice that are common to most other examples, such as fear, distrust, envy, and lack of knowledge. The class should evaluate each group's conclusions.

b. Have students do research on the farming methods the Mormons employed. They should investigate whether other desert areas of the world have been transformed into cropland.

Support Materials

Assignments can include:

1. Chapter Review, pp. 320–321
2. Vocabulary and Comprehension Master V53
3. Test 7-2, p. CT41
4. Enrichment Master E41

UNIT 7

CHAPTER 3   The Spanish in California

Overview   The Spanish were the first white settlers in California, which at the time was part of Mexico. The Spanish administrators showed little interest in California until it appeared that Russia and Great Britain might claim the territory. Starting with efforts of Gaspar de Portolá and Father Junípero Serra, the Spanish administrators and priests built 21 missions from 1769 to 1823. Near the missions were presidios (forts) and pueblos (towns). The main purpose of the missions was to convert the Native Americans to Christianity. At the missions, priests also taught the Native Americans to raise cattle and crops and to work at trades. The Native Americans learned much from the Spaniards, but their lives at the missions were often hard. The mission lands were sold off to rancheros after Mexico became independent of Spain in 1821. The Native Americans were used as workers on the ranches, and they were not well treated.

Objectives

1. To identify the role of the missions in Spanish California.
2. To explain how Native Americans were treated at the California missions.
3. To describe how the rancheros used the mission lands after 1821.

Developing the Chapter

1. Motivation: Show students the picture of the Santa Barbara mission on page 323. Explain that this is how many of the present-day cities south of San Francisco, California, looked when they were founded as missions. Tell them places like this are the main focus of the chapter.

2. Introduction

a. Write the chapter vocabulary words on the chalkboard. Explain why three of them are of Spanish origin. Ask students to pronounce Gaspar de Portolá and Junípero Serra aloud.
b. Have students read the chapter title and the Objective question.
c. Have students read the rest of the chapter.

3. Review and Recall

a. Ask students who Father Serra and Portolá were and what they did.
b. Ask students what the Native Americans did in the missions.

c. Ask what happened to the missions after Mexico became independent.
d. Have students reread and answer the Objective question.

4. Building Social Studies Skills

a. Have students study the picture of the Santa Barbara mission on page 323. Have them notice each part of the mission and explain what its function was. Ask them to identify the groups of people shown and explain what they did at the mission.
b. Have students look at a map of California and locate the missions. Students can then calculate the distance between each one and locate El Camino Real, the road joining the missions. Discuss why such a road was built. On a present-day road map, have students locate the road that most closely follows the route of El Camino Real.

5. Extension

a. Have students build a model of a mission, working in small groups. Possible roles are: architect, drafter, builder, researcher.
b. Have students research those California missions that are still in existence and learn what takes place there.
c. Have students investigate other evidence of the influence of the Spanish in California and report to the class. They might make a list of cities and town with names of Spanish origin and give their meanings in English. Ask them to explain why almost all of these names are south of San Francisco.

Support Materials

Assignments can include:

1. Chapter Review, pp. 326–327
2. Vocabulary and Comprehension Master V54
3. Test 7-3, p. CT42
4. Enrichment Master E42

UNIT 7

CHAPTER 4   The War with Mexico

Overview   The Americans in Texas, which was part of Mexico, had religious and political differences with that country. General Santa Anna became dictator of Mexico in 1834, and a year later the Americans declared their independence. Although the Americans were defeated at the Alamo, they won the decisive Battle of San Jacinto and set up the independent republic of Texas. In 1845 Texas became a state of the United States. Boundary disputes between the United States and Mexico led to war. The War with Mexico, 1846–1848, resulted in victory for the United States. In the Treaty of Guadalupe Hidalgo ending the war, the United States gained a huge territory in the Southwest from Mexico called the Mexican Cession. Additional territory was added through the Gadsden Purchase.

Objectives

1. To identify problems that developed between Mexico and the Americans in Texas.
2. To outline the steps that Texans took to gain independence.
3. To describe the causes of the War with Mexico, the military action, and the results of the war.

Developing the Chapter

1. Motivation: Tell the students to imagine that they are a small group of people who live and own property in a foreign country. The language, religion, and customs of this country are different from their own. A dictator becomes the ruler of the country and tries to force the group to obey laws that they object to. Ask the students to discuss what choices of action the group has. Explain that this is the situation that Americans living in Mexican-held Texas in the 1830s faced and that this chapter will describe what they did.

2. Introduction

a. Write the chapter vocabulary words on the chalkboard. Have students find the words in the text and note their meanings as given there. Ask volunteers to use each vocabulary word in a sentence.

b. Tell the students to read the chapter title and the Objective question.

c. Have students read the chapter.

3. Review and Recall: After the students have read the chapter:

a. Ask them for the causes of the War with Mexico. List them on the chalkboard.

Ask: Was there any way that the War with Mexico could have been avoided?

b. Have students write the names Scott, Taylor, and Kearny on paper. Ask them to fill in a contribution of each. Students might then compare their list with a partner's.

4. Building Social Studies Skills

a. Draw a time line on the board with the years 1820, 1825, 1830, 1835, 1840, and 1845. Then ask students to fill in the dates 1821, 1830, 1836, 1845, and an event for each of these years.

b. Have students study the map of the War with Mexico on page 331. Have them use the map scale to note distances between battles that were American victories. Have them trace the movements of the American generals' troops. Ask why General Scott landed in Veracruz. Make sure the students understand from the map that all the action in the war was on Mexican territory or disputed territory.

5. Extension

a. Explain to students that there was considerable opposition in the United States to the War with Mexico. Have students research the question of differences of opinion about the war and prepare a report for class presentation.

b. Ask students to use their imaginations and library research to write on one of these topics: an insider's account of what happened at the Alamo; a Mexican's eyewitness story of what went on in Santa Fe during Kearny's attack on the city; a conversation between two American plantation owners in Texas in 1834; a discussion between a Northerner and a Southerner on whether the United States should declare war on Mexico.

Support Materials

Assignments can include:

1. Chapter Review, pp. 332–333
2. Vocabulary and Comprehension Master V55
3. Test 7-4, p. CT43
4. Map Transparency Activity Sheet A15
5. Enrichment Master E43

UNIT 7

CHAPTER 5   California Becomes a State

Overview   The Gold Rush brought many types of people to California. Mining camps sprang up in the gold fields, and some became boom towns. Among the newcomers were Chinese men who worked hard, washing clothes and cooking food in mining camps, yet who were subjected to harsh treatment by the miners. Many Chinese worked on the transcontinental railroad that was being built. California's population grew rapidly. California applied for statehood, prompting a dispute between the North and the South. The Compromise of 1850 was agreed to, under which California came in as a free state in exchange for stricter laws against fugitive slaves.

Objectives

1. To describe the routes to the Gold Rush region of California.
2. To identify what life was like for the "forty-niners" who came to California.
3. To describe how California became a state.

Developing the Chapter

1. Motivation: Ask students to read paragraph 1 of the chapter. Then describe living conditions in the gold region—rough housing, boom towns, minimum law enforcement, high prices. Then ask students what they think they would have done when they heard about the discovery of gold in California. Ask them to remember their decision and compare it with what they might decide after reading the chapter.

2. Introduction

a. Write the vocabulary words on the board. Have students use the glossary to look up the words they do not know and write the definitions in their notebooks.

b. Use these advance organizers: tell students they will find out about how miners got the gold from streams by reading paragraph 7, what the life of a gold digger was like by reading paragraph 8, and how California became a state from paragraphs 10 and 11.

c. Have students read the chapter.

3. Review and Recall: After students have read the chapter:

a. Have them ask one another questions about the content of the chapter.

b. Have them reread each subhead question and answer it.

c. Have students describe one method of prospecting for gold.

4. Building Social Studies Skills: Have students draw two routes to the California gold fields on a map of the United States. Suggest they use paragraphs 2 and 3 for reference and compare their routes with a classmate's. Ask them whether they know what later developments made travel to California much easier [the transcontinental railroad and the Panama Canal].

5. Extension

a. Have students work in groups of four to simulate going to California together during the Gold Rush. Each group will choose its mode of travel, by boat or by wagon. Students have only 15′ by 6′ of space if they choose to go by wagon, and 15′ x 10′ if they go by boat. Each group will make a list of the items to take on the trip and list them in order from "must have" to "would like." Have one speaker from each group tell the class the top six items on that group's list. Then have groups compare their lists.

b. Have students go to the library to research one of the towns that sprang up during the Gold Rush. They should cover the way the town was established, what life there was like, who were the leading people, what kinds of businesses there were, what happened to the town after the Gold Rush was over and what the town is like today. They should be ready to report to the class on their findings.

Support Materials

Assignments can include:

1. Chapter Review, pp. 338–339
2. Vocabulary and Comprehension Master V56
3. Test 7-5, p. CT 44
4. Map Transparency Activity Sheet A16
5. Enrichment Master E44

UNIT 7

CHAPTER 6   Settlers Move into the Great Plains

Overview   Miners, ranchers, and farmers moved into the Great Plains between the 1850s and the 1890s. The 1850s and 1860s brought prospectors for gold and silver to Colorado, South Dakota, Nevada, and other western regions. Then, with railroads offering cheap land along their right of way, thousands flowed onto the plains to become ranchers and farmers. In 1862 the Homestead Act brought the ''homesteaders'' west. They lived in sod houses, using the new steel plow to cut through the thick sod and plant crops. The life there was difficult for many.

Objectives

1. To compare the part miners, ranchers, and farmers played in opening the Great Plains.
2. To describe the reasons why miners came to the Rocky Mountains in the 1850s and 1860s.
3. To evaluate the role of the railroads in the settling of the Great Plains.
4. To describe the way farmers on the Great Plains lived and worked and the hardships they faced.

Developing the Chapter

1. Motivation: Ask students to imagine that they have just come to the Great Plains to settle there as farmers. Describe the land—treeless, windy, dry, with soil heavily covered with grass so thick that it could not be cut with an ordinary plow. Tell them that this was the land that thousands of Americans and people from foreign countries came to, beginning in the 1860s. Ask students to speculate how, by the 1890s, the Great Plains had become the ''breadbasket of America.''

2. Introduction

a. Ask students to locate the new vocabulary words in the text of the chapter. Have them write each word and its definition in their notebooks.
b. Read the chapter title and Objective question aloud.
c. Have students read the chapter.

3. Review and Recall: After the students have read the chapter:

a. Divide the class into three groups: miners, ranchers, farmers. Have each group answer these questions: why they came to the Great Plains, where they settled, problems they faced, how they solved these problems.

b. Ask the students to explain how inventions helped Great Plains farmers.
c. Have students review the role of railroads in settling the Great Plains.

4. Building Social Study Skills:

a. Remind students that using a scale of distance is an important map skill that helps them understand how far places are from one another. Have the students use the scale on the map on page 342 to estimate the length of the cattle trails and of the railroads shown. They may also measure the greatest distances east and west and north and south of the cattle-raising region and compare it with the Great Plains area as a whole.

b. Have students research the Homestead Act and make a chart of the number of acres (or hectares) homesteaded in 1862, 1867, 1872, 1877, 1882, 1887, 1907, 1927, 1947, and 1986. They should understand that much of the homesteading after 1900 took place in Alaska.

5. Extension

a. Have students use an encyclopedia or other source to work on one of these projects: 1. Sod houses. Suggest that students may construct a miniature sod house of their own and bring it to class. 2. Finding western songs (e.g., ''Sweet Betsy from Pike'' and ''She'll Be Comin' 'Round the Mountain''). Have students transcribe the words for the class so that all can sing.

b. Have students pretend to be a Scandinavian woman who has settled on the Great Plains with her husband to farm. She writes a letter to her parents in the old country telling about their new life in the United States. Have volunteers read their letters aloud to the class.

Support Materials

Assignments can include:

1. Chapter Review, pp. 344–345
2. Vocabulary and Comprehension Master V57
3. Test 7-6, p. CT45
4. Enrichment Master E45

UNIT 7

CHAPTER 7   The Decline of Native Americans on the Great Plains

Overview   The settlement of the Great Plains by white people resulted in great changes in the lives of the Native Americans for whom it had been home for hundreds of years. Conflicts occurred when the United States government tried to take land from the Native Americans and force them to live on reservations. In Minnesota, a Sioux chief, Red Cloud, led his people in a successful fight to protect Sioux hunting grounds, while in South Dakota, Crazy Horse and Sitting Bull routed General Custer, only to be captured later. In the Southwest, Geronimo led the Apaches on raids but later was captured also.

Objectives

1. To describe why conflict between the Native Americans and the white people who came to the Great Plains developed.
2. To describe how the arrival of miners, ranchers, and farmers affected the Native Americans and their culture.
3. To explain how the culture of the Great Plains Native Americans was changed as a result of the coming of the white people.

Developing the Chapter

1. Motivation: Read the chapter introduction to the students, or paraphrase it, and discuss the situation the Native Americans found themselves in as white people began encroaching on their lands. Discuss with the students the questions raised in the paragraph with reference to decisions the Native Americans had to make.

2. Introduction

a. Have the students locate the new chapter vocabulary words in the text. Ask them to write each word and its definition in their notebooks.
b. Read the chapter title and Objective question aloud.
c. Have the class read the chapter.

3. Review and Recall: After the students have read the chapter:

a. Have them analyze the reasons for the clashes between the whites who were coming to the Great Plains and the Native Americans. Have them review the nature of the clashes. Ask the students to discuss whether solutions other than

warfare and settling the Native Americans on reservations could have been worked out.
b. Write these names on the chalkboard: Red Cloud, George Custer, Sitting Bull, Crazy Horse, Geronimo, Chief Joseph. Ask the students to identify each person, describe what action he was involved in, and explain what role this action played in the decline of the Native Americans of the Great Plains.

4. Building Social Studies Skills: Explain to students that an important part of being able to read a map is identifying the cardinal directions—east, west, north, and south—on a map and observing the relative position of some of the information given on a map. Have the students study the map on page 347 and answer the following questions and similar ones that you may make up: Along which river were most of the farming tribes found? Name the hunting tribe that hunted just west of the Ponca tribe. Which farming tribe was located north of the Sioux? Which is the northernmost farming tribe shown on the map? Name three hunting tribes located just east of the Rocky Mountains.

5. Extension

a. Divide the students into two groups. Ask one group to assume the role of white settlers on the Great Plains and argue that they were right in driving the Native Americans from their homelands. Ask the other group to assume the role of Native Americans and present arguments against the whites and in favor of their continued occupation of the land.
b. Have students investigate whether there have been recent instances of one people trying to take over the land of another people and what the outcomes have been.

Support Materials

Assignments can include:

1. Chapter Review. pp. 350–351
2. Vocabulary and Comprehension Master V58
3. Test 7-7, p. CT46
4. Enrichment Master E46

UNIT 8

Slavery Tears the Nation Apart

Unit Overview   At the beginning of the 1800s, differences between North and South that threatened the country's unity became more apparent. While slavery became more firmly entrenched in the Southern states, it was gradually phased out in the North. Also, the growth of factories resulted in a more industrial North that contrasted sharply with the agricultural South. These divisions became critical as debates increased over the extension of slavery to the new territories. By the 1830s, the antislavery movement had gained momentum in the Northern states, while some Southerners were starting to think that leaving the Union was the only way they could preserve their way of life.

Unit Objectives

1. To understand the growth of slavery in the colonies and the young nation.
2. To learn about how Southern planters began to rely more on and more on slaves for labor.
3. To learn how African slaves resisted slavery.
4. To learn about the growth of factories in the North.
5. To understand how slavery drove the North and the South further apart.

Unit Introduction

1. Motivation: Call on groups of students to role-play the following situation: A shopkeeper from New York City, who is opposed to slavery, travels to South Carolina. There he meets a plantation owner, who owns one hundred slaves. The time is 1830, when many people in the North are becoming more vocal about their hatred of slavery and their belief that it should be ended. The two have a discussion about the issue, and several onlookers join in. Before beginning the role-plays, ask students questions such as: What arguments against slavery do you think the New York shopkeeper would give? Why would he have thought it was wrong? Why would the Southern planter think it important to keep his slaves? After the presentations, explain that as they read Unit 8 they will learn more about how Northerners and Southerners felt about slavery in the 1800s.

2. Visual: The unit opening painting shows life on a Southern plantation in about the mid-1800s. Ask students what the attitude of the artist about plantation life seems to be. (The plantation looks very peaceful and calm.) What type of work is shown here (cotton farming)? Why might large numbers of people be needed to do this type of work? Tell students that they will learn now the cotton farming in the South came to depend on slave labor.

3. Time Line: Have the class read the events on the unit time line, pages 354–355. Ask students to identify any events they are familiar with.

Ask: What events on this time line do you think are related to the Civil War?

Encourage students to refer to the time line as they study Unit 8 to keep events in perspective.

4. Historical Points of View: Have students read the introductory paragraph in this feature.

Ask: Why do you think "slavery created sharp divisions among Americans"? Was there any way to settle the issues without a war?

Have students read the first selection.

Ask: What does the author mean when he says the enslaved African's "powers have never yet been fully tried"? What "difficulties and discouragements" do you think the enslaved Africans had to struggle against?

Have students read the second selection.

Ask: How does this speaker think that the slaves feel about their condition? What does he consider to be the purpose of slaves?

Unit Activities

1. Cooperative Learning: Have students work in small groups to create an illustrated time line that includes the major events discussed in this chapter, from the slave code passed by the Virginia legislature in 1680 to John Brown's raid in 1859. Students can use magazine or newspaper pictures as well as their own illustrations to complete the time line.

2. Research: Have students write news accounts of five or six key events discussed in Unit 8. These articles should be written as if they were to be published in newspapers of the period. Students will need to research the events they choose to write about. Remind them to answer the questions *who, what, when, where,* and *why* in the first paragraph of their articles.

Support Materials

Assignments can include:

1. Unit 8 Review, pp. 394–395
2. Unit Vocabulary and Comprehension Masters V67–V68
3. Unit 8 Test, pp. UT15–UT16

UNIT 8

CHAPTER 1   Slavery in the Colonies and the Young Nation

Overview   Enslaved Africans were brought to the New World to perform hard work in the West Indies and in South America. Africans first arrived in the English colonies in the early 1600s; however, at first the English colonists used indentured servants more than enslaved Africans. This practice changed with the growth of tobacco plantations in the South in the 1700s. Strict laws called slave codes were passed to control African slaves. While slavery declined in the North, it increased in the South as a result of the rise of cotton plantations in the early 1800s.

Objectives

1. To learn how free Africans were captured and brought to the New World.
2. To understand how slavery spread in the South in the 1700s.
3. To learn about the slave codes that were passed to control the lives of enslaved Africans.
4. To explain how some African slaves became free and to understand what their lives were like.
5. To understand how slavery was affected by the spread of cotton farming in the South.

Developing the Chapter

1. Motivation: Ask students to recall any accounts of the lives of enslaved African Americans that they might have read, seen on television, or seen in the movies.

Ask: How do you think Africans felt when they first arrived in this strange new land? In what ways had their experiences and lives in Africa been different from those of the people whom they would encounter in the New World? How were the enslaved Africans treated? Why do you think they were treated this way?

Explain that as they read this chapter students will learn more about slavery in the colonies.

2. Introduction

a. Write the chapter vocabulary words on the chalkboard. Have students write each word and its glossary definition in their vocabulary notebook. Ask volunteers to use each vocabulary word in an original sentence. Call on volunteers to read aloud their sentences without the vocabulary words. Ask other students to complete the sentences with the correct vocabulary words.

b. Have students read the chapter title and the Objective question.

c. Ask students to look at the map on page 360 and note the states that are included in what became known as the "cotton kingdom."

d. Have students read the chapter.

3. Review and Recall: After the students have read the chapter:

a. Have them reread and answer the Objective question.

b. Have them reread and answer each section question.

c. Have them make up questions based on the material in each section and quiz one another.

d. Have them find the main idea in each section.

e. Write the following chart heading on the chalkboard: *Spread of Slavery in the Colonies.* Under this heading, write: *Type of Worker; Where Slavery Was Used; Why Slavery Spread.* On the left hand side of the chart, list the following: *1600s; 1700s; 1800s.* Have students complete the chart with information from the chapter.

4. Building Social Studies Skills: Use the map on page 360 to briefly review map-reading skills with the students. Point out the key, the scale, and the compass rose. Ask students to locate the following cities on the map: Richmond, Virginia, and New Orleans, Louisiana. Have them name the cities found along the Mississippi River. Have students use the distance scale to determine the distance between Savannah, Georgia, and Charleston, South Carolina.

5. Extension

a. Ask students to write a series of three journal entries from the point of view of either an enslaved African who has just arrived in America or a Southern plantation owner who had just purchased more slaves to work on his farm.

b. Have students write editorials for either a Northern or a Southern colonial newspaper of the early 1800s, commenting on the continued use of enslaved Africans in America.

Support Materials

Assignments can include:

1. Chapter Review, pp. 362–363
2. Workbook, pp. 48, 52
3. Vocabulary and Comprehension Master V61
4. Test 8-1, p. CT47
5. Enrichment Master E47

CHAPTER 2 Southern Planters, Farmers, and African Slaves

Overview Although most Southerners were small farmers who could not afford to own slaves, they supported the slave system. However, slaves were still essential to the owners of the large plantations for the day-to-day existence of their plantations, where cash crops such as tobacco, sugar cane, and cotton were grown. The powerful plantation owners controlled every facet of the lives of their slaves. Despite these brutal conditions, enslaved African Americans struggled to keep their own culture alive.

Objectives

1. To compare and contrast the lives of small farmers and large plantation owners in the South before 1860.
2. To describe the life of enslaved Africans on a Southern plantation.
3. To understand how work was organized on a plantation.
4. To understand how African slaves kept their own culture and traditions alive.

Developing the Chapter

1. Motivation: Read to students the selection from Solomon Northrup's *Twelve Years a Slave: Narrative of Solomon Northrup* on page 366 of their textbooks.

Ask: How were the enslaved Africans who worked in the fields treated? Why do you think they were treated so harshly? What do you think that life on a Southern plantation was like?

Explain that as they read this chapter, students will learn about life in the South before the Civil War.

2. Introduction

a. Write the chapter vocabulary words on the chalkboard. Have students write each word and its glossary definition in their vocabulary notebook. Have volunteers write on the chalkboard a synonym and an antonym for each vocabulary word. Ask another student to identify the correct vocabulary word that corresponds to the words on the chalkboard.

b. Have students read the chapter title and the Objective question.

c. Have students preview the chapter visuals.

Ask: What do these illustrations tell you about life in the South in the period before the Civil War?

d. Have students read the chapter.

3. Review and Recall: After the students have read the chapter:

a. Have them reread and answer the Objective question.

b. Have them reread and answer each subhead question.

c. Write these headings on the chalkboard: *House Slave; Field Slave.* Call on students to volunteer information about the life of each group of enslaved Africans, and write their answers in list form under the appropriate heading.

d. Have students make up crossword puzzles using words and ideas from the chapter. After they have written all the Down and Across clues, they can try to solve each other's puzzles.

4. Building Social Studies Skills: Remind students that outlines are a useful way to organize information. Point out that topical outlines have a simpler format than sentence outlines because they use phrases rather than complete sentences. Briefly review the use of main headings, headings, and subheadings in an outline. Write the following headings on the chalkboard and have students fill in appropriate subheadings, using information from the chapter:

I. Life in the South Before 1860
  A. Life on a small farm
  B. Life on a large plantation
  C. The life of an enslaved African American

5. Extension

a. Have students use their school encyclopedias to research life on a pre-Civil War plantation. They should summarize their findings in written reports. The reports should include diagrams of the various buildings on a Southern plantation of this period.

b. Have students write newspaper accounts of a slave auction held during the period before the Civil War. Remind them to answer the journalistic questions *who, what, where, when,* and *why* in the first paragraph. Ask them to do additional research if necessary.

Support Materials

Assignments can include:

1. Chapter Review, pp. 368–369
2. Workbook, p. 53
3. Vocabulary and Comprehension Master V62
4. Test 8-2, p. CT48
5. Enrichment Master E48

UNIT 8

CHAPTER 3 African Slaves Resist Slavery

Overview   Enslaved Africans showed their hatred of slavery in many ways. Some defied their masters; others ran away; in some instances armed rebellion took place. African slaves were supported in their search for freedom by citizens of industrial Northern states. However, most of the white opponents of slavery wanted a gradual emancipation. Some runaway slaves reached freedom with the help of the "underground railroad." As a result of armed uprisings by African slaves, more restrictive laws were passed by Southern states.

Objectives

1. To learn the ways in which enslaved African Americans resisted slavery.
2. To describe the major slave rebellions in the South.
3. To learn about the underground railroad.
4. To understand how many citizens of Northern industrial states felt about slavery.
5. To explain how the new slave codes further restricted enslaved African Americans.

Developing the Chapter

1. Motivation: Direct students' attention to the map of the underground railroad on page 374 of their textbook. Explain that this organization worked to help enslaved Africans to escape to safety in Canada. Ask students to estimate how long it would take escaping slaves to reach their final destination on the railroad.

Ask: What do you think the people who worked for this group were like? Why did they want to help the slaves to gain freedom?

2. Introduction

a. Write the chapter vocabulary words on the chalkboard. Have students write each word and its glossary definition in their vocabulary notebook. Ask students to write an original sentence for each vocabulary word. Divide the students into pairs. Have each pair exchange papers and complete each other's sentences with the appropriate vocabulary words.

b. Have students read the chapter title and the Objective question.
Ask: How do you think enslaved Africans might have shown their hatred of slavery?

c. Have students preview the chapter visuals.
Ask: What can you tell about the life of slaves in the South during this period?

d. Have students read the chapter.

3. Review and Recall: After the students have read the chapter:

a. Have them ask each other questions about the content of each section.

b. Have them reread the Objective question and answer it.

c. Have them reread each subhead question and answer it.

d. Have them create a time line for the major events discussed in this chapter.

e. Divide the class into teams to play "Who Am I?" based on the people discussed in this chapter. The student pretending to be a historical figure of this period must answer yes-or-no questions posed by the other team until the team guesses the identity of the figure.

f. Write the following chart headings on the chalkboard: *Leader of Slave Revolt, Date, Results*. Have students complete the chart with appropriate information about the slave revolts discussed in this chapter.

4. Building Social Studies Skills: Explain that being able to tell the differences between facts and opinions is an important skill. Review the definitions of *fact* and *opinion*. A fact is a true statement that can be proved. An opinion is that which a person or a group of people think or believe to be true. An opinion cannot be proved to be true. Then have students identify two facts each from paragraphs 3 and 8. Ask them to write two examples of opinions based on information in these paragraphs.

5. Extension

a. Have students research and write a report on the underground railroad. Their reports should include information about the "conductors" who guided escaping Africans to freedom.

b. Have pairs of students role-play interviews between a modern reporter and one of the people from the chapter. Subjects for the interviews might be Harriet Tubman, Nat Turner, or Denmark Vessey.

Support Materials

Assignments can include:

1. Chapter Review, pp. 374–375
2. Vocabulary and Comprehension Master V63
3. Test 8-3, p. CT49
4. Enrichment Master E49

CHAPTER 4   Factories Grow in the Northeast

Overview   The invention of new machines such as the spinning frame and the power loom changed life in the North in the early 1800s. Goods began to be manufactured in factories rather than in small workshops. By 1860 many Northern cities had become associated with particular industries, such as textiles and meat packing. About 20 percent of Northern workers had a manufacturing job. The distinction between the industrial North and the agricultural South strengthened the divisions between these two areas of the country.

Objectives

1. To identify new machines that revolutionized the ways goods were produced.
2. To learn how the North became an industrial center of the country.
3. To describe the work and the living conditions of factory workers in the North.
4. To understand the growing differences between the industrial North and the agricultural South.

Developing the Chapter

1. Motivation: Point to an article of clothing worn by one of the students (such as running shoes) and ask the class how the item was made.
Ask: How do you think a pair of pants or shoes would have been made in 1700? Explain that it wasn't until the late 1700s that new textile-making machines were brought to the United States from England.
Ask: How do you think the new factories where these machines were used changed the life of the towns and cities where they were built? What do you think working conditions were like for these early factory workers?

   Point out that as they read the chapter students will learn more about these early factories.
2. Introduction
a. Write the chapter vocabulary words on the chalkboard. Have students write each word and its glossary definition in their vocabulary notebook. Write sentences on the chalkboard using each vocabulary word from the chapter. Have students try to determine the word's meaning from context clues.
b. Have students read the chapter title and the Objective question.

Ask: Can you think of any reasons why the Northeast became the manufacturing center of the United States?
c. Have students preview the chapter visuals.
   Ask: What can you learn about life in these early factories by studying these pictures?
d. Have students read the chapter.
3. Review and Recall: After the students have read the chapter:
a. Have them reread and answer the Objective question.
b. Have them reread and answer each subhead question.
c. Have students identify the main idea in each section.
d. Write the following heading on the chalkboard: *Life in the United States—1800.* Under this main heading, write: *Northern United Staes; Southern United States.* On the left side of the chart, in list form, write: *Economy; Kinds of Workers.* Then ask students to complete the chart with information from the chapter.

4. Building Social Studies Skills: Review with students the importance of using a time line to arrange the events in a chapter in chronological order. Help students to make a time line of the key events discussed in this chapter. They might also add dates such as those of the following inventions: the sewing machine (1846); the steam engine (1769); the cotton gin (1793); the steam-powered loom (1780s).

5. Extension
a. Have students research one of the machines invented between the late 1700s and the early 1800s. Their reports should include information on how the machine was operated, its effect on industry, and a picture that explains how it worked.
b. Have students create a poster to advertise jobs in one of the new factories in a Northeast town or city in the early 1800s. The posters should include both text and illustrations.

Support Materials
Assignments can include:
1. Chapter Review, pp. 380–381
2. Vocabulary and Comprehension Master V64
3. Test 8-4, p. CT50
4. Enrichment Master E50

UNIT 8

CHAPTER 5 Slavery Causes Bitter Feelings

Overview   Slavery became a divisive issue in the early 1800s. During this period, states entered the Union as either "slave" or "free." The Missouri Compromise temporarily settled the problem of allowing slavery in the territories. However, the North and the South continued to disagree over other issues, such as tariffs on imported goods. Meanwhile, Northern abolitionists such as William Lloyd Garrison spoke out against slavery, declaring it morally wrong. Their attitude angered Southerners, and the gulf between North and South widened.

Objectives

1. To learn about the events leading to the Missouri Compromise.
2. To understand how the issue of tariffs further divided North and South.
3. To learn how the abolitionists worked to end slavery.
4. To identify the issues that divided the North and the South by the 1830s.

Developing the Chapter

1. Motivation: Ask students to imagine themselves living in the United States at the beginning of the 1800s. A new state is about to enter the Union. Should it allow slavery within its borders or not? Have students explain their answers.

Ask: Do you think the federal government should have been able to tell citizens of a particular state whether or not they could own slaves?

Point out that Americans had different views on this question during the beginning of the 1800s. Explain that by reading this chapter students will learn how this issue was dealt with.

2. Introduction

a. Write the chapter vocabulary words on the chalkboard. Have students write each word and its glossary definition in their vocabulary notebooks. Ask volunteers to use each vocabulary word in a sentence.
b. Have students read the chapter title and the Objective question.
c. Have students preview the chapter visuals. Direct students' attention to the map on page 384. After studying the title and the map key, ask students to explain what the Missouri Compromise line was.

d. Have students read the chapter.

3. Review and Recall: After the students have read the chapter:

a. Have them reread and answer the Objective question.
b. Have them reread and answer each subhead question.
c. Have them ask each other questions about the chapter's content.
d. Have volunteers identify a fact from each section. Have other students present opinions based on the same information.
e. Divide the class into teams to play "Who Am I?" based on the persons in the chapter. The person pretending to be a historical figure must answer yes-or-no questions posed by the other team until the team guesses his or her identify. The team that correctly guesses the most identities wins.

4. Building Social Studies Skills: Remind students that readers often can use the context of a word to figure out its meaning. Point out that the words around an unfamiliar word often contain a definition of that word; at other times, the reader can figure out the meaning by what the other words say. Direct students' attention to the word *compromise* in paragraph 5. Ask them to find in the next sentence the definition of the word.

Ask: What does the word mean (an arrangement in which all sides agree to give up some of their demands)?

Repeat the procedure with *tariff,* in paragraph 6.

5. Extension

a. Have students create political cartoons that would have appeared in either a Northern or a Southern newspaper of the period. Possible topics include the Missouri Compromise, the abolitionist cause, the issue of tariffs.
b. Have students write an exchange of letters between two friends in 1825. One writer lives in New York, the other in Mississippi. The writers should focus on the events of the day and their hopes and fears for the future.

Support Materials

Assignments can include:

1. Chapter Review, pp. 386–387
2. Vocabulary and Comprehension Master V65
3. Test 8-5, p. CT51
4. Writing Workshop, pp. W9–W12
5. Enrichment Master E51

UNIT 8

CHAPTER 6   The North and South Grow Further Apart

Overview   The North and the South remained divided over the issue of slavery during the pre-Civil War period. The Compromise of 1850 attempted to settle the slavery issue in the lands gained by the United States through the Mexican cession. However, as the *Dred Scott* decision and the conflict in "bleeding Kansas" proved, there was no common ground for the troubled nation that could satisfy both pro- and antislavery forces. A new anti-slavery party, the Republicans, was created in 1854. Lincoln and Douglas debated the issue in 1858. The following year, John Brown's raid stirred strong emotions throughout the country.

Objectives

1. To learn how Congress tried to deal with the issue of slavery in new territories.
2. To describe the battle over slavery in Kansas.
3. To understand the effects of the Dred Scott decision.
4. To learn about the formation of the Republican party.

Developing the Chapter

1. Motivation: Explain that a new antislavery party, the Republican party, was formed in 1854. A series of important debates between Republican Abraham Lincoln and Democrat Stephen Douglas took place in 1858. Both men were candidates for senator from Illinois. Have students pretend to be members of the audience during one of these debates. Then read to the class the two excerpts from the Lincoln–Douglas debates on page 391.

Ask: Which speaker believed that the Union divided into slave and free States could last forever? What do the opinions expressed in these two speeches tell you about the mood of the country during this period before Civil War?

Explain that as they read this chapter, students will learn more about the events that led up to the war.

2. Introduction

a. Write the chapter vocabulary words on the chalkboard. Have students write each word and its glossary definition in their vocabulary notebook. Then have students make up word-search puzzles with all the vocabulary words in the unit. The words can be hidden horizontally, vertically or diagonally. Ask students to exchange papers and to solve each other's puzzles.

b. Have students read the chapter title and the Objective question.

c. Have students preview the chapter visuals.

d. Have students read the chapter.

3. Review and Recall: After the students have read the chapter:

a. Have them ask each other questions about each section of the chapter.

b. Have them reread and answer each subhead question.

c. Have them reread and answer the Objective question.

d. Have them make up a time line with the key events discussed in the chapter.

e. Write names, events, and terms from Chapter 6 on file cards. Divide the class into two teams. Have a member of the first team select a file card from a box and identify the name, the event, or the term.

4. Building Social Studies Skills: Review with students the use of an encyclopedia. Explain that an encyclopedia contains articles about a variety of topics. The entries are arranged in alphabetical order. The encyclopedia index includes the location of all the articles about a particular topic. Ask students to provide a list of entries, including page numbers and volumes, for the following topics: Dred Scott, Compromise of 1850, John Brown, Mexican cession, "bleeding Kansas."

5. Extension

a. Have students write news accounts of John Brown's trial for a newspaper of the period. They should answer the questions *who, what, where, when,* and *how* in the first paragraph. Suggest that students do additional research in their school libraries on the trial.

b. On an outline map of the United States, ask students to indicate the states that were "free" and the states that were "slave" in 1860. Have students do additional research to find the necessary information. Remind them to include a map legend that explains the symbols on their maps.

Support Materials

Assignments can include:

1. Chapter Review, pp. 392–393
2. Workbook, pp. 49, 50–51
3. Vocabulary and Comprehension Master V66
4. Test 8-6, p. CT52
5. Enrichment Master E52

UNIT 9

The Civil War and Reconstruction

Unit Overview   With the election of Abraham Lincoln as President in 1860, the nation moved toward Civil War as seven Southern states seceded, later to be joined by four others. The ensuing conflict lasted four years and cost more than 600,000 lives. It ended when Lee surrendered to Grant at Appomattox in 1865. African Americans did vote for a time in the South during Reconstruction. However, in the post-Reconstruction period, beginning in 1877, numerous laws ensuring racial segregation were passed. This principle of "separate but equal" was upheld by the Supreme Court in 1896.

Unit Objectives

1. To understand the causes of the Civil War.
2. To identify key events in the Civil War.
3. To learn about the Reconstruction period.
4. To understand the treatment of African Americans after Reconstruction.

Unit Introduction

1. Motivation: Point to the map of Union and Confederate states on page 402 of the textbook. Elicit any information students already have about the Civil War.
Ask: What do you think our lives would be like today if our country were now divided into two separate nations? What effect would this have on your daily lives? What differences would you expect between the two countries?
2. Visual: The unit opening visual is a contemporary print of the Battle of Lookout Mountain in November 1863. A Union victory, it was one of the key battles in the Union campaign to take Chattanooga. Ask students what they can infer about Civil War fighting from the picture.
3. Time Line: Have the class read the events on the time line. Ask them to identify events they are already familiar with and share their information with the rest of the class. Have them pinpoint events they are unfamiliar with. Write these events on the chalkboard and have students identify them as they read the unit.
4. Historical Points of View: Have students read the introductory paragraph in this feature. When they are finished, ask them to explain what secession is. Then have students read the first point of view.

Ask: According to this writer, what happens to citizens of states that have seceded from the Union? How does this writer view acts of resistance to a government? What does this writer think would happen in a nation where the opposite point of view was upheld? Do you agree or disagree with these opinions? Explain your answers.

Point out that in the second selection in this feature, the opposite point of view is presented. Have students read the selection.
Ask: What does this writer mean by the statement, "We have timber and gold enough to make another" (line 3)? According to the writer, what steps do the Southern states have to take to "have" their rights? Why do you think this writer refers to the war as a "war of revenge"? If the writers of these two editorials met one another, what do you think they would say?

Unit Activities

1. Creative Writing: Have students select one of the historical figures mentioned in this unit and do additional research on his or her life and the part that the individual played in the Civil War. Then ask students to write a series of diary entries that might have been written by that individual.
2. Cooperative Learning: Have students work in small groups to construct an illustrated time line that highlights major events from the election of Abraham Lincoln in 1860 to the *Plessy v. Ferguson* decision in 1896. Students can use as illustrations pictures cut from magazines or newspapers in addition to their own drawings.

Support Materials

Assignments can include:
1. Unit 9 Review, pp. 430–431
2. Unit Vocabulary and Comprehension Masters V74–V75
3. Unit 9 Test, pp. UT17–UT18

UNIT 9

CHAPTER 1   The Civil War Begins

Overview   The question of slavery was the primary issue of the election of 1860. After Lincoln's victory, with only 40 percent of the total popular vote, the Southern states seceded from the Union and formed a new national government. Jefferson Davis was chosen president of the Confederacy. The Civil War began on April 12, 1861, when Confederate forces fired on United States soldiers in Fort Sumter. Each side had certain advantages in fighting the war and hoped for an early victory. However, the difficult fighting at the Battle of Bull Run in July 1861 indicated that the war would be long and bloody.

Objectives

1. To learn about the presidential election of 1860.
2. To understand the factors that led to the formation of the Confederacy.
3. To learn how the Civil War began.
4. To identify the advantages and the disadvantages of each side in the Civil War.
5. To learn about the leaders of the Civil War.

Developing the Chapter

1. Motivation: Point to the pictures of Abraham Lincoln on pages 398 and 401. Elicit any information that students already have about Lincoln. Explain that between the time of his election and his taking office, seven Southern states seceded from the Union. Read students the selection from Lincoln's inaugural address on pages 401–402 of their textbook, in which he appeals to the South not to secede. Ask students to describe their reactions to Lincoln's words. Explain that students will learn what happened after Lincoln's election as they read this chapter.

2. Introduction

a. Write the chapter vocabulary words on the chalkboard. Have students write each word and its glossary definition in their vocabulary notebook. Ask volunteers to use each vocabulary word in a sentence. Call on volunteers to read aloud their sentences, without the vocabulary word. Have other students complete the sentences with the correct vocabulary word.

b. Have students read the chapter title and the Objective question. Ask students to predict how the Civil War will begin. Write their answers on the chalkboard. Refer back to students' predic-

tions as the class reads the chapter.

c. Have students preview the chapter visuals. Encourage them to volunteer their reaction to the picture of Jefferson Davis on page 399.

d. Have students read the chapter.

3. Review and Recall: After the students have read the chapter:

a. Have them reread and answer the Objective question.

b. Have them reread and answer each section question.

c. Have them complete a two-column, two-row chart that shows strengths and weaknesses of North and South.

d. Divide the class into teams to play "Who Am I?" based on the people discussed in the chapter. The person pretending to be a Civil War figure must answer yes-or-no questions posed by the other team until the team guesses the identity of the figure. The team that makes the most correct guesses wins.

4. Building Social Studies Skills: Have students study the map on page 402. Briefly review map-reading skills, including the use of the map legend (key), the compass rose (direction indicator), the scale, and longitude and latitude markings. Then have students use the map to identify the states that voted for the different candidates in the election of 1860.

5. Extension

a. Have students pretend to be citizens of either a Union or a Confederate state on April 12, 1861, when the Civil War began. Have them write letters to friends on the other side in which they describe their feelings at the start of the Civil War.

b. Have students write newspaper accounts of one of the events described in this chapter. Possible topics include the firing on Fort Sumter, the Battle of Bull Run, or the election of 1860. Remind students to write a headline for their article and to answer in the first paragraph the journalistic questions who, what, where, when, and why.

Support Materials

Assignments can include:

1. Chapter Review, pp. 404–405
2. Workbook, p. 54
3. Vocabulary and Comprehension Master V69
4. Test 9-1, p. CT53
5. Enrichment Master E53

UNIT 9

CHAPTER 2 The Early Years of the Civil War

Overview   Both North and South had specific military strategies for winning the war. The Union planned to blockade the South, to split the Confederacy along the Mississippi, and to take Richmond. The South's goal was to resist until the North was convinced that it could not win the war. The major battles of 1862 included the Peninsular Campaign, New Orleans, the Second Battle of Bull Run, Antietam, and Shiloh. During the summer of 1862, President Lincoln issued the Emancipation Proclamation, which declared that all Africans who were held as slaves in the Confederacy would be free on January 1, 1863.

Objectives

1. To understand the military strategies developed by the North and the South to win the war.
2. To learn about the early battles of the war.
3. To learn about the Emancipation Proclamation.

Developing the Chapter

1. Motivation: Have students look at the picture of the Battle of Lookout Mountain on pages 396–397 of the textbook. After students have had an opportunity to study the picture, elicit their response to it by asking questions such as the following: How does this picture make you feel about the Civil War? What can you learn about the war by studying it? How do you think United States citizens of the period would have responded to it?

2. Introduction

a. Write the chapter vocabulary words on the chalkboard. Have students write each word and its glossary definition in their vocabulary notebook. Then write sentences using each word. Have students try to determine the words' meanings from context clues.

b. Have students read the chapter title and the Objective question. Based on their knowledge of the geography and the economy of the North and the South, ask them to predict how each side might have planned to win the Civil War. Write their predictions on the chalkboard.

c. Have students preview the chapter visual.

Ask: What can you learn about the battle of the Monitor and the Merrimack from the picture of this event on page 406 of your textbook?

d. Have students read the chapter.

3. Review and Recall: After students have read the chapter:

a. Have students ask each other questions about the content of each section.

b. Have students reread and answer the Objective question.

c. Have students reread and answer each section question.

d. Have students identify one fact from each section. Ask other students to volunteer one opinion about the same material.

e. Have students make a time line of the major events discussed in this chapter.

f. Write the following chart title on the board: *Early Battles of the Civil War.* Then write the following headings at the top of the chart: *Peninsular Campaign, New Orleans, Second Battle of Bull Run, Antietam, Shiloh.* Write the following on the left side of the chart in list form: *Date, Casualties, Victor, Significance.* Have students complete the chart with information from the chapter.

4. Building Social Studies Skills: Remind students of the importance of taking accurate and concise notes. Each note card should be titled, and notes should be listed in abbreviated form. These notes should focus on the key points of the selection. Ask students to take notes on paragraphs 3–8 on file cards. Have volunteers read their note cards to the class.

5. Extension

a. Point out that the issues that divided the nation in the Civil War divided families and friends as well. Divide the class into small groups. Ask each group to dramatize a meeting between a Union and a Confederate soldier after one of the battles described in this chapter. The soldiers are brothers. This is the first time they've met since the Civil War began. Ask different groups to present their dramatizations to the class.

b. Ask students to prepare a diary entry written by an eyewitness to one of the historical events described in this chapter.

Support Materials

Assignments can include:

1. Chapter Review, pp. 410–111
2. Workbook, pp. 55–57
3. Vocabulary and Comprehension Master V70
4. Test 9-2, p. CT54
5. Map Transparency Activity Sheet A20
6. Enrichment Master E54

UNIT 9

CHAPTER 3 The North Wins the Civil War

Overview The battles of Gettysburg and Vicksburg in July 1863 were the turning point of the Civil War. The Confederacy collapsed in 1865, and General Robert E. Lee surrendered his army to General Ulysses Grant at Appomattox on April 9, 1865. During the Civil War, African Americans enlisted in both the Union army and the navy and helped to win the war for the North. Women also played important roles in the war effort by managing family farms in the absence of husbands and sons and by working in factories. The Civil War increased the power of the federal government and promoted the idea of equality.

Objectives

1. To learn about the main battles of 1863–1865.
2. To understand the contributions of African Americans to the war effort.
3. To understand the contributions of women to the war effort.
4. To describe the results of the war.

Developing the Chapter

1. Motivation: Show a videotape of Edward Zwick's 1989 film *Glory* or John Huston's 1951 film *The Red Badge of Courage*.
Ask: How do soldiers seem to feel in these battles? What do you think it would have been like to take part in such battles for four years?

Next, read students the excerpts from the Gettysburg Address on page 413 of the textbook.
Ask: How would you compare Lincoln's view of the war with what you saw in the film?

2. Introduction
a. Write the chapter vocabulary words on the chalkboard. Have students write each word and its glossary definition in their vocabulary notebook. Ask volunteers to use each word in original sentences. Have pairs of students exchange papers and complete them.
b. Have students read the chapter title and the Objective question. Ask students to predict how the war will affect people's lives in both the Union and the Confederacy.
c. Have students read the chapter.

3. Review and Recall: After the students have read the chapter:
a. Have them reread and answer the Objective question.
b. Have them reread and answer each section question.
c. Ask students to list the contributions of African Americans and women to the Civil War.
d. Ask students to make a time line of the important events discussed in this chapter.
e. Write the following on file cards: *April 9, 1865; General Grant; General Lee; Battle of Gettysburg; Battle of Vicksburg; Chancellorsville; General George G. Meade; Gettysburg Address; Abraham Lincoln; Chattanooga; General Sherman; Richmond; "March to the Sea"; Appomattox Court House; 54th Massachusetts; Clara Barton; "Angel of the Battlefield."* Divide the class into two teams. Ask each team member to select a file card and to identify the item on the card. Each correct identification is worth five points. The team with the most points after all the cards have been drawn is the winner.

4. Building Social Studies Skills: Remind students of the difference between a primary source and a secondary source. Have students identify the primary source included in this chapter (excerpt from the Gettysburg Address). Ask them to identify three primary sources and three secondary sources that they would use to learn about the final years of the Civil War. (Primary sources include letters and diaries, newspaper accounts, and battle maps. Secondary sources include history books, biographies, and historical atlases.)

5. Extension
a. Have students write imaginary diary entries from the point of view of a woman living in the Union or in the Confederacy during the Civil War. In the entries the writer will talk about her feelings about the war, how she has contributed to the war effort, and her hopes for the future.
b. Ask students to read the full text of Lincoln's Gettysburg Address. Then have them write editorials for either a Union or a Confederate newspaper in which they comment on Lincoln's speech and on the progress of the war.

Support Materials

Assignments can include:
1. Chapter Review, pp. 416–417
2. Workbook, p. 58
3. Vocabulary and Comprehension Master V71
4. Test 9-3, p. CT55
5. Map Transparency Activity Sheet A21
6. Enrichment Master E55

CHAPTER 4   Reconstruction

Overview   The Reconstruction period lasted from 1865 to 1877. After Lincoln's death, Andrew Johnson, who became president, tried to complete Lincoln's plans for restoring the South to the Union. However, the radical Republicans who controlled Congress took over the plans for Reconstruction and implemented a policy of rights for African Americans and power for the Freedman's Bureau. Johnson vetoed many of the laws passed by Congress, and in 1868 the House of Representatives impeached him. He was tried by the Senate and found not guilty. Ulysses S. Grant was elected President in 1868. By 1877, with the reassertion of white control in the South, Reconstruction ended.

Objectives

1. To understand how Andrew Johnson tried to complete Lincoln's plans for Reconstruction.
2. To describe the radical Republicans' plans for rebuilding the South and how Congress clashed with President Johnson.
3. To learn about the Constitutional amendments that were ratified during Reconstruction.
4. To identify the accomplishments of the Reconstruction governments in the South.
5. To learn what led to the end of Reconstruction and how this affected African Americans.

Developing the Chapter

1. Motivation: Tell students that you are going to read a description of Georgia after the war. Then read them the following description:

It looked for many miles like a broad, black streak of ruin and destruction—the fences all gone; lonesome smokestacks surrounded by dark heaps of ashes and cinders, marking the spots where homes had stood, the fields along the road wildly overgrown with weeds.

Ask: If you lived in the South after the Civil War, how would you have felt about the destruction that the war had caused to your land? Imagine yourself as the president or a member of Congress during this period. How would you have gone about rebuilding the South? What problems do you think would have to be solved first? How would you have gone about bringing the South back into the Union?

2. Introduction

a. Write the chapter vocabulary words on the chalkboard. Have students write each word and its glossary definition in their vocabulary notebook. Then ask students to use each word in an original sentence.

b. Have students read the chapter title and the Objective question. Have students identify potential problems involved in bringing the South back into the Union. Refer to their predictions as you read the chapter.

c. Have students preview the chapter visuals. **Ask:** What do these illustrations tell you about life in the South during this period?

d. Have students read the chapter.

3. Review and Recall: After the students have read the chapter:

a. Have them reread each subhead question and answer it.

b. Have them reread the Objective question and answer it.

c. Have them make up questions based on each section and quiz one another.

d. Have students make a time line of key events.

4. Building Social Studies Skills: As a group activity, help students make a chart that explains President Johnson's plans for Reconstruction and the plans of the radical Republicans. Begin by titling the chart and deciding the headings to appear at the top. Then call on volunteers to complete the chart with information from the chapter.

5. Extension

a. Have students write imaginary diary entries from the point of view of one of the following individuals: a Confederate soldier who returns home to find his house destroyed; a former slave freed by the North's victory in the Civil War who is now living in a Southern state during the Reconstruction period; Andrew Johnson on the eve of his impeachment trial.

b. Have students write editorials for either a Northern or a Southern newspaper commenting on the Reconstruction plans of the radical Republicans.

Support Materials

Assignments can include:

1. Chapter Review, pp. 422–423
2. Workbook, p. 59
3. Vocabulary and Comprehension Master V72
4. Test 9-4, p. CT56
5. Enrichment Master E56

CHAPTER 5 From Slavery to Segregation

Overview After the Civil War, many African Americans were treated harshly, and their efforts to obtain legal and social equality were not rewarded. Freed African Americans in the South labored as sharecroppers without hope of owning the land they worked. Their rights were further abridged by the racial segregation laws that were first passed in the South in the early 1880s. These laws were later upheld by the Supreme Court, with only Justice Harlan dissenting. Other laws were passed to deny African Americans the right to vote. Booker T. Washington and W.E.B. DuBois were the most important African American leaders during this difficult period.

Objectives

1. To learn what life was like in the South after Reconstruction.
2. To understand the new agricultural labor system in the South during this period.
3. To learn about the racial segregation laws that were passed after Reconstruction.
4. To identify the contributions of Booker T. Washington and W.E.B. DuBois.

Developing the Chapter

1. Motivation: Explain that in 1896 the Supreme Court upheld a law that took away many rights of African American citizens. Only one justice, John Harshall Harlan, who was himself a Southerner, argued against racial segregation. Then read students the excerpt from Harlan's dissent on page 425 of their textbook. (Alternatively, you might want to read the entire dissent to the class.)

Ask: How do you think African Americans would have felt when they read what Justice Harlan said? How do you think many Southerners at the end of the nineteenth century would have reacted to his words? Why is it so important for the constitution of any country to be "color blind"? What do these words mean to you?

2. Introduction

a. Write the chapter vocabulary words on the chalkboard. Have students write each word and its glossary meaning in their vocabulary notebook. Then have students make up word-search puzzles with all the vocabulary words in the unit. The words can be hidden horizontally, vertically, or diagonally. Ask students to exchange papers and circle the words in each other's word search puzzles.

b. Have students read the chapter title and the Objective question.
   Ask: How do you think African Americans were treated after Reconstruction? In what ways do you think they faced setbacks in their struggle for equality? Write students' answers on the chalkboard, and refer back to their predictions as you read the chapter.

c. Have students preview the chapter visuals.
   Ask: What can you learn from these pictures about life in the South after Reconstruction?

d. Have students read the chapter.

3. Review and Recall: After the students have read the chapter:

a. Have them reread and answer the Objective question.

b. Have them reread and answer each section question.

c. Have students make up a crossword puzzle using words and ideas from the chapter. After they have written all the Down and Across clues, they can solve each other's puzzles.

4. Building Social Studies Skills: Remind students that outlines are a useful way to organize information. Briefly review the use of the main headings, headings, and subheadings. Point out that topical outlines are easier and more concise than sentence outlines. Then have students make outlines of paragraphs 1–7.

5. Extension

a. Ask students to research the history of the Populist party. Then have them make up posters that might have been used by the Populists to encourage small farmers and sharecroppers to vote for Populist candidates. The posters should include both illustrations and text.

b. Have students write editorials either in support of or in opposition to the *Plessy v. Ferguson* decision.

Support Materials

Assignments can include:

1. Chapter Review, pages 428–429
2. Vocabulary and Comprehension Master V73
3. Test 9-5, p. CT57
4. Enrichment Master E57

UNIT 10

The United States Becomes an Industrial Nation

Unit Overview   The United States developed into an industrialized nation in the late 1800s. New inventions revolutionized agricultural and industrial production. Improvements in rail and water travel enabled goods to be shipped to more customers more quickly. Business empires created by industrialists such as Andrew Carnegie and John D. Rockefeller flourished. Many of the poorest workers were European and Asian immigrants who flocked to the United States in record numbers seeking a better life. Increased population was one of the many factors that contributed to the growth and the development of cities during this period. Living conditions in urban areas were difficult for the poorest citizens; however, middle-class citizens enjoyed the benefits of city life.

Unit Objectives

1. To understand how the United States became an industrial nation between the end of the Civil War and the beginning of the twentieth century.
2. To explain the rise of big business during this period.
3. To learn about the large numbers of immigrants who came to the United States.
4. To identify the factors that contributed to the growth of cities in the late 1800s.
5. To learn about city life during this period.

Unit Introduction

1. Motivation: Bring in photographs or illustrations of an American city, such as New York or San Francisco before the Civil War and at the turn of the twentieth century. Elicit students' reactions to these two urban scenes.
Ask: How has life in this city changed in only fifty years? What do you think is responsible for these changes in the way people lived?

Point out that in a relatively short period of time, peoples' lives and life-styles can change dramatically. Have students speculate on what life will be like in 50 years.
2. Visual: Ask students to look at the painting that opens Unit 10 and to comment on how the artist shows the drama and excitement of industry through color and swirling lines. Point out that in the late 1800s, large-scale manufacturing was new and had a more glamorous image than it has today.

Ask students to speculate on aspects of industry that might have appealed to people in the 1800s.
3. Time Line: Have the class read the events on the unit time line (pp. 432–433). Ask if any of them are familiar with the events shown there. Call on volunteers to share any prior knowledge.
Ask: What do many of the events from 1790 to 1879 relate to?

Encourage students to refer to the unit time line as they study the unit.
4. Historical Points of View: Have students read the introductory paragraph of this feature.
Ask: Which factor was responsible for the change in the way Americans lived? Ask students to read the first point of view.
Ask: What were the living conditions of the family like? What was the woman's job? Why was it so difficult for her to work?

Then have students read the second point of view.
Ask: Why does the author of this article think that cities are the best place to conduct business? How does he describe city life during this period?

If the authors of these two articles could meet each other, what do you think they would say? How do you account for the difference in the point of view of these two articles? How do you feel about the last statement from "A Professor's View"?

Unit Activities

1. Cooperative Learning: Have students work together to create an illustrated time line that highlights major events that took place in the period covered in this unit. Encourage them to use pictures from old magazines or drawn by students to illustrate the time line.
2. Research: Have students research what life was like in American cities in the late nineteenth century. Ask each student to select a particular city to research. Then have them pretend to be city planners of the period and draw a map of a proposed community within the city that would include the facilities most needed by the citizens who lived there. Encourage students to be as thoughtful as possible as they construct their neighborhoods.

Support Materials

Assignments can include:
1. Unit 10 Review, pp. 466–467
2. Unit Vocabulary and Comprehension Masters V81–V82
3. Unit 10 Test, pp. UT19–UT20

T91

UNIT 10

CHAPTER 1   The Growth of Industry to 1860

Overview   Prior to the Civil War, American industry developed significantly. These industrial advances were facilitated by new and improved systems of transportation and communication. In addition, inventions such as the reaper, the thresher, and the sewing machine, as well as Eli Whitney's concept of interchangeable parts, improved agricultural and industrial production. Factory-made goods that were cheap and accessible changed the way Americans lived. Increased industrial production also resulted in urban pollution and harsh conditions for many workers.

Objectives

1. To identify the inventions that affected travel and communication prior to the Civil War..
2. To identify the inventions that affected agriculture and industry prior to the Civil War.
3. To understand how the iron and textile industries developed.
4. To learn how agricultural and industrial jobs were changed by the development of new technology.
5. To learn how industrial development changed the way Americans lived.

Developing the Chapter

1. Motivation: Bring in a box of nails and show them to the students.

Ask: What do we use nails for?

Point out that cheap nails cut by machines weren't available in our country until after 1830. Similarly, many of the inventions that changed the way Americans lived and led to the development of the country as we know it today were created at the beginning of the nineteenth century. Ask students to name and discuss inventions that are useful to them in their daily lives.

How would you preserve your food or cook your meals?

Explain that in this chapter students will learn how inventions such as the machine-produced nail, changed American life.

2. Introduction

a. Write the chapter vocabulary words on the chalkboard. Have students write each word and its glossary definition in their vocabulary notebooks. Ask students to use each word in an original sentence. Call on volunteers to read aloud each sentence without the vocabulary word. Have other students identify the word that will correctly complete the sentence.

b. Have students read the chapter title and the Objective queston.

Ask: How do you think the American industry developed before the Civil War?

c. Have students preview the chapter visuals.

Ask: What can you deduce about railroad travel from the chart on page 440? What does this tell you about how life changed during this period?

d. Have students read the chapter.

3. Review and Recall: After the students have read the chapter:

a. Have them reread the Objective question and answer it.

b. Have them reread each section question and answer it.

c. Have one student identify a change in industrial or agricultural life. Call on another student to identify one effect of this change.

d. Call on students to identify characteristics of a particular industrial or agricultural invention. Other students in the class must then identify the invention being described.

4. Building Social Studies Skills: Review with students the importance of making a time line to organize historical events in chronological order. Help students make a time line of the inventions discussed in this chapter. When they have finished, ask them to identify the decades in which major changes that affected transportation, communication, and industry took place.

5. Extension

a. Have students select one of the inventions discussed in this chapter. Ask them to make up an advertisement for the device that would appeal to American consumers of the period. Their ads should include both pictures and text.

b. Ask students ot select one of the inventions described in this chapter and make a model or a diagram that explains its use.

Support Materials

Assignments can include:

1. Chapter Review, pp. 440–441
3. Vocabulary and Comprehension Master V76
4. Test 10-1, p. CT58
5. Enrichment Master E58

UNIT 10

CHAPTER 2   An Industrial Nation

Overview   In the latter half of the nineteenth century, the United States became the world's leading industrial nation. The number of railroad-track miles in 1900 was six times what it had been just forty years before. New industries and sources of energy developed. Steel replaced iron as the main industrial metal. Inexpensive electrical power was widely used. The gasoline engine led to the development of the automobile and with it a new emphasis on methods of mass production. As a result of these advances, assembly lines were introduced that changed the work of many Americans.

Objectives

1. To identify how the United States became the leading industrial nation in the world.

2. To learn how railroad growth contributed to the country's industrial boom.

3. To identify the new industries that developed.

4. To identify the new sources of energy that shaped American industry.

5. To learn how the lives of American workers were changed by this new technology.

Developing the Chapter

1. Motivation: Bring in a picture of an early Model T Ford. Explain that this Ford car was mass-produced in the United States in the early 1900s. **Ask:** How do you think the automobile changed the way Americans lived?

Discuss with students the importance of continually inventing products that change the way we live.

Ask: What would you invent to change our method of transportation today? Encourage students to be as creative as possible in thinking about their inventions. Point out that without this never-ending process of inventing, the United States would never have become a great industrial leader.

2. Introduction

a. Write the chapter vocabulary words on the chalkboard. Have students write each word and its glossary definition in their vocabulary notebooks. Ask students to make up a synonym and an antonym for each vocabulary word. Call on other students to identify the vocabulary word that matches the synonym and the antonym.

b. Have students read the chapter title and the Objective question. Ask them how they think the

United States became an industrial nation.

c. Have students preview the chapter visuals. **Ask:** Based on the information on the chart on page 445, what were some of the most important inventions of the late 1800s?

d. Have students read the chapter.

3. Review and Recall: After the students have read the chapter:

a. Have them ask each other factual questions about the chapter's content.

b. Play "What Am I?" with the class. Call on one student to give four or five clues about a particular invention. The other students must identify the invention being described.

c. Have students make up a crossword puzzle using words and ideas from the chapter. After they have written all the Down and Across clues, they can try to solve each other's puzzles.

4. Building Social Studies Skills: Review map-reading skills with students. Refer to the compass rose, the scale of distance, and the title of the map on page 444 of the chapter. Ask a series of questions about key locations on the map.

Ask: What were the main cities where steel making was an important industry? In what areas of the country was steel making an important industry? Have students use the scale of distance to determine the number of miles from as specific steel-producing city to another city on the map.

5. Extension

a. Point out that although mass production was important, some people believe that it's important to create products by hand because of the skill involved. Stage a class debate between students representing Henry Ford and a watchmaker who still makes timepieces by hand.

b. Have students do additional research about the early assemble line. Then have them write letters from workers in a factory of the period. The letters should reflect the workers' feelings about the conditions in the factories.

Support Materials

Assignments can include:

1. Chapter Review, pp. 446–447

2. Workbook, pp. 60, 64

3. Vocabulary and Comprehension Master V77

4. Test 10-2, p. CT59

5. Enrichment Master E59

UNIT 10

CHAPTER 3   The Rise of Big Business

Overview   Between 1865 and 1900, business empires led by powerful men such as John D. Rockefeller and Andrew Carnegie controlled American industry. The growing power of big business in the form of giant corporations and trusts frightened many Americans. The ICC was the first governmental commission set up to regulate an industry. Congress also tried, unsuccessfully, to break up the trusts by passing the Sherman Anti-Trust Act of 1890. The "Panic of 1893" left millions out of work.

Objectives

1. To understand the role of big business in America's industrial econlmy.
2. To learn about influential business leaders such as Andrew Carnegie and John D. Rockefeller.
3. To learn how the government tried to regulate big business.
4. To explain what happened during the depression of 1893.
5. To understand how American business found new ways to sell its low-priced goods.

Developing the Chapter

1. Motivation: Ask students to imagine that they are owners of a small business; for example, they design and manufacture a T-shirt with a special design or logo. A large clothing manufacturer produces the same style T-shirt at a lower price.
Ask: Why would it be difficult to compete with the bigger clothing corporation?

Point out that at the turn of the century in this country, large corporations were able to control an entire industry. In the following chapter, students will learn how it was done.

2. Introduction
a. Write the chapter vocabulary words on the chalkboard. Then write sentences on the chalkboard using each vocabulary word from the chapter. Have students try to determine the words' meanings from context clues. When they have finished, have them look up each work in the glossary. Then ask them to write the word and its definition in their vocabulary notebook.
b. Have students read the chapter title and the Objective question.
Ask: How do you think that big businesses controlled industries in America during this period?
c. Have students preview the chapter visuals.

Ask: How is a large corporation organized?
d. Have students read the chapter.

3. Review and Recall: After students have read the chapter:
a. Ask them to reread the chapter Objective question and answer it.
b. Have them reread each section question and answer it.
c. Have them reread the first sentence in the Outlook section and find five examples from the chapter that supports this statement.
d. Write the following heading on the chalkboard: *Government Attempts to Regulate Big Business.* Ask students to complete the chart with appropriate information from the chapter.
e. Ask students to identify one fact from each section and to write an opinion based on this fact.

4. Building Social Studies Skills: Review with students the importance of using the library card catalogue to find books for a research report on a particular topic. Have them select an individual or an event discussed in this chapter. Ask them to find six books in the card catalogue that they could use to research the report. Ask them to note the following information about each book on the bibliography file card: title, author, publisher, and date of publication. Ask students with the same research topic to compare the books they found.

5. Extension
a. Have students research and write a report on the lives and life-styles of the robber barons of the period. Possible topics include John D. Rockefeller, Andrew Carnegie, Henry Clay Frick, or Cornelius Vanderbilt. Their reports should include information on how their business empires began and flourished.
b. Have students role-play an interview between a contemporary journalist and one of the business tycoons discussed in this chapter. The questions should focus on the subject's business practices and opinions of American business during this period. Call on different teams of students to present their interviews to the class.

Support Materials

Assignment can include:
1. Chapter Review, pp. 452–453
2. Workbook, p. 65
3. Vocabulary and Comprehension Master V78
4. Test 10-3, p. CT60
5. Enrichment Master E60

UNIT 10

CHAPTER 4   Immigrants Bring New Ways of Life to America

Overview   Immigrants came to the United States in record numbers after the Civil War, seeking a better life. Prior to the 1890s, most immigrants had come from northern and western Europe. In the last years of the century, people came from southern and eastern Europe. Immigrants worked in the most menial jobs, where working conditions were harsh. Native-born Americans reacted angrily and sometimes violently to the immigrant workers. As a result, the government passed laws to limit immigration from certain countries.

Objectives

1. To identify the immigrants who came to the United States at the end of the 1800s.
2. To understand where immigrants lived.
3. To learn about the employment opportunities for immigrants.
4. To explain how native-born Americans felt about the immigrants.

Developing the Chapter

1. Motivation: Bring in pictures of the Statue of Liberty and Ellis Island. Elicit any information students might have about the history of the monument. Explain that the giant statue is 225 tons (202.5 t). It is a steel-reinforced, copper female figure. It stands 152 feet (45.6 m) high and faces the Atlantic Ocean from Liberty Island in New York Harbor. The statue was a gift to this country from the French nation in honor of the alliance of the two countries in the American Revolution and their continuing friendship. The statue was accepted by President Grover Cleveland in 1886. It was the welcome that greeted European immigrants to the country when they arrived at their entry point on Ellis Island.

Ask: What feelings does the poet express about the Statues of Liberty? How do you think immigrants to this country felt when they first saw the statue? What did it mean to them? What do these words mean to you now?

2. Introduction

a. Write the chapter vocabulary words on the chalkboard. Have students write each word and its glossary definition in their vocabulary notebook. Ask volunteers to use each vocabulary word in a sentence.

b. Have students read the chapter title and the Objective question. Elicit any information they might have about the people who immigrated to the United States at the end of the 1800s.

c. Have students review the chapter visuals. **Ask:** What do you think life was like for these immigrants?

d. Have students read the chapter.

3. Review and Recall: After the students have read the chapter:

a. Have them reread the Objective question and answer it.

b. Have them reread each section question and answer it.

c. Write the following chart headings on the chalkboard: *Country of Origin, Date of Immigration, Occupation, Living Conditions.* Have students complete the chart with appropriate information about immigrant life from this chapter.

4. Building Social Studies Skills: Review the difference between primary and secondary sources. A primary source is written by someone who has actually experienced the event first-hand. A secondary source is written by someone who did not witness an event but has researched primary sources of the period for information. Have students identify the primary sources in this chapter. Ask students to identify primary sources they would use to find out about the immigrant experience (diaries, letters, eyewitness accounts, photographs, interviews, court records and other legal documents).

5. Extension

a. Have students research and write reports on the working conditions of immigrant workers at the turn of the century. Their reports should include information about a typical workday of the period and how and where the immigrants worked.

b. Have students write editorials that might have appeared in newspapers of the early twentieth century about the recent influx of immigrants to the country.

Support Materials

Assignments can include:

1. Chapter Review, pp. 458–459
2. Workbook, p. 61
3. Vocabulary and Comprehension Master V79
4. Test 10-4, p. CT61
5. Enrichment Master E61

UNIT 10

CHAPTER 5   The Growth of Cities

Overview   The rapid industrialization of the United States resulted in the growth and development of its cities. The largest cities were often located near major waterways and important mineral resources. By the end of the nineteenth century, many of America's large cities were battling overcrowding and serious health problems. City governments took steps to improve the quality of urban life. Private citizens such as Jane Addams started settlement houses to provide training, advice, and recreation for the poor. For the middle class, cities offered increased cultural and economic opportunities.

Objectives

1. To understand how industrialization, geographical features, and improved transportation systems led to the growth and the development of cities in the United States.
2. To learn about living conditions in American cities.
3. To study the ways in which city governments improved life for their citizens.
4. To learn about the benefits of city life.

Developing the Chapter

1. Motivation: Bring in photographs that illustrate city life at the turn of the century. Elicit students' reactions.

Ask: What do you think life was like for people who lived in poor neighborhoods?

Point out that while the middle class enjoyed a comfortable life, slum dwellers faced unsanitary and often dangerous living conditions. Explain that students will learn more about city life at the turn of the century as they read the chapter.

2. Introduction

a. Write the chapter vocabulary words on the chalkboard. Have students write each word and its glossary definition in their vocabulary notebooks. Then have students make up word-search puzzles with all the vocabulary words in this unit. Ask students to exchange papers and solve each other's puzzles.

b. Have students read the chapter title and the Objective question.

Ask: Can you think of any factors that would have contributed to the growth and the development of cities at the end of the nineteenth century?

Write students' answers on the chalkboard. Refer to their predictions as you read the chapter.

c. Have students read the chapter.

3. Review and Recall: After the students have read the chapter:

a. Ask them to reread and answer the Objective question.

b. Have them reread and answer each subhead question.

c. Make two columns on the chalkboard: *Problems; Solution.* Have students identify the problems that faced cities during this period and how city governments attempted to solve them. List their answers on the board in the appropriate column.

4. Building Social Studies Skills: Review with students the importance of using outlines to organize information. Briefly discuss the use of main headings, headings, and subheadings in standard outlines. Point out that topical outlines that do not use full sentences to present the factual information have a simpler format. Then have students read sections 2–5 and use them to make an outline of these paragraphs. Use the following as a start.

I. Factors contributing to urbanization
   A. Industrialization
   B. Geography

5. Extension

a. Have students research the twelve largest cities in the United States in 1900. Then have them locate the cities on an outline map of the country. Their map should also include the important industries in the country during this period. Ask them to include a map legend that explains the symbols on their map. When they have finished, they should be able to correlate the geographical and the industrial influences on the growth of cities during this period.

b. Have students pretend to be reporters for turn-of-the-century city newspapers. Ask them to write a news account based on one aspect of city life discussed in this chapter.

Support Materials

Assignments can include:

1. Chapter Review, pp. 464–465
2. Workbook, pp. 62–63
3. Vocabulary and Comprehension Master V80
4. Test 10-5, p. CT62
5. Enrichment Master E62

UNIT 11

Reform Movements

Unit Overview   In the late nineteenth and early twentieth centuries, Americans tried to improve society through governmental reforms and private initiative. As America became more industrialized, labor unions were created to help workers achieve better working conditions. The most successful union was the American Federation of Labor (AFL), founded in 1886. The Grange and the Populist party tried to help farmers, many of whom faced financial ruin at the end of the nineteenth century. The crusade for women's rights began in 1848. By the end of the century, women had made major gains in rights to equal education and employment. Other reformers worked to make changes in the educational, health care, and prison systems. The Populist party sought to make the government more responsive to the needs of the citizens.

Unit Objectives

1. To describe the ways in which reformers tried to better the lives of Americans.
2. To identify the role played by unions in the nineteenth and early twentieth centuries.
3. To explain how farmers were helped by the Grange and the Populist party.
4. To explain the aims of the women's rights movement.
5. To describe the changes in the educational, health care, and prison systems in this period.
6. To list the goals and accomplishments of the Progressive party.

Unit Introduction

1. **Motivation:** Explain that journalists who wrote exposés about political and social injustices at the turn of the century were called *muckrakers*. One of the most famous was Lincoln Steffens, a magazine writer who exposed corruption in business and government.

Ask: Why do you think life was so harsh for many Americans during this period? If you had lived at this time, what would you have done to change the way people lived? Explain that this was a time when groups of people, called Progressives, got together to make important changes in American life.

2. **Visual:** Direct students' attention to the unit opening picture of workers.

Ask: What do you think it was like to work as these men were? Why do you think people wanted to improve working conditions in factories and other work places?

3. **Time Line:** Ask the class to read the time line on pages 468 and 469 and to look for familiar names and events.

Ask: From the events included on this time line, which groups of people do you think the reformers tried to help during this period?

4. **Points of View:** Have the students read the first paragraph of the introduction and make sure that they understand why American society was in such turmoil at this time. Then explain that there were different points of view as to how the country's problems could be addressed. Have them read Professor Sumner's point of view and contrast it with that of Theodore Roosevelt. Ask students which position they agree with. Point out that they will come across the same kinds of differences of opinion when they read about the Great Depression of the 1930s.

Unit Activities

1. **Cooperative Learning:** Divide the class into small groups of students. Ask each group to select an event from the chapters and dramatize it. Suggest that students do additional research where necessary to find out more information about their incident. Encourage them to consult such primary sources as autobiographies of historical figures to give them a more personal sense of the era.

2. **Creative Writing:** Ask students to imagine that they can go back in time and participate in one of the reform movements discussed in this unit. Have them write a first-person narrative in which they describe what they, as reformers, are doing to bring about change and how they feel about the likelihood of their bringing about change. Reform movements that they might choose to write about include women's rights, the Populist movement, the Progressive party, the Grange, health care, and education.

Support Materials

Assignments can include:

1. Unit Review, pp. 502–503
2. Unit Vocabulary and Comprehension Masters V88–V89
3. Unit 11 Test, pp. UT21–UT22
4. Map Transparency Activity Sheet A23

UNIT 11

CHAPTER 1 Unions Help Workers

Overview As the United States became an industrialized nation, unions were organized to improve working conditions in factories. The first unions were organized in the 1800s. However, the early unions, such as the National Labor Union, had limited success. The Knights of Labor, with 700,000 members by 1886, was more successful in achieving gains from industry. The power of the Knights of Labor declined after a series of strikes that were marked by violence. The American Federation of Labor (AFL), founded in 1886, won important gains for its members in terms of improved working conditions and higher pay.

Objectives

1. To describe what the early labor unions in the United States were like.
2. To identify the achievements of the national labor unions.
3. To explain how some strikes resulted in violence.
4. To identify the achievements of the AFL.

Developing the Chapter

1. Motivation: Bring in a sweater or another piece of clothing that has a union-made label in it and show it to the class. Elicit whatever information students already have about what unions are and how they operate. Then read to students the excerpt from Arthur Burgoyne's eyewitness account of the Homestead strike on page 474 of their book. **Ask:** Do you think that the owners of the steel company should have hired new workers to replace the striking workers? Why do you think it was so difficult for many industries to accept unions? Can you think of any recent strikes in your city or state? Point out that students will learn more about the history of the labor-union movement in this country as they read the chapter.

2. Introduction

a. Write the chapter vocabulary words on the chalkboard. Have students write each word and its glossary definition in their vocabulary notebook. Then ask them to use each word in an original sentence. Call on students to read aloud their sentences without the vocabulary word. Have other students supply the missing word based on context clues.

b. Have students read the chapter title and the Objective questions.

c. Have students preview the chapter visuals. Based on these pictures, what do they think working conditions in the early days of the labor-union movement were like?

d. Have students read the chapter.

3. Review and Recall: After the students have read the chapter:

a. Have them answer the Objective question.

b. Have them answer each section question.

c. Have them ask one another factual questions based on each section.

d. Have students make up a crossword puzzle using words and ideas from the chapter. After they have written all the clues, they should try to solve each other's puzzles.

4. Building Social Studies Skills: Remind students of the importance of taking accurate and concise notes on their reading. These notes will help them review for tests and write research reports. Review basic notetaking skills with the class: notes should be taken on file cards; notes should be written in phrases, rather than in sentences, to save space; notes should reflect the most important facts about a topic; each note card should have a topic heading. Ask students to reread and take notes on Sections 1 through 6 of the chapter. Compare note cards that were written by different students about the same material.

5. Extension

a. Have students write editorials for a contemporary newspaper about one of the events described in this chapter. They can choose to write for a paper that is either pro-union or pro-industry. Have volunteers read editorials aloud that reflect different points of view.

b. Have students make up posters that encourage workers to join an early labor union. Their posters should include illustrations as well as text. Display the posters in the classroom.

Support Materials

Assignments can include:

1. Chapter Review, pp. 476–477
2. Workbook, p. 66
3. Vocabulary and Comprehension Master V83
4. Test 11-1, p. CT63
5. Enrichment Master E63

UNIT 11

CHAPTER 2 Farmers Face Hard Times

Overview Farmers faced a harsh economic reality at the end of the nineteenth century. Overproduction resulted in a sharp decrease in prices for agricultural products, bringing many farmers to financial ruin. High railroad rates compounded the problem. The Grange, founded in the 1860s, provided information and social contacts for farmers. Later, farmers helped to form the short-lived Populist party. However, the influence of the farmers continued to decline as more people moved from rural to urban areas.

Objectives

1. To outline the problems faced by American farmers at the end of the nineteenth century.
2. To describe how the Grange tried to help the struggling farmers.
3. To explain the reasons for the rise and the decline of the Populist party.

Developing the Chapter

1. Motivation: Bring in recent newspaper or magazine articles about the economic difficulties faced by farmers.

Ask: What would you do if you were a farmer faced with these problems? How would you go about trying to resolve them?

Elicit any information that students may have about the situation and the reasons for these economic problems.

Ask: Are there new problems, or have farmers always faced problems like these? What do you think was different about farmers' problems a hundred years ago?

Confirm that one hundred years ago, American farmers also faced problems. Explain that in this chapter students will learn more specific details about the difficulties faced by American farmers at the end of the nineteenth century and what they did about them.

2. Introduction
a. Write sentences on the chalkboard using each vocabulary word from the chapter. Have students try to determine the meanings of the words from context clues.
b. Have students read the chapter title and the Objective question.
c. Have students read the chapter.

3. Review and Recall: After the students have read the chapter:
a. Have them answer the Objective question.
b. Have them answer the section questions.
c. Have some students cite specific events discussed in each section. Have other students cite effects brought about by each event.
d. Have students make up a time line for the events discussed in this chapter. When they have finished, ask volunteers to cite either the event that took place in a particular year or the year in which a particular event took place.

4. Building Social Studies Skills: Review with students the importance of using the library catalog to develop a bibliography on a particular research topic. Ask students to find five books for a report on the Populist party and make a file card for each one. Remind them to look up the topic in the subject index of the catalogue. Each file card should include the title, author, publisher, and date of publication.

5. Extension
a. Have students research the life of William Jennings Bryan and write a report about this three-time presidential candidate. Their reports should focus on Bryan's presidential campaigns as the Populist candidate. Call on volunteers to summarize the key points of their reports for the class.
b. Have students pretend to be farmers at the end of the nineteenth century who are experiencing the events described in this chapter. Ask them to write a letter to a friend or a relative in which they describe their feelings about the difficulties they have experienced and their hopes for the future.
c. Have students do additional research on the Grange. Then ask them to role-play a Grange meeting at which farmers discuss their problems and receive advice from Grange leaders on how to deal with their problems.

Support Materials

Assignment can include:

1. Chapter Review, pp. 482–483
2. Vocabulary and Comprehension Master V84
3. Test 11-2, p. CT64
4. Enrichment Master E64

UNIT 11

CHAPTER 3   Women's Rights

Overview   The women's rights convention at Seneca Falls, New York, in 1848 was the beginning of the feminist movement in the United States. Initially, the fight for women's rights produced few changes, although individual women did achieve prominence in certain fields. Gradually, greater educational and employment opportunities opened for American women. By 1900 they enjoyed many legal rights that had been denied to them half a century earlier. However, they did not achieve one of their most important goals, the right to vote, until the Nineteenth Amendment was passed in 1920.

Objectives

1. To explain the reasons why women sought equality.
2. To identify the leading feminist leaders and to recognize their contributions.
3. To describe the importance of the Seneca Falls Convention and Declaration.
4. To explain how opportunities for women increased in the late 1800s.
5. To describe the struggle for women's suffrage.

Developing the Chapter

1. Motivation: Read to students the excerpt from the Seneca Falls Declaration on page 486 of their textbook. Preface your reading with a description of this meeting as a milestone in the history of the women's rights movement.

Then ask: From the injustices listed in this excerpt, what do you think women's lives were like in the middle of the nineteenth century in the United States? In what ways are women's lives different today? Which rights are women still struggling to attain? Explain that students will learn more about the women's rights movement in this country as they read this chapter.

2. Introduction

a. Write the chapter vocabulary words on the chalkboard. Have students write each word and its glossary definition in their vocabulary notebook.

b. Have students read the chapter title and the Objective question.

Ask: How do you think women tried to gain equality in American society? Write their answers on the chalkboard and refer to them as you read the chapter.

c. Have students read the chapter.

3. Review and Recall: After the students have read the chapter:

a. Ask them to answer the Objective question.

b. Ask them to answer each section question.

c. Have students play "Who Am I?" based on the people discussed in the chapter. (Instructions for playing this game are given in the teacher's notes for Unit 1.)

d. Have students reread the first sentence in the Outlook sections and identify at least five key events that took place between the two events mentioned, the Seneca Falls Convention and the adoption of the women's suffrage amendment.

4. Building Social Studies Skills: Review with students the importance of interpreting an illustration or a photograph as a means of acquiring important information about an event. Direct students' attention to the picture on page 484.

Ask: What does the picture tell you about what women in the United States were trying to accomplish during this period?

5. Extension

a. Have students pretend to be twentieth-century reporters who have been transported back in time to the Seneca Falls convention. Ask different groups to role-play interviews between the reporters and some of the men and the women who attended the convention.

b. Have students create political cartoons about the suffragist movement at the beginning of the twentieth century.

c. Have students research and write a report on one of the causes that the early feminists fought so hard for. Possible topics include the right to vote, coeducational schools, and the rights of divorced women.

d. Have students read the full text of the Seneca Falls Declaration and write their own version as it applies to contemporary American life. Call on students to read aloud their "declarations."

Support Materials

Assignments can include:

1. Chapter Review, pp. 488–489
2. Workbook, pp. 67–69
3. Vocabulary and Comprehension Master V85
4. Test 11-3, p. CT65
5. Enrichment Master E65

UNIT 11

CHAPTER 4 Americans Improve Their Lives

Overview   Reformers of the nineteenth century worked to change American society in several significant areas. In the late 1800s, there was an increase in the number of secondary schools, colleges, and universities. Advancements in medical care, including the care and training of the handicapped and the mentally ill, were other important achievements. Although there were some attempts at prison reform, they met with little success.

Objectives

1. To describe how education improved in the nineteenth century.

2. To identify the changes in medical treatment in nineteenth century.

3. To describe how care for the mentally ill and the handicapped improved.

4. To identify attempts at prison reform.

Developing the Chapter

1. Motivation: Read students the selection by Horace Mann on page 491 of the chapter.

Then ask: When do you think these words were written? Explain that this excerpt came from a report on education written by Horace Mann in the nineteenth century.

Ask: Do you think Mann's words are still appropriate today? Explain that in the early nineteenth century there were few public schools in the United States and that many people could not read or write. Explain that in the chapter they are about to read students will learn how this situation began to change.

2. Introduction

a. Write the vocabulary words from the chapter on the chalkboard. Ask students to write the words and their glossary definitions in their vocabulary notebook. Then write a phrase that defines each word. Have students match the words with the correct phrases and use the vocabulary words in original sentences.

b. Have students read the chapter title and Objective question.

Ask: What social reforms were brought about in the nineteenth century?

c. Have students preview the chapter visuals: they should study the picture of the one-room schoolhouse.

Then ask: What can you learn about late nineteenth-century education from this picture? What do you think attending a school with children of all ages and grades in the same room was like? Ask similar questions after students have studied the other visuals of the chapter.

d. Have students read the chapter.

3. Review and Recall: After students have read the chapter:

a. Ask them to answer the Objective question.

b. Ask them to answer the section questions.

c. Write the following heading on the chalkboard: *Reforms: Education, Health, Prisons.* Then have students complete the chart with appropriate information from the chapter.

d. Have some students mention an accomplishment of one of the reformers discussed in the chapter. Have other students identify the person being described.

4. Building Social Studies Skills: Remind students that encyclopedias are important sources of information on a wide variety of topics. Review the fact that encyclopedias are organized alphabetically and that they usually have a separate volume with an index. Then have the students consult an encyclopedia to locate articles on each of the following topics: education in the United States, prison reform, care of the mentally ill, care of the handicapped, Horace Mann, Dorothea Dix, and Thomas Gallaudet.

5. Extension

a. Ask a group of students to discuss this topic: How important is education in keeping the United States a world leader?

b. Have students research and write a report on the life and accomplishments of one of the following: Dorothea Dix, Horace Mann, Thomas Gallaudet, or Samuel Gridley Howe.

c. Have students write newspaper editorials in which they advocate a particular social reform that would be of benefit to our society.

Support Materials

Assignments can include:

1. Chapter Review, pp. 500–501

2. Workbook, p. 70

3. Vocabulary and Comprehension Master V86

4. Test 11-4, p. CT66

5. Enrichment Master E66

UNIT 11

CHAPTER 5 The Progressive Movement

Overview The Progressive movement was active in the United States from the late 1890s to about 1920. This reform movement sought to make the government and society in general more responsive to the needs of its citizens. The injustices that the Progressives fought were publicized in newspapers, magazines, and books written by muckrakers. Many cities and states changed their form of government during the Progressive era. At the federal level, President Theodore Roosevelt supported reforms in business and public health and conservation. President Woodrow Wilson continued the Progressive mandate.

Objectives

1. To identify the goals of the Progressive movement.
2. To describe how the Progressives brought about changes in city and state governments.
3. To identify the Progressive measures adopted under Theodore Roosevelt and Woodrow Wilson.
4. To describe the ways in which American society changed during the Progressive period.

Developing the Chapter

1. Motivation: If possible, obtain a copy of Upton Sinclair's *The Jungle* and read selections to the class. If the book is not available, describe some of the appalling conditions in the meat-packing industry that Sinclair revealed. Explain to students that his revelations shocked the nation and led President Roosevelt to press for passage of the Pure Food and Drug Act. Tell students that today we are used to having laws that protect us from unsanitary products, but that the Pure Food and Drug Act was the first step in this direction and was a radical departure for government.
Ask: What kind of struggle do you think took place when people tried to get the government to protect them from business practices like these? Can you think of any current practices that should be changed to protect consumers?
2. Introduction
a. Write the chapter vocabulary words on the chalkboard. Have students write each word and its glossary definition in their vocabulary notebook. Then have students make up crossword puzzles that contain all the vocabulary words of the chapter. Ask students to exchange and complete each other's puzzles.
b. Have students read the chapter title and the Objective question. Ask the students to predict how the Progressives tried to change American society. Write their predictions on the chalkboard and refer back to them as the class studies the chapter.
c. Have students read the chapter.
3. Review and Recall: After the students have read the chapter:
a. Have them answer the Objective question.
b. Have them answer the section questions.
c. Have students play "Who Am I?" working with the names of the historical figures discussed in this chapter.
4. Building Social Studies Skills: Remind students of the importance of making a time line to organize a sequence of events in chronological order. Help students make a time line of the major events in this chapter. Then ask them questions about the chronological relationship between key events.
5. Extension
a. Ask students to research and write reports about the lives of one of the following: Upton Sinclair, Frank Norris, Lincoln Steffens, Ida Tarbell, or Thomas Lawson.
b. Ask students to create political cartoons that might have appeared in newspapers of the period that comment on some of the conditions that the Progressives were trying to improve.
c. Have a group of students do a report on the life and career of Theodore Roosevelt, emphasizing the years before he became President. Interesting aspects of career include his teens, when he was sent west for his health; his years as police commissioner of New York City; his service in the Spanish-American War; his big-game hunting expeditions; and his writing (he authored more books than any other President).

Support Materials

Assignments can include:
1. Chapter Review, pp. 500–501
2. Workbook, p. 71
3. Vocabulary and Comprehension Master V87
4. Test 11-5, p. CT67
5. Writing Workshop, pp. W13–W16
6. Enrichment Master E67

UNIT 12

The United States as a World Leader

Unit Overview   America's emergence as world leader took place at the end of the nineteenth century. As a result of the Spanish-American War, the United States gained possession of the Philippines, Puerto Rico, and Guam. In addition, the United States began to trade with Japan and instituted the Open Door policy in China. With the construction of the Panama Canal, the United States entered into a period of strained relations with the countries of Latin America. However, despite its expansionist policy, this country remained neutral at the onset of World War I and did not enter the conflict until 1917. At the end of the war, the United States advocated an isolationist policy.

Unit Objectives

1. To explain the steps taken by the United States to become a world leader.
2. To explain about the Spanish-American war.
3. To describe United States relations with Latin America at the beginning of the twentieth century.
4. To describe how the United States expanded in the Pacific.
5. To explain about the United States' participation in World War I and the aftermath of this international conflict.

Unit Introduction

1. Motivation: Point to a map of the United States at the end of the Civil War (page 416 in students' textbook).
Ask: Did the United States own any land outside its mainland at that time (no)?

Next, point to the map of the Pacific Rim on page 522 in the students' textbook. Ask students to identify new possessions outside the continental United States. Explain that the Philippines, Puerto Rico, Guam and Midway Islands, Alaska, and Hawaii were acquired by the United States at the end of the nineteenth century and the beginning of the twentieth century.
Ask: Why do you think the United States was looking beyond its own natural boundaries for more territory? How do you think it acquired this land?
2. Visual: Have students read the titles of the unit and the chapters. Then have them look at the visuals on pages 504–507.

Ask: What evidence do you find that shows that the United States has become a world power?
3. Time Line: Have the class read the events on the time line (pages 504–505). Elicit any information that students might have about the names and the events listed there. Ask students to identify the wars that were fought during this period.
Ask: How did the United States obtain Alaska and Midway? Encourage students to refer to the time line as they read the unit.
4. Historical Points of View: Ask students to read the introductory paragraph in this feature.
Ask: Do you think Britain, France, and the United States were right to follow a policy of imperialism? Have students read the first selection, ''The Case for American Expansion.''
Ask: Whose feelings and opinions does Senator Beveridge not consider when he crusades for America's expansionism overseas? How do you think people living in other countries might feel about his policy?

Then ask students to read the second selection.
Ask: Why does this speaker think that imperialism is ''hostile to liberty and tends toward militarism''? Which position do you feel is correct?

Unit Activities

1. Cooperative Learning: Have students work together to produce a newspaper of the period. As they read the chapters in this unit, class members should write news accounts and editorials about key events. Other students can contribute political cartoons, which present a visual commentary on the events of the period. Encourage students to do additional research so that their articles will be factually accurate.
2. Creative Writing: Ask students to create a fictional character who lives in the United States and experiences many of the events discussed in this chapter. As an ongoing activity, have them write a series of diary entries in which this individual records his or her feelings about what has happened.

Support Material

Assignments can include:

1. Unit 12 Review, pp. 538–539
2. Unit Vocabulary and Comprehension Masters V95–V96
3. Unit 12 Test, pp. UT23–UT24

UNIT 12

CHAPTER 1   The Spanish-American War

Overview   The United States's declaration of war against Spain in April 1899 signaled the beginning of an expansionist foreign policy. The United States entered the war after the battleship *Maine* was blown up in Havana harbor. The Spanish-held Philippines had been seized by Admiral George Dewey weeks earlier. As a result of the peace treaty that ended the Spanish-American War, the United States became a world power and pursued an imperialistic foreign policy.

Objectives

1. To identify the causes of the Cuban war for independence against Spain.
2. To explain United States involvement in the Spanish-American War.
3. To describe the results of the Spanish-American War.
4. To describe relations between the United States and the Philippines, Puerto Rico, and Cuba after the Spanish-American War.
5. To explain how and why the United States developed an expansionist foreign policy.

Developing the Chapter

1. Motivation: Tell students that in January 1898, the United States Navy sent the battleship *Maine* on a "friendly" visit to Cuba. At that time the Cubans were fighting a civil war against Spain. On February 15, an explosion aboard the *Maine* sank the ship in Havana harbor, killing more than 250 sailors. Explain that you will read an excerpt from an editorial that appeared in the *New York World* following the destruction of the *Maine*: "Regardless of any question of Cuban independence . . . the destruction of the *Maine* by foul play should be the occasion of ordering our fleet to Havana and demanding proper amends within 48 hours under threat of bombardment. If Spain will not punish the cowards who did it, we must punish Spain."

Ask: How do you think people felt about Spain after reading editorials such as this one? What do you think the United States did after the battleship *Maine* was sunk?

Explain that by reading the chapter students will learn more about this episode in American history.

2. Introduction

a. Write the chapter vocabulary words on the chalkboard. Have students write each word and its glossary definition in their vocabulary notebook. Ask volunteers to share original sentences that use the vocabulary words.

b. Have student read the chapter title and the Objective question.

c. Have students preview the chapter visuals. Based on these illustrations, ask them to draw conclusions about the course of United States foreign policy during this period.

d. Have students read the chapter.

3. Review and Recall: After the students have read the chapter:

a. Have them answer the Objective question.

b. Have them ask each other factual questions based on the content of each selection. They may ask the section question if they wish.

c. Write the following headings on the chalkboard: *Causes of the Spanish-American War; Results of the Spanish-American War*. Ask students to complete the chart with appropriate information from the chapter.

4. Building Social Studies Skills: Remind students that using time lines helps to keep historical events in perspective. Ask students to make a time line that includes the major events from 1898 to 1917 described in this chapter. Suggest that they add brief explanations about the events.

5. Extension

a. Have student write editorials that might have appeared in newspapers of the period about the Spanish-American War and the change in United States foreign policy. Reread and discuss the editorial from the motivational activity as a model. Call on students to read aloud their editorials.

b. Stage a class debate on the following topic: The United States had no right to rule the Philippines after the Spanish-American rule. The debaters should represent the views of scholars and government leaders from the period. Students in the audience should be prepared to ask the debaters questions.

Support Materials

Assignments can include:

1. Chapter Review, pp. 512–513
2. Vocabulary and Comprehension Master V90
3. Test 12-1, p. CT68
4. Map Transparency Activity Sheet A24
5. Enrichment Master E68

UNIT 12

CHAPTER 2 Relations with Latin America

Overview   The Panama Canal, the much-needed link between the Atlantic and the Pacific oceans, was completed in 1914. In order to obtain the rights to the land, the United States had supported a Panamanian uprising against Colombia. The United States's continued presence in Latin America during this period reflected Theodore Roosevelt's corollary to the Monroe Doctrine. Taft's efforts to protect United States investments in Latin America resulted in military intervention. Franklin Roosevelt tried to improve United States relations with Latin America by instituting the Good Neighbor Policy in 1933.

Objectives

1. To explain how the United States acquired the right to build a canal across Panama.
2. To describe United States policies toward Latin America in the early 1900s.
3. To describe how Latin Americans responded to these policies.
4. To explain Franklin Roosevelt's attempts to improve relations of the United States with Latin America.

Developing the Chapter

1. Motivation: Show students a map of Latin America. Point to the isthmus of Panama. Have students identify the country you are indicating.
Ask: What do you think is the advantage of building a waterway here to link the Atlantic and the Pacific oceans?

Explain that in the early twentiethth century, the United States wanted to build a canal across this land.
Ask: How do you think the United States acquired the land? What are some of the problems the builders might have faced in constructing the canal?

List students' predictions on the chalkboard. Refer to them as you read the chapter. Tell students that, as they read this chapter, they will learn about the Panama Canal.
2. Introduction
a. Write the chapter vocabulary words on the chalkboard. Write sentences on the chalkboard using each vocabulary word from the chapter. Have students try to determine the words' meanings from context clues. Then, have students write each word and its glossary definition in their vocabulary notebook.
b. Ask students to read the chapter title and the Objective question. Have them volunteer possible answers to the Objective question.
c. Have students read the chapter.

3. Review and Recall: After the students have read the chapter:
a. Ask them answer the Objective question.
b. Have them answer each subhead question.
c. Play "Who Said This?" with the students. Ask students to review the information about Presidents Theodore Roosevelt, Howard Taft, Woodrow Wilson, and Franklin Roosevelt. Then call on students to make a statement about United States–Latin American policy that might have been made by one of these United States presidents. Call on other students to identify the president who would have made the statement.

4. Building Social Studies Skills: Explain to students that they can learn important information about a particular historical event or person by interpreting an illustration or a photograph. Ask students to turn to the picture of the building of the Panama Canal on page 514 of their textbook.
Ask: What does this illustration teach you about the construction of the Panama Canal? What do you think working on this project was like? What might be some problems?

5. Extension
a. Ask students to do additional research about the construction of the Panama Canal and to prepare a diagram that illustrates how the Canal operates.
b. Ask students to do background research on the problems faced by the builder of the Panama Canal, including the poor living conditions of the workers, many of whom became ill from malaria or yellow fever. Have students write two diary entries from the point of view of one of the builders in which these conditions are described.

Support Materials

Assignments can include:

1. Chapter Review, pp. 518–519
2. Workbook, p. 72
3. Vocabulary and Comprehension Master V91
4. Test 12-2, p. CT69
5. Enrichment Master E69

UNIT 12

CHAPTER 3   Opening the Pacific

Overview   Although the United States had begun to trade with China at the end of the eighteenth century, Japan remained closed to foreigners until Commander Perry's fleet arrived there in 1853. Secretary of State John Hay's Open Door Policy encouraged equal trading rights for all countries in China. Other Pacific lands that came under United States control included Alaska, Hawaii, and Midway, the Philippines, Guam, Wake Island, and part of Samoa.

Objectives

1. To explain why the United States became interested in Pacific lands.
2. To explain how the United States developed trade with Japan and China.
3. To detail the events leading to the United States takeover of other Pacific lands.
4. To analyze how the Pacific peoples felt about United States intervention in their lives.

Developing the Chapter

1. Motivation: Read or reproduce this excerpt from a letter written by Millard Fillmore to the emperor of Japan:

I send you this public letter by Commodore Matthew C. Perry. . . . I am desirous that our two countries should trade with each other for the benefit of both Japan and the United States.

We know that the ancient laws of Your Imperial Majesty's government do not allow of foreign trade except with the Dutch. But as the state of the world changes, . . . it seems to be wise from time to time to make new laws. [President Fillmore then asks that shipwrecked sailors be treated fairly and that United States ships be allowed to refuel and resupply in Japan.]

We have directed Commodore Perry to beg Your Imperial Majesty's acceptance of a few presents. They are of no great value in themselves, but some of them may serve as specimens of the articles manufactured in the United States, and thy are intended as tokens of our sincere and respectful friendship.

Ask: What did the United States want from Japan? What did the United States offer Japan? Why did the United States want this? How do you think the Japanese reacted?

Explain that in this chapter students will learn more about United States expansion in the Pacific.

2. Introduction

a. Write the chapter vocabulary words on the chalkboard. Have students write each word and its glossary definition in their vocabulary notebook. Ask volunteers to use each vocabulary word in a sentence.

b. Have students read the chapter title and the Objective question. Ask students to list possible reasons to explain the importance of the Pacific lands to the United States. Save their predictions by writing them on the chalkboard.

c. Ask students to preview the chapter visuals. **Ask:** What do you think some of the important events of this chapter will be?

d. Have students read the chapter.

3. Review and Recall: After the students have read the chapter:

a. Have them answer the Objective question.

b. Have them answer the section questions.

c. Compare the students' predictions with the actual reasons for United States expansion that they learned about in the chapter.

d. Write the following headings on the chalkboard: *Japan; China; Hawaii; Alaska.* On the left side of this chart, write the following: *Reason for U.S. interest; How Acquired; Date Acquired; Result.* Ask students to complete the chart.

4. Building Social Studies Skills: Review students' basic map-reading skills. Have students turn to the map on page 522 of their textbook. Ask them to identify the location of Tokyo, Honolulu, Manila, and Anchorage by giving the longitude and the latitude of each city's location.

5. Extension

a. Have students write the first two or three pages of a historical novel or story based on one of the events discussed in this chapter. Encourage them to do additional research if necessary.

b. Have students write about the arrival of Americans in one of the Pacific lands discussed in this chapter from the point of view of a person who is a native of that country. Call on volunteers to read aloud their narratives.

Support Materials

Assignments can include:

1. Chapter Review, pp. 524–525
2. Workbook, p. 73
3. Vocabulary and Comprehension Master V92
4. Test 12-3, p. CT70
5. Enrichment Master E70

UNIT 12

CHAPTER 4 World War I

Overview   The system of political alliances created throughout pre-World War I Europe resulted in tensions that exploded with the assassination of the heir to the Austria-Hungary throne in 1914. By August of that year, Germany and Austria-Hungary were allied against Britain, France, and Russia. By late 1914, the war was at a standstill, and trench warfare began. President Woodrow Wilson favored neutrality. However, in April 1917, he reversed this position and the United States joined the war.

Objectives

1. To analyze the origins of World War I.
2. To describe the early fighting in the war.
3. To explain why the United States stayed out of the war initially.
4. To identify the events that resulted in the United States's entrance into the war.

Developing the Chapter

1. Motivation: Read students the excerpt from Woodrow Wilson's address to Congress in the chapter. Explain that the president had initially wanted the United States to stay out of the war. **Ask:** Why did Wilson believe that the United States had to enter the war? What do you imagine was the reaction of most Americans to Wilson's speech?

Explain that as they read the chapter students will learn more about Woodrow Wilson and the early history of World War I.

2. Introduction

a. Write the chapter vocabulary words on the chalkboard. Have students write each word and its glossary definition in their vocabulary notebook. Ask volunteers to use each vocabulary word in an original sentence.
b. Have students read the chapter title and the Objective question.

Ask: Why do you think the United States tried to stay out of the European conflict?

Write their predictions on the chalkboard. Refer to them as students read the chapter.
c. Have students preview the chapter visuals. Elicit any information they might have about the sinking of the *Lusitania* and its effect on the course of the war.
d. Have students read the chapter.

3. Review and Recall: After the students have read the chapter:
a. Have them answer each subhead question.
b. Have them answer the Objective question.
c. Have students make a time line of the events discussed in this chapter.
d. Ask students to identify each of the following terms or names in one or two sentences: Archduke Franz Ferdinand, Allies, Central Powers, trench warfare, neutrality, William Jennings Bryan, British blockade, *Lusitania*.

4. Building Social Studies Skills: Review with students requirements of a topical outline. Remind them that topical outlines list information in phrases rather than complete sentences. Have students complete the following topical outline with appropriate information from the chapter. Have them add subtopics with necessary information.

I. Beginning of World War I
  A. Causes
      1.
      2.
      3.
  B. Alliances
      1.
      2.
  C. Trench Warfare
  D. American Neutrality

5. Extension

a. Ask your librarian for a copy of the complete text of Wilson's speech to Congress that is excerpted in this chapter. Have students read it aloud. Then have them role-play interviews in which reporters question different Americans about their reaction to the speech.
b. Have students in small groups create TV news programs about the events described in this chapter. If necessary, ask them to do additional research in their class or school encyclopedias. Possible topics include: the assassination of Archduke Franz Ferdinand; the sinking of the *Lusitania;* America's entrance into the war.

Support Materials

Assignments can include:

1. Chapter Review, pp. 530–531
2. Workbook, p. 74
3. Vocabulary and Comprehension Master V93
4. Test 12-4, p. CT71
5. Map Transparency Activity Sheet A25
6. Enrichment Master E71

CHAPTER 5   America Goes to War

Overview   Participation of the United States in World War I required the cooperation of its citizens to raise and equip a fighting force of millions of men. Industrial and agricultural production was increased. By spring 1918, 2 million American troops arrived in France. Their much-needed support helped to defeat the Germans at the Second Battle of the Marne, the turning point in the war. The armistice was signed in November 1918, and the allied leaders met in Versailles a month later to negotiate the terms of the peace plan. The United States Senate rebuffed Wilson's support of the League of Nations, thus leading the nation back into isolationism.

Objectives

1. To explain how the United States prepared for war.
2. To analyze how the United States helped with the war.
3. To describe the Treaty of Versailles.
4. To define the course of United States foreign policy after the war.

Developing the Chapter

1. Motivation: Read to the students the following excerpt written by a soldier about war in the trenches:

> . . . *you could not show a finger by daylight, and by night every path by which you might be supposed to move was raked by machine-guns which had been trained on it by day. The entrance . . . was under continuous shell-fire. If you could reach your funk-hole, and crouch in it, there was a fair chance of your coming out of it alive next day. . . . In your funk-hole, with no room to move, no hot food, and no chance of getting any, there was nothing worse to suffer than a steady drizzle of wintry rain and a temperature just above freezing-point . . . you could do nothing. There was no fighting . . . the combatants could not get at one another. . . .*

Ask: How would you describe the battlefield conditions? How would you feel if you had been fighting in the trenches?

Explain that in this chapter students will learn about World War I and the role of the United States during and after the war.

2. Introduction

a. Write the chapter vocabulary words on the chalkboard. Have students write each word and its glossary definition in their vocabulary notebook. Conduct a vocabulary bee. Use other words from the unit, if necessary.

b. Have students use the visuals to prepare a list of questions about the chapter that they want answered.

c. Have students read the chapter.

3. Review and Recall: After the students have read the chapter:

a. Have them answer the Objective question.

b. Have them answer each section question.

c. Have students make up a time line of important events in this chapter.

d. Have students reread the first sentence in the Outlook section. Ask them to provide at least three facts from the chapter that support the statement.

4. Building Social Studies Skills: Point out that encyclopedias have indexes that list all the articles containing information on a topic. Ask students to list the volume and the page number of articles about the following topics: World War I, the Treaty of Versailles, Woodrow Wilson, The League of Nations, isolationism, and General John J. Pershing.

5. Extension

a. Stage a class debate on whether or not the United States should join the League of Nations. Ask students debaters to imagine themselves to be Americans in the period directly after World War I.

b. Have students create posters that encourage Americans to support the war effort in a variety of ways: buying Liberty Bonds, increasing industrial production, increasing agricultural production, contributing money, or enlisting in the armed services. Their posters should include illustrations a well as slogans. Have students display their completed posters in the classroom.

Support Materials

Assignments can include:

1. Chapter Review, pp. 536–537
2. Workbook, pp. 75–77
3. Vocabulary and Comprehension Master V94
4. Test 12-5, p. CT72
5. Writing Workshop, pp. W17–W20
6. Enrichment Master E72

UNIT 13

Peace, Depression, and Another War

Unit Overview   The period between the two world wars was a time of change for all Americans. The 1920s was a period of prosperity that ended with the crash of the stock market and the beginning of the Great Depression. During the next ten years, millions of workers faced unemployment, banks closed, and businesses failed. When Franklin D. Roosevelt became President in 1933, the period known as the New Deal began, when many laws were passed to ease the suffering of the American people and to help the economy recover. The United States entered World War II in December 1941. After the defeat of the Axis powers four years later, the world looked forward to a period of peace. The formation of the United Nations was an important step in this direction.

Unit Objectives

1. To explain what American life was like in the 1920s.
2. To identify the causes of the Great Depression and how it affected millions of Americans.
3. To describe the New Deal.
4. To explain World War II and the United States' role in the war.
5. To describe the aftermath of World War II as the countries of the world returned to peace.

Unit Introduction

1. Motivation: Elicit any information that students already have about the United Nations. Bring in recent newspaper or magazine articles that pertain to the United Nations and display them to the class. Point out that the United Nations was established at the end of World War II.

Ask: Why do you think the countries of the world felt that an organization like the United Nations was necessary? What do you think it was like to live in a world that had just endured a world war?

Explain that students will learn about World War II and the events that preceded it as they read this unit.

2. Visual: Direct students' attention to the unit-opening painting of an employment office during the Great Depression. Have them discuss the mood of despair that the painting conveys.

3. Time Line: Have the class read the events on the unit time line (pp.540–541). Ask students whether they are familiar with any of the events

listed there, and have them share their knowledge with the class. Encourage students to refer to the unit time line as they study the unit to help them put events in perspective.

Ask: What do many of the events on the time line pertain to (World War II)?

4. Points of View: Have students read the first paragraph in this feature.

Ask: What are the two points of view that will be expressed in these selections? Then have students read the first selection.

Ask: Why did President Hoover believe that the government should not become involved in the peacetime economy? Why do you think he believed that ''it would impair the very basis of liberty and freedom . . . ''? What are some of the objections to governmental involvement in the economy that Hoover discussed? Do you agree with him? Why or why not? Now have students read the second selection.

Ask: What did President Roosevelt believe was the government's greatest task? How did he believe that this task could be accomplished? Do you agree or disagree with this point of view? Explain your answer.

Unit Activities

1. Cooperative Learning: Have students work in small groups to construct an illustrated time line that highlights major events from the end of World War I in 1917 to the formation of the United Nations in 1945. Encourage students to use pictures cut out from old magazines or drawn by students to illustrate the time line.

2. Creative Writing: Have students write a short example of historical fiction set during the period covered by this unit and related to one of the events discussed in the chapters. Help students to select the event that they will use as the setting of their short story. Suggest that students do additional research to make sure that their work is historically accurate.

Support Materials

Assignments can include:

1. Unit 13 Review, pp. 574–575
2. Unit Vocabulary and Comprehension Masters V102–V103
3. Unit 13 Test, pp. UT25–UT26

UNIT 13

CHAPTER 1 America in the 1920s

Overview   The 1920s was a period of change that affected the lives of all Americans in both positive and negative ways. From 1923 to 1929, business prospered. Movies and radio—relatively new forms of entertainment—changed Americans' use of their leisure time. Women had the right to vote for the first time. However, other Americans, including African Americans and immigrants, were subjected to discrimination. The Ku Klux Klan gained new strength. In 1919 and 1920, thousands of people were arrested on the suspicion that they were political radicals.

Objectives

1. To describe how Americans lived in the 1920s.
2. To explain why business prospered.
3. To identify America's new leisure-time activities.
4. To describe how women's lives changed in the 1920s.
5. To explain the negative feelings against African Americans, immigrants, and political radicals.
6. To describe the lawlessness and crime of this period.

Developing the Chapter

1. Motivation: Point to several of the illustrations in this chapter and elicit any information that students might have about the 1920s. Then read the poem by the African American poet, Langston Hughes, one of the best-known writers of the Harlem Renaissance.

Ask: What does this poem tell you about feelings toward African Americans that existed during the 1920s? Think about the last line, "I, too, am American." What do you think Hughes is talking about here? Explain that students will learn more about the 1920s as they read this chapter.

2. Introduction

a. Write the chapter vocabulary words on the chalkboard. Have students write each word and its glossary definition in their vocabulary notebook. Ask volunteers to use each vocabulary word in an original sentence.

b. Have student read the chapter title and the Objective question.

Ask: What do you think that Americans of the 1920s were seeking? Remind students that the country was still recovering from World War I.

c. Have students preview the chapter visuals.

d. Have students read the chapter.

3. Review and Recall: After the students have read the chapter:

a. Have them ask each other questions about the content of each section.

b. Have them answer the Objective question.

c. Have them answer each section question.

d. Have the make a time line of the key events in the chapter.

e. Divide the class into teams to play "Who Am I?" based on the people discussed in the chapter. One person pretends to be a historical figure from this period. The other teams asks yes-or-no questions until the team guesses the identity of the figure. The team that makes the most correct identifications wins.

4. Building Social Studies Skills: Explain that being able to tell the differences between a fact and an opinion is an important skill. Remind students that a fact is a true statement that can be proven. An opinion is what a person or a group thinks or believes; it cannot be proven to be true. Then have students identify two facts from paragraphs 4, 7, 8, and 10. Ask them to write opinions based on the same materials.

5. Extension

a. Have students write a diary entry from the point of view of one of the following: an African American, an immigrant worker, an assembly-line worker, a businessperson, and a political radical. The entry should reflect the individual's thoughts and feelings about his or her life in the United States in the 1920s.

b. Have students bring to class other poems by Langston Hughes. Volunteers should read them aloud and discuss the feelings Hughes displays in them.

Support Material

Assignments can include:

1. Chapter Review, pp. 548–549
2. Workbook, p. 78
3. Vocabulary and Comprehension Master V97
4. Test 13-1, p. CT73
5. Map Transparency Activity Sheet A26
6. Enrichment Master E73

CHAPTER 2 The Great Depression and the New Deal

Overview With the collapse of the stock market in October 1929, the Roaring Twenties ended, and the Great Depression began. A major cause of this economic collapse was the production of goods that people could not afford to buy, coupled with the failure of many banks. With the election of Franklin Delano Roosevelt in 1932, the federal government enacted a series of New Deal laws designed to help many Americans. Some of the most significant included the establishment of the Social Security system, the establishment of the WPA and TVA, and the passage of laws that regulated banks and the stock market.

Objectives

1. To identify the causes of the Great Depression.
2. To describe the hardships faced by Americans during the Great Depression.
3. To identify the ways in which government responded to the Great Depression.
4. To explain how the New Deal changed American society.

Developing the Chapter

1. Motivation: Ask if any students have their Social Security card yet. Elicit any information students already have about the Social Security system. Point out that this system was established during the Great Depression of the 1930s as part of President Franklin D. Roosevelt's New Deal.
Ask: If you were the President during this period, how would you have created jobs for unemployed people? What would you have done to provide income for people who couldn't find work? Write students' answers on the chalkboard. Refer to them as students read this chapter.

2. Introduction
a. Write the chapter vocabulary words on the chalkboard. Write sentences on the chalkboard using the vocabulary words from the chapter. Have student try to determine the words' meanings from context clues. Have student write each word and its glossary definition in their vocabulary notebook.
b. Have students read the chapter title and the Objective questions.
c. Have student preview the chapter visuals.

Ask: What do these illustrations tell you about life in America during the Depression?
d. Have student read the chapter.
3. Review and Recall: After students have read the chapter:
a. Have student answer each subhead question.
b. Have students answer the Objective question.
c. Have student identify the main idea in each section.
d. Call on students to identify an event in each section that caused a particular result. Have another student identify the result or the effect of this causative action.
e. On the chalkboard write the names of major New Deal laws. Ask student to describe each one and tell what it accomplished. Write this information on the board.

4. Building Social Studies Skills: Point out that the words surrounding an unfamiliar word often contain a definition of that word; other times, the context can help readers to infer the meaning by what the other words say. Direct students' attention to the words "Great Depression" in Section 2. Have students find the definition in the next sentence. Repeat the process with "evicted" in Section 5 and "pensions" in Section 9.

5. Extension
a. Divide the class into small groups of students. Have each group role-play an interview between a newspaper reporter and a man or a woman on the street after the stock market crash of 1929. Call on different groups to role-play their vignettes in front of the class.
b. Have students research one of the New Deal laws that were discussed in this chapter and write reports in which they explain how the new legislation helped Americans during this era.
c. Have students interview one or more grandparents about their memories of the Great Depression. If possible, use tape recorders to record the interviews, so that they can later be played in class.

Support Materials

Assignments can include:
1. Chapter Review, pp. 554–555
2. Workbook, p. 79
3. Vocabulary and Comprehension Master V98
4. Test 13-2, p. CT74
5. Enrichment Master E74

UNIT 13

CHAPTER 3 World War II Begins

Overview A series of international events took place in the 1920s and 1930s that propelled the nations of the world toward another war. In Italy, Germany, and the Soviet Union, dictators rose to power and created totalitarian states. In 1931 Japan invaded Manchuria, and by 1937 Japanese forces occupied much of China's territory. The policies of appeasement toward Hitler adopted by Britain and France failed to stop Nazi aggression in Europe. After German armies attacked Poland in 1939, Britain and France declared war on Germany. The early years of the war brought heavy casualties among the Allied powers. The United States entered World War II in December 1941.

Objectives
1. To explain how dictators came to power in Europe.
2. To explain why Japan seized lands in Asia.
3. To identify the events that led to the outbreak of World War II.
4. To describe the early years of the war.

Developing the Chapter

1. Motivation: Elicit any information that students might have about World War II from what they may have seen on television or in the movies or learned from relatives. Explain that World War II was similar to World War I in that Great Britain and France fought Germany in both wars, but the events leading up to World War II were quite different. Also, explain that many more nations were involved in World War II and that hundreds of thousands of civilians as well as soldiers lost their lives.

2. Introduction

a. Write the chapter vocabulary words on the chalkboard. Have students write each word and its glossary definition in their vocabulary notebook. Divide the students into pairs. Have each student make up original sentences for the vocabulary words. Ask students to exchange papers, and have each student in a pair complete the other's sentences with the correct words.

b. Have students read the chapter title and the Objective question.

c. Have students preview the chapter.

3. Review and Recall: After the students have read the chapter:

a. Have them reread and answer the Objective question.

b. Have them reread and answer each section question.

c. Have students identify a fact in each section; then ask them to make up an opinion based on the same materials.

d. Write on the chalkboard the heading Causes of World War II. Then have students list the causes of the war.

e. Ask students to identify each of the following names, terms, or events in one or two sentences: *totalitarian state, Mussolini, Hitler, Joseph Stalin, isolationism, Rome-Berlin-Axis, Munich Conference, appeasement, Battle of Britain, blitzkrieg.*

4. Building Social Studies Skills: Review with students the use of a time line to record events in chronological order. Work with students to make up a time line of the major events discussed in this chapter beginning in 1921, when Mussolini established a fascist dictatorship, and ending in 1941, when the United States entered World War II.

5. Extension

a. Ask students to draw political cartoons based on one of the events discussed in this chapter.

b. Have students stage a debate between two teams: one of the teams represents the isolationist view of international politics that existed in the United States before the country entered World War II; the other team represents a group of United States citizens who favors the country's participation in World War II.

c. Have students research and compare the most important of the dictators who came to power between the world wars: Mussolini in Italy, Stalin in the Soviet Union, Hitler in Germany, and Franco in Spain. In what ways were these dictators alike? How were they different from each other?

Support Materials

Assignments can include:
1. Chapter Review, pp. 560–561
2. Vocabulary and Comprehension Master V99
3. Test 13-3, p. CT75
4. Enrichment Master E75

CHAPTER 4 The United States in World War II

Overview The Japanese attack on Pearl Harbor on December 7, 1941, resulted in a declaration of war by the United States. Between 1942 and 1944 the Allied forces launched attacks in North Africa, Europe, and the Pacific. They captured Paris in August 1944, while the Soviets took Berlin in April 1945. President Roosevelt died suddenly in April 1945, and Vice-President Harry S. Truman succeeded him. In August 1945 the United States dropped atomic bombs on the Japanese cities of Hiroshima and Nagasaki. The Japanese surrendered on August 14.

Objectives

1. To describe the events that led to a declaration of war by the United States.
2. To explain how Americans mobilized for war.
3. To list the major conflicts leading to an Allied victory in Europe and the Pacific.
4. To describe the events leading to Japan's surrender.

Developing the Chapter

1. Motivation: Explain to students that the United States entered World War II quite suddenly after the Japanese attacked Pearl Harbor in December 1941. Have students imagine themselves living in the United States during this period.

Ask: What steps do you think the country should have taken to prepare for war? How would you have reacted? What would you have done to contribute to the war effort? Explain that students will learn more about the United States in the war in this chapter.

2. Introduction

a. Write the chapter vocabulary words on the chalkboard. Have students write each word and its glossary definition in their vocabulary notebook. Ask volunteers to use each vocabulary word in a sentence.
b. Have students read the chapter title and the Objective question.
c. Have students preview the chapter visuals and read the captions.
   Ask: What information about World War II can you find out by studying the illustrations and the captions in this chapter?
d. Have students read the chapter.

3. Review and Recall: After the students have read the chapter:
a. Have them ask each other questions about the content of specific paragraphs.
b. Have them reread and answer the Objective question.
c. Have them reread and answer each section question.
d. Copy the following headings on the chalkboard: *War Is Declared; Americans Mobilize for War; The Drive to Victory.* Then ask students to place the following items under the correct heading: *"A date which will live infamy"; Relocation camps; D-Day; Island-hopping; Hiroshima; V-J Day.*

4. Building Social Studies Skills: Briefly review the main points of outlining, specifically the use of headings and subheadings. Then ask students to reread Section 8, 9, and 10. Have them outline the material, using the following format as a started:

I. The Drive to Victory
   A. Allied attacks in North Africa, Europe, and the Pacific
      1.
      2.
   B. D-Day
      1.
      2.

5. Extension

a. Have students work together to prepare an illustrated time line of the major events of World War II, from the bombing of Pearl Harbor to the Japanese surrender.
b. Have students write diary entries from the point of view of the Japanese Americans who were interned during the World War II in which they express their feelings about what had happened to them.

Support Materials

Assignments can include:

1. Chapter Review, pp. 556–567
2. Workbook, pp. 80–83
3. Vocabulary and Comprehension Master V100
4. Test 13-4, p. CT76
5. Map Transparency Activity Sheets A27–A28
6. Enrichment Master E76

UNIT 13

CHAPTER 5   The World Returns to Peace

Overview   More than 55 million soldiers and civilians died in World War II. Many of Europe's cities lay in ruins. Hitler's ''final solution'' had resulted in the slaughter of six million Jews, as well as other groups. While the Allies decided what should be done with Germany and Japan, the United Nations was beginning its work as an international peacekeeping organization.

Objectives

1. To identify the problems that faced the Allies at the end of World War II.
2. To describe the Holocaust and explain how the Allies sought to punish war criminals.
3. To describe why the United Nations was established and how it worked.
4. To identify the goals of nations in the postwar era.

Developing the Chapter

1. Motivation: Explain to students that Anne Frank was a young Dutch girl who was forced to go into hiding with her family and several friends because they were Jewish. They lived in an attic over her father's place of business in Amsterdam. During World War II Holland was occupied by Nazis, and any Jews who could be found were sent to concentration camps. Anne wrote in a diary her feelings during this period. The diary was found after she, her family, and their friends were finally captured by the Nazis and sent to concentration camps. Anne, her older sister, and their mother died there. She was fifteen years old. Only her father survived the war. Read to students a selection from *The Diary of a Young Girl.*

Ask: What are your reactions to Anne Frank's words? How did she feel about what was happening in the world around her? How would you have felt in her place?

Point out to the class that Anne Frank's diary has been published in many languages and has been read by millions of people throughout the world. Explain that her diary brought home to many people after the war how the Nazi policies towards Jews affected individuals.

2. Introduction

a. Write the chapter vocabulary words on the chalkboard. Have students write each word and its glossary definition in their vocabulary note-

book. Then have students make up crossword puzzles with all the vocabulary words in this unit. The words can be hidden horizontally or vertically. Ask students to exchange papers and solve each other's puzzles.

b. Have students read the chapter title and the Objective question.

c. Have students preview the chapter visuals.

d. Have students read the chapter.

3. Review and Recall: After the students have read the chapter:

a. Have them reread and answer the Objective question.

b. Have them reread and answer each section question.

c. Have them identify an event in each paragraph that caused a particular action. Have other students identify the result produced by the action.

4. Building Social Studies Skills: Remind students that an encyclopedia is a set of reference books that includes articles, arranged in alphabetical order, on a wide variety of topics. The index volume lists all the entries, with page and volume number, about a particular subject. Ask students to find and read the entries for the following topics in their class or school encyclopedia: United Nations, atomic bomb, Holocaust, and Ralph Bunche.

5. Extension

a. Have students work in small groups to research and report on key components of the United Nations, such as the General Assembly, the Security Council, UNICEF, UNESCO, the World Health Organization, and the Universal Postal Union. Have students make charts for classroom display showing what these agencies do and how they operate.

b. Have students read *The Diary of a Young Girl* by Anne Frank. Then have small groups of students dramatize different episodes from the book and present their dramatizations to the class.

Support Materials

Assignments can include:

1. Chapter Review, pp. 572–573
2. Vocabulary and Comprehension Master V101
3. Test 13-5, p. CT77
4. Enrichment Master E77

UNIT 14

The United States Becomes a Superpower

Unit Overview　America's military, economic, and political strength reached its zenith after World War II. However, as the Soviet Union gained more control over Eastern European countries, a Cold War developed between the superpowers that has influenced Soviet–American policy ever since. The struggle of the United States to contain communism resulted in America's involvement in the Korean War in the early 1950s and in the Vietnam War ten years later. The latter conflict was especially unpopular, and many Americans opposed it. The 1970s was a period of détente with the Soviet Union and Communist China. However, the Cold War resumed in the early 1980s, and the United States also became involved in conflicts in the Middle East. In the late 1980s the Soviet Union sought to improve relations with the United States.

Unit Objectives

1. To understand how the United States became a superpower after World War II.
2. To understand the beginnings of the Cold War and its influence on United States foreign policy.
3. To learn about United States involvement in wars in Korea and Vietnam.
4. To understand why the United States has become involved in conflicts in the Middle East.
5. To understand the steps the United States has taken to try to end the Cold War.

Unit Introduction

1. **Motivation:** Bring in several headlines from recent newspapers or magazines that refer to one of the superpowers. Display them in class. Elicit any information students might have about the Cold War and how it affects world politics. Point to the headlines.

Ask: In what ways do these recent events seem to be related to the Cold War that has existed since the end of World War II? How are you affected by events that take place in other countries?

Next, read to students a passage from President John Kennedy's speech on page 605.

Ask: Do you agree or disagree with President Kennedy's sentiments? Explain your answer. Think about the recent events we've just discussed. Do you think the leaders of the Soviet Union have adopted the "enlightened attitude" that President Kennedy mentioned in his speech?

2. **Visual:** Ask students to look at the unit opener photograph and explain why the moon landing was "a great step" for humanity. Ask students to discuss why Americans are so interested in space travel. Have them think about the expression "space: the final frontier" from a popular television and movie series. Ask them how space exploration might be similar to the opening of the Western frontier in the nineteenth century.

3. **Time Line:** Direct the students' attention to the unit time line (page 608). Ask them to read the events named. Elicit any prior knowledge about these events that students might have.

4. **Historical Points of View:** Ask students to read the introductory paragraph in this feature.

Ask: Why do you think the United States and the Soviet Union were such bitter enemies during this period? How would you characterize the relationship between the two countries now?

Have students read the first selection.

Ask: What does this government official think the United States is committed to? Why does he think our country and the Soviet Union are rivals?

Have students read the second selection.

Ask: How does the Soviet leader view the United States? What do these two selections show you about the reason why the Cold War continues?

Unit Activities

1. **Creative Writing:** Have students select one of the events discussed in this unit and use it as the basis for a short piece of historical fiction. Remind them that this genre is fiction set against a historical background. Therefore, students should do additional research before they begin to write so that their stories will be historically accurate. Call on volunteers to read aloud their completed stories.

2. **Cooperative Learning:** Ask students to work together to create a "Meet the Press" type of television program. There should be two panels with representatives from eastern and western block countries as well as a team of "reporters." The subject of the discussion should be "The Cold War: Past, Present, and Future."

Support Materials

Assignments can include:

1. Unit 14 Review, pp. 610–6111
2. Unit Vocabulary and Comprehension Masters V109–V110
3. Unit 14 Test, pp. 000–000

UNIT 14

CHAPTER 1   Postwar America

Overview   America's conversion to a peacetime economy after World War II resulted in a postwar economic boom. After the death of President Roosevelt, President Truman based his political agenda on his predecessor's "economic bill of rights." He was reelected in a surprise victory in 1948. A widespread fear of communism in the United States resulted in the rise of Senator Joseph McCarthy. But McCarthy's televised hearings in 1954 led to his censure by the Senate. During this postwar period, United States factories and farms were operating at optimum efficiency. The United States was also a world leader in medical research. The Salk vaccine was introduced in 1953.

Objectives

1. To understand how the United States maintained a strong postwar economy.
2. To identify the main issues during Harry Truman's presidency.
3. To understand the rise and fall of Senator Joseph McCarthy.
4. To learn about the United States' position as a powerful world leader after the war.

Developing the Chapter

1. Motivation: Explain to students that after the death of President Franklin D. Roosevelt, his vice-president, Harry S. Truman, became president. Truman introduced an economic program based on what President Roosevelt had called an "economic bill of rights." Read students an excerpt from President Truman's speech to congress, which is reprinted on page 582 of their textbook.
Ask: Which of these rights do you consider to be the most important? Based on the "economic bill of rights," how would you characterize the mood and the spirit of the country after the war? How many of these basic rights still have not been accomplished today?

2. Introduction
a. Write the chapter vocabulary words on the chalkboard. Have students write each word and its glossary definition in their vocabulary notebook. Ask students to make up a synonum for each of the vocabulary words. Call on students to volunteer one synonym from their lists. Have other students identify the correct vocabulary word that matches it.

b. Have students read the chapter title and the Objective question.
Ask: Can you predict the ways in which the United States became a great power in the period after World War II?
Write their predictions on the chalkboard. Refer to them as students read the chapter.
c. Have students preview the chapter visuals. Based on these visuals, have students identify some of the key events of the period.
d. Have students read the chapter.

3. Review and Recall: After the students have read the chapter:
a. Have them reread and answer the Objective question.
b. Have them reread and answer each section question.
c. Have them ask each other factual questions based on the content of each section.
d. Have students identify a fact from each section. Then have other students volunteer opinions based on this fact.
e. Have students make up a crossword puzzle using words and ideas from the chapter. After they have written all the Down and Across clues, they can try to solve each other's puzzles.

4. Building Social Studies Skills: Remind students of the importance of using a time line to organize information about important events in chronological order. Have students make a time line of the key events of the period.

5. Extension
a. Have students role-play an interview between a newspaper reporter and a United States citizen on the day World War II ended. During the interview the reporter should elicit the person's feelings about the future of the United States in the postwar period. Call on different pairs of students to present their dramatizations.
b. Ask students to research and to write a report on one aspect of American life in the period immediately following the war. Possible topics include the economy, medical and scientific research, housing, and radio and television.

Support Materials

Assignments can include:
1. Chapter Review, pp. 584–585
2. Vocabulary and Comprehension Master V104
3. Test 14-1, p. CT78
4. Enrichment Master E78

UNIT 14

CHAPTER 2   The Cold War

Overview   After World War II, Eastern European countries bacame Soviet satellites and the era of the Cold War in international politics began. To protect Turkey and Greece from Soviet domination, the Truman Doctrine, which sought to contain communism, was introduced. At the same time, the Marshall Plan to help European countries recover from the ravages of the war was announced. A Soviet blockade of Berlin resulted in a massive airlift of supplies by the United States, Britain, and France. In 1949 Germany was divided into two countries. That same year the NATO alliance, which provided for military assistance in the event of a Soviet attack, was formed.

Objective

1. To learn how the Soviet Union took control of Eastern Europe after World War II.
2. To identify key points of American foreign policy after the war, including the Truman Doctrine and the Marshall Plan.
3. To understand the origins of the Cold War.
4. To understand how and why Germany was divided after the war.
5. To learn about the NATO alliance and what it hoped to achieve.

Developing the Chapter

1. Motivation: Bring in newspaper or magazine clippings about recent political events that involve the United States and the Soviet Union. Ask students factual question to elicit any information they might have about these events. Then point to the map "Cold War Divides Europe" on page 588 of their textbook. Ask them to identify the countries that joined NATO and those that were Warsaw Pact members.

Ask: What do you know about the Cold War? How do you think it began? How would you describe the relationship between the United States the the Soviet Union now?

2. Introduction

a. Write the chapter vocabulary words on the chalkboard. Have students write each word and its glossary definition in their vocabulary notebook. Ask volunteers to use each word in original sentences.

b. Have students read the chapter title and the Objective question.

c. Have students preview the chapter visuals and the main headings. Ask them to identify some key events that will be discussed in the chapter.

d. Have students read the chapter.

3. Review and Recall: After the students have read the chapter:

a. Have them reread and answer the Objective question.

b. Have them reread each subhead question and answer it.

c. Have them provide one- or two-sentence identifications for the following terms, events, and names: *Cold War, Iron Curtain, Truman Doctrine, Marshall Plan, Berlin Airlift, George C. Marshall,* and *NATO.*

d. Write the following chart title on the chalkboard: *Ways the United States Helped Europe.* Write the following heading at the top of the chart: *Truman Doctrine; Marshall Plan; Berlin Airlift; NATO.* Ask students to complete the chart with information that describes each topic.

4. Building Social Studies Skills: Briefly review the outline form, including the use of headings for main ideas and subheadings for supporting ideas. Have students complete the following outline, adding other headings and subheadings.

I. The Communist Threat After World War II
  A. Beginning of the Iron Curtain
  B. Truman Doctrine
  C. Marshall Plan
  D. Berlin Airlift

5. Extension

a. Ask students to research and write a report on the form of government that exists in the Soviet Union today and how it operates.

b. Ask students to keep a current-events log for one week in which they clip newspaper and magazine articles that focus on Soviet–United States relations. Have different students track specific stories involving both countries. Ask them to write five-minute news-style documentaries in which they summarize the key events of these stories.

Support Materials

Assignments can include:

1. Chapter Review, pp. 590–591
2. Workbook, p. 84
3. Vocabulary and Comprehension Master V105
4. Test 14-2, p. CT79
5. Map Transparency Activity Sheet A29
6. Enrichment Master E79

UNIT 14

CHAPTER 3 Conflict in Asia

Overview After North Korea invaded South Korea in 1950, soldiers from many nations, including the United States, fought the invaders under the United Nations flag. A truce ended the war in 1953. In 1961 our country again became involved in a conflict in Asia, helping South Vietnam resist communism. The war escalated under the administration of President Johnson. However, the war was unpopular with many Americans, who believed that the United States should not become involved in another country's civil war. A peace treaty was signed in 1973. In August 1974, following the Watergate investigation by a congressional committee, President Richard Nixon resigned.

Objectives

1. To understand the origins of the Korean War and how the United States became involved in the conflict.
2. To learn about the involvement of the United States in the Vietnam War.
3. To learn about the Watergate scandal and President Nixon's resignation.

Developing the Chapter

1. **Motivation:** Bring in a picture of the Vietnam memorial in Washington, D.C., and show it to the students. Elicit any information students might already have about the memorial and its significance. Explain that it includes the names of all the American men and women who died in Vietnam.
Ask: In what ways was this war different from other wars that our country had fought in the 1900s? Why do you think this war was so unpopular with United States citizens?

   Explain that students will learn more about the Vietnam War and other events that took place in the 1960s and early 1970s as they read this chapter.
2. **Introduction**
a. Write the chapter vocabulary words on the chalkboard. Have students write each word and its glossary definition in their vocabulary notebook. Write sentences on the chalkboard using each vocabulary word from the chapter. Have students try to determine the words' meanings from context clues.
b. Ask students to read the chapter title and the Objective question. Ask them to suggest reasons why the United States fought wars in both Ko-

rea and Vietnam against Communist armies. Write their answers on the chalkboard under the headings *Korea* and *Vietnam*. Refer to their answers as you read the chapter.
c. Have students preview the chapter visuals. Ask them to identify key events from the illustrations that are included that will be discussed in this chapter.
d. Have students read the chapter.
3. **Review and Recall:** After students have read the chapter:
a. Ask students to reread and answer the Objective question.
b. Ask students to reread and answer each section question.
c. Divide the class into teams to play "Who Am I?" based on the people discussed in this chapter. The person pretending to the the historical figures must answer yes-or-no questions posed by the other team until the team guesses the identity of the figure. The team that makes the most correct identifications wins.
4. **Building Social Studies Skills:** Review map-reading skills with students, using the maps on page 596 of this chapter. Include the following points in your review: map title, map legend, distance scale, compass rose, and lines of longitude and latitude. Ask students to identify key cities according to their longitude and latitude, and to use the map legend to interpret map symbols.
5. **Extension**
a. Have students write letters from soldiers in either the Vietnam or the Korean wars to friends or relatives in the United States. These letters should reflect their feelings about their participation in the war. Suggest that students do additional research on the history of both wars.
b. Have students do additional research about the Watergate break-in and subsequent investigation. When they have finished, have teams of students present "Meet the Press" type interviews between a team of reporters and one or two of the key participants in the scandal.

Support Materials

Assignments can include:

1. Chapter Review, pp. 596—597
2. Workbook, p. 85
3. Vocabulary and Comprehension Master V106
4. Test 14-3, p. CT80
5. Enrichment Master E80

CHAPTER 4   The United States and the Middle East

Overview   Because it is dependent on oil from the Middle East, the United States has become involved in political events in that part of the world. For many years the United States has supported Israel with arms, money, and technical assistance. To punish the United States for supporting Israel in the 1973 Arab–Israeli war, Arab oil countries placed an embargo on oil shipments to the United States. The result was a serious oil shortage and high inflation. In 1978 President Jimmy Carter helped to negotiate the Camp David agreement between Israel and Egypt. A year later Americans were taken hostage by young Iranians in Teheran.

Objectives

1. To understand the importance of the Middle East to the United States.
2. To learn about the wars between the Israelis and the Arabs and how the United States has supported Israel.
3. To identify the effects of the Arab oil embargo on the United States.
4. To learn how the United States was affected by events in Iran.
5. To understand how the war between Israel and Lebanon involved the United States.

Developing the Chapter

1. Motivation: Direct students' attention to the picture of Americans waiting in long lines to buy gasoline on page 598. Explain that this situation existed in the United States as a result of Arab nations cutting off oil supplies in 1973.

Ask: In what other ways have Americans been affected by events in the Middle East? Why do you think there have been so many problems and conflicts in that area?

2. Introduction

a. Write the chapter vocabulary words on the chalkboard. Have students write each word and its glossary definition in their vocabulary notebook. Call on students to make up a one-sentence definition of each word. Have volunteers read aloud their definitions. Ask other students to identify the vocabulary word that is being defined.

b. Have students read the chapter title and the Objective question.

c. Have students preview the chapter visuals, focusing on the information provided by the map in the geographical feature.
   Ask: Why do you think the actions of the OPEC members have such an impact on Western nations, such as the United States?

d. Have students read the chapter.

3. Review and Recall: After the students have read the chapter:

a. Have them reread and answer the Objective question.

b. Have them reread and answer each section question.

c. Have them make a time line of the important events discussed in this chapter.

d. Write the following headings on the chalkboard: *Israel; Saudi Arabia; Egypt; Iran; Lebanon.* On the left-hand side of the chart, write the following in column form: *Event; Effect on U.S.* Have students complete the chart with appropriate information from the chapter. The completed chart should include the event that took place in each Middle Eastern country and the impact of the event on the United States.

4. Building Social Studies Skills: Review with students the importance of taking accurate and concise notes on their reading. Ask students to take notes on Sections 2 through 7 in their chapters. Call on volunteers to aloud their note cards.

5. Extension

a. Have students write news accounts of one of the historical events described in this chapter. Possible topics include the Arab oil embargo, the Camp David peace treaty, and the release of the Iranian hostages. Ask them to do additional research on the topic before writing the article.

b. Have students role-play interviews between a television or newspaper reporter and one of the people discussed in this chapter. The interviews should take place immediately after an important event in which the historical figure played a key role. Call on different teams of students to present their role-plays to the class.

Support Materials

Assignments can include:

1. Chapter Review, pp. 602–603
2. Workbook, p. 86
3. Vocabulary and Comprehension Master V107
4. Test 14-4, p. CT81
5. Enrichment Master E81

UNIT 14

CHAPTER 5 America Works for Peace

Overview   The Cold War has continued to affect United States–Soviet relations. During the Cuban missile crisis in October 1962, the world feared that the superpowers were on the brink of World War III. In the 1970s, President Nixon improved relations with Communist China and the Soviet Union. President Carter signed the SALT II treaty with Soviet leader Leonid Brezhnev. However, President Carter's criticism of human-rights violations in the Soviet Union coupled with the Soviet invasion of Afghanistan cause a setback in superpower relations. Mikhail Gorbachev's policy of glasnost has resulted in better relations with the United States.

Objectives

1. To understand the causes and the consequences of the Cuban missile crisis.
2. To trace the course of Soviet–American and Sino–American relations in the 1970s.
3. To trace the course of the Cold War in the 1980s.

Developing the Chapter

1. Motivation: Ask students what they would think if during school, a loud buzzer went off and they had to file out of class to the basement. These were not fire drills but air-raid drills students in the late 1950s and 1960s had to do. Explain to students that they will read in this chapter how the Cold War has greatly affected international and domestic affairs.

2. Introduction: Write the chapter vocabulary words on the chalkboard. Have students write each word and its glossary definition in their vocabulary notebook. Then have students make up word-search puzzles with all the vocabulary words.

3. Review and Recall: After students have read the chapter:

a. Ask students to reread and answer the Objective question.

b. Ask students to reread and answer the section questions.

c. Write the following events, names, and key terms on index cards: *Cuban missile crisis, Cuban blockade, hot line, John F. Kennedy, Nikita Khrushchev, détente, Richard Nixon, superpowers, Henry Kissinger, Jimmy Carter, human rights, Afghanistan, 1980 Olympic games, Grenada, glasnost,*

Mikhail Gorbachev, Solidarity, George Bush. Divide the class into two teams. Have each team member take one of the index cards and correctly identify the printed name or event in one or two sentences. Assign a score of five points for each correct identification. The team with the most points at the end of the game is the winner.

d. Have a student identify one fact from each section. Ask another student to volunteer an opinion based on this fact.

4. Building Social Studies Skills: Remind students of the importance of preparing a bibliography of sources when researching a report about a specific topic. Review the use of the subject, the title, and the author divisions of the card catalogue in your school library. Point out the correct form to be used in making up a bibliography index card. Have students make up six bibliographical cards that could be used in writing reports on one of the following topics: the Cuban missile crisis, President John F. Kennedy, the Cold War, and Solidarity.

5. Extension

a. Have students write fiction stories set in the future. The premise of the stories is a confrontation that threatens the planet between the two superpowers. Students can develop the plot in any way they choose. They should decide on the final outcome: either peace, or war that destroys the planet. The stories should give reasons for the final outcome they chose. Call on volunteers to read aloud their stories to the rest of the class.

b. Have students write editorials in which they comment on one of the historical events described in this chapter. Their editorials can represent the views of a Soviet or an American writer. Call on students who have written editorials about the same event, but from different points of view, to read aloud their paragraphs. Encourage additional research.

Support Materials

Assignments can include:

1. Chapter Review, pp. 608–609
2. Workbook, pp. 87–89
3. Vocabulary and Comprehension Master V108
4. Test 14-5, p. CT82
5. Enrichment Master E82

UNIT 15

Americans Strengthen Their Nation

Unit Overview The second half of the 20th century has been a period of change for the United States. Groups such as African Americans, women, Hispanic Americans, Native Americans, the elderly, and the disabled have worked to receive their full civil rights. All these groups were helped by judicial decisions and federal legislation. At the same time the social fabric of the nation has been changed by new immigrants from Asia, Eastern Europe, and Latin America. Meanwhile, cities have struggled with problems of crime, drugs, and protecting the environment. Under Presidents Reagan and Bush, the nation pursued conservative ecomonic and governmental policies while improving relations with the Soviet Union and nations of Eastern Europe.

Unit Objectives

1. To describe how different groups of Americans achieved their civil rights.
2. To identify the problems and achievements of America's cities.
3. To describe the domestic and foreign policies of Presidents Reagan and Bush.
4. To explain how science and technology have changed the United States.
5. To learn how different groups of people have changed our country.
6. To list ways of protecting the environment.

Unit Introduction

1. Motivation: Have students imagine that they are creating a time capsule to be opened one hundred years from today. In the capsule they would include information about the most important achievements and problems that have taken place recently in the following areas: civil rights; the environment; science and technology; politics; world events.
Ask: What are some events that you would choose to include in each category? Explain that students will learn about changes and achievements in these areas and their effects on life in the United States since World War II as they read this unit.
2. Visual: Direct students' attention to the unit-opening photograph on pages 612 and 613 of the bicentennial celebration of the United States Constitution in 1987. Explain that this was a proud moment for most Americans because it meant that the United States had been governed by the Constitution for two centuries. Point out that they will learn about the progress in fulfilling the promise of equality for all implied in the Constitution.
3. Time Line: Have students review the time line on pages 610 and 611 of their textbooks for familiar names and events.
Ask: In general, what do many of the events included in this time line deal with? (achievements in the area of civil rights)
4. Points of View: Have students read the introductory paragraph in this feature. Ask students to name some of the accomplishments that the United States can take pride in and some of the problems that still remain to be solved. Have students read the first selection.
Ask: What problems does this writer see for minority groups living in the United States today? Do you agree or disagree? Explain your answer. Now have students read the second selection.
Ask: What is the most important thing that this writer looks forward to in the future? Do you agree or disagree? Explain your answer.

Unit Activities

1. Cooperative Learning: Have students work in small groups to create an illustrated time line that includes major events discussed in this unit and more recent events that reflect achievements in the areas of civil rights, environmental protection, science and technology, and politics. Have students use material from magazines and newspapers as well as their own photographs and illustrations.
2. Research: Have students select a topic that is discussed in this unit, such as an environmental or civil rights issue. Have them collect newspaper and magazine articles about the topic for a two-week period. Ask students to present their findings to the class in a five-minute oral presentation.
3. Creative Writing: Have students write science fiction stories set in the United States 100 years from today. Their stories should focus on one of the areas discussed in this Unit—civil rights, politics, environmental protection, science and technology, the population, and so on.

Support Materials

Assignments can include:

1. Unit Review, pp. 670–671
2. Unit Vocabulary and Comprehension Master V121
3. Unit 15 Test, pp. UT29–UT30
4. Map Transparency Activity Sheet A32

UNIT 15

CHAPTER 1   Equal Rights for African Americans

Overview   On December 1, 1955, the civil rights movement began in Montgomery, Alabama. Protesters were led by Dr. Martin Luther King who advocated a nonviolent strategy. The civil rights movement continued to grow in the 1960s. Important goals were voting rights for African Americans and an end to segregation. Decisions by the Supreme Court extended civil rights of African Americans and other minorities. Federal legislation also strengthened people's civil rights.

Objectives

1. To describe the forms of segregation that existed prior to the civil rights movement.
2. To understand the strategies and goals of the civil rights movement.
3. To describe Dr. Martin Luther King's contributions to the civil rights movement.
4. To explain how the Supreme Court and Congress aided equality for African Americans.
5. To evaluate the gains made by African Americans as a result of the civil rights movement.

Developing the Chapter

1. Motivation: Read or play students a selection from Dr. Martin Luther King's "I Had a Dream" speech, delivered at the Lincoln Memorial during the March on Washington in 1963.
Ask: What is the most important message of the speech? How do you think the people in the crowd felt as they listened? How does this speech make you feel today?

Explain that students will learn more about the achievements of the civil rights movement in this chapter.

2. Introduction
a. Write the chapter vocabulary words on the chalkboard. Have students write each word and its glossary definition in their vocabulary notebooks. Ask volunteers to use each vocabulary word in a sentence.
b. Have students read the chapter title and the Objective question.
c. Have students preview the chapter visuals.
   Ask: What do these illustrations tell you about the problems facing African Americans during this period?
d. Have students read the chapter.

3. Review and Recall: After the students have read the chapter:
a. Have them answer the Objective question.
b. Have them answer each section question.
c. Have students identify the main idea in each of the sections.
d. Divide the class into teams to play "Who Am I?" based on the people discussed in the chapter.
e. Have students identify the following in one or two sentences: Jackie Robinson, Rosa Parks, civil rights movement, passive resistance, Southern Christian Leadership Conference, Dr. Martin Luther King, Jr., Congress of Racial Equality, freedom riders, sit-ins, "Black Power," *Brown vs. the Board of Education of Topeka,* affirmative action, Jesse Jackson.

4. Building Social Studies Skills: Remind students of the importance of making up a bibliography of sources to be used in researching reports and projects. Each source should be listed separately on a file card with the following information: title, author, publisher, date of publication. Ask students to use their school library catalogue to make up bibliographical cards for books about the following topics: the March on Washington; civil rights movement; Martin Luther King, Jr.

5. Extension
a. Have students do additional research on the March on Washington. Then have them write a first-person narrative about the March from the point of view of a participant in this historic event.
b. Have teams of students role-play interviews between a reporter and one of the civil rights figures discussed in this chapter.

Support Materials

Assignments can include:
1. Chapter Review, pp. 620–621
2. Vocabulary and Comprehension Master V111
3. Test 15-1, p. CT83
4. Map Transparency Activity Sheet A30
5. Enrichment Master E83

CHAPTER 2 Equal Opportunities for Women

Overview As women's roles in society changed in the 1950s and 1960s, women became more vocal in demanding equality in a "man's world." Women began to lobby for newer, more effective laws to protect their interests. Although the Equal Rights Amendment was passed by Congress, it was not ratified by the states. Despite this setback, women have continued to press for progress in other areas. In 1972, the Equal Employment Opportunities Act was passed. In recent years women have become leaders in professions that were once dominated by men. However, other goals, including equal pay and improved day care, have yet to be met.

Objectives

1. To describe how women's roles in society changed in the 1950s and 1960s.
2. To explain how groups lobbied for changes in the legal system to protect women's rights.
3. To define the Equal Rights Amendment.
4. To identify the goals to be achieved in order for women to have equal opportunity.
5. To identify the areas in which women have made progress since World War II.

Developing the Chapter

1. Motivation: Elicit any information that students might already have about the women's rights movement and its achievements.

Ask: In what ways have your lives been affected by the women's rights movement? Do you consider these effects to be positive or negative? Imagine yourself explaining the roles that men and women play in our society to someone who was totally unfamiliar with our culture—what would you say? In what ways do you think these roles still have to be changed? If you could suggest five goals for the women's rights movement for the next 50 years, what would they be?

2. Introduction

a. Write the chapter vocabulary words on the chalkboard. Have students write each word and its glossary definition in their vocabulary notebooks. Ask students to write fill-in-the-blank sentences for each word. Have students exchange papers and complete each other's sentences with the correct vocabulary words.

b. Have students read the chapter title and the Objective question.

Ask: What does the title "Equal Opportunities" mean to you?

c. Have students preview the chapter visuals.

Ask: What can you learn about the women's rights movement from these illustrations?

3. Review and Recall: After the students have read the chapter:

a. Have them answer the Objective question.

b. Have them answer each section question.

c. Have them make up a time line of the major events discussed in the chapter.

d. Have them identify the main idea in each section.

e. Divide the class into teams to play "Who Am I"? based on people discussed in this chapter.

4. Building Social Studies Skills: Review the difference between a fact an opinion: A fact is a true statement that can be proven. An opinion is what a person or a group of people think or believe; it cannot be proven to be true. Have students reread section 10. Ask them to find examples of two facts. Then have them write two opinions based on the material in this section.

5. Extension

a. Have students work in small groups to create posters that provide a visual overview of an issue or issues related to the women's rights movement. Students can use illustrations and headlines from newspapers and magazines as well as create their own pictures for the posters.

b. Have students read all or part of Betty Friedan's *The Feminine Mystique* and write a report on the book. In their reports ask students to identify the ways in which women's lives have changed since the book was published.

c. Have students interview an older female relative or family friend about the attitudes regarding women's roles that existed in her generation. If possible, ask students to tape-record the interviews and play them back in class. Alternatively, have students summarize their findings in writing.

Support Materials

Assignments can include:

1. Chapter Review, pp. 626–627
2. Workbook, p. 91
3. Vocabulary and Comprehension Master V112
4. Test 15-2, p. CT84
5. Enrichment Master E84

CHAPTER 3 Opportunities for All Americans

Overview In the 1960s and 1970s, both Hispanic Americans and Native Americans worked to achieve equal rights in American society. To achieve better working conditions for farm laborers, Cesar Chavez started the National Farm Workers Association. Other Hispanic Americans have worked to gain full voting rights. Similarly, Native Americans have sought political equality. The Indian Civil Rights Act of 1968 finally granted full civil rights to all Native Americans. As a result of Native American pressure, the Indian Self-Determination Act of 1976 was passed. Native Americans have also won important legal victories that resulted in repayment for the lands they lost.

Objectives

1. To describe the progress made by Hispanic Americans in achieving equal rights.
2. To explain how Native Americans organized and fought for equal rights.
3. To identify the legal and political results of the Native Americans' civil rights struggles.

Developing the Chapter

1. Motivation: Read students the "Declaration" on page 631 of their textbooks.

Ask: What group do you think was responsible for writing this statement of purpose? What were these people forced to give up? What are they determined to hold on to? In what ways is it similar to and different from the *Declaration of Independence,* that you studied about earlier?

Point out to students that they will learn more about the struggles of Native Americans and Hispanics for civil rights as they read this chapter.

2. Introduction

a. Write the chapter vocabulary words on the chalkboard. Have students write each word and its glossary definition in their vocabulary notebooks. Ask volunteers to use each vocabulary word in an original sentence.
b. Have students read the chapter title and the Objective question.
c. Have students preview the chapter visuals.
   Ask: What can you learn from these illustrations about the struggles of Hispanic Americans and Native Americans to achieve equality in American society?

d. Have students read the chapter.

3. Review and Recall: After the students have read the chapter:
a. Have them answer the Objective question.
b. Have them answer each section question.
c. Have students create a time line of the major events discussed in this chapter.
d. Ask students to identify the following: La Raza; Wounded Knee; Reies Lopez; National Farm Workers Association; American Indian Chicago Conference; Indian Self-Determination Act; Cesar Chavez; Indian Civil Rights Act; Lauro Cavazos.
e. Have students use the chart on page 668 to compare the numbers of Hispanic Americans in 1975 and 1990.
   Ask: How many more Hispanic Americans are living in the United States in 1990 than in 1960?

4. Building Social Studies Skills: Use the map on page 632 to briefly review map reading skills with the class, including the key, scale, and direction indicator (compass rose). Based on the map, ask students to identify the areas with the greatest Hispanic population in the United States today.

5. Extension
a. Have students do additional research on the strike against the grape growers in Delano, California and the takeover of Wounded Knee by Native Americans. Then ask them to write a protest song or statement from the point of view of participants in either incident. Call on volunteers to read their protests to the class.
b. Have groups of students write a "Declaration of Purpose" similar to the one on page 00 of their textbook that summarizes the feelings of Hispanic Americans or another ethnic group living in the United States.

Support Materials

Assignments can include:
1. Chapter Review, pp. 632–633
2. Vocabulary and Comprehension Master V113
3. Test 15-3, p. CT85
4. Map Transparency Activity Sheet A31
5. Enrichment Masters E85

UNIT 15

CHAPTER 4   A Changing America

Overview   The composition of the U.S. population reflects the growing importance and political awareness of different groups of people in our society. The country of origin of many immigrants is now Asia rather than Europe. In addition, political pressure by the United States has resulted in a greater number of Soviet immigrants than ever before. The elderly and handicapped are two other groups in the population that are actively voicing their right to participate fully in society.

Objectives

1. To identify the changes in the immigrant population of the United States.

2. To understand the impact of older Americans on our society.

3. To learn about the ways the handicapped are participating in our society.

4. To understand how changing population trends are changing the face of our society.

Developing the Chapter

1. Motivation: Call on volunteers to identify the county of origin of their parents or grandparents. Write their answers on the chalkboard. Discuss with students the contributions that people from other cultures have made to their immediate community or city.

Ask: What are some of the different ethnic restaurants in the area? Are there any speciality or clothes stores that sell merchandise made in other countries? What would our lives be like if people from other countries were not permitted to settle here? (note: The discussion should stress the positive effects of such ethnic diversity on the community.) Can you identify other groups who contribute to our community? (older Americans; the handicapped) Explain that students will learn more about the changing face of American society as they read this chapter.

2. Introduction

a. Write the chapter vocabulary words on the chalkboard. Have students write each word and its glossary definition in their vocabulary notebooks. Have students create crossword puzzles. Remind students words must be written horizontally and vertically. They should use their definitions as clues. Have students exchange and complete one another's puzzles.

b. Have students read the chapter title and the Objective question.

c. Have students preview the chapter visuals.
  Ask: What information about the chapter do these illustration give you?

d. Have students read the chapter.

3. Review and Recall: After the students have read the chapter:

a. Have them answer each subhead question.

b. Have them answer each Objective question.

c. Have them identify the main idea in each section.

d. Write the following chart headings on the chalkboard: Older Americans; Handicapped. On the left side of the chart, write: Goals; Achievements. Have students complete the chart with appropriate information from the chapter.

4. Building Social Studies Skills: Review with students how to take accurate notes on notecards when reviewing material or preparing a report. Remind them to write a heading that identifies the topic at the top of each notecard. Also, the notes should be written in phrases rather than complete sentences to save space. Have students reread sections 2, 6, 7, and 9 and take notes on their reading. Call on volunteers to read their notecards aloud to the class.

5. Extension

a. Have students investigate the community services available for older Americans and the handicapped in their community. Have them summarize their research in an illustrated pamphlet. Encourage students to give their pamphlets to someone who could benefit from the research.

b. Have pairs of students make posters or collages that reflect the ethnic diversity of their community. Suggest that they use magazine or newspaper illustrations and photographs in their work.

Support Materials

Assignments can include:

1. Chapter Review. pp. 638–639

2. Workbook, p. 90

3. Vocabulary and Comprehension Master V114

4. Test 15-4, p. CT86

5. Enrichment Master E86

UNIT 15

CHAPTER 5   A Nation of Cities

Overview   The majority of Americans are urban dwellers. Although American cities are vital centers of culture and education, they are plagued with problems. The plight of the homeless remains a chronic situation, and many city schools are old and in need of repair. Overcrowding and high drop-out rates are two dilemmas facing public schools in urban areas. In addition, the quality of life in many cities has been seriously undermined by the high crime rate and availability of drugs.

Objectives

1. To identify the opportunities that cities provide for Americans.
2. To describe the problems that exist in city schools and housing and the ways in which American cities are coping with them.
3. To identify the effects of drugs and crime on America's cities.
4. To understand how some business leaders are working to lower the school dropout rate.

Developing the Chapter

1. Motivation: Begin by asking students to identify the cultural and educational opportunities that their city provides for its citizens. Then have students identify the most serious problems that plague their city.
Ask: How could the city solve the problems it faces today? List the suggested solutions on the board. Explain that students will learn more about American's cities, including their problems and their achievements, as they read this chapter.

2. Introduction
a. Write the chapter vocabulary words on the chalkboard. Have students write each word and its glossary definition in their vocabulary notebooks. Conduct a vocabulary bee. Use vocabulary words from previous chapters, if necessary, to determine a winner.
b. Have students read the chapter title and the Objective question.
c. Have students preview the chapter visuals.
   Ask: Which illustration best represents today's cities? Why?
d. Have students read the chapter.

3. Review and Recall: After the students have read the chapter:
a. Have them answer the Objective question.

b. Have them answer each section question.
c. Have them identify the main idea in each section.
d. Write the following heading on the chalkboard: Cities' Problems, Cities' Solutions. Then have students complete the chart with appropriate information from the chapter.

4. Building Social Studies Skills: Remind students that readers can often use the context of a word to determine its meaning. Point out that the words around an unfamiliar word often contain a definition of that word; other times, the context can help readers infer the meaning by what the other words say. Direct students' attention to the word *homesteading* in section 7. Ask students to find the definition of the word that is provided in the next sentence. Repeat the procedure with *dropouts* in section 15.

5. Extension
a. Have students make up a map of an "ideal" city in the future. Their city should be an interesting, exciting place to live and free of the most common problems that plague America's urban areas. Their maps should include areas for public buildings, housing, entertainment, and medical and educational centers. Ask students to consider what the American city of the future will look like—will it be at all similar to the cities that exist today? What kind of housing will its citizens live in? What will the transportation system be like? Ask students to write an explanation of the choices they made in creating their own cities. Call on volunteers to display their maps in the classroom.
b. Ask students to work in small groups to create an advertising campaign for either print or television that alerts citizens to one of the urban problems discussed in this chapter.

Support Materials

Assignments can include:
1. Chapter Review, pp. 644–645
2. Workbook, pp. 92–93
3. Vocabulary and Comprehension Master V115
4. Test 15-5, p. CT87
5. Enrichment Masters E87

CHAPTER 6   New Leaders for the Nation

Overview   Both Presidents Reagan and Bush implemented conservative policies and programs that favored reducing government control of business and industry. During the Reagan administration, personal and business tax rates were lowered; however, Reagan also favored cutting many social programs and increasing military spending. President Bush promised to carry on President Reagan's economic policies and not to raise taxes. Both Presidents were deeply concerned about the growing drug problem in the United States.

Objectives

1. To describe President Reagan's economic and governmental policies.
2. To identify President Bush's goals and plans for the United States.
3. To explain the social and economic problems that Presidents Reagan and Bush had to deal with during their administrations.

Developing the Chapter

1. **Motivation:** Suggest that students imagine themselves running for President.
Ask: What economic and social goals would you want to achieve during your presidency? What problems facing our country today would you want to correct? How would you go about it? Do you think the federal government should have greater or less control over business and industry? Would you spend tax dollars on social programs or on military funding?

   Have students explain their answers. Point out that students will learn more about the Reagan and Bush presidencies in the chapter.
2. **Introduction**
a. Write the chapter vocabulary words on the chalkboard. Have students write each word and its glossary definition in their vocabulary notebooks. Ask students to use each vocabulary word in a sentence. Call on students to read their sentences aloud, leaving out the vocabulary word. Have other students supply the vocablary word that completes the sentence correctly.
b. Have students read the chapter title and the Objective question.
c. Have students preview the chapter visuals. Ask volunteers to read the captions and suggest connections to the chapter content.
d. Have students read the chapter.
3. **Review and Recall:** After the students have read the chapter:
a. Have them answer the Objective question.
b. Have them answer each section question.
c. Have them identify in two or three sentences the following people, events, or topics: Ronald Reagan; John Hinckley; George Bush; deregulation; recession; budget deficit; Gramm-Rudman-Hollings Act; Sandra Day O'Connor; Antonin Scalia; Anthony Kennedy; drug lords.
d. Write the following chart headings on the chalkboard: Economy; Social Issues; Relations with Congress. On the left side of the chart, in list form, write the following: President Reagan; President Bush. Then have students complete the chart with appropriate information from the chapter.
4. **Building Social Studies Skills:** Remind students of the importance of making a time line to arrange important events in chronological order. Help students make a time line of the key events discussed in this chapter, beginning with Ronald Reagan's first inauguration in 1981 and ending with George Bush's election in November 1988.
5. **Extension**
a. Have students write a news account of one of the key events described in this chapter. Possible topics include the following: the assassination attempt on President Reagan, George Bush's election, Sandra Day O'Connor's appointment to the Supreme Court.
b. Ask groups of students to role-play a press conference with either President Reagan or President Bush and a group of television and newspaper reporters. Each student ''journalist'' should have a list of six questions to ask the president. Call on groups to present their role-play in front of the class.

Support Materials

Assignments can include:

1. Chapter Review, pp. 650–651
2. Vocabulary and Comprehension Master V116
3. Test 15-6, p. CT88
4. Enrichment Master E88

UNIT 15

CHAPTER 7   Dealing with Other Nations

Overview   During the Reagan administration the first significant thaw in the Cold War with the Soviet Union took place, a political development encouraged by Mikhail Gorbachev's policy of glasnost, or openness. However, the United States was drawn into conflicts in both Central America and the Middle East. Congress suspended President Reagan's support of the Salvadoran rebels in 1988, and officials in his administration took part in an illegal arms deal with Iran. The United States faced strong economic competition from both Japan and Europe. By 1989, the demand for liberty resulted in governmental reforms throughout the Soviet bloc.

Objectives

1. To explain how the United States improved relations with the Soviet Union.
2. To identify the problems faced by the United States in Central America and the Middle East.
3. To explain how economic growth in both Europe and Japan affected American trade.
4. To explain the governmental reforms that swept Communist bloc countries in the 1980s.

Developing the Chapter

1. Motivation: Elicit any information that students already have about Mikhail Gorbachev, the Soviet leader, and his policy of glasnost, or openness. Then remind students that during the Reagan administration relations between the United States and the Soviet Union began to improve. Do you think improving relations with the Soviet Union are good or bad for the United States and the world? Explain that students will learn more about foreign policy during the Reagan and Bush years in this chapter.

2. Introduction

a. Write sentences on the chalkboard using each vocabulary word from the chapter. Have students try to determine the words' meanings from context clues. Then have students write each word and its glossary definition in their vocabulary notebooks.

b. Have students read the chapter title and the Objective question.

c. Read the captions of the chapter visuals and ask students to add related information.

d. Have students read.the chapter.

3. Review and Recall: After the students have read the chapter:

a. Have them answer the Objective question.

b. Have them answer each section question.

c. Have students make up a time line of the major events discussed in this chapter.

d. Call on students to review each section and identify a cause for a particular action. Have another student identify the result of that action. Then reverse the process and have one student identify a result and another volunteer identify the cause that produced it.

4. Building Social Studies Skills: Review the difference between primary and secondary sources with the students. Have students reread the excerpt from President Reagan's speech in their textbooks.

Ask: Is this a primary or secondary source? (primary).

Then have students suggest two other primary sources and two secondary sources they could use to write a report on the Reagan–Gorbachev meeting. (Primary: photographs, news footage, interviews with an eyewitness, eyewitness accounts in magazines or newspapers; secondary: books, magazine articles written after the event.)

5. Extension

a. Have student select one country in the Soviet bloc that has experienced major governmental reforms. Each student should write a one- or two-page report in which these reforms are summarized. The report should compare the government of the country today with the type of government that existed in the mid-eighties.

b. Have students work in small groups to create oral presentations about current problems that the United States faces in dealing with other governments in the world today. Suggest that they use audiovisual materials to enhance their presentations.

Support Materials

Assignments can include:

1. Chapter Review, pp 656–657
2. Workbook, p. 94
3. Vocabulary and Comprehension Master V117
4. Test 15-7, p. CT89
5. Enrichment Masters E89

CHAPTER 8   Science and Technology

Overview   Since the introduction of microchips to the American public in 1971, new discoveries in science and technology have revolutionized the way people live. Advancements in computer technology have changed the nature of jobs in both business and industry. While automation has decreased the number of blue-collar jobs in America, it has created new opportunities for workers with white-collar skills. Computers and advanced medical tools, such as CT scanners, x-rays, and magnetic resonance imaging, have also improved the quality of health care in the United States.

Objectives

1. To explain how the use of computers has changed the way people work.
2. To describe the new medical tools that have improved health care.
3. To identify the ways in which new technology has changed American life.

Developing the Chapter

1. **Motivation:** Begin by demonstrating a hand-held calculator and asking if any students know what makes it operate (microchips). Explain that a microchip is a piece of electronics smaller than a thumbnail containing tens of thousands of transistors.

Ask: What other equipment that we use in our daily lives operates through the use of microchips? (FAX machines, CDs, microwave ovens, etc.) Imagine that you awoke to find that microchips were no longer being produced. How would your daily lives be changed? Explain if the change would be for the better or for the worse.

Explain that students will learn more about new advancements in science and technology as they read this chapter.

2. **Introduction**
a. Write the chapter vocabulary words on the chalkboard. Have students write each word and its glossary definition in their vocabulary notebooks. Ask students to write an original sentence that uses vocabulary word. Have volunteers read their sentences aloud without the vocabulary word. Ask other students to fill in with the correct vocabulary word.
b. Have students read the chapter title and the Objective question.

c. Have students preview the chapter visuals.
   Ask: What can you learn about the contents of the chapter from the illustrations?
d. Have students read the chapter.

3. **Review and Recall:** After the students have read the chapter:
a. Have them answer the Objective question.
b. Have them answer each section question.
c. Ask students to identify and tell the importance of the following: shorter work week; more leisure time; microchips; greater variety of farm produce; automation; white-collar jobs; x-rays; blue-collar jobs; CT-scanners; Optacon; EPCOT center; magnetic resonance imaging.

4. **Building Social Studies Skills:** Point out that topical outlines are a useful way of organizing information. Review the use of main headings and subheadings. Then have students review the information in sections 10–14 and use it to complete an outline of those paragraphs. Suggest the following as topics to be included: Medical Advancements, Use of computers, New medical tools, x-rays, CT-scanners.

5. **Extension**
a. Ask students to write a science fiction story set in a futuristic society. Their stories should focus on the role played by new inventions and technologies in this world of the future.
b. Have students imagine themselves living in their community in the year 2100.

Ask: What new inventions would be developed by that date? In what way would your daily lives be significantly different from the way they are today? Have small groups of students discuss possible inventions and their effects. Then ask each group to create a print ad for one of the new technological advancements discussed.

Support Materials

Assignments can include:

1. Chapter Review, pp. 662–663
2. Vocabulary and Comprehension Master V118
3. Test 15-8, p. CT90
4. Enrichment Master E90

UNIT 15

CHAPTER 9   Protecting the Environment

Overview   The public's awareness of the need for environmental protection was sparked by the publication of Rachel Carson's *Silent Spring* in 1961. Today, air pollution that damages the ozone layer and produces a "greenhouse effect" continues to be an important environmental issue. In addition, steps have been taken to prevent the dumping of toxic waste and other pollutants. Oil spills, such as the Exxon Valdez disaster in 1989, continue to endanger fish and wildlife. However, the government has implemented more stringent regulations to reduce car exhaust fumes and acid rain.

Objectives

1. To describe the beginning of the current environmental protection movement.
2. To explain the effects of air and water pollution.
3. To explain our country's new environmental policy.

Developing the Chapter

1. Motivation: Elicit any information students already have about environmental problems. Begin by asking them to identify the most important problems we currently face in protecting the world we live in. Write their responses on the chalkboard. **Ask:** What steps do you take to protect the environment? Do you take metal cans to a neighboring recycling center? Do you make an effort to use biodegradable products?

Point out that public awareness sparked the movement to protect the environment. **Ask:** What do you think the world will be like in 100 years if we do not protect our environment? Explain that students will learn more about environmental protection as they read this chapter.

2. Introduction

a. Write the chapter vocabulary words on the chalkboard. Have students write each word and its glossary definition in their vocabulary notebooks. Conduct a vocabulary bee. Use other words from the unit, if necessary, to determine the winner.
b. Have students read the chapter title and Objective question. Ask them to volunteer different ways in which Americans can protect the environment. List their answers on the chalkboard.
c. Have students preview the chapter visuals.

Ask: What do these illustrations show you about the environment?
d. Have students read the chapter.

3. Review and Recall: After the students have read the chapter:

a. Have them answer the Objective question.
b. Have them answer each section question.
c. Write the following chart title on the chalkboard: *Protecting Our Environment*. Then write the following headings: *Problems, Solutions*. Have students complete the chart with information from the chapter.

4. Building Social Studies Skills: Remind students that the encyclopedia is a multivolume reference book that lists information about a wide variety of topics in alphabetical order. The index volume identifies all the articles about a particular topic that are included in the encyclopedia. Have students list all the entries in your class or school encyclopedia that relate to the following topics: acid rain; Rachel Carson; pesticides; air pollution.

5. Extension

a. Have groups of students work together to research the steps being taken by their community or city to protect the environment. Have each group make up a chart summarizing its findings.
b. Have students write editorials in which they advocate a strong environmental protection program. Call on volunteers to read their editorials aloud. Encourage students to submit their editorials to the school and local newspaper.

Support Materials

Assignments can include:

1. Chapter Review, pp. 668–669
2. Vocabulary and Comprehension Master V119
3. Test 15-9, p. CT91
4. Enrichment Masters E91

ANSWER KEY TO CHAPTER REVIEWS

UNIT 1 ❧ CHAPTER 1
VOCABULARY REVIEW
1. estimate 2. ancestors 3. migrated 4. glaciers 5. nomads 6. archaeologists 7. maize 8. irrigate

SKILL BUILDER: PREVIEWING
Students might benefit from practice in previewing one or two paragraphs as a class. Some more discerning readers may notice that this textbook helps them preview by using the device of asking a question before they begin a selection, as a way of telling what the focus will be.

SKILL BUILDER: CRITICAL THINKING AND COMPREHENSION
I. Introduction to the Main Idea
1. b 2. c 3. a 4. d

USING PRIMARY SOURCES
Students should discover that the speaker is talking directly to natural phenomena, asking them to intervene for his or her child (having the belief that the phenomena could hear, make choices, and act consciously).

ENRICHMENT
1. Students might share their poem and song discoveries with the class. **2.** Native American lore is filled with myths that explain the origins of seasons, heavenly bodies, etc. After students have told the stories they invented, they might enjoy hearing some of the authentic tales found in anthologies and collections. **3.** Some petroglyphs easily overlooked are those we still make, in decorations on buildings, tombstones, and the walls of abandoned houses.

UNIT 1 ❧ CHAPTER 2
VOCABULARY REVIEW
1. i 2. f 3. d 4. a 5. h 6. b 7. j 8. g 9. c

SKILL BUILDER: MAKING A CHART

	INUIT	PACIFIC NORTHWEST	HAWAIIANS
Location	4,000 miles from western Alaska to Greenland	Pacific coast and inland	8 Pacific islands in a chain
Culture	hunting and fishing	salmon fishing, hunting sea mammals	farming and fishing
Houses	tents in spring and summer, igloos in winter	wooden houses seasonal moves	(housing: doesn't tell us, but some students may have seen pictures of Hawaiian grass shacks)

	INUIT	PACIFIC NORTHWEST	HAWAIIANS
Food	caribou meat, fish, whale meat and blubber	fish and whale meat	mainly fish and vegetables
Types of Boats	kayaks	30-ft. wooden canoes	double canoes with sails
Other Facts	wore skins, rocks, wood, and animal parts used to make tools	shamans, totem poles, potlatches	powerful gods and goddesses, strict chiefs

SKILL BUILDER: CRITICAL THINKING AND COMPREHENSION
I. Main Idea

a. 14 b. 4 d. 6 e. 8 f. 14 g. 12
II. Facts versus Opinion

a. F b. O c. F d. O

USING PRIMARY SOURCES
Students' guesses about the figures on the totem pole will vary.

ENRICHMENT
1. The Inuits' lives would be different, depending on the season. Make sure students don't mix up summertime's dwelling, clothes, and activities with wintertime's lifestyle.
2. Students should be able after their research to describe how to build an igloo. An excellent account is given in Peter Freuchen's story of life in Greenland, and the activity is captured on film and video for students who are interested.
3. Students should mention beaver, otter, whales, walruses, polar bears, seals, caribou, sea lions, and should note use of animal products for food, clothing, and tools.

UNIT 1 ❧ CHAPTER 3
VOCABULARY REVIEW
1. i 2. b 3. e 4. h 5. c 6. g 7. a 8. d

SKILL BUILDER: INTERPRETING A PHOTOGRAPH
1. The poles are used for setting up a teepee.
2. Teepee covers, clothing, and equipment made from buffalo hide and bone.
3. European-style wheeled carriage at right; horses (introduced by Spanish).

SKILL BUILDER: CRITICAL THINKING AND COMPREHENSION
I. Main Idea
1. Their main crops were squash, beans, and corn. These nations usually raised extra food and traded it with the buffalo-hunting tribes for meat and animal hides.

T131

2. Horses allowed them to move across the huge area of the Great Plains faster and more easily. As a result, hunters on horseback could kill as many buffalo in one day as they had killed before in a week.

3. Some houses had as many as 800 rooms. The only way of entering these houses was up a ladder that led to an opening in the roof.

4. The Navajos lived in hogans, or one-room houses, made of poles covered with packed earth and brush. The Apaches continued to hunt and were among the most skilled and feared fighters in the Southwest.

CLASSIFYING

	PLAINS NATIONS	SOUTHWEST NATIONS
Farming Nations	Mandan, Pueblo, Hidatsa, Navajo, Arikara	Mogollon, Hohokam, Hopi
Hunting Nations	Arapahoe, Blackfoot, Cheyenne, Comanche, Crow, Kiowa, Sioux, Apache	other Anasazi

USING PRIMARY SOURCES

The Pueblo people believed the kachinas had the power to bring rain and a bountiful harvest. Plains people would probably ask for the same things and help in buffalo hunts.

ENRICHMENT

1. Students' summaries of myths will vary, as will their choice of tribes to research.

2. Students should discover very recent work by archaeologists and anthropologists using airplanes to trace the trails in direct lines from Anasazi village ruins to a sun temple at their hub. Other research involves microscopic examination of garbage heaps to learn what the people ate (and thus what plant life grew then) and the size of their population. Others study the oral traditions of descendants.

3. Students' listing of artifacts from their present-day culture should evoke a lively discussion of what these items reveal about the way we live. The activity can lead in to a number of spin-off activities, such as a discussion of what the class hopes will be found out about us by future archaeologists.

UNIT 1 ✍ CHAPTER 4

VOCABULARY REVIEW

1. league 2. wigwam 3. confederation 4. long house

USING PRIMARY SOURCES

Not speaking in unison wastes energy and blurs the message—tribes must unite to have their message heard.

SKILL BUILDER: READING A MAP

1. Inuit   2. Meskito
3. Micmac, Mohegan, Pequot, Creek, Seminole, Delaware
4. Sauk, Fox, Erie, Iroquois, or Miami
5. Illinois, Chickasaw, Osage, or Delaware

SKILL BUILDER: CRITICAL THINKING AND COMPREHENSION

I. Introduction to Classifying

1. Algonquian Language: 2, 4, 6. Iroquois Language: 1, 3, 5
2. Food: 1, 2, 4, 5, 6. Clothing: 1. Tools and Other Uses: 1, 3, 5

II. Main Idea
Telegrams will vary.

ENRICHMENT

1. Research on pottery will yield varied results. 2. Native American recipes will vary. 3. Research on dwellings will vary.

UNIT 1 ✍ CHAPTER 5

VOCABULARY REVIEW

1. Astronomy 2. tribute 3. steles 4. quipus 5. domesticated 6. glyphs 7. Terraces

SKILL BUILDER: USING CONTEXT CLUES

1. expedition—organized trip to explore; came upon, companions. 2. civilization—society of people living together in an organized way; great city, Mayan. 3. sacrifices—something killed and offered to a god in a ritualistic way; sacrificed (action verb), human.

SKILL BUILDER: CRITICAL THINKING AND COMPREHENSION

I. Classifying

	MAYAN	AZTEC	INCA
Writing System	glyphs	no information	no writing system
Important Crops	corn, beans, squash, sweet potatoes, cotton	no information	no information
Religion	gift of animals and crops to the many gods	human sacrifice to many gods	emperor was one of many gods
War Customs	no information	captives for sacrifices and slaves	integrated conquered people into Inca culture
Buildings	pyramids	pyramids	pyramids

2. Aztecs: a, b, c, f, g. Incas: a, d. Mayas: a, c, e, g.

II. Main Idea
Paragraph 3: The Mayas built great cities, which were centers of their religion. Paragraph 10: The Aztecs believed their lives were shaped by the will of the gods. Paragraph 15: The Incas were excellent builders and engineers.

USING PRIMARY SOURCES

Mothers warmed the bathwater by holding it in their mouths.

ENRICHMENT

1. Drawings will vary but should show babies' arms tied to their sides. 2. Reports will vary.

UNIT 2 ✍ CHAPTER 1

VOCABULARY REVIEW

1. monopoly 2. caravans 3. Islamic 4. Muslims 5. navigator 6. caravels 7. compass 8. astrolabe

SKILL BUILDER: USING A CHART

1. Name the new land "Greenland" to attract food growers.
2. Travel in a caravan to have safety in numbers.
3. Find a new way to get to the East, perhaps by water.

4. Invent a compass to use when it's cloudy, and an astrolabe to plot directions using stars as points.
5. Invent a ship like the caravel that can sail into the wind.

SKILL BUILDER: CRITICAL THINKING AND COMPREHENSION

I. Summarizing
1. b. **2.** c. **3.** a
II. Classifying
Explorers: Eric the Red, Leif Ericson, Marco Polo.
Improvements that Made Sailing Safer:
astrolabe, compass, caravel.
Products from the East: cinnamon, silk, ginger, figs, nutmeg, jewels.

USING PRIMARY SOURCES

Items on the list: silk, medicines, gold, rubies, sapphires, topazes, amethysts, and garnets. Items not costly today: ginger, pepper, nutmegs, cloves, and other spices.

ENRICHMENT

1. Students' sketches should picture the compass and astrolabe, and their oral reports should describe the use of these two instruments.
2. Students in small groups or pairs should discuss the discoveries of Marco Polo.

UNIT 2 🐾 CHAPTER 2

VOCABULARY REVIEW

1. d **2.** c **3.** a **4.** f **5.** e

SKILL BUILDER: USING AN ENCYCLOPEDIA

Answers will vary, but each student should have two facts that clearly reflect diversity, as coming from different sections of a long article.

SKILL BUILDER: CRITICAL THINKING AND COMPREHENSION

I. Summarizing
1. Summary might include the following details: left from Spain, 90 sailors, 3 ships, Canary Islands, 33 days of wind, sailors need calming, reach Bahamas. **2.** Columbus describes Arawaks to King and Queen as naked, tall, timid, unarmed, generous, gullible, and eager to please. **3.** Columbus led 17 ships and over 1,200 settlers in 3 trips over 12 years to set up colonies in what is now Honduras, Panama, Costa Rica, and Nicaragua. **4.** Columbus goes to Portugal but the naval council votes against funding, so he goes to Spain and after 4 years is successful. **5.** The Bahamas, Cuba, Hispaniola, Honduras, Panama, Costa Rica, Nicaragua, Jamaica, and Trinidad are claimed by Spain. **6.** Columbus used the wood from the *Santa María* to build a trading post where the ship sank at Hispaniola.
II. Classifying
1. Students should list facts about the discovery of the Bahamas, Cuba, Hispaniola, Honduras, Panama, Costa Rica, Nicaragua, Jamaica, and Trinidad. **2.** Columbus rides on *Santa María*, *Pinta* has rudder trouble, third ship is *Niña*. **3.** Columbus showed Europe another hemisphere, charted shortest and safest routes across the Atlantic, increased people's knowledge of plants, animals, and of Native Americans' ways of life.
4. Born in Italy, became sailor, then map maker, captain of ships, geographer, student of explorations. **5.** Self-educated

sailor, commanded ships after experience, but studied map making at Henry the Navigator's school and exploration lore by reading widely. **6.** Holy Savior, Indians, Little Spain.

USING PRIMARY SOURCES

Europeans would not be accustomed to seeing people without clothing on, without weapons, fearful of strangers smaller than they, and who gave away their possessions just for the asking.

ENRICHMENT

Students' responses will be varied.

UNIT 2 🐾 CHAPTER 3

VOCABULARY REVIEW

1. northwest passage **2.** circumnavigate **3.** conquistadores **4.** atlas **5.** isthmus **6.** territory **7.** strait **8.** line of demarcation

SKILL BUILDER: READING A MAP

1. a. North America and South America
b. Pacific Ocean and Atlantic Ocean
c. Indian Ocean and Pacific Ocean
2. a. Atlantic Ocean
b. Atlantic, Indian Ocean, and Arabian Sea
c. Atlantic Ocean
d. Atlantic and Pacific oceans
3. Columbus, Cabot, Verrazano, Cartier, DaGama, and Magellan sailed west. Cabral and Dias sailed east.

SKILL BUILDER: CRITICAL THINKING AND COMPREHENSION

I. Summarizing
1. Balboa heard from Native Americans that another ocean was nearby, so he led a band of men across 45 miles of jungle and swampland that took 3 weeks to cross. He finally saw the Pacific Ocean. **2.** Cabot, an Italian, was sent by England to find a route to Indonesia. His two voyages allowed England to claim most of North America. Cabot died on the second voyage.
II. Classifying
1. Explorers for France: Verrazano, Cartier.
2. Explorers for Spain: Balboa, Ponce de Leon, Magellan.
3. Explorers from Portugal: Magellan.
4. Important Discoveries: Pacific Ocean, La Floridá, Hudson River.

USING PRIMARY SOURCES

America is named for Amerigo (Vespucci, its discoverer) but changed to end in *a* because other continents were named for women.

ENRICHMENT

1. Students' opinions about who took greater risks—Magellan or Columbus—will vary. **2.** Students' reasons for why settlers ought to come to the West Indies should be based upon the knowledge of the West Indies that people had at the time, not our present-day knowledge of Puerto Rico or other Caribbean vacation spots.

UNIT 2 🐾 CHAPTER 4

VOCABULARY REVIEW

Sentences will vary, but should correctly use:
1. delegate **2.** veteran **3.** alliance **4.** massacre, and
5. convert, according to Glossary definitions.

SKILL BUILDER: USING A TIME LINE

1. 492 years **2.** 35 years **3.** 4 years **4.** 1 year **5.** 21 years

SKILL BUILDER: CRITICAL THINKING AND COMPREHENSION

I. Generalizing
1. c **2.** b **3.** c
II. Summarizing
1. Summaries should mention Cortés's greed at hearing of golden cities, his knowledge of the disunity of the Aztec Empire, and his ability to use slaves and other unhappy conquered peoples for his own ends. **2.** Montezuma expected Cortés to come because of an old Aztec belief. He agreed to give Cortés all he owned because he wanted to obey his people's rightful king. **3.** Summaries should mention the role of De Soto helping to subdue the Incas in Peru, and to describe how Pizarro tricked Atahualpa and took him hostage. **4.** Doña Marina had learned the Aztec language and quickly learned Spanish. She taught Cortés about Aztec life and became his interpreter.

USING PRIMARY SOURCES

The letter to the Spanish king should assure him that the Aztecs await his authority and are ready to give him everything they own.

ENRICHMENT

1. The two Native American leaders should have quite similar stories to relate about their impression of the Spaniards and the way they were taken captive, the way their warriors failed to merely elect new leadership and carry on the resistance, and the way their empires fell when confronted by the Spaniards' superior weaponry. **2.** Students' maps should use three colors or kinds of lines to distinguish the three voyages.

UNIT 2 🐚 CHAPTER 5

VOCABULARY REVIEW

1. b. **2.** a **3.** d **4.** c

SKILL BUILDER: INTERPRETING A MAP

1. Coronado
2. De Vaca and Coronado
3. Narváez was lost at sea. De Vaca led a small group back to Mexico City.
4. De Soto and Narváez

SKILL BUILDER: CRITICAL THINKING AND COMPREHENSION

I. Generalizing
1. b. **2.** b
II. Summarizing
1. Fray Marcos lied about the richness of the Seven Cities of Cíbola. His only truth was that the houses are made of stone. **2.** Estevanico was a black slave from Morocco who served as guide to Cabeza de Vaca and to Mendoza through northern Mexico and southern Arizona. Native Americans from one of the Seven Cities executed him as a spy. **3.** Cabeza and his companions pretended to be medicine men and thus walked safely from village to village across Texas to Mexico.

USING PRIMARY SOURCES

Coronado expected to find seven cities built with gold brick and decorated in turquoises. He found stone houses five stories high in seven little villages.

ENRICHMENT

1. Students' drawings should resemble a Pueblo complex, with adobe apartments reached by ladders from the roof below, up to five stories high. **2.** The two explorers should describe the bayous, plains, and deserts of the United States from the Mississippi River to Arizona, mention the societies of Native Americans growing corn and fishing or hunting there, and exaggerate the wealth of these people. **3.** Students' reports should feature only the geography and climate of Spanish America.

UNIT 2 🐚 CHAPTER 6

VOCABULARY REVIEW

Students should have used these words correctly according to their Glossary definitions: **1.** encomienda **2.** missions **3.** census **4.** missionaries

SKILL BUILDER: READING A MAP

1. Santa Elena **2.** Tegesta **3.** Rio Grande, Mississippi River **4.** Central Camino Real **5.** Mexico City **6.** Shortage of food and water; heat **7.** Western Camino Real

SKILL BUILDER: CRITICAL THINKING AND COMPREHENSION

I. Generalizing
1. Settler's demand for land for livestock, new silver mines, and water drew them north. **2.** The Spanish moved in and settled permanently in a fort at St. Augustine to supply their troops fighting the French. **3.** The purpose of the missions was to convert Native Americans to Christianity and teach them European ways of life.
II. Summarizing
1. Spaniards came to the New World to gain wealth and status. Although they were few, they governed a large empire in southwestern North America. The skills, crops, and animals the Spaniards brought became a part of the culture of the area. **2.** The Spanish founded their own settlement in Florida and drove the French out. **3.** At the missions, Native Americans learned Christianity and other European ways, and received protection from warring neighbors. **4.** Las Casas convinced the king of Spain to pass laws to improve the treatment of Native Americans by Spanish settlers. When few Spanish obeyed, Las Casas suggested using African slaves instead, but they also suffered.

USING PRIMARY SOURCES

Father Kino believed converting Native Americans would protect them from their enemies and pacify them, enabling Spain to conquer new territory (and peoples) more easily, thus spreading Spanish and Christian influence.

ENRICHMENT

1. Reports should mention the foods that helped Europeans reduce starvation and increase population: potatoes and corn. Indigo became a valuable cash crop, as did chocolate. For many decades, Europeans did not eat tomatoes, thinking them poisonous. **2.** Persons and events chosen will vary. **3.** Settlements will vary, ranging from towns like Santa Fe to missions.

UNIT 2 🐚 CHAPTER 7

VOCABULARY REVIEW

1. tributary **2.** pelts **3.** portaged **4.** Jesuit

SKILL BUILDER: MAKING A CHART

	LANDS EXPLORED	DATE EXPLORATION BEGAN
Champlain	Maine coast, New Hampshire coast	1603
	Quebec shore	1608
	Ontario rivers, Vermont, Lake Champlain, upstate New York	1609
	Lake Huron, Lake Ontario, St. Lawrence River valley	1615
Marquette and Joliet	Wisconsin River, Mississippi River to Arkansas River.	May 1673
La Salle	Ohio River valley, Mississippi River valley, Lake Ontario, Lake Michigan	1666
	Louisiana and mouth of the Mississippi River	December 1681; 1685

SKILL BUILDER: CRITICAL THINKING AND COMPREHENSION

I. Generalizing
1. The survival of New France depended upon the fur trade.
2. La Salle's discoveries gave France claim to all of the midwestern part of America to wall in the English in the East and shut out the Spanish in the South. 3. The knowledge of the direction of the Mississippi River helped France plan to spread into the fur regions by planning the best sites for forts and trading posts. 4. Champlain courted the Huron nation and sewed up the fur region the Hurons controlled, keeping it from exploitation by the English, who were friendly with the Hurons' enemies, the Iroquois.
II. Sequencing
Order should be: 4., 1., 3., and 2.

USING PRIMARY SOURCES

The French would advise the Spaniards to make it mutually advantageous to the Native Americans to co-exist with the Europeans, by providing goods in return for labor, by ensuring peace through protection from their rivals, and by learning their customs in order to interfere as little as possible.

ENRICHMENT

1. Students should include drawings and interviews in their articles about French explorers, fur traders, or Huron-Iroquois conflicts. 2. Students will need to use a wall map of the eastern half of the United States in their oral reports. 3. Students should refer to books about seventeenth-century fashions, decorative arts, formal gardens, and paintings and sculpture for full coverage of Versailles life during the reign of Louis XIV.

UNIT 2 ✍ CHAPTER 8

VOCABULARY REVIEW
1. h 2. i 3. g 4. a 5. c 6. b 7. e 8. d 9. f

SKILL BUILDER: READING A TIME LINE
1. 20 years 2. 9 years 3. 57 years 4. Spain

SKILL BUILDER: CRITICAL THINKING AND COMPREHENSION

I. Sequencing
The order of events should read: 2., 4., 6., 1., 3., and 5. (The month Africans arrived may have been earlier in 1619 than declaration of Virginia as a royal colony in July of that year, but technically the Africans did not arrive as slaves but, rather, as indentured servants).
II. Generalizing
1. Smith organized the tasks needed for survival and enforced rules made for the benefit of the group. 2. Some English people treated Native Americans fairly and other did not, and vice versa. Because of the marriage, there was a time of peace. 3. The colony probably failed because no supplies arrived from home and the colonists ran out of food and medicines.

USING PRIMARY SOURCES

The English "expected they would destroy us." The Native Americans knew the English were starving and were "no less in doubt of my intent" (to trade for food).

ENRICHMENT

1. Students should mention climate, living conditions, food shortage, strict rules, (self-government, later), Pocahontas and other friendly Native Americans. 2. Students will construct models of timber huts. 3. Diary entries might feature a cataclysmic event, such as raid by Native Americans, hurricane, starvation, or death by disease.

UNIT 3 ✍ CHAPTER 1

VOCABULARY REVIEW
1. f 2. j 3. c 4. d 5. i 6. h 7. a 8. g 9. b 10. e

SKILL BUILDER: MAKING A TIME LINE

Students have been provided dates and events to rank in consecutive order.

SKILL BUILDER: CRITICAL THINKING AND COMPREHENSION

I. Generalizing
1. The generalization is a poor one because only one of the paragraphs discusses economic reasons and the second of the two states that the most important is the religious reason. 2. Religion was important to the early colonists.
II. Sequencing
In order of occurrence: a. 1604 f. Sept. 1620 c. between Sept. and Nov. 1620 e. Nov. 1620 b. 1630 d. 1691

USING PRIMARY SOURCES

We share the idea that we join together into a government to achieve law and order and safety, and we obey our laws because they are for the general good.

ENRICHMENT

Students' role-plays, reports on Squanto, and compacts will vary.

UNIT 3 ❧ CHAPTER 2

VOCABULARY REVIEW

1. dissenter **2.** banished **3.** royal colony **4.** Fundamental Orders

SKILL BUILDER: MAKING A TIME LINE

Students should have events with the following numbers placed at the dates indicated: **1.** Oct. 1635 **2.** 1638 **3.** 1637 **4.** 1639 **5.** 1644

SKILL BUILDER: CRITICAL THINKING AND COMPREHENSION

I. Sequencing
b., e., c., a., d.
II. Cause and Effect
1. e **2.** a and e **3.** b and f **4.** c **5.** d

USING PRIMARY SOURCES

Students' opinions about the source of Europeans' racism may vary, but should mention the roles of ignorance, fear, and the Puritans' belief in their own superiority.

ENRICHMENT

1. Students' self-images of themselves as dissenters will vary.
2. The most important events in Hutchinson's life will differ.

UNIT 3 ❧ CHAPTER 3

VOCABULARY REVIEW

1. proprietary colony **2.** proprietor **3.** Quakers **4.** traitors

USING PRIMARY SOURCES

We share with Penn the ideal that all religious beliefs should be allowed and respected.

SKILL BUILDER: INTERPRETING A GRAPH

1. 40,000
2. over 400,000
3. 175,830; 314,578
4. 1700 to 1720
5. Students should predict that the population rises sharply by 1740 based on the trend of increase illustrated by the graph.

SKILL BUILDER: CRITICAL THINKING AND COMPREHENSION

I. Summarizing
1. Three sentences together should mention all of these topics: English, Swedes, Dutch, Scots, Irish, French, and Germans. Sentences should not include Native Americans or African Americans. **2.** The sentences should mention New York, New Jersey, Pennsylvania, and Delaware (the latter given through the Duke of York). **3.** Sentences should describe William Penn's purposes for founding his colony.
II. Generalizing
The generalization is not good. Students should note that paragraphs 6, 9, and 12 describe the varied nationalities of settlers in British colonies.
III. Cause and Effect
1. b **2.** a **3.** c

ENRICHMENT

Student's responses to all four activities will vary.

UNIT 3 ❧ CHAPTER 4

VOCABULARY REVIEW

1. Maryland **2.** owe **3.** poor **4.** plantations **5.** Fall Line **6.** bridges **7.** head of navigation

SKILL BUILDER: READING A MAP

1. Georgia
2. New Hampshire
3. Southern Colonies
4. Southern and Middle Colonies
5. Pennsylvania
6. The Spanish

SKILL BUILDER: CRITICAL THINKING AND COMPREHENSION

I. Sequencing
Events should appear in this order: **c.** 1619; **e.** 1632; **d.** 1634; **b.** 1712; **a.** 1729; **f.** 1733.
II. Cause and Effect
1. Roman Catholic **2.** indentured servants **3.** slavery

USING PRIMARY SOURCES

Students should point out that land and slaves are sold in the same ad and for the same currency (ready money or tobacco).

ENRICHMENT

1. Student interviews should elicit more information about contemporary colonial life than offered in the text, and specifically mention emotions about the Native American's trip to England. **2.** Differences between indentured servitude and slavery certainly should point out that slavery was from birth until death, extended to one's offspring and their offspring, etc., and as an institution gave the master control of life and death over his slave. Indentured servants could also be "sold" (for the time remaining to be served), but usually could refuse permission to be sold to an owner from another region away from their families. Their children were born free and did not have to serve parents' unfulfilled time when parents could not continue working.

UNIT 4 ❧ CHAPTER 1

VOCABULARY REVIEW

Students' original sentences must contain the following words: back country, Breadbasket colonies, cash crops, drought, girdling, imported, indigo, Piedmont, subsistence farmers, Tidewater.

USING PRIMARY SOURCES

Students should mention that colonists ate bread and puddings made from corn and fed corn to their animals. Because Native Americans knew about corn already, they must have had a similar diet before Europeans came. Because they grew corn, they must have had a settled life near their crops and storage pits, must have eaten cooked food, and must have made planting and harvesting tools.

SKILL BUILDER: READING A MAP

1. Maryland, Virginia, North Carolina, South Carolina, Georgia
2. Maryland, Virginia, and North Carolina

3. South Carolina and Georgia
4. Georgia, North Carolina, and Virginia
5. Virginia, North Carolina

SKILL BUILDER: CRITICAL THINKING AND COMPREHENSION

I. Introduction to Comparing and Contrasting

New England: thin, rocky; long, cold winters; subsistence; corn, peas, beans, pumpkins. Middle Colonies: fertile; warmer, longer growing season, sometimes low rainfall; cash crop, including livestock and fruits; wheat, potatoes, oats, barley, rye, vegetables, plus what New England grew. Southern Colonies: fertile; warmest of the three regions, longest growing season; cash crop and subsistence (latter in Piedmont); tobacco, rice, indigo, cotton, flax, subsistence crops like corn and other vegetables.

II. Cause and Effect

1. Girdling resulted in (a) the land becoming cleared and (b) girdled trees were burned, producing ash for fertilizer.
2. Richer soil and warmer climate meant (a) a greater variety of crops could be grown, (b) extra crops could be produced and then sold, (c) the colonies became prosperous as their farmers prospered, (d) other colonies less fortunate could be provided with food, and (e) America became less dependent upon England for its needs.
3. The growth of the plantation system meant (a) tobacco could be produced in ever-increasing quantities to supply the demand for it, (b) more and more field workers (slaves) were needed in this low-populated region to make the system profitable, (c) more and more land was needed to add size to such profitable farms, and (d) with plantation farming so profitable, young people chose plantation administrating as a career rather than law, medicine, teaching, or business.

ENRICHMENT

1. Students will teach a variety of colonial skills. 2. Differences students notice between regions on their trips should reflect the contrasts shown on the preceding chart. Some students might include differences noticed in lifestyles implied by the different political or religious philosophies discussed in the previous Unit.

UNIT 4 ❧ CHAPTER 2

VOCABULARY REVIEW

1. true 2. Mercantilism was a system that encouraged colonies to IMPORT manufactured goods. (or, . . . export RAW MATERIALS) 3. Naval supplies are goods used in SHIP-BUILDING. 4. The triangular trade involved trade routes between the American colonies, WEST AFRICA, AND THE WEST INDIES 5. true

SKILL BUILDER: COMPLETING A TABLE

PLACE EXPORTED FROM	EXPORTS
New England	dried fish, whalebone and oil, ivory, furs, beaver hats (at first, until the Hat Act), lumber, rum, guns, cloth
Middle Colonies	wheat, oats, barley, furs
Southern Colonies	tobacco, indigo, rice, sugar.

SKILL BUILDER: CRITICAL THINKING AND COMPREHENSION

I. Comparing and Contrasting

Pilgrims and Africans both rode below deck, were seasick in bad weather, had a long trip, became homesick, and were afraid of rough seas, storms, and the unknown life awaiting them. Differences were: Africans were chained, couldn't move, sit up, or roll over, lay in their own excrement and vomit, were in terror for their lives at the moment and in the future, couldn't get in touch with family members, ate unaccustomed food, and did not understand the language of their captors or even of the persons who lay next to them. If a person one was chained to died, the body remained there to rot and stink.

II. Cause and Effect

1. Merchants went to the West Indies to sell lumber and dried fish. Merchants went to the West Indies to buy sugar and molasses. 2. Colonists wanted to make the manufacturer's profit on beaver hats, rather than merely the fur-trapper's profit on beaver pelts. The British hat industry could not compete, since they had to add not only trading-goods costs but the cost of shipping the pelts to England before they could set the price of their hats. 3. Plantations needed more workers than the colonial population could provide. West African slave traders demanded guns and rum, and would pay for these manufactured goods in slaves they had captured already. 4. Farming was not profitable. Most of New England is coastal. Plentiful forests made shipbuilding profitable. 5. Rural colonists needed goods brought from England to trade centers. Towns were needed as crafts centers to provide essential goods and services for colonists isolated from overseas industries and guilds. Trading ports grew with the volume of trade.

USING PRIMARY SOURCES

The colonists had developed a successful trade in the manufactured item, and did not see why they should give the profits of hat making to other British people instead. If all English manufacturers were able to keep all colonial manufacturers from making items from their own raw materials, the colonists would always have to spend more to buy goods than they made from selling the materials the goods were made from. British interference with colonial attempts at self-advancement would cause resentment.

ENRICHMENT

1. Students' whaling stories will vary. 2. Students will select a variety of ways to present the saga of a Middle Passage. Perhaps presentations could be repeated for other classes to see.

UNIT 4 ❧ CHAPTER 3

VOCABULARY REVIEW

1. a 2. a 3. a 4. a 5. c 6. b 7. b

SKILL BUILDER: INTERPRETING A TIME LINE

1. 1647 2. 1636 3. 1730s-1740s 4. 1689 5. 1688 6. 20 7. 41

SKILL BUILDER: CRITICAL THINKING AND COMPREHENSION

I. Cause and Effect

1. Groups of new churches began, schools were started, people began to help orphans and the poor, people began to believe

everyone is born equal, African American churches began
2. a. 2 b. 3, c. 1

II. Comparing and Contrasting

	GIRLS	BOYS	SLAVES
Subjects	reading, sewing, writing, cooking, and Bible	English, math, law, theology, and surveying	plantation skills, metal work, wood work, and some reading of Bible
Where they learned	dame schools	public & private schools, universities, and private tutors	self taught, craftsmen, and willing individuals

USING PRIMARY SOURCES

Education was presented through religious teachings. School was very strict.

ENRICHMENT

Plays and oral reports or debates will vary.

UNIT 4 ❧ CHAPTER 4

VOCABULARY REVIEW

1. royal colony **2.** executive **3.** council **4.** Bacon's Rebellion **5.** veto **6.** self-governing colony **7.** libel **8.** proprietary colony **9.** legislature **10.** assembly

SKILL BUILDER: MAKING A CHART

	EXECUTIVE	COUNCIL	ASSEMBLY
Duties	enforces the law, calls assembly meetings, leads army, orders forts built, grants land, appoints judges, controls trade	serves as court, approves laws, helps executive	passes laws, votes salary of executive and judges, approves taxes
How Got Job	appointed by king or trading company, or elected by white, male, propertied (taxpaying) voters in colony	appointed by executive	elected by voters

	EXECUTIVE	COUNCIL	ASSEMBLY
Challenges to Authority	king or company could remove, assembly could fail to authorize salary	executive could dismiss, assembly could fail to approve payment of salaries	members could fail to be reelected by voters, governor could veto laws passed, governor could ignore (not enforce) laws passed, laws passed needed approval by council.

SKILL BUILDER: CRITICAL THINKING AND COMPREHENSION

I. Comparing and Contrasting

1. Bacon's style: took up arms against the governor. Zenger's style: fought with words to change governor's policies.
2. Royal: governor appointed by the king. Proprietary: governor appointed by the trading company owners. Self-governing: governor elected by the voters.

II. Introduction to Drawing Conclusions

b. The governor was a man with many responsibilities.

USING PRIMARY SOURCES

Similarities: all townspeople could attend; clerks record the meetings; local business, such as fixing roads, is voted on; every town has a meeting frequently and regularly scheduled. Differences: in colonial times, only white men, usually property or business owners, could vote; today, most problems concerning rivers, fishing, and larger roads are decided by state or federal government after studies by the EPA, Dept. of Interior, Dept. of Transportation, etc., and the money to pay for solving the problem is not voted on at a local level.

ENRICHMENT

1. Student dramas of the Zenger trial should be based upon material other than what appears in this textbook.
2. Town meetings should reflect real problems in their town as the students perceive them.
3. Student reports of other rebellions will vary.

UNIT 4 ❧ CHAPTER 5

VOCABULARY REVIEW

1. The "king's daughters" were women sent to New France to marry French colonists and begin to increase the population.
2. true **3.** true **4.** true **5.** The habitants' chief sources of income were extra crops and livestock. (Or: The coureurs de bois's chief source of income was the fur trade.)

SKILL BUILDER: MAKING AN OUTLINE

A. Coureurs de bois: wore snowshoes, trapped beaver, hunted animals, traded fur for goods. **B.** Intendant: helped business grow. **C.** Habitant: raised wheat and oats, cleared land, eventually owned land.

USING PRIMARY SOURCES

The French learned how to make portable birchbark canoes and bark shelters. If the French had not learned to travel on the waterways, settlement would have depended on people's ability to clear land for roads, and travel would have stopped in winter. Frenchmen would not have been able to set up widespread trading posts to gain profit from Native American fur trapping, and the French king would not have been able to claim the Louisiana Territory. French settlers would not have been enticed to come to the New World. The French would not have gained the respect or friendship of the Native Americans and perhaps would have been driven off this continent.

SKILL BUILDER: CRITICAL THINKING AND COMPREHENSION

I. Drawing Conclusions
First set of facts: There could be a good fur trade between France and New France. Second set of facts: Catholic nuns and priests were important to New France.
II. Comparing and Contrasting
See bottom of page for chart.

ENRICHMENT

1. The best arguments should probably base on humanitarian grounds—Native Americans cannot physically tolerate alcohol, and they will lose their dignity and pride as a people. An economic argument can be made for the injury to the fur trade profits for the French, as more and more animals are over-trapped to feed the Native Americans' increasing addiction to alcohol, culminating in physical inability of trappers to attend their lines or care about future income. A missionary would also use the argument that one cannot teach religion or anything else to someone who is drunk.
2. Dialogues should base upon new information beyond that given in the textbook.

UNIT 4 ❧ CHAPTER 6

VOCABULARY REVIEW

1. c **2.** b **3.** d **4.** a **5.** h **6.** j **7.** i **8.** k **9.** g **10.** e **11.** m **12.** n **13.** l

SKILL BUILDER: READING A MAP

1. Livestock ranching
2. Gold and Silver
3. Sugar
4. Veracruz was a chief port

SKILL BUILDER: CRITICAL THINKING AND COMPREHENSION

I. Drawing Conclusions
1. b **2.** b **3.** b; **1.** b **2.** b **3.** b

USING PRIMARY SOURCES

Reasons for staying in Spain or emigrating to the New World will vary.

ENRICHMENT

Activities will vary.

UNIT 4 ❧ CHAPTER 7

VOCABULARY REVIEW

1. Cumberland Gap **2.** Wilderness Road **3.** Old Southwest
4. Great Wagon Road

SKILL BUILDER: STUDYING FOR A TEST

Students might benefit from peer review and suggestions by classmates who could evaluate each other's made-up tests for appropriateness and degree of difficulty.

SKILL BUILDING: CRITICAL THINKING AND COMPREHENSION

I. Compare and Contrast

	PIONEER	PLANTATION OWNER	SLAVE
Homes	log cabin	stone house	dirt-floor shack
Food	what was caught and grown	livestock raised for meat, garden vegetables	cornbread, beans, and rice, some pork

CHART FOR UNIT 4, CHAPTER 5, II. COMPARING AND CONTRASTING

	ORIGINS OF SETTLERS	GOVERNMENT	MAJOR ECONOMIC ACTIVITIES	RELIGION	EXAMPLES OF DAILY LIFE
New France	France	royal province with governor and intendant chosen by the king	furs and farming	Roman Catholicism	coureurs de bois or habitant
New England	England	self-governing colonies	furs, farming, fishing, shipbuilding, and trade	Protestant Christianity	subsistence farmer, craftsperson, fisher, sailor
Middle Colonies	Britain and some Europeans	royal colonies and proprietary colonies	farming and manufacturing	Protestants and Catholics	craftsperson or farmer
Southern Colonies	Britain, some French and Spanish, and African slaves	royal colonies and self-governing colonies	cash crop farming.	Protestants and Catholics	plantation owner, subsistence farmer, or slave.

	PIONEER	PLANTATION OWNER	SLAVE
Work	farming and hunting	administrating, overseeing, and planning	hard labor, crafts, house work
Dangers	attacks by Native Americans, exposure, accidents	slave uprisings	death or injury from mistreatment, overwork, accidents
Social Class	middle and lower classes	aristocracy and upper middle class	not in class system.

2. Answers will vary.

II. Introduction to Predicting

Predictions should mention mud, tree stumps, rocks, and flooded roadways. Some students may intuit unnecessary winding and hilliness.

ENRICHMENT

Answers will vary.

UNIT 5 ❧ CHAPTER 1

VOCABULARY REVIEW

1. e 2. c 3. a 4. d 5. b

SKILL BUILDER: OUTLINING

A. 1. The French had a well-trained army with a skilled commander. **B. 2.** Defending the area would be difficult because trading posts and army forts were scattered hundreds of miles apart. **C. 2.** The powerful Iroquois nation supported the British. **D.** Problems the British faced.

USING PRIMARY SOURCES

Students should mention the independent nature of the American colonists, who were not content to obey orders from across the ocean.

SKILL BUILDING: CRITICAL THINKING AND COMPREHENSION

I. Drawing Conclusions
The best conclusion is b.
II. Predicting
1. The students' answers will vary but all should mention moving into the new territory now that the French and Native Americans are not such a threat. **2.** Answers may vary but should include the lack of unity among Native American nations who had chosen opposite sides in the French and Indian War.

ENRICHMENT

Opinions and illustrations will vary.

UNIT 5 ❧ CHAPTER 2

VOCABULARY REVIEW

debt, money owed by one person or organization to another
Proclamation of 1763, an order by King George III that closed off the lands west of the Appalachian Mountains to American settlers
smuggled, transported goods across a border illegally

trade laws, laws that control trade with other countries
customs officers, officials who inspect and collect taxes on imported goods
Sugar Act, a tax imposed by Parliament in 1764 on molasses and sugar imported from the French West Indies
Quartering Act, an act that required American colonists to provide British troops with food and shelter

SKILL BUILDER: READING A MAP

1. Mississippi River
2. Spain
3. England
4. A portion of Guianas, St. Dominique, and some other islands in the West Indies
5. Fort Duquesne was located west of the Proclamation Line

USING PRIMARY SOURCES

Students should use the primary source to discover that the British government wanted only to protect the settlers from unpacified Native Americans. An argument that Britain really wanted to avoid the cost of another war cannot be supported by the source.

SKILL BUILDER: CRITICAL THINKING AND COMPREHENSION

I. Drawing Conclusions
1. None of the conclusions can be made from the statement. Conclusion a is true, but students would not have any way of knowing this. **2.** a **3.** d **4.** f
II. Understanding Points of View
1. British **2.** American **3.** American **4.** British

ENRICHMENT

1. Students should mention that it is unfair (as stated in their text) to keep colonists penned up along the eastern coast.
2. Renditions of Grenville's beliefs will vary.

UNIT 5 ❧ CHAPTER 3

VOCABULARY REVIEW

1. f 2. b 3. g 4. e 5. d 6. c 7. a

SKILL BUILDER: COMPLETING A TABLE

INDIVIDUAL OR GROUP	FORM OF RESISTANCE
Crispus Attucks	Group of protesters provoked soldiers.
Sons of Liberty	Threatened tax collectors, burned governor's house, boycotted taxed goods.
Daughters of Liberty	Made homespun cloth, boycotted British goods.
Stamp Act Congress	Sent petition to Parliament, sent delegates to colonial protest meeting.
Samuel Adams	Made speeches against Parliament, against redcoats, and against Britain.
Committees of Correspondence	Kept each colony informed of what was happening in other colonies.

SKILL BUILDER: CRITICAL THINKING AND COMPREHENSION

I. Predicting
1. Students either will believe that the colonists would have obeyed the Townsend Acts or will assume that the colonists would look for another reason not to obey them. 2. Students' paragraphs will vary, but should use facts from the chapter to support their opinions.
II. Identifying Fact versus Opinion
1. O 2. F 3. O 4. F 5. F

USING PRIMARY SOURCES

The colonists had to win the argument that no one can be taxed except by those he consents to tax him. Otherwise there would be no end to the governmental bodies that could levy taxes, and the taxpayer could not un-elect the men who voted to tax him.

ENRICHMENT

1. Students' accounts of the Boston Massacre should not conflict with accounts given in primary sources. 2. Students might not convict the redcoats who shot the protesters, if the students believe that the redcoats shot in self-defense or thought that the protesters' sticks were guns.

UNIT 5 ❧ CHAPTER 4

VOCABULARY REVIEW

1. intolerable 2. Minutemen 3. declaration

SKILL BUILDER: READING A BAR GRAPH

1. 300,000
2. 2,200,000
3. 1,900,000
4. 7 times

SKILL BUILDER: CRITICAL THINKING AND COMPREHENSION

I. Predicting
1. Students probably will predict that the colonists will keep meeting, trying new ways to protest, until the laws are rescinded. Examples from the text are the escalating means use to protest the Stamp Act: threaten the tax collectors, petition Parliament, make declarations, harass redcoats, organize, boycott. 2. Students' answers will vary.
II. Fact versus Opinion
1. F 2. O 3. F 4. O 5. O 6. F 7. O

USING PRIMARY SOURCES

Patrick Henry believed that the lack of peace (the constant rebellions and riots) showed that the war had already begun.

ENRICHMENT

1. Students' speeches should mention what action the colonies should take, why or why not a boycott is a good action to take, what rights colonists should have guaranteed to them, and why these rights should exist.
2. Students' posters should be persuasive and contain a slogan.

UNIT 5 ❧ CHAPTER 5

VOCABULARY REVIEW

1. Continental Army 2. Battle of Bunker Hill 3. Hessians

SKILL BUILDER: READING A PIE GRAPH

1. 2,200 2. 3,500 3. 260 4. 350 5. 1,300

SKILL BUILDER: CRITICAL THINKING AND COMPREHENSION

I. Predicting
1. Students should guess that the colonists would have worked toward winning self-government as separate states within the British Empire (similar to the way Canada and Australia are now). 2. The rebels would have been hanged as traitors. The king had already sent soldiers to arrest them. 3. Students' predictions will vary.
II. Fact versus Opinion
1. F 2. O 3. O

USING PRIMARY SOURCES

Paine says that all of the debating has not stopped people from dying to defend their points of view, and that once people have been driven to die for a belief, events can't be held back from their logical progression.

ENRICHMENT

1. The list of acts the Declaration blames on the king includes actions taken by Parliament and sometimes representatives of Parliament in the colonies. The king's list of acts is shorter.
2. Students' answers will vary.

UNIT 5 ❧ CHAPTER 6

VOCABULARY REVIEW

retreat, to go back or withdraw
alliance, an agreement between nations to help each other
campaign, a series of military operations carried out to gain a particular objective
advance, to move forward

SKILL BUILDER: MAKING A TIME LINE

Students should make a time line with events inserted at the appropriate dates.

SKILL BUILDER: CRITICAL THINKING AND COMPREHENSION

I. Fact versus Opinion
1. F 2. O 3. F 4. O 5. F 6. F 7. F 8. F 9. O 10. F
II. Point of View
1. George Washington 2. French leaders 3. British leaders 4. British people 5. Americans

USING PRIMARY SOURCES

Washington feared that the Continental Congress was too weak to demand financial support from the new states, and without money the Continental Army would lose the war.

ENRICHMENT

1. Students' descriptions of British-held New York City will vary. 2. Students should mention the important contributions of each of the three leaders.

UNIT 5 ❧ CHAPTER 7

VOCABULARY REVIEW

1. Loyalists 2. Treaty of Paris 3. Patriots 4. Loyalists 5. Treaty of Paris

SKILL BUILDER: MAKING AN OUTLINE

I. How American Women Helped the War
  A. Women took over the farms during the war.
  B. Women acted as spies and helped on the battlefield.
II. How African Americans Helped the War
  A. African Americans fought in all major battles.
  B. James Armistead was a spy for the American army.
III. How the War Divided Americans
  A. Patriots and Loyalists hated each other.
  B. Nearly 100,000 Loyalists left the United States.

SKILL BUILDER: CRITICAL THINKING AND COMPREHENSION

I. Fact versus Opinion
1. a. F b. O **2.** a. O b. F **3.** a. F b. O
4. a. O b. F **5.** a. F b. O **6.** a. F b. O
II. Point of View
1. P **2.** L **3.** L **4.** P **5.** P **6.** P and L

USING PRIMARY SOURCES

Abigail Adams' translation of ''no laws without consent'' to ''no obedience without our choosing to comply'' is a direct application to the situation faced by females of her time.

ENRICHMENT

1. The British were more class conscious, and a freed slave had a better chance of rising above the lowest rung on the status ladder under democratic American laws and customs.
2. Role-playing discussion topics will vary.
3. Women lost most of the power they had gained when the men were at war.

UNIT 6 ❧ CHAPTER 1

1. c **2.** c **3.** b **4.** a **5.** b

SKILL BUILDER: COMPLETING A CHART

a. one **b.** 9 **c.** true **d.** one **e.** true **f.** No President

SKILL BUILDER: CRITICAL THINKING AND COMPREHENSION

I. Point of View
1. British general **2.** western settlers **3.** creditors **4.** Daniel Shays **5.** Congressman Henry Knox
II. Fact versus Opinion
1. Students who think the former soldiers were right might cite the fact that they were having their farms confiscated by tax collectors because they didn't have the money and thus couldn't pay their own debts. Students who disagree might cite the example of George Washington, who took no pay for serving in the war.
2. When people have been ruled by a despotic government that used troops to enforce Parliament's laws, taxed people without their consent, and arrested people and then sent them away to be tried by unsympathetic strangers, it is natural to create a weak government to replace the despotic one.

USING PRIMARY SOURCES

The states can give powers or take them away from the national government. The central government has no powers except those the states give it. The central government's role is to safeguard the defense of the states, to secure the people's liberties (religious, trade, etc.) against attacks against any state (implying that states are separate and independent).

ENRICHMENT

1. Answers will vary according to where a student lives. Some students may understand that regional opinions would not be overridden by national laws—for example, citizens of Utah might still be allowed to practice polygamy, and southern states would be able to have laws enforcing racial segregation or prohibiting intermarriage between races. The Civil War would not have occurred.
2. Students' research will uncover the fact that Dickinson feared conflict and chaos so much that he refused to sign the Declaration of Independence. Later he would champion the U.S. Constitution because the Articles didn't give enough power to the central government to enforce civil order.
3. Students should mention that the farmers saw the government (which levied higher taxes) and the courts (which took their property as payment of taxes owed) as partners working against them.

UNIT 6 ❧ CHAPTER 2

1. e **2.** g **3.** a **4.** c **5.** d **6.** b **7.** h **8.** i

SKILL BUILDING: INTERPRETING A CARTOON

1. The states
2. A Federalist and an Anti-Federalist
3. Strong national government versus states' rights
4. Constitution
5. The addition of the Bill of Rights
6. Before the ratification of the United States Constitution
I. Making Judgments
3. The Connecticut Plan; it satisfied both large and small states by letting them be equal in one house and letting majority rule minority in the other house.
II. Point of View
Federalist: The United States needs a strong central government. Anti-Federalist: states should have their own right to make the laws people of that region want. A Bill of Rights is needed to protect individual freedoms.

USING PRIMARY SOURCES

The Constitution was need to protect the nation from enemies outside and from mobs within and to provide strong backing for enforcing laws it enacts.

ENRICHMENT

Journal entries and speeches will vary.

UNIT 6 ❧ CHAPTER 3

VOCABULARY REVIEW

1. b **2.** c **3.** a **4.** f **5.** d **6.** e **7.** h

SKILL BUILDER: INTERPRETING A CHART

1. true **2.** A bill is sent to the house it originated in after the committee reviews it and makes changes in it. **3.** true **4.** If both houses of Congress approve the final version of a bill, the President can veto it. **5.** true

SKILL BUILDER: CRITICAL THINKING AND COMPREHENSION

I. Making Judgments
1. Students' answers may vary, but they should offer good reasons for keeping or extending the length of a President's term.
2. Students who disagree should say who should take over, and why that choice is better than having a vice-president.
3. Students who disagree should say why they want this power removed from the Supreme Court, and if the power should be kept, where the power should reside. **4.** Students who argue against a life term for justices of the Supreme Court should use

reasonable examples of why that check on the executive and legislative branch is too powerful.

II. Point of View

1. Jefferson 2. Hamilton 3. Washington

USING PRIMARY SOURCES

Students should mention the following present-day examples: speech—pro-choice (abortion rights) and right-to-life (laws forbidding abortion); press—for or against the right to publish pornography; assembly—the right of neo-Nazis to march through Jewish neighborhoods, or the right of demonstrators to picket abortion clinics, or the right of people with AIDS to rally outside Congress to demand more money for research and medicines; petition—the right to petition appropriate legislative bodies for or against any of the above issues, or for more police protection in one's neighborhood, or for a traffic light at an intersection, or lower taxes.

ENRICHMENT

1. Some students may use the example of other countries where Bill of Rights freedoms are not protected. **2.** Reports should mention details not provided in the text.

UNIT 6 🐌 CHAPTER 4

VOCABULARY REVIEW

1. b **2.** f **3.** e **4.** d **5.** g **6.** c **7.** a

SKILL BUILDER: READING A MAP

1. Hudson River
2. Albany and Buffalo
3. By road: Ohio River to Mississippi River to Illinois River to Illinois and Michigan Canal
4. Northeast
5. Pennsylvania, Indiana, Ohio, Illinois, Virginia or West Virginia
6. Vandalia, Illinois

SKILL BUILDER: CRITICAL THINKING AND COMPREHENSION

I. Point of View
1. S **2.** T **3.** S
II. Making Judgments
1. The students who say Congress was right might argue that since Tecumseh himself said no one can own the land, then a treaty is not needed by anyone to settle on it.
2. Answers will vary.

USING PRIMARY SOURCES

Tecumseh wants Native Americans to band together and fight back.

ENRICHMENT

1. Students' research should lead them to learn about the role barges played in westward expansion; others might read about those who moved into the Northwest Territories on foot and horseback.
2. Students may be able to visit the display about the Shawnee tribe in a museum in Rochester, NY, or the American Indian museum as part of the Smithsonian on the Mall in Washington, D.C. Plays will differ.

UNIT 6 🐌 CHAPTER 5

VOCABULARY REVIEW

1. surplus crops **2.** right of deposit **3.** Louisiana Territory **4.** strict constructionist **5.** judicial review

SKILL BUILDER: INTERPRETING A MAP

1. True **2.** From the Mississippi River to the Rocky Mountains **3.** True **4.** West of St. Louis **5.** True **6.** True

SKILL BUILDER: CRITICAL THINKING AND COMPREHENSION

I. Main Idea
1. Plants and Animals; Native People; Terrain; Weather; Miscellaneous and Unusual Sights.
2. I. C. York
    D. Toussaint Charborneau
    E. Sacajawea
  II. A. recorded names, numbers, and customs of tribes
    C. gave peace offerings, traded goods and trinkets
  III. Accomplishments of Lewis and Clark's Expedition
    C. collected unknown plants and animals for study
    E. brought back dinosaur bones
II. Classifying
1. Meriwether Lewis, William Clark, Zebulon Pike
2. Missouri, Arkansas, Columbus
3. bear cubs, maps, dinosaur bones

USING PRIMARY SOURCES

The Expedition needed horses, game, knowledge of what plants and animals encountered were edible and how to catch or find them.

ENRICHMENT

Students' travel accounts will vary.

UNIT 6 🐌 CHAPTER 6

VOCABULARY REVIEW

1. g **2.** f **3.** h **4.** a **5.** j **6.** b **7.** c **8.** e **9.** d
10. i

SKILL BUILDER: USING A CHART

1. U.S.S. *Erie*, *Thames River*, and *Chesapeake* **2.** Battle of Thames River **3.** U.S.S. *Chesapeake* **4.** The Americans

SKILL BUILDER: CRITICAL THINKING AND COMPREHENSION

I. Classifying
1. Oliver Hazard Perry **2.** Embargo Act **3.** Jefferson
4. at Washington, D.C. **5.** James Monroe
II. Main Idea
1. a **2.** a **3.** b

USING PRIMARY SOURCES

The speech implies that African Americans were spoken to sarcastically, were thought of as "adopted children," and needed to be protected from situations in which they would compare (unfavorably) with whites; it implies, also, that African Americans could be brave and would deserve the same reward (bounty) as whites.

ENRICHMENT

1. Students' radio plays will vary. **2.** Students' descriptions of Lafitte's character will vary.

UNIT 6 & CHAPTER 7

VOCABULARY REVIEW

nationalism, devotion to the interests of one's own nation
Rush-Bagot Agreement, an agreement by the United States and Great Britain to limit warships on the Great Lakes
49th Parallel, the boundary line between the United States and Canada west of the Great Lakes
American System, an 1816 plan to encourage American manufacturing, develop roads, and make other internal improvements
Era of Good Feelings, the period from 1816 to 1825, when political differences in the United States faded in importance
Adams-Onis Treaty, an 1819 agreement between Spain and the United States, in which the United States received Florida and land in Alabama and Mississippi along the Gulf of Mexico for $5 million
Monroe Doctrine, a policy issued by President James Monroe warning European nations against trying to retake their former colonies in Latin America
midnight appointment, during President John Adams's administration, the last-minute appointment of an official before Adams left office
commission, a document that makes an appointment official
Marbury vs. Madison, the court case that established the right of the Supreme Court to decide whether laws are unconstitutional
states' rights, the theory that the power of a state government is or should be greater than that of the federal government.

SKILL BUILDER: READING A TIME LINE

1. 7 years.
2. Adding new territory; creation of national bank; closing of Federalist party.
3. U.S. buys Florida, Alabama, Mississippi.

SKILL BUILDER: CRITICAL THINKING AND COMPREHENSION

I. Classifying
1. Democratic-Republican   **2.** Democratic-Republican
3. Federalist **4.** Federalist **5.** Federalist
II. Summarizing
1. The United States promised to stay out of the affairs of Europe or any existing colony of a European nation. The United States would defend Latin American nations against invasion or new colonization. **2.** *Marbury vs Madison* established the right of judicial review. That means that the federal government courts can overcome state government laws. **3.** America had a strong sense of nationalism after the War of 1812. The decade after the war was known as the "Era of Good Feelings." **4.** Henry Clay's American System protected young American manufacturers from European competition. It set up a system whereby the South and West would ship raw materials to the East, and the East would sell finished goods to the West.

USING PRIMARY SOURCES

Any European attempt to extend its influence in this hemisphere would be viewed as unfriendly.

ENRICHMENT

1. Students' editorials will vary, but should reflect the idea of national power over states' rights. **2.** Students' scripts will vary. They might enjoy comparing the actions of Jackson with contemporary United States' actions in Grenada and Panama. **3.** Students' campaign will vary, as will their predictions about the winner.

UNIT 6 & CHAPTER 8

VOCABULARY REVIEW

1. Jacksonian Democracy **2.** nominating convention **3.** Removal Act **4.** "Trail of Tears" **5.** spoils system

SKILL BUILDER: MAKING A TIME LINE

1. 1828 **2.** December, 1829 **3.** 1830 **4.** 1831 **5.** 1832

SKILL BUILDER: CRITICAL THINKING AND COMPREHENSION

I. Summarizing
Sentences 2 and 3 support the main idea.
II. Generalizing
1. The factory workers and their unions in the eastern cities soon demanded the same rights as their neighbors in the West.
2. Jackson started the spoils system, the nominating convention, and universal white male suffrage, crushed the National Bank that stifled frontier growth, and fought the Court to promote democratic interests. **3.** Jackson got the Native Americans to sell their land cheap and remove to a place outside the present boundaries of any state. **4.** Jackson fought Congress and the courts to get his way.
III. Drawing Conclusions
Students' opinions about military candidates will vary.

USING PRIMARY SOURCES

Keeping Native Americans near white settlements weakens their resources and lessens their population, just as it has already destroyed tribes from the East.

ENRICHMENT

1. Students' accounts of the "trail of tears" will vary.
2. Charts should give dates for voting rights for women, African Americans, people 18-21, and residents of D.C. **3.** Candidates' speeches will vary.

UNIT 7 & CHAPTER 1

VOCABULARY REVIEW

1. a **2.** b **3.** c **4.** b **5.** a **6.** a **7.** c

SKILL BUILDER: MAKING A CHART

NAME OF TRAIL	LENGTH OF TRAIL	CITY AT START OF TRAIL	DESTINATION AT END OF TRAIL	STATES THAT FORMED ALONG THE TRAIL	YEARS WHEN HEAVY TRAVEL BEGAN
Santa Fe Trail	780 miles (1,250 km)	Independence	Santa Fe	Kansas, Colorado, New Mexico	1846–1860s
Oregon Trail	2,000 miles (3,200 km)	Independence	Portland	Nebraska, Idaho, Oregon	Peak use: 1840s
Old Spanish Trail	700 miles (1,120 km)	Santa Fe	Los Angeles	Colorado, Utah, California	no information given

SKILL BUILDER: CRITICAL THINKING AND COMPREHENSION

I. Sequencing
Order of events: a (1821), e (1837), c (1843), b (1846), and d (1847 or 1848)

II. Generalizing
1. They all shared a love of the wilderness and a desire to live freely. They often covered as much as 3,000 miles (about 4,800 km) through the forests and streams of the mountains. **2.** Many of them also went west to escape the Panic of 1837, a depression that had hit the eastern United States. Those people now were eager to start a new life in the West, where land was cheap. **3.** Many women went to the Northwest on the Oregon Trail. **4.** Wars between Native Americans were still going on at this time, as well as wars between settlers and Native Americans.

USING PRIMARY SOURCES

Amelia Knight regrets being on the journey, but students attuned to nuance might guess that she has kept her sense of humor and is merely telling about a particularly bad day.

ENRICHMENT

1. Students' maps should show its size when first settled, when it became a territory, and when it became a state. **2.** Students' interviews will vary. **3.** Role-plays will vary.

UNIT 7 CHAPTER 2

VOCABULARY REVIEW

1. c **2.** d **3.** a. **4.** b

SKILL BUILDER: READING A MAP

1. 9 states
2. 1,100 miles (1,760 km)
3. South Pass
4. Utah and Idaho
5. Answers will vary: Used river for water supply; used river as a trail reference or guide
6. The Colorado River

SKILL BUILDER: CRITICAL THINKING AND COMPREHENSION

I. Sequencing
1. b, c, a **2.** c, a, b **3.** a, b, c

II. Cause and Effect
2. Joseph Smith was killed. **3.** Smith published the writings in *The Book of Mormon.* **4.** Smith moved his followers again, this time to Nauvoo, Illinois. **5.** Utah was finally allowed to become a state.

USING PRIMARY SOURCES

We are striving and working hard, and it is bringing us only joy because of our singleminded focus.

ENRICHMENT

1. Mormons still believe in hard work and doing good, avoiding doing bad things. Nowadays they do not practice polygamy, and some are not farmers anymore. **2.** Students should base their arguments on First Amendment freedom of religion. Some may argue that the Mormons are good citizens, are hardworking. **3.** Oral reports will vary.

UNIT 7 CHAPTER 3

VOCABULARY REVIEW

1. d **2.** e **3.** f **4.** a **5.** b **6.** g

SKILL BUILDER: INTERPRETING A PICTURE

I. Generalizing
1. He is punishing the Native Americans.
2. This shows further the harsh discipline or servitude under Spanish rule.
3. They are giving the Native Americans work orders.
4. The Native Americans were treated like slaves.

SKILL BUILDER: CRITICAL THINKING AND COMPREHENSION

I. Compare and Contrast
1. Pueblo: community of nonreligious farmers growing food for soldiers in presidio. Mission: community of friars and the Native Americans to whom they teach crafts and Christianity. Native Americans supply food to themselves and the friars as well as to traders offshore. **2.** Missions: grew and made everything used by people there. Land was a schoolroom for teaching farming methods. Rancheros: grazed cattle on grasslands. **3.** Similarities: hard work, harsh treatment. Differences: mission focus on religion and self-sufficiency; ranches were profit-making, left Native Americans in debt.
II. Cause and Effect
1. Missionaries taught the skills and created demand for the products. **2.** Spain's claims to California were endangered by Russia and England. **3.** Portolá and Father Serra set out to found missions and presidios. **4.** After Mexico won its independence from Spain, ranchers bought the old mission lands.

USING PRIMARY SOURCES

Serra was humane, didn't want to exploit Native Americans, thought them equal to white sailors, wanted them to be free to come and go at the end of their contract.

ENRICHMENT

Reports on missions, Russian presence, daily life at missions, and students' plays will vary.

UNIT 7 ❧ CHAPTER 4

VOCABULARY REVIEW

1. dictator **2.** Manifest Destiny **3.** annexed **4.** Alamo **5.** Mexican Cession **6.** Gadsden Purchase

SKILL BUILDER: DRAWING A TIME LINE

Order should read: 1820—Moses Austin in Texas, 1821—Mexico wins independence from Spain, Santa Fe Trail opens, 1830—Smith starts Mormon Church, 1836—Texans from Mexico at the Alamo, 1844—Smith killed, 1846—War with Mexico begins, 1847—Mormons reach Great Salt Lake Basin, 1848—U.S. annexes 535,000 sq. mi. (1,385,100 sq. km)

SKILL BUILDER: CRITICAL THINKING AND COMPREHENSION

I. Drawing Conclusions
1. a, b, c, d, f **2.** b, c **3.** a, b
II. Comparing and Contrasting
2. Mexican: Santa Anna won at the Alamo, later was captured. Texan: William B. Travis was greatly outnumbered, fought to the death. **3.** Mexican: slavery is outlawed. Texan: proslavery. **4.** Mexican: 6,000 men. Texan: 187 men.

USING PRIMARY SOURCES

Students should recognize Travis's sense of loyalty and total commitment.

ENRICHMENT

1. Reports will vary. **2.** Focus should be on arguments of prowar and antiwar speakers.

UNIT 7 ❧ CHAPTER 5

VOCABULARY REVIEW

1. c **2.** f **3.** d **4.** a **5.** g **6.** b

SKILL BUILDER: READING A MAP

1. Northern Pacific; answers will vary: weather conditions, length of railroad, terrain, etc.
2. Duluth, Butte, Tacoma: *Northern Pacific*
Los Angeles, El Paso, San Antonio, Houston, New Orleans: *Southern Pacific*
San Francisco, Ogden: *Central Pacific*
Ogden, Omaha: *Union Pacific*
Los Angeles, Santa Fe: *Atlantic & Pacific*

Santa Fe, Kansas City, St. Louis: *Atchison, Topeka & Santa Fe*
El Paso; Fort Worth, Vicksburg: *Texas & Pacific*
Ogden, Pueblo: *Denver, Rio Grande*
Denver, Kansas City: *Kansas Pacific*
3. 15,000 miles (24,000 km)—estimates will vary. The cities grew quickly in areas that were near or came into direct contact with the railroads.

SKILL BUILDER: CRITICAL THINKING AND COMPREHENSION

I. Drawing Conclusions
1.–4. Students' answers will vary because there are no specific sentences in the text to illustrate these ideas. The paragraph about relations between Chinese and Americans will vary but should have racism as the central topic.
II. Predicting
1. Students should discuss the nature of gold when found in sand and water. **2.** Answers will vary but should include service businesses such as blacksmithing to repair tools and wagons, restaurants, boarding houses, bars, laundries, and entertainment. **3.** Answers will vary **4.** If you found gold you might attempt to buy your freedom. Your life as a slave away from other slaves or the structure of the plantation system would be very different, specially if you were working one-on-one with your master. **5.** Students should describe the trip to and across the isthmus of Panama and then up the west coast by boat.

USING PRIMARY SOURCES

Answers will vary but should include topics of homesickness, lack of stable family life, and fear of racial abuses.

ENRICHMENT

Activities will vary.

UNIT 7 ❧ CHAPTER 6
VOCABULARY REVIEW

1. rustlers **2.** T **3.** T **4.** homesteaders **5.** T **6.** T

SKILL BUILDER: COMPARING PICTURES

a. type of home: Settlers—sod house, permanent; Native Americans—tepee, movable
b. style of dress: Settlers—made of cloth; Native Americans—made of animal skins
c. use of horses: Settlers—to pull wheeled vehicles; Native Americans—to ride on
d. other: Settlers—note plough, indicating farming; Native Americans—note spears and animal skin being worked on

SKILL BUILDER: CRITICAL THINKING AND COMPREHENSION

I. Fact versus Opinion
1. F **2.** O **3.** F **4.** F **5.** O **6.** F **7.** O **8.** O
II. Predicting
1. b **2.** c **3.** b

USING PRIMARY SOURCES

Answers will vary.

ENRICHMENT

1. Letters should include information from the text about the following: work, weather, diet, lifestyle. **2. and 3.** Activities will vary.

UNIT 7 ❧ CHAPTER 7

VOCABULARY REVIEW

1. c **2.** a **3.** a **4.** b

SKILL BUILDER: MAKING A TIME LINE

Events and dates are provided for students.

SKILL BUILDER: CRITICAL THINKING AND COMPREHENSION

I. Fact versus Opinion
A. 1. paragraphs 3 and 14 **2.** paragraphs 2, 3, 4, 7, 8, 12, 14, 15, 16 **3.** paragraph 6 **4.** paragraph 5 **B.** Opinions will vary. **C. 1.** Miners trespassed on Native Americans' land. **2.** Fact **3.** The United States Army put down the Sioux rebellion. **4.** Fact **5.** General Custer was made into a hero. **6.** Fact
II. Points of View
A. 1. Chief Joseph **2.** Black Elk **B. 1.** Custer **2.** Chief Joseph **3.** Geronimo

USING PRIMARY SOURCES

His people would not have lived even if he had won.

ENRICHMENT

Admirable qualities will vary; eyewitness accounts should be based upon documented reports; opinions about government policy will vary.

UNIT 8 ❧ CHAPTER 1

VOCABULARY REVIEW

1. a **2.** b **3.** c **4.** c

SKILL BUILDER: USING AN ENCYCLOPEDIA

1. Paragraphs should mention the "seasoning system" in the West Indies and the failure to enslave Native Americans profitably. **2.** Working conditions will vary. **3.** Life in the servants' quarters in the mansion was different from life in the slave quarters. **4.** Paragraphs will vary.

SKILL BUILDER: CRITICAL THINKING AND COMPREHENSION

I. Classifying
1. Free—Pennsylvania, Massachusetts, New Jersey, Connecticut.
Slave: South Carolina, Tennessee, Maryland.
2. Good for growing cotton: 200 frost-free days, rain during growing season, dry weather during harvest.
Bad for growing cotton: rain during harvest, frost before harvest, frost during growing season, sandy soil
II. Making Judgments
1. legal **2.** legal **3.** illegal **4.** illegal

USING PRIMARY SOURCES

1. Answers may vary depending on map scales and students'

ENRICHMENT

1. Role-plays should mention good results: growth of textile industry, expansion westward of America, and bad: slavery expanded and became less humane, textile factories brought sooty air and child labor. **2.** Posters will vary. **3.** Dramas should feature Suleiman's capture, escape, and return to Africa. **4.** Reports should stick to colonial subjects.

UNIT 8 ❧ CHAPTER 2

VOCABULARY REVIEW

1. planter **2.** patrols **3.** overseer **4.** spirituals

SKILL BUILDER: READING A MAP

1. Florida, Georgia, Alabama, Louisiana, Mississippi, Texas, Arkansas, Tennessee, Kentucky, South Carolina, North Carolina, Virginia, Maryland
2. Illinois, Indiana, Ohio, Pennsylvania, New Jersey
3. Texas
4. Areas with the most cotton crop had the most slaves.

SKILL BUILDER: CRITICAL THINKING AND COMPREHENSION

I. Fact versus Opinion
1. O **2.** O **3.** O **4.** F **5.** F
II. Making Judgments
1. Answers will vary. **2.** Answers about "pleasant" slavery versus freedom will vary.
III. Point of View
1. S **2.** S **3.** P **4.** P

USING PRIMARY SOURCES

The words are a disguised prayer, asking God to tell the masters to free their slaves.

ENRICHMENT

1. Tales of slave life will vary. **2.** Reports on staple crops should mention tobacco, sugar cane, and cotton, wheat crops were exported, and what jobs were connected with each. Other facts will show greater depth of research.

UNIT 8 ❧ CHAPTER 3

VOCABULARY REVIEW

1. a **2.** d **3.** b **4.** f **5.** c

SKILL BUILDER: READING A MAP

1. Sea
2. Cairo, Chester, Evansville, Springfield, Quincy
3. Illinois
4. Tennessee and Kentucky
5. Marietta to Cleveland, Ohio across Lake Erie to Canada

SKILL BUILDER: CRITICAL THINKING AND COMPREHENSION

I. Generalizing
1. When slaves tried to become free and failed, they were beaten and whipped, fitted with leg chains, and sometimes sold to other states far from their wives and children. **2.** If a group was caught planning armed revolt, its members were usually killed. **3.** Most escaped slaves headed for Canada.
II. Cause and Effect
they attempted to lead an armed revolt. frightened. Slavery is cruel and Africans want to be free at all costs.
III. Predicting
1. It will die because Africans do not want to go to Liberia. Most were born here and do not know what to expect or how to survive in Africa. **2.** Yes, because the antislavery movement is growing rapidly. **3.** No, because Southern slaveowners are frightened of revolts.

USING PRIMARY SOURCES

1. Answers may vary depending on map scales and students'

imagination. If Randol knew that his escape by sea could be arranged in Charleston, South Carolina, he would have to travel approximately 400 miles (640 km). If Randol could arrange for his own escape at the closest sea route or body of water, he would be within a few miles (kilometers) of an attempt.

ENRICHMENT

Activities will vary.

UNIT 8 ✎ CHAPTER 4

VOCABULARY REVIEW

Industrial Revolution The change that took place in the late 1700s and early 1800s from making goods in small workshops to making goods with machines in factories.
famine A severe and widespread shortage of food.
blight A disease that kills plants.
mills Buildings used for grinding grain into flour or for manufacturing.
textile Cloth

SKILL BUILDER: INTERPRETING A DRAWING

1. The running water is a source of power for the machinery.
2. The main shaft
3. A machine with rollers covered with wire teeth, used to brush, clean, and straighten fibers of wool, cotton, etc.
4. Workers worked long hours on dangerous machines. Many of the workers were inexperienced.

SKILL BUILDER: CRITICAL THINKING AND COMPREHENSION

I. Generalizing

1. Sentences should feature roles of rural women and immigrants in the mills. **2.** Sentences should mention New England or the Northeast. **3.** The British forbade revealing the secret to Americans. **4.** Twelve hours a day, six days a week, low wages, child labor. **5.** The potato famine was causing many to starve or to lose their farms. **6.** Many native-born Americans hated and feared the Irish.
II. Cause and Effect
1. The United States developed a domestic textile industry. **2.** Mills were located in New England. **3.** The potato crop was blighted. **4.** All members of a family had to work because wages were so low.

USING PRIMARY SOURCES

Advantages were a chance to earn money for one's labor, to see other places, and to buy goods in stores instead of making them.

ENRICHMENT

1. Role-plays will vary. **2.** Letters should mention the advantages of wage earning and tell about long hours and low pay.
3. Models or drawings will vary.

UNIT 8 ✎ CHAPTER 5

VOCABULARY REVIEW

1. tariffs **2.** compromise **3.** abolitionists

SKILL BUILDER: USING A TIME LINE

1. *Walker's Appeal* **2.** 11 years **3.** No, Vesey's revolt was 7 years earlier. **4.** No **5.** 9 years **6.** 16 years **7.** Titles will vary but should mention antislavery.

SKILL BUILDER: CRITICAL THINKING AND COMPREHENSION

I. Sequencing
b, c, a, e, d
II. Comparing and Contrasting
1. Northern senator: set an end date for slavery in Missouri. Southern senator: Congress had no right to tell a state's citizens what they can own. **2.** Northern: We need to prevent cheap European goods from competing with our factories' products. Southern: We want cheaper goods no matter who made them, and we don't want Europe punishing us by putting tariffs on our cotton, tobacco, and sugarcane. **3.** Northern: perhaps feel guilt, perhaps be angry that slaves are sold to do jobs that free people could be employed to do. Southern: fear, and a new resolve to justify the rightness of slavery by religious means (Bible passages in favor of it) or by belief in white racial superiority.

USING PRIMARY SOURCES

Walker says the slaves will revolt.

ENRICHMENT

1. Debates should mention arguments in paragraphs 8-13.
2. Abolitionists will vary. **3.** Sentences should use words *murderers, monsters, a horrible mockery, crushing the arm of power, wretchedness and misery, deliver us from under you.*

UNIT 8 ✎ CHAPTER 6

VOCABULARY REVIEW

1. b **2.** b **3.** a **4.** b

SKILL BUILDER: MAKING A TIME LINE

Students should create a time line showing the events listed on page 392 at appropriate time intervals.

SKILL BUILDER: CRITICAL THINKING AND COMPREHENSION

I. Drawing Conclusions
1. b **2.** a and b **3.** a and b
II. Points of View
1. a—Lincoln b—Douglas **2.** a—abolitionists b—planter

USING PRIMARY SOURCES

Students' summaries should mention the following: Lincoln—slavery is wrong, we should stop it from spreading, we should set an end date for owning slaves. Douglas—each state has the right to decide for itself, it's more important not to break up the Union than not to stop slavery.

ENRICHMENT

1. Stories of slave life will vary. **2.** Opinions about the Lincoln-Douglas debates will vary. **3.** Dred Scott's letter should mention his feelings about losing his court case.

UNIT 9 ✎ CHAPTER 1

VOCABULARY REVIEW

1. c **2.** b **3.** d **4.** a **5.** e

SKILL BUILDER: TIME LINE

1860—Lincoln elected
Feb. 1861—Confederacy is formed, seven states secede
March 1861—Lincoln inaugurated as president
Apr. 1861—Confederate troops fire on Ft. Sumter
July 1861—Battle of Bull Run

SKILL BUILDER: CRITICAL THINKING AND COMPREHENSION

I. Predicting
1. The South seceded from the Union. **2.** The North won the Civil War. **3.** Lincoln won the election of 1860.
II. Point of View
1. Lincoln **2.** Breckinridge **3.** Davis **4.** Douglas

USING PRIMARY SOURCES

Lincoln is quoting from the Constitution's list of Executive duties in the Oath of Office.

ENRICHMENT

1. Letters from Davis to Lincoln will vary. **2.** Sketches should show Ft. Sumter, weapons, and uniforms of the time with accuracy. **3.** Reports should describe the following: campaign of 1860, speeches, advertising, news reports, and rallies.

UNIT 9 ❧ CHAPTER 2

VOCABULARY REVIEW

1. blockade shut off a nation's ports from trade **2. emancipate** grant freedom to enslaved people **3. peninsula** land surrounded on three sides by water
Students' sentences will vary.

SKILL BUILDER: READING A MAP

1. 4 Confederate victories; 11 Union victories; 3 indecisive battles
The Union was winning the war in 1862.
2. The South was the scene of the largest number of battles. The North planned to blockade the South, win control of the Mississippi to split the Confederacy, and capture Richmond. The South, having declared its independence, did not intend to fight battles in the North—it only wanted to hold out against Northern attacks, reasoning that the North would soon grow tired of fighting. This is why most of the battles took place in the South.
3. Most battles were fought at or near seaports. The North's main strategy was to cut off the South's trade with Europe, thereby cutting off its money for weapons and supplies.
4. The seaport at Charleston probably was least affected by the Union blockade, since the Confederates won the battle there.
5. The Battle of Antietam; no one won this indecisive battle.
6. Grant will probably attack New Orleans. The Confederacy would strongly defend this port, since it was the major port of trade for the South.

SKILL BUILDER: CRITICAL THINKING AND COMPREHENSION

I. Fact versus Opinion
1. F **2.** F **3.** O **4.** O **5.** O **6.** O
II. Making Judgments
1. Important—largest city in the South, main Confederate seaport. Not important—there were many other cities in the South, so the North could have won without New Orleans. **2.** Not a mistake—Europe might have joined the North, slaves might have revolted, owning slaves was always morally wrong, before and after the Emancipation Proclamation. A mistake—would not have actually freed any slaves, so would have been a pointlessly antagonistic act. **3.** Freeing the slaves—slavery was morally indefensible. Saving the Union—a dissolved union would have resulted in complete chaos and no real government.

USING PRIMARY SOURCES

The ideas in the excerpt should not be changed in meaning and should all be present in the paraphrased version.

ENRICHMENT

1. Maps and battle accounts will vary. **2.** Editorials should show both Northern and Southern views of freeing African slaves. **3.** Descriptions of the *Monitor-Merrimack* battle will vary only in some details.

UNIT 9 ❧ CHAPTER 3

VOCABULARY REVIEW

1. b **2.** a

SKILL BUILDER: READING A MAP

1. False **2.** True **3.** False **4.** False
5. False **6.** True **7.** False

SKILL BUILDER: CRITICAL THINKING AND COMPREHENSION

I. Summarizing
1. Nearly 186,000 African Americans fought in the Union army. Many African Americans fought in the Union navy. More than 20 African American soldiers and sailors were given the Medal of Honor for their great bravery. **2.** Women did jobs men used to do, African Americans were free. The federal government was stronger than the states. **3.** The Civil War is a test to see whether the Union can endure; the men who died to keep the Union going as a place of freedom and equality should not have died for nothing.
II. Comparing and Contrasting
1. North: worked in factories, sewed uniforms in factories, worked in government, worked as nurses, fought in battles, spied. South: worked in factories, wove and sewed clothing, worked as nurses, fought in battles, spied. **2.** Africans were not treated fairly in the Union army. In the Confederacy, many were forced to help the Confederate army. **3.** Sherman's war methods: total war. Grant's war methods: hold cities under siege.
III. Generalizing
1. More than 600,000 Americans had been killed in the four long years of fighting. **2.** For example, they usually did not receive equal pay. African American soldiers often were given difficult, dirty jobs like digging trenches and building earthen forts. **3.** Before the war, women had been restricted to certain jobs. Many women on both sides worked long hours in factories.

USING PRIMARY SOURCES

Recitations of the Gettysburg Address should not vary in language.

ENRICHMENT

1 and 2. Students' plays and news reports will vary.

UNIT 9 ❧ CHAPTER 4

VOCABULARY REVIEW

1. Reconstruction **2.** vetoed **3.** corrupt (carpetbaggers is also correct) **4.** scalawags **5.** black codes **6.** carpetbaggers **7.** freedmen **8.** Radical Republicans **9.** impeached **10.** Freedmen's Bureau

SKILL BUILDING: GIVING AN ORAL REPORT

Oral reports may vary.

SKILL BUILDING: CRITICAL THINKING AND COMPREHENSION

I. Main Idea
1. Acts to Help Freedmen Obtain Rights
2. Reconstruction Acts to Prepare South for Statehood
3. Reconstruction Government's Acts to Improve Lives

II. Sequencing
e, c, a, d, f, b.

III. Drawing Conclusions
Students' conclusions will vary.

USING PRIMARY SOURCES

Answers will vary.

ENRICHMENT

Activities will vary.

UNIT 9 ❧ CHAPTER 5

VOCABULARY REVIEW

1. h 2. a 3. f 4. d 5. g 6. b 7. e 8. c 9. j
10. i

SKILL BUILDER: READING A MAP

1. churches, schools, stores
2. Railroad tracks
3. Whites live near more stores, a library, more schools, and public roads. African Americans live near farms, factories, and few services.

SKILL BUILDER: CRITICAL THINKING AND COMPREHENSION

I. Main Idea
1, 2, and 3. Students' rewrites can vary.

II. Cause and Effect
1. They had no money to rent land or buy tools. 2. African Americans lost many of the rights they had gained.

III. Predicting
Examples of changes in history if segregation had been outlawed will vary, but some might guess that de facto segregation would exist as it did in the North where segregation was not the law.

USING PRIMARY SOURCES

Students lacking in self-confidence may want to recite in unison.

ENRICHMENT

1. Role-plays should indicate that the former master still needs workers on his land, and the kinder masters might be respected by former slaves. 2. The letters should mention that Washington wanted former slaves to learn practical trades, and DuBois wanted them to train as professionals and become leaders.

UNIT 10 ❧ CHAPTER 1

VOCABULARY REVIEW

1. e 2. d 3. c 4. b

SKILL BUILDING: READING A GRAPH

1. 1855 and 1860 2. 10,000 miles 3. There is about ten times as much 20 years later 4. they nearly double every five years (or, they more than triple every 10 years)

SKILL BUILDER: CRITICAL THINKING AND COMPREHENSION

I. Sequencing
1. 1798 (first), 1830 2. 1853, 1807 (first) 3. 1840, 1830 (first) 4. 1822 (first), 1836

II. Classifying
Transportation and Communication: *Tom Thumb, Clermont,* canals, newspapers, telegraph, locomotives
Industry: Lowell workers, division of labor, locomotives, newspapers, telegraph

III. Drawing Conclusions
Conclusions will vary but should feature the sewing machine, cooking stoves, mass-produced rugs and furniture.

USING PRIMARY SOURCES

Problems listed will vary but should include respiratory diseases, sooty living quarters, eye irritation, and emotional depression.

ENRICHMENT

Drawings and poems will vary.

UNIT 10 ❧ CHAPTER 2

VOCABULARY REVIEW

1. c 2. a 3. f 4. b 5. e 6. d 7. g

SKILL BUILDER: INTERPRETING A PHOTOGRAPH

1. The car broke down. The driver has tools on hand to repair the car.
2. The road is not paved.
3. He might be grateful that his horse and carriage are working.

SKILL BUILDER: CRITICAL THINKING AND COMPREHENSION

I. Classifying
1. Matzeliger—I 2. Vanderbilt—T 3. Ford—T 4. Bessemer—I 5. Duryeas—I

II. Predicting
1. cut down to make ties 2. anything it wants, free from regulation 3. more steel

III. Point of View
1. worker 2. owner 3. owner 4. worker

USING PRIMARY SOURCES

Students should guess that the early automobiles needed many improvements, and many owners were would-be inventors themselves and couldn't resist tinkering.

ENRICHMENT

1 and 2. Students' answers and book reports will vary in subject matter.

UNIT 10 ❧ CHAPTER 3

VOCABULARY REVIEW

1. b 2. f 3. h 4. e 5. g 6. a 7. k 8. c 9. l
10. i 11. j

SKILL BUILDER: MAKING A TIME LINE

Students should create a time line showing the events listed on page 452 at appropriate time intervals.

SKILL BUILDER: CRITICAL THINKING AND COMPREHENSION

I. Generalizing

1. A depression has hit **2.** Department stores grew in size and number.
II. Fact versus Opinion
1. F **2.** O **3.** F **4.** O
III. Cause and Effect
1. a. cause **b.** effect **2. a.** effect **b.** cause

USING PRIMARY SOURCES

Love is supplying a market that exists. African Americans were probably motivated to work harder for someone who respected them and gave them a chance for a promotion, which shows Love's loyalty and faith in his people.

ENRICHMENT

1. Interviews with strikers or marchers will vary but should mention the violence encountered by both groups. **2.** Trademarks, brand names, and products will vary.

UNIT 10 ❧ CHAPTER 4

VOCABULARY REVIEW

1. ghettoes **2.** pogroms **3.** padrone **4.** scapegoats
5. tenements **6.** labor unions **7.** picket lines

SKILL BUILDER: READING A MAP

1. Scandinavia
2. Germany
3. There were not many immigrants from Mexico and Canada during the period shown on the map.
4. The number of immigrants from Ireland and Italy is roughly the same.

SKILL BUILDER: CRITICAL THINKING AND COMPREHENSION

I. Compare and Contrast
1. Contrasts: Before—life was rural, children were unschooled and often hungry. After—life was urban, children might work but probably had a chance for a good education. **2.** Lists should include: poor English, work is good and play is a waste of time, old customs are good even though they don't relate to present-day life.
II. Generalizing
1. Sentences should mention the desire to improve the future possibilities for their children. **2.** unskilled jobs, doing hard, dirty, and dangerous work. **3.** crowded, airless bedrooms in tenements without indoor running water and toilets.
III. Main Idea
The answer is b.

USING PRIMARY SOURCES

Answers will vary because not all children grew up to realize that their parents were sacrificing for them.

ENRICHMENT

1. Accounts might mention the Statue of Liberty and Ellis Island. **2.** Students should have discovered the difference in ethnicity between immigrants of then and now.

UNIT 10 ❧ CHAPTER 5

VOCABULARY REVIEW

1. c **2.** d **3.** a **4.** f **5.** b **6.** h **7.** g **8.** e **9.** i

SKILL BUILDER: USING A TIME LINE

1. 9 years **2.** 33% **3.** 50% **4.** Conditions in the tenements were often crowded and unhealthful.

SKILL BUILDER: CRITICAL THINKING AND COMPREHENSION

I. Classifying
1. r **2.** s **3.** s **4.** l **5.** s **6.** r **7.** s **8.** s **9.** l
II. Sequencing
1. a **2.** b **3.** c **4.** f **5.** e **6.** d (c and f may be reversed)
III. Drawing Conclusions
The answer is 3.

USING PRIMARY SOURCES

The agent would be asked today about schools and, in some states, about water supply and commuter railroad connections near big cities. But today agents would be asked about how far the house was from factories, heavily congested roads, and garbage dumps.

ENRICHMENT

1. Reports should include changes in rules and uniforms.
2. Book report subjects will vary.

UNIT 11 ❧ CHAPTER 1

VOCABULARY REVIEW

1. craft union **2.** strike **3.** labor union **4.** federation
5. collective bargaining **6.** recognize

SKILL BUILDER: INTERPRETING A CARTOON

1. As fat and greedy, in control of American industry
2. As hardworking, giving everything to monopolists
3. Monopolists
4. Attacks capitalists and sympathizes with the working class

SKILL BUILDER: CRITICAL THINKING AND COMPREHENSION

I. Fact *versus* Opinion
1. F **2.** O **3.** O **4.** F
II. Cause and Effect
1. b **2.** a **3.** d **4.** c
III. Generalizing
1. Workers in the late 1800s were exploited and powerless.
2. The AFL concentrated on trying to improve the lot of workers rather than trying to change government to be more friendly to labor.

USING PRIMARY SOURCES

Account seems fair, doesn't try to lay blame until the end when labor's feelings are expressed as fact, and guards are labeled "strangers." Owners would be angry that report doesn't tell how many guards were shot. Strikers would be angry that report mentions their having weapons.

ENRICHMENT

1. Statistics should show small percentage of union members.
2. Accounts will vary.

UNIT 11 ❧ CHAPTER 2

VOCABULARY REVIEW

1. d **2.** a **3.** b **4.** c **5.** f **6.** e

SKILL BUILDER: COMPLETING A TABLE

FACTOR	HELPED THE FARMER	HURT THE FARMER
Cooperatives	helped by lowering costs.	
Railroad Monopoly		hurt farmers with no other way to ship goods
High Production		hurt the farmer by lowering food prices
Railroad Land Grants	helped by making land cheap and available for sale	hurt by overpopulating the land and thus causing too much production.

SKILL BUILDER: CRITICAL THINKING AND COMPREHENSION

I. Point of View
1. Great Plains farmer 2. railroad tycoon 3. Granger 4. Great Plains farmer 5. Granger 6. Populist party member 7. Great Plains farmer
II. Classifying
1. the Grange 2. Grange, Populist party 3. Populist party 4. Populist party 5. the Grange 6. Populist party 7. the Grange 8. Grange, Populist party 9. Populist party
III. Sequencing
b, d, e, a, c

USING PRIMARY SOURCES

Opinions about the Grange will vary.

ENRICHMENT

1. Current population figures should be located. 2. Drawings should be based on descriptions on text pages 479–480. 3. Current statistics should be cited. 4. Students should mention all these: inflation, deflation, mortgage, land values, and crop values.

UNIT 11 ♣ CHAPTER 3

VOCABULARY REVIEW

1. b 2. c 3. c 4. a

SKILL BUILDER: READING A TIME LINE

1. 1852 2. 1920 3. The Seneca Falls Declaration 4. 50 years 5. The passage of the 15th Amendment in 1870. Women are citizens and have the right to vote.

USING PRIMARY SOURCES

Women had no control over their own wages.

SKILL BUILDER: CRITICAL THINKING AND COMPREHENSION

I. Drawing Conclusions
The best conclusion is b.
II. Summarizing
1. Women win right to vote 2. First women's rights convention held 3. First American woman doctor graduates
III. Making Judgments
1. London antislavery meeting—unfair 2. many states' laws—unfair 3. the right to assemble—fair

ENRICHMENT

Posters, statistics, and reports will vary.

UNIT 11 ♣ CHAPTER 4

VOCABULARY REVIEW

1. c 2. d 3. b 4. f 5. e 6. a 7. g

SKILL BUILDER: MAKING A TIME LINE

1873—first nursing schools, 1817—Gallaudet opens school for the deaf, 1831—Howe offered job running school for the blind, 1832—Perkins Institute opens, 1860—people knew germs caused diseases, 1820—prison reforms began

SKILL BUILDER: CRITICAL THINKING AND COMPREHENSION

I. Predicting
1. Children won't learn to be good citizens, and our democracy will fall. 2. More people who serve time will be rehabilitated and won't return to prison again. 3. The special needs of handicapped people won't be filled.
II. Generalizing
1. A good generalization about this paragraph—it explains a new philosophy about how to treat those who commit crimes.
2. "Public Education Improved" is a good title because it gives examples; "Students Have Greater Chances to Learn" is a good title because it shows increase in length of school term and in number of schools nationally.
III. Cause and Effect
1. Surgery could be done now that used to be too painful for the patient. 2. People didn't want tax money spent on rehabilitation. 3. States founded colleges and universities paid for by taxes to make education cheaper for their citizens.

USING PRIMARY SOURCES

Students' opinions will vary.

ENRICHMENT

Problems, reports, and resources will vary.

UNIT 11 ♣ CHAPTER 5

VOCABULARY REVIEW

1. d 2. f 3. h 4. i 5. e 6. a 7. g 8. j 9. b 10. k 11. c

USING PRIMARY SOURCES

McClure means that wrongs not corrected today will bring revolution in our children's time that will destroy our democracy.

SKILL BUILDER: COMPLETING A TABLE

1890—Sherman Antitrust Act: government can dissolve trusts.
1906—Pure Food and Drug Act: required food labeling
1913—16th Amendment: authorized an income tax.
1913—17th Amendment: provided direct election of senators.
1913—Federal Reserve Act: created regional banks so Western states had access to credit.
1914—Clayton Antitrust Act: outlawed rebates and price cutting.
1919—18th Amendment: prohibited sale of alcoholic beverages.
1920—19th Amendment: gave women the vote.

SKILL BUILDER: CRITICAL THINKING AND COMPREHENSION

I. Classifying

Tarbell, Teddy Roosevelt, McClure—Business Reform
Wilson—Labor Reform
Teddy Roosevelt—Conservation
Wilson—Banking   Sinclair—Health
Du Bois, Wells-Barnett, Terrell—Racial Discrimination

II. Sequencing

a and c in 1906. Then f, b, h, g, e, d.

III. Comparing and Contrasting

Roosevelt: Republican at first, hero, conservationist, strenuous life, militant. Wilson: Democrat, concerned with banking system, child labor, and workers.

USING PRIMARY SOURCES

McClure means that wrongs not corrected today will bring revolution in our children's time that will destroy democracy.

ENRICHMENT

Answers will vary.

UNIT 12 ❧ CHAPTER 1

VOCABULARY REVIEW

1. c **2.** a **3.** c **4.** a

SKILL BUILDER: READING A MAP

1. United States Navy and the Filipino nationalists
2. April 30
3. 10 islands
4. Spain and the U.S. wanted control of countries in the Pacific.

SKILL BUILDER: CRITICAL THINKING AND COMPREHENSION

I. Summarizing

1. Cubans fought a guerrilla war for ten years. Then the United States joined by declaring war on Spain. **2.** Spain gave Guam, Puerto Rico, and the Philippines to the United States.

II. Cause and Effect

1. Americans invaded Cuba. **2.** The United States now had an overseas empire.

III. Point of View

1. Spaniards **2.** Puerto Ricans **3.** Filipinos **4.** Cubans
5. Americans

USING PRIMARY SOURCES

Martí is referring to the martyrs who died for the cause.

ENRICHMENT

Responses will vary.

UNIT 12 ❧ CHAPTER 2

VOCABULARY REVIEW

1. c **2.** b **3.** b

SKILL BUILDER: MAKING AN OUTLINE

I. **A.** The United States offers Colombia $10 million.
   B. American warships help Panamanian rebels defeat Colombia.
II. Panamanian rebels decide to break away.
   B. American warships keep Colombian ships from landing troops.
III. **A. 1.** The United States pays Panama $10 million for a canal zone.

2. The United States agreed to pay rent of $250,000 a year.
B. The United States later paid $425 million to Colombia.

SKILL BUILDER: CRITICAL THINKING AND COMPREHENSION

I. Generalizing

1. Facts: U.S. military rule in Cuba; Teddy Roosevelt kept Colombia from putting down rebellion in Panama; United States protected investors against just arrest and convictions and even against loss of trade in Latin American countries. **2.** Puerto Rican immigrants are usually unskilled and poor, and they further face discrimination because many of them are black.

II. Compare and Contrast

Countries	SIMILARITIES	DIFFERENCES
Panama	1. U.S. armed forces involved	1. encouraged rebellion
	2. U.S. paid Panama for the canal zone.	2. asked for American assistance
	3. U.S. paid Colombia for the injustice.	3. negotiated a treaty
Mexico	1. U.S. armed forces involved	1. tried to stay out
	2. United States sends troops to Mexico during the Mexican Revolution to protect American property there.	2. did not ask for American assistance
	3. United States kicks Europeans out of Mexico before the Mexican-U.S. War.	3. did not negotiate a treaty

There were more differences than similarities because the Panamanians saw much to gain from U.S. involvement. The Mexicans were resentful about U.S. involvement.

III. Point of View

Postcards will vary.

USING PRIMARY SOURCES

Answers should show students' understanding of why Latin Americans distrust United States' strength and potential for policing them.

ENRICHMENT

Answers will vary.

UNIT 12 ❧ CHAPTER 3

VOCABULARY REVIEW

1. b **2.** a

SKILL BUILDER: INTERPRETING A TIME LINE

1. 1899 **2.** 1900 **3.** 1893 **4.** 1900 **5.** 1898

SKILL BUILDER: CRITICAL THINKING AND COMPREHENSION

I. Fact versus Opinion

1. F **2.** O **3.** O **4.** O **5.** O **6.** F

II. Cause and Effect

1. The United States bought or occupied stepping-stone islands. **2.** The Boxer Rebellion **3.** The United States overthrew her government.

III. Classifying

Answers will vary, but the following is one way to complete the text chart:

	JAPAN	CHINA	HAWAII
Opened to Trade	forced open the market	carved out a sphere of influence	started up industries in Hawaii to trade with the continental United States
Dealt with Government	coercion of ruler	paid off the local warlords	dethroned the queen
Create Market for Our Goods	opened country to western ideas and demand followed	sent missionaries to westernize people	sent missionaries

USING PRIMARY SOURCES

Opinions will vary.

ENRICHMENT

Activities will vary.

UNIT 12   CHAPTER 4

VOCABULARY REVIEW

1. alliance **2.** Triple Entente **3.** Triple Alliance **4.** tsar **5.** Central Powers **6.** Allies

SKILL BUILDER: READING A MAP

1. France, Italy, Romania
2. Estonia, Latvia, Poland, Czechoslovakia, Lithuania, Finland, Yugoslavia
3. Russia, United Kingdom, Austria-Hungary, Germany. Because of treaties and the forming of new alliances

SKILL BUILDER: CRITICAL THINKING AND COMPREHENSION

I. Sequencing
a, c, g, f, e, d, b

II. Comparing and Contrasting

	WAR OF 1812	WORLD WAR I
Allies		Britain, France, Italy, the United States
Where Fought	Great Lakes, East Coast of America, New Orleans	France, Russia, German ports, Atlantic sea routes, So. Africa.

	WAR OF 1812	WORLD WAR I
Methods of Fighting	ships' guns, Native American attacks, blockades	trench warfare, submarines, mustard gas, cannon, blockades.
Who Won	The United States	the Allies
Outcomes of the War	Americans expanded north and west, Native Americans weakened, Britain increased efforts to dominate Latin America	Europe was devastated, Germany lost all its colonies, France exacted harsh reparations on Germany.

Similarities: wars for empire and trade, use of blockade and control of the seas.
Differences: many more participants, many more lives lost in WW I.

III. Making Judgments
Opinions will vary but should include topics of freedom of the seas, colonization, democracies allied against undemocratic regimes.

USING PRIMARY SOURCES
The statement falls into almost everyone's value system.

ENRICHMENT
Activities will vary.

UNIT 12   CHAPTER 5

VOCABULARY REVIEW

1. Communication designed to promote certain ideas and attitudes **2.** an agreement to stop fighting **3.** payments by a defeated nation for damages or losses suffered during a war **4.** policy of not becoming involved in world affairs **5.** an interest-earning certificate that promises to pay the owner a certain amount of money when due **6.** list of war aims drawn up by President Wilson during World War I

SKILL BUILDER: USING A TIME LINE

1. two **2.** three **3.** 1920 **4.** one and one-half years

SKILL BUILDING: CRITICAL THINKING AND COMPREHENSION

I. Cause and Effect
1. The League of Nations was part of the treaty. **2.** Money was needed for munitions. **3.** Women took their places. **4.** He devised a League of Nations.

II. Classifying
Supporting the war effort: buying Liberty Bonds, producing uniforms and tanks, conserving food, getting millions of men into the military.
Creating a peace treaty: ending secret agreements among nations, making the seas free for all, League of Nations.

III. Drawing Conclusions
1. Allies will push into Germany **2.** The Senate will not confirm the Treaty of Versailles

USING PRIMARY SOURCES
Opinions will vary.

ENRICHMENT
Activities will vary.

UNIT 13 ❧ CHAPTER 1

VOCABULARY REVIEW

1. Red Scare **2.** quota system **3.** Prohibition Amendment **4.** Harlem Renaissance **5.** bootleggers **6.** bribed

SKILL BUILDER: READING A MAP

1. population and population increase
2. New Orleans, Washington, New York
3. Chicago, Detroit, Cleveland
4. Because of the large numbers of African Americans migrating from the South to the North

SKILL BUILDER: CRITICAL THINKING AND COMPREHENSION

I. Generalizing

1. The boom in auto sales gave a boost to other industries. The housing industry boomed as people moved out of the crowded cities into suburbs. **2.** Many factory workers and miners earned so little money that they could barely provide their families with the basics of life. Farm workers such as Mexican Americans in the Southwest earned low wages and so could not afford the new consumer goods. **3.** Garvey's ideas offered hope for a brighter future. A magnetic speaker, he told African Americans to be proud of their race and themselves as human beings.

II. Comparing and Contrasting

	BEFORE WORLD WAR I	AFTER WORLD WAR I
Women's hairstyles	long hair	short "bobbed" hair
Where many African Americans lived	rural South	urban North
Heroes and Heroines	presidents, inventors like Henry Ford	Charles Lindbergh, movie stars, sports figures, jazz musicians
Where most Americans lived	rural areas	cities
Roads in the U.S.	dirt roads	highways
Women's right to vote	not at all in most states, and not in national elections	equal voting rights with men

USING PRIMARY SOURCES

African Americans were beginning to feel equal to whites and to expect an end to discrimination.

ENRICHMENT

Students' activities will vary.

UNIT 13 ❧ CHAPTER 2

VOCABULARY REVIEW

1. The TVA was set up to end floods and provide electricity in the Tennessee Valley. **2.** true **3.** The main purpose of public works programs is to put people to work **4.** The New Deal was President Roosevelt's program to hire the jobless, end the banking crisis, and help the poor. **5.** true **6.** true for some people.

SKILL BUILDER: INTERPRETING A PHOTOGRAPH

1. The Great Plains region
2. The dust storms have buried the fencing, the house, and probably all the crops.
3. They are probably farmers.

SKILL BUILDER: CRITICAL THINKING AND COMPREHENSION

I. Classifying
Causes of the Great Depression: 1, 2
Things that Happened During the Great Depression: 1, 3, 4, 5, 6
II. Predicting
Predictions will vary.

USING PRIMARY SOURCES

Students' explanations of the song will vary.

ENRICHMENT

Students' answers will vary.

UNIT 13 ❧ CHAPTER 3

VOCABULARY REVIEW

1. c **2.** f **3.** h **4.** d **5.** b **6.** g **7.** e **8.** j **9.** k **10.** a

SKILL BUILDER: MAKING A TIME LINE

1922—Mussolini seizes power. 1931—Japan invades Manchuria. 1933—Hitler becomes dictator. 1936—Rome-Berlin Axis formed.
1938—Hitler annexes Austria. Sept. 1, 1939— Germany invades Poland. Sept. 3, 1939—Britain and France declare war on Germany.
1941—Hitler invades Soviet Union.

SKILL BUILDER: CRITICAL THINKING AND COMPREHENSION

I. Main Idea
1. Hitler soon seized the rest of Czechoslovakia. Then without warning, on September 1, 1939, German forces poured into Poland and overwhelmed it. Using airplanes, tanks, and heavy guns, Nazi forces crushed Denmark, Norway, Holland, and Belgium.
2. In Italy, an ambitious leader, Benito Mussolini, seized power in 1922. In 1933, Hitler became dictator of Germany. In the Soviet Union, another dictator, Joseph Stalin, held power in the 1930s.
3. At the Munich Conference in 1938, Britain and France agreed to Hitler's demand for part of Czechoslovakia. Ignoring his promise, however, Hitler soon seized the rest of Czechoslovakia. His next goal was Poland.
II. Predicting
1. Hitler is stopped. **2.** Hitler can't attack countries close to Russia.
III. Cause and Effect
1. Germany invades Poland. **2.** Japan has a depression. **3.** Americans didn't send troops to help British in the Battle of Britain.

USING PRIMARY SOURCES
Answers will vary.

ENRICHMENT
Students' activities will vary.

UNIT 13 ❧ CHAPTER 4

VOCABULARY REVIEW
1. D-Day 2. Atlantic Charter 3. Lend-Lease Act 4. island hopping 5. arsenal

SKILL BUILDER: INTERPRETING A MAP
1. New Guinea, Guam, Philippines, Taiwan, Iwo Jima, Okinawa
2. Midway, Okinawa, Iwo Jima, Wake

SKILL BUILDER: CRITICAL THINKING AND COMPREHENSION

I. Summarizing
1. Plans should mention island-hopping and direct bombing of Japan's cities. 2. Sentences should include the places Hope went. 3. Sentences should mention that women took men's jobs.

II. Comparing and Contrasting
1. Roosevelt led the nation at war; Truman dropped the atom bomb. 2. Normandy Beach: allied forces cross English Channel to begin land invasion of German-held France. Pearl Harbor: Japan attacks U.S.-held Hawaii by air. 3. Europe: allied forces push across France into Germany. Japan: U.S. island-hops across Pacific while bombers attack Japan's cities.

III. Drawing Conclusions
1. Americans lost protection from attacks from the west. 2. Full-scale conversion of peacetime production to military goods. 3. Americans were frightened of the threat from Japan and Japan's swift conquest of the Pacific, and Americans were also racist enough to think that what they did to Japanese Americans and Japanese aliens was justified.

USING PRIMARY SOURCES
Pyle lived on the front lines with the enlisted men.

ENRICHMENT
Written reports, interviews, and oral reports will vary.

UNIT 13 ❧ CHAPTER 5

VOCABULARY REVIEW
1. b 2. c 3. c

SKILL BUILDER: MAKING A TIME LINE
Events should appear on the time line as follows: 1939—WW II begins; 1941—Lend-Lease Act, America enters WW II; 1944—D-Day; 1945—United Nations charter is drawn up, first atomic bomb is dripped, Japan surrenders; 1948—Ralph Bunche becomes UN mediator in Palestine

SKILL BUILDER: CRITICAL THINKING AND COMPREHENSION

I. Generalizing
1. a 2. c.

II. Point of View
1. Hitler—he will rebuild Germany into a great power.
2. FDR—people must co-exist in peace.

III. Making Judgments
Students' opinions may vary.

USING PRIMARY SOURCES
Students should sense the utter devastation of Europe.

ENRICHMENT
Responses will vary.

UNIT 14 ❧ CHAPTER 1

VOCABULARY REVIEW
1. boom 2. inflation 3. vaccine 4. consumer 5. demobilization 6. demagogue 7. censure

SKILL BUILDER: USING AN ENCYCLOPEDIA
Reports on inflation, President Truman, the Cold War, polio, Joseph McCarthy, and Josef Stalin will vary.

SKILL BUILDER: CRITICAL THINKING AND COMPREHENSION

I. Generalizing
1. People looked forward to normal lives again. 2. People were tired of sacrificing. 3. They were enjoying prosperity.

II. Cause and Effect
1. There is full employment. 2. People had money to spend on goods they couldn't get during wartime. 3. U.S. farmers became prosperous supplying the world's food.

III. Point of View
1. The Fair Deal is good because it is more of Roosevelt's New Deal left unfinished because of the war. I'm tired of worrying about the poor—I want to spend my earnings on a new car. 2. If people can continue buying, they can keep people employed to produce more things to buy. If people keep buying, they will reach a point where they need nothing more, and employment will slow down. 3. McCarthy is trying to protect us from our enemies. McCarthy is more un-American than our enemies are because of his methods.

USING PRIMARY SOURCES
The right to education allows everyone the opportunity to learn skills that put other goals within their reach.

ENRICHMENT
Answers will vary.

UNIT 14 ❧ CHAPTER 2

VOCABULARY REVIEW
1. Western 2. with ideas and words 3. discouraged 4. cargo planes 5. a superpower 6. Western 7. forbidden

SKILL BUILDER: READING A MAP
1. Soviet
2. Soviet Union, Poland
3. France
4. Oder and Neisse Rivers
5. The combined Allied zones.

SKILL BUILDER: CRITICAL THINKING AND COMPREHENSION

I. Summarizing
1. The Truman Doctrine aimed to help any country that resisted communism. 2. The Marshall Plan aimed to help the economy of every country in Europe. 3. NATO was formed to

meet the threat of attack on a European country by the Soviets.
4. The Cold War started because the Soviet Union wanted to
spread its control over European countries that the allies wanted
to be democratic. **5.** Germany was divided into two nations because the allies allowed free elections in their sectors and the Soviets didn't in theirs.

II. Cause and Effect
1. The U.S. sent aid to governments that were threatened by
communism. **2.** The war-torn countries of Europe were too
devastated to recover without help. **3.** Germany became divided.
III. Fact versus Opinion
1. O **2.** F **3.** O **4.** O

USING PRIMARY SOURCES

Marshall didn't want any superpower to feel threatened by our
interference, so he said the world needed us to help Europe
prevent new wars.

ENRICHMENT

Debates will vary.

UNIT 14 ॐ CHAPTER 3

VOCABULARY REVIEW
1. b **2.** e **3.** a **4.** d **5.** c

SKILL BUILDER: READING A MAP

1. Tumen and Yalu rivers
2. South Vietnam, Cambodia, Laos
3. Answers will vary. Because of its strategic location
4. Saigon, now Ho Chi Minh City

SKILL BUILDER: CRITICAL THINKING AND COMPREHENSION

I. Comparing and Contrasting
1. Vietnam: the communist army tried to overthrow the South
Vietnamese government; the U.S. helped South Vietnam resist;
the U.S. withdrew and let the Viet Cong take over. Korea:
communist troops from North Korea invaded South Korea; the
UN sent troops to help the U.S. resist; Chinese troops helped
the North Koreans; the war ended in a stalemate.
2. Americans were increasingly against United States involvement in Vietnam. World War II was supported wholeheartedly.
II. Point of View
1. We need to resist the North Koreans' invasion because we
must stop the advance of communism in Asia. We just fought a
war and now it is someone else's turn to solve the world's
problems. **2.** We need to stop the advance of communism in
Vietnam or the other poor countries near it will fall, too. We
can't win the war and the government we are propping up there
hasn't even the support of the South Vietnamese.
III. Making Judgments
1. Yes, because the Constitution states that our civilian President
controls the military. **2.** From his point of view, many Americans also supported the war. Johnson thought they were in the
majority, and he thought they were the responsible citizens rather
than student radicals. **3.** Nixon was right to get out because he
couldn't have defended himself in an impeachment trial against
the evidence Congress had.

USING PRIMARY SOURCES

Congress was afraid that if Vietnam fell to Communists other
countries in the region would, too.

ENRICHMENT

Students' activities will vary.

UNIT 14 ॐ CHAPTER 4

VOCABULARY REVIEW
1. f **2.** c **3.** b **4.** a **5.** d

SKILL BUILDER: MAKING AN OUTLINE

I. The Arab-Israeli conflict affects the United States
II. The United States has had both success and failure in the
Middle East

SKILL BUILDER: CRITICAL THINKING AND COMPREHENSION

I. Cause and Effect
1. The U.S. helped Israel in the Arab-Israeli War of 1973.
2. Iranian radicals took 52 American hostages in Tehran.
3. Israel invaded Lebanon in 1982 to wipe out the PLO.
II. Sequencing
In order from earliest to latest: i, f, d, e, b, g, h, c, and a
III. Predicting
1. The Ayatollah might not have won power from the less-ex-
treme and westernized Iranians. **2.** Carter might have won re-
election.

USING PRIMARY SOURCES

Our energy supplies depend on OPEC's goodwill.

ENRICHMENT

Activities will vary.

UNIT 14 ॐ CHAPTER 5

VOCABULARY REVIEW
1. e **2.** c **3.** d **4.** a **5.** f **6.** b

SKILL BUILDER: MAKING A TIME LINE

1962—Cuban Missile Crisis. 1972—Nixon visits China and the
Soviet Union. 1974—Nixon resigns. 1979—Soviet Union invades Afghanistan. 1979—Carter and Brezhnev sign the SALT II
treaty.

USING PRIMARY SOURCES

Kennedy isn't sure differences can be resolved but believes peace
is possible.

SKILL BUILDER: CRITICAL THINKING AND COMPREHENSION

I. Making Judgments
Answers will vary. Students should give reasons for their answers.
II. Drawing Conclusions
Students should choose a different way to handle each of the two
problems.
III. Compare and Contrast
1. Nixon opened China to trade, and a policy of detente
defused the Cold War. **2.** Nixon didn't tie his detente policy to
concern for human rights in the Soviet Union.

ENRICHMENT

Students' activities will vary.

VOCABULARY REVIEW

1. the idea that African Americans should live apart from whites **2.** movement to overturn practices that denied rights to minorities **3.** peacefully disobeying a law to show that it is unjust **4.** bus trips to protest segregation on interstate buses **5.** self-help through racial pride, solidarity, and economic enterprises **6.** hiring program to correct past racial injustices **7.** protesting segregation by sitting in a segregated area and refusing to move

SKILL BUILDER: READING A MAP

1. New York **2.** Northeast **3.** California
4. Georgia and Florida **5.** sixteen states

SKILL BUILDER: CRITICAL THINKING AND COMPREHENSION

I. Cause and Effect

1. Few African Americans could vote before 1960. **2.** It made African Americans inferior because if anything must be kept separate that implies inequality and thus inferiority. **3.** Rosa Parks refused to give up her seat on the bus to a white.

II. Fact versus Opinion

1. O **2.** F **3.** F **4.** O

III. Comparing and Contrasting

1. Malcolm X was a separatist, and King was not. Malcolm X didn't always believe in nonviolent protest, and King did.
2. The 1964 act outlawed all racial segregation in employment, education, and use of public places. The 1954 decision declared it unconstitutional to segregate schools on the basis of color.
3. Before 1960, African Americans seldom held office, and in many states they could not even vote. Now they vote, are routinely elected even in districts with white majorities, and have run for president.

USING PRIMARY SOURCES

Opinions will vary.

ENRICHMENT

1. Activities will vary.

UNIT 15 ❧ **CHAPTER 2**

VOCABULARY REVIEW

1. abridged **2.** leaves **3.** lobbied

SKILL BUILDING: READING A GRAPH

1. 19 million, 55 million **2.** 26 million, 36 million **3.** 1970–1980 **4.** 23 million, 12 million **5.** moving toward equal numbers of men and women **6.** there will be a few million more men than women

SKILL BUILDING: CRITICAL THINKING AND COMPREHENSION

I. Cause and Effect

1. labor-saving devices freed their time and energies **2.** women filled jobs left by men who went to war **3.** some women feared losing protection for themselves and support of children by divorced husbands; men who feared equality or didn't want to pay higher wages to women insist there are already laws to protect women's rights **4.** TV programs help people see how others live and thus reduce fear and distrust of strangers, and TV helps people get used to new ideas

II. Compare and Contrast

1. Schlafly—women will lose child support and special treatment from men, and the traditional family will break down if roles change. Friedan—women will never win equal rights until they act independently and demand them. **2.** Women in the 1950s were often housewives who had held men's jobs during the war and didn't want to give up the status and the income. Women in the 1980s gained equal pay in many areas and began to demand equal opportunity to be promoted, to borrow money for mortgages, and to hold jobs requiring physical strength. **3.** White women have been successful more quickly because they don't have to cross the color barrier presented by existing prejudice. African American women are far behind in gains.

III. Drawing Conclusions

1. Women have not yet achieved full equality. Some students may notice that the third fact listed does not say "parents have difficulty finding affordable daycare" but rather, "women" do, implying that women have the ultimate responsibility for child care. **2.** Women are breaking down barriers.

USING PRIMARY SOURCES

Opinions will vary.

ENRICHMENT

1–2. Activities will vary.

UNIT 15 ❧ **CHAPTER 3**

VOCABULARY REVIEW

ethnic studies—The study of history, philosophy, language, literature, and art forms of an ethnic group.
American Indian Chicago Conference—A meeting in 1961 of 500 Native Americans from 67 tribes that began the Native American Movement.
Indian Civil Rights Act—A law passed in 1968 granting full civil rights to all Native Americans.
Indian Self-Determination Act—A law passed in 1976 giving Native Americans a greater voice in the management of reservations.
La Raza—Spanish for "the race"; refers to all Spanish-speaking people in the Western Hemisphere.
National Farm Workers Association—The first labor union for farm workers, organized in 1965.
Freedom Airlift—Transportation by airplane of 4,000 Cubans to the United States in 1965.
Mariel boat people—A group of about 125,000 Cubans who in 1980 were allowed to leave Cuba by boat.

SKILL BUILDER: READING A MAP

1. California
2. about 3,700,000
3. Most Hispanic Americans live in the Southwest, where they can find jobs as farm workers.

SKILL BUILDER: CRITICAL THINKING AND COMPREHENSION

I. Comparing and Contrasting

Native American—militant organizations, sit-ins, marches, took over Alcatraz, the Bureau of Indian Affairs, and the town of Wounded Knee, SD; went to court to get money owed.
Hispanic American—organized farm workers and struck, organized voting registration to get Hispanic Americans elected.

II. Fact versus Opinion

a. F **b.** O **c.** O **d.** F

III. Making Judgments

Opinions will vary.

USING PRIMARY SOURCES

The basic right is to keep their own spiritual and cultural values that allow them to have a unique identity. Anglo-Americans took these rights away and took away also their entire continent of North America.

ENRICHMENT

Responses will vary.

UNIT 15 ❧ CHAPTER 4

VOCABULARY REVIEW

The definitions for these words can be found in the glossary on pages 681, 683, 679, 678, 685, and 682.

SKILL BUILDER: INTERPRETING A GRAPH

1. 1940
2. 15 million, 25 million
3. About 34 million; 2.5 million
4. 1960-1980
5. The over-65 population will increase.

SKILL BUILDER: CRITICAL THINKING AND COMPREHENSION

Paragraphs should mention the forming of an organization to get laws passed to fight discrimination. The Grey Panthers have had some success. The Black Panthers were less successful because racial discrimination is more deep-seated than age discrimination.

II. Fact versus Opinion

1. F 2. O 3. F 4. O 5. F

III. Making Judgments

Opinions may vary about accepting Russian immigrants, requiring citizens to vote, and the need to speak English to be considered a good citizen.

USING PRIMARY SOURCES

1. The government must legislate acceptable standards of education because the handicapped can't rely on the good-will of all administrators to provide it. **2.** It's important for voters to be able to monitor the activities of the people they elect to represent them.

ENRICHMENT

1–3. Students' activities will vary.

UNIT 15 ❧ CHAPTER 5

VOCABULARY REVIEW

1. addicts—People who are physically dependent on a drug.
2. homesteading—Settling on free land offered by the government under the Homestead Act.
3. suburbs—Small communities on the outskirts of a city.
4. subsidize—To give money, often by a government, as support or assistance.
5. pollution—Chemicals and other impurities in the air, water, and elsewhere in the environment.
6. recycling—Processing glass, metal, paper, and other substances so that they can be used again.

SKILL BUILDER: READING A MAP

1. Northeast

2. San Francisco, San Jose, Los Angeles, San Diego
3. Houston, New Orleans, San Antonio
4. Houston, Dallas, San Antonio, El Paso, Phoenix

SKILL BUILDER: CRITICAL THINKING AND COMPREHENSION

I. Predicting

1. Ideas can include limiting traffic, providing shuttle buses, recycling glass, plastic, and paper, and limiting the amounts and types of packaging allowed, among others. **2.** They can't get good-paying jobs and will stay poor or become poorer. **3.** It will become more impersonal and boring, and the people involved in the arts and those who support the arts will leave to create interesting communities elsewhere.

II. Fact versus Opinion

1. O 2. F 3. O 4. O

III. Making Judgments

1. Opinions will vary. **2.** Students should support their judgments with strong arguments.

USING PRIMARY SOURCES

Students' views will vary.

ENRICHMENT

Activities will vary.

UNIT 15 ❧ CHAPTER 6

VOCABULARY REVIEW

1. budget deficit **2.** social programs **3.** recession **4.** deregulation

SKILL BUILDER: INTERPRETING A CARTOON

1. Ronald Reagan
2. Because they affect his family directly
3. Because Republicans usually cut social programs to reduce government spending.
4. Reagan wanted to restore school prayer
5. Responses will vary

SKILL BUILDER: CRITICAL THINKING AND COMPREHENSION

I. Generalizing

1. Reagan wished to reduce the role of government in people's lives, lower taxes on businesses, cut the federal budget, increase military spending, and cut social programs. **2.** He cut expenditures for such social programs as welfare, food stamps, Medicaid, and aid to education. **3.** Bush convened a conference on the nation's schools and signed a tough bill to curb air pollution.

II. Drawing Conclusions

1. Reagan cut social programs. Bush warned he could not launch an expensive antidrug program, and he declared the states and local governments would have to pay for changes in education. **2.** Reagan appointed Sandra Day O'Connor and other conservatives to the Supreme Court. Bush also named conservatives to the Court, including Clarence Thomas. **3.** Bush named a drug czar to coordinate an antidrug campaign, proposed heavy jail sentences for drug dealers, and offered to help drug users get treatment.

III. Making Judgments

Students' opinions will vary.

ENRICHMENT

Reports will vary.

UNIT 15 ❧ CHAPTER 8

VOCABULARY REVIEW

1. use of systems of machines to do routine work **2.** to imitate **3.** an electronic machine that processes, retrieves, and stores data **4.** pieces of silicon smaller than a thumbnail that store information in a computer **5.** a hand-held machine that changes letters on a page into raised symbols, to aid the blind in reading **6.** an intense, amplified beam of light **7.** the ability to understand and operate computers **8.** jobs that do not require manual labor, such as managers, technicians, and sales people. **9.** a machine that x-rays a patient from different angles **10.** a machine that uses magnets and sounds in place of x-rays, eliminating exposure to radiation. **11.** a computer that translates spoken words into written form 12. narrow glass tubing that transmits light

SKILL BUILDER: READING A GRAPH

1. 42,000
2. 1984–1985
3. The use of robots will increase

SKILL BUILDER: CRITICAL THINKING AND COMPREHENSION

I. Generalizing
1. The multibillion-dollar computer industry has created many new jobs. Technology is helping doctors identify, prevent, and treat disease. New medical tools are making some handicapped people's lives easier. **2.** These people argue that automated machines take away jobs. Others feel that automation has contributed to workers' feeling unappreciated and dehumanized, or machine like.
II. Predicting
Students' predictions will vary but should all be in the direction of technological innovation.
III. Fact versus Opinion
Students' statements will vary.

USING PRIMARY SOURCES

Students' opinions about the need for personal accomplishment will vary.

ENRICHMENT

Activities will vary.

UNIT 15 ❧ CHAPTER 7

VOCABULARY REVIEW

1. c 2. d 3. b

SKILL BUILDER: USING AN ENCYCLOPEDIA

1. Malaysia, Indonesia, Amazon River Basin **2.** Brazil, Colombia **3.** Bolivia **4.** Central and South America, Central Africa **5.** Japan, Korea, and Taiwan

SKILL BUILDER: CRITICAL THINKING AND COMPREHENSION

1. D **2.** D **3.** M **4.** M **5.** M **6.** D
II. Summarizing
1. Supporters of funding warned that Nicaragua would become the center for Soviet influence in Central America. Opponents of funding insisted that Nicaragua was not a threat to the United States. **2.** Foreign-made goods poured into the country. By 1987, imports exceeded exports by $140 billion. **3.** Newspapers and television stations could now discuss their government openly, and non-Communist Party candidates were allowed to run for office.
III. Comparing and Contrasting
1. U.S. in Central America in 1980s: Americans sent economic and military aid to Nicaraguan rebels; advisors, weapons, and aircraft to El Salvador; and troops to Honduras to train Salvadorean and Honduran soldiers. U.S. role in Southeast Asia in the 1960s: began the same way as in Central America but escalated into a war involving mostly American troops, requiring a military draft for servicemen to fight, and a costly defense budget to tax for.
2. China enforced population control and strict censorship and employment laws. An attempt to ease restrictions resulted in a popular effort to gain even more freedom, causing a government backlash to restore order. The Soviet Union relaxed control and allowed more political freedom, but clamped down on ethnic groups that tried for greater local control. **3.** U.S.-Europe economic competition is similar to U.S.-Japan competition, resulting in a severe trade imbalance. **4.** Soviet-U.S. relations improved so rapidly in the late 1980s that the Cold War of the 1950s seemed almost totally turned around.

USING PRIMARY SOURCES

Students should understand the concept that to Americans liberty is more important than peace, and the Soviet Union had not yet granted total freedom to its people.

UNIT 15 ❧ CHAPTER 9

VOCABULARY REVIEW

1. destruction of forests **2.** polluted air often in cities, caused by auto exhaust **3.** the gradual warming of the earth because of too much carbon dioxide in the air **4.** a scientist who studies underwater plants and animals **5.** layer of gas that shields the earth from harmful ultraviolet rays **6.** scientists who study the relationship between organisms and the environment **7.** chemicals sprayed on food crops to kill harmful bugs and organisms

8. chemicals that destroy the ozone layer **9.** rainfall with heavy acid content **10.** toxic fumes released into the air from manufacturing plants

SKILL BUILDER: READING A CHART

1. Health and Human Services received the most money in 1990
2. Defense received the second largest amount of money in 1990
3. 170.8 billion
4. 3.6 billion
5. Two departments—Agriculture and Housing and Urban Development—got less money in 1990 than in 1985
6. From most money received to least—Health and Human Services, Defense, Treasury, Agriculture, Transportation, Labor, Education, Housing and Urban Development, Energy, Justice, Interior, State, Commerce.

SKILL BUILDER: CRITICAL THINKING AND COMPREHENSION

I. Predicting
Predictions will vary.
II. Point of View
1. Big Business **2.** Environmentalists **3.** Environmentalists, and some Big Business would agree **4.** Big Business
III. Making Judgments
Opinions will vary.

USING PRIMARY SOURCES

Opinions may vary, but even if other points of view are not supported they should be referred to.

ENRICHMENT

Activities will vary.

ANSWER KEY TO AMERICA'S PEOPLE FEATURES

UNIT 1 ❧ CHAPTER 2, *Page 14*
1. They reached the islands in double canoes with sails from Tahiti.
2. A powerful king or chief ruled each of the four island kingdoms. They were skilled in farming and fishing. They lived under a strict system of laws set down by chiefs and priests. They believed in powerful gods and goddesses.

UNIT 2 ❧ CHAPTER 6, *Page 74*
1. New Spain offered a chance to become wealthy by mining gold and silver. Land was cheap and opportunities for employment plentiful in the newly settled towns.
2. Most of the gold and silver mines were located in Mexico and Peru. Because these areas were more heavily settled, they were safer.

UNIT 3 ❧ CHAPTER 3, *Page 110*
1. The Portuguese captured the settlement. 2. Stuyvesant was prejudiced against Jews. The Dutch West Indies Company would not allow him to force Jews out because Jewish investors had helped to found the colony. 3. Answers will vary but should mention anti-Semitic prejudice.

UNIT 4 ❧ CHAPTER 2, *Page 134*
1. Africans were forced to come to America. Many had been captured or kidnapped and all were treated like mere cargo on the passage. Other colonists came because they hoped for a better life; the Africans had no such hope.
2. Answers will vary.

UNIT 5 ❧ CHAPTER 7, *Page 216*
1. They supported independence, and wanted to contribute to America's success.
2. Answers will vary.

UNIT 6 ❧ CHAPTER 5, *Page 282*
1. The early French travelers to the United States were fur trappers, traders, Catholic missionaries, and the Huguenots, French protestants who fled France for reasons of religious persecution.
2. In the French Revolution of 1789, the French king and nobles were overthrown. Many of these nobles, fearing for their lives and fortunes, fled to America as political refugees. In 1815, when the French king regained power, it was Napoleon's followers who fled to America.

3. The French influence is seen today in the United States in Louisiana, a former French colony.
4. At one time, the French had colonized so much of the United States, it was called "New France."

UNIT 7 ❧ CHAPTER 5, *Page 336*
1. Since 1849.
2. Through hard work, they helped build the first transcontinental railroad; they opened shops, restaurants, and other businesses; they worked in factories.

UNIT 8 ❧ CHAPTER 4, *Page 378*
1. The Irish came to the United States in the 1840s because of the potato famine.
2. The Irish gained acceptance after the Civil War because of their loyal service as soldiers and generals.

UNIT 9 ❧ CHAPTER 3, *Page 414*
1. American students would not go to kindergarten, take gym, or have vocational training.
2. German immigrants would have to learn to speak English and participate in a democratic system.

UNIT 10 ❧ CHAPTER 4, *Page 456*
1. The Italians, like the Irish, lived in cities under rather harsh conditions when they first came. Both groups experienced prejudice when they first arrived but later gained acceptance. Both groups contributed significantly to politics and the professions. Since the largest group of Italians came later in the 1800s, the cities were even more crowded and living conditions even more unhealthy until the cities were improved.
2. The padrone helped the immigrants get jobs. Since many of the immigrants were not familiar with ways of life in the United States and did not speak English, the padrone could easily trick the immigrants.
3. Education was important to the newcomers so that they could get jobs with higher pay and improve their living conditions.

UNIT 11 ❧ CHAPTER 5, *Page 498*
1. Limitation of immigration was a result of racial prejudice and intolerance by some Americans and fear that the immigrants were an economic threat. Students may disagree as to whether immigration should be limited.
2. Students may answer that the Japanese wanted official recognition that they had been wronged during World War II. Money payments were a lesser consideration. Students may disagree as to whether the Japanese requests were reasonable.

UNIT 12 ❧ CHAPTER 2, *Page 516*

1. Puerto Ricans enjoy a mixture of Spanish, African, and Native American culture in addition to the later American influence. They speak Spanish and English.

2. Puerto Ricans face prejudice and discrimination in the continental United States. Often, they must start from the bottom of the social and economic ladder.

UNIT 13 ❧ CHAPTER 5, *Page 570*

1. Mexican Americans joined the U.S. population by having lived in areas acquired from Mexico and by immigration.

2. Among their handicaps were lack of knowledge of English, poor education, and low-paying jobs. Their achievements include increasing numbers who enter the mainstream of American life, who hold high government positions, business people, and entertainers.

UNIT 14 ❧ CHAPTER 3, *Page 594*

1. The first wave of Koreans were all men; no women were allowed to come. The men moved to Hawaii to harvest sugar cane.

2. The Korean and Vietnam Wars caused greater numbers of Asians to immigrate to the United States than were previously allowed.

UNIT 15 ❧ CHAPTER 2, *Page 630*

1. To escape from Fidel Castro's communist Cuba.

2. Through determination, hard work, and the Cuban custom of helping one another, they achieved positions of prominence in local, state, and federal government.

3. Answers may vary. Students may point to the fact that many Cuban Americans came from backgrounds in business and the professions and the desire to make a new life as Americans.

ANSWER KEY TO LINKING GEOGRAPHY AND HISTORY FEATURES

UNIT 1 ❧ CHAPTER 3, *Page 20*
1. The mesas are shown in green, while the canyons are shown in beige; **2.** in Cliff Canyon; **3.** Indian cornfield demonstration plot, national park headquarters, picnic area, park roads.

UNIT 2 ❧ CHAPTER 2, *Page 50*
1. On his second voyage, Columbus visited Puerto Rico and other islands in the Caribbean.
2. Columbus landed on the continent of South America during his fourth voyage.
3. The winds and currents move in the same direction.

UNIT 3 ❧ CHAPTER 4, *Page 116*
1. The Fall Line separates the Piedmont from the Coastal Plain.
2. Savannah River
3. James River
4. Answers vary: Students might mention overcrowding, flooding, economic problems relating to trade.

UNIT 4 ❧ CHAPTER 7, *Page 164*
1. Potomac River, Shenandoah River, Susquehanna River
2. The American pioneers had to travel over ridge after ridge of the Appalachians while the French could travel west by water.
3. Answers will vary. Students should suggest that the mountains allowed only the most adventurous and the bravest to go west. The barrier encouraged differing life styles.

UNIT 5 ❧ CHAPTER 6, *Page 210*
1. The battles of Long Island and White Plains were fought in and around New York City.
2. The United States would have won control of the St. Lawrence River and Lake Champlain. The victory would have prevented the British army from advancing into New York.

UNIT 6 ❧ CHAPTER 4, *Page 276*
1. Six states—Minnesota, Wisconsin, Illinois, Indiana, Ohio, and Michigan—were formed from the Northwest Territory.
2. 36 sections make up a township. Each section is one mile (1.6 km) square and covers 640 acres (3 sq. km).
3. The one-mile square sections used in the township and range survey system made it easy to subdivide the land (into half-sections, quarter-sections, or even smaller units). The latitude-longitude grid used in the township and range survey system made the land easy to locate (by section number).

UNIT 7 ❧ CHAPTER 6, *Page 342*
1. In the central portion of the Great Plains; east and west;
2. The Goodnight-Loving Trail went to Cheyenne, Wyoming; the Chisholm Trail went to Ellsworth and Abilene, Kansas; The unnamed trail went to Ogallala, Nebraska; **3.** The grassy plains at the southern end of the Great Plains provided ample food for the cattle, unlike the drier northern portion of the Great Plains.

UNIT 8 ❧ CHAPTER 1, *Page 360*
1. In 1801, the main cotton-growing areas were North and South Carolina. Virginia and Georgia also grew cotton.
2. Large areas in Georgia, Alabama, Mississippi, Louisiana, Arkansas and eastern Texas, as well as parts of northern Florida, were planted with cotton between 1801 and 1860.
3. The best cotton-growing soils are in the Mississippi and Red River valleys, in eastern Texas, and in central Alabama.

UNIT 9 ❧ CHAPTER 2, *Page 408*
1. Each side in a war needs to protect its land and break up the enemy's defenses. Answers to the second question will vary, but yes is a reasonable answer since a defense of territory or defeat of an enemy would have positive results.
2. Gettysburg was close to Washington, D.C. The Southern army could have captured the capital if it had won at Gettysburg.

UNIT 10 ❧ CHAPTER 2, *Page 444*
1. Youngstown, Ohio and Pittsburgh, Pennsylvania are located within the coal field area; Sandusky and Cleveland, Ohio and Erie, Pennsylvania are close by.
2. Duluth, Minnesota and Ashland, Wisconsin developed close to the Lake Superior iron ore fields. Sault Ste. Marie, in Canada, might also be mentioned.
3. Movement of coal and iron ore on the Great Lakes helped the lakeshore cities grow.

UNIT 11 ❧ CHAPTER 2, *Page 480*
1. Banking, insurance, selling of capital goods such as farm equipment, and other financial functions, as well as some rail-roading; **2.** Receiving grain to be fed to animals in the stock-yards and livestock to be slaughtered and packed for shipment out of the city; **3.** Chicago was a rail center, where railroad lines from the West and Midwest brought their farm and manufactured products to be processed and/or shipped by railroads going to the East and South. The lines from the East also brought manufactured products to Chicago for shipment to the West and Midwest.

UNIT 12 ❧ CHAPTER 3, *Page 522*
1. The Panama Canal drastically reduced the distance between the Atlantic and the Pacific oceans, making travel to Hawaii from the eastern United States much shorter.
2. The Hawaiian Islands provided a strategic location in the middle of the Pacific. The islands also could be used as a protective outpost for the west coast of the United States.
3. Alaska provides a location that controls the northern part of the Pacific and an outpost close to Asia.

UNIT 13 ❧ CHAPTER 2, *Page 552*

1. Nebraska, Kansas, Oklahoma, Texas, New Mexico, and Colorado; **2.** Areas outside of the line usually received enough rain for normal farming, while areas that received less than 20 inches (50 cm) received too little rain. **3.** Answers will vary. Students who think farming was good for the Dust Bowl region may state that the region has enough rainy years for farmers to do well there. Students who believe farming was bad for the region may point to the hardship caused farmers in dry years and the loss of the soil in dust storms.

UNIT 14 ❧ CHAPTER 4, *Page 600*

1. Most of the oil fields and tanker terminals are around the Persian Gulf.
2. Iraq, Iran, Saudi Arabia, Kuwait, Qatar, Bahrain, Oman, United Arab Emirates
3. Iraq, Iran, Kuwait, Saudi Arabia, Qatar, United Arab Emirates

UNIT 15 ❧ CHAPTER 5, *Page 642*

1. About 75 miles (about 120 km); **2.** About 60 miles (about 96 km); **3.** Benefits include ability to avoid the congestion of a central city and access to recreational facilities and varied physical environment. Harmful effects are the need to travel long distances on crowded freeways to jobs, the cost of fuel for such travel, and the resulting pollution of the air from automobiles.

Page 246,   column 2
1. "We the people of the United States . . . ."
2. Answers will vary.

Page 248,   column 1
1. At least 25 years old, a U.S. citizen for seven years, live in state from which elected.
2. Because it makes the laws of the nation.

Page 248,   column 2
1. On the basis of the state's population.
2. Because he or she presides over the House.

Page 249,   columns 1 and 2
1. Be at least 30 years old, be a U.S. citizen for nine years, live in the state from which elected.
2. House 435 members, Senate 100 members; House 2 years, Senate six years; House at least 25 years old and a citizen for seven years; Senate at least 30 years old and a citizen for nine years.

Page 250,   column 1
1. Each house decides on its members.
2. So that there is a clear understanding of the rules in case of disputes.

Page 250,   column 2
1. So that they may feel free to say what they believe is important without fear of being sued or arrested for their statements.
2. So that they may devote all their time to being legislators and to avoid any possible conflict of interest between their responsibilities as legislators and allegiance to outside work or individuals.

Page 251,   column 2
1. Congress may override the veto by a two-thirds vote.
2. So that the exact procedure is understood by all, thus avoiding the likelihood of disputes about procedure.

Page 252,   column 2
1. Levy taxes and borrow money.
2. Because the Articles of Confederation gave the Congress little or no power with respect to money and because the raising and issuing of money is an important function of the federal government.

Page 253,   column 1
1. By passing laws.
2. Without such laws, the powers cannot be exercised.

Page 254,   column 1
1. An appropriations law must be passed.
2. Answers will vary.

Page 254,   column 2
1. Punish a person without a trial, pass ex post facto laws, pass laws allowing persons not to carry out contracts, make persons nobles.

2. Because a person has a right to know whether an act that he or she may not be punished for is legal at the time the act is committed.

Page 255,   column 2
1. Carry out the laws passed by Congress.

Page 256,   column 1
2. Because, in addition to carrying out the laws, he or she conducts foreign policy and appoints persons to important positions in the Executive Branch and the Judicial Branch.

Page 256,   column 2
1. Be at least 35 years old, be a native-born citizen, and have lived in the U.S. for at least 14 years.
2. So that Congress cannot punish a President by lowering his or her salary or reward a President by increasing it.

Page 257,   column 2
1. Appointment of ambassadors to foreign countries and justices of the Supreme Court.
2. Because he or she is the one individual who represents or stands for the United States in the eyes of the public and foreign countries.

Page 258,   column 2, top
1. The President may suggest laws that he or she would like to have enacted and he or she has to sign or veto bills passed by Congress.
2. Answers will vary.

Page 258,   column 2, middle
1. If convicted of treason, bribery, or other serious crimes.

Page 260,   column 1
1. The Judicial Branch is made up of the Supreme Court and the lower federal courts. Its main duty is to hear cases involving U.S. laws.
2. The Supreme Court is the highest court of appeal and rules on issues of constitutionality.

Page 260,   column 2
1. Because it involves betrayal of one's country and might result in the country's defeat and/or loss of life of one's fellow citizens.
2. Have the testimony of at least two people to the crime.

Page 261,   column 2
1. The country would no longer be a nation of "united" states and persons who are favored by one state's laws might move to that state, to the loss of the original state.
2. Request the return of a person charged with a crime who has fled to another state.
3. The federal government would order the state legislature reinstated.

Page 262, column 2, bottom
1. The state law is nullified.

Page 263, column 1
1. The Constitution would not have gone into effect.

Page 264, Amendment 1
1. Freedom of religion, speech, press, right to hold meetings, ask the government to correct wrongs.
2. To prevent the government from depriving people of the liberties listed, some of which were denied under British rule.

Page 264, Amendment 2
1. Because the courts have decided that the amendment applies only to state militias.

Page 265, Amendment 4
1. Obtain a warrant.
2. They protect citizens from practices of the British under colonial rule.

Page 266, Amendment 5
1. A person cannot be tried for a federal crime unless accused of it by a grand jury, cannot be forced to give evidence against himself or herself, cannot be deprived of life, freedom, or property without due process of law.
2. Pay for the property.

Page 266, Amendment 6
1. Public trial, held in a reasonable time, in the part of the state where the crime occurred, with the accused able to hear witnesses, have a lawyer, and call witnesses.

Page 266, Amendment 9
1. No, because the amendment states that the fact that a right is not mentioned in the Constitution does not mean that an individual may not have that right.

Page 267, Amendment 10
1. Yes, because the amendment provides for the states to have those rights that are not given to the federal government.
2. Increases the power of the states because they have all powers not specifically given to the federal government. Students should understand, however, that this amendment does not give the states unlimited powers. Thus, for example, the states may not exercise their powers in such a way as to endanger the federal government, as they would if they decided to tax the federal government.

Page 268, Amendment 12, column 1, top
1. The House of Representatives chooses the President, the Senate chooses the Vice-President.
2. The separation of electors' votes for President and Vice-President prevents the situation that arose in the 1800 election from arising again. In that election, no distinction was made between candidates for President and Vice-President, with the result that Thomas Jefferson, who was assumed to be the presidential candidate, and Aaron Burr, who was thought to be running for Vice-President, received the same number of electoral votes, and the election was thrown into the House of Representatives. Under the amendment, electors know which candidate has run for which office.
3. Because, in the event of the President's death, he or she would be succeeded by a Vice-President with broadly the same political point of view as the deceased Chief Executive.

Page 268, Amendment 13, column 1, bottom
1. It forbids slavery.
2. Criminals, as part of their punishment.

Page 269, Amendment 14, column 2, top
1. Gave freed slaves citizenship and provided that rights of citizens could not be taken away without due process of law.
2. Because until the end of the Civil War, when slavery was abolished and thousands of former slaves became free, there had been no need to define the rights of citizens and how these rights had to be safeguarded. Students may be interested in knowing that Native Americans were not granted citizenship until 1924.

Page 269, Amendment 15, column 2, mid-page
1. It gave them the right to vote.

Page 269, Amendment 16, column 2, bottom
1. To allow the federal government to raise more money than it was able to under its taxing power in existence until then.

Page 270, Amendment 17
1. By allowing the people to decide for themselves whom to vote for, instead of allowing state legislators to decide for them.
2. Hold a special election or appoint a person to fill the seat until the next senatorial election.

Page 270, Amendment 19
1. Because most states did not allow women to vote in any elections, and, although women could vote in a number of states, in these states, they could not vote for national offices.

Page 271, Amendment 20
1. The Vice-President-elect.

Page 272, Amendment 22, column 1
1. Because the amendment applied to Presidents who came after Roosevelt.

Page 272, Amendment 24, column 2
1. With the poll tax outlawed, the number of voters in these states increased substantially.

Page 273, Amendment 25, column 2, mid-page
1. Name a person as Vice-President, subject to approval by a majority of both houses of Congress

Page 273, Amendment 26, column 2, bottom
1. Answers will vary.

UNIT 1, *Pages 4-5*
❧ Two Attitudes Toward the Land
1. Native Americans believed that people were part of nature and shared it with other creatures. Non-Indians believe in using nature to their own advantage, even if, regrettably, it results in setting a river on fire.
2. Answers will vary. Students may point out that the Native American view does not encourage the development of society beyond the subsistence level, while non-Indians believe that people should take advantage of the potential for improving life that is available in nature.

UNIT 2, *Pages 40-41*
❧ A New World Appears
1. Depends on the route chosen from point of origin.
2. The value of the land for mining and farming was probably exaggerated. Although it would prove to be true, Columbus would have no way of knowing this at such an early stage of exploration. Exaggeration enhanced the prestige of his discovery.

UNIT 3, *Pages 94-95*
❧ Toleration For and Against
1. People who listen to heretics must pay a fine. Heretics themselves could be exiled, sent to prison, and fined.
2. Freedom of conscience to worship as one believed was necessary for happiness. In Pennsylvania, anyone believing in one almighty God could worship in freedom.

UNIT 4, *Pages 124-125*
❧ The American Colonies and Their Future
1. De Crèvecoeur felt that America would be great because there were no noble families, there was not too much difference between rich and poor, government was fair, people worked hard, and people would become united. Burnaby felt that America would fail because of slavery, the great differences between people from different backgrounds and religions, and the different interests of the colonies.
2. Answers will vary: Students might point out that Burnaby was an Englishman who might have been reacting to the resentment the colonists felt toward Great Britain. De Crèvecoeur, a Frenchman, might have seen America as an example of an ideal society that was opposite of the France of the time.

UNIT 5, *Pages 172-173*
❧ Taxation Without Representation
1. They believed that control of the right of taxation was "essential to the freedom of a people."
2. The British government held to the belief that it was superior in all matters affecting the colonies.
3. A serious conflict seems very likely.

UNIT 6, *Pages 224-225*
❧ Deciding on a New Form of Government
1. He felt that unless Americans took strong action to unify the country, a tyrant might seize power in the growing confusion and/or a monarchy might replace democracy in America.
2. He praised it as having been strong enough to have carried the country through a long and dangerous war.

3. He felt a central government that had more power than the states was dangerous. He believed that the state governments, and not the people, were the soul of the government.

UNIT 7, *Pages 308-309*
❧ Settlers and Native Americans
1. He wanted others to settle in California.
2. Answers may vary, but should include these major points: Settlers would think of the land as something to use and to transform to their needs, unlike the Native Americans, who believed that the land was a part of nature and should not be abused.

UNIT 8, *Pages 356-357*
❧ Slavery Is Debated
1. Charles Burleigh thinks that it is wrong because enslaved people are robbed of basic rights such as their dignity as human beings, education, and legal marriage. James Henry Hammond thinks that slavery is good because he believes the African race is inferior to the white race and, for that reason, is well adapted to slavery.
2. Burleigh thinks that African Americans seem inferior because they are working at a disadvantage; they have always had to struggle against difficulties that white people have not had. Hammond thinks that the African Americans are inferior because he thinks that the African race itself is inferior to the white race.

UNIT 9, *Pages 398-399*
❧ Secession
1. Secession is a crime because it is a violation of the law.
2. Secession must take place so that an independent government can right the wrongs that the state has been subjected to. The "wrongs" are not specified, but they almost certainly have to do with federal, and particularly Republican party, claims to precedence over state governments.

UNIT 10, *Pages 434-435*
❧ City Life in Industrial America
1. Manufacturers can carry on their work more profitably if they group together in the same area.
2. The Boston writer would probably point out that "the best in life" was not available to all people.

UNIT 11, *Pages 470-471*
❧ How to Deal with America's Problems
1. The changes may not work and may not be reversible.
2. Religious and moral teaching, education to train people for service, fair division of industry's profits, government to share in promoting these goals.
3. Answers will vary.

UNIT 12, *Pages 506-507*
❧ American Expansion—For and Against
1. Beveridge states that Americans are creating more agricultural

and industrial products than they can consume so they must trade. In addition, American culture, law, and government must be spread throughout the world. People who might agree would be the industrialists, cash crop farmers, those owning transportation systems, and others who stood to benefit from increased trade.

2. Schurz feels that imperialism is contrary to the basic ideas of liberty that the United States was founded upon. Imperialism was anti-democratic because people would not be allowed to participate in the decision-making process. People who would agree with Schurz would be many of the citizens of countries in danger of being taken over and those who believed strongly in the ideas of the Declaration of Independence and the Constitution.

UNIT 13, *Pages 542-543*
Government and the Economy
1. Hoover. He believed such a government would hurt liberty and freedom, increase abuse and corruption, discourage the development of leadership, hamper people's mental and spiritual energies, and end the spirit of liberty and progress.
2. Answers will vary. Based on Roosevelt's use of laws to help move the country out of the Great Depression, some students may conclude that he would want to support laws to save the environment. Other students may disagree, claiming that, for example, the environmental crisis is not as severe as the depression and would not require legislative action.

UNIT 14, *Pages 578-579*
The Cold War of Words
1. Truman accuses the Soviet Union of taking away the freedom of part of Europe, and of trying to bring the rest of the continent under its control.
2. Zhdanov says that the Marshall Plan is part of a larger United States strategy to expand its control throughout the world.

UNIT 15, *Pages 614-615*
Looking to Tomorrow
1. Some similar problems are drugs, the homeless and poor, racism, and education. Opinions and reasons will vary.
2. Opinions and reasons will vary.
3. Opinions and answers will vary.

ANSWER KEY TO UNIT REVIEWS

UNIT 1 ❧ REVIEW, *Pages 36-37*

SKILL BUILDER: READING A MAP

1. by fishing and gathering seeds and acorns
2. in the Subarctic
3. Eastern Woodlands, Southeast, Plains
4. maize
5. Plains, Arctic

SKILL BUILDER: CRITICAL THINKING AND COMPREHENSION

I. Comparing and Contrasting
1. Plains Indians: buffalo; Subarctic: caribou.
2. Southeast Woodlands: maize, tobacco, and cotton; Southwest: maize
3. Plains Indians: tepees; Subarctic: igloos
4. Eastern Woodlands: long houses; Pacific Northwest Coast: frame houses

II. Main Idea
1. Chapter 5   2. Chapter 2   3. Chapter 3
4. Chapter 1   5. Chapter 4

ENRICHMENT

1. Commercials will vary but should reflect an understanding of the people chosen based on the text.
2. Pictures and talks will vary.

UNIT 2 ❧ REVIEW, *Pages 90-91*

SKILL BUILDER: READING A MAP

1. Santo Domingo
2. Hispaniola
3. Atlantic Ocean, Caribbean Sea, Gulf of Mexico
4. Guadalajara
5. Travel by water was easier than travel by land. Much of the interior of the continent was unexplored at the time shown on this map.

SKILL BUILDER: CRITICAL THINKING AND COMPREHENSION

I. Generalizing
1. Spain's influence in the New World was strong because the Spanish had claimed large areas of land by 1614.
2. Christopher Columbus's discoveries in the New World were very important. They led to the exploration and settlement of two huge continents that had been unknown to Europeans of Columbus's time.

II. Summarizing
Answers will vary, depending on the person chosen. Be sure students focus on the main ideas in their summaries.

III. Classifying
French: Marquette, Champlain, La Salle
Spanish: de Las Casas, Cortés, De Soto
English: Sir Walter Raleigh, Queen Elizabeth I, Captain John Smith
Native American: Montezuma, Pocahontas, Doña Marina

ENRICHMENT

1. The conversation should reflect a knowledge of events surrounding the Spanish conquest of Mexico and the relatively cordial relationship between the French and the Huron.

2. Answers will vary, depending on the settlement chosen. The letters should reflect appropriate historical details from Unit 2 relating to each location.
3. Answers will vary, but should reflect knowledge of the contributions of the explorer chosen.

UNIT 3 ❧ REVIEW, *Pages 120-121*

SKILL BUILDER: READING A MAP

1. Mexico City, Acapulco, Veracruz
2. England
3. Most were located on the east coast because transportation, trade, and communication were more easily accomplished.

SKILL BUILDER: CRITICAL THINKING AND COMPREHENSION

I. Classifying
1. d 2. e 3. f 4. b 5. c 6. a 7. g, h

II. Generalizing
1. Sentences will vary.
2. Sentences will vary.
3. Sentences will vary.

ENRICHMENT

1. Colonies will vary.
2. Reports will vary.
3. Answers will vary. Students should recognize that both documents set up rules for the colonies. The Act of Toleration dealt with freedom of worship, while the Mayflower Compact established a form of government.

UNIT 4 ❧ REVIEW, *Pages 168-169*

SKILL BUILDER: READING A MAP

1. Light orange
2. The Dutch (Netherlands)
3. Spain
4. France

SKILL BUILDER: CRITICAL THINKING AND COMPREHENSION

I. Main Idea
1. **Main idea:** Religious beliefs were very important in the colonies of the New World
Details: New Spain was greatly influenced by the Roman Catholic Church. The New England colonies did not allow religious freedom for all citizens. In Pennsylvania, all citizens who believed in Jesus were allowed to worship freely. All thirteen colonies had Blue Laws that prohibited work or. Sunday.
2. **Main idea:** Trade was an important source of income for American colonies.
Details: Fur trappers in New France collected furs to be sent to Europe. New England sent dried fish to many European nations. Spain imported silver and other products from her colonies to the New World. Great Britain wanted forest products and tobacco from the thirteen colonies.

II. Classifying

New England: fur trading, farming, education, triangular trade, whaling, colleges

Middle Colonies: farming, royal colony, religious tolerance, education, cash crops

Southern Colony: royal colony, large farms/plantations, triangular trade, slavery, tobacco, indigo

New France: fur trading, farming, Roman Catholic Church

New Spain: farming, Roman Catholic Church, strict social classes, mining

ENRICHMENT

1. The television news programs will vary.
2. The secret communiques will vary. Evaluations should be based on facts.

UNIT 5 ✍ REVIEW, *Pages 220-221*

SKILL BUILDER: READING A MAP

1. British North America.
2. Great Britain
3. The Mississippi River.
4. Spain.
5. Spain; New Orleans controlled the mouth of the Mississippi River.
6. Spain.

SKILL BUILDER: CRITICAL THINKING AND COMPREHENSION

I. Predicting

Answers will vary, but should be backed up with facts. The likeliest reason to predict conflict along the border is the history of conflict during the Revolution. The likeliest reason to predict friendly relations is the similarity in background of the two peoples.

II. Point of View

1 and 2. Paragraphs will vary, but should demonstrate a basic understanding of the event being described.

ENRICHMENT

1. Articles should follow the basic journalistic guidelines, as specified, but the more important consideration is that they be historically accurate.
2. Arguments should be based on the experience of the colonies as discussed in these chapters as well as in other sources the students may consult.

UNIT 6 ✍ REVIEW, *Pages 304-305*

SKILL BUILDER: READING A MAP

1. The states of Mississippi, Alabama, Missouri, Illinois, Maine, and Indiana joined the Union after 1812.
2. The Louisiana Territory was acquired in 1803.
3. Explorers could reach the Louisiana Purchase and the Oregon Territory by following the Missouri River westward.
4. Louisiana was the only state west of the Mississippi before 1820.
5. All of Texas, New Mexico, Arizona, California, Nevada, Utah, and parts of Wyoming, Colorado, Oklahoma, and Kansas belonged to Mexico in 1825.

SKILL BUILDER: CRITICAL THINKING AND COMPREHENSION

I. Point of View

1. a. Federalists favored a national bank which, they argued, would help the government to collect taxes, control trade, and support the nation's defense. Anti-Federalists opposed a national bank which, they argued, would spend instead of save the people's money.

b. Federalists supported a strong central government over state governments; anti-Federalists wanted only a loose confederation of states, with state governments having more power than the national government.

2. Henry Clay and his supporters (mainly western settlers and Southerners) wanted war, arguing it was the only way to uphold America's honor on the seas. They also saw war as a way to gain valuable lands in British Canada and Spanish Florida. President Monroe and northeastern farmers and merchants opposed war.

II. Summarizing

1. Western farmers needed a port on the Gulf of Mexico from which to ship their surplus crops east. Spain granted them a right of deposit in New Orleans, which was threatened when France took this territory from Spain. Then Napoleon, looking for a way to raise money to pay his army and win his war for control of Europe, astounded President Jefferson by offering to sell the Louisiana Territory to the United States.

2. The government passed an ordinance that broke up the Northwest Territory into townships. It used a survey system that made it easy to give out land to settlers and to locate land. This Northwest Ordinance also told how the territory would be governed, with a bill of rights for white male settlers and provided monies for each township's public schools. Congress built the National Road to carry settlers westward and speed the movement of people and goods.

ENRICHMENT

1. Answers will vary.
2. Answers will vary.
3. Answers will vary. Students should note that British-American relations were poor before the War of 1812, and greatly improved after the war.

UNIT 7 ✍ REVIEW, *Pages 352-353*

SKILL BUILDER: READING A MAP

1. California
2. six
3. Minnesota Territory, New Mexico Territory, Utah Territory, Oregon Territory, Indian Territory, Indian Country
4. Mexico
5. Great Britain.
6. Florida
7. In 1850 U.S. territory extended to the Pacific, with large areas having been acquired from Mexico; in 1850, all areas east of the Mississippi were now states; in 1825, only two states west of the Mississippi, in 1850, six states.

I. Comparing and Contrasting

1. At Spanish missions Native Americans were taught farming and trades. On the other hand, the Native Americans were often treated harshly and were made to convert to Christianity. In the period of the Spanish missions, the number of Native Americans under Spanish control diminished markedly. The U.S. government made no attempt to teach Native Americans. In fact, by killing off the buffalo, Americans deprived Native Americans of the Great Plains of their main source of food and tools. By moving Native Americans onto reservations, the government forced them to change their ways of life.

2. The Mormons always kept their strong faith in their way of life and were able to adapt to the new places in which they lived. In Nauvoo, for example, they built a prosperous community and in Utah they transformed the desert into rich farmland. Native Americans in their contact with settlers and other white people were deprived of the most basic aspects of their traditional culture such as food sources and ideas about the land and had great difficulty adapting to new ways of living.

3. Texas broke away from Mexico, of which it had been a part, and became an independent republic. It then asked to be admitted as a state of the United States. California was also a part of Mexico, but it became part of the United States by the treaty that ended the War with Mexico. After the Gold Rush, California became a state.

II. Drawing Conclusions

1. c. The Mormons were not Native Americans.

ENRICHMENT

1 and 2. Pictures and stories will vary.

UNIT 8 REVIEW, *Pages 394-395*

SKILL BUILDER: READING A MAP

1. 18 free states; 15 slave states
2. Between Missouri and Arkansas
3. Washington, Utah, New Mexico, Nebraska, Kansas, Unorganized Territories
4. Kansas became a free state. The principle of popular sovereignty was applied in New Mexico and Utah. These areas, together with Washington and Nebraska, might be more likely to become free states than slave states, since their climate would not be appropriate for crops that depended on slave labor.

SKILL BUILDING: CRITICAL THINKING AND COMPREHENSION

I. Contrasting and Comparing

1. Answers will vary, but should include the following: African American slaves had no opportunities for formal education, in fact in many states it was illegal for them to learn to read and write; factory workers could legally obtain education, but might have limited opportunities to do so because of child labor. Working conditions were poor for both groups; a field slave worked outdoors doing hard physical labor, while a factory worker worked indoors, doing monotonous tasks over and over. A factory worker was free to change jobs whereas a slave had to do whatever job he or she was assigned. Neither group would have much time to enjoy their families because of long working hours; in addition, slave marriages were not legally recognized in the south, and members of the same family could be sold to separate owners.
2. Answers might include the following: Neither group of African Americans could vote or testify against a white person in court in most states. Free African Americans could receive pay for their work, own property, legally marry, and travel where they pleased. Slaves had none of these rights.

II. Making Judgments

1. Students might make the judgment that the main cause of differences of opinion about slavery was the fact that the powerful owners of large southern plantations were economically dependent on African American slave labor.
2. Many southern planters made the judgment that slaves were better off under slavery because they believed that African Americans were inferior to other Americans and were not able to care for themselves.
3. Many Northerners made the judgment that protecting the way of life that existed in the South was less important than abolishing slavery, which they felt was an evil that should not be tolerated.

III. Cause and Effect

1. Either of these effects would be acceptable: Cotton farming became more profitable; or, slavery grew rapidly.
2. effect: Many Southern farmers moved west, and the question of slavery in the territories grew in importance.

3. cause: New machinery was developed that made cotton manufacturing easier and faster.
4. cause: John Brown, a Northern abolitionist, led a raid at Harper's Ferry, Virginia, for which he was convicted and hanged.

ENRICHMENT

1. Letters or diary entries should include descriptions of working and living conditions for African American plantation slaves such as: long working hours, lack of freedom to move around without owner's permission, punishments such as whipping for disobedience or not meeting work quotas. Students might also describe African music and folklore that was preserved and handed down by African Americans in the New World.
2. Posters might include biographical details that would demonstrate either man's qualifications to speak on abolitionist themes; slogans or phrases stressing the evils of slavery might also be included.
3. Answers will vary.

UNIT 9 REVIEW, *Pages 430-431*

SKILL BUILDER: READING A MAP

1. 37
2. Washington, Idaho, Montana, Dakota, Wyoming, Utah, Colorado, Arizona, New Mexico, and the Indian Territory (Oklahoma).
3. Alaska.
4. The Pacific Ocean; the border with Mexico, as established by the Texas Annexation, the Mexican Cession, and the Gadsden Purchase; the Atlantic Ocean.
5. Controlled by Great Britain: British Honduras, Jamaica, British Columbia, the eastern tip of North America (Newfoundland and Labrador, not labeled), and a number of islands in the Arctic Ocean. Controlled by Spain: Cuba and Puerto Rico.

SKILL BUILDER: CRITICAL THINKING AND COMPREHENSION

I. Summarizing

Summaries will vary, but should reflect the following basic information:
a. Union forces under Grant took Vicksburg on July 4, 1863, after a six-week siege. The victory assured Union control of the entire length of the Mississippi River.
b. In 1865, the Confederacy collapsed. On April 9, 1865, Lee met Grant at Appomattox and surrendered his army to Grant.
c. Jefferson Davis was chosen as first president of the Confederate States and inaugurated at Montgomery, Alabama, then the Confederate capital, in February 1861.
d. Blanche K. Bruce, who escaped from slavery in 1861 and became wealthy after the Civil War, was elected to the Senate from Mississippi in 1874 and sworn in the following year. He was the first African American to serve a full term as senator.
e. Booker T. Washington believed that what was most important for African Americans was developing economic skills, and to that end founded Tuskegee Institute in Alabama.
f. At his inauguration in 1861, Lincoln said that no state had the right to secede. He asked the Southern states to return to the Union.

II. Point of View

1. The likely author is Booker T. Washington. The strongest evidence is the second sentence. Every other reference to working hard and starting at the bottom may also be taken as a clue.
2. Du Bois would be likely to oppose these views. He believed that African Americans had rights as United States citizens and should not have to "prove" themselves in any way to claim those rights. **3 and 4.** Paragraphs will vary.

ENRICHMENT

1. Students' letters should demonstrate an understanding of the basic issues of the Civil War, and they should clearly reflect either a Union or a Confederate point of view. **2.** Reports of this research may be either oral or written.

UNIT 10 ⅍ REVIEW, *Pages 466-467*

SKILL BUILDER: READING A MAP

1. In Pennsylvania, West Virginia, and Kentucky; in Illinois and nearby states in the Midwest; and in the west, in Wyoming and the states directly north of it.
2. Alabama
3. the Great Lakes; also in Canada, on the northern Atlantic Ocean.
4. Quebec and Labrador. Iron from these fields would probably not have been used for steel by the United States in 1900, because iron was plentiful in the United States in areas much closer to the U.S. coal deposits.

SKILL BUILDER: CRITICAL THINKING AND COMPREHENSION

I. Point of View
1. John D. Rockefeller
2. Jane Addams
3. John D. Rockefeller, Henry Ford
4. Henry Ford
5. Jane Addams
II. Predicting
1. b. I will place an ad for my store in the newspaper.
2. b. The peasant goes to America, gets a job, and later sends for his family.

ENRICHMENT

1. Answers will vary, depending on the invention chosen.
2. Answers will vary.

UNIT 11 ⅍ REVIEW, *Pages 502-503*

SKILL BUILDER: READING A MAP

1. Newfoundland, British Honduras
2. Puerto Rico
3. Bahamas
4. Alaska
5. Canada: Maine, New Hampshire, Vermont, New York, Michigan, Minnesota, North Dakota, Montana, Idaho, Washington. Mexico: Texas, New Mexico, Arizona, California
I. Generalizing
1. "Farmers, still troubled by hard times, helped form the Populist party in the 1890s." (Chapter 2, paragraph 8.) "Almost from the time factories were first set up in the United States, workers united to improve working conditions." (Chapter 1, paragraph 2)
2. "After Mott and Stanton returned from London in 1840, they began organizing the women's rights movement." (Chapter 3, paragraph 3) "By 1900 women had gained many rights that had been denied them in the 1840s." (Chapter 3, paragraph 8) "It was a long road from Seneca Falls to the adoption of the Nineteenth Amendment, which gave women the right to vote." (Chapter 3, paragraph 13)
II. Comparing and Contrasting
1. The student paragraphs may include the following:
Rural life was hard because of the low prices farmers received for their crops and the railroads' unfair treatment. The Grange helped farmers by providing social life and information on how to improve their farming methods. Farmers helped form the Populist party to improve their economic condition. Life for city workers was also hard. Wages were low and they had to work long hours. They were subject to injuries in the factories and were not paid for time lost from work. To improve their lot, they formed unions, which served a roughly similar purpose for workers as the Grange did for farmers. Through the unions workers were able to get a shorter work day and other improvements in working conditions. Although the Knights of Labor had political goals, as did the farmers' Populist party, the more successful labor organization, the American Federation of Labor, avoided political activity.
2. The chart should include the following:
corrupt government, unfair business practices, monopolies, child labor, production of unhealthful food, prison reform, care of the mentally ill, immigration.
III. Making Judgments
1. Answers will vary. Students who believe unions properly represented their members may point to the gains unions achieved in working conditions, hours of work, and wages. Students who take the opposite position may point out that the while unions were responsible for improvements, there was still much to be done for working people. Wages, although higher than before, were still low, hours were still long compared to today's working day, and many unions resorted to strikes that were sometimes violent and antagonized the general public.
2. Any event may be selected provided the student supports the choice with a plausible reason or reasons.

ENRICHMENT

Answers will vary.

UNIT 12 ⅍ REVIEW, *Pages 538-539*

SKILL BUILDER: READING A MAP

1. green
2. Kamerun, Namibia, German East Africa
3. Mexico

SKILL BUILDER: CRITICAL THINKING AND COMPREHENSION

I. Point of View
1. A Cuban
2. A Puerto Rican
3. An American
4. A Filipino
5. A Panamanian
6. A Hawaiian
II. Comparing and Contrasting
1. Answers will vary. Some similarities: both involve American efforts to open trade in Asia; on occasion U.S. employed the military. Some differences: U.S. opened trade with Japan; in China, Europe had already carved out large areas of influence; In Japan, the U.S. showed military force but in China they fought the Boxers along with European troops.
2. Some similarities: Both wars fought on foreign soil; newspapers stirred up feelings. Differences: U.S. wanted to free Cuba from Spain; U.S. involvement in WW I occurred because of financial considerations, German submarine warfare, and dislike of German aggression in Belgium; trench warfare, submarines, gas used in WW I not in Spanish American war.

ENRICHMENT

1. Plays will vary.
2. Letters to the editor will vary.

UNIT 13 ❧ REVIEW, *Pages 574-575*

SKILL BUILDER: READING A MAP

1. The Allies and the Axis
2. The Axis; Europe
3. Great Britain
4. part of China, the countries of Southeast Asia, and the Dutch East Indies
5. Sweden, Portugal, Spain, Switzerland
6. North America, South America, Australia

I. Main Idea
1. d is the main idea; a, b, and c are supporting details.
2. b is the main idea; a, c,, and d are supporting details.

II Fact versus Opinion
1. Opinion
2. Fact
3. Fact
4. Opinion
5. Opinion

ENRICHMENT

1.–2. Radio plays and diary entries will vary.

UNIT 14 ❧ REVIEW, *Pages 610-611*

SKILL BUILDER: INTERPRETING A MAP

1. In Europe: mainly in the middle, but also at the far northern and southeastern extremities; also in Asia, at the eastern end of Turkey.
2. Cuba (near Florida) and the Soviet Union (near Alaska).
3. Paragraphs will vary, but should reflect the fact that Greenland and Canada lie directly between the two superpowers and so are important areas in any missile defense. Cuba, as the CEMA country nearest the continental United States, was a much greater threat as a base for missiles.

SKILL BUILDER: CRITICAL THINKING AND COMPREHENSION

I. Cause and Effect
Answers will vary, but should reflect awareness of the following:
1. The United States helped western Europe recover from World War II and later formed a series of military alliances to contain the Soviet Union.
2. The United States (along with its neighbor Canada) was the only part of the industrialized world to emerge from World War II with its industry and economy intact.
3. Large numbers of Americans died in a seemingly stalemated war, with the eventual result that most Americans turned against the war.
4. Changes within the Soviet Union made it seem less of a threat.

II. Making Judgments
Judgments will vary, but should reflect awareness of the following:
1. To most people at the time, the threat of communists in the United States government was real. However, McCarthy was never able to prove any of his specific accusations.
2. The "domino effect" was the fear that the fall of one country to communism would lead directly to the fall of its neighbor, and so to the fall of another, and so on in a continuing series. By 1990 it had not proved true in Southeast Asia.
3. The basic question is whether greater security is gained by reducing armaments worldwide or by striving to remain stronger than any possible attacker.

ENRICHMENT

1. Suggest that students concentrate their research on interviewing adults who remember the Vietnam War. Reports on this research may be either oral or written.
2. Students should be prepared to give brief explanations of the significance of each photo.
3. Some students can include in their reports a discussion of how these categories have held up into the 1990s. What countries appear to be moving from one "world" to another?

UNIT 15 ❧ REVIEW, *Pages 670-671*

SKILL BUILDER: READING A MAP

1. The European community, Japan, Canada
2. Canada
3. Almost 140 billion dollars
4. Answers will vary. Students should note that a large trade deficit can cause serious economic problems for the country.
5. South America
6. Answers will vary. Students might note that trade involves less than a billion dollars.

SKILL BUILDER: CRITICAL THINKING AND COMPREHENSION

I. Making Judgments
1. Answers and reasons will vary. Better choices are African Americans and women.
2. Grades will vary. Students should recognize some effort has been made but not outstanding effort.

II. Comparing and Contrasting
Similarities: All groups organized themselves. All carried on some kind of collective action.
Differences:
African Americans-used passive resistance and black separatism, many national organizations, forced the Supreme Court to declare many discriminatory laws unconstitutional, served as a model for other groups, organized collective actions on a national level, some violence involved occasionally, poverty still a problem
Women-organized NOW, faced strong opposition within own group, *The Feminine Mystique*, lobbied for changes, were unsuccessful with ERA, some laws passed, equal pay and child care still problems
Native Americans-demanded civil rights and return of property, based organizations on Black Power model, established Red Power, used direct action, some laws returning property passed, effective in law suits
Hispanic Americans-national boycott, organized a union, formed new political parties, became more political, organized groups by national background
Older Americans-Grey Panthers, demands for health care and protection of rights, some effective law suits
Handicapped Americans-demands for educational opportunities and mainstreaming, some laws passed, demand special equipment, etc., increasing public awareness, special Olympics

ENRICHMENT

1. Newspapers will vary.
2. Issues and presentations will vary.

Annotated Teacher's Edition

EXPLORING AMERICAN HISTORY

 GLOBE BOOK COMPANY
A Division of Simon & Schuster
Paramus, New Jersey

JOHN R. O'CONNOR

B.A., St. Francis College; M.A., University of Pittsburgh. Mr. O'Connor taught social studies for many years before becoming a principal in the New York City school system. He is widely known for his lectures and articles on reading skills in the social studies. In addition to this book, Mr. O'Connor has coauthored other Globe textbooks: *Exploring World History, Exploring the Urban World, Exploring American Citizenship,* and *Unlocking Social Studies Skills.* He has edited Globe's *Exploring a Changing World* and *Exploring the Non-Western World.*

Acknowledgements of quoted matter begin on page 697. Acknowledgements of illustrations begin on page 698.
Photo Editor: Joan Scafarello
Graphs on page 404 and Diagrams on pages 75, 380, and 428 by Mark Stein Studios

The reading on page 308 is reprinted with permission of Charles Scribner's Sons, an imprint of Macmillan Publishing Company, from *John Marsh, Pioneer,* by George D. Lyman. Copyright 1930 Charles Scribner's Sons; Copyright renewed © 1958 Dorothy Van Sickler Lyman.

Maps: General Cartography, Inc.
      Patricia A. Rodriguez, M.A.

Cover Pictures: "The Return" by Richard Yarde; The Museum of Fine Arts, Boston; Sophie Friedman Fund
      "Vaqueros in a Horse Corral" by James Walker; The Gilcrease Museum, Tulsa, Oklahoma
      "The Old Scout's Tale" by William Tylee Ranney; The Gilcrease Museum, Tulsa, Oklahoma (detail)

ISBN: 835-90630-2

Printed in the United States of America
    5 6 7 8 9 0 97 96 95

GLOBE BOOK COMPANY
A Division of Simon & Schuster
Paramus, New Jersey

CONSULTANTS AND REVIEWERS

Frank de Varona
Superintendant for Region I
Dade County Public Schools
Miami, Florida

Dr. D. William Tinkler
Coordinator for Secondary Social Studies
Fulton County Schools
Atlanta, Georgia

Leon T. Hairston
Principal
Anderson Sixth Grade School
Petersburg, Virginia

Robert L. Clark
Social Studies Consultant - Writer
Eastchester, New York

A KEY TO SYMBOLS USED IN EXPLORING AMERICAN HISTORY

Recognizing Main Idea: Identifying the most important idea in a paragraph.

Classifying: Organizing facts into categories based on what they have in common.

Summarizing: Giving the main idea of a group of paragraphs in a brief form.

Generalizing: Making a statement that links several facts.

Sequencing: Putting a series of events in the correct time order.

Recognizing Cause and Effect: Matching the action or event that makes something happen to what happens as a result.

Comparing and Contrasting: Recognizing similarities and differences.

Drawing Conclusions: Making a statement that explains the facts and evidence.

Predicting: Guessing what will happen on the basis of clues and facts.

Identifying Fact Versus Opinion: Specifying whether information can be proven or whether it expresses feelings or beliefs.

Understanding Points of View: Recognizing why people have different attitudes about the same thing.

Making Judgments: Stating a personal opinion based on historical facts.

Cooperative Learning: Activities noted with this symbol can be used as cooperative learning activities.

Historical Method: This symbol identifies some of the tools that historians use to research and analyze historical events.

iii

Take charge of your studies.

You'll learn more and get the most enjoyment from reading about American history when you know how to use this book. Read these six pages first. They'll show you the best way to use all the study aids and Special Features you'll find in EXPLORING AMERICAN HISTORY.

Take a good look at the two pages that start each Unit. They'll give you a better understanding of what you'll be learning in the Unit.

The Unit title and the list of Chapter titles give you a quick outline of the people, places, and events you'll be studying.

Pictures at the beginning of each Unit introduce scenes and people from American history and give you a feeling for the time and the events you'll study in the Unit.

UNIT 5

AMERICA WINS INDEPENDENCE

Chapter

1 The French and British Fight 174

2 Britain Tightens Its Grip 180

3 The Colonists Resist Taxation Without Representation 186

4 "Give Me Liberty or Give Me Death" 192

5 Independence Is Declared 198

6 The New Nation Wins Its Independence 208

7 The Revolutionary War Changes American Life 214

UNIT OVERVIEW   Unit 5 will help you understand what caused the 13 colonies to turn against Great Britain and fight to win their rights as an independent nation.

UNIT SKILLS OBJECTIVES   In Unit 5, three critical thinking skills are emphasized:
- Drawing Conclusions: Making a statement that explains the facts and evidence.
- Predicting: Telling what you think will happen on the basis of clues and facts.
- Identifying Fact versus Opinion: Specifying whether information can be proved or whether it expresses feelings or beliefs.

You will also use two important social studies skills: Using Time Lines   Reading a Bar Graph

170

▲ The British suffered heavy losses at the Battle of Bunker Hill, the first major battle of the American Revolution.

171

Read the Unit Objective. It will give you a good idea of what you should think about as you read the Unit and help you relate the Chapters to one another.

Read the Unit Skills Objectives. They tell you the Critical Thinking Skills and the Social Studies Skills you will use in the Unit to help you learn and think more about American history.

The Unit Time Line shows the time span and the major events in American history covered in the Unit.

Points of View helps you understand how people in the past felt about important issues and ideas in American history. These different ways of thinking show you the reasons for the historical events you will study in the Unit.

You learn about major events in American history and why people who lived in these years often had strong and contrasting opinions about them.

The questions at the end of these pages let you check what you learned and prepare you to study the Unit content.

Historical documents give the actual words each person used to express their thoughts and feelings.

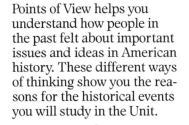

Points of View

The people of Great Britain had struggled for hundreds of years to limit the power of their kings. By the 1700s, the lawmaking body in England called Parliament was more powerful than the king. One of Parliament's most important powers was the power to pass tax laws. The American colonists

NO TAXES BUT WITH THEIR OWN CONSENT

The Congress . . . esteem it [believe it is] our . . . duty to make the following declarations . . . respecting [about] the . . . rights and liberties of the colonists . . .

That His Majesty's . . . subjects in these colonies are entitled to all the . . . rights and liberties of his natural born subjects within the kingdom of Great Britain.

That it is . . . essential to the freedom of a people, and the undoubted right of Englishmen, that no taxes should be imposed [placed] on them, but [except] with their own consent [agreement], given personally or by their representatives.

"Taxation Without Representation"

believed that their rights as British citizens meant that only their lawmaking bodies, the colonial assemblies, had the right to tax them. In 1765 the 13 colonies sent members to the Stamp Act Congress in New York City. The Congress forcefully stated the colonists' point of view.

SUBJECTS TO THE CROWN OF GREAT BRITAIN

Be it declared. . . . That the . . . colonies . . . in America have been, are, and of right ought to be, subordinate unto [under the power of] and dependent upon the imperial crown [the king] and Parliament of Great Britain [England]. And that . . . Parliament . . . had, has, and by right ought to have, full power and authority to make laws . . . to bind [keep] the colonies and people of America subjects to the crown [king] of Great Britain in all cases whatsoever.

And be it further declared . . . that all resolutions, votes, order, and proceed-

George III was king of Great Britain during the American Revolution. To colonists he symbolized the injustice of British rule.

Using Primary Sources

1. Why did the colonists believe so strongly in the idea of "no taxation without representation"?

2. Why was the English government so strongly against the idea of "no taxation without representation"?

3. What do you think could happen because the colonists and England held such very different points of view?

173

CHAPTER 1

The French and British Fight

OBJECTIVE: Why did rival claims to western land lead to war between the French and the British colonists?

1. Deep in the wilderness, 800 French soldiers and 400 Native American warriors had the tiny British force of 150 men surrounded. The British were led by a 22-year-old American colonel. The British force had gone west from Virginia into the Ohio Valley to find out what the French were doing there. They learned that the French had a large fort called Fort Duquesne in the area. The young American officer had hurriedly ordered his men to build a small fort. Now they were huddled behind its walls as musket fire ripped into them. Then rain began to fall and the fort flooded. The colonel, barking out commands, slogged through the deep mud over wounded and dying men. His force was doomed, and he knew it. With great relief the colonel accepted the French commander's offer to let him and his men surrender and return to Virginia. The young colonel's name was George Washington.

Rival land claims How did the struggle for the Ohio Valley lead to war between France and Britain?

2. Great Britain and France were the two most powerful nations in Europe in the 1700s with important colonies in North America. **New France** covered a much larger area than Britain's 13 colonies. It included Canada and

the land around the Great Lakes. France also claimed all the land west of the Appalachian Mountains. This land reached from the Ohio Valley to the Gulf of Mexico and as far west as the Rocky Mountains.

3. The French carried on a rich trade in beaver and other furs. This trade brought

Discuss: Briefly review with the class Unit 2, Chapter 7, which discusses the early explorers who established France's claim to New France. Have students study the map below to locate the areas of New France explored by these trailblazers.

large profits to the French traders and the French king. To protect this trade, France in the 1750s sent more soldiers to America and built new forts in the Ohio Valley.

4. Britain's colonies also were interested in the Ohio Valley and took steps to claim it for themselves. In Virginia and Pennsylvania, colonial families had begun to move across the Appalachians to settle in these western lands. They were encouraged to move there by **land companies**. Land companies bought western land and sold it to people who wanted to settle there. British fur traders also began to move into the Ohio Valley. As more and more British colonists entered the region, the threat of a showdown between France and Britain grew.

France against Britain What advantages did each side have in fighting the French and Indian War?

5. Britain and France did not declare war until 1756, but fighting had begun in the Ohio

Valley in 1754 near Fort Duquesne. In Europe this war between Britain and France was called the Seven Years War. In North America the war became known as the **French and Indian War**. Each country had reasons to think that it would win the war.

6. The French had a well-trained army with a skilled commander. In addition, the French had as allies most of the Native American tribes in North America. Most of the Native Americans distrusted the British colonists, for they knew the colonists wanted to settle in their lands. The French trappers, on the other hand, did not threaten the Native Americans' lands or way of life. In what ways could these tribes aid the French?

7. Though New France was huge, only 80,000 French settlers lived there. This was a disadvantage in the war. Except for Montreal and Quebec in Canada, there were few settlements. Instead, trading posts and army forts were scattered hundreds of miles apart. Defending New France would be difficult.

MAP SKILL BUILDER: A map key explains the meaning of the colors and symbols used on a map. Always study the key before looking at a map such as the one below. 1. What color stands for French lands about 1750? 2. What areas on the map have the most forts? Why?

▲ George Washington battled the French near Fort Duquesne three times during the French and Indian War.

The French and Indian War

- British lands about 1750
- French lands about 1750
- ---- Frontier
- British advances
- ▼ British forts
- French advances
- French forts
- French lands

0 200 miles
0 300 kilometers

In Chapter 1 you will apply these critical thinking skills to the historical process:
▶ **Predicting:** Telling what you think will happen on the basis of clues and facts.
▶ **Drawing Conclusions:** Making a statement that explains the facts and evidence.

174

Key History Words you should know are highlighted in boldface type.

You can find the main idea of every paragraph in the first or second sentence.

Every Chapter begins with an Objective that poses an important question. Focus on answering the question as you read, and you'll develop a good understanding of the Chapter.

The Introduction to the Chapter helps you relate history to your own life and to events taking place today.

Colored symbols mark critical thinking questions that will help involve you in the reading.

Each Section in the Chapter begins with an important question to direct your reading. Finding the answer to that question helps you understand what you've read.

Special Features show American history in action.

Every Chapter is filled with interesting details on the people, places, and ideas that have shaped America's history. As you read the Features, you'll build Social Studies skills and master important facts from the Chapter, too.

Linking Geography and History—Explore the relationship between geography and history. You'll see how understanding geography helps you understand the course of American history.

People in History—The history of our nation is filled with extraordinary people. You'll learn how their ideas and actions helped shape the course of American history.

The President's Corner—You will meet some of America's leaders and get to know what was happening in the years when each of them was in office.

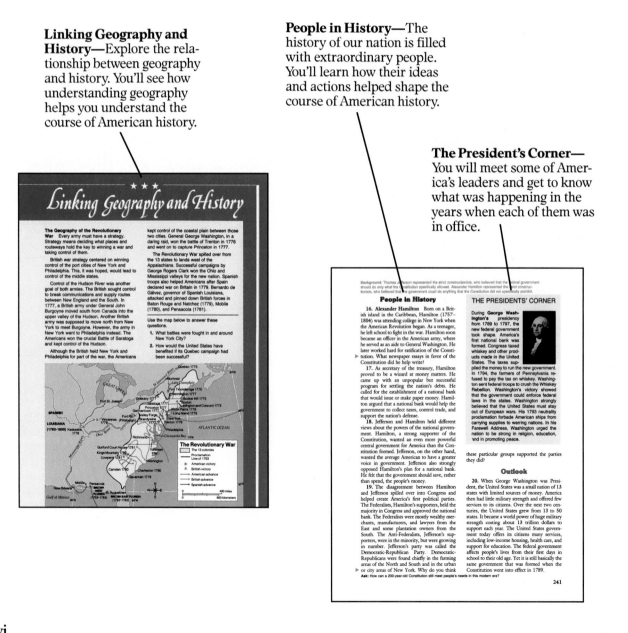

America's People—The people who built America came here from all over the world. You'll learn about these important groups, their struggles and achievements, and the rich contributions they have made to American life.

Spotlight on Sources—American history comes alive as you read the actual ideas and views of people who have influenced America's growth.

Map Skill Builders—Maps are important in studying American history, and you'll find opportunities like these to practice and improve your skills of reading and using maps.

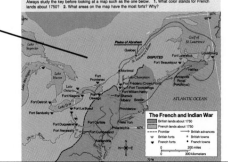

Check your understanding and develop skills.

Two pages of review and skill-building activities at the end of each Chapter and again at the end of each Unit help you check what you've learned. Review pages will help you master the important information from the Chapter and Unit, develop proper study habits, and build history skills.

A second Skill Builder section challenges you to think critically about what you've learned in the Chapter.

Begin your review with a check of the Key History Words you learned in the Chapter.

Use the Study Hints to improve your understanding of the Chapter and to help you get better grades on tests.

CHAPTER REVIEW

STUDY HINT Use an outline map of North America to develop a color code showing the British and French land claims in America. Then list the causes of the French and Indian War and the results.

VOCABULARY REVIEW

Write each number and term on a sheet of paper. Then write the letter of the definition next to the term it defines.

1. land companies
2. Albany Plan of Union
3. New France
4. militia
5. French and Indian War

a. Canada, the land around the Great Lakes, and the land west of the Appalachian Mountains
b. Conflict between Great Britain and France in North America
c. Proposal for the colonies to join together under one government
d. Volunteer army
e. Companies that bought western land and sold it to people who wanted to settle there
f. British army

SKILL BUILDER: OUTLINING

The following is an incomplete outline about the advantages and disadvantages of each side in fighting the French and Indian War. Copy the outline on a sheet of paper. Then fill in the blanks with subheads or supporting details from the list below. Refer to paragraphs 6–9 in this chapter if you need help.

Defending the area would be difficult
Problems the British faced

Iroquois nation supported them
Had a well-trained army with a skilled commander

I. Advantages and disadvantages of each side in the French and Indian War
  A. Reasons the French thought they could win the war
    1. _____
    2. Native American tribes were their allies.
  B. Problems the French faced
    1. There were only 80,000 settlers in New France.
    2. _____

C. Great Britain's advantages in North America
  1. Its colonists outnumbered those of the French.
  2. _____
  3. Britain's navy controlled the Atlantic.
D. _____
  1. The 13 colonies often quarreled with one another about boundaries and claims to western lands.
  2. To help defend themselves, they would have to learn to work together.

USING PRIMARY SOURCES

Why do you think Benjamin Franklin thought a ". . . voluntary union entered into by the colonies themselves, . . ." would be preferable to one imposed by Parliament"?

178

SKILL BUILDER: CRITICAL THINKING AND COMPREHENSION

I. Drawing Conclusions

Read each of the following groups of statements. Think carefully about each group. Then, from the list of possible conclusions, choose the conclusion that best fits the facts.

Statements:

1. In 1754, Benjamin Franklin proposed the Albany Plan of Union to unite the colonies under one government.
2. The government created by the Albany Plan of Union would collect taxes from the colonies to pay for a volunteer army.
3. Colonial assemblies were not willing to give up their power to a new joint government.
4. The 13 colonies were not able to unite to fight against the French. They had to depend on Great Britain to provide the armies and weapons needed to fight the French and Indian War.

Possible Conclusions:

a. The rejection of the Albany Plan of Union weakened Britain's hold over the colonies.
b. The rejection of the Albany Plan allowed Britain to have complete leadership in the war.
c. Since the colonies rejected the Albany Plan, it was unlikely that they would ever unite in the future.

II. Predicting

When you predict, you tell what you think will happen in the future. A prediction is not just guesswork. It is most likely to be correct when it is based on facts and clues.

Because Britain won the French and Indian War, its empire in North America doubled in size. The western lands were no longer occupied by French soldiers.

1. What do you think the colonists would want to do now that the war was over?
2. How do you think Native American nations would react?

Write your prediction on a sheet of paper. Tell also your evidence is. In other words, tell what facts and clues you used in making your prediction.

ENRICHMENT

1. Suppose you are a Native American living in New France. A French trapper approaches your people. He wants you to help France in the war against Britain. How do you feel about fighting in this war? Write about your reactions to what the trapper says.
2. Research Benjamin Franklin's *Poor Richard's Almanac*. Copy some of the sayings that were published in the Almanac. Choose two of these sayings to write down and illustrate on a poster board. Explain to the class why you like these sayings and what they mean to you.

179

In the first Skill Builder section, you review the content of the Chapter and practice your Social Studies skills.

Learn more about American history by making your own discoveries. Enrichment activities take what you've learned in the chapter and ask you to use it in new, creative ways.

The activities in the Unit Review cover all the Chapters together, so you'll see how they connect to each other. Read the Summary first to help you remember important information you read in the Unit.

The second Skill Builder section applies your critical thinking skills to people, places, and events throughout the Unit.

UNIT REVIEW

SUMMARY

In the 1750s, conflicts in the valley of the Ohio River led to the French and Indian War between Great Britain and France. When the war ended in 1763, France had been driven from North America.

In the years following the war, strong disagreements arose between Great Britain and its American colonies. The main issue was taxes. The British government believed that it had the right to tax the colonies. Colonists believed that only their own colonial assemblies could tax them. The colonies protests against the British taxes led to increasing unity of the colonies. Sometimes the protests also led to violence, as in the Boston Massacre of 1770 and the Boston Tea Party of 1773.

The Continental Congress, with delegates from every colony, met in 1774 and again in 1775. When fighting broke out in 1775 at Lexington and Concord, the Congress appointed

George Washington as head of the colonial army. A year later, on July 4, 1776, Congress declared that the colonies were now free and independent.

The new country had to fight a war to win its independence. The British forces had many advantages over the small and poorly equipped Continental Army. However, the Continental Army stayed together, thanks mainly to the leadership of George Washington. With French aid, the Americans finally were victorious.

The last important battle of the American Revolution took place at Yorktown, Virginia, in 1781. Two years later, the Treaty of Paris set the boundaries of the United States. Now the new nation would be faced with the task of forming a government on which all the colonies would agree. The new nation also would have to choose a leader to run the new government. What laws do you think would be important to the new nation?

SKILL BUILDER: READING A MAP

North America in 1783

1. What territory was to the north of the United States?

2. Which European country controlled this territory?

3. What river formed the western boundary of the United States?

4. What European country controlled the territory to the west of this boundary?

5. What country controlled New Orleans? Why was control of this city important?

6. To what country did Florida belong in 1783?

SKILL BUILDER: CRITICAL THINKING AND COMPREHENSION

I. Predicting

At the end of the Revolutionary War, Great Britain remained in control of Canada. The United States and Canada shared a long border, stretching from the Atlantic coast through the Great Lakes to the source of the Mississippi River. Predict how this border will affect relations between Great Britain and the United States. Will relations along the border be peaceful and friendly, or hostile and unfriendly? Write a paragraph that states your prediction and gives your reasons for it.

II. Point of View

1. Select one of the major events described in Unit 5. Write a paragraph describing the event from the point of view of an American. The American may be either taking part in the event or standing on the sidelines watching it.

2. Write a second paragraph describing the same event from a British point of view.

ENRICHMENT

1. Choose an event discussed in the unit. Read about the details of this event in your library. Then write a newspaper article telling about the event. Begin the article with a paragraph that includes the five Ws of newspaper articles: who, what, when, where, why. When your article is finished, write a headline for it. OPTIONAL: Draw an illustration for the article.

2. Suppose that it is June 1776. You are a member of the Second Continental Congress. The Congress is trying to decide whether it is a good idea to declare independence from Great Britain. Prepare a speech that you will give at the next meeting of the Congress. Your speech should argue for one of these points of view and against the other two:
   a. The colonies should declare independence, and the sooner the better.
   b. Independence is the goal that the colonies should work toward. However, declaring it now would be dangerous.
   c. Independence would probably create more problems than it solves. The colonies should instead try to work out their problems with Great Britain.

221

The first Skill Builder section uses maps to review important places and developments in the Unit.

Enrichment activities challenge you to explore facts and ideas from the Unit in greater depth. For some activities, you will have to look for information in places other than your textbook.

ix

CONTENTS

UNIT 9   THE CIVIL WAR AND RECONSTRUCTION 396

UNIT 10   THE UNITED STATES BECOMES AN INDUSTRIAL NATION 432

UNIT 11   REFORM MOVEMENTS 468

PEOPLE IN HISTORY

PRESIDENTS' CORNER

The Five Elements of a Map

The map below is a **political map** of the United States and its neighbors. The map has five basic elements:

1. Title. The title tells the subject of the map. What is the title of the map below?

2. Map Key. The map key tells what the colors and symbols used on the map represent. In the map below, since the states of the United States are not continuous, a color is used for the United States and is explained in the key.

3. Latitude and Longitude. Imaginary lines called latitude lines (parallels) and longitude lines (meridians) are used to locate places on the globe. Latitude lines run east and west and

are parallel to each other. Longitude lines run north and south and meet at the North Pole and the South Pole.

4. Map Scale. Maps of small areas, like the map on the facing page, show distance with a map scale. A map scale relates distances on the map to real distances on the earth. Maps of large areas like hemispheres or the entire world distort distances and cannot have an accurate map scale. The map below has a triangle of distances. How far is Fairbanks, Alaska, from Washington, D.C.?

5. Compass Rose. The compass rose shows direction. The north arrow on a compass rose always points to the North Pole.

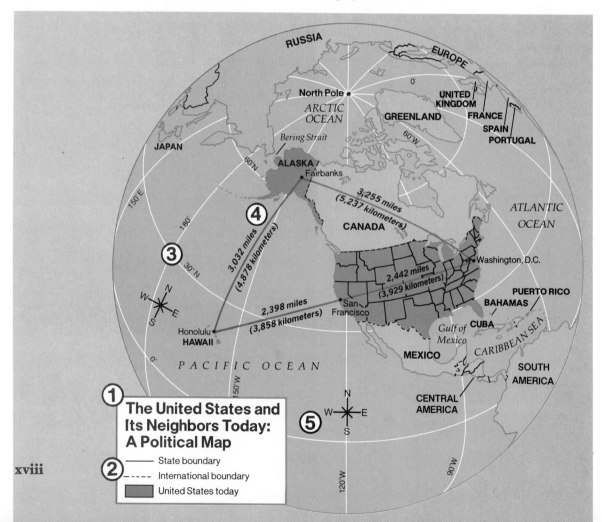

History Through Maps

The United States: A Physical-Political Map

The map below is a **physical-political map** of the United States today. The map shows such physical features as rivers and height of the land as well as international and state borders.

A key element of the physical environment found on a physical-political map is **elevation,** or height of the land above sea level. On the map below, colors divide the land into five elevation levels above sea level. A sixth color distinguishes lands below sea level. The diagram at the top is a cross-section of the land of the United States at about the latitude of San Francisco, California.

Physical-political maps show at a glance where the main lowlands and highlands are located. Notice on the map below how much of the United States is located below the 2,000-foot (610-meter) level. The two principal lowlands are the Coastal Plain bordering the Atlantic Ocean and the Gulf of Mexico and the Central Plains along the Mississippi River and Great Lakes. The principal highlands above 10,000 feet (2,050 meters) are in the West and in Alaska.

The **Continental Divide** is also shown on the map below. The Continental Divide is a highland area that separates rivers flowing to the Pacific Ocean from rivers flowing to the Atlantic Ocean and the Gulf of Mexico.

Political information on the map below includes the United States international and state borders. Larger physical-political maps, such as the United States map on pages 674-675, also include the names of states, capitals, and other cities.

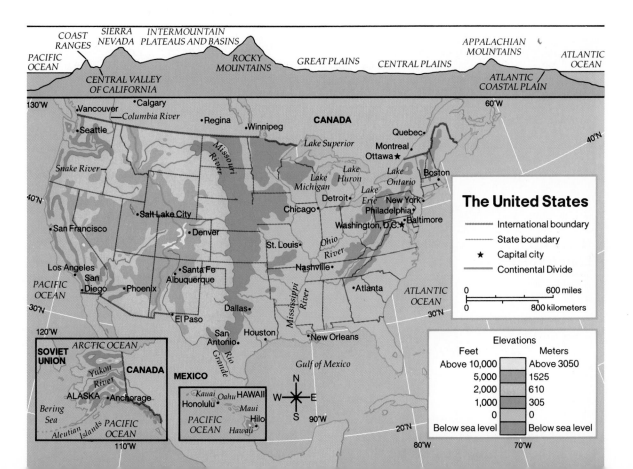

North America: A Landform Regions Map

Five types of landforms are shown on the **landform regions map** below. Two of the five landform types are **mountains.** The other three landform types are **lowlands, interior plains,** and **plateaus** or **table lands.**

Mountains are landforms with steep slopes and elevations above 1,000 feet (305 meters). The Appalachian Upland and Interior Highland (Ozarks and Ouachitas) are old, worn-down mountains. Old, worn-down mountains have lower elevations than young, rugged mountains found in western North America, such as the Rocky Mountains.

Plateaus are flat lands at high elevations with steep-sided river valleys. The Canadian Shield, at elevations of 500 to 2,000 feet (152 to 610 meters), is the largest North American

plateau. Many smaller plateau regions are located between the western mountain ranges.

Lowlands are flat lands at low elevations with shallow river valleys. The largest lowland in North America is the Coastal Plain. What bodies of water does the Coastal Plain border? Smaller lowlands occur in the mountainous western half of the continent.

Interior Plains lie inland at higher elevations than coastal plains. The Central Plains section of the Interior Plains lies mostly between 500 feet and 2,000 feet (152 and 610 meters). The Great Plains section of the Interior Plains lies between 2,000 feet and 5,000 feet (610 and 1524 meters).

Locate these five landform regions on the map below.

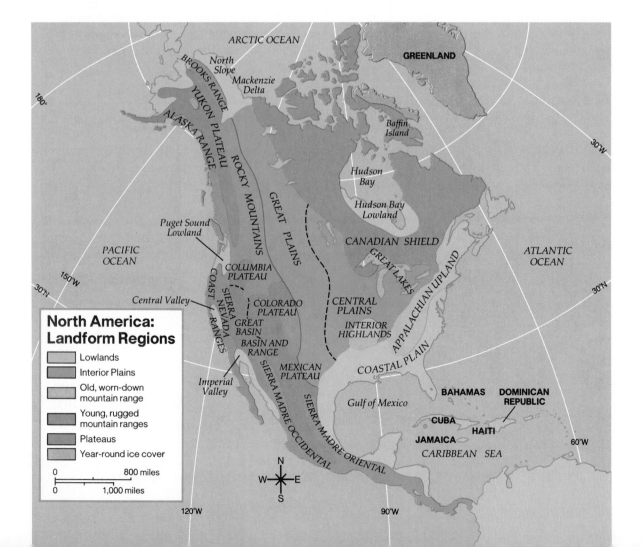

The United States: An Historical Map

Historical maps connect places and historical events. The map below is an historical map tracing the territorial growth of the United States. The expansion transformed the United States from a small nation first to a continental power and then to a world power.

The historical core of the United States lies in the 13 British colonies founded along the Atlantic Coast. Great Britain granted independence to the colonies and interior lands to the Mississippi River in 1783.

Southward expansion into Spanish lands along the Gulf of Mexico began in 1795. As a result of the War of 1812, East and West Florida became part of the United States.

American westward expansion began with the purchase of the Louisiana Territory from France. The Louisiana Purchase doubled the size of the young United States. When did the United States gain control of the vital Mississippi River waterway?

Territorial expansion continued rapidly after 1803. The boundary with Canada was fixed in 1818 and 1842. Then Texas, after declaring its independence from Mexico in 1836, joined the United States in 1845. In 1846, the Oregon Territory was added to the United States. The Mexican Cession in 1848 and the Gadsden Purchase in 1853 brought other lands to the United States. By 1853, American control of lands now in the 48 present-day lower mainland states was complete.

Until 1959 the United States was a country of 48 connected states. Then in 1959, Alaska and Hawaii became the 49th and 50th states. Alaska has no land connection with the other states of the United States. Hawaii is the only state not located on the North American continent. As a result of these additions, new terms were needed to describe the United States. The 48 pre-1959 states are called the **lower mainland** or **conterminous states.** The 48 conterminous states plus Alaska are called the **mainland states.** All 50 states make up the United States.

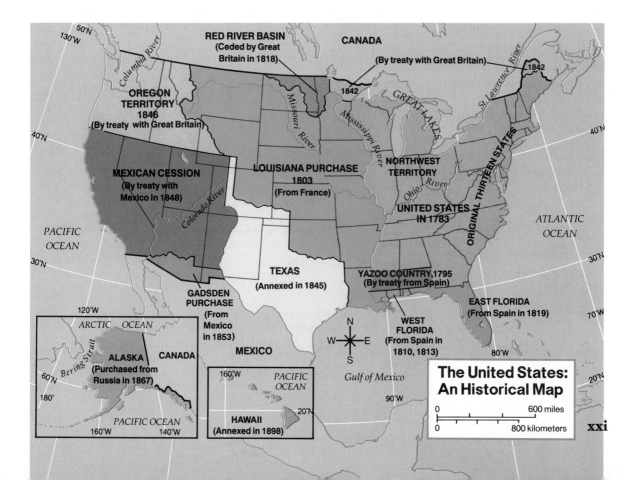

The United States: An Historical Map

xxi

Historical Methods

How Historians Learn About the Past

In this book you will read the story of your country from its beginnings to the present day. The people who tell this story are called historians. You may wonder how historians find out what happened in the past. Historians are like detectives. They use many kinds of clues to learn about the way people lived and what they did in years gone by. The pictures and descriptions on these two pages show you some of the ways historians find evidence that has helped them write *Exploring American History*.

▲ **Diaries and letters** written by people of the past tell historians what individuals did, what they knew, and what their feelings were. The picture above shows a diary that William Clark kept on the Lewis and Clark expedition that explored the Louisiana Territory. From it historians have learned a great deal about this vast region.

▲ **Artifacts** help historians learn how people of the past lived. An artifact is an object made by people and used by them in their lives. This picture shows a slave who was forced to wear bells on her head to discourage her from running away. Such an artifact gives historians an idea of how American slaves were treated.

◄ **Manuscripts** of important speeches and other documents tell historians what people of the past said in public. This picture shows the manuscript of one of President Abraham Lincoln's great speeches. In this speech, he dedicated the cemetery at Gettysburg, Pennsylvania, in memory of the soldiers who fought at the Battle of Gettysburg during the Civil War.

▲ **Business documents** help historians find out what people of the past spent their money on and what prices were like. The picture shows a receipt for the purchase of an African American slave woman and her child for the equivalent of about $300.

Posters give historians an idea of what people thought was important and what they wanted the public to know. This 1851 poster shows that African Americans in Boston were in danger of being kidnapped and sent into slavery. ▶

▲ **Archaeologists** are scientists who study how people of the past lived. They do this by uncovering the ruins and other remains of old societies. Here archaeologists are digging to find evidence of what life was like in the city of Williamsburg, Virginia, in the 1700s.

▲ **Cartoons** are drawings that appear in newspapers and magazines that show how the artist feels about what is happening in the country. Often a cartoon also reflects the public's opinion about events. From this 1966 cartoon historians can get an idea of how serious the problem of city slums appeared to some Americans.

Newspapers are an important source of information for historians. Newspapers record important events of the day soon after they happen. The newspaper at the right gives historians details about the assassination of President Lincoln. ▶

UNIT 1

THE EARLY PEOPLE OF THE AMERICAS

Chapter

UNIT OVERVIEW   Unit 1 will help you understand how the early people reached North America, how they spread across the continent, and how their ways of life differed.

UNIT SKILLS OBJECTIVES   In Unit 1, two critical thinking skills are emphasized:

▲ **Recognizing the Main Idea:** Identifying the most important idea in a paragraph

▷ **Classifying:** Organizing facts into categories based on what they have in common.

You will also use two important social studies skills:
Reading a Map   Completing a Table

Migration across Beringia begins c. 30,000 B.C.

End of Ice Age c. 10,000 B.C.

2   **ESL/LEP Strategy:** Have students leaf through the unit to find vocabulary words for which to prepare illustrated glossary entries. Then ask them to exchange their entries with classmates to assess one another's knowledge.

▲ The early Native Americans used nature as a source of food and shelter, but they were careful to preserve its beauty and wealth.

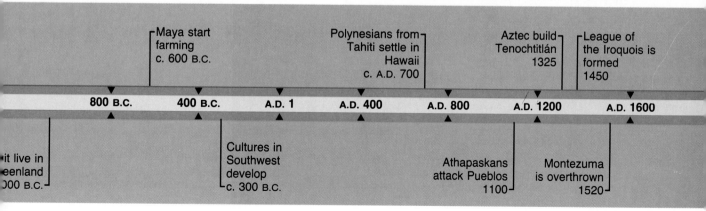

Maya start
farming
c. 600 B.C.

Polynesians from
Tahiti settle in
Hawaii
c. A.D. 700

Aztec build
Tenochtitlán
1325

League of
the Iroquois is
formed
1450

| 800 B.C. | 400 B.C. | A.D. 1 | A.D. 400 | A.D. 800 | A.D. 1200 | A.D. 1600 |

it live in
eenland
000 B.C.

Cultures in
Southwest
develop
c. 300 B.C.

Athapaskans
attack Pueblos
1100

Montezuma
is overthrown
1520

3

Points of View

Native Americans were the first people to live on the continents of North and South America. For thousands of years, the Native Americans lived in the natural surroundings of the land. They did very little to change the land. The Native Americans thought of the land as a mother who provides people with life and food. They wanted to protect the land. The Europeans, who first came to the Americas in the 1500s, thought of the land as something to be owned, tamed, and developed for housing, businesses, and industry.

▲ This is how the Cuyahoga River region in northeastern Ohio looked not long after Native Americans had left the area and white settlers had begun to move in.

LUTHER STANDING BEAR

❝ The Indian was a true naturist—a lover of nature. He loved the earth and all things of the earth, the attachment growing with age. The old people came literally to love the soil and they sat or reclined [leaned back] on the ground with a feeling of being close to a mothering power. It was good for the skin to touch the earth. . . . Kinship [relationship] with all creatures of the earth, sky, and water was a real and active principle. For the animal and bird world there existed a brotherly feeling that kept the [Indian] safe among them, and so close did some of the [Indians] come to their feathered and furred friends that in true brotherhood they spoke a common tongue. The [Indian] was wise. He knew that man's heart away from nature becomes hard; he knew that lack of respect for growing, living things soon led to lack of respect for humans too. ❞

—from *Touch the Earth*, T. C. McLuhan, ed.

Two Attitudes Towards the Land

The two passages below explain the deep feelings of the Native Americans for the land. In the first passage, Luther Standing Bear, an Oglala Sioux, tells about the special relationship Native Americans had with the land and nature. In the second passage, Vine Deloria, Jr., a modern-day Standing Rock Sioux, contrasts the Native Americans' respect for the land with other people's idea that changing the environment is a sign of progress. He points out that such changes often have harmed the earth. Ask yourself whether progress is worth its cost.

VINE DELORIA, JR.

"Every now and then I am impressed with the thinking of the non-Indian. I was in Cleveland [Ohio] last year and got to talking with a non-Indian about American history. He said that he was really sorry about what had happened to Indians, but that there was good reason for it. The continent had to be developed and he felt that Indians had stood in the way and thus had had to be removed. 'After all,' he remarked, 'what did you do with the land when you had it?' I didn't understand him until later when I discovered that the Cuyahoga River running through Cleveland is inflammable [can be burnt]. So many combustible pollutants [things that poison and can burst into flames] are dumped into the river that the inhabitants have to take special precautions during the summer to avoid accidentally setting it on fire. After reviewing the argument of my non-Indian friend [that the Indians had not put the land to good use], I decided that he was probably correct. Whites had made better use of the land. How many Indians could have thought of creating an inflammable river?" —*We Talk, You Listen*, Vine Deloria, Jr.

▲ In 1952, flammable material that had been dumped into the Cuyahoga River began to burn. What was Native Americans' view of this use of nature?

Using Primary Sources

1. How do the Indians' and non-Indians' attitudes differ?

2. Explain why either view may not be completely right or completely wrong.

The First People of the Americas

OBJECTIVE: Who were the first people of the Americas and what were their lives like?

1. The air was freezing cold. Icy winds howled out of the north. Much of the land from the Arctic Circle to south of the Great Lakes was covered by enormous sheets of moving ice. These ice sheets are called **glaciers** (GLAY-shurz). Prehistoric animals, such as huge woolly mammoths, short-faced bears, and saber-toothed tigers, roamed the land. This was what the first people who came to the Americas saw. Historians think that the first people of America walked here from Asia across a land bridge. The land bridge connected Siberia in Asia with Alaska in North America. These people were following the herds of animals that were their main source of food.

Land Bridge to the Americas How did a land bridge link Asia and North America during the Ice Age?

2. Over the past 400 years, many people have tried to explain the origins of the first Americans. For 2,000 years, Europeans had read about Atlantis. This continent, it was said, had sunk into the Atlantic Ocean with all its people. In 1552, a Spanish writer said that people from Atlantis must have escaped westward to become the first Americans. Other writers said that the first Americans were Asians who came from another "lost" continent called

▲ The first people to live on the North American continent are thought to have walked across the Bering Strait from Asia. How would you describe the clothing of these people?

Lemuria (luh-MOO-ree-uh) in the Pacific Ocean. However, no one has proved that either Atlantis or Lemuria ever existed.

3. Some Europeans looked to ancient peoples of the Middle East to explain the **ancestors** (AN-ses-turz) of the first Americans. An ances-

In Chapter 1 you will apply this critical thinking skill to the historical process:
▲ **Recognizing the Main Idea:** Identifying the most important idea in a paragraph.

tor is a family member in the past. Some Europeans said the Phoenicians (fuh-NEE-shuhnz), a great sailing people, were the first to come to the Americas. Others said the ancient Egyptians first settled the Americas. They compared the great pyramids of Egypt to the pyramids of the Aztec, Inca, and Maya. Still others believed that the first Americans were ancient Hebrews from the Ten Lost Tribes of Israel. This theory is accepted by a religious group in America known as the Mormons.

4. A Spanish scholar named José de Acosta (hoh-SAY day ah-KOHS-tah) wrote in 1589 that the first Americans came from Asia. Scientists now believe that Acosta was correct. They have discovered that a land bridge long ago connected Asia and North America. The first Americans probably entered America across this land bridge during the Ice Age.

5. Scientists **estimate** (ES-tim-ayt) that the Ice Age ended about 10,000 years ago. To estimate is to make a guess based on facts.

During the Ice Age, temperatures dropped, and glaciers moved south as far as the present-day states of Illinois and Missouri. However, there were other areas, especially along the coastlines, that the glaciers did not cover. These coastal areas actually grew during the Ice Age, because as ocean waters froze, the water level dropped by as much as 330 feet (100 m). The Bering Strait, a narrow body of water that separates Siberia and Alaska, became a land bridge, called Beringia (beh-RING-gee-uh). Look at the map on this page. Which continents were connected by Beringia?

6. Most scientists agree that people from northeastern Asia followed herds of animals across Beringia about 30,000 years ago. These hunters and their families came in small groups over thousands of years, rather than all at once. Historians call these people Paleo-Indians. (Paleo is a Greek word that means very old). The Paleo-Indians were the first people in North and South America.

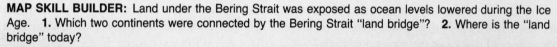

MAP SKILL BUILDER: Land under the Bering Strait was exposed as ocean levels lowered during the Ice Age. **1.** Which two continents were connected by the Bering Strait "land bridge"? **2.** Where is the "land bridge" today?

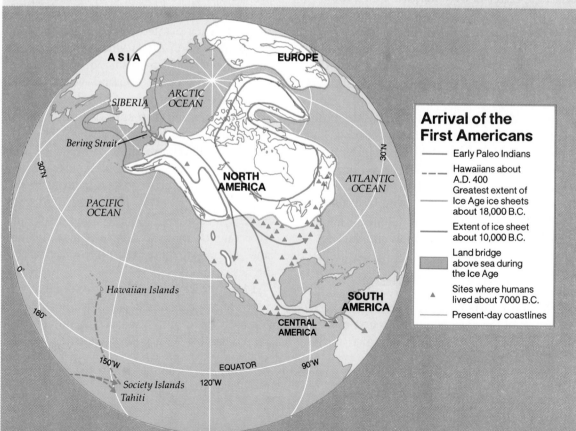

Paths of Migration   How did the early people spread through North and South America?

7. The first hunters from Asia probably stayed in the area of present-day Alaska for thousands of years. They lived by hunting in freezing subarctic lands. Eventually, groups of Paleo-Indians moved to the south and east of Alaska. These groups probably used paths that opened up when the glaciers moved apart. One path led to the west coast of what is today the United States. A second path led along the ridge of the Rocky Mountains. A third path brought Native Americans into the central part of North America. Find these paths on the map on page 7.

8. Over thousands of years, groups of early Native American peoples **migrated** (MY-gray-tuhd) across North and South America. To migrate means to move from one place to another. Gradually, some groups moved into Central America and South America. Others crossed in small boats to islands in the Caribbean Sea. By 8000 B.C., Native Americans had reached the southern tip of South America. ▶ Why do you think Native Americans took so long to spread out over the two continents?

The Early Native Americans   What was life like for the earliest people of the Americas?

9. The first Native Americans were **nomads** (NOH-madz). Nomads are people who move about in search of food. Early Native Americans spent most of their days hunting, fishing, and gathering wild plants. They used simple tools made of stone and wood. Sharpened pieces of stone attached to the end of wooden poles served both as weapons and tools. The animals they killed were cut up for meat, and the animal hides were used to make clothes and shelters.

People in History

10. **The Clovis People** We do not know the names of the early people who first came to North America because they left no written records. However, scientists have found important clues about these people from **artifacts** (AHR-tuh-fakts). Artifacts are objects such as tools made or used by people. Artifacts of one group of early people were found at Clovis, New Mexico, in 1932. From the weapons scientists found there, they think the Clovis people hunted using heavy spears with stone points. To make these points, the Clovis people chipped hard stones to give them sharp and pointed edges. Then the points were tied tightly with strips of animal skin to strong sticks that were split at one end. What kind of tools do you ◄ think they used for fishing?

11. The Clovis people hunted large and dangerous animals. One was the giant bison, which stood 14 feet (4 m) tall and had long, sharp tusks. Another was the saber-tooth tiger, an animal larger than any lion today. Killing these great beasts was not easy. The Clovis people often hunted them by setting grass fires that drove the animals over cliffs. Then the hunters, working in groups, used spears and clubs to kill those that had not died from the fall.

12. Farming was one of the most important discoveries made by early Native Americans. Around 5000 B.C., some Native Americans in present-day Mexico learned how to plant seeds for food. They planted crops of squash, beans, and **maize** (MAYZ), another name for corn. Later, they learned to plant potatoes and lima beans. Over several thousand years, farming spread southward into Central and South America. Farming also spread northward into what today is the United States.

13. The development of farming led some groups to change from nomadic life to village life. With a supply of food on hand from their crops, no longer was it necessary to move endlessly in search of food. In some areas, canals were dug to **irrigate** (IR-ruh-gayt) the farm land. To irrigate means to supply water through ditches or canals.

14. For early Native Americans, religion and daily life could not be separated. They believed that each force of nature, such as sun and rain, was controlled by a god or spirit. As a result,

8

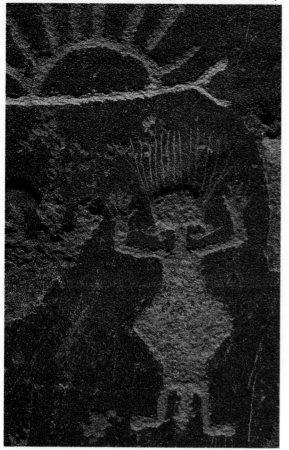

▲ Petroglyphs, such as this one done by Native Americans in Arizona, give archaeologists clues about the life and beliefs of the first Americans. What might this symbol represent?

they worshiped many gods of nature. For example, most tribes worshiped a sun god. They hoped that by pleasing the sun god, they could make sure that the sun would rise each morning.

15. One way that **archaeologists** (ahr-kee-OL-uh-jists) have learned about Native Americans is by studying their religious buildings. Archaeologists are scientists who study the life and culture of ancient peoples. Native Americans often built temples as mounds of solid earth. The largest group of Native American mounds north of Mexico is at Cahokia, Illinois on the Mississippi River, near present-day St. Louis, Missouri. Around 1000 A.D., 120 mounds stood at this site. Some of the mounds were temples. Other mounds were used to bury

the dead or to protect the village. Another group of Native Americans built mounds in the shape of animals. Perhaps the most famous mound is the Great Serpent Mound in Adams County, Ohio. This mound looks like a large snake with its mouth open. It is more than 1,300 feet (about 400 m) long. Can you guess ◄ what was the purpose of this mound?

Spotlight on Sources

16. Native Americans used spoken words to save and pass along their beliefs and history. They did this by having older members of Native American groups tell stories, poems, and prayers over and over again to the children. Here is a prayer said when a child was born:

> Ho! Sun, moon, and stars,
> All you that move in the
> heavens, listen to me!
> Into your midst new life
> has come.
> Make its path smooth.
> Ho! Winds, clouds, and rain,
> you that move in the air.
> Into your midst
> new life has come.
> Make its path smooth!
> —Omaha tribe prayer on the birth of a child

What does the prayer tell you about the belief of ▲ Native Americans in the power of the sun, moon, and stars?

Outlook

17. During the Ice Age, about 30,000 years ago, people from Asia moved across a land bridge over the Bering Strait into North America. These early people were following the herds of animals they hunted for food. Gradually, these Native Americans moved farther and farther into the Americas. By 8000 B.C., they had reached the southern tip of South America. During the next several thousand years, early people who settled across North and South America developed different ways of life. Why ◄ did these Native American cultures vary?

Activity: Draw a picture of nomadic life during the Ice Age. What kind of clothing would the people wear? What tools would they use? Then draw a picture of village life. What differences would your pictures show?

CHAPTER REVIEW

VOCABULARY REVIEW

▶ Write each of the following sentences on a sheet of paper. Then fill in the blanks with the word from the list below that best completes each sentence.

glaciers   nomads

ancestors   maize

estimate   irrigate

migrated   archaeologists

1. Scientists _____ that the Ice Age began about 3 million years ago.

2. It is believed that the _____ of the Native Americans came to America from Asia.

3. People from northeastern Asia _____ across the Bering Strait to what is now Alaska.

4. During the Ice Age, a large part of the earth was covered with _____ .

5. The first Native Americans were hunting and fishing _____ before they learned how to farm.

6. Scientists who study the life and culture of ancient peoples are _____ .

7. Around 5000 B.C., Native Americans living in present-day Mexico planted squash, beans, and _____ .

8. Native Americans dug canals to _____ their farm land.

SKILL BUILDER: PREVIEWING

How do you choose a book from the library to read? Probably you look through its pages to get an idea of what it is about. When you look over a book or selection before reading it, you are **previewing** that book or selection. Previewing is a skill that helps you understand what a book or selection is going to be about.

There are some steps you can follow when you preview a selection.

1. Read the **title** of the selection. The title tells you what the selection is about. Look at this first.

2. Read any headings that are printed in boldface, or heavy, type. They may help you to better understand what the selection is about.

3. Pay attention to key words or phrases that are in boldface type in a selection. They will give you more information about the selection.

4. Read the topic sentences of the paragraphs. In this book, a topic sentence is usually the first sentence of a paragraph. Think of some questions that you think the paragraph might answer.

▶ Practice the steps of previewing by applying them to this chapter of your textbook.

SKILL BUILDER: CRITICAL THINKING AND COMPREHENSION

▲ I. Introduction to the Main Idea

A **main idea** is the most important idea in a paragraph. It tells what the paragraph is about. Often, the main idea is in the first sentence of the paragraph.

▶ Choose the sentence that best expresses the main idea of each paragraph from the three sentences given here. Write the sentences on a separate sheet of paper.

1. The main idea of paragraph 2:
   a. No one has been able to prove that Atlantis or Lemuria existed.
   b. Many people have tried to explain the origins of the first Americans.
   c. Some Europeans suggested the first Americans came from "lost" continents.

2. The main idea of paragraph 6:
   a. Bands of people came in waves over thousands of years rather than as one large group at the same time.
   b. Skilled hunters and their families came in small groups or bands.
   c. Most scientists agree that people from northeast Asia followed herds of animals across Beringia and into a new world.

3. The main idea of paragraph 13:
   a. As Native Americans learned to farm, they began to live in villages.
   b. Villages, then towns, began to develop and grow.
   c. In some areas, Native Americans dug canals to irrigate the land.

4. The main idea of paragraph 15:
   a. Native American mounds have been found near St. Louis, Missouri.
   b. The Great Serpent Mound in Adams County, Ohio, is more than 1300 feet (about 400 m) long.
   c. Archaeologists are scientists who study the life and culture of ancient peoples.
   d. Religious buildings tell us much about Native Americans.

USING PRIMARY SOURCES

▶ Reread the Spotlight on Sources on page 9. How does the source show that the Native Americans were close to nature? How does the source show that nature was a part of their religious beliefs?

ENRICHMENT

1. Many songs and chants by Native Americans express a feeling of special closeness with nature. Research some Native American songs and chants and write them on a separate sheet of paper.

2. Imagine that you are an early Native American. Using religion to explain nature, tell a story about why the seasons change. Then have another student tell the same story, but tell it in a slightly different way. Have a few students do this.

3. Find photographs of many different petroglyphs and try to explain what each one tells you about the people who made them.

CHAPTER 2

Native Americans of the North and the Pacific Coast Regions

OBJECTIVE: What ways of living developed among native peoples of the North and the Pacific Coast regions?

1. Young Matka was very excited to be on his first whale hunt. His people, the Nootka, were proud of their skill in hunting these giant sea animals in open water. Whales were the Nootka's chief source of food and most of their belongings. They feasted on the whale's delicious meat and fat. The Nootka women used the whale's sinews to make long ropes. They used the animal's intestines to make containers. Just as important, they used the oil from the whale's fat to heat and light their homes. Matka knew that one day he would become the chief harpooner, or spear thrower, like his father. He would need to be very strong to drive the long harpoon into the whale.

2. The many different groups of Native Americans developed special ways of living that suited their needs. In each region of the Americas, the early people developed new **cultures.** Culture is a people's way of life. A culture includes people's beliefs and customs, the way they organize their society, their language, their buildings and art, and many other things.

▲ An Inuit carefully builds his igloo, or winter home, of blocks of snow. The Inuit have been building winter shelters like this for hundreds of years.

The Inuit How were the Inuit's lives shaped by their environment?

3. The **Inuit** (IN-yoo-wit) lived in a huge region stretching 4,000 miles (about 6,400 km) from western Alaska to Greenland. The Inuit are also known as Eskimos, a name given to them later by Europeans. The environment in which the Inuit lived was very harsh. The treeless, frozen ground of their homeland was nearly always covered by snow. However, the waters around their lands were filled with fish, seals, walruses, and whales. Large animals, like

In Chapter 2 you will apply this critical thinking skill to the historical process:
▲ **Recognizing the Main Idea:** Identifying the most important idea in a paragraph.

12

polar bears and **caribou** (KAR-ih-boo), a kind of large deer, roamed across the frozen lands.

4. The land where the Inuit lived had fewer **natural resources** than other parts of North America. Natural resources are things found in nature such as trees, soil, coal, oil, water power, and minerals. The Inuit used rocks, driftwood, and animal parts to make their tools, weapons, and sleds. For clothing, the Inuit used the skins of animals, especially the caribou.

5. The ancestors of the Inuit were the last of the hunting groups from Asia to arrive in the Americas. By about 2000 B.C., some of these people had walked as far as Greenland. Like their ancestors, the Inuit were skilled hunters. In the spring, they hunted the seals that lay on the ice sheets sunning themselves. In the summer, they went after caribou herds on land and whales and walruses in the waters. In the winter, they broke holes in the ice and caught fish. The Inuit's hunting boat, the **kayak** (KY-ak), was a covered canoe with a small opening for the paddler. The boat's frame was made from driftwood with sealskin stretched over it.

6. The Inuit way of living varied, depending on the season. During the spring and summer months, the Inuit lived in tents made of animal skins. When winter arrived, they built snowhouses, known as **igloos** (IG-looz). An igloo is a round building made of blocks of packed snow. A tunnel entrance led to the inside of the snowhouse. How do you think the Inuit learned ◄ to make an igloo?

Peoples of the Northwest Pacific Coast

What kind of society was formed by the people of the Pacific Northwest?

7. Several Native American nations lived in the Pacific coastal region. The land there has a rocky coastline. Behind the coastline are hills and thickly forested mountains. The temperature is mild, and rainfall is heavy.

8. The lives of the Pacific Coast nations were closely tied to the water. They fished especially for the great schools of salmon that swam in the rivers each spring. They also hunted seals, sea lions, sea otters, and whales. One of the nations, the Nootka, were great whale hunters. They went to sea in 30-foot (10-m) wooden hunting canoes.

9. The Northwest Pacific Coast nations lived in two village sites during each year. In the summer, they lived in villages along the coast. They built wooden frame houses there, to which they attached roofs and sides also made of wood. When bad winter weather set in along the coast, these tribes moved inland to their other village. They left behind the frames of their summer houses. However, they carried with them the wood of the roof and the sides, which they used on the frames of their inland houses.

MAP SKILL BUILDER: Culture regions are land areas where people share similar cultures or lifestyles. **1.** How many culture regions are named on the map? **2.** In which culture region are the Cree? The Nootka?

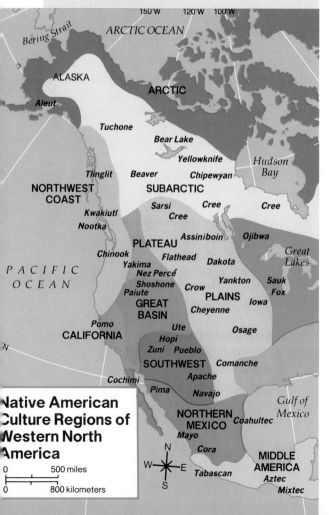

Native American Culture Regions of Western North America

0 _____ 500 miles

0 _____ 800 kilometers

13

America's People

THE HAWAIIANS

Hawaii is a chain of eight islands in the Pacific Ocean. It is about 2,400 miles (3,682 km) southwest of the mainland United States and about 5,000 miles (8,045 km) east of Asia. The earliest people of Hawaii were the Polynesians (pah-luh-NEE-zhuhnz). They were people who came from the Marquesas Islands farther south and west in the Pacific. The Polynesians were not related to the early peoples who lived in North and South America. Around A.D. 700, a second group of Polynesian explorers from Tahiti, sailing in giant double canoes with sails, settled in Hawaii. According to legend, they brought with them hogs, dogs, and chickens. They also introduced such basic food plants as coconuts and bananas to the islands. Because there were few animals to hunt in Hawaii, the Hawaiians ate mainly fish and vegetables.

Eventually, the eight islands of Hawaii were formed into four kingdoms, or chiefdoms. A powerful king or chief ruled each island. These chiefs believed they owned all the land, everything on the land, and even the fish in the sea. As a result, warfare between their kingdoms was common.

▼ The Hawaiians used double canoes like this one to reach the Hawaiian Islands from other Pacific islands. The rowers in the picture are wearing the special dress associated with one of the Hawaiian gods.

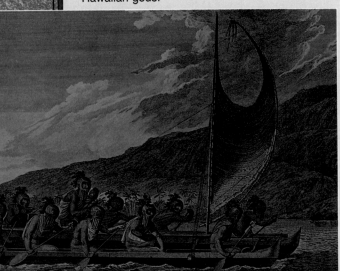

The early people of Hawaii were isolated from the rest of the world. They developed their own lifestyle based on their beliefs and the natural resources of the islands. These people were highly skilled in farming and fishing. Their chiefs and priests set down a strict system of laws that the people closely followed. In addition, they believed in powerful gods and goddesses. The Hawaiians never developed a written language. Instead, legends, traditions, and oral, or spoken, stories are the sources of information about Hawaii's early history.

Hawaii's modern history dates from 1778. In that year, Captain James Cook, a British naval officer, visited the island. After that, Hawaii was open for contact with the rest of the world.

Hawaii became an American possession in 1898 and joined the United States as the fiftieth state in 1959. Today, Hawaii is the home of people from many parts of the world. The descendants of the early Polynesians make up about 15 percent of the population and are called Hawaiians. The rest of the population are descendants of people who came to Hawaii from China, Japan, Korea, the Philippines, Europe, and mainland America. Although English is the most widely spoken language, the languages of the early Hawaiians and other peoples are also heard. The culture of the early Hawaiians still is part of the rich heritage of the state. However, in other ways Hawaii is becoming like the other American states. For example, in this state of beautiful beaches and majestic mountains, most people live in cities. Many Hawaiians work in the states' busy tourist industry. Others work in the sugar and pineapple industries.

Now answer the following questions:

1. How did the early Polynesians reach the islands and where did they come from?

2. Describe the culture of the early Hawaiians.

▲ The symbol for the Thunderbird is atop this totem pole. What do you think the second figure on the totem pole symbolizes?

People in History

10. Shamans The people of the Pacific Northwest Coast believed that **shamans**, or medicine men, had magical powers. They believed shamans could cure sickness, bring good weather, and ensure a large catch of salmon. Shamans were thought to have the power to chase away evil forces and to bring the nation victory in war. Both men and women were shamans. In some Pacific Northwest nations, the most powerful shamans were women.

11. The nations of the Pacific Northwest believed shamans were able to communicate with the spirits that ruled everything in the world. One of the greatest of these spirits was the Thunderbird, a great creature who lived on top of the highest mountain. With its great wings, the Thunderbird was believed to make rain fall. Shamans carried on many religious ceremonies to ask the Thunderbird for rain.

12. One of the most important ceremonies of the Northwest Pacific Coast peoples, in which one clan honored another clan, was the **potlatch** (POT-lach). This event took its name from a Nootka word meaning "to give." Chiefs and other leaders invited guests to a potlatch. During this festival, villagers would sing, dance, and tell stories about the history of their tribe. The host also would give many presents to the invited guests to show off his wealth and power.

Spotlight on Sources

13. One rich source about the history of Native Americans of the Northwest Pacific Coast is their **totem poles**. A totem pole is a carved pillar of wood. Each group's totem pole would have an animal as its most important symbol. Other carved images on the totem pole stood for people, spirits, or animals that had aided the group in the past. These images helped a group to remember and tell about its history.

The People of California What ways of life developed among the many Native American people in California?

14. The present-day state of California was the home of the largest Native American population north of Mexico. About 300,000 Native Americans lived there. They were organized into more than 100 different nations. California was so rich in natural sources of food that tribes there never needed to develop farming. The mild climate and plentiful supply of food allowed most of the nations to live together in peace.

Outlook

15. The early people of the North and the Pacific Northwest Coast lived in very different regions. Their ways of life centered largely on the natural resources available to them. What were some reason why Native Americans developed many different cultures? What do you think these early people valued most?

15

CHAPTER REVIEW

VOCABULARY REVIEW

▶ Write each word on a separate sheet of paper. Then write the letter of the definition next to the word it defines.

1. caribou
2. Inuit
3. kayak
4. totem pole
5. potlatch
6. culture
7. igloo
8. shamans
9. natural resources

a. a carved pillar of wood

b. a people's way of life

c. things of nature such as bees and minerals

d. a canoe with a small opening for the paddler

e. a round building made of blocks of packed snow.

f. people who live in the region from western Alaska to Greenland.

g. medicine men and women of the Pacific Northwest.

h. festival of the Northwest Indians in which one clan honor another clan.

i. a kind of a large deer

j. an ice house

SKILL BUILDER: MAKING A CHART

▶ Copy the chart below on a separate sheet of paper. Then write in the information about these Native American peoples you have read about in this chapter.

	Inuit	Pacific Northwest	Hawaiians
Location			
Culture			
Houses			
Food			
Types of Boats			
Other Facts			

SKILL BUILDER: CRITICAL THINKING AND COMPREHENSION

▲ I. Main Idea

▶ The main idea tells what a paragraph is about. On a separate sheet of paper, write the number of the paragraph in the text of this chapter that gives the main idea.

Main Idea

a. The tribes of the Pacific Northwest never needed to develop farming.

Paragraph Number

Main Idea	Paragraph Number

b. The Inuit depended on hunting animals for food and clothing.

c. The Pacific Northwest Coast tribes were peaceful.

d. The Inuit way of living varied depending on the season.

e. The life of Pacific tribes was closely connected to the water.

f. The Native Americans of California led peaceful lives.

g. The potlatch was an important ceremony among Northwest Pacific Coast peoples.

II. Fact *versus* Opinion

▶ Some of the following statements are facts, others are opinions. On a separate sheet of paper, write *F* if a statement is a fact, *O* if it is an opinion.

a. The Inuit were skilled hunters.

b. The Pacific Northwest people should never have used shamans to cure people of illness.

c. The custom of the potlatch was a way a Pacific Coast chief could show others how rich he was.

d. Some historians believe the Pacific Coast people had a more advanced culture than the Inuit.

USING PRIMARY SOURCES

▶ Look again at the picture of the totem pole on page 15. Why do you think the makers of pole chose the figures represented on the pole?

ENRICHMENT

1. Reread the chapter. Describe a day in the life of an Inuit family. What would they eat? What would their home look like? What animals would they see?

2. Find out how the Inuit built their igloos and make a presentation to your class of what you have learned.

3. Describe the animals that were most important to the Inuit and the tribes of the Northwest Pacific Coast. In what ways were these animals important to these people?

CHAPTER 3

Native Americans of the Mid-Continent

OBJECTIVE: How did the Native Americans of the Mid-Continent develop their rich cultures?

1. The two cowboys rode their horses slowly along the trail. Snow was beginning to fall, and they still had not found their lost cattle. As the cowboys rode their horses into the snowy valley, they saw a sight they would never forget. There, in the walls of the canyon, high above them, were stone houses. As they looked more closely, they were even more amazed. The stone houses were part of a village that people had built far above the valley. On that snowy afternoon in December 1888, these cowboys discovered Mesa Verde. This village in southern Colorado had been built nearly 600 years earlier by early Native Americans called the Anasazi.

Peoples of the Great Plains What ways of living developed among the Native Americans on the Great Plains?

2. The Great Plains are in the central part of the United States. This huge area of grasslands has few trees except in its river valleys. Enormous herds of buffalo and antelope once roamed across the Great Plains. Elk and deer were also found there.

3. Two different ways of living, farming and hunting, developed among the Native American nations of the Great Plains. The farming nations, such as the Mandan (MAN-dan), Hidatsa (hy-DAH-tsuh), and Arikara (uh-REE-kuh-

▲ Each year the Mandans had a four-day ceremony called Okipa. The ceremony celebrated the creation of the Mandan people. Young men had to go through a series of tortures. When exhausted, they were said to see their life goals in visions.

ruh), lived on the eastern side of the Great Plains. Their main crops were squash, beans, and corn. These peoples usually raised extra food and traded it with the buffalo-hunting nations for meat and animal hides.

In Chapter 3 you will apply this critical thinking skill to the historical process:
▲ **Recognizing the Main Idea:** Identifying the most important idea in a paragraph.

4. The Native Americans in most parts of the rest of the Great Plains were nomadic buffalo-hunting peoples. They are the nations that historians often call the Plains Indians. There were about 30 Plains Indian nations. The most powerful were the nations we know as the Arapahoe (uh-RAP-uh-hoh), Blackfoot, Cheyenne (shy-EN), Comanche (kuh-MAN-chee), Crow, Kiowa (KY-oh-wuh), and Sioux (SOO). These names of the nations were given to them by later Europeans. The way of life of these Plains nomads differed greatly from the life of the farming peoples. They moved from place to place hunting buffalo and living in tents called **tepees.** Tepees were made of poles covered with buffalo hides. They could easily be taken apart and carried when the people moved.

5. Later, horses introduced by the Spanish were used by the Plains nations. Horses allowed them to move across the huge area of the Great Plains faster and more easily. As a result, hunters on horseback could kill as many buffalo in one day as they had killed before in a week.

People of the Southwest How did Native Americans in the Southwest live?

6. Three important cultures developed in the American Southwest after 300 B.C. They were the Mogollon (MOH-goh-yahn), Hohokam, (hoh-HOH-kuhm), and Anasazi (an-uh-SAH-zee) cultures. The Southwest is hotter and drier than the Great Plains. This region has a desert climate with little rainfall.

7. The Mogollon people lived in the rugged mountain land of present-day eastern Arizona and western New Mexico. There they grew beans, corn, and squash for food. Hohokam culture, centered in present-day southern Arizona, was also a farming culture. Because so little rain fell in the area, the Hohokam dug canals that sent river water to their farm fields.

8. The Anasazi lived in the Four Corners area of the Southwest, where present-day Arizona, New Mexico, Colorado, and Utah meet. Anasazi means the "old ones." The Anasazi were expert builders. Anasazi villages were located on the sides of steep cliffs high above river valleys. There they were safe from attack by enemies. The Anasazi lived in large apartment-like houses. Many were several stories high. Some houses had as many as 800 rooms. The only way of entering these houses was up a ladder that led to an opening in the roof. If they were attacked, the people of the village only had to pull the ladders up to be safe.

9. Sometime around 1300, the Anasazi left their cliff villages. No one is sure why. Perhaps a terrible drought or a water shortage forced them to leave. Almost all of the Anasazi moved toward the southeast, where they resettled in the area of the Rio Grande in what is now New Mexico. However, one group, the Hopi, stayed in northern Arizona and kept its farming way of life. For protection, the Hopi now built their villages on the top of great rocky plateaus, called **mesas** (MAY-suhz). How would this location ◄ protect the Hopi? The Hopi village of Oraibi is still in use today. People have lived there longer than in any other town in the United States.

10. Other descendants of the Anasazi now live along the Rio Grande in villages of stone and **adobe** (uh-DOH-bee) houses. Adobe is a mixture of clay and straw that makes a long-lasting building material. The Spanish called these farming people the **Pueblo** (PWEB-loh), a Spanish word meaning "village." Pueblo villages had special underground rooms called **kivas** (KEE-vuhz), where Pueblo men held religious ceremonies. In the floor of the kiva was a small hole to allow powerful spirits called **kachinas** (kuh-CHEE-nuhz) to enter.

Spotlight on Sources

11. The Pueblo people believed that kachinas had the power to bring rain and a full harvest. In Pueblo ceremonies dancers wore masks and pretended they were kachinas. At the end of a dance, one of the men made a farewell speech to a kachina:

> When you go home and get to your parents and sisters and the rest of your relatives who are waiting for you, tell them

Background: The Spaniards' arrival changed the ways of life for the Native Americans in the Southwest. Not only did Spanish soldiers bring horses and written history, they brought guns, slavery, and a new religion.

19

The Geography of Mesa Verde National Park Geography is the study of places and how their physical (natural) and human features interact. Study the map below to compare how the physical features of Mesa Verde were developed by prehistoric Native Americans and by Americans of today.

Landforms in the park have steep-sided canyons (brown) and high and fairly flat-topped mesas or tablelands (green). The brown contour lines show altitude and are numbered in feet above sea level. Slopes are steep where contour lines are close together and gentle where they are far apart.

The climate is too dry for permanent rivers. Melting snows and some rain fill up the non-permanent rivers in the spring, but the rivers are short-lived and soon dry up. Vegetation is more plentiful on the flat mesa tops than in the canyons. This vegetation provides food and cover for wildlife.

From A.D. 700 to 1200, the mesa tops were densely populated with Native Americans. At first these Native American inhabitants of

Mesa Verde lived on the mesa tops. They lived in pithouses dug out of the ground and roofed with woven logs and twigs. About A.D.1000, they built stone apartment-like buildings or "pueblos." Then, about 1200, the mesa-top dwellings were suddenly abandoned. The people moved into hard-to-reach cliff dwellings built high on the sides of the mesas along canyon walls. No one knows why they moved. Finally, about 1300, the cliff dwellings, too, were abandoned, and the people moved away.

Today, few Americans live year-round in Mesa Verde. Modern Americans see the land as too dry, too rugged, and too isolated for farming or settlement. Instead, they value the land as a national park.

Now use the map to answer these questions:

1. How are the mesas and canyons shown?

2. Where are most cliff dwellings?

3. What human features on the map are park-related?

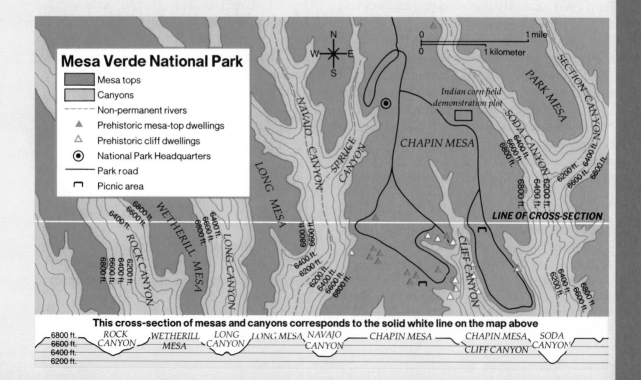

This cross-section of mesas and canyons corresponds to the solid white line on the map above

People in History

12. He-e-e Among the Native Americans of the Southwest, there are many legends about great warriors. One legend tells of He-e-e, a Hopi warrior girl. One day He-e-e's mother was combing and fixing her daughter's hair. Without warning, enemies attacked the village. He-e-e's hair was half-finished, with one side hanging loose, when the attack came. Quickly picking up her bow and arrows, He-e-e climbed the village wall and, showing no fear, shot her arrows at the attackers. Not expecting such a strong and fearless fighter, the attackers fled. Ever since, the Hopis have believed this girl was a kachina. Many drawings and dolls have been made of He-e-e, with one part of her hair up and the other side hanging down.

13. In about 1100, the Pueblos were attacked by bands of Athapaskan (a-thuh-PAS-kuhn) Indians from western Canada. The newcomers attacked the peaceful Pueblo villages, stealing their animals and crops. Later, the Athapaskans split into two different tribes that lived in the Southwest. These were called the Navajos (NAH-vuh-hohz) and the Apaches (uh-PACH-eez). The Navajos lived in **hogans** (HOH-gnz), or one-room houses, made of poles covered with packed earth and brush. They raised sheep and other animals and farmed the land. The Apaches continued to hunt and were among the most skilled and feared fighters in the Southwest. They lived in huts called **wickiups** (WIK-ee-ups), made of grass, twigs, and tree branches.

Outlook

14. Two groups of Native Americans lived on the Great Plains. The nations of the eastern plains were farming people. The Plains Indians were nomadic people, who wandered across vast areas of the land to hunt buffalo. In the Southwest, the Pueblo and the Navajo were farmers, while the Apaches were hunters. What ◀ things do you think were most important in shaping the lives of different Native American tribes?

▲ Native Americans of the Southwest held elaborate ceremonies like the kachina dance shown here to bring the rain they needed to grow their crops.

all the words that I am going to tell you. Tell them that they should not wait, but let them come at once and bring rain to our fields. We may have just a few crops in our fields, but when you bring the rain they will grow up and become strong. Then if you will bring some more rain on them, we will have more corn, and more beans, and more watermelons, and all the rest of our crops. . . .

So now, this will be all. Now go back home happily, but do not forget us. . . .
—from *Americas' Fascinating Heritage*

▶ What did the Pueblos expect the kachina to bring? What do you notice about the way the speaker talked to the kachina?

Activity: Many Native Americans tribes faced the constant threat of attack from other tribes. Write why you think these fights occurred. How do you think this changed with the arrival of Europeans?

21

CHAPTER REVIEW

VOCABULARY REVIEW

▶ On a sheet of paper, write the numbered words below. Then write the letter and the definition next to the word it defines.

1. pueblo
2. kiva
3. mesas
4. teepee
5. hogan
6. wickiup
7. kachina
8. adobe

a. a spirit
b. place where Pueblo men met to hold religious ceremonies
c. house made of poles covered with earth and brush
d. a building material
e. rocky plateau
f. cowboy of the Southwest
g. an Apache home
h. a movable tent
i. Spanish word for village

SKILL BUILDER: INTERPRETING A PHOTOGRAPH

▶ Look at the photograph below. Then answer these questions on a sheet of paper.

1. What are the long poles used for in this photograph of a Great Plains Native American mother and her children?

2. What evidence do you see that buffalo were an important resource to these people?

3. Where do you see the influence of European cultures in these Native Americans' lives?

SKILL BUILDER: CRITICAL THINKING AND COMPREHENSION

I. Main Idea

Did you ever talk to someone who never "came to the point"? The "point" in talking or reading is the same as the main idea. It is the idea which all the other ideas support or are about.

▶ Reread the paragraphs noted below. The main idea of each paragraph is given. On a sheet of paper, write two or three facts from the paragraph that support the main idea.

1. **Paragraph 3:** Farming provided most of the food needed by the eastern Great Plains tribes.

2. **Paragraph 5.** The introduction of horses by the Spanish brought about improvements in Plains Indians' lives.

3. **Paragraph 8:** The Anasazi built houses several stories high on the sides of cliffs.

4. **Paragraph 13:** The Athapaskans split into two tribes.

II. Classifying

When you classify, you sort items into groups. Copy the following chart on a piece of paper. The chart classifies the Native American nations discussed in this chapter. Complete the chart by writing each nation in the correct box.

	Plains Nations	Southwest Nations
Farming Nations		
Hunting Nations		

USING PRIMARY SOURCES

▶ Reread the Spotlight on Sources on pages 19 and 21. Why did the Pueblo people have a kachina ceremony? If the Plains nations had a similar ceremony, what would they expect from their kachina?

ENRICHMENT

1. Find early Native American myths, legends, or stories that explain how the world began or how their way of life was created. Write a short summary of the myth and tell something about the way of life of the people.

2. Read how historians found out about the Anasazi, who did not leave written records. Prepare a report for the class about the research of scientists who studied the Anasazi.

3. Visit a Native American history museum or find books in your library. List the types of artifacts made by early Native Americans. Tell where the artifacts were found, the dates these artifacts were believed to have been made or used, and which tribes they came from. Using this method of historical research, list a few artifacts from your everyday life. What do they reveal about the way you live?

23

CHAPTER 4

Native Americans of the Eastern Woodlands

OBJECTIVE: How did Native Americans in the Eastern Woodlands live?

1. Sixty men on each team were lined up, ready for the game to start. Each player held two sticks with a webbed loop at the end for catching a leather ball. The object of the game was to catch a ball and throw it between the opposing team's goal posts. As the game began, the players dashed about the field trying to get the ball. They tackled each other and kicked and hit as hard as they could. This game, similar to lacrosse today, was played by the Muskogee (mus-KOH-gee) people during their harvest celebration. The game was taken seriously as practice for fighting in war. As part of the harvest celebration, the Muskogee also went without food, took steam baths, and drank dark herb tea. Then at the end they lighted new fires and roasted the first green ears of corn. This harvest celebration was very important to the Muskogee, for they were celebrating their first crop of the year. Like many other Native Americans of the Eastern Woodlands, the Muskogee were skilled farmers.

▲ This is a picture of a Algonquin village in North Carolina. What does the picture tell you about the lifestyle of this people?

Peoples of the Northeast Woodlands What kinds of societies were formed by the Iroquois and the Algonquin?

2. The vast area between the Northeast Atlantic Coast and the Mississippi River was the home of the Northeast Woodlands people. These Northeast Woodland nations belonged to two large groups, the Iroquois (IH-ruh-kwoy) and the Algonquin (al-GAHNG-kwin). The Iroquois were the more powerful group. The Iroquois included the Mohawk, Seneca, Cayuga (ky-OO-guh), Onondaga (oh-nahn-DAH-gah), and Oneida (oh-NY-duh) tribes. The Iroquois lived in present-day New York State.

In Chapter 4 you will apply these critical thinking skills to the historical process:

📁 **Classifying:** Organizing facts into categories based on what they have in common.

▲▲ **Recognizing the Main Idea:** Identifying the main idea in a paragraph.

Algonquin nations lived along the Atlantic coast from Canada to Virginia and around the Great Lakes. The main Algonquin nations were the Naragansett (na-ruh-GAN-set), Pequot (PEH-kwaht), Delaware, Mohegan (moh-HEE-gun), and Powhatan (POW-ha-tan).

3. The thick forests that covered the Northeast Woodlands were important to the Native Americans who lived there. They depended on these forests for their food and shelter. They used logs and branches to make their houses, canoes, tools, and weapons. Deer, beaver, and moose provided them with meat for food, hides for clothing and moccasins, and bones to make tools. Northeast Woodlands peoples also gathered nuts and fruit from the forest and fished in the rivers and streams. What does this tell you about how Native Americans lived in harmony with nature?

4. The Native Americans of the Eastern Woodlands were farmers as well as hunters. The men cleared the forests to make farmland, but women did most of the farming. The main crops were corn, beans, and squash. The Iroquois called these crops "the three sisters," and they gave thanks to the spirits for them in religious ceremonies. Like most Native Americans, the Northeast Woodlands nations believed spirits were in all parts of nature.

5. The Northeast Woodlands nations lived in small villages protected by fences made of wooden stakes. The people's houses were built close together. These houses were made of wooden poles tied together to make a frame. Layers of tree bark were used for the walls and roof. The Algonquin houses, called **wigwams,** had a round or oval shape and a domed roof. Iroquois homes, called **long houses,** were larger dwellings. A long house often measured 50 to 100 feet (about 15 to 30 m) long. It was divided into a central hall with rooms on both sides of this hall. Eight to ten families lived in each long house, which was the property of the women who lived there.

6. In the Iroquois nations, women had a very important role. Women owned the farmland and tended the crops. Family membership was traced through the mother's side of the family. Iroquois women were in charge of raising the children. Children stayed with their mothers until seven or eight years of age. Then boys went off with the men, and girls stayed with the women. Boys and girls then learned hunting and farming skills from the men and women of the nation. After an Iroquois girl married, she and her husband lived in her mother's long house. In this way, the long house became the home of each mother's family. How did this custom show the importance of Iroquois women?

The Iroquois League How did the Iroquois tribes form a powerful union?

7. About 1450, the five Iroquois nations joined together to form the **League** (LEEG) **of the Iroquois.** A league is an association of groups or individuals united for common interest or goals. The purpose of this powerful League was to end fighting among the nations and to set up a strong government.

People in History

8. Hiawatha and Deganawidah No one knows for sure when the Iroquois League began or who founded it. Like other Native Americans, the Iroquois had no written history. However, they did pass down stories in which they told how the League began. One of these stories says that the Iroquois League was founded by Hiawatha (hy-uh-WAH-thuh) and Deganawidah (duh-gan-uh-WY-duh). Deganawidah is said to have been a Mohawk chief or even to have come from the spirits. Hiawatha was probably an Onondaga chief. According to Iroquois legend, these two chiefs were upset by the bloody wars being fought among the Iroquois nations. They decided they must end this warfare. The Iroquois League was set up to bring peace to the nations and help them defend themselves against other enemies. Hiawatha's and Deganawidah's ideas were to be used later by the leaders of the colonies.

Activity: Have students read Chapters 2–4 from *The Book of Indians* by Holling C. Holling, which is a fictionalized account of woodland life, or other books available from the library about the woodland tribes.

Spotlight on Sources

9. Iroquois legend also recounts the speech that Hiawatha made when the Iroquois League was founded. Hiawatha spoke these words to his people:

> Friends and Brothers: You begin as members of many tribes. . . . The voice [danger] of war has aroused [upset] you. You are afraid [for] your homes, your wives, and your children. . . . We must unite ourselves into one common band of brothers. We must have but one voice. Many voices make confusion. We must have one fire, one pipe, and one war club [weapon]. This will give us strength.
>
> —from *The Jesuit Relations and Allied Documents,* ed. by Reuben G. Thwaites

---

▼ This Native American is covering his canoe with birch bark. Canoes were used on the Eastern Woodlands' many streams and lakes.

How would you state the main idea of Hiawatha's speech? What is your opinion of Hiawatha's goals?

10. The Iroquois League was headed by a council made up of **50** chiefs from the five Iroquois nations. This council helped the nations to settle their disputes with one another and learn to live in peace. The council also helped the nations to unite and prepare for war with other nations. Each Iroquois nation also had its own chief and controlled its people's affairs. The League worked so well that the Iroquois became the most powerful group among the Northeast Woodlands nations. Later, the Tuscorora nation also joined the Iroquois League.

Native Americans of the Southeast Woodlands

What ways of living developed among the Creek, Natchez, and other nations?

11. The Southeast Woodlands stretched north to south from present-day Tennessee to the Gulf of Mexico. East to west it stretched from the Atlantic coast to the lower Mississippi valley. Among the nations of the Southeast Woodlands were the Creek, Natchez, Seminole, Cherokee, Choctaw, and Chickasaw. The people of the Southeast Woodlands nations were skilled farmers. They lived in farming villages near rivers and streams. The climate of the Southeast Woodlands was mild and good for growing crops. Their chief crop was corn, but they also grew beans, squash, pumpkins, and tobacco. Women did most of the farming, though men also sometimes worked in the fields. Men also fished and hunted turkey, deer, and other animals to provide food for the people of the village.

12. The importance of farming among the nations of the Southeast Woodlands was shown in their ways of living. Villages were moved often to new lands after the old soil had worn out. The ashes of dead trees were used to fertilize the soil. By cutting into the trunk of the tree, they could kill it and then burn it. Fish were also used to fertilize the soil. Crops were

Background: Another source of information about Native American society was Benjamin Franklin. Franklin published records of assemblies and negotiations with Native Americans. Indian Commissioner during the 1750s, he learned about the League of the Iroquois and recommended that the colonies follow its example.

26

▲ The Southeastern Native Americans had to protect their corn crops from blackbirds and crows. One woman is hitting an object to make loud noises and the other woman is waving a piece of cloth to scare away the birds. At night the Native Americans built bonfires to keep the birds away.

planted in common fields, which everyone helped to care for. The crops from these fields were for public use by the entire village. Families planted their own gardens as well, and they owned the crops they grew there.

13. The Creek, who lived in the present-day states of Alabama and Georgia, were an important Southern Woodland nation. The Creek lived in villages that were joined together in a **confederation,** or league. The Creek Confederation was organized for both war and peacetime. Within the Creek Confederation there were "red towns" and "white towns." Red towns took charge of Creek warfare. White towns were towns of peace. The chief of the Creek Confederation always came from a white town. The chief who led the Creek in fighting came from a red town. How was the Creek Confederation different from the Iroquois League?

14. Another kind of government among Southern Woodland nations was found among the Natchez. The Natchez were the only North American nation to have an absolute ruler. This ruler was called the Great Sun, and he had power of life and death over the people. The Great Sun's feet were not allowed to touch the ground, so he was carried everywhere. He lived in a special dwelling at the top of an earthen mound in the center of the village. On a nearby mound was his temple.

15. The Natchez nation was divided into several classes. The highest class was the small group of people who were related to the Great Sun. In the next class were the nobles and a group called the Honored Ones. At the bottom were the common people, called Stinkards.

Outlook

16. The people of the Northeast Woodlands and the Southeast Woodlands developed important well-organized cultures. Most depended on farming and lived a settled village life. The Iroquois and the Creek formed leagues to help keep peace among their nations. In all of the Eastern Woodlands, Native Americans developed ways of living that blended with the land and climate. Why do you think Native Americans did not try to change the land?

Ask: Why do you think some tribes built mounds for their temples and chiefs? Encourage students to explore different reasons such as the following: to symbolize their higher status; to be closer to the sun, their source of power; to provide a higher vantage point from which to see more of their land and people; to continue traditions.

27

CHAPTER REVIEW

VOCABULARY REVIEW

▶ Use these words to complete the sentences below.

confederation   long house   wigwam   league

1. Nations often formed an alliance or _____ with other nearby groups who had simi.
   interests.

2. Young men would help put up the poles for the framework of the _____ .

3. A _____ is another word for a league.

4. The _____ was where many families lived, it had a long central hall, with rooms along
   both sides.

USING PRIMARY SOURCES

▶ Reread the Spotlight on Sources on pages 25–26. What does Hiawatha mean when he says,
"We must have but one voice"?

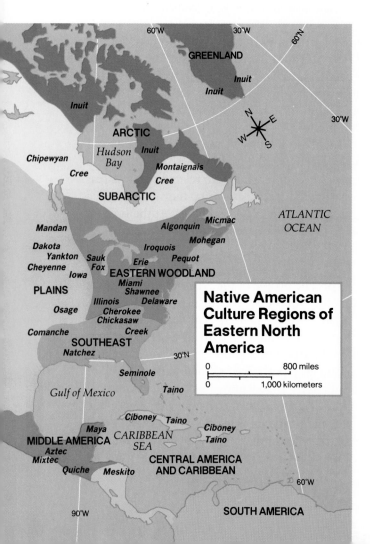

Native American Culture Regions of Eastern North America

SKILL BUILDER: READING A MAP

▶ The map at the left shows the major Native American culture regions of eastern North America. As you answer these questions on a sheet of paper, think of how each nation's lifestyle may have been influenced by the geography of the land.

1. What people lived in the most northern part of the continent?

2. What nation lived in the most southern part of the continent?

3. Name nations who lived close to the Atlantic Ocean in North America.

4. Name at least three nations who lived near the Great Lakes.

5. Name at least two neighbors of the Cherokee.

SKILL BUILDER: CRITICAL THINKING AND COMPREHENSION

I. Introduction to Classifying

When you listen to music, how do you know what type it is? You can tell by listening to the tempo, rhythm, and beat. Sometimes, you can also tell by what the lyrics are saying, and how they are sung. Is it rock, pop, jazz, gospel, or classical? Or is it country? **Classifying** things helps you put things together that have something in common. If you heard Michael Jackson's *Bad*, you would classify it with your pop albums. If you heard Dolly Parton's songs, you would classify them as country music.

1. On a piece of paper set up two columns. Title one column *Algonquin Language* and the other *Iroquois Language*. Then classify the following nations under the correct language.

   1. Oneida
   2. Delaware
   3. Mohawk
   4. Mohican
   5. Seneca
   6. Powhatan

2. Divide another piece of paper into three columns. Title the columns *Food*, *Clothing*, and *Tools and Other Uses*. Classify the following list according to the way the Native American used them. Some items may be classified in more than one column.

   1. deer
   2. corn
   3. trees
   4. nuts
   5. fish
   6. beans

II. Main Idea

▶ Imagine that you had to send three telegrams that had the main idea of each of the paragraphs that are numbered below. Write the telegrams on a sheet of paper. Use no more than 25 words for each telegram.

Paragraph 4

Paragraph 14

Paragraph 15

ENRICHMENT

1. Find information on how Native Americans in the Eastern Woodlands made their pottery and what their pottery looked like. Follow their methods to make your own pottery.

2. Research various ways Native Americans used corn, squash, beans, and wild food sources such as fruits, nuts, and seeds. Prepare dishes that have a Native American origin and share them with the class as lunch or a snack.

3. Imagine you are a newspaper reporter asked to write about the kinds of houses used by Native Americans of the Eastern Woodlands. Write an article using what you have learned about the houses in this chapter and information from other books and encyclopedias.

CHAPTER 5

Native Americans of Latin America

> OBJECTIVE: What were the main features of the Mayan, Aztec, and Inca civilizations?

1. One day in 1839, an American named John Lloyd Stephens was on an expedition deep in the rain forests of Central America. Suddenly, in the dense jungle, Stephens and his companions came upon the ancient city of Copán. It was overgrown with trees and creeping vines. Yet everywhere Stephens saw huge stones and carved pillars where great buildings had once stood. "All was mystery," Stephens later wrote. The great city of Copán was in ruins. The only sounds he heard were "the scrambling of monkeys and the chattering of parrots." After Stephens's discovery, scientists and historians began to study this great city and the Maya people who had built it. The Mayan civilization was one of three great Native American civilizations that developed in Latin America.

The Maya What were some achievements of the Mayan civilization?

2. The Maya lived in Yucatán, a peninsula along the Gulf of Mexico. Yucatán includes present-day Guatemala, Belize, and part of Mexico. Here, about 600 B.C., the Maya developed a settled way of life based on farming. They were one of the earliest people to raise corn. They cleared rain forests to grow this crop as well as beans, squash, and sweet potatoes. They also grew cotton, which they wove into cloth.

▲ The steps of this Mayan pyramid lead up to the temple on top. Only priests and the ruler were allowed into the temple.

3. The Maya built great cities, which were centers of their religion. Copán, whose ruins Stephens discovered in 1839, was one of these cities. Only priests and noble families lived in Mayan cities. The rest of the people lived in farming villages. The priests of the city ruled the people of the nearby villages.

In Chapter 5 you will apply these critical thinking skills to the historical process:

📁 **Classifying:** Organizing facts into categories based on what they have in common.

▲ **Recognizing the Main Idea:** Identifying the main idea in a paragraph.

4. The largest city was Tikal, the capital. All the buildings in Tikal had a religious purpose. In the center of the city were great stone pyramids, with steps leading to a temple at the top. In the huge square in front of the pyramids, religious ceremonies were held. Near the pyramids were stone shafts called **steles** (STEE-leez), carved with pictures of priests and gods.

5. The Mayan religion included belief in many gods. All of the gods were connected with nature and the corn harvest. Each god had to be honored in great ceremonies to ensure that the corn would grow and people would have food. Village people brought animals and crops to the priests, who gave them to the gods as gifts.

6. Mayan priests shaped the culture of their people in many important ways. They made interesting discoveries in **astronomy** (as-TRAH-nuh-mee). Astronomy is the science that studies the planets and the stars. Using this knowledge, Mayan priests worked out a calendar that was more accurate than the one used in Europe at the time of Columbus.

7. The priests developed a system of numbers. They also invented a system of writing. This writing used picture symbols called **glyphs** (GLIFS). Historians do not yet know what the glyphs mean. However, they know the Mayan priests used this writing to keep records of the sun's movements and religious events. Why ◀ would arithmetic and writing be useful to astronomers?

The Aztec What were some important features of Aztec culture?

8. The Aztec were another important group of Native Americans who developed a great civilization in Mexico. About 1200, Aztecs moved into central Mexico. About 1325, they built a beautiful capital city, Tenochtitlán (tay-nahch-tee-TLAN), by building islands in a lake. Tenochtitlan was a beautiful city with bridges to the mainland by day. At night or during an enemy attack the bridges could be lifted to protect the city. Mexico City today stands where this ancient capital was built. Nearly 100,000 people lived in Tenochtitlán, making it one of the largest cities in the world at the time.

9. The Aztec were a warlike people. In a short time, they brought most of central Mexico under their control. All the conquered peoples were forced to give the Aztec corn, gold, cotton, or slaves as **tribute** (TRIB-yoot). Tribute is a payment that a nation demands from a conquered people.

10. Like the Maya, the Aztec worshiped many gods. The Aztec believed their lives were shaped by the will of the gods. For example, they believed that the sun god made the sun rise and set each day. To please and strengthen the gods of the sun and war, the priests made human sacrifices. In fact, many Aztec wars were fought in order to capture warriors who were later sacrificed to the gods.

MAP SKILL BUILDER: A map key explains what the colors and symbols on a map mean. Always study the key when using a map. **1.** What color locates the Aztec civilization? **2.** What was the capital city of the Maya?

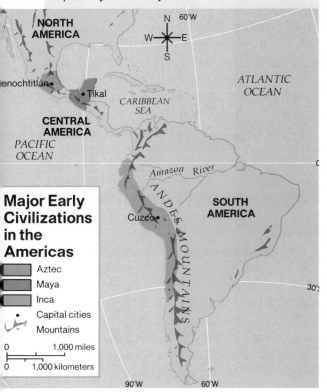

NORTH AMERICA

60°W
N
W—E
S

enochtitlán•
• Tikal
CARIBBEAN SEA

ATLANTIC OCEAN

CENTRAL AMERICA

PACIFIC OCEAN

Amazon River

ANDES

SOUTH AMERICA

Cuzco•

MOUNTAINS

90°W   60°W

Major Early Civilizations in the Americas

- Aztec
- Maya
- Inca
- • Capital cities
- Mountains

0   1,000 miles
0   1,000 kilometers

Background: English has several words derived from Latin American languages of the early peoples. Most of them are names of plants or animals previously unknown to Europeans. Nahuatl, the language of the Aztec, has given us *chocolate, ocelot,* and *tomato.* From the Inca language of Quechua come *llama, quinine,* and *vicuña.*

31

▲ Aztec traders buy and sell corn in the marketplace of Tenochtitlán, now Mexico City. On the main market days, as many as 60,000 buyers and sellers would gather here.

People in History

11. Montezuma II   The best-known Aztec ruler was Montezuma II (mahn-tuh-ZOO-muh), who ruled from 1502 to 1520. As ruler, Montezuma chose all the officials of the government and received tribute from conquered people. He also was a strong warrior-leader. Montezuma followed the Aztec tradition of taking thousands of prisoners to be sacrificed to the gods of the sun and war. Visitors had to walk barefoot and keep their eyes on the ground, for no one was allowed to look directly at Montezuma's face. During his reign the Aztec empire was at its height. The Aztec also met Europeans for the first time during his reign.

The Inca   What were some of the achievements of Inca civilization?

12. The Inca built a great empire high in the rugged Andes Mountains. At the peak of its power in the early 1500s, their empire stretched over almost all of the western coast of South America. It covered more than 2,500 miles (4,000 km) from north to south. Although only a small amount of their mountainous land could be used for farming, the Inca produced large amounts of crops. As a result, Inca farmers were able to grow the food needed to support nearly 15 million people. Inca farmers dug canals to bring water to their crops. They built **terraces** (TER-uh-suhz), or platforms of earth rising like steps up the mountainsides. The terraces allowed them to gain more farmland. The Inca also **domesticated** (doh-MES-tuh-kay-tuhd), or tamed, llamas. The llama looks like a small camel. The Inca used llamas to carry goods and as a source of wool, meat and milk.

13. The Inca emperor was thought of as a god who had total power. He was believed to come from the sun god, and the people obeyed his every order and command. They also paid heavy taxes by giving the emperor part of their crops each year. In return, the Inca emperor gave the people food when crops failed, and his officials helped people who were sick or poor.

Activity: There are many Spanish narratives about the cultures they discovered in America. Among the best known are Diego de Landa, Bernal Diaz, and Francisco de Xerez. Garcilaso de la Vega's writings include descriptions of the royal gardens in Cuzco, the building of suspension bridges, and the messenger system.

14. The Inca built their empire both by conquest and by wise rule. To unite their empire, the Inca made the people they conquered use the Inca language and follow Inca customs. They built roads covering thousands of miles to link all parts of the Inca Empire together. Runners carrying orders from the emperor and his officials used these roads to reach all parts of the Inca Empire. Since the Inca had no writing system, the runners had to memorize the orders they brought from the emperor. Each runner carried a **quipu** (KEE-poo), which was made of knotted pieces of string in different colors. The position of the knots helped the runners remember the messages they were to deliver.

15. The Inca were excellent builders and engineers. The Inca capital of Cuzco (KOOS-koh), built in the high Andes Mountains, had stone palaces and pyramid-shape temples. A huge fortress guarded the city. It was built with huge stones weighing several tons. They fit together so perfectly that Inca walls have lasted thousands of years, even through earthquakes.

Spotlight on Sources

16. Spanish soldiers conquered the Inca in the 1530s. Afterwards, many Spaniards married Inca women. The son of such a marriage was Garcilaso de la Vega (gahr-see-LAH-soh day lah VAY-gah). When he was an old man living in Spain, he wrote a famous book called *Royal Commentaries of the Inca.* In it, he described the Inca way of life. Here he tells how Inca children were brought up:

> Children were brought up severely. . . . From birth, they were washed in cold water every morning. . . . However, really tender, attentive mothers took [warmed] the water in their mouths before washing their babies. This custom of a cold dip [bath] was said to strengthen the child's legs and arms and provide greater resistance to [help the child survive] harsh mountain climate. The baby's arms were kept tightly bound until the age of four months. . . . The child remained attached night and day to a netting . . . which was stretched across a chest [a trunk] with only three legs, to make it rock like a cradle.
> —*The Meas,* by Garcilaso de la Vega

What does this tell you about some hardships of ◄ living in the high Andes Mountains?

Outlook

17. The Maya, Aztec, and Inca built great civilizations in Latin America. The Maya were skilled in astronomy. They developed an accurate calendar, a numbering system, and a system of writing. All three peoples had great skill as builders. The people of these civilizations were ruled by powerful priests or emperors. Yet the Aztec and the Inca were themselves conquered by Europeans in the early 1500s. What other ◄ achievements might they have made if the Spaniards had not conquered their land?

▼ To this day archaeologists wonder how the Inca brought the cut stone used to build the city of Machu Picchu from the valley below. What do you think?

CHAPTER REVIEW

VOCABULARY REVIEW

▶ Select one of the words from the following list to complete each of the numbered sentences.

steles

astronomy

glyphs

tribute

domesticated

quipus

terraces

1. _____ is the science that studies the planets and the sun.

2. A ruler may demand that a conquered nation make a payment called _____ .

3. Stone shafts carved with Mayan symbols were called _____ .

4. Inca runners carried _____ to help them remember messages.

5. _____ animals are animals tamed by humans.

6. Mayan writing was done with picture symbols called _____ .

7. _____ , carved into the mountainsides, greatly increased farmable land.

SKILL BUILDER: INTRODUCING CONTEXT CLUES

Suppose you come across an unfamiliar word or phrase in your reading. Sometimes you can figure out the meaning of the unfamiliar word by thinking about the meanings of the words around it. When you do this, you are using context clues. **Context** means the setting in which the unfamiliar word is placed. Context also means the words around a word or phrase that can throw light on the word or phrase.

1. **a.** Find the word *expedition* in paragraph 1 on page 30.
   b. Reread the first two sentences of that paragraph.
   c. Now use context clues to explain the meaning of *expedition* on your paper. What word clues helped you?

2. **a.** Find the word *civilization* in paragraph 1 on page 30.
   b. Reread the last 3 sentences of that paragraph.
   c. Now use the context clues to explain the meaning of *civilization* on your paper. What word clues helped you?

3. **a.** Find the word *sacrifices* in paragraph 10 on page 31.
   b. Reread the paragraph.
   c. Now use the context clues to explain the meaning of *sacrifices* on your paper. What word clues helped you?

SKILL BUILDER: CRITICAL THINKING AND COMPREHENSION

I. Classifying

Classifying means putting things that are alike together.

1. Copy the table below on a sheet of paper and fill in the table with information from the chapter. Put an **X** in the spot if no information was given.

	Mayan	**Aztec**	**Inca**
Writing System			
Important Crops			
Religion			
War Customs			
Buildings			

2. On a sheet of paper make three columns titled 1. MAYA, 2. AZTEC, 3. INCA. Classify the following statements under the correct titles. Some statements may apply to all three civilizations.

a. worshiped many gods

b. sacrificed humans to their gods

c. the gods were honored to ensure good crops

d. the emperor was a god with total power

e. animals and food were given as gifts to the gods

f. they worshiped gods of sun and war

g. the priests kept records of religious events

II. Main Idea

▶ Reread the paragraphs listed below. Then take one sentence from each paragraph that states the main idea. On a sheet of paper, write each main idea.

Paragraph 3   Paragraph 10   Paragraph 15

USING PRIMARY SOURCES

▶ Reread the "Spotlight on Sources" on page 33. According to Garcilaso de la Vega, how did some mothers warm their babies' baths?

ENRICHMENT

1. Draw a picture to illustrate how an Inca mother cared for her baby.

2. In 1911 Hiram Bingham found the Inca city of Machu Picchu (MAH-choo-PEE-choo) in the mountains of Peru. In an encyclopedia or other reference work, read about Bingham and Machu Picchu. Report to the class on what you have learned.

UNIT REVIEW

SUMMARY

For many years, no one knew the origin of the earliest people of North America. Now scientists have discovered evidence that proves the first people to settle in America came from Asia. About 30,000 years ago, people began to migrate over a land bridge that connected Asia and North America. These people were ancestors of the Native Americans.

These early people spread out in the Americas in different directions. Some went east to the cold regions around the Arctic Ocean. Most of the others went south. They settled along the Northwest Pacific Coast and California. Other early people settled the Great Plains, in the Southwest, and in the Eastern Woodlands. Still others went farther south to what is now Central and South America.

As time went on, each group developed its own way of living. All of them lived in ways that were suited to the land and climate of their region. On the Great Plains, for example, where there were hundreds of thousands of buffalo, the

Native Americans came to rely on these animals for their food and materials for clothing, tools, and weapons. With few trees in this region, they built their homes of buffalo skins and carried them with them as they moved about in search of the buffalo. In the Pacific Northwest, where fish were plentiful, the Native Americans used the fish as their main source of food. Here wood was readily available, and, since they did not have to move about in search of food, they built large houses of the wood.

Each group of Native Americans had its own way of governing itself. One of the most advanced forms of government was the Iroquois League of the Eastern Woodlands. The league was formed by five tribes of the Eastern Woodlands to assure peace among themselves.

The lives of Native Americans began to change greatly after Europeans landed on the shores of the Americas. Native Americans fought to save their way of life, but in the end they lost the battle.

SKILL BUILDER: READING A MAP

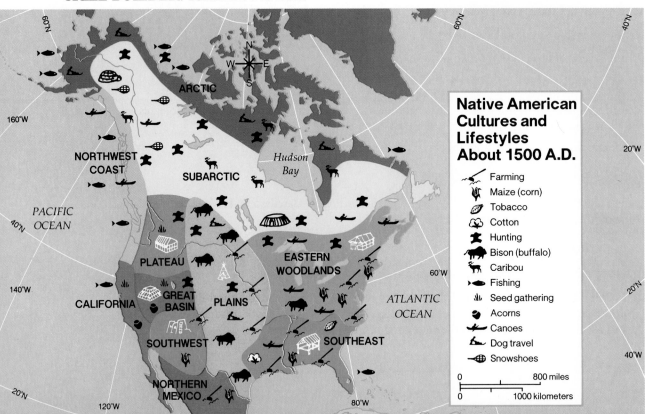

Native American Cultures and Lifestyles About 1500 A.D.

- Farming
- Maize (corn)
- Tobacco
- Cotton
- Hunting
- Bison (buffalo)
- Caribou
- Fishing
- Seed gathering
- Acorns
- Canoes
- Dog travel
- Snowshoes

0   800 miles
0   1000 kilometers

► Look at the map on the opposite page. Then answer these questions on a sheet of paper.

1. How did the California Indians get their food?

2. Where did Indians use snowshoes?

3. Which three groups did the most farming?

4. What crop did the Eastern Woodlands people raise?

5. Where did people travel by means of dogs?

SKILL BUILDER: CRITICAL THINKING AND COMPREHENSION

I. Comparing and Contrasting

► Use the map to answer these questions.

1. Contrast the animals hunted by the Plains Indians with those hunted by the Subarctic group.

2. Compare the crops of the Native Americans of the Southeast Woodlands with the crops grown by Native Americans of the Southwest.

3. Contrast the homes of the Plains Indians with those of the Inuit in the Subarctic lands.

4. Compare the houses of the Eastern Woodlands Native Americans with the houses of Native Americans of the Pacific Northwest Coast.

II. Main Idea

► Below are five items that could be headlines in a newspaper. Each expresses the main idea of a chapter in this unit. Match each headline with the chapter where that main idea is found. Use a sheet of paper for your answers.

1. Tribes Attack Neighbors and Build a Rich Empire

2. In Freezing Climate, Tribes Fish and Hunt to Live

3. Indians Use Buffalo to Meet Their Needs

4. People Cross a Land Bridge to New Homelands

5. Tribes Form a Confederation to Bring Peace

ENRICHMENT

1. Work in groups of three or four students. Each group should write a short radio commercial that tries to attract tourists to visit one of the Native American people described in this unit. Read the commercials in class and vote on which one is the most convincing.

2. Many Native American people were skilled in making paintings, carvings, jewelry, or other forms of art. Investigate the artwork of one of the people and bring to class pictures of their art. Use the pictures as the basis for a short talk on this Native American art.

37

UNIT 2

EUROPEANS EXPLORE THE AMERICAS

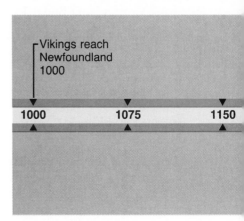

Chapter

UNIT OVERVIEW   In this unit you will learn how people from Europeans nations explored a New World and settled there.

UNIT SKILLS OBJECTIVES   In Unit 2, two critical thinking skills are emphasized:

▲ **Summarizing:** Giving the main idea of a group of paragraphs in a brief form.

○ **Generalizing:** Making a statement that links several facts.

You will also use two important social studies skills:
   Using an Encyclopedia   Making a Chart

Vikings reach
Newfoundland
1000

| 1000 | 1075 | 1150 |

ESL/LEP Strategy: Ask students to discuss what it would have been like to be an explorer arriving in the Americas or a settler already living there in the 1500s and early 1600s. Students should include these people's thoughts and feelings.

▲ The Spaniards were the first Europeans to claim land in the Americas. How do you think the Europeans seemed to the Native Americans who lived there?

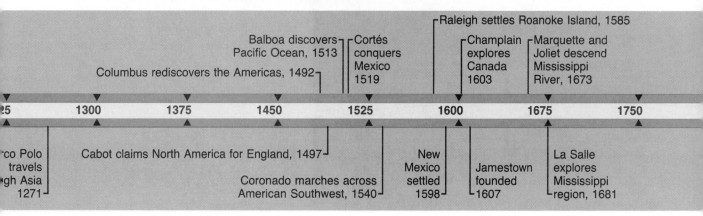

Raleigh settles Roanoke Island, 1585

Balboa discovers
Pacific Ocean, 1513

Cortés conquers Mexico 1519

Champlain explores Canada 1603

Marquette and Joliet descend Mississippi River, 1673

Columbus rediscovers the Americas, 1492

| 25 | 1300 | 1375 | 1450 | 1525 | 1600 | 1675 | 1750 |

co Polo travels gh Asia 1271

Cabot claims North America for England, 1497

Coronado marches across American Southwest, 1540

New Mexico settled 1598

Jamestown founded 1607

La Salle explores Mississippi region, 1681

Points of View

Can you name the seven continents? If you lived in the 1400s, you would say there were only three: Europe, Africa, and Asia. During this period, a new spirit of exploration swept the world. Small groups of adventurers boldly sailed across unknown seas, exploring new continents. The two letters that follow present "before" and "after" viewpoints about these European voyages of exploration. In the first, written in 1474, an Italian map maker named

▲ The Atlantic Ocean was once thought to be full of sea monsters. What basis in fact might these legends have had?

BEFORE

"Paul, the Physician to Cristobal Columbus greeting. I perceive your magnificent and great desire to find a way to where the spices grow [Asia] and . . . I send you the copy of another letter which I wrote . . . to a friend . . . of the . . . King of Portugal. . . .

I have already spoken with you respecting a shorter way to place of spices [Asia] than that which you take by Guinea [sailing around Africa]. . . . I have determined to show that way by means of a sailing chart. . . . made by my own hands, on which are delineated [shown] your coasts and islands, whence [from where] you must begin to make your journey always westward . . . and through how . . . many miles you should arrive at those most fertile places full of all sorts of spices and jewels [Asia]. You must not be surprised if I call the parts where the spices are west, when they usually call them east, because to those always sailing west, those parts are found by navigation on the under side of the earth. . . .

—*The Journal of Christopher Columbus and Documents Relating to the Voyages of John Cabot and Gaspar Corte Real,* trans. and ed. by Clements R. Markham

A New World Appears

Toscanelli makes a bold claim. Toscanelli assures Christopher Columbus that a westward sea passage from Europe to the Indies [Asia] is possible. The second letter is Columbus's own slightly exaggerated report about his first voyage to the New World. It was written in 1493 to an advisor to the King and Queen of Spain. During the next four years, this letter was printed 16 times throughout Europe. It is the first modern description of the Americas.

AFTER

"I write you this, by which you should know that in 33 days I passed over the Indies with the fleet which the . . . King and Queen gave me; where I found very many islands . . . and, of them all, I have taken possession for their Highnesses. . . . There are many havens [safe places] on the sea-coast . . . and plenty of rivers, so good and great that it is a marvel. . . . [There] are palm trees wondrous to see for their beautiful variety . . . and fruits, and plants. . . . [In] the earth there are many mines of metals . . . the mountains and hills, and plains, and fields, and the soil, so beautiful and rich for planting and sowing, for breeding cattle of all sorts, for building of towns and villages. There could be no believing without seeing, such harbors. . . . as well as the many great rivers, and excellent waters, most of which contain gold. . . . [There] are many spiceries, and great mines of gold and other metals. . . . This is a land to be desired and once seen never to be relinquished [given up]."

—*The Northmen, Columbus, and Cabot, Nine Eighty-Five to Fifteen Three: Original Narratives of Early American History*, ed. by Julius E. Olson and Edward G. Bourne

▲ When Columbus first landed in America, he had no idea that he had come upon an entire continent that was unknown to Europeans.

Using Primary Sources

1. How does Toscanelli persuade Columbus to sail west to Asia?

2. In Columbus's report, which remarks seem exaggerated? Why might he want to exaggerate the beauty and value of the lands he discovered?

CHAPTER 1

The Earliest Explorations

OBJECTIVE: Why did Europeans begin to explore new lands across the oceans?

1. The door of the space rocket slides shut. The astronauts are strapped in their chairs, waiting for liftoff. An astronaut knows the danger a trip into outer space can hold. Yet astronauts know a lot about what to expect in space. The Europeans who first sailed west from Europe on the Atlantic Ocean did not know what they would find. Some believed that the sea was filled with monsters and whirlpools that sucked ships into the deep. Others thought that they could reach Japan, China, and other lands of Asia if they would sail west. The early European explorers did not have the accurate maps that sailors use today. They did, however, have the courage to explore the unknown.

Viking Explorers How did the early Viking explorers reach Greenland and the coast of North America?

2. The Vikings were the first Europeans to reach the shores of North America. These fierce warriors lived in Scandinavia, in the north of Europe. Each summer, the Vikings sailed south from their shores looking for food and riches. By the 900s, the Vikings were among the finest ship builders and sailors in the world. Viking sailors figured out directions by observing the positions of the sun and stars. They used their knowledge of the habits of sea birds and ocean currents to help them find their way.

▲ Viking warships were often over 65 feet (20 meters) in length. They were powered by 15–30 pairs of oars.

3. Viking explorers made voyages of discovery to the west of Scandinavia. Because the population of Scandinavia was growing, the Vikings wanted good, fertile land to settle and farm. In the 800s, a group of Vikings settled in Iceland, an island west of Norway. In the 900s, another group, led by the Viking leader Eric the

In Chapter 1 you will apply these critical thinking skills to the historical process:

▲ **Summarizing:** Giving the main idea of a group of paragraphs in brief form.

⇒ **Recognizing Cause and Effect:** Recognizing the action or event that makes something happen; identifying the result of an action or event.

Red, explored a large island in the Atlantic Ocean. Because he wanted to attract farmers to this distant place, Eric named the new island "the Greenland." His idea worked. In the late 900s, Eric brought over 400 Scandinavian settlers to Greenland to start new lives.

4. Around the year 1000, Leif Ericson sailed 500 miles (800 km) west of Greenland to North America. The Vikings established several small settlements in a place they called Vinland. Some scientists think that Vinland was on the eastern tip of Newfoundland, Canada. Traces of a Viking settlement were found there in 1960. The settlements at Vinland did not last long. The reasons for this remain a mystery. The Vikings probably did not have an organized plan to settle Vinland.

Trade with Asia   Why did Europe's growing trade with Asia lead to a search for ocean trade routes?

5. Soon after Viking explorers sailed toward new lands in the West, other Europeans began looking toward the East. To the East lay the rich lands they called "the Indies." The area known as the Indies included India, China, Indonesia, and Japan. From the 1200s to the 1400s, these lands became more important as sources of spices and fruits. Europeans liked to use spices from Indonesia, such as cinnamon, ginger, and nutmeg, in their cooking. Figs, oranges, and other tropical foods were prized for their delicious flavors. Throughout Europe, nobles bought rubies, emeralds, and other precious stones from the East. They also bought silk from China to replace their uncomfortable woolen clothing.

6. Much of the Indies was controlled by the **empire** of the Mongols. An empire is a group of countries controlled by one government. The Mongols were a warlike people from east Asia. At its height, under Kublai Khan, the Mongol empire stretched from the Pacific Ocean all the way to the eastern edge of Europe. It included China and neighboring lands. East of the Mediterranean Sea, between Europe and the Indies,

were a powerful group of **Islamic** states. Islam is the religion based on the teaching of the prophet Muhammad. Its followers are called **Muslims.** Led by the Turks, these Islamic states controlled a large area.

7. By the 1100s, the Italian cities of Genoa and Venice had begun a profitable trade with both Muslims and Mongols. Although Genoa and Venice were rivals, they worked together to keep a **monopoly** (muh-NOP-oh-lee) over this trade. A monopoly is complete control over a product or service. Genoa and Venice developed special ways of working with Islamic and Mongol rulers. Only merchants from these two cities were allowed to trade directly with these nations.

8. Bringing the products of the East to Europe was hard and cost a lot of money. The goods had to be moved over both land and sea. Traders from Venice shipped wheat and other European products to the large trading city of Constantinople. Traders from Genoa shipped their goods to Islamic ports on the Mediterranean Sea. These ports were connected by land routes to trading centers in the East. Italian merchants used **caravans** (KAR-uh-vanz) to carry their products along the land routes. A caravan is a large group of people who travel together for safety. Goods for trading were carried by camels. The caravans traveled across the deserts and over the mountains of Persia, now known as Iran. From there they went to India, and beyond to China. There the Europeans traded their goods for silk, fruits, and spices from the East. The traders returned to the port cities with their treasures by the same land routes. From the ports, the products from the East were carried by sea to Italy and then to markets throughout Europe.

9. The river of trade between the East and Europe became a flood during the 200 years of the Crusades. The Crusades were a series of attempts by Christian rulers in Europe to recapture the Holy Land (Palestine) from Muslims. Crusaders captured Jerusalem and held it for many years, but eventually they were driven out by the Turks. The Crusades

43

had two important effects. Beginning with the First Crusade in 1096, the Italian cities grew richer by transporting and supplying the European soldiers. The Crusades also speeded up contact between the East and Europe.

Spotlight on Sources

10. The amazing adventures of Marco Polo, a young man from Venice, also helped to bring Europe closer to the East. In 1271, when Marco Polo was 17 years old, he left Italy to visit the great Kublai Khan in China. When he returned home 24 years later, Polo had seen more of Asia than any other European of his time. Marco Polo told about the sights he saw in his book called *Description of the World*.

> The country produces in great abundance [amounts], silk, ginger, and many drugs [medicines] that are nearly unknown in our part of the world. . . . The country abounds with [is full of] rich commodities [products]. Pepper, nutmegs . . . cloves, and all the other valuable spices and drugs, are the produce of this island. . . . The quantity of gold exceeds all calculations [cannot be counted] and belief. . . . The island produces more beautiful and valuable rubies than are found in any other part of the world, and likewise sapphires, topazes, amethysts, and garnets, and many other precious and costly stones.
>
> —from *The Travels of Marco Polo, the Venetian*, Manuel Komroff

Which groups of people might be especially ◄ interested in the description given above?

11. Marco Polo told about other exciting discoveries in Asia. He wrote about strange animals called elephants, giraffes, and rhinoceroses. Marco Polo also introduced gunpowder, paper money, spaghetti, the use of coal as a heating fuel, and printing to the West.

12. Soon after Marco Polo's book was finished, several events had a major impact on European trade. The powerful Kublai Khan died in 1297. Without his leadership, the Mon-

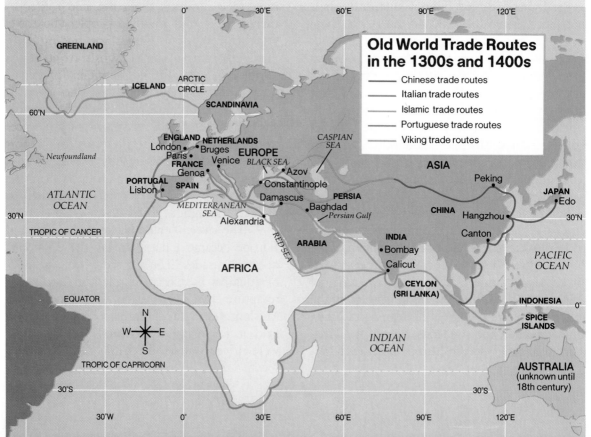

MAP SKILL BUILDER: In the 1400s, Europeans wanted to trade directly with other lands. **1.** Which countries controlled the trade routes to India? **2.** Which countries controlled the trade routes to China?

Old World Trade Routes in the 1300s and 1400s

— Chinese trade routes
— Italian trade routes
— Islamic trade routes
— Portuguese trade routes
— Viking trade routes

gol Empire fell apart in the 1300s. In 1453, the Turks conquered Constantinople and took control of all eastern caravan routes. How did the Islamic takeover of these trade routes affect the fortunes of Genoa and Venice? Right away the Turks limited the number of caravans that could travel to the East. Because fewer caravans brought back products, the prices of spices, silks, and jewels rose. These developments caused other Europeans to search for a cheaper, better way to get products from the East. Some thought that finding a direct sea route to the East would be the best solution.

Portuguese Explorers   How did Prince Henry the Navigator help Portuguese explorers discover sea routes to Asia?

13. Finding an all-sea route to Asia meant sailing far from known shores. Only with a major effort could another European country change Italy's control of Eastern trade.

People in History

14. **Prince Henry the Navigator**   Portugal had the right person to set up and direct daring sea explorations. This person was Prince Henry, the third son of the king of Portugal. When he was 19, Prince Henry led an expedition to capture an important Islamic trading center on the coast of Africa. This experience opened the eyes of the young prince to the treasures of Africa. At Sagres, near the southern tip of Portugal, Prince Henry started a great school for training sailors. Because of his interest in sailing, Prince Henry was given the nickname "the **Navigator**" (NAV-uh-gay-tur).

15. Like the Vikings, Prince Henry knew that good sailing skills were needed for ocean travel. Sailors had to be able to sail safely in the open ocean, far from land. To reach this goal, Henry invited sea captains, instrument makers, and mathematicians from all over the world to his school. Prince Henry encouraged sailors to keep careful records of their trips. He also encouraged the use of instruments such as the **compass** and **astrolabe** (AS-troh-layb). The compass had a magnetic needle that always pointed toward the north. The astrolabe was used to measure the angles formed by the stars and the horizon. Both of these instruments helped sailors be more sure of their direction.

16. Under Prince Henry's leadership, Portugal also became the center of shipbuilding in Europe. Portuguese shipbuilders developed the **caravel** (KAR-uh-vel), an improved type of sailing ship. The caravel had a new kind of sail that allowed explorers to sail into the wind. No longer did sailors have to depend on sailing with the wind at their backs. This saved valuable time on ocean voyages.

17. Armed with excellent maps and instruments, Portuguese explorers began to explore the coastline of Africa. At different points along the way they built trading posts to carry the wealth of Africa back to Portuguese ports. The wealth gained from this trade in gold, ivory, spices, and slaves paid for more Portuguese voyages. One such voyage to Africa was commanded by Bartholomeu Dias. Several weeks into his journey down the coast of Africa, Dias was caught in a terrible storm. On February 13, 1488, Dias's ships reached the safety of a new harbor. Only then did Dias realize that the powerful storm had driven his ships around the southern tip of Africa. He had found a direct sea route from Portugal to the lands of the East.

Outlook

18. The remarkable voyages of Prince Henry's explorers opened a new world of trade for Portugal. Soon, Spain and other European nations began important ocean voyages of their own. New knowledge about the size and shape of the world was carefully recorded on maps and charts. In this way, the early European explorers helped to make sea travel much easier for those who would soon cross the "Green Sea of Darkness," the Atlantic Ocean. What benefits did ocean exploration bring to Europe?

Ask: Have students study the map on page 44 to locate Scandinavia and Portugal. Ask them what geographical advantages these places gave to early Viking and Portuguese explorers.

45

CHAPTER REVIEW

VOCABULARY REVIEW

▶ Copy the paragraph below on a sheet of paper. Choose the correct word from the list to fill in the blanks.

Muslim(s)   caravan(s)   navigator(s)   caravel(s)

astrolabe(s)   monopoly(s)   compass(es)   Islamic

At first, the cities of Genoa and Venice had a ___1___ on trade with the East. Only merchants from these Italian cities were allowed to send their ships and ___2___ over the long routes to the East, which were controlled by Mongols and ___3___ people, or ___4___ . In time, however, ships from Portugal found an all-sea route to the East. Portuguese sailing expeditions were directed by Prince Henry, who was called the ___5___ because of his interest in sailing. The Portuguese sailors' success was partly because of their well-designed ships, called ___6___ . The use of improved instruments such as the ___7___ and the ___8___ helped the sailors find their way when sailing in unknown seas.

SKILL BUILDER: USING A CHART

▶ Copy the chart below onto a separate sheet of paper. Complete the chart by filling in the solutions to the problems. You may refer to the paragraph listed if you need help.

Problem	Solution
1. Eric the Red needs to convince Vikings to settle in a land far from their home. (paragraph 3)	
2. Transporting goods over deserts is dangerous. (paragraph 8)	
3. After 1453, only a limited number of caravans could go by land to China. (paragraph 12)	
4. Sailors need better instruments to help them be sure of their direction. (paragraph 15)	
5. On sea voyages, much time is lost because the ships cannot sail into the wind. (paragraph 16)	

SKILL BUILDER: CRITICAL THINKING AND COMPREHENSION

▲ **I. Summarizing**

Did you ever write a post card to someone? If you have, you know that you had room to put down only a few thoughts. They were probably the most important things you had to say. Or, imagine that you are writing an advertisement for a new type of sports equipment. You would want to select only the most important facts about that product to include in the ad. Writing a **summary** is much the same thing. A summary is a short version of a longer story or piece of information.

To write a summary, you need to select the most important facts about a situation. Summaries are written as sentences or paragraphs, rather than as lists, phrases, or outlines. Writing summaries will help you analyze what you have read. You need to decide what facts or conclusions are most important. Why might writing a summary be a good way to study for a test?

▶ The sentences below are summaries of paragraphs in Chapter 1. Reread each paragraph, then select the sentence that best summarizes that paragraph.

1. Which sentence is the best summary of paragraph 8?
   a. Caravans carried goods by camel from the East to Europe.
   b. Bringing products from the East to Europe was complicated and expensive.
   c. European goods were shipped to Constantinople.

2. Which sentence is the best summary of paragraph 9?
   a. The Crusades did not achieve their main goal.
   b. The Crusades lasted for 200 years.
   c. The Crusades made Italian cities richer and brought Europe and the East closer.

3. Which sentence is the best summary of paragraph 7?
   a. Two Italian cities, Genoa and Venice, controlled trade between the East and Europe in the 1100s.
   b. Genoa and Venice were rivals.
   c. Other cities were jealous of Genoa and Venice.

II. Classifying

▶ Copy these three categories on a sheet of paper: "Explorers," "Improvements that Made Sailing Safer" and "Products from the East." Classify the people and things listed below under each heading.

Eric the Red	silk	Marco Polo	nutmeg	compass	astrolabe
cinnamon	Leif Ericson	figs	jewels	caravel	ginger

USING PRIMARY SOURCES

▶ Reread the description of Marco Polo's travels, paragraph 10. What does this paragraph tell you about what was considered valuable in the 1200s? If a list of valuable items were drawn up today, what items from Marco Polo's account would be on it? What would probably not?

ENRICHMENT

1. Many improvements in tools and instruments helped sailors find their way in the unknown seas. Find out about the compass and astrolabe. Sketch these instruments and make a short oral report to the class about how they were used in the 1400s.

2. Work with other classmates to find out more about Marco Polo's discoveries. Use encyclopedias or other reference books. Present your findings to the rest of the class. Include in your report an answer to this question: In what ways was the East more advanced than Europe in the 1200s?

CHAPTER 2

Columbus Sails West

> **OBJECTIVE:** What lands in the Western Hemisphere did Columbus explore, and why were his voyages important?

1. From his lookout position on board the *Pinta,* Rodrigo de Triana stared at the Atlantic Ocean. Strong light from the nearly full moon revealed only crashing waves, not land. Directly above, Rodrigo heard the canvas sails snapping in the winds. These powerful winds had blown his tiny ship across unknown waters for 33 days. Rodrigo looked back over his shoulder. He could see the lantern lights of the *Niña,* and behind her, the outline of the *Santa María.* Rodrigo turned forward, straining his eyes. He saw a flash of light. He rubbed his eyes, then looked up again. Yes, that was it! Off in the distance, Rodrigo saw a cliff shining in the moonlight. "Tierra! Tierra! Land! Land!" he shouted. The *Pinta's* cannon passed the good news to the other ships. The admiral of the group, Christopher Columbus, heard the cry with relief. They had reached the rich lands of the Indies! Little did the sailors realize that instead of the Indies, they had come upon a whole "new world" unknown to Europeans.

▲ Columbus's crew came close to revolting during his first voyage across the Atlantic. With great relief, they finally sighted land.

Columbus's Plan How did Columbus try to interest the rulers of Portugal and Spain in exploring for lands overseas?

2. Christopher Columbus began planning his first voyage west several years before it actually took place. Columbus knew that Portuguese rulers had tried to find a sea route around Africa to Asia. Like many explorers of his day, Columbus wanted to solve this problem. Unlike many, however, he looked west rather than east for the way to Asia. Columbus was well educated and knew the world was round. However, he thought that the world was

In Chapter 2 you will apply these critical thinking skills to the historical process:
○ **Generalizing:** Making a statement that links several facts.
▱ **Classifying:** Organizing facts into categories based on what they have in common.

much smaller than it actually is. At that time the huge continents that lay between Europe and Asia were still unknown to Europeans. Columbus believed that a ship could sail west from Europe across the Atlantic Ocean to reach the eastern shores of Asia. There, he would build a large trading post to exchange European products for the spices, silk, and gold of the Indies. To test his bold idea, Columbus had to get the ships and sailors needed for a long ocean trip. He therefore turned to the richest people he knew, the kings and queens of Europe.

People in History

3. Christopher Columbus Born about 1451 in Genoa, Italy, Christopher Columbus went to sea at an early age. As a young man, Columbus was shipwrecked off the coast of Portugal. He swam to shore near Cape St. Vincent, the home of Henry the Navigator's school. There, Columbus became a skilled chart maker. Soon he was commanding ships to and from Portuguese trading posts on the western coast of Africa. A brave sailor, Columbus was also a **geographer** (ghee-OG-ruh-fur). A geographer is a person who studies the surface of the earth. Columbus read the works of ancient Greek, Egyptian, and Roman geographers. He also studied with interest Marco Polo's writings about the Indies.

4. Because Portugal was the leading center of European sailing, Columbus presented his plan first to King John II of Portugal. The king liked Columbus's idea, but his naval council voted against the plan. The council believed that Columbus's proposed voyage was too dangerous.

5. Columbus spent the next several years asking other European rulers to support his trip. From Portugal, Columbus traveled to Spain, where he tried to win the support of Queen Isabella and King Ferdinand. The Spanish rulers, however, were fighting a war against the **Moors,** Muslims from North Africa who for many years occupied parts of Spain. Four years later, in the spring of 1492, Spain finally

defeated the Moors. In April of that year, the king and queen agreed to pay for Columbus's first voyage.

Columbus's Four Voyages   What lands in the Americas did Columbus explore for Spain?

6. Columbus spent the rest of the spring and early summer choosing the best ships and supplies for his voyage. To encourage sailors to join his expedition, Columbus had to promise them extra money. Why might a sailor of that time be afraid to join Columbus's voyage across the Atlantic Ocean?

7. On August 3, 1492, Columbus set sail from Palos, Spain. His group included 90 sailors and three small ships, the *Niña,* the *Pinta,* and the *Santa María.* After stopping for five weeks in the Canary Islands to repair the *Pinta's* rudder, the ships continued on. During the 33-day trip, the three ships were pushed across the Atlantic Ocean by strong, constant winds. As the weeks wore on, the sailors grew restless. It took all of Columbus's skill to keep them calm. On the morning of October 12, 1492, Columbus dropped anchor near a small island in the Bahamas. The Spaniards later named this island San Salvador, meaning "holy Saviour."

8. Although the sailors were happy to find land, Columbus was disappointed. Instead of the riches of the Indies, he saw only wooden huts. Although he saw few signs of gold and spices, Columbus still thought that he had reached the Indies. He named the land he had discovered the West Indies. He called the friendly people who lived on the island "Indians."

9. For the next three months, Columbus sailed through the Caribbean Sea, searching for the gold and spices that would prove he had found Asia. Instead of finding these riches, Columbus made other important discoveries. He claimed the Bahama Islands for Spain. He explored the island of Cuba, then found and named the island of Hispaniola, or Little Spain. When the *Santa María* ran into a chain of rocks and sank, Columbus gathered the wood from the ship. With the wood he built a trading post

Background: In 1485, after declining to finance Columbus's expedition, King John II authorized two other sailors to survey a western water route to Asia. The sailors left Lisbon in 1487, ran into harsh Atlantic storms, and were lost at sea.

Linking Geography and History

The Atlantic Basin When Columbus landed in America in 1492, he did not come upon what is now the United States. Instead, he landed on a tiny island in the Bahamas, just off the Florida coast. On his second and third trips, Columbus sailed even farther south. The Vikings had visited areas far to the north of the United States many years earlier. The Atlantic coast of the United States was the last to be discovered. It was not discovered until several years after the first voyage of Columbus. Why did it take longer for Europeans to find the coast of the United States?

You can discover part of the answer to this question by looking at the map below. The coastlines of North America, South America, and Europe form a circular area known as the Atlantic Basin. Remember that sailing ships depended on wind, not engines, for power. Ships were small, and it was hard to sail against the wind.

The white arrows on the map show the wind patterns over the North Atlantic. In the south, winds blow from Spain to the West Indies. In the north, winds blow from Europe to Canada. But in the ocean between, from Europe to the Atlantic coast of the United States, winds blow from west to east. For this reason, ships coming to North America found it easier to sail to the south or far to the north. But ships returning to Europe sailed across the middle ocean.

The blue arrows on the map show the ocean currents of the North Atlantic Ocean. On the first leg of all four voyages, Columbus sailed southwest with the Canary Current to the Canary Islands. At the Canaries, other ocean currents carried his tiny ships south and west across the ocean. The Gulf Stream, on the west side of the Atlantic basin, aided the return trip.

Now answer the following questions.

1. What countries did Columbus visit on his second voyage?

2. On which voyage did Columbus first land on the continent of South America?

3. Look at the ocean currents shown on the map. Compare the ocean currents with the direction of the winds.

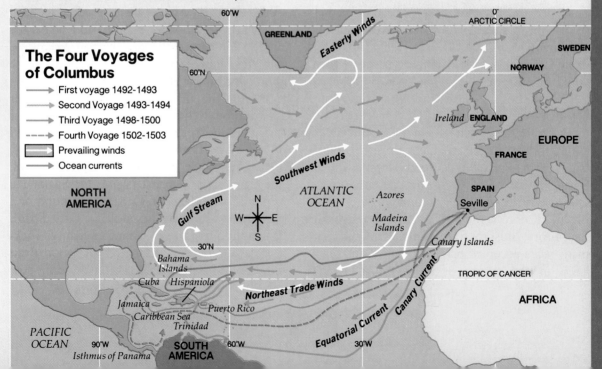

The Four Voyages of Columbus

→ First voyage 1492-1493
→ Second Voyage 1493-1494
→ Third Voyage 1498-1500
---→ Fourth Voyage 1502-1503
▢ Prevailing winds
→ Ocean currents

on Hispaniola. This became the first European settlement in the Americas since the Vikings had settled Vinland nearly 500 years before.

🦅 Spotlight on Sources

10. On his return trip to Spain, Christopher Columbus wrote to Queen Isabella and King Ferdinand of Spain. In his letter, the explorer described the friendly Arawaks that he met on Cuba and Hispaniola.

> All go naked [without clothes], men and women, as their mothers bore them. . . . Although they were well-built people of handsome stature [attractive height], they are wonderfully timorous [easily frightened]. They have no other arms [weapons] than arms of canes, and they dare not make use of these. . . . Of anything they have, if you ask them for it, they never say no; rather they invite the person to share it, and show as much love as if they were giving their hearts. . . . They believe very firmly that I, with these ships and people, came from the sky . . . how easy it would be to convert these people [make them Christians]—and to make them work for us.
>
> —"Columbus's Letter on His First Voyage,"
> April, 1493

▶ What might an Arawak think of this letter?

11. Columbus made three more trips to the newly discovered lands over the next 12 years. In 1493 he led a second group of ships to set up a **colony** (KAHL-uh-nee) in Hispaniola. A colony is a group of people who settle in a new land but are still under the rule of the country from which they came. On this trip, Columbus led 17 ships and over 1,200 settlers across the Atlantic Ocean. Among the islands he discovered were Puerto Rico and the Virgin Islands. Both of these islands are now part of the United States. On his third and fourth voyages, Columbus explored the coast of Central and South America. He discovered and claimed many other new lands for Spain. These included the present-day countries of Honduras, Panama,

Costa Rica, and Nicaragua. Columbus also discovered Jamaica and Trinidad.

Columbus's Achievement Why was Columbus's "discovery" of America so important?

12. Although he did not discover a western sea route to the Indies, Columbus discovered lands that no Europeans knew about. In fact, Columbus showed to Europeans the Western **Hemisphere** (HEM-uh-sfihr), or the western one-half of the earth. Columbus was a brilliant navigator. He charted the best sea routes from Europe to the Americas and discovered the shortest and safest routes back. Even today, Columbus's sea routes are thought to be the best way to sail from Europe to the Caribbean Sea. The discovery of the New World, as the new lands were called, led to an increase in many branches of knowledge. As Europeans explored the new lands, they were brought into contact with new types of plants and animals. As they settled there, they learned new ways of life from the Native Americans.

13. Columbus also made possible the Spanish **conquest** (KON-kwest) of the Americas. A conquest is the act of winning a people or place by war. In addition, Columbus began Spain's profitable trade across the Atlantic Ocean. By 1506, the year Columbus died, ships from the West Indies were already unloading gold and silver in Spanish ports.

Outlook

14. Columbus never realized the full importance of his trips. After his discoveries, however, other rulers were willing to pay for explorations to what was soon called the New World. Because of Columbus, Spain became very rich and powerful in the 1500s. If Columbus had lived for a few more years, he would have seen his prediction come true. "I have placed under the sovereignty [rule] of the King and Queen," Columbus wrote, "an Other World, whereby Spain . . . is to become the richest of all countries." Why did Columbus demand the title ◀ of "The Admiral of the Ocean Sea?"

CHAPTER REVIEW

VOCABULARY REVIEW

▶ Write each of the chapter vocabulary words on a separate piece of paper, then match each word with its definition.

1. geographer
2. colony
3. hemisphere
4. Moors
5. conquest

a. half of the earth
b. group of people called together for advice
c. group of people who settled in a distant land under the rule of their native country
d. person who studies the surface features of the earth
e. the act of winning by war
f. Muslim people from North Africa

SKILL BUILDER: USING AN ENCYCLOPEDIA

▶ Choose one of the topics below. Go to an encyclopedia and look up the article on that topic. If the article is long, it will be divided into sections. Write one or two facts from each section of the article.

1. Moors
2. San Salvador
3. Queen Isabella
4. Christopher Columbus
5. Prince Henry the Navigator

SKILL BUILDER: CRITICAL THINKING AND COMPREHENSION

▲ I. Summarizing

To summarize means to write the main ideas of something you have read or heard in a few sentences of your own. A summary is a good technique to use when you want to remember a main idea or when you have only a little time or space to write. For example, imagine that you read a long newspaper review of a new movie. You want to tell a friend about what you read so the two of you can decide if you want to go to the next show. You would not copy the entire article for your friend, but you might write a summary, or general restatement of the most important information in the review. That way you both can make a decision that is based on facts.

▶ Now look at the headlines below. These headlines announce events from the late 1400s. Copy three of them onto a sheet of paper. Leave space after each. Then go back to the paragraphs shown, and write a short summary that refers to each.

1. Columbus Reaches West Indies (paragraph 7)
2. Columbus Meets Arawaks (paragraph 10)

3. Colony Heads for New World (paragraph 11)

4. Columbus Continues Search for Funding (paragraphs 4 and 5)

5. Columbus Claims New Lands for Spain (paragraphs 9 and 11)

6. Columbus Builds Trading Post (paragraph 9)

II. Classifying

▶ Write the headings below on a sheet of paper, leaving space after each. Look at the paragraphs shown to find two or three facts you could classify under each heading and write them in.

1. Places Columbus Claimed for Spain (paragraphs 7, 9, and 11)

2. Columbus's Ships (paragraphs 1 and 7)

3. Results of Columbus's discoveries (paragraph 12)

4. Columbus's Background (paragraphs 2 and 3)

5. The Education and Skills of Columbus (paragraph 3)

6. Names Given by Columbus to new Places and People (paragraphs 7, 8, and 9)

USING PRIMARY SOURCES

▶ Reread the Spotlight on Sources on page 51. Think about the qualities of the Arawaks that Columbus described. Can you think of reasons why these qualities might have seemed unusual to a European?

ENRICHMENT

1. Read more about one of Columbus's four voyages to the Americas in reference books or in encyclopedias. Then, imagine you are Columbus. Write several journal entries during one voyage that express your hopes, fears, and dreams about your mission.

2. Work with another student to prepare a mock conversation between an Arawak and a noble in the Spanish court. The noble might ask the Arawak about reactions on seeing Europeans for the first time and the Arawak's impressions of the court. The Arawak might ask the noble about European customs, including dress and manners. Rehearse your conversation. Then present it to the class.

3. Use encyclopedias and other reference books to find out more about Columbus's life before and after his famous voyages. Present your findings to the class in a brief oral report. Use drawings, charts, graphs, or other illustrations to make your report more interesting.

CHAPTER 3

Explorers Sail the World

OBJECTIVE: How did the search for a sea route to Asia lead to the exploration of America?

1. Imagine that you are living in Europe during the early 1500s. People everywhere are discussing Columbus's "other world," a new land discovered between Europe and Asia. Adventurers, merchants, and rulers are planning new voyages to explore and claim these unknown lands. What might cause you to take part in such a voyage? If you are a sailor, you might want the excitement of discovering new lands. A trader might describe the wealth to be gained from finding a new sea route to Asia. If you are a ruler, you would probably say that successful sea voyages can lead to rich overseas colonies. Whoever you are, you would probably thank Columbus, who had discovered a brand new world. Now it would be up to you to discover what secrets were hidden there.

▲ The map above, made in 1590, shows Magellan's ship in full sail. What land would not appear on this map if it had been made in 1490?

Exploring America Which explorers came to America and claimed land there for England and France?

2. Christopher Columbus's discoveries caused the rulers of France and England to organize their own trips to the new lands. King Henry VII of England hired John Cabot, a sea captain from Genoa, Italy, to explore and claim new land in America for England. Cabot was also asked to find a **northwest passage** to the Spice Islands of Indonesia. The northwest passage was thought to be a sea route leading through North America to Asia.

3. John Cabot made two voyages to the new world for England. In 1497, Cabot sailed to the eastern tip of North America and claimed this land for England. During his second voyage to North America in 1498, Cabot was lost at sea.

In Chapter 3 you will apply these critical thinking skills to the historical process:

▲ **Summarizing:** Giving the main idea of a group of paragraphs in a brief form.

◢ **Making Judgments:** Stating a personal opinion based on historical facts.

Cabot did not find the northwest passage he was looking for. The lands he discovered, however, gave the English a reason to claim most of North America.

4. England's claim to North America was soon questioned by France, England's long-time rival. In 1524, the King of France, Francis I, supervised France's first voyage of discovery to America. The leader of this trip was Giovanni da Verrazano (zhuh-VAHN-ee dah vair-uh-ZAH-noh), a sailor from Florence, Italy. French silk merchants, who wanted a shorter, less expensive sea route to the silk centers of China, gave much of the money for this trip. Verrazano expected to sail directly from France to Asia. He reached the coast of North America instead. He might have landed at what is now South Carolina. Because he did not find a northwest passage through these shores, Verrazano turned north. He reached New York harbor and may have discovered the Hudson River. Verrazano sailed north to Nova Scotia before returning to France. Because of Verrazano's skill, France claimed more than 2,000 miles of North American coast, from South Carolina to Newfoundland. How might the claims that England and France made in North America cause later problems between these two countries?

5. Jacques Cartier (zhak kahr-TYAY), a sailor from northern France, led the next major French expeditions to America. Between 1533 and 1535, Cartier made two trips to present-day Canada. Like the explorers before him, Cartier searched for a northwest passage. Like them, too, he failed to find one. Cartier's explorations, however, had a lasting effect on the settlement of North America. Cartier discovered and named the St. Lawrence River. He also claimed for France the future locations of Quebec (kwih-BEC) City and Montreal (mahn-tree-AHL). After Cartier, France sent no other expeditions to America for nearly 60 years.

🦅 Spotlight on Sources

6. The naming of America was an accident, just as its discovery was. Between 1499 and 1504, an Italian sailor named Amerigo Vespucci (ah-may-REE-goh ves-POO-chee) headed up several trips to the New World for both Spain and Portugal. In 1505, five letters, believed to be written by Vespucci, were printed in Europe. These letters described Vespucci's discovery of a new continent. Amazed by this news, a geographer in France named Martin Waldseemüller (VAHLD-zay-myoo-luhr) included maps of this new continent in an **atlas** (AT-luhs) that he was preparing. An atlas is a book of maps and charts. Waldseemüller named the new land after the sailor who he believed had discovered it. The atlas became a best-seller in Europe, and the name was accepted.

> Now, these parts of the earth [Europe, Africa, Asia] have been more extensively [thoroughly] explored and a fourth part has been discovered by Amerigo Vespucci. . . . Inasmuch as [Because] both Europe and Asia received their names from women, I see no reason why any one should justly object to calling this part Amerige [from Greek "ge" meaning "land of"], i.e., the land of Amerigo, or America, after Amerigo, its discoverer, a man of great ability.
>
> —*The Cosmographiae Introductio*,
> Martin Waldseemüller

If the land Waldseemüller described were named after its true discoverer, what would America be called?

Spanish Explorers   What lands in the Caribbean did Balboa and Ponce de León explore?

7. In contrast to the early French and English explorations, Spanish trips to the New World had results right away. In 1496, Spanish soldiers defeated the Native Americans of Hispaniola. Soon after, Spanish ships began to bring colonists to Hispaniola. These ships returned to Spain filled with gold, cotton, and pearls. These products helped to raise money for other Spanish trips. Soon the ships from Spain

Background: Sailors at sea often contracted scurvy, a serious disease caused by a lack of vitamin C. Although they did not understand its causes, ships' officers often carried private stores of dates, figs, and other dried fruits to ward off the illness.

55

were bringing a new type of Spanish explorer, the **conquistador** (kahn-KEES-tuh-dawr), or conquerer. Conquistadores were from the noble families of Spain. They came to the West Indies to seek fame and riches. From Hispaniola and newer Spanish colonies, these "soldiers of fortune" explored and conquered the lands of the Caribbean and beyond for Spain.

8. Vasco Nuñez de Balboa (VAHS-koh NOO-nyayth day bal-BOH-uh) was a conquistador who began a successful colony located on the **Isthmus** (IS-muhs) of Panama. This isthmus is a long, narrow strip of land that joins North and South America. Balboa heard tales from the Native Americans about another ocean only several days' journey away. Finally, Balboa thought, here was proof of the hidden sea passage to Asia. Balboa quickly got together a small exploration party to find this new ocean.

9. The journey of "several days" turned into a three-week nightmare. The explorers cut through 45 miles (72 km) of steaming jungle. They crossed swamps, battled Native American armies, and fought off snakes and diseases. Finally, on September 25, 1513, Balboa stood on a mountain peak and gazed at the Pacific Ocean. He was the first European to see the Pacific Ocean from the shores of North America.

10. While Balboa was marching across the Isthmus of Panama, Juan Ponce de León (hwahn PAWN-say day lay-AWN), another conquistador, was searching for a "fountain of youth." This fountain was said to lie on an island north of Cuba. According to local legends, water from this fountain could "make old people young again." In March 1513, Ponce de León sailed from Puerto Rico to search for this fountain. What de León found instead was a large area of land, which he named "La Floridá" and claimed for Spain. "Floridá" means "full of flowers."

▲ A European legend about a fountain of youth was similar to the story the Spanish explorers heard from Native Americans.

Portuguese Explorations What were the results of Portuguese explorations after Columbus?

11. When Columbus returned from his first voyage, an argument broke out between Spain and Portugal. The king of Portugal denied Spain's claims to the newly discovered lands. In 1493, the pope proposed that an imaginary line be drawn through the new land. Portugal could claim lands east of the line. Spain could claim lands west of the line. This line came to be known as the **Line of Demarcation**, or line of separation. Why would the ruler of Portugal have been especially interested in claiming lands in the area Columbus had discovered?

12. Portuguese sailors continued their search for an eastern sea route to the Indies. In 1498, a Portuguese sailor, Vasco da Gama (VAS-koh duh GAH-muh) sailed around the tip of Africa and across the Indian Ocean to India. Da Gama's new route opened up the Indian Ocean to Portuguese trade.

Background: Balboa named the ocean he discovered "Mar del Sur," or the great South Sea, because he had traveled south from Hispaniola and again south across the Isthmus of Panama. Magellan's sailors named it El Pacifico, or Pacific. They sailed almost four months and 12,000 miles upon it without encountering a single storm.

56

13. During Portugal's second eastern sea voyage to India, Pedro Álvares Cabral (PAY-throo AHL-vuh-reesh kuh-BRAHL) discovered Brazil by accident. Cabral followed da Gama's sailing instructions, but his group of a dozen ships sailed off course. On April 22, 1500, Cabral sighted land, which he claimed for Portugal. This new **territory** later became the Portuguese colony of Brazil. A territory is an area of land that is claimed by a country.

People in History

14. Ferdinand Magellan Columbus's goal of reaching the Indies by sailing west was reached by Ferdinand Magellan, a skilled Portuguese sea captain. Magellan wanted to find a passage to the Pacific through South America. From there he would sail west across the Pacific Ocean to the Spice Islands. Like Columbus before him, he gained support for his plan from the king of Spain. In 1519, Magellan set sail from Spain with five ships.

15. Near the southern tip of South America, Magellan found a **strait** (STRAYT) and entered the Pacific Ocean. A strait is a narrow body of water that joins two larger ones. Magellan sailed for 14 weeks over unknown waters of the Pacific before seeing new land. During this long journey, four ships were lost. The food on the ships ran out and the sailors had to eat rats and leather goods in order to keep alive. Finally, they reached the Philippines, where they were able to rest and get fresh supplies for their ships. Unfortunately, they also became involved in a local battle. Magellan was killed, and the group continued on its way without him.

16. Three years later, one of Magellan's ships returned to Spain. The captain was Juan Sebastian Del Cano, who had taken charge of the ships after Magellan's death. On board were only 18 of the original band of over 200 sailors. The ship was filled with a cargo of pepper, nutmeg, and cloves from the Spice Islands. Magellan's crew had finished their mission. They had **circumnavigated** (sir-kum-NAV-uh-gayt-uhd), or traveled completely around, the

Activity: Trace Magellan's route on a globe. Refer to the map on page 58 for guidance.

▲ Once Magellan's expedition was completed, navigators finally had an accurate idea of the size of the earth.

globe. This brave voyage gave people their first true idea of the size of the world.

Outlook

17. The early English and French explorers to North America did not realize that lands they discovered were worth a great deal. They saw plenty of fish, lumber, and fur-bearing animals, but they found no gold, spices, or precious jewels. Spanish adventurers, though, quickly found valuable products. Money made from the sale of gold and silver paid for further Spanish trips to the Caribbean Sea, the Pacific Ocean, and the Gulf of Mexico. How did the ▲ exploration of America change the way people thought about the world?

CHAPTER REVIEW

VOCABULARY REVIEW

▶ Copy the sentences below on a separate piece of paper. Then fill in each blank with the correct vocabulary word.

northwest passage	territory	strait
isthmus	line of demarcation	conquistador(es)
circumnavigate	atlas	

1. English and French explorers searched for a(n) _____ through North America to Asia.

2. Juan Sebastian Del Cano was the first sailor to _____ the world.

3. Spanish _____ explored and conquered new lands in the West Indies.

4. A(n) _____ contains maps, plus valuable information about winds and distances.

5. A(n) _____ connects two larger areas of land.

6. Cabral claimed a large _____ for Portugal that later became Brazil.

7. A(n) _____ connects two larger bodies of water.

8. A(n) _____ divided the New World into parts that could be claimed by Spain and parts that could be claimed by Portugal.

SKILL BUILDER: READING A MAP

▶ Look at the map below. Then answer the questions on page 59 on another sheet of paper.

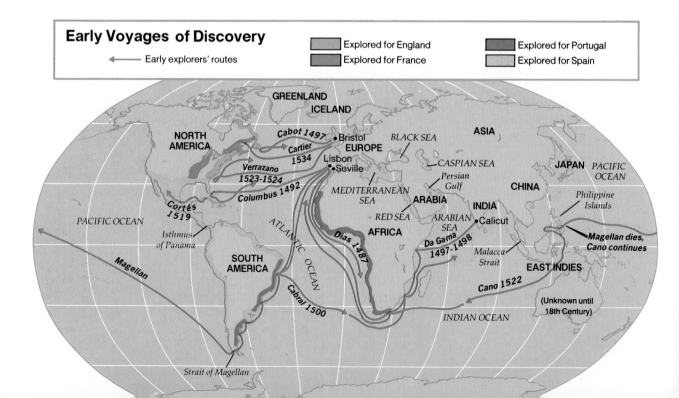

Early Voyages of Discovery

← Early explorers' routes

Explored for England

Explored for France

Explored for Portugal

Explored for Spain

1. What two bodies of water or land do the following connect?
   a. Isthmus of Panama
   b. Strait of Magellan
   c. Malacca Strait

2. Trace the routes of the following explorers on the map. List the major bodies of water that each explorer traveled through.
   a. Dias
   b. Da Gama
   c. Cabot
   d. Magellan

3. Which explorers sailed west, toward the continents of North and South America? Which explorers sailed east, toward Asia?

SKILL BUILDER: CRITICAL THINKING AND COMPREHENSION

▲ I. Summarizing

1. Reread paragraphs 8 and 9. These paragraphs give an account of Balboa's discovery of the Pacific Ocean. Write a summary of these paragraphs.

2. Reread paragraphs 2 and 3. These paragraphs describe the exploration of John Cabot. Write a summary of these paragraphs.

II. Classifying

▶ Write Headings 1–4 on a sheet of paper. Then write the names and items from the **Classify** list under the appropriate headings. Some might go under more than one heading.

1. Explorers for France
2. Explorers for Spain
3. Explorers from Portugal
4. Important Discoveries

Classify

Ferdinand Magellan	La Floridá	Juan Ponce de León
Pacific Ocean	Giovanni da Verrazano	Jacques Cartier
Vasco da Gama	Vasco Nuñez de Balboa	Hudson River

USING PRIMARY SOURCES

▶ Reread the passage about the naming of America in paragraph 6. Write a short paragraph describing how America got its name.

ENRICHMENT

1. Use reference books to find out more about Magellan's trip around the world. Present a report to the class. In your report, include details not covered in the textbook. Give your opinion on this question: "Who took greater risks—Magellan or Columbus?"

2. Develop an advertising campaign to attract Spanish settlers to the West Indies. Work in groups of three. One person could be the person organizing the colony. A poster artist and copywriter should create a sales pitch and a slogan. Develop a strategy that you feel would motivate people to make the trip and start a new life halfway around the world. Present your sales pitch to the rest of the class and see how many settlers you can attract.

CHAPTER 4

Spain Conquers an Empire

OBJECTIVE: How did the Spanish conquistadores gain an empire in Mexico and South America?

1. It was 1622, and the *Atocha* was sailing from Cuba to the Spanish port of Cádiz. It carried a fortune in gold, precious stones, and silver. Six hundred pounds of gold, together with 2,300 emeralds, were locked below deck. Sailors guarded the mountain of 1,038 silver bars and 100,000 coins from Spanish colonies in Mexico and Bolivia. But hurricane winds attacked the fleet, and the *Atocha* sank without a trace. The wreck and its valuable cargo lay under the sea for 363 years. Then, in 1985, divers working for an American company discovered the *Atocha* off the coast of Florida. Experts valued the treasure at a steep $183 million. The *Atocha* was only one of thousands of Spanish ships that pumped riches from the New World into the Spanish treasury.

The Aztecs Why did Cortés conquer the Aztecs and use their lands to enrich Spain?

2. The Spaniards who conquered the Caribbean and South America fought to explore and claim new territory for Spain. Each wanted to **convert** (kon-VERT) Native Americans to Christianity. To convert is to change from one religion to another. Each conquistador also had a goal of wealth and glory. Hernando Cortés (kohr-TEZ), a noble from Spain, was no exception. Cortés had been rewarded for his role in

▲ The painting above shows an Aztec version of Cortés's invasion. Based on evidence in the painting, how do you think the Aztecs viewed the Spanish conquerers?

the conquest of the island of Cuba in 1511. The young soldier then turned his attention to the shores of what is now Mexico. He listened to Spanish explorers who returned to Cuba with tales of a rich empire on the mainland.

3. Cortés thought that these tales were true and formed an expedition to conquer that em-

In Chapter 4, you will apply these critical thinking skills to the historical process:
○ **Generalizing:** Making a statement that links several facts.
◣ **Comparing and Contrasting:** Recognizing similarities and differences.

pire. Starting in 1519, Cortés sailed up the coast of Mexico and set up a base at Veracruz. During the months he spent building his town, Cortés received Aztec **delegates** (DEL-uh-gayts) who were sent by an emperor called Montezuma (mahn-tuh-ZOO-muh). A delegate is a person who acts for another person. From these Aztecs, Cortés learned about the wealth of the Aztec Empire. This empire, he was told, covered land from the Gulf of Mexico to the Pacific Ocean. The Aztec Empire governed over three million people. Throughout the empire were cities with gold-plated buildings. The delegates asked Cortés to leave Mexico, but the conquistador had other plans.

4. From the non-Aztec peoples of the Gulf Coast, Cortés had learned that the Aztec Empire rested on a weak base. The empire was really a loose group of great cities and tribes who had been conquered by the Aztec army. Each tribe had to pay a yearly tribute of gold and slaves to Montezuma. Many of the conquered people were **sacrificed**, or killed, in Aztec religious ceremonies. Cortés listened to these facts. He knew that his army of fewer than 600 Spaniards was too small to win against the Aztecs. He also knew that many tribes within the Aztec Empire hated their rulers, but were not strong enough to defeat them. Cortés therefore decided to form **alliances** (uh-LY-uhn-sez) with the non-Aztec peoples of the empire. An alliance is an agreement among nations to help each other. Cortés talked the non-Aztec chiefs into believing that he was their only hope of destroying Montezuma.

People in History

5. Doña Marina Without the help of Doña Marina, Hernando Cortés would probably have failed to conquer the Aztecs. The daughter of a powerful Native American chief, Doña Marina had been sold into slavery upon her father's death. She was given to Cortés as a gift by the Gulf Coast Native Americans and quickly became a valuable member of Cortés's group. Doña Marina spoke the Aztec language and understood Aztec life. She quickly learned Spanish and became Cortés's teacher and interpreter. She also was Cortés special delegate to Native American chiefs. During the two-year Spanish expedition in Mexico, Doña Marina kept the Spaniards from getting into trouble many times.

6. From his settlement at Veracruz, Cortés began a 250-mile march across deserts and tropical forests, and over high mountain ranges. His march led to the Aztec capitol, Tenochtitlán (tay-nahch-tee-TLAHN), a beautiful city built on a large, shallow lake. As Cortés traveled westward, he persuaded non-Aztec Native Americans to join his march on the Aztec capitol. These Native Americans gave Cortés's army food and advice. In addition, many of them joined his march toward Tenochtitlán.

Spotlight on Sources

7. Montezuma welcomed Cortés into Tenochtitlán on November 8, 1519. According to Aztec beliefs, a fair-skinned god with a beard was supposed to return from the East. By chance, Cortés arrived in Mexico during the year this god was to return. The weapons and horses that Cortés's army brought into Mexico gave the Aztecs the idea that these were powerful people. Horses were unknown in that part of the world. In the passage below, Montezuma tells about how Cortés was thought to be a god.

> We have known for a long time . . . that . . . I and those who inhabit [live in] this country were . . . brought to these parts by a lord, whose vassals [servants], they all were, and who returned to his native country. And we have always held that those who descended from him [his children and grandchildren] would come to subjugate [conquer] this country . . . and according to the direction from which you say you come . . . and . . . what you tell us of your great lord, or king [Charles I of Spain], who has sent you here, we believe . . . that he is our rightful sovereign [king]. . . . Hence you may be sure that we shall

Ask: For Native Americans, gold and silver were valued only as materials for making art and jewelry. Ask what might have happened had the Aztecs and Incas shared European ideas about gold and silver.

61

obey you . . . and throughout the country you may command at your will, because you will be obeyed, and recognized, and all we possess [own] is at your disposal [is yours].

—*The Five Letters*, Hernando Cortés

▶ Why might the Aztec's view of Cortés have made them hesitate to fight his army?

8. Hernando Cortés however, had come to Mexico for treasure and glory, not kind words. He took Montezuma prisoner and demanded a tribute from every city and tribe in the Aztec Empire. How might this demand for treasure have made Cortés's Native American allies feel? Cortés told his soldiers to destroy Aztec temples. They were also ordered to melt into solid bars all the gold statues and jewelry they could find. This angered the Aztec priests and warriors. In 1520, they attacked the Spanish. Montezuma, who was still a prisoner of the Spanish, was killed, and Cortés had to retreat.

9. Cortés gathered his forces later in 1520 and attacked Tenochtitlán again. During the four-month battle, nearly 240,000 Aztecs died defending their capitol. Tenochtitlán was destroyed by the fighting. Finally, European weapons, powerful non-Aztec allies, and help for Cortés from Cuba proved too much for the Aztecs. By 1521, the conquest of Mexico was over. Cortés quickly rebuilt Tenochtitlán and named it Mexico City. He opened mines and shipped gold and silver to ports in Cuba and Hispaniola, and then on to Spain. In 1522, Cortés was made governor and captain-general of New Spain, a colony that included all Spanish lands north of Panama.

The Incas How did Pizarro defeat the Incas in South America?

10. Francisco Pizarro (pee-ZAHR-oh), a **veteran** (VET-er-un) of several expeditions,

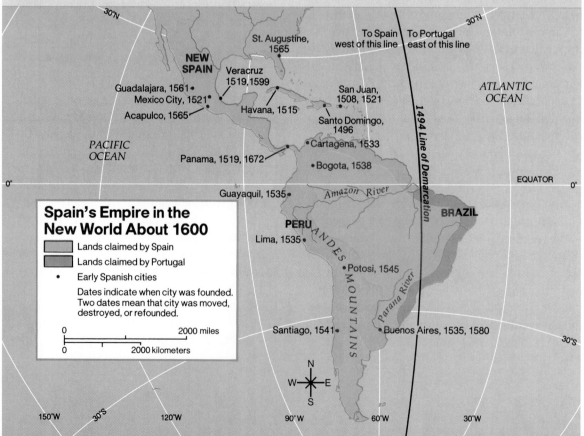

MAP SKILL BUILDER: Meridians are the north–south lines on a map that indicate longitude east and west of England. **1.** What meridian is closest to Buenos Aires? **2.** What meridian is closest to Mexico City?

Spain's Empire in the New World About 1600

- Lands claimed by Spain
- Lands claimed by Portugal
- Early Spanish cities

Dates indicate when city was founded. Two dates mean that city was moved, destroyed, or refounded.

had heard tales of a rich empire south of Panama. A veteran is a person with experience, especially experience in battle. Pizarro sailed down the coast of South America past Ecuador to Peru. There, he got in touch with the Incas, members of a powerful Native American empire. Inca nobles brought Pizarro gifts of gold, jewelry, and valuable stones. Pizzaro was convinced that he had discovered an empire even richer than Mexico.

11. In the early 1530s, Pizarro led another expedition south from Panama into Peru. When he reached Peru, he was joined by another conquistador, Hernando De Soto. Together, these two explorers faced an army of thousands of Inca warriors. Pizarro learned that the Inca emperor, Atahualpa (ah-tah-WAHL-pah), was camped high in the Andes Mountains. When Pizarro reached the place where Atahualpa was camped, he sent a greeting and invited the emperor to come to the Spanish camp for a meeting. Believing that 200 Spanish soldiers were no match for his powerful army, Atahualpa accepted the friendly-sounding invitation. In doing so, he walked into a dangerous trap.

12. The following day, Atahualpa, with several thousand unarmed guards, met with Pizarro. The Spanish forces made a surprise attack and **massacred** (MAS-suh-kurd) the Incas. To massacre is kill a number of people without mercy. Pizarro captured Atahualpa and demanded a large amount of gold and silver for his freedom. Without their war chief to lead them, the Inca army failed to fight back. Neither could they keep Pizarro from executing Atahualpa the following year and declaring himself ruler of Peru. Pizarro founded the capital city of Lima (LEE-muh) in 1535 and ruled the new Spanish colony of Peru for the next six years. Peru was rich in silver and gold, and soon large mines were set up. In what ways was the conquest of Peru like the conquest of Mexico?

Outlook

13. The conquest of Mexico and South America brought many benefits for Spain. Colonies were set up to mine gold and silver. The

▲ The large buildings of Tenochtitlán were completely destroyed by the Spanish soldiers and the Native Americans who had joined Cortés.

colonies of New Spain and Peru were to become important sources of power and wealth for Spain. The search for treasure, however, meant great suffering to the Native Americans. In fewer than 50 years, two of the world's great empires, the Aztecs and the Incas, were destroyed. The Spaniards brought diseases such as smallpox, typhoid, and yellow fever, which were unknown to the Native Americans. The Native Americans had no defense against these diseases, and many of them died. At the time of Cortés's conquest, more than 25 million people lived in Mexico. By 1605, less than 100 years later, warfare and disease had killed 95 per cent of these Native Americans. What example did Spain's conquest of Mexico and South America set for later European settlements in America?

63

CHAPTER REVIEW

VOCABULARY REVIEW

▶ On a separate piece of paper, write each of the following words in a sentence of your own. Use the Glossary at the back of the book to check each definition.

1. delegate
2. veteran
3. alliance

4. massacre
5. convert

SKILL BUILDER: USING A TIME LINE

▶ Study the time line below. Then answer the questions on a separate sheet of paper.

```
┌Vikings    ┌Leif Ericson              Columbus reaches the┐    ┌Balboa sees
 sail        reaches North                West Indies, 1492│     the Pacific
 900         America           Turks limit caravan routes to┐    Ocean
             1000                             Asia, 1453│         1513

   900     1000    1100    1200    1300    1400    1500    1600

                         First Crusades              Dias finds new    Columbus sets
                         begin                        route around      up first colony
                         1096                          Africa           in New World
                                                       1488┘           └1493
```

1. How many years after Leif Ericson reached North America did Columbus reach the West Indies?

2. How many years after the Turks limited caravan routes did Dias find a sea route around Africa?

3. How soon after Dias discovered a new route around Africa did Columbus reach the West Indies?

4. How long did it take for Columbus to set up a colony after he discovered the New World?

5. How many years after Columbus reached America did Balboa first see the Pacific Ocean?

SKILL BUILDER: CRITICAL THINKING AND COMPREHENSION

I. Generalizing

A **generalization** is a statement that combines different events or facts into one idea. A generalization states what is the same about these facts, not what is different. For example, suppose you had a friend who watches football on TV, reads football magazines, and plays football in his or her free time. You might generalize about this friend by saying that he or she is a football fan.

Which of these sentences is a generalization?

a. Doña Marina helped the Spaniards in the New World.

b. Doña Marina was able to translate the Aztec language into Spanish.

c. Doña Marina served as Cortés's delegate to Native American chiefs.

Sentence **a** is the generalization. It makes a broad statement that covers the facts given in the other two sentences.

▶ Read the following groups of sentences. In each group, one of the sentences is a generalization. Choose the generalizations and write them on a separate sheet of paper.

1. **a.** Cortés demanded a tribute from every Aztec city.
   b. Cortés told his soldiers to melt all Aztec statues into gold bars.
   c. Many of Cortés's actions were aimed toward gaining wealth for Spain.

2. **a.** Atahualpa, the Inca leader, was executed by Pizarro's soldiers.
   b. Many Incas were killed by the Spaniards.
   c. Spanish forces massacred Incas in a surprise attack.

3. **a.** Montezuma's friendship with Cortés cost Montezuma his life when enemy forces attacked the Spanish explorers.
   b. Spanish soldiers executed Atahualpa.
   c. Native American rulers lost their lives when the Spanish conquered South America.

▲ **II. Summarizing**

▶ Choose one of the topics below. Write a short summary two or three sentences long about the topic. Reread the paragraphs listed after each topic to review the facts before you write the summary.

1. Cortés's plans to conquer the Aztecs (paragraphs 3 and 4)

2. Montezuma's thoughts about Cortés (paragraph 7)

3. Pizarro's conquest of the Inca Empire (paragraphs 11 and 12)

4. The part Doña Marina played in the Spanish conquest of Mexico (paragraph 5)

USING PRIMARY SOURCES

▶ Reread the quotation by Montezuma in paragraph 7. Write a short letter to King Charles I of Spain. Summarize what Montezuma has promised. Give your opinion about what his words mean.

ENRICHMENT

1. Role-play a meeting between Atahualpa and Montezuma. Compare your opinions about the Spaniards and the way your people were treated.

2. Use library resources to learn more about Pizarro's three voyages to South America. Then, draw a map that shows the routes that Pizarro followed down the coast of South America and across the Andes Mountains. Display your map for the class.

CHAPTER 5

Spanish Explorers Move North

OBJECTIVE: Why did Spanish explorers continue to search for gold in the lands north of Mexico?

1. A dusty column of soldiers winds across the southwest desert. The luckier ones ride thin, tired horses. The majority, wearing torn leather boots, are marching on foot. The soldiers are hundreds of miles from home, hungry, and puzzled. Most have given up hope of finding the lost Cities of Gold. Yet they keep following the conquistador to whom they have promised their loyalty. During the 1500s, rugged Spaniards tried to carve out personal empires in the unexplored lands north of Mexico. Some searched for the famed lost cities of gold. Others hunted for a water route through North America. These explorers added to the Spanish Empire much of what is now the southern part of the United States.

Explorers of the Southwest Where did Spanish explorers search for the Cities of Gold?

2. After the conquest of Mexico and Peru, Spaniards turned their attention to the deserts and mountains north of Mexico. There, they were told, lay the Seven Cities of Cíbola (SEE-buh-luh). These cities had riches more valuable than those discovered by Cortés and Pizarro. Excited by new discoveries of gold and silver in northern Mexico, the conquistadores began trips even farther to the north.

3. Panfílo de Narváez (narh-VAH-ayth) led

▲ Dreams of glory and riches caused explorers such as Francisco Vásquez de Coronado to risk crossing the harsh deserts of the Southwest.

the first expedition in search of the Seven Cities. In 1527, Narváez sailed from Cuba with an army of 600 soldiers and colonists. Narváez intended to conquer and colonize the lands along the Gulf of Mexico. This area stretched from Florida to the border of New Spain. In April 1528, Narváez reached the west coast of

In Chapter 5, you will apply these critical thinking skills to the historical process:

▲ **Identifying Fact versus Opinion:** Specifying whether information can be proved or whether it expresses feelings or beliefs.

◯ **Generalizing:** Making a statement that links several facts.

Florida, near what is now Tampa Bay. Without a guide, Narváez marched north to find his fortune, but he discovered only Native American villages and swamps. By midsummer, Narváez decided to return home. Because he could not find his ships, Narváez built five rafts to carry his troops. The flimsy rafts were separated by storms in the Gulf of Mexico, and Narváez was lost at sea.

4. Alvar Núñez Cabeza de Vaca (ka-BAY-tha thay VAH-kah), the police officer of Narváez's fleet, led three other men to safety. Cabeza, along with 40 other explorers, had been rescued by Native Americans. After a year of living as a slave among them, Cabeza escaped. He met three other men from the Narváez expedition, and together the four decided to walk back to Mexico. For safety, they pretended to be **medicine men**. Medicine men are people who are thought to have magic powers in curing disease. Cabeza's group became known among the Native Americans as great healers. They were led safely from one village to the next, across what is now Texas. On reaching northern Mexico, the men were greeted by Spanish soldiers. The travelers then made another 800-mile (1,280-km.) trip to Mexico City.

5. On July 25, 1536, eight years after starting their voyage, the four men were welcomed into the capital. These men were the first Europeans to explore much of the Gulf Coast. The tales they told of the Seven Cities—places which they had never seen—caused other explorers to follow in their footsteps. Why were the Spaniards so quick to believe the tales of the Seven Cities?

De Soto's Explorations   How did De Soto explore Florida and the Mississippi River?

6. In 1539, Hernando De Soto, another Spanish explorer, sailed from Cuba to begin another search for the lost cities. De Soto, you may remember, had helped Pizarro conquer the Inca Empire. Upon landing in Florida, De Soto took the same route that Panfilo Narváez had taken 11 years earlier. After spending six

months searching for the Cities of Gold, De Soto decided to look west. This began a long trip through what is now the southern United States. First, De Soto crossed into Georgia and led his army over the Blue Ridge Mountains. Then he marched south and spent the winter of 1540–1541 in what is now Louisiana.

7. In the spring of 1541, De Soto reached the Mississippi River. De Soto and his men built four barges and crossed the river near present-day Memphis, Tennessee. They were the first Europeans to cross this river. In March of 1542, De Soto gave up his dream of finding gold and decided to return to Cuba. Believing that the Gulf of Mexico lay to the west, the soldiers marched in that direction by mistake. They found themselves once more at the banks of the Mississippi River. This discovery broke De Soto's spirit. A few days later, he caught a fever and died. His band of soldiers buried him secretly in the Mississippi River. Why did De Soto's soldiers try to hide their leader's death from the Native Americans? The new leader of the group, Luis de Moscoso, brought the remaining soldiers back to Mexico. De Soto's expedition added nearly 350,000 square miles (906,500 sq. km.) of new land to the Spanish Empire.

8. While Hernando De Soto was planning his three-year voyage in Cuba, the **viceroy** (VYS-roy) of New Spain, Antonio de Mendoza, was planning another expedition. A viceroy is person sent by a ruler to govern another region or country. In 1539, Mendoza asked a Franciscan **friar**, or monk, named Fray Marcos de Niza to find out more about the people and lands north of Mexico. Fray Marcos was also told to find the Seven Cities of Cíbola.

People in History

9. Estevanico   Viceroy Mendoza chose Estevanico (es-tay-vahn-EE-koh), an experienced guide, for the expedition. Three years before, Estevanico, an African slave from Morocco, had returned with Cabeza de Vaca after traveling through these same lands. Estevanico led Fray Marcos's group through northern Mexico and

▲ De Soto's journey took him through what later became nine states, from Florida in the east to as far west as Louisiana.

into southeastern Arizona. When Estevanico was traveling ahead of the group as a scout, he discovered a city. He believed that this city was one of the Seven Cities of Cíbola. As he came close to the city, however, he was taken prisoner. The Native American chiefs believed that Estevanico was a Spanish spy and executed him. Estevanico was the first explorer from a European expedition to travel through southern Arizona and western New Mexico.

Coronado's Journeys   What lands did Coronado explore for Spain?

10. Although Estevanico died on his scouting trip, Fray Marcos returned to Mexico City with glowing reports of the Seven Cities. These reports led to a new expedition to search for gold in the lands north of Mexico. The new expedition was led by Francisco Vásquez de Coronado (kor-oh-NAH-thoh). In February of 1540, Coronado led a colorful group of 230 cavalry, 32 foot soldiers, and 1,000 Native Americans north into what is now the Southwestern United States.

Spotlight on Sources

11. After traveling for many weeks, Coronado caught sight of Shi-uo-na (shee-YOUO-nah), the capital of the Zuñi Native American **confederacy**. A confederacy is a union of people, groups, or tribes. Shi-uo-na was the city that Estevanico had discovered. Far from being a golden city, Shi-uo-na was a pueblo. Coronado attacked Shi-uo-na and captured its people. After the battle, Coronado wrote a letter to Viceroy Mendoza. In it, he describes the battle and tells how he felt about Fray Marcos's claims.

> I ordered the musketeers and crossbowmen [soldiers] to . . . drive back the enemy from the defenses. . . . It now remains for me to tell about this city and kingdom and province of which the Father Provincial [Fray Marcos] gave your Lordship an account. In brief, I can assure you that in reality he has not told the truth in a single thing he has said, except the name of the city and the large stone houses. For, although they are not decorated with turquoises [valuable blue stones], nor made of . . . gold bricks, nevertheless they are very good houses, with three and four and five stories [levels] . . . the Seven Cities are seven little villages, all having the kind of houses I have described.
> —*The Journey of Coronado, 1540–1542*

What did Coronado find that was valuable to his soldiers?

12. Coronado used the conquered city as a base for his activities. Next, he split his army into three groups to increase his chances of finding the "real" Cíbola. Each group traveled

Background: Spanish explorers considered 5 to 6 miles a good day of traveling, and 10 to 12 miles an excellent day.

▲ The ruins pictured above show that the Zuñi were skilled builders. This site can be visited today in New Mexico. What parts of these buildings fit Coronado's description of Shi-uo-na?

in a different direction. The first group went west and discovered the Grand Canyon. The second group marched east through present-day New Mexico and Texas. Coronado himself led the third group to a large pueblo. Here, Coronado heard tales of a rich city to the east, called Gran Quivira. The following spring, Coronado marched across Texas and Oklahoma and into the great plains of central Kansas. To his disappointment, Coronado learned that Gran Quivera was merely a small village of beehive-shaped huts, populated by the Wichita Native American people. Instead of finding gold and silver, Coronado saw a sea of tall grass and thousands of strange animals, called "buffalo" (bison). Coronado returned to Mexico, believing that his journey was a failure.

Exploring the Pacific Coast How did the search for a sea passage enlarge Spain's empire?

13. Just as the conquistadores searched for the Seven Cities of Cíbola, Spanish sea explorers searched for a strait, the Strait of Anian. This sea passage was said to link the Atlantic and Pacific Oceans. Why would the discovery of this strait be valuable to Spain? In 1542, Juan Rodríguez Cabrillo led an ocean expedition up the coast of California. Cabrillo sailed north and anchored in a sheltered bay, near present-day Los Angeles. Then he continued north, missing the entrance to San Francisco Bay. In January 1543, Cabrillo died from an injury. Bartolomé Ferrelo took over the voyage of discovery. Ferrelo may have gone as far north as Oregon. He claimed the new lands for Spain and returned to Mexico

Outlook

14. The early Spanish explorers of North America covered many miles of unknown territory. They did not, however, find riches like those of Mexico and South America. The Spanish government lost its interest in exploration north of Mexico. Soon, ranchers and colonists would follow the trails blazed by these early explorers. What career opportunities would attract Spaniards to settle in the New World? ◄

Activity: Using a string, a ruler, and a wall map, ask volunteers to determine the distances traveled by the conquistadores.

69

CHAPTER REVIEW

VOCABULARY REVIEW

▶ Write each of the vocabulary words on a separate piece of paper. Then match each word with its correct definition.

1. medicine man

2. friar

3. viceroy

4. confederacy

a. a monk
b. a person supposed to have magical powers to cure disease
c. a union of people, groups, or states for a specific purpose
d. a person sent by a ruler to govern another country
e. a Native American village in the southwestern United States

SKILL BUILDER: INTERPRETING A MAP

▶ At the bottom of the map below you will find a map key. This key tells you what the different lines on the map stand for. Use the key to answer these questions on a separate sheet of paper.

1. Whose expedition covered more miles, Coronado's or De Soto's?

2. Which two explorers crossed the Rio Grande River?

3. What is the significance of the arrow that shows Narváez's trip turning into a dotted line in the Gulf of Mexico?

4. Which explorers might have followed the same trail for a while in Florida?

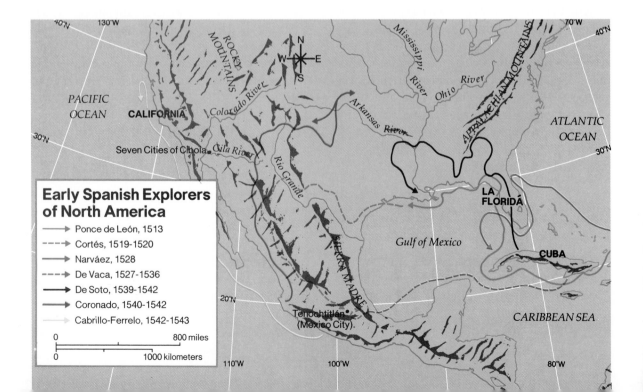

Early Spanish Explorers of North America

→ Ponce de León, 1513
---→ Cortés, 1519-1520
→ Narváez, 1528
---→ De Vaca, 1527-1536
→ De Soto, 1539-1542
→ Coronado, 1540-1542
→ Cabrillo-Ferrelo, 1542-1543

0   800 miles
0   1000 kilometers

SKILL BUILDER: CRITICAL THINKING AND COMPREHENSION

I. Generalizing

A generalization is a statement that links, or connects, several facts.

1. Reread paragraph 2 at the beginning of this chapter. Which statement makes the best generalization about facts presented in that paragraph?

   a. The story of the Seven Cities of Cíbola interested the conquistadores.

   b. The promise of wealth inspired the conquistadores to explore areas north of Mexico.

   c. Gold and silver were discovered in northern Mexico.

2. Reread paragraph 12. Which statement makes the best generalization about facts presented in this paragraph?

   a. Coronado was glad to find new plants and animals.

   b. Coronado believed that his journey of exploration was a failure.

   c. Coronado traveled through much of the present-day United States.

II. Summarizing

1. Reread the Spotlight on Sources, paragraph 11. Summarize Coronado's report in one or two sentences.

2. Reread the People in History feature, paragraph 9. In one or two sentences, summarize what you know about Estevanico.

3. Reread paragraph 4. In one or two sentences, summarize how Cabeza reached safety.

USING PRIMARY SOURCES

▶ Reread the Spotlight on Sources, paragraph 11, then answer the following question. How was what Coronado found different from what he expected to find?

ENRICHMENT

1. Imagine what the Seven Cities of Gold might have looked like, and draw a picture of them. Use your picture as part of a poster calling for volunteers to join the exploration.

2. Imagine that two of the explorers from the chapter meet. Write a dialogue between these explorers, describing their adventures and discoveries. Before writing, ask yourself what kind of information an explorer might choose not to share with a competitor.

3. Use library resources to learn more about the geography and climate of the North American territories discovered by the Spaniards. Share what you learn with the class.

71

CHAPTER 6

Spanish Settlers Move North

> **OBJECTIVE:** How was Spain able to settle the large region north of Mexico?

1. Church bells announced the news. Outside the Palace of Governors, in Santa Fe, excited colonists were unloading wagons. On the ground sat boxes of clothing, hardware, and farm tools. There were other goods, too. Crates of candlesticks, pottery, rugs, and coffee would bring comfort to the harsh lives of the frontier settlers. The mule-drawn wagons that carried these goods had traveled 1,500 miles (2,400 km) from the more developed areas of New Spain. Every three or four years a wagon train arrived at the capital city. It carried supplies, settlers, and news about the outside world to the lonely Spanish communities of New Mexico.

Spain Settles La Floridá How did Spain force French settlers to leave Florida?

2. After Juan Ponce de León claimed Florida in 1513, other Spaniards strengthened Spain's claim to the area. Florida at that time included all the lands along both the Gulf of Mexico and the Atlantic Ocean. Because Florida had no gold or silver, Spain was not interested in settling it at first. The first colonies did not last. In 1526, Lucas Vázquez de Ayllón took about 600 settlers from Hispaniola to the coast of what is now Georgia. The new colony, named San Miguel de Guadalupe, soon failed. Two-thirds of the colonists died from illness and hunger, and the others returned to Hispaniola.

▲ The earliest forts in St. Augustine, Florida, were made of wood. In the 1600s, work was begun on the stone Castillo de San Marco.

3. The first Spanish colony that lasted was built in 1565. The Spanish became worried when a group of French people arrived to settle on the northeast coast of Florida. Right away Spain sent ships to drive out the French. On September 8, 1565, the Spanish, led by Pedro Menéndez de Avilés, landed in Florida. They

In Chapter 6, you will apply these critical thinking skills to the historical process:

➡ **Recognizing Cause and Effect:** Recognizing the action or event that makes something happen; identifying the result of an action or event.

⭕ **Generalizing:** Making a statement that links several facts.

founded St. Augustine, now the oldest city in the United States. The Spaniards then fought successfully against the French in present-day Florida, Georgia, and South Carolina. This quick action protected Spain's control over Florida and stopped French settlement there.

The Southwest
How did Spain settle the regions that are now the states of New Mexico, Arizona, and Texas?

4. Following Coronado's disappointing reports in 1542, Spain waited 50 years to settle the American Southwest. Meanwhile, thousands of Spaniards came to the north of Mexico to mine silver. Along with the miners came sheep and cattle ranchers, who took over large areas for grazing livestock. The settlers' demands for land and water pushed the frontier of Mexico north. The growth of Spanish settlements threatened Native Americans, who
▶ fought to defend their communities. How did the reaction of the Native Americans compare to Spain's reaction to French settlers in Florida?

5. The leaders of New Spain decided to start a new colony north of Mexico. This colony would protect the silver mines and ranches against Native American attacks. In 1598, Spanish settlers, led by Juan de Oñate, reached northern New Mexico and built the village of San Juan de los Caballeros. Several years later, the city of Santa Fe was built.

6. When the settlers came to the Southwest, Spanish officials also sent **missionaries** (MISH-un-ayr-eez). A missionary is a person sent by a church to teach a religion to a group of people. In the 1690s, a Spanish priest, Father Kino (KEE-noh), built eight **missions** in Arizona. A mission is a religious center where members of a church teach their religion to others. The missionaries taught the Native Americans to read and write in Spanish and in their own languages. Native Americans living on the missions also learned European methods of farming and craftsmaking. The last remaining Spanish mission in Arizona is San Xavier de Bac, built in 1700, near what is now Tucson.

Spotlight on Sources

7. The aim of the missionaries was to convert the Native Americans to Christianity. Father Kino and others also wanted the missions to improve life for the Native Americans. In the following letter, Father Kino tells how the missions can help bring peace among the Native Americans.

> For many years this province of Sonora [Arizona] has suffered very much from its . . . enemies, the Hocomes, Janos, and Apaches [enemies of the local Native Americans]. . . . But by founding very good missions for them . . . a great restraint [control] can be placed upon their [the Native Americans'] enemies . . . not only will the Christian settlements . . . have more protection . . . but at the same time a way will be opened to many other new conquests and new conversions, in many other more remote new lands . . . of this still somewhat unknown North America.
>
> —from *Original Narratives of Early American History: Spanish Exploration in the Southwest, 1542–1706* ed. by Herbert E. Bolton

What benefit did Father Kino think the missions would bring to the Native Americans? ◀

8. Spanish priests also built missions in the area that later became Texas. As early as 1682, the mission at El Paso provided safety for people driven out of New Mexico by the Native Americans. The Spaniards also built a string of mission-forts. The most successful of these became the modern city of San Antonio.

9. Many of the Spanish settlements in Arizona and Texas were not very successful. The Native Americans bravely fought to keep their lands in the Southwest. Their attacks caused many Spaniards to leave.

Life for the Native Americans
How did the Spanish officials treat the Native Americans?

10. The Spanish officials forced Native Americans to do much of the work in the

Ask: Horses escaping from Spanish herds became the wild mustangs and broncos used by Native Americans to hunt migrating herds of bison.

SPANIARDS

Why did Spaniards come to the New World in the 1500s and 1600s? In Spain, traders and craftspeople found few chances to gain wealth in crowded towns and villages. Many Spaniards did not have enough money to buy their own farms. Tales of the rich treasures of gold and silver found in New Spain attracted many. The New World offered Spaniards a chance to increase their wealth and improve their places in society. Missionaries came to New Spain to teach Christianity to the Native Americans. The missions they built offered protection to Native Americans and Spaniards alike.

Upon reaching New Spain, some Spaniards struck it rich by mining silver or gold. Others settled in frontier regions where land could be bought cheaply. Many others served the crown as army officers, judges, or tax

▼ The buildings of Mission San Jose, one of several missions near San Antonio, were planned by Spaniards skilled in building design.

collectors. Skilled workers created fine silver and leather products and supplied the colonists with tools, furniture, and cloth.

During Spain's early period of colonization, a surprisingly small number of people emigrated to the New World. Over a period of 250 years, only 300,000 Spaniards settled in New Spain and Peru. In 1560, the first Mexican **census**, or official counting of people, counted only 28,000 Spanish emigrants. In 1760, there were only 7,666 Spanish males in the Kingdom of New Mexico. Population figures show that the Spanish were the smallest group in New Spain. They made up only 2 percent of the total population. African slaves made up 3 percent, and Native Americans made up nearly 95 percent of the population. Yet, even with this small number of people, Spain was able to govern a huge empire in the New World. Even in later years, few Spaniards entered the United States. Instead, they traveled farther south, to Latin America.

The Spanish settlers who came to the area that is now the southwestern United States brought many new crops. These included wheat, oats, barley, rye, and sugar cane. They also brought farm animals, such as sheep, pigs, cattle, burros, and horses. These crops and animals were new to the continent and brought important changes to the lives of the Native Americans.

The Spanish also brought with them their excellent knowledge of building design. The results of their work can still be seen in the mission buildings, churches, and forts that remain in the American Southwest today.

Now answer the following questions.

1. Why might life in New Spain seem attractive to some Spaniards in Europe?

2. Why might it have been easier to become wealthy by settling in Mexico or Peru rather than in the settlements in North America?

A SPANISH MISSION

▲ A Spanish mission in the American Southwest was a nearly self-sufficient community. Why might soldiers' barracks be needed?

colonies. They set up a system called **encomienda** (en-koh-mee-EN-dah). Under this system, the colonists demanded payment from Native Americans. This payment was made in food, in gold, or by hard physical work. Native Americans were forced to dig silver ore from deep underground mines. Others worked under hard conditions on farms and ranches. Although the Spanish officials were supposed to provide clothing, housing, and health care, few did. Tens of thousands of Native Americans died from these harsh working and living conditions and from diseases introduced by Europeans.

People in History

11. Bartolomé de Las Casas Many of the missionaries did not agree with the way some Spanish treated the Native Americans. Las Casas (lahs KAH-sahs), a missionary priest, saw that the Native Americans often were treated cruelly under the encomienda system. Las Casas asked King Charles I of Spain to pass laws that would protect the Native Americans. The king passed these laws, but few Spaniards obeyed them. Why do you think most Spaniards did not obey these laws?

12. Las Casas had another idea to help the Native Americans. He suggested that African slaves be brought to do the work that the Native Americans were doing. The settlers agreed. Later, Las Casas was sorry that his idea had been accepted. He saw that the Africans suffered as much as the Native Americans had.

Outlook

13. After the explorations of the conquistadores, Spanish settlers moved into Florida and the Southwest. Many Native Americans died from diseases introduced by the Spaniards and from forced labor in the colonies. In addition, Native Americans were not pleased to see the Spaniards taking over lands the Native Americans had held for years. The Native Americans fought to keep these lands and drove many Spaniards away. What might have been done to promote friendship between these groups?

Activity: Organize students into small groups and have them develop "What if?" questions and answers. For example, "What if Native Americans had been less successful in fighting the Spanish?"

CHAPTER REVIEW

VOCABULARY REVIEW

▶ Use each of the following words in a sentence of your own. You may look up the words in the Glossary at the back of the book to check each definition.

1. encomienda

2. missions

3. census

4. missionaries

SKILL BUILDER: READING A MAP

▶ Use the key at the top of the map below to answer the following questions. Write your answers on a sheet of paper.

1. Which settlement on the east coast of the Atlantic Ocean was the farthest north?

2. What is the settlement farthest south in Florida?

3. What major rivers did the Eastern Camino Real cross?

4. Which overland trail was San Juan de los Caballeros, in New Mexico, closest to?

5. If you were to travel south on any of the overland trails, in what city would you end your trip?

6. Imagine that you were traveling north on the Eastern Camino Real. What difficulties do you think you might come across on your trip to St. Augustine? Hint: Remember much of Mexico and present-day Texas is desert.

7. To reach California from Santa Fe, which overland trail would you take?

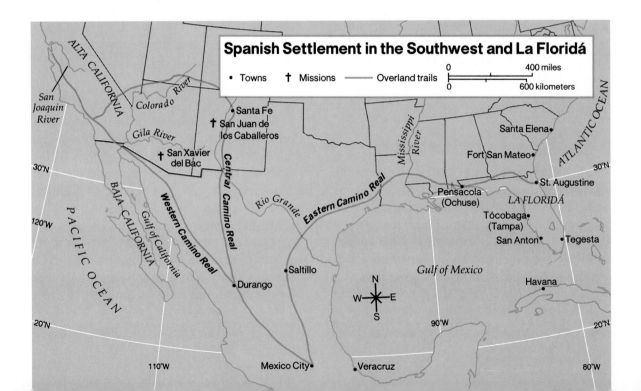

Spanish Settlement in the Southwest and La Floridá

• Towns   † Missions   — Overland trails

0   400 miles
0   600 kilometers

SKILL BUILDER: CRITICAL THINKING AND COMPREHENSION

I. Generalizing

▶ Write the following generalizations on a sheet of paper. Read the paragraph listed after each statement if you need to review the facts.

1. Make a generalization about why the people of New Spain moved to the north of Mexico. (paragraph 4)

2. Make a generalization about how the Spanish solved the problem of French settlements in Florida. (paragraph 3)

3. Make a generalization about the purpose of the missions. (paragraph 6)

II. Summarizing

Choose one of the following topics to write a summary about. Before you begin to write your summary, review the material by rereading the paragraphs listed after each topic.

1. Reread the "America's People: Spaniards" feature. Write a summary of this feature. (page 74)

2. Summarize in one or two sentences the Spanish exploration and settlement of Florida. (paragraphs 2 and 3)

3. Summarize the contribution that missions played in helping Spaniards and Native Americans in the early American Southwest. (paragraphs 6, 7, 8, and 11)

4. Summarize the role that Bartolomé de Las Casas played in improving life for the Native Americans. (paragraphs 11 and 12)

USING PRIMARY SOURCES

▶ Reread the Spotlight on Sources section, paragraph 7. How did Father Kino think the missions could help the Spanish settlers?

ENRICHMENT

1. Prepare a brief written report on the important agricultural products that Native Americans shared with Spanish settlers. In your report, discuss how these new food sources contributed to Spain's success in the New World. (Sample products: corn, tomatoes, potatoes, indigo, cacao beans for chocolate)

2. A historical novel is a work of fiction based on people or events of the past. Choose a person or event from this chapter and write the opening page of a historical novel about your subject.

3. Choose one of the Spanish settlements that you studied in this chapter. Use encyclopedias and other reference books to find out more about this settlement. Work with other students to create a poster designed to attract new settlers. You might include drawings of buildings in the settlement and information about the climate and typical activities there.

CHAPTER 7

The French Explore North America

OBJECTIVE: How did French explorers gain a vast empire for France in North America?

1. The small army of French explorers and Native American families stood on the banks of the mighty river. Salty breezes blew from the Gulf of Mexico, several miles downstream. The explorers saluted their distant ruler with shouts of "Long Live the King!" Then, the commander of the expedition planted the French flag in the warm spring soil. "In the name of the most high, mighty, invincible, and victorious Prince, Louis the Great . . . King of France . . . ," he announced, "I, this ninth day of April, one thousand six hundred and eighty-two . . . have taken, and do now take, in the name of his majesty and of his successors to the crown, possession of this country of Louisiana." With these few words, France made its claim to a giant slice of North America—from the Great Lakes south to the Gulf of Mexico, and from the Appalachian Mountains west to the Rockies.

▲ This painting from the 1800s shows the chief of the Taensa Native Americans receiving La Salle in 1682.

Champlain Founds New France   How did Champlain set up trading posts and explore the Great Lakes?

2. As you have read, Jacques Cartier claimed for France the lands of North America between New England and the Gulf of St. Lawrence. Cartier failed to discover either a sea route to China or the valuable metals needed to pay for other voyages of exploration. France lost inter- est in North America for nearly 50 years. The only French on the continent were fishermen who lived on the eastern coast and traded goods with Native Americans. In 1590, King Henry IV awakened France's interest in the New World. The king gave fur-trading monopolies in New France to merchants who promised to

In Chapter 7, you will apply these critical thinking skills to the historical process:

Sequencing: Putting a series of events in the correct time order.

Understanding Points of View: Recognizing why people have different attitudes about the same thing.

settle colonists there. In 1603, a merchant company set up the small trading post of Port Royal, in Nova Scotia. Samuel de Champlain (sham-PLAYN) was the company's geographer.

3. For three summers, Champlain sailed from Port Royal, mapping the coastlines of what are now Maine and New Hampshire. In 1608, Champlain sailed up the St. Lawrence River to search for a water route to China. Champlain landed near a place where the great river became narrow. He built a trading fort called Quebec on its northern shore.

Spotlight on Sources

4. From his Native American guides, Champlain learned that the land around Quebec was held by the Huron. The Huron were Native Americans who spoke one of the Algonquian family of languages. Champlain traveled by canoe throughout Huron lands. He studied Huron customs and made peace treaties with their leaders. He encouraged the Hurons to sell beaver skins to his company at Quebec. In his book *The Voyages*, Champlain discusses his travels among the Huron. He also explains how he made them his trading partners.

> They [Huron chiefs] signaled their satisfaction, saying that no greater good could come to them than to have our friendship, and that they desired to live in peace with their enemies, and that we should dwell in their land, in order that they might in future more than ever before engage in hunting beavers, and give us part of them in return for our providing them with things which they wanted. . . . I presented them with hatchets, paternosters [prayer beads], caps, knives . . . when we separated from each other. All the rest of this day and the following night . . . they did nothing but dance, sing, and make merry, after which we traded for a certain number of beavers.
>
> —from *The Voyages of Samuel de Champlain, 1604–1618: Original Narratives of Early American History*, ed. by W. C. Grant

Under this trading agreement, what did each side agree to? ◄

5. To prove his friendship with the Huron, Champlain joined them in war against the Iroquois, their enemies to the south. In 1609, Champlain traveled with a Huron war party through what is now Vermont to what is now the state of New York. At a large lake there, which he named for himself, Champlain helped the Huron defeat the Iroquois. Crossing Lake Huron and Lake Ontario six years later, Champlain joined the Huron in an unsuccessful battle against the Iroquois. How would the Iroquois think of the French after these early French–Huron raids? As a result of these attacks, the powerful Iroquois Nation became bitter enemies of the French settlers. For many years, the unfriendly Iroquois kept French from moving out of the St. Lawrence River valley into the area beyond.

6. Champlain worked hard to attract French merchants and settlers to Quebec. In 1627, the king named Champlain governor of New France. The king also gave a fur-trading monopoly to the Company of New France. The company agreed to bring 300 new settlers to New France each year. However, settlers in New France faced many problems. The oak, maple, and birch forests were difficult to cut and clear for planting. In addition, many colonists felt cut off from the rest of the world. Winter ice on the St. Lawrence River prevented contact with France for six months each year. By 1663, only 2,500 people from France, a nation of 16 million people, had settled in New France. Most of these settlers lived on a strip of land along the St. Lawrence River, in three main settlements. These settlements were Quebec, Trois-Rivières (twah-riv-YAIR), and Montreal.

Marquette and Joliet How did these French explorers expand French control of North America?

7. In 1663, King Louis XIV began a great effort to colonize New France. The king made

Activity: Moderate a class debate on the following statement: "The fur trade was as profitable for Native Americans as it was for French merchants." Help students develop clear, logical arguments based upon facts.

79

New France a royal colony and put its government under his direct control. To end the danger from the Iroquois, the king sent French troops to invade their lands. How would this act help French exploration? When peace was declared in 1666, the French were finally free to explore the interior of North America. By 1670, **Jesuit** missionaries had built missions at Green Bay, Wisconsin, and at Sault Ste. Marie (soo saynt mar-EE), where Lake Huron joins Lake Superior. Jesuits were members of the Society of Jesus, a Roman Catholic religious order founded in 1534. From the Native Americans, the Jesuits learned of a great river to the west. This river was said to lead to the Pacific Ocean and China. Here at last, they thought, was the famous strait across North America.

8. In May 1673, Louis Joliet (zhoh-lee-AY) and Father Jacques Marquette (mahr-KET) set out to see if the story of the strait was true. Joliet was a soldier and fur trader. Father Marquette was a Jesuit missionary. From Lake Michigan, the two explorers **portaged** (PORT-ijd), or carried their canoes overland, to the Wisconsin River. Marquette and Joliet traveled down this river, which flowed into the Mississippi River. For three weeks they paddled southward, finally stopping near the mouth of the Arkansas River. Here, they saw that the Mississippi River did not turn to the west. Rather, it flowed south, emptying into the Gulf of Mexico. Fearing capture by Spanish troops who controlled that territory, Marquette and Joliet returned to Quebec.

La Salle   How did La Salle's exploration of the Mississippi region gain Louisiana for France?

9. Marquette and Joliet did not find a strait to the Pacific Ocean. However, the governor of New France was very pleased with their discoveries. Their expedition led him to plan to set up a series of trading forts. These forts would be

MAP SKILL BUILDER: Early French explorers followed water routes deep into the interior of North America.   **1.** How did French explorers reach the Great Lakes?   **2.** How did French explorers reach the Mississippi?

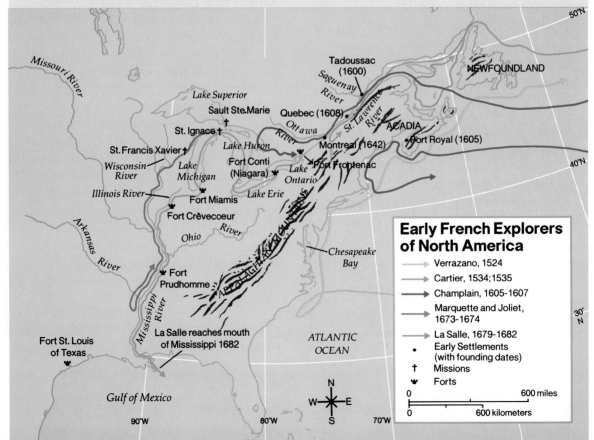

Early French Explorers of North America

- Verrazano, 1524
- Cartier, 1534; 1535
- Champlain, 1605-1607
- Marquette and Joliet, 1673-1674
- La Salle, 1679-1682
- • Early Settlements (with founding dates)
- † Missions
- ☙ Forts

0   600 miles
0   600 kilometers

located along the Mississippi River and the smaller **tributary** (TRIB-yoo-tayr-ee) rivers that flowed into it. They would serve as fur warehouses and provide shelter for the French fur traders who would work in the area. Why did the governor feel that forts, as well as trading posts, were necessary?

People in History

10. Robert La Salle To lead this important project, the governor chose Robert Cavalier de La Salle (luh SAL), an experienced explorer and wealthy fur trader. Born and educated in France, La Salle came to Montreal in 1666 and entered the fur trade. La Salle learned some of the Native American languages and became friendly with many Algonquian tribes in New France. La Salle explored the Ohio and Mississippi river valleys and built trading forts on Lake Ontario and Lake Michigan. He became convinced that the Mississippi River flowed into the Gulf of Mexico.

11. In December 1681, with 23 French and 31 Native Americans, La Salle set out on his boldest adventure. Because it was winter, La Salle built wooden sleds to pull his canoes across frozen lakes and rivers. After a difficult journey, he reached the Mississippi River and began the trip downstream. Along the way, La Salle became friendly with Native American tribes, who gave him guides and food. On April 9, 1682, he reached the mouth of the Mississippi River. La Salle claimed the land for France. He named the new land Louisiana in honor of the French king, Louis XIV. What La Salle called Louisiana was the entire middle section of North America.

12. King Louis was so pleased that he sent La Salle back to the mouth of the Mississippi River three years later. La Salle intended to build a fort there and seize control of Spanish lands near the Gulf of Mexico. But his mission was a failure. His ships lost their way and landed on the shore of present-day Texas. La Salle then set out with a small group to find the Mississippi. He was killed by rebels from his troop in March 1687.

New France Why did the fur trade enable France to build a new empire in North America?

13. French explorers made huge profits from **pelts,** or skins of fur-bearing animals. In Europe, beaver pelts were used to make fashionable hats and warm clothing. To be sure of a steady supply of pelts, French fur trappers and traders followed Native American trails and rivers deeper into North America. These adventurers were protected by French soldiers, who kept control over these new lands.

14. New France depended for survival on its fur trade. The fur trade in turn depended on the safety of the river routes that led to fur-rich lands of the South and West. The French sought the friendship of the Huron, who controlled these trading highways. This friendship, however, made the more powerful Iroquois angry. They began to trade pelts for guns with merchants from Holland and England. In 1633, the Iroquois began a war against Huron and French settlements. This war had a lasting effect on the future settlement of North America.

Outlook

15. Samuel de Champlain knew that a profitable fur trade was the key to French success in the New World. Fur trade was the main reason for the exploration and settlement of New France. It also helped to shape France's early relationships with Native Americans. At the same time, the fur trade caused conflicts between French merchant companies and French settlers. Fur traders did not want the farmers to clear forests and drive off the wild animals. Many settlers felt unwelcome in New France, and chose not to settle there. As a result, France was not able to colonize much of the territory it claimed in North America. With few people and weak defenses, New France became an easy target for other European nations building settlements in North America. How might Native Americans and English settlers have felt about France's claims in the New World?

Background: A single French colonist could cut and clear only two acres of land annually. Only after the tree stumps rotted, several months later, could he or she remove them to plow fields and plant crops.

CHAPTER REVIEW

VOCABULARY REVIEW

▶ For each sentence below, fill in the blank with the correct word from the vocabulary list.

Jesuit   tributary   portaged

warehouses   pelts

1. Marquette and Joliet realized that the Missouri River was a _____ of the Mississippi River.

2. The quest for beaver _____ brought French fur traders into the interior of North America.

3. Marquette and Joliet _____ their canoes to the Wisconsin River.

4. Daring _____ priests helped to explore and settle new lands in North America.

SKILL BUILDER: MAKING A CHART

▶ Making a chart is a good way to summarize names, dates, and other facts for study. For example, in Chapter 7 you read about several French explorers. Make a chart showing their names, the dates of their explorations, and the places they explored. The chart has been started for you below. Copy it over and fill it in using information from the chapter.

Explorer	Lands Explored	Date Exploration Began
Champlain		
Marquette and Joliet		
La Salle		

SKILL BUILDER: CRITICAL THINKING AND COMPREHENSION

I. Generalizing

▶ Choose one of the following topics. Write a generalization about the topic on a sheet of paper.

1. The importance of the fur trade to New France (paragraphs 13 and 14)

2. The contributions of La Salle to French influence in the New World (paragraphs 10 and 11)

3. The achievements of Marquette and Joliet (paragraphs 8 and 9)

4. The achievements of Champlain (paragraphs 3 through 6)

II. Sequencing

Sequencing is the skill of putting facts in their correct order in time. In order to make a time line, you need to understand sequencing. When arranging events in their correct sequence, ask yourself: Which event came first? Which came second? Which came next? Often you will need to check on the exact date in order to figure out the correct sequence.

For example: Suppose you were asked to read the following paragraph and then put some of the events from the paragraph in the correct order.

Alice graduated from high school in 1984 and began studying at the University of Southern California the same year. She married Jorge in 1986. Alice took five years to graduate from U.S.C. The summer after graduation, Alice started work as a waitress. She stayed at the restaurant for a year. Then she began her successful career as a journalist on television.

If you were asked to put the following events in order, how would you figure it out?

A. Alice graduates from the University of Southern California.
B. Alice begins her job as a professional television journalist.
C. Alice marries Jorge.
D. Alice works as a waitress.

You know that Alice graduated from U.S.C. five years after she started. That would be 1989 because she started college in 1984. She started working at the television station in 1990, a year after she graduated. She married Jorge in 1986. She started working as a waitress the same year that she graduated. That year you already know was 1989.

Therefore, you know that the correct order is C, A, D, B.

▶ Write the following events from Chapter 7 in the order in which they occurred. If you need to look up the date, check the paragraph number given after each event.

1. The Iroquois begin a war against French settlements (paragraph 14)

2. La Salle reaches the mouth of the Mississippi River (paragraph 11)

3. Marquette and Joliet begin exploration of the Mississippi River (paragraph 8)

4. A small trading post is established in what is now Nova Scotia (paragraph 2)

USING PRIMARY SOURCES

▶ Reread the passage in paragraph 4. What advice do you think the French fur traders would have given to the Spanish conquistadores about dealing with the Native Americans?

ENRICHMENT

1. Work with other students to develop a newspaper article that might have appeared in New France. Report on the return of Marquette and Joliet to Quebec in 1673 or on some other topic from the chapter. Include drawings and interviews as well as factual reports.

2. Give a brief oral report about the geography of New France. In it, explain how the region's abundant streams and rivers were used as freight lanes during the 1600s.

3. Use history books or encyclopedias to compare and contrast Louis XIV's palace of Versailles, near Paris, with settlements in New France of the same period. Using visual aids, share your findings with the class.

CHAPTER 8

England Founds a Colony

OBJECTIVE: Where was the first permanent English colony started in America and how was it established?

1. The new governor glanced at his six advisors. "Surely," he thought, "they are as uncomfortable as I am." Indeed, the inside of the church was too hot to bear. Yet, it was the only building in the town large enough to hold this important meeting. The governor shook his head at the bare, dirty floor. "Why did I leave the comfort of England for this primitive land?" he wondered. The governor raised his hand. At this signal 20 planters, two from each of the colony's ten settlements, walked into the church. Each man pledged his loyalty to King James I of England and took his seat. It was July 30, 1619. With the first meeting of the Virginia General Assembly, self-government in North America had begun.

England against Spain How did England end Spain's control of the seas?

2. By 1580, Spain was the most powerful country in the world. Spain controlled important areas of Europe, including the Netherlands and parts of Italy. The Spanish Empire stretched east to the Philippine Islands and west to New Spain and Peru. Huge sums of money were needed to defend and govern these lands. In spite of the riches coming in from New Spain, the government continued to spend too much. In time, the empire began to crumble.

▲ The House of Burgesses formed part of the early government of Virginia. Only free white men could take part in elections for this assembly.

3. As the Spanish Empire weakened, England rose to power under the strong leadership of Queen Elizabeth I. Elizabeth gained the throne in 1558. The queen allowed English sailors, called **sea dogs**, to attack Spanish ships in the West Indies and trade with Spanish colonies there. Queen Elizabeth's actions made

In Chapter 8, you will apply these critical thinking skills to the historical process:

Understanding Points of View: Recognizing why people have different attitudes about the same thing.

Generalizing: Making a statement that links several facts.

King Philip II of Spain angry. In 1588, he assembled a great **armada** (ahr-MAHD-uh) to invade and destroy England. The fleet of 130 armed ships set out for England from Lisbon, Portugal. However, the skilled English navy, together with fierce storms off the English coast, destroyed the armada. The 76 Spanish ships that sailed home marked an end to Spain's control of the seas. England could now send ships to North America without Spanish attacks.

The First English Colonies   How did England attempt to settle North America?

4. In the 1580s, Queen Elizabeth had allowed Sir Walter Raleigh to explore the east coast of North America. Raleigh named the land Virginia. Using his own money, he tried tc set up a colony there in 1585. This first colony did not last. In 1587, Raleigh sent another group of 100 colonists to Roanoke Island, off the coast of what is now North Carolina. However, England was at war with Spain, and for three years no supply ships could reach the colony. When a ship finally arrived at Roanoke Island, no settlers could be found.

5. English merchants found a new way to raise money for future colonies. They borrowed the idea of the **joint-stock company** from the Dutch. Under this plan, several people could buy part of the ownership of a company. As partial owners, they helped to run the company and share in its successes as well as its failures. In 1606, a group of merchants founded a joint-stock company called the London Company. They asked the new English King, James I, for a **charter** (CHAR-tur) to establish a trading colony in Virginia. A charter is a document that gives the right to set up a colony.

6. The London Company hired 104 employees, promising to pay their way to Virginia. In return, the settlers agreed to send back any gold or silver they found and any crops they grew on the company's land. The settlers sailed from England in December 1606. Four months later, they reached the mouth of the Chesapeake Bay. They entered a wide river, which they named for King James I. The settlers chose a site 60 miles (96 kilometers) upstream for their settlement.

The Jamestown Colony   What were some of the problems the colony faced?

7. From the start, life at Jamestown was filled with problems. The leaders failed to build proper shelters or to plant crops for food. Instead, the settlers spent their time looking for gold and silver and exploring the rivers for a route to China. Half of the settlers were nobles who were not used to physical work. They expected the London Company to provide them with food. As a result, they quickly ate all the food they had brought from England. Without proper nutrition, the settlers easily fell sick. By September 1607, one-half had died. The rest were saved by Native Americans, who shared their fall harvest with the starving colonists.

Spotlight on Sources

8. John Smith, an experienced soldier, made friends with the Native Americans. He traded iron tools for corn, squash, and beans. In his book, *A True Relation,* Smith describes the friendly actions of the Native Americans.

> It pleased God to move the Indians to bring us Corne [corn] . . . when we rather expected they would destroy us . . . the Indians brought us great store both of Corne and bread ready made . . . and later . . . as at this time most of our chiefest men either sicke or discontented . . . our vituals [food] now being 18 days spent [gone], I was sent . . . to trade for Corne. . . . The Indians thinking us neare famished [starving], with carelesse kindnes, offred us little pieces of bread and small handfulls of beanes or wheat, for a hatchet or a piece of copper . . . with fish, oysters, bread, and deere, they kindly traded with me and my men, beeing no lesse in doubt of my intent, then I of theirs.
> —from *Narratives of Early Virginia: 1606–1625,*
> ed. by Lyon Gardiner Tyler

Activity: Have students investigate the lost Roanoke colony. Point out that historians now believe the settlers abandoned the colony and intermarried with the mainland Chesapeake people. All were probably wiped out, however, in local Native American wars.

85

▶ Why did John Smith think the Native Americans would kill the settlers?

9. John Smith took charge of Jamestown, setting strict rules to help the colony survive. He set up working parties to build new houses, plant crops for the winter, and bring fresh water to the colony. Jamestown lost its able leader in 1609, when a gunpowder accident forced John ▶ Smith to return to England. Why were strict rules needed in Jamestown?

10. The same year, the London Company changed the government of Jamestown. A royal governor was appointed to bring leadership and security. The company also sent 500 new colonists, including women and children, to Jamestown. However, a hurricane scattered the settlers' ships, and only 400 people arrived in Jamestown that autumn. By then, it was too late to plant new crops. The colony's **surplus**, or extra supply, of food was not large enough to feed the new settlers. The winter of 1609–10 was called "the starving time" because so many people died from starvation and disease.

The Virginia Colonies Why did English settlements in Virginia begin to succeed?

11. In the spring of 1610, sixty survivors set out from the troubled colony to begin the long trip back to England. They were met several miles downriver by the new governor, who brought three ships loaded with supplies and new colonists to Jamestown. This help gave the colony a new beginning. Under the next governor, Sir Thomas Dale, colonists built ten new settlements along the James River. Dale assigned a small plot of land to each person to farm. Then John Rolfe, one of the settlers, found that tobacco could be grown in Virginia. Popular in England, tobacco became a source of money for the colony. Tobacco was planted in every possible space, including the town streets.

People in History

12. **Pocahontas** Native Americans did not all agree with each other about the English settlers. Some thought the settlers were enemies. Others tried to make peace, teaching the English how to clear forests and grow their own food. Pocahontas (poh-kuh-HAHN-tus), the daughter of a local chief, tried to live in peace with the Jamestown settlers. Pocahontas is reported to have saved John Smith's life twice. The English rewarded Pocahontas's kindness by kidnapping her. They held her as a **hostage** (hahs-tej) to prevent Native Americans from attacking Jamestown. A hostage is a person held prisoner until certain demands are met.

13. During her captivity, Pocahontas became a Christian and took the name Rebecca. She and John Rolfe fell in love and were married in 1614. The couple traveled to England, and for ten months they were treated like royalty. In 1617, on the way home, Pocahontas

MAP SKILL BUILDER: Inset maps (see upper left) are used to show information that the main map cannot. **1.** What is on the inset map that is not on the main map? **2.** What is on the main map that is not on the inset map?

The First English Settlements

- Settlement (date when founded)

Note: two dates mean that colony failed and was refounded.

```
0          80 miles
0       100 kilometers
```

NORTH AMERICA
Jamestown
40°N
20°N
120°W   80°W

Rappahannock River
York River
James River
Jamestown, 1607
Chesapeake Bay
ATLANTIC OCEAN
Chowan River
Albemarle Sound
Roanoke, 1585 (1587 failed)
Pamlico Sound
Croatoan
Cape Hatteras
38°N
36°N
76°N

Background: King James I objected to tobacco, claiming it, "Lothsome to the eye, hateful to the Nose, harmfull to the braine, daungerous to the Lungs." By 1630, however, 500,000 pounds of the leaf were being shipped every year to England. How does King James' objection compare to the Surgeon General's warning today?

▲ In 1619, a group of about 100 women arrived at Jamestown from England. Men who had settled there earlier married and began families. This was important in making Jamestown a stable and successful colony.

caught smallpox and died. For six years, the marriage between Pocahontas and John Rolfe brought peace between the Native Americans and the English settlers. What does Pocahontas's life show about the early relations between Native Americans and English colonists?

14. By 1619, peace and profits from the sale of tobacco brought important changes to Virginia. As their colony grew stronger, the settlers demanded a greater voice in their government. The London Company sent a new governor, Sir George Yeardley, to call together a general assembly. Yeardley asked colonists to elect **burgesses** (BUR-juh-sez) to this assembly. A burgess was a person elected to represent a town. The Virginia Assembly gave settlers the right to privately own more farmland.

15. Larger farms needed more workers. **Indentured servants** (in-DEN-churd) filled this need. These were people who paid with their labor to get to Virginia. Indentured servants worked without pay for three to seven years. After that time, they were free. In 1619 a Dutch ship brought 20 Africans to Virginia as indentured servants. Soon, more Africans would be brought to Virginia as slaves.

16. Although the Virginia colonies were growing, they were still not making enough money for the London Company. In addition, King James I was not pleased with the way the colony was being managed. In 1624, the king made Virginia a **royal colony**, owned and governed by the king or queen.

Outlook

17. At first, Jamestown was a trading post. Only when settlers were allowed to farm their own land did the colony succeed. Although the king appointed royal governors, many found it hard to rule without the help of the Virginia Assembly. Early on, the Virginia colonists began to guide their own government. As time went on, the experience Virginians had gained in self-government would help them gain their independence from Great Britain.

Activity: Show students an outline map of North America. Have volunteers define, label, and color in lands claimed by Spain, France, and England in 1625.

CHAPTER REVIEW

VOCABULARY REVIEW

▶ Write the following vocabulary words on a separate sheet of paper. Then, match each word with its correct definition.

1. sea dogs

2. armada

3. joint-stock company

4. charter

5. surplus

6. burgess

7. indentured servant

8. hostage

9. royal colony

a. legal right to establish a colony

b. representative of an elected assembly

c. extra amount or supply

d. a person held prisoner until certain demands are met

e. worker who pays in labor for a passage to America

f. governed directly by the king or queen

g. business plan to raise money for overseas colonies

h. English sea raiders

i. a large fleet of armed ships

SKILL BUILDER: READING A TIME LINE

▶ Look at the time line below. Then answer the questions that follow.

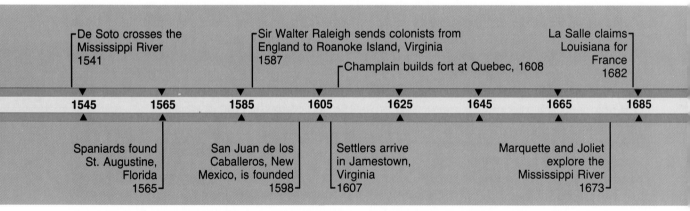

De Soto crosses the Mississippi River 1541

Sir Walter Raleigh sends colonists from England to Roanoke Island, Virginia 1587

Champlain builds fort at Quebec, 1608

La Salle claims Louisiana for France 1682

1545   1565   1585   1605   1625   1645   1665   1685

Spaniards found St. Augustine, Florida 1565

San Juan de los Caballeros, New Mexico, is founded 1598

Settlers arrive in Jamestown, Virginia 1607

Marquette and Joliet explore the Mississippi River 1673

1. How many years after Sir Walter Raleigh sent colonists to Roanoke Island did the first settlers arrive in Jamestown?

2. How many years passed between Marquette and Joliet's exploration of the Mississippi River before La Salle claimed Louisiana for France?

3. How many years after De Soto crossed the Mississippi was the first settlement in New Mexico founded?

4. What country founded the first settlement in what is now the United States?

88

SKILL BUILDER: CRITICAL THINKING AND COMPREHENSION

I. Sequencing

▶ Sequencing is putting events in order according to time. The earliest date comes first, then the later dates. A list of events is given below. Write them on a sheet of paper in the correct sequence. All of these events are mentioned in Chapter 8, with their dates.

1. John Rolfe married Pocohantas.

2. Queen Elizabeth I came to the throne.

3. King James I made Virginia a royal colony.

4. The Spanish Armada was destroyed.

5. The first Africans came to Virginia.

6. Settlers from the London Company sailed from England to America for the first time.

II. Generalizing

▶ Choose one of the following topics to write a generalization about. Write your generalization on a separate sheet of paper.

1. Generalize about ways that John Smith helped the settlers of Jamestown. (paragraphs 8 and 9)

2. The marriage between Pocahontas and John Rolfe had an effect on relationships between the Native Americans and the English. Make a generalization about what this effect was. (paragraphs 12 and 13)

3. Make a generalization about why the "lost colony" of Sir Walter Raleigh might have failed. (paragraph 4)

USING PRIMARY SOURCES

▶ Reread the Spotlight on Sources in paragraph 8. Do you think the Native Americans or the English were more secure about the motives of the other side? Give a quotation from the passage to support your answer.

ENRICHMENT

1. Imagine you are a Jamestown settler. Write a letter to a friend back in England. Express your opinion about the benefits and hardships of living in this frontier colony. Comment on the government of the colony and on the Native Americans you have met.

2. Houses at Jamestown had timber frames, walls of branches and mud, and thatched roofs. Find out more about these houses by reading about Jamestown in other history books or encyclopedias. Then build a small model of a house to display for the class.

3. Imagine that you are a member of the lost colony at Roanoke Island. Write a diary account of the last day of the colony.

UNIT REVIEW

SUMMARY

The first Europeans to reach the Western Hemisphere were the Vikings. The Vikings explored the North American coast almost 1,000 years ago but did not establish lasting settlements. Nearly 500 years later, Christopher Columbus sailed west in 1492 with the goal of reaching Asia. Instead, he discovered a half of the world that was unknown to Europeans at that time. Spain, France, and England soon were competing to establish empires in this New World. Spain claimed the gold-rich lands of Central America, South America, and many of the Caribbean Islands. Much of what later became the southern and western United States was conquered by Spain as well. Although the Spanish gained the richest lands, before long England and France had also established settlements in the New World. Life in the early settlements was difficult and often dangerous. However, the New World offered opportunities for freedom and wealth not available in Europe. If these settlers had not been willing to take risks, North and South America would have remained a wilderness.

SKILL BUILDER: READING A MAP

▶ Look at the map, then answer the questions below.

1. What city shown on the map was settled first?

2. What island shown on the map was settled first?

3. Near what bodies of water are the earliest settlements shown on the map?

4. Which city is farthest west?

5. Why are there so few settlements that are not near a large body of water?

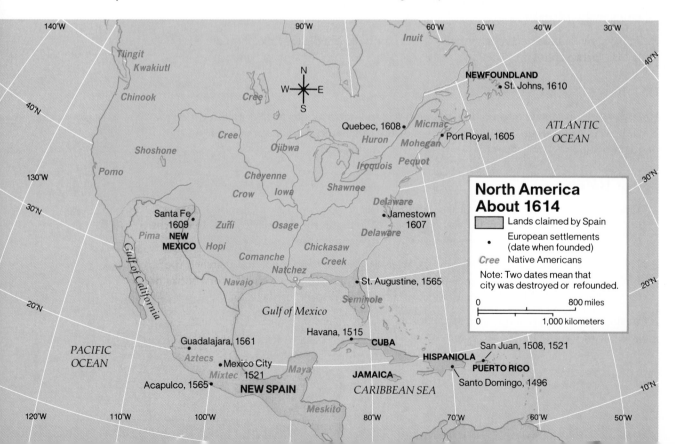

SKILL BUILDER: CRITICAL THINKING AND COMPREHENSION

○ **I. Generalizing**

1. Look at the map on the opposite page. Make a generalization about the influence of Spain in the New World.

2. Make a generalization about the importance of Christopher Columbus's discoveries in the New World.

▲ **II. Summarizing**

▶ Choose the person from the "People in History" features in this unit that interests you the most. Review the feature, then write a summary of that person's achievements. Include a statement about the importance of these achievements in your summary.

▢ **III. Classifying**

▶ A list of people that you studied in Unit 2 is given below. Classify each according to whether the person was French, Spanish, English, or Native American.

Sir Walter Raleigh	Montezuma
Marquette	La Salle
de Las Casas	Queen Elizabeth I
Champlain	Pocahontas
Cortés	Captain John Smith
De Soto	Doña Marina

ENRICHMENT

1. Role-play a conversation between a Huron who had met French explorers and an Aztec member of Montezuma's court. Compare your impressions of the Europeans and the treatment your people received.

2. Review the facts given in Chapters 6–8 about life in the earliest New World settlements. Choose one of the towns, trading posts, forts, or missions. Imagine that you are an early settler and write a letter to a relative in Europe about your impressions of your new home. You might describe the scenery, the Native Americans in your area, and other settlers. Include an account of some events that took place. Add drawings to your letter if you wish.

3. Many of the early explorers did not find what they set out to find. In some cases, they discovered lands and resources that proved far more valuable that what they were looking for. Columbus, De Soto, and others did not realize the true importance of their discoveries. Choose one of these explorers and write him a note. Congratulate him and give an explanation of why his efforts were appreciated by those who came later. If you prefer, present your statement as an oral report to the class.

UNIT 3

COLONIES IN THE AMERICAS PROSPER AND GROW

Chapter

UNIT OVERVIEW   You will learn the reason why the original 13 colonies were founded. Discover the colonists' attitudes about religious freedom, toleration, and self-government.

UNIT SKILLS OBJECTIVES In Unit 3, three critical thinking skills are emphasized:

Classifying: Organizing facts into categories based on what they have in common.

Generalizing: Making a statement that links several facts.

Predicting: Telling what you believe will happen on the basis of clues and facts.

You will also use two important social studies skills:
Using a Chart   Reading a Map

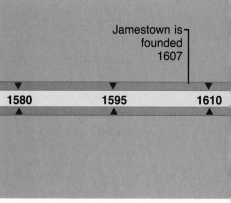

Jamestown is founded 1607

1580	1595	1610

ESL/LEP Strategy: After students complete the unit, have them work in teams to role play one of the major events that occurred during the colonial era such as the arrival of the Pilgrims or the arrival of the first Africans in the colonies.

▲ The Pilgrims come ashore at Plymouth Rock after a difficult voyage from England.

┌Maryland is founded, 1634
┌Carolina is founded 1663
┌Carolina is divided into two colonies 1712
grims d at ymouth ck, 1620
┌Rhode Island and Connecticut are founded, 1636

| 625 | 1640 | 1655 | 1670 | 1685 | 1700 | 1715 | 1730 |

└Massachusetts Bay Colony is founded, 1628

New Jersey is founded 1660

Pennsylvania is founded 1682

Georgia is founded 1733┘

└Dutch found New Amsterdam, which becomes New York, 1624

Points of View

Today, Americans accept the idea that people have the right to worship in whatever church they choose. That was not the case in many colonies in the 1600s. Even though colonists such as the Puritans crossed the ocean in search of religious freedom for themselves, they did not tolerate other religious groups. To some, religious freedom meant practicing their religion freely. At the same time, they banned people who did not have the same religious

▲ In Connecticut and other Puritan settlements, when dissenters, people who disagreed about religious ideas, spoke up, the majority often put them on trial, as in this painting.

FROM THE LAWS OF CONNECTICUT (1672)

❝ That no person in this colony shall give any unnecessary entertainment [attention] unto any Quaker, Ranter, Adamite, or other notorious heretic [someone who goes against the teachings of the established Church], upon penalty of *five pounds* [English money] for every such persons entertainments, to be paid by him that shall so entertain them. . . . That it shall be in the power of the governor . . . to order that all such heretics be committed to prison, or sent out of this colony; and no person shall unnecessarily fall into discourse [conversation] with any such heretic upon the penalty of *twenty shillings* [English money]. ❞

—from *American History Told by Contemporaries*, Albert Hart, ed.

Toleration: For and Against

beliefs. To others, it included tolerating people with different beliefs. In fact, the intolerance of the Puritans was one reason new settlements were formed.

The two selections that follow show the different views on toleration. The first selection comes from the laws of Connecticut in 1672. The second selection comes from the Charter of Liberties that William Penn drew up in 1701 for his Pennsylvania colony.

FROM WILLIAM PENN'S CHARTER OF LIBERTIES

" Because no people can be truly happy, though under the greatest enjoyment of civil liberties, if abridged [denied] the freedom of the consciences, as to their religious profession and worship . . . , I do hereby grant and declare that no person or persons, inhabiting in this province or territories, who shall confess and acknowledge *One* almighty God, . . . shall be in any case molested or prejudiced in his or their person or estate because of his or their conscientious [religious] persuasion or practice. . . . "

—from *The Making of American Democracy,* Ray Billington

▲ William Penn, pictured here, considered his colony a "Holy Experiment." Any one who believed in "one Almighty and Eternal God" was permitted to worship openly.

Using Primary Sources

1. How did the laws of Connecticut limit freedom of religion?

2. Why did William Penn think freedom of conscience was necessary? What one religious qualification did people have to meet to enjoy freedom of conscience in Pennsylvania?

CHAPTER 1

Europeans Settle in New England

OBJECTIVE: Why did the Pilgrims and Puritans come to America?

1. The *Mayflower* had pitched and rolled across the Atlantic Ocean for nine long weeks. Ever since they left England, the passengers had lived crammed below deck along with their chickens and pigs. Finally, in early November 1620, they sighted land in North America. A few days later, the *Mayflower* dropped anchor in the bay of what is now Cape Cod. Some of the passengers left the ship. Those passengers were members of a religious group called the Pilgrims. As soon as they reached shore, the people fell to their knees and thanked God for getting them to this new land. Here they would be free to live as English settlers and follow their religion as they wished.

The Pilgrims   Why did the Pilgrims leave England for America?

2. The need to earn a better living was one reason why the Pilgrims left England to travel to an unknown land. The 1500s was a time of high **inflation**, or a rapid rise in prices, in England. By 1600, food prices were four times higher than they had been in 1500. Yet people's pay had hardly risen at all. Many farmers found they were not able to support their families. Some of them decided to leave England and seek a better life.

3. The freedom to practice their religion was the most important reason why the Pilgrims left

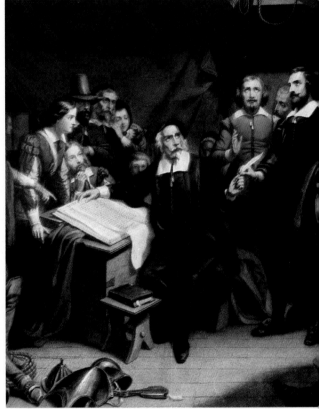

▲ William Bradford (center, seated) helped write the *Mayflower Compact*, setting up a colonial government. After the Compact was written, each of the Pilgrim families signed it.

England. There, all citizens had to worship in the Church of England. However, some groups, like the Pilgrims, did not want to belong to this church. These groups were known as **Separatists** because they wanted to leave or separate from that church. Separatists

In Chapter 1 you will apply these critical thinking skills to the historical process:

○ **Generalizing:** Making a statement that links several facts.

▯ **Sequencing:** Putting a series of events in the correct time order.

felt the Church of England could never be changed into the true church of Christ. They felt their souls were in danger. Their ideas sounded like rebellion to King James I (1603–1624), who was the leader of the Church of England. He decided to punish the Separatists. One group of Separatists then fled to the Netherlands to escape **persecution** (per-suh-KU-shun). Persecution is making people suffer for their beliefs. In the Netherlands, the Separatists started to call themselves **Pilgrims**. Pilgrims are people traveling on a holy journey.

4. The Pilgrims stayed in the Netherlands for twelve years. Yet they were unhappy there, even though they were allowed to practice their religion. First of all, they wanted a place of their own to live. Second, they wanted their children to grow up English, not Dutch.

5. In 1620, the Pilgrims decided to leave the Netherlands and settle in America. Their leaders, William Brewster and William Bradford, gained permission from the Virginia Company for them to travel to the Virginia colony as settlers. The Virginia Company was a trading and settlement company. The Pilgrims planned to settle near the mouth of the Hudson River, which was then a part of Virginia. On September 16, 1620, they set sail for Virginia. During the stormy voyage across the Atlantic, their ship, the *Mayflower*, was blown north of the Hudson River. On November 9, 1620, the Pilgrims sighted land in Massachusetts. They decided to land in a place that became Provincetown. Later, on December 11, an exploring party found Plymouth Harbor. The Pilgrims decided to build a village there.

6. While aboard the *Mayflower*, some people who were not Pilgrims were getting restless. The Pilgrim leaders feared that there might be trouble. Since the colonists had not landed in Virginia, there were no laws to govern them. The Pilgrim leaders believed that some rules or laws were needed. Right on board the *Mayflower*, they drew up a document that described the kind of government they wanted. In this document, known as the *Mayflower Compact*, the men swore their loyalty to the English king.

They also agreed that some citizens in Plymouth Colony could take part in government. They promised to obey all the laws the new government might pass. The *Mayflower Compact* did not actually set up a permanent government for Plymouth Colony. However, it was an important step on the road to democracy.

Spotlight on Sources

7. The Pilgrim leaders drew up the *Mayflower Compact* which 41 heads of families signed. The *Mayflower Compact* stated:

> We . . . do solemnly . . . in the presence of God and one another . . . combine [join] ourselves together into a civil body politick [government], for our better ordering [law and order] and preservation [safety] . . . And by virtue hereof do enact . . . such just and equal laws, ordinances [rules], acts, constitutions, and offices . . . as shall be thought most meet [needed] and convenient [easy to follow] for the general good of the colony; unto which we promise all due submission [to follow] and Obedience.

Why do you think that the Pilgrims felt they ◀ must set up a new government?

People in History

8. Squanto The Pilgrims would not have lived long at Plymouth without help from Native Americans. When they arrived at Plymouth in December, it was too late to plant crops. The weather caused terrible hardships. By spring, half the *Mayflower* passengers were dead. Then in March 1621, help arrived. Squanto (SKWAN-toh) was a Native American of the Patuxet tribe. To the Pilgrims' surprise, Squanto could speak English. In 1604, he had been captured by an English sea captain and had lived in England for nine years.

9. Squanto helped the Pilgrims learn how to live in their new land. The food Squanto shared with the Pilgrims helped them to live through the first winter. Then he taught the settlers how

▲ Without Squanto's help the Plymouth Colony probably would have failed. Here Squanto is showing the Pilgrims that fish make an excellent fertilizer for growing corn.

to plant corn, how to hunt, and how to fish. He even showed them the best streams for fishing. When Squanto died of a fever in 1622, the ► settlers knew they had lost a great friend. Why do you think Squanto was willing to help the Pilgrims even though other Native Americans were unhappy that the Pilgrims had come to stay?

Plymouth Colony   What steps did the Pilgrims take to establish a settlement in America?

10. At first, the Pilgrims tried to farm the land together and share the crops. They worked common fields and stored food in a common storehouse to be shared equally among families.

However, most of the young men and women wanted their own land. In 1623, the government of the Plymouth Colony gave families their own plots of land. After 1623, some settlers made their living by trading with Native Americans and England.

11. Left alone by the English kings, the people of Plymouth Colony learned to govern themselves. However, the colony was not a **democracy** (deh-MOK-ruh-see), or a government by the people. Every year a governor and his assistants were elected. However, not everyone could vote. Only fathers of families who owned a large amount of property could vote. The voters usually chose the same leaders year after year. Then, in 1691, the Plymouth colony was combined with the larger and richer colony to the north, Massachusetts Bay Colony. Why ◄ do you think the English kings did not bother much with the Pilgrims?

The Puritans   Why did the Puritans come to America?

12. Unlike the Pilgrims, the Puritans did not want to leave the Church of England. The Puritans wanted to **reform** (ruh-FORM), or change, and purify the church by simplifying it. They wanted to get rid of bishops' **vestments**, or religious robes. They also wanted to get rid of most church ceremonies. These practices reminded the Puritans of the Catholic Church and seemed to get in the way of the more direct approach to God they were seeking. However, King Charles I believed the Church of England did not need more reform. For this reason, he persecuted the Puritans, just as his father, James I, had persecuted the Pilgrims.

13. Besides religious problems, the Puritans also faced the same difficult economic problems as the Pilgrims had faced. Rising prices and loss of farmland made earning a living difficult. In addition, Puritans disliked the way the rich English lords lived. Then in 1629, King Charles began to rule without calling a **Parliament** (PAR-luh-ment), or an assembly of people who help govern. The king also made the people pay new taxes. The Puritans decided that they could never establish "heaven on earth" in England.

14. By 1630, the Puritans felt that America was the place to set up their new community. The Pilgrims already had proven that Europeans could live on the rocky soil of New England. Puritan leaders like John Winthrop and John Cotton wanted to set up a holy Christian colony that lived by the teachings of Christ. Winthrop called the settlement that the Puritans dreamed of "a city upon a hill."

The Massachusetts Bay Colony What steps did the Puritans take to build the Massachusetts Bay Colony?

15. In 1630, the Great Migration from England to New England began. A **migration** is a movement of people from one place to another. Fifteen ships carried over 1,000 Puritans to

▼ Rules for behavior were very strict in the colonies of New England. People who broke the law could be put in the pillories as these people have or in a dunking stool.

Massachusetts Bay. By 1634, there were over 10,000 settlers. Nine years later, when the migration ended, the population of New England included over 20,000 colonists.

16. All along the Massachusetts coast, Puritans established small towns such as Salem, Charlestown, Boston, Concord, and Sudbury, among others. Here people used the ideas of God's law in every part of daily life. At the center of the towns stood Puritan **meeting houses.** These buildings were usually dark and unheated and furnished with hard benches. At first, these meeting houses served mainly as places of worship. In time, though, they also became the gathering place for town meetings where people talked about local problems.

17. Puritans did not always agree about everything, but in matters of religion they rarely disagreed. Although fair-minded in other ways, Puritan leaders did not welcome questions about their faith. People who questioned the religion often had to leave the colony. The voyage to America had not changed Puritan beliefs. As one leader put it, "We have only changed our climate, not our minds." Why do you think a group that left England to escape religious persecution would not tolerate, or allow, dissenters?

Outlook

18. In the early 1600s, the Pilgrims and Puritans started a new life in Massachusetts. Both groups had come to America in search of religious freedom. Other English settlers followed during the Great Migration of the 1630s and 1640s. Yet the Puritans and the Pilgrims did not welcome other religions in their colonies. Likewise, they did not believe that Native Americans had rights. What problems do you ◄ think Puritan and Pilgrim attitudes might cause? At first, only a select few could participate in government, but other settlers demanded a say in government. The leaders gave in. It was a first step toward democracy. Much of what the Pilgrims and Puritans started in Massachusetts became the base for later developments in government and individual rights.

Background: The meetinghouse was the center of the community. It was always the first building to be built. The law prohibited the clergy from holding public office, but pastors had great authority in advising officials of God's will for the community.

99

CHAPTER REVIEW

VOCABULARY REVIEW

▶ On a sheet of paper, copy the following vocabulary words. Next to each word, write the letter of its definition.

1. vestments
2. Separatists
3. migration
4. democracy
5. reform
6. inflation
7. persecution
8. meeting houses
9. Pilgrims
10. Parliament

a. making people suffer
b. name Separatists gave themselves when they decided to move to the New World
c. movement from one place to another
d. government by the people
e. a governing body
f. religious robes
g. buildings where people worshipped and held town meetings
h. a sizable and continuing rise in prices
i. change
j. people who wanted to separate from the Church of England
k. a Native American who helped the Pilgrims

SKILL BUILDER: MAKING A TIME LINE

▶ On a sheet of paper, copy the time line below. Then read the dates and events that follow. Add them to your time line in the places where they belong.

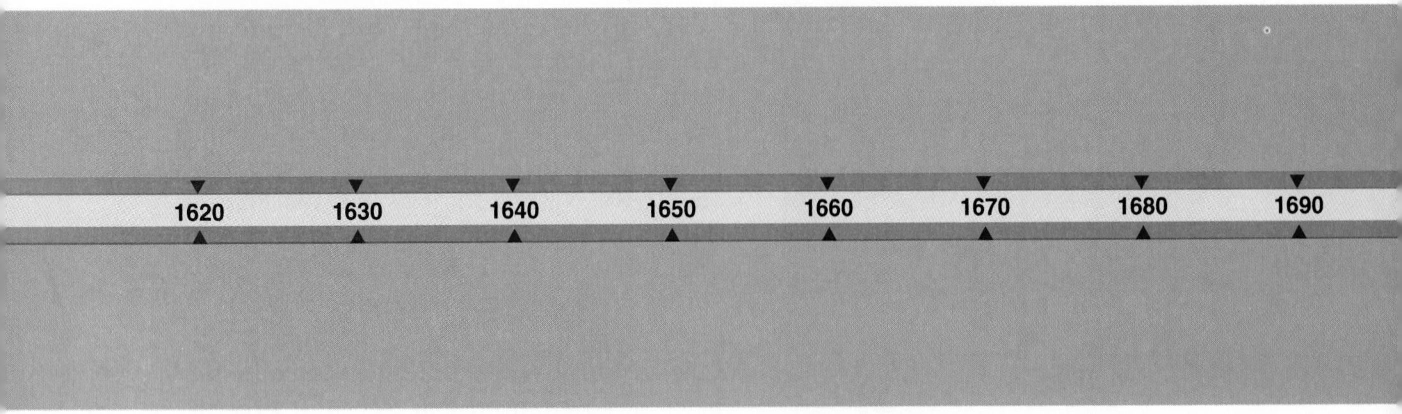

1620	1630	1640	1650	1660	1670	1680	1690

1643 Number of settlers in New England reaches over 16,000.
1623 Pilgrim families are assigned their own plots of land.
1691 Plymouth Colony is combined with the Massachusetts Bay Colony.
1620 The *Mayflower* lands in North America.

| 1657 | Governor William Bradford dies. | 1621 | Squanto helps the Pilgrims. |
| 1630 | The Great Migration begins. | 1649 | King Charles I dies. |

SKILL BUILDER: CRITICAL THINKING AND COMPREHENSION

I. Generalizing

1. Read paragraphs 2 and 3 in the chapter. On a sheet of paper, write why you think the following generalization is either a good or poor generalization about the paragraphs.

Economic pressure was the main reason the Pilgrims left England for America.

2. Make a generalization about the early colonization of America from the following facts.
   a. The Separatists, later called Pilgrims, left England because they wanted religious freedom.
   b. The Puritans wanted a close tie between church and state.
   c. Places of worship also became the scenes of town meetings.

II. Sequencing

▶ On a separate sheet of paper, write the following events with their dates in the order in which they occurred.

   a. Squanto lived in England for nine years.

   b. The Great Migration brought many new settlers to America.

   c. The *Mayflower Compact* was signed by Pilgrim leaders.

   d. The Plymouth Colony was combined with the Massachusetts Bay Colony.

   e. The Pilgrims arrived in America after nine weeks on the sea.

   f. The Pilgrims set sail for Virginia.

USING PRIMARY SOURCES

▶ Reread the Spotlight on Sources on page 97. What ideas do you share with the writers of the *Mayflower Compact*? What ideas from the *Mayflower Compact* has the United States used?

ENRICHMENT

1. With another member of your class, role play a Pilgrim and a Puritan having a conversation. Tell why you came to America and how you feel about the Church of England. For example, if you are playing the Pilgrim, explain why you want to reject the Church of England completely.

2. Imagine that your classroom is a ship and that you and your classmates are headed for an unknown land. Together, draw up a compact like the *Mayflower Compact* that will determine the rules you will live by in your new home.

3. Find a book on Squanto in your school or local library. How had he come to live in England? Write a few paragraphs on his life. Explain what you find most interesting about him.

CHAPTER 2

Champions of Religious Freedom

OBJECTIVE: How did the search for religious freedom lead to the founding of new colonies in New England?

1. The stern faces of 50 Puritan fathers stared at the young pastor as he was asked if he would give up his false beliefs. "Never!" he answered. Roger Williams believed religion could not be forced on people, but people should believe in their own way. As punishment, Williams was thrown out of Plymouth Colony. Through deep snow, he made his way to the friendly Narragansett (nair-a-GANN-sut) tribe, who took care of him. They also gave him land. Williams soon founded a colony that allowed everyone freedom of religion.

New Settlements Why did the Puritans expand beyond the Massachusetts Bay Colony?

2. Both practical and religious reasons caused Puritans to leave the Massachusetts Bay Colony and start new towns. Some people left because they did not like the lack of freedom under Puritan government. These people hoped that in a new settlement they would have a chance to take part in government. Others disagreed with the teachings of the Puritan church. Some disapproved of the church's strict control over the way people behaved. Others felt the church was not strict enough.

3. The Puritans were sure they knew God's truth, and they believed everyone should accept

▲ The Narragansett Indians came to Roger Williams aid when he was thrown out of Plymouth Colony. What did the Narragansett Indians wear on their feet to get through the snow more easily?

that truth. However, some people, such as Roger Williams, did not agree with the Puritans. They were called **dissenters** (dih-SENT-urs), or people who disagreed. Roger Williams spoke out against the Massachusetts Bay Colony for trying to put the Ten Commandments into

In Chapter 2 you will apply these critical thinking skills to the historical process:

Sequencing: Putting a series of events in the correct time order.

Recognizing Cause and Effect: Recognizing the action or event that makes something happen, identifying the result of an action or event.

law. Williams also questioned the Puritans' right to rule the colony. The settlers had purchased only part of the land from the Native Americans. The rest of the colonists had simply taken the land. In October 1635, the Puritans **banished** (BAN-ishd), or expelled, Williams from the colony. With some of his followers, Williams fled to Narragansett Bay and started a colony at Providence, Rhode Island.

4. After his experience in the Massachusetts Bay, Williams felt more strongly that religious freedom was important. He welcomed all sincere Protestants to Rhode Island. He also welcomed Quakers, Catholics, Jews, and people who did not believe in the God of the Bible. In addition, Williams helped Native Americans become Christians, but only if they asked.

⚜ Spotlight on Sources

5. While most white settlers feared and hated Native Americans, Williams respected Native Americans. He explained:

> [I have found] courtesy even amongst these wild Americans, both amongst themselves and toward strangers. . . . Nature knows no difference between Europe and Americans in blood, birth, bodies.
> —from *Roger Williams: His Contribution to the American Tradition*, Perry Miller

People in History

6. Anne Hutchinson Rhode Island soon became a safe place for dissenters and independent thinkers. One important dissenter who escaped to Rhode Island was Anne Hutchinson. She had arrived in Massachusetts Bay in 1634 with her husband and 13 children. Like Roger Williams, she was against forcing people to go to church, but for a different reason. Hutchinson thought that going to church would not prepare people to find the way of God. For Hutchinson, all that was needed to find God was personal desire. People did not need a church for that. The Puritan leaders could not accept this different view about salvation. They threw Hutchinson and her family out of the

colony. The Hutchinson family then moved to Portsmouth, Rhode Island, in 1638. There, she and Roger Williams built a colony based on religious freedom and study.

7. In 1644, Rhode Island became an official English colony through a charter from King Charles I. The charter gave men the right to choose their own government and make their own laws. The charter also said that Rhode Island's government could pass no laws about religious matters. In addition, the church could have no say in government. Why was separation ◄ of church and state important in Rhode Island?

Other New England Settlements Why were settlements established in Connecticut, New Hampshire, and Maine?

8. While some settlers who formed new colonies were religious dissenters, others wanted richer farm lands and less government.

▼ Anne Hutchinson got into trouble with the Puritan leaders when she started preaching sermons about her beliefs in her house in Boston.

Background: A rich London merchant, Theophilous Eaton, and his life-long friend, Rev. John Davenport, wanted to found a true "Bible commonwealth" of their own. However, the location they chose was not as good as they thought. New Haven did not become the commercial center they hoped for but became an agricultural settlement instead.

103

In 1637, the Reverend John Wheelwright was driven from Massachusetts for disagreeing with the Puritans. He and his followers settled in New Hampshire. Other settlers went farther north to Maine. However, some settlers were not driven out but wanted to spread the Puritan way of religion to new settlements. From 1633 to 1635, three Puritan groups marched 120 miles (about 192 km) from the Massachusetts Bay Colony to the valley of the Connecticut River. The Connecticut Valley had the most fertile farmland in all of New England. There they founded the towns of Hartford, Windsor, and Wethersfield. Another Puritan group founded New Haven in 1639.

9. In 1639, a group of the Connecticut settlers got together and wrote a plan of government called the **Fundamental** (fuhn-duh-MENT-ul) **Orders**. The Fundamental Orders created a more democratic government than the Massachusetts Bay Colony's. In Connecticut, every man who owned land could take part in government no matter what religion he believed in. Women as usual could not take part in government. The ideas of self-government in Fundamental Orders helped form the basis for Connecticut's government for nearly 200 years.

10. The last two New England colonies had been started in 1622 by land grants from King James I. These grants stretched from the Merrimack River to the Kennebec River. The southwestern part of this territory became New Hampshire and the northeastern part, Maine. In 1677, Maine was sold to the Massachusetts Bay Colony. Maine remained a part of Massachusetts for the next 143 years. In 1679, New Hampshire was sold to the king. It then became a **royal colony**. A royal or crown colony did not have its own elected government. The governor was chosen by the king of England.

Native Americans and Puritans Why did conflict grow between Native Americans and Puritans?

11. As more and more English settlers spread out through New England, a bitter

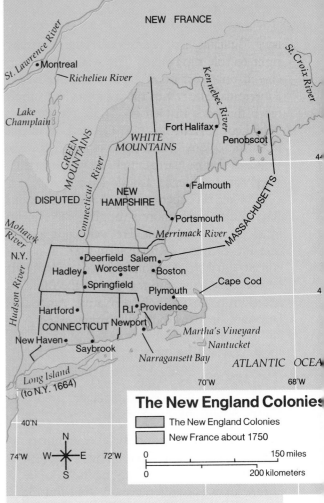

The New England Colonies

☐ The New England Colonies
☐ New France about 1750

0   150 miles
0   200 kilometers

MAP SKILL BUILDER: Parallels are the east–west lines on a map that show latitude north and south of the Equator. **1.** What is the approximate latitude of Boston? **2.** What city is located at approximately 43°N on the coast of Massachusetts?

struggle grew between them and the Native Americans. From the beginning, most Puritans had looked down on the Native Americans. They did not want Native Americans to live in the English colonies. The English colonists believed that Native Americans who did not become Christians should be forced to leave their lands and move west. Only a few people like Roger Williams believed that Native Americans should be treated fairly.

12. At first, relations between the Native Americans and the colonists were friendly. The English settlers traded with the Native

Background: The coastal Native Americans whom the English met were generally weaker tribes on the fringe of more powerful tribes farther west, such as the Iroquois and the Susquehannas.

Americans. Traders exchanged cloth, blankets, pots, and firearms for food and furs. The Puritans also bought land from Native American tribes. Some Native Americans became Christians. These "praying Indians," as the English called them, lived alongside their English neighbors.

13. In 1637, the peaceful relations ended. The Pequots (PEE-kwaht) were angered about losing their land and the increasingly unfriendly ways of the new settlers. Other Native American tribes, who hated the Pequots, joined the settlers in the war. The Puritans and their allies burned down a Pequot fort, killing 400. The Pequot tribe was almost completely destroyed. Most of the Pequots who lived were sold as ▶ slaves. Why would this kind of treatment lead to future problems?

14. Even though there were 40 years of peace after the Pequot War, relations between the Native Americans and settlers grew worse. Fur trade with the Native Americans slowed. Now, the colonists were growing their own food. They had less need for Native American goods. The Massachusetts Bay Colony tried to force Native Americans to follow its laws. There were also many fights over land. Native Americans believed that a brave could hunt on land his tribe had sold, but the colonists did not agree. In addition, English settlers often took land set aside for Native Americans.

15. In 1675, Native Americans tried desperately to stop the settlers. Metacomet (ME-tuh-kahm-et), chief of the Wampanoags (wahm-puh-NOH-ahgz), brought together almost all of the tribes of New England. These tribes waged a fierce fight against their longtime English neighbors. This war was called King Philip's War because the Puritans had given Metacomet the name Philip. Fighting lasted for two years before the Puritans won. The power of the Wampanoags and other New England tribes was destroyed forever. New Englanders could now continue their settle- ▶ ments westward. Why would defeat of the Native American tribes allow the colonists to move west and settle?

▲ Metacomet was chief of the Wampanoag Indians. He was among the first of the Native American leaders to recognize that the European settlers were a serious threat to his people's way of life.

Outlook

16. By 1700, the New England settlements had been organized into four colonies: Massachusetts Bay, Rhode Island, Connecticut and New Hampshire. Some of these new colonies were started by people who disagreed with the Puritans of the Massachusetts Bay Colony. These dissenters did not want the church to rule over government. This desire to keep state and church separate would be an important idea for democracy in America. Settlement would continue for about 200 years. After King Philip's War, the struggle between the Native Americans and the colonists grew. The struggle was to become a war between the English and the French. On which side do you think ◀ Native Americans would fight when the English faced the French across battle lines? Why?

105

CHAPTER REVIEW

VOCABULARY REVIEW

▶ On a sheet of paper, copy the paragraph below. Then fill in the blanks with the word or phrase that best completes each sentence.

dissenter

banished

royal colony

Fundamental Orders

Some settlers wanted more religious freedom. Roger Williams was a ___**1**___ . Williams believed in freedom of religion for all people. He was ___**2**___ from the Massachusetts Bay Colony for his ideas. He settled in Rhode Island. Unlike New Hampshire, Rhode Island was not a ___**3**___ . Other colonies had religious freedom. The ___**4**___ of Connecticut allowed more freedom in government. Any white man who owned land could take part in government no matter what religion he believed in.

SKILL BUILDER: MAKING A TIME LINE

▶ Place the following events on the timeline.

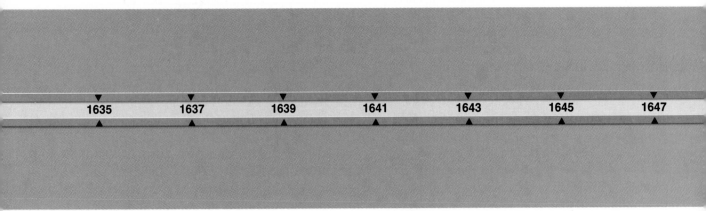

| 1635 | 1637 | 1639 | 1641 | 1643 | 1645 | 1647 |

1. The year Roger Williams was banished from the Massachusetts Bay Colony.

2. The year Anne Hutchinson moved to Rhode Island.

3. The year Wheelright settled New Hampshire.

4. The year the first official government was started in Connecticut.

5. The year Rhode Island became an official colony.

SKILL BUILDER: CRITICAL THINKING AND COMPREHENSION

I. Sequencing

▶ Write the following events in the order in which they occurred.

  a. Maine is sold to Massachusetts Bay Colony.

  b. Roger Williams starts the colony of Rhode Island.

  c. King Philip's War begins.

  d. New Hampshire is sold to the king and becomes a royal colony.

  e. About 400 Pequots are killed and their fort burned.

II. Cause and Effect

A **cause** is an action or event that makes something happen. An **effect** is what happens as a result of that action or event. For example, religious persecution and the lack of religious freedom in England was the cause of the Separatists' unhappiness. The effect or result of the persecution was the Separatists' leaving England.

▶ Write each cause on a sheet of paper. After each cause, write the effect that matches it. Some causes may have more than one effect.

Causes

1. Religious dissent and the need for new farm land arise in the Puritan colony.

2. Anne Hutchinson questions the rules set by the Bay Colony's leaders.

3. Native Americans become angry about the growing number of English settlers.

4. New Hampshire is sold to the king.

5. Maine is sold to Massachusetts Bay Colony.

Effects

a. She is banished from the Bay Colony.

b. In 1675, the tribes of New England wage war on the English.

c. This colony becomes a royal colony in 1679.

d. It did not become a separate state until 1820.

e. Groups leave the Bay Colony to establish other colonies.

f. The Pequot tribe attacks the settlers in the Connecticut Valley.

USING PRIMARY SOURCES

▶ Reread the Spotlight on Sources on page 103. Why do you think other Puritans did not share Williams's opinion of Native Americans?

ENRICHMENT

1. If you had been living in the Massachusetts Bay Colony when Roger Williams arrived, would you have agreed with his criticisms? If you had agreed with him, would you have said so publicly? Would you have followed Williams to Narragansett Bay? Write your answers on a sheet of paper. Then hold a vote in your class. Discuss reasons.

2. Imagine that you are Anne Hutchinson. Using a book from your school or local library, write a short autobiography. Describe the most important events in your life.

CHAPTER 3

Europeans Settle in the Middle Colonies

OBJECTIVE: Why and how were settlements started in New York, New Jersey, Pennsylvania, and Delaware?

1. The Delaware tribes knew that this strange man from across the ocean was bringing settlers to live among them. The English person had been a top runner and jumper in his school days. The Delaware were delighted because he could run and jump like a warrior! Perhaps they could trust him. The Delawares' faith in this white man was not misplaced. When William Penn drew up laws for his new colony, Pennsylvania, he protected the rights of Native Americans in his colony. Pennsylvania was one of several new colonies that were founded in the late 1600s.

▲ Peter Minuit, the first governor of New Amsterdam, bought Manhattan Island from the Man-a-hat-ta Indians for twenty-four dollars worth of goods. What kinds of goods were probably exchanged?

New Sweden and New Netherlands Why did the Swedes and the Dutch settle in the Delaware and Hudson valleys?

2. Besides the English, other Europeans settled along North America's Atlantic coast. First to arrive were the Dutch, who settled in the Hudson River Valley of present-day New York in 1621. Seeking the fur trade, the Dutch set up their first trading post at Fort Orange, where the Mohawk River flows into the Hudson River. A few years later, the Dutch started another trading post, New Amsterdam. New Amsterdam was located at the southernmost tip of an island where the Man-a-hat-ta tribe lived. Man-a-hat-ta means "Island of the Hills."

3. The Dutch named their colony New Netherland. Soon it included all the land from the Connecticut River on the east to the Delaware River on the west. The Dutch also built permanent settlements, called New Amsterdam and Bergen, in New Jersey. Bergen became Jersey City. By 1655 New Netherland included

In Chapter 3 you will apply these critical thinking skills to the historical process:
○ **Generalizing:** Making a statement that links several facts.

➡ **Recognizing Cause and Effect:** Recognizing the action or event that makes something happen, identifying the result of an action or event.

the settlements of New Sweden. In 1638 the New Sweden Company had sent an expedition of 50 colonists to America. The Swedes settled near the site of what is now Wilmington, Delaware, and in southern New Jersey. The Swedes were quickly taken over and ruled by the Dutch.

4. After only 40 years, Dutch rule disappeared from North America. By 1664, England and the Netherlands were almost at war. King Charles II of England decided to drive the Dutch out of North America. A powerful English fleet sailed to Manhattan Island to force the Dutch to hand over their colony. The Dutch did not have the power to stop the English navy. England gained control over all the colonies from Maine to Carolina.

The Duke of York's Grant How did New York and New Jersey develop as English Colonies?

5. In 1660 King Charles II decided that any new colony would be a **proprietary** (proh-PRY-e-tair-ee) **colony**. A proprietary colony began as a grant of land given to one of the king's supporters. A **proprietor** (proh-PRY-e-tor) is the ruler of a proprietary colony. By giving land to his friends, the king could reward their loyalty and keep close control over the colonies. The king made his brother James, the Duke of York, the proprietor of New Netherlands in 1664. One of the first things James did was rename the colony New York. The second thing he did was to give the land between the Hudson and Delaware rivers to his friends, Lord John Berkeley and Sir George Carter. What colony did that area become? ◄

6. James granted religious freedom for all colonists. People from Scotland, France, and other European countries hurried to settle in New York. Besides the Europeans, Native Americans and African Americans lived in New York. Most of the African Americans were indentured servants, not slaves.

MAP SKILL BUILDER: New York City is the only city in the world at 40° 40′ North latitude and 73° 50′ West longitude. **1.** What city is located at 42° 40′ N, 73° 49′ W? **2.** What city is located at 40° N, 75° 50′ W?

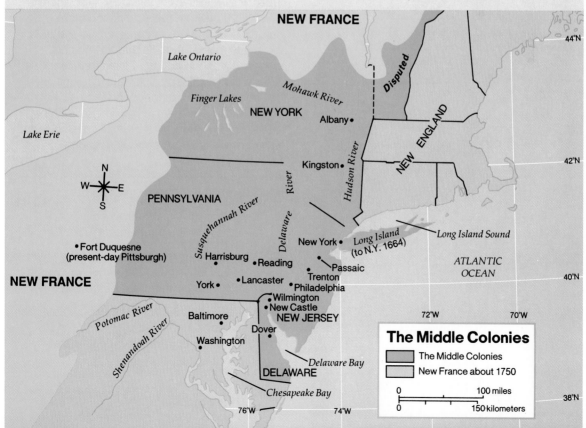

The Middle Colonies

- The Middle Colonies
- New France about 1750

0 — 100 miles
0 — 150 kilometers

THE JEWS

In 1654 a group of 23 Dutch Jews arrived in New Amsterdam from Brazil. United only by their ancient customs and religion, Jews had no single national identity. They were often persecuted by the countries in which they lived. The Dutch tolerated the Jews; the Portuguese did not. When the Portuguese captured the Dutch settlement in Brazil, they drove out the Jews who were living there. Forced to leave all their possessions behind, these Dutch Jews became the first group of Jews known to have settled in North America.

When they arrived in New Amsterdam the Jews were not welcomed. Peter Stuyvesant, the governor, was prejudiced against the Jews. However, he used their poverty as an excuse for not wanting them in New Amsterdam. The Dutch West Indies Company had set up New Netherland to make money, and the colony was not doing well enough to support the newcomers. Stuyvesant asked the Dutch West Indies Company to allow him to

tell the Jews "in a friendly way to depart." The company directors informed Stuyvesant that much of the money used to set up the colony had come from Jewish investors in The Netherlands. Therefore, the newcomers should be allowed to stay. After hearing about the plight of the newcomers, a group of Jews in The Netherlands sent money to help them get started. This experience is another example of how America became a safe haven for some oppressed peoples.

The most successful of the Jews who had settled in New Amsterdam was Asser Levy. Over the next ten years, Levy became well-do-do through selling finished goods imported from Amsterdam. He was the first Jew to fight for the right to serve in the colony's militia. In 1661 he was the first Jew to own a house in the North American colonies. Ten years later he was the first Jew to sit on a colonial jury.

As more Jews came to America, they benefitted from the freedom and economic opportunities in the colonies. By 1750 there were 2,500 Jews in the American colonies. In their roles as traders, shipowners, merchants, and craftspeople, they helped the colonial economy grow. In addition, their traditional belief in human liberty and equality supported the American spirit of independence. Although the Jews remained small in number until the 1830s, they continued to be active participants in the growth of the American economy and the American nation.

▼ This Synagogue, built in Newport, R.I. in 1763, shows the beauty of New England colonial architecture. Newport was the location of the second Jewish settlement in America.

Now answer the following questions.

1. Why were the Dutch Jews from Brazil forced out of their settlement?

2. Why did Peter Stuyvesant want the Jews to leave New Netherland, and why was he unable to force them out of the colony?

3. Why do you think some colonists, such as Asser Levy, had to struggle more than other colonists to gain political rights?

Pennsylvania and Delaware Who were the Quakers and why did they come to America?

7. While the Dutch were losing New Amsterdam to the English, William Penn, the founder of Pennsylvania, was living in England. Although Penn came from a wealthy family, religion was more important to him than money. When he was 22 years old, Penn became a member of the **Quakers** (KWA ker), a religious group. The Quakers, also known as the Society of Friends, were a group of Separatists. They were called Quakers because the founder, George Fox, said they should "tremble [quake] at the Word of the Lord." Quakers were against all types of religious ceremony and they did not accept the power of ministers or priests. Quakers believed that people should be guided by an "inner light" from God. Equality was so important to them that they refused to bow or remove their hats to officials. Quakers were strongly against slavery. They believed in peace and would not fight in wars or to protect themselves. Their beliefs seemed dangerous to English officials who persecuted the Quakers as **traitors** (TRA-tor). A traitor is someone who turns against his or her country.

8. William Penn wanted a place of peace and safety for the Quakers. Penn learned that King Charles II owed a large sum of money to Penn's father. Penn suggested that the king give him a grant of land in North America in return for the debt. The king, who had much more land than money, agreed. The land given to Penn became known as Pennsylvania. William Penn came to Pennsylvania in 1682 to start his colony. Although he had a charter giving him the land, he still felt he should pay the Delaware Indian tribes for it. He wanted to live in peace and friendship with them. The peace treaty Penn wrote was never broken during his lifetime.

🦅 Spotlight on Sources

9. Penn opened his colony to all religious groups and granted these rights to all the people who settled in Pennsylvania.

> . . . I hereby grant and declare, That no Person or Persons inhabiting in [living in] this Province . . . shall be . . . molested [hurt] or prejudiced [treated unfairly], in his or their Person or Estate [home or business] . . . contrary [against] to their religious Persuasion . . .
> —from *Deputyes and Libertyes: The Origins of Representative Government in Colonial America*, Michael Kammen, ed.

Why do you think many people from England, ◀ Ireland, Scotland, and Germany flocked to Pennsylvania?

10. Soon Penn saw that the colony needed ports on the Atlantic. He got the Duke of York to give him an added land grant along the eastern shore of Delaware Bay. The area was known as the Three Lower Counties. The Three Lower Counties became the colony of Delaware.

People in History

11. Hannah Penn After his first wife died, William Penn married Hannah Callowhill in 1695. Hannah Penn soon became her husband's closest business partner. When William Penn suffered a severe illness in 1712, Hannah handled all his business affairs until his death in 1718. In his will, Penn left the Pennsylvania and Delaware proprietorship to his four sons by Hannah. Because the sons were not yet grown, Hannah Penn kept the colonies well managed for them.

Outlook

12. By 1664, Great Britain had gained control of North America's Atlantic coast from Maine to Carolina. Like the New England colonies, the Middle Colonies were farming and trading settlements. However, the Middle Colonies had a much greater variety of religions and nationalities among its peoples. To the south of the Middle Colonies, a different kind of society developed. The South was developing an economy based largely on big farms that grew crops to sell for a profit.

Ask: "The real homeland of religious liberty was not New England but the Middle Colonies." Is this statement true or false? Why?

CHAPTER REVIEW

VOCABULARY REVIEW

▶ On a sheet of paper, copy the sentences below, completing each one with the correct word or term from the following list.

proprietary colony   Quakers   Dutch

proprietors   traitors

1. King Charles II made Pennsylvania a _____ .

2. A _____ was the ruler of a colony that began as a land grant from the king.

3. _____ were strongly against slavery.

4. English officials persecuted people they believed were _____ .

USING PRIMARY SOURCES

▶ Reread the Spotlight on Sources on page 111. What ideas and beliefs do present-day Americans share with William Penn?

SKILL BUILDER: INTERPRETING A GRAPH

▶ On a sheet of paper, answer the following questions using the graph. When asked for a number, your answer may be approximate.

1. What was the population of the colonies in 1640?

2. What was the population of the colonies one hundred years later?

3. How much did the United States population grow between 1660 and 1700? Between 1680 and 1720?

4. What twenty-year period saw the most growth in population?

5. What do you predict happens to the population in 1740? Why?

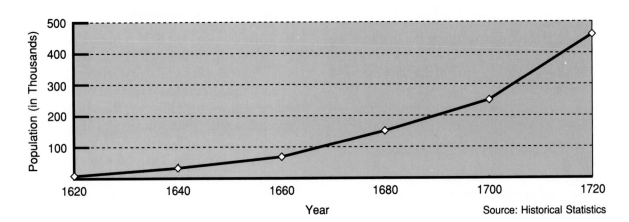

COLONIAL POPULATION GROWTH, 1620–1720

Source: Historical Statistics

SKILL BUILDER: CRITICAL THINKING AND COMPREHENSION

▲ I. Summarizing

▶ Summarize the information in Chapter 3 by writing two or three sentences about each newspaper headline.

1. Europeans Settle in Middle Colonies

2. King Charles II Says, "There will be proprietary colonies!"

3. Quakers Arrive in America!

○ II. Generalizing

▶ Review the chapter. On a sheet of paper, write why you think the following generalization is either a good or poor generalization about colonization.

The British discouraged people from other countries from settling in their colonies.

⇨ III. Cause and Effect

A cause is an action or event that makes something happen. An effect is what happens as a result of that action or event.

▶ On a sheet of paper, match the cause or causes with each of the following effects.

Causes	Effects
1. A powerful English fleet sailed to Manhattan Island on King Charles II's orders.	a. People from many religious groups and of different nationalities came to Pennsylvania.
2. William Penn promised freedom of worship and cheap land in Pennsylvania.	b. The Dutch gave up New Amsterdam without a fight.
3. King Charles II owed William Penn's father a large sum of money.	c. William Penn was given land that was to become Pennsylvania.

ENRICHMENT

1. Use library resources to write a report on why England and the Netherlands were angry at one another in 1664.

2. Identify and research Peter Stuyvesant and write an opinion paper about him.

3. With a small group of students, select one of the Middle Colonies to research. Using a map and other sources, categorize location names in your colony according to their European origin.

4. Find and draw pictures of things, people, places, or ideas that are associated with log cabins. Assemble your illustrations into a booklet for elementary students. The booklet will explain why log cabins were important to the colonists. As you write your text, be sure that you use simple words so your audience can understand your booklet. Do not forget a title, a title page, and a table of contents for your booklet.

113

CHAPTER 4

Europeans Settle in the Southern Colonies

OBJECTIVE: Why were colonies founded in the south?

1. On a spring day in 1734, people swarmed into the streets of London. Everyone wanted to see the Creek Indian chief, Tomo-chi-chi, who had just arrived from the New World. King George II invited him to the palace. When Tomo-chi-chi went to Eton, a famous boys' school, the king asked the head of the school to declare a holiday. All this was good news to General James Oglethorpe, who had brought Tomo-chi-chi to England. Oglethorpe wanted to draw more settlers to the new colony of Georgia.

Maryland How did the Calvert family found a refuge for Roman Catholics?

2. The earliest proprietary colony in the South was Maryland. You will recall that the rulers of England sometimes gave large grants of land to their friends. These people became the proprietors, or owners, of land in America. George Calvert, the first Lord Baltimore, was a friend of King Charles I and a Catholic. The Catholics were another religious group in England who were persecuted for their beliefs. Calvert wanted to start a colony for Catholics who then would be able to practice their religion in peace. In 1632 Lord Baltimore became the proprietor of land in northern Virginia.

3. The settlers started Maryland's first settlement, called St. Mary's, in 1634. Soon other settlements were formed, and the colony be-

▲ The first group of Catholics to come to Maryland blessed the land and the freedom from persecution. What do you think the Native Americans thought of the newcomers' religious ceremonies?

came known as Maryland. Maryland was named for King Charles's wife, Henrietta Maria.

4. The Calvert family believed in **toleration** (tal-uhr-AY-shun), and they allowed people to practice different religions in Maryland. Lord Baltimore insisted that Protestants be treated

In Chapter 1 you will apply these critical thinking skills to the historical process:

Sequencing: Putting a series of events in the correct time order.

Recognizing Cause and Effect: Recognizing the action or event that makes something happen, identifying the result of an action or event.

the same as Catholics. Two years before Roger Williams founded Rhode Island, Maryland was a place where settlers could worship freely.

People in History

5. Margaret Brent The spirit of toleration in Maryland may have helped Margaret Brent have the courage to become North America's first feminist. Brent believed that a woman could be equal with a man in both economics and politics. Brent received 70½ acres (about 29 hectares) from Lord Baltimore and became the first woman to own land in Maryland. Because she was a landowner, Brent demanded the right to vote in the Maryland Assembly. She was probably the first woman in the colonies to demand the right to vote. Although the Assembly turned her down, Brent started an idea that women would bring up again and again. Why ▶ were women kept from voting?

The Carolinas How were the Carolinas colonized?

6. Carolina, the next southern colony to be founded, was also a proprietary colony. In 1663, King Charles II gave a piece of land south of Virginia to eight friends. In 1670, they founded a settlement at Charleston along the coast of southern Carolina. The early Carolina settlers built large **plantations** (plan-TAY-shunz). Plantations are large farms that grow one main cash crop, such as tobacco, rice, or cotton. Plantation owners soon began to rely on slave labor in order to be able to afford the cost of plantations. African slaves had been used for many years in the sugar plantations in the Caribbean. Soon traders were bringing Africans to the Southern colonies for plantation owners to buy. In the 17th century, Carolina had more slaves than any other American colony.

7. In 1712, the Carolina colony split into two parts, North and South Carolina. The parts had always been different. They had different governors and different economies. The north was mostly small farms while the south was

large tobacco plantations. The southern part also grew much faster than the north. The Carolina settlers felt the proprietors were not governing fairly. Finally, in 1729, the proprietors sold their land back to the British king who then made North and South Carolina into two separate royal colonies.

Georgia How was Georgia different from the other Southern colonies?

8. Georgia, founded in 1733, was the last of the original 13 British colonies in North America. General James Oglethorpe paid the Creek Indians for the land where he built the first settlement, called Savannah. Oglethorpe's purpose in starting Georgia was to give English **debtors** (DET-herz) a new start in life. Debtors are people who cannot pay their bills. In 18th century England, debtors were thrown into jail until their debts were paid.

9. Oglethorpe's plans for Georgia did not attract many colonists. Oglethorpe had set up tough rules, thinking these were needed for debtors to live better lives. No farm could be larger than 500 acres (about 200 hectares). Colonists could not own or buy slaves, so large plantations could not be started. Oglethorpe also made settlers grow silkworms, even though no one ever had any success doing this. Drinking liquor was not allowed. Some of the settlers who had come to Georgia gave up and left for South Carolina. By 1750, the rules had changed. Slavery became legal. In 1752, believing he had failed, Oglethorpe returned the colony to King George II. Georgia became a royal colony. Most of the rules started by Oglethorpe were dropped. The colony then began to grow slowly.

African Americans Why did the role of African Americans change in the Southern colonies during the mid-1700s?

10. The first Africans came to the English colonies in 1619. They arrived before most of the Europeans, who came after 1682. Most early

Background: The first ship carrying Africans to Jamestown docked in 1619. But it is not known whether they were slaves or indentured servants. Historical records for the first years of the Virginia colony are few and not always clear.

115

The Fall Line in Colonial America Many waterfalls are found along rivers flowing east from the Appalachian Mountains to the Atlantic Ocean. In the Middle and Southern colonies, these waterfalls occur at the **Fall Line**. The Fall Line separates the hard, old rock base of the Piedmont region from the younger, softer rock base of the Coastal Plain. The water falls that mark the Fall Line are formed where streams pass from the rocky soil to the soft plain.

The lowest **bridging point** of most rivers flowing east from the Appalachians occurs at the Fall Line. Bridges can be easily built at the bridging point because there the banks of the river are close together. Many colonial towns, such as Richmond, Virginia; Baltimore, Maryland; and Fort Augusta, South Carolina, grew up around the bridging points.

Fall Line towns also had an advantage, being at the **head of navigation** (nav-uh-GAY-shun). The head of navigation is the farthest point inland that ships can travel. Trade is busy wherever goods are transferred from river to land transportation. Colonial products such as pottery, tobacco, and furs

were brought there for shipment to Britain or the West Indies. Needed tools, household goods, and foods such as coffee and spices from Europe were unloaded at Fall Line towns. Philadelphia and Baltimore were among the most important Fall Line port cities.

Fall Line locations were also important sites for early industry. In the days before steam engines and electricity, falling water powered mills. Fall Line cities that developed early textile mills included Newark, New Jersey, and Columbia, South Carolina. Birmingham, Alabama, a Fall Line city, became the leading iron and steel center in the South.

Use the map of the Southern colonies below to answer the following questions.

1. Which landform regions does the Fall Line separate?

2. On the Fall Line of what river is Fort Augusta located?

3. On the Fall Line of what river is Richmond located?

4. What problems or difficulties might a Fall Line city face?

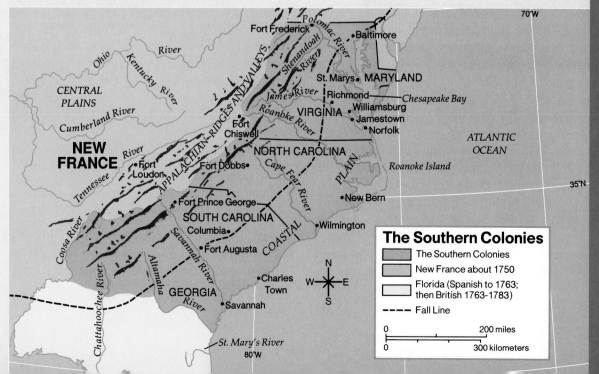

The Southern Colonies

- The Southern Colonies
- New France about 1750
- Florida (Spanish to 1763; then British 1763-1783)
- - - - Fall Line

0 — 200 miles
0 — 300 kilometers

Africans were indentured servants in the Northern colonies. But by the 1750s, most Africans were slaves in the Southern colonies.

11. For most of the 1600s, slave labor was not needed because farms were small in both the Northern and Southern colonies. The usual farm was about 100 acres (about 40 hectares). These farms could usually be worked by the family with one or two indentured servants.

12. By about 1680, farming changed and so did the type of farm labor. In the South, more and more large plantations ranging in size from 1000 to 6000 acres (400 to 2400 hectares) were started. Plantation owners needed a work force of 50 to 100. Indentured servants were too costly for the plantation owners to pay. There were also not enough indentured servants to fill the plantations' needs. By the 1650s slave traders began to bring many Africans to the colonies. They and their children after them became slaves for life.

13. The slave trade became big business. In the Northern colonies, African slaves were about 4 to 5 percent of the total population. But African slaves made up three quarters of the population in the Southern colonies. About one fifth of the total population of the colonies in North America were African slaves.

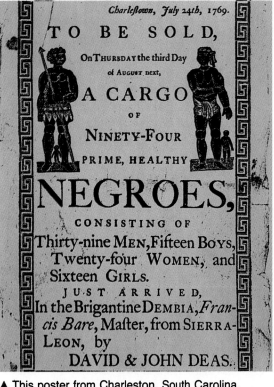

▲ This poster from Charleston, South Carolina, announces the sale of Africans into slavery. From what area of Africa were they coming?

pays ready Money or Tobacco, shall have Five per cent Discount. Any Person that chooses to make a Purchase of the said Land or any of the Slaves, before the Day of Sale, may know the Terms. . . .

From this advertisement, what can you tell ◄ enslaved Africans were considered the same as? What could be used instead of money?

Spotlight on Sources

14. As slaves, Africans were thought to be property and not human beings with rights and freedoms. This advertisement was printed in *The Virginia Gazette* on September 19, 1755.

To be SOLD, on the Second Tuesday in October next, at Prince-George Court-House. Ten choice slaves, most of them Virginia born: Credit will be given till the Second Tuesday in December next, the Purchaser giving Bond and Security. And on Wednesday following, will be sold at the same Place, Nineteen Acres of Land, adjoining [next to] the Town of Bland-ford, pleasantly situated [located] for carrying on Business of any Kind. Whoever

Outlook

15. By 1773, Great Britain had established 13 colonies along the Atlantic Coast of North America from Georgia to Massachusetts. The population of these colonies had grown from 27,000 in mid-1600 to almost 1 million people by the mid-1700s. More and more people were coming with the great hope that they could build better lives for themselves than they had in Europe. As you will read in Unit 4, the regions began to develop different ways of life.

Ask: Have students decide which of the 13 colonies they would have chosen to colonize. Discuss the reasons for their choices.

117

CHAPTER REVIEW

VOCABULARY REVIEW

▶ Copy the following sentences on a separate sheet of paper, changing each italicized word to make the statements true.

1. Toleration was important to the people in *New England*.

2. Debtors are people who *lend* money.

3. To come to America, a *rich* person would become an indentured servant and work for the person who paid his or her passage.

4. The early Carolina settlers built large *cities*.

5. The line that separates the hard, old rock base of the Piedmont region from the softer rock base of the Coastal Plain is called the *bridging point*.

6. A bridging point is where *canals* can be built.

7. The *Fall Line* is the farthest point inland ships can travel on a river.

SKILL BUILDER: READING A MAP

▶ Study the map. Then answer the questions that follow.

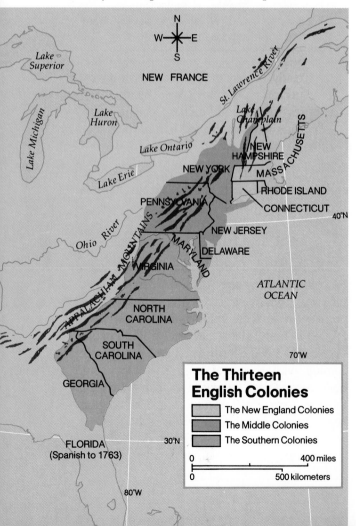

1. What is the southernmost of the English colonies?

2. What is the northernmost of the English colonies?

3. Which region—New England, Middle, or Southern—had the largest number of colonies?

4. Through which colonies did the Appalachian Mountains range?

5. Which colony had no boundary on the Atlantic Ocean?

6. Who owned Florida?

SKILL BUILDER: CRITICAL THINKING AND COMPREHENSION

I. Sequencing

▶ Rewrite the following events in the correct order as they happened. Add the dates when they happened.

a. North Carolina and South Carolina become royal colonies.

b. The Carolina colony splits.

c. Africans arrive in the English colonies of North America.

d. The first settlements are started in Maryland.

e. George Calvert becomes proprietor of Maryland.

f. Georgia, last of the 13 British colonies, is founded and settled.

II. Cause and Effect

▶ Write the following statements on a sheet of paper and fill in the blanks.

1. Cause: George Calvert became a _____ .
Effect: He wanted to found a colony that would be a place of safety for others of his religion.

2. Cause: Many people who wanted to come to America could not afford to do so.
Effect: They became _____ , paying for the price of their passage with work.

3. Cause: In the Chesapeake region, the small farm was being replaced by large plantations.
Effect: The institution of _____ grew with the need for workers.

USING PRIMARY SOURCES

▶ Reread the Spotlight on Sources on page 117. How does this advertisement show that African slaves and land were treated alike? What do you think of this attitude? Why do you think some people felt that way?

ENRICHMENT

1. With a partner, write a television interview with Tomo-chi-chi. Ask about his life in America. Also find out how Tomo-chi-chi felt during his trip to England. Do some library research, and also use your imagination. Did Tomo-chi-chi enjoy his visit with the king? What did he think of the students at Eton? Present your interview to the class.

2. Imagine you are poor and live in England without hope for a better future. Write a letter to your parents explaining why you have decided to become an indentured servant and go to America. Tell how you feel about the hard work you will have to do and your loss of freedom for several years. What are the differences and similarities between indentured servants and slavery?

UNIT REVIEW

SUMMARY

Both the search for religious freedom and economic prosperity led to the English colonization of North America. The Pilgrims and the Puritans arrived in New England in the 1600s, escaping the religious persecution that arose from their differences with the Church of England. Eventually the two groups formed one colony, known as the Massachusetts Bay Colony.

People who disagreed with the colony's leaders left the community to establish their own colonies. Roger Williams, for example, founded the Colony of Rhode Island and Providence Plantations. As the colonists spread, tension with Native Americans grew.

Meanwhile the English achieved dominance on the Atlantic coast. The Dutch colony of New Amsterdam became New York under English rule. Pennsylvania, the Carolinas, New Jersey and Georgia emerged as proprietary colonies, or colonies that the King of England gave one or more friends to control. Unlike the New England colonies, many of these colonies allowed freedom of worship.

SKILL BUILDER: READING A MAP

▶ Use the map below to answer the following questions:

1. What are three cities that were once a part of New Spain?

2. New Spain controlled the most territory in 1641. Which European nation controlled the next largest area?

3. Where were most of the settlements and colonies located in 1641? Why?

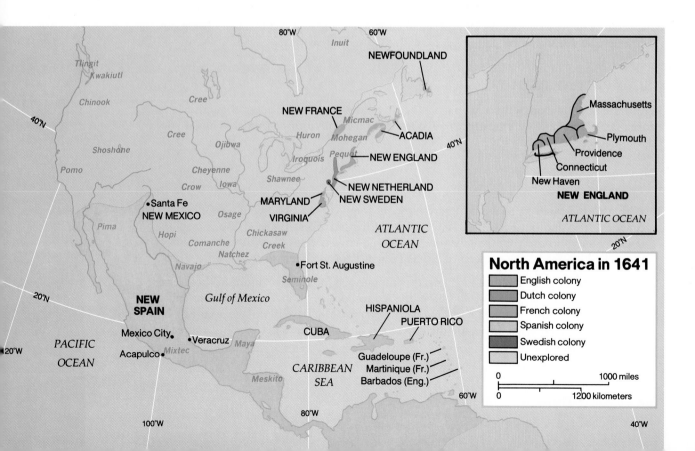

I. Classifying

▶ Number on a sheet of paper from one to seven. Write the letter or letters of the person that each of the following statements describes.

1. Native American who helped the Pilgrims

2. founded the colony of Georgia

3. founded the Colony of Rhode Island and Providence Plantations

4. a Quaker who founded Pennsylvania

5. a Catholic who founded Maryland

6. one of the Pilgrim leaders

7. the two proprietors of the Province of New Jersey

a. William Bradford

b. William Penn

c. George Calvert

d. Squanto

e. James Oglethorpe

f. Roger Williams

g. George Carteret

h. John Berkeley

i. King Charles

II. Generalizing

▶ Read the following generalizations. Find sentences from the unit that support them. Write each generalization and the sentences that support it on a sheet of paper.

1. Proprietary colonies, while also formed as investments, were often considered by the proprietors as a means to religious freedom.

2. Religious groups that wanted religious freedom for themselves refused to give it to people who disagreed with them.

3. The Middle colonies and the Southern colonies had more religious toleration than those in New England.

ENRICHMENT

1. Imagine King James II has given you and two or three other people a proprietary colony on the Atlantic Coast. What would you call your colony? How would you run it and what kind of people would you seek as colonists? Would you follow the example of William Penn, Roger Williams, or James Oglethorpe? Write your responses on a sheet of paper. Where would you locate your colony? What rules would you create about religion? Give reasons for your choices.

2. Find a book on the Pilgrims or the Puritans in your school or local library. Write a one to two page report on their religious beliefs. Include similarities and differences between what they believed and what people today believe.

3. Research in the library the *Mayflower Compact* and Maryland's Act of Toleration. How are they similar in their purpose? How are they different? Use quotes from each document.

UNIT 4

LIFE IN COLONIAL AMERICA

Chapter

UNIT OVERVIEW   In this unit, you will learn about how people lived in the English, French, and Spanish colonies in the Americas. Discover the similarities and differences in the lives of colonists and the ways that they met the challenges they faced.

UNIT SKILLS OBJECTIVES   In Unit 4, three critical thinking skills are emphasized:

Recognizing Cause and Effect: Recognizing the action or event that makes something happen, identifying the result of an action or event.

Sequencing: Putting a series of events in the correct time order.

Predicting: Telling what you believe will happen on the basis of clues and facts

You will also use two important social studies skills:
Using a Map   Using a Chart

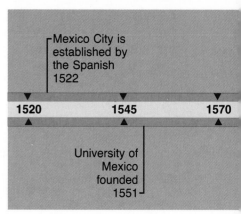

Mexico City is established by the Spanish 1522

| 1520 | 1545 | 1570 |

University of Mexico founded 1551

122   **ESL/LEP Strategy:** Have students preview the unit to choose a subject for a visual display depicting farming, trade, religion, government, or education in colonial America. After completing the unit, they should prepare the display and then compare the way of life shown there to life today.

▲ Daniel Boone knew the Appalachian Mountains very well. He led many settlers, his wife and daughter included, across the mountains into Kentucky.

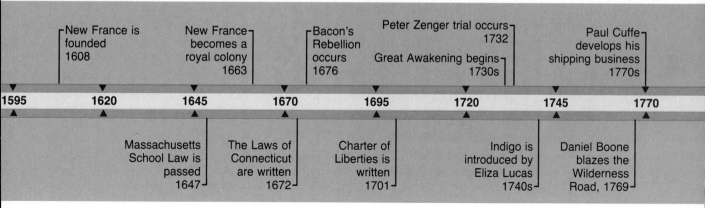

New France is founded 1608

New France becomes a royal colony 1663

Bacon's Rebellion occurs 1676

Peter Zenger trial occurs 1732

Great Awakening begins 1730s

Paul Cuffe develops his shipping business 1770s

1595   1620   1645   1670   1695   1720   1745   1770

Massachusetts School Law is passed 1647

The Laws of Connecticut are written 1672

Charter of Liberties is written 1701

Indigo is introduced by Eliza Lucas 1740s

Daniel Boone blazes the Wilderness Road, 1769

Points of View

During the 1600s and 1700s, many Europeans visited the 13 American colonies. They had heard new and interesting things and wanted to see for themselves how the colonists lived. Among these newcomers was a Frenchman named Jean de Crèvecoeur (krev-KOOR). He first came to the colonies in 1759, and, after traveling in New York State, Pennsylvania, and the Carolinas, he settled down in New York State. As you will read in the first selection below, he found a great deal to admire in the colonies.

▲ Independence Hall in Philadelphia, or Old State House, was the scene of some of the most important events in American History.

WHAT IS AN AMERICAN?

❝[America] is not composed [made up], as in Europe, of great lords, who possess everything, and a herd of people who have nothing. Here are no aristocratic [noble] families, no [royal] courts, no kings. . . . The rich and the poor are not so far removed [apart] from each other as they are in Europe. . . .

[The colonists] are . . . united by . . . mild [a good] government, all respecting [obeying] the laws because they are equitable [fair]. [The colonists] are all animated with [have] the spirit of an industry [the will to work hard]. . . .

What then is the American? . . . *He* is an American who, leaving behind him all his ancient prejudices [ideas] and manners, receives new ones from the new modes [ways] of life he has embraced [accepted], the new government he obeys, and the new rank he holds. . . . Here [in the colonies] individuals of all nations are melted into a new race of men, whose labors and posterity [people born after him] will one day cause great changes in the world. ❞

—*Letters from an American Farmer,*
Hector St. Jean de Crèvecoeur

The American Colonies and Their Future

Andrew Burnaby was another visitor to the colonies. He was a young Englishman who had recently graduated from Cambridge University. He spent two years traveling in New England, the Middle Colonies, and Virginia and, in 1760, wrote a book about his experiences on his return home. Burnaby recognized that America wanted to be a model for the rest of the world, but he did not think it would work. You will see from the second selection below that he had quite a different view of the colonies and how people lived there than de Crèvecoeur.

AMERICA'S WEAKNESSES

" In a course [trip] of 1,200 miles, I saw . . . weaknesses which will necessarily prevent its [America's] being a potent state [strong nation].

The mode of cultivation [way of farming] by slavery is another insurmountable [very great] cause of weakness. The number of Negroes [African Americans] in the Southern colonies is . . . nearly equal . . . to that of the white men. . . . Their condition is truly pitiable; their labor excessively hard, their diet [food] poor and scanty, their treatment cruel and oppressive.

The Northern colonies . . . [also] have . . . real disadvantages. . . . They are composed of people of different nations, different manners, different religions, and different languages. They have a mutual [common] jealousy of each other. . . . In short, such is the difference of character, of manners, of religion, [and] of interest of the different colonies, that I think [if] they were left to themselves, there would soon be a civil war from one end of the continent to the other. . . . "

—*Travel Through the Middle Settlements in America in the Years 1759 and 1760,* Andrew Burnaby

▲ Although George Washington as a farmer and plantation owner had slaves, he freed all of them in his will.

Using Primary Sources

1. What reasons does de Crèvecoeur give to support his view that America will become a great nation? What reasons does Burnaby give to support his view that Americans could not build a strong nation?

2. Why do you think the two writers had such different ideas about America and its future?

125

CHAPTER 1

Farming in the Colonies

OBJECTIVE: How did farming differ in the New England, Middle, and Southern colonies?

1. It was still dark outside when the young farm girl awoke. She wanted to sleep, but she knew her chores had to begin. For everyone in her family, work began at dawn and finished at night. That morning, her mother wanted her to search the farmyard to find eggs. Then she had to milk the cows, weed the garden, and carry water to the house. She and her sister helped their mother cook, make soap, and spin wool into yarn. Her three brothers plowed, planted, harvested, and cut firewood. The boys also hunted or fished. The day ended at dark, often with Bible reading. By night, she looked forward to falling into her corn-husk mattress for a well-earned rest. Families throughout the 13 colonies worked hard on their farms, but the crops and animals they raised were different, depending on where they lived.

▲ New England farmers cultivated small areas of land. They grew food and raised animals in an effort to make themselves self-sufficient.

Farming in New England What challenges did New England farm families face?

2. Learning farming methods from Native Americans helped white farming families in New England to face the many hardships. Winters were long, so the growing season was short. The soil was thin and full of rocks. Trees grew everywhere. To clear trees, farm families used the Native American method of **girdling** (GERD-ling). That is, they removed the bark around the trunk of a tree. The trees were girdled in the summer. Over the winter, the girdled trees would die. Settlers used a few simple tools to remove stumps and remaining thick roots. Crops were planted between the dead trunks. Fallen trunks were burned, and the ash became another source of fertilizer. What ◄ problems might these difficulties have caused farming families?

3. Most New England families grew enough for their own needs, but not enough to sell to others. This kind of farmer is called a **subsistence** (sub-SIS-tuhns) **farmer**. New England

In Chapter 1 you will apply these critical thinking skills to the historical process:
 Recognizing Cause and Effect: Recognizing the action or event that makes something happen, identifying the result of an action or event.

Comparing and Contrasting: Recognizing similarities and differences.

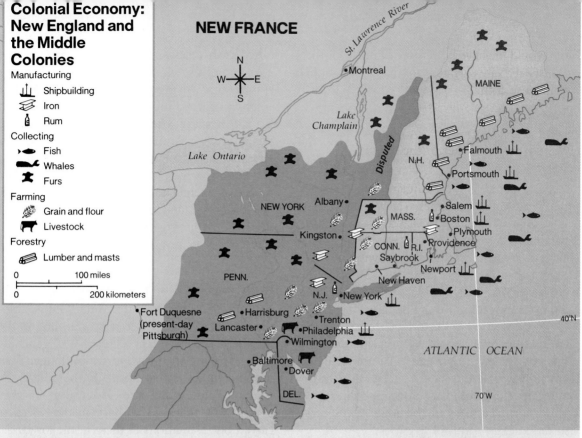

Colonial Economy: New England and the Middle Colonies

Manufacturing
- Shipbuilding
- Iron
- Rum

Collecting
- Fish
- Whales
- Furs

Farming
- Grain and flour
- Livestock

Forestry
- Lumber and masts

0   100 miles
0   200 kilometers

NEW FRANCE

St. Lawrence River
Montreal
Lake Champlain
Lake Ontario
MAINE
Falmouth
N.H.
Portsmouth
NEW YORK
Albany
Salem
Boston
MASS.
Kingston
Plymouth
Providence
CONN. R.I.
Saybrook
New Haven
Newport
N.J.
New York
40°N
Fort Duquesne (present-day Pittsburgh)
Harrisburg
Trenton
Lancaster
Philadelphia
PENN.
Wilmington
Baltimore
Dover
DEL.
70°W
ATLANTIC OCEAN
Disputed

MAP SKILL BUILDER: Using economic symbols on a map. The economic symbols used on this map to describe the colonial economy are explained in the map key. **1.** What did New England produce in colonial days? **2.** What products came from the Middle Colonies?

farms were generally small, but families grew a variety of crops such as corn, peas, beans, and pumpkins. Besides growing their own food, farm families made their own clothing, furniture, and even tools. At times, they might trade corn or furs for salt or iron nails. Everyone worked from dawn to dusk. Men and boys plowed the land or hunted wild turkeys and other game in the forest. Women and girls made butter, soap, and candles or spun wool and ► wove cloth. Why do you think chores were so rigidly divided between men and women?

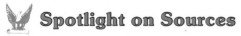 **Spotlight on Sources**

4. Native Americans had taught the settlers to raise corn. The colonists came to depend on corn. They used it to make bread and puddings and fed it to their farm animals. In the 1750s, a Swedish scientist, Peter Kalm, visited the En-

glish colonies and wrote *Travels in North America*. In it, he described the importance of corn.

> Now I will come to the uses of maize [corn], which are so numerous. I doubt if any other species of grain exists which alone may be used for so many purposes both for man and animals.
>
> In most of the English colonies the farmers make their bread from maize. In Maryland even the aristocracy and the wealthy eat hardly any other bread. If a stranger comes to them, they place before him both wheat and maize bread, allowing him the freedom to choose whichever he prefers; they themselves prefer the maize bread. . . .
>
> From the American [Native American] the Europeans have learned to make a grit soup. . . . The English [call it] Hommony [hominy].

ESL/LEP STRATEGY: Have partners define *subsistence farming, cash crops, plantations.* Using the maps on pages 127 and 130, discuss the geography of the regions and the different crops and kinds of farms that developed in the New England, Middle, and Southern Colonies.

Background: When the Dutch colonized New Amsterdam, they granted large estates to wealthy men, called patroons. Patroons then paid for farmers from Europe to come work the land. In return for their passage, the farmers had to give the patroon a percentage of their crops. This system of tenant farming continued after the English conquered New Amsterdam. Kilaen Van Rensselaer, a wealthy patroon, owned a vast estate near what is today Albany.

▶ How would life have been more difficult for the colonists if Native Americans had not taught them to use corn?

Farming in the Middle Colonies What kinds of crops did farm families in the Middle colonies raise?

5. Compared to New England, the geography of the Middle colonies—New York, New Jersey, Pennsylvania, and Delaware—was more favorable to farmers. The soil was fertile. The climate was warmer, and the growing season was longer. Most farms in the Middle colonies were larger than those in New England. A few families had great estates on the Hudson River.

6. Settlers in New York, New Jersey, Delaware, and Pennsylvania grew a greater variety of crops than New Englanders. Farmers raised many kinds of fruits and vegetables. Native Americans introduced the settlers to potatoes as well as corn. Farmers in the Middle colonies also raised many kinds of livestock.

7. Many of the farms in the Middle colonies were more than subsistence farms. The farmers raised **cash crops,** such as wheat, oats, barley, rye, and livestock. Cash crops are crops or animals that are grown to be sold. The Middle colonies shipped food to other colonies and to Britain. Because wheat was the chief cash crop, the Middle colonies became known as the **Breadbasket Colonies**. Like other colonial farmers, however, they faced problems. The problems included drought, or lack of rain, poor harvests, and insect or animal pests that destroyed their crops.

Farming in the South What two patterns of farming developed in the Southern colonies?

8. As in New England and the Middle colonies, geography helped to shape farming in the Southern colonies. The climate was generally warm, making the growing season longer than in the colonies farther north. In the South, the coastal plain, called the **Tidewater**, reaches about 200 miles (323 km) inland. Settlers carved out plantations in these fertile lowlands. You will remember that a plantation is a large farm on which one main product is usually

▼ A Virginia planter and his clerk oversee the packing of tobacco leaves by slaves for shipment to Great Britain.

grown. Southern planters grew cash crops. With the profits from selling their crops, some wealthy planters built large, comfortable homes. They also bought silver, gold, lace and other special goods from Britain. Why did the colonists buy products from Britain?

9. Tobacco was the most important crop in Virginia and Maryland. Rice and **indigo** were important cash crops for South Carolina planters. Indigo is a plant that can be processed to make a blue dye. To raise these crops, Southern landowners **imported** increasing numbers of slaves. To import is to bring something in from another place. African American slaves worked at planting, weeding, and harvesting.

People in History

10. **Eliza Lucas** When she was only 16 years old, Eliza Lucas's father left her in charge of his three plantations in South Carolina. Eliza Lucas was determined to find crops that would make her father's land profitable. She tried growing ginger, alfalfa, and cotton, but with little success. In 1742, her father sent her indigo seeds. Within a few years, this energetic and practical young woman was successfully cultivating the new plant.

11. Lucas did not stop with growing her own crops. She gave indigo seeds to her neighbors and showed them how to make the blue dye from the plant. After introducing indigo, Lucas continued to experiment with new crops. She grew mulberry trees, which were important in making silk. She also began to grow flax, a plant used in the making of linseed oil and linen. ▶ What do you think are the advantages of introducing people to products new to them?

12. Later, Lucas married Charles Pinckney and helped him manage his plantation. Their children would play important roles in the founding of the new American nation.

13. In the **Piedmont** region of the South, subsistence farming developed. The Piedmont is the area between the Tidewater and the Appalachian Mountains. The Piedmont was often called the **back country**. Here, another way of

▲ Plantations in Maryland and North Carolina grew tobacco. In South Carolina and Georgia plantations produced rice. What crop did Virginia plantations like this one grow?

farming developed. The land was fertile, but the climate was cooler than on the coast. In the 1700s, settlers pushed west, carving out small subsistence farms in the hilly, forest-covered lands of back country. Some families grew tobacco along with corn, potatoes, and the other foods they ate themselves. Life in the back country was a struggle, and back country farmers often resented the wealth of coastal planters.

Outlook

14. Because of differences in geography, the colonists developed different ways of life. The difficulties of farming led many New Englanders to find other ways of earning a living. Conditions in the South favored the growing of cash crops. As a result, the plantation system, which needed large numbers of workers, took hold. Increasingly, planters turned to slave labor to make their lands profitable.

Activity: Ask why planters settled along waterways. Point out that it made transporting their crops easier. Because there were few, if any, roads, rivers served as highways to coastal ports.

CHAPTER REVIEW

VOCABULARY REVIEW

▶ Use the following vocabulary words to write original sentences that give information about farming in the 13 colonies.

girdling	imported
subsistence farmers	indigo
cash crops	back country
Breadbasket colonies	Piedmont
Tidewater	drought

USING PRIMARY SOURCES

▶ Reread Spotlight on Sources on page 127. How important was corn to the early colonists? What does the fact that Native Americans showed the colonists how to grow and use corn tell you about Native Americans?

SKILL BUILDER: READING A MAP

▶ Study the map below. Then answer these questions.

1. List the colonies shown on the map.

2. Which of the Southern colonies produced tobacco?

3. Which of the Southern colonies produced rice?

4. In which of the Southern colonies were furs produced?

5. What Southern colonies manufactured iron?

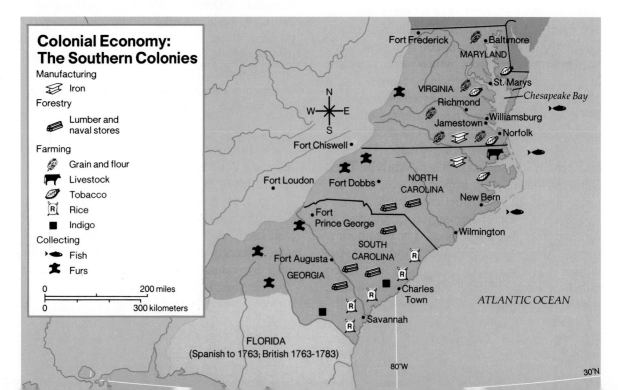

Colonial Economy: The Southern Colonies

Manufacturing
- Iron

Forestry
- Lumber and naval stores

Farming
- Grain and flour
- Livestock
- Tobacco
- R Rice
- Indigo

Collecting
- Fish
- Furs

0   200 miles
0   300 kilometers

STUDY HINT Make a chart with three rows and four columns. Label the rows, New England, Middle Colonies, Southern Colonies. Label the columns, size of farm, kinds of crops, climate, soil. Complete the chart using the information in the chapter.

SKILL BUILDER: CRITICAL THINKING AND COMPREHENSION

I. Introduction to Comparing and Contrasting

When you **compare** two things, you tell how they are alike. If you were comparing milk and soda, you might say they both are liquid, and they both are for drinking. When you contrast two things, you tell how they are different. To **contrast** milk with soda, you could say that milk is more nutritious than soda. You also could say that milk is a natural product, while soda is manufactured.

▶ The chart below is set up to compare and contrast the three regions of the British colonies. Copy the chart and review the chapter to fill in the boxes with facts about each category in each region. After the chart is complete write a paragraph explaining which two of the three regions are most similar and why.

	New England	Middle Colonies	Southern Colonies
Soil			
Climate			
Type of Farming			
Crops Grown			

II. Cause and Effect

▶ Sometimes one cause can have more than one effect. Give two effects for each of the causes below.

1. The process of girdling resulted in
   Effect 1: ______
   Effect 2: ______
2. The richer soil and warmer climate of the Middle Colonies resulted in
   Effect 1: ______
   Effect 2: ______
3. The development of plantations in the Southern Colonies resulted in
   Effect 1: ______
   Effect 2: ______

ENRICHMENT

1. Prepare a "how to" lesson that explains how to make a colonial product or raise a colonial crop. Research how settlers made candles, soap, wool, linen, or leather, or how colonial farmers grew rice, tobacco, indigo, wheat, or corn. Make pictures, charts, or diagrams to illustrate important steps in the process. Then, teach the class about your new "skill."
2. Imagine you were an English visitor to the 13 colonies in the 1750s. Write two postcards to your friends back home about the differences you noticed in your travels.

CHAPTER 2

Colonial Trade and Shipping

> **OBJECTIVE:** Why were the colonies' trading and shipping strictly controlled by Great Britain?

1. In the 1770s on market days, farmers brought produce from outlying areas to sell in the growing colonial cities. For Rebecca, a farm girl from outside Philadelphia, visiting the city on market day was exciting. She enjoyed the shouting peddlers selling tasty food and fashionable clothes in the streets, but she ignored the pigs that hunted through muddy streets for rotting garbage. Along different streets she watched many skilled craft workers, including tailors, weavers, and silversmiths. Most of all Rebecca loved the goods from Great Britain —hats, buttons, boots, needles, lace. Trading goods with Great Britain helped colonial towns like Philadelphia grow.

Britain and Its Colonies Why did Great Britain want to manage economic life in the colonies?

2. Like other European countries in the 1600s and 1700s, Britain followed a plan known as **mercantilism**. Mercantilists believed a nation grew rich and powerful by controlling trade. The colonies would be markets for English goods and would supply Britain with raw materials. British officials wanted the colonies to be profit-making businesses for Great Britain. What were the advantages and the disadvantages of mercantilism for the colonists?

▲ Philadelphia was the largest colonial port city. It had a population of 28,000 which made it bigger than most British cities in the 18th century.

Colonial Trade What products did the colonists have for trade?

3. The colonists were expected to send raw materials as **exports** to Britain. Exports are goods sent to other countries for sale. Among the chief exports were forest products. Britain

In Chapter 2 you will apply these critical thinking skills to the historical process:
Recognizing Cause and Effect: Recognizing the action or event that makes something happen, identifying the result of an action or event.
Comparing and Contrasting: Recognizing similarities and differences.

needed them for **naval supplies**. Naval supplies are goods used in shipbuilding such as timbers for ships and masts.

4. In New England, where farming was difficult, many colonists turned to the sea for food and for goods to trade. Settlers used trees from the huge forests to start a shipbuilding industry. Besides building ships, New Englanders caught rich harvests of fish. Then they dried the fish and sold them to the other colonies and to Great Britain. Whaling offered New Englanders another source of income from the sea. Whale oil was used to light lamps. Whale bone and ivory were used for buttons.

People in History

5. Paul Cuffe Like other boys from Massachusetts, Paul Cuffe earned success at sea. Cuffe was the son of a free African American father and a Nantucket Indian mother. Cuffe had no formal schooling. He taught himself to read and write. At the age of 16, Cuffe went to sea on a whaling ship. After several trips, he set up his own business. Through hard work, he finally bought six ships and traded from New England to Great Britain to South America.

6. Cuffe helped other African Americans. He hired crews of Africans Americans and Native Americans to sail his ships. Since he owned land, he had to pay taxes, but because he was African American, he was not allowed to vote. Cuffe fought against this injustice and won voting rights for free African American taxpayers in Massachusetts.

7. The Middle and Southern colonies exported mainly farm goods. The Middle Colonies exported wheat, oats, and barley to New England and parts of the South. The South produced indigo, rice, sugar, and tobacco to sell to Great Britain and Europe. Since these crops could not be grown there, the British were happy to buy them. In fact, the demand for smoking tobacco increased quickly in Britain and Europe after people learned to use it. By the late 1600s, Virginia was exporting as much as 28 million pounds of tobacco each year.

8. Another source of income was the fur trade. In Europe, wealthy people wore fur coats and fur hats. Colonists traded Native Americans tools, guns, or cloth for animal skins. By 1770, the fur trade was worth almost $700,000 a year. What problems for the environment of America ◄ would you predict because of the great demand for fur in Europe?

Spotlight on Sources

9. By the 1700s, the colonists had developed a successful trade in hats made from beaver skins and other furs. British mercantilists did not want competition from their own colonies. The British government passed the Hat Act of 1732 to stop colonists from exporting hats.

> Whereas the art and mystery of making hats in Great Britain hath arrived to great perfection . . . be it enacted by the king's most excellent Majesty . . . that no hat . . . shall be shipt, loaden, or put on board any ship or vessel in any place or parts within any of the British plantations [colonies] . . . to be exported, transported, shipped off, carried or conveyed out of any of the said British plantations . . . to any other place.

How would you have responded to such a law if ◄ you were a colonial hat maker? What group of tradesmen in Britain do you think were particularly happy with this law?

The Triangular Trade What products and routes made up the profitable triangular trade?

10. Despite Britain's tight control of colonial trade, New England merchants built up many profitable trade routes. One series of routes was called the **triangular** (try-ANG-gyoo-luhr) **trade** because goods were exchanged at three points. These places were New England, the West Indies, and Africa. First, New England merchants sent fish and lumber to the West Indies. On the return voyage, ships

Background: In the early 1800s, Cuffe helped free African Americans settle in Africa. At his own expense, he took 38 free African Americans to Sierra Leone on the west coast of Africa. Cuffe had a small farm in Westport, Massachusetts. Because the town had no school, Cuffe built a school and gave it to the town. He worked for abolition of slavery.

133

America's People

AFRICANS

"We stood in arms, firing on the revolted slaves, of whom we kill'd some and wounded many," wrote John Barbot, captain of a slave ship in 1701. "[M]any of the most mutinous leapt overboard," he added, "and drowned themselves in the ocean. . . ." Barbot stood to make a profit on the sale of every man, woman, and child he carried safely to America. But for the people, stolen from their homelands in Africa, what lay ahead?

At least 11 million Africans were brought to the Americas during the years of the slave trade. Most of them were captured in wars and slave raids ordered by African rulers. Some African rulers tried to stop the slave trade. Others wanted European-made goods, especially guns, in return for slaves. Where did the slaves come from? Some were captured as they farmed the land or herded cattle along the coast of West Africa. Others were rounded up from inland villages and forced to march to the coast. There slave captains loaded their valuable human cargo. The nightmare voyage across the Atlantic Ocean was known as the Middle Passage. Chained in pairs at their ankles and wrists, the Africans were packed in airless spaces below decks. They could not stand or move about.

Europeans needed cheap labor especially for the rich farmlands of the New World. In Africans, they found strong people who were skilled at farming and used to hard work. Thousands of Africans worked as slaves on the plantations of the South. In the North the slave population was smaller, and more free blacks could be found. Free or slave, African Americans also became skilled craft workers. Without African labor, the colonies of the New World probably would not have been as economically successful as they were.

In addition to its economic growth, African Americans contributed to the cultural and scientific growth of America. Slaves such as Phillis Wheatley, Juniper Hammon, and Gustavus Vasa wrote poetry and non-fiction. African Americans saved and shared African folk tales and music among themselves. Often they were heard singing as they worked in the fields. Other African Americans became scientists and inventors. A free African named Benjamin Banneker was a scientist and inventor. Banneker carved a clock that kept time for more than 50 years. He also helped plan the city of Washington, D.C.

Barbot quotation is cited in Vincent Harding, *There is a River: The Black Struggle for Freedom in America.*

▼ In slave ships like the one shown here, Europeans brought about 11 million Africans to North America, the Caribbean islands, and Brazil from the 1500s to the 1800s.

Now answer the following questions:

1. What was the main difference in the way Africans came to America and the way other people did?

2. Which African contribution to American culture do you think is most important? Explain your answer.

carried sugar and molasses to New England. There, the molasses was made into rum. Other ships carried rum, guns, and cloth from New England to West Africa. At West African ports, New England ship captains exchanged their **cargoes** (KAHR-gohz) for Africans who had been captured to be sold into slavery. Cargo is the goods that a ship carries. The ships then took the Africans to the West Indies, where they were sold. With the profits from these sales, captains bought more sugar and molasses to carry back to New England. While New Englanders owned few slaves themselves, some of them made huge profits selling Africans as slaves to planters in the West Indies.

▶ Why do you think that most colonists accepted slavery?

___

Towns and Cities How did colonists make a living in the towns and cities?

11. Although more than 90 percent of colonists lived on farms in the 1700s, a grow-

ing number of people lived in towns. Some made money from local and overseas trade. Others manufactured goods needed by the colonists. The largest colonial cities were the busy ports of Boston, Philadelphia, New York, and Charleston, South Carolina. In New York, more than a dozen languages were spoken by sailors and merchants visiting from many lands. Why did a profitable trad- ◀ ing business increase the colonists' desire for independence?

Outlook

12. In the 1700s, trade within the colonies and with England increased. New industries helped the colonists take care of themselves. The colonists did not need British goods as much as they had. However, the British still wanted to control the economy of the colonies. As you will discover in Unit 5, the colonists' economic success set the stage for trouble with Britain.

MAP SKILL BUILDER: Triangular trade routes linked colonial Americans with Europe, Africa, and the West Indies. **1.** What did the colonies sell in Africa? **2.** What did the colonies buy from the West Indies?

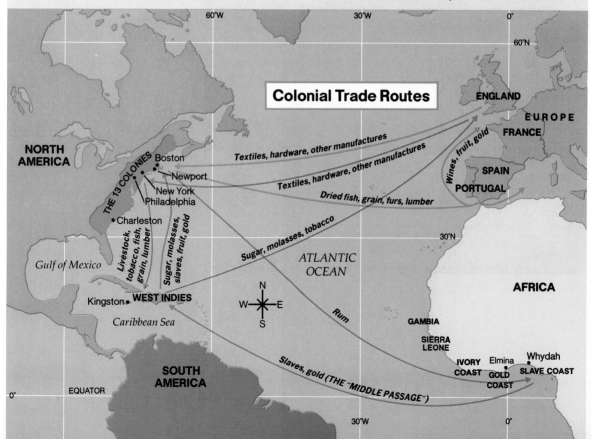

Colonial Trade Routes

CHAPTER REVIEW

▶ Decide if the following statements are true or false. If the statement is false, rewrite it to make it true.

1. Exports are goods that are sent to other countries for sale.

2. Mercantilism was a system that encouraged colonies to export manufactured goods.

3. Naval supplies are goods that were used in the slave trade.

4. The triangular trade involved a series of trade routes between the American colonies and England.

5. Cargo is the goods that a ship carries.

SKILL BUILDER: COMPLETING A TABLE

▶ Copy the table below on to a separate sheet of paper. Complete the table by filling in the goods that were exported from each of the regions. After the table is complete, write a paragraph explaining why there were regional differences in exports.

Place Exported from	Exports
New England	
Middle Colonies	
Southern Colonies	

SKILL BUILDER: CRITICAL THINKING AND COMPREHENSION

I. Comparing and Contrasting

As you already know, when you compare things, you show how they are similar. When you contrast two things, you tell how they are different.

▶ Compare and contrast the trip of the Pilgrims with the trip of the Africans to the New World. On a clean piece of paper, list two ways the trips were similar. Then list two ways the trips were different.

II. Cause and Effect

▶ Give at least two causes for the following effects.

1. **Cause:** _____
   Cause: _____
   Effect: Merchants going to the West Indies.

2. **Cause:** _____
   Cause: _____
   Effect: The British passed the Hat Act of 1732.

3. **Cause:** _____
   Cause: _____
   Effect: Africans were brought as slaves to the colonies.

4. **Cause:** _____
   Cause: _____
   Effect: New England developed an economy based on the sea.

5. **Cause:** _____
   Cause: _____
   Effect: The population of colonial towns increased.

USING PRIMARY SOURCES

▶ Reread the Spotlight on Sources on page 133 and then answer the questions. Why do you think the Hat Act caused resentment among the colonists? Why might this law cause problems for Britain later on?

ENRICHMENT

1. Read stories and articles about life on a whaling ship. You might even watch the film *Moby Dick*. Then write a story about the most exciting and the most frightening times in the life of a whaler.

2. Prepare a dramatic oral report on the Middle Passage, the terrible voyage that slaves had to survive from Africa to the Americas. You might wish to work with other students and write a play. You might want to tape record a dramatic reading. You could create an audio-visual presentation or a mural with an oral story.

CHAPTER 3

Religion and Education in the Colonies

OBJECTIVE: What was the importance of religion and education in the colonists' lives?

1. Religion strongly influenced the lives of most colonists. The Bible was the most widely read book in the colonies. In Puritan New England, the **Sabbath** (SAB-eth), or Sunday, was kept strictly as a day of worship. If a child was caught playing on the Sabbath, the child's parents had to pay a fine. This fine was greater than a day's pay. Every colony had "blue laws." Under these laws, everyone had to attend church. No work was to be done on Sunday. People were punished for swearing or for being drunk on Sunday. The religious beliefs of the ▶ settlers greatly shaped their way of life. What "blue laws" are there today?

Puritan New England How did Puritan beliefs affect education and daily life in New England?

2. Because many New England settlers were Puritans, their church helped shape the New England way of life. The Puritans taught their people to strictly obey God's laws, which they interpreted from the Bible. They valued hard work and lived simply. They disapproved of being lazy and having a good time, such as playing music and dancing. They saw these activities as evil.

3. At the center of every town was the church, or meeting house. Puritans strictly ob-

▲ Puritan churches were unheated in the winter. The people stood during prayers that could last for an hour.

served the Sabbath. The whole family spent Sunday at the meeting house. There, they prayed and listened to long sermons about the punishment awaiting sinners. How does your ◀ life seem to be different from that of a Puritan?

4. The Puritan settlers wanted their children to learn to read and write so they could study

In Chapter 3 you will apply these critical thinking skills to the historical process:

138

➡ **Recognizing Cause and Effect:** Recognizing the action or event that makes something happen, identifying the result of an action or event.

▌ **Comparing and Contrasting:** Recognizing similarities and differences.

the Bible. In 1647, just a few years after arriving in Massachusetts, Puritans passed the Massachusetts School Law. As a result of this law, the first public schools in North America were set up. The Massachusetts School Law said that every town with 50 or more families had to hire a schoolmaster. A larger town had to set up a grammar school that would prepare students for the **university** (yoo-nuh-VER-suh-tee). A university is a school of higher learning. Harvard College, established in Massachusetts in 1636, was the first university in the colonies. Its founders wanted to be sure that Puritan ministers were well educated. In 1701, Yale College in Connecticut was founded for similar reasons.

▶ How do religious beliefs affect life today?

🦅 Spotlight on Sources

5. Many children learned to read and write by studying the Bible. The first textbook was printed in the colonies as early as 1688. It was called the *New England Primer*. For more than 100 years, school children said these verses to learn the ABC's.

In **A**dam's fall
We sinned all.

Thy life to mend
This **B**ook attend.

The **C**at doth play
And after slay.

The idle **F**ool
Is whipt at school.

Besides teaching the alphabet, what do you think these rhymes taught? How were children expected to behave?

The Middle Colonies How did the variety of religious beliefs in the Middle Colonies affect education?

6. Immigrants to the Middle Colonies came from many countries. As a result, the people practiced many religious faiths and were more tolerant than colonists in New England. By the

1700s, immigrants had set up Lutheran, Catholic, Presbyterian, Baptist, and Methodist churches. Jews settled around Rhode Island and New York. French Protestants, known as Huguenots (HEW-guh-nahts), found freedom from persecution there. New England Puritans also moved into the Middle Colonies. In Pennsylvania, of course, the Quakers were powerful.

7. The Middle Colonies were slower to set up schools than New England. This was due in part to the many different languages and people who settled there. Early Dutch settlers in New Amsterdam set up schools, but these schools closed after the English took over the colony. The Anglican Church, as the official Church of England is called, set up some private schools. Although New Jersey passed laws asking towns to set up public schools, most schools in New Jersey and elsewhere were run by churches. In Pennsylvania, the Quakers organized a number of schools. Quaker schools mostly taught useful subjects such as English, mathematics, and **surveying** (sir-VAY-ing). Surveying is measuring and plotting land. Higher education for training ministers and others was available in the Middle Colonies also in universities like Princeton (1746) and Columbia (1754).

The South What role did religion play in the South?

8. The Anglican Church was the official church in the five Southern colonies. In Virginia, wealthy planters and families supported the Anglican Church. Because the church was established by British law, everyone had to pay taxes to the church. Non-Anglicans, such as the Catholics in Maryland, were angry about having to pay such taxes.

9. African American slaves were expected to attend the church of their owners. Sitting in a special, separate section of the church, they were told weekly by the minister to obey their master. Some African American slaves, however, were able to meet secretly and worship in their own way. Their religious leaders often told them that

Background: Puritans prepared food for Sunday meals on Saturday. Penalties for swearing and drunkenness on Sunday could be twice what they were on any other day.

139

▲ Girls often attended dame schools. There they were taught the basics of reading and writing by a woman in her own home.

God would end slavery. This belief gave many African Americans hope. That hope was sometimes expressed in religious songs called spirituals, which the African Americans sang as they worked.

Other Ways of Learning How did children who did not attend school learn basic skills?

10. In general, schools were for boys. In New England, girls might attend one of the "dame schools" that a woman ran out of her house. More often, girls learned to read, write, sew, and cook at home. Their families thought that these skills would make them good wives and mothers.

11. African Americans who were slaves had almost no chance to get an education. If they worked as house servants, they might receive some training or even be taught to read the Bible. Slave owners feared that if an African

American slave was educated, he or she would see the unfairness of slavery and fight back. Free African Americans faced **prejudice** (PREJ-oo-dis), or hatred because of one's race, when it came to schooling. Some, like Paul Cuffe, were self taught. Others found people willing to educate them.

12. Instead of classroom education, many boys and some girls learned useful skills by becoming **apprentices** (uh-PREN-uh-suhz). An apprentice was a person who worked without pay for a master craftsperson in order to learn a trade or a skill. Some slaves learned crafts, such as metal work and wood working, that were necessary for plantation life. But they were not allowed to become free craftspeople. They were too valuable. Usually the master craftsperson agreed to teach the apprentice reading, writing, and arithmetic as well. At the end of the training period, which was usually seven years, the apprentice could take a job for pay.

Changing Views of Religion Why did religious toleration grow in the colonies in the 1700s?

13. By the late 1600s, the power of the Puritan and Anglican churches in New England and the Southern colonies weakened. Immigrants with different faiths flooded into the colonies. These changes led to a growth in religious **toleration** (tah-luh-RAY-shuhn), that is, the willingness to allow differing religious views. Slowly, the strict Puritan laws against fancy clothing and certain kinds of entertainment were eased. But everyone still had to go to church every Sunday. Even in Great Britain, people became more tolerant of other religions. In 1689 Parliament passed the Toleration Act, giving religious freedom to most Protestants, although not to Catholics and Jews.

14. In the 1730s and 1740s, the **Great Awakening** swept through the colonies. The Great Awakening was a religious movement that strongly affected the colonists. In this movement, Methodist and Baptist preachers, not part of the established churches, wandered

Background: Children who lived on farms far from a town or school learned from their parents. A woman would teach her children to read the Bible. Her husband would show them how to clear the land and mend or make the tools they needed on the farm.

140

the countryside. Through their fiery speeches, they stirred people to a state of religious experience that they believed would help them be less sinful. Through the Great Awakening, people were taught that all who repented could be saved. The Great Awakening led people to want a greater say in their religious practices and beliefs. The power of the established churches weakened as groups split from the Anglican Church and started new churches.

15. The Great Awakening brought other changes in education, manners, and equal rights. Education became a way to teach about new beliefs, so the groups started schools. The Great Awakening encouraged kindness to others. Some people began to help orphans and the poor. The idea that all people could be saved brought some people to the belief in equal rights. The leaders of the movement worked hard to convert African Americans as well as whites. The Great Awakening even inspired

some people to oppose slavery. Because of the Great Awakening, it became more acceptable for African Americans to have their own churches. As a result, the church grew to be the central support for African Americans.

People in History

16. Jonathan Edwards Among the best-known preachers of the Great Awakening was Jonathan Edwards. Edwards was a Congregational minister in Northampton, Massachusetts. He believed that the world had been created for God's glory and that through God alone could people be saved. Only through strong feelings for God and Jesus, believed Edwards, could people turn away from sin and toward God.

17. Through his preaching, Edwards fanned the fires of the Great Awakening in New England. He frightened listeners with pictures of their sinful souls in a terrible Hell. In his most famous sermon, he pictured God as holding sinners "over the pit of Hell much as one holds a spider or some loathsome insect over the fire." People were greatly moved by Edwards. Hundreds of people accepted Edwards's preaching, and the Great Awakening movement spread quickly. Why do you think people were so ◀ greatly moved by Edwards?

Outlook

18. Religion shaped the lives of the colonists in many ways. Education started in the colonies because the children needed to know how to read the Bible. Many colonial laws, including some about the home and community, were based on religious principles. In addition, a variety of religious groups came to America because religious differences were often better tolerated. The Great Awakening brought a new way of religious practice that was based more on the individual and less on the established churches. This movement also added to the idea of separation of church and state. Another idea from the Great Awakening, religious tolerance, continues today, making the United States a country with a great variety of religions.

▼ Jonathan Edwards led a religious revival that spread throughout the country and served as a missionary to Native Americans in Massachusetts.

Ask: What does separation of church and state mean? How did the early colonies mix church and state? How did the growing number of religious groups in America lead to the idea that church and state should be separate?

CHAPTER REVIEW

VOCABULARY REVIEW

▶ Select the word or term that best completes each sentence. Number your paper and write the correct letter by each answer.

1. Another word for Sabbath is
   a. Sunday.　　b. feast.　　c. holiday.

2. A university is
   a. a school of higher learning.
   b. large hotel.
   c. football stadium.

3. After a student learned surveying, he could
   a. measure land.　　b. paint a house.
   c. write letters.

4. A boy or girl became an apprentice in order to
   a. learn a trade.
   b. avoid going to school.
   c. achieve salvation.

5. Religious toleration means
   a. religious freedom for Catholics only.
   b. the separation of church and state.
   c. a willingness to allow different religious views.

6. The Great Awakening led to
   a. stricter enforcement of religious laws.
   b. the growth of new religious groups.
   c. harsher punishments for lawbreakers.

7. Persons who are prejudiced
   a. like other people.
   b. hate people because of their race.
   c. make good teachers.

SKILL BUILDER: INTERPRETING A TIME LINE

▶ Copy the timeline below on to a separate sheet of paper. Then answer the questions based on the timeline.

1. The year the law was passed that said that every town with 50 or more families had to hire a schoolmaster.

2. The year Harvard College was founded.

3. A year during the Great Awakening.

4. The year Parliament passed an act giving religious freedom to most Protestant groups.

5. The year the first textbook was printed in the colonies.

6. How many years did the Great Awakening last?

7. How many years after Massachusetts town had to establish schools was the first Primer printed?

Harvard College was established 1636　　English Toleration Act passed by Parliament 1689　　Great Awakening swept through the colonies 1730–1750

1640　1660　1680　1700　1720　1730　1750

Massachusetts School Law passed 1647　　Approximate year the first New England Primer was published 1688

SKILL BUILDER: CRITICAL THINKING AND COMPREHENSION

I. Cause and Effect

1. Use paragraphs 14 and 15 in the text to help you list four effects of the Great Awakening of the 1730s and 1740s. Write the effects on a separate sheet of paper.

2. Look at the lists of causes and effects below. Decide which effects belong with each cause. Write your choices on another sheet of paper. You might find the same effects from different causes, and some are not effects of these causes.

Causes

a. desire to study the Bible

b. keeping the Sabbath holy

c. religious toleration in Middle colonies

Effects

1. many religious faiths

2. establishing schools

3. paying heavy fines for drunkenness on Sunday

II. Comparing and Contrasting

▶ Reread paragraphs 4 and 11. Below is a chart that asks you to fill in subjects and places of learning in early New England. Copy the chart on to a separate sheet of paper, and fill it in.

	Girls	Boys	Slaves
Subjects			
Where They Learned			

USING PRIMARY SOURCES

▶ What can you tell about education in New England from the verses on page 139?

ENRICHMENT

1. Find out about life in a colonial school. Write a play showing what life was like such a in school.

2. Prepare an oral report on the Salem witchcraft trials. Explain why they occurred and their results (or turn this into a debate activity).

CHAPTER 4

Government in the Colonies

OBJECTIVE: How were the British colonies governed? What rights did the colonists have?

1. "No free man shall be captured, or imprisoned, . . . except by the lawful judgment of his peers or by the law of the land." That idea appeared in the Magna Carta, or Great Charter, signed in 1215 by the English ruler King John. American colonists strongly believed in their rights as British citizens. They also believed in the right to fight for fairness if power was used badly by government. Americans struggled to create government and laws that would correct too much control and unfairness. From the Mayflower Compact, to Connecticut's Fundamental Orders to today's Constitution, Americans have believed it important to keep government from using power unfairly.

Colonial Governments What three kinds of government were set up in the British colonies?

2. By the mid-1700s, there were three kinds of colonial government: **royal**, **proprietary**, and **self-governing**. In a royal colony, the governor was appointed by the king. In a proprietary colony, the governor was appointed by the trading company or proprietor who founded the colony. In a self-governing colony, the governor was elected by the voters or citizens of the colony. The governor's power was greater in the royal and proprietary colonies.

▲ All voters could take part in a New England town meeting. Sometimes the debates in a town meeting became very lively.

3. In all colonies, the governor served as the **executive** (ek-ZEK-yoo-tiv). The executive enforces and carries out the law. Besides enforcing the laws, the governor had other powers. The governor called the assembly to meet, and he could dismiss it. The governor could **veto** (VEE-toh), or reject, decisions made by the

In Chapter 4 you will apply these critical thinking skills to the historical process:
◣ **Comparing and Contrasting:** Recognizing similarities and differences.
◤ **Drawing Conclusions:** Making a statement that explains the facts and evidence.

assembly. The governor led the colony's army forces and built forts to protect the colony. He granted land, appointed judges, and controlled the colony's trade.

4. To carry out these jobs, the governor had the help of his **council** (KOWN-suhl). The council was made up of leading citizens in the colony who usually were chosen by the king or governor. The governor's council also served as the highest court in the colony.

5. Most colonies had a two-house **legislature** (LEH-jus-lay-chur). The legislature is the lawmaking body of a government. The governor's council served as the upper house. The **assembly** served as the lower house. Each colony had an elected assembly such as the House of Burgesses in Virginia or the House of Representatives in Massachusetts. Only white men who owned a certain amount of property were allowed to vote. In some colonies, voters also ▶ had to be members of the established church. Why do you think women, Native Americans, and African Americans were not permitted to vote?

6. The main job of the colonial assemblies was to serve the people who voted for them. Members talked about and voted on matters that came before the assembly. At first, colonial assemblies only had the right to approve laws written by the executive. In time, they had the right to make new laws as well. The assembly had the right to vote on the money paid to the governor and to judges. Colonial assemblies used that power to make the governor pay attention to their wishes. What government ◀ body in the United States acts like this today?

Spotlight on Sources

7. Each town or county in a colony had its own local government. In New England, white colonial townspeople could speak out at the town meeting. But only property owners could vote. Town clerks kept records about the meetings. Here is the plan for the March 3, 1766, Braintree, Massachusetts, town meeting.

> First, to choose all such town officers for the ensuing [following] year as the law

---

▼ In most colonial legislatures, a law was passed after being approved by both houses of the legislature. A bill needed to pass in the lower house before it went to the upper house for final approval.

Background: In the 1700s, voting requirements included: Connecticut—an estate worth 40 shillings each year or £40 of personal property; Georgia—50 acres of land; Pennsylvania—50 acres of land or £50 of personal property.

▲ Until the Revolution Bacon's Rebellion was the largest and most powerful uprising against a government in the history of the colonies. What problems did it bring to light?

directs, also a county treasurer and a register of deeds [person who keeps legal records], for said county.

Secondly, to make provision [look out] for leasing [renting] out the town's lands, as the present leases are nigh expired [almost run out] . . .

Thirdly, to see if the town will repair the highways within said town in the same manner it was done the last years.

Fourthly, to see if the town will allow the surveyors [people who map land] that served for the year 1764 a reward for their extraordinary [great] service.

Fifthly, to consider of and resolve [decide] upon some effectual [way to get done] means for a passage for the fish called alewives up Monotaquot River (so called).

▶ What do these agenda items show citizens of Braintree were concerned about? What concerns do people today share with them?

Bacon's Rebellion Why did discontent lead to uprisings in the late 1600s?

8. Unrest in Virginia led to the outbreak of **Bacon's Rebellion** (ruh-BEL-yun) in 1676. A rebellion is a violent action by people who are angry or fed up. Bacon's Rebellion pitted backcountry farmers against Governor William Berkeley. The rebellion had several causes. Farmers in the backcountry suffered from poor harvests and low prices. They were angered by the wealth and power of planters along the coast. The farmers felt that Berkeley, a wealthy landowner, did not care about their needs. Most important, backcountry farmers were angry at the governor for failing to protect them from attacks by Native Americans.

9. Nathaniel Bacon, who served on the governor's council, sided with the frontier farmers. On his own, he brought together a band of fighters and attacked the Native Americans. The governor called Bacon a rebel. In September 1676, Bacon's forces burned Jamestown and

▲ The trial of John Peter Zenger took place in New York City. Andrew Hamilton successfully defended Zenger against a charge of libel.

tried to divide the land more fairly among people. When Bacon died a month later, Berkeley hanged many of the rebels.

10. The rebellion showed how unhappy the common people were with the few wealthy landowners who ruled the colony. It also showed that the people would fight what they felt was unfair use of power. In the years after Bacon's Rebellion, Virginia governors slowly had to grant more rights to the common people.

People in History

11. John Peter Zenger Unlike Nathaniel Bacon in Virginia, John Peter Zenger found a peaceful way to fight a New York governor. Zenger, who came to America from Germany, was the publisher of the *New York Weekly Journal*. The newspaper printed articles that pointed out the weaknesses of New York's governor, William Cosby. In 1734, the governor had Zenger arrested and charged with **libel** (LY-bul). Libel is a false statement that is made for the purpose of hurting the good name and reputation of a person.

12. The Zenger trial drew much attention. Many people saw Zenger as being unfairly attacked by the governor. At the trial, Zenger was charged with printing articles that made people unhappy and angry with the government. Zenger's lawyer replied that what Zenger had printed was true and that the truth is not libel. In the end, the jury found Zenger not guilty. In time, the Zenger trial became a symbol of freedom of the press. How would the ◄ United States be different if freedom of the press were not a right?

Outlook

13. Colonists believed strongly in the liberties, or rights, they enjoyed as British citizens. These included the right to trial by jury, like the Zenger trial, and the right to approve taxes. During the late 1600s and early 1700s, the colonies grew rapidly, and the settlers slowly gained more say over their own affairs. However, when Britain began to tighten its controls on the colonies in the mid-1700s, the colonists protested loudly.

Ask: What is libel? Can a statement be libel if it is truthful? What did the jury in the Zenger case decide on this issue?

CHAPTER REVIEW

VOCABULARY REVIEW

▶ Select the word or term that best completes each sentence. Number your paper and write the correct word by each number.

council	proprietary colony	veto	libel
assembly	charter	legislature	self-governing colony
royal colony	executive	Bacon's Rebellion	

1. In a _____ , the English monarch appointed the governor and his council.

2. The _____ is the person who has the responsibility of enforcing the law.

3. The _____ was made up of leading citizens chosen by the king or governor.

4. The uprising against Virginia governor William Berkeley was known as _____ .

5. A colonial governor had the power to _____ , or reject, laws passed by the assembly.

6. In a _____ , citizens elected the governor.

7. Someone who prints malicious or false statements that might injure another person's reputation can be accused of _____ .

8. In a _____ , a group of individuals owned the land but they recognized the authority of the English ruler.

9. In the colonies, the _____ was made up of the governor's council and the assembly.

10. The lower house of colonial legislatures was the _____ .

SKILL BUILDER: MAKING A CHART

A chart can help you organize information that you have read. You can use the chart to study for a test or write an essay.

▶ Make a chart about the three branches of colonial government: the executive, the council, the assembly. Make a column for each branch. List the duties of each beneath the proper heading. Make another row that tells how people in each branch got their jobs. Make a third row that gives examples of challenges to the authority of each branch. You may not have examples for all branches.

	Executive	Council	Assembly
Duties			
How Got Job			
Challenges to Authority			

SKILL BUILDER: CRITICAL THINKING AND COMPREHENSION

I. Comparing and Contrasting

1. What is the difference between Bacon's and Zenger's style of protesting?

2. Contrast the three types of colonial governments. Read paragraph 2, and write the contrasts on a separate piece of paper.

II. Introduction to Drawing Conclusions

A **conclusion** is a reasoned judgement. It is something you figure out after you learn all the facts. To draw a conclusion, you study different events or ideas, decide what the facts tell you about the subject. For example, Nathaniel Bacon's fighters attacked Native Americans. Bacon is called a rebel. Many rebels were hanged. You conclude Bacon's rebellion failed.

▶ Read these facts. Then decide which of the list of conclusions fits the facts best. Write the facts and your conclusion on a separate sheet of paper.

Facts

1. The governor enforced laws.

2. The governor vetoed decisions of the assembly.

3. The governor built forts.

Conclusions

a. The governor had the same job in all states.

b. The governor was a man with many responsibilities.

c. The governor was a friend of the king.

USING PRIMARY SOURCES

▶ Read the Spotlight on Sources on pages 145 and 146 again. How is the Braintree, Massachusetts, council meeting similar to city council meetings today? How is it different?

ENRICHMENT

1. The Zenger trial raised an important question about what is libel. Use encyclopedias and books to find out more about the trial. Then, in a group, prepare a play about the trial. Before you begin to write the script, brainstorm in the following categories: facts you know about the trial, arguments that support the government's case, arguments that support Zenger. Then write an informal outline of your script. Use your research books again to find out about New York's courts during the colonial period. Use what you found to add details to the setting to make it realistic.

2. Imagine what a town meeting would be like in your community. Then prepare an agenda and conduct a town meeting. What are the issues important in the community? Determine what the requirements for citizenship are. Be sure to decide beforehand who will be allowed to speak and to vote on the issues that are raised.

3. Virginia was not the only colony where people revolted against the government. Prepare an oral report on the causes and effects of one of these rebellions: Culpepper's Rebellion in North Carolina; Leisler's Rebellion in New York; Coode's Rebellion in Maryland.

CHAPTER 5

Colonial Life in New France

OBJECTIVE: What ways of life did settlers in New France develop?

1. The young French women stepped ashore eagerly. They were glad to be on land after so many weeks crossing the ocean. The women were not put off by the crowds of men who watched their arrival. Within weeks, each of the women would marry one of these strangers. King Louis XIV of France wanted his colony of New France to grow. He sent the women to marry the colony's bachelors and have families. The young women were known as the **kings's daughters** because the king paid their way to New France. When they married, he gave them gifts of household goods. Getting people to settle in New France was one of many challenges facing the colony.

Treasures of the Forest How did the fur trade affect life in New France?

2. As you know, French explorers found a treasure in the forests of New France. The treasure was not gold but fur-bearing animals such as beaver, mink, and otter. In the early 1600s, the French started a way of trading with Native Americans that would last for 150 years.

3. The fur trade shaped life in New France. Each spring as the ice in the St. Lawrence River melted, weathered fur traders in bark canoes appeared at Quebec. Shouting and singing, they unloaded their furs and traded them in town. These bold adventurers were known as **coureurs de bois** (koo-ROOR duh BWAH),

▲ French fur traders used snowshoes and dog sleds to move quickly through the snowy wilderness in winter. What do you think they are carrying in the dog sleds?

or runners of the forest. From Native Americans, they learned to canoe through white water rivers into the unexplored western wilderness. There, they traveled on snowshoes to trap beaver and hunt other animals. After living through the bitter winter, they returned to the French

In Chapter 5 you will apply these critical thinking skills to the historical process:

150 ◣ **Comparing and Contrasting:** Recognizing similarities and differences. ◢ **Drawing Conclusions:** Making a statement that explains the facts and evidence.

settlements with their load of furs. In late summer, the coureurs de bois loaded their canoes with trade goods, such as tools and gunpowder, and headed into the wilderness.

Governing New France How was New France governed?

4. During the middle 1600s, the French king took greater direct control of New France. For many years, several trading companies had controlled New France. They developed the fur trade rather than bringing settlers to the colony. In 1663, however, King Louis XIV made New France a royal province, or colony. He chose a governor and an **intendant** (ahn-tahn-DAWNT) to rule the colony. The governor had to take care of defending the colony. The intendant took care of economic growth and made sure the laws were followed. Unlike the English colonies, New France did not have a body of elected representatives.

5. Louis XIV pushed the colony to grow by giving rewards to colonists. For example, Louis sent soldiers to fight the Iroquois tribes, who were allies of the English in the fur trade. The king offered the soldiers land in New France as payment. Also, Jean Talon, the first intendant, brought people to New France by offering rewards to parents who had large families. A father had to pay a fine if his son was not married by 20 or his daughter by 16. These policies helped the population grow from about 3,200 in 1666 to 6,700 in 1673. Talon also tried to improve the economy by setting up industries such as lumbering and shipbuilding.

The Church in New France What role did the Catholic Church play in New France?

6. Priests and nuns from the Catholic Church took a leading role in the building of New France. Black-robed priests paddled in canoes alongside the French explorers. The

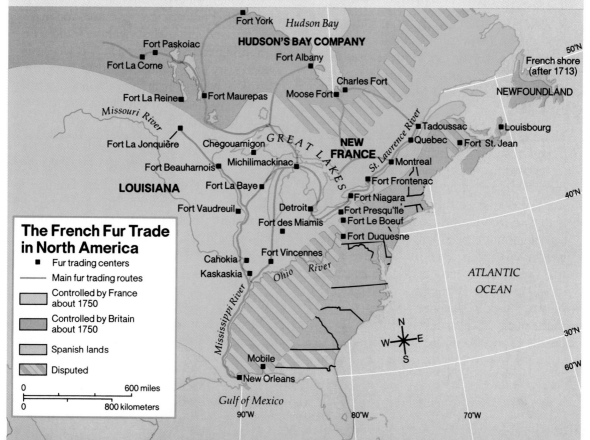

MAP SKILL BUILDER: Trade in furs made New France prosperous. A chain of forts protected the valuable trade. **1.** From what areas were furs collected? **2.** Which was larger, the area controlled by France or by Britain? **3.** How do you think most fur traders traveled?

The French Fur Trade in North America

- ■ Fur trading centers
- — Main fur trading routes
- Controlled by France about 1750
- Controlled by Britain about 1750
- Spanish lands
- Disputed

0   600 miles
0   800 kilometers

priests had one goal—to bring Christianity to Native Americans. Nuns, too, joined in the work of building the colony. Women such as Sister Jeanne Mance spent their lives helping the sick and wounded and teaching the daughters of settlers. The missionaries helped New France grow by exploring deep into Indian lands. They set up missions that soon grew into trading posts and then settlements.

7. The Catholic Church influenced both religious and political development in New France. While the English colonies had a variety of Protestant religions, the Catholic Church was the only religion in New France. The Church controlled the way people lived and acted. It owned large amounts of land. In the growing settlements, the Church built hospitals and schools run by priests and nuns. For settlers in New France, the Church was a place to discuss non-religious concerns. The Church was also an important political force. The bishop of New France was as powerful as the governor and had

▶ influence with the king. What were the advantages and disadvantages of the government of New France?

FATHER MARQUETTE AND HIS SYMBOL OF PEACE.

▲ Jacques Marquette was one of the Catholic priests who traveled far to bring Christianity to Native Americans. What is he doing here?

🦅 Spotlight on Sources

8. Like the coureurs de bois, missionary priests learned to live in the wilderness. They traveled everywhere by canoe. In the late 1600s, Father Galinée (gah-lee-NAY) wrote about life on the trail as he traveled from Quebec to the Great Lakes.

> These [canoes] are . . . about 20 feet [about 6 meters] long and two feet [.6 meter] wide, strengthened inside with cedar floors and gunwales [upper part of a ship], very thin, so that one man carries it with ease, although the boat is capable of carrying four men and 800 or 900 pounds' weight of baggage. . . . Although it is a true saying that when a person is in one of these vessels he is always, not a finger's breath, but the thickness of five of six sheets of paper, from death [very thin sides on the canoes separated passengers from

> the rough water]. . . . When the weather is fine, after unloading your canoe, you make a fire and go to bed without otherwise housing yourself; but when it is wet, it is necessary to go and strip some trees, the bark of which you arrange upon four small forks, with which you make a cabin to save you from the rain. . . .
>
> —from "Exploration of the Great Lakes, 1669–1770 . . . Galinée's Narrative and Map," ed. by James H. Coyne

From whom do you think Father Galinée and ◀ other priests learned the skills to live in the wilderness? What clues for your answer do you find in the primary source?

Settlers of New France What was life like for the colonists?

9. New France grew much more slowly than the English colonies to the south for several reasons. The climate was often cold and snowy. In the early years, many colonists died of disease and starvation or were killed by Native Americans. Non-Catholics could not settle in the colony. Then, too, the fur trade caused the sons of many settlers to leave farming. They wanted to try the dangerous and adventurous life of a coureur de bois. They also knew that the furs brought in a lot of money.

10. Besides the coureurs de bois, priests, and nuns, there were two main groups of settlers— farmers and large landowners. To bring in farmers, the French government divided land along the St. Lawrence into large pieces called **seigneuries** (sen-yoo-REE). Landowners, called seigneurs, had to clear and develop their land. The seigneurs attracted settlers by offering them good deals to farm the land. The farmers of New France were called **habitants** (ah-bee-TAWNT). They raised wheat and oats and grazed cattle, sheep, and pigs. As the habitants cleared more land, they began producing more than enough to meet their needs.

11. Although some landowners were French nobles, the settlers had more rights than they would have had in France. Because there were few farmers, the habitants won many rights from landowners that French peasants did not have. The early habitants developed a spirit of independence. Some habitants rose within the small colonial society to become wealthy and
▶ respected landowners. As people become wealthy and independent, what do you predict they would want from the government?

People in History

12. **Michel Sarrazin** A young French doctor, Michel Sarrazin (sah-rah-ZAN), was one of the first white men to sail the St. Lawrence River. Sarrazin was with the army Louis XIV sent to New France in 1685 to fight the Iroquois, the only tribe not friendly with the French. He held the title "surgeon to the troops."

13. Besides his interest in medicine, Sarrazin was also interested in the plants, animals, and minerals of New France. He studied and wrote

Ask: How did the fur trade limit economic growth in New France?

about animals native to the Americas. The skunk, however, he left alone because "it had a frightful smell, capable of making [that could make] a whole canton [area] a desert." Sarrazin used what he had learned about living things to help him in his work as a doctor. This knowledge helped other doctors and scientists.

Outlook

14. French explorers and fur traders had found the rich forest land of New France. However, the settlers and their Native American allies had to defend the frontiers of New France against the larger population to the south. By the mid-1700s, land-hungry British colonists were pushing west from their coastal settlements. As you will read in Unit 5, New France and her Native American allies were unable to stop the British threat.

▼ One day, a Native American gave Sarrazin an insect-eating plant. Sarrazin sent a drawing of it to France, where it caused a sensation. The plant was named sarracenia in his honor.

CHAPTER REVIEW

VOCABULARY REVIEW

▶ Decide if each of the following statements is true or false. If a statement is false, rewrite it to make it true.

1. The "king's daughters" were nuns who went to New France to convert Native Americans.

2. Coureurs de bois lived in the wilderness, hunting and trapping fur-bearing animals.

3. An intendant was an official appointed by the king of France to supervise the economic affairs of the colony.

4. Seigneuries were large tracts of land given to French settlers.

5. The habitants' chief source of income was the fur trade.

SKILL BUILDER: MAKING AN OUTLINE

▶ Let's say you wanted to write a job description for each of the persons listed below. You would outline it first, putting in different activities. Put the heading on a piece of paper, as you see below. Then copy the activities under the right heading. Note: some activities don't belong under any job description.

Headings

A. Coureurs de Bois Job Description

B. Intendant Job Description

C. Habitant Job Description

Activities

1. raised wheat and oats

2. wore snowshoes

3. built railroads

4. trapped beaver

5. cleared land

6. ate otter

7. enforced laws

8. wrote loving reports

9. helped business grow

10. hunted animals

11. traded fur for goods

12. was in charge of defense

13. eventually owned land

USING PRIMARY SOURCES

▶ Read the Spotlight on Sources on page 152 again. What did the French learn from the Native Americans in Canada? If the French had not learned from Native Americans, how would New France have been different? Would life have been easier or more difficult? Give examples to support your opinion.

STUDY HINT Write the questions that introduce each section in the chapter on a piece of paper. Underneath each question, jot down short phrases that answer the question.

SKILL BUILDER: CRITICAL THINKING AND COMPREHENSION

I. Drawing Conclusions

A conclusion is a judgment, decision, or opinion formed after careful investigation or thought. When you draw conclusions, you reason from the facts. For example, historians put together information to draw conclusions about a past civilization.

Now copy the sets of facts below on to a separate sheet of paper. Pick the better conclusion for each set of facts. Write the conclusion.

Facts

1. There were many minks and otters in the forests of New France.

   People in New France liked fur.

2. Catholic priests and nuns built hospitals in New France.

   Catholic nuns taught daughters of the settlers.

Conclusions

1. **a.** There could be a good fur trade between France and New France.

   b. Not many people wanted to go where there are wild animals.

2. **a.** Catholic priests and nuns liked to do different things.

   b. Catholic nuns and priests were important to New France.

II. Comparing and Contrasting

The chart below helps you to compare life in New France to life in the English colonies. Copy the chart and fill in the boxes with the facts you have learned in Chapters 1–5.

	New France	New England	Middle Colonies	Southern Colonies
Origins of Settlers				
Government				
Major Economic Activities				
Religion				
Examples of Daily Life				

ENRICHMENT

1. French traders often exchanged a keg of brandy for furs that Native Americans had spent an entire winter gathering. Priests opposed selling alcohol to Native Americans because of its terrible effects on individuals and their families. Write to the king of France to ask for a law banning the sale of liquor to Native Americans.
2. Many sons of habitants dreamed of becoming coureurs de bois. Find out more about the life of both habitants and coureurs de bois. With a partner, write a dialogue between a boy who wants to go live in the wilderness and his habitant father who opposes the boy's dream. Perform the dialogue for the class.

CHAPTER 6

Colonial Life in New Spain

OBJECTIVE: How did Spain organize and govern its colony of New Spain?

1. In 1716, pirate Henry Jennings captured a Spanish galleon (treasure ship) off the coast of Florida. Imagine the shouts of delight when he and his crew found 350,000 pieces of eight in the ship's storerooms. These famous pieces of eight or pesos were silver Spanish coins worth about a dollar. This was a lot of money to an average seaman, who usually earned about three dollars a month. The fleets of Spanish treasure ships that left Veracruz twice a year were tempting targets for pirate attacks. These ships were filled with great riches taken from gold and silver mines in the New World. Spain became rich from the wealth of its New World colonies.

The Economy of New Spain How did people in New Spain make a living?

2. A major source of income for both colonists and Spain was mining. In fact, Spain's main interest in its colonies was the riches in gold and silver that could be found. Many colonists went to New Spain hoping to get rich by finding new sources of gold and silver. To find the workers needed to dig in the mines, they turned to Native Americans. The Native Americans were forced from their villages and endured terrible conditions in dangerous underground shafts. Tens of thousands died digging out the riches of the land.

▲ In 1545, silver was discovered in a part of New Spain called Cerro Potosí, now in Bolivia. Soon it was one of the world's richest mines.

3. Besides mining, farming and ranching were important economic activities. Large farms that grew one or two cash crops were called **haciendas** (ah-see-EN-dahs). Native Americans worked the land for the **hacendados** (ah-sen-DAH-dohs), or landowners. They grew crops such as wheat, corn, sugar, or rice. Most haci-

In Chapter 6 you will apply these critical thinking skills to the historical process:

▶ **Drawing Conclusions:** Making a statement that explains the facts and evidence.

▱ **Classifying:** Organizing facts into categories based on what they have in common.

endas were **self-sufficient**, which means they grew or made almost everything the landowner and workers needed. In New Mexico, Texas, and California, Spanish settlers began **ranchos** (RAHN-chohs), or large land areas where cattle were raised. **Vaqueros**, or cowboys, were hired to look after the cattle.

4. Many Spaniards settled in New Spain's towns or cities and became skilled craftsworkers. They turned out fine silver and leather goods. Weavers, potters, and candle makers also sold their goods in city markets. People especially loved the **mantas**, or blankets woven by Native Americans. A new culture developed, blending Native American and Spanish customs, language, ideas, and dress.

Spotlight on Sources

5. Early in the 16th century, Andre Agric (AH-grik) arrived in Mexico City with little money. He became a trader, buying goods from Native Americans and selling them to other Native Americans or to Spanish settlers. In the letter that follows, Agric writes to his nephew in Spain to come take over his business.

Nephew, I live in Mexico City in the tianguiz [market] of San Juan, among the shops of Tegada. I deal in Campeche wood and cotton blankets and wax, and I also have a certain business in cacao [the bean from which chocolate is made] in Soconusco. But now, nephew, I am advanced in years [older] and can no longer take care of all this. I wish, if it please God, that you would come to this land. . . . I am married here to a woman very much to my taste. And though there in Spain it might shock you that I have married an Indian woman, here one loses nothing of his honor, because the Indians are a nation held in much esteem [honor and respect] . . . [S]he is of the opinion that if God our Lord brings you to this land, we should leave you our property. . . .
— from *Letters and People of the Spanish Indies*, edited by James Lickhart et. al.

From this letter, what was important in life to Agric? What values do you share with him?

Government of New Spain How did Spain govern its colonies in the New World?

6. New Spain included Mexico, Central America, and a large part of North America. Find New Spain on the map on page 160. The heart of New Spain was Mexico. In some areas of New Spain, Spanish settlers and Native Americans lived and worked together. Mexico City, for example, had a large population of both Native American and Spanish settlers. In other communities, there were few Spanish settlers, and the Native Americans knew very little about the Spanish.

7. The Spanish king kept tight control over his empire in the New World through a group of governors and judges. He appointed a **viceroy**, or governor, to rule New Spain. The viceroy carried out royal laws, was in charge of the military, controlled the treasury, and watched over local matters. Under the viceroy were regional governors and five **audiencias** (ow-dee-en-SEE-ahs), or courts made up of committees of judges.

A Powerful Influence What role did the Catholic Church play in New Spain?

8. The conquistadores came to American for gold, but the priests of the Catholic Church came to save souls. The priests succeeded because they explained Christianity to Native Americans in a way they could understand and accept. Some ideas from native religions mixed together with Catholic beliefs and changes in both happened. The Spanish priests came to believe that the Aztec god Quetzalcoatl was the apostle Thomas. They believed that Thomas came to the New World to lead Native Americans to Jesus. Likewise, Mexicans believed that some Catholic saints were their local gods. For example, the Mexican "Our Lady Spirit" became the patron saint of Mexico—the Virgin of Guadalupe.

Background: By 1742, the population of Mexico was divided as follows: peninsulares—9,814; criollos—391,512; mestizos—249,368; Indians—1,540,256; blacks—20,131; mixed black & Spanish or black and Indian—266,196. Unlike slaves in the English colonies, those in New Spain had the right to choose their spouses and to marry.

9. Much of the priests' success happened because they taught that faith and honest belief were more important than formal practices. Their understanding attitude and acceptance of Native American practices helped them to try to change the cruel Spanish policies of encomienda you read about in Unit 2.

10. Because of its many activities, the church was a major force in colonial life. The missions often were the center of community life. Church officials advised members of the government. Priests and nuns converted Native Americans. Priests and nuns ran hospitals and took care of orphans. In addition, the church owned huge amounts of land and had the right to collect special taxes to support its work.

11. The church also brought Spanish culture to the New World. The church paid artists to create paintings and statues to decorate churches and other religious buildings. The church directed education. Spanish schools

taught children of all races. In 1551, the church also set up the first university in the Americas in Mexico City. What are the advantages and ◄ disadvantages of a church or religious group having so much power and influence?

People in History

12. **Juana Inés de Abasje** At the age of three, Juana Inés de Abasje (HWAH-nah ee-NAYS duh ah-BAHS-yeh) could read. By the time she was eight, she had written a short play. Juana Inés de Abasje was born in 1651 in New Spain. By the time she was nine, she was living in Mexico City and writing fine poems in Latin. Juana Inés longed to study at the University of Mexico, but women were not allowed. She decided to study on her own. At age 16, she was invited to be a lady-in-waiting to the viceroy's wife. The nobles in the viceroy's court were amazed at her learning.

13. Juana Inés did not like being at court. She soon entered a **convent**, a community of nuns, and gave her life to prayer, study, and writing. As Sister Juana Inés de la Cruz, she gathered a huge library of 4,000 books and wrote plays, poems, and essays. She wrote to many educated people throughout Europe and the New World. Her interest in learning and her complaints about unequal treatment of women brought objections from some church leaders. In 1694, she sold her books, gave the money to the poor, and gave her life to her faith. A year later, she died while looking after victims of an illness that swept New Spain. Why do you think ◄ Sister Juana might have protested unequal treatment of women?

▼ Sister Juana Inés, one of the most learned women in New Spain, gave up the life of learning to helping the poor and the ill.

Social Classes How were the people of New Spain divided into social classes?

14. In the years after the Spanish conquest, a class system developed in New Spain with the **peninsulares** (pay-neen-soo-LAH-res) on top. The peninsulares were the settlers who were born in Spain. Only the peninsulare men could have the highest jobs in government and the

Background: Indian peasants, called peons, who worked on haciendas were paid a daily wage, but the wage was so low that they were always in debt to the landowner. Under the law, peons had to stay on the hacienda until they repaid their debts. Since they never earned enough to do so, they were virtually slaves.

158

▲ Mestizos, people of mixed Spanish and Native American background, were the fastest growing group in New Spain in the 1600s and 1700s.

▶ church. Why do you think the Spanish government allowed only Spaniards to hold these jobs?

15. Next came the **criollos** (kree-OH-yohs), or people born in the Americas to Spanish parents. The criollos were often rich landowners or lawyers, doctors, teachers, and priests. Although they lived comfortable lives, criollos were not allowed to hold top government or ▶ church jobs. If you had been a criollo, how would you feel about the class system?

16. The people in the third class were the **mestizos** (mehs-TEE-zohs), or people of mixed Spanish and Native American background. This class grew fast because many Spanish settlers married Native American women. The mestizos made up a lower middle class. Some mestizos were in charge of workers on haciendas, in

mines, and on ranches. Others farmed their own land or were store owners in the towns.

17. The great majority of people in New Spain were Native Americans. They ranked low in the class system. Many Native Americans worked on the land owned by peninsulares and criollos or in the missions run by the Church. Many others lived in their villages, farming as they had for hundreds of years.

18. As the Native American population grew smaller in the 1500s, the Spanish brought slaves from Africa to work their land. From 1519 to 1605 the Native American population in New Spain dropped from about 25 million to one million. Forced labor and disease were the main reasons. The Native Americans died from diseases such as smallpox and measles brought by the Spanish. African slaves ranked lower than the Native Americans in the class system. On sugar plantations in the Caribbean, there were more slaves than whites or mestizos. However, after slaves were brought to New Spain, another class of people arose. They were called **mulattoes,** and they were born of African and Spanish parents. Mulattoes ranked higher than the slaves but lower than the mestizos.

Outlook

19. Before England and France started their small, starving colonies in North America, New Spain had successful cities, a system of missions, several universities, and a literary and artistic culture of its own. The culture of New Spain, like that of Mexico today, was a mix of Native American and Spanish customs, language, ideas, and dress. Because of the large Native American population, the emerging culture also blended many Native American traditions and beliefs. However, it was a society that was also cruel to human beings. It existed because of forced labor by Native Americans Then, after the Native Americans died off from disease and overwork, slaves imported from Africa did the work. For New Spain, this cruel practice caused problems in later times. What sort of problem would you expect this practice to cause?

Ask: How was a hacienda in New Spain similar to a plantation in the Southern Colonies?

159

CHAPTER REVIEW

VOCABULARY REVIEW

▶ Match each word in Column 1 with the correct definition in Column 2. Number your paper and write the correct letter by each number.

Column 1

1. ranchos
2. mulattoes
3. mantas
4. convent
5. viceroy
6. audiencias
7. peninsulares
8. criollos
9. mestizos
10. haciendas
11. hacendados
12. vaqueros
13. self-sufficient

Column 2

a. a community of nuns
b. people of Spanish and African parents
c. large areas where cattle were raised
d. blankets woven by Native Americans
e. large estates
f. oil
g. people of mixed Spanish and Indian background
h. governor
i. Spanish-born people in New Spain
j. courts made up of committees of judges
k. people descended from Spanish settlers
l. growing or making everything that people living in a place need
m. landowners
n. cowboys

SKILL BUILDER: READING A MAP

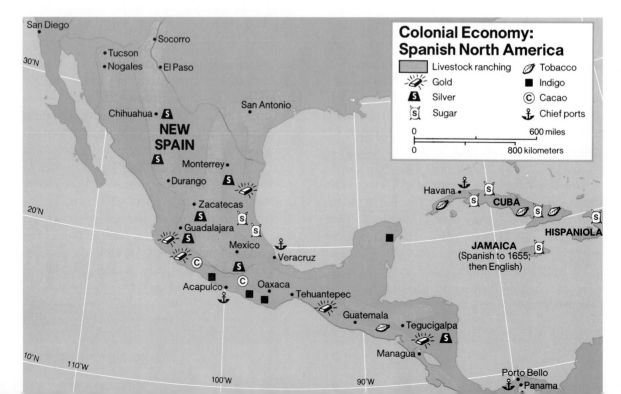

The Economy of Colonial Spanish North America

▶ Study the map on the opposite page. Then answer these questions.

1. The land in the interior of New Spain is use to produce what product?

2. What are the two types of mining done in New Spain?

3. What is produced near Zacatecas?

4. Why was Veracruz an important city?

SKILL BUILDER: CRITICAL THINKING AND COMPREHENSION

▶ **I. Drawing Conclusions**

▶ Read these facts. Then decide which conclusion fits the facts best. Write the facts and your conclusion on a separate sheet of paper.

Facts

1. Priests and nuns taught in schools.

2. Church officials advised members of government.

3. The church owned huge amounts of land.

Conclusions

a. Many cities were named after Spaniards.

b. The church was a major force in the colonial life of New Spain.

1. Many Native Americans worked on land owned by criollos or church-run missions.

2. Native Americans died of disease, hunger, and overwork.

3. Spanish rulers granted encomiendas, which included Native American laborers.

a. The colony of New Spain existed for the benefit of the parent country.

b. Native Americans ranked low in the social class of New Spain.

USING PRIMARY SOURCES

▶ Read Spotlight on Sources on page 157. If you were Andre Agric's nephew, would you travel to the New World to take over the business? Give your reasons why or why not.

ENRICHMENT

1. Many priests and nuns were horrified at the terrible death rate among the Indians and their treatment at the hands of the conquistadors. Imagine you are a priest or a nun, and write a letter to King Charles I of Spain urging him to pass reforms.

2. With group of three or four others, research life on a hacienda. Look in books and encyclopedias for information. Write a script for an eyewitness news report about life on a hacienda in New Spain. Present the news program to the class.

CHAPTER 7

Colonial Life on the Frontier

OBJECTIVE: How did pioneers adapt to life on the frontier?

1. The young man watched as another line of wagons lumbered west from Philadelphia, Pennsylvania. Those high covered wagons could carry four to six tons of goods. Their tall wheels allowed the wagons to cross rain-swollen streams and bump over rough roads. He admired the bright blue sides with red trim, the jangling bells, and the teams of strong horses. He knew that another group was on its way to the backcountry. Some day, he imagined, he too might be one of those heading west in a covered wagon.

The Frontier   What was the frontier?

2. Land west of the colonial settlements was called the frontier. In 1700, the English colonies were in only a narrow strip of land along the Atlantic coast of North America. The boundaries of the colonies were not clear. To the west lay thousands of miles of forests, mountains, and plains. Although the colonists thought of this land as unsettled land, many Native American tribes lived on this land. Many colonists thought that the frontier would be too hard to settle mainly because the Appalachian Mountains were a huge barrier. Yet Native Americans had been crossing the Appalachian ► Mountains for hundreds of years. Why do you think the colonists thought of Native American lands as unsettled?

▲ Women did their share of the hard work of running a home on the western frontier. Even supplying a family's water needs was not easy. How did this family draw water from its well?

Moving Westward   What brought colonists into the lonely wilderness before 1776?

3. Colonists came to the frontier for reasons such as adventure and a desire for more land. Some settlers simply wanted to find out what

In Chapter 7 you will apply these critical thinking skills to the historical process:
❯ **Predicting:** Telling what you believe will happen on the basis of clues and facts

◩ **Comparing and Contrasting:** Recognizing similarities and differences.

lay beyond the next hill or valley. Others thought they could have a better life where they would be able to choose the land they wanted. Many younger sons moved west because they would not inherit the family land in the East. Because colonial farming methods wore out the soil, many people moved west to start again on fertile land. Still others wanted to get away from settled areas which they thought were too crowded.

4. By the 1700s, the pioneers were settling the Piedmont region, also known as the backcountry. As you may recall, the Piedmont is rolling land between the coastal plains and the Appalachian Mountains. One of the most important early pioneers who settled in the Piedmont Region of North Carolina was Daniel Boone. It was Daniel Boone who learned the secret of crossing the Appalachians.

People in History

5. Daniel Boone A wanderer, a pathfinder, a bold wilderness man, Daniel Boone was always searching for new places to explore and settle. By the time he died, he had lived in what are today the states of Pennsylvania, North Carolina, Virginia, Kentucky, West Virginia, and Missouri. Boone was born of Quaker parents in a log cabin in Pennsylvania in 1734. While growing up, he learned a great deal about hunting from friendly Native Americans who lived nearby. As Pennsylvania grew more crowded, Boone and his family decided to move to the frontier in North Carolina.

6. It was from North Carolina, in 1769, that Boone set out on one of his many explorations. For a long time he had wanted to find a way to the lands beyond the Appalachians. He had heard that those lands were full of beaver, flocks of turkeys, herds of buffalo, and other game. He also had heard of a Native American trail called the Warrior's Path. Boone and his partners found the Warrior's Path, which led them to the **Cumberland Gap**. The Cumberland Gap is an opening through the Cumberland Mountains. Find the Cumberland Gap on the map on page

164. In 1775, Boone led a group of settlers through the Cumberland Gap into the land today called Kentucky. He and a group of men built a fort and cabins and named it Boonesborough.

Frontier Roads   How did roads help open up the frontier?

7. In colonial days, roads were rough, narrow, and slow. Many followed old Native American trails and were hardly more than paths through the wilderness. Rocks and tree stumps dotted the way. Wagons could not get through the roads in winter because of the ice and snow. In spring, wagons sank axle deep into the mud. Often, settlers traveled by boat or canoe along rivers and streams rather than suffer life on the road.

8. By the 1750s, probably the most useful road was the **Great Wagon Road**. It ran west from Philadelphia in Pennsylvania to Lancaster. Then it turned south to York and into the Piedmont region of Virginia and North Carolina. Hundreds of pioneers took the Wagon Road to settle the Piedmont Region of Virginia, North Carolina, and South Carolina. A second road that pushed back the frontier was the **Wilderness Road** blazed by Daniel Boone. The Wilderness Road opened the way for the settlement of the **Old Southwest**, the present-day states of Kentucky and Tennessee.

Frontier Life   What problems did frontier families face?

9. Life on the frontier offered only a few benefits. Land was cheap. There was no shortage of wood for building and fuel. Game was plentiful, and frontier families hunted for the food they put on the table. However, hardships on the frontier were many. Parents and children worked from dawn to dusk. Frontier settlements seldom had schools. The only medical care was the knowledge the settlers had themselves or what they had learned from friendly Native American tribes.

The Appalachian Mountains The Appalachian Mountains are located between the Piedmont Region on the east and the Central Lowland on the west. Today people drive across the Appalachian on interstate highways in less than four hours. Jet airplanes fly over this mountain range in minutes. Early pioneers, however, found the Appalachian Mountains a more difficult barrier to cross.

The Appalachians extend in a southwest-northeast direction from central Alabama to Quebec in Canada. They are about 1,200 miles (1,920 km) long and between 200 and 300 miles (160 and 480 km) wide. Lowlands along the Hudson and Mohawk rivers are the only lowland gap. The French and the Native Americans controlled this natural opening until the 1760s.

The Appalachian Mountains are not the highest mountain range in the United States. Many parts rise only between 1,000 and 1,500 feet (305 and 475 m) above sea level. Even Mt. Mitchell, the highest point, is only 6,684 feet (2,037 m) high.

Rows of long narrow ridges along the spine of the Appalachian Mountains make east–west travel difficult. The ridges, which run from southwest to northeast, blocked the path of westward-moving pioneers. The Appalachian Mountains were also difficult to cross because they are a "divide." The uplands separate rivers flowing to the Atlantic Ocean from rivers flowing to the Gulf of Mexico. Early pioneers could follow the rivers inland to their source or "headwaters." Then they had to cross up and over the divide to find river valleys leading to the west.

One well-travelled pioneer route followed the Susquehannah River and its tributaries inland. The route then crossed over to the headwaters of the Ohio River. Another early pioneer route followed the Potomac River and then went south along the Shenandoah River or north toward the Ohio River. Many pioneers from the Southern colonies travelled inland along the Roanoke and James rivers. They crossed the divide to headwaters of the Cumberland and Tennessee rivers.

Now use the map below to answer these questions.

1. What rivers flowing to the Atlantic Ocean begin near headwaters of the Ohio River?

2. Why did American pioneers face more difficulties traveling west than French pioneers living along the St. Lawrence River?

3. In what ways do you think the Appalachian barrier affected American history?

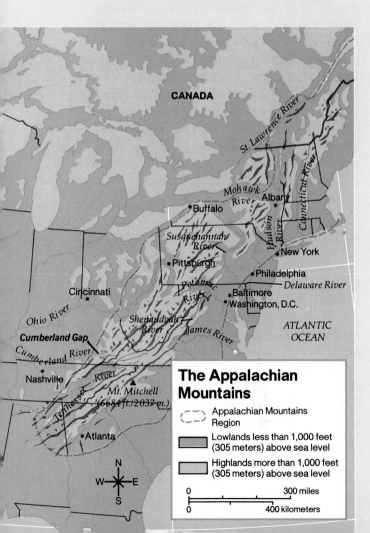

The Appalachian Mountains

- - - Appalachian Mountains Region

☐ Lowlands less than 1,000 feet (305 meters) above sea level

☐ Highlands more than 1,000 feet (305 meters) above sea level

0 — 300 miles
0 — 400 kilometers

▲ This family is resting after a hard day of making its way through the Appalachians in a covered wagon. Hundreds of families like this one headed west in a search for land and a better life.

10. The frontier was sometimes a violent place. The westward move of white settlers pushed the Native Americans from their lands. More and more Native American tribes fought back to save their land. In Kentucky, for example, the Shawnee tribe attacked pioneers to stop them from settling on their land. What do you think you would have thought about the pioneers if you had been a Shawnee?

Spotlight on Sources

11. Settlers had to be sturdy and self-reliant. In 1711, the Reverend John Urmstone moved to the backcountry of North Carolina. In a letter home he described what life was like on the frontier.

I am forced to work hard with axe, hoe, and spade. I have not a stick to burn for any use but what I cut down with my own hands. I am forced to dig a garden, raise beans, peas, etc. . . . He or she that cannot do all these things . . . will have but a bad time of it; for help is not to be had. . . .

What tasks does the writer have to perform? ◄ How can you tell that he is not used to doing this kind of work?

Frontier Democracy   How did life on the frontier break down social barriers?

12. The demands of frontier life broke down social barriers. In the East, there was a system of social classes based on money and on who a person's parents were. On the frontier, everybody had to work hard. They did not expect others to wait on them. How might this social equality contribute to a democratic spirit?

Outlook

13. The frontier movement had important effects on American society. If the government tried to force too much control over the lives of the pioneers, they resisted or they moved on. As you will learn in Unit 5, this growing spirit of independence would clash with British plans and goals for the colonies.

Background: Because iron was scarce, families saved the nails from their homes when they moved on to new ones. They often burned down their old homes (wood was plentiful) and then collected the nails from the ashes.

165

CHAPTER REVIEW

VOCABULARY REVIEW

► Fill in the blanks with the vocabulary word that correctly completes each sentence.

Cumberland Gap   Wilderness Road   Appalachian Trail

Great Wagon Road   Old Southwest

1. The _____ is an opening in the mountains with Kentucky on the other side.

2. Daniel Boone helped blaze the _____ by following an old Native American path.

3. The states of Kentucky and Tennessee were once known as the _____ .

4. Farmers used the _____ to send crops from western Pennsylvania to Philadelphia.

SKILL BUILDER: STUDYING FOR A TEST

Many of you may worry when you know you must take a test. However, if you study ahead of time and are prepared, it is not difficult to succeed in taking your tests. The first step in studying well is knowing what you need to study. Usually your teacher will tell you ahead of time what subjects will be covered on a test. It is important to begin studying about a week ahead of time. Then you will not be nervous or miss anything.

Try to resist the temptation to turn on the television or call a friend when it is time to study. You will gain much more from your study time if you do it while you are alert, rather than waiting until it is past your bedtime. Find the quietest place possible so that you will not be disturbed. Following these simple rules will help you take the best advantage of your study time.

► Write an outline about the topics that will be on the test. This will guide you as you begin to study. Collect the books, notes, and materials you need. Set aside a certain period of time each day to study. Try to make up sample tests and questions and answer them. Look up the correct answers to any question you are unsure about. You may need to ask your teacher to explain any answer you do not understand. Exchange sample tests with a friend for additional practice.

1. Make up a sample test for Chapter 7. Include the following:
   a. multiple choice questions
   b. matching exercises
   c. fill-in-the-blank questions
   d. essay questions.

2. Write an answer key.

3. Exchange your test with that of a classmate and take the test.

4. Correct your partner's test.

5. You and your partner should review the incorrect answers and determine which areas of the chapter you need to restudy.

SKILL BUILDERS: CRITICAL THINKING AND COMPREHENSION

I. Compare and Contrast

1. Compare the life of a pioneer to the life of a wealthy Southern plantation owner and to the life of a slave. After you have copied and completed the chart, write a paragraph explaining which life style you would have preferred and why.

	Pioneer	Plantation Owner	Slave
Homes			
Food			
Work			
Dangers			
Social Class			

2. Compare the Great Wagon Road and the forms of transportation used on it to the interstate highways of today. What are the advantages and disadvantages of each type of travel? What do you think the highways of the future will be like?

II. Introduction to Predicting

Have you ever looked up at the sky on a cold, gray day? You may have thought to yourself that snow was sure to fall. What you were doing was predictiong, or guessing what might happen next. Predicting is a critical thinking skill of guessing what will happen based on facts and clues that you know. For example, the cold and the gray clouds were clues that you recognized that helped you predict snow.

▶ Reread paragraphs 1, 7, and 8 carefully. Then make a prediction about what a trip west along one of the frontier roads would be like. Write your prediction on a sheet of paper. List three clues or facts you used to make the prediction.

ENRICHMENT

1. Many songs and poems have been written about Daniel Boone. Read more about Boone's childhood and his career as a frontiersman. Then write a song or poem about some incident in his life.

2. Imagine you and your family are about to leave your farm in Virginia to head west in 1770. In a group, make a list of the goods you will take with you. Then research what the pioneers actually took to see how well you prepared for your "journey."

167

UNIT REVIEW

SUMMARY

In the 1600s and 1700s, settlers poured into the thirteen English colonies. Most of the newcomers were farmers. They learned to adjust to the climate and soil of the land, whether in New England, the Middle Colonies, or the South.

In order to make profits from its colonies, England passed laws that regulated colonial trade. Despite the laws, colonies prospered from trade in fish, lumber, and other goods.

Each of the thirteen colonies developed its own way of life. Religion was a powerful force in the early colonies. Although colonial governments varied, each colony had its own governor and an assembly made up of elected representatives.

By the 1700s, settlers were pushing west across the Appalachian Mountains. While the English colonies expanded along the Atlantic seaboard, settlers from France and Spain developed their own ways of life in New France and New Spain. For many years, the fur trade dominated the life of New France. New Spain included a huge area extending from Mexico through present-day California. In both colonies, the Catholic Church played an important role.

As these three groups grew and prospered, it became inevitable that conflicts would develop between them. Problems brewing in Europe would spill over into the Americas. An unforeseen result of these conflicts was the colonists' growing dissatisfaction with the mother country.

SKILL BUILDER: READING A MAP

▶ Use the map below to answer the following questions:

1. New Spain is represented by what color on the map?

2. What European nation controlled the least amount of territory in 1750?

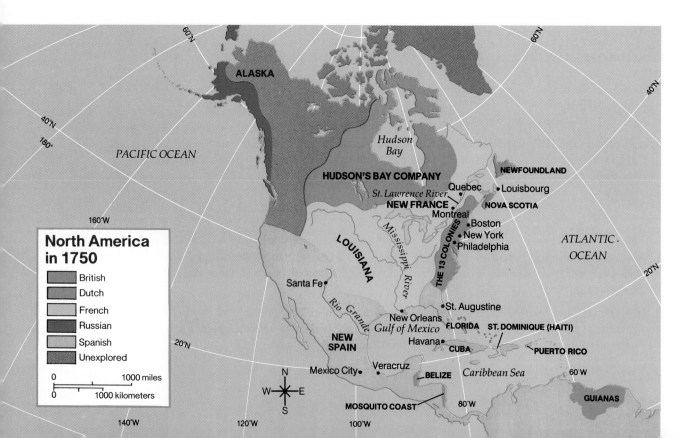

3. Which country claimed land on both the Atlantic and Pacific coasts?

4. Which nation claimed most of the great river valleys?

SKILL BUILDER: CRITICAL THINKING AND COMPREHENSION

I. Main Idea

▶ Read the sentences in each group below. Decide which sentence in each group is the main idea and which sentences are details about that idea. Write each group of sentences on your paper with the main idea first and the details below.

1. The sentences in this group are about religion in the colonies.
 a. New Spain was greatly influenced by the Roman Catholic Church.
 b. The New England Colonies did not allow religious freedom for all citizens.
 c. In Pennsylvania, all citizens who believed in Jesus were allowed to worship freely.
 d. All thirteen colonies had Blue Laws that prohibited work on Sunday.
 e. Religous beliefs were very important in the colonnies of the New World.

2. The sentences in this group are about the economy.
 a. Fur trappers in New France collected furs to be sent to Europe.
 b. Trade was an important source of income for American colonies.
 c. New England sent dried fish to many European nations.
 d. Spain imported silver and other products from her colonies in the New World.
 e. Great Britain wanted forest products and tobacco from the thirteen colonies.

II. Classifying

▶ Classify each of the following items according to whether it has to do with New England, the Middle Colonies, the Southern Colonies, New France, or New Spain. Some items may relate to more than one group of colonies.

fur trading	cash crops	strict social classes	tobacco
farming	religious tolerance	triangle trade	mining
royal colony	Roman Catholic Church	slavery	indigo
education	large farms/plantations	whaling	colleges

ENRICHMENT

1. Work with a group of three of four other students. You will write a television news program about the colonies of the New World. You will need to present "current events," business news, special features about daily life, and an interview with a real or imaginary settler.

2. Imagine that you are a spy sent by your government to discover the strengths and weaknesses of all the colonies developing in the New World. Write a secret communique to your leaders that tells what you have uncovered. Be sure you evaluate the government, the economy, and the way of life for you report.

169

UNIT 5

AMERICA WINS INDEPENDENCE

Chapter

UNIT OVERVIEW   Unit 5 will help you understand what caused the 13 colonies to turn against Great Britain and fight to win their rights as an independent nation.

UNIT SKILLS OBJECTIVES   In Unit 5, three critical thinking skills are emphasized:

▶ **Drawing Conclusions:** Making a statement that explains the facts and evidence.

❭ **Predicting:** Telling what you think will happen on the basis of clues and facts.

⊿ **Identifying Fact versus Opinion:** Specifying whether information can be proved or whether it expresses feelings or beliefs.

You will also use two important social studies skills:
Using Time Lines   Reading a Bar Graph

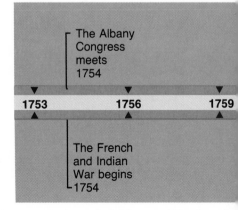

The Albany Congress meets 1754

1753   1756   1759

The French and Indian War begins 1754

ESL/LEP Strategy: Have teams of students preview the unit to identify a person to be studied. After completing the unit, they should discuss the person's accomplishments and prepare an oral report comparing that person with an historic figure from their country of origin or of that of family members.

▲ The British suffered heavy losses at the Battle of Bunker Hill, the first major battle of the American Revolution.

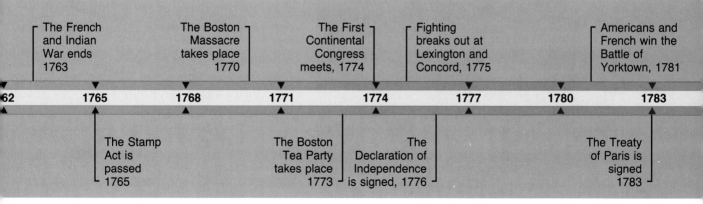

The French and Indian War ends 1763

The Boston Massacre takes place 1770

The First Continental Congress meets, 1774

Fighting breaks out at Lexington and Concord, 1775

Americans and French win the Battle of Yorktown, 1781

62   1765   1768   1771   1774   1777   1780   1783

The Stamp Act is passed 1765

The Boston Tea Party takes place 1773

The Declaration of Independence is signed, 1776

The Treaty of Paris is signed 1783

Points of View

The people of Great Britain had struggled for hundreds of years to limit the power of their kings. By the 1700s, the lawmaking body in England called Parliament was more powerful than the king. One of Parliament's most important powers was the power to pass tax laws. The American colonists

▲ The Stamp Act was the beginning of Britain's efforts to tax the colonies. Here colonists burn stamps as a protest against the Stamp Act.

NO TAXES BUT WITH THEIR OWN CONSENT

❝ The Congress . . . esteem it [believe it is] our . . . duty to make the following declarations . . . respecting [about] the . . . rights and liberties of the colonists. . . .

That His Majesty's . . . subjects in these colonies are entitled to all the . . . rights and liberties of his natural born subjects within the kingdom of Great Britain.

That it is . . . essential to the freedom of a people, and the undoubted right of Englishmen, that no taxes should be imposed [placed] on them, but [except] with their own consent [agreement], given personally or by their representatives.

That the people of these colonies are not, and . . . cannot be represented in [Parliament]. . . That the only representatives of the people of these colonies are persons chosen therein [in the colonies] by themselves; and that no taxes ever have been, or can be constitutionally [lawfully] imposed on them but [except] by their respective [own] legislatures [lawmaking bodies]. ❞

Henry Steele Commager, ed. Documents of American History (N.Y.: Appleton, Century, Crofts, 1971)

believed that their rights as British citizens meant that only their lawmaking bodies, the colonial assemblies, had the right to tax them. In 1765 the 13 colonies sent members to the Stamp Act Congress. The Congress forcefully stated the colonists' point of view, which the king soon rejected.

SUBJECTS TO THE CROWN OF GREAT BRITAIN

"Be it declared. . . . That the . . . colonies . . . in America have been, are, and of right ought to be, subordinate unto [under the power of] and dependent upon the imperial crown [the king] and Parliament of Great Britain. And that . . . Parliament . . . had, has, and by right ought to have, full power and authority to make laws . . . to bind [keep] the colonies and people of America subjects to the crown [king] of Great Britain in all cases whatsoever.

And be it further declared . . . that all resolutions, votes, order, and proceedings, in any of the said colonies . . . whereby [in which] the power and authority of the Parliament of Great Britain to make laws . . . is denied [rejected] or drawn into question, are, and are hereby declared to be, utterly [completely] null and void [of no value] to all intents and purposes [for any purpose] whatsoever."

Henry Steel Commager, ed. Documents of American History (N.Y.: Appleton, Century, Crofts, 1971)

▲ George III was king of Great Britain during the American Revolution. To colonists he symbolized the injustice of British rule.

Using Primary Sources

1. Why did the colonists believe so strongly in the idea of "no taxation without representation"?

2. Why was the English government so strongly against the idea of "no taxation without representation"?

3. What do you think could happen because the colonists and England held such very different points of view?

173

CHAPTER 1

The French and British Fight

OBJECTIVE: Why did rival claims to western land lead to war between the French and the British colonists?

1. Deep in the wilderness, 800 French soldiers and 400 Native American warriors had the tiny British force of 150 men surrounded. The British were led by a 22-year-old American colonel. The British force had gone west from Virginia into the Ohio Valley to find out what the French were doing there. They learned that the French had a large fort called Fort Duquesne in the area. The young American officer had hurriedly ordered his men to build a small fort. Now they were huddled behind its walls as musket fire ripped into them. Then rain began to fall and the fort flooded. The colonel, barking out commands, slogged through the deep mud over wounded and dying men. His force was doomed, and he knew it. With great relief the colonel accepted the French commander's offer to let him and his men surrender and return to Virginia. The young colonel's name was George Washington.

▲ George Washington battled the French near Fort Duquesne three times during the French and Indian War.

Rival land claims How did the struggle for the Ohio Valley lead to war between France and Britain?

2. Great Britain and France were the two most powerful nations in Europe in the 1700s with important colonies in North America. **New France** covered a much larger area than Britain's 13 colonies. It included Canada and the land around the Great Lakes. France also claimed all the land west of the Appalachian Mountains. This land reached from the Ohio Valley to the Gulf of Mexico and as far west as the Rocky Mountains.

3. The French carried on a rich trade in beaver fur and other furs. This trade brought

In Chapter 1 you will apply these critical thinking skills to the historical process:
❯ **Predicting:** Telling what you think will happen on the basis of clues and facts.
▶ **Drawing Conclusions:** Making a statement that explains the facts and evidence.

large profits to the French traders and the French king. To protect this trade, France in the 1750s sent more soldiers to America and built new forts in the Ohio Valley.

4. Britain's colonies also were interested in the Ohio Valley and took steps to claim it for themselves. In Virginia and Pennsylvania, colonial families had begun to move across the Appalachians to settle in these western lands. They were encouraged to move there by **land companies**. Land companies bought western land and sold it to people who wanted to settle there. British fur traders also began to move into the Ohio Valley. As more and more British colonists entered the region, the threat of a showdown between France and Britain grew.

France against Britain   What advantages did each side have in fighting the French and Indian War?

5. Britain and France did not declare war until 1756, but fighting had begun in the Ohio

Valley in 1754 near Fort Duquesne. In Europe this war between Britain and France was called the Seven Years War. In North America the war became known as the **French and Indian War**. Each country had reasons to think that it would win the war.

6. The French had a well-trained army with a skilled commander. In addition, the French had as allies most of the Native American tribes in North America. Most of the Native Americans distrusted the British colonists, for they knew the colonists wanted to settle in their lands. The French trappers, on the other hand, did not threaten the Native Americans' lands or way of life. In what ways could these tribes aid the French?

7. Though New France was huge, only 80,000 French settlers lived there. This was a disadvantage in the war. Except for Montreal and Quebec in Canada, there were few settlements. Instead, trading posts and army forts were scattered hundreds of miles apart. Defending New France would be difficult.

MAP SKILL BUILDER: A map key explains the meaning of the colors and symbols used on a map. Always study the key before looking at a map such as the one below.   **1.** What color stands for French lands about 1750?   **2.** What areas on the map have the most forts? Why?

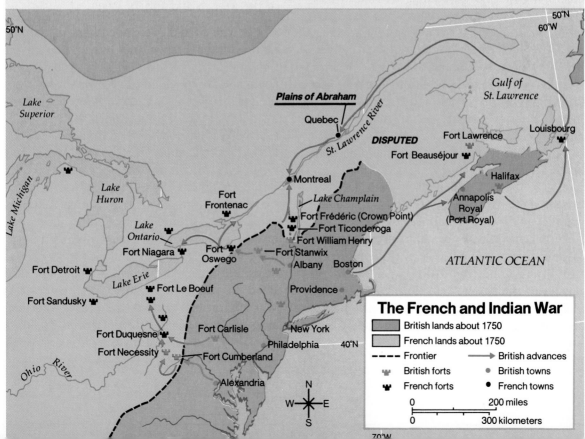

The French and Indian War

- British lands about 1750
- French lands about 1750
- ---- Frontier
- → British advances
- ⚜ British forts
- ● British towns
- ⚜ French forts
- ● French towns

0 — 200 miles
0 — 300 kilometers

8. Great Britain had more colonists, some Native American support, and a powerful navy. Great Britain's colonists greatly outnumbered the French. The 13 colonies had a population of more than 1 million people who would fight to defend their families and their colonies. Although most groups of Native Americans supported the French, the powerful Iroquois nation supported the British. In addition, Britain's large navy controlled the Atlantic. In this way, Britain was able to prevent France from sending more troops to America.

9. The British colonies were not united as they went into the war. The 13 colonies had often quarreled with one another about their boundaries and their claims to western land. Each colony was concerned with its own problems and took little interest in the other colonies. How would this lack of unity be a disadvantage in a war with the French?

People in History

10. Benjamin Franklin Even before war was declared, Benjamin Franklin suggested a plan to help the 13 colonies unite. For years, colonists had enjoyed reading Franklin's *Poor Richard's Almanac.* This book each year gave useful information on farming and the weather. It also was full of clever sayings, like "Early to bed and early to rise makes a man healthy, wealthy, and wise." In addition, Franklin was known for his inventions and scientific experiments. He was the first person to prove that lightning is a form of electricity. A self-taught man, Franklin was one of the outstanding leaders in the colonies.

11. In 1754, at Albany, New York, Franklin proposed the **Albany Plan of Union** to join the colonies under one government. The idea for this joint government was borrowed from the Iroquois nation. The government would command the **militia** (mih-LISH-uh) in each colony. The militia was a volunteer army that helped defend the colonies. The government also would collect taxes from the colonies to pay for the militia.

Spotlight on Sources

12. This is how Franklin explained the purpose of the Albany Plan of Union:

". . . A union of the colonies is certainly necessary to us all. A voluntary [freely chosen] union entered into by the colonies themselves, I think, would be preferable to [better than] one imposed [required] by Parliament. Were there a general council formed by all the colonies, everything relating to the defense of the colonies might properly be put under its management [control]."

The Papers of Benjamin Franklin,
Leonard Labaree, ed.

13. The colonies turned down the Albany Plan. Franklin hoped the Albany Plan would strengthen the colonies to fight the coming war. However, the colonial assemblies were not willing to give up their power. Each colony insisted on keeping its right to tax itself and control its own affairs. As a result, the British colonies would not join together to fight the French.

Fighting the War What were the major battles of the French and Indian War?

14. The French were successful in the first battles of the French and Indian War in the Ohio Valley. In July 1755, a British army commanded by General Edward Braddock headed for Fort Duquesne. Braddock's army included a force of 500 colonial soldiers led by George Washington. General Braddock had just arrived from Britain. He did not know how wars were fought on the American frontier. Braddock ignored Washington's warning that the French troops and their Native American allies would attack from behind trees and bushes. Braddock insisted on marching his soldiers in their bright red uniforms into open fields. He expected the British soldiers to then stand in rows and shoot at the enemy. As Washington had warned, the French and their allies made a surprise attack. General Braddock was killed, and most of his army was destroyed.

Background: Franklin based his Albany Plan partly on the organization of the six Iroquois nations. The Iroquois Confederation, or league, included the Seneca, Mohawk, Onondaga, Oneida, Cayuga, and Tuscarora. The close cooperation of their chiefs in keeping peace among these tribes and working together in their own defense also probably later influenced the framers of the Constitution.

176

Washington then took command and ordered what was left of the British army to retreat. After this defeat and for another two years, France seemed to be winning the war.

15. In 1757, a new leader named William Pitt took charge of Britain's government and helped turn around the war. Pitt chose able new generals and increased the size of the army. He promised that Britain would pay the colonies for their costs of fighting the war. Pitt's efforts turned the war in Britain's favor. During 1758 and 1759, the British armies won several important victories. First, Fort Duquesne finally was captured. Soon after, General James Wolfe captured Louisbourg, France's main outpost in northeastern Canada.

16. The deciding battle of the war took place at Quebec, the capital of New France. There, in September 1759, Wolfe's army faced the larger French forces led by General Louis de Mont-

calm (mahnt-KAHM). After sneaking up a cliff at night, the British army launched a surprise attack and overwhelmed the French. Both Wolfe and Montcalm were killed in this battle. The capture of Quebec meant that Britain had won the war. However, the fighting lasted another year, until Montreal fell to the British. In 1763, France and Britain signed the peace treaty that formally ended the French and Indian War.

Results of the War What lands did Britain gain, and how did the war affect the American colonists?

17. Britain's victory in the war gained it a huge new empire in North America. France was forced to give up nearly all of its territory in America. Britain now ruled Canada and all the land east of the Mississippi River except New Orleans. This land included Florida, which Britain got from France's ally Spain. New Orleans and the large territory of Louisiana west of the Mississippi were given to Spain. What problems ◄ do you think Britain might have in ruling its great new empire?

18. The British colonists gained from the war in several important ways. They had learned new ways of fighting and winning battles. More important, the colonists were no longer surrounded by French and Spanish colonies. The western lands were open to settlement. British colonists could now look forward to moving into the Ohio Valley.

Outlook

22. The 13 colonies had not been able to unite to fight against the French. They had depended on Great Britain to provide the armies and weapons needed to win the French and Indian War. As a result of the war, Britain's empire in North America now doubled in size. How do you think the colonists felt when ◄ the war ended? Do you think Britain might now decide to change the way it ruled the 13 colonies?

▼ By climbing this steep bluff near Quebec, Wolfe's troops surprised the French. The battle that followed lasted less than 15 minutes.

CHAPTER REVIEW

VOCABULARY REVIEW

Write each number and term on a sheet of paper. Then write the letter of the definition next to the term it defines.

1. land companies
2. Albany Plan of Union
3. New France
4. militia
5. French and Indian War

a. Canada, the land around the Great Lakes, and the land west of the Appalachian Mountains

b. Conflict between Great Britain and France in North America

c. Proposal for the colonies to join together under one government

d. Volunteer army

e. Companies that bought western land and sold it to people who wanted to settle there

f. British army

SKILL BUILDER: OUTLINING

The following is an incomplete outline about the advantages and disadvantages of each side in fighting the French and Indian War. Copy the outline on a sheet of paper. Then fill in the blanks with subheads or supporting details from the list below. Refer to paragraphs 6–9 in this chapter if you need help.

Defending the area would be difficult

Problems the British faced

Iroquois nation supported them

Had a well-trained army with a skilled commander

I. Advantages and disadvantages of each side in the French and Indian War
   A. Reasons the French thought they could win the war
      1. _____
      2. Native American tribes were their allies.
   B. Problems the French faced
      1. There were only 80,000 settlers in New France.
      2. _____

C. Great Britain's advantages in North America
   1. Its colonists outnumbered those of the French.
   2. _____
   3. Britain's navy controlled the Atlantic.
D. _____
   1. The 13 colonies often quarreled with one another about boundaries and claims to western lands.
   2. To help defend themselves, they would have to learn to work together.

USING PRIMARY SOURCES

Why do you think Benjamin Franklin thought a ". . . voluntary union entered into by the colonies themselves, . . ." would be preferable to one imposed by Parliament."?

SKILL BUILDER: CRITICAL THINKING AND COMPREHENSION

▶ I. Drawing Conclusions

▶ Read each of the following groups of statements. Think carefully about each group. Then, from the list of possible conclusions, choose the conclusion that best fits the facts.

Statements:

1. In 1754, Benjamin Franklin proposed the Albany Plan of Union to unite the colonies under one government.

2. The government created by the Albany Plan of Union would collect taxes from the colonies to pay for a volunteer army.

3. Colonial assemblies were not willing to give up their power to a new joint government.

4. The 13 colonies were not able to unite to fight against the French. They had to depend on Great Britain to provide the armies and weapons needed to fight the French and Indian War.

Possible Conclusions:

a. The rejection of the Albany Plan of Union weakened Britain's hold over the colonies.

b. The rejection of the Albany Plan allowed Britain to have complete leadership in the war.

c. Since the colonies rejected the Albany Plan, it was unlikely that they would ever unite in the future.

❯ II. Predicting

▶ When you predict, you tell what you think will happen in the future. A prediction is not just guesswork. It is most likely to be correct when it is based on facts and clues.

Because Britain won the French and Indian War, its empire in North America doubled in size. The western lands were no longer occupied by French soldiers.

1. What do you think the colonists would want to do now that the war was over?

2. How do you think Native American nations would react?

▶ Write your prediction on a sheet of paper. Tell also what your evidence is. In other words, tell what facts and clues you used in making your prediction.

ENRICHMENT

1. Suppose you are a Native American living in New France. A French trapper approaches your people. He wants you to help France in the war against Britain. How do you feel about fighting in this war? Write about your reactions to what the trapper says.

2. Research Benjamin Franklin's *Poor Richard's Almanac*. Copy some of the sayings that were published in the Almanac. Choose two of these sayings to write down and illustrate on a poster board. Explain to the class why you like these sayings and what they mean to you.

CHAPTER 2

Britain Tightens Its Grip

OBJECTIVE: Why did Great Britain pass laws to tax the colonists and to control colonial trade?

1. Daniel Boone first explored Kentucky in 1767 on a hunting trip. He had always liked to hunt, and he was fascinated by life on the frontier. In fact, 12 years earlier he had served in General Braddock's western army. Boone had then returned to North Carolina, where he married and raised a family. Yet he still was drawn to frontier lands. He went on hunting trips into western Virginia and Tennessee that lasted several months. Finally, in 1769, Boone and some friends set out across the Appalachians to explore Kentucky. He was amazed by the beauty of the forests and the large herds of bison there. He also was sure that its rich soil would make Kentucky a fine home for settlers from back east. Daniel Boone knew that Britain had made it unlawful to settle in these western lands. Even so, he decided to ignore the law and open Kentucky to colonial settlers.

▲ On the frontier west of the Appalachians, settlers cleared the land to plant crops. How might Native Americans feel about this activity?

Peace Returns What were the colonists' hopes when the French and Indian War ended?

2. When the French and Indian War ended in 1763, the colonists looked forward to enjoying the benefits of peace. They had helped Britain win the war. Now they were especially happy that French armies were no longer a danger on their western border. Colonists would now be able to settle in the rich farming land of the Ohio Valley. They also would be able to hunt there for valuable furs. However, problems soon arose between Great Britain and its colonies.

3. The British government had borrowed huge amounts of money to fight the French and Indian War. Its **debt** had doubled as a result.

In Chapter 2 you will apply these critical thinking skills to the historical process:
▶ **Drawing Conclusions:** Making a statement that explains the facts and evidence.
❯ **Predicting:** Telling what you believe will happen on the basis of clues and facts.

Debt is money owed to individuals and banks. In addition, Britain's empire in North America now cost more to govern, because it had grown much larger. Who do you think should have paid these expenses? Where would Britain get the money that it needed? Even before Britain could begin to solve these problems, it faced another serious challenge.

___

Pontiac's Rebellion How did Pontiac's Rebellion cause Britain to issue the Proclamation of 1763?

4. In May 1763, Pontiac, chief of the Ottawa tribe in the Ohio Valley, led an uprising against the British. The Native Americans took this strong action in order to protect their lands. They feared that colonists would cross the Appalachians and seize their lands. To prevent this, they made surprise attacks on British forts along the western frontier. This uprising is known as Pontiac's Rebellion.

People in History

5. Pontiac The leader of the Ottawa nation, Pontiac was a skilled and brave fighter. In 1762 he formed an alliance with the Miami, the Chippewa, the Delaware, and several other Native American nations. In the spring of 1763, Pontiac and his allies attacked and captured eight British forts along the western frontier. However, Pontiac was not able to capture the important fort at Detroit. As a result, some of his allies tired of the fighting and went home. In 1766, Pontiac signed a peace treaty with the British.

6. Pontiac's Rebellion alarmed the British government and forced it to issue the **Proclamation of 1763**. This was an order by King George III that closed off all the lands west of the Appalachians. American colonists were now forbidden to settle in these western lands. Even colonial hunters and fur traders were not allowed there. How would Native Americans benefit from this policy? What would be the advantages to Great Britain?

Spotlight on Sources

7. The Proclamation of 1763 was set forth in these words:

> It is essential to the security of the colonies that the several nations or tribes of Indians [Native Americans] should not be disturbed in territories [lands] reserved to them as their hunting grounds. All the land lying to the westward of the [Appalachians] we do strictly forbid all our subjects [the colonists] from making any purchase or settlement.

However, the British government said the proclamation would last only until peace was made with the Native Americans in the western lands.

8. The Proclamation of 1763 angered the American colonists. They remembered that the colonies had been given these lands in their charters. More important, they did not believe the British government's reasons for this law. Instead, the colonists feared that England was trying to keep them crowded together in the East. How would such a policy be an advantage to Great Britain? Owners of land were especially upset, since they now would not be able to sell their western lands to new settlers. Families that were eager to settle in the West disliked the law even more. Because of the Proclamation of 1763, American colonists began to distrust Britain and its actions in the colonies.

___

Trade Laws What were the Navigation Acts, and why did Britain try to enforce them?

9. King George III, who came to the throne in 1760, was determined to find new ways of obtaining money. Great Britain still had to pay off its large war debt, and it needed money to pay for governing the American colonies. The king chose George Grenville, an expert in money matters, to head the government.

10. George III and Grenville believed that colonists should pay a greater share of the costs of governing their colonies. British taxpayers had paid huge sums to defend the colonies in

Background: The colonists' suspicion that the Proclamation Line was meant to keep them in the East had some merit. Britain was eager to keep the colonies as a market for its manufactured goods. If the colonies spread westward, the cost of transporting goods there might add enough cost to stimulate local manufactures.

181

▲ Thousands of ships carried goods between Great Britain and the colonies. These ships are in the harbor of Charleston, South Carolina.

the war with France. British soldiers had defended the colonies again by putting down Pontiac's Rebellion. Yet a colonial assembly would send its militia and vote funds only when the colony itself was in danger. Even then, Britain still paid most of the costs. Now the colonies must pay a larger share.

11. Grenville decided that one quick way to raise money was to enforce the Navigation Acts. These acts were **trade laws**. Trade laws are laws that control trade with other countries. The Navigation Acts had been passed in the 1600s. They required the colonists to sell certain goods only to Britain. The colonists had to buy all their manufactured goods only from Britain. Certain other products that came from other countries had to go first through Britain. Colonists were supposed to pay taxes on all these ▶ goods. Who benefited most from this kind of trade law?

12. For many years, colonists had broken the Navigation Acts by **smuggling** goods into the colonies. To smuggle is to bring goods in illegally, without paying taxes on them. The

British government had not tried to stop the smuggling, because Britain was getting rich from trade with America even when it did not enforce the laws.

13. Then, in 1764, Grenville sent **customs officers** to the colonies to enforce the Navigation Acts. Customs officers were British officials whose job was to collect taxes on imported goods. They soon began to arrest colonial merchants who were caught smuggling. Merchants arrested as smugglers were then tried by special British courts in the colonies. Grenville also added many products to the list of goods on which taxes had to be paid. By enforcing the Navigation Acts and by making them stronger, Grenville expected to gain more money for Britain. He also wanted to show that Britain was able to control the colonies.

14. Once again, Britain's policies angered many colonists, who believed that Grenville's plan to tax and control their trade was unfair. Colonists felt that they had already done their part in helping Britain in its war with France. They also knew that British traders and manu-

Background: Grenville and his advisors estimated it would now cost Britain 70,000 pounds a year to govern the colonies. This was five times more than in 1754. Yet British taxpayers were insisting on relief from the heavy wartime taxes they had been paying.

182

facturers made money in America. Yet now Britain was forcing the colonists to help pay British debts. Even worse, Britain was interfering in the colonies and threatening the colonists' rights.

New Taxes   What new taxes did Britain try to make the American colonists pay?

15. To increase its income from the colonies, Grenville's government passed the **Sugar Act** in 1764. Molasses and sugar from the French West Indies had become one of the New England colonies' most profitable trade items. The Sugar Act required a tax to be paid when these items entered the colonies. Customs officers were stationed in Boston, New York, Philadelphia, and other colonial ports to see that the new law was enforced. Once again, the actions of the British government angered American colonists, who saw the Sugar Tax as part of a British plan to take away their rights.

16. The **Quartering Act** of 1765 required colonists to provide food and housing for Brit-

ish troops in their colony. Grenville had just sent 10,000 soldiers to the colonies. The British government said they were needed to keep peace on the western frontier. Yet many of these soldiers were stationed in eastern colonial towns, such as New York and Boston. Colonists resented having to pay the expense of housing and feeding the British troops.

Outlook

17. After Britain's victory in the French and Indian War, its relations with the American colonies began to change. Britain tightened its control over the colonies' trade. It also passed new trade laws. The British government believed these steps were needed to raise money for governing the colonies. Many colonists, however, began to believe that Britain wanted only to rule them more strictly. What might have caused this misunderstanding between Britain and the 13 colonies? What new problems might arise because of this difference of opinion?

▼ Protests against the Stamp Act sometimes became violent. Here a group of colonists take out their feelings on one of the king's tax collectors.

CHAPTER REVIEW

VOCABULARY REVIEW

▶ Write each of the following words on a sheet of paper. Then write the correct definition for each word. Use the glossary on pages 678–688 to help you.

debt   smuggled   Sugar Act   trade laws

Proclamation of 1763   customs officers   Quartering Act

SKILL BUILDER: READING A MAP

▶ The map below shows North America in 1763, at the end of the French and Indian War. Use the key at the bottom to answer these questions.

1. What was the boundary between British North America and New Spain?

2. What country controlled New Orleans?

3. What country controlled Florida?

4. Does the map show any French possessions? If so, where?

5. Which direction from the Proclamation Line was Fort Duquesne?

USING PRIMARY SOURCES

▶ Reread the Spotlight on Sources on page 181. What do you think was more important to the British in issuing the Proclamation of 1763: protecting the settlers, or avoiding the cost of another war? Why?

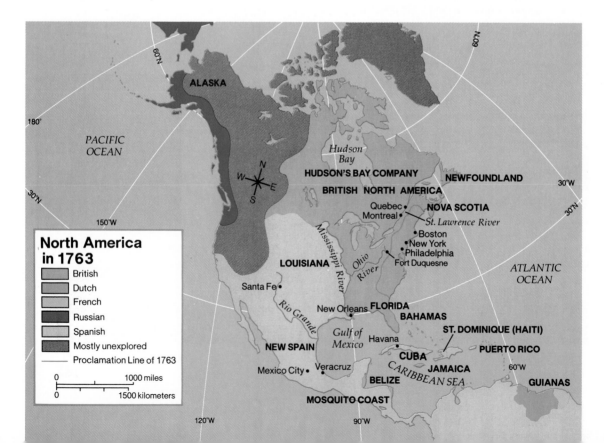

SKILL BUILDER: CRITICAL THINKING AND COMPREHENSION

I. Drawing Conclusions

▶ Read each of the following groups of statements. Think about them carefully. Then choose the possible conclusions that best fit the statements.

Statements

1. The Proclamation of 1763 closed all the lands west of the Appalachians to the colonists.

2. Daniel Boone knew that Britain had made it unlawful to settle in Kentucky, but in 1769 he decided to ignore the law and open the land to settlers.

Possible Conclusions

a. The Proclamation of 1763 was difficult to enforce.

b. Britain did not want the Proclamation of 1763 to be enforced.

c. Most settlers had never heard of the Proclamation of 1763.

Statements

3. Colonists had broken the Navigation Acts for years by smuggling goods into the colonies.

4. Britain had a large war debt, and it needed money to pay for governing the American colonies.

Possible Conclusions

d. Britain would continue to allow colonists to disobey the Navigation Acts.

e. The colonists would decide to stop smuggling in order to help Britain pay its debts.

f. Britain would enforce the Navigation Acts.

II. Understanding Points of View

A point of view is an attitude, belief, or opinion that a person holds. It is a certain way of looking at a situation, and it largely depends on a person's past experiences. For example, this statement shows the point of view of a British person: "The colonies should always be made to serve Britain, the mother country."

▶ Read the following statements. Identify the point of view of each statement as either American or British. Be prepared to explain your choices.

1. Native Americans should not be disturbed in the territories reserved to them.

2. Britain should not expect colonists to pay the British debt.

3. Soldiers should not have the right to move into the houses of colonists.

4. Money spent governing the colonies should be paid by the colonies themselves.

ENRICHMENT

1. Imagine that you are Daniel Boone. Write a description of your feelings as you explore Kentucky. Include your opinion on why the Proclamation of 1763 should be ignored.

2. Find a biography of George Grenville in your school or local library. Read about his opinion of the colonists. Write a short play in which Grenville explains his position on the trade laws and defends himself against the colonists' complaints. Include at least two colonists in the play. With a group of your classmates, enact the play in front of the class.

CHAPTER 3

The Colonists Resist Taxation without Representation

OBJECTIVE: What new tax laws did the British government pass for the colonies, and what did the colonists do about them?

1. It was a cold, snowy evening in early March. A group of protesters slowly moved toward a group of British soldiers. These soldiers had been sent to Boston to help collect taxes from colonists. A young African American sailor named Crispus Attucks was one of the protesters. They began to call the soldiers names and to throw snowballs at them. At first, the soldiers were angry. Then their anger turned to fear as the protesters began to throw sticks. Suddenly a fight broke out. Attucks grabbed a soldier's rifle. Someone gave the order to fire. The fighting lasted only a few minutes. When it ended, Crispus Attucks and four other colonists were dead. This attack, which came to be known as the Boston Massacre, took place on March 5, 1770. As you read this chapter, trace the events that led up to the Boston Massacre. What were those events? Could the massacre have been avoided? What might happen as a result of the massacre?

▲ British Redcoats fire on the people of Boston in the Boston Massacre. Do you think the people and the soldiers would actually have been so close together? Why are they shown that way?

The Stamp Act   What was the Stamp Act, and why did colonists oppose this new tax?

2. In March 1765, **Parliament** passed a tax law called the Stamp Act. Parliament was the lawmaking body of Great Britain. The Stamp Act required colonists to pay taxes on newspapers, almanacs, playing cards, and all legal papers. Britain hoped to raise a large amount of money from this tax. The Stamp Act was Britain's first attempt to tax colonists directly. How was this different from earlier British taxes on the colonists?

In Chapter 3 you will apply these critical thinking skills to the historical process:
❯ **Predicting:** Telling what you believe will happen on the basis of clues and facts.

▲ **Identifying Fact *versus* Opinion:** Specifying whether information can be proved or whether it expresses feelings or beliefs.

3. The American colonists refused to obey the Stamp Act. Immediately, newspaper editors, lawyers, and printers spoke out strongly against it. People paraded and held protest marches. Colonial assemblies met to protest the Stamp Act. A leader of the Virginia assembly named Patrick Henry declared that George III was acting like a **tyrant**. A tyrant is a strong ruler who treats the people harshly and ignores their rights.

4. During the summer of 1765, American colonists increased their protests against the Stamp Act. In Massachusetts, groups of men who called themselves Sons of Liberty threatened stamp tax collectors. They burned the British governor's house. In Pennsylvania and New Hampshire, colonists burned copies of the Stamp Act. Merchants in the colonies signed agreements to **boycott** British goods. To boycott is to refuse to buy certain goods or to buy from certain people. How would a boycott hurt British businesses? Finally, colonists decided to hold a meeting to plan what other action they could take together.

5. In October 1765, nine colonies sent delegates to a meeting, known as the Stamp Act Congress, in New York City. This meeting showed that colonists were able to work together to protect their interests. The delegates to the congress drew up a declaration that explained their views. It stated that the colonists were loyal subjects of the British king. However, it firmly declared that only the colonial assemblies elected by the colonists had the power to tax the colonies. Therefore, the taxes passed by Parliament would not be acceptable to the colonies.

Spotlight on Sources

6. The Stamp Act Congress called on Parliament to remove the stamp tax. It sent this petition, or formal written request, to Parliament:

It is essential to the freedom of a people, and the right of Englishmen [British citizens] that no taxes be imposed [put] on them but [except] with their own consent. No taxes ever can be constitutionally [lawfully] imposed on them but [except] by their respective [own] legislatures [assemblies].

What does the petition say is the basic right of Englishmen? Why did the colonists think that this right applied to them?

7. In March 1766, Parliament voted to end the Stamp Act. The colonies had won their fight against this tax. However, to show that it did not agree with the colonists' views about its power to tax, Parliament passed a law called the Declaratory Act. This law declared that Parliament was the highest lawmaking body in Great Britain and in the colonies. Thus, Parliament had the power to pass any law it wished "to bind the colonies and people of America." Colonists were so pleased by Parliament's ending the Stamp Act that they overlooked the Declaratory Act. What trouble do you think this newest law might cause the colonies in the future?

Taxation and Representation How did the American colonies' ideas of a just government clash with British views?

8. The colonists' ideas were summed up in the slogan "no taxation without representation." This idea was very different from Britain's views. The colonists believed that British citizens should have the right to elect the people who taxed them. Yet colonists were not allowed to vote for members of Parliament. Therefore, the colonists believed that Parliament had no right to tax them. How do the words "no taxation without representation" sum up this idea?

9. Grenville and George III believed that Parliament acted for all British citizens, including those in the colonies. Most people in Britain lacked the right to vote. In fact, only men who owned a certain amount of property could vote in elections for members of Parliament. Yet Parliament passed laws and taxes for the whole nation. Britain's leaders believed that Parliament represented the people in Britain's colonies the same way.

The Townshend Acts   What were the Townshend Acts, and why did these laws anger the colonists?

10. Because the British government still needed money, Parliament in 1767 passed the Townshend Acts. These laws taxed manufactured goods shipped to the colonies, such as paper, glass, and paints. There was also a tax on tea. Britain would use the money from these taxes to pay for governing the colonies, including paying the salaries of British governors and tax collectors. Colonial assemblies, which up to now had paid these salaries, would have less control over the actions of these officials. The British government was determined to enforce these new laws. Tax collectors could now use **writs of assistance**. Writs of assistance were legal documents that allowed tax collectors to search colonists' homes and businesses for smuggled goods. With a writ of assistance, the tax collector could make these searches without first obtaining a search warrant.

11. The Townshend Acts caused more and more colonists to protest British taxes. Some colonists even began to ask if Britain had the right to rule the colonies. Samuel Adams of Boston warned that Parliament wanted to take away the colonists' rights and freedoms. Other colonial leaders, such as John Dickinson of Pennsylvania, were less extreme. Dickinson declared that Parliament must stop meddling in the colonies and allow the colonial assemblies to tax the colonists.

12. During the next three years, merchants in colonial cities set up boycotts against all British goods. People in all the colonies supported these boycotts. For example, colonists agreed not to buy British tea or woolen cloth.

People in History

13. Daughters of Liberty   To aid the boycott, women formed groups called **Daughters of Liberty**. Rather than buy British-made cloth, the Daughters of Liberty spun and wove their

▼ British troops land at Boston in 1768. The British government sent these troops in order to reinforce the writs of assistance.

Background: Charles Townshend, whom George III chose to replace Grenville, was scarcely the person to deal with the mistrustful colonies. "Champagne Charlie" was, as his nickname suggests, more interested in social life than in politics, and he had little talent for government.

own cloth. They used this cloth to make clothing for their families. They held spinning contests to speed up their output of this homemade cloth. Daughters of Liberty also helped lead the boycott against British tea. They served coffee instead, or they made tea from herbs that they grew themselves.

The Boston Massacre   How did the Townshend Acts lead to bloodshed in Boston?

14. The seaport city of Boston now became the center of the trouble between Britain and its colonies. The British government had sent soldiers there to end the unrest caused by the Townshend Acts. However, Samuel Adams continued to stir up the colonists' angry feelings toward Britain and these British soldiers.

15. On March 5, 1770, the fight that became the Boston Massacre broke out between a group of young colonial men and some British **Redcoats**. British soldiers were called Redcoats because of the bright red uniforms they wore. As you remember, when the fighting ended, Crispus Attucks and four other colonists had been killed. The news of the Boston Massacre quickly spread throughout the British colonies. Many colonists now feared that Britain was prepared to take almost any steps to enforce its rule of the colonies.

16. Lord Frederick North, the new leader of the British government, asked Parliament to end the Townshend Acts. In April 1770, Parliament agreed to Lord North's request. Once again the colonists had forced Britain to back down. However, North and Parliament kept the tax on tea. They did this to show that Britain still had the right to tax its colonies.

American Unity Grows   How did the American colonies begin to unite during the years 1770–1773?

17. The American colonists welcomed the end of the Townshend Acts. They were tired of protests and unrest. Now the boycotts ended,

▲ There were other protests in the colonies besides the Boston Massacre. What do you think these colonists are protesting?

and people could buy the goods they needed. Merchants began to make profits again. The British government, too, seemed glad to see peaceful times return to the colonies. Parliament wisely did not pass any new tax laws.

18. Leaders in Massachusetts and Virginia set up **committees of correspondence** so that each colony would know about events in the other colony. A committee of correspondence was a group of citizens who wrote about what was happening in their colony. Messengers on horseback then carried this news to the other colonies. Soon committees were set up in nearly all the colonies. As a result, each colony now learned quickly about important events in other colonies. In this way, the colonies became more able to work together.

Outlook

19. Great Britain found that ruling its American colonies was more and more difficult. The colonists protested each new tax law. Even more important, the colonists and Britain came to hold very different views of each other's rights. What might happen if each side was constantly making demands to protect its rights?

189

CHAPTER REVIEW

VOCABULARY REVIEW

▶ Write each number and word on a sheet of paper. Then write the letter of the correct definition for that word.

1. boycott

2. tyrant

3. committees of correspondence

4. writs of assistance

5. Parliament

6. Redcoats

7. Daughters of Liberty

a. Groups of women who spun and wove cloth so that they would not have to buy cloth from Great Britain

b. A strong ruler who treats the people harshly and ignores their rights

c. British soldiers

d. The lawmaking body of the British government

e. Legal documents that allowed tax collectors to search colonists' homes and businesses for smuggled goods

f. To refuse to buy certain goods or to buy from certain people

g. Groups of citizens who reported what was happening in their colonies

SKILL BUILDER: COMPLETING A TABLE

▶ On a sheet of paper, copy the table below. Then complete it by writing how the individual or group resisted Britain.

COLONIAL RESISTANCE

Individual or Group	Form of Resistance
Crispus Attucks	
Sons of Liberty	
Daughters of Liberty	
Stamp Act Congress	
Samuel Adams	
Committees of Correspondence	

SKILL BUILDER: CRITICAL THINKING AND COMPREHENSION

❭ I. Predicting

Colonists believed that they had the right to elect the people who taxed them. Because the colonists were not allowed to vote for members of Parliament, the colonists believed that Parliament had no right to tax them. Suppose that colonists had been given the right to elect members of Parliament. Suppose, too, that the British members of Parliament had passed the Townshend Acts, even though every American member of Parliament voted against them.

1. What action do you think the colonists would have taken against the acts?

2. Write a paragraph predicting what would have happened. Then write a second paragraph supporting your opinion with facts from the chapter.

II. Identifying Fact *versus* Opinion

A **fact** is something that can be proved. You can check in other sources to see if the fact is true. For example, *The Boston Massacre took place on March 5, 1770* is a fact. An **opinion** is a statement that tells what someone believes about something. An opinion cannot be proved. For example, *The Boston Massacre was the most terrible night of that year* is an opinion. Why do you think it is important to be able to tell the difference between a fact and an opinion?

▶ On a sheet of paper, copy the following statements. Then decide whether each one is a fact or an opinion. Label each statement *F* for fact or *O* for opinion.

1. The Daughters of Liberty deserve our admiration for their boycott of British cloth.

2. In March 1765, the British Parliament passed the Stamp Act.

3. The colonists should not have been taxed by the British government.

4. Crispus Attucks was one of the colonists killed in the Boston Massacre.

5. Patrick Henry declared that George III was acting like a tyrant.

USING PRIMARY SOURCES

Reread the Spotlight on Sources on page 187. Why was winning the fight against the stamp tax important for the nine colonies in America?

ENRICHMENT

1. The Boston Massacre stirred up the colonists' anger against Britain. Imagine that you were living in Boston at the time and that you had seen the fight from your window. Write a letter to your cousin in Virginia. In the letter, describe what you saw, and tell how you felt about it.

2. Hold a trial of the British troops involved in the Boston Massacre. The teacher or a student can be the judge. Students play the roles of prosecuting attorney, the defense attorney, and three defendants. Three or four witnesses can tell what they saw. The rest of the class will be the jury. Compare your verdict with the decision in the actual trial.

CHAPTER 4

"Give Me Liberty or Give Me Death!"

> OBJECTIVE: What actions of the British government caused the American colonies to unite and to move toward independence?

1. The people on the Boston docks were excited and happy. They cheered and shouted their support for the busy people on the ships. It was unusual to see Native Americans aboard ships in Boston harbor. However, the people watching from the docks knew that the "Native Americans" really were colonists from Boston. They had dressed up as Native Americans to disguise themselves, because they were breaking the law against destroying property. They already had broken the law by boarding the British ships. Now they were lifting heavy chests full of tea up to the ships' railings and throwing the tea overboard into the water. During this night in December 1773, these colonists dumped nearly 350 chests of tea into the harbor. They had held this "Boston Tea Party" to show the British government what they thought of its new Tea Act.

▲ Colonists chop open cases of tea on board a British ship during the Boston Tea Party. Do you think the British were fooled by the Native American costumes that the colonists wore?

The Boston Tea Party What was the Tea Act, and how did the colonists in Boston protest this law?

2. In May 1773, the British Parliament passed the Tea Act to help the British East India Company. This trading company now was allowed to sell its tea directly to the American colonies. The company did not even have to pay any tax on the tea. As a result, the East India Company would be able to supply tea to the colonies at a low price. Tea was the colonists' favorite drink. Lord North, the leader of the British government, expected the colonies to provide a large and profitable market for the

In Chapter 4, you will apply these critical thinking skills to the historical process:

 Predicting: Telling what you believe will happen on the basis of clues and facts.

▲ **Identifying Fact _versus_ Opinion:** Specifying whether information can be proved or whether it expresses feelings or beliefs.

company's tea. At the same time, North expected the Tea Act to help the many members of Parliament who owned shares in the East India Company. How would the Tea Act help these members of Parliament?

3. The Tea Act worried the American colonists, who did not trust North. Merchants in the colonies were especially worried. They were not interested in lower tea prices if this meant that Parliament could make laws to favor British businesses. If the colonists put up with the Tea Act, Parliament could give the same kind of advantages to other British companies, and other colonial merchants would suffer. Committees of Correspondence in the colonies began to plan how colonists could resist this new law.

4. In November 1773, when British ships arrived with tea, the colonists were ready. In New York and Philadelphia, they forced the ships to return to England. In Boston, after the British governor allowed the tea ships into the harbor, colonists took even stronger action. As you have read, a group of men dressed as Native Americans threw all the tea into Boston harbor. This event became known as the Boston Tea Party.

The Intolerable Acts   What was the purpose of the Intolerable Acts, and how did colonists react to them?

5. The British government decided that Boston must be punished for the Boston Tea Party. The news of this event had shocked George III and North. They decided to make laws so harsh that the other colonies would learn a lesson ▶ from Boston's example. How successful would you expect this kind of policy to be?

6. In March 1774, Parliament passed several laws that the American colonists soon named the Intolerable Acts. **Intolerable** means too severe to put up with. What were the colonists showing by their use of this word? These acts closed the port of Boston to all trading. No ships were allowed to enter or leave. Massachusetts also lost many of its rights to govern itself.

General Thomas Gage, the commander of British troops in the 13 colonies, became governor of Massachusetts. The people of Boston had to pay for the British soldiers who were sent there.

7. Another of the Intolerable Acts, called the Quebec Act, set up a new government for Canada. The Quebec Act made the lands west of the Appalachians part of Canada. American settlers were again barred from the western lands.

8. The Intolerable Acts convinced many colonists that Britain was acting to end colonists' rights and freedom. North's government had expected that strong laws would cause the colonies to accept the authority of Parliament. Instead, the colonies now united to defend their liberty. The people of Boston resisted in every way they could. Other colonies quickly showed their support. Colonists as far away as the Carolinas sent food and supplies to Massachusetts. Why would the other colonies act in this ◀ way?

People in History

9. Mercy Otis Warren A leader in the struggle against Britain, Mercy Otis Warren wrote poems and plays attacking the British government and citizens of Boston who were loyal to it. Earlier Warren had helped set up the Massachusetts Committee of Correspondence. Her home became a meeting place where Samuel Adams and John Adams planned how to resist British tax laws. Her role was especially remarkable because she acted at a time when women were not expected to take part in politics.

The First Continental Congress   What was the purpose of this meeting, and what actions did it take?

10. In September 1774, the colonies sent delegates to a meeting called the First Continental Congress. The meeting took place in Philadelphia. The delegates agreed that the colonists must stand together against the Intolerable Acts. They called for a boycott of all British

Activity: The Quebec Act was intended to provide a strong government for Britain's new colony in Canada. Yet the 13 colonies saw it as an attempt to take away their western lands. Discuss why people interpret events in different ways and how such points of view shape history.

193

products until these laws were ended. They also set up groups in each colony to see that this boycott was carried out.

11. An important step of the First Continental Congress was the writing of a Declaration of Rights. A **declaration** is a formal announcement. This declaration stated the colonists' rights as British citizens. These included the rights to tax themselves and to manage their own affairs. The Congress rejected all tax laws that Parliament had passed since 1763. It accepted only Parliament's power over colonial trade. It agreed to meet again if Parliament did not end the Intolerable Acts.

The Road to Revolution How did the fighting at Lexington and Concord begin the struggle for American independence?

12. The British government refused to give in to the colonies. When George III learned

about the acts of the First Continental Congress, he told North that the colonies were rebelling. Britain decided to use force to keep control of the 13 colonies.

Spotlight on Sources

13. Many Americans now feared that war was about to begin. As support for Massachusetts grew in other colonies, these colonies began to form their own armies of citizens. In March 1775, Patrick Henry spoke to the Virginia assembly:

> The war is inevitable [cannot be prevented]—and let it come. Gentlemen may cry peace, peace! But there is no peace. The war is actually begun! Our brethren [brothers] are already in the field [at war]. Why stand we idle here? I know not what course others make take, but as for me, give me liberty or give me death.

SKILL BUILDER MAP: The map is divided into boxes, labeled A, B, C, D, E, and F (top) and 1, 2, 3, and 4 (sides). **1.** In what box is Boston located? **2.** What places are shown in Box A1?

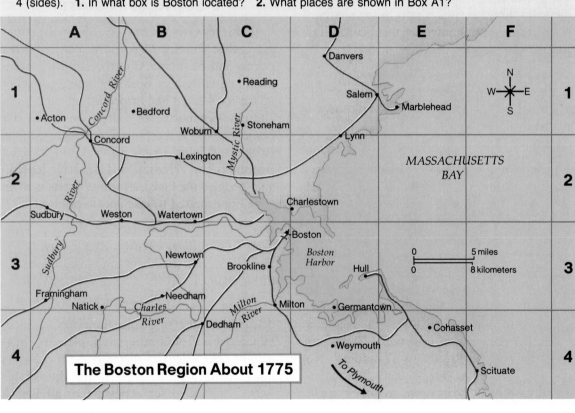

The Boston Region About 1775

▲ The war for American independence was begun by the 77 Minutemen who met the British at Lexington. They had been warned that the British were coming by Paul Revere, who brought the news from Boston during the night.

▶ What two choices did Patrick Henry say the colonies faced? Do you think he was right in his belief?

14. By spring of 1775, the American colonists were preparing to resist the British forces. Colonists in Massachusetts took the lead. They armed themselves and practiced their skills in using guns and muskets. They called themselves **Minutemen**. A Minuteman was a citizen soldier who was prepared to fight on a minute's warning. Some of the Minutemen began to collect weapons and ammunition at Concord, a town near Boston. When Gage learned of this action, he decided to send British soldiers there to seize the weapons. He also ordered the arrests of Samuel Adams and John Hancock, another leader of the colonists, who were in nearby Lexington.

15. On April 19, 1775, the first shots of the Revolutionary War were fired. That morning, when Gage's 700 soldiers arrived at Lexington, they were met by a small group of Minutemen. At first, both sides tried to remain calm. Then, suddenly, someone fired a weapon. Minutes later, eight Americans were dead. The British troops then marched to Concord. There they were met by a much larger group of Minutemen, and more fighting took place. As the British soldiers returned to Boston, angry farmers shot at them from close range. At the end of the day, more than 250 British soldiers and nearly 100 colonists had been killed.

Outlook

16. After the Tea Act was passed, Britain and the colonies moved farther and farther apart. The Intolerable Acts, which were intended to punish Boston, instead caused the American colonies to unite. Colonists now strongly stated their right to tax and govern themselves. George III and North decided they must use force to rule the colonies. The fighting at Lexington and Concord was the result. What ◀ other policy by the British might have been more successful? What do you think each side would do next? If there were a war, what would colonists be fighting for?

Background: Some members of Parliament spoke out against the British government's policy. Edmund Burke and William Pitt urged Parliament to seek conciliation with the colonies by repealing the Intolerable Acts and renouncing taxation of the colonies. However, their eloquent warnings were outvoted.

CHAPTER REVIEW

VOCABULARY REVIEW

▶ Write the sentence below on a piece of paper. Fill each blank space with one of the vocabulary words.

intolerable   declaration   Minutemen   representation

1. Colonists thought it was _____ to have to pay taxes imposed by Parliament.

2. The _____ were ready to fight on short notice.

3. A _____ is a formal written statement.

SKILL BUILDER: READING A BAR GRAPH

Between 1700 and 1775, the population of the colonies grew at an amazing rate. By 1775, when the population of England was about 6.7 million, the population of the colonies was about a third of that number and growing fast. The bar graph below shows the population growth of the colonies between 1700 and 1775.

▶ After studying the bar graph, answer the questions that follow. Write your answers on a separate sheet of paper.

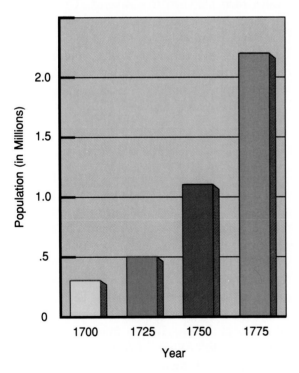

Colonial Population Growth, 1700–1775

Source: Historical Statistics

1. About how many people lived in the colonies in 1700?

2. About how many people lived in the colonies in 1775?

3. How many more people were there in the colonies in 1775 than there were in 1700?

4. Did the population grow more than 5 times, more than 7 times, or more than 10 times between 1700 and 1775?

SKILL BUILDER: CRITICAL THINKING AND COMPREHENSION

I. Predicting

Because of the Boston Tea Party, the British Parliament passed several laws that the colonists called Intolerable Acts. The First Continental Congress then met to discuss what to do about these laws.

1. What would you expect the Continental Congress to do if Parliament continued the Intolerable Acts? Write your prediction on a sheet of paper. Use examples of how the colonists had reacted to earlier laws.

2. Why do you think the British government did not successfully predict how the colonists would react to its new laws?

II. Fact *versus* Opinion

A fact is information that can be proved. An opinion is a belief or judgment. It is important to be able to tell the difference between facts and opinions.

▶ Read the statements below. Decide whether each statement is a fact or an opinion. Write the letter of each statement on a sheet of paper. Label each statement *F* for fact or *O* for opinion.

1. General Thomas Gage was the commander of British troops in the 13 colonies.

2. With the Intolerable Acts, Britain was trying to destroy all the colonists' rights.

3. Mercy Otis Warren helped set up the Massachusetts Committee of Correspondence.

4. Every colonist in Boston was happy about the Boston Tea Party.

5. The British believed that strong laws would cause the colonies to accept the authority of Parliament.

6. Colonists as far away as the Carolinas sent food and supplies to Boston.

7. Colonists had the right to tax themselves and to manage their own affairs.

USING PRIMARY SOURCES

▶ Reread the Spotlight on Sources on page 194. Why did Patrick Henry believe that war was sure to happen?

ENRICHMENT

1. Imagine that you are a delegate to the First Continental Congress. You must give a speech to the congress explaining your colony's point of view. Write a speech about the action you believe the colonies should take against the Intolerable Acts. Do you support a boycott? What rights would you wish included in a Declaration of Rights? Be sure to give reasons to support your point of view.

2. The Boston Tea Party was an exciting moment in American history. Colonists dressed up as Native Americans to keep their identities secret. They boarded British ships and threw chests of tea into the water. Make a political poster about this event. The poster should encourage colonists to continue resisting Britain. Include a slogan on the poster.

CHAPTER 5

Independence Is Declared

OBJECTIVE: Why did the American colonies declare their independence from Great Britain?

1. All week long, it had been very hot in Philadelphia. The room where the men were meeting was large, but it was very warm. The men were tired and becoming more restless each day. For several weeks now, this group of men had been discussing what the colonies should do. These men included some of the most important leaders in the colonies. They had been sent to Philadelphia to represent the people of the 13 colonies. On July 2, these members of the Second Continental Congress agreed to take a final vote. As they voted, each member knew that this was the most important vote he would ever cast. Why? The Congress was voting on whether the colonies "must be free and independent states." As the name of each state was called, the members voted in favor of independence. Then, two days later, they voted again. This time they cast their votes for the great document that formally declared America's independence. This document is called the Declaration of Independence.

▲ The Declaration of Independence is presented to the Continental Congress. Thomas Jefferson, author of the Declaration, is the tallest of the five men standing near the desk.

The Second Continental Congress How did this congress try both to keep peace and at the same time to prepare for war?

2. In May 1775, the Second Continental Congress met in Philadelphia. All the colonies sent representatives. The fighting at Lexington and Concord was very much on the minds of the members of the Congress. They knew they must act immediately to defend the colonies. What British actions were they afraid of? ◄

3. The Second Continental Congress decided to act as a government for all 13 colonies.

In Chapter 5 you will apply these critical thinking skills to the historical process:

198

❯ **Predicting:** Telling what you believe will happen on the basis of clues and facts.

▲ **Identifying Fact *versus* Opinion:** Specifying whether information can be proved or whether it expresses feelings or beliefs.

In this new role, it took several important actions. It chose George Washington to take command of the colonial army. It asked all the colonies to furnish soldiers and money for an American army. This army was called the **Continental Army**. At the same time, the members of the congress tried to work for peace. They knew that most colonists still hoped to keep their ties with Great Britain. Most colonists did not yet favor full independence. Instead, they hoped to govern themselves while remaining loyal subjects of the British king.

4. In June 1775, fighting broke out again near Boston in the **Battle of Bunker Hill**. General Gage led his British troops in an attack on the colonial militia. This militia was made up of farmers and merchants, among whom were free African Americans. The Americans fought well, but they had to retreat when they ran out of ammunition. Even so, the American citizen-soldiers had proved that they were able to fight ▶ the trained British army. How might this knowledge be useful in the months and years ahead?

5. The next month, the Second Continental Congress appealed to George III to stop the fighting. The members of the Congress blamed Parliament, not the king, for what had happened. By showing loyalty to the king, they also showed that they still thought of themselves as loyal to Great Britain. They wanted the right to govern themselves, but they also wanted to remain British citizens. However, when George III received this appeal from the Continental Congress, he tore it up. He told North that the American colonists were "in open rebellion."

6. George III was determined to defeat the rebellion in the colonies. The British government prepared to send 25,000 more soldiers to America. Then, in January 1776, the colonists learned that George III had hired thousands of trained German soldiers to fight in America. These German soldiers were called **Hessians** (HESH-unz), because they came from a part of Germany called Hesse. The Hessians were to be paid for each colonial soldier they killed or wounded. The king also ordered the British

navy to close off the American colonies to all trade with other countries. How would this policy affect the colonies? Many colonists who had wanted to avoid a split with Great Britain now lost hope.

Common Sense   How did Thomas Paine's writings help the colonists decide on independence?

7. At this same time, a booklet called *Common Sense* helped the American colonists decide in favor of independence. This booklet was written by Thomas Paine, an Englishman who had just come to the colonies. *Common Sense* told the colonists that George III was a tyrant who did not deserve their loyalty. In strong but simple words, Paine inspired Americans to fight for their freedom and become an independent nation.

Spotlight on Sources

8. In *Common Sense,* Paine wrote that the time for arguments about independence was past. He said that the time had come when the colonies must rebel against Britain:

> Volumes [books] have been written on the subject of the struggle between England and America. The period of debate is closed. I challenge the warmest advocate [strongest supporter] for reconciliation [making peace] to show a single advantage that the colonies can reap [gain] by being connected with Great Britain. Everything that is right and reasonable pleads for separation. The blood of the slain cries 'TIS [it is] TIME TO PART.

What did Paine mean when he wrote, "The period of debate is closed"? What does he mean ◀ by "the blood of the slain"?

9. More than 150,000 copies of *Common Sense* were sold in the early months of 1776. During these months, colonists also grew angrier as the fighting with Britain continued. Most now agreed that it was time for the colonies to become a separate, independent nation.

Background: The appeal to George III—the so-called Olive Branch Petition—had considerable support, especially in the Middle Colonies. The king's stubborn insistence on ending colonial resistance eroded the moderates' position and ultimately led to the revolution that the king was determined to prevent.

▲ This political cartoon shows the American "horse" getting rid of its British "rider." Is this an American cartoon or a British one? How can you tell?

10. In June 1776, members of the Second Continental Congress began to discuss independence. Assemblies in several colonies had urged their representative at Philadelphia to vote for independence. In addition, Washington's armies had been winning some important victories against the British. The Continental Congress decided to ask Benjamin Franklin, John Adams, and three other members to write a statement explaining why the colonies must be independent. Thomas Jefferson, the youngest member of the Congress, wrote the first draft of the Declaration. Benjamin Franklin suggested a few changes in it, and the Congress made a few more. However, the Declaration is mainly the work of Jefferson.

People in History

11. Thomas Jefferson A young lawyer from Virginia, Thomas Jefferson, had served as a member of the Virginia Assembly for seven years. He also had helped form the Committee of Correspondence in that colony. In 1774,

Jefferson had written a booklet in which he argued that Parliament had no right to pass laws for the colonies. The colonies must have the right to govern themselves. At that time, Jefferson also had said that the colonies should remain loyal to the king. Now, however, he was writing the document that would bring that loyalty to an end. Jefferson was a quiet man. Unlike many other members of the Continental Congress, he was not a skilled speaker. However, he was one of the greatest writers and thinkers in the American colonies.

12. The first part of the Declaration of Independence gives reasons why the American people should form their own nation. This opening part is called the Preamble. It states that Americans, like people everywhere, have certain human rights. These rights of life, liberty, and trying to achieve happiness should never be taken away by any ruler. The purpose of all governments is to make sure that people enjoy these rights. When any government unjustly limits or takes away these rights, the people have a duty to replace this government.

Background: Jefferson explained what he sought to achieve in the Declaration: "I did not consider it any part of my charge to invent new ideas, but to place before mankind the common sense of the subject, in terms so plain and firm as to command their assent. . . . It was intended to be an expression of the American mind."

Therefore, the colonists must do away with British rule and set up a new government that will protect their rights.

13. The next part of the Declaration gives a long list of the things George III had done that failed to protect the colonists' rights. Why would such a list be included in the Declaration? By acting in these ways, the king actually had tried to destroy the people's rights. Therefore, the colonists no longer had to obey him. The Declaration points out that for years the colonists had protested the king's unjust actions. Yet he had never listened to their protests. Instead, George III kept on acting like a tyrant. The Declaration ends with the statement that the colonies are now a free and independent nation.

▼ After independence was declared, a crowd in New York pulled down the city's statue of George III. Later, the statue was melted down and used to make bullets.

14. The Second Continental Congress adopted the Declaration on July 4, 1776. Members of the Congress then signed their names to the Declaration. By doing so, they knew they were founding a new nation. They also knew they must first fight and win a war before this nation could be safe.

15. The Declaration of Independence sets forth ideals that have guided the American people ever since. These ideals include the people's right to "life, liberty, and the pursuit of happiness." They also include the duty of government to rule "with the consent of the governed." These ideals have formed the foundation for freedom and democracy in America for more than 200 years. As ideals, they have not been completely achieved. Yet they have provided goals that Americans continually try to reach.

16. A main idea of the Declaration of Independence is that "all men are created equal." Thus, all people should have equal rights and equal opportunities. However, in 1776, the signers of the Declaration used these words to refer only to white male colonists. Over the years, the meaning of this idea has changed and grown to include men and women of all races. Like other ideals, this ideal has not been fully achieved. Yet because of it, the Declaration of Independence remains a powerful force in the lives of people everywhere in the world. Why ◀ would this American document be important to people outside the United States? You can read the Declaration of Independence in this textbook on pages 204–207.

Outlook

17. The Second Continental Congress worked to avoid war with Great Britain. However, George III and his government saw the colonists as rebels and sent soldiers to crush them. Instead of giving in, the colonists adopted the Declaration of Independence. What dangers do you think the American peo- ◀ ple now faced? What might happen if they lost their fight for independence?

CHAPTER REVIEW

VOCABULARY REVIEW

▶ On a sheet of paper, copy the paragraph below. When you come to a blank, write in the word or phrase that best completes the sentence.

Hessians   Battle of Bunker Hill   Continental Army

In May 1775, the Second Continental Congress asked all the colonies to furnish soldiers and money for an American army. This army was called the ___1___. In June 1775, British troops attacked colonial militia in the ___2___. The Americans had to retreat, but they fought well. By January 1776, George III had hired thousands of trained German soldiers to fight in America. These German soldiers were called ___3___ after the part of Germany that they were from. They were to be paid for each colonial soldier that they killed or wounded.

SKILL BUILDER: READING A PIE GRAPH

▶ The pie graphs below show the English and American losses at the Battle of Bunker Hill. Study the graphs. On a sheet of paper, write your answers to the questions that follow the graphs.

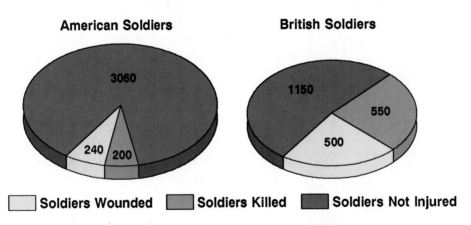

THE BATTLE OF BUNKER HILL

American Soldiers

3060

240 200

British Soldiers

1150

550

500

☐ Soldiers Wounded   ☐ Soldiers Killed   ■ Soldiers Not Injured

1. How many men fought on the British side at the battle of Bunker Hill?

2. How many Americans fought at the battle of Bunker Hill?

3. How many more British soldiers than Americans were wounded in the battle?

4. How many more British soldiers than American were killed in the battle?

5. How many more American soldiers than British fought in the battle?

SKILL BUILDER: CRITICAL THINKING AND COMPREHENSION

▶ I. Predicting

1. In July 1775, the Second Continental Congress appealed to George III to stop the fighting. George refused. What do you think would have happened in the colonies if he had accepted? Write your answer on a sheet of paper.

2. In January 1776, the British government sent soldiers to fight the colonists. What do you think would have happened to the signers of the Declaration of Independence if Great Britain had won the war? On a sheet of paper, write your answer and the facts that support it.

3. The Declaration of Independence dedicates the United States to the idea that "all men are created equal." What would America be like today if that idea had not been included? Would there be another American Revolution? Write your answer on a sheet of paper.

II. Fact *versus* Opinion

▶ On a sheet of paper, write three statements of fact based on information you have read in this chapter. Then write a statement of opinion about each of the facts. For example:

Fact: The Second Continental Congress voted that the colonies "must be free and independent states."

Opinion: The vote by the Second Continental Congress was a brave and courageous act.

▶ The statements below are from paragraph 8 in this chapter. On a sheet of paper, identify each statement as a fact or as an opinion.

a. Volumes have been written on the subject of the struggle between England and America.

b. Everything that is right and reasonable pleads for separation.

c. The blood of the slain cries 'TIS TIME TO PART.

USING PRIMARY SOURCES

▶ Reread the Spotlight on Sources on page 199. Why did Thomas Paine believe that it was not possible to make peace between the American colonists and Great Britain?

ENRICHMENT

1. In your school or local library, read a biography of George III. List the actions that George took in the British struggle with the colonists. Next, turn to the Declaration of Independence on pages 204–207 of this book. Read the list of acts that the Declaration blames on the king. Compare the two lists. Which items are on one list but not on the other? Write a paragraph explaining the difference.

2. Hold a discussion on the idea, "All men are created equal." Do you feel that Americans are now treated equally? Why, or why not? Suggest ways in which equality can be achieved.

The Declaration of Independence is one of the greatest documents in American history. Its meaningful words inspired the colonists in their fight for independence. The great ideals stated in the Declaration also have given hope to Americans ever since. Many people in other nations too have been guided by its words in their struggle for freedom.

The Declaration of Independence was written to explain why the American colonists were rebelling against Great Britain. In July 1776, when the Declaration was signed, the colonists knew that they faced a great danger. They had been fighting for their freedom for more than a year. They knew that the American colonies no longer could hope to settle their struggle against the British government peacefully. Therefore, the Second Continental Congress, acting as the colonists' representatives, decided to declare America's independence. The members of the Congress knew that this bold action might lead to a long, bloody war. Yet they believed that the colonies must become a free and independent nation.

Preamble

WHEN IN THE COURSE OF HUMAN EVENTS, it becomes necessary for one people to dissolve the political bands which have connected them with another, and to assume among the powers of the earth, the separate and equal station to which Laws of Nature and of Nature's God entitle them, a decent respect to the opinions of mankind requires that they should declare the causes which impel them to the separation.

Principles of Democracy

We hold these truths to be self-evident, that all men are created equal, that they are endowed by their Creator with certain unalienable Rights, that among these are Life, Liberty and the pursuit of Happiness.—That to secure these rights, Governments are instituted among Men, deriving their just powers from the consent of the governed,—That whenever any Form of Government becomes destructive of these ends, it is the Right of the People to alter or to abolish it, and to institute

---

Understanding the Declaration of Independence

Preamble

The introduction of the Declaration explains why it was written. It states that events may force a people to break away from the nation ruling them. When this happens, the people need to tell the world the reasons for their action. In fact, one of the aims of the Declaration was to gain the support of France and other nations as America's allies against Great Britain.

Principles of Democracy

The second part of the Declaration expresses the great ideals of the new American nation. Many consider it the most important part of the document. It proudly states that all people are created equal. All people also are born with the same basic human rights. The most important of these rights are the right to "life, liberty, and the pursuit of happiness." These basic human rights come from God, and no government can

204

new Government, laying its foundation on such principles and organizing its powers in such form, as to them shall seem most likely to effect their Safety and Happiness. Prudence, indeed, will dictate that Governments long established should not be changed for light and transient causes; and accordingly all experience hath shewn that mankind are more disposed to suffer, while evils are sufferable, than to right themselves by abolishing the forms to which they are accustomed. But when a long train of abuses and usurpations, pursuing invariably the same Object evinces a design to reduce them under absolute Despotism, it is their right, it is their duty, to throw off such Government, and to provide new Guards for their future security.—Such has been the patient sufferance of these Colonies; and such is now the necessity which constrains them to alter their former Systems of Government. The history of the present King of Great Britain is a history of repeated injuries and usurpations, all having in direct object the establishment of an absolute Tyranny over these States. To prove this, let Facts be submitted to a candid world.

Reasons for Independence

He has refused his Assent to Laws, the most wholesome and necessary for the public good.

He has forbidden his Governors to pass Laws of immediate and pressing importance, unless suspended in their operation till his Assent should be obtained; and when so suspended, he has utterly neglected to attend to them.

He has refused to pass other Laws for the accommodation of large districts of people, unless those people would relinquish the right of Representation in the Legislature, a right inestimable to them and formidable to tyrants only.

He has called together legislative bodies at places unusual, uncomfortable, and distant from the depository of their Public Records, for the sole purpose of fatiguing them into compliance with his measures.

He has dissolved Representative Houses repeatedly, for opposing with manly firmness his invasions on the rights of the people.

He has refused for a long time, after such dissolutions, to cause others to be elected; whereby the Legislative Powers, incapable of Annihilation, have returned to the People at large for their exercise; the State remaining in the mean time exposed to all dangers of invasion from without, and convulsions within.

He has endeavoured to prevent the population of these States; for that purpose obstructing the Laws of Naturalization of Foreigners; refusing to pass others to encouraging their migrations hither,

---

take them away. If any government tries to do so, the people have a right to rebel. In fact, all governments are formed by the people and must rule with the support of the people. If any government takes away the rights of the people, the people have a duty to set up a new government. The new government will rule with the people's consent. These ideas about government in the Declaration later helped shape the Constitution of the United States.

Reasons for Independence

The third part of the Declaration lists British actions that took away the colonists' rights.

Many of these things actually had been done by the Parliament, but King George III was blamed for them. Jefferson pictured King George as an evil tyrant who destroyed local self-government on purpose. Some of the things the king is blamed for are:

- not approving laws passed by the colonists; dissolving some colonial governments

- discouraging settlement in the West by raising the price of land

- allowing judges to serve only as long as the king approves of their decisions

and raising the conditions of new Appropriations of Lands.

He has obstructed the Administration of Justice, by refusing his Assent to Laws for establishing Judiciary Powers.

He has made Judges dependent on his Will alone, for the tenure of their offices, and the amount and payment of their salaries.

He has erected a multitude of New Offices, and sent hither swarms of Officers to harass our People, and eat out their substance.

He has kept among us, in times of peace, Standing Armies without the Consent of our legislatures.

He has affected to render the Military independent of and superior to the Civil Power.

He has combined with others to subject us to a jurisdiction foreign to our constitution, and unacknowledged by our laws; giving his Assent to their Acts of pretended legislation:

For quartering large bodies of armed troops among us:

For protecting them, by mock Trial, from punishment for any Murders which they should commit on the Inhabitants of these States:

For cutting off our Trade with all parts of the world:

For imposing Taxes on us without our Consent:

For depriving us in many cases, of the benefits of Trial by Jury:

For transporting us beyond the Seas to be tried for pretended offences:

For abolishing the free System of English Laws in a neighbouring Province, establishing therein an Arbitrary government, and enlarging its Boundaries so as to render it at once an example and fit instrument for introducing the same absolute rule into these Colonies:

For taking away our Charters, abolishing our most valuable Laws and altering fundamentally the Forms of our Governments:

For suspending our own Legislatures, and declaring themselves invested with power to legislate for us in all cases whatsoever.

He has abdicated Government here, by declaring us out of his Protection and waging War against us.

He has plundered our seas, ravaged our Coasts, burnt our towns, and destroyed the lives of our people.

He is at this time transporting large Armies of foreign Mercenaries to compleat the works of death, desolation and tyranny, already begun with circumstances of Cruelty & perfidy scarcely paralleled in the most barbarous ages, and totally unworthy the Head of a civilized nation.

He has constrained our fellow Citizens taken Captive on the high Seas to bear Arms against their Country, to become the executioners of their friends and Brethren, or to fall themselves by their Hands.

He has excited domestic insurrections amongst us, and has endeavoured to bring on the inhabitants of our frontiers, the merciless Indian Savages, whose known rule of warfare, is an

---

- keeping British soldiers in the colonies after the French and Indian War

- demanding total authority over the colonies for the king and Parliament

- restricting trade with other countries

- hiring soldiers to fight the colonists

The colonists had protested these unjust acts, but the British government always had refused to listen. Jefferson was not only trying to inspire the American colonists. He was also trying to convince other nations, such as France, that the colonists were justified in fighting for independence.

Formal Declaration

The last part of the Declaration is the formal declaration of independence from Great Britain. Great Britain was a great military power. If Britain put down the Revolution, the signers of the Declaration could be found guilty of treason and executed. Their formal declaration stated that they were free and had every right to be free. The delegates promised to give their lives, their money, and their honor to the struggle.

undistinguished destruction of all ages, sexes and conditions.

In every stage of these Oppressions We have Petitioned for Redress in the most humble terms: Our repeated Petitions have been answered only by repeated injury. A Prince, whose character is thus marked by every act which may define a Tyrant, is unfit to be the ruler of a free people.

Nor have We been wanting in attention to our Brittish brethren. We have warned them from time to time of attempts by their legislature to extend an unwarrantable jurisdiction over us. We have reminded them of the circumstances of our emigration and settlement here. We have appealed to their native justice and magnanimity, and we have conjured them by the ties of our common kindred to disavow these usurpations, which, would inevitably interrupt our connections and correspondence. They too have been deaf to the voice of justice and of consanguinity. We must, therefore, acquiesce in the necessity, which denounces our Separation, and hold them, as we hold the rest of mankind, Enemies in War, in Peace Friends.

Formal Declaration

We, therefore, the Representatives of the united States of America, in General Congress Assembled, appealing to the Supreme Judge of the world for the rectitude of our intentions, do, in the Name, and by Authority of the good People of these Colonies, solemnly publish and declare, That these United Colonies are, and of Right ought to be Free and Independent States; that they are Absolved from all Allegiance to the British Crown, and that all political connection between them and the State of Great Britain, is and ought to be totally dissolved; and that as Free and Independent States, they have full Power to levy War, conclude Peace, contract Alliances, establish Commerce, and to do all other Acts and Things which Independent States may of right do.—And for the support of this Declaration, with a firm reliance of the protection of Divine Providence, we mutually pledge to each other our Lives, our Fortunes and our sacred Honor.

John Hancock	Thos. Nelson jr.	Tho M:Kean
Button Gwinnett	Francis Lightfoot Lee	Wm. Floyd
Lyman Hall	Carter Braxton	Phil. Livingston
Geo Walton.	Robt. Morris	Frans. Lewis
Wm. Hopper	John Adams	Lewis Morris
Joseph Hewes,	Robt. Treat Paine	Richd. Stockton
John Penn	Elbridge Gerry	Jno Witherspoon
Edward Rutledge.	Step. Hopkins	Fras. Hopkinson
Thos. Heyward Junr.	William Ellery	John Hart
Thomas Lynch Junr.	Benjamin Rush	Abra Clark
Arthur Middleton	Benja. Franklin	Josiah Bartlett
Samuel Chase	John Morton	Wm: Whipple
Wm. Paca	Geo Clymer	Saml. Adams
Thos. Stone	Jas. Smith.	Roger Sherman
Charles Carroll of Carrollton	Geo. Taylor	Saml. Huntington
George Wythe	James Wilson	Wm. Williams
Richard Henry Lee	Geo. Ross	Oliver Wolcott
Th: Jefferson	Caesar Rodney	Matthew Thornton
Benja. Harrison	Geo Read	

CHAPTER 6

The New Nation Wins Its Independence

OBJECTIVE: How did Americans fight and win their war for independence?

1. The American spies in New York City were amazed—and frightened. As they watched, a fleet of nearly 30 warships and 400 other ships sailed into New York harbor and docked. An army of 32,000 soldiers came ashore, along with 10,000 sailors. Then followed an endless stream of cannons and weapons for this huge army. On orders from their commander, the men set up camp and began to prepare for the battles ahead. The British had sent this great army to crush the American states. George Washington now knew that his Continental Army faced an enemy more than twice its size. Yet when the British sent a letter to Washington asking him to surrender, he refused to accept it. Americans were not afraid to face even this powerful British force. They were fighting for their independence.

The 13 Colonies Against Great Britain What advantages and what problems did each side have in fighting the war?

2. At the start of the Revolutionary War, Great Britain was much more powerful than the 13 states. Britain had a larger army. British soldiers were well trained, and they had the weapons and supplies they needed to fight a war. The mighty British navy controlled the seas. British ships could cut off trade and move British armies from one state to another.

▲ George Washington on horseback reviews his ragged troops at Valley Forge. How might these harsh winter conditions actually have strengthened the Continental Army?

3. Despite its powerful army and navy, Great Britain had many problems fighting a war in America. One problem was that Britain was about 3,000 miles (about 4,800 kilometers) from the colonies. Why would this be a disadvantage in fighting a war? Another problem was

In Chapter 6 you will apply these critical thinking skills to the historical process:

▲ **Identifying Fact *versus* Opinion:** Specifying whether information can be proved or whether it expresses feelings or beliefs.

Understanding Points of View: Recognizing why people have different attitudes about the same thing.

that British generals were used to methods of fighting that were not suited to America. They did not understand how to use forests and hills to make surprise attacks. Finally, the war was not strongly supported by the British people. Many of them were unhappy because Parliament had raised their taxes to help pay for the war. Also, many of them believed that the American colonies were right.

4. The American states also had difficult problems in fighting the war. Forming a strong army was the greatest problem. The state militias, or citizen-soldiers in each state, were weak. The Continental Army, commanded by George Washington, seldom had more than 5,000 soldiers. They were untrained and had never before fought in battles. Most of the officers who commanded these soldiers had little military training.

5. The Continental Congress lacked the powers it needed to carry on the war. It had no power to tax the states or the people. Instead, it had to ask the state assemblies for money to fight the war. Often the soldiers were ▶ not paid. Why do you think the states refused to give the Continental Congress the power to tax them?

🦅 Spotlight on Sources

6. George Washington knew how weak the Continental Congress was, and he worried about it. In a letter, Washington wrote:

> Certain I am that unless they [the Continental Congress] are vested with [given] powers competent to [needed for] the great purposes of war, and unless they act with more energy than they hitherto have done, our cause is lost.
>
> —*The Writings of George Washington,*
> ed. by John C. Fitzpatrick

7. The American states did have some important advantages over the British in the Revolutionary War. Americans believed in their cause and were willing to die for it. They also were fighting to defend their homes and families. In addition, Americans knew the land. They were familiar with its forests, trails, hills, and coastlines.

8. The huge size of the 13 states helped the Americans. British armies could capture important cities or take control of large parts of a state. Yet many other cities and the other states were able to keep on fighting.

9. The Americans who led the struggle for independence during the Revolutionary War were an outstanding group of leaders. The Continental Congress included such able men as Benjamin Franklin, Thomas Jefferson, and John Adams. However, no one was more important in winning the Revolutionary War than George Washington. Without his skilled leadership and unselfish courage, the Continental Army could not have held together until it finally won.

People in History

10. George Washington Born into a wealthy family of Virginia tobacco planters, George Washington became interested in the colony's western frontier lands when he was a young man. In 1754 he led a small British force into the Ohio Valley, and a year later he again went west with General Braddock. In 1758, he was elected to the Virginia assembly. In 1774, he was selected as a member of the First Continental Congress. In 1775, he became commander-in-chief of the Continental Army. He served in that job without pay for the next six years, until the American victory. Washington's good judgment and his selfless devotion to the American cause made him the most admired man in America. More than anything else, it was the force of his character that held the Continental Army together.

New York City to Saratoga What were the results of the key battles of 1776 and 1777?

11. The first year of the war brought both defeats and victories for the Americans. In August 1776, a large British army led by General William Howe took New York City. Washington then drew back his small army of 5,000

209

Linking Geography and History

The Geography of the Revolutionary War Every army must have a strategy. Strategy means deciding what places and routes hold the key to winning a war and taking control of them.

British war strategy centered on winning control of the port cities of New York and Philadelphia. This, it was hoped, would lead to control of the middle states.

Control of the Hudson River was another goal of both armies. The British sought control to break communications and supply routes between New England and the South. In 1777, a British army under General John Burgoyne moved south from Canada into the upper valley of the Hudson. Another British army was supposed to move north from New York to meet Burgoyne. However, the army in New York went to Philadelphia instead. The Americans won the crucial Battle of Saratoga and kept control of the Hudson.

Although the British held New York and Philadelphia for part of the war, the Americans kept control of the coastal plain between those two cities. General George Washington, in a daring raid, won the battle of Trenton in 1776 and went on to capture Princeton in 1777.

The Revolutionary War spilled over from the 13 states to lands west of the Appalachians. Successful campaigns by George Rogers Clark won the Ohio and Mississippi valleys for the new nation. Spanish troops also helped Americans after Spain declared war on Britain in 1779. Bernardo de Gálvez, governor of Spanish Louisiana, attacked and pinned down British forces in Baton Rouge and Natchez (1779), Mobile (1780), and Pensacola (1781).

Use the map below to answer these questions.

1. What battles were fought in and around New York City?

2. How would the United States have benefited if its Quebec campaign had been successful?

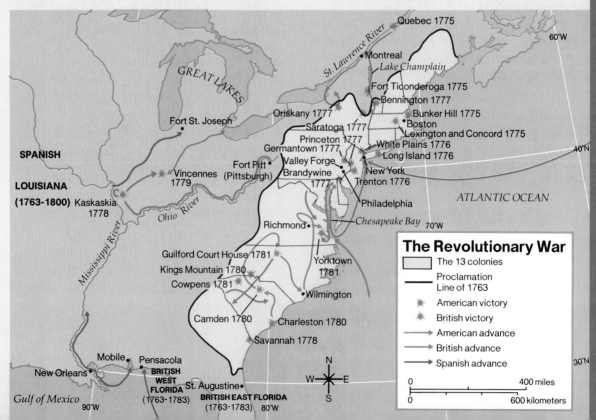

The Revolutionary War

Background: Spain, too, became an ally in 1779. Even earlier, Spain had secretly funnelled money and supplies to America through a dummy trading company. Spanish funding played a vital part in winning the Revolutionary War. Diego de Gardoquí, a wealthy Spanish banker, helped direct this money to the Continental Congress.

into New Jersey. It seemed that the war might be lost. However, in December 1776, Washington made a surprise attack against Hessian soldiers at Trenton and captured the city. A week later, he won against British forces at Princeton. However, New York City remained in British hands for the rest of the war.

12. The Saratoga **campaign** was the turning point of the Revolutionary War. A campaign is a series of movements and battles. In 1777, General John Burgoyne (bur-GOYN) led a British army south from Canada into New York state. An American army, led by General Horatio Gates, moved to meet Burgoyne. Militia from many New England towns joined Gates's army. Together they defeated the British. The first victory, at Bennington, Vermont, was followed by two victories at Saratoga, New York. On October 17, 1777, Burgoyne surrendered his entire army.

13. The American victory at Saratoga brought France into the war. Leaders of the French government now believed that the American states could win their fight for independence. The French government already had secretly given money and weapons to the Continental Army. Now France signed an alliance with the Continental Congress. France promised to send additional weapons and supplies to the Continental Army. France also agreed to send soldiers to America. This French aid played a very important part in helping America win the war.

14. At this same time, the Continental Army was facing its worst months of the war. In September 1777, General Howe had moved his army from New York City to Philadelphia. Washington's small army was forced to **retreat** to the small Pennsylvania town of Valley Forge. To retreat is to pull back. During the severe winter of 1777–1778, these soldiers suffered terrible hardships. They were short of food and supplies. They nearly froze as blasts of icy wind and snow beat against their tents. Still, Washington refused to give up. In fact, he used these months at Valley Forge to make the Continental Army stronger. In doing this, he had important

help from Frederick von Steuben (STOO-ben), a German general who took charge of training the soldiers. By spring, the Continental Army was again prepared to fight the British.

From Saratoga to Yorktown What major battles were fought from 1778 to 1781?

15. After Saratoga, most of the important fighting took place in the southern states. British leaders believed that most people in the South still supported George III. Even though this belief proved to be wrong, the British spent the rest of the war mainly in the South. In 1778, they captured Savannah, Georgia. They planned to take other seaports in the South. In this way, the British navy could supply their troops and also keep supplies from reaching the Americans. In 1780, fighting was mainly in the Carolinas. Small bands of daring Americans now began to make swift surprise raids against the British. In 1781, Charles Cornwallis, the British commander, decided to move north into Virginia.

16. Cornwallis's decision led to the end of the Revolutionary War. In September, Washington and his army had arrived at Yorktown, Virginia, from New York. A French army led by General de Rochambeau (roh-shom-BOH) joined the Americans there. The French navy blocked the British navy from aiding Cornwallis. Why would this make a difference in the outcome of the battle? Cornwallis held out against the American and French armies for almost two weeks. Finally, on October 17, 1781, the British army surrendered. The Battle of Yorktown was the last important battle of the war.

Outlook

17. The Revolutionary War lasted from 1775 until 1781. Saratoga was the turning point of the war, for this important victory led to France's joining the Americans. Aided by the French, Americans won their independence after four more years of fighting. What do you think was the most important reason why America won the war?

Activity: Have the class read accounts of the winter of 1777–1778 at Valley Forge. Then ask them to imagine that there had been television news reporting in the Revolutionary War. Have class members write brief newscasters' descriptions of conditions at Valley Forge.

CHAPTER REVIEW

VOCABULARY REVIEW

▶ On a sheet of paper, copy the following vocabulary words. Check the chapter or use your glossary to be sure of each word's definition. Then write a sentence that uses the word.

retreat	campaign
alliance	advance

SKILL BUILDER: MAKING A TIME LINE

▶ On a sheet of paper, copy the time line below. Then read the dates and events that follow. Add each event to the time line in the correct place.

1770	1773	1776	1779	1782	1785

1774 First Continental Congress meets.

1775 Battles of Lexington and Concord; Second Continental Congress meets; Washington becomes commander of the Continental Army.

1776 Declaration of Independence is adopted.

1777 Washington's army retreats to Valley Forge; British are defeated at Saratoga.

1778 France enters alliance with United States; British capture Savannah, Georgia.

1780 British capture Charleston, South Carolina.

1781 Americans and French defeat the British at Yorktown.

SKILL BUILDER: CRITICAL THINKING AND COMPREHENSION

I. Fact *versus* Opinion

▶ Write the following statements on a sheet of paper. Decide whether each statement is a fact or an opinion. Next to each statement, write **F** if it is a fact or **O** if it is an opinion.

1. Great Britain is about 3,000 miles (4,800 km) from the United States.

2. No one was more important in winning the Revolutionary War than George Washington.

3. In August 1776, the British took New York City.

4. The United States would not have won the Revolutionary War without France.

5. The Battle of Yorktown was the last important battle of the Revolutionary War.

6. British leaders believed that most people in the South supported George III.

7. At the start of the Revolutionary War, Britain's navy controlled the seas.

8. Soldiers in the Continental Army often were not paid.

9. A good soldier should not care whether he is paid.

10. France entered the war after the American victory at Saratoga.

II. Point of View

A point of view is an attitude, belief, or opinion that a person holds. People with different points of view see things differently. For example, Consuela and Eddie recently reviewed *Field of Dreams,* a film about baseball. Here are parts of the two articles. Who wrote each one?

. . . The subject of the movie caused me to yawn. Who cares about some baseball players who died a long time ago? I found the "magic" elements of *Field of Dreams* corny and completely unrealistic. This is NOT a movie for those of you who like real action.

. . . *Field of Dreams* is a film that warms the hearts of the audience. Anyone who loves baseball (and don't we all?) will love this movie. However, the movie is about more than our national sport. The magical return of the famous Black Sox symbolizes the hopes and dreams that all people have. See this movie and come away feeling wonderful.

You know that Consuela enjoys baseball so she would like the subject. This is the point of view in the second review. You can logically guess she wrote it. You also know that Eddie does not like the game. The first review was written from that point of view. You correctly decide Eddie wrote the first one.

▶ The following statements are points of view held by people mentioned in Chapter 6. Write the numbers of the statements on a piece of paper. Then identify the person or people who held that point of view. Write the correct name after the number.

1. The Continental Congress should be given more power, or the Revolutionary War will be lost.

2. The Americans' victory at Saratoga proved they could win the war.

3. Most colonists in the South supported George III.

4. Parliament should not have raised British taxes to pay for the war against the colonists.

5. Surprise attacks that make use of forests and hills are the best way to fight a war.

USING PRIMARY SOURCES

▶ Reread the Spotlight on Sources on page 209. What was George Washington worried about? What would he have liked the Continental Congress to do?

ENRICHMENT

1. You are an American spy in British-held New York City. Write a letter to George Washington about what is happening in the city. Use books in your school or local library to help you describe what the city was like at that time.

2. Benjamin Franklin, Thomas Jefferson, John Adams, and George Washington made outstanding contributions to the Revolutionary War. In a small group, research each leader's contributions and important accomplishments. Then use your research to write a short play about these people. Have them meet on the street, talk together at a party, or watch a football game together. Present the play to the class.

CHAPTER 7

The Revolutionary War Changes American Life

OBJECTIVE: Who contributed to victory in the American Revolution, and how did it change the lives of Americans?

1. The young American soldier carefully aimed his musket and fired. A short distance away, a Redcoat officer fell wounded. The soldier and the other men in the 4th Massachusetts Regiment then charged into the British lines. Soon Robert Shirtliffe was in the midst of the fighting. Then suddenly, Shirtliffe himself staggered and fell to the ground. Other men rushed to his aid, but the young soldier refused their help. Then he fainted from the pain. When Shirtliffe awoke, he was in an army hospital. There he quietly took a surgeon's knife and removed the bullet from his own leg. After another week, he was well enough to return to his regiment. No one had discovered Shirtliffe's secret. Robert Shirtliffe was really Deborah Sampson, a woman dressed as a man. She was one of many women who helped the Continental Army win the Revolution.

▲ Mary Ludwig Hays was a hero of the Battle of Monmouth in 1778. The soldiers called her "Molly Pitcher." Why did they give her that nickname?

Women in the Revolution In what ways did American women help in winning the war?

2. Many American women helped to win the Revolutionary War by taking over men's jobs. With thousands of men off fighting the war, wives and daughters managed the shops and stores that men had always run before. Even more important, women learned to run the families' farms. They planted and harvested crops and sold them to earn money. In this way, women were able to feed their families and earn their own living during the war.

3. Women helped make possible the Continental Army's victories on the battlefield. Many women who managed farms during the Revolution gave or sold their crops to the army for

In Chapter 7 you will apply these critical thinking skills to the historical process:

▲ **Identifying Fact *versus* Opinion:** Specifying whether information can be proved or whether it expresses feelings or beliefs.

Understanding Points of View: Recognizing why people have different attitudes about the same thing.

food. Women also wove the cloth and sewed the uniforms worn by American soldiers. Women collected money to send to the Continental Army. They gave their own pewter or brass bowls, trays, and candlesticks for the army to melt down for ammunition. They made the bandages that were used to save the lives of wounded soldiers.

4. Other women went with their husbands to army camps. One of them was Mary Ludwig Hays, who followed her husband to his camp in the Continental Army. Hays became famous at the Battle of Monmouth in 1778. Through much of the battle, she carried water to the tired and thirsty troops. Then, when her husband fell by his cannon, she took his place. For the rest of the battle she loaded the cannon, keeping it in action and thus helping the Continental Army gain its victory. After the war, she received a soldier's pension for her services.

5. Women acted as spies to help Washington learn about British army plans. Some took jobs cooking and serving food to British officers. They listened as these officers talked about their orders and battle plans. Then they reported the plans to the Continental Army. In this way, women helped win several major battles.

🦅 Spotlight on Sources

6. Many American women believed that they had earned the right to be treated as equals with men. Abigail Adams was one of these women. Here is part of a letter she wrote to her husband, John Adams, when he was a member of the Continental Congress:

> In the new code of laws which I suppose it will be necessary for you to make, I desire [ask] you to remember the ladies and be more generous and favorable to them. If particular care and attention is not paid to the ladies, we will not hold ourselves bound by [will not have to obey] any laws in which we have no voice or representation.
>
> —from *The Book of Abigail and John,*
> ed. Lyman H. Butterfield

What advice does Abigail Adams offer to the ◄ Continental Congress? How many years do you think would pass before American women could vote or hold government office?

African Americans in the Revolution How did African Americans help win the American Revolution?

7. African Americans fought in the major battles of the Revolution, from Lexington to Yorktown. During the war, more than 5,000 African Americans served in the American army. Many of these soldiers were from New England. In Rhode Island, African Americans formed a black regiment. These soldiers helped win the Battle of Newport in 1778 and were praised for their brave actions against the British army.

8. Some of the African Americans who fought in the war were free, but many of them were slaves. When the war began, the Continental Army did not allow slaves to enlist. Then, in 1775, the British army offered freedom to slaves who would fight on its side. Many slaves decided to join the British to gain freedom. In January 1776, the Continental Army changed its policy and agreed to accept slaves as soldiers. Why would the British policy cause the Conti- ◄ nental Army to change its policy? African Americans then formed a large regiment of soldiers in Maryland. Others served in the American army in Virginia, South Carolina, and Georgia.

People in History

9. James Armistead A slave from Virginia named James Armistead took an important part in the Battle of Yorktown. When Washington's army arrived in Virginia in 1781, Armistead's master allowed him to join it. Armistead went to work for Lafayette, the young French general who was serving in the American army. Many times, Lafayette sent Armistead into the British camp to learn about the plans of the British. His reports of the British army's plans helped the French and American armies end the war at Yorktown. Armistead later was honored for his

Background: A few American leaders, including Patrick Henry and Benjamin Franklin, strongly favored abolishing slavery. Franklin founded an abolitionist group in Philadelphia. Others, like Washington and Jefferson, supported the ideal of abolition but continued as slaveowners. Washington freed his slaves in his will.

215

America's People

EUROPEAN ARMY OFFICERS

During the Revolutionary War, the Americans were helped by army officers from Europe. Though few in number, they were important contributors to the Americans' success.

The best-known of these foreigners was a young French nobleman, the Marquis de Lafayette (lah-fah-YET). Lafayette came to the United States in 1777 and served for four years as a general in the Continental Army. Washington admired the young man greatly and came to think of him almost as a son. After the Revolutionary War he returned to France, and later he played an important part in the fight for freedom in his own country.

Another hero in two countries was the Polish officer Thaddeus Kosciusko (kah-see-US-koh). Kosciusko, who came to America in 1776, had been trained in Europe.

Kosciusko's work helped win several battles. Kosciusko later became a hero in Poland.

Germany contributed Frederick von Steuben and Johann de Kalb to the Continental Army. Steuben joined the Continental Army during its winter at Valley Forge. His training turned Washington's raw troops into an orderly army.

A Spanish general, Bernardo de Gálvez (GAHL-vez), also aided the American cause. As governor of Spanish-held Louisiana, he led Spanish forces against the British on the Mississippi and the Gulf of Mexico.

Now answer the following questions.

1. Why did European officers fight in the Revolutionary War?

2. Which of these officers do you think made the most important contribution?

▼ Left, General von Steuben teaches military basics to the Continental Army at Valley Forge. At the right, Bernardo de Gálvez, on horseback, leads his troops into battle.

service. He also gained his freedom after the war and took the name Lafayette.

10. When the war ended, the new state governments granted freedom to most slaves who had fought in the Continental Army. Yet most African Americans had not taken part in the fighting. Thus, most African Americans still were slaves when the war ended.

Patriots against Loyalists How did the Revolution divide the colonists, and what happened to the Loyalists?

11. Some Americans did not want to separate from Britain and become an independent nation. Americans who stayed loyal to George III during the war were called **Loyalists**. Those Americans who supported the war and fought against the British called themselves **Patriots**. Patriots and Loyalists hated each other. Patriots feared that Loyalists would aid the British army. They believed all Loyalists were spies and traitors. However, although some Loyalists did help the British, many just tried to stay out of the fighting.

12. Loyalists suffered many hardships during and after the American Revolution. Many Loyalists lost their homes and their lands. Many were put in prison. As a result, nearly 100,000 Loyalists left the United States. They moved to Canada, the West Indies, and England. Many were lawyers, doctors, landowners, and business people. When they left, the United States lost an important group of educated and able people.

Results of the War What did Americans gain from the peace settlement with Britain?

13. The **Treaty of Paris**, which ended the war in 1783, was very favorable to Americans. In this treaty, Britain recognized the 13 former colonies as an independent nation. Britain agreed to withdraw its soldiers from the United States. The treaty also gave the new nation more territory. The United States now reached north to Canada and west all the way to the Mississippi River. Britain also agreed to return East

▲ When James Armistead Lafayette was an old man, this portrait of him was painted as a gift for General Lafayette.

and West Florida to Spain. See the map on page 220 to locate the new boundaries.

14. In the Treaty of Paris, Great Britain received two promises from the United States. The United States promised to ask the new 13 states to pay the debts their citizens owed to British businesses. It also promised to ask the states to pay for lands taken from colonists who had been loyal to Britain during the war.

Outlook

15. The American Revolution deeply affected the lives of all Americans. Loyalists lost their homes, and many fled to other lands. Women helped win the war and proved they were able to handle men's jobs. African Americans fought for America's freedom. Do you ◄ think women and African Americans would work more strongly for equality in the future?

Activity: Have the class role-play Patriots and Loyalists on the eve of war. Have each group explain what it thinks colonists should do. Each group should also be prepared to rebut the other's arguments.

217

CHAPTER REVIEW

VOCABULARY REVIEW

▶ Write each of the following sentences on a sheet of paper. Fill the blank with the word or phrase that best completes the sentence. Some words or phrases may be used in more than one sentence.

Treaty of Paris   Loyalists   Patriots

1. Americans who sided with Britain during the Revolutionary War were called _____ .

2. The _____ ended the Revolutionary War in 1783 and gave the United States new boundaries.

3. Americans who fought against the British were called _____ .

4. Nearly 100,000 _____ left the United States during and after the Revolutionary War.

5. In the _____ , Britain agreed to return Florida to Spain.

SKILL BUILDER: MAKING AN OUTLINE

▶ On a separate sheet of paper, make an outline of the chapter using the main heads and subtopics below. First locate the topic sentences that will become the main heads labeled I., II., and III. Then select the subtopics and place them under the correct main head. Label the subtopics A, B, C, etc.

Women took over the farms during the war.

Women acted as spies and helped on the battlefield.

How African Americans Helped the War.

How American Women Helped the War.

African Americans fought in all the major battles.

How the War Divided Americans.

Nearly 100,000 Loyalists Leave the United States.

James Armistead was a spy for the American army.

Patriots and Loyalists hated each other.

SKILL BUILDER: CRITICAL THINKING AND COMPREHENSION

I. Fact *versus* Opinion

▶ In each of these pairs, one statement is a fact and one is an opinion. Identify the fact, and write the statement on a sheet of paper.

1. a. More than 5,000 African Americans served in the Continental Army.
   b. The African Americans were the bravest soldiers in the Revolutionary War.

2. a. It was wrong of the British to offer freedom to slaves who fought on their side.
   b. In 1775 the British army offered freedom to slaves who would fight on its side.

3. a. Americans who supported the Revolutionary War and fought against the British were called Patriots.
   b. Patriots fought on the right side in the Revolutionary War.

4. a. Loyalists deserved to lose their homes and lands.
   b. After the war, many Loyalists lost their homes and lands.

5. **a.** Few women fought on the battlefield.
   b. Only men belong on the battlefield.

6. **a.** Women managed farms so their husbands could fight in the war.
   b. Women make better managers than men.

II. Point of View

Point of view means the way someone looks at things. Different people can have different points of view about the same thing. For example, one person may see something as good that another person sees as bad.

▶ Read the following statements. On a sheet of paper, write the numbers of each statement. Write *P* if the statement gives a Patriot point of view and *L* if it gives a Loyalist point of view.

1. Good people are loyal to the country where they live.

2. Good people are loyal to their king.

3. It would be better to live in Canada than in an independent United States.

4. People who don't like it here should get out.

5. Traitors do not deserve to keep their property.

6. We must stand up for our beliefs, even if it costs us everything we own.

USING PRIMARY SOURCES

▶ Reread the Spotlight on Sources on page 209. What warning did Abigail Adams make to her husband and the other members of the Continental Congress? How is this warning like the anger of the colonists to Great Britain?

ENRICHMENT

1. In 1775, the British army offered freedom to slaves who would fight on its side. In 1776, the Continental Army also decided to accept slaves as soldiers. When the Revolutionary War ended, the new state governments granted freedom to most slaves who had fought in the Continental Army. In an essay, explain why you think a slave would have fought in the Continental Army rather than in the British army. Use books on the roles of African Americans in the Revolutionary War for your sources.

2. With another student, role-play a Loyalist and a Patriot having a heated discussion. Tell whether your discussion takes place before, during, or after the Revolutionary War. Have each character show how he or she is reacting to the events of the period. Each character should also show why he or she chose to be either a Patriot or a Loyalist.

3. You are a woman whose husband has been away fighting in the Revolutionary War. While he was away, you ran the farm, made all the planting decisions, and sold the crops. Now he has returned. You cannot make the decisions any more, and he disagrees with anything you suggest. In a letter to your sister, explain how you feel about your husband's return. How do you feel about giving up your responsibilities? Have your feelings for your husband changed?

UNIT REVIEW

SUMMARY

In the 1750s, conflicts in the valley of the Ohio River led to the French and Indian War between Great Britain and France. When the war ended in 1763, France had been driven from North America.

In the years following the war, strong disagreements arose between Great Britain and its American colonies. The main issue was taxes. The British government believed that it had the right to tax the colonies. Colonists believed that only their own colonial assemblies could tax them. The colonies protests against the British taxes led to increasing unity of the colonies. Sometimes the protests also led to violence, as in the Boston Massacre of 1770 and the Boston Tea Party of 1773.

The Continental Congress, with delegates from every colony, met in 1774 and again in 1775. When fighting broke out in 1775 at Lexington and Concord, the Congress appointed George Washington as head of the colonial army. A year later, on July 4, 1776, Congress declared that the colonies were now free and independent.

The new country had to fight a war to win its independence. The British forces had many advantages over the small and poorly equipped Continental Army. However, the Continental Army stayed together, thanks mainly to the leadership of George Washington. With French aid, the Americans finally were victorious.

The last important battle of the American Revolution took place at Yorktown, Virginia, in 1781. Two years later, the Treaty of Paris set the boundaries of the United States. Now the new nation would be faced with the task of forming a government on which all the colonies would agree. The new nation also would have to choose a leader to run the new government. What laws do you think would be important to the new nation?

SKILL BUILDER: READING A MAP

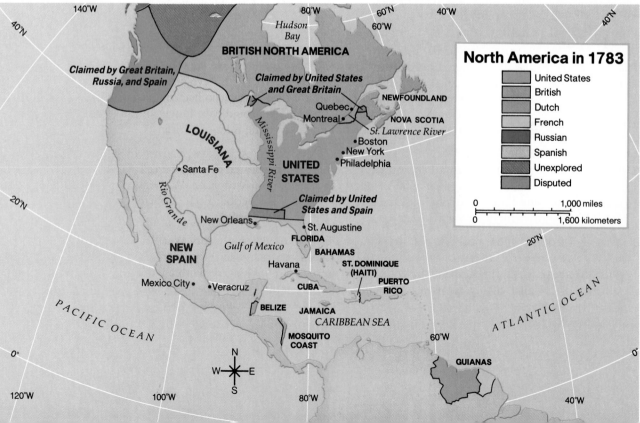

1. What territory was to the north of the United States?

2. Which European country controlled this territory?

3. What river formed the western boundary of the United States?

4. What European country controlled the territory to the west of this boundary?

5. What country controlled New Orleans? Why was control of this city important?

6. To what country did Florida belong in 1783?

SKILL BUILDER: CRITICAL THINKING AND COMPREHENSION

❯ I. Predicting

At the end of the Revolutionary War, Great Britain remained in control of Canada. The United States and Canada shared a long border, stretching from the Atlantic coast through the Great Lakes to the source of the Mississippi River. Predict how this border will affect relations between Great Britain and the United States. Will relations along the border be peaceful and friendly, or hostile and unfriendly? Write a paragraph that states your prediction and gives your reasons for it.

II. Point of View

1. Select one of the major events described in Unit 5. Write a paragraph describing the event from the point of view of an American. The American may be either taking part in the event or standing on the sidelines watching it.

2. Write a second paragraph describing the same event from a British point of view.

ENRICHMENT

1. Choose an event discussed in the unit. Read about the details of this event in your library. Then write a newspaper article telling about the event. Begin the article with a paragraph that includes the five Ws of newspaper articles: who, what, when, where, why. When your article is finished, write a headline for it. OPTIONAL: Draw an illustration for the article.

2. Suppose that it is June 1776. You are a member of the Second Continental Congress. The Congress is trying to decide whether it is a good idea to declare independence from Great Britain. Prepare a speech that you will give at the next meeting of the Congress. Your speech should argue for one of these points of view and against the other two:
   a. The colonies should declare independence, and the sooner the better.
   b. Independence is the goal that the colonies should work toward. However, declaring it now would be dangerous.
   c. Independence would probably create more problems than it solves. The colonies should instead try to work out their problems with Great Britain.

UNIT 6

A NEW GOVERNMENT, A GROWING NATION

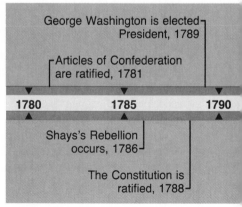

Chapter

UNIT OVERVIEW   Unit 6 will help you see how the United States grew in size and strength after the War for Independence.

UNIT SKILLS OBJECTIVES   In Unit 6, two critical thinking skills are emphasized:

Understanding Points of View: Recognizing why people have different attitudes about the same thing.

Making Judgments: Stating a personal opinion based on historical facts.

You will also use two important social studies skills:
Using a Chart   Reading a Map

George Washington is elected President, 1789

Articles of Confederation are ratified, 1781

| 1780 | 1785 | 1790 |

Shays's Rebellion occurs, 1786

The Constitution is ratified, 1788

ESL/LEP Strategy: On separate index cards, write the major events that occurred in the United States as it grew in the years after gaining its independence. After students complete the unit, have them identify these events and put them in chronological order.

▲ George Washington, standing at right, watches as state delegates step up to sign the Constitution of the United States on September 17, 1787.

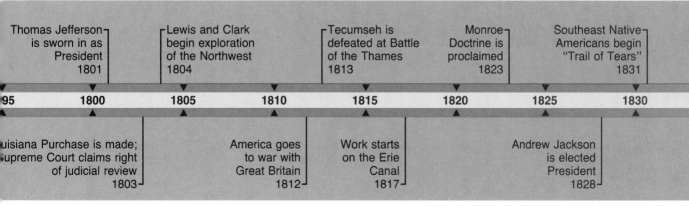

Thomas Jefferson is sworn in as President 1801

Lewis and Clark begin exploration of the Northwest 1804

Tecumseh is defeated at Battle of the Thames 1813

Monroe Doctrine is proclaimed 1823

Southeast Native Americans begin "Trail of Tears" 1831

95   1800   1805   1810   1815   1820   1825   1830

uisiana Purchase is made; upreme Court claims right of judicial review 1803

America goes to war with Great Britain 1812

Work starts on the Erie Canal 1817

Andrew Jackson is elected President 1828

Points of View

After the War of Independence, Americans set up a loose union of states with a central government. The central government was not very powerful. Even though the nation had a war debt of $40 million, the central government did not have the power to tax. Some states helped pay the war debt, while other states did not. Some states taxed goods coming into their state from another state. Massachusetts had the highest government debt of all the states. To pay for this debt Massachusetts had high taxes. People who could not pay their taxes were put in debtors' prison. Finally, in 1786, a group of Massachusetts

▲ By the 1780s, many farmers in the new United States had become quite successful. What protection might a strong central government offer to a farm such as the one pictured?

IN FAVOR OF THE CONSTITUTION

❝ Mr. President, . . . there was a black cloud [Shays's Rebellion] that rose in the east last winter, and spread over the west. . . . People that used to live peaceably, and were before good neighbors, got distracted [carried away], and took up arms against government. . . . [I]f you went to speak to them, you had the musket [shotgun] of death presented to your breast. They would rob you . . . , threaten to burn your houses. . . .

Our distress [upset] was so great that we should have been glad to [grab] at anything that looked like a government. . . . So that you see that anarchy [complete absence of government] leads to tyranny. . . .

Some gentlemen say, don't be in a hurry; take time to consider [think]; and don't take a leap in the dark. I say, take things in time—gather the fruit when it's ripe. . . . Now is the time to reap the fruit of our labor. And if we won't do it now, I am afraid we never shall have another opportunity. ❞

—*New York Journal and Weekly Register,*
November 8, 1787

Deciding on a New Form of Government

people led by Daniel Shays decided to rebel against the state government. While Shays's Rebellion did not succeed, it made George Washington and other leaders uneasy. Washington felt that power struggles among the states would not be happening if the central government were stronger.

In the first passage below, Jonathan Smith, who owned a small farm, agrees with Washington that a stronger central government is needed. In the second passage, Patrick Henry, a Virginia leader, argues against the proposed Constitution, which would make the national government stronger.

AGAINST THE CONSTITUTION

"The [Articles of] Confederation, this despised [hated] government, merits [deserves] in my opinion the highest [praise]. It carried us through a long and dangerous war [with Great Britain]; it rendered [made] us victorious in that bloody conflict with a powerful nation. It has secured [gained] us a territory greater than any European monarch possesses [owns]. And shall a government which has been thus strong . . . be accused of imbecility [weakness] . . . ?

I am sure [the delegates to the Constitutional Convention] were fully impressed with the necessity of forming a great consolidated [central] government instead of a confederation [union] [of states]. . . . [T]he danger of such a [central] government is, to my mind, very striking [obvious]. I have the highest [regard] for those gentlemen [the convention delegates], but, sir, give me leave [allow me] to demand: What right had they to say, *We, the people . . .* instead of, *We, the states?* States are the . . . soul of a confederation."

—*Virginia Ratifying Convention,*
June 4, 1788

▲ Patrick Henry, whose speeches had inspired Americans before the Revolution, played an active role in debating the Constitution.

Using Primary Sources

1. Why did Jonathan Smith fear Americans would never have another chance to change their form of government?

2. What did Patrick Henry think of the government under the Articles of Confederation?

3. Why was Patrick Henry against the new Constitution?

225

CHAPTER 1

The New Nation Stumbles

OBJECTIVE: Why did the Confederation government fail to build a strong new nation?

1. John Dickinson of Delaware stared out the window of the meeting hall of the Second Continental Congress. He was remembering the words of a British officer, spoken after the colonists had won the War for Independence: "These United States will not last." Already the officer's prediction seemed to be coming true. The 13 states were arguing over many issues, including slavery, voting rights, and claims to western lands. Dickinson, like other American leaders, knew that if the nation were to last, the states had to band together. He and the other members of the Second Continental Congress were about to take an important vote. The vote would decide the plan of government for the new United States.

▲ John Dickinson, Delaware's state delegate to the Second Continental Congress, prepared the first draft of the Articles of Confederation.

The Articles of Confederation What plan of government did the United States adopt after the Revolutionary War?

2. In 1777, the Second Continental Congress wrote a plan of government for the United States called the **Articles of Confederation** (kun-fed-uh-RAY-shun). The plan called for a loose union of states with a limited central government. The Articles were adopted in 1781 by all 13 states.

3. The Articles formed just one branch of government—the Congress. Under the Articles, states elected from two to seven men to the Congress, but each state had only one vote in Congress. For example, tiny Rhode Island had an equal vote with Virginia, which was larger and had many more people. Was this a fair ◄ system of representation? The approval of 9 of the 13 states was needed to pass most laws.

In Chapter 1 you will apply these critical thinking skills to the historical process:

Understanding Points of View: Recognizing why people have different attitudes about the same thing.

Identifying Fact *versus* Opinion: Specifying whether information can be proved or whether it expresses feelings or beliefs.

Changes to the Articles, however, needed the approval of all 13 states. Usually, getting that many states to agree was very hard.

4. The Articles of Confederation gave few powers to the new government. The Congress, not the states, took care of all foreign affairs. Foreign affairs are matters between countries such as trade, war, and peace. The duties of Congress ranged from making war and arranging treaties to coining money and supplying postal services. Yet because the memory of "taxation without representation" was strong, Congress had no power to raise money by collecting taxes. Congress could only ask the states for money.

5. Unlike the United States government today, the Confederation government had no President to carry out the laws. Nor was there a national system of courts to protect peoples' rights. How did the lack of a strong government threaten the new freedom of the United States?

▚ Spotlight on Sources

6. The first three articles of the Articles of Confederation stress that the new government was, above all, a union of states:

ARTICLE I. The stile [name] of this confederacy [union] shall be "The United States of America."

ARTICLE II. Each State retains [keeps] its sovereignty [power], freedom and independence, and every power, jurisdiction [limits of power], and right, which is not by this confederation expressly [given] to the United States Congress assembled.

ARTICLE III. The said states hereby severally [together] enter in a firm league [union] of friendship with each other for their common defense, the security [safety] of the liberties and their mutual [joint] and general welfare; binding themselves to [help] each other against all force offered to, or attacks made upon them, on account of religion, sovereignty, trade, or any other pretense [excuse] whatsoever.

Was the power of the states reduced or ◀ strengthened by Article III? In what way?

Weaknesses of the Confederation How well did the new nation deal with problems in Europe and at home?

7. The Confederation government had mixed results in foreign policy. After the American Revolution, it worked out the Treaty of Paris, by which Great Britain recognized American independence. Two years later it made a treaty with Spain, opening up American trading rights with the Spanish West Indies. Foreign governments, however, soon saw that the Congress lacked power both at home and in Europe.

▼ Great Britain broke the Treaty of Paris by refusing to leave its forts in the Northwest. Fort Washington (below) was one of the few forts there over which the American flag flew.

Activity: Tell students the first set of rules was called the Articles of Confederation. If you like, make an analogy between the problems Americans faced in creating a government to the problems students face in forming a student council or club. Ask how they decide what rules to make, when and where to meet, and so on.

227

For example, it could not raise money for a navy to defend American trading ships against pirates on the Mediterranean Sea. Many American ships were seized and hundreds of American sailors taken prisoner. Nor could Congress enforce the treaties it made. Great Britain broke the Treaty of Paris by keeping ports and fur-trading posts in the American Northwest territory. Yet, without a strong army, Americans were unable to take from Britain what had become rightfully theirs.

8. Settlers in the western territories complained bitterly about the Confederation government. These settlers said the trade treaty with Spain gave up their rights to ship goods on the Mississippi River. They also said the Congress failed to protect them from Native American attacks.

9. The Congress promised the western settlers the right to elect a law-making body. In 1785, a land **ordinance** (OR-duh-nens), or law, divided the Northwest Territory into townships. Two years later, a law called the Northwest Ordinance divided the territory into future states. This law said that settlers could elect territorial **legislatures** (LEJ-uh-slay-cherz), or lawmaking bodies. It also said territories could ask for statehood when their population reached 60,000. New states would be equals of the original states. (You will read more about the Northwest Ordinance in Chapter 4.)

10. Perhaps the biggest failure of Congress, however, was in getting money from the states. The states had Revolutionary War debts of their own to repay, and tax collectors had been unpopular since the Revolution. Therefore, the states never gave Congress the full money it needed. The government had so little money by 1783 that Revolutionary War soldiers marched on Congress to demand their back pay. Members of Congress in Philadelphia had to scatter to their homes to avoid the soldiers. Neither could Congress pay its own war debts. This failure caused the paper money it had printed during wartime, called "Continentals," to drop in value. "Not worth a Continental" became a popular saying of the times for something worthless.

▼ At first, states issued their own currency, such as the Georgia four dollar banknote, 1777, on the left. Later, Congress got the power to coin money, such as the United States Continental Currency twenty dollar banknote, 1778, on the right.

Shays's Rebellion How did a farmers' revolt show the need for a stronger government?

11. The most dramatic sign of public unrest under the Confederation was an uprising by farmers in Massachusetts called Shays's Rebellion. Small farmers in western Massachusetts and other states were being pressed by **creditors** (KRED-uh-terz) to repay their debts. Creditors are people who lend money or to whom money is owed. At the same time, state governments were raising the farmers' taxes. The courts took the farm animals and land of farmers who could not pay their debts. In 1786 armed bands of angry farmers led by Daniel Shays tried to seize an **arsenal** (AR-suh-nul) in Springfield that was filled with rifles. An arsenal is a place for making or storing weapons. The Massachusetts army protected the arsenal and arrested the leaders of the rebellion.

People in History

12. Daniel Shays As a captain in the Revolutionary War, Daniel Shays fought at Bunker Hill. After the war he became a farmer in Pelham, Massachusetts. There, other farmers looked to him for leadership in their struggle against the creditors.

13. By the end of 1786, Shays had become a leader around whom many farmers rallied. Angered by court rulings that took lands from small farmers, Shays led armed bands on raids that closed down the courts. Shays said he was "sorry he ever engaged in the scrape," but he "had his hand to the plough and could not now look back." In the skirmish at Springfield, 4 farmers were killed and 20 wounded. Shays was sentenced to death, but he fled from the Massachusetts military across the border to Vermont. In later years, he made his peace with Massachusetts and was pardoned.

14. Shays's Rebellion frightened many Americans, especially merchants and wealthy property holders. Why would these people have been especially frightened by the revolt? If Congress had had troops and power, some

▲ Daniel Shays's followers seized a Massachusetts court in 1786. Shays and other small farmers were angered by court rulings that took their lands as debt repayment.

people argued, the farmers would not have rebelled. Many Americans called for a stronger government to protect lives and property.

Outlook

15. The Confederation government lacked the power to solve the many difficult issues it faced. Most Americans did not really know much about their national government. Only white men who owned property had voting rights. Most citizens felt far closer to their state governments, whose officials they did elect and whose actions affected their daily lives. But the states often quarreled among themselves. A stronger central government seemed necessary. Soon a movement would begin to strengthen the central government. But could the 13 states overcome their fears and set aside their disagreements to become a truly united nation?

Activity: We tend to talk mostly about the failures of the Articles of Confederation. Have students make a list of its successes and discuss why some people defended this form of government.

229

CHAPTER REVIEW

VOCABULARY REVIEW

▶ Number your paper from 1 to 4. Then complete each of the following sentences by writing the letter of the phrase that best explains the underlined word or words.

1. The Articles of Confederation established
   a. American independence from Great Britain.
   b. a strong central government.
   c. a union of states.

2. In 1785, Congress passed an ordinance that
   a. protected settlers from attacks by Native Americans.
   b. raised farmers' taxes.
   c. divided the Northwest Territory into townships.

3. In the 1780s, farmers were pressed by their creditors
   a. to increase their debts.
   b. to pay back their debts.
   c. to seek government loans.

4. In 1786, an armed band of farmers led by Daniel Shays tried to seize an arsenal in Springfield that was filled with
   a. rifles.
   b. farm animals.
   c. money.

5. The Northwest Ordinance allowed the settlers to elect territorial legislatures to
   a. coin money.
   b. make laws for the territory.
   c. apply for statehood.

SKILL BUILDER: COMPLETING A CHART

▶ Copy the chart below onto a sheet of paper. The statements in the chart refer to the government under the Articles of Confederation. The underlined part makes the statement true or false. If the statement is false, change the underlined part to make the statement true.

PLAN OF GOVERNMENT UNDER
THE ARTICLES OF CONFEDERATION

a. Three branches of government

b. Approval of 13 states needed to pass most laws

c. Two to seven delegates elected to Congress from each state

d. Two congressional votes per state

e. Approval of 13 states needed to make changes to the Articles

f. One President to carry out the laws

SKILL BUILDER: CRITICAL THINKING AND COMPREHENSION

I. Point of View

▶ Who am I? On a sheet of paper, identify the person from the list below who might have made each of the following statements in the 1780s.

Daniel Shays	Congressman	Henry Knox
British general	western settler	creditors

1. We insist on keeping a fort in the American Northwest Territory, in spite of the Treaty of Paris.

2. We don't like giving up our right to ship goods on the Mississippi.

3. We take the farm animals of farmers who can't pay their debts.

4. I fled to Vermont after attacking the Springfield arsenal and later made my peace with the government.

5. If Congress had the power to raise an army, there never would have been a Shays's Rebellion.

II. Fact *versus* Opinion

▶ Read each statement of fact below. Each statement is followed by a question that asks you what you think about the event. Write your opinion on a sheet of paper. Where you can, use facts from this chapter to support your opinion.

1. In 1783, American soldiers who fought in the Revolutionary War marched on Congress to demand their back pay. Were they right to take this action? Why?

2. The Articles of Confederation gave few powers to the national government. Was this a good decision? Why?

USING PRIMARY SOURCES

▶ Reread the Spotlight on Sources on page 227. How did the first three Articles limit the powers of the new central government? Write your answer on a sheet of paper.

ENRICHMENT

1. Suppose the United States government still operated under the Articles of Confederation. Write a brief essay suggesting how your state might be different if it had remained more independent from other states.

2. Read the photo caption on page 226. Do library research to gather information on John Dickinson's life and times. Then write a speech from Dickinson's point of view, explaining why the Articles of Confederation was a good plan of government.

3. Imagine that you are Daniel Shays. Your rebellion against the state government has collapsed, and you have fled from your state. Prepare a statement for the newspapers to explain what your rebellion was all about.

CHAPTER 2

Forming a New Plan of Government

OBJECTIVE: What were the problems in writing the new plan of government, and how were they solved?

1. Imagine that not enough members of the Student Council came to the meetings. You might want to change the rules so that people who skipped two meetings in a row couldn't belong anymore. How would you go about changing the rules? Would you write a new rule and then vote on it? In the 1700s, many Americans thought the rules of their government needed changing, too. So 55 of the most famous men in the new nation got together to write a new set of rules that would last—the United States Constitution.

The Constitutional Convention Why was this meeting held and who attended?

2. The Constitutional Convention met at Philadelphia in May 1787 to discuss ways to strengthen the federal government. Many of America's smartest leaders were among the 55 delegates to the convention. Well-educated and wealthy lawyers, merchants, and planters, they represented the people who had the power to make changes in America. However, Native Americans, African Americans, and women of all races were not allowed to have a say in forming the new government. George Washington agreed to serve as president of the convention. Elderly Benjamin Franklin was a delegate. So were the bright young lawyer

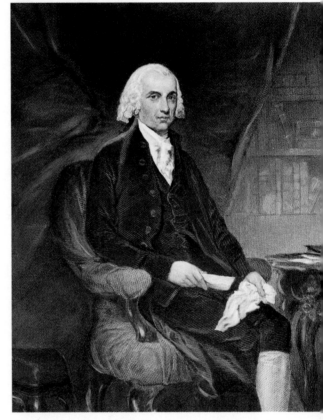

▲ James Madison's wide knowledge of history and philosophy helped him become an expert at solving political problems.

Alexander Hamilton and the well-educated, soft-spoken James Madison.

People in History

3. James Madison Virginia's delegate, James Madison not only studied history, he also

In Chapter 2 you will apply these critical thinking skills to the historical process:
Making Judgments: Stating a personal opinion based on historical facts.

Understanding Points of View: Recognizing why people have different attitudes about the same thing.

put it to use. By studying the governments of nations, past and present, he learned how governments should work. He used this knowledge in forming a new plan of government for the Confederation.

4. Madison wanted to establish a **federal** (FED-uh-ruhl) **government** with the power divided between the national government and the states. Madison's plan offered a middle ground between a national government that has all the power and one that has almost none. Therefore, the delegates were quick to support the plan.

5. The Virginia Plan, as Madison's idea was called, divided power among three independent branches of the federal government. The **legislative** (LEJ-uh-slay-tiv) **branch** would make laws. A chief executive, called the President, would head the **executive** (ek-ZEK-yoo-tiv) **branch** and would carry out the laws. The **judicial** (joo-DISH-uhl) **branch,** or the nation's court system, would judge the meaning of laws. The courts would also judge the way the laws are carried out.

6. Madison took an active role in urging the states to ratify the Constitution that the delegates had written. Madison wrote many of the newspaper essays known as *The Federalist Papers.* Drawing from his understanding of past governments, Madison told in these essays how he thought the new Constitution would work. Later, Madison devoted his life to the new government he had helped to form. He became a leader in the House of Representatives and then served as secretary of state under President Thomas Jefferson. Later he served two terms as President of the United States.

The Great Compromise What conflicts threatened to block the convention, and how were they resolved?

7. The convention almost broke down over a disagreement between the large and small states. Madison's Virginia Plan stated that Congress, the legislative branch, have a lower house and an upper house. It urged that the states be represented in Congress based on the size of

▼ The chart below shows the makeup of the three branches of government as they exist in the United States today. Which positions in the executive branch are filled by elected politicians? Among all three branches, which elected politicians serve the longest term?

THE THREE BRANCHES OF THE FEDERAL GOVERNMENT

Executive Branch	Legislative Branch	Judicial Branch

PRESIDENT
VICE-PRESIDENT
  (elected every 4 years)
CABINET OF DEPARTMENT HEADS
  (chosen by President subject
  to Senate's approval)
DEPARTMENTS:
• State • Health and Human
• Treasury   Services
• Justice • Housing and Urban
• Interior   Development
• Agriculture • Transportation
• Commerce • Energy
• Labor • Education
• Defense • Veterans Affairs
	CONGRESS
	SENATE
	  100 elected members
	  Serve 6-year terms
	  2 Senators per state
	
	HOUSE OF REPRESENTATIVES
	  435 elected members
	  Serve 2-year terms
		SUPREME COURT
		  9 Supreme Court justices
		  appointed for life
		LOWER COURTS
		• 12 U.S. Courts of Appeals
		• U.S. Court of Appeals for
		  the Federal Circuit
		• 91 U.S. District Courts
		SPECIAL COURTS
		• U.S. Claims Court
		• U.S. Court of International Trade
		• U.S. Court of Military Appeals
		• U.S. Tax Court

Activity: Have students write short essays about delegates to the Convention not mentioned in the text (e.g., George Mason, Elbridge Gerry, Edmund Randolph, William Paterson, Roger Sherman, Charles Pinckney, Governeur Morris).

their populations. States with large populations, such as Virginia, would have more members in Congress than smaller states, such as New Jersey. The small states could not accept this plan. Instead, the small states offered the New Jersey Plan, under which all states would be equally represented. How was this solution unfair to the larger states? Neither side would give in to the other. Then Connecticut suggested a plan that came to be called the **Great Compromise** (KAHM-pruh-myz), which met the demands of both sides. A compromise is the give and take to arrive at a solution both sides can live with. In the lower house, the House of Representatives, the states would have representation based on the size of their population. In the upper house, the Senate, all states large or small would have two representatives. The Great Compromise was accepted by the convention.

8. James Madison believed that the issue of slavery was a greater threat to the success of the convention. While slavery was allowed in all states, the greatest number of slaves were in the South. African American slaves were the chief source of labor on Southern plantations. It was clear that slave states would never join a union that failed to protect their property.

9. The Northern and Southern states disagreed over whether to count slaves as part of the population. If slaves were counted, the Southern states would send more representatives to the House of Representatives than the Northern states. The Northern states argued that because slaves were "property" in the South and could not vote, they should not be counted. Finally a compromise was reached. The **Three-Fifths Compromise** said that three-fifths of the slaves would be counted when figuring taxes and the number of a state's representatives. Another disagreement over slavery arose when Northerners wanted the Constitution to put an end to the slave trade. Southerners argued that if they could no longer import slaves, their whole plantation system would be destroyed. Again, a compromise was reached. Northern and Southern delegates agreed to allow the slave trade to continue until 1808. After that,

Congress would be free to put an end to the slave trade. The Constitution never uses the word "slaves." It refers only to "other persons" and persons "held to service." Why do you think the Constitution avoided the word "slave"?

Spotlight on Sources

10. The purpose of the Constitution is stated in its **Preamble** (PREE-am-buhl), or introduction. The Preamble states that the Constitution would create a "more perfect union" than the Articles of Confederation. This would be not just a union of states but a union of "people of the United States." As you read the Preamble, find the six reasons for having a United States Constitution.

> We the people of the United States, in Order to form a more perfect Union, establish Justice, insure domestic Tranquility [protect peace at home or in the nation], provide for the common defense, promote the general Welfare [every citizen's well-being], and secure the Blessings of Liberty to ourselves and our Posterity [descendants], do ordain [order] and establish this Constitution for the United States of America.

Why do you think each of the six points are important?

Ratifying the Constitution What key issues were debated between supporters and opponents of the Constitution?

11. The delegates to the Constitutional Convention completed the new plan for a government of the United States in September 1787. The plan called for a democracy, a type of government in which the people hold the ruling power through elected representatives. Now it was up to the states to decide whether they would **ratify** (RAT-uh-fy), or vote for, the Constitution. The Constitution was to take effect after it had been ratified by 9 of the 13 states.

▲ A silk painted banner carried in the parade for the ratification of the Constitution read "solid and pure." Americans celebrated the unity of their new plan of government.

12. Soon the country was divided for or against the Constitution. Federalists believed the Constitution provided the strong national government that the United States needed. Among the Federalists were such leaders as George Washington, James Madison, and Alexander Hamilton. Those who were against the Constitution became known as Anti-Federalists. Anti-Federalists such as Patrick Henry and Samuel Adams placed their trust in state government. They wanted a loose confederation of the states. They objected to the fact that there was no Bill of Rights in the Constitution. A Bill of Rights was needed, they argued, to define and protect the rights of citizens. To win Anti-Federalist support, Federalists promised to add a Bill of Rights to the Constitution once the new government was ratified.

13. The nation watched closely as states struggled to approve or reject the Constitution. Smaller states believed that much had been achieved at the Philadelphia convention, and most of them ratified the Constitution right away. The major struggle took place in the larger states. For example, Anti-Federalist feel-ings ran strong in New York and Virginia. But Virginia's Federalists finally won. In June 1788 Virginia became the ninth state to ratify the Constitution, which allowed it to become law. Not wanting to be left out of the union, New York ratified the Constitution a month later. Only two states, Rhode Island and North Carolina, waited to join the Union until after the new government had begun.

Outlook

14. The Constitution, with the addition of the Bill of Rights, established a democratic government to protect Americans' rights. Ideally, in a democracy, all people should have the right to vote. Why could America only be ◄ considered a limited democracy in 1788? Is America still a limited democracy? Why? Today the Constitution continues to protect the liberty of Americans. People in some areas of the world still look to the United States as their hope for freedom. The success of the Constitution is a tribute to the hard work done by those who gathered in Philadelphia in 1787.

Background: In addition to slaves, those who could not vote but were counted for representation included women, children, and men who owned no property.

CHAPTER REVIEW

VOCABULARY REVIEW

▶ Write each number and word on a sheet of paper. Then write the letter of the definition next to the word it defines.

1. federal government

2. Great Compromise

3. ratify

4. Preamble

5. executive branch

6. legislative branch

7. judicial branch

8. Three-Fifths Compromise

a. to vote for
b. the branch of government that makes laws
c. the introduction to the Constitution
d. the branch of government that carries out laws
e. a type of government where power is divided between the national government and the states
f. the part of the Constitution guaranteeing the rights of citizens
g. the plan for Congress that was accepted by the Constitutional Convention
h. the branch of government that interprets laws
i. agreement reached at the Constitutional Convention to count a percentage of slaves as part of a state's population when figuring taxes and the number of its representatives

SKILL BUILDER: INTERPRETING A CARTOON

▶ Reread paragraph 12. Then look at the cartoon at the bottom of this page. Answer the questions about the cartoon on a sheet of paper.

1. Who is the "jury"?

2. What men are arguing?

3. Why are they arguing?

4. What paper is in their hands?

5. How was the argument settled?

6. When did the argument take place?

SKILL BUILDER: CRITICAL THINKING AND COMPREHENSION

I. Making Judgments

When you make a judgment, you make a decision by examining the facts. When you go to the cafeteria and decide not to have a particular food for lunch, you are making a judgment. Maybe you had that food before and didn't like it. Or, imagine you are on a jury listening to the story of a crime. You listen to evidence for and against the person accused of the crime. Then you make a judgment of guilty or not guilty.

▶ Which of the following plans discussed at the Constitutional Convention offered the best solution to the problem of state represention in Congress? Write your judgment on a sheet of paper, and give a reason for your decision.

1. The Virginia Plan: States would be represented in Congress according to the size of their populations.

2. The New Jersey Plan: All states would be equally represented in Congress.

3. The Connecticut Plan: States would be represented in the House according to the size of their populations. Every state, regardless of size, would have two representatives in the Senate.

II. Point of View

▶ Imagine that you were sent to Philadelphia by your local newspaper to write about the Constitutional Convention. Your boss told you to find out about the points of view of people for and against the Constitution. On a sheet of paper, write the point of view of Federalists and then of Anti-Federalists. Reread paragraph 12 if you need help.

USING PRIMARY SOURCES

▶ The purpose of the Declaration of Independence was to free the colonists from the strong government of Great Britain. Reread the Spotlight on Sources on page 234. What was the purpose of the Constitution?

ENRICHMENT

1. James Madison kept an important journal about the activities of the Constitutional Convention. Imagine that you were a delegate to the convention. Write a journal entry of your thoughts about the delegates and the issues they debated.

2. In the ratifying convention, arguments were voiced for and against the Constitution. What reasons would Patrick Henry give for opposing the Constitution? How would James Madison respond? Do library research, then write a speech from the point of view of either Madison or Henry arguing for or against ratification.

237

CHAPTER 3

A Federal Government Is Formed

OBJECTIVE: What plan of government did the authors of the Constitution give the United States?

1. When the Constitution was signed after the long, hot summer of 1787, no one was more pleased than Benjamin Franklin. Franklin, at 81, was the oldest delegate to the convention. On the back of George Washington's chair was painted a picture of the sun. Franklin said he had always wondered if that sun was coming up or going down. "But now," he said, "I have the happiness to know that it is a rising and not a setting Sun." He was right. That day, the delegates had created a system of government that is still in use today, over 200 years later.

Three Branches of Government   What are the powers of Congress, the President, and the courts?

2. In June 1788, the Constitution became the supreme law of the land. The shapers of the Constitution were forward-looking. They saw that disagreements might someday arise between the state constitutions and the new federal laws. To protect their hard work, they wrote a statement in the Constitution that made the laws of the federal government supreme. In other words, federal laws would be obeyed over state laws.

3. In addition to giving the United States a federal government, the Constitution divided that government into three separate parts or

▲ Flower girls greet General George Washington on his way to his inauguration as the first President of the United States.

branches. These branches of government are the legislative, the executive, and the judicial. Although each branch has certain powers, the Constitution was careful to keep any one branch from becoming too strong. This system is called **separation of powers.** How does this system ◄ protect the people?

238

In Chapter 3 you will apply these critical thinking skills to the historical process:

◢ **Making Judgments:** Stating a personal opinion based on historical facts.

Understanding Points of View: Recognizing why people have different attitudes about the same thing.

4. Article I of the Constitution describes Congress, the legislative branch of the United States government. The chief job of Congress is to make laws. Congress has the power to coin money and set taxes, to raise an army and navy, and to declare war. It also controls trade with foreign countries and sometimes between states.

5. The executive branch of the federal government enforces the laws passed by Congress. The President, as head of the executive branch, is commander in chief of the armed forces. Choosing cabinet members, federal judges, and ambassadors and making treaties with foreign nations are among the President's powers.

6. The Constitution set the length of term a President serves at four years. With no limit placed on reelection, a President could be reelected as often as the people wanted. Was that a good or bad idea? Why? Also, the Constitution protects the presidency in case the President dies, resigns, or becomes unable to perform the job. In such cases, the Vice-President takes on the role of President until the next presidential election.

7. The third branch of the national government interprets or explains the federal laws. This branch is made up of the Supreme Court and a number of lower federal courts. The Supreme Court plays an especially important role in the national government. It settles disagreements over the meaning of laws passed by Congress. It also has the power to declare a law **unconstitutional** (un-kahn-stuh-TOO-shun-uhl). In other words, it can rule that a law passed by Congress conflicts with the Constitution and is therefore not acceptable.

8. The nine **justices,** or judges, who sit on the United States Supreme Court are the most important judges in the court system. They handle cases that cover federal laws, the United States government, foreign ambassadors, and treaties with foreign countries. The justices are chosen by the President and serve on the Court ▶ for life. How does a lifetime appointment protect the justices from political pressure and help them to make fair decisions? What are some negative results of a lifetime appointment?

Checks and Balances How does the Constitution keep any one branch of government from becoming too powerful?

9. The members of the convention adopted a system of **checks and balances** among the three branches of government. In other words, they gave each branch of government powers to serve as a check on the other branches. In this way, no one branch can become too powerful. For example, the President (executive branch) can veto a bill passed by Congress (legislative branch) and keep it from becoming law. In turn, Congress can refuse to pass laws that the President supports. The Supreme Court (judicial branch) can check both the President and Congress by declaring a law unconstitutional. How does a system of checks and balances make ◀ a government more fair?

Amending the Constitution How can changes be made in America's plan of government?

10. The Constitution is a living document because it can be changed. These changes, or additions, are called **amendments** (uh-MEND-ments). A convention to propose an amendment can be called by Congress or two-thirds of the state legislatures. Each house of Congress must pass the amendment by a two-thirds vote before it goes to the states for approval. If three-fourths of the states approve the change, it is added to the Constitution.

The Bill of Rights What rights are guaranteed to all Americans?

11. As you recall, the Anti-Federalists ratified the Constitution on condition that a Bill of Rights would be added later on. During the first meeting of the House of Representatives in June 1789, the Federalists kept their promise. James Madison proposed the first ten amendments to the Constitution, called the **Bill of Rights.** These amendments guarantee every American the right to speak, write, and worship freely anywhere in the United States. The Bill of

Rights protects Americans from unreasonable search of their homes. It guards them against the taking of their belongings by police or other government officials. The Bill of Rights forbids courts from making people give evidence, or proof of wrongdoing, against themselves. It also promises every citizen a speedy and public trial, and prohibits "cruel and unusual punishments." You can read the Bill of Rights ▶ on page 260. How important is the addition of a Bill of Rights to the Constitution?

🦅 Spotlight on Sources

12. The First Amendment to the Constitution states some of the most important rights of Americans. It guarantees freedom of speech and of the press. It forbids the establishment of an official religion and protects the people's right to worship as they please.

> Congress shall make no law respecting [about the] establishment of religion, or prohibiting the free exercise thereof; or abridging [limiting] the freedom of speech, or of the press; or the right of the people peaceably to assemble, and to petition the government for a redress [righting] of grievances [wrongs].

◀ Why is the separation of church and state important?

Washington and the Federalists How did the United States grow stronger under the presidency of George Washington?

13. When George Washington took the oath of office in New York City on April 30, 1789, the world took note. Since countries usually were ruled by a king or queen, people everywhere were curious. Could a country headed by a President who was an ordinary citizen succeed?

14. It is easy to see why Washington won a landslide election as the first President of the United States. This Revolutionary War hero had earned the trust and respect of the Ameri-

can people. As president of the Constitutional Convention, he well understood the new law of the land. When he took office, Washington was perhaps the man best prepared to head the new government. At this time in American history, there were no political parties.

15. The first President of the United States appointed able and experienced advisors. Thomas Jefferson, the secretary of state, gave Washington advice in matters about foreign nations. Alexander Hamilton, as secretary of the treasury, gave advice on money matters. Washington supported Hamilton's bold, far-seeing budget plans, which helped to pay war debts and secure the new nation's money system. Edmund Randolph, the first **attorney general,** advised the President on matters of law. Washington's old army friend, General Henry Knox, served as secretary of war.

▼ When the Constitution was passed, Federalists held a victory parade in New York City. What role did Alexander Hamilton play in ratification?

Activity: Have students do library research on the Electoral College. Then hold a class discussion on the following issue: Should the president be elected directly by popular vote and not by the Electoral College?

240

People in History

16. Alexander Hamilton Born on a British island in the Caribbean, Hamilton (1757–1804) was attending college in New York when the American Revolution began. As a teenager, he left school to fight in the war. Hamilton soon became an officer in the American army, where he served as an aide to General Washington. He later worked hard for ratification of the Constitution. ▶ What newspaper essays in favor of the Constitution did he help write?

17. As secretary of the treasury, Hamilton proved to be a wizard at money matters. He came up with an unpopular but successful program for settling the nation's debts. He called for the establishment of a national bank that would issue or make paper money. Hamilton argued that a national bank would help the government to collect taxes, control trade, and support the nation's defense.

18. Jefferson and Hamilton held different views about the powers of the national government. Hamilton, a strong supporter of the Constitution, wanted an even more powerful central government for America than the Constitution formed. Jefferson, on the other hand, wanted the average American to have a greater voice in government. Jefferson also strongly opposed Hamilton's plan for a national bank. He felt that the government should save, rather than spend, the people's money.

19. The disagreement between Hamilton and Jefferson spilled over into Congress and helped create America's first political parties. The Federalists, Hamilton's supporters, held the majority in Congress and approved the national bank. The Federalists were mostly wealthy merchants, manufacturers, and lawyers from the East and some plantation owners from the South. The Anti-Federalists, Jefferson's supporters, were in the minority, but were growing in number. Jefferson's party was called the Democratic-Republican Party. Democratic-Republicans were found chiefly in the farming areas of the North and South and in the urban ▶ or city areas of New York. Why do you think these particular groups supported the parties they did?

THE PRESIDENTS' CORNER

During **George Washington's** presidency from 1789 to 1797, the new federal government took shape. America's first national bank was formed. Congress taxed whiskey and other products made in the United States. The taxes supplied the money to run the new government. In 1794, the farmers of Pennsylvania refused to pay the tax on whiskey. Washington sent federal troops to crush the Whiskey Rebellion. Washington's victory showed that the government could enforce federal laws in the states. Washington strongly believed that the United States must stay out of European wars. His 1793 neutrality proclamation forbade American ships from carrying supplies to warring nations. In his Farewell Address, Washington urged the nation to be strong in religion, education, and in promoting peace.

Outlook

20. When George Washington was President, the United States was a small nation of 13 states with limited sources of money. America then had little military strength and offered few services to its citizens. Over the next two centuries, the United States grew from 13 to 50 states. It became a world power of huge military strength costing about 13 trillion dollars to support each year. The United States government today offers its citizens many services, including low-income housing, health care, and support for education. The federal government affects people's lives from their first days in school to their old age. Yet it is still basically the same government that was formed when the Constitution went into effect in 1789.

Ask: How can a 200-year-old Constitution still meet people's needs in this modern era?

CHAPTER REVIEW

VOCABULARY REVIEW

▶ Write each number and word on a sheet of paper. Then write the letter of the definition next to the word it defines.

1. separation of powers
2. justices
3. unconstitutional
4. checks and balances
5. amendments
6. Bill of Rights
7. attorney general

a. contrary to the rights guaranteed by the Constitution
b. the system of giving branches of government different powers
c. the judges on the Supreme Court
d. changes to the Constitution
e. the first ten amendments to the Constitution
f. the system that gives each branch of government the power to serve as a check on the other branches
g. the introduction to the Constitution
h. the chief law officer of the nation who advises the President on legal matters

SKILL BUILDER: INTERPRETING A CHART

▶ Read the chart below on "How a Bill Becomes a Law." Then decide whether the statements that follow it are true or false. Rewrite the false statements to make them true.

HOW A BILL BECOMES A LAW

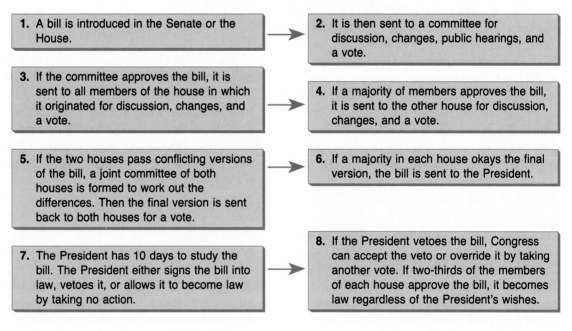

1. A bill is introduced in the Senate or the House.

2. It is then sent to a committee for discussion, changes, public hearings, and a vote.

3. If the committee approves the bill, it is sent to all members of the house in which it originated for discussion, changes, and a vote.

4. If a majority of members approves the bill, it is sent to the other house for discussion, changes, and a vote.

5. If the two houses pass conflicting versions of the bill, a joint committee of both houses is formed to work out the differences. Then the final version is sent back to both houses for a vote.

6. If a majority in each house okays the final version, the bill is sent to the President.

7. The President has 10 days to study the bill. The President either signs the bill into law, vetoes it, or allows it to become law by taking no action.

8. If the President vetoes the bill, Congress can accept the veto or override it by taking another vote. If two-thirds of the members of each house approve the bill, it becomes law regardless of the President's wishes.

1. A bill can be introduced in either the House of Representatives or in the Senate.

2. A bill is sent to both houses of Congress before it goes to a committee for review.

3. A majority of members of one house in Congress must approve a bill before it can go to the other house in Congress for a vote.

4. If both houses of Congress approve the final version of a bill, the President cannot veto it.

5. If the President vetoes a bill, there must be a two-thirds majority of both houses of Congress in order to override the President's veto.

SKILL BUILDER: CRITICAL THINKING AND COMPREHENSION

I. Making Judgments   When you make a judgment, you make a decision by examining the facts.

▶ Do you think the following laws are good, fair laws? Write your decisions on a sheet of paper. Be sure to give reasons for your judgments.

1. The term of office for a President is limited to four years.

2. If the President is unable to fulfill his duties, the Vice-President takes over as President until the next presidential election.

3. The Supreme Court can declare a law unconstitutional.

4. Justices are appointed to the Supreme Court for life.

II. Point of View

▶ List the person or persons from the chapter who might have made each of these statements.

1. "As a member of Washington's Cabinet, I want the average American to have an even greater voice in government. I am against the establishment of a national bank. The government should conserve, not spend, the people's money."

2. "I disagree with the secretary of state. A national bank will help the government to collect taxes, regulate trade, and provide for the national defense."

3. "I heartily endorse the bold, far-seeing financial plans of the secretary of the treasury."

USING PRIMARY SOURCES

▶ Reread the Spotlight on Sources on page 240. The First Amendment guarantees freedom of speech to all Americans. How important is it that Americans have the right to speak out without being punished for what they say or believe? What present-day examples of First Amendment controversies can you describe?

ENRICHMENT

1. Write a dramatic story about what American society might be like without the Bill of Rights.

2. From the library, select a book about Thomas Jefferson or Alexander Hamilton. After you have read the book, give a brief report to the class on his life.

We the People

of the United States, in Order to form a more perfect Union, establish Justice, insure domestic Tranquility, provide for the common Defence, promote the general Welfare, and secure the Blessings of Liberty to ourselves and our Posterity, do ordain and establish this Constitution for the United States of America.

Article. I.

Section 1. All legislative Powers herein granted shall be vested in a Congress of the United States, which shall consist of a Senate and House of Representatives.

Section 2. The House of Representatives shall be composed of Members chosen every second Year by the People of the several States, and the Electors in each State shall have the Qualifications requisite for Electors of the most numerous Branch of the State Legislature.

No Person shall be a Representative who shall not have attained to the Age of twenty five Years, and been seven Years a Citizen of the United States, and who shall not, when elected, be an Inhabitant of that State in which he shall be chosen.

Representatives and direct Taxes shall be apportioned among the several States which may be included within this Union, according to their respective Numbers, which shall be determined by adding to the whole Number of free Persons, including those bound to Service for a Term of Years, and excluding Indians not taxed, three fifths of all other Persons. The actual Enumeration shall be made within three Years after the first Meeting of the Congress of the United States, and within every subsequent Term of ten Years, in such Manner as they shall by Law direct. The Number of Representatives shall not exceed one for every thirty Thousand, but each State shall have at Least one Representative; and until such enumeration shall be made, the State of New Hampshire shall be entitled to chuse three, Massachusetts eight, Rhode Island and Providence Plantations one, Connecticut five, New York six, New Jersey four, Pennsylvania eight, Delaware one, Maryland six, Virginia ten, North Carolina five, South Carolina five, and Georgia three.

When vacancies happen in the Representation from any State, the Executive Authority thereof shall issue Writs of Election to fill such Vacancies.

The House of Representatives shall chuse their Speaker and other Officers; and shall have the sole Power of Impeachment.

Section 3. The Senate of the United States shall be composed of two Senators from each State, chosen by the Legislature thereof, for six Years; and each Senator shall have one Vote.

Immediately after they shall be assembled in Consequence of the first Election, they shall be divided as equally as may be into three Classes. The Seats of the Senators of the first Class shall be vacated at the Expiration of the second Year, of the second Class at the Expiration of the fourth Year, and of the third Class at the Expiration of the sixth Year, so that one third may be chosen every second Year; and if Vacancies happen by Resignation, or otherwise, during the Recess of the Legislature of any State, the Executive thereof may make temporary Appointments until the next Meeting of the Legislature, which shall then fill such Vacancies.

No Person shall be a Senator who shall not have attained to the Age of thirty Years, and been nine Years a Citizen of the United States, and who shall not, when elected, be an Inhabitant of that State for which he shall be chosen.

The Vice President of the United States shall be President of the Senate, but shall have no Vote, unless they be equally divided.

The Senate shall chuse their other Officers, and also a President pro tempore, in the Absence of the Vice President, or when he shall exercise the Office of President of the United States.

The Senate shall have the sole Power to try all Impeachments. When sitting for that Purpose, they shall be on Oath or Affirmation. When the President of the United States is tried, the Chief Justice shall preside: And no Person shall be convicted without the Concurrence of two thirds of the Members present.

Judgment in Cases of Impeachment shall not extend further than to removal from Office, and disqualification to hold and enjoy any Office of honor, Trust or Profit under the United States: but the Party convicted shall nevertheless be liable and subject to Indictment, Trial, Judgment and Punishment, according to Law.

Section 4. The Times, Places and Manner of holding Elections for Senators and Representatives, shall be prescribed in each State by the Legislature thereof; but the Congress may at any time by Law make or alter such Regulations, except as to the Places of chusing Senators.

The Congress shall assemble at least once in every Year, and such Meeting shall be on the first Monday in December, unless they shall by Law appoint a different Day.

Section 5. Each House shall be the Judge of the Elections, Returns and Qualifications of its own Members, and a Majority of each shall constitute a Quorum to do Business; but a smaller Number may adjourn from day to day, and may be authorized to compel the Attendance of absent Members, in such Manner, and under such Penalties as each House may provide.

Each House may determine the Rules of its Proceedings, punish its Members for disorderly Behaviour, and, with the Concurrence of two thirds, expel a Member.

Each House shall keep a Journal of its Proceedings, and from time to time publish the same, excepting such Parts as may in their Judgment require Secrecy; and the Yeas and Nays of the Members of either House on any question shall, at the Desire of one fifth of those Present, be entered on the Journal.

Neither House, during the Session of Congress, shall, without the Consent of the other, adjourn for more than three days, nor to any other Place than that in which the two Houses shall be sitting.

Section 6. The Senators and Representatives shall receive a Compensation for their Services, to be ascertained by Law, and paid out of the Treasury of the United States. They shall in all Cases, except Treason, Felony and Breach of the Peace, be privileged from Arrest during their Attendance at the Session of their respective Houses, and in going to and returning from the same; and for any Speech or Debate in either House, they shall not be questioned in any other Place.

No Senator or Representative shall, during the Time for which he was elected, be appointed to any civil Office under the Authority of the United States, which shall have been created, or the Emoluments whereof shall have been encreased during such time; and no Person holding any Office under the United States, shall be a Member of either House during his Continuance in Office.

Section 7. All Bills for raising Revenue shall originate in the House of Representatives; but the Senate may propose or concur with Amendments as on other Bills.

Every Bill which shall have passed the House of Representatives and the Senate, shall, before it become a Law, be presented to the President of the

The Constitution is the plan for the government of the United States. To help you study the Constitution, the text as written is presented first. Then after each part is a summary that you may find easier to read. Headings have been added to the Constitution to tell you what each article and section is about. Blue lines are used to cross out parts of the Constitution that have been changed by amendments or other laws.

Preamble

WE THE PEOPLE of the United States, in order to form a more perfect union, establish justice, insure domestic tranquility, provide for the common defense, promote the general welfare, and secure the blessings of liberty to ourselves and our posterity, do ordain and establish this Constitution for the United States of America.

This opening part lists the reasons why the Constitution was written. It clearly says the Constitution expresses the will of the American people ["We the people"]. The people's representatives who wrote this great document had six major goals. These goals are (1) to set up a government better than the government of the Articles of Confederation [to form a more perfect Union], (2) to have fair and just laws, (3) to keep peace and order in the nation [to insure domestic tranquility], (4) to take measures to defend the nation, (5) to provide services to help the people [to promote the general welfare], and (6) to make sure Americans will always have freedom.

1. What words in the Constitution show it is based on the will of the American people?
2. Which goal or goals do you think are the most important to Americans today?

▲ The Capitol is home of the Legislative Branch of the federal government.

Article I The Legislative Branch

Section 1 *Congress*

All legislative powers herein granted shall be vested in a Congress of the United States, which shall consist of a Senate and House of Representatives.

Section 2 *The House of Representatives*

1. How a Representative is elected. The House of Representatives shall be composed of members chosen every second year by the people of the several States, and the electors in each State shall have the qualifications requisite for electors of the most numerous branch of the State Legislature.

2. Who may be a Representative? No person shall be a representative who shall not have attained to the age of twenty-five years, and been seven years a citizen of the United States, and who shall not, when elected, be an inhabitant of that State in which he shall be chosen.

This article describes Congress. Congress is one of the three main branches of the federal government. Congress makes the laws for the United States. Congress has two parts, or houses, called the House of Representatives and the Senate.

247

The House of Representatives is elected directly by the people. Its members are selected every two years. Members must (1) be at least 25 years old, (2) be a citizen for at least seven years, and (3) live in the state from which they are chosen.

1. What three qualifications must all members of the House of Representatives have?
2. Why is Congress so important in the federal government?

3. The number to be chosen. Representatives [and direct taxes] shall be apportioned among the several States which may be included within this Union, according to their respective numbers, [which shall be determined by adding to the whole number of free persons, including those bound to service for a term of years, and excluding Indians not taxed, three fifths of all other persons].[1] The actual enumeration shall be made within three years after the first meeting of the Congress of the United States, and within every subsequent term of ten years, in such manner as they shall by law direct. The number of Representatives shall not exceed one for every thirty thousand, but each state shall have at least one representative; [and until such enumeration shall be made, the state of New Hampshire shall be entitled to choose three; Massachusetts, eight; Rhode Island and Providence Plantations, one; Connecticut, five; New York, six; New Jersey, four; Pennsylvania, eight; Delaware, one; Maryland, six; Virginia, ten; North Carolina, five; South Carolina, five; and Georgia, three].

4. Filling vacancies. When vacancies happen in the representation from any State, the Executive authority thereof shall issue writs of election to fill such vacancies.

5. The House officers; their power to impeach. The House of Representatives shall choose their Speaker and other officers; and shall have the sole power of impeachment.

The number of Representatives each state has is based on the size of the state's population. Every 10 years each state's population is counted in a census to decide the number of Representatives it should have. The way of counting up the total

number of members described here was later changed. The size of the House of Representatives was limited to 435 members in 1929.

When a Representative dies or is not able to complete his or her term in office, the governor ["the executive authority"] of the state calls for a special election to select a new Representative.

When a new Congress meets every two years, the members of the House of Representatives choose a Speaker and other officers. The Speaker is the leader of the House of Representatives. Only the House has the power to charge high government officials with wrongdoing ["impeachment"].

1. How is the number of each state's Representatives decided?
2. Why is the Speaker of the House an important officer?

Section 3 *The Senate*

1. Each state has two Senators; term of office. The Senate of the United States shall be composed of two Senators from each state, [chosen by the legislature thereof][2] for six years, and each Senator shall have one vote.

2. One-third of the Senate is elected every two years. Immediately after they shall be assembled in consequence of the first election, they shall be divided as equally as may be into three classes. [The seats of the Senators of the first class shall be vacated at the expiration of the second year, of the second class at the expiration of the fourth year, and of the third class at the expiration of the sixth year,] so that one third may be chosen every second year; [and if vacancies happen by resignation, or otherwise, during the recess of the legislature of any State, the Executive thereof may make temporary appointments until the next meeting of the legislature, which shall then fill such vacancies].[3]

3. Who may be a Senator? No person shall be a Senator who shall not have attained to the age of thirty years, and been nine years a citizen of the United States, and who shall not, when elected, be an inhabitant of the State for which he shall be chosen.

4. The President of the Senate. The Vice-President of the United States shall be President of the

[1] Changed by the 14th Amendment.

[2] Method of election changed by the 17th Amendment
[3] Changed by the 17th Amendment.

248

Senate, but shall have no vote, unless they be equally divided.

5. The Senate chooses its officers. The Senate shall choose their other officers, and also a President pro tempore, in the absence of the Vice-President, or when he shall exercise the office of President of the United States.

6. The Senate tries impeachments. The Senate shall have the sole power to try all impeachments. When sitting for that purpose, they shall be on oath or affirmation. When the President of the United States is tried, the Chief Justice shall preside; and no person shall be convicted without the concurrence of two thirds of the members present.

7. What punishment may be given for conviction. Judgment in cases of impeachment shall not extend further than to removal from office, and disqualification to hold and enjoy any office of honor, trust or profit under the United States; but the party convicted shall nevertheless be liable and subject to indictment, trial, judgment and punishment, according to law.

The Senate is the other house of Congress. All states are represented equally in the Senate. Each state has two members. The members of the Senate are elected for six-year terms. One-third of the Senate is up for election every two years. Senators were chosen by the law-making bodies of their state until 1913. Senators now are elected by the voters in each state.

Senators must (1) be at least 30 years old, (2) be a citizen for at least nine years, and (3) live in the state from which they are chosen.

The Vice-President of the United States presides at meetings of the Senate. He or she can vote only if there is a tie. The members of the Senate choose the other officers of the Senate.

Only the Senate can bring to trial high officials who are impeached. If a President is on trial for impeachment, the Chief Justice of the Supreme Court will preside at the Senate trial. Two-thirds of the Senators voting must agree before a person is found guilty. If the Senate finds a person guilty, it can remove the official from office. However, it cannot punish the person. If the guilty person has broken laws, he or she may only be punished by the regular courts.

1. What three qualifications must Senators have?

2. Compare the number of members, the term of office, and the qualifications of members of the Senate with members of the House of Representatives.

Section 4 *Election of Senators and Representatives*

1. Rules for holding elections. The times, places and manner of holding elections for Senators and Representatives shall be prescribed in each State by the Legislature thereof; but the Congress may at any time by law make or alter such regulations, except as to the places of choosing Senators.

2. Congress meets once a year. The Congress shall assemble at least once in every year, [and such meeting shall be on the first Monday in December unless they shall by law appoint a different day].[4]

Section 5 *Rules of Procedure for Both Houses*

1. How the Houses are organized. Each House shall be the judge of the elections, returns and qualifications of its own members, and a majority of each shall constitute a quorum to do business; but a smaller number may adjourn from day to day, and may be authorized to compel the attendance of absent members, in such manner, and under such penalties, as each House may provide.

2. Each House makes its own rules. Each House may determine the rules of its proceedings, punish its members for disorderly behavior, and, with the concurrence of two thirds, expel a member.

3. Each House keeps a journal. Each House shall keep a journal of its proceedings and from time to time publish the same, excepting such parts as may in their judgment require secrecy; and the yeas and nays of the members of either House on any question shall, at the desire of one fifth of those present, be entered on the journal.

4. Closing. Neither House, during the session of Congress, shall, without the consent of the other, adjourn for more than three days, nor to any other place than that in which the two Houses shall be sitting.

[4] The time of meeting was changed by the 20th Amendment.

Each state may decide when, where, and how its Senators and Representatives are to be elected. However, Congress can pass laws that replace these state laws. Congress must meet once each year.

Both the Senate and House of Representatives have the power to decide if their members are qualified and have been elected fairly. To carry on their work, both houses of Congress must have at least half their members ["a quorum"] present.

The House of Representatives and the Senate both may make rules for carrying on their work. They can punish members who do not obey these rules. If two-thirds of the members agree, they can force a member to resign.

Both houses of Congress must keep a public record of what they do at their meetings and show how their members voted. (This public record is now printed in the *Congressional Record*.) Both houses also must meet in the same city. They cannot let more than three days pass without holding a meeting when Congress is in session.

1. Who decides if members of Congress are qualified and elected fairly?
2. Why does the Constitution carefully set up these rules about Congress?

Section 6 *Privileges and Restrictions of Members*

1. The members of Congress are paid. The Senators and Representatives shall receive a compensation for their services, to be ascertained by law, and paid out of the Treasury of the United States. They shall in all cases except treason, felony and breach of the peace, be privileged from arrest during their attendance at the session of their respective houses, and in going to and returning from the same; and for any speech or debate in either house, they shall not be questioned in any other place.

2. Members of Congress cannot hold other offices. No Senator of Representative shall, during the time for which he was elected, be appointed to any civil office under the authority of the United States which shall have been created, or the emoluments whereof shall have been increased during

such time; and no person holding any office under the United States shall be a member of either house during his continuance in office.

Senators and Representatives are to be paid for serving in Congress. When Congress is meeting, members of Congress cannot be arrested or sued for anything they say. However, they can be arrested if they commit a major crime.

Senators and Representatives cannot hold other offices in the federal government while they are serving in Congress.

1. Why is the freedom of speech of members of Congress protected?
2. Why are members of Congress not permitted to hold other federal jobs?

Section 7 *How Laws Are Made*

1. Money bills start in the House. All bills for raising revenue shall originate in the House of Representatives; but the Senate may propose or concur with amendments as on other bills.

2. How a bill becomes a law. Every bill which shall have passed the House of Representatives and the Senate shall, before it becomes a law, be presented to the President of the United States; if he approves he shall sign it, but if not he shall return it, with his objections, to that house in which it shall have originated, who shall enter the objections at large on their journal, and proceed to reconsider it. If after such reconsideration two-thirds of that house shall agree to pass the bill, it shall be sent, together with the objections, to the other house, by which it shall likewise be reconsidered, and if approved by two-thirds of that house, it shall become a law. But in all cases the votes of both houses shall be determined by yeas and nays, and the names of the persons voting for and against the bill shall be entered on the journal of each house respectively. If any bill shall not be returned by the President within ten days (Sundays excepted) after it shall have been presented to him, the same shall be a law, in like manner as if he had signed it, unless the Congress by their adjournment prevents its return, in which case it shall not be a law.

3. The President's part in lawmaking. Every order, resolution, or vote to which the concurrence of the Senate and House of Representatives may be necessary (except on a question of adjournment) shall be presented to the President of the United States; and before the same shall take effect, shall be approved by him, or being disapproved by him, shall be repassed by two-thirds of the Senate and House of Representatives, according to the rules and limitations prescribed in the case of a bill.

All bills, or proposed laws, for raising money [revenue] must start in the House of Representatives. The Senate can then ask for changes in the bill.

To become a law, a bill must be passed by both houses of Congress. Then it is sent to the President. The bill becomes a law (1) if the President signs it within ten days after receiving the bill, (2) if the President does not sign it but does not veto it in this ten-day period, or (3) if the President vetoes the bill but Congress passes the bill over this veto by a two-thirds vote.

When a bill is passed in the last ten days Congress is meeting and the President does not sign this bill, it does not become a law. (When the President acts in this way, the bill has received a "pocket veto.")

All orders and resolutions passed by Congress, as well as laws, need to be signed by the President before they go into effect. The President can veto these orders and resolutions, but Congress may then override this veto. However, Congress can end its meetings for the year without the President's agreeing to it.

1. How can a bill become a law if the President vetoes the bill?
2. Why does the Constitution explain so carefully what must be done before a bill becomes a law?

Section 8 *The Powers of Congress*
The Congress shall have power
1. To lay and collect taxes, duties, imposts, and excises, to pay the debts and provide for the common defence and general welfare of the United States; but all duties, imposts, and excises shall be uniform throughout the United States;

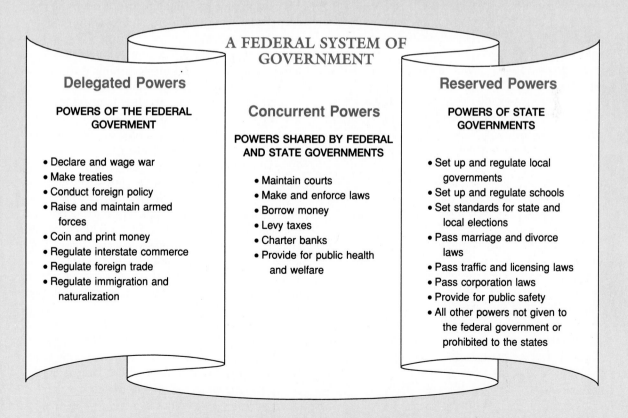

A FEDERAL SYSTEM OF GOVERNMENT

Delegated Powers

POWERS OF THE FEDERAL GOVERMENT

- Declare and wage war
- Make treaties
- Conduct foreign policy
- Raise and maintain armed forces
- Coin and print money
- Regulate interstate commerce
- Regulate foreign trade
- Regulate immigration and naturalization

Concurrent Powers

POWERS SHARED BY FEDERAL AND STATE GOVERNMENTS

- Maintain courts
- Make and enforce laws
- Borrow money
- Levy taxes
- Charter banks
- Provide for public health and welfare

Reserved Powers

POWERS OF STATE GOVERNMENTS

- Set up and regulate local governments
- Set up and regulate schools
- Set standards for state and local elections
- Pass marriage and divorce laws
- Pass traffic and licensing laws
- Pass corporation laws
- Provide for public safety
- All other powers not given to the federal government or prohibited to the states

2. To borrow money on the credit of the United States;

3. To regulate commerce with foreign nations, and among the several States, and with the Indian tribes;

4. To establish a uniform rule of naturalization, and uniform laws on the subject of bankruptcies throughout the united States;

5. To coin money, regulate the value thereof, and of foreign coin, and fix the standard of weights and measures;

6. To provide for the punishment of counterfeiting the securities and current coin of the United States;

7. To establish post offices and post roads;

8. To promote the progress of science and useful arts by securing for limited times to authors and inventors the exclusive right to their respective writings and discoveries;

Congress has many important powers that help it carry out the duties of the federal government.

Congress has the power to raise and collect taxes, to spend money to pay for the costs of the federal government, to defend the nation, and to provide services to help the people ["the general welfare"].

Congress has the power to borrow money for the federal government.

Congress has to the power to control all trade ["commerce"] with other countries as well as trade among the states.

Congress has the power to pass laws allowing people born in other countries to become American citizens ["naturalization"]. It also has the power to pass laws that deal with businesses or persons who cannot pay their debts ["bankruptcies"].

Congress has the power to print and coin money and say how much it is worth. It also has the power to say how much foreign money is worth and to set up a system of weighing and measuring things.

Congress has the power to punish anyone who makes fake money or fake government bonds or stamps ["counterfeiting"].

Congress has the power to set up post offices and to handle mail.

Congress has the power to pass laws to help inventors and writers protect their work by means of patents and copyrights.

1. Name two ways Congress can raise money for the federal government.
2. Why do you think many of the powers of Congress are about money?

9. To constitute tribunals inferior to the Supreme Court;

10. To define and punish piracies and felonies committed on the high seas and offences against the law of nations;

11. To declare war, [grant letters of marque and reprisal,] and make rules concerning captures on land and water;

12. To raise and support armies, but no appropriation of money to that use shall be for a longer term than two years;

13. To provide and maintain a navy;

14. To make rules for the government and regulation of the land and naval forces;

15. To provide for calling forth the militia to execute the laws of the Union, suppress insurrections, and repel invasions;

16. To provide for organizing, arming, and disciplining the militia, and for governing such part of them as may be employed in the service of the United States, reserving to the States respectively the appointment of the officers, and the authority of training the militia according to the discipline prescribed by Congress;

17. To exercise exclusive legislation in all cases whatsoever, over such district (not exceeding ten miles square) as may, by cession of particular States, and the acceptance of Congress, become the seat of the government of the United States, and to exercise like authority over all places purchased by the consent of the legislature of the State, in which the same shall be, for the erection of forts, magazines, arsenals, dockyards, and other needful buildings; and

18. To make all laws which shall be necessary and proper for carrying into execution the foregoing powers, and all other powers vested by this Constitution in the government of the United States, or in any department or officer thereof.

Congress has the power to set up a system of federal courts.

Congress has the power to make laws about crimes that take place at sea ["piracies and felonies"]. It also has the power to pass laws to punish those who break treaties or international law.

Congress has the power to declare war.

Congress has the power to set up and supply an army. However, Congress cannot provide money for the army for longer than two years.

Congress has the power to set up and supply a navy.

Congress has the power to make rules to organize and control the army and navy.

Congress has the power to order the National Guard ["the militia"] in each state to help enforce federal laws, to put down rebellions, and to push back enemy invaders.

Congress has the power to help organize and arm the National Guard, but the states have the duty to choose the officers and train them.

Congress has the power to govern the nation's capital city (now Washington, D.C.), and other federal lands used as forts, dockyards, and weapons centers.

Congress has the power to pass the laws needed to carry out the powers given to it by the Constitution. (This clause is important because it enables Congress to do many things not specifically listed in the Constitution.)

1. How does Congress carry out the powers listed in the Constitution?
2. Why do you think Congress was given the power to pass laws that may be needed to carry out its powers?

Section 9 *Powers Denied to the Federal Government*

[1. The migration or importation of such persons as any of the States now existing shall think proper to admit, shall not be prohibited by the Congress prior to the year one thousand eight hundred and eight, but a tax or duty may be imposed on such importation, not exceeding ten dollars for each person.]
2. The privilege of the writ of habeas corpus shall not be suspended, unless when in cases of rebellion or invasion the public safety may require it.

3. No bill of attainder or ex post facto law shall be passed.
[4. No capitation, or other direct tax, shall be laid, unless in proportion in the census or enumeration herein before directed to be taken.]
5. No tax or duty shall be laid on articles exported from any State.
6. No preference shall be given by any regulation of commerce or revenue to the ports of one State over those of another: nor shall vessels bound to, or from, one State be obliged to enter, clear, or pay duties in another.
7. No money shall be drawn from the Treasury, but in consequence of appropriations made by law; and a regular statement and account of the receipts and expenditures of all public money shall be published from time to time.
8. No title of nobility shall be granted by the United States: and no person holding any office of profit or trust under them shall, without the consent of the Congress, accept of any present, emolument, office, or title, of any kind whatever, from any king, prince, or foreign state.

Congress is not permitted to do certain things, as listed in this section.

Until 1808, Congress was not permitted to ban the importation of slaves ["such persons"]. Congress cannot arrest people or put them in jail without holding a hearing on the charges against them ["the writ of habeas corpus"] except when the United States is in danger from an enemy invasion or faces a rebellion. Congress cannot pass a law to punish a person without a trial in a court of law ["a bill of attainder"]. Congress cannot pass a law to punish a person for doing something that was not against the law when that person did it ["an ex post facto law"]. Congress cannot tax the goods or products sent from one state to another state.

Congress cannot pass laws that favor the trade ["commerce"] carried on by any one state.

No government money can be spent unless Congress passes a law for that purpose ["appropriations"]. Records must be kept of all government spending and be reported to the people.

The federal government cannot make anyone a noble (such as a duke, a duchess, or a countess). No person in the federal government can be made a noble by any other country unless Congress allows it.

Section 10 *Powers Denied to the States*

1. No State shall enter into any treaty, alliance, or confederation; grant letters of marque and reprisal; coin money; emit bills of credit; make any thing but gold and silver coin a tender in payment of debts; pass any bill of attainder, ex post facto law, or law impairing the obligation of contracts, or grant any title of nobility.

2. No State shall, without the consent of the Congress, lay any imposts or duties on imports or exports, except what may be absolutely necessary for executing its inspection laws; and the net produce of all duties and imposts, laid by any State on imports or exports, shall be for the use of the Treasury of the United States; and all such laws shall be subject to the revision and control of the Congress.

3. No State shall, without the consent of Congress, lay any duty of tonnage, keep troops, or ships of war in time of peace, enter into any agreement or compact with another state, or with a foreign power, or engage in wars, unless actually invaded, or in such imminent danger as will not admit of delay.

The states are forbidden to do certain things, and they can do some things only if Congress approves their actions.

The states cannot make treaties with other countries or become a part of another country. States cannot allow their citizens to attack other countries ["grant letters of marque and reprisal"]. States cannot make their own paper money or coins. States cannot pass a law to punish a person without a trial in a court of law ["a bill of attainder"]. States cannot pass a law to punish a person for doing something that was not against the law when that person did it ["an ex post facto law"]. States cannot pass a law allowing people not to carry out lawful agreements. States cannot pass a law to make anyone a noble.

States cannot tax goods or products being sent to or from other countries unless Congress allows them to do so.

States cannot do any of the following things unless Congress allows them to do so. States (1) cannot tax ships, (2) cannot have soldiers (except the National Guard) or warships in peacetime, (3) cannot make treaties with other states or a foreign country, and (4) cannot go to war unless they are invaded or about to be invaded by another country.

Article II The Executive Branch

Section 1 *President and Vice-President*

1. The President is elected for four years. The executive power shall be vested in a President of the United States of America. He shall hold his office during the term of four years, and together with the Vice-President, chosen for the same term, be elected as follows:

2. The President is chosen by electors. Each State shall appoint, in such manner as the legislature thereof may direct, a number of electors, equal to the whole number of Senators and Representatives to which the State may be entitled in the Congress; but no Senator or Representative, or person holding an office of trust or profit under the United States, shall be appointed an elector.

3. Election of the President. [The electors shall meet in their respective States, and vote by ballot for two persons, of whom one at least shall not be

▲ The White House is the home of the president, who heads the Executive Branch of the federal government.

an inhabitant of the same State with themselves. And they shall make a list of all the persons voted for, and of the number of votes for each; which list they shall sign and certify, and transmit sealed to the seat of government of the United States, direct to the President of the Senate. The President of the Senate shall, in the presence of the Senate and House of Representative, open all the certificates, and the votes shall then be counted. The person having the greatest number of votes shall be the President, if such number be a majority of the whole number of electors appointed; and if there be more than one who have such majority, and have an equal number of votes, then the House of Representatives shall immediately choose by ballot one of them for President; and if no person have a majority, then from the five highest on the list the said house shall in like manner choose the President. But in choosing the President the votes shall be taken by States, the representation from each State having one vote; a quorum for this purpose shall consist of a member or members from two-thirds of the States, and a majority of all the States shall be necessary to a choice. In every case, after the choice of the President, the person having the greatest number of

votes of the electors shall be the Vice-President. But if there should remain two or more who have equal votes, the Senate shall choose from them by ballot the Vice-President.][5]

The President and Vice-President are in charge of the Executive Branch of the federal government. This branch has the power to carry out the laws of the United States.

The President is given the power to carry out the laws passed by Congress. The President has a four-year term in office. The Vice-President also serves for a four-year term.

Both the President and the Vice-President are chosen by a group of people called electors. The legislatures, or law-making bodies, in each state decide how the electors are to be chosen. Each state has the same number of electors as it has Senators and Representatives. No member of Congress or an official of the federal government can be an elector.

1. What is the main duty of the Executive Branch?

[5] Changed by the 12th Amendment.

255

2. Why is the President so important in the federal government?

---

4. Date of elections. The Congress may determine the time of choosing the electors, and the day on which they shall give their votes; which day shall be the same throughout the United States.

5. Who may be President? No person except a natural born citizen, [or a citizen of the United States, at the time of the adoption of this Constitution,] shall be eligible to the office of President; neither shall any person be eligible to that office who shall not have attained to the age of thirty-five years, and been fourteen years a resident within the United States.

6. The Vice-President succeeds the President in certain cases. In case of the removal of the President from office or of his death, resignation, or inability to discharge the powers and duties of the said office, the same shall devolve on the Vice-President, and the Congress may by law provide for the case of removal, death, resignation, or inability, both of the President and Vice-President, declaring what officer shall then act as President, and such officer shall act accordingly, until the disability be removed, or a President shall be elected.

7. The President shall be paid. The President shall, at stated times, receive for his services, a compensation, which shall neither be increased nor diminished during the period for which he shall have been elected, and he shall not receive within that period any other emolument from the United States, or any of them.

8. The President takes an oath of office. Before he enters on the execution of his office, he shall take the following oath or affirmation:—"I do solemnly swear (or affirm) that I will faithfully execute the office of President of the United States, and will to the best of my ability, preserve, protect and defend the Constitution of the United States."

Congress decides the date when electors are chosen and when the electors are to meet to vote for the President and Vice-President. The date must be the same in all the states.

To be elected President, a person (1) must have been born a citizen, (2) must be at least 35 years old, and (3) must have lived in the United States for at least 14 years.

If both the President and the Vice-President are not able to serve in office, Congress has the power to say what official will become President. (In 1947, Congress named the Speaker of the House of Representatives as next in line.)

The President is paid a salary ["compensation"] while in office. This salary cannot be increased or decreased during a President's term in office. The President cannot receive any other payment ["emolument"] from the federal government or from state governments.

The President must take an oath to promise to carry out the duties of this office and to make sure the Constitution is obeyed.

1. What three qualifications must a person have to become President?
2. Why do you think a President's salary may not be changed while he or she is in office?

Section 2 *Powers of the President*

1. The President is in charge of the armed forces. The President shall be commander in chief of the army and navy of the United States, and of the militia of the several States, when called into the actual service of the United States; he may require the opinion, in writing, of the principal officer in each of the executive departments, upon any subject relating to the duties of their respective offices, and he shall have power to grant reprieves and pardons for offences against the United States, except in cases of impeachment.

2. The President makes treaties and appointments. He shall have power, by and with the advice and consent of the Senate, to make treaties, provided two-thirds of the Senators present concur; and he shall nominate, and by and with the advice and consent of the Senate, shall appoint ambassadors, other public ministers and consuls, judges of the Supreme Court, and all other officers of the United States, whose appointments are not herein otherwise provided for, and which shall be established by law; but the Congress may by law vest the appointment of such inferior officers as they think proper, in the President alone, in the courts of law, or in the heads of departments.

The President is commander-in-chief of all the armed forces of the nation, including the states'

National Guard ["the militia"] when it is called into federal service.

The President as the head of the Executive Branch can ask the leaders of the executive departments for their ideas ["opinion"] on important matters.

The President can pardon persons who are guilty of federal crimes or delay their being punished ["a reprieve"]. However, the President cannot use this power in cases where a person has been charged with wrongdoing ["impeached"].

The President can make treaties with other countries, but these treaties must be approved by a vote of two-thirds of the Senate.

The President selects ambassadors, justices of the Supreme Court, and many other officials in the federal government. The Senate must approve the persons appointed by a two-thirds vote.

Congress can pass laws allowing the Presi-

dent, the courts, or the heads of the executive departments to select less important officials in the federal government.

The President can select people to fill vacancies in important federal offices when Congress is not meeting.

1. What important duties of the President must be approved by a vote of two-thirds of the Senate?
2. Why do you think the President is often regarded as the most important official in the United States?

---

3. The President fills vacancies. The President shall have power to fill up all vacancies that may happen during the recess of the Senate, by granting commissions which shall expire at the end of their next session.

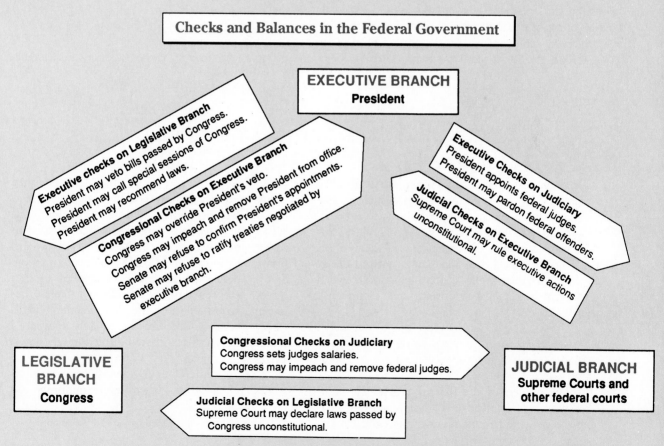

Checks and Balances in the Federal Government

EXECUTIVE BRANCH
President

Executive checks on Legislative Branch
President may veto bills passed by Congress.
President may call special sessions of Congress.
President may recommend laws.

Congressional Checks on Executive Branch
Congress may override President's veto.
Congress may impeach and remove President from office.
Senate may refuse to confirm President's appointments.
Senate may refuse to ratify treaties negotiated by executive branch.

Executive Checks on Judiciary
President appoints federal judges.
President may pardon federal offenders.

Judicial Checks on Executive Branch
Supreme Court may rule executive actions unconstitutional.

Congressional Checks on Judiciary
Congress sets judges salaries.
Congress may impeach and remove federal judges.

LEGISLATIVE BRANCH
Congress

Judicial Checks on Legislative Branch
Supreme Court may declare laws passed by Congress unconstitutional.

JUDICIAL BRANCH
Supreme Courts and other federal courts

257

The President may fill important positions that normally require Senate approval while Congress is not in session. However, the Senate must vote on these appointments after Congress meets.

Section 3 *Duties of the President*

The President reports to Congress once a year. He shall from time to time give to the Congress information of the state of the Union, and recommend to their consideration such measures as he shall judge necessary and expedient; he may, on extraordinary occasions, convene both houses, or either of them, and in case of disagreement between them with respect to the time of adjournment, he may adjourn them to such time as he shall think proper; he shall receive ambassadors and other public ministers; he shall take care that the laws be faithfully executed, and shall commission all the officers of the United States.

The President must speak to Congress regularly about the condition of the United States ["the state of the Union"]. The President also may suggest laws that Congress should pass. The President can ask Congress or either house of Congress to hold a special meeting to deal with an emergency.

The President meets with ambassadors from other countries and deals with those countries.

The President makes sure that the laws of the United States are followed ["faithfully executed"].

The President approves all officers chosen for military service.

1. What part does the President have in making laws?
2. What do you think is the President's most important duty?

Section 4 *Removal from Office*

Officers of the United States may be impeached. The President, Vice-President and all civil officers of the United States shall be removed from office on impeachment for, and conviction of treason, bribery, or other high crimes and misdemeanors.

This section states that the President and other federal officials may be accused of certain wrongdoings, or impeached, and removed from office if convicted.

1. For what reasons may a President be removed from office?

Article III   The Judicial Branch

Section 1 *The Federal Courts*

The judicial power of the United States shall be vested in one Supreme Court, and in such inferior courts as the Congress may from time to time ordain and establish. The judges, both of the Supreme and inferior courts, shall hold their offices during good behavior, and shall, at stated times, receive for their services, a compensation, which shall not be diminished during their continuance in office.

Section 2 *Powers of the Federal Courts*

1. **The powers of the federal courts.** The judicial power shall extend to all cases, in law and equity, arising under this Constitution, the laws of the United States, and treaties made or which shall be made, under their authority; to all cases affecting ambassadors, other public ministers and consuls; to all cases of admiralty jurisdiction; to controversies to which the United States shall be a party; to controversies between two or more States; [between a State and citizens of another State,] between citizens of different States, between citizens of the same State claiming lands under grants of different States, and between a State, or the citizens thereof, and foreign states, citizens or subjects.[6]

2. **The Supreme Court's powers.** In all cases affecting ambassadors, other public ministers and

---

[6] This clause has been modified by the 11th Amendment.

▲ The Supreme Court building houses the highest court in the Judicial Branch of the federal government.

consuls, and those in which a State shall be a party, the Supreme Court shall have original jurisdiction. In all the other cases before mentioned, the Supreme Court shall have appellate jurisdiction, both as to law and fact, with such exceptions, and under such regulations as the Congress shall make.

3. How trials are held. The trial of all crimes, except in cases of impeachment, shall be by jury; and such trial shall be held in the State where the said crimes shall have been committed; but when not committed within any State, the trial shall be at such place or places as the Congress may by law have directed.

This article describes the Judicial Branch of the federal government. The Judicial Branch is made up of the Supreme Court and the lower federal courts. It has the power to hear and decide cases involving the laws of the United States.

The power to hear and decide law cases is given to the Supreme Court and to the system of lower ["inferior"] courts set up by Congress. The judges who sit on these courts hold office for life unless they are impeached and found guilty. They are to be paid a salary, and their salary cannot be decreased while they are members of the court.

The federal courts hear and decide cases that involve the Constitution, the laws of the United States, treaties, ambassadors or officials of other countries, or ships on the oceans ["admiralty and maritime jurisdiction"]. Federal courts also try cases that involve the United States government and cases that involve two or more states. In addition, federal courts try cases that involve a state or the citizens of a state and a foreign government or its citizens.

The Supreme Court acts as the trial court in cases involving ambassadors or officials of foreign countries ["original jurisdiction"] and cases

259

involving the states. All other cases are first tried in the lower courts, but then may be appealed to the Supreme Court ["appellate jurisdiction"].

In all cases in the federal courts, the accused person has the right to a trial by a jury. The trial must be held in the state where the crime took place.

1. What is the Judicial Branch and what is its main duty?
2. In what ways is the Supreme Court the country's most important court?

Section 3 *Treason*

1. The meaning of treason. Treason against the United States shall consist only in levying war against them, or in adhering to their enemies, giving them aid and comfort. No person shall be convicted of treason unless on the testimony of two witnesses to the same overt act, or on confession in open court.

2. The effect on relatives. The Congress shall have power to declare the punishment of treason, but no attainder of treason shall work corruption of blood or forfeiture except during the life of the person attainted.

Treason is the crime by an American citizen of making war against the United States or helping enemies of the United States ["giving them aid and comfort"]. No person can be found guilty of treason unless two people swear the person is guilty or unless the person confesses to this crime.

Congress can decide how a person guilty of treason should be punished. However, the family or the children of the guilty person cannot be punished.

1. Why do you think treason is such a serious crime?
2. What must the government do to prove a person has committed treason?

Separation of Powers in the Federal Government

Executive Branch	Legislative Branch	Judicial Branch
PRESIDENT	**CONGRESS**	**SUPREME COURT & FEDERAL COURTS**
Powers to:	**Powers to:**	**Powers to:**
• Enforce Laws	• Pass laws	• Rule on the constitutionality of all laws
• Manage the government	• Levy taxes	• Interpret the meaning of laws
• Manage the armed forces	• Coin and print money	
• Conduct foreign policy	• Borrow money	
• Make treaties	• Declare war	
• Grant pardons to federal offenders	• Regulate foreign trade	
• Veto bills passed by Congress	• Set standards of weights and measures	
• Appoint Supreme court justices and judges of the federal courts	• Impeach and remove the President and other high officials from office	
• Appoint Cabinet members	• Senate can approve or reject President's nominees for high government office	
• Appoint ambassadors	• Senate can approve or reject treaties	

Article IV The States and the Federal Government

Section 1 *State Records*

Full faith and credit shall be given in each State to the public acts, records, and judicial proceedings of every other State. And the Congress may by general laws prescribe the manner in which such acts, records, and proceedings shall be proved, and the effect thereof.

Section 2 *Rights of Citizens*

1. Privileges. The citizens of each State shall be entitled to all privileges and immunities of citizens in the several States.

2. Extradition. A person charged in any State with treason, felony, or other crime, who shall flee from justice, and be found in another State, shall, on demand of the executive authority of the State from which he fled, be delivered up, to be removed to the State having jurisdiction of the crime.

[**3. Runaway slaves.** No person held to service or labor in one State, under the laws thereof, escaping into another shall in consequence of any law or regulation therein, be discharged from such service or labor, but shall be delivered upon claim of the party to which such service or labor may be due.]

Section 3 *New States and Territories*

1. How a new State is admitted. New States may be admitted by the Congress into this Union; but no new State shall be formed or erected within the jurisdiction of any other State; nor any State be formed by the junction of two or more States, or parts of States, without the consent of the legislatures of the States concerned, as well as of the Congress.

2. The power of Congress over territories and lands. The Congress shall have power to dispose of and make all needful rules and regulations respecting the territory or other property belonging to the United States; and nothing in this Constitution shall be so construed as to prejudice any claims of the United States, or of any particular State.

Section 4 *Guarantees to the States*

The United States shall guarantee to every State in this Union a republican form of government, and shall protect each of them against invasion; and on application of the legislature, or of the executive (when the legislature cannot be convened) against domestic violence.

All states must accept the laws ["public acts"], the records, and the findings of the courts ["judicial proceedings"] of other states.

All states must give the citizens of other states the same rights ["privileges and immunities"] they give their own citizens.

If a person accused of a crime flees to another state, that state must return the person if the governor ["executive authority"] of the state where the crime took place asks for the person's return.

New states can be added to the United States. However, new states cannot be formed by dividing up a state or by joining parts of states unless Congress and those states agree to it.

Congress has the power to sell land and property that belongs to the United States. Congress also can make laws to govern these lands.

The federal government promises that states will have governments in which the people elect their representatives ["a republican form of government"]. The federal government also promises to protect all states from invasion by other countries and to help the states to put down rebellions or riots.

1. What would happen if each state gave its citizens special rights that citizens of other states did not have?
2. Under this article, what is the governor of a state required to do?
3. What would happen if the governor of a state tried to get rid of the state legislature and rule alone?

261

Article V   Methods of Amendment

The Congress, whenever two thirds of both houses shall deem it necessary, shall propose amendments to this Constitution, or, on the application of the legislatures of two thirds of the several States, shall call a convention for proposing amendments, which, in either case shall be valid to all intents and purposes, as part of this Constitution, when ratified by the legislatures of three fourths of the several States, or by conventions in three fourths thereof, as the one or the other mode of ratification may be proposed by the Congress, provided that [no amendments which may be made prior to the year one thousand eight hundred and eight shall in any manner affect the first and fourth clauses in the ninth section of the first article; and that] no State, without its consent, shall be deprived of its equal suffrage in the Senate.

There are two steps in amending, or changing, the Constitution. First, an amendment must be proposed. Then, it must be approved.

An amendment may be proposed in two different ways: (1) two-thirds of both houses of Congress can propose an amendment, or (2) two-thirds of the state legislatures can ask Congress to call a national convention to propose an amendment. The proposed amendment must then be approved by three-fourths of the state legislatures or by special meetings in three-fourths of the states.

1. In what two ways may an amendment be proposed?
2. In what two ways may an amendment be approved?

Article VI   General Provisions

1. The public debts will be paid. All debts contracted and engagements entered into, before the adoption of this Constitution, shall be as valid against the United States under this Constitution, as under the Confederation.

2. The Constitution is the highest law of the land. This Constitution, and the laws of the United States which shall be made in pursuance thereof; and all treaties made, or which shall be made, under the authority of the United States, shall be the supreme law of the land; and the judges in every State shall be bound thereby, anything in the Constitution or laws of any State to the contrary notwithstanding.

3. The oath of office; no religious test. The Senators and Representatives before mentioned, and the members of the several State legislatures, and all executive and judicial officers, both of the United States and of the several States, shall be bound by oath or affirmation, to support this Constitution; but no religious test shall ever be re-quired as a qualification to any office or public trust under the United States.

The federal government agrees to accept all debts and all treaties ["engagements"] of the Confederation government made before the Constitution was adopted.

The Constitution, the laws of the United States based on the Constitution, and treaties made by the federal government are the highest law of the nation ["the supreme law of the land"]. State judges must follow this highest law even if their state laws or constitutions go against it.

All federal and state officials must promise to support the Constitution of the United States. However, no religious test can be set up for holding any office or job in the federal government.

1. What do you think happens when a state law goes against a law passed by Congress?

Article VII Ratification of the Constitution

The ratification of the conventions of nine States shall be sufficient for the establishment of this Constitution between the States so ratifying the same.

DONE in Convention by the Unanimous Consent of the States present the Seventeenth Day of September in the Year of our Lord one thousand seven hundred and Eighty seven and of the Independence of the United States of America the Twelfth. IN WITNESS whereof We have hereunto subscribed our Names.

George Washington—
President and deputy from Virginia

New Hampshire
John Langdon
Nicholas Gilman

Massachusetts
Nathaniel Gorham
Rufus King

Connecticut
William Samuel Johnson
Roger Sherman

New York
Alexander Hamilton

New Jersey
William Livingston
David Brearley
William Paterson
Jonathan Dayton

Pennsylvania
Benjamin Franklin
Thomas Mifflin
Robert Morris
George Clymer
Thomas FitzSimons
Jared Ingersoll
James Wilson
Gouverneur Morris

Delaware
George Read
Gunning Bedford, Jr.
John Dickinson
Richard Bassett
Jacob Broom

Maryland
James McHenry
Daniel of St. Thomas Jenifer
Daniel Carroll

Virginia
John Blair
James Madison, Jr.

North Carolina
William Blount
Richard Dobbs Spaight
Hugh Williamson

South Carolina
John Rutledge
Charles Cotesworth Pinckney
Charles Pinckney
Pierce Butler

Georgia
William Few
Abraham Baldwin

Amendments to the Constitution

In the more than 200 years since the Constitution was adopted, only 26 amendments have been added to the Constitution. The first ten amendments are called the Bill of Rights. They were added to the Constitution by the first Congress in 1791. The Bill of Rights protects the rights of the people and limits the power of the federal government. The remaining 16 amendments were added between the years 1798 and 1971.

AMENDMENT 1 Freedom of Religion, Speech, Press, Assembly, and Petition

adopted 1791

Congress shall make no law respecting an establishment of religion, or prohibiting the free exercise thereof; or abridging the freedom of speech, or of the press; or the right of the people peaceably to assemble, and to petition the government for a redress of grievances.

Congress cannot pass any law setting up an official religion or preventing people from following their own religious beliefs.
    Congress cannot pass laws that take away ["abridging"] the people's freedom of speech or freedom of the press. Congress cannot take away the people's right to hold peaceful meetings ["peaceably to assemble"] or to ask the government to correct something that is wrong ["petition for a redress of grievances"].

1. What great freedoms are protected by the First Amendment?
2. Why do you think the First Amendment was needed?

AMENDMENT 2 Right to Keep Arms

adopted 1791

A well-regulated militia, being necessary to the security of a free State, the right of the people to keep and bear arms, shall not be infringed.

The people have a right to keep a militia, or National Guard, to protect their state. The courts have generally interpreted this amendment to mean that the government may restrict private ownership of weapons.

1. Under this amendment as interpreted by the courts, explain why your state would be free to pass a law controlling the sale of guns.

AMENDMENT 3 Sheltering of Troops

adopted 1791

No soldier shall, in time of peace, be quartered in any house, without the consent of the owner; nor in time of war, but in a manner to be prescribed by law.

People cannot be forced to shelter and feed soldiers in their homes during peacetime. During a war, Congress may order this done.

AMENDMENT 4 Search and Seizure; Warrants

adopted 1791

The right of the people to be secure in their persons, houses, papers, and effects, against unreasonable searches and seizures, shall not be violated, and no warrants shall issue but upon probable cause, supported by oath or affirmation, and particularly describing the place to be searched, and the persons or things to be seized.

People's homes cannot be searched or their property taken away unless a judge issues an official order ["warrant"] to do so. This court order can only be given for good reasons, and the order must tell where the search is to be made and name the person or property to be taken.

1. Under Amendment 4, what do the police need before they can search a person's home?
2. Why do you think Amendments 3 and 4 were needed?

AMENDMENT 5 Rights of Persons Accused of Crimes

adopted 1791

No person shall be held to answer for a capital, or otherwise infamous, crime, unless on a presentment or indictment of a grand jury, except in cases arising in the land or naval forces, or in the militia, when in actual service in time of war or public danger; nor shall any person be subject for the same offense to be twice put in jeopardy of life or limb; nor shall be compelled in any criminal case to be a witness against himself; nor be deprived of life, liberty, or property, without due process of law; nor shall private property be taken for public use without just compensation.

No person can be put on trial for any important crime unless a grand jury accuses the person. A person cannot be put on trial again ["be twice put in jeopardy"] by a federal court after he or she has been found innocent of a crime. However, the person may also be tried in a state court if the crime is a crime under state laws.

No person can be forced to give evidence ["be a witness"] against herself or himself in a federal court.

The federal government cannot take a person's life, freedom, or property except by following the laws that tell exactly how this may be done ["by due process of law"]. The federal government cannot take people's property for its own use unless it pays them a fair price ["just compensation"].

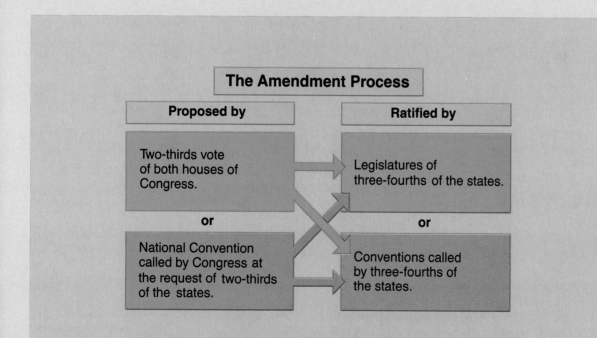

The Amendment Process

Proposed by	Ratified by
Two-thirds vote of both houses of Congress.	Legislatures of three-fourths of the states.
or	**or**
National Convention called by Congress at the request of two-thirds of the states.	Conventions called by three-fourths of the states.

1. How does the Fifth Amendment protect the rights of a person accused of a crime?
2. What must the government do if it needs a person's property for its own use?

AMENDMENT 6 Speedy, Public, and Fair Trial by Jury

adopted 1791

In all criminal prosecutions, the accused shall enjoy the right to a speedy and public trial, by an impartial jury of the State and district wherein the crime shall have been committed, which districts shall have been previously ascertained by law, and to be informed of the nature and cause of the accusation; to be confronted with the witnesses against him; to have compulsory process for obtaining witnesses in his favor, and to have the assistance of counsel for his defense.

A person accused of a crime has a right to a public trial by jury. The trial should be held within a reasonable time after the person is accused of the crime. The trial should be held in the part of the state where the crime took place. The accused person must be told what crime he or she is on trial for. The accused person has a right to hear the witnesses who speak at the trial. The accused person has the right to have a lawyer ["counsel"] and the right to call witnesses and make them give evidence.

1. Under the 6th Amendment, what rights are given to a person accused of a crime to make sure he or she has a fair trial?

AMENDMENT 7 Jury Trials for Property Disputes

adopted 1791

In suits at common law, where the value in controversy shall exceed twenty dollars, the right of trial by jury shall be preserved, and no fact tried by a jury shall be otherwise re-examined in any court of the United States than according to the rules of the common law.

In cases where a lawsuit involves $20 or more, a jury trial must be held.

AMENDMENT 8 Bail and Fines, Cruel Punishments

adopted 1791

Excessive bail shall not be required, nor excessive fines imposed, nor cruel and unusual punishments inflicted.

Bail is the money an accused person puts up to guarantee that he or she will appear for trial. Bails, fines, and punishments of persons found guilty must not be unreasonably severe.

AMENDMENT 9 Rights Kept by the People

adopted 1791

The enumeration in the Constitution of certain rights shall not be construed to deny or disparage others retained by the people.

The fact that many important rights are listed and protected in the Constitution does not mean they are the only rights people have or that their other rights are less important.

1. If a right is not mentioned in the Constitution, does this mean that a person may not have this right? Explain.

AMENDMENT 10 Powers Left to the States and the People

adopted 1791

The powers not delegated to the United States by the Constitution, nor prohibited by it to the States, are reserved to the States respectively, or to the people.

All powers not given to the federal government or not withheld from the states are left to the states or to the people.

266

1. Under the 10th Amendment, is it possible for a state to have a power that the federal government does not have? Explain.
2. Do you think the 10th Amendment increases the power of the federal government or the state governments?

AMENDMENT 11 Lawsuits Against the States

adopted 1798

The judicial power of the United States shall not be construed to extend to any suit in law or equity, commenced or prosecuted against one of the United States by citizens of another State, or by citizens or subjects of any foreign state.

When a state is sued by citizens of other states or of foreign countries, the trial must be held in a state court, not a federal court.

AMENDMENT 12 Election of President and Vice-President

adopted 1804

The electors shall meet in their respective States, and vote by ballot for President and Vice-President, one of whom, at least, shall not be an inhabitant of the same State with themselves; they shall name in their ballots the person voted for as President, and they shall make distinct lists of all persons voted for as President, and of all persons voted for as Vice-President, and of the number of votes for each, which lists they shall sign and certify, and transmit sealed to the seat of government of the United States, directed to the President of the Senate; the President of the Senate shall, in the presence of the Senate and House of Representatives, open all the certificates and the votes shall then be counted; the person having the greatest number of votes for President shall be the President, if such number be a majority of the whole number of electors appointed; and if no person have such majority, then from the persons having the highest numbers not exceeding three on the list of those voted for as President, the House of Representatives shall choose immediately, by ballot, the President. But in choosing the President, the votes shall be taken by States, the representation from each State having one vote; a quorum for this purpose shall consist of a member or members from two thirds of the States, and a majority of all the States shall be necessary to a choice. And if the House of Representatives shall not choose a President whenever the right of choice shall devolve upon them [before the fourth day of March next following] then the Vice-President shall act as President, as in the case of the death or other constitutional disability of the President. The person having the greatest number of votes as Vice-President, shall be the Vice-President, if such number be a majority of the whole number of electors appointed, and if no person have a majority, then from the two highest numbers on the list, the Senate shall choose the Vice-President; a quorum for the purpose shall consist of two thirds of the whole number of Senators, and a majority of the whole number shall be necessary to a choice. But no person constitutionally ineligible to the office of President shall be eligible to that of Vice-President of the United States.

This amendment changed the way the electors vote for the President and Vice-President as described in Article II, Section 1. The people added this amendment to make sure that the Vice-President belongs to the same political party as the President.

The electors are to meet in their states and cast separate votes for President and Vice-President. The votes for each office are to be counted and listed separately. The results of the voting by the electors in each state are to be signed, sealed, and sent to the Senate. A meeting of both houses of Congress then counts the votes from all the states.

The person who receives the majority, or more than half, of the votes becomes President. However, if no one gets a majority of the votes, the House of Representatives must choose the President from the three persons with the most votes. When the House of Representatives votes, each state has only one vote. The person with the majority of these votes becomes President.

267

The person who receives the majority of the electors' votes for Vice-President becomes Vice-President. However, if no one gets a majority of the votes, the Senate must then choose the Vice-President from one of the two persons with the most votes. The person who receives the majority of the votes in the Senate then becomes Vice-President.

A person must meet the same qualifications as the President to be elected Vice-President.

1. Which house chooses the President and which house chooses the Vice-President if no person receives a majority of the electors' votes?
2. Why do you think it is important that electors separate their voting for President from their voting for Vice-President?
3. Why do you think it is important that the President and Vice-President belong to the same political party?

AMENDMENT 13 Slavery Abolished

adopted 1865

Section 1 *Slavery Is Ended*
Neither slavery nor involuntary servitude, except as a punishment for crime whereof the party shall have been duly convicted, shall exist within the United States, or any place subject to their jurisdiction.

Section 2 *Enforcement*
Congress shall have power to enforce this article by appropriate legislation.

Slavery is forbidden in the United States or in any American territory. No person can be given forced labor, or forced to work ["involuntary servitude"], unless that person is being punished for a crime. Congress has the power to pass laws to enforce this amendment.

1. What does the Thirteenth Amendment say about slavery?
2. Who are the only persons who may be forced to work?

AMENDMENT 14 Rights of Citizens

adopted 1868

Section 1 *Who Is a Citizen?*
All persons born or naturalized in the United States, and subject to the jurisdiction thereof, are citizens of the United States and of the State wherein they reside. No State shall make or enforce any law which shall abridge the privileges or immunities of citizens of the United States, nor shall any State deprive any person of life, liberty, or property, without due process of law; nor deny to any person within its jurisdiction the equal protection of the laws.

Section 2 *The Number of Representatives to Be Chosen*
Representatives shall be apportioned among the several States according to their respective numbers, counting the whole number of persons in each State, excluding Indians not taxed. But when the right to vote at any election for the choice of electors for President and Vice-President of the United States, Representatives in Congress, the executive and judicial officers of a State, or the members of the legislature thereof, is denied to any of the male inhabitant of such State, being twenty-one years of age, and citizens of the United States, or in any way abridged, except for participation in rebellion, or other crime, the basis of representation therein shall be reduced in the proportion which the number of such male citizens shall bear to the whole number of male citizens twenty-one years of age in such State.

Section 3 *How Citizens May Lose Some Rights*
No person shall be a Senator or Representative in Congress, or Elector of President and Vice-President, or hold any office, civil or military, under the United States, or under any State, who, having previously taken an oath, as a member of Congress, or as an officer of the United States, or as a member of any State legislatures, or as an executive or judicial officer of any State to support the Constitution of the United States, shall have engaged in insurrection or rebellion against the

same, or given aid or comfort to the enemies thereof. But Congress may by vote of two thirds of each house, remove such disability.

Section 4 *The Public Debt of Rebels against the United States*

The validity of the public debt of the United States, authorized by law, including debts incurred for payment of pensions and bounties for services in suppressing insurrection or rebellion, shall not be questioned. But neither the United States nor any State shall assume or pay any debt or obligation incurred in aid of insurrection or rebellion against the United States, or any claim for the loss or emancipation of any slave; but all such debts, obligations, and claims shall be held illegal and void.

Section 5 *Enforcement*

The Congress shall have power to enforce by appropriate legislation the provisions of this article.

The 14th Amendment has several major parts. (1) It gave citizenship to people who had been slaves and protected their rights. (2) It overturned Article I, Section 2, that counted slaves as part of the population in electing Representatives. (3) It punished Confederate officers. (4) It promised to pay the debt owed by the Union and refused to pay the debt of the Confederacy.

All persons born in the United States are citizens. Persons born in other countries who are naturalized become citizens.

No state can pass laws that limit or take away any of the rights of citizens. No state can take a person's life, freedom, or property except by following the laws that tell exactly how this may be done ["due process of law"]. All persons living in a state must be protected equally by all laws.

In counting a state's population to decide how many Representatives it has, every person must be counted. If a state prevents adult males from voting, its number of members in the House of Representatives will be decreased.

No person who held federal or state office before the Civil War and then fought for the Confederacy can serve in any office in a state government or in the government of the United States, unless Congress permits it.

All debts the United States owes as a result of fighting for the Union in the Civil War must be paid. However, the United States will not accept or pay any debts owed by the Confederacy.

1. How did the 14th Amendment protect the rights of the freed slaves?
2. How can you tell this amendment was passed soon after the Civil War ended?

AMENDMENT 15 Right of Voting
adopted 1870

Section 1 *Former Slaves' Right to Vote*

The right of citizens of the United States to vote shall not be denied or abridged by the United States or any State on account of race, color, or previous condition of servitude.

Section 2 *Enforcement*

The Congress shall have power to enforce this article by appropriate legislation.

A person's right to vote cannot be limited or taken away ["denied or abridged"] by the federal government or by the states because of his or her race or color, or because he or she was once a slave ["previous condition of servitude"].

1. In what way does the 15th Amendment add to former slaves' rights?

AMENDMENT 16 Income Tax
adopted 1913

The Congress shall have power to lay and collect taxes on incomes, from whatever source derived, without apportionment among the several States, and without regard to any census or enumeration.

Congress has the power to pass tax laws and collect taxes on incomes without following the method of collecting income taxes set out in Article I, Section 9.

1. Why do you think the 16th Amendment was added to the Constitution?

269

AMENDMENT 17 Direct Election of Senators

adopted 1913

Section 1 *How a Senator Is Elected*

The Senate of the United States shall be composed of two Senators from each State, elected by the people thereof, for six years, and each Senator shall have one vote. The electors in each State shall have the qualifications requisite for electors of the most numerous branch of the State legislatures.

Section 2 *Filling Vacancies*

When vacancies happen in the representation of any State in the Senate, the executive authority of such State shall issue writs of election to fill such vacancies: *Provided* that the legislature of any State may empower the executive thereof to make temporary appointments until the people fill the vacancies by election as the legislature may direct.

[Section 3 *Effect on Senators Elected Earlier*

This amendment shall not be so construed as to affect the election or term of any Senator chosen before it becomes valid as part of the Constitution.]

The people of the states are to elect the members of the United States Senate. Before, Senators were chosen by the state legislatures.

A vacant Senate seat may be filled by a special election in the state. Or the governor ["executive authority"] of the state may choose someone to serve as Senator until an election is held.

1. In what way does this amendment increase people's democratic rights?
2. If a Senator dies, what may the governor of his or her state do to fill the office?

[AMENDMENT 18 National Prohibition

adopted 1919

Section 1 *Alcoholic Drinks Banned*

After one year from the ratification of this article the manufacture, sale, or transportation of intoxicating liquors within, the importation thereof into, or the exportation thereof from the United States and all territory subject to the jurisdiction thereof for beverage purposes is hereby prohibited.

Section 2 *Enforcement*

The Congress and the several States shall have concurrent power to enforce this article by appropriate legislation.

Section 3 *Limited Time for Approval*

This article shall be inoperative unless it shall have been ratified as an amendment to the Constitution by the legislatures of the several States, as provided in the Constitution, within seven years from the date of the submission hereof to the States by the Congress.][7]

This amendment made it unlawful to make, sell, or carry alcoholic drinks ["intoxicating liquors"] in the United States.

AMENDMENT 19 Women May Vote

adopted 1920

Section 1 *Women's Right to Vote*

The right of citizens of the United States to vote shall not be denied or abridged by the United States or by any State on account of sex.

Section 2 *Enforcement*

The Congress shall have power to enforce this article by appropriate legislation.

Citizens of the United States cannot be prevented from voting because of their sex.

1. Why do you think it was necessary to add this amendment to the Constitution?

AMENDMENT 20 The "Lame Duck" Amendment

adopted 1933

Section 1 *When the Terms of the President, Vice-President, and Members of Congress Begin*

The terms of the President and Vice-President shall end at noon on the 20th day of January, and

---

[7] This amendment was repealed by the 21st Amendment.

the terms of Senators and Representatives at noon on the 3rd day of January, of the years in which such terms would have ended if this article had not been ratified, and the terms of their successors shall then begin.

Section 2 *Meetings of Congress*
The Congress shall assemble at least once in every year, and such meeting shall begin at noon on the 3rd day of January, unless they shall by law appoint a different day.

Section 3 *Who Succeeds the President?*
If, at the time fixed for the beginning of the term of the President, the President-elect shall have died, the Vice-President elect shall become President. If a President shall not have been chosen before the time fixed for the beginning of his term, or if the President elect shall have failed to qualify, then the Vice-President elect shall act as President until a President shall have qualified, and the Congress may by law provide for the case wherein neither a President-elect nor a Vice-President-elect shall have qualified, declaring who shall then act as President, or the manner in which one who is to act shall be selected, and such person shall act accordingly until a President or a Vice-President shall have qualified.

Section 4 *Choice of a President by the House*
The Congress may by law provide for the case of the death of any of the persons from whom the House of Representatives may choose a President, whenever the right of choice shall have devolved upon them, and for the case of the death of any of the persons from whom the Senate may choose a Vice-President whenever the right or choice shall have devolved upon them.

[Section 5 *Effective Date*
Sections 1 and 2 shall take effect on the fifteenth day of October following the ratification of this article.

Section 6 *Time Limit for Approval*
This article shall be inoperative unless it shall have been ratified as an amendment to the Constitution by the legislatures of three fourths of the several States within seven years from the date of its submission.]

The President and Vice-President take office at noon on January 20th. Senators and Representatives take office at noon on January 3rd.
Congress must meet at least once a year.
If the President-elect dies before taking office, the Vice-President elect becomes President.

1. If the President-elect dies on January 19, who takes office as President the next day?

AMENDMENT 21 Repeal of Prohibition
adopted 1933

Section 1 *Repeal of the 18th Amendment*
The eighteenth article of amendment to the Constitution of the United States is hereby repealed.

Section 2 *States Protected*
The transportation or importation into any State, territory or possession of the United States for delivery or use therein of intoxicating liquors in violation of the laws thereof, is hereby prohibited.

[Section 3 *Ratification*
This article shall be inoperative unless it shall have been ratified as an amendment of the Constitution by conventions in the several States, as provided in the Constitution, within seven years from the date of the submission hereof to the States by the Congress.]

This amendment repealed the 18th Amendment. However, states can forbid the use of alcoholic drinks ["intoxicating beverages"].

AMENDMENT 22 Two-Term Limit for President
adopted 1951

Section 1 *The Presidential Term Limited to Two Terms*
No person shall be elected to the office of the President more than twice, and no person who has

held the office of President, or acted as President, for more than two years of a term to which some other person was elected President shall be elected to the office of the President more than once. [But this article shall not apply to any person holding the office of President when this article was proposed by the Congress, and shall not prevent any person who may be holding the office of President, or acting as President, during the term within which this article becomes operative from holding the office of President, or acting as President during the remainder of such term.

Section 2 *Ratification*
This article shall be inoperative unless it shall have been ratified as an amendment to the Constitution by the legislatures of three-fourths of the several States within seven years from the date of its submission to the States by the Congress.]

No person can be elected President more than two times. No person who serves more than two years of another President's term may be elected more than one time.

1. President Franklin D. Roosevelt was elected President four times, from 1932 to 1944. Explain why he did not violate this amendment in being elected more than twice.

AMENDMENT 23 Presidential Vote for the District of Columbia
adopted 1961

Section 1 *Electors for the District of Columbia*
The district constituting the seat of government of the United States shall appoint in such manner as the Congress may direct: A number of electors of President and Vice-President equal to the whole number of Senators and Representatives in Congress to which the district would be entitled if it were a State, but in no event more than the least populous State; they shall be in addition to those appointed by the States, but they shall be considered, for the purpose of the election of President and Vice-President, to be electors appointed by a State; and they shall meet in the district and per-

form such duties as provided by the twelfth article of amendment.

Section 2 *Enforcement*
The Congress shall have power to enforce this article by appropriate legislation.

The people who live in the District of Columbia, the nation's capital, can vote for President and Vice-President. They can vote for as many electors as the state with the smallest population has.

AMENDMENT 24 Poll Tax
adopted 1964

Section 1 *Poll Tax Banned in National Elections*
The right of citizens of the United States to vote in any primary or other election for President or Vice-President, for electors for President or Vice-President, or for Senator or Representative in Congress shall not be denied or abridged by the United States or any state by reason of failure to pay any poll tax or other tax.

Section 2 *Enforcement*
The Congress shall have power to enforce this article by appropriate legislation.

No person can be forced by the federal government or the states to pay a poll tax or any other tax in order to vote in a federal election.

1. People in some states had to pay a poll tax before this amendment was passed. What effect do this think this amendment had on the number of people who voted in such states?

AMENDMENT 25 Presidential Succession
adopted 1967

Section 1 *When the Vice-President Can Take Over the Presidency*
In case of the removal of the President from office or his death or resignation, the Vice-President shall become President.

Section 2 *Appointment of a New Vice-President*

Whenever there is a vacancy in the office of the Vice-President, the President shall nominate a Vice-President who shall take the office upon confirmation by a majority vote of both houses of Congress.

Section 3 *How the President Can Transmit Powers to the Vice-President*

Whenever the President transmits to the President pro tempore of the Senate and the Speaker of the House of Representatives his written declaration that he is unable to discharge the powers and duties of his office, and until he transmits to them a written declaration to the contrary, such powers and duties shall be discharged by the Vice-President as Acting President.

Section 4 *How the Vice-President Can Take Over the Powers of the President*

Whenever the Vice-President and a majority of either the principal officers of the executive departments, or of such other body as Congress may by law provide, transmit to the President pro tempore of the Senate and the Speaker of the House of Representatives their written declaration that the President is unable to discharge the powers and duties of his office, the Vice-President shall immediately assume the powers and duties of the office as Acting President.

Thereafter, when the President transmits to the President pro tempore of the Senate and the Speaker of the House of Representatives his written declaration that no inability exists, he shall resume the powers and duties of his office unless the Vice-President and a majority of either the principal officers of the executive departments, or of such other body as Congress may by law provide, transmit within four days to the President pro tempore of the Senate and the Speaker of the House of Representatives their written declaration that the President is unable to discharge the powers and duties of his office. Thereupon Congress shall decide the issue, assembling within 48 hours for that purpose if not in session. If the Congress, within 21 days after the receipt of the latter written declaration, or, if Congress is not in session, within 21 days after Congress is required to assem-

ble, determines by two-thirds vote of both houses that the President is unable to discharge the powers and duties of his office, the Vice-President shall continue to discharge the same as Acting President; otherwise, the President shall resume the powers and duties of his office.

If the President dies, resigns, or is removed from office, the Vice-President becomes President. When there is no Vice-President, the President names a Vice-President with the approval of a majority in each house of Congress.

If the President feels unable to carry out the duties of President, the Vice-President then takes over. When the President feels ready to carry out the duties again, he or she can tell Congress. However, if the Vice-President and the majority of the heads of the executive departments do not agree that the President is ready, Congress must decide whether the President can take up the duties of office. Congress must decide within 21 days by a two-thirds vote.

1. Under the 25th Amendment, what may a President do if the Vice-President has died in office?

AMENDMENT 26 Voting Age Lowered to 18

adopted 1971

Section 1 *Those Eighteen Years of Age or Older May Vote*

The right of citizens of the United States, who are eighteen years of age or older, to vote shall not be denied or abridged by the United States or by any State on account of age.

Section 2 *Enforcement*

The Congress shall have power to enforce this article by appropriate legislation.

The right of all citizens 18 years or older to vote cannot be limited or taken away ["denied or abridged"] by the federal government or the states.

1. Under this amendment, in what year will you be able to vote?

CHAPTER 4

Settling Western Lands to the Mississippi

OBJECTIVE: How did Americans settle the lands between the Appalachians and the Mississippi?

1. Has your family or someone you know moved recently? People move for many reasons. If they take a job in another state, often they must move to be closer to the new job. Sometimes people believe their health will be better in a different state because the climate is warmer. Other times people move just because they are ready for a change. In the 1780s, Americans had many such reasons for moving west.

Westward Expansion What steps did the federal government take to encourage people to move west?

2. After the American Revolution, the Confederation needed money to pay off its war debts. One way to raise this money was to sell off the northwestern lands American had won from Britain. These lands reached from the Ohio River to the Great Lakes, and as far west as the Mississippi River.

3. In 1785, the government began to prepare the territory for sale and settlement. Congress had passed a land ordinance that broke up the territory into squares of land called townships. Two years later Congress passed the **Northwest Ordinance,** which told how the territory would be governed.

4. The Northwest Ordinance included a bill of rights for the white male settlers of the

▲ Troops led by General Anthony Wayne forced Native Americans from their lands. In 1775, several tribes were forced to sign a treaty giving up their lands in Ohio and Indiana.

territory. It guaranteed them freedom of speech, freedom of worship, and the right to trial by jury. It also set aside a section of land in each township. The money from the sale of that land paid for the township's public schools.

In Chapter 4 you will apply these critical thinking skills to the historical process:
▥ **Understanding Points of View:** Recognizing why people have different attitudes about the same thing.

◢ **Making Judgments:** Stating a personal opinion based on historical facts.

The Early Settlements   How were the lands above and below the Ohio River settled?

5. At the signing of the Articles of Confederation, all but two pieces of the western lands were given to the national government. Connecticut kept the **Western Reserve,** a section of land in northeastern Ohio along Lake Erie. Virginia kept the Virginia Military District, in southeastern Ohio. Virginia gave parts of the Military District to Virginia veterans of the Revolutionary War. The rest of the land was sold to a **land company.** These companies made a profit by buying large tracts of land and reselling them in small parcels. Connecticut gave parts of the Western Reserve to Connecticut persons whose towns had been destroyed by the British during the war. In 1796, Connecticut sold the rest of the Reserve to the Connecticut Land Company.

People in History

6. Moses Cleaveland   A director of the Connecticut Land Company, Moses Cleaveland (1754–1806) led the first survey party of the Western Reserve. Cleaveland had served as a captain in George Washington's army during the Revolutionary War. He was later a member of the Connecticut state legislature that ratified the Constitution. In the summer of 1796, Cleaveland's survey party set off for the shores of Lake Erie. Shortly after, he founded the city that bears his name on the Cuyahoga River. The spelling was changed to Cleveland in 1832 when the "a" was dropped to fit the word in a newspaper headline.

7. Farmers were especially attracted to the rich soils of the Northwest. They fenced in the land and cut down the trees of many Native American hunting grounds. Why were the first settlements built near military forts?

8. Farmers from the South moved west to the lands south of the Ohio River. In the 1790s, there was a growing demand for cotton. Yet one slave could clean only a single pound of cotton by hand in one day. With the invention of the cotton gin (JIN) in 1793, the seeds from 100 pounds (45.36 kilograms) of cotton could be cleaned in one day. Because of the cotton gin, more cotton could be grown. However, cotton quickly wore out the soils of many plantations east of the Appalachians. Southern plantation owners, searching for richer soils for large-scale cotton planting, moved west into the territories of Alabama and Mississippi.

Native Americans   How were Native Americans treated by the government?

9. The national government and the pioneers badly treated the Native American tribes who lived between the Appalachians and the Mississippi River. After the American Revolution, treaties with Congress promised Native Americans that they would not be forced from their lands. Such treaties were largely ignored by the pioneer settlers. Wherever Native Americans defended their lands, the federal government sent in troops forcing them to move off their lands farther west. Congress drew up new treaties of sale and made Native Americans sign them.

Spotlight on Sources

10. Tecumseh (1768–1813), a leader of the Shawnee nation, spoke out against the new treaties. Like most Native Americans, he believed that no one owned the land or had the right to sell it. He met with William Henry Harrison, a former army general, in August 1810 to explain how Native Americans felt.

Once there was no white man on this continent. It then all belonged to red men, children of the same parents, placed on it by the Great Spirit that made them, to keep it, to traverse [travel] it, to enjoy its productions [all that is made from the land], and to fill it with the same race. Once a happy race. Since made miserable by the white people, who are . . . always encroaching [trespassing].

Activity: Help the students identify Native American names on the maps of present day Mississippi and Ohio. In addition, have them search for Native American names on the map of their own state.

275

Logic on the Land   Middle America when viewed from an airplane is a pattern of straight roads and square or rectangular fields. A survey system invented by the United States in 1785 explains this dramatic human imprint on the land.

In 1785, Congress needed a way to divide up the Northwest Territory. The delegates decided on a survey system based on the earth's grid of east–west latitude lines and north–south longitude lines. Surveyors surveyed the east–west base line. Using this as a starting point, they marked off rows of east–west lines parallel to the base line 6 miles (9.6 km) apart. Cutting across the east–west lines they surveyed parallel rows of north–south lines 6 miles apart.

The two sets of lines crossed each other every 6 miles to form squares. Townships were formed in each 6-mile square. The townships were 36 square miles (about 94 sq. km). Each township was subdivided into 36 numbered sections. Each section was one mile (1.6 km) square and covered 640 acres (about 3 sq. km).

The new survey system was an easy way to give out land to settlers. The one-mile square sections were easy to subdivide into half-sections (320 acres), quarter-sections (160 acres), or even smaller units. However small, each piece of land was easily located by section number.

The township and range system, as the survey is called, marked off townships from the Appalachians to the Pacific coast. Everywhere the system was used the same straight roads and square and rectangular patterns were fixed permanently upon the land.

Now use the map and diagram below to answer these questions.

1. What present-day states have been formed from the Northwest Territory?

2. How many sections make up a township and how large is each section?

3. What are some of the advantages of the township and range survey system?

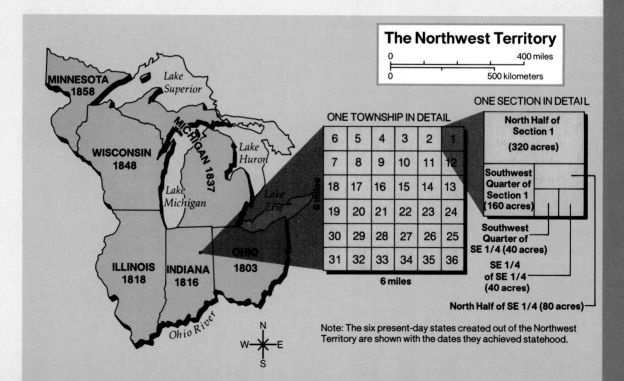

The Northwest Territory

Note: The six present-day states created out of the Northwest Territory are shown with the dates they achieved statehood.

The way, and the only way to check and stop this evil, is for all the red men to unite in claiming a common and equal right in the land, as it was at first and should be yet. For it never was divided, but belongs to all, for the use of each. That no part [no Native American individual] has a right to sell, even to each other, much less to strangers—those who want all and will not do with less. The white people have no right to take the land from the Indians who had it first; it is theirs.

—From *Great Documents in American Indian History,* ed. by Wayne Moquin Praeger, 1973. Used by permission.

▶ What is the "evil" to which Tecumseh refers? After delivering his speech, Tecumseh made his point of view even clearer: He took his seat on the bench, pushing Harrison to the edge. When Harrison complained, Tecumseh pointed out that he was only doing to Harrison what white settlers had done to Native Americans.

Building Roads and Canals How did the new roads and waterways help the nation grow?

11. By the turn of the century, new roads were being built to speed the movement of people and goods. Private companies built **turnpikes,** roads on which tolls are collected at several points. Every few miles, a wooden pole, or pike, blocked these roads until a toll was paid. In 1802 Congress voted money to build the **National Road.** Opened in 1818, it wound through western Maryland and Pennsylvania into Ohio and Illinois. What effect do you think ◀ the National Road had on the westward movement?

12. The nation's network of water routes grew quickly after the **Erie Canal** was built. Work on the canal began in 1816 and ended nine years later. With a pick and shovel, each worker dug about 16 feet (5 meters) per week. The 400 mile (640 kilometers) canal linked the Hudson River with the Great Lakes. This all-water route lowered the price of carrying a ton (907 kilograms) of goods from Buffalo to New York by almost $100. By the 1830s, more than 3,000 miles (4,800 kilometers) of canals had been built in the United States.

Outlook

13. By the 1830s, new roads and waterways linked the cities of the East with the frontier settlements. However, there was a cost for this "progress." The growth of new settlements in the western territories tore apart the Native American society. In less than 50 years, the white settlers outnumbered the Native Americans. The greater military strength of the United States army drove the Native Americans from their lands.

▼ Tecumseh, whose name means "shooting star," was a strong warrior and orator. He urged Native Americans to band together and defend their lands from invasion by whites.

Activity: On a current map of the United States, have volunteers trace Route 40 to follow the path of the National Road. **Ask:** What similarities and differences can you see between the early American roads and modern highways?

CHAPTER REVIEW

VOCABULARY REVIEW

▶ Write each number and word. Then write the letter of the definition next to the word it defines.

1. cotton gin

2. land company

3. Northwest Ordinance

4. Western Reserve

5. turnpikes

6. National Road

7. Erie Canal

a. linked the Hudson River and the Great Lakes

b. made large-scale cotton planting possible

c. linked Maryland and western Pennsylvania with Ohio and Illinois

d. Connecticut's land in Ohio

e. law that told how the Northwest Territory would be governed

f. made profits by buying large areas of land and reselling them in smaller pieces

g. toll roads

h. law that provided for surveys of Native American lands

SKILL BUILDER: READING A MAP

▶ Read the map at the bottom of this page. The key tells you which lines are canals and which are roads. Use the key to answer the questions that follow. Write your answers on a sheet of paper.

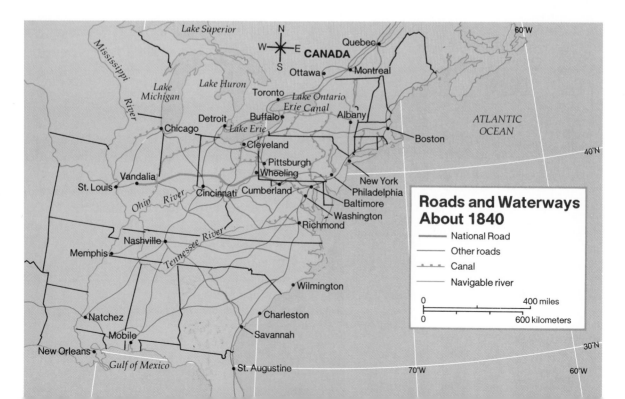

Roads and Waterways About 1840

— National Road
— Other roads
∙∙∙∙∙ Canal
— Navigable river

0   400 miles
0   600 kilometers

STUDY HINT

Geography plays an important role in history. Examine the map on page 276 as you read this chapter. How did mountains and rivers affect the migration west?

1. What all-water route on this map links New York City to Lake Erie?

2. Name two cities of New York through which the Erie Canal passes.

3. How were goods shipped from Cincinnati to Chicago?

4. Which section of the United States had the most canals—the Northeast, Northwest, Southeast, or Southwest?

5. Name three states through which the National Road passed.

6. Which city on the National Road is farthest west?

SKILL BUILDER: CRITICAL THINKING AND COMPREHENSION

I. Point of View

Understanding how another person feels about something can help you better understand a problem or conflict. Answer the following questions to better understand the conflict that developed between Native Americans and the early frontier settlers. On a separate sheet of paper, write *T* if the statement expresses Tecumseh's point of view. Write *S* if the statement expresses the white settlers point of view.

1. The wheels of progress keep turning and more and more roads will be needed for these wheels to travel on.

2. You did not make the land. The land has always been. What right do you have to claim it as your own and to sell it?

3. This country will be great once all of its land is farmed, new towns are built, and money is made.

II. Making Judgments

Answer these questions on a separate sheet of paper.

1. Was Congress right in taking away the land from Native Americans, with or without a treaty? Why?

2. What do you think of the idea of ownership of land? Do you agree or disagree with the Native American view that land belongs to everyone and not to one person? Why?

USING PRIMARY SOURCES

Reread the Spotlight on Sources on page 275. How does Tecumseh want to stop the white people from taking Native American lands?

ENRICHMENT

1. Before the new roads and canals were built, traveling west was a nightmare. Wagons often sank to their axles in mud. Huge potholes in the dirt roads broke wheels and jarred passengers from their seats. Find out more about how people traveled and give a brief report on your findings to the class.

2. Do library research on the Shawnee nation. Write a play about the customs and beliefs of the nation and its early contacts with white settlers.

CHAPTER 5

Adding the Louisiana Territory

OBJECTIVE: How did the United States obtain the vast land between the Mississippi and the Rocky Mountains?

1. You have probably seen prairie dogs, woolly mountain goats, badgers, muskrats, and grizzly bears in a zoo. Imagine what it was like to meet these animals in the wild. Lewis and Clark did just that as they explored the Louisiana Territory in 1804. They saw beautiful animals such as the red fox with black and white markings on its back. They also faced the frightening grizzly bears that chased them even after being shot at several times. Lewis described a bird with a wingspread of about nine feet (3 meters). That bird is known today as the California condor. As the nineteenth century began, the lands between the Mississippi and the Pacific Ocean were about to become a part of the United States.

Gulf of Mexico   Why was this gulf important to the United States?

2. The Mississippi River was the major highway of trade for American farmers living in the western territories. By the 1790s, these farmers were raising more crops than they needed. They wanted to sell these extra crops, or **surplus** (SER-plus) **crops,** to the markets in the East. However, it took money and time to send crops overland across the Appalachians. Western farmers needed a port on the Gulf of Mexico from which to ship their goods.

▲ Sacajawea, York, Lewis, Clark, and others greet Native Americans from the Northwest Coast on the lower Columbia River. Why was the Lewis and Clark Expedition important?

3. In 1795, the federal government formed a treaty with Spain that gave Americans the **right of deposit** in New Orleans. Find New Orleans on the map on page 284. On what river is New Orleans located? The right of deposit allowed Americans to unload their

In Chapter 5 you will apply these critical thinking skills to the historical process:

▲ **Recognizing Main Idea:** Identifying the most important idea in a paragraph.

📁 **Classifying:** Organizing facts into categories based on what they have in common.

goods at New Orleans and later load them on ocean-going vessels.

4. Americans were worried that they would lose the right of deposit in 1800 when France took the **Louisiana Territory** from Spain. Trace the borders of this territory on the map on page 284. Unlike Spain at the time, France was a mighty nation. The thought of having French troops stationed along America's western border alarmed the new President, Thomas Jefferson. Also, closing the port of New Orleans to Americans would cripple the western trade. Therefore, Jefferson offered $10 million to buy New Orleans from France. No one, not even Jefferson, expected France to take this offer seriously.

The Louisiana Purchase
How did Jefferson obtain the vast Louisiana Territory from France?

5. Napoleon Bonaparte, the ruler of France, stunned Jefferson by offering to sell all the Louisiana Territory to the United States. Napoleon wanted to control all of Europe and he had been seeking a way to raise money to pay his army. When Jefferson offered $15 million for the Louisiana Territory, Napoleon accepted. In 1803, the western lands between the Mississippi and the Rocky Mountains became part of the United States. This event is known as the Louisiana Purchase.

The Lewis and Clark Expedition
What were the results of Lewis and Clark's exploration of the Louisiana Territory?

6. President Jefferson sent two United States army captains, Meriwether Lewis and William Clark, to explore the Louisiana Purchase. Their orders were to carve a path across the continent to the Pacific Ocean. They were to take careful note of the plants and animals—especially those ▶ not known in the United States. Why do you think Jefferson wanted Lewis and Clark to keep detailed records of everything they saw? Jefferson also ordered Lewis and Clark to record the names, customs, and numbers of Indian tribes in the territory.

7. The Lewis and Clark expedition set out from St. Louis, Missouri, in May 1804. Among the party of exploration was an African slave named York, who belonged to William Clark. They traveled northwest along the Missouri River about 1,600 miles (2,500 kilometers) to what is now South Dakota. There they hired a French-Canadian fur trader named Toussaint Charborneau and his wife, a Shoshone woman named Sacajawea (sak-uh-juh-WEE-uh). Taking their new-born son with them, Sacajawea and her husband guided the expedition through the wilderness. What were some of the skills a ◀ guide probably would need? The party reached the base of the Rocky Mountains almost a year later.

Spotlight on Sources

8. This account is from Meriwether Lewis's journal, dated July 27, 1805.

> We begin to feel considerable anxiety [fear] with respect to the . . . Indians. If we do not find them or some other nation who have horses I fear the success . . . of our voyage will be very doubtful. . . . We are now several hundred miles within . . . this wild and mountainous country, where game [animals hunted for food] may rationally [reasonably] be expected shortly to become scarce [hard to find]. . . . However, I still hope for the best, and intend [plan] taking a tramp [walk] myself in a few days to find these [Indians] if possible. . . . If any Indians can subsist [survive] in the form of a nation in these mountains with the means they have of acquiring [getting] food, we can also subsist.
>
> —*The Journals of Lewis and Clark*, ed. by Bernard DeVoto

How did the expedition depend on the help of ▲ Native American tribes?

9. During their adventure west, Lewis and Clark met peaceably with over 50 Native Amer-

THE FRENCH

The French discovered and colonized so much of the United States that, at one time, part of America was called New France. Many American cities have French names—for example, Des Moines, LaSalle, St. Louis, New Orleans, and Detroit. The early French travelers to America were adventurous fur trappers, traders, and Catholic missionaries. An important group of early French immigrants was the Huguenots (HYOO-guh-nahts). The Huguenots, or French Protestants, were forced out of France by religious persecution. About 15,000 Huguenots came to America between 1685 and 1760. Some became colonial leaders—among them Paul Revere; John Jay, the first Chief Justice of the Supreme Court; and Francis Marion, a Revolutionary War hero from South Carolina.

▼ This painting shows the removal of the Acadians from Nova Scotia by the British in 1755. Why were the Acadians forced to move? Where did they resettle?

Some of the French Huguenots settled in Acadia, the French name for Nova Scotia in Canada. When the British seized this island in Canada, they demanded that the French Acadians swear loyalty to the British king. Those who refused were forced to move out of Acadia in 1755. Several thousand Acadians resettled in Southwest Louisiana, then a French territory. The Creoles and Cajuns of present-day Louisiana and eastern Texas are the descendants of the French Huguenots from Acadia.

In the late 1700s and early 1800s, another group of people came to the United States from France. When the French Revolution of 1789 succeeded in overthrowing the French king and the nobles, some French nobles escaped. Fearing for their lives and fortunes, they fled to America. In 1815, the French king regained power. An even larger group of French political refugees fled to America—the followers of the fallen Napoleon.

The French brought to America their great love of the arts, of music, painting, theater and literature. In Louisiana, a former French colony, the French started many popular festivals, including **Mardi Gras** (MAR-dee GRAH). Since Mardi Gras was started in 1766, people from all over the world have come to New Orleans to celebrate in this colorful carnival.

Now answer the following questions.

1. Who were the early French travelers to the United States?

2. What political developments in France caused people to emigrate to the States?

3. Where is the French influence seen in the United States today?

4. Why was the United States once called "New France"?

ican tribes. They gave out silver medals with a picture of President Jefferson on them as peace offerings. They traded goods and trinkets for fresh horses and supplies. The explorers rode across the Rocky Mountains to the Columbia River, where they made canoes from tree bark and paddled downstream. On the Pacific Slope, they met the Shoshones and their new chief, Sacajawea's brother. During the long trek west, many Native Americans were drawn to the white men's camp out of curiosity over York, William Clark's slave.

People in History

10. York A man called York was the first African American to set foot on the western frontier. York was a powerfully built man whose great hunting and fishing skills supplied much of the food for the expedition. His skin color and strength impressed the Native Americans. "All flocked round him and examined him from top to toe," Clark noted in his journal. York was freed at the end of the trip. Why do you think he was freed?

11. Lewis and Clark reached their goal on November 7, 1805, when the expedition sighted the Pacific Ocean. In September 1806, the explorers returned to St. Louis. They had been gone for two years and had traveled 8,000 miles (12,800 kilometers).

12. The expedition had carried out Jefferson's directions and opened the Louisiana Territory for settlement. Lewis and Clark had explored the uncharted Missouri and Columbia rivers and made maps that showed how to get to the Pacific Ocean. They had collected unknown plants and animals for study, including medicinal herbs and roots used by Native Americans. From the large supply of fur-bearing animals in the territory, they brought back two bear cubs for President Jefferson. Jefferson kept the cubs on the White House lawn. The explorers told of 122 kinds of birds, mammals, and reptiles they had discovered. They also brought back the bones of a 45-foot (13.5 meter) dinosaur unearthed at one of their campsites.

THE PRESIDENTS' CORNER

Thomas Jefferson was President from 1801 to 1809. With his election, the young Democratic-Republican Party took control of the government for the first time. Jefferson was known as a **strict constructionist.** That meant he didn't believe in giving the federal government any more power than is given to it in the Constitution. Jefferson lowered taxes and the national debt. He sent the navy to the Mediterranean to defend American merchant ships from Barbary pirates. Jefferson introduced a less formal style to the presidency. Washington and Adams had bowed to the people. Jefferson shook hands.

Pike's Expedition What parts of the Louisiana Territory did Pike explore?

13. In July 1806, United States Army lieutenant Zebulon Pike set out from St. Louis to explore the southwest land of the Louisiana Purchase. 23 white men and 51 Native Americans made up the scouting party. Pike was stopped by a peak of the Rocky Mountains later named in his honor. From Colorado, Pike traveled south to explore the border between the Louisiana Territory and the Spanish-held lands.

Outlook

14. The Louisiana Purchase doubled the size of the United States and opened a rich new territory to farmers and fur traders. In time, all or part of 13 states would be carved from these new lands. Yet within a few years of the Lewis and Clark expedition, the amazing adventures of the early pioneers were put on hold. What happened in 1812 to slow the westward march of the United States?

Background: Pike was arrested as a spy in Spanish territory and brought before the governor of Spanish New Mexico in Santa Fe. He was later released, but the Spanish officials kept the valuable journals of his explorations of Texas and the plains country. Nevertheless, Pike was able to write a book about his explorations that added much to the knowledge of the Louisiana Purchase, its land and resources.

283

CHAPTER REVIEW

VOCABULARY REVIEW

▶ Write the following paragraph on a sheet of paper. Then fill in the blanks with the words that best complete the paragraph.

judicial review   uncharted   surplus crops   Louisiana Territory

strict constructionist   right of deposit   expedition

   By the 1790s, western settlers needed an outlet in the Gulf of Mexico from which to ship their ___1__ to market. The federal government struck a treaty with Spain that gave Americans the ___2__ in New Orleans. This right was threatened when France took the port and other lands from Spain. To safeguard western trade, Thomas Jefferson purchased the ___3__ from France in 1803. Because he was a ___4__ , Jefferson worried that the Constitution did not give him the power to buy land. During Jefferson's first term of office, the Supreme Court expanded its power by setting forth the right of ___5__ .

SKILL BUILDER: INTERPRETING A MAP

▶ Study the map at the bottom of the page. Then decide whether the following statements are true or false. If a statement is false, rewrite it to make it true.

1. The Louisiana Purchase doubled the size of the United States.

2. The Louisiana Purchase extended the United States boundary to the Pacific Ocean.

3. Lewis and Clark traveled into the Oregon territory.

4. Pike's explorations took him north from St. Louis.

5. Lewis and Clark traveled in a northwest direction.

6. Pike traveled through land that is now part of Mexico and Texas.

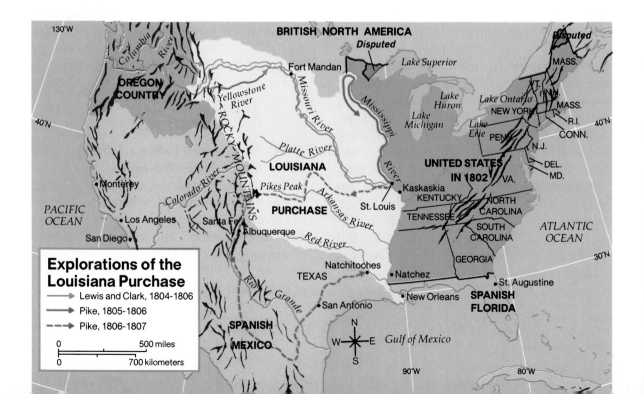

Explorations of the Louisiana Purchase
→ Lewis and Clark, 1804-1806
→ Pike, 1805-1806
- - → Pike, 1806-1807

0   500 miles
0   700 kilometers

The United States purchased the Louisiana Territory to solve a problem: reopening the port of New Orleans to western settlers. List other reasons why the Louisiana Purchase became important to the United States.

SKILL BUILDER: CRITICAL THINKING AND COMPREHENSION

▲ I. Main Idea

1. Write 5 main topics that William Clark probably wrote in his journal during the journey across the Louisiana Territory.

2. Supply the missing main ideas and supporting details to complete the following outline on the Lewis and Clark expedition. Write the completed outline on a sheet of paper. (Refer to the paragraph numbers in parentheses if you need help.)

  I. Key Members of the Expedition (paragraph 7)
    A. Meriwether Lewis
    B. William Clark
    C. _____
    D. _____
    E. _____

  II. Dealings with Native American Tribes (paragraphs 6, 8–9)
    A. _____
    B. traded with tribes for fresh horses and supplies
    C. _____

  III. _____ (paragraph 12)
    A. explored Missouri and Columbia rivers
    B. made maps showing way to Pacific Ocean
    C. _____
    D. discovered new kinds of birds, mammals, and reptiles
    E. _____

📂 II. Classifying

▶ On a sheet of paper, group the items listed below into the following categories: **1. explorers, 2. rivers, 3. things brought back by Lewis and Clark.**

Meriwether Lewis	bear cubs	dinosaur bones
Missouri River	Columbia River	Zebulon Pike
Arkansas River	William Clark	maps

USING PRIMARY SOURCES

▶ Reread the Spotlight on Sources on page 281. What did the Lewis and Clark Expedition need from the Native American tribes?

ENRICHMENT

Using *The Journals of Lewis and Clark*, tracing paper, and a modern road map, trace Lewis and Clark's route across the Louisiana Territory. Then plan a modern-day expedition along the same route. Decide on a means of transportation, what supplies to take, where to stop, and what to bring back. Write a brief travel plan to share with the class.

CHAPTER 6

America *vs.* Britain: The War of 1812

OBJECTIVE: Why did the United States fight a second war with Great Britain, and what were the results?

1. All night, the British had bombarded Fort McHenry. Aboard a British warship, where he had gone to exchange prisoners, the American Francis Scott Key had not slept while the battle raged. But now, at dawn's break, the smoke was starting to clear. Key leaned over the ship's rail, trying to make out who had won the battle. To his joy, he saw the American flag, torn and battered, still flying over the fort. On the back of a letter he carried, Key began to write the words to a song to tell the great feeling he felt. In a matter of minutes, he had written "The Star-Spangled Banner," the song that would later become America's national anthem.

▲ Because cannon balls seemed to bounce off its wooden hull, the American warship *Constitution* was called "Old Ironsides." It sank Britain's *Guerrière* in the War of 1812 (pictured above).

War in Europe What effect did war in Europe have on the United States?

2. In 1803, Napoleon declared war in Europe. By 1807, French soldiers had driven British troops from the European continent and defeated Britain's European allies. Napoleon controlled most of Europe. A French victory seemed likely, even though the strong British navy still "ruled the waves."

3. Many American merchants enjoyed a rich trade selling war supplies to both France and Great Britain. However, in 1807 Great Britain tried to cut off the American trade with France.

America was France's major source of supply. The British Parliament passed the **Orders in Council,** laws forbidding American ships to enter French-controlled ports. What did the ◄ British hope to gain by passing the Orders? Also, the British navy illegally stopped and

In Chapter 6 you will apply these critical thinking skills to the historical process:
▲ **Recognizing Main Idea:** Identifying the most important idea in a paragraph.
📁 **Classifying:** Organizing facts into categories based on what they have in common.

searched American merchant ships on the open seas. During these searches for French-bound cargo, many American sailors born in England were accused of having deserted the British navy. The British kidnapped these sailors and forced them to serve in the British navy. The British policy of **impressment**, or seizure, of American sailors deeply offended America's national pride.

4. In reaction to the Orders in Council, Napoleon declared a **blockade** (blah-KAYD) against Great Britain. A blockade is a shutting off of a nation's ports by the troops or ships of the enemy. In a series of orders, Napoleon forbade all nations to trade with Great Britain. Also, France threatened to seize any ship carrying British cargo that entered French ports.

5. Despite the British Orders and Napoleon's orders, the United States refused to take sides, preferring to remain **neutral** (NOO-truhl) in the European war. The United States felt its ships were free to sail the open seas. Therefore, American merchants took up the risky practice of blockade running. When ships run blockades, they continue to do trading but at the risk of being attacked.

6. In the summer of 1807, a British attack on the *U.S.S. Chesapeake* off the coast of Virginia angered many Americans. The captain of the *U.S.S. Chesapeake* refused to allow the soldiers of the British ship *Leopard* on board. The *Leopard* opened fire. 20 American sailors were wounded, 3 killed, and 4 kidnapped.

7. Faced with this action against American rights, President Thomas Jefferson sought peaceful ways to protect American ships from enemy attack. He closed American ports to the British navy. He suggested an **embargo** (em-BAR-goh), an order forbidding any trade with foreign countries. The **Embargo Act** of 1807, which forbade American merchants to trade with foreign nations, removed American ships from the open seas. New England farmers, unable to sell their crops to foreign markets, lost money, and many American sailors were put out of work. As a result, American merchants pressured Congress to **repeal** the Embargo Act.

Congress gave in to the pressure on March 1, 1809, a few days before Jefferson left office.

8. With the repeal of the Embargo Act, more American sailors were seized by the British. In response, some Americans pushed so strongly for war, they earned the name **War Hawks.** Western settlers favored war as a way to stop the British from lending support to Native Americans in the Northwest. They also sought to win Canada in a war. Southerners favored war as a way to push the Spanish, who were allies of Britain, out of Florida.

9. One group of War Hawks strongly protested the impressment of sailors. They were led by representative Henry Clay of Kentucky and Peter B. Porter of western New York. They demanded that Congress uphold America's honor on the seas by forcibly removing the British forts that remained in America's Northwest. The War Hawks wanted land in British Canada and Spanish Florida for the United States. They accused the British in Canada of encouraging Native Americans to attack American settlers of the Northwest.

10. If either Britain or France lifted its blockade, President James Madison promised to stop trade with the other nation. When Napoleon agreed to lift the French blockade, Madison stopped trade with Great Britain. But British manufacturers strongly demanded the British government end the Orders of Council. Britain had suffered from poor harvests and badly needed American grain. On June 23, 1812, the British withdrew their Orders of Council, but their action came too late. On June 18, the United States had declared war.

The War of 1812 How successful were the British and American campaigns?

11. The Americans won an important early victory on Lake Erie. The British, who controlled the Great Lakes, had attacked the American cities of Buffalo and Detroit. The American navy sent a fleet led by Commodore Oliver Hazard Perry to stop the British ships at Lake Erie. Look at the map on page 288. Why was it ◀

important that Americans regain control of this lake? During the spring and summer of 1813, Perry and a small group of local volunteers built a fleet of 9 ships. On September 10, 1813, Perry's fleet was launched to battle the British fleet of 6 warships. After a pitched battle, the Americans won. Upon victory, Perry sent a famous message to the American people: "We have met the enemy, and they are ours." The British were forced to retreat to Canada as a result of the American victory.

12. American soldiers followed the British into Canada. However, their attack on Montreal was unsuccessful, and they had to withdraw from York (now Toronto) occupying it for a few days. In fact, the Americans were able to win only one major battle on Canadian soil. Under General William Henry Harrison the American troops won the Battle of the Thames River. In this battle, the Shawnee warrior Tecumseh was killed alongside the British troops. When Tecumseh died, the movement for Native American unity died with him.

People in History

13. Tecumseh As the Shawnee's powerful leader, Tecumseh had tried to unite the tribes of the Northwest Territory region. He got many of these tribes to agree not to sign treaties selling their lands to Congress or to white settlers. Tecumseh did not want war—he wanted only to stand up for Native American rights. The settlers wanted Tecumseh's land and were prepared to use force to get it. In 1811 army troops commanded by General William Henry Harrison attacked Tecumseh's people at Tippecanoe in Indiana while Tecumseh was away. Tecumseh and the Native American survivors of the battle fled north into Canada. Tecumseh sided with the British in the War of 1812. As a general in the British army, he won a number of battles against the Americans. When he died in the Battle of the Thames, his warriors buried him in a secret grave.

14. In 1814 the British began a campaign aimed at the nation's capital in Washington,

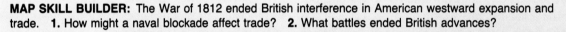

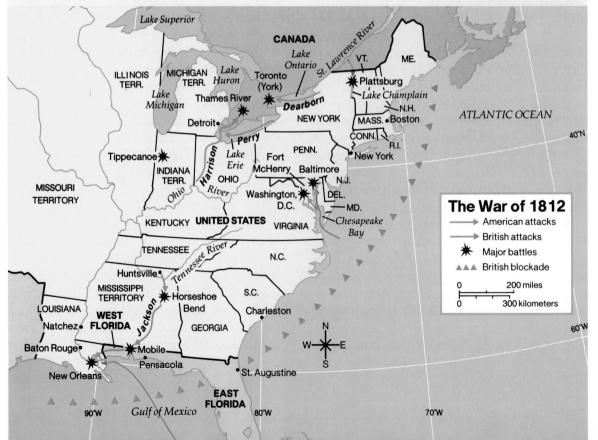

MAP SKILL BUILDER: The War of 1812 ended British interference in American westward expansion and trade. **1.** How might a naval blockade affect trade? **2.** What battles ended British advances?

The War of 1812

→ American attacks
→ British attacks
✴ Major battles
▲▲▲ British blockade

0 — 200 miles
0 — 300 kilometers

D.C. and Baltimore, Maryland. The powerful British navy, which had blockaded American ports along the Atlantic coast, landed at Chesapeake Bay. British troops entered Washington, D.C. in August, 1814. The President and Congress, who had heard about the British attack only hours before, fled the city. The British marched through the capitol and set fire to the President's mansion, the Capitol, and other government buildings. The British ships then sailed to Baltimore and fired throughout the night at Fort McHenry. Yet, at dawn, the American flag still flew over the fort, which inspired Francis Scott Key to write "The Star-Spangled Banner." At the same time, an American victory at Lake Champlain kept the British from entering New York.

The War Ends   How did the War of 1812 come to a close and who won the war?

15. By 1814, neither Great Britain nor the United States was clearly winning the war. Madison sent government officials to discuss peace with the British at Ghent (GENT), a city in Belgium. There, both countries agreed to end the war. Peace was struck when both nations signed the **Treaty of Ghent** in December 1814.

16. Because news traveled slowly from Europe, the final battle of the war took place after the treaty was signed. In January 1815, an American force led by General Andrew Jackson defeated the British in the **Battle of New Orleans.** The battle was won by volunteers. Jackson's forces included army troops, frontiersmen, pirates, Hispanics, Native Americans, and free African Americans. The victory led Americans to believe that they had actually won the war.

Spotlight on Sources

17. This appeal from Andrew Jackson, on September 21, 1814, drew many free African Americans into the fight.

As sons of freedom, you are now called upon to defend our most inestimable [valuable] blessing. As Americans, your country looks with confidence [sureness] to her adopted children, for valorous [brave] support, as a faithful return for the advantages enjoyed under her mild and equitable [fair] government. As fathers, husbands, and brothers, you are summoned [called] to rally round the standard of the Eagle . . .

To every noble-hearted, generous, freeman of color, volunteering to serve during the present contest with Great Britain, and no longer, there will be paid the same bounty [prize] in money and lands, now received by the white soldiers of the [United] States, viz. [that is] one hundred and twenty-four dollars in money, and one hundred and sixty acres of land. . . .

Due regard will be paid to the feelings of freemen and soldiers. You will not, by being associated [in contact] with white men in the same corps, be exposed to improper comparisons or unjust sarcasm [ridicule]. As a distinct [separate], independent battalion or regiment, pursuing the path of glory, you will, undivided, receive the applause and gratitude of all your countrymen.

—*Niles Weekly Register*, VII, 1815

What promises did Jackson make? Which promise do you think was the most successful in drawing African Americans into the war?

Outlook

18. The War of 1812 is sometimes called the Second War for Independence. Americans had to defend the freedom they had won in the War for Independence almost 30 years before. They took great pride in the victories of their navy, and Andrew Jackson became a hero of the nation. The people now saw the need for a strong government that could protect their country in time of war. What leaders, events, and decisions strengthened the growing nation in the coming years?

CHAPTER REVIEW

VOCABULARY REVIEW

▶ Write each number and word on a sheet of paper. Then write the letter of the definition next to the word it defines.

1. War Hawks

2. embargo

3. Treaty of Ghent

4. neutral

5. blockade

6. Embargo Act

7. repeal

8. impressment

9. Orders in Council

10. Battle of New Orleans

11. Battle of Tippecanoe

a. impartial; not taking sides

b. Jefferson's failed solution to the conflict with Great Britain on the seas

c. to end or take back

d. British laws forbidding American ships to enter French ports

e. the British policy of seizing American sailors suspected of desertion from the British navy

f. an order forbidding any trade with foreign countries

g. supporters of war

h. peace treaty ending the War of 1812

i. battle won by a volunteer army led by Andrew Jackson

j. a shutting off of a nation's ports by the troops or ships of the enemy

SKILL BUILDER: USING A CHART

▶ Use the chart at the bottom of this page, to answer the following questions about the War of 1812. Write your answers on a sheet of paper.

1. Which battles took place on or near water?

2. Which battle took place in Canada?

3. On what ship did the *Leopard* open fire?

4. Who won the battle of Fort McHenry?

Battle	Results
Lake Erie	General Perry defeated the British
Battle of Thames River	Shawnees sided with the British; Tecumseh was killed
U.S.S. Chesapeake vs. Leopard	*Leopard* opened fire; Embargo Act was passed
Fort McHenry	The American flag still flew at dawn

SKILL BUILDER: CRITICAL THINKING AND COMPREHENSION

I. Classifying

▶ Copy items 1 through 5 onto a sheet of paper. Then circle the item in each group that doesn't belong.

1. American generals: William Henry Harrison, Andrew Jackson, Oliver Hazard Perry

2. British policies: Orders in Council, impressment, Embargo Act

3. Americans who favored war: Jefferson, settlers, War Hawks

4. American victories: at Thames, at New Orleans, at Washington, D.C.

5. Americans who opposed war: Henry Clay, northeast merchants, northeast farmers, James Monroe

II. Main Idea

▶ Choose the headline that best expresses the main idea of each paragraph identified below. Reread the paragraph first and then write your answers on a sheet of paper.

1. Paragraph 4
   a. Napoleon Declares Blockade
   b. France and Britain Still at Odds
   c. British Cargo Ships Seized in French Ports

2. Paragraph 9
   a. War Hawks Want British Forts Removed
   b. The United States Faces War
   c. War Hawks and Clay Fight Monroe

3. Paragraph 15
   a. U.S. Wins the War
   b. Peace at Ghent for Britain and U.S.
   c. British, Near Defeat, Ask for Peace

USING PRIMARY SOURCES

▶ Reread the Spotlight on Sources on page 289. What does this speech tell you about the treatment of African Americans in the early 1800s?

ENRICHMENT

1. At the library, select a book on the life of President James Madison or First Lady Dolley Madison. Read the section of the book on the War of 1812. Write a radio play about the Madisons during the British invasion of Washington in 1814. Assign classmates roles and read the play to the class.

2. The pirate Jean Lafitte led the party of seamen who joined forces with General Andrew Jackson in the Battle of New Orleans. Do library research on Jean Lafitte. Then write a brief character study of this famous pirate to share with the class.

291

CHAPTER 7

A New Nationalism Takes Shape

OBJECTIVE: Why did Americans take new pride in their country after the War of 1812?

1. How did the cartoon character Uncle Sam become a symbol for the United States? During the War of 1812, a businessman named Samuel Wilson sold barrels of beef to the American army. The barrels were stamped "U.S." to show that they belonged to the United States government. Soldiers began joking that "U.S." really stood for "Uncle Sam." In 1813, a newspaper in Wilson's hometown picked up this story. Soon after, "Uncle Sam" became the nickname for the United States. Uncle Sam's style of dress—a long-tailed coat and top hat—showed how men ▶ dressed after the War of 1812. Why do you think Americans stopped wearing the old colonial wigs and clothes? An act of Congress in 1961 made Uncle Sam a national symbol.

The Era of Good Feelings Why was the United States a stronger, more unified nation after the War of 1812?

2. Americans celebrated the peace with a renewed sense of **nationalism,** or pride in their country's strength and independence. The war had taught them to survive without the help of Europe. It also helped manufacturing develop in the United States. During the war, the American people could not get manufactured goods from Europe. As a result, they started factories in New England to supply the nation

▲ This painting of the House of Representatives shows many leading political figures of the 1820s. Chief Justice John Marshall stands seventh from the left in the top row.

with needed goods such as clothing and tools. Americans felt proud about standing up to Great Britain. They showed great courage in battling the strongest naval power in the world. Finally, the nations of Europe began to look upon the United States with more respect.

In Chapter 7 you will apply these critical thinking skills to the historical process:

292

Classifying: Organizing facts into categories based on what they have in common.

Summarizing: Giving the main idea of a group of paragraphs in a brief form.

3. Relations between Great Britain and the United States improved after the war. In the **Rush-Bagot Agreement** of 1817, both nations pledged to remove their warships from the Great Lakes. In 1818, long-held boundary disputes between the United States and British Canada were resolved. Both sides agreed to make the **49th Parallel** (PAYR-uh-lel) the boundary line between the United States and Canada west of the Great Lakes.

4. Freed from worries over European affairs, Americans devoted their energies to building a better, stronger nation. House Speaker Henry Clay put forward an ambitious economic plan called the **American System.** The plan included tariffs to protect the new American textile mills in Lowell and other Massachusetts towns. The taxes on foreign goods would allow more products manufactured in the East to be sold in the South and West. The South and West would supply the textile mills of the East with food and raw materials. What were the advantages of binding the nation together economically in this way? Clay sponsored a second national bank to promote financial order. All government money would be kept in it for safekeeping. He also proposed a federal program of internal improvements, such as the building of roads and canals with national funds.

5. Political divisions faded in the years 1816 to 1825, which are known as the **"Era of Good Feelings."** The Democratic-Republican candidate for President in 1816, James Monroe, easily defeated his Federalist opponent, Rufus King. Monroe offered Americans the best of the old and the new America. A former senator, governor, and diplomat, the tall and stately Monroe was a symbol of the nation's newfound strength. As the last President to wear a powdered wig and breeches, he also reminded Americans of their Revolutionary War days. In 1820, Monroe ran for reelection unopposed. Americans now considered themselves Democratic-Republicans. The Federalist party ceased to exist. What would be the advantages of a period of one-party rule? What would be the disadvantages?

Florida   How was Florida added to the United States?

6. By the end of the War of 1812, the United States claimed all land east of the Mississippi except Florida. Florida was still under Spanish control. However, the Spanish empire in the Americas was rapidly collapsing. Inspired by the American and French revolutions, many Latin Americans rebelled against Spanish rule.

7. In 1818, President Monroe sent General Andrew Jackson to drive the Seminole Indians of Spanish Florida from American lands. The Seminoles often crossed the border into United States territory and attacked American settlements. Contrary to orders, the impulsive, headstrong Jackson pursued the Seminoles into Florida and captured two Spanish forts there. In

MAP SKILL BUILDER: Florida, divided into East and West Florida, was annexed by the United States in stages.   **1.** What river divided East and West Florida?   **2.** When did the United States annex Mobile?

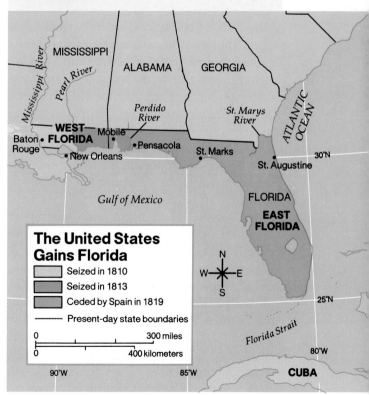

The United States Gains Florida

- Seized in 1810
- Seized in 1813
- Ceded by Spain in 1819
- Present-day state boundaries

0 — 300 miles
0 — 400 kilometers

Background: Not all sections of the country supported Clay's ideas for a national bank. Westerners feared that a bank in the East would not respond to their needs for credit.

Florida, his troops hanged two British subjects suspected of stirring Indian raids. These actions angered both Great Britain and Spain.

8. There was much angry protest of Jackson's actions from the Spanish government and from President Monroe's cabinet as well. But Monroe and his Secretary of State, John Quincy Adams, claimed Jackson's actions were necessary to keep order in Florida and to control the Seminoles. Adams threatened to invade Florida and take it if Spain could not keep order. Spain was too weak to defend Florida. In the **Adams-Onís Treaty,** Spain agreed to give up Florida to the United States for $5 million. However, the United States never paid this money to Spain, a country that had once assisted the thirteen American colonies in their struggle for independence. Claiming losses from the Seminole raids, the United States government paid this money to Americans in Georgia instead.

The Monroe Doctrine   What warning did President Monroe issue to European nations in 1823?

9. In the 1820s, the United States and Great Britain applauded when many Spanish colonies in Latin America won their freedom. The revolts against Spanish rule reminded Americans of their own earlier struggle for independence. The British, meanwhile, established a thriving trade with the new Latin American nations.

10. The British would lose money if any other power closed the door on its profitable Latin American trade. The tariffs of the American Plan had reduced Britain's trade with the United States. When Spain asked European nations to help it win back its colonies, both Great Britain and the United States objected. Why did the United States want the Latin American colonies to remain free?

11. The British proposed that the Americans join them in a combined effort to keep other European nations out of Latin America. Secretary of State Adams objected. Why do you think he wanted the United States to set its own, independent policy toward Latin America?

12. President Monroe agreed with Adams, and in 1823, issued a policy statement known as the **Monroe Doctrine.** The Monroe Doctrine stated that the United States would prevent all nations from setting up new colonies in the Americas. The United States promised to stay out of European affairs as well as the affairs of any existing colony. The United States would, however, defend the new Latin American nations against invasion.

Spotlight on Sources

13. Presidents today use their annual "State of the Union" messages to propose ways to deal with national problems. On December 2, 1823, President Monroe delivered this annual message to Congress, outlining the Monroe Doctrine.

> The American continents, by the free and independent condition which they have assumed [taken] and maintain, are henceforth not to be considered as subjects for future colonization by any European powers. . . . In the wars of the European powers, in matters relating to themselves, we have never taken any part. . . . With the movements in this hemisphere, we are, of necessity, more immediately connected. . . . We owe it, therefore, to candor [frankness], and to the amicable [friendly] relations existing between the United States and those [European] powers to declare, that we should consider any attempt on their part to extend their system to any portion of the hemisphere, as dangerous to our peace and safety. With the existing colonies or dependencies of any European power, we have not interfered, and shall not interfere. But with the governments who have declared their independence, and maintained it, and whose independence we have . . . acknowledged, we could not view any interposition [interference] for the purpose of oppressing them, or controlling, in any other manner, their destiny, by any European power, in any other light than as the manifestation

Background: In reality, the United States lacked a strong navy to enforce this doctrine. Ironically, it depended on the British navy to preserve and enforce Latin American independence.

294

[sign] of an unfriendly disposition [attitude] toward the United States.
—*House Documents, 1823–1824*, Volume I

▶ How is the Monroe Doctrine still in effect in Latin America today?

Marshall's Supreme Court How did Chief Justice Marshall's decisions increase the power of the Supreme Court?

13. In addition to setting foreign policy, Americans were deciding on laws and policies at home. John Marshall was the chief justice of the Supreme Court from 1801 to 1835. He made important rulings that expanded the power of the Court, and of the federal government over the states. His rulings have had a lasting effect on how America is governed.

People in History

14. John Marshall A Virginian like his cousin Thomas Jefferson, John Marshall (1755–1835) fought in the Revolutionary War, and then practiced law. Later, Marshall served as secretary of state under President John Adams. In his last weeks in office, President Adams appointed Marshall, a Federalist, chief justice of the Supreme Court. Marshall, who held the post for 35 years, was chief justice under 5 Presidents—Thomas Jefferson, James Madison, James Monroe, John Quincy Adams, and Andrew Jackson.

15. In addition to Marshall's appointment, President Adams made other appointments to keep the Federalist stamp on the courts. Shortly before Jefferson was sworn in, the Judiciary Act of 1801 was passed, creating several new openings for judges. Adams quickly filled these posts
▶ with Federalists. Why do you think these appointments were called **"midnight appointments"**? The last-minute appointments angered the Democratic-Republican supporters of President Jefferson. The new Secretary of State, James Madison, flatly refused to deliver the **commissions**, which were the documents that made the appointments official. One Federalist

appointee, William Marbury, then sued, and the case went to the Supreme Court.

16. Chief Justice John Marshall expanded the Supreme Court's power in the case of *Marbury v. Madison* in 1803. He decided Marbury was entitled to receive the commission, but that the Court lacked the power to deliver it. The Judiciary Act that allowed the commissions, Marshall explained, conflicted with the Constitution. The Act was, therefore, not legal. With this ruling, the Court claimed the right of judicial review, which you read about in Chapter 5.

17. When Thomas Jefferson took the presidential oath in 1801, control of the executive branch and Congress passed to the Democratic-Republicans. Yet in the judicial branch, many Federalist judges still served life terms. Marshall and his cousin sharply disagreed on most issues. President Jefferson believed in a limited national government and **states' rights.** This principle puts the power of the states above the power of the federal government. Marshall was a **nationalist,** someone who puts the power of the national government above the power of the states. Jefferson disagreed with Marshall that the Court had the power to declare acts of Congress unconstitutional. Jefferson complained about the "crafty chief judge," but he could not reverse Marshall's decisions. In what ▲ recent cases has the Supreme Court ruled on laws passed by states?

Outlook

18. Early in the nineteenth century, a spirit of nationalism captured the nation. Americans fought Great Britain and preserved their independence a second time. The Constitution, as interpreted by the Marshall Court, was stronger than ever. President Monroe delivered a strong message to European powers against interference in the Western Hemisphere. Political divisions faded as the Republican Party adopted many of the views of the Federalists. By 1824, more people were gaining a voice in government. Chapter 8 will tell you how.

Background: On July 4, 1826, the fiftieth anniversary of the Declaration of Independence, both John Adams and Thomas Jefferson died.

295

CHAPTER REVIEW

VOCABULARY REVIEW

▶ On a sheet of paper, define each of the following terms. Then check your answers in the glossary in the back of this book.

nationalism

Rush-Bagot Agreement

49th Parallel

American System

"Era of Good Feelings"

Adams-Onís Treaty

Monroe Doctrine

"midnight appointments"

commissions

Marbury v. Madison

states' rights

nationalist

SKILL BUILDER: READING A TIME LINE

▶ Study the time line below, which shows events in American history from 1816 to 1825. These years were known in America as the "Era of Good Feelings." Then use the time line to answer the questions that follow. Write your answers on a sheet of paper.

1. How long after Monroe first became President was the Monroe Doctrine issued?

2. What events shown on the time line might be used to support re-election of Monroe as President?

3. Which event on the time line increased the size of the United States?

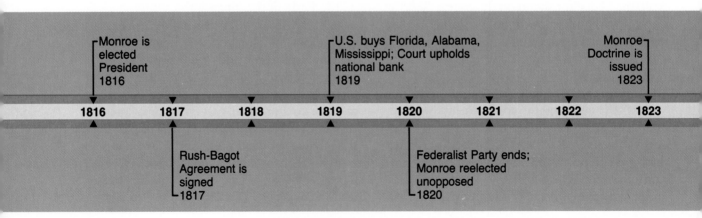

Monroe is elected President 1816

U.S. buys Florida, Alabama, Mississippi; Court upholds national bank 1819

Monroe Doctrine is issued 1823

| 1816 | 1817 | 1818 | 1819 | 1820 | 1821 | 1822 | 1823 |

Rush-Bagot Agreement is signed 1817

Federalist Party ends; Monroe reelected unopposed 1820

SKILL BUILDER: CRITICAL THINKING AND COMPREHENSION

I. Classifying

▶ Classify the following American leaders according to their political party—*Federalist Party* or *Democratic-Republican Party* . Write each name with the correct party label on a separate sheet of paper.

1. James Monroe

2. Thomas Jefferson

3. John Adams

4. William Marbury

5. John Marshall

II. Summarizing

▶ On a sheet of paper, write two or three sentences that summarize the following topics presented in this chapter.

1. The Monroe Doctrine

2. *Marbury v. Madison*

3. America after the War of 1812

4. The American System

USING PRIMARY SOURCES

▶ Reread the Spotlight on Sources on pages 294–295. According to President Monroe, what action would destroy the friendly relations between the United States and Europe, and why?

ENRICHMENT

1. An editorial is a piece of writing that gives a personal opinion, or point of view, about an issue. Write a newspaper editorial on the case of *Marbury v. Madison*, either supporting or opposing Marshall's ruling. Do library research on the case before you begin to write.

2. Reread paragraphs 6, 7, and 8 in this chapter. Imagine the reaction in President Monroe's Cabinet when they received word of General Jackson's actions in Florida. Write a script for a play in which the Cabinet debates the pros and cons of Jackson's actions. Assign roles to classmates and present the play to the class.

3. Do library research on the presidential election of 1816. Make campaign posters for the two candidates, James Monroe and Rufus King. Then write a list of the promises each candidate made during his campaign. Also describe each candidate's views of government. When your report is finished, read it to your classmates and have them debate which candidate would win the election if it were being held today.

CHAPTER 8

The Influence of the West

OBJECTIVE: How did frontier democracy influence the rest of America and help expand voting rights for more Americans?

1. Have you ever wondered how the donkey became the political symbol of the Democratic party? During the election campaign of 1828, Andrew Jackson's opponents called him an impolite name for a donkey. Instead of reacting in anger, Jackson used his ever-ready sense of humor to make a point. He had new campaign posters made showing a donkey kicking up its heels. Sure enough, Jackson stomped his opponent at the polls and to this day, the donkey is a symbol of the Democratic Party. Jackson, the seventh President of the United States, became one of our nation's most popular Presidents.

The Right To Vote How did western farmers and factory workers gain a stronger voice in government?

2. In the 1820s, America loosened its voting rules. Before, only white men who owned property or were wealthy could vote. When people moved west, however, they faced a hard and dangerous life. They had to band together to survive in the wilderness. A sense of social equality soon developed among the frontier settlers. They allowed *all* white males the right to vote and to hold office in their state legisla-
▶ tures. Why do you think voting still was not opened up to African Americans and white women?

▲ As this painting shows, President Andrew Jackson was truly the "people's choice." Hundreds of people gathered at the White House in 1829 to celebrate his inauguration.

3. The factory workers and their unions in the eastern cities soon demanded the same rights as their neighbors in the West. They, too, wanted a greater voice in government. By the 1828 election, all white males over the age of 21 could vote and hold public office. Throughout

In Chapter 8 you will apply these critical thinking skills to the historical process:
▲ **Summarizing:** Giving the main idea of a group of paragraphs in a brief form.
◯ **Generalizing:** Making a statement that links several facts.

America, however, the right to vote was still denied to women, African Americans, and Native Americans. By 1830, only a few New England states allowed African Americans to vote.

Jacksonian Democracy How did democracy grow during Jackson's Presidency?

4. Andrew Jackson was the first man from the West to be elected President of the United States. Jackson was a frontier settler, Indian fighter, and hero of the Battle of New Orleans. Born in a Carolina frontier log cabin, Jackson fought in the Revolutionary War at age 13. After the war, Jackson moved west to Tennessee to make his fortune. He became a lawyer and was elected to Congress when Tennessee became a state. Jackson had fought in duels and lived a rough-and-tumble life. He kept in touch with the hardy people who were settling the land. Like the pioneers and factory workers who voted for him, Jackson was a self-made man who had little formal schooling.

5. The inaugural celebration in 1829 showed that Jackson was truly the "people's choice" as President. Westerners in homespun clothing came to watch "their" President take the oath of office. People in muddy boots stood on the elegant White House chairs to see Jackson. When the new President was nearly crushed in the excitement, his aides took action. They placed a huge punchbowl on the White House lawn to get people outside. Most people of wealth and property were shocked by the crowd's behavior.

6. One of Jackson's first presidential acts was to dismiss many of the old federal officeholders. Jackson thought that it was time for a change in the government. He did not have faith in the honesty of many of those office holders. Jackson replaced them with friends who had helped in his campaign. This practice of giving jobs to faithful party workers is known as the **spoils system**. Spoils are loot or goods taken from an enemy in war. When his political opponents complained, Jackson argued that all people

THE PRESIDENTS' CORNER

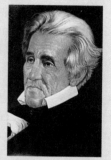

Andrew Jackson, President from 1829 to 1837, was called "Old Hickory" because he was as tough as hickory wood. Jackson jumped into politics early. In 1796, he was elected Tennessee's first member of the House of Representatives. He later became a senator and a state supreme court judge. Jackson won fame as a general in the Tennessee militia, putting down Native American rebellions. He became a national hero by winning the Battle of New Orleans. Jackson was old and in poor health by the time he won the presidency. Yet he proved a strong President, often fighting with Congress and the courts to get his way. Jackson's forceful actions and support of the common people made him one of the nation's most popular Presidents.

should have the chance to hold public office. Do you agree with Jackson that all people should have the chance to hold office? Why?

7. While in office, Jackson started a more democratic way of choosing presidential candidates. He believed that common people should have a greater say in choosing the leaders of their government. For a long time, small groups of congressmen held private meetings to decide who should run for President. Jackson opposed these private meetings. Instead, he called for a **nominating convention** (kun-VEN-shun), or large meeting where delegates from all the states could choose the candidates. Presidential candidates have been chosen in this way since 1840.

8. During his first term as President, Jackson disagreed with the Supreme Court over the constitutionality of the National Bank. Jackson felt the Bank had too much power. The Bank controlled loans made by state banks. The Bank placed limits on the amount of money these banks could lend. Many people in the South and

Background: Andrew Jackson was known for his sense of humor. A notoriously poor speller, he often joked that he was smarter than good spellers because he could think of more than one way to spell a word.

West who needed to borrow money to buy land could not get loans. Westerners feared that banks run by wealthy Easterners would ignore their needs for money. Jackson agreed, saying that the Bank was unconstitutional. What 1819 Court ruling was Jackson going against?

9. Despite strong support for the National Bank in Congress, Jackson won. He vetoed the 1832 bill that would have renewed the Bank's charter. The President's veto became the chief issue in his reelection campaign. Jackson was reelected by a landslide vote. Why do you think so many people voted for Jackson?

Jackson's Policy of Indian Removal   How were Native Americans treated under Jacksonian Democracy?

10. In 1830, Jackson ordered the forced removal of Native Americans from their homes in the South. The Southern states wanted to buy land from Native American tribes. However, the Cherokees, Creeks, Choctaws, Chickasaws, and Seminoles did not want to sell their homes. In 1828, the Cherokees wrote a constitution declaring themselves an independent nation within the state of Georgia. When the state of Georgia refused to recognize this constitution, the Cherokee people took their case to the Supreme Court. Chief Justice Marshall sided with the Cherokees, but Jackson refused to support the ruling. Instead, he got Congress to pass the **Removal Act**, which forced eastern Indians to sell their lands cheaply. Jackson then sent the army to remove the tribes to dry lands far west of the Mississippi.

11. In the winter of 1831, the Cherokees began their long march to the territories west of the Mississippi River. Leaving their homes in Georgia, the Cherokees traveled for hundreds of miles to what is now Arkansas and Oklahoma. They were allowed to take only what they could carry. Thousands died along the way from cold, hunger, and sickness. Why do you think their path westward became known as the "**Trail of Tears**"? Within 10 years, the United States government had moved more than 70,000 Native Americans across the Mississippi.

MAP SKILL BUILDER: The compass rose shows where north, south, east, and west are on a map.
1. In what direction did the Cherokee travel?   **2.** In what direction did the Seminoles travel?

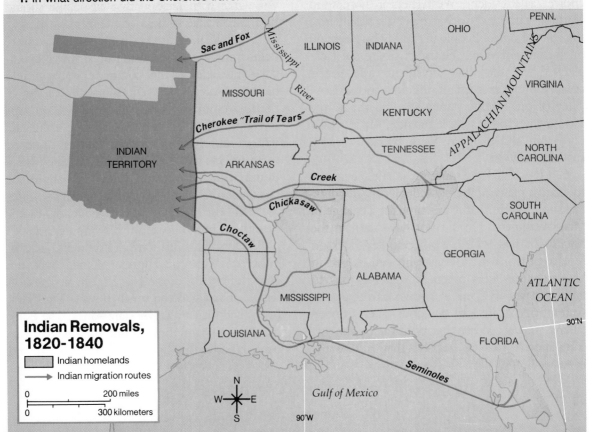

Indian Removals, 1820–1840
- Indian homelands
- → Indian migration routes
- 0   200 miles
- 0   300 kilometers

People in History

12. Sequoyah The Cherokees were able to write a constitution because they had developed a writing system of their own by 1821. In fact, they were the only Native American nation at the time to have a writing system. This system was invented by a Cherokee hunter named Sequoyah (suh-KWOI-uh). He first got the idea for a writing system about 1809 to strengthen his nation against the invading white

▶ settlers. How might this help unite the Cherokee people against the invading settlers? At first, Sequoyah tried a method that used a separate symbol for each word, but there were too many symbols. Then he decided to create symbols for a small number of sounds or syllables. The syllables could be grouped together to make many different words. Sequoyah completed his **syllabary**, or syllable-based writing system, 12 years later in 1821. Soon the Cherokees started a weekly newspaper. Tribal history, beliefs, and treaties were written down in this paper, which was called the *Cherokee Phoenix*. The paper also kept Cherokees informed of events in the world of white people. Because of Sequoyah's work, within two years thousands of Cherokees learned to read and write. Sequoyah is remembered by Native Americans for dedicating his life to advancing his people. Some want to bring back his writing system. The redwood tree of the Pacific coast, the sequoia, was named in honor of Sequoyah.

Spotlight on Sources

13. In Jackson's State of the Union message to Congress on December 8, 1829, he defended his policy toward Native Americans. He argued that the Removal Act was for the Cherokees' own good.

> Our conduct [behavior] toward these [Native American] people is deeply interesting to our national character. Their present condition, contrasted with what they once were, makes a most powerful appeal to our sympathies. Our ancestors found them un-

controlled possessors [owners] of these vast [huge] regions. By persuasion and force, they have been made to retire from river to river, and from mountain to mountain; until some of the tribes have become extinct [passed away], and others have left but remnants [small traces], to preserve, for a while, their once terrible names. Surrounded by the whites, with their arts of civilization, which, by destroying the resources of the savage, doom [condemn] him to weakness and decay; the fate of the Mohegan, the Narragansett, and the Delaware, is fast overtaking the Choctaw, the Cherokee, and the Creek. That this fate surely awaits them if they remain within the limits of the States, does not admit of a doubt. Humanity [kindness] and national honor demand that every effort should be made to avert [stop] so great a calamity [disaster] . . . I suggest, for your consideration [that you think about], the propriety [rightness] of setting apart an ample [large enough] district West of the Mississippi, and without the limits of any State or Territory, now formed, to be guaranteed [promised] to the Indian tribes.
>
> —*Senate Documents, 1829–1830,* Volume I

What is Jackson's main defense of his Indian ◀ policy? What are the flaws in his argument?

Outlook

14. Jacksonian Democracy, as the President's policies were called, gave more people a greater voice in American politics and government. Jackson opened land in the South to planters and small farmers. He crushed the powerful Bank of the United States and served as the "voice of the people" against Congress and the courts. How did American democracy grow from the time of the Articles of Confederation through the end of the Jacksonian period? What groups of people still did not have full rights as citizens, and how would they gain these rights?

Background: Jackson and his followers were being called Democrats by about 1830, although historians aren't really sure why. Perhaps it was because Jackson and his policies appealed to such a wide variety of voters.

CHAPTER REVIEW

VOCABULARY REVIEW

▶ Write each of the following sentences on a sheet of paper. Then fill in the blank with the word that best completes each sentence.

syllabary	"Trail of Tears"	Removal Act
spoils system	nominating convention	Jacksonian Democracy

1. _____ refers to the presidential policies of Andrew Jackson that gave more Americans a greater voice in government.

2. Since 1840, presidential candidates have been chosen by a _____ .

3. Native Americans of the Southeast were forced to sell their homelands and relocate west by the _____ .

4. Along the _____ to barren lands far west of the Mississippi, many Native Americans suffered and died.

5. Jackson started the _____ in American politics by rewarding loyal party members with government jobs.

SKILL BUILDER: MAKING A TIME LINE

▶ Copy the time line at the bottom of this page onto a sheet of paper. Then write the following events where they belong on the time line.

1. Andrew Jackson is elected the first President from the West.

2. Jackson delivers a State of the Union message to Congress, defending his policy toward Native Americans.

3. Under Jackson's pressure, Congress passes the Removal Act.

4. The "Trail of Tears" begins.

5. Jackson vetoes the National Bank.

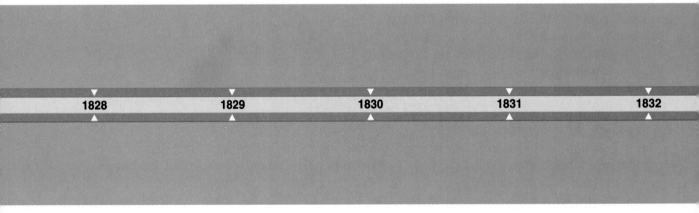

| 1828 | 1829 | 1830 | 1831 | 1832 |

SKILL BUILDER: CRITICAL THINKING AND COMPREHENSION

▲ **I. Summarizing**

▶ Reread paragraph 7 on page 299. Which of the following sentences support the main idea of paragraph 7? Write the numbers of the supporting sentences on a sheet of paper.

1. Jackson opposed the party caucuses.

2. Presidential candidates have been chosen by a nominating convention since 1840.

3. Jackson wanted all the state delegates to choose the presidential candidate.

4. For a long time, small groups of congressmen decided who should run for President.

○ **II. Generalizing**

▶ Support each of the following generalizations with facts from the chapter. Write the number of the generalization and its supporting facts on a separate sheet of paper.

1. Frontier democracy influenced the rest of America.

2. Andrew Jackson was the "voice of the people."

3. Native Americans suffered at the hands of Jacksonian Democracy.

4. Jackson was a strong President.

▶ **III. Drawing Conclusions**

▶ Andrew Jackson was a great military leader during the War of 1812. Why have Americans often selected military leaders (such as George Washington, Ulysses S. Grant, and Dwight D. Eisenhower) for President? Write your conclusion on a sheet of paper.

USING PRIMARY SOURCES

▶ Reread the Spotlight on Sources on page 301. In what ways did Andrew Jackson believe his Indian policy would actually help the Native Americans?

ENRICHMENT

1. Imagine you and your family are Cherokees at the time of the passing of the Removal Act. Write a dramatic account of your experiences on the "trail of tears." Do library research, if you wish, to make your account more vivid.

2. Use the Constitution beginning on page 244 to determine when these groups of people gained the right to vote: women, African Americans, young people aged 18, residents of the District of Columbia. Then make a chart on the history of voting rights in America to post on your classroom bulletin board.

3. Conduct a Presidential election in class. Hold a nominating convention to select the two candidates. Have student candidates give brief campaign speeches, have supporters speak on each candidate's behalf, and have the class cast votes.

UNIT REVIEW

SUMMARY

After winning the War for Independence, the American people faced a new challenge. They had to decide which powers to give to their new central government. Federalists supported a strong central government over the powers of the state. Anti-Federalists favored states' rights. Both sides finally agreed on a federal government that had three separate branches. A system of checks and balances kept any one branch from becoming too powerful. When the Constitution was ratified in 1788, the new plan of government took effect. The courage Americans showed in the War of 1812 finally earned them the respect of Europe. A spirit of nationalism took shape in America.

Explorers opened up new territory for settlement west of the Mississippi. Old political divisions faded for a time as everyone became Democratic-Republicans. The Supreme Court expanded its power and more Americans won the right to vote. Americans demanded, and got, a greater say in choosing presidential candidates. Democracy was growing in the states, but only for white men. Native Americans were forcibly removed from their homes as white settlers made their way west. Women and African Americans continued to be denied the right to vote. The Federalist Party died during this era, and the Democratic-Republican and Democratic parties were born.

SKILL BUILDER: READING A MAP

▶ Study the map at the bottom of this page, which describes North America in 1825. The dates on the map show when the new states and territories joined the Union. The map also gives you an idea of the land size of these new states and territories. Using the information from the map, write answers to the questions that follow on a separate sheet of paper.

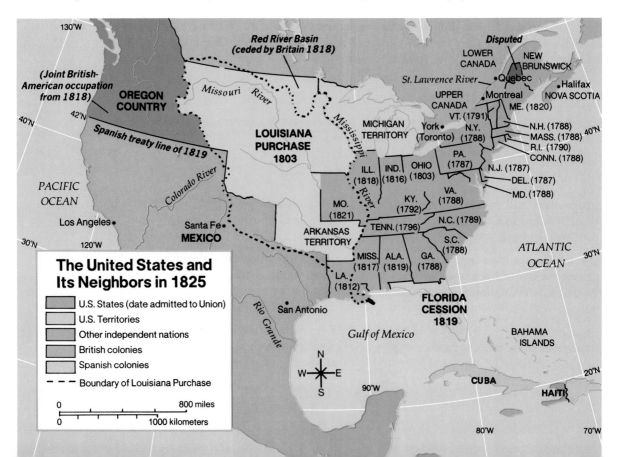

The United States and Its Neighbors in 1825

1. What new states joined the Union after 1812?

2. What new territory was acquired in 1803?

3. What western lands could explorers reach by following the Missouri River westward?

4. What state existed west of the Mississippi River before 1820?

5. Compare this map to the historical map of the United States on page xxi and the current map of the United States on page 674. What present-day states belonged to Mexico in 1825?

SKILL BUILDER: CRITICAL THINKING AND COMPREHENSION

I. Point of View

1. As the young United States tried to form a government, many debates and disagreements took place between Federalists and Anti-Federalists. On a sheet of paper, list their differing points of view on:
   a. the establishment of a national bank
   b. the power of the federal government *versus* the power of the states

2. Later in American history, people debated whether to go to war with Britain a second time. Identify the differing points of view on this issue of Henry Clay and his supporters *versus* President James Monroe and the northeastern farmers and merchants.

II. Summarizing

▶ Answer one of the following questions. Write your summary on a separate sheet of paper.

1. Write a summary of the events which led up to the purchase of the Louisiana Territory. Discuss western farmers' needs, right of deposit, France getting the territory from Spain, and Napoleon's plans for Europe.

2. Summarize the steps taken by the federal government to encourage settlers to move west. Discuss the Northwest Ordinance and the building of new roads.

ENRICHMENT

1. Compare and contrast Tecumseh's speech on page 275 with Jackson's message to Congress on page 301. Each man offers a different solution to the same problem. Which do you think was the better solution, and why?

2. Find out more about one of the following famous American military heroes mentioned in this unit: Commodore Oliver Hazard Perry, General William Henry Harrison, General Andrew Jackson. Give a brief biographical sketch to the class explaining why the man was considered a legend in his time.

3. Prepare a report for a television special on relations between America and Great Britain before and after the War of 1812. Mention the Treaty of Paris, the British policy of impressment, the Embargo Act, the Treaty of Ghent, and the Rush-Bagot Agreement in your report.

UNIT 7

AMERICANS MOVE WESTWARD

Chapter

UNIT OVERVIEW   Unit 7 will help you understand how and why the West was settled, who settled there, and what happened to the Native Americans who lived there.

UNIT SKILLS OBJECTIVES   In Unit 7, three critical thinking skills are emphasized:

Sequencing: Putting a series of events in correct time order.

Recognizing Cause and Effect: Recognizing the action or event that makes something happen; identifying the result of an action or event.

Drawing Conclusions: Making a statement that explains the facts and evidence.

You will also use two important social studies skills:

Making a Chart   Drawing a Time Line

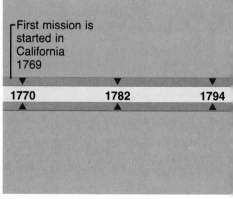

First mission is started in California 1769

1770	**1782**	**1794**

306   **ESL/LEP Strategy:** Have student teams preview the vocabulary words in this unit and arrange them in these categories: *Names, Foreign Words, Compound Words, Words with Prefixes or Suffixes.* Then ask students to write what they think the words mean and check their guesses after they have read the unit.

▲ A train of covered wagons slowly plods its way west in a journey that may take eight months to complete.

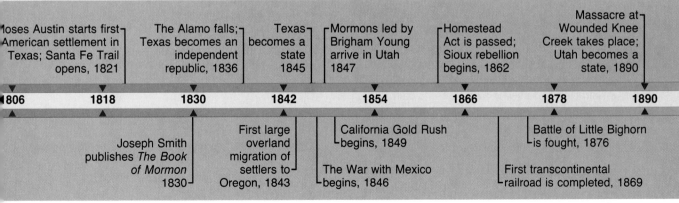

Moses Austin starts first American settlement in Texas; Santa Fe Trail opens, 1821

The Alamo falls; Texas becomes an independent republic, 1836

Texas becomes a state 1845

Mormons led by Brigham Young arrive in Utah 1847

Homestead Act is passed; Sioux rebellion begins, 1862

Massacre at Wounded Knee Creek takes place; Utah becomes a state, 1890

806 1818 1830 1842 1854 1866 1878 1890

Joseph Smith publishes *The Book of Mormon* 1830

First large overland migration of settlers to Oregon, 1843

California Gold Rush begins, 1849

The War with Mexico begins, 1846

Battle of Little Bighorn is fought, 1876

First transcontinental railroad is completed, 1869

Points of View

Native Americans, who had lived in the West for hundreds of years, had very different ideas about settlement than the white settlers. As the settlers poured into the western lands, conflicts arose. Native Americans fought bravely to defend what was theirs. However, they were finally forced to give up their homelands.

One of the western settlers was John Marsh, who went from Missouri to California in 1836. There he started a cattle ranch in the rich San Joaquin

▲ Peaceful, fertile valleys like this one in California attracted settlers who were eager to start new lives far from the crowded lands back east.

VIEW OF A WESTERN SETTLER

July 3, 1840

❝Dear Sir:
Pray [please tell me], what has become of all the zeal [excitement] for emigration [moving] to this country [the West]? . . . I see by the papers that great preparations [plans] are making [being made] in the United States for settling the Oregon, and that population must eventually [finally] extend to this place [California], as this is beyond all the finest country and the finest climate. The only thing we lack here is a good government. But for my part I have but little cause to complain. I have got as much land as I want. . . . What we want most here is more people. . . . I live near the mouth of the rivers Sacramento and St. Joaquin and the whole country south and east is unoccupied [unsettled].❞

—*John Marsh, Pioneer*, G. D. Lyman

(wah-KEEN) Valley. Although California was still owned by Mexico at the time, Marsh and other settlers wanted it to become part of the United States. Marsh wrote many letters like the following one to newspapers back East to persuade other Americans to move to the West. Then three statements by Native Americans are presented. These Native Americans were among the many thousands who faced being driven off their land and being forced to change their ways of living.

VIEWS OF NATIVE AMERICANS

" A Comanche Chief:
Why do you ask us to leave the rivers, the sun, and the wind, and live in houses? Do not ask us to give up the buffalo for the sheep. The young men have heard talk of this, and it has made them sad and angry.

Kiowa Chief Satanta:
I love to roam the wide prairie, and when I do it, I feel free and happy. But when we settle down, we grow pale and die.

An Elder Sioux:
They [the United States government] made us many promises, more than I can remember, but they never kept but one; they promised to take our land and they took it. "

—from *History of the Indian Wars*, Robert M. Utley and Wilcomb E. Washburn

▲ Hunters like these, who roamed the plains freely for hundreds of years, in the 1800s had to give way to settlers who used the land to raise cattle and farm.

Using Primary Sources

1. Why did Marsh point out that so much land in California was still not settled?

2. Keeping in mind Marsh's letter and the Native Americans' statements, how do you think the settlers differed from the Native Americans in their ways of life and their ideas about the land?

309

CHAPTER 1

Pioneer Trails to the West

OBJECTIVE: How and why did American traders and settlers move into the Far West?

1. A joyful celebration was being held by the Crow people. Crow warriors had just brought back a large supply of buffalo meat after raiding a Cheyenne village. The Crow people now would have enough food for the winter. Morning Star, one of the greatest Crow braves, had led this daring raid. However, he was actually James P. Beckwourth, a Virginian who had been born a slave. He was one of a courageous band of men who came to the mountains of the West long before the settlers arrived. These **mountain men** came to hunt, to trade, to fight, to explore. Some, like Beckwourth, spent years with the Native Americans. The mountain men in the West were the first sign that the American nation was moving toward the Pacific. Soon large numbers of settlers would move into the West. Soon Native Americans would be forced from much of their land.

▲ One of the most famous mountain men was James P. Beckwourth. Born a slave, he later hunted beaver in the West and lived with the Crow tribe of Native Americans.

The Mountain Men   How did pioneer explorers and trappers help to open the West?

2. Furs first drew pioneers to the West. In the early 1800s, the furs of wild animals, especially beavers, were popular. They were used for clothing and men's hats in the United States and Europe. Fur trappers traveled deep into the wilderness beyond the Rocky Mountains to help meet the demand for furs. Some of these mountain men were French Canadians. Others were British, Irish, and Mexicans, as well as Americans. One of these "men" was actually a woman, named Marie Dorion. Some mountain men were young and inexperienced, looking for adventure. Some were criminals escaping cities

In Chapter 1, you will apply these critical thinking skills to the historical process:
Sequencing: Putting a series of events in correct time order.
Generalizing: Making a statement that links several facts.

and punishment. Yet they all shared a love of the wilderness and a desire to live freely.

3. Life for the mountain men was hard but exciting. For much of the year they hunted beaver. They often covered as much as 3,000 miles (about 4,800 kilometers) through the forests and streams of the mountains. Then in the fall, the mountain men brought their animal skins to trading posts. These trading posts were owned by companies like John Jacob Astor's American Fur Company. There the mountain men traded the skins for goods they would need for the next hunting season. These goods included horses, guns, traps, and blankets.

4. Mountain men explored many places that had been known only to Native Americans before them. One mountain man, Jim Bridger, was the first white man to sail the Great Salt Lake of present-day Utah. Another, Jedediah Smith, was the first white man to discover a pass through the Rocky Mountains in Wyoming. James Beckwourth explored a pass through the Sierra Nevada Mountains that led to the Sacramento Valley. These explorations were used by the later pioneers who headed west.

5. By the early 1840s, the day of the mountain men was over. Most of the beavers had been killed off, and the fur trade was no longer profitable. Many mountain men chose to live on with their Native American friends rather than return to the life style of the East. Some mountain men, such as Kit Carson and Jim Bridger, became guides. They helped the United States Army. They also guided the new settlers who were moving west. Often these settlers came west because of the stories they had heard from ▶ old mountain men. Why do you think people enjoyed hearing colorful stories about the lives of the mountain men?

The Santa Fe Trail   How did the Santa Fe Trail open the Southwest to settlers?

6. The **Santa Fe Trail**, the first major trail to the Far West, began as a trading route. It was opened by trader William Becknell in 1821. Becknell carried manufactured goods on horse-

back from Independence, Missouri, overland to Santa Fe. Santa Fe was then still a part of Mexico. Here, Becknell exchanged his goods for furs, mules, and silver and gold from Mexico. The Santa Fe Trail was 780 miles (1,255 kilometers) long. It was one of the longest trading routes in the United States at that time.

7. Gradually settlers began moving west along the Santa Fe Trail. In its first 20 years, the trail was used by only 80 wagons a year. By the late 1860s, however, over 5,000 wagons were traveling on it each year. This huge increase in traffic took place after the United States had gained a large part of the Southwest from Mexico. After the Mexican War of 1846, settlers from the East and Midwest swarmed into the Southwest. Some settlers went on past Santa Fe into Arizona and Southern California. They traveled along an added part of the Santa Fe Trail known as the **Old Spanish Trail**.

The Oregon Trail   How and why did American settlers move along the Oregon Trail into the Far Northwest?

8. The most famous trail to the Far West, called the **Oregon Trail**, also started from Independence, Missouri. The Oregon Trail wound 2,000 miles (about 3,200 kilometers) to the Pacific Northwest. Find the Oregon Trail on the map on page 312.

9. Word of the rich soil in the Willamette (wil-AH-met) Valley spread quickly back east in the United States. So fertile was the valley, Easterners heard, that crops could grow there almost overnight. A flood of settlers, swept up in "**Oregon fever**," headed west on the Oregon Trail in the early 1840s. Many of them also went west to escape the Panic of 1837, a **depression** (de-PRESH-un), that had hit the eastern United States. A depression is a time when businesses do poorly and many people are out of work. Those people now were eager to start a new life in the West, where land was cheap. Besides this, eastern cities were becoming overcrowded. Finally, the British, who owned Canada, were threatening to take over

Background: One of the most famous of the mountain men was Jedediah (Jed) Smith. He might have had a great career as a guide and explorer in the West if he had not been killed by Comanches in 1831.

the Pacific Northwest. The United States government encouraged settlers to go to Oregon to strengthen the American claim to Oregon.

10. Life on the Oregon Trail was filled with danger. The journey took as long as six months. The settlers traveled by covered wagons that were organized in wagon trains. Some of these trains had as many as 120 wagons. The trains left Independence, Missouri, in the spring and tried to average about 15 miles (24 kilometers) a day. This was fast enough to reach Oregon before the snow began to fall in the mountains. However, the settlers faced many dangers—attacks from Native Americans, deadly diseases like **cholera** (KAHL-uh-ruh), and possible starvation. Rivers were often flooded and water holes poisoned. It is believed that 34,000 people died on the Oregon Trail. Most people, however, survived the journey and arrived in the Willamette Valley. Here they built log cabins
▶ and farmed the rich soil. How would you have felt about traveling the Oregon Trail?

11. In 1843, about 1,000 Americans settled in the Willamette Valley. The hundreds who came each year after 1843 helped the United States gain control of Oregon. The British agreed to establish the **49th parallel** of latitude as the border between Canada and the United States in 1846. The United States of America now stretched from coast to coast.

People in History

12. Narcissa and Marcus Whitman Not everyone who went west on the Oregon Trail did so mainly to find a new home. Some wanted to take Christianity to the Native Americans in the Northwest. Narcissa Whitman and her husband Marcus were missionaries who went to Oregon in 1837. You have read that missionaries are people who take their religion to those who are not members of their faith. Narcissa was only 28 years old when she made the difficult journey. She and a traveling companion

MAP SKILL BUILDER: Measure the map scale to find out how many inches on the map stand for 200 miles on the ground. **1.** How many miles is Bent's Fort from Santa Fe? **2.** On what early trail was Bent's Fort?

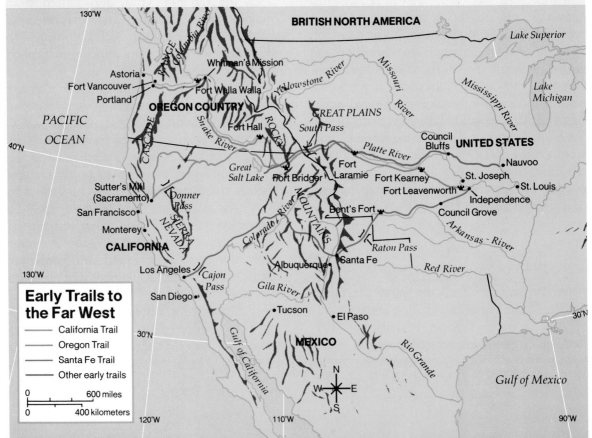

Early Trails to the Far West
— California Trail
— Oregon Trail
— Santa Fe Trail
— Other early trails

0 — 600 miles
0 — 400 kilometers

▲ As soon as the pioneers arrived in Oregon, they set to work building their homes and farming the rich soil.

were the first white women to travel the length of the Oregon Trail.

13. Narcissa and Marcus Whitman settled at a place the Native Americans called Waiilatpu, which means "Place of the Rye Grass." This is now part of Washington state. They built a mission and a school for Native American children. At the mission the Whitmans taught and cared for many of the people who traveled to the Willamette Valley. They lived in peace here for 11 years. Then in November 1847 members of the Cayuse tribe caught smallpox from the new settlers. Many Cayuse children died from the disease. The Cayuse blamed all white people for the deaths. Out of anger and grief, they attacked the mission and killed Narcissa, Marcus, and 12 others. The remaining settlers struck back and wiped out a number of Cayuse villages. Within a year of the Cayuse attack, Oregon became a territory of the United States. A territory is a region controlled by the United

States that has not yet become a state. Why do ◀ you think making Oregon a territory might help prevent other massacres?

Spotlight on Sources

14. Many brave women followed Narcissa Whitman along the Oregon Trail in the 1840s and 1850s. One of them was Amelia Knight. With her husband and seven children, she left Iowa in 1853 for the Northwest. Here is how she described one day on the Oregon Trail:

> Cold and cloudy this morning and everybody out of humor [cranky]. Seneca [one of her children] is half sick. Almira [another child] says she wished she was at home and I say ditto [the same]. Have to eat cold supper. We are creeping along slowly, one wagon after another, out of one mud hole and into another. Them that eat the most breakfast eat the most sand. It has been raining all day long. The men and boys are all soaking wet and look sad and comfortless [unhappy]. The little ones and myself are shut up in the wagons from the rain. Take us all together we are a poor looking set, and all this for Oregon.
> —from "Diary," *Transactions*, Amelia Knight

Why do you think Amelia Knight and her ◯ family did not turn around and go home?

Outlook

15. The explorers, trappers, traders, and settlers who decided to explore and settle the West came for many different reasons. Some were looking for adventure and wealth. Others wanted to start a new life for themselves and their families. Still others came to bring Christianity to the Native Americans. All of these men and women helped the United States gain the vast lands of the West. Without these pioneers, the United States might not be as large as it is today. Some Native American tribes might have their own nations on western lands. In ◀ what areas do present-day Americans show the same spirit of adventure as the settlers today?

Activity: Perhaps the most famous account of life on the Oregon Trail was *The Oregon Trail* written by historian Francis Parkman in 1847. It describes Parkman's journey with a friend the previous year on the trail to Wyoming, where he lived with the Sioux. Read excerpts from *The Oregon Trail* and have students compare it to Amelia Knight's diary.

313

CHAPTER REVIEW

VOCABULARY REVIEW

▶ Select the word that best completes each sentence. Number your paper from 1 to 7 and write the correct letter next to each number.

1. The first group of people to explore the Far West were fur trappers known as _____ .
   a. mountain men
   b. pioneers
   c. traders

2. The first major trading route to the Far West was the _____ .
   a. Oregon Trail
   b. Santa Fe Trail
   c. Old Spanish Trail

3. The route that settlers took into Arizona and Southern California was the _____ .
   a. Oregon Trail
   b. Santa Fe Trail
   c. Old Spanish Trail

4. The route that settlers took to settle in the Willamette Valley was the _____ .
   a. Independence Trail
   b. Oregon Trail
   c. Santa Fe Trail

5. A severe _____ left many people in the East out of work and helped them decide to head westward.
   a. depression   c. war
   b. winter

6. Many settlers in the West died as a result of _____ .
   a. cholera   c. capital
   b. parallels

7. The British and Americans set the border between the United States and Canada at the _____ .
   a. Willamette Valley
   b. Oregon Trail
   c. 49th parallel

SKILL BUILDER: MAKING A CHART

▶ Copy the chart below on a separate piece of paper. Then fill in the information based on the map on page 312 and the content of the chapter.

Name of Trail	Length of Trail	City at Start of Trail	Destination at End of Trail	States That Formed Along the Trail	Years When Heavy Travel Began
Santa Fe Trail					
Oregon Trail					
Old Spanish Trail					

314

SKILL BUILDER: CRITICAL THINKING AND COMPREHENSION

I. Sequencing

▶ On a separate sheet of paper, write the following in the order in which they took place.

a. William Becknell opened the Santa Fe Trail.

b. When the United States first stretched from coast to coast.

c. The first settlers arrived in the Willamette Valley.

d. Narcissa and Marcus Whitman were killed by the Cayuse tribe.

e. The Whitmans set out for Oregon.

II. Generalizing

1. Find sentences from paragraphs 2 and 3 that support the following generalization and write them on a sheet of paper:

   Mountain men were not like most people who stayed in the cities.

2. Find sentences from paragraph 9 that support the following generalization and write them on a sheet of paper:

   The need for money was one of the reasons people went west.

3. Make a generalization about the people who went west to live from these facts from paragraphs 12 through 14. Write your generalization on a sheet of paper.
   a. Narcissa Whitman and her husband Marcus were missionaries who went to Oregon.
   b. With her husband and children, Amelia Knight left Iowa for the Northwest.

4. Make a generalization about Native Americans from the following statements from the text. Write your generalization on a sheet of paper.
   a. Morning Star, one of the greatest Crow braves, had led this daring raid. However, he was actually James P. Beckwourth, a Virginian who had been born a slave.
   b. They [the Cayuse] attacked the mission and killed Narcissa, Marcus, and 12 others. The remaining settlers struck back and wiped out a number of Cayuse villages.

USING PRIMARY SOURCES

▶ Reread the Spotlight on Sources on page 313 and answer this question: Do you think Amelia Knight regretted ever having started the long journey to Oregon? Explain your answer.

ENRICHMENT

1. Draw a map of the Oregon Territory, showing how it changed in size. Show its borders when it was first settled, when it became a territory, and when it became a U.S. state.

2. Read a biography of Narcissa Whitman. Then write an imaginary interview with her at her mission in the Oregon territory.

3. Role play with other students a meeting between Native Americans and settlers on a trail leading west.

CHAPTER 2

The Mormons Settle Utah's Salt Lake Basin

OBJECTIVE: Who were the Mormons, and why did they set up their home in the desert land of Utah?

1. The young man walked slowly alongside the covered wagon in the hot, sweltering sun. He wiped the sweat from his eyes and gazed out at the scene before him. In every direction lay **desert** and mountains. A desert is a barren, dry region of land with little rainfall. Was this the promised land he and his family had traveled 1,400 miles (about 2,250 kilometers) to reach? The man was a member of a religious group called the Mormons. What brought him and hundreds of other Mormons to the desert land of Utah in 1847? To understand, you need to go back in time 24 years to a place over 2,000 miles (about 3,200 kilometers) away.

The Mormons   What caused the Mormons to settle in Illinois?

2. In 1823, in the town of Palmyra, New York, another young man had a religious experience. His name was Joseph Smith, and he believed that he had been visited by an angel named Moroni. Smith said Moroni had told him about a set of golden plates. On these plates, was a description in an ancient language of a lost tribe of Israel. Supposedly this tribe had lived in North America thousands of years before. Later, Smith said, the angel led him to the plates, which he then translated into English. In 1830, Smith published these writings

▲ After being attacked at their first settlement by people who did not trust or understand the Mormon religion, the Mormons moved farther and farther west to find peace.

as *The Book of Mormon*. That same year he started the Mormon Church or the Church of Jesus Christ of Latter-day Saints. The church's Christian beliefs were based on this book. In 1831, Smith founded a Mormon community in Ohio. Smith was such a forceful religious leader

In Chapter 2, you will apply these critical thinking skill to the historical process:

Sequencing: Putting a series of events in correct time order.

Recognizing Cause and Effect: Recognizing the action or event that makes something happen; identifying the result of an action or event.

that within a year his church had grown to have more than 10,000 members.

3. Many Americans were troubled by the growth of Smith's church. They believed that Mormons put their loyalty to their religion and to Joseph Smith over that to the United States. Mormons also worked and lived together, sharing their wealth, unlike most other Americans. Finally, they practiced **polygamy** (poh-LIG-uh-mee). Polygamy is the practice of a man having two or more wives at the same time.

4. Wherever they went, the Mormons found that people were prejudiced against them and judged them unfairly. The Mormons were attacked and even killed for their beliefs. In 1837, Smith moved his followers from Ohio to Missouri to get away from prejudiced people. Two years later, they moved to Nauvoo, Illinois, which soon became the largest city in the state. Why might Nauvoo have grown so fast?

Brigham Young Why did the Mormons and their leader seek a new home in the West?

5. Under Smith's leadership, the Mormons became a powerful group in Illinois. They even formed their own private army. The non-Mormons of Illinois were afraid the Mormons would take over their state. In 1844, Smith and other Mormon leaders were arrested and jailed. A mob then attacked the jail and killed Smith and his brother. The Mormon Church might have come to an end at this time if not for one man—Brigham Young. In what other, more peaceful ways do you think non-Mormons might have learned to live with the Mormons?

People in History

6. Brigham Young In 1801 Brigham Young was born in Vermont. Young grew up in western New York State, where he was a neighbor of Joseph Smith. After studying Smith's teaching, Young joined the Mormon Church at the age of 31. Young worked tirelessly for the church. He served as a missionary in Great Britain and brought many new con-

▲ The Mormons, led by Brigham Young, turned the Great Salt Lake Basin from a desert into excellent farmland. To this day the largest number of Mormons in the United States live in Utah.

verts into the church. You have read that a convert is a person who changes from one religion to another.

7. After Smith's death, Brigham Young became the leader of the Mormon Church. Young knew that to survive, the Mormons had to find a new home, far away from their enemies. That place, Young decided, was the Great Salt Lake Basin beyond the Rocky Mountains. The Great Salt Lake Basin is in what is now Utah.

The Mormons in Utah How did the Mormons build a new home in Utah?

8. Many historians call the Mormons's western journey the best-planned migration of any

Activity: Ask the class to name groups of people in America today who are victims of prejudice, as the Mormons were. What are these prejudices based on? How might they be corrected?

317

group of Western pioneers. Brigham Young led 3,500 Mormons out of Illinois in 1846. An advance party led by Young arrived in the Great Salt Lake Basin on July 23, 1847. According to Mormon belief, when Young saw the Salt Lake Valley from the mountains he had a religious vision. He cried out, "This is the place!"

9. Some Mormons may well have questioned their leader's judgment. The Salt Lake Valley hardly seemed a place to build God's kingdom on earth. It was dry, treeless, and covered with salt, sand, and hot sulfur springs. Although the soil proved to be fertile, the valley lacked enough rain or water to make crops grow. The Mormons' first winter in Utah was harsh, and the spring brought a new problem—crickets. Millions of these insects swarmed into the valley, eating the grain the Mormons had worked so hard to grow.

10. Just when things looked darkest, the Mormons' luck changed. Seagulls flew in from the Great Salt Lake, 20 miles (32 kilometers) to the north, and ate the crickets. The grain was saved, and the Mormons called it a "miracle."

Today, the seagull is the state bird of Utah. Encouraged by the action of the seagulls, Young decided to build an **irrigation** (ir-i-GAY-shun) system so that the Mormon farmers could grow more crops. Irrigation is the watering of land through ditches and canals in order to grow crops. Using irrigation, the Mormons turned the Utah desert into a fertile garden.

11. Under Young's leadership, the Mormons built homes, schools, factories, roads, and bridges. They even built a telegraph system, one of the first in the Far West. In 1850, the United States government set up the Territory of Utah and appointed Brigham Young as its governor.

12. Soon the same prejudice that had driven the Mormons from the East and Midwest caught up with them in Utah. Non-Mormons in the territory complained to the federal government, and in 1857 a non-Mormon governor replaced Brigham Young. The Mormons rebelled, and President James Buchanan sent federal troops into Salt Lake City. The "Mormon War" that followed was largely bloodless. The next year, Young agreed to accept a new gover-

▼ The Mormons journeyed hundreds of miles to find freedom of worship, just as the Pilgrims and Puritans had in the 1600s. Look at their method of transportation. About how many miles do you think the Mormons traveled each day?

Background: The Mormons applied for statehood in 1849 but were turned down by the United States government. Congress felt they first had to end their practice of polygamy. It also believed the state the Mormons wanted was too big an area. It would have included all of Utah, Arizona, Nevada, and parts of five other states.

▲ Thousands of seagulls saved the Mormons' grain crop from being eaten by the crickets. Why do you think the Mormons called this event a "miracle"? Why do you think the seagulls arrived at just the right moment?

nor in return for a full pardon for all Mormons who had broken the law.

13. By the time of his death in 1877, Brigham Young had helped found over 200 communities in Utah, with over 100,000 people. In 1896, six years after the Mormons agreed to end polygamy, Utah became the forty-fifth state of the United States. Why do you think Utah had to wait so long before becoming a state?

🦅 Spotlight on Sources

14. Many Mormons who traveled west to Utah were converts from Europe. Here is a poem written by William Clayton, a British convert, written on the trail west in 1847:

> Come, come ye Saints, no toil no labor
> fear,
> But with joy wend your way [travel].
> Though hard to you this journey may
> appear,
> Grace [goodness] shall be as your day.
> 'Tis better far for us to strive [try]

Our useless cares from us to drive;
Do this, and joy your hearts will swell—
All is well! All is well!
> —from *The Mormons*, Kathleen Elgin

Although Clayton is a convert to the Mormon Church, he is just as eager about the journey to Utah as someone who was born a Mormon. How does his poem show his eagerness?

Outlook

15. The Mormons and their leader, Brigham Young, played a major part in opening up the Far West for settlement. They were the first group of people to use irrigation successfully in the United States. They spread education and learning in the West by opening schools. In addition, the Mormons followed the American tradition of believing in freedom of worship. The Mormons's hard work, determination, and courage helped to shape the state of Utah. Even today the state of Utah is the center for the Mormon religion. How is the Mormons' experience a good example of the spirit of America?

Ask: Ask students to discuss how Clayton's poem reflects the spirit and character of not just the Mormons but all Western pioneers.

CHAPTER REVIEW

VOCABULARY REVIEW

▶ Write each number and word on a sheet of paper. Write the letter of the definition next to the word it matches.

1. irrigation
2. desert
3. converts
4. polygamy

a. people who adopt a religion
b. having more than one wife at a time
c. the watering of land with ditches and canals
d. dry, barren land with little rainfall
e. forming an opinion without judging fairly

SKILL BUILDER: READING A MAP

▶ Study the map below. Then answer the questions that follow.

1. The Mormons had wanted to establish the state of Deseret in 1849. How many of today's states would have been part of Deseret?

2. Using the scale of miles and kilometers, find how far the Mormons traveled from Nauvoo to Salt Lake City.

3. Which pass did the Mormons use to get through the Rocky Mountains?

4. In which states are the chief Mormon areas located today?

5. Why do you think a large section of the Mormon Trail followed the Platte River?

6. Which river passes through today's chief Mormon area? What do you think this might indicate about the rest of the Mormon area?

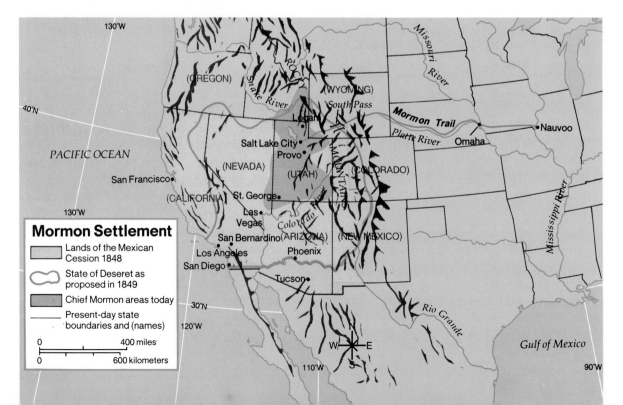

Mormon Settlement

- Lands of the Mexican Cession 1848
- State of Deseret as proposed in 1849
- Chief Mormon areas today
- Present-day state boundaries and (names)

0   400 miles
0   600 kilometers

SKILL BUILDER: CRITICAL THINKING AND COMPREHENSION

I. Sequencing

▶ Write the events in each of the following sets in the order in which they took place. Use a separate sheet of paper.

1. **a.** Brigham Young joins the Mormon Church.
   b. Joseph Smith publishes *The Book of Mormon*.
   c. The Mormon Church grows to 10,000 members.

2. **a.** Joseph Smith is killed after being put in jail.
   b. The Mormons arrive at the Great Salt Lake Valley in Utah.
   c. The Mormons move from Missouri to Nauvoo, Illinois.

3. **a.** Brigham Young becomes governor of the Territory of Utah.
   b. Mormons agree to end their practice of polygamy.
   c. Utah becomes the forty-fifth state of the United States.

II. Cause and Effect

▶ Write the following statements on a sheet of paper and supply the missing cause or effect. The first one is done for you.

1. **Cause:** The Mormon leaders were jailed and attacked by a mob in Illinois.
   Effect: Brigham Young led the Mormons west out of Illinois.

2. **Cause:** _____
   Effect: Brigham Young became the leader of the Mormons.

3. **Cause:** An angel showed Joseph Smith a set of golden plates, which he translated.
   Effect: _____

4. **Cause:** In 1837, Mormons in Missouri were attacked and killed for their beliefs.
   Effect: _____

5. **Cause:** In 1896 the Mormons agreed to end polygamy.
   Effect: _____

USING PRIMARY SOURCES

▶ Reread the Spotlight on Sources on page 319 and explain what William Clayton means when he writes, "All is well! All is well!"

ENRICHMENT

1. Read a book or article about the Mormons today. How are they similar to the Mormons of Brigham Young's day? How are they different?

2. Write a letter to the editor of an imaginary newspaper in Illinois in the 1840s. Tell why you think the Mormons should be allowed to stay in the state.

3. With other students, prepare an oral report on the Mormons trip to the West. Each student should play the role of one of the travelers.

321

CHAPTER 3

The Spanish Settle California

OBJECTIVE: What part did the missions play in settling California?

1. The Spanish governor looked at the priest's red, swollen leg. "Father," he said, "you are not well enough to make the long journey with me up the California coast." The priest smiled and shook his head. "Your Excellency, I have waited so long to start this journey. I cannot turn back now. Bringing God's word to the people of this Spanish territory is more important than my bad leg." The governor shook his head. "As you wish," he said. "I will help you in every way I can." The stubborn priest was Father Junípero Serra (hoo-NEE-pay-roh SAY-rah). In that year of 1769, Serra would not allow anything to stop him from his goals. He dreamed of expanding the reach of Christianity by setting up religious settlements in the still untamed and unsettled territory of California.

California   How did the leaders of New Spain "rediscover" California?

2. What we call California was one of the last areas in the Western Hemisphere to be settled by Spain. In 1533, Hernando Cortés, the conqueror of Mexico, sent an expedition that discovered Baja (BAH-hah), California. Nine years later, Juan Rodríguez Cabrillo (wahn rod-REE-gez kah-BREE-yoh) sailed north along the coast of Alta, or Upper, California. There he claimed all the lands he discovered for Spain.

▲ Father Junipero Serra and the Spanish governor of California gaze down on San Diego, where they will soon set up the first Catholic mission.

Few people in New Spain, however, were interested in Cabrillo's claim. They did not want a land that had no gold and silver. In those years, sailing north from Mexico against the winds and ocean current along the Pacific coast was very difficult. Besides, Spain was already busy exploring the vast territories north and east of

In Chapter 3, you will apply these critical thinking skills to the historical process:

▌ **Comparing and Contrasting:**
Recognizing similarities and differences.

⇢ **Recognizing Cause and Effect:**
Recognizing the action or event that makes something happen; identifying the result of an action or event.

Mexico. For these reasons, Spain ignored California for the next two centuries.

3. Then, in 1765, José de Gálvez (hoh-SAY day GAHL-vez) stirred Spain's interest in California. Gálvez was a high official of New Spain. He dreamed of building Spanish settlements throughout Alta California. Gálvez convinced the Spanish government that Spain's claims to California were threatened. He pointed out that Russian fur hunters already had built trading posts along the northern California coast. Gálvez warned that England, too, would soon send explorers there from Canada. Establishing new settlements in California would give Spain control of California. Then this yet untapped area would supply Spain with much-needed **revenue**, or income, and keep the Russians and the English away from New Spain.

People in History

4. Gaspar de Portolá To start the new settlements in California Gálvez chose Captain Gaspar de Portolá (GAHS-pahr day pawr-toh-LAH). Portolá was a Spanish soldier and a skilled **administrator**. An administrator is a person who manages a large group of people. Portolá also was made governor of California. On May 15, 1769, Portolá and Father Junípero Serra, a Catholic priest, together with a few soldiers, began a 1,000-mile (1,600-km) expedition up the coast of California. Their goal was to build a mission and a **presidio** (pre-SID-ee-oh), or small fort, at San Diego. After the presidio and mission were built, they moved north, almost as far as San Francisco, before turning back. On the return journey, they faced many hardships, especially a terrible shortage of food. Portolá's men were even forced to kill their mules and eat the meat of the animals.

5. The following year Portolá and Father Serra set out again and started a mission and a presidio at Monterey. Traveling to the north, Portolá found San Francisco Bay, and became the first white man to see this beautiful harbor. Now California was firmly in Spanish hands. Portolá, however, never again set eyes on the territory he had settled in New Spain. In 1776, he was made governor of the city of Pueblo in Mexico. Later, in 1784, he returned to Spain.

Missions Why were the missions so important in New Spain?

6. Few Spanish colonists were willing to endure the hardships of building new settlements in California. As a result, officials of New Spain decided to build missions in California, as they had done earlier in the Southwest. Spanish priests saw this as an opportunity to convert a new population of Americans to Christianity. These Native Americans provided the labor and grew crops needed at the mission. In this way, many more Native Americans came under the rule of New Spain. The missions, in time, became the main centers of Spanish settlement in California.

7. The first California mission that Father

▼ This painting shows the mission church in Santa Barbara, California, and the Native Americans who lived and worked there.

Background: In June 1579, Sir Francis Drake made an emergency stop on the California coast, near San Francisco. Drake repaired his ship, the *Golden Hind*, there and claimed the territory for Queen Elizabeth of England.

323

Serra founded in 1769 soon grew to chain of 21 missions. Each mission was one day's journey from the next. They stretched from present-day San Diego to Sonoma north of San Francisco. The road connecting the missions was called *El Camino Real* (el kah-MEE-noh ray-AHL), or ▶ the royal highway. Why do you think it was given this name? The Spanish built presidios near many missions to protect them. They also founded small, non religious farming communities called **pueblos** (PWEB-lohz) to supply the presidio soldiers with food.

8. The missions became the key to the success of Spanish rule in California. Each mission was a **self-sufficient** religious center and farming community. That is, the people there produced all the food, clothing, and shelter they needed to survive. The Native Americans brought to the missions did most of this work. They tended the cattle and grew corn, wheat, and grapes. They also wove cotton cloth and made leather from cowhides. Native Americans at the missions sold goods to traders from New ▶ York and Boston. Do you think Native Ameri-

cans benefitted from this trade? Some Native Americans living at the mission were so skilled that often only a few Spaniards were needed to oversee their work.

Spotlight on Sources

9. In founding the California missions, Father Junípero Serra wanted to protect the Native Americans. In this letter to a Spanish official in Mexico City, Serra describes his plans:

> During the year, their [the Native Americans'] pay should be on the same basis as [equal] that of the [Spanish] sailors at San Blas. And in the missions they should receive free rations [food]. And if at the end of the first year they wish to stay a second year, the same treatment should be continued. If they prefer [wish] to return to San Blas, . . . they should be granted their request and others [Native Americans] should . . . take their place."
> —from *Writing of Junípero Serra*, Vol. 1, ed. by Antonine Tibesar

▼ To protect their missions, the Spanish set up a series of forts, or presidios. After Mexican independence in 1821, the presidios became less important as military stations. The presidios at Monterey and San Francisco have been used by the United States Army.

▶ What parts of Father Serra's plan show that he intended to treat the Native Americans well?

10. Unfortunately, few of Father Serra's ideas about treating Native Americans fairly were carried out. Treatment of Native Americans did not change much from that in New Spain in the 1600's and early 1700's. Those who broke the strict rules of the missions were punished. Some Native Americans were treated as slaves while others died from diseases. During the period of mission activity in California, the Native American population fell from 72,000 to only 18,000. What were the advantages and disadvantages of mission life for Native Americans?

▲ California had over 800 ranches like this one in the years after 1821, when Mexico became free of Spain. Many of the ranches had been missions before then.

Decline of the Missions   Why did the mission system in California come to an end?

11. By the time Mexico won its independence from Spain in 1821, the missions were losing their importance. To the Mexicans, the missions represented the Spanish rule they had resented. The Mexican government then began selling mission property. Wealthy Mexicans who owned large ranches knew the grassy mission lands were perfect for grazing their cattle. These owners of large ranches, who were called **rancheros** (rahn-CHAIR-ohs), persuaded the government to sell them mission property. As a result, many missions closed, and the Native Americans who lived there went to work for the rancheros.

12. The ranches were huge properties that proved to be very profitable for the rancheros. They grew wealthy selling cattle hides for leather and tallow. Under the rancheros, the Native Americans received only food, clothing, and shelter for their labor. Since they received no wages, they were forced to borrow money from their masters. As a result, many Native Americans were always in debt and were unable to leave the ranches. Making their lives even worse was the prejudice they faced from the Mexicans and other people. For the Native Americans in California, life was no easier now than it had been for earlier Native Americans at the missions.

Outlook

13. New Spain stretched from Mexico into the Southwest and California. Power there was in the hands of a few people, and Spanish settlements were too far apart to build a strong society. In California, missions became the main centers of Spanish settlement where the Spanish tried to convert Native Americans to Christianity. However, many Native Americans suffered hardship under New Spain's rule. After Mexico became independent, the missions began to disappear and ranches took their place. Before long, other settlers would arrive in the Southwest. How do you think the arrival of settlers ◀ from the United States would affect Spanish rule in North America?

325

CHAPTER REVIEW

VOCABULARY REVIEW

▶ Write each number and word on a sheet of paper. Write the letter of the definition next to the word it matches.

1. pueblo
2. ranchero
3. presidio
4. revenue
5. self-sufficient
6. administrator

a. money
b. able to get along without help
c. a cowboy
d. a small farming community
e. the owner of large ranches
f. a small fort
g. a manager

SKILL BUILDER: INTERPRETING A PICTURE

▶ Look at the picture below made by a Native American artist under Spanish rule. Answer the questions about the picture on a sheet of paper.

a. What is the man in the lower right doing?

b. Why is the Native American on the top right shown carrying a Spaniard?

c. What are the other Spaniards doing?

d. What does this picture tell you about the life of these Native Americans?

chalchicueyecā

SKILL BUILDER: CRITICAL THINKING AND COMPREHENSION

I. Compare and Contrast

▶ Use a separate sheet of paper to answer the following questions:

1. How was a pueblo like a mission? How was it different?

2. How was the land used by missions and how was the land used by rancheros?

3. How were Native Americans' lives the same on the missions and on the ranches? How were they different?

II. Cause and Effect

▶ Write the three sets of "effects" below on a sheet of paper. Then next to each set write what caused these things to happen.

1. Effects:
   a. Native Americans wove cotton cloth.
   b. Native Americans made leather from cowhides.
   c. Native Americans tended cattle.

2. Effects:
   a. Twenty-one missions were started from San Diego to Sonoma.
   b. Native Americans were converted to Christianity.

3. Effects:
   a. Men were forced to kill their mules for food.
   b. San Francisco Bay was discovered.

4. Effects:
   a. Many ranches were set up in California.
   b. Native Americans owed money to ranch owners.

USING PRIMARY SOURCES

▶ Reread the Spotlight on Sources on page 324. From what you learn about Father Serra in his letter, what can you say about him as a person?

ENRICHMENT

1. Prepare a report on the missions of California. Include information on where they were located and which missions are still there today.

2. Imagine you are a Native American who is living at one of the missions. Write an account of your daily life there, including information on how you are treated by the priests.

3. Write a short play about the journey of Portolá and Father Serra in 1769 to set up the first missions. Include speeches that show how the two men got along together and how some of their views were different.

4. The text mentions the fact that Russian fur hunters were building trading posts in California. Research the activities of the Russians in California. Find out whether there is any evidence of the Russians' presence in California today.

CHAPTER 4

The War Between the United States and Mexico

> **OBJECTIVE:** Why did the United States fight a war with Mexico, and what were the results of this war?

1. In 1847, General Winfield Scott had a difficult task before him. Fighting in the War with Mexico, Scott and his troops had just captured the Mexican city of Veracruz. Now he was marching his men toward the capital, Mexico City. To get there as quickly as possible, however, Scott had to cross over dangerous passes in the mountains. Scott decided to put a young officer from Virginia in charge of building bridges over the passes. After the bridges were built, American troops were able to reach Mexico City. Soon after, they captured it and brought the war to an end. General Scott gave much of the credit for the American victory to the young officer. General Scott also promoted the young man and described him as "the greatest military genius in America." Fourteen years later, in the Civil War, this officer commanded the Confederate army. The officer's name was Robert E. Lee.

▲ General Winfield Scott led his soldiers through high mountain passes in order to reach Mexico City. After a fierce battle Scott and the American soldiers marched into Mexico City.

Americans Settle in Texas What problems developed between Mexico and the Americans in Texas?

2. The first large group of Americans settled in Texas in the 1820s. In 1820, the Spanish government allowed Moses Austin, a Missouri banker, to start an American settlement there. Austin died soon after. However, his son, Stephen Austin, led a group of 300 American families to land along the Brazos River in 1821. The success of Austin's colony soon brought other Americans into Texas. These settlers were given land grants by Mexico, which had won its independence from Spain in 1821. By 1830, the

In Chapter 4, you will apply these critical thinking skills to the historical process:
▶ **Drawing Conclusions:** Making a statement that explains the facts and evidence.
◢ **Comparing and Contrasting:** Recognizing similarities and differences.

number of Americans in Texas was over 20,000.

3. The Mexican government became worried about the growing number of Americans in Texas. It was afraid that if more Americans settled in Texas, the United States would try to **annex** (uh-NEX) the territory. When a country annexes land, it adds or joins that territory to its existing land. In 1830, the Mexican government refused to allow more Americans into Texas. Despite this, many Americans continued to enter Texas.

4. Gradually, hard feelings developed between the Americans and the Mexican government. While most of the Americans were Protestants, a Mexican law said they had to go to Catholic church services. The Mexicans also expected the Americans to obey a Mexican law forbidding slavery. However, the American plantation owners in Texas refused to obey it. The Texans began to think seriously about becoming independent from Mexico. Then, in 1834, an ambitious general named Antonio López de Santa Anna became **dictator** (DIK-tay-tuhr) of Mexico. A dictator is a ruler who takes total power over the people. The Texans were now ready to fight for their independence.

▶ Why would the Texans want to be free of a dictator in Mexico?

Texans Win Independence How did Texas gain its independence from Mexico?

5. In 1835 the Texans formed their own army. The next year, a force of 187 Texans under William B. Travis was attacked at San Antonio. Travis faced a Mexican army of 6,000 men led by Santa Anna. The Texans retreated to an old Spanish mission called the **Alamo**. Greatly outnumbered, the men in the Alamo held off the Mexicans for two weeks. Finally, on March 6, 1836, the Alamo fell. Every man inside died in the fighting, including such famous Americans as Davy Crockett and Jim Bowie. Among the defenders of the Alamo were nine Mexican Americans. "Remember the Alamo" became the battle cry for Texans in their fight for freedom from Mexico.

▲ The men at the Alamo believed so strongly in independence for Texas that they were willing to die rather than surrender to Santa Anna.

Spotlight on Sources

6. This message, from William B. Travis, gives you an idea of how the Texans at the Alamo felt:

Fellow Citizens and Compatriots:

I am besieged [attacked] by a thousand or more of the Mexicans under Santa Anna. I have sustained [undergone] a continued bombardment for 24 hours and have not lost a man. The enemy have demanded a [our] surrender; otherwise the garrison [the Texans] is to be put to the sword [killed] if the place is taken. I have answered the [Mexican] summons [demand] with a cannon shot, and our flag still waves proudly from the walls. I shall never surrender or retreat. . . . I am determined [know I must] to sustain [defend] myself as long as possible and die like a soldier

Activity: Suggest that students use a biography or encyclopedia to research the life of one of the Alamo's defenders—William Travis, Davy Crockett, or Jim Bowie. Why was this person at the Alamo fighting for Texas?

329

who never forgets what is due to his own honor and that of his country. Victory or death.

—from *History of Texas*, by Henderson Yoakum

▶ What words would you use to describe Colonel Travis and his men?

7. Santa Anna's victory at the Alamo, however, was one of his few successes in the war. In 1836, the main Texas army, led by Sam Houston, took the Mexicans by surprise at the Battle of San Jacinto (juh-SIN-toh). Santa Anna was captured and his army defeated by the Texans. He was forced to sign a treaty granting Texas its independence. Texas now became an independent republic. It elected Sam Houston its first president. The Vice-President was a Mexican named Lorenzo de Zavala.

People in History

8. **Sam Houston** Before coming to Texas in the 1830s, Sam Houston had led a life full of adventure. At the age of 15, he ran away from home and lived with the Cherokee for three years. Later, he was a soldier, a lawyer, a member of Congress, and governor of Tennessee. When Texas became independent, Houston served twice as its president. Houston wanted Texas to become part of the United States, and he worked hard to achieve this goal. After Texas became a state, he served as a United States senator for 13 years. He was elected governor of Texas in 1859. The city of Houston was named in his honor.

Texas Joins the Union Why did admitting Texas to the Union lead to war with Mexico?

9. Texans had strong reasons for wanting to join the United States. The republic of Texas had little money to run its government. Its army was too small and weak to protect it from raids by Mexicans, Comanches, and Apaches. Besides, most Texans had been Americans before they settled in Texas, and they wanted to remain

MAP SKILL BUILDER: Often rivers become natural boundaries between states or nations. **1.** What did the Rio Grande separate in 1845? **2.** What does the Rio Grande separate today?

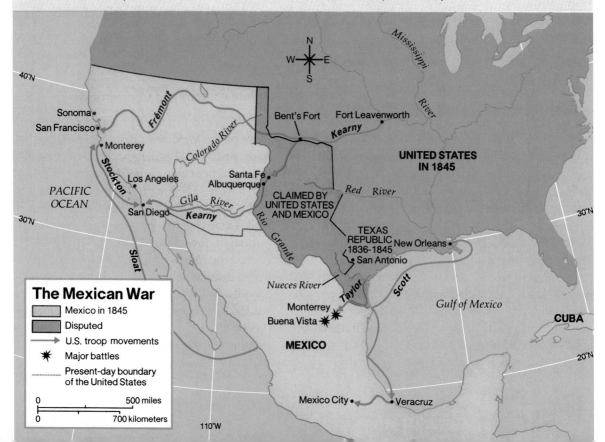

The Mexican War

- ▢ Mexico in 1845
- ▢ Disputed
- → U.S. troop movements
- ✳ Major battles
- ---- Present-day boundary of the United States

0   500 miles
0   700 kilometers

Americans. In the United States, though, people did not agree on whether Texas should be admitted as a state. Many Northerners were against it because Texas was a slaveholding region. Others feared that Mexico would declare war on the United States if it accepted Texas as a state. Finally, in December 1845, after nearly ten years of independence, Texas became the twenty-eighth state of the United States. Did Northerners or Southerners gain the most when Texas was admitted as a state?

10. As expected, Mexico was upset with the United States over the annexation of Texas. To begin with, Mexico had never accepted the idea of an independent Texas. Also, Mexico disagreed with Texas about its southern border. Texas claimed its southern boundary was the river called the Rio Grande. The Mexican government insisted the boundary was farther north at the Nueces River.

11. For its part, the United States had reasons to be on bad terms with Mexico. Mexico owed American citizens several million dollars in unpaid debts. Many Americans also believed in the idea of **Manifest Destiny** (MAN-i-fest DES-ti-nee), or the right of the United States to rule all of North America. This would include Mexico and its lands. The stage was set for war. In April 1846, Mexican soldiers attacked American forces along the Rio Grande in territory claimed by both Texas and Mexico. The United States used this attack as a reason to declare war.

The War with Mexico What military action took place in the war?

12. From the American point of view, the War with Mexico was unusual in two ways. One was that American armies had to cover great distances. The other was that the American forces fighting the war were quite small. In the Southwest, General Stephen Kearny led an army of only about 1,700 men from Fort Leavenworth, Kansas, nearly 800 miles (1,290 km) to Santa Fe. Kearny captured Santa Fe with hardly a shot being fired, giving him control of New Mexico. He then marched part of his small

army another 900 miles (about 1,450 km) farther west to southern California. There he defeated a Mexican army near San Diego and Los Angeles. The territory of California was now in American hands.

13. Meanwhile, General Zachary Taylor was invading Mexico. He marched 300 miles (about 490 km) into northern Mexico, defeating the Mexicans at Monterrey and Buena Vista. When Mexico refused to make peace, in March 1847 General Winfield Scott landed his army at the port of Veracruz and captured the city. Less than six months later, Scott captured Mexico City and ended the war.

Results of the Mexican War What new lands did the United States gain?

14. In February 1848, the Americans and Mexicans signed the Treaty of Guadelupe Hidalgo (gwah-day-LOO-pay ee-DAHL-goh) that ended the War with Mexico. In this treaty the United States gained over 535,000 square miles (1,385,650 sq. km) of new territory, for which it paid Mexico $15 million. This territory was known as the **Mexican Cession.** The United States promised to give the Mexicans in the Mexican Cession full citizenship rights and to respect their property. Five years later, the United States bought the **Gadsden Purchase** for $10 million. Find the Gadsden Purchase and the Mexican Cession on the map on page xxi.

Outlook

15. With the annexation of Texas, the land won in the Mexican Cession, and the Gadsden Purchase, the United States gained most of its present-day boundaries. The new territories of the Southwest would bring rich natural resources and provide new homes for thousands of Americans moving west. Yet the slavery issue in these territories would weaken the growing nation. It would help cause a terrible war, not with foreign enemy, but within the nation itself. This bloody conflict, called the Civil War, pitted Americans against one another.

Background: With the Gadsden Purchase of 1853, Mexico lost more territory—29,000 square miles (75,110 square kilometers). All told, Mexico lost nearly one third of its land to the United States between 1848 and 1853.

331

CHAPTER REVIEW

VOCABULARY REVIEW

▶ Write each of the following sentences on a sheet of paper. Then fill in the blank with the word that best completes each sentence.

Mexican Cession   Manifest Destiny   dictator

annexed   Gadsden Purchase   Alamo

1. General Santa Anna became _____ of Mexico in 1834.

2. According to the ideas of _____, the United States had a right to expand its borders.

3. The United States _____ Texas and made it a state in 1845.

4. The _____ was a Spanish mission in which 187 brave Texans fought Santa Anna's army to the death.

5. The _____ resulted in the United States gaining all of California, Utah, and Nevada, as well as other territory.

6. Through the _____, the United States bought a strip of land in what is today southern Arizona and New Mexico.

SKILL BUILDER: DRAWING A TIME LINE

▶ Draw a time line on a separate sheet of paper. Find the dates for the following events in this unit. Then write each event and the date it happened on the time line. Copy the time line below as your base.

1820	1825	1830	1835	1840	1845	1850	1855

Joseph Smith starts the Mormon Church

Moses Austin settles in Texas

Joseph Smith is killed

Mormons reach the Great Salt Lake Basin

Texans die at the Alamo

The United States annexes 535,000 square miles (1,385,100 sq. km) of land from Mexico

The War with Mexico begins

Mexico wins independence from Spain

The Santa Fe Trail opens

SKILL BUILDER: CRITICAL THINKING AND COMPREHENSION

▶ **I. Drawing Conclusions**

▶ Each conclusion below has a set of facts that follow it. Some facts support the conclusion, while others do not. For each conclusion, write the letters of the correct facts.

1. **Conclusion:** Hard feelings developed between Mexico and the early settlers in Texas.
   Facts:
   a. Texas was part of Mexico.

b. Texans had to worship at Catholic churches in Mexico.

c. Texans wanted slavery.

d. Mexico forbade slavery.

e. Mexicans spoke a different language.

f. Texans were thinking of becoming independent.

2. **Conclusion:** There were strong reasons why the Texas wanted to join the Union.
   Facts:
   a. Texans did not like the Mexicans.
   b. Most Texans were American citizens.
   c. Texans wanted the protection of the United States Army.

3. **Conclusion:** Some Americans were not sure they wanted Texas to become a state.
   Facts:
   a. Texans had slaves.
   b. Mexico might declare war on the United States.
   c. Mexico never accepted Texas as an independent republic.

II. Comparing and Contrasting

▶ After each "compare" and "contrast" statement below, write a statement a Mexican and a Texan might make on that subject. Use a separate sheet of paper. The first answer is given.

1. Contrast the views on the boundaries of Texas in the 1830s.
   Mexican: The boundary is at the Nueces River.
   Texan: The boundary is at the Rio Grande.

2. Compare the two leaders of the armies of Texas and Mexico.
   Mexican: _____
   Texan: _____

3. Contrast the views on slavery in 1830.
   Mexican: _____
   Texan: _____

4. Contrast the size of the two armies at the Alamo.
   Mexican: _____
   Texan: _____

USING PRIMARY SOURCES

▶ Reread the Spotlight on Sources on pages 329 and 330. What can you learn from Colonel Travis's statement about why the Alamo is such an important event in Texas history?

ENRICHMENT

1. Do research on some of the well-known Americans who opposed the war with Texas and prepare a report on what you learn.

2. Have a class debate on this question: Was the United States right in going to war with Mexico in 1846?

CHAPTER 5

California Becomes a State

OBJECTIVE: How did the discovery of gold change the course of California's history?

1. On January 28, 1847, James Marshall, dripping wet and wild-eyed, rushed into the office of his employer, John Sutter. Sutter was surprised to see Marshall, who managed Sutter's sawmill in the Sacramento Valley nearly 40 miles (64 kilometers) away. Excitedly, Marshall reached into his pocket and carefully removed a large nugget of yellow metal. It weighed about a quarter of an ounce and was the size of a dime. John Sutter knew at once what it was—gold! Marshall had found the nugget at Sutter's Mill. In a few months, news of the discovery of gold in California spread like wildfire across the United States and other parts of the world. The California Gold Rush was on.

The Gold Rush What routes did Americans take to reach California and search for gold?

2. The Gold Rush began in California in 1849. Thousands of Americans left their jobs, families, and homes to go west to strike it rich. Doctors, lawyers, farmers, and factory workers rushed to the gold fields. For most Americans, the journey to California was long and dangerous. People living in the middle part of the country came by land. They traveled over well-worn pioneer trails in covered wagons. They faced the same hardships that thousands of pioneers before them had faced.

▲ Women were among the thousands of Forty-niners who came to California in search of gold. These miners are using a cradle to filter out the gold from the mud.

3. For Easterners the route to California was by sea. Many traveled by ship around South America and then north up the Pacific Ocean to San Francisco. From there it was a short distance to the gold fields. However, this ocean voyage took many months. A faster route was

In Chapter 5, you will apply these critical thinking skills to the historical process:

▶ **Drawing Conclusions:** Making a statement that explains the facts and evidence.

▶ **Predicting:** Telling what will happen on the basis of clues and facts.

by boat to the **Isthmus** of Panama in Central America. An isthmus (IS-muhs) is a narrow strip of land with water on either side that connects two larger land areas. Then the gold seekers traveled across the Isthmus of Panama and took a ship up the Pacific coast to San Francisco. The Panama crossing, however, had its own dangers. A thick jungle had to be crossed, and travelers could catch deadly tropical diseases such as malaria. Even so, none of these dangers stopped the flood of gold seekers.

▶ Why could the gold seekers in those years not travel across Panama by boat?

People in History

4. John Sutter A Swiss immigrant named John Sutter came to America in 1834. He wanted to be a rancher in California. In 1841, he bought a piece of rich land in the Sacramento Valley from the Mexican governor of California. Here, Sutter built a fort which became an important stopover place for settlers coming to northern California. Later, he built a sawmill that James Marshall ran for him.

5. When Marshall showed Sutter the gold he had found near the mill, Sutter was not happy. He feared the Gold Rush would destroy his land, and he was right. Thousands of gold seekers, including his own workers, soon overran his property. They even stole Sutter's cattle and butchered them for food. A broken man, Sutter later moved to Pennsylvania. He died in Washington, D.C., in 1880, while making an appeal to Congress for help. The gold that had made others rich was the ruin of John Sutter.

The Forty-Niners What was life like in the gold fields and mining towns of California?

6. The first group of gold seekers reached San Francisco by steamship on February 28, 1849. Why do you think they were called "Forty-niners"? A more mixed group of **prospectors**, or people searching for gold, could not be imagined. Many of them had never done a day's worth of labor in their lives. Most of them had no experience mining. Some thought all they had to do was pick gold nuggets off the ground. Among the prospectors were runaway slaves and African American sailors who jumped ship when they heard of the gold strike. Some African Americans came as slaves but earned enough in the mines to buy their freedom.

7. The two main ways of prospecting, or searching for gold, were **panning** and using a **cradle**. In panning, a prospector scooped up the dirt and sand from a stream using a metal pan. The prospector would then wash out the sand with water until only heavier gold flakes were left on the bottom of the pan. Using a cradle was a faster and easier way to find gold. It looked like a wooden cradle but had an iron

---

▼ Here in a boom town, a judge chosen by the miners is using his own cabin to hold the trial of an accused horse thief. What does this tell you about law and order in the mining towns?

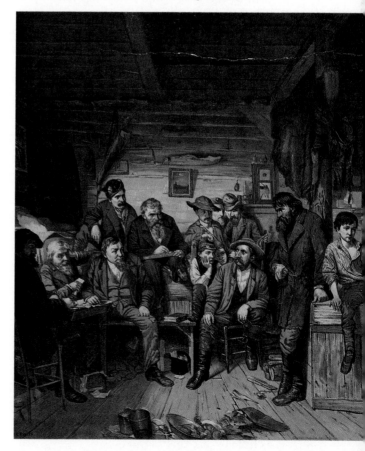

THE CHINESE

The Gold Rush brought gold seekers from many other countries, including China, to California. The gold-rich California that was advertised in the large cities of China seemed like a dream. Many Chinese came to California to find their riches and return home wealthy. Over 20,000 Chinese came to California in the first three years of the Gold Rush. While some became miners, others took whatever work they could find, mostly in service work. Many washed clothes and cooked food in the mining camps.

The customs and culture of the Chinese were vastly different from those of the Americans. To protect themselves from prejudiced Americans and preserve their culture, most Chinese lived in separate communities called "Chinatowns," both in the mining camps and in towns and cities.

▼ The Chinese in the United States became known for the backbreaking work they did helping to build the first transcontinental railroad.

When the Gold Rush ended, many Chinese stayed on in California. They opened their own shops, restaurants, and other businesses to meet the growing state's needs. Other Chinese worked in factories and on farms.

One of the greatest achievements of the Chinese in America was the work they did in building the **transcontinental** (trans-kon-tuh-NEN-tuhl) railroad in the 1860s. Transcontinental means across a continent. The Chinese worked on the Central Pacific, the western part of the transcontinental railroad, that crossed the Rocky Mountain region. It took 10,000 workers to build the Central Pacific, and 9,000 of them were Chinese. Many Chinese died performing dangerous tasks that other workers would not do.

In the 30 years after the Gold Rush, over 250,000 Chinese came to California. While most stayed on in the land they helped build into a major state, the Chinese population spread to other states. In 1882, however, as the Chinese became stronger economically, anti-Chinese feeling grew in the United States. Congress passed the Chinese Exclusion Act that prohibited Chinese from immigrating into the United States. It was not until after World War II, when China was an ally of the United States, that this law was repealed.

Now answer the following questions.

1. How long have the Chinese been immigrating to the United States?

2. What contributions have the Chinese made to life in the United States?

plate dotted with holes on top. Miners shoveled dirt from the stream's bottom onto the cradle. Then they rocked it while pouring water on its iron plate. The gravel and rocks rolled off the cradle, while the sand and gold dust went through the holes. Inside, the gold dust became trapped between strips of wood. The sand and water were washed out an open end.

8. Mining camps sprang up around every stream or creek where gold was found. Miners lived in tents while they searched for gold. They gave their camps colorful names like Coffee Gulch, Hog Eye, and You Bet. When a camp grew big and successful enough, it turned into a **boom town**. A boom town was a fast-growing community in a mining area. Stores, saloons, and even hotels and theaters were built in most boom towns. The prices of store goods often were sky high because they had to be shipped around South America from the East. Flour could cost as much as $800 a barrel! When all the gold had been mined, a boom town often disappeared as quickly as it had sprung up.

🦅 Spotlight on Sources

9. Among the newcomers who arrived in California in the days of the Gold Rush were Chinese men. Life in their new home was hard and often strange for the Chinese. Here is how one Chinese immigrant, Lee Chew, described his experience in California:

> I went to Hong Kong with five other boys and we got passage on a steamer [steamship], paying $50 each. A man got me work as a house servant in an American family, and my start was the same as that of almost all the Chinese in this country. . . . We were three years with the railroad [as laundrymen] and then went to the mines, where we made plenty of money in gold dust, but had a hard time. Many of the miners were wild men who carried revolvers [guns] and after drinking would come into our place to shoot and steal shirts, for which we had to pay. One of these men hit his head against a flat iron, and all the

miners came and broke up the laundry, chasing us out of town. . . . We lost all our property and $365 in money. . . .
> —from *The Life Stories of Undistinguished Americans As Told by Themselves*, by Hamilton Holt

Why do you think the miners attacked the ◀ Chinese workers?

California Joins the Union How did California become a state as part of a compromise over slavery?

10. Californians were eager to see their territory become a state. The Gold Rush brought in many people who stayed on and settled in the region. The population of California grew from about 26,000 in 1848 to 200,000 in 1850. When the people of California had to decide in 1850 if they wanted to allow slavery there, they voted against slavery.

11. Americans in the North and the South were bitterly divided over whether California should be admitted as a free state or a slave state. Henry Clay, an important leader in Congress, proposed the Compromise of 1850. You remember that a compromise is the settlement of a dispute in which both sides give up something. The proslavery Southern states agreed to allow California to enter the Union as a free state. In return, the antislavery Northern states supported stricter laws against runaway slaves. The compromise allowed California to become the thirty-first state of Union.

Outlook

12. Only a few lucky prospectors struck it rich in the California Gold Rush. Yet those who did not find gold found other riches when they looked around them. They discovered a land with rich soil and a growing population that needed many goods and services. Many of them stayed in California and became successful in businesses and farming. With both coasts settled, Americans then began to move into the vast middle region of the country known as the Great Plains.

Background: The mining camps were models of democracy in action. John Borthwick, a Scottish author who lived among the miners, had this to say about a trial he observed: "A jury of miners was the highest court known, and I must say I never saw a court of justice with so little humbug about it."

337

CHAPTER REVIEW

VOCABULARY REVIEW

▶ Write each number and word on a sheet of paper. Write the letter of the definition next to word it matches.

1. boom town
2. cradle
3. prospectors
4. isthmus
5. transcontinental
6. panning

a. a narrow strip of land with water on either side.

b. a way of separating gold from dirt and water.

c. fast-growing communities that sprang up near mines.

d. people searching for gold

e. settlement of a dispute by both sides giving up something

f. a tool for finding gold

g. across a continent

SKILL BUILDER: READING A MAP

▶ Use the map of the transcontinental railroad routes to answer the following questions.

1. Which railroad, the Northern Pacific or the Union Pacific, do you think was more difficult to build? What may have been some of the natural obstacles faced in each case?

2. List the cities that were railroad stops and the railroad lines that passed through them.

3. Estimate the amount of railroad track laid between 1870–1890. What does this tell you about the growth of cities in the West?

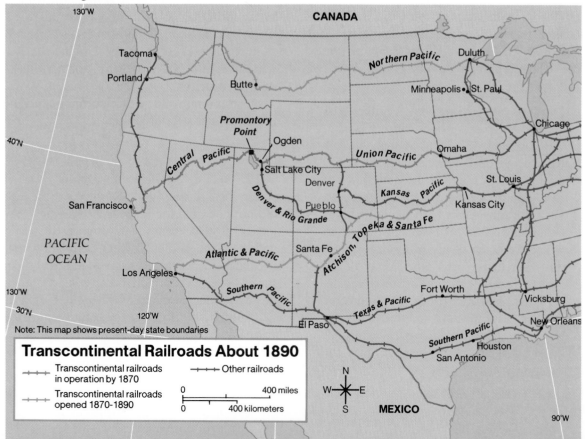

Transcontinental Railroads About 1890

— Transcontinental railroads in operation by 1870

— Transcontinental railroads opened 1870-1890

— Other railroads

0   400 miles

0   400 kilometers

Note: This map shows present-day state boundaries

SKILL BUILDER: CRITICAL THINKING AND COMPREHENSION

I. Drawing Conclusions

▶ The statements below tell an aspect of life in California during the Gold Rush period. For each statement, on a separate sheet of paper write a few sentences describing the problems that may have arisen as a result.

1. Prospectors usually did not bring their families with them to California.

2. Many prospectors were uneducated people who had never worked before.

3. Chinese opened restaurants and laundries in the mining towns.

4. California was admitted as a free state, rather than a slave state.

▶ What conclusions can you draw about the relationship between the Chinese and Americans in early California? Write a brief paragraph explaining your ideas.

II. Predicting

▶ Write the each statement on a sheet of paper and write your prediction below it.

1. You are a prospector who has just found gold. Predict what you would have to learn to mine your gold.

2. Your mining camp is starting to grow. Predict the kind of business you would start there to make a lot of money.

3. You are a Chinese immigrant in California in 1849. Predict what you would do to try to find work.

4. You are an African American slave brought to California by your owner. Predict how your life might change here.

5. You are an Easterner who wants to prospect for gold in California. Predict what steps you would take to get to California.

USING PRIMARY SOURCES

▶ Reread the Spotlight on Sources on page 337. Do you think Lee Chew was glad he came to the United States? Explain your answer.

ENRICHMENT

1. Draw a poster to make Easterners want to join in the California Gold Rush.

2. Imagine a meeting between John Sutter and a wealthy prospector who struck it rich shortly after the Gold Rush ended. With another student, write what these two men might have said to each other. Read your conversation to the class.

3. Research the history of the Chinese in California after the Gold Rush ended with a small group of classmates. Why were some Californians prejudiced against them? How did the Chinese try to overcome this prejudice? Prepare a group report on your findings.

CHAPTER 6

Settlers Move into the Great Plains

OBJECTIVE: What part did miners, ranchers, and farmers play in opening the Great Plains?

1. Thousands of eager pioneers lined up at the starting line on the dusty prairie. Here, on April 22, 1889, on the border of the Indian Territory that is now Oklahoma, they were waiting for a signal. At noon, the sound of a signal gun cracked the air, and the land rush was on. In a cloud of dust pioneers in wagons, on horseback, on bicycles, on a railroad train, and on foot all raced ahead. Their goal was to claim the free land the government had promised them. When these settlers came to a piece of land they liked, they pounded a stake into the ground to claim it. By that evening, 50,000 people had moved into Oklahoma.

2. This dry prairie had been used by the United States government to relocate at least 30 Native American tribes. Under pressure from settlers eager for land, the United States government had pushed back the Native Americans living in this territory. Then it opened a part of the Oklahoma Territory to white farmers and ranchers. Five large tribes, who had lived in the Oklahoma Territory, lost hope that they would ever have their own state.

▲ On April 22, 1889, thousands of settlers tore into the Oklahoma territory to claim the free land the government was offering. A year later the government reported that there was no longer a frontier line.

Miners Why did miners flock to the Rocky Mountains in the 1850s and 1860s?

3. After the Gold Rush in California ended, many prospectors decided to head for the Rocky Mountains. They went there to search for the gold that had been discovered in Colorado and the Black Hills of South Dakota. Other prospectors went to Idaho, Nevada, Montana, Utah, Wyoming, and New Mexico.

4. Along with gold, miners found another precious metal in many of these places—silver.

In Chapter 6, you will apply these critical thinking skills to the historical process:

▲ **Identifying Fact *versus* Opinion:** Specifying whether information can be proved or whether it expresses feelings or beliefs.

❯ **Predicting:** Telling what you believe what will happen on the basis of clues and facts.

Unlike gold mining, silver mining took heavy machines to dig out the ore and then remove the silver in the ore from other minerals. Mining companies were formed in the 1860s and 1870s, making mining a big business. The mining industry soon created thousands of jobs. New towns and cities grew up around the mines. Three of the most famous were Denver, Colorado; Deadwood, South Dakota; and Virginia City, Nevada.

Railroads   What part did the railroads play in opening the Great Plains?

5. As you read in Chapter 5, the transcontinental railroad was finished in 1869. To draw passengers, the railroad companies made a tempting offer. They would sell farmland along the railroad's **right of way** to new farmers at $2.50 an acre. The right of way is the land along the tracks owned by the railroads. Thousands of settlers flocked into the Great Plains to buy this land. The railroad provided safe, cheap, and fast
▶ transportation to their new homes. What other reasons might the railroads have had for offering land so cheaply?

Ranchers   How did cattle ranchers use the Great Plains in the 1870s?

6. Ranchers found the grasslands of the Great Plains good for their growing herds of Mexican longhorn cattle. After the Civil War, the North's economy was expanding quickly, and so was its demand for beef. The ranchers could get a good price there for their cattle. But how could they get their herds to the eastern markets? The railroad was the answer. All the ranchers had to do was drive their cattle north on a cattle trail. Cattle trails went to Abilene, Dodge City, and Wichita in Kansas, as well as several other growing "cow towns." Here, the cattle could be loaded onto trains and shipped east to be market.

7. Cowboys had the job of getting the cattle herds to the cow towns, hundreds of miles away. The lives of these young, tough cattle-herders were colorful but also dangerous. A cowboy had to guard 4,000 or more head of cattle from wild animals, bad weather, and **rustlers** (RUS-luhrs), or cattle thieves. At night, a single gunshot or the sound of thunder could start a **stampede** (stam-PEED). A stampede is a sudden rush of frightened cattle running wild, and crushing everything in their path.

People in History

8. Nat Love   One of the most famous cowboys was a young African American named Nat Love. Love was born in Tennessee in 1854. When he was 15, Love set out for Dodge City, Kansas, to become a cowboy.

9. For 20 years, Love worked on the long cattle drives north from Texas. He became a skilled rider and sharpshooter. On the Fourth of July in 1876, he entered a cowboy contest in Deadwood, South Dakota. He was judged the best rider, cow roper, and sharpshooter. From that day on, other cowboys respectfully called him "Deadwood Dick." By 1889, the cattle drives were ending, and Deadwood Dick settled down to a job on the railroad.

10. The years of the cowboys and the cattle kingdom they watched lasted only a short time. Farmers and sheep ranchers soon came west and quickly put an end to the open range. Farmers fenced off their land with barbed wire, which was invented in 1874. The sheep ranchers let their animals graze freely on the pastureland of the cattle ranchers. The sheep cropped the grass there down to its roots, leaving nothing for the cattle to eat. The cattle ranchers also allowed their herds to become too large. The grassland on the plains could not support so many cattle. By 1885, many cattle ranchers had been replaced by farmers on the Great Plains. Why did farmers need less land than cattle ranchers?

Farmers   How did the Homestead Act help farmers to the Great Plains?

11. In 1862, the United States government passed the Homestead Act. This law offered

Activity: Suggest that students read selections from the autobiography of Nat Love or another cowboy or Western personality. Are the facts of this person's life exaggerated? How can they tell?

341

Settling the Great Plains All lands have advantages and disadvantages for human settlement. Cattle ranchers and farmers who settled the Great Plains learned to adapt to the advantages and disadvantages of that dry, flat, grassy land with few trees.

For settlers coming from the eastern United States, the treeless grasslands of the Great Plains were strange and new. Water was hard to find. Rainfall was only half that of the lands east of the Mississippi River. Winds roared across the plains, blowing dry soil into dust and cold snow into blizzards. Summer temperatures regularly rose above 100 degrees Fahrenheit (38 degrees Celsius). Winter temperatures in the northern plains often stayed below freezing for days.

Cattle ranchers first saw the possibilities of the grassy plains. The map below shows how cattle ranchers made use of the difference in climate between the southern and northern Great Plains. In the milder climate of the southern plains, they bred cattle. Then they drove the cattle north "on the hoof" to summer pastures or to railroads for shipment to market.

Farming on the Great Plains began more slowly than cattle ranching. The soils, bound by grass roots, were rich but hard to plow before the steel plow was invented. The rainfall also varied greatly from year to year. When there was enough rainfall, crops of wheat and corn grew well, and farmers prospered. When the dry years came, as they often did, farmers watched their crops die and winds blow away the bared soils. Cattle ranchers sometimes added to the farmers' woes when their herds trampled the growing crops.

Gradually, farmers learned to cope with these advantages and disadvantages of the Great Plains. They set up fences of barbed wire to keep cattle out. They planted varieties of wheat and barley that were able to survive all but the driest years. New ways of plowing kept soils from blowing away. Windmills pumped up water trapped deep in the ground. Huge new tractors and harvesting combines worked especially well on the flat plains. Hard work, new machinery, and hardier seeds brought success. The American farmers turned the Great Plains into one of the world's great farming regions.

Now answer these questions.

1. Where are the railroads and in which direction do they run?

2. What cattle trails are shown on the map, and where did they go?

3. Why are most of the cattle trails at the southern end of the Great Plains?

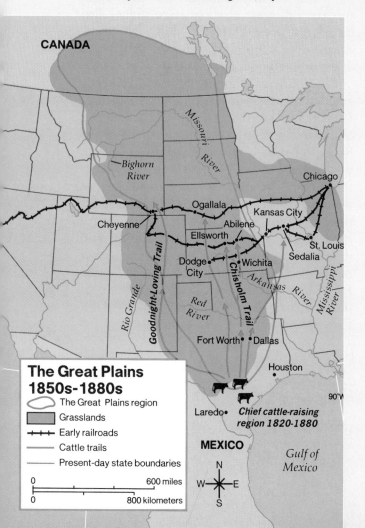

The Great Plains 1850s–1880s

◯ The Great Plains region
▨ Grasslands
+++ Early railroads
— Cattle trails
— Present-day state boundaries

Chief cattle-raising region 1820-1880

| 0 | 600 miles |
| 0 | 800 kilometers |

160 acres (65 hectares) of land free to anyone who farmed it for five years. Thousands of settlers took the offer and became known as **homesteaders**. They came not only from the eastern United States, but also from European countries, such as Sweden, Norway, and Germany. In the first six months after the Homestead Act passed, nearly 250,000 acres (about 101,000 hectares) of land were claimed in Kansas and Nebraska alone.

12. Farmers found the soil of the Great Plains fertile but hard to plow. It was covered by **sod**, a top layer of earth with thick grass. However, the steel plow, invented by John Deere in 1837, helped farmers to cut through the sod and plant their crops. Since timber was hard to find on the Great Plains, settlers used the sod to build houses. These **sod houses** kept their owners cool in the hot summers and warm in the freezing winters. Many homesteaders came to choose their sod houses over wooden ones even after they were able to buy lumber from the East.

13. Homesteaders used other ways of making their lives easier. On the Great Plains, most of the water was found under the ground. Windmills powered by the constant winds were used to pump water from springs deep below the ground. Barbed wire kept wandering cattle from destroying crops.

Spotlight on Sources

14. Not all the people who came west liked their life on the Great Plains. Here is part of a diary kept by Mollie Sanford, a teacher, who lived for a while with a family of homesteaders:

> Their manner of living is so different from ours that it just about used me up. For breakfast we had corn bread, salt pork, and black coffee. For dinner, greens, wild ones at that, boiled pork, and cold corn bread washed down with 'beverage' [something to drink]. The 'beverage' was put upon the table in a wooden pail and dished out in tin cups. When asked if I would have some . . . I said 'yes,' thinking it perhaps

▲ These settlers in Nebraska dug their home into the side of a hill and roofed it over with sod. A load of fresh sod for repairs is in the wagon.

> was cider, but found out it was vinegar and brown sugar and warm creek water.
> —from *Mollie: Journal of Mollie Dorsey Sanford in Nebraska & Colorado Territories, 1857–1866,* by Mollie Sanford

What is Mollie Sanford's opinion of the homesteaders' meals? ◄

Outlook

15. The people who came to the Great Plains from the 1850s to the 1880s began to turn its vast grassland into prosperous farms, towns, and cities. The miners and ranchers brought business and industry. The farmers built homes and communities. The railroad made it easier for all these groups to move there. However, all these changes brought great hardships to many Native Americans. Native American tribes had lived on the Great Plains for many hundreds of years. They would not give up homelands without a long and bitter fight.

343

CHAPTER REVIEW

VOCABULARY REVIEW

▶ Number your paper from 1 to 6. In each of the sentences that follow, the underlined word or words make the sentence true or false. If the sentence is true, write *T* after the number of the sentence. If it is false, write the word or words that would make it true.

1. Thieves who stole cattle were called *cowboys*.

2. Railroads sold land to settlers along the *right of way*.

3. The houses of settlers on the Great Plains were called *sod houses*.

4. The people who acquired land under the Homestead Act were called *rustlers*.

5. New gold *strikes* were made in Great Plains territories.

6. The new steel plows helped farmers cut the *sod* on their land.

SKILL BUILDER: COMPARING PICTURES

▶ Look at the two pictures below. On a separate sheet of paper, compare the people in the pictures in terms of their:

a. type of home   **b.** style of dress   **c.** use of horses   **d.** other

▶ In a paragraph, describe how they are the same and how they are different.

SKILL BUILDER: CRITICAL THINKING AND COMPREHENSION

I. Fact *versus* Opinion

▶ Read each of these sentences and decide whether it states a fact or an opinion. On a sheet of paper, write 1 to 8. If a statement is a fact, write **F** next to the letter of the sentence. If it is an opinion, write **O** next to the letter of the sentence.

1. The soil of the Great Plains was fertile.

2. The homesteaders were very brave people.

3. The soil of the Great Plains was hard to plow.

4. Barbed wire kept cattle from wandering.

5. Barbed wire was cruel to animals.

6. Sod houses were cool in summer and warm in winter.

7. Homesteaders should not have settled on the Native Americans' lands.

8. Homesteaders were very clever to use sod to build their houses.

II. Predicting

▶ Read the following statements. Then predict which of the events listed below each statement is likely to happen. Write your prediction on a sheet of paper and explain why you chose it. More than one prediction can be made for some statements.

1. Land next to the railroads in the West goes on sale for $2.50 an acre. You predict:
   a. People will think something is wrong with the offer. No one will buy the land.
   b. People will think it is a good offer. Many people will buy land.

2. There are many herds of cattle in the West, and many people in the East like beef. You predict:
   a. People in the West will start to raise something else.
   b. People in the East will change their tastes.
   c. People will find a way to get cattle from the West to the East.

3. A gunshot goes off near a herd of cattle. You predict:
   a. Cattle are used to hearing guns go off, so nothing will happen.
   b. The cowboys who take care of the cattle will be busy making sure the cattle do not stampede.

USING PRIMARY SOURCES

▶ Reread the Spotlight on Sources on page 343. What does Mollie Sanford's description of her meals tell you about homesteaders' lives?

ENRICHMENT

1. Imagine you are a homesteader on the Great Plains. Write a letter to a friend back East about your new life.

2. Make a map showing where the major gold and silver strikes took place in the West after the California Gold Rush.

3. Write to the Golden Spike National Historic Site in Promontory, Utah, or a railroad museum for more information about the building of the first transcontinental railroad.

CHAPTER 7

The Decline of Native Americans on the Great Plains

OBJECTIVE: Why were Native Americans forced to give up their lands on the Great Plains?

1. Imagine you and your parents are living in the house that your great-grandparents had built. Suppose that one day an agent of the United States government comes to your home. The agent says you and your family must move out of the house and give it to another family from far away. Not only that, but you have to leave your town and move to another state where you know no one. How would you feel? Would you agree to leave, or would you refuse? If you stayed, would you be prepared to fight the people who were going to take your home? This was what happened to Native Americans on the Great Plains when white settlers started moving into their lands in the 1860s.

Arrival of Settlers How were Native Americans' lives changed by the arrival of miners, ranchers, and farmers on the Great Plains?

2. Most white settlers who moved into the Great Plains did not care about the rights of the Native Americans who lived there. Yet, many treaties, or agreements, had been made between the United States government and the Native Americans. These treaties said the Native Americans would keep their lands "as long as the rivers shall run and the grass shall grow." Miners, looking for gold and silver, ignored the

▲ These are typical homes of the nomadic Plains Indians. What can you learn about Plains Indians from this picture?

treaties and trespassed on Native Americans' lands. Farmers and ranchers took over Native American hunting grounds for homesteads and grazing land. The government wanted to avoid conflicts between whites and Native Americans. Therefore, it tried to buy the land from Native Americans and move them to **reservations.**

In Chapter 7, you will apply these critical thinking skills to the historical process:

▲ **Identifying Fact *versus* Opinion:** Identifying whether information can be proved or whether it expresses feelings or beliefs.

Understanding Points of View: Recognizing why people have different attitudes about the same thing.

Reservations are lands set aside for Native Americans to live on.

3. The Great Plains tribes, especially the Sioux, did not want to live on reservations. Their lives depended on hunting the huge herds of buffalo on the open plains. In this way, the Sioux were nomads. Nomads are people who wander from place to place. Yet, on the reservation they were expected to live in one place and farm the land. The Sioux, however, refused to change their lives and give up the land that was rightfully theirs. Were the Sioux right in refusing to change their way of living?

4. The government's failure to keep its treaties and promises to the Great Plains tribes led to war. In 1862, the first of many conflicts

> **MAP SKILL BUILDER:** Humans interact with the earth according to their skills, knowledge, tools, traditions, and values. **1.** How did lifestyles of Plains Indians vary? **2.** Why did those lifestyles vary based on the earth around them?

between the United States army and Native Americans took place. In that year, the Sioux on their reservation in Minnesota did not receive the money promised them by the government. The money was payment for land. Not permitted to hunt, they had no food. Many nearly starved to death that winter. Angry, they left the reservation and raided homesteaders' land. Many settlers were killed and their homes burned. The United States army was called in to put down the rebellion.

5. Red Cloud, a powerful Sioux chief, took up the fight to protect his people's land. Miners on the way to the Montana gold fields used a trail that crossed the Sioux hunting grounds. To protect the whites traveling this trail, the army built three forts. For two years, Red Cloud led attacks on the forts. Finally, in 1868, the government agreed to give up the forts and leave Sioux territory. In return, the Sioux agreed to move to a reservation in the Black Hills of South Dakota. Red Cloud became the first, and last, Native American to win a war against the United States government. However, the peace did not last long.

Native American Warfare What was the result of the Native Americans' fight to defend their land?

6. In 1874, the government once more broke a treaty with the Sioux. Lieutenant Colonel George Custer, a proud, headstrong soldier, led a group of miners looking for gold into the Black Hills of South Dakota. When they found gold there, the government knew that many more miners would soon arrive. Once again, the government told the Sioux they would have to move out and make way for white people. The Sioux had had enough of broken promises. Under their leaders Crazy Horse and Sitting Bull, they gathered into a large war party. In June 1876, Custer led his soldiers into Sioux territory in Montana to arrest the Sioux leaders. Custer did not know that his forces were greatly outnumbered by the Sioux. With 264 soldiers, he rode boldly into the valley of the Little

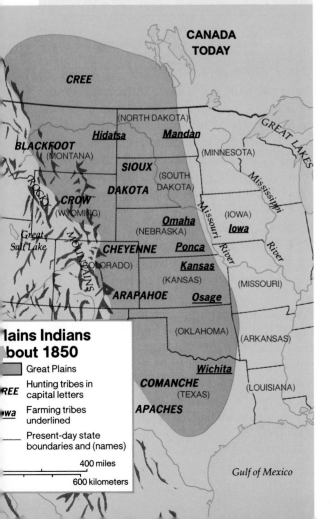

CANADA TODAY

CREE

(NORTH DAKOTA)

GREAT LAKES

Hidatsa   *Mandan*

BLACKFOOT
(MONTANA)   (MINNESOTA)

SIOUX
(SOUTH
DAKOTA)   *Mississippi*

DAKOTA   DAKOTA

CROW
(WYOMING)   (IOWA)

*Great
Salt Lake*   *Omaha*
(NEBRASKA)   *Iowa*

CHEYENNE   *Ponca*   *Missouri River*

(COLORADO)

Kansas
(KANSAS)   (MISSOURI)

ARAPAHOE   *Osage*

(OKLAHOMA)   (ARKANSAS)

**Plains Indians
about 1850**

Great Plains

CREE   Hunting tribes in capital letters

wa   Farming tribes underlined

Present-day state boundaries and (names)

Wichita

COMANCHE
(TEXAS)   (LOUISIANA)

APACHES

400 miles

600 kilometers

Gulf of Mexico

▲ In the early morning hours of September 1864, American soldiers surrounded a peaceful Cheyenne camp and attacked and massacred 200 Cheyenne. This Sand Creek Massacre in Colorado was one of several massacres that contributed to the destruction of Native American tribes in the 1860s and 1870s.

Bighorn River. Suddenly, Custer's army was surrounded by over 2,000 Sioux warriors. Custer and all his men were killed in what came to be called "**Custer's Last Stand**."

7. For the Sioux, however, this victory did not last long. The United States army sent many soldiers to fight against them. The Sioux tribes soon were forced to split up. In the fall of 1876, Sitting Bull fled to Canada with a small group of warriors. Crazy Horse surrendered early in 1877. The Sioux now were forced to give up their lands and move to reservations.

8. In the Southwest, however, the fighting continued. In 1877, the Apaches, left their reservation in Arizona. They were led by Geronimo (juh-RON-uh-moh), whose Apache name means "the smart one." Geronimo outsmarted the United States army, hiding out in Mexico's Sierra Madre mountains. From there, the Apaches made raids on settlers in Arizona, then fled back across the border to Mexico. Geronimo was finally captured in 1886, and conflict ended in the Southwest.

People in History

9. Chief Joseph The Nez Percé were an important tribe of Native Americans in the Northwest. Like many other tribes, by the 1870s the Nez Percé were being driven from their homeland by land-hungry white settlers. In 1877, the United States government forced them to leave Oregon's Wallowa Valley and move to a reservation in Idaho. However, some of the Nez Percé, led by Chief Joseph, refused.

10. Chief Joseph realized after several battles with American troops that his warriors could not win. He and his followers decided to flee to Canada, where they hoped to join Sitting Bull and his Sioux. Chief Joseph then led the Nez Percé on an amazing march across 1,700 miles (2,735 km) of mountains and wilderness. The army chased them but was unable to catch them. Colonel Nelson Miles, however, made up his mind to stop the Nez Percé. Forty miles (64 km) from the Canadian border, Miles and his troops surprised the Nez Percé. For six days, the

Background: Geronimo actually returned to the reservation several times during the ten-year period he fought the army. He was finally captured when one of his own Apaches led soldiers to his hiding place.

Native Americans fought bravely in the freezing snow. On October 5, 1877, Chief Joseph decided his people had suffered enough, and he surrendered to Colonel Miles. The courage of Chief Joseph and the Nez Percé deeply moved many Americans. They began to ask for better treatment for Native Americans.

🦅 Spotlight on Sources

11. In defeat, Chief Joseph kept his courage and dignity. His famous surrender speech in 1877 was written down by a soldier who was there. Here is a part of it:

> I am tired of fighting. Our chiefs are killed. . . . It is cold and we have no blankets. The little children are freezing to death. My people, some of them, have run away to the hills and have no blankets, no food. . . . Hear me, my chiefs! I am tired. My heart is sick and sad. From where the sun now stands, I will fight no more forever.

▶ What does Chief Joseph mean when he says he will fight "no more forever"?

The Dawes Act   What did Congress do to relocate Native Americans?

12. With most Native Americans now forced to live on reservations, the United States government tried to break up the tribes. In 1887, Congress passed the **Dawes Act**, which broke up tribal lands into small plots. Each family was allowed about 160 acres (65 hectares) to live on. Any reservation land that was left was then open for whites to buy and settle.

13. The Native Americans were given seeds and tools to farm the poor soil of their land on the reservation. Most Native Americans had been hunters and had never grown crops or farmed. As a result, their farms often failed. In addition, Native Americans who produced good crops were often cheated out of their ▶ profits by greedy white men. Why do you think some members of Congress voted against the Dawes Act?

Native American Cultures   How did the rich culture of the Plains Indians change?

14. The life of Native Americans on the reservations was very different from their life on the Great Plains. As you have read, before white settlers came, the Plains peoples were nomads, following and hunting the buffalo herds. In the 1870s and 1880s, however, white hunters killed millions of buffalo for their skins. By 1890, the buffalo were gone from the Great Plains.

15. The Sioux were one of the tribes that found life on the reservations very difficult. As a result, many Sioux turned to new religions for comfort. One of these, the Ghost Dance Religion, promised its followers that the buffalo would return and that white settlers would be removed from Sioux lands. Sitting Bull, now living on a reservation, became one of the leaders of the Ghost Dancers. In 1890, the United States government, fearing Sitting Bull would lead an uprising, sent reservation police to arrest him. He resisted and was killed. Two weeks later, the army arrived at Wounded Knee Creek in South Dakota. In the **Battle of Wounded Knee**, 290 of Sitting Bull's followers were killed or wounded by the United States army. Even unarmed men, women, and children were killed. This terrible event brought the wars with Native Americans to an end. Black Elk, a Sioux, later looked back on that dark day and said, "A people's dream died there."

Outlook

16. The Native Americans of the Great Plains were a proud people. They refused to live the way the United States government wanted them to live. For nearly 30 years, they fought bravely for their ways of life. Even in defeat, they did not forget their past. Today, over 1.4 million Native Americans live in the United States. Nearly half of them live on reservations. They have preserved many of their tribal customs while they farm, raise livestock, and work in tribal-owned businesses. They take great pride in keeping alive their rich cultures.

Activity: If possible, invite a Native American representative from a reservation in your area or state to come speak to the class. Or, as an alternative, take students on a field trip to a nearby reservation.

349

CHAPTER REVIEW

VOCABULARY REVIEW

▶ Select the word that best completes each sentence. On a sheet of paper, write each sentence, completing it with the correct word.

1. The Sioux had a great victory at Little Bighorn. The battle is often referred to as _____ .
   a. the Battle at Wounded Knee
   b. the Battle at Sand Creek
   c. Custer's Last Stand

2. The Dawes Act forced Native Americans to _____ .
   a. farm
   b. hunt
   c. retreat

3. A large group of Sioux were killed in _____ .
   a. the Battle at Wounded Knee
   b. Custer's Last Stand
   c. the chase to Canada's border.

4. Today, about half of all Native Americans live on _____ .
   a. riverbanks
   b. reservations
   c. mountains

SKILL BUILDER: MAKING A TIME LINE

▶ Copy the time line below onto a separate sheet of paper. Then position the events that follow in the correct place on the time line. If the events are close in time, write one above and one below the line.

1840	1850	1860	1870	1880	1890

1849 First group in the Gold Rush reaches San Francisco.

1850 California becomes a state.

1862 Homestead Act is passed.

1868 Sioux tribe wins war against United States government.

1869 Transcontinental railroad is completed.

1876 Custer's Last Stand.

1877 Crazy Horse and Chief Joseph surrender.

1886 Geronimo surrenders.

1887 Dawes Act is passed.

1890 The frontier comes to an end.

SKILL BUILDER: CRITICAL THINKING AND COMPREHENSION

I. Fact *versus* Opinion

A. On a separate sheet of paper, write a fact about each of the following.
  1. buffalo
  2. reservations
  3. General Custer
  4. Red Cloud

B. Now write a statement of opinion about each of the above.

C. On a separate sheet of paper, identify each of the following statements as a fact or an opinion. Rewrite each opinion as a fact.

  1. Miners should not have trespassed on the land of Native Americans.

  2. Over half of all Native Americans live on reservations today.

  3. The United States Army was right to put down the Sioux rebellion.

  4. The white settlers wiped out the buffalo on the Great Plains.

  5. General Custer should not have been made into a hero.

  6. For Native Americans, life on the reservation was different from life on the Great Plains.

II. Points of View

A. On a separate sheet of paper, write the name of the person who made each of these statements.
  1. "I am tired of fighting. . . . It is cold and we have no blankets."
  2. "A people's dream died here."

B. Now read the following statements that might have been made by people you have been reading about. Write the name of the person who made each statement.
  1. "I'll get those Sioux if it's the last thing I do."
  2. "We'll go to Canada to find peace."
  3. "I refuse to stay on this reservation any longer."

USING PRIMARY SOURCES

▶ Reread the Spotlight on Sources on page 349. Why do you think Chief Joseph finally surrendered?

ENRICHMENT

1. Read a biography of one of the Native American chiefs discussed in this chapter. What qualities made this person a good leader of his people? Share your findings with the class.

2. Imagine you are a TV news reporter at Custer's Last Stand or at Wounded Knee Creek. Write a short eyewitness account of what you see.

3. Have a class debate about the United States government's policy toward the Native Americans on the Great Plains. Was it fair to Native Americans? What other policies might have prevented war and helped preserve the Native Americans' way of life?

UNIT REVIEW

SUMMARY

Before 1840, most people in the United States still lived east of the Mississippi River. Much of the vast region that stretched from the Mississippi to the Pacific coast was the homeland of many Native American tribes. The mountain men were among the first non-Native Americans to explore the West. Americans soon learned about the rich soil, the mighty mountains, and the endless land of the West. By about 1840, American settlers began streaming west over the Santa Fe Trail and the Oregon Trail. Some settled in the Great Plains to farm the rich soil there. Others pushed still farther, into the Northwest, settling in the fertile valleys in Oregon and Washington. Then others—whites, African Americans, and Chinese—moved into the former Spanish territory of California to search for gold. Texas, another former Spanish land, also drew new American settlers to its ranches and plantations. This great flood of people, willing to face great hardships of pioneer life, opened the West during the years from the 1850s to 1880s. However, this settlement of the West also caused great suffering for Native Americans. It nearly destroyed the ways of life of the Native Americans there. Native Americans were forced to give up their lands and move to reservations.

SKILL BUILDER: READING A MAP

▶ Study the map below, then answer these questions.

1. Which state had joined the Union most recently?

2. How many states were there west of the Mississippi?

3. Name the parts of the United States that were not states.

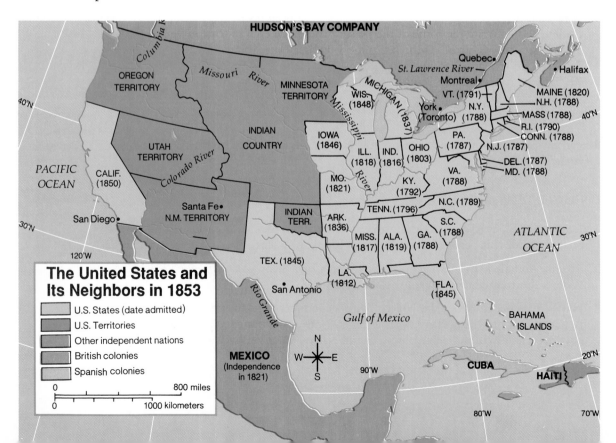

The United States and Its Neighbors in 1853
- U.S. States (date admitted)
- U.S. Territories
- Other independent nations
- British colonies
- Spanish colonies

4. Which independent country bordered the United States?

5. Which European country owned territory that bordered on the United States?

6. Which state was nearest to a Spanish colony?

7. Compare this map with the map on page 304. Name three changes that took place in the United States between 1825 and 1850.

SKILL BUILDER: CRITICAL THINKING AND COMPREHENSION

I. Comparing and Contrasting

▶ Use a separate sheet of paper to answer the following questions.

1. Compare and contrast the way Native Americans were treated at Spanish missions in California with the way they were treated by the United States government. What was similar and what was different?

2. The Mormons and the Native Americans were both people who were driven out of their homelands. How were their experiences different?

3. Compare the way Texas and California became states.

II. Drawing Conclusions

▶ The conclusion below has a set of facts that follow it. Some of the facts support the conclusion, while others do not. On a separate sheet of paper, select the number of the fact that does not support the conclusion. Then explain why it does not.

1. **Conclusion:** Much of the land of the United States west of the Mississippi was taken from Native Americans or gained from Mexico.

Facts

a. Americans carried out the idea of Manifest Destiny.

b. After the Homestead Act of 1862 was passed, large numbers of white settlers staked claims to the lands of the Great Plains.

c. United States Army troops were sent to put down the Mormon protests of 1857.

d. The United States government failed to keep its promises to the Sioux.

ENRICHMENT

1. Find or draw pictures of the different kinds of people who came to California. Label each picture.

2. Make up a story about an African American cowboy. Include facts of his life on the range and his relations with white cowboys.

UNIT 8

SLAVERY TEARS THE NATION APART

Chapter

> **UNIT OVERVIEW**   In this unit you will learn why the Northern and Southern states grew farther apart in the early 1800s.

UNIT SKILLS OBJECTIVES   In Unit 8, three critical thinking skills are emphasized:

Recognizing Cause and Effect: Recognizing the action or event that makes something happen; identifying the result of an action or event.

Making Judgments: Stating a personal opinion based on historical facts.

Comparing and Contrasting: Recognizing similarities and differences.

You will also use two important social studies skills:
Interpreting a Drawing   Making a Time Line

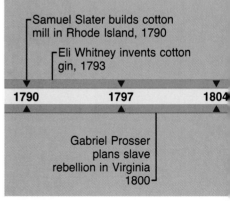

Samuel Slater builds cotton mill in Rhode Island, 1790

Eli Whitney invents cotton gin, 1793

| 1790 | 1797 | 1804 |

Gabriel Prosser plans slave rebellion in Virginia 1800

ESL/LEP Strategy: Have students work in teams to prepare lists of words or terms that describe the lives of enslaved African Americans. After students complete the unit, they should review these terms and decide which are appropriate, adding others as desired.

▲ Plantation owners in the South developed a way of life dependent on the work of African slaves. Most slaves had no say in where they lived or worked.

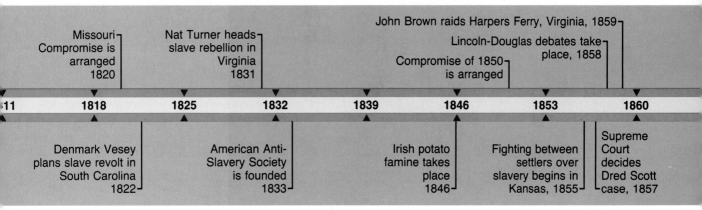

John Brown raids Harpers Ferry, Virginia, 1859

Missouri Compromise is arranged 1820

Nat Turner heads slave rebellion in Virginia 1831

Lincoln-Douglas debates take place, 1858

Compromise of 1850 is arranged

| 11 | 1818 | 1825 | 1832 | 1839 | 1846 | 1853 | 1860 |

Denmark Vesey plans slave revolt in South Carolina 1822

American Anti-Slavery Society is founded 1833

Irish potato famine takes place 1846

Fighting between settlers over slavery begins in Kansas, 1855

Supreme Court decides Dred Scott case, 1857

355

Points of View

What social issues do people in America argue about today? The rising crime rate, the shortage of affordable housing, and civil rights for minorities might come to your mind. Everyone agrees that these are problems, but many disagree about the solutions. Between the American Revolution and the Civil War, no issue caused hotter debate than slavery. Slavery created sharp divisions among Americans. Growing numbers of people in the North

ANTI-SLAVERY MEETING ON THE COMMON.

▲ Northerners against slavery frequently met in small groups to express their views and win support for the antislavery movement.

A NORTHERNER'S VIEW

❝The question of slavery is undeniably [no doubt] . . . the great question of the age. . . . Here are three million slaves in a land calling itself free; three millions of human beings robbed of every right, and, by statute [law] and custom . . . held as brutes [animals]. Knowledge is forbidden and . . . the sanctity [sacredness] of marriages is denied. . . . If slavery be [is] wrong in every way . . . let it be abolished [done away with] at once. . . . What if the black man [person] is inferior to [lower than] the white? It does not follow that he always must be. . . . His powers have never yet been fully tried [tested], for he has always had to struggle against difficulties and discouragements which white men [people] do not meet.❞

—*Slavery and the North*, Charles C. Burleigh

Slavery is Debated

attacked slavery, while white Southerners often defended it. The conflict over slavery eventually led to a civil war.

The following selections show two opposing points of view about slavery. In the first, a Northerner named Charles Burleigh gives reasons for his opposition to slavery. The second passage is a speech by James Henry Hammond, a Southern Senator and plantation owner who defended slavery.

A SOUTHERN PLANTER'S VIEW

" In all social systems there must be a class to do the mean [ordinary] duties, to perform the drudgery [hard physical work] of life. . . . Fortunately for the South, she found a race adapted to that purpose. . . . [We] call them slaves. . . . We do not think that whites should be slaves either by law or necessity. Our slaves are black, of another and inferior [lower] race. . . . They are elevated from the condition in which God first created them, by being made our slaves. . . . They are happy, content, unaspiring [without ambition], and utterly incapable, from intellectual weakness, ever to give us any trouble. **"**

—*Congressional Globe*, March 4, 1858

▲ Southern plantation families became dependent on African slaves for both farm and household work.

Using Primary Sources

1. What does Charles Burleigh think is bad about slavery? What does James Henry Hammond think is good about slavery?

2. What reasons does each writer give for believing that African slaves are inferior to white people?

357

CHAPTER 1

Slavery in the Colonies and the Young Nation

OBJECTIVE: How did slavery develop in colonial times and in the early years of the nation?

1. Suppose that tomorrow morning on your way to school, you are stopped by a curious-looking group of people. They are pale, strangely dressed, and speak a language you have never heard before. The odd-looking group throws a net over you and kidnaps you. You are taken to another planet where you are forced to work many hours a day. You cannot move around freely. If you try to escape, you are beaten severely. Other humans who have been taken to this planet help you get used to the strange ways of life there. You marry and have a family. When your children begin to grow up, however, they are taken away from you and you never see them again. Today you would see a story like this only in a science fiction or horror movie. Less than 200 years ago, however, thousands of Africans had experiences like this when they were brought to America.

Slavery Takes Root Why were free Africans captured and brought to the American colonies?

2. Slavery existed in the American colonies almost from their beginnings. As you have read, Africans first arrived in the English colonies in the early 1600s. As time went on, more and more Africans were brought to the colonies as slaves. By the time the colonies won their

▲ African poets, craftworkers, mathematicians, and inventors contributed in many ways to the growth of the young United States.

independence, about one out of every six people in America was a slave. Slavery was far more common in the plantation colonies of the South than in the farming colonies of the North.

3. African people were taken to the New World to perform hard work. By the early 1600s, Europeans had brought African slaves to

In Chapter 1 you will apply these critical thinking skills to the historical process:
Comparing and Contrasting: Recognizing similarities and differences.
Classifying: Organizing facts into categories based on what they have in common.

their colonies in the West Indies and in South America. The African slaves worked in mines and on plantations. Ships that brought African slaves to these colonies often brought them north to English colonies as well.

4. For most of the 1600s, English colonists did not buy many African slaves. They more often used indentured servants. Indentured servants signed a contract to work for a master for a certain period of time. Unlike a slave, an indentured servant was freed at the end of the term of service. The cost was less to bring over an indentured servant than to buy a slave. Many of the indentured servants brought to the colonies were white people from Europe. Others were Africans.

5. Most colonists did not think that there was anything wrong with owning African slaves. Africans spoke different languages and had different ways of life from the English. The colonists did not understand African culture. Many thought that the African race was **inferior** (in-FEER-ee-ur) to, or lower than, their own race. These opinions caused the colonists to **justify** (JUS-tuh-fy) holding Africans as slaves. To justify is to have an explanation for why people think something is right.

6. As you have read already, many Africans died on the way to the American colonies. Those who survived this terrible journey began a life in which everything was strange and new.

People in History

7. Ayuba Suleiman   Suleiman was the son of an African merchant and religious leader. He followed the Muslim religion and could read and write in the Arabic language. In 1730, at the age of about 30, Suleiman was captured and put aboard a slave ship. He was taken to Maryland, where he was sold to a tobacco plantation owner. Suleiman soon escaped from the plantation, but he was captured and jailed. While in jail Suleiman met Thomas Bluett, a lawyer from England. Bluett was impressed with the African slave's intelligence and helped him escape. In 1734, Suleiman returned to his

home in Africa. How might Suleiman's early background in Africa have helped him gain freedom? Suleiman's success shows that escape from slavery was possible with the help of white people.

8. African slaves who had lived for a time in the American colonies helped newly arrived Africans get used to their new lives. Africans learned the English language, and many became Christians. They did not, however, forget their African heritage. They kept many African folk tales, songs, and customs alive by passing them down to their children and grandchildren.

The Southern Colonies   Why did slavery spread in the South during the 1700s?

9. In the 1700s, plantations in the South grew larger. New tobacco plantations began in Virginia and Maryland. Along the coast of South Carolina, planters grew rice and indigo. As the plantations grew, so did the demand for African slaves. Partly because it was getting more costly to bring over indentured servants, planters began to buy African slaves instead. They purchased thousands of African people from colonies in the West Indies and thousands more directly from Africa. By the time of the American Revolution, four out of ten people in Virginia and South Carolina were African slaves.

Slave Codes   What laws were passed to control the lives of African slaves?

10. Most of the American colonies passed special laws to control African slaves. These laws became known as **slave codes**. The slave codes allowed owners to punish African slaves by whipping. The codes made it against the law for African slaves to run away from their owners or travel without permission. The owners could break up African slave families by selling members of the same family to different owners. African slaves could not own property. They were not allowed to vote and could not testify against a white person in court.

The Cotton Kingdom   A region is the basic unit of geographic study. Regions are defined by qualities they have in common. The Cotton Kingdom was a region united by cotton growing.

Cotton plants need a long growing season. The plants do best in areas that have at least 200 days free from frost. This limits large-scale cotton growing to areas where there are no frosts for at least seven months a year. Look at the map below. Study the line that joins places with a 200-day frost-free season. This line marks the northern limit of lands where cotton can be safely grown year after year. Growing cotton north of this line is risky.

Cotton also needs plenty of water while growing and a dry fall for the cotton bolls, or pods, to ripen. Growing cotton where rainfall totals less than 25 inches (38 centimeters) of rain a year is risky unless crops can be irrigated. More than 25 inches (38 centimeters) of rain falls each year across all parts of the South except western Texas. Most of the rain falls in summer when the cotton plants need it most. Also, the fall season is usually dry in the South, so that cotton ripens properly. Only areas along the Gulf of Mexico, where

hurricanes are common in the fall, get too much rain for cotton to ripen.

Cotton is very hard on the soil. As the soil wore out, cotton growers moved farther west to clear new lands. The spread of cotton fields across the Southwest gave unity to the region called the Cotton Kingdom.

A large labor force and much hard work was needed to grow cotton in the days before farm machinery. To obtain this labor, cotton growers bought more and more African slaves to work in the cotton fields. The plantation system of white owner and African worker spread westward along with cotton before the Civil War. The plantation system gave a social unity to the region called the Cotton Kingdom.

Now answer the following questions.

1. Where were the main cotton-growing areas in 1801?

2. What new areas were planted with cotton between 1801 and 1860?

3. Where are the best cotton-growing soils?

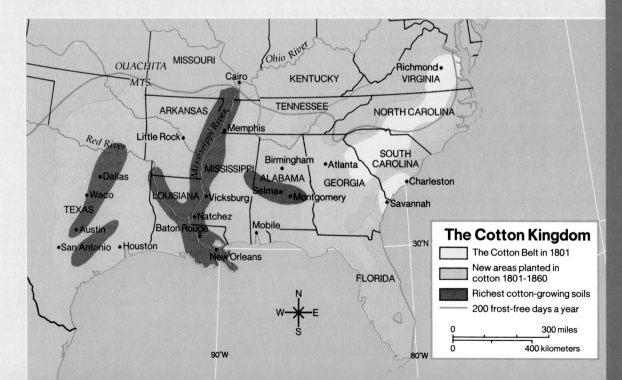

The Cotton Kingdom

- ☐ The Cotton Belt in 1801
- ☐ New areas planted in cotton 1801-1860
- ■ Richest cotton-growing soils
- — 200 frost-free days a year

0 — 300 miles
0 — 400 kilometers

Spotlight on Sources

11. The following law, passed by the Virginia colonial legislature in 1680, was part of the colony's slave code.

> . . . it shall not be lawfull for any negroe or other slave to carry or arme himself with any club. . . . gunn, sword or any other weapon . . . nor to goe or depart from . . . his masters ground without a certificate from his master, mistris or overseer, and such permission not to be granted but upon perticuler [special] and necessary occasions; and every negroe or slave soe offending not haveing a certificate . . . shalbe sent to the next constable [policeman], who is . . . required to give the said negro twenty lashes on his bare back well layd on, and soe sent home to his said master. . . .
>
> —from *The Statutes at Large,*
> ed. by William Walter Heming

▶ Why did owners want to prevent their African slaves from traveling without permits?

Free African Americans How did African slaves become free, and what were the lives of free African Americans like?

12. Although most of the African people in the American colonies lived their entire lives as slaves, some managed to win their freedom. A few ran away and began new lives as **freedmen**, or free people. Others were given their freedom by their masters. During the American Revolution, some slave owners began to think that it
▶ was wrong to enslave others. Why might the Revolution have caused the owners to think in this way? As time went on, more Northerners came to believe slavery was both unjust and unprofitable. In the 1780s and 1790s, many Northern states passed laws to do away with slavery. By the early years of the 1800s, all states from Pennsylvania north had agreed to free the African slaves within their borders.

13. The lives of free Africans were different from those of slaves in some ways, but like them in others. Unlike slaves, free Africans could legally marry and travel as they pleased. They could receive pay for their work and own property. Quite a few free Africans owned small farms or shops. Free Africans, however, were forced to live under many restrictions. Like Africans who were slaves, they could not vote or testify in court against white people in most states. Free Africans were also in danger of being kidnapped and sold into slavery.

The Cotton Kingdom How did the spread of cotton farming affect slavery in the South?

14. At the same time slavery was decreasing in the North, it was increasing in the South. The main reason for this was the increase of cotton growing in the South. Until about 1800, not much cotton was grown in the South. The climate and soil in the South were ideal for growing cotton. However, the tiny cotton seeds had to be separated by hand from the fiber, the part used to make thread. Separating the seeds by hand took a long time. In 1793, Eli Whitney invented the cotton gin, a machine that removed the seeds quickly. Cotton growing became very profitable. The planters became rich and bought more African slaves to work in the cotton fields.

15. In the early 1800s, some Southerners moved west to set up more cotton plantations. The climate in the new states of Georgia, Tennessee, Alabama, and Mississippi was also ideal for growing cotton. By about 1820, cotton was the most important crop in the South. Southern planters began to depend even more heavily on African slave labor.

Outlook

16. At the time the Cotton Kingdom was growing in the South, slavery was ending in the North. The nation was dividing into free states and slave states. Before long, the presence of slavery in only part of the nation would become a source of conflict. Why did the South have a greater interest in keeping slavery?

Discuss: Locate West Africa and Europe in relation to the United States on a wall map. Compare a voyage of African immigrants to America with that of European immigrants. Remind students of the Triangle Trade, studied in Unit 4 Chapter 2.

361

CHAPTER REVIEW

VOCABULARY REVIEW

▶ Choose the best definition for each of these words.

1. inferior
   a. lower than
   b. without feeling
   c. higher than
   d. below ground level

2. justify
   a. to explain fully
   b. to have an explanation for why something is right
   c. to figure out
   d. to be mistaken

3. slave codes
   a. codes of honor among African slaves
   b. codes used to pass secret messages between free African Americans and slaves
   c. laws passed in the American colonies to control African slaves
   d. codes used in the education of young slaves

4. freedmen
   a. men who worked to free slaves
   b. people brought over on ships to work in the colonies
   c. free African Americans
   d. indentured servants

SKILL BUILDER: USING AN ENCYCLOPEDIA

▶ Use an encyclopedia to find more information on one of the topics below. Take notes from the encyclopedia article. Use your notes to write a paragraph or two on the topic you chose.

1. beginnings of slavery in the New World

2. working conditions of African slaves

3. living conditions of African slaves

4. religion, education, and culture of African slaves

SKILL BUILDER: CRITICAL THINKING AND COMPREHENSION

I. Classifying

1. Classify the following states according to whether they were free states or slave states.

Pennsylvania

Massachusetts

South Carolina

Tennessee

New Jersey

Connecticut

Maryland

2. Classify the following conditions as "good for growing cotton" or "bad for growing cotton." Review the "Linking Geography and History" feature, page 360, if you need help.

long cool summers

sandy soil

200 frost-free days

rain during growing season

rain during harvest

frost before harvest

frost during growing season

dry weather during harvest

II. Making Judgments

▶ Imagine that you are a judge in North Carolina in 1805. Read the cases below. Make a judgment about whether the action described is legal or not.

1. George Abbot, an African American slave from Raleigh, North Carolina, traveled to Charleston, South Carolina. He did not have written permission from his master. His master found him in Charleston and had him whipped.

2. Amity Abbot, George's 12-year-old daughter, was sold to a planter in Tennessee.

3. The master freed Herbert Abbot, George's 21-year-old son. Herbert votes in the next North Carolina election.

4. Philip Abbot, George's 18-year-old son, carries a gun at all times for protection.

USING PRIMARY SOURCES

▶ Reread the passage from Virginia's slave code in paragraph 11. Imagine that you are an African American slave in the late 1600s who has learned about this code. Write down your reactions in a letter to a friend.

ENRICHMENT

1. Imagine that Eli Whitney, the inventor of the cotton gin, has come back to life. Work with another student to role-play a conversation with Whitney. Tell Whitney about the good and bad results that came from his invention.

2. Reread the information about slave codes in paragraphs 10 and 11. Design a poster warning slaves of these rules. Illustrate your poster with drawings.

3. Reread the feature about Ayuba Suleiman, paragraph 7. Work with other students to create a drama based on his experiences. Use your imagination to create conversations he might have had with the people who captured him in Africa, the Maryland plantation owner who bought him, and Thomas Bluett, who helped escape. End with a scene showing his arrival back in Africa.

4. Use encyclopedias, books about African American history, and other reference books to find out more about contributions of African Americans to colonial life. You might choose Jupiter Hammon or Phyllis Wheatley, both poets; James Derham, a physician in New Orleans; or Benjamin Banneker, a scientist and mathematician who helped plan the city of Washington, D.C. Write out your report and read it to the class.

CHAPTER 2

Southern Planters, Farmers, and African American Slaves

> **OBJECTIVE:** How did the people of the South live before 1860?

1. The sale of property from a household is usually an interesting neighborhood event. People gather around, curious about how much items from the household will bring. For African slaves in the 1800s, however, the selling of household property could bring tragedy. The slaves themselves were part of that property. When Josiah Henson was about six years old, his family was part of the property sold from anestate. First his brothers and sisters, then his mother, were sold. When Josiah's turn came, hismother "pushed through the crowd, while the bidding for me was going on, to the spot where Riley [the person who bought Josiah's mother] was standing. She fell at his feet, and clung to his knees, entreating [begging] him in tones that a mother could only command, to buy her baby as well as herself, and to spare to her one, at least, of her little ones. . . ." Riley answered Josiah's mother by kicking her away. "As she crawled away from the brutal man I heard her sob out, 'Oh, Lord Jesus, how long, how long shall I suffer this way!'" Scenes such as this were not rare in the 1800s. Because slaves were thought to be property, they were completely dependent on the wishes of their owner. Some owners respected the feelings of their slaves, and some did not. Not all Southerners owned slaves, but in different ways, slavery touched the lives of nearly everyone in the South.

▲ Many white Southern landowners thought owning African American slaves was a mark of respectability as well as a profitable investment.

Small Farmers How did small farmers in the South make a living, and why did they support slavery?

2. Most of the white people in the South were small farmers who could not afford to own slaves. Members of these farm families did all

In Chapter 2 you will apply these critical thinking skills to the historical process:

▲ **Identifying Fact *versus* Opinion:** Specifying whether information can be proved or whether it expresses feelings or beliefs.

▰ **Making Judgments:** Stating a personal opinion based on historical facts.

the chores around their home themselves. They worked in the fields, growing corn and other vegetables to feed themselves and their work animals. They had chickens and pigs that they raised for food, and they hunted and fished. Many of them also grew small crops of cotton or tobacco, which they sold to make money. Some small farmers owned a few African slaves, but these farmers' lives were very different from those of plantation owners. These small farmers worked alongside their slaves and sometimes shared the same cabin with them. Many small farmers in the South lived near plantations. They often attended the same church and shopped at the same stores as the plantation owners. Even so, the plantation owners looked down on the smaller farmers. Farmers who did not own slaves resented the superior attitudes of the plantation owners.

3. Few small farmers in the South, however, wanted to do away with slavery. Almost all of these farmers had lived in slave states nearly all their lives. They were used to a system in which some people owned other people. Many hoped one day to own slaves themselves. Like other Southern whites, they also feared that the African's hatred of slavery might explode in violent rebellion. White men who did not own slaves often served on **patrols**, or groups responsible for catching runaway slaves.

Plantations Why were large plantations important to Southern life?

4. Between 1800 and 1860, about half of the Africans in the South lived as slaves on plantations. Plantations were large farms where many slaves worked growing cash crops. Cash crops, you will remember, are crops that are grown to be sold. Tobacco was the most important cash crop in Maryland, Virginia, North Carolina, Kentucky, and Tennessee. Sugar cane was grown in parts of Louisiana. Nearly everywhere else, cotton was king. By the 1830s, cotton had become the most important export of the entire United States. Far more African slaves worked growing cotton than any other cash crop.

What are some cash crops produced in the ◀ United States today?

5. Planters, or plantation owners, were a small minority of the Southern white population, but they were very powerful. Only about one out of 20 white people in the South were planters or members of plantation families. Those few people owned the most fertile land in the South and most of the slaves. Each planter owned at least 20 slaves, and some owned more than 100.

6. Ownership of Africans as slaves made it possible for planters and their families to live without working the land themselves. In fact, many planters had little to do with the day-to-day operations of farming. Instead, they hired **overseers** to supervise their enslaved workers. The planters sold their crops. The planters' wealth allowed them to travel, gain a higher education, and hold political offices. These experiences were beyond what most people in the South could afford. Planters' wives and daughters also had African slaves who worked for them as household servants. They cooked, cleaned, did laundry, and took care of children. The planters' wives and daughters supervised the work of these household servants and saw that their huge households ran smoothly.

African American Slaves of the Plantation What were the lives of African slaves like?

7. The lives of African slaves differed greatly from the lives of even the poorest white people. Whether they worked in the field or the planter's house, these enslaved people were denied the right to make many decisions about their everyday lives. Their owners told them how to work and where to live. Most of the food they ate and the cabins they lived in were supplied by their owners. African slaves were not allowed to come and go as they pleased. They could not marry and establish families without their owners' permission. Although some slaves lived in families, their owners could separate husbands from their wives and parents from their children. African slaves could at any time be sold

Ask: In what ways were the lives of African American plantation slaves different from the lives of white owners of small farmers in the South? In what ways were they similar?

365

to another owner or moved to another state. When that happened, they had to leave their family and friends behind. Few African slaves escaped the pain of forced separation from their loved ones.

8. African slaves did nearly all the hard physical labor on the plantations. They worked long hours, usually every day except Sunday, and received no pay for their work. They had to obey all commands from their owner or overseer. Disobedience brought severe punishment, usually by whipping. On some plantations, at least one slave was whipped almost every day. On other plantations, whippings were rare. But all African slaves worked under the constant threat of punishment.

People in History

9. Frederick Douglass Although it was against the law to teach African slaves to read and write, a few had the chance to learn. Frederick Douglass was an African slave in Maryland. As a boy of eight, he taught himself to read and write with the help of his master's wife. When Douglass was 21, he escaped to Massachusetts. In the 1840s, Douglass began to speak at antislavery meetings. He soon became well known for his strong speeches against slavery. Douglass spent many years working to free African Americans from slavery. His autobiography, *Narrative of the Life of Frederick Douglass,* gives a detailed account of his early years in slavery.

10. On plantations most of the African slaves worked in the fields. On a typical day, a field slave rose at dawn, ate breakfast, and worked until about noon. At breakfast and lunch, the food was usually the same: cornbread, molasses, and a little bacon. After a short rest and lunch, work began again and continued until dark. Women who were slaves worked beside the men, and children often began field work as early as age ten. The overseers kept close watch over all the work. They punished slaves that they thought worked too slowly or carelessly.

Spotlight on Sources 🦅

11. Solomon Northrup, a former slave, described the work of field slaves on a cotton plantation in Louisiana. The cotton fields, he explained, were hoed four times a season to remove weeds. The hours were long and the pace of work was backbreaking.

> During all these hoeings the overseer or driver [supervisor] follows the slaves on horseback with a whip. . . . The fastest hoer takes the lead row. He is usually about a rod [sixteen feet] in advance of his companions. If one of them passes him, he is whipped. If one falls behind or is a moment idle, he is whipped. . . . The hoeing season thus continues from April until July, a field having no sooner been finished once, than it is commenced [started] again. . . . In the latter part of August begins the cotton picking season. . . . An ordinary day's work is two hundred pounds [of picked cotton]. A slave who is accustomed to [used to] picking, is punished, if he or she brings in a less quantity than that.
>
> —from *Twelve Years a Slave: Narrative of Solomon Northrup,* Solomon Northrup

How did the overseers make sure the slaves ◀ were working hard?

12. African house slaves had very different duties from those of their friends and relatives who worked in the fields. Their work as house servants kept them in close contact with the planter's family. As a result, Africans who were house slaves sometimes became close to their owners. Their working conditions might be better than those of field slaves, but house slaves were still slaves. They were still considered to be the property of their owners.

African Americans Culture   How did African Americans keep their own traditions alive?

13. African American slaves did not simply accept their owner's control over their lives.

They hated slavery and looked forward to a day when they could be free. They could not express those ideas openly, but they found ways to do so in private. Why do you think slaves had to hide their true feelings about slavery?

14. Some masters did not allow their slaves to gather together in groups, for fear of revolt. Others, however, encouraged them to attend religious meetings with other slaves and to become Christians. African slaves developed their own understanding of the Bible. To them, the "promised land" of the Old Testament was a world in which they would be free. They created songs or **spirituals** (SPIR-i-choo-uhlz) that expressed their longing to be free. Many African American spirituals are still sung today. The words to one of these songs are:

> Go down, Moses,
> Way down in Egypt's land.
> Tell old Pharaoh
> To let my people go.

15. African slaves struggled to protect their families. The laws of Southern states did not consider marriage between slaves as legal. However, many slaves had marriage ceremonies that they and their owners regarded as binding, even if the law did not. African parents loved their children, and did what they could to protect them. Sometimes they took into their own families children who had been separated from their parents. Family life was important in Africa, and Africans in America continued to value their families.

16. Within the harsh rules of slavery, Africans enjoyed a few privileges. At Christmas, most slaves were allowed to visit friends and relatives nearby. Many plantation owners allowed their slaves to tend their own gardens or raise chickens or pigs. Slaves could eat the vegetables and meat they raised or earn a little money by selling them. These small privileges sometimes made the hard lives of enslaved Africans easier to bear. Nevertheless, they wanted to be free, so that their lives would not be under the control of their owners.

▲ An overseer supervises African field slaves. Do you think that the artist who did this painting thought that the overseer had a hard job?

Outlook

17. Slavery affected everyone who lived on the farms and plantations of the South. The Southern planters benefited from slavery and praised it as a good thing. Most white farmers who did not own African slaves also seldom questioned it. Enslaved Africans, however, hated slavery and wanted to be free. As time passed, growing numbers of people in the North also came to oppose slavery. Both Southerners and Northerners would soon be forced to either defend slavery or join the struggle to do away with it. Why did Southern planters feel that their way of life would be destroyed if slavery was abolished?

367

CHAPTER REVIEW

VOCABULARY REVIEW

▶ Select the word that best completes each sentence. On a clean sheet of paper, write the complete sentence. Underline twice the word you selected.

planter(s)   overseer(s)

patrol(s)   spiritual(s)

1. A Southern _____ was the owner of a large farm and many slaves.

2. _____ were groups of white people who tried to capture runaway slaves.

3. Supervisors who directed the labor of field slaves were called _____ .

4. Slaves often expressed their desire for freedom in songs known as _____ .

SKILL BUILDER: READING A MAP

▶ The map below shows the population of African slaves in the United States about ten years before the outbreak of the Civil War. Study the map. Then answer the questions that follow.

1. What states had places where more than 50 percent of the population was made up of African slaves?

2. Which states were free, that is, they had no slaves?

3. What is the area farthest west that had African slaves as part of its population?

4. Compare this map with the map on page 360. Make a generalization about the relationship of cotton growing and African slave population.

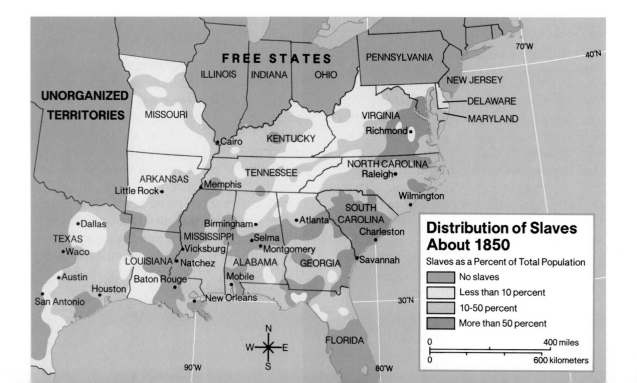

Distribution of Slaves About 1850

Slaves as a Percent of Total Population

- No slaves
- Less than 10 percent
- 10-50 percent
- More than 50 percent

SKILL BUILDING: CRITICAL THINKING AND COMPREHENSION

I. Fact *versus* Opinion

▶ Number your paper from 1 to 5. Read the sentences below. Decide which are fact and which are opinion. Write an *F* beside the number if the statement is a fact, an *O* if it is an opinion.

1. Anyone who wants to own a slave should be allowed to buy one.

2. It would have been better if the planters had not allowed their farms to grow so big.

3. Plantation owners should have worked in the fields with their slaves.

4. Some small farmers worked in the fields alongside their slaves.

5. Frederick Douglass became famous for his skill in speaking.

II. Making Judgments

▶ Answer the questions below on a separate sheet of paper.

1. Do you think the life of the average house slave was better than the life of the average field slave? Why or why not?

2. If a planter and his family were kind to their slaves, were the slaves better off than if they had been free? Why or why not?

III. Point of View

▶ Number your paper from 1 to 5. Read the statements below. If the statement reflects the point of view of the planters, write a *P* next to the number. If it reflects the point of view of the slaves, write an *S* next to the number.

1. Slaves should be allowed to travel without special permission.

2. We can only express our opinions about slavery freely in songs.

3. A planter should sell a troublesome slave if possible, even if it means breaking up the slave's family.

4. It is better to not give the slaves any legal rights. They are not educated well enough to use these rights responsibly.

USING PRIMARY SOURCES

▶ Review the lines from the song in paragraph 14. What do the words to this song mean?

ENRICHMENT

1. Imagine that you are an African American slave who has escaped from a plantation to the North. A reporter for a newspaper wants to know what your life as a slave was like. Make some notes to prepare for your interview. Then present the information to the class.

2. Find out more about staple crops that were grown in the South. What were tobacco, sugar cane, and cotton used for? Which crops were exported to Europe? What types of jobs were connected with growing each crop?

CHAPTER 3

African American Slaves Resist Slavery

OBJECTIVE: How did slaves show their hatred of slavery?

1. Can you imagine yourself in a package that was mailed from state to state? Henry "Box" Brown was. Brown, an African American slave, put himself in a wooden box and had himself mailed from Virginia to Pennsylvania. The trip was uncomfortable, but when he got out of the box, he was a free man. If African Americans did or said anything that showed that they disliked slavery, they faced severe punishment. For attacking a white person or starting a revolt, slaves were usually punished by death. But they still found many ways to resist slavery.

African American Slave Resistance How did African Americans show their dislike of slavery?

2. African American slaves resisted slavery in many ways. For example, a slave might pretend not to understand a command. A group of African American slaves might agree to slow down the pace of work in the fields. At times slaves damaged crops or broke tools and claimed that it was an accident. In these ways, slaves were able to make trouble for their owners without being found out.

3. Some African American slaves tried to gain their freedom by running away. After escaping their owners, many began the long, risky trip to a Northern free state. Others tried to live by themselves in the woods or swamps,

▲ Runaway African American slaves faced many risks as they traveled toward freedom. What risks are shown in this painting?

and still others pretended they were free. Some traveled west or south to live with Native American tribes such as the Seminoles of Florida. Whatever escape method was chosen, the way to freedom was difficult and dangerous. An escaped slave was considered to be a criminal. This person would immediately become a

In Chapter 3 you will apply these critical thinking skills to the historical process:
○ **Generalizing:** Making a statement that links several facts.

⇨ **Recognizing Cause and Effect:** Recognizing the action or event that makes something happen; identifying the result of an action or event.

fugitive (FYU-jih-tiv) from the law. A fugitive is a runaway. Fugitives had a better chance of escaping if they traveled alone. For this reason, escape usually meant leaving family and friends behind. The fugitives also had to be able to survive in the woods and avoid patrols set up to capture them.

4. Not many fugitives escaped slavery for long. Hunger, fear, and loneliness led some runaways to return to their owners. Other fugitives were caught by patrols or slave-catchers. Once in a while, a runaway who had been living as a free person for a long time would be captured and returned to slavery.

Spotlight on Sources

5. Newspapers in the South regularly carried notices about fugitive African American slaves. If you were reading a newspaper in Raleigh, North Carolina, in 1818, you might have seen this advertisement:

FIFTY DOLLARS REWARD Ran Away from the subscriber, living in Franklin county, a Negro Man named Randol about 26 or 27 years of age, between 5 and 6 feet high, rather yellow complected [has yellow-colored skin]; appears humble when spoken to. It is expected he has some marks of shot about his hips, thighs, neck and face, as he has been shot at several times. His wife belongs to Mr. Henry Bridges, formerly of this county, who started [out] with her about the 14th. instant [December 14], to South-Carolina, Georgia or Tennessee. It is supposed he will attempt to follow her. This is to caution all persons harboring or trading for said Negro. And all masters of vessels [ships] are forbid having anything to do with him.

—*Register* [Raleigh, NC], February 20, 1818

What does this notice tell you about why Randol probably wanted to escape from slavery? Why do you think Randol was "shot at"?

6. Although most runaways did not succeed in gaining their freedom, some did. At least

several thousand African slaves reached the free states or Canada, where they began new lives. Dozens of successful runaways spoke and wrote against slavery. A few published books telling about their lives in bondage and their escape to freedom. Frederick Douglass, whom you read about in Chapter 2, was the most famous of these former slaves.

White Opponents of Slavery Why did some white people support freedom for African slaves in the late 1700s and early 1800s?

7. Enslaved and free Africans were not the only Americans opposed to slavery in the late 1700s and early 1800s. Some white people also wanted to see slavery ended. Most of these people lived in the industrial Northern states. Northerners had freed their African American slaves in the years after the American Revolution. In addition, some Southerners were convinced that slavery was wrong and freed their slaves. Many white people against slavery were members of religious groups such as the Quakers that thought slavery was immoral.

8. Most of the white opponents of slavery during this period did not want to see African Americans **emancipated** (ih-MAN-suh-pay-tud) all at once. To emancipate means to set free. Antislavery whites usually wanted to have African American slaves in the South set free over a period of many years. The Northern states had freed their African slaves in this way. Some opponents of slavery wanted freed slaves to be sent from the United States to Africa. A group called the **American Colonization Society** was formed in 1817 to ship freed slaves to Africa. Five years later, they began sending freed African Americans to a new African country called Liberia. But few of the former slaves wanted to go to Africa. Why do you think freed Africans would hesitate to return to Africa?

The Underground Railroad How were slaves helped to escape to freedom in the North?

9. Some Northerners helped escaped slaves to reach freedom. They allowed runaways to

Ask: If slaves wanted to be free so badly, why did they not start more revolts or run away more often than they did?

371

hide in their homes and sometimes guided them to other free states or Canada. The network of Northerners who helped slaves escape slavery ▶ was called the **underground railroad**. Why do you think it was given this name? The "conductors" on the underground railroad put themselves in great danger. It was illegal to help slaves escape. The Fugitive Slave Law, passed by Congress in 1793, required that slaves who escaped to the North be captured and returned to their owners. Slaves could not be completely sure of their freedom until they reached Canada.

People in History

10. Harriet Tubman A former slave who guided other slaves to freedom, Harriet Tub-

▼ Harriet Tubman was called "Moses" by some of her fellow African Americans. Why might she have been given this nickname?

man was a very important conductor of the underground railroad. Tubman was born a slave in Maryland around 1821. In 1849, she ran away from her owner and escaped to Philadelphia with the help of several white abolitionists. In the following years Tubman made about twenty trips into the South. From there she led about 300 slaves to new lives in the North. She even managed to rescue her own parents. Tubman was hated by Southern slaveholders and Northerners who opposed the antislavery movement. Southern slaveowners offered a $40,000 reward for her capture. In 1860, Tubman was attacked by a Northern mob and beaten badly. But she outsmarted her enemies to live a long and full life.

African Slave Revolts What African slave uprisings took place in the early 1800s?

11. From time to time, groups of Africans tried to win their freedom by force. Revolts required large numbers of African slaves and careful planning. It was hard for large numbers of African slaves to meet and to keep their plans secret. Some uprisings were discovered before they could take place. In 1800, an African slave named Gabriel Prosser planned a major uprising in the area around Richmond, Virginia. More than 1,000 African slaves learned about the plan through word of mouth. Several hundred had weapons and were ready to fight in Prosser's revolt. Before the plot could be carried out, some African slaves who knew of the plan informed city officials in Richmond. Many African slaves were captured, and about 20, including Prosser, were executed.

12. In 1822, South Carolina was stunned by the discovery of plans for another slave revolt. The plot was organized by Denmark Vesey, a free African American who lived in Charleston. Vesey and several friends secretly planned to **recruit** (ree-KROOT), or gather together, an army of African slaves to attack Charleston. Probably several thousand African slaves knew of the plot. Vesey's plans, however, were discovered, and the revolt never took place. The leaders of the revolt received swift punishment. Vesey and over thirty others were hanged.

13. In 1831, an African slave revolt took place in Virginia that shocked the entire South. It was led by an African slave named Nat Turner. Turner believed that God had instructed him to lead an uprising against slavery. One August night, Turner and five other African slaves began to attack farm owners and their families in Virginia. They were soon joined by about 60 other African slaves. It took two days for a large group of armed white men to stop the revolt. By this time, about 60 whites had been killed. Once again, the captured Africans faced terrible penalties. Turner was hanged. Over 100 African slaves lost their lives because of the revolt.

Stronger Slave Codes

What stronger slave laws were passed to prevent slave revolts, and how did they affect the slaves?

14. The revolts led by Vesey, Turner, and others caused Southern whites to try to prevent other uprisings. As a result, Southern states passed new slave codes that were harsher than before. Some of the new laws made it a crime for groups of slaves to meet together unless there was a white person present. Other new laws aimed at preventing slaves from reading antislavery books. Some states made it a crime to send such books into the state. It also became illegal for a slave to learn to read and write. Some Southerners believed that free blacks were a bad influence on slaves. For this reason, many states passed laws that made it more difficult for owners to set their slaves free. The changes in the slave codes brought new restrictions to the lives of all African Americans.

15. The fear of slave revolts also caused slave owners to be suspicious of slaves who did not seem rebellious. Many masters tightened their control over their slaves. Sometimes they stopped allowing slaves to leave the plantation to go to church or visit friends. Other times, they were quicker to punish slaves who worked slowly or refused to carry out orders.

▲ Nat Turner, shown here with a group of his followers, was a convincing speaker who had learned to read and write.

Outlook

16. The resistance of slaves to slavery had important results. By running away and rebelling, slaves showed their hatred of slavery and their desire for freedom. Their opposition helped convince many people in the North that slavery was wrong. As a result, Northern opposition to slavery grew stronger. The slaves' resistance had different effects in the South. Slaveholders and other white people grew nervous that the slaves would start violent revolts. They kept close watch over their slaves and criticized Northerners who opposed slavery. What ideas about African Americans in the 1800s were challenged by the slave revolts? ◄

373

VOCABULARY REVIEW

▶ Match the word on the left with its correct definition on the right.

1. fugitive

2. emancipate

3. American Colonization Society

4. underground railroad

5. recruit

a. a person running away from the law

b. an organization that wanted to send freed slaves to Africa

c. to gather a group together

d. to set free

e. a famous slave revolt in the 1800s

f. the network of Northerners who helped slaves escape slavery

SKILL BUILDER: READING A MAP

▶ Use the map below to answer these questions.

1. Does the escape route from South Carolina go by land or by sea?

2. If you were a slave in Louisiana, what cities would be the closest links to the North?

3. Name a state that had four or more Underground Railway routes.

4. What states would a slave from Georgia have to pass thorugh before reaching north?

5. Describe a route from Kentucky to Canada that goes partly by land and partly by water.

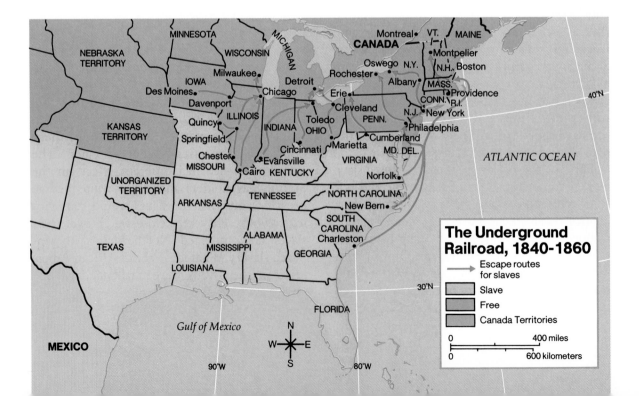

The Underground Railroad, 1840-1860

SKILL BUILDER: CRITICAL THINKING AND COMPREHENSION

○ I. Generalizing

▶ Make generalizations to answer the following questions. Write your answers in complete sentences.

1. What happened when slaves tried to become free and failed?

2. What happened if a group of slaves were caught planning armed revolt?

3. Where did most slaves want to go when they escaped?

➡ II. Cause and Effect

▶ Imagine that you bought a newspaper in 1815. One of the articles was ruined when you got caught in the rain. Copy the article on a separate sheet of paper and fill in the missing parts.

SLAVE REVOLTS

Denmark Vesey and others were hanged today because _____ . This could be another effect of books such as that encourage rebellion. Because of the increase in slave rebellions, Southern slave-owners are _____ . Many Northerners, however, have a different view. The increase in slave revolts has convinced them that _____ .

❯ III. Predicting

▶ Answer the questions below by making predictions. Give a reason for each prediction based on information from Chapter 3.

1. What will happen to the American Colonization Society in the 1830s?

2. Will more antislavery literature be published in the North in the 1830s?

3. Will slave codes become more lenient by 1850?

USING PRIMARY SOURCES

▶ Reread paragraph 5. Franklin County is the county northeast of Raleigh. Look at a map of North Carolina. If Randol wanted to escape by sea, how far would he have to travel?

ENRICHMENT

○○ 1. Work with several of your classmates to prepare a skit about slaves planning an escape. Compare the attractions of possible freedom with the dangers of becoming a fugitive.

2. Use the map on the opposite page to plan an escape route from the northern border of Kentucky to Canada.

CHAPTER 4

Factories Grow in the Northeast

OBJECTIVE: How did the Northeast become the nation's manufacturing center?

1. The spinning machine, invented in 1769, was one of the most complicated machines in the world. A 21-year-old Englishman, however, had it memorized down to the last part. He had worked on these machines since he was 14. Now he was in America, where he offered to build a spinning machine for some New England factory owners. The owners were thrilled. They had been trying to figure out how to make these machines for years. In 1790, the young Englishman, Samuel Slater, built the first successful spinning machine in the United States.

Textile Machinery What machines were invented in England and America to produce factory-made cloth?

2. Slater's success was part of a change that was taking place in the way goods were manufactured. Before, people made goods such as cloth, shoes, and clocks at home or in small workshops. Now, they began to manufacture goods using machinery in large factories. This change came to be known as the **Industrial Revolution**.

3. The invention of new machines in the late 1700s and early 1800s changed the way cloth was made. Before that time, all the steps in making cloth were done by hand, usually by women working in their homes. In the 1700s,

▲ This scene from a textile mill in the early 1800s shows part of the process of spinning cotton into thread.

English inventors created a machine called the spinning frame. This machine could spin yarn many times faster than the spinning wheels that had been used for hundreds of years. The new machine was powered by water moving over a mill wheel. Factories that produced yarn with these machines were called **mills**. Around 1815,

In Chapter 4 you will apply these critical thinking skills to the historical process:
○ **Generalizing:** Making a statement that links several facts.

➡ **Recognizing Cause and Effect:** Recognizing the action or event that makes something happen; identifying the result of an action or event.

the invention of the power loom changed the way cloth was made. Before, factory-made yarn had to be woven on hand looms. These new machines made it possible to make cloth much faster and more cheaply.

People in History

4. Samuel Slater The first person to build the new machines in America was Samuel Slater. The British government had passed laws to keep the machines in England. They could not be exported, and no plans or drawings of them could leave the country. It was even forbidden for **textile** workers to leave the country. Textile is another word for cloth. Slater disguised himself as a farm boy and left England in 1798. The factory owners who hired Slater opened the first spinning mill in the United States in Pawtucket, Rhode Island. Slater also taught other people how to set up textile factories. How did Slater's work increase the demand for cotton in the South?

Early New England Factories   Why were the first factories built in New England?

5. New England had many advantages as a region where textile mills and other industries could succeed. New England had swiftly flowing rivers that could provide water power for the machinery. Some New Englanders were wealthy enough to buy machinery and hire workers. Often the owners joined together to build large mill towns with housing for workers. In addition, New England had plenty of workers. Most of these were children or young women from farm families.

6. Textiles were not the only products made in New England factories. By the early 1800s, shoes, guns, clocks, and other items were being made there. Some of the new factories depended on machinery, but others did not. Before the rise of shoe factories, one skilled worker would make a pair of shoes from start to finish. But a factory-made shoe was put together by many different workers, with each worker doing

only one or two tasks. Factory owners could hire less skilled workers at lower wages and produce goods more cheaply than a skilled craftmaker could. As a result, many craftworkers faced hard times when they had to compete with large factories.

Northern Industries   How did the North come to depend on textiles and other industries?

7. New industries developed rapidly in the North between about 1800 and 1860. Different types of industries arose in different parts of the North. Textile and shoe factories were found mainly in New England. Buffalo, New York, and Chicago, Illinois, became flour milling centers. Cincinnati, Ohio, was known for meatpacking. Pittsburgh, Pennsylvania, was a steel and glass center. Although most Northerners during this time still worked on farms, the number of industrial workers grew rapidly. By 1860, about one out of five workers in the North had a job in manufacturing.

Spotlight on Sources

8. Northerners took jobs in factories for different reasons. Many workers in cotton mills were young people from nearby farms and small towns. Some of them had worked their whole lives on a farm and were ready for a change. In some parts of the Northeast, there was little land available for young men and women who wanted to set up their own farms. A large number of immigrants also became factory workers. Why would immigrants be likely to take jobs in factories? In the following passage, a woman recalls how life changed for young women who left small towns for the mill.

> It was an all-day ride, but that was nothing to be dreaded. It gave them a chance to behold [see] other towns and places, and see more of the world than most of their generation had ever been able to see. They went in their plain, country-made clothes, and, after working several months, would come home for a visit, or perhaps to be

Ask: Using a wall map, ask students to locate the cities mentioned in paragraph 7. What advantage did each city have that would help industry grow there? (Examples might be nearness to natural resources, crops such as wheat, and available water transportation.)

377

THE IRISH

Today more people of Irish descent live in the United States than in all of Ireland. In colonial times, small numbers of Irish craftspeople and farmers sailed to America. More Irish came in the 1820s and 1830s, attracted by well-paying jobs building canals. The great migration of the Irish to America, however, did not begin until the 1840s. This migration was caused by the failure of a single crop—the potato.

By 1840, the potato was the main source of food for almost half of Ireland's nine million people. These were tenant farmers who rented small plots of land and cottages from wealthy landlords. Growing potatoes was practical. The crop required little land, labor, or equipment. In the summers of 1845 and 1846, disaster struck. A **blight**, or disease, caused the potato crops to rot in the ground. A terrible **famine** (FAM-uhn) spread throughout Ireland. A famine is a severe shortage of food. Families unable to pay their rent were turned out of their farms. Homeless and hungry, they easily became sick. By the time the potato crops returned to normal in 1850, 750,000 people had died of starvation or disease. For thousands of Irish, leaving the country was their only hope for survival.

Although they had been farmers in the old country, most Irish immigrants became city dwellers here. Few had the money to buy land or farm equipment. The newcomers quickly found jobs in Northern cities, especially Boston and New York. Irish men became dock workers or factory workers. Irish women often worked as servants. Those Irish who went west became laborers. Many helped to build the early railroads.

All too often, the Irish met hardships. Since they had to live near their jobs, they crowded into city slums. Epidemics of disease killed thousands. Rather than helping the Irish, many native-born Americans reacted in fear. "No Irish Need Apply" appeared on many "help wanted" ads. On the stage, the Irish were made fun of as people who liked to brag and fight.

The Civil War did much to do away with this anti-Irish feeling. During the war, Irish Americans furnished at least six generals and more than 150,000 men to the Union Army. After the war, Irish Americans began to assume leadership roles throughout the country. Some entered politics and won elections in many cities. Others gained leadership positions in the Roman Catholic church and in trade unions. Their success inspired others to come to the United States. Irish immigration continued strong well into the 1900s.

▼ Irish people are boarding the coach to leave for America. This drawing was done in the 1860s. What mood do you think the artist was trying to communicate through this drawing?

Now answer the following questions.

1. Why did large numbers of Irish come to the United States in the 1840s?

2. Why did the Irish gain acceptance after the Civil War?

married, in their tasteful city dresses, and with more money in their pockets than they ever owned before.

—*The History of Sutton, New Hampshire,*
Augusta Harvey Worthen

▶ Why would a young person leave the farm to work in a mill?

9. Factory work brought new hardships along with new opportunities. Hours of work were long. Most factory workers worked about twelve hours a day, six days a week. The work was often very dull. Accidents were common with inexperienced workers using dangerous machines. Wages were usually too low to support a family if only one family member worked. Some factories hired entire families, including children as young as five. If a factory closed, the workers were left without jobs. People who left farm life for factory work found their lives changed in many ways. Once they had worked to the rhythm of the sun, seasons, and weather. Now machines and timeclocks set the pace of

▶ work. In what other ways did factory work differ from farm work?

10. The growth of factories was a sure sign that the North and South were developing in different ways. While industry was becoming important to the economy of the North, the South had very few of the nation's factories. Plantation farming remained the backbone of the Southern economy. The South sold large amounts of its cotton to the Northern textile factories. While Northern cities grew in both number and size, Southern cities lagged behind. In 1860, only one of the nation's ten largest cities, New Orleans, was located in the South. The people who lived in each section were also different. As you have seen, by the 1820s there were African slaves all over the South and hardly any slaves in the North. The community leaders of the North were wealthy factory owners. The richest and most powerful people in the South were the plantation owners. Many Northerners were factory workers, but only a few Southerners were. In addition, most of the new immigrants to the United States settled in the North instead of the South.

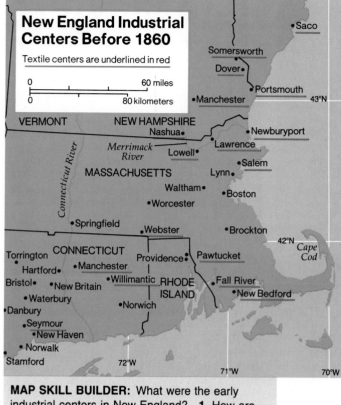

MAP SKILL BUILDER: What were the early industrial centers in New England? **1.** How are textile centers shown on the map? **2.** What textile cities were in Rhode Island?

Outlook

11. In the late 1700s, new textile-making machines were brought to the United States from England. As a result, life in the North changed. Cloth and other goods began to be made in factories rather than in small workshops. The factories opened up new jobs for young people. Many European immigrants also found jobs in the growing factory towns. As industry grew in the North, the differences between North and South became greater. The political leaders in the North were interested in protecting the factory owners. The political leaders in the South were interested in protecting the plantation owners. These differences would lead to rising disagreements among politicians and ordinary citizens alike as the middle of the 1800s approached.

CHAPTER REVIEW

VOCABULARY REVIEW

► Copy the words given below on a sheet of paper. Then write the correct definition for each word. Use the glossary at the back of the book if you need help.

Industrial Revolution

famine

blight

mills

textile

SKILL BUILDER: INTERPRETING A DRAWING

► Study the drawing below. Then answer the questions that follow.

1. Why was it important for mills to be built near running water?

2. As the water goes over the wheel, what does the wheel turn?

3. What was the purpose of the carding machine? Why were these machines needed?

4. Why might a textile mill have been a dangerous place to work?

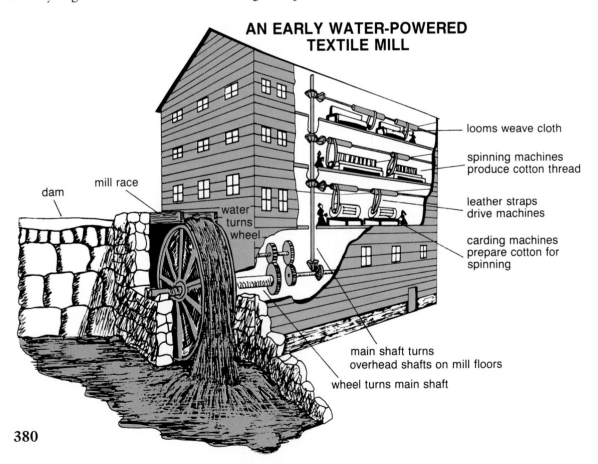

AN EARLY WATER-POWERED TEXTILE MILL

dam

mill race

water turns wheel

looms weave cloth

spinning machines produce cotton thread

leather straps drive machines

carding machines prepare cotton for spinning

main shaft turns overhead shafts on mill floors

wheel turns main shaft

STUDY
HINT

Write an answer to the chapter objective, page 376. If you need help, review the first three sections of the chapter.

SKILL BUILDER: CRITICAL THINKING AND COMPREHENSION

I. Generalizing

▶ Write a sentence or two that makes a generalization about each of the following topics.

1. the types of people who worked in the textile mills in the 1800s

2. the parts of the country where most early textile mills were found

3. the attitude of the British government about sharing plans for the new textile-making machines

4. working conditions in the early New England factories

5. conditions in Ireland that caused immigration to America in the mid-1800s

6. reactions to the Irish when they first arrived in the United States

II. Cause and Effect

▶ For each cause listed below, write an effect.

1. **Cause:** Samuel Slater memorized the plans for the spinning machine and offered to build a machine in New England.
   Effect: _____

2. **Cause:** New England had swiftly flowing rivers that could supply water power for mills.
   Effect: _____

▶ For each effect given below, write a cause.

3. **Cause:** _____
   Effect: A famine spread throughout Ireland.

4. **Cause:** _____
   Effect: Children often worked in factories.

USING PRIMARY SOURCES

▶ Reread the passage about the young women who went to work for the mills, paragraph 8. Make a list of the advantages of working in the mill as described in this passage.

ENRICHMENT

1. Imagine that in 1800, Samuel Slater meets his former boss from England at a party in Boston. Role-play the conversation that might take place.

2. Imagine that you have just left your home on a farm in New England to work in a textile mill. Write a letter to your family explaining why you took the job and what your work is like.

3. Do additional research on the textile-making machines that were developed in the late 1700s and early 1800s. Build a simple model of one of these machines, or prepare a detailed drawing with labels describing what each part does.

CHAPTER 5

Slavery Causes Bitter Feelings

OBJECTIVE: Why did slavery become a serious problem as the United States grew in size?

1. On the first day of the year 1831, a new newspaper appeared in America. There had never been anything quite like it. "Many object to the severity [harshness] of my language," wrote the editor, "but is there not cause for severity . . . ? I am in earnest . . . I will not excuse—I will not retreat a single inch—and I will be heard!" This angry writer was William Lloyd Garrison, his newspaper was *The Liberator*, and his hatred was for slavery. Garrison called owners of African slaves "murderers" and "monsters" and the United States "a horrible mockery of freedom." No one had ever attacked slavery with such language. With harsh words like Garrison's, the debate over slavery reached new heights of anger. As tempers flared, tension rose between the North and the South.

Slavery Spreads How did slavery spread into new lands in the South and the West?

2. Between about 1790 and 1820, thousands of Southern farmers and planters looked to the West for new land. The farm land of the South was becoming worn out from years of use. Rich land suitable for farming lay in neighboring territories, however. The territories of Alabama and Mississippi were especially attractive, because their soil and climate were good for growing cotton. Many Southern planters

▲ This drawing shows the Boston police breaking up an antislavery meeting in 1860. The speaker was Frederick Douglass. What groups of people are shown attending this meeting?

brought African slaves to work on the plantations. Before long, slavery was firmly established in new Southern territories. Between 1790 and 1819, five new "slave states" entered the Union: Kentucky, Tennessee, Alabama, Mississippi, and Louisiana.

In Chapter 5 you will apply these critical thinking skills to the historical process:

Sequencing: Putting a series of events in the correct time order.

Identifying Fact *versus* Opinion: Specifying whether information can be proved or whether it expresses feelings or beliefs.

3. Farmers from the Northeastern states also moved west to neighboring states to set up new farms. Hardly any slaves and very few free African Americans moved to the Northern territories. There were two main reasons for this. First, in 1787, Congress had passed a law prohibiting slavery in any territory within certain boundaries. These boundaries were to the north of the Ohio River and to the east of the Mississippi River. Second, the climate of the Northern territories was not right for crops usually grown in the South by slave laborers. When the Northern territories joined the Union as states, they all prohibited slavery. Between 1790 and 1819, four new "free states" entered the Union: Ohio, Indiana, Illinois, and the New England state of Vermont.

The Missouri Compromise   What laws were passed by Congress about slavery in the new states?

4. Not many had objected when some territories east of the Mississippi River became slave states and others became free states. But the territories west of the Mississippi River were another matter. Congress had made no laws about slavery in that region. In one of those territories, Missouri, Southerners had brought in thousands of African American slaves. In 1819, Missouri applied to join the Union as a slave state. But many Northern congressmen opposed the idea of slavery spreading farther west. They would not let Missouri become a state unless it agreed to end slavery after a period of years. Southern congressmen, joined by some Northerners, disagreed. They responded that Congress had no right to prevent people in Missouri from owning slaves if they wanted to. A long debate arose in Congress.

5. In 1820, Congress finally reached a **compromise** to settle the argument over Missouri. A compromise is an arrangement in which all sides agree to give up some of their demands. Under the Missouri Compromise, Missouri entered the Union as a slave state. To keep a balanced number of slave states and free states, Maine joined the Union as a free state. Congress also passed a law designed to prevent future disputes about slavery in the western territories. The law proposed that an imaginary line divide the territories. The line would reach from the southern boundary of Missouri (36°30′)west across the rest of the Louisiana territory. Slavery was forbidden in any territory north of that line. The Missouri Compromise cooled the debate over slavery in the territories. As you will later see, however, it did not solve the problem for long. Why do you think arguments over slavery might break out again? ◄

The Fight over the Tariff   Why did the North favor a tax on imports and why was the South against the tax?

6. The North and South disagreed on other issues, that were not directly related to slavery. One of these was the **tariff,** or tax on imports. Tariffs were one of the ways the federal government raised money. Many Northerners were in favor of high tariffs on manufactured goods shipped into America from other countries. They reasoned that these taxes would raise the price of imported products. This would allow goods manufactured in America to be sold for less. The people in New England and in the Middle Atlantic states thought this would help American factories. Why do you think Northerners would be likely to favor taxes that helped factories? ◄

7. Most people in the South objected to high tariffs. The South, which had little manufacturing, imported many manufactured products. Southerners did not want to pay higher prices for imported goods. Southerners also feared that foreign governments would react by raising tariffs on items the South exported. That would hurt Southern farmers and planters who exported cotton, tobacco, and sugarcane. Differences over the tariffs were often resolved by compromises in Congress. But these taxes remained an important source of disagreement between North and South.

Activity: Using a wall map, ask volunteers to locate the slave states and free states that entered the Union between 1790 and 1819.

The Antislavery Movement Grows How did some Northerners work to end slavery?

8. During the 1820s, some Northerners began to criticize slavery harshly. Men and women called **abolitionists** believed that Southern slavery was an evil that harmed the whole nation. They called upon slaveholders to free their slaves at once. Others warned that slave revolts would become more common unless slavery was ended in the South.

🦅 Spotlight on Sources

9. David Walker, a free African American, published a book in 1829 called *Walker's Appeal*. The book urged slaves to resist slavery by force. It warned white Americans that slavery was unjust and wrong in the eyes of God. The book caused fierce arguments. Slaveholders were outraged. A group of men in Georgia even offered a reward to anyone who would capture or kill Walker. This is what Walker wrote:

Remember, Americans, that we [African Americans] must and shall be free . . . will you wait until we shall, under God, obtain our liberty by crushing the arm of power? Will it not be dreadful for you? I speak Americans for your good. We must and shall be free I say, in spite of you. You may do your best to keep us in wretchedness [suffering] and misery, to enrich you and your children, but God will deliver us from under you. And woe, woe, will be to you if we have to obtain our freedom by fighting. Throw away your fears and prejudices then, and enlighten us and treat us like men [human beings] . . . and tell us now no more about colonization [to Africa], for America is as much our country, as it is yours.

—from *Walker's Appeal*, by David Walker

Why did Walker oppose plans to send free African Americans to Africa?

10. By the early 1830s, the abolitionists were beginning a national campaign against

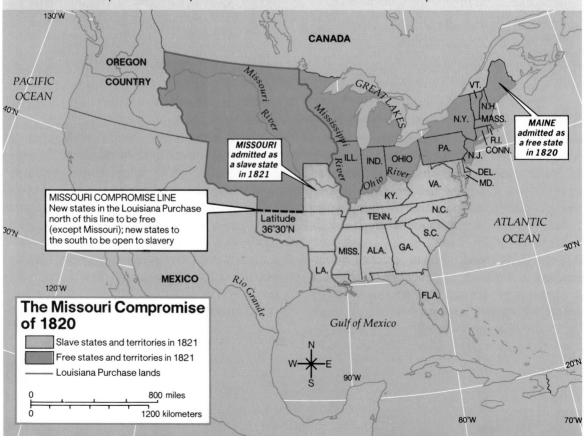

MAP SKILL BUILDER: What was the Missouri Compromise Line and how was it defined? **1.** What did the Missouri Compromise Line separate? **2.** What was the latitude of the Compromise Line?

MAINE admitted as a free state in 1820

MISSOURI admitted as a slave state in 1821

MISSOURI COMPROMISE LINE
New states in the Louisiana Purchase north of this line to be free (except Missouri); new states to the south to be open to slavery

Latitude 36°30′N

The Missouri Compromise of 1820

- Slave states and territories in 1821
- Free states and territories in 1821
- Louisiana Purchase lands

0 — 800 miles
0 — 1200 kilometers

slavery. In 1833, they formed an organization called the **American Antislavery Society**. Its leader was William Lloyd Garrison, the man who published *The Liberator*. This society and others like it included both men and women, and African Americans as well as whites. African Americans such as Frederick Douglass and Henry Highland Garnet were active in the new antislavery cause. So were women like Susan B. Anthony and Elizabeth Cady Stanton, who would later become women's rights leaders.

People in History

11. Sojourner Truth Among the women who worked to abolish slavery was a former slave named Isabella Baumfree. Baumfree was an African American slave in New York State. She escaped slavery in 1827, when she was about 30 years old. A year later, the state of New York outlawed slavery. In the 1840s, Baumfree felt that God was calling her to preach and teach. She took the name Sojourner Truth. Truth joined the abolitionist movement and soon began to give antislavery speeches throughout the North. Although Sojourner Truth had no formal education, her speeches were clear, logical, and convincing. Truth also worked hard to support the cause of women's rights. Throughout her life, however, she never stopped her efforts to gain equal rights for African Americans.

12. The influence of the abolitionists was far greater than their numbers. Abolitionists gave speeches throughout the North and in parts of the South. They also tried to persuade slaveholders to free their slaves by mailing them ▶ antislavery books and letters. Do you think many Southerners were convinced by the actions of the abolitionists?

13. Southern whites were surprised and angered by the growing antislavery movement in the North. They strongly disagreed with the abolitionists' belief that slavery was morally wrong. Southerners pointed out that slavery had existed in many societies in the past, including ancient Greece and Rome. Some Southern-

▲ Sojourner Truth was one of the most famous abolitionists of the time. Why might her speeches have been especially convincing?

ers tried to justify slavery by what they called "scientific" reasoning. They argued that black people were inferior to white people. As a result they thought it was proper that Africans be held as slaves.

Outlook

14. By the 1830s, slavery had become an issue that divided the North from the South. At the same time, Americans also understood that people in the two sections had a lot in common. Most Americans wanted to avoid conflicts that would tear the Union apart and lead to a civil war. As more territories became states, however, arguments over the spread of slavery continued. Events in the next 20 years would widen divisions between the North and South.

CHAPTER REVIEW

VOCABULARY REVIEW

▶ Use the words below to fill in the blanks in the paragraph. Use the glossary at the back of the book if you need help.

compromise(s)

abolitionist(s)

tariff(s)

During the early years of the 1800s, differences between the Northern and Southern states grew. These disagreements centered mainly on slavery. Other issues, however, such as helping northern factories by raising ___1___ , caused conflict as well. Many of these issues were resolved by ___2___ . Led by people known as ___3___ , a national campaign against slavery began in the North.

SKILL BUILDING: USING A TIME LINE

▶ Use the time line to answer the questions that follow.

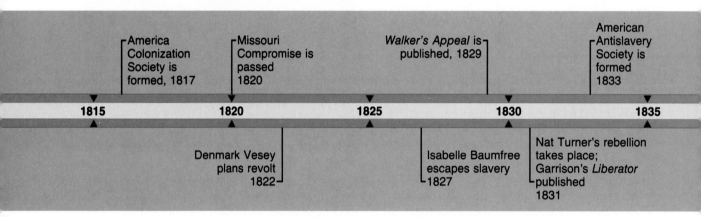

1. What publication might have encouraged Nat Turner to plan a rebellion?

2. How long after the Missouri Compromise did Turner's rebellion take place?

3. Could Denmark Vesey have read *Walker's Appeal* before planning his revolt?

4. Did the American Antislavery Society exist when Isabelle Baumfree escaped slavery?

5. How many years passed between Vesey's plot and Turner's rebellion?

6. How many years after the American Colonization Society was formed was the American Antislavery Society founded?

7. Make up an appropriate title for this time line.

SKILL BUILDER: CRITICAL THINKING AND COMPREHENSION

I. Sequencing

▶ Write the following events in the order that they happened. Begin with the earliest event and end with the latest one. Include the dates in your list.

  a. Missouri Compromise is agreed to.

  b. Congress declares that no slavery is allowed in territories north of the Ohio River.

  c. Missouri applies to join the union as a slave state.

  d. American Antislavery Society is formed.

  e. *The Liberator* is published for the first time.

II. Comparing and Contrasting

▶ Choose one of the comparisons below and write your answer on a sheet of paper.

  1. Missouri has applied for statehood. Contrast the viewpoint of a Northern senator with the viewpoint of a Southern senator.

  2. A debate is going on in Congress about tariffs. Contrast the opinion of a Northern senator with the opinion of a Southern senator.

  3. A booklet from the American Anti-Slavery Society has just arrived in the mail. Contrast the reaction of the Northern factory worker who reads it with the reaction of a Southern plantation owner to it.

USING PRIMARY SOURCES

▶ Reread the "Spotlight on Sources" section, paragraph 9. What does Walker think will happen if slavery is not abolished?

ENRICHMENT

  1. Work with other classmates to stage a debate. One side should play the role of the abolitionists. The other side should play the role of Southern supporters of slavery. Review paragraphs 8–13 as you plan your debate.

  2. Use library books or encyclopedias to find out more about Henry Highland Garnet, Elizabeth Cady Stanton, or another abolitionist. Present a brief oral report to the class about the person you choose.

  3. Writers who want to convince their readers to change their point of view sometimes use exaggerated, highly emotional language. Reread the passages and phrases from *The Liberator*, paragraph 1, and *Walker's Appeal*, paragraph 9. Make a list of words and phrases that seem to be included because of their emotional appeal. Using these phrases as a model, write a few sentences about something you feel strongly about. Read your sentences to the class and invite them to pick out words or phrases which you might have included in order to add to the emotional appeal of your argument.

CHAPTER 6

The North and South Grow Farther Apart

OBJECTIVE: What events in the 1840s and 1850s brought the North and the South closer to conflict?

1. The year was 1856. Disagreements over slavery were dividing the country. Violence had broken out in Kansas. The senator from Massachusetts, Charles Sumner, was deeply angered by these actions as he took the Senate floor. Lashing out at proslavery politicians, Sumner was especially sharp in his criticism of Andrew Butler, an elderly senator from South Carolina. Two days later, Congressman Preston Brooks, Butler's nephew, stormed into the Senate. To the shock of everyone, Brooks beat Sumner with a heavy cane. In moments, Sumner lay on the floor, bloody and unconscious. Sides were taken. Southerners blamed Sumner and sent canes as gifts to Brooks to show their support for him. Northerners were angry. They saw the attack as proof that slavery caused violence ▶ among Americans. Why were angry debates about slavery still going on in the 1850s?

The Mexican Cession Why did the North and South disagree over slavery in the new lands won from Mexico?

2. When the United States gained lands reaching to the Pacific through the Mexican Cession, new arguments broke out about slavery. Americans disagreed about whether to allow slavery in the Mexican Cession. There were three main opinions about what to do.

▲ This cartoon of 1856 shows Congressman Brooks beating Senator Sumner. Whom do you think the cartoonist was in sympathy with—Brooks or Sumner?

Many Southerners believed that the federal government had no right to stop slavery from spreading into any new territory. Many Northerners believed that slavery should be forbidden in all new territories. Many people believed instead that white settlers in a territory should decide for themselves whether to have slavery or

In Chapter 6 you will apply these critical thinking skills to the historical process:
Understanding Points of View: Recognizing why people have different attitudes about the same thing.

Making Judgments: Stating a personal opinion based on historical facts.

not. This idea was called **popular sovereignty** (SOV-ruhn-tee).

3. For months, Congress debated different ideas about slavery in the Mexican Cession. The atmosphere was tense. A few Southern lawmakers warned that the South might **secede** (sih-SEED) from the Union unless slavery were allowed in all new territories. To secede from is to leave an organization or political group. Some Northern lawmakers accused the South of secretly wanting to bring slavery back into the free states in the future. As long as these angry discussions were going on, none of the new territories could become states. Many Congressmen feared that the slavery issue was getting out of control.

The Compromise of 1850   What were the terms of the Compromise of 1850, and why did it fail?

4. Led by Senator Henry Clay of Kentucky, a group of Congressmen pushed through several laws that they hoped would satisfy both Southerners and Northerners. These laws were known as the Compromise of 1850. California entered the Union as a free state, which was what the Californians wanted. In the territories of New Mexico and Utah, popular sovereignty would be applied. White settlers would decide later whether to allow slavery. To satisfy antislavery Northerners, the slave trade was abolished in the District of Columbia. To satisfy proslavery Southerners, a stronger fugitive slave law was passed. This law made it easier for slaveholders to recapture slaves who ran away to the North. It also increased the punishment for anyone who helped runaway slaves escape. Senator Clay and other Congressmen hoped the Compromise of 1850 would prevent further disputes about slavery.

5. The compromise, however, did little to ease the tension between North and South. Southerners who wanted the government to allow slavery in all the new territories were angry at the compromise. Most people in the South also opposed Congress's ending the slave trade in the District of Columbia. Abolitionists and many other Northerners were angered by the new fugitive slave law. Some Northern states even passed laws to try to protect runaway slaves. Do you think the Compromise of 1850 was a fair compromise?

"Bleeding Kansas"   What were the results of the struggle over slavery in Kansas?

6. Four years after the Compromise of 1850, Congress faced the issue of slavery in the territories again. Under the Missouri Compromise, slavery was forbidden in the territories of Kansas and Nebraska. This law was challenged by a bill that Senator Stephen Douglas of Illinois introduced into Congress. The new bill would apply the popular sovereignty principle in Kansas and Nebraska. This meant that slaveholders could bring in slaves to those areas. The settlers themselves would eventually vote on whether to allow slavery to continue. A heated debate broke out in Congress. Antislavery Northerners were furious. They saw the bill as part of a Southern plot to spread slavery into areas where it had been outlawed. In spite of the protests, enough Northern Congressmen voted with Southern Congressmen to pass Douglas's bill.

7. After the new act was passed, a violent struggle began in the Kansas territory. Slaveholders from neighboring Missouri and other slave states moved into Kansas. So did nonslaveholders from Northern free states. Conflicts erupted between proslavery and antislavery settlers. For a time, Kansas had two groups claiming to be the government of the territory. One had a constitution that allowed slavery, the other a constitution that prohibited slavery. Armed attacks by supporters of one group against the other were common. Dozens of people lost their lives in "**Bleeding Kansas.**" Because antislavery settlers outnumbered proslavery settlers, Kansas eventually became a free state. But the violence in Kansas showed how serious the fight over slavery had become. Why did the principle of popular sovereignty fail to work in the Kansas territory?

Background: Congress could end the slave trade in the District of Columbia (Washington, D.C.) because the District of Columbia was not a state (then as now) and Congress had authority to make laws for it.

389

The Dred Scott Case   How did this ruling by the Supreme Court drive the North and South further apart?

8. Not long after the battles in Kansas, the Supreme Court ruled on an important case, the Dred Scott case. Dred Scott was a slave whose owner had lived in Missouri. Scott's owner had taken him to Illinois and Minnesota, where slavery was illegal. Scott claimed that he should be freed because he had lived in a free state. He brought a lawsuit in Missouri trying to win his freedom. He lost the case, but appealed, and in 1857 it was heard by the Supreme Court.

9. The majority of judges on the Court ruled against Scott. They said that because Scott was an African American he had no legal right to start a lawsuit. The judges also ruled that Congress had no power to prohibit slavery in any territory. The Dred Scott decision angered Northerners who opposed the spread of slavery.

▶ Which part of the decision might have alarmed the North the most?

People in History

10. Harriet Beecher Stowe   Thousands of Northerners learned about slavery by reading a popular book written by a woman named Harriet Beecher Stowe. Born in Massachusetts in 1811, Stowe came from a family of ministers. Stowe believed strongly that slavery was a moral wrong. Hoping to persuade others, she wrote a story called *Uncle Tom's Cabin*. It was a dramatic story about the lives of slaves on a plantation in Kentucky. Published as a book in 1852, *Uncle Tom's Cabin* became a huge success and sold 300,000 copies in a single year. The book convinced many Northerners who had never visited the South or met a slave that slavery was wrong and should be abolished.

The Lincoln–Douglas Debates   What political parties did Lincoln and Douglas represent, and what were their views on slavery?

11. An important result of the disagreement over slavery was the growth of a new antislavery

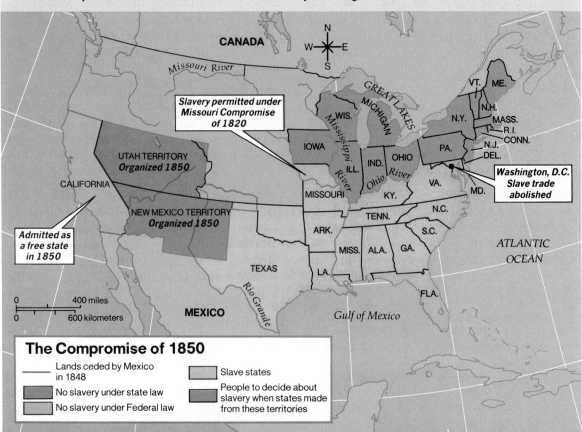

MAP SKILL BUILDER: Study the map below. Then decide if these statements are true or false.
1. California joined the Union as a free state.   **2.** Slavery was illegal west of the Rio Grande.

The Compromise of 1850

—— Lands ceded by Mexico in 1848	Slave states
No slavery under state law	People to decide about slavery when states made from these territories
No slavery under Federal law	

political party. Beginning in the 1840s, many antislavery politicians in the North were unhappy with the views of the two major political parties. Those parties were called the Democrats and the Whigs. By 1856, most Northern Whigs and some Northern Democrats had joined a new party, the **Republicans**. The new party was committed to stopping the spread of slavery into new territories. Unlike the Democrats, who had supporters in both the North and South, the Republican party was strong only in the Northern states.

 ## Spotlight on Sources

12. Abraham Lincoln was one of the members of the new Republican party. In 1858, Lincoln was a candidate for senator from Illinois. His opponent was Stephen Douglas, a Democrat. Before the election, the two men traveled around the state and held debates before large crowds. The debates often touched on the candidates' views about slavery. The candidates also spoke for the views of their political parties. The Republicans saw slavery as wrong. Lincoln said,

> [Republicans] insist that it [slavery] should, as far as may be, *be treated* as a wrong; and one of the methods of treating it as a wrong is to *make provision that* [make sure that] *it shall grow no larger*. They also desire a policy that looks to a peaceful end of slavery at some time.

Douglas had different views:

> [The country] can endure forever, divided into free and slave States, . . . each State having the right to prohibit [forbid], abolish, or sustain [keep] slavery, just as it pleases. . . . I would not endanger the perpetuity [survival] of this Union . . . for all the negroes that ever existed.
>
> —from *Documents of American History*, ed. by Henry Steele Commager

Which speaker believed that the Union would be in danger if slavery were not allowed to remain in the South?

John Brown Why did John Brown's raid stir deep feelings in both the North and South?

13. In October 1859, just one year after the Lincoln–Douglas debates, an event took place that shook the nation. A white Northerner named John Brown led a band of 18 armed African Americans and whites on a daring raid at Harpers Ferry, Virginia. They seized the weapons at a federal arsenal there. An arsenal is a storage place for guns and other weapons. Brown expected that slaves near Harpers Ferry would join his army. He then hoped to establish a new free state in the mountains of western Virginia. But his plan failed badly. Brown and his followers were soon surrounded by United States Army troops. Many of the raiders were killed in the fighting, and Brown was forced to surrender. During his trial, Brown pleaded not guilty and declared that his acts were morally right. He was convicted and hanged.

14. Brown's raid stirred strong emotions. For white Southerners, Brown's raid seemed like a nightmare come true. Southerners were especially fearful and angry after they found out that Northern abolitionists had secretly given Brown money. Many Northerners saw Brown as a hero. How would you react if you were ◄ living in 1859 and heard about Brown's raid?

Outlook

15. John Brown's raid showed that it was becoming harder to settle the conflict over slavery peacefully. Every passing year during the 1850s seemed to increase the tension between North and South. As the conflict between the two sections grew stronger, the new Republican party gained strength in the North. Southerners began to talk openly about separating from the United States and forming their own country. The career of Abraham Lincoln indicates how rapidly times were changing. Lincoln lost his campaign for the Senate in 1858 to Stephen Douglas. Just two years later he was back, however, this time as a winning candidate for President of the United States.

CHAPTER REVIEW

VOCABULARY REVIEW

▶ Choose the best definition for each term.

1. popular sovereignty
   a. granting African Americans the right to vote
   b. the idea that the white settlers of a new territory should decide whether to allow slavery in that territory
   c. arguments among the people
   d. free elections of a ruler
   e. a movement to abolish slavery

2. secede
   a. to win or accomplish a given task
   b. to leave or separate from a political group
   c. to agree by compromise
   d. to repeal an existing policy
   e. to convince by argument or debate

3. Republicans
   a. a new antislavery political party formed in the 1850s
   b. a group that opposed high tariffs
   c. a group that supported popular sovereignty
   d. a group that supported debates
   e. a political party formed in the 1850s that supported slavery

4. "Bleeding Kansas"
   a. a disease caused by lack of fresh fruits
   b. the name given to a state because of the violence taking place there
   c. a name abolitionists gave to the territory of Kansas
   d. the name given to any territory where disputes took place
   e. a name given to arguments in Congress about slavery

SKILL BUILDING: MAKING A TIME LINE

▶ Create a time line to show the events listed below. The time line should begin in 1820 and end in 1860. Draw a line and mark it at every inch. An inch will equal ten years. Label every inch mark with the year it represents. Then place the events on the time line.

1820   Missouri Compromise is agreed to

1850   Compromise of 1850 is agreed to

1857   Dred Scott decision is made

1852   *Uncle Tom's Cabin* is published

1845   Potato blight strikes in Ireland

1831   *The Liberator* begins to be published

SKILL BUILDING: CRITICAL THINKING AND COMPREHENSION

I. Drawing Conclusions

▶ Read the facts and possible conclusions below. Select the best conclusion that could be drawn from these facts. Write the conclusion on a sheet of paper.

Facts

1. Charles Sumner, a Northern senator, criticized Senator Butler for Butler's pro-slavery views. Two days later, Sumner was attacked and beaten unconscious.

2. Harriet Tubman, a leader of the Underground Railroad, was attacked and beaten by a Northern mob.

3. In Kansas, armed groups for and against slavery often attacked each other.

Conclusions

a. The Compromise of 1850 did not solve all the conflicts about slavery.

b. Persons who took strong positions on slavery were sometimes attacked physically.

c. It was dangerous to be for slavery in the 1800s.

II. Point of View

▶ Answer the questions below on a separate sheet of paper.

1. Which point of view below would have been held by Abraham Lincoln? Which would have been held by Stephen Douglas?
   a. Slavery should be kept from spreading further into the territories and into new states.
   b. There is no reason why slavery cannot continue forever in the United States.

2. Which point of view below would have been held by an abolitionist? Which would have been held by a Southern planter?
   a. If we spread the truth about slavery, it will gradually stop.
   b. It might be better for the Southern states to secede from the United States rather than give up slavery.

USING PRIMARY SOURCES

▶ Reread the quotations from the Lincoln–Douglas debates, paragraph 12. Write a summary in your own words of the position of each candidate on slavery.

ENRICHMENT

1. Imagine that you are going to write a story similar to *Uncle Tom's Cabin*. What facts would you select about slave life to demonstrate that slavery is wrong? Choose some of these facts and write a paragraph for your planned story.

2. Find out more about the Lincoln–Douglas debates. Then role-play a conversation between two people listening to these debates. Take opposite sides and give your opinion of Abraham Lincoln and Stephen Douglas as speakers and debaters.

3. Dred Scott was sold and was granted his freedom by his new owner shortly after the Supreme Court handed down its unfavorable decision. Pretend that you are Scott and write a letter to a relative giving your reactions to the decision.

UNIT REVIEW

SUMMARY

In the early 1800s, the North and South grew apart. The plantation owners in the South came to rely more and more on African American slave labor. In the North, slavery existed as well, but it was gradually ended. The North became more industrial because of the growth of textile mills and other factories. The sources of wealth and income of the people in the North and South differed. Because of this, the political viewpoints in the two sections differed as well.

As new states farther west entered the Union, bitter arguments arose over whether or not these states should allow slavery. In the 1830s, the antislavery movement grew stronger in the North. Northerners helped escaping slaves and gave support to slave resistance. Some Southerners began to believe that the only way to protect slavery was to break away from the United States. Is it likely that a similar situation would ever arise in our nation again? Why or why not?

SKILL BUILDER: READING A MAP

▶ Study the map. Then answer the questions on a sheet of paper.

1. In 1860, how many free states were there? How many slave states were there?

2. Between what two states does the 36°30′ line fall?

3. Name the territories that had not yet become states in 1860.

4. Based on what you have read in Unit 8, which territories would be likely to allow slavery? Which would be more likely to forbid slavery?

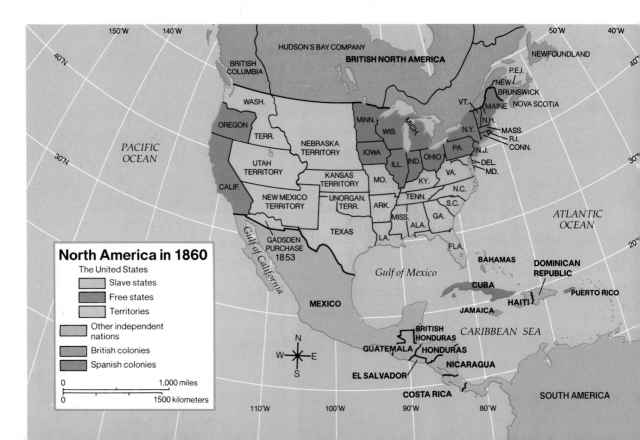

North America in 1860

The United States
- Slave states
- Free states
- Territories
- Other independent nations
- British colonies
- Spanish colonies

0 — 1,000 miles
0 — 1500 kilometers

I. Contrasting and Comparing

1. Contrast the life of a white factory worker in the North with the life of an African field slave in the South. Consider the following in your answer: opportunities for education, working conditions, and family life.

2. Compare the rights of a freed African American in the South with the life of an African slave in the South.

II. Making Judgments

1. Using facts from Unit 8, make a judgment about the main cause of the differences of opinion about slavery that were common in the 1850s.

2. What judgment did many Southern planters make about the rights of African slaves?

3. What judgment did many Northerners make about the importance of protecting the way of life that existed in the South?

III. Cause and Effect

Read the following statements. For each cause given, write down at least one effect on a separate sheet of paper.

1. **Cause:** Eli Whitney invented the cotton gin, a machine that made it much easier and faster to clean seeds from cotton.
   Effect:

2. **Cause:** The soil in some parts of the South became worn out from overuse.
   Effect:

For each effect given below, write at least one cause.

3. **Cause:**
   Effect: Northern factories bought more cotton for cloth.

4. **Cause:**
   Effect: John Brown became a hero to Northerners who were opposed to slavery.

ENRICHMENT

1. Imagine that you are a British teenager visiting your cousin on a plantation in Georgia. Write a letter or diary entry describing your impressions of the African American slaves on the plantation.

2. Design a poster advertising a lecture by a famous abolitionist such as Frederick Douglass or William Lloyd Garrison.

3. Find examples of African spirituals or work songs from the South. Work with a small group of classmates to learn to sing the songs and perform them for the class.

THE CIVIL WAR AND RECONSTRUCTION

Chapter

UNIT OVERVIEW   Unit 9 will help you understand the issues that led to the Civil War, how the North won the war, and how Reconstruction affected Southerners, especially African Americans.

UNIT SKILLS OBJECTIVES   In Unit 9, three critical thinking skills are emphasized:

❯ **Predicting:** Telling what you believe will happen on the basis of clues and facts.

▲ **Summarizing:** Giving the main idea of a group of paragraphs in a brief form.

Understanding Points of View: Recognizing why people have different attitudes aobut the same thing.

You will also learn two important social studies skills:
Reading a Map   Using Time Lines

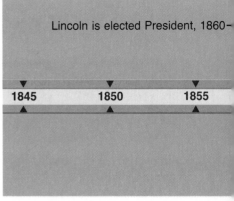

Lincoln is elected President, 1860–

| 1845 | 1850 | 1855 |

ESL/LEP Strategy: Before they study the unit, tell students they will be asked to write an article that might have appeared in a newspaper during the Civil War or Reconstruction. Remind students to think about the assignment as they read.

▲ In 1862 David Farragut won an important Union naval victory at Mobile Bay.

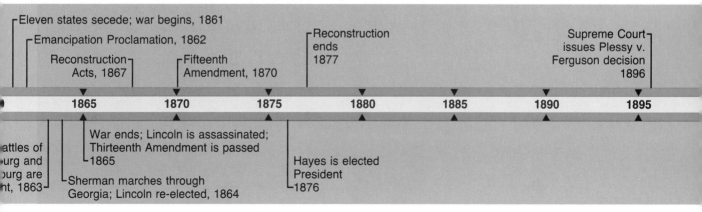

Eleven states secede; war begins, 1861

Emancipation Proclamation, 1862

Reconstruction
Acts, 1867

Fifteenth
Amendment, 1870

Reconstruction
ends
1877

Supreme Court
issues Plessy v.
Ferguson decision
1896

1865   **1870**   **1875**   **1880**   **1885**   **1890**   **1895**

War ends; Lincoln is assassinated;
Thirteenth Amendment is passed
1865

Hayes is elected
President
1876

attles of
urg and
urg are
nt, 1863

Sherman marches through
Georgia; Lincoln re-elected, 1864

Points of View

In 1860 and 1861, 11 states decided to secede, or break away, from the United States. The two selections that follow show opposing views of secession. In the first, a Tennessee newspaper editor in 1860 compares secession to a crime committed by a person. In the second selection, a Georgia

▲ Abraham Lincoln looked like this near the end of his first term as President. His election in 1860 led seven (later eleven) Southern states to secede.

A SOUTHERNER AGAINST SECESSION

❝Secession, therefore, by the people of a State, is a nullity in law [has no legal meaning], and every citizen of the State continues, in spite of secession, still a citizen of the Union, liable to [bound by] the penalties of the laws of the Union; and every act of resistance to the laws of the government, either by one man or one hundred thousand, is a crime, and can only be made innocent by the people of the United States. The contrary doctrine [opposite beliefs] would give us a government without law, without order, without safety either for life, liberty, or property—just no government at all. The violation [breaking] of a law by a single individual is simply a crime; if there be organized resistance to the law by many, it may be rebellion; and if by a State, it is called secession.❞

—"DAILY NASHVILLE PATRIOT," November 19, 1860

Secession

newspaper editor tells readers that states have a right to secede. What would your view of secession have been? Did a state have the right to withdraw from the United States? Or was seceding an illegal act that had to be put down, by a war if necessary?

A SOUTHERNER FAVORING SECESSION

"Let us not raise the cry of a disgraced and dishonored [shamed] South, for secession would be but backing from a blow [only backing off from an attack], not revenging it, and is not the final remedy [cure] if we have wrongs to punish.

Simply stand by our rights, and if the Union be not a safe ark [strongbox] for our law, we have timber and gold enough to make another. We know our rights, and they are all plainly laid down [written out]. We will have them, and all that is needful [needed] to do is to ask for them of the great partners of the Union [the other states], and quit doing business with those that refuse. We say that if we do not get all we desire [want] by sending an ultimatum [demand], then we must resist, and will have to secede before we can resist.

If we want a war of revenge, we must get out first, and get a Congress of our own, empowered to declare war and contract [make] alliances."

—"THE DAILY CONSTITUTIONALIST," Atlanta, Georgia, December 1, 1860

▲ Jefferson Davis, a strong supporter of secession, was elected president of the Confederate States of America early in 1861.

Using Primary Sources

1. Why does the writer of the first statement view secession as a crime?

2. Why does the writer of the second statement believe that secession is the first step in punishing wrongs? What "wrongs" do you think this writer meant?

CHAPTER 1

The Civil War Begins

OBJECTIVE: How did the Civil War begin, and what were the strengths and weaknesses of the North and the South?

1. The history of America changed forever in the dark, early dawn of April 12, 1861. The sky over Fort Sumter was suddenly on fire. A terrifying sound pierced the air. Soldiers threw themselves flat on the ground just as a shell exploded. Fort Sumter was a United States government fortress on an island in the harbor of Charleston, South Carolina. Now it was under attack from heavy cannons on the shore. South Carolina had announced that it was no longer part of the United States, and it wanted the United States army to leave. The bombardment lasted nearly two days. Finally, Fort Sumter surrendered. Surprisingly, no lives were lost. In a brief and bloodless battle, the long and bloody Civil War had begun.

Lincoln Becomes President Why did Lincoln's election lead Southern states to form the Confederacy?

2. The presidential election of 1860 showed how deeply the slavery issue had divided the United States. The Republican Party chose Abraham Lincoln as its candidate for President. The Democratic Party split into two parts, and a new Constitutional Union party was formed. This meant that there was a four-way race for the presidency. The Northern Democrats chose Stephen Douglas, and the Southern Democrats

▲ A Confederate shell explodes inside Fort Sumter. After two days of this kind of attack, the Union forces in the fort surrendered.

chose John C. Breckinridge. Douglas was against slavery in the states. However, he favored the right of people in the territories to decide the slavery issue for themselves. Breckinridge favored slavery in both the states and the territories. Lincoln was against slavery anywhere, but he knew it would be hard to end it in

In Chapter 1 you will apply these critical thinking skills to the historical process:

❯ **Predicting:** Telling what you believe will happen on the basis of clues and facts.

Understanding Points of View: Recognizing why people have different attitudes about the same thing.

the states. He believed that it would be fair to keep slavery from spreading to the territories. John Bell, the candidate of the Constitutional Union party, tried to ignore the slavery question. Why do you think slavery was such an important issue?

3. Lincoln won the election of 1860. However, he won only the votes of the states in the North and West. He did not win any states in the South. In fact, Lincoln received only 40 percent of the total votes Americans cast in the election. Even so, Lincoln received a half million more votes than Douglas, who was second in the race. Lincoln clearly owed his victory to Northern voters.

4. Lincoln's election to the Presidency alarmed many Southern leaders. They were certain that Lincoln would take steps to end slavery in the South. However, they insisted that decisions about slavery were a question of **states' rights**. States' rights are matters that the Constitution allows the states to decide for themselves, without the involvement of the federal government. During the election campaign, Southern leaders had warned that their states would **secede** (see-SEED), or withdraw, from the Union if Lincoln were elected. Seceding, they believed, was one of their states' rights.

5. In the months after Lincoln's election, seven Southern states voted to secede from the United States. South Carolina was first, followed by Mississippi, Florida, Alabama, Georgia, Louisiana, and Texas. In February 1861, a month before Lincoln took office, these states formed a new national government. They called their nation the Confederate States of America, or the **Confederacy** (kun-FED-uh-ruh-see). They called on the other slave states to join the Confederacy. Later they would be joined by Virginia, North Carolina, Tennessee, and Arkansas, bringing the Confederacy to 11 states. The Confederate States chose Jefferson Davis, a former Senator, as President.

6. In March 1861, when Lincoln took office as President, the nation faced the greatest challenge in its history. Southern states had declared their independence and formed a new national

THE PRESIDENTS' CORNER

Abraham Lincoln's presidency, from 1861 to 1865, was entirely taken up with the Civil War. Lincoln began with very little. He had almost no schooling, but he loved to read and taught himself many subjects. As an adult, he became a successful lawyer. In 1858, a series of debates with Douglas made him nationally famous. Lincoln tried to prevent the Civil War, but when war came, he lead the Union with skill and vision.

government. Would Lincoln allow the South to leave the United States? In his **inaugural address** (ih-NAW-gyoo-rul uh-DRES), Lincoln gave his answer. An inaugural address is the speech given by a President just after taking the oath of office. The new President told the people that no state had the right to secede. He said the Constitution had created a lasting union of all the states. Lincoln also made it clear that he did not want a war. He appealed to the Southern states to return to the **Union**. The Union was the name for the Northern and border states that remained loyal members of the United States.

Spotlight on Sources

7. In his March 4, 1861, inaugural address, Lincoln made this appeal to the South:

> In your hands, my dissatisfied [unhappy] fellow-countrymen, and not in mine, is the momentous issue [very great question] of civil war. The government will not assail [attack] you. You can have no conflict [war] without being yourselves the aggressors [attackers]. You have no oath [promise] registered in heaven to destroy the

401

government, while I shall have the most solemn one to "preserve, protect, and defend" it.

▶ What was President Lincoln telling the Southern states? How would you expect the Southern states to respond?

8. The leaders of the Confederacy refused to listen to Lincoln, and war seemed certain. On April 12, 1861, when Confederate forces fired on United States soldiers in Fort Sumter, the war began. This war is called the Civil War or, sometimes, the War between the States.

The North and South at War What advantages did each side have in fighting the war?

9. The North had several important advantages on its side in the Civil War. The population of the North was 22 million. The South had only 9 million people, including 3.5 million slaves. Do you think these slaves would fight for the Confederacy? The North had most of the

nation's factories and industries. As a result, Northern factories could make the guns and other weapons needed for war. Most of the railroads also were in the North. Therefore, the North was able to send soldiers and war supplies to the battle front quickly. Finally, the North had the United States Navy and owned nearly all the nation's ships. It could use this sea power to keep the South from getting food and war supplies.

10. The South had some important advantages in fighting the Civil War. The South had more of the good generals. The military skill of Southern generals helped win many battles against larger Northern armies. Because it was fighting for its independence, the Confederacy was ready to fight for a long time. In addition, white Southerners were fighting to defend their land and their way of life. For these reasons, Southerners expected to keep fighting. They hoped that sooner or later the North would get tired of fighting and let the Southern states go. Southerners also believed that European na-

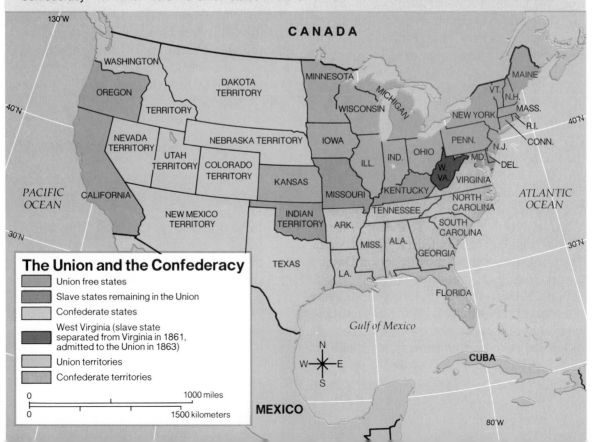

MAP SKILL BUILDER: Study the map key to answer these questions about the Union and the Confederacy. **1.** Which were the Union states in the Civil War? **2.** Which were the Confederate states?

The Union and the Confederacy

- Union free states
- Slave states remaining in the Union
- Confederate states
- West Virginia (slave state separated from Virginia in 1861, admitted to the Union in 1863)
- Union territories
- Confederate territories

tions would aid them, just as France and Spain had aided the United States during the American Revolution. Europe needed cotton, and cotton was the South's chief source of wealth. The South would use the money from cotton to buy the weapons and other war supplies it needed from Europe.

Fort Sumter to Bull Run   How did the Battle of Bull Run dash both sides' hopes for an early end to the war?

11. After Fort Sumter fell, both the North and the South hoped that an early victory would win the war. The first thing to do was to build up each side's army. President Lincoln asked the Northern states to sign up 75,000 men for the Union army. Jefferson Davis called on the Southern states to form a Confederate army.

People in History

12. Robert E. Lee   The commander of the Confederate army in Virginia was General Robert E. Lee. Lee graduated from West Point in 1829. He became an officer in the army, serving in many parts of the United States and brilliantly in the Mexican War. Before Virginia left the Union, Lee was offered command of the Union army. He turned the offer down because he would not fight against Southern states, even though he did not himself believe in either slavery or secession. However, when Virginia joined the Confederacy, he decided he must fight for his home state. In 1862 he became commander of the Army of Northern Virginia and led it to the end of the war. Lee's skilled and daring leadership helped the Confederacy win many victories.

13. In July 1861 the first battle of the war was fought at Bull Run in northern Virginia, near Washington, D.C. Many people from Washington, including members of Congress, came to watch what they expected to be an easy Union victory. Instead, after a full day of hard fighting, the battle ended as a Confederate victory. The hard fighting at the Battle of Bull

▲ Robert E. Lee's leadership of Confederate forces made him the most famous general in the Civil War. His army often defeated much larger Union enemies.

Run suggested that the war would be a long and bloody struggle.

Outlook

14. After Lincoln was elected President, eleven Southern states decided to secede and form their own nation, the Confederate States of America. Lincoln acted to preserve the Union. Soon the two parts of the country were at war. Both sides expected the war to be over quickly. In fact, people from Washington had come to watch the Battle of Bull Run so as not to miss the war. Do you think that the Civil War ◄ could have been prevented? Would you expect it to end quickly?

Activity: Have class members conduct research on the Confederacy and its leaders. Assign one group to report on the type of government it set up. Assign another group to tell how Jefferson Davis was chosen. A third group should tell about Davis's life, including decisions he made as leader of the Confederacy.

403

CHAPTER REVIEW

VOCABULARY REVIEW

▶ Write each number and word on a separate sheet of paper. Then write the letter of the definition next to the word it defines.

1. states' rights

2. secede

3. Confederacy

4. inaugural address

5. Union

a. speech that one gives after taking an oath of office

b. withdraw from

c. questions that the Constitution allows state governments to decide

d. the government of Southern states that withdrew from the United States

e. the Northern and border states that remained loyal to the United States

SKILL BUILDER: TIME LINE

▶ Copy the time line below and complete it by placing the events listed and their dates in the correct position on the time line.

Battle of Bull Run

Confederacy is formed

Lincoln inaugurated as President

Lincoln elected

Confederate troops fire on Ft. Sumter

Seven states secede

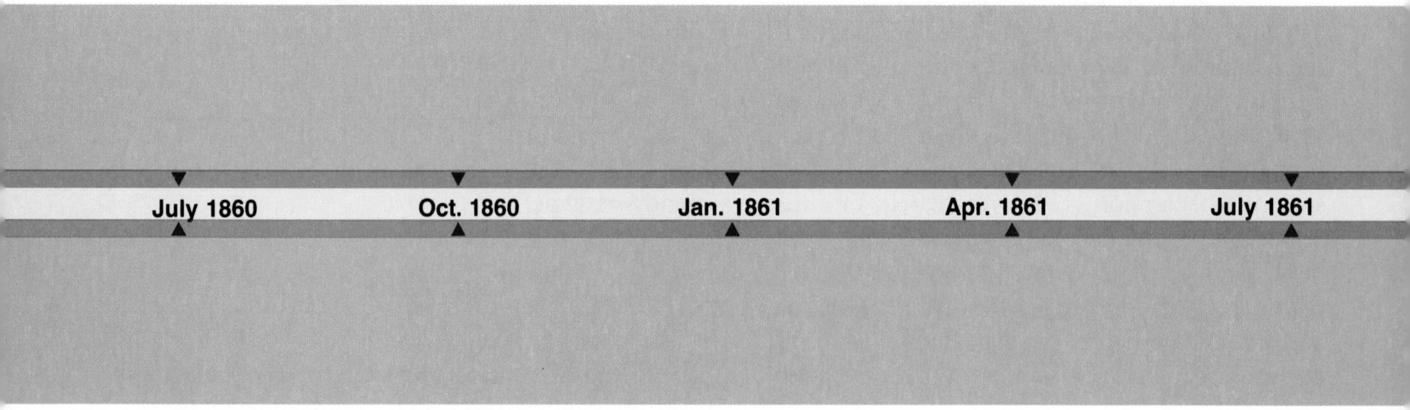

July 1860	Oct. 1860	Jan. 1861	Apr. 1861	July 1861

SKILL BUILDER: CRITICAL THINKING AND COMPREHENSION

❱ I. Predicting

▶ Read the following facts. On a separate sheet of paper, predict the result or outcome.

1. **Facts:**
   The South wanted to keep slavery.
   Lincoln opposed slavery.
   Lincoln was elected President.

2. **Facts:**

The North had a much larger population than the South.

The North had nearly all of America's factories and industries.

The North had the railroads and navy to transport food and military supplies.

3. **Facts:**

Presidential candidate Lincoln had the solid support of the Republican party and anti-slavery Northern voters.

The candidates of the Democratic party were divided.

The Northern states had a much bigger voting population than the South.

II. Point of View

▶ Read the following points of view. From the list below, choose the person that best fits the point of view. On a separate sheet of paper, write your selection.

President Lincoln

Stephen Douglas

Jefferson Davis

John C. Breckinridge

1. Viewed slavery as an evil that must not be allowed to spread anywhere.

2. Favored slavery in both states and territories.

3. Believed that a Confederate army needed to be assembled as quickly as possible.

4. Opposed slavery but believed that the territories should decide for themselves.

USING PRIMARY SOURCES

▶ Reread the Spotlight on Sources selection on page 401. Why did Lincoln say that he had made a solemn oath to "preserve, protect, and defend" the nation? (Refer to the Constitution, page 244–273, to help you answer this question.)

ENRICHMENT

1. Conduct library research on Jefferson Davis and his opinion of secession. Then imagine you are Davis. You have just read a copy of President Lincoln's inaugural address. You know Lincoln; he knows you. You want to avoid war, but you also do not want to anger the people who elected you. Write a letter to Lincoln telling him your views and feelings.

2. Create a drawing or painting showing the fall of Fort Sumter. Before you begin, do research in the library to help you show buildings, weapons, and soldiers accurately. Then, before completion, show your teacher a rough sketch of what you intend to draw or paint.

3. As an individual or as a group, tell what the 1860 presidential election was like. Use library resources. Present an oral report to the class that includes the following: campaigning, speeches, advertising, news reporting, rallies.

CHAPTER 2

The Early Years of the Civil War

OBJECTIVE: What were the plans of the North and the South to win the Civil War?

1. The young sailors of the Union navy did not believe their own eyes. A strange-looking ship was sailing directly toward them. It was low to the water and had sloping sides, like the roof of a house. An instant later, the ship's heavy guns began firing. Then it rammed into a Union ship. The wooden ships of the Union navy were no match for this Confederate ship, called the *Virginia* but better known by its earlier name, the *Merrimack*. Why? The *Merrimack,* was covered with iron plates. Shells from the Union Ships just bounced off the iron plates. When the battle ended, the *Merrimack* had sunk two ships of the Union navy.

2. The next day, the *Merrimack* again attacked. However, this time, the Union sent an even stranger looking ship, the *Monitor*, to meet it. The *Monitor* looked like a round box on a raft. It, too, had sides of iron and carried powerful cannon. The two ironclads battled fiercely for several hours. At the end of the day, neither ship had won. However, the two strange ships introduced a new kind of warship, and navies would never be the same again.

▲ Near Hampton Roads, Virginia, Union soldiers rescue sailors from a sinking Union ship as the *Monitor* and the *Merrimack* battle in the background.

Military Strategies How did the North and the South each plan to win the Civil War?

3. The North believed it had to reach several important goals in order to win the war. First, the North had to blockade the South. The chief aim of the Northern blockade was to cut off the South's trade with Europe. The Union navy would keep the South from shipping cotton and tobacco to European nations. As a result, the South could not earn money to buy the weapons and supplies it needed from those nations.

In Chapter 2 you will apply these critical thinking skills to the historical process:

▲ **Identifying Fact *versus* Opinion:** Specifying whether information can be proved or whether it expresses feelings or beliefs.

◤ **Making Judgments:** Stating a personal opinion based on historical fact.

The North soon set up a tight blockade around Southern seaports, from Virginia all the way to Texas. Why would this blockade become one of the North's most important weapons against the South?

4. The second important goal in the North's war plan was to split the Confederacy. By winning control of the Mississippi River, the North could cut Texas, Louisiana, and Arkansas off from the rest of the Confederacy. The North also planned to capture Chattanooga (chat-uh-NOO-guh), Tennessee. Chattanooga was a major city where key railroads, roads, and rivers met. If it fell, Union armies could cut off Tennessee, Mississippi, and Alabama.

5. The last goal in the North's plan to win the war was to capture Richmond, Virginia. If Union armies captured Richmond, they would deal a heavy blow to the Confederacy. It might even cause the South to ask for peace.

6. The South believed its armies could hold out against Northern attacks. Southerners felt that the North would soon grow tired of fighting. Then the North would be forced to accept the Confederacy as an independent nation. Therefore, the South's main aim was to convince the North that the North could not win the war. Another aim was to gain help from Europe. To do this, Southerners would have to convince Britain and France that the Confederacy was here to stay.

Early Campaigns   What were the major battles in 1862?

7. In the East, the goal of the Union's Army of the Potomac was to capture Richmond. General George McClellan spent many months training this large Union army. In April 1862, his huge army was taken by ship to a **peninsula** southeast of Richmond. A peninsula is an area of land surrounded on three sides by water. In just a few weeks, Union soldiers were only 10 miles (16 kilometers) from Richmond. Then, in a series of battles from May to July 1862, Confederate forces under Lee and Jackson defeated McClellan's Union army and drove it

back to its ships. These battles are called the Peninsular Campaign after the peninsula where they took place.

8. Lee's Army of Northern Virginia now seemed close to winning the war. In August 1862, Jackson and Lee won another important victory at the Second Battle of Bull Run. Lee then decided to strike into the North. In September 1862, Confederate forces crossed the Potomac River into Maryland. However, on September 17, 1862, McClellan stopped Lee's armies at Antietam (an-TEE-tum) Creek in Maryland. In the bloodiest single day of the entire war, the two sides lost more than 26,000 men. The North claimed the victory, since Lee was forced to retreat to Virginia. However, McClellan failed to follow up his victory with another attack on Lee's army, so Lee's army survived to fight again.

9. Early in the war, the Union army had greater success in the West. There, in February 1862, a Union army under General Ulysses S. Grant won a key battle at Fort Donelson, near Nashville, Tennessee. In April he won another important battle at Shiloh (SHY-loh), also in Tennessee. Grant then occupied Memphis, an important city on the Mississippi River. These victories gave the Union armies control of much of Tennessee and of long stretches of the Mississippi.

People in History

10. David Farragut   Another great Union victory took place at the mouth of the Mississippi with David Farragut's capture of New Orleans in April 1862. New Orleans was the largest city in the South and the main Confederate seaport. Farragut, the commander of a fleet of the Union navy, skillfully ran his ships past the powerful forts defending New Orleans. Farragut, who as a young boy had seen action in the War of 1812, became the greatest Northern naval hero of the war. Later, he was made the first admiral in the nation's history. Farragut was one of many Hispanic Americans who fought in the Civil War.

Activity: Ask the class to imagine that Lee had won the Battle at Antietam and then had captured Washington, D.C. Have them write a short paragraph predicting what might have happened after that.

Linking Geography and History

Strategic Targets of the Civil War In a war, each side has to have two strategies: one to protect its territory, and the other to attack the enemy. Both the Union and the Confederacy had plans involving each strategy.

Each side had a problem protecting territory, especially its capital. Washington, D.C., the capital of the Union, was just across the river from Virginia, a Confederate state. To protect Washington, the Union built forts all around the capital. Richmond, the Confederate capital, was also exposed because it was just 120 miles (192 km) from Washington.

For each side, an important part of its strategy was to capture the other's capital. For much of the war, armies of the two sides moved back and forth between Richmond and Washington.

The second strategy involved the break-up of the other's defense and supply lines. In this, the North had an advantage. The South depended on selling cotton to Europe, particularly England, and on buying European manufactured goods. The Union sent a naval force to stop the ships sailing across the Atlantic to and from the South.

Each side tried to cut the other's territory in two. For the North that meant, first of all, moving down the Mississippi River. Union forces were successful with this strategy and moved to control the Mississippi. Union forces then moved up the Tennessee Valley, cutting Kentucky and Tennessee in two. Finally, they divided the South again by driving across Georgia to the sea at Savannah.

The Confederate forces countered by a plan to move into the North. They used the broad valley of the Shenandoah River, west of the Blue Ridge Mountains, as their route to Maryland and Pennsylvania. The Confederate drive was stopped at Gettysburg, the most famous battle of the war.

Now answer the following questions:
1. Why are two strategies (protect and strike) needed to win a war? Could the South have won the war if it succeeded at one of these strategies?
2. Why was Gettysburg so critical geographically? If the Southern forces were not defeated there, what would their next move have been?

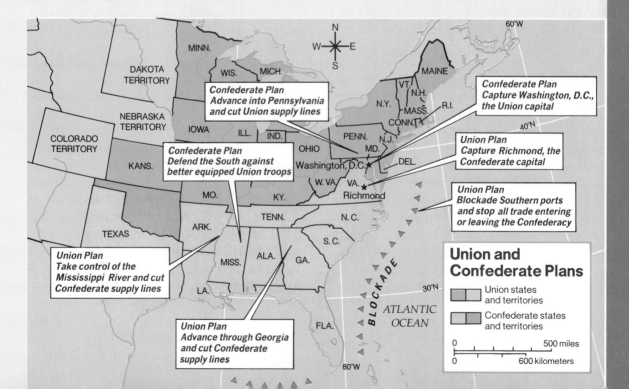

▲ After Farragut ran his fleet past the forts that defended the lower Mississippi, New Orleans fell easily to the Union forces.

The Emancipation Proclamation   Why did Lincoln declare freedom for the slaves in the Confederacy?

11. During the summer of 1862, President Lincoln decided to free the Africans who were still slaves in the Confederacy. When the Civil War began, four states with slavery had stayed in the Union. These slave states in the Union were called border states. Because he needed the support of these states, Lincoln had not acted against slavery up to this time. However, as the Civil War went on, many slaves fled from their owners and asked for freedom. They demanded the right to fight with the Union armies. Lincoln now believed that **emancipating** (ee-MAN-sih-pay-ting) some of the African slaves would help the Union win the war. To emancipate is to grant freedom to enslaved people.

12. In September 1862, after the Battle of Antietam, Lincoln issued the Emancipation Proclamation. The Emancipation Proclamation declared that all African Americans held as slaves in the Confederacy would be free on January 1, 1863. However, the proclamation did not free the African Americans held as slaves in the border states or in parts of the South under Union control. Even so, the Emancipation Proclamation gave the North a new purpose in the war. It now was fighting for the freedom of African Americans as well as to save the Union. Fighting for this cause also gained the support of European nations for the North.

Spotlight on Sources

13. The Emancipation Proclamation includes these words:

> I, Abraham Lincoln, President of the United States . . . on the first day of January, 1863, order and declare that all persons held as slaves within said [those] states . . . in rebellion against the United States shall be then, thenceforth [from then on], and forever free. . . .
>
> And upon this act, sincerely believed to be an act of justice, warranted [allowed] by the Constitution upon military necessity [in order to win the war], I invoke [ask] the considerate judgment [favorable opinion] of mankind, and the gracious favor of Almighty God.

What "military necessity" did Lincoln have in mind? How would the Emancipation Proclamation help the Union in the war?

Outlook

14. When the Civil War began, both the North and the South believed they would win. In 1862, Confederate armies won major battles in the East, and Union forces won important victories in the West along the Mississippi. Then, in January 1863, Lincoln's Emancipation Proclamation went into effect. The Civil War became a great struggle for freedom and justice. What effect would this change have? ◄

409

CHAPTER REVIEW

VOCABULARY REVIEW

▶ Write each of the following words on a sheet of paper. Then write the definition of each word. Finally, use each word in a sentence of your own.

1. blockade

2. emancipate

3. peninsula

SKILL BUILDER: READING A MAP

▶ The map below shows the major battles of the Civil War from 1861 to 1862. Use this map to answer these questions.

1. Count the number of Confederate victories and of Union victories from 1861 to 1862. Then count the number of "indecisive" battles. Who was winning the war in 1862?

2. What part of the country was the scene of the largest number of battles? Why were they fought there?

3. Did the greatest number of battles occur inland or near seaports? Why?

4. Which seaport would you guess was least affected by the Union blockade? Why?

5. Where was the most northern battle fought between 1861 and 1862?

6. What town seems likely to be the next place Grant will attack? How strongly would you expect the Confederacy to defend this place? Why?

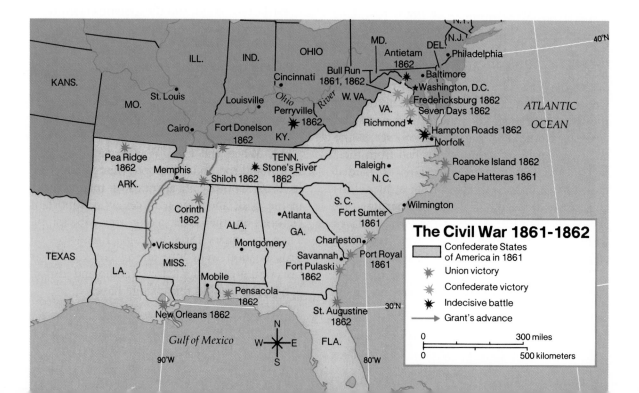

SKILL BUILDER: CRITICAL THINKING AND COMPREHENSION

I. Fact *versus* Opinion

▶ Decide whether each of the following statements is a fact or an opinion. Write each statement on a sheet of paper. Next to each statement, write *F* for fact or *O* for opinion.

1. The chief aim of the Northern blockade was to cut off the South's trade with Europe.

2. Richmond, Virginia, was the key city in Lee's war plans in the east.

3. The South had a stronger belief in its cause than did the North.

4. Robert E. Lee was the greatest general of that time.

5. Lincoln was right not to free the slaves at the beginning of the Civil War.

6. When Lincoln did issue the Emancipation Proclamation, the North had even more cause for its fighting.

II. Making Judgments

▶ Using your ability to make a judgment, answer these questions on a separate sheet of paper.

1. How important was David Farragut's capture of New Orleans for the Union's war effort?

2. Was it a mistake for Lincoln not to free the slaves at the beginning of the Civil War?

3. What was more important to the North's cause: fighting for the freedom of the slaves, or saving the Union?

USING PRIMARY SOURCES

▶ Reread the Spotlight on Sources excerpt on page 409. As one might expect, Lincoln's language in the Emancipation Proclamation is formal and official. If you had written the Emancipation Proclamation, you would use words more natural to yourself. Rewrite the selection in your own words, trying to keep the same basic meaning.

ENRICHMENT

1. Select one of the battles discussed in the chapter. Conduct library research to determine locations and movements of the opposing armies. Then draw a map showing the battle and its results. Show day-by-day battle actions leading up to final results. Color codes and arrows will be helpful in showing progress of the battle.

2. Lincoln's Emancipation Proclamation was published in Northern newspapers on September 23, 1862. Assume the role of a newspaper editorial writer. First write an editorial from the point of view of a big-city Northern newspaper. Then write another editorial, this time from the point of view of a rural Southern newspaper.

3. Imagine you are a teenager in 1862 who has witnessed the battle of the *Monitor* and the *Merrimack*. In a dramatic role-playing presentation, tell your family (the class) what you have just seen. Be sure to convey appropriate details and feelings.

CHAPTER 3

The North Wins the Civil War

OBJECTIVE: What battles ended the Civil War, and how did the war affect people's lives in the North and South?

1. The two men sat facing each other at a table in the old farmhouse. Both men were tired after the many battles they had fought. General Grant held out his hand when General Lee finished signing the paper. Then Grant shook Lee's hand as they both stood up. The date was April 9, 1865. Lee had surrendered his army and asked for peace. Within days, all the other Confederate generals would follow his example. The North had won the Civil War, but both sides had paid a terrible price. More than 600,000 Americans had been killed in the four long years of fighting.

Chancellorsville to Appomattox What were the main battles in the last years of the Civil War?

2. The turning point of the Civil War came in the first days of July 1863 with the battles of Gettysburg and Vicksburg. The Battle of Gettysburg took place north of Washington, D.C., in Pennsylvania. Two months earlier, a Confederate army under Robert E. Lee had won a major victory at Chancellorsville in Virginia. Lee then decided to again invade the North. He hoped that if the South could win another great victory, the North might be ready to quit.

3. On July 1, 1863, Lee's army and a Union army under General George G. Meade met at Gettysburg. The battle lasted through three

▲ The 54th Massachusetts Infantry was the first African American regiment in the Union army. It won lasting fame for its heroism in a battle near Charleston, South Carolina.

days of bitter fighting. On the first day, Union forces were pushed back. On the second and third days, however, they held their ground against fierce Confederate attacks. Finally, late on the third day, Lee sent 13,000 troops in one charge against the Union lines. Almost half the

In Chapter 3 you will apply these critical thinking skills to the historical process:

▲ **Summarizing:** Giving the main idea of a group of paragraphs in a brief form.

○ **Generalizing:** Making a statement that links several facts.

attackers were killed, and the rest were driven back. Lee had lost the battle, and his plan to end the war had failed. Why was the Battle of Gettysburg a turning point in the war?

4. One day later, on July 4, 1863, Confederate forces at Vicksburg, Mississippi, surrendered to a Union army under Grant. Grant had had the city under **siege** (SEEJ) for six weeks. In a siege, an army surrounds a city and prevents food and supplies from reaching it. This victory gave the North control of the entire Mississippi River. The North had completed an important part of its war plan.

🦅 Spotlight on Sources

5. Several months later, Lincoln visited the battlefield at Gettysburg. In a short speech, he praised the brave soldiers who died there and dedicated the country to a better future. Here is part of Lincoln's Gettysburg Address:

> Four score and seven [eighty-seven] years ago, our fathers [the nation's founders] brought forth on this continent, a new nation, conceived [begun] in Liberty, and dedicated to the proposition [idea] that all men [people] are created equal.
>
> Now we are engaged in [fighting] a great civil war, testing whether that nation . . . can long endure [continue to exist]. . . . We here highly resolve [decide] that these dead shall not have died in vain [without results]; that this nation, under God, shall have a new birth of freedom; and that government of the people, by the people, for the people, shall not perish [be wiped out] from the earth.

What did Lincoln mean by "government of the people, by the people, for the people"? How might war bring "a new birth of freedom"?

6. In November 1863, Grant won two battles near Chattanooga, in eastern Tennessee. Northern soldiers were now in position to march south into Georgia. The North clearly was winning the Civil War. However, hard fighting continued for more than a year.

7. In March 1864, Lincoln put Grant in charge of all the Union armies. Grant selected General William Tecumseh Sherman to lead the Union army in the West. Grant himself commanded the Union army in the East. In May 1864, Grant and his army began their campaign against Richmond. Lee's army was driven back to the area around Richmond, where it built a series of trenches and forts around the city. Grant's soldiers spent the next nine months there, holding Richmond under siege.

8. While Grant moved against Richmond, General Sherman's army left Chattanooga and fought its way into Georgia. After a summer of difficult fighting, Sherman's army captured Atlanta in September 1864. Then Sherman led the Union army toward Savannah, on the coast. For several weeks, Sherman's army burned farms and destroyed crops in its "March to the Sea" across Georgia. Sherman was waging **total war**. In total war, an army destroys everything the enemy army can use to feed and supply its soldiers. In December 1864, Sherman's army entered Savannah.

9. In 1865, the Confederacy collapsed. In February 1865, Sherman and his Union army marched north into South Carolina, where they again destroyed farmlands and burned cities. By March 1865, Sherman's forces were in North Carolina, heading for Virginia. Meanwhile, in Virginia, Lee could no longer hold Richmond. On April 9, 1865, Lee met Grant at the small Virginia town of Appomattox Court House and surrendered his army to Grant. Within a month, all the other Confederate armies also surrendered. The South had been defeated. The Civil War was over.

African Americans How did African Americans help fight the Civil War?

10. African American soldiers had an important part in winning the war for the North. Nearly 186,000 African Americans fought in the Union army. More than half these soldiers had escaped from slavery in the Confederate states. African American regiments like the 54th

GERMANS

In the Union army, many regiments were made up of German immigrants. Both before and after the Civil War, vast numbers of people came to America from Germany. The first group came in colonial times. In 1683, a group of 34 immigrants established Germantown in Pennsylvania to escape religious persecution. By 1776, some 225,000 Germans had sailed to America.

In the nineteenth century, economic and political trouble in Germany brought a steady flow of immigrants. By 1832, well over 10,000 Germans a year were coming to the United States. Teachers, professors, farmers, doctors, lawyers, and craft workers arrived to build a new life—and new communities. St. Louis, Milwaukee, and Chicago all owed their growth to German-Americans. After an outbreak of revolution in Germany in 1848, the tides of immigration increased. They came not just to escape civil strife; they had a hunger for democracy. Among them was Carl Schurz. Schurz became one of Lincoln's most important supporters and was eventually named a general for the Union side.

The new Americans from Germany brought ideas and practices soon taken up by the whole country. German music and styles of celebrating Christmas caught on with all Americans. Kindergarten, a German word for "garden of children," and gymnasiums were ideas adopted nationwide. Vocational training was another German educational idea.

Now answer the following questions:

1. How would American education be different today without ideas contributed by German-Americans?

2. What adjustments would an immigrant from Germany have to make after arriving in the United States in the 1850s?

▼ German immigrants brought their customs and ways of life to many parts of the United States in the 1800s. These Germans settled a section of Texas about the time of the Civil War.

Massachusetts were honored for their courage in battle. Many African Americans also served in the Union navy. In fact, African Americans made up about one-quarter of the Union navy. More than 20 African American soldiers and sailors were given the Medal of Honor for their great bravery.

11. African Americans who served in the Union armies faced many hardships. As you have learned, African Americans who lived in the North did not have the same rights as white Northerners. It is not surprising, then, that they were not treated fairly in the Union army. For example, they usually did not receive equal pay. Many white Union soldiers did not accept African American soldiers as their equals. African American soldiers often were given difficult, dirty jobs like digging trenches and building earthen forts. Nevertheless, nearly 40,000 African American soldiers and sailors gave their lives for the Union cause.

12. In the Confederacy, many enslaved African Americans were forced to help the Confederate army. Some went as servants when their masters joined the army. Others built the army's forts, dug its field trenches, and did much other hard labor for the South's armies.

Women in the War   How did women in the North and the South take part in the war?

13. The Civil War tore families apart, forcing many Northern and Southern women to take on new roles. Before the war, women had been restricted to certain jobs. However, during the war they were needed to replace men who had left for the battlefield. Many women on both sides worked long hours in factories. Some women made guns and ammunition. Others worked in government jobs as clerks and managers. In this way, women learned many new skills as they helped support the Union or the Confederacy.

14. Women were important to both the Union and Confederate armies. In the South, many women wove and sewed clothing in their homes for the Confederate army. Northern women worked in factories where they sewed shirts and uniforms for Union soldiers. In both the North and the South, women took care of sick and wounded soldiers in army hospitals. They also were nurses on the battlefield, helping wounded and dying men. Some women even disguised themselves as men and fought in the war. Others became spies to learn military plans of the Union or the Confederacy.

People in History

15. Clara Barton   When the Civil War began, Barton was working as a clerk in Washington, D.C. Each day she saw hundreds of wounded soldiers carried to the nation's capitol, with few nurses available to care for them. Clara Barton decided that something had to be done to help the wounded. She organized a group of women to nurse the wounded soldiers and bring them blankets, food, and clothing. During the war, Clara Barton risked her own life by going on to the battlefields to aid and comfort the wounded. She became known as the "Angel of the Battlefield." After the Civil War, while visiting Europe, she learned of the work of the International Red Cross in helping victims of wars. Returning to the U.S., Barton founded the American Red Cross. She served as its president for 22 years.

Outlook

16. The Civil War had important and lasting effects on the United States. While African Americans were no longer slaves, in the years ahead, they would struggle to try to achieve equality. The Civil War also increased the power of the federal government. No state or group of states ever again could claim the right to leave the Union. Finally, the war left many people in both the North and the South bitter and angry. Old ideas and opinions died hard. What do you think the government should do ◄ to help the country, and especially the South, recover from the war? What do you think were some of the problems former slaves faced when the war ended?

CHAPTER REVIEW

VOCABULARY REVIEW

▶ Write the words in the left-hand column on a piece of paper. Then write the letter of the definition next to the word it matches.

1. siege

2. total war

a. the destruction of everything an enemy army can use

b. the army's prevention of food and supplies from reaching an enemy city

SKILL BUILDER: READING A MAP

▶ Study the map of the major Civil War battles 1863–1865 carefully. Then tell whether each of the following statements is true or false. Number your paper and write TRUE or FALSE.

1. Sherman began his advance by taking Port Hudson.

2. Control of the Gulf of Mexico coast was an important element in a Union victory.

3. The northernmost battlesite during the Civil War from 1863–1865 was Philadelphia.

4. Five seaports fell under Union control between 1863–1865.

5. In Sherman's "March to the Sea," his army destroyed most of the Union's food supply in Alabama.

6. The battles of Franklin and Nashville were the last Union victories west of the Appalachian Mountains.

7. Fighting in the Civil War never got as far south as Florida.

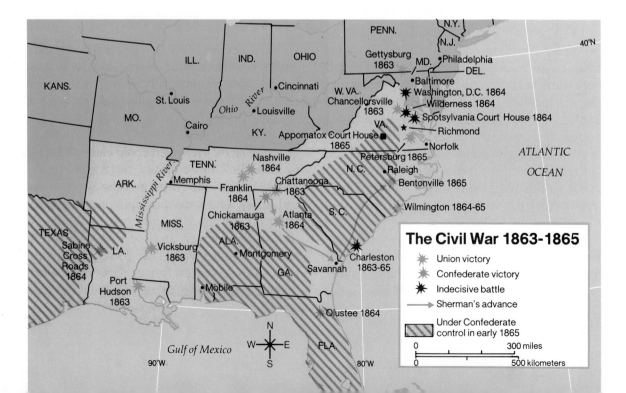

SKILL BUILDER: CRITICAL THINKING AND COMPREHENSION

▲ I. Summarizing

▶ On a separate sheet of paper, write two or three sentences that summarize each of the topics below.

1. The role of African Americans in the Civil War

2. The changes brought about by the Civil War

3. The message of the Gettysburg Address by Lincoln

◣ II. Comparing and Contrasting

▶ On a separate sheet of paper, compare and contrast the following.

1. Compare the work of women in the North for the Union army and the work of women in the South for the Confederate army.

2. Contrast the role of African Americans in the Civil War for the Union and the Confederacy.

3. Compare the war methods used by General Sherman and General Grant.

◯ III. Generalizing

▶ Find sentences from the the chapter that support the following generalizations. Write the sentences on a separate sheet of paper.

1. Both sides paid a terrible price for the Civil War.

2. African Americans faced the problem of racism from both the Union and the Confederacy.

3. Women's lives in America were greatly changed by the war.

USING PRIMARY SOURCES

▶ Reread the Spotlight on Sources on page 413. Using library resources, find a complete version of Lincoln's Gettysburg Address. Recite it aloud to your class, or tape record a version for your teacher to hear. Be sure to pronounce words properly and rehearse until your reading makes sense to you. Consult a dictionary if you are not sure of meaning or pronunciation. Some students may want to memorize the entire speech.

ENRICHMENT

1. Reread the opening scene describing Lee's surrender, in paragraph 1. Write a short play describing the words and feelings of these two proud men. Try to show how awkward and difficult this meeting must have been for all involved.

2. Prepare and record an audio program about one of the Civil War's key battles. Make it like a radio news report approximately two minutes' long. Before recording, make notes. Then write a script and rehearse it. Use sound effects and "live" interviews with soldiers. You might first want to listen to radio news programs to get a sense of how to proceed.

417

CHAPTER 4

Reconstruction

OBJECTIVE: What serious problems did the nation face in bringing the South back into the Union?

1. The President and Mrs. Lincoln were enjoying their evening out. They were relaxed and happy as they watched the play at Ford's Theater. They did not hear the man opening the door behind them. The man fired a pistol directly at President Lincoln's head. Lincoln died the next day, April 15, 1865. Less than a week after Lee's surrender, the nation had lost its great leader. The man who shot him, John Wilkes Booth, had favored the Confederacy. This terrible deed was a clear sign that the bitterness between the North and the South would not end soon.

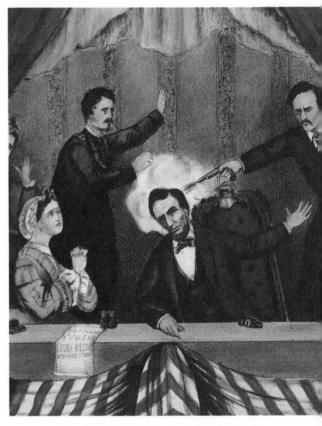

▲ While enjoying an evening away from the cares of state, President Lincoln was assassinated by John Wilkes Booth, an actor whose sympathies lay with the Confederacy.

Rebuilding the Nation What plans were made to help the freed slaves and deal with the Southern states?

2. The period of rebuilding the nation after the Civil War is called **Reconstruction** (ree-kun-STRUK-shun). Reconstruction lasted from 1865 to 1877. Before his death, Lincoln had begun to plan for Reconstruction. He hoped that the Southern states would quickly rejoin the Union after the war. He planned to offer their leaders easy terms to come back into the United States. Vice President Andrew Johnson, who became President, tried to complete Lincoln's plans for Reconstruction. Under Johnson's plan, states had to free their slaves and agree not to pay any part of the Confederacy's debts. Voters had to swear that they were loyal to the Union. By December 1865, most of the Southern states had formed new governments and accepted Johnson's terms.

3. These new governments in the Southern states were made up entirely of white men, including some of the men who had been leaders of the Confederacy. The new Southern state governments passed harsh **black codes.** Black codes were laws that kept many important rights from the **freedmen.** Freedmen were the

In Chapter 4 you will apply these critical thinking skills to the historical process:

 Recognizing Main Idea: Identifying the most important idea in a paragraph.
Sequencing: Putting a series of events in the correct time order.

▶ **Drawing Conclusions:** Making a statement that explains the facts and evidence.

African American men, women, and children who had been slaves. African Americans could not vote, hold government offices, or serve on juries. The new black codes also forced most freedmen to work as farm laborers. Republicans in Congress refused to allow the Southern states with these governments back into the Union.

Radical Republicans   What was the plan of the Radical Republicans for Reconstruction?

4. When Congress met in December 1865, it decided to take over planning for Reconstruction. Congress was now controlled by the **Radical Republicans**. Radical Republicans believed in equal rights for African American citizens. They believed the federal government had a duty to help the freedmen. They did not want white Southerners to have power in the South. Instead, they believed the South should be treated like a conquered nation. They were determined that white Southerners who had favored the Confederacy must not be allowed to vote or hold government office.

5. The Radical Republicans took steps to guarantee the rights of African Americans. In 1865, they were successful in having the Thirteenth Amendment added to the Constitution. This amendment ended slavery in the United States. Then, in June 1866, Congress passed the Fourteenth Amendment and sent it to the states for their approval. The Fourteenth Amendment stated that freedmen were citizens who were protected by laws equally with all other citizens. The amendment also said that freedmen's rights to life, liberty, and property could not be limited or taken away by the states. Congress also gave more power to the **Freedmen's Bureau**, which helped African Americans find homes and jobs and get an education.

6. President Johnson believed that the Radical Republicans were taking actions that were unwise and unlawful. Johnson **vetoed**, or turned down, the bill to renew the Freedmen's Bureau. Later he vetoed a civil rights bill intended for freedmen. However, Congress passed these bills over Johnson's vetoes. The Radical Republicans and the President were heading for a showdown over Reconstruction.

7. Victories in the 1866 Congressional election enabled the Radical Republicans to move forward with their Reconstruction plan. In March 1867, Congress passed a new set of laws, called the Reconstruction Acts, over President Johnson's vetoes. These laws set up army rule in the South. The South was divided into five military districts. Army commanders in each district would prepare the states to rejoin the Union. In each state, all male citizens, black and white, were to choose delegates who would write a new constitution for the state. This constitution had to grant the right to vote to African Americans. White Southerners who had supported the Confederacy were not allowed to vote or to take part in these governments. Why ◄ did Northerners want to keep supporters of the Confederacy out of state governments? When a state carried out all these terms, it would be accepted back into the Union.

8. During the next few years, all the Southern states rejoined the United States. By 1868, the Fourteenth Amendment was ratified. Two years later, the Radical Republicans added the Fifteenth Amendment to the Constitution. This amendment provided that no state could deny the right to vote to citizens because of their race or color, or because they had once been slaves.

9. The Radical Republicans tried to get rid of President Johnson. Early in 1868, the House of Representatives **impeached** the President. To impeach means to accuse an official of criminally breaking the law. Johnson was accused of "high crimes" in refusing to carry out laws passed by Congress. In March, Johnson was tried by the Senate. By a margin of only one vote, the Senate found Johnson not guilty. Even so, Johnson now had little power. Later that year the Republicans nominated Ulysses S. Grant, who went on to win election as President. Grant had supported the Radical Republicans and their ideas on Reconstruction.

Background: Thaddeus Stevens urged that freedmen be given land in the South. He proposed that the large plantations be confiscated and the land redistributed. Only in this way, he argued, would African Americans have the economic strength to survive.

Reconstruction Government Which groups supported new governments in the South, and what did the governments achieve?

10. The Reconstruction governments in the South helped improve many people's lives. They set up free public schools for all children. They built public hospitals and clinics. These governments also improved conditions in prisons. They made taxes fairer and used tax money to build new roads and railroads. Industries, such as cotton and steel, were encouraged to build new factories in the South and to provide jobs.

 Spotlight on Sources

11. Many Northern teachers were sent by the Freedmen's Bureau to teach in the South during Reconstruction. The following is a letter from one school teacher describing how important education was to the freedmen:

It is surprising to me to see the amount of suffering which many people endure for the sake of sending their children to school. . . . They are anxious to have the children "get on" in their books and do not seem to feel impatient if they lack comforts themselves. A pile of books is seen in almost every cabin, though there is no furniture except a poor bed, a table, and two or three broken chairs.

—from *The American Freedman*, April 1869

What details suggest how important education ◄ was to the freedmen? Does education have the same importance today?

12. African American Southerners played a key part in the Reconstruction governments of the South. In five Southern states, African American voters were in the majority. African Americans were elected as local officials, state officials, and as members of state lawmaking bodies. Seventeen African Americans served as Representatives and Senators in Congress.

MAP SKILL BUILDER: After the Civil War, the defeated South was divided into military districts.
1. In which military district was South Carolina?   **2.** Which was the largest military district?   **3.** When was Mississippi readmitted to the Union?

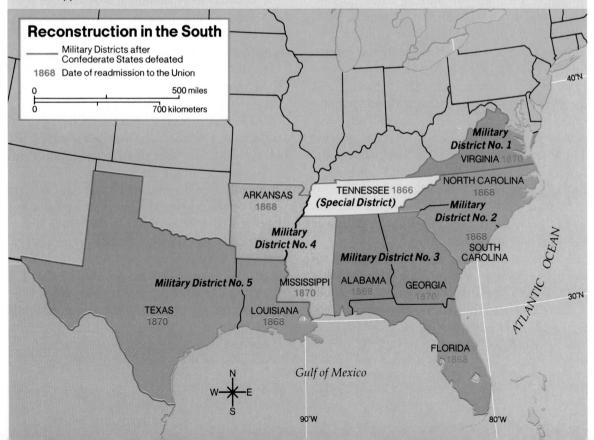

Reconstruction in the South

Military Districts after Confederate States defeated
1868 Date of readmission to the Union

0   500 miles
0   700 kilometers

Military District No. 1
VIRGINIA 1870

TENNESSEE 1866 (Special District)

NORTH CAROLINA 1868

ARKANSAS 1868

Military District No. 2

Military District No. 4

1868 SOUTH CAROLINA

Military District No. 3

Military District No. 5

MISSISSIPPI 1870   ALABAMA 1868   GEORGIA 1870

TEXAS 1870

LOUISIANA 1868

FLORIDA 1868

Gulf of Mexico

ATLANTIC OCEAN

40°N

30°N

90°W   80°W

N
W — E
S

▲ After the Civil War, the Freedmen's Bureau set up over a thousand schools throughout the South where former slaves were taught to read and write.

People in History

13. Blanche K. Bruce One of two African Americans who were elected during Reconstruction to the United States Senate was Blanche K. Bruce. He was the first African American who served a full six-year term in the Senate. Born a slave in Virginia, Bruce had escaped to Hannibal, Missouri. There he had worked as a printer and set up a school for African Americans. He attended Oberlin College in Ohio. After the Civil War, Bruce moved to Mississippi. There he became a wealthy planter and entered politics. Elected to the Senate from Mississippi in 1874, Bruce worked to help poor African Americans and Native Americans. Bruce later served as an official in the Treasury Department.

14. Besides African Americans, white Northerners were an important group in the South. Some were business leaders. Others were teachers or soldiers. White Southerners disliked these people and called them **carpetbaggers**, after a kind of suitcase they sometimes carried. White Southerners also claimed that the carpetbaggers were **corrupt**. A corrupt person is one who gets rich in illegal or immoral ways. In fact, however, most of them were honest and hardworking. They did their best to improve Southern governments and to improve conditions for African Americans.

15. Some white Southerners worked with the state governments of the Reconstruction era. These white Southerners were called **scalawags** by other white Southerners. Some were Southerners who had sided with the Union during the Civil War. Others were people who believed that helping the Reconstruction governments would aid their state's economy. Like the carpetbaggers, the scalawags often were accused of being corrupt. In fact, most of them were honest people.

16. In the 1870s, the Reconstruction governments in the South weakened. The Amnesty Act of 1872 allowed most white Southerners who had supported the Confederacy to vote and hold office once again. They soon took control of the governments in the Southern states. They were aided by secret groups like the Ku Klux Klan, which used terror and violence against African Americans to keep them from voting. Finally, in 1877, the federal government withdrew the last of its troops from the South. When these soldiers left, Reconstruction ended. To this day, the reversal of the gains African Americans had made during Reconstruction is strongly felt. For African Americans, the struggle for equality would continue for many years.

Outlook

17. Reconstruction lasted from 1865 to 1877. During these years, Radical Republicans tried to rebuild the South. Freed African Americans in the South made important gains. Yet they were not able to enjoy these gains for long. Why did Reconstruction policies fail to bring ◀ lasting equality to African Americans?

Background: The Civil Rights Acts of 1886 and 1875 were all but invalidated by court rulings after Reconstruction. However, they became important legal precedents and foundations for the civil rights legislation of the 1960s.

CHAPTER REVIEW

VOCABULARY REVIEW

▶ Select the word or phrase that best completes each sentence. Number your paper and write the correct word by each number.

freedman   Freedmen's Bureau   carpetbaggers

Reconstruction   vetoed   scalawags

black codes   corrupt   civil rights

Radical Republicans   impeached

1. _____ refers to the period of rebuilding the nation after the Civil War.

2. Andrew Johnson _____ many laws that displeased him.

3. White Southerners felt the Northerners who came South were _____ .

4. _____ were white Southerners who supported the state governments in the South after the Civil War.

5. _____ were laws that kept many important rights from African American freedmen.

6. Northerners who played a key role in Southern governments were called _____ .

7. After the Civil War, former slaves became known as _____ .

8. Those in Congress who wanted to be sure that ex-slaves were treated fairly were known as _____ .

9. Andrew Johnson was _____ , but he remained in office.

10. The _____ was set up to help freed slaves find homes and jobs.

SKILL BUILDER: GIVING AN ORAL REPORT

Presenting a report in class causes everyone some anxiety. However, following a few simple steps will help you to relax. It will also help you to present a better report. Read the following steps. They will help you to practice making reports in class.

1. Narrow your topic by focusing on a specific topic instead of a too general one. It will make your job easier, and it will be easier on your listeners.

2. Take notes.

3. Make an outline from your notes.

4. Practice by yourself by looking in a mirror as you speak.

5. Revise your talk.

6. Practice with an audience. Ask your audience to give you feedback about how clear you were, how often you looked at them, and how interesting your talk was.

SKILL BUILDER: CRITICAL THINKING AND COMPREHENSION

▲▲ I. Main Idea

▶ Writing a title is a good way to express a main idea. On a separate sheet of paper, write titles to express the main ideas in the chapter.

1. paragraph 5

2. paragraph 7

3. paragraph 10

II. Sequencing

Sequencing involves putting information in proper time order. Although time lines are a good way of understanding sequencing, other ways are available.

▶ On a separate sheet of paper, write the following events in the order in which they occurred.

a. Andrew Johnson is impeached.

d. Ulysses S. Grant is elected President.

b. The last federal soldiers leave the South.

e. President Lincoln is assassinated.

c. Congress passes the Reconstruction Acts.

f. The Fifteenth Amendment is ratified.

III. Drawing Conclusions

▶ Reread the following paragraphs. On a separate sheet of paper, write your own conclusions about what you have read.

1. African Americans in the Civil War: paragraphs 10–12.

2. Women in the Civil War: paragraphs 13–15.

USING PRIMARY SOURCES

▶

Reread the Spotlight on Sources in paragraph 11. Why was education important to freedmen?

ENRICHMENT

1. Design a mural on the Reconstruction era. First, list people, place or events that you want to show. Then sketch scenes that depict these aspects of Reconstruction.

2. Historians continue to debate the Reconstruction era. Participate in a debate on the following topic: Resolved, Reconstruction eventually delayed the progress of African Americans. Debaters should be prepared to argue the affirmative or the negative view of the statement.

3. Choose one of the following dates. Create a newspaper front page that tells what happened on that important day in history. You are free to add fictional details to support the basic facts.
a. Abraham Lincoln's assassination
b. Andrew Johnson defeats impeachment
c. The Fourteenth Amendment becomes law

CHAPTER 5

From Slavery to Segregation

OBJECTIVE: How were African Americans treated after Reconstruction, and why did they face setbacks in their struggle for equality?

1. The Civil War was over, and a public meeting was being held in Yorktown, Virginia. An African American named Bayley Wyatt rose to speak. Former slaves, he argued, had a right to own land. "Didn't we clear the lands and raise the crops of corn, of cotton, of tobacco, of rice, of sugar, of everything?" he cried. "And then didn't large cities in the North grow up on the cotton and the sugars and the rice that we made? Yes! I appeal to the South and to the North if I haven't spoken the words of truth. I say they have grown rich and my people are poor." Now that slavery was dead, former slaves looked forward to living the lives of free people—to getting an education, to voting, to owning land. They had heard rumors that each former slave would get "40 acres and a mule." But it was not to be. Less than ten years after the first exciting rush of freedom, most of them were again raising cotton—in conditions little better than those they had known in slave days.

▲ Two young women pick cotton in a Southern field in the years after the Civil War. How did their lives differ from their parents' lives under slavery?

African American Sharecroppers Who were the sharecroppers, and what hardships did they face?

2. After the Civil War, many of the large plantations in the South were broken up into small farms. Poor white farmers rented some of these farms from the planters. These farmers were called **tenant farmers.** Tenant farmers paid rent for using the land, but they supplied their own seeds, farm tools, and labor.

3. Most of the small farms in the South were farmed by the freed African Americans. The freedmen had no money to rent land or to buy tools and supplies. Why wouldn't they have ◄

In Chapter 5 you will apply these critical thinking skills to the historical process:
▲ **Recognizing Main Idea:** Identifying the most important idea in a paragraph.
Recognizing Cause and Effect: Recognizing the action or event that makes something happen; identifying the result of an action or event.

money? For this reason, these farmers came to be called **sharecroppers** (SHAYR-krah-purz). Instead, the planters who owned the land gave them seeds, farm tools, a mule, and a small farmhouse. In return, farmers gave a share of their crops to the planters as rent. Sharecroppers got the food and other supplies they needed at a store. They promised another part of their crops to pay for these supplies.

4. Each year, sharecroppers went more and more into debt. Each year, they had to give a large part of their crops to the planter. Often, sharecroppers' harvests did not cover the amount they owed the planter or the store owner. No matter how hard they worked, they could never grow enough cotton or tobacco to pay back what they owed. State laws prevented people who had debts from leaving their land. In this way, African American sharecroppers were forced to stay on the land they farmed. ▶ Why did some sharecroppers feel their lives had not improved much after slavery?

African Americans Lose Their Rights   What new laws in the South took away freedom from African Americans?

5. After federal troops left the South in 1877, African Americans lost many of the rights they had gained. By the early 1880s, Southern states began to pass **racial segregation** (seg-ruh-GAY-shun) laws. Racial segregation separates people of different races. Soon all the Southern states had segregation laws. These laws made African Americans ride in separate streetcars and railroad cars. They could not stay at the same hotels or eat in the same restaurants with whites. Their children had to attend separate schools. The laws passed in the 1880s and 1890s that required racial segregation in the South were called **Jim Crow** laws. Jim Crow was originally a character in a song sung in shows that made fun of African Americans.

6. The Supreme Court upheld the laws that took away the rights of African American citizens. The court ruled that the segregation laws of the Southern states were not against the Constitution. The most famous of these Supreme Court rulings was *Plessy v. Ferguson* in 1896. In this case, the court said African Americans could be forced to ride in separate cars on railroad trains. The court added that these separate cars must be equal in quality to the train cars for whites. The Supreme Court's **separate but equal rule** allowed racial segregation to become even stronger in the South. Why might ◀ the court have believed that "separate but equal" was a fair system?

Spotlight on Sources

7. Justice John Marshall Harlan was the only Supreme Court justice who argued against racial segregation. His **dissent**, or disagreeing opinion, in *Plessy v. Ferguson* strongly upheld the equality of African American citizens. Harlan, a Southerner himself, wrote these important words:

> The white race deems [believes] itself to be the dominant [superior] race in this country. But in view of the Constitution, there is in this country no superior [better] class of citizens. Our Constitution is color-blind. In respect of civil rights, all citizens are equal before the law. The law regards man [people] as man [people], and takes no account of his color when his civil rights as guaranteed [protected] by the supreme law of the land are involved [affected].

What does Harlan say is the white race's opin- ◀ ion of itself? Does Harlan believe that the Constitution supports this point of view?

8. One of the few white groups that tried to help African Americans was the Populist party. This new political party promised to help the poor small farmers and sharecroppers both black and white. Southern planters, however, tried to stop the growing power of the Populists. First, they gained the support of many poor white farmers by appealing to racial prejudices. They said that if the Populist party won, African American sharecroppers would soon rule the South. They said white farmers should

vote for the Democratic party, which was controlled in part by the planters.

9. Beginning in the 1880s, Southern states passed laws to deny African Americans the right to vote. The Fifteenth Amendment had said that no state could keep African American men from voting. Even so, the new laws found several ways to **disenfranchise**, or deny the right to vote to, African Americans. One way was a **poll tax** for all voters. A poll tax was a small sum of money voters had to pay to vote. Since most African Americans had little money, they could not pay the poll tax. Many states also required voters to pass a **literacy** (LIT-er-uh-see) **test**. A literacy test was supposed to prove that a voter knew how to read and write. Many African Americans had never attended school, and they could not pass such a test.

10. Several states also passed **grandfather clauses** which allowed voting only for persons whose fathers or grandfathers had voted in 1867. African American citizens had not been able to vote in 1867. Since their fathers or grandfathers could not vote, neither could they. Poll taxes, the literacy test, and the grandfather clause all kept most Southern African Americans from voting. Do you think there should be any limits on the right to vote? Why or why not?

African American Leaders How did Booker T. Washington and W.E.B. DuBois work for African Americans?

11. During these difficult years, Booker T. Washington was a very important African American leader. Washington taught that African Americans had to accept racial segregation. He said that Southern African Americans were too poor to struggle for equal rights. Instead, he believed the most important thing African Americans should do was learn skills needed for jobs. He founded Tuskegee (tus-KEE-gee) Institute in Alabama to teach job skills for industry and farming. Washington believed when African Americans were educated and had good jobs, they would be able to gain equal rights.

▼ Some African Americans, like this family, moved to the West, where they could acquire their own farmland under the Homestead Act. Why did Southern sharecroppers not take advantage of this opportunity?

Background: The *Plessy v. Ferguson* separate but equal ruling stood until 1954, when the Supreme Court overturned it in *Brown v. Board of Education of Topeka*. The 1954 ruling marked the beginning of a new era in civil rights.

▲ At Tuskegee Institute, founded by Booker T. Washington, African American students work in a chemistry laboratory. The director of this laboratory was George Washington Carver, one of America's most famous scientists.

12. Booker T. Washington's ideas were accepted by many African Americans in the South. His school brought hope to some African Americans. White leaders of the Southern states also supported Washington. Why do you think they did so? However, many African Americans were still unable to improve their lives. Most remained poor sharecroppers.

People in History

13. W.E.B. DuBois   A great African American leader in the early 1900s was W.E.B. DuBois (doo-BOYS). He was born in Great Barrington, Massachusetts. He was a brilliant student who studied at Harvard University. DuBois was the first African American to receive a doctorate degree from Harvard. After teaching at several northern colleges, he went to Atlanta University in Georgia, where he taught from 1897 to 1910. DuBois wrote many books, including *The Souls of Black Folk.*

14. During his years in Georgia, DuBois saw how racist ideas caused African Americans to suffer. He then decided to speak out against the ideas of Booker T. Washington. DuBois insisted that segregation both in the North and the South must be ended. He urged African Americans to fight for equal rights. He also believed that they must be well educated and become teachers, doctors, and lawyers. In this way, African Americans would have strong leaders in their struggle for equality.

Outlook

15. After Reconstruction, African Americans in the South lived through years of great hardship. Most of them became poor sharecroppers. African Americans in the North and the South were treated as second-class citizens. Segregation laws kept African Americans from mixing with whites in the South. African Americans also were kept from voting. However, their leaders worked to win equality for their people. Why do you think Booker T. Washington and W.E.B. DuBois had such different views? Do these two different views still appear today?

CHAPTER REVIEW

VOCABULARY REVIEW

▶ Write each number and word on a sheet of paper. Then write the letter of the definition next to the word it defines.

1. sharecroppers
2. racial segregation
3. tenant farmers
4. separate but equal
5. literacy test
6. Jim Crow laws
7. poll tax
8. grandfather clauses
9. disenfranchise
10. dissent

a. separation of people of different races
b. laws depriving blacks' civil rights
c. laws that allowed whites to vote because their ancestors did
d. Supreme Court view allowing segregation
e. sum of money required to vote
f. one who rents land but supplies own seeds and equipment
g. obstacle to voting for uneducated freedmen.
h. farmers whose harvest helped pay for land, seed, tools
i. disagreement
j. take away the right to vote
k. to take away the right to own land

SKILL BUILDER: READING A MAP

▶ Look at the map below. It shows segregation in an imaginary small Southern town in the 1880s. Answer the questions below.

1. Which buildings or places are separate for African Americans and whites?
2. What divides African Americans and whites into two areas of the town?
3. What advantages do whites have? What disadvantages do African Americans have?

A SEGREGATED SOUTHERN TOWN IN THE 1880s

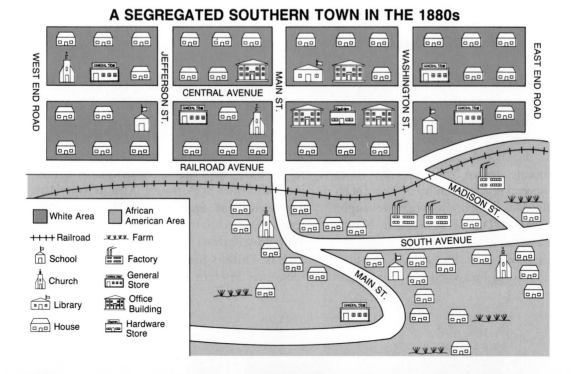

SKILL BUILDER: CRITICAL THINKING AND COMPREHENSION

▲ I. Main Idea

▶ Each of the paragraphs in this chapter begins with a topic sentence. The topic sentence expresses the main idea. There are often several ways of expressing the same idea. Rewrite in your own words the following topic sentences from the chapter. You may simply want to use synonyms or simpler sentences. If you wish, you may break a topic sentence into two sentences.

1. Each year, sharecroppers went more and more into debt. (paragraph 4)

2. The Supreme Court upheld the laws that took away the rights of African American citizens. (paragraph 6)

3. Several states also passed **grandfather clauses** to keep African Americas from voting. (paragraph 10)

➡ II. Cause and Effect

▶ On a separate sheet of paper, write the cause or effect for the following.

1. **Cause:** _____
   Effect: The African American freedmen became sharecroppers.

2. **Cause:** Federal troops left the South.
   Effect: _____

❯ III. Predicting

▶ You have read how the Supreme Court ruled in 1896 in the *Plessy v. Ferguson* case. The court allowed "separate but equal," making segregation legal. Historically, separate was almost never equal. Predict what might have happened if the court had ruled against separate but equal. How might history have changed if segregation had been outlawed some 58 years earlier than it was? Give specific examples and reasons.

USING PRIMARY SOURCES

▶ Many people are familiar with a number of famous speeches. Some people memorize portions of these speeches. Memorization is a valuable learning tool. Memorize Justice John Marshall Harlan's words on page 425. Some students may want to recite the passage before the class. (Library resources will help you if you want to use a more complete version of the speech.)

ENRICHMENT

1. Role-play a situation involving a former slave who meets his former master on a downtown street. Act out a scene between the two. What might the two say to each other? What would have influenced their opinions of each other?

2. Imagine you are W.E.B. DuBois. Write a letter about your views to Booker T. Washington. Then write the response that Booker T. Washington might have given.

UNIT REVIEW

SUMMARY

The Civil War ripped the United States into two warring sides. Slavery had always divided Americans, but in the 1850s, North and South were on a collision course over it. The election of Abraham Lincoln in 1860 forced the issue. Before Lincoln was sworn in as President, seven states declared that they had seceded from the Union. Later four others followed them. The seceded states joined to form the Confederate States of America. The question now was whether there would be one nation or two.

Each side hoped for an early victory in the war, but it was not to be. The fighting raged on for four years, from 1861 to 1865. In the early years of the war, Confederate forces won important battles. However, after 1863, when Grant took Vicksburg and Lee was halted at Gettysburg, the tide turned in favor of the North. Lincoln's Emancipation Proclamation turned the war into a moral crusade by the North and its supporters. By the time of Lee's surrender to Grant at Appomattox in 1865, Lincoln had begun plans for restoring the South to the Union and for rebuilding the lives of former slaves.

After Lincoln's death, Radical Republicans enacted a plan for Reconstruction over President Johnson's opposition. For a time, African Americans voted throughout the South, and some held office. However, by the time Reconstruction ended in 1877, white Southerners had found ways to deprive African Americans of many of their rights. After so much bloodshed and hardship, African Americans had yet to gain the full rights of citizenship.

SKILL BUILDER: READING A MAP

▶ Refer to the map to answer these questions.

1. How many states had been admitted to the Union by 1870?

2. Name areas that still were territories in 1870.

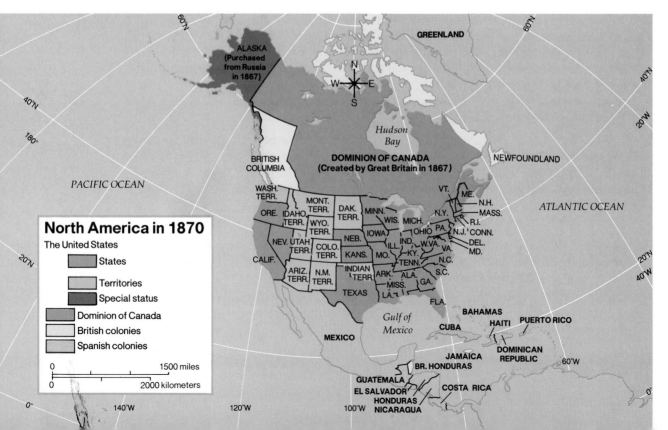

North America in 1870

The United States

- States
- Territories
- Special status
- Dominion of Canada
- British colonies
- Spanish colonies

0   1500 miles
0   2000 kilometers

3. What area had a special status under the United States government?

4. What was the western boundary of the United States? The Southern boundary? The Eastern?

5. In 1870, what areas in North America and the Caribbean does the map show as colonies of European countries? Which European countries controlled these areas?

SKILL BUILDER: CRITICAL THINKING AND COMPREHENSION

▲ I. Summarizing

▶ Summarize information in the unit by writing three or four sentences about each of the following headlines.

a. Grant Takes Vicksburg

b. Lee Surrenders

c. Jefferson Davis Inaugurated

d. Blanche Bruce Sworn in as Senator

e. Booker T. Washington Sets up New School

f. Lincoln Inaugurated

II. Point of View

▶ Read the passage below. Then answer the questions that follow it.

Our greatest danger is that, in the great leap from slavery to freedom, we may overlook the fact that the masses of us are to live by the productions of our hands. . . . It is at the bottom of life we must begin, and not at the top. . . . Progress in the enjoyment of all the privileges that will come to us must be the result of severe and constant struggle rather than of artificial forcing. . . . It is important and right that all privileges of the law be ours, but it is vastly more important that we be prepared for the exercise of these privileges. The opportunity to earn a dollar in a factory just now is worth infinitely more than the opportunity to spend a dollar in an opera house.

1. These words were published in the 1890s, after Reconstruction had ended. Who is the likely author? What clues in the passage help you conclude who the author is?

2. Of Booker T. Washington or W.E.B. DuBois, which one would *oppose* the views in the selection. Why?

3. Rewrite the selection in your own words.

4. Write a paragraph that takes an opposing point of view.

ENRICHMENT

1. Suppose you have lived in West Virginia during the Civil War. You have relatives who died for the North, and others who died for the South. Write an imaginary journal entry for April 16, 1865. You have just received word of Lincoln's death. Tell about your feelings and your thoughts for the future on this day.

2. Research the role of your state during and after the Civil War. Include the following: part taken in the war, notable persons or events, effects of the war.

UNIT 10

THE UNITED STATES BECOMES AN INDUSTRIAL NATION

Chapter

UNIT OVERVIEW   In this unit you will learn how industrialization, immigration, and the growth of cities changed life in America in the late 1800s.

UNIT SKILLS OBJECTIVES   In Unit 10, two critical thinking skills are emphasized:

○ **Generalizing**: Making a statement that links several facts.

❯ **Predicting**: Telling what you believe will happen on the basis of clues and facts.

You will also use two important social studies skills:
Reading a Graph   Interpreting a Photograph

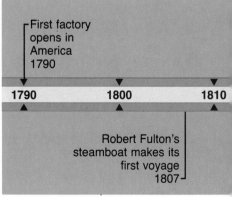

First factory opens in America 1790

| 1790 | 1800 | 1810 |

Robert Fulton's steamboat makes its first voyage 1807

ESL/LEP Strategy: Write the vocabulary terms from this unit on the chalkboard. Ask students to write the definitions of those words they are familiar with. Have them guess the meanings of the other terms and check after they have studied the unit.

▲ Improvements in industry during the 1800s changed the way many Americans lived.
This painting shows a dramatic moment in the steel-making process.

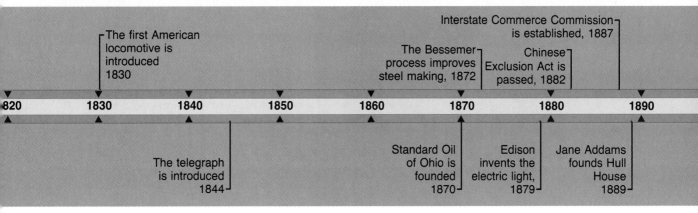

Interstate Commerce Commission
is established, 1887

The first American
locomotive is
introduced
1830

The Bessemer
process improves
steel making, 1872

Chinese
Exclusion Act is
passed, 1882

820   1830   1840   1850   1860   1870   1880   1890

The telegraph
is introduced
1844

Standard Oil
of Ohio is
founded
1870

Edison
invents the
electric light,
1879

Jane Addams
founds Hull
House
1889

433

Points of View

When the 1800s began, most Americans were guided in their daily lives by the rising and setting of the sun and by the weather. By the time the century ended, though, many Americans were listening for the factory whistle and following the motion of machines. The rise of industry created a strange new America. Nowhere was the change more striking than in the nation's growing

▲ For many who had little money, city life meant living in crowded, unhealthy conditions such as these.

A REFORMER'S VIEW

❝The first building we entered faced a narrow street. The hallway was as dark as the air was foul [smelly] or the walls filthy [dirty]. . . . After ascending [climbing] several flights of stairs, we entered a room of undreamed-of wretchedness [awfulness]. On the floor lay a sick man. . . . For more than two years he had been paralyzed in his lower limbs. . . . There . . . he had lain on a wretched pallet [poor bed] of rags, seeing his faithful wife tirelessly sewing, hour by hour, day by day, and knowing full well that health, life and hope were hourly slipping away from her. This poor woman supports her invalid [sick] husband, her two children and herself, by making pants for Boston's clothiers [clothing manufacturers]. No rest . . . a perpetual [unending] grind from early dawn often till far into the night; and what is more appalling [horrifying] . . . the long months of semi-starvation and lack of sleep have brought on rheumatism [a painful disease of the joints], which had settled in the joints of her fingers, so that every stitch means a throb of pain. . . .❞

—*Civilization's Inferno, or, Studies in the Social Cellar*, B. O. Flower

cities. In the cities, the contrast between living conditions for the wealthy and for the poor was all too evident. Here are two views of city life in America during the 1890s. The first selection is from a book by a writer who was troubled by what he saw in Boston. The second is from a magazine article by a professor who believed in the importance of cities.

A PROFESSOR'S VIEW

" . . . [T]he best place to . . . carry on any kind of business is where that business is already being done. For that reason we see different kinds of manufacturers grouping themselves together—textiles in one place, metals in another . . . and so on. The reason of this is obvious [easy to see]. In a community where a certain kind of business is carried on, the whole population become, to a certain extent, experts. . . .

We must remember, too, that cities . . . have vastly improved within half a century. About fifty years ago neither New York nor Boston had public water, and very few of our cities had either water or gas, and horse railroads had not been thought of. . . .

It would seem, then, (1) that for economic reasons a large part of the work of the world must be done in cities, and the people who do that work must live in cities.

(2) That almost everything that is best in life can be better had in the city than elsewhere. . . . "

—*Journal of Social Science*, volume XXXIII, November, 1895

▲ City families who were well off enjoyed many benefits of city life, including shopping in the newly created department stores.

Using Primary Sources

1. Reread point (1) in the second selection. What does the professor mean by "economic reasons?"

2. What would the Boston writer say about point (2) in the professor's article?

CHAPTER 1

The Growth of Industry to 1860

OBJECTIVE: How did American industry begin to develop in the early 1900s?

1. Stockton and Stokes, owners of the stage-coach company, did not think much of the new steam locomotive called "Tom Thumb." On this day in 1830, Tom Thumb was making its first run. As it steamed toward Baltimore, the stage-coach owners were waiting—with a strong gray horse pulling a car. The race was on! The horse got off to a quick start, but Tom Thumb got up steam, and soon the locomotive had caught up with the horse. The passengers cheered. Tom Thumb was ahead! Suddenly a drive belt slipped, and the horse went on to victory. It did not matter. Tom Thumb had pulled 42 people at the surprising speed of 18 miles an hour. The train had proved its worth. The future no longer belonged to the stage coach. It belonged to the railroad.

Transportation and Communication What inventions speeded travel and communication?

2. The chain of turnpikes and canals connecting cities in the east was improved and expanded in the early 1800s. By 1852, the National Road was lengthened from the town of Wheeling, on the Ohio River, to Vandalia, Illinois. The nation's network of water routes expanded rapidly after the Erie Canal was finished in 1825. Travel by both land and water was still slow and difficult, however.

▲ People in frontier villages welcomed each locomotive that passed through carrying visitors, farm products, and manufactured goods.

3. In the early 1800s, the invention of the steamboat made traveling by water much faster. Robert Fulton's steamboat, the *Clermont*, appeared on the Hudson River in 1807. Powered by a British steam engine, the *Clermont* paddled its way from New York City to Albany and back. Fulton's new boat was a huge success. A

In Chapter 1, you will apply these critical thinking skills to the historical process:
❯ **Predicting:** Telling what you believe will happen on the basis of clues and facts.
◤ **Drawing Conclusions:** Making a statement that explains the facts and evidence.

few years later, steamboats began carrying passengers and freight up and down the Ohio and the Mississippi Rivers. By 1853, a steamboat could travel upstream from New Orleans, Louisiana, to Louisville, Kentucky, in five days.

4. In the 1830s, the "iron horse," or locomotive, gave manufacturers an easier way to transport goods than by canal. Railroads were better than canals in several important ways. They were cheaper to build and did not freeze in the winter. What was another advantage railroads had over canals? By 1840, when Europe had 2,000 miles of track, 3,000 miles had already been laid in the United States. In the next twenty years, the American total reached 30,000 miles.

5. The telegraph and other new ways of communicating joined railroads and canals in tying the nation together. In 1837, Samuel Morse invented the telegraph, a machine that could send messages over electric wires. Seven years later, Morse proved that the telegraph would work. He sent a message over a "talking wire" from Washington D.C. to Baltimore, Maryland. In his own code he tapped out the words, "What hath God wrought [done]!?" Newspaper reporters put the telegraph to good use. Interesting stories quickly became national news. Morse's invention also helped railroad companies direct trains over great distances.

Early Factories and Industry   How did the iron and textile industries develop?

6. Better transportation helped industries grow by moving goods to customers more cheaply and quickly. As roads improved, raw materials such as cotton could reach manufacturers more easily. Finished products, like cotton cloth, could reach many more customers. Manufacturers saw that selling to many more people would bring greater profits. They looked for ways to produce greater amounts of goods.

7. The new spinning machines and power looms, which you read about in Unit 8, provided a way to make cloth more quickly. Because of these machines, textile makers were

some of the first manufacturers to build large factories. The new machines were expensive and needed water power to operate them. In 1813, Francis Cabot Lowell built a large textile mill at Waltham, Massachusetts, beside a waterfall on the Charles River. Lowell's mill was one of the first that put all of the machines needed to produce cloth in one place. Raw cotton was carried into Lowell's factory and bolts of cotton cloth were carried out.

8. As industry grew, more iron was needed for machinery and tools. Orders from railroad companies for iron rails were pouring in. Iron workers were kept busy making tools and machines for the nations's workshops, factories, and farms. Iron workers made nails, bolts, anchors, cannons, chains, and barrel hoops. As the frontier moved west, there was a need for guns, plows, axes, and kettles. By the 1840s, the center of the iron industry had shifted to western Pennsylvania. Coal from the Great Valley of the Appalachians had taken the place of charcoal as furnace fuel for making iron.

Farmers and Workers   How did farm work and manufacturing jobs begin to change?

9. Better farm equipment helped American farmers produce bigger crops. In 1834, Cyrus McCormick introduced a **mechanical reaper** (muh-KAN-ih-kul REEP-ur), a machine for cutting grain. At the time, a farmer swinging a scythe from daybreak to sunset could harvest about one acre of wheat. Using McCormick's new machine, the same farmer could harvest six acres a day. A new type of steel plow could cut through the hard earth of the western prairies. Another important invention was the thresher, which separated wheat kernels from the plant's husk. Farmers were eager to buy the new machinery, add land to their farms, and increase their harvests. Why were farmers sure that their grain could reach buyers in cities many miles away?

10. Just as farmers' work was changed by the development of new machines, city workers' jobs also changed. In 1798, Eli Whitney intro-

Background: Despite the advantages that railroads enjoyed over canals, the volume of freight carried by railroads did not exceed that carried by canals until after the Civil War.

duced the idea of **interchangeable parts** (in-ter-CHAYNJ-uh-bul), or parts so much alike that one could be used in place of another. Interchangeable parts were made by machine. They did not have to be filed by hand until they fit. Making and using interchangeable parts led to a division of labor in workshops and factories. As you learned in Unit 8, the work of making a product, such as a clock, was divided into simple tasks. Each task was given to a different worker. Soon clocks and many other products were being made quickly and cheaply by workers with very little training. How do you think skilled workers felt about the division of labor?

People in History

11. The Lowell Workers In 1822, the company started by Francis Cabot Lowell opened a five-story mill beside the Merrimack River in Massachusetts. Other mills were built nearby, and the town of Lowell grew up around them. Most of the workers in the Lowell mills were women or children. Farm families in the area did not send their sons to the mills because boys were needed for field work. The "mill girls" lived in boarding houses, usually watched over by older women with children of their own. A library was provided. Mill owners even urged the workers to put out a newspaper and write poetry. Wages were low, but housework, sewing, and teaching paid even less than mill work. There were few other jobs open to women at that time. Why do you think women have more opportunities open to them in the United States today?

12. As the years passed, life in Lowell and other textile towns grew harder. Workers were packed two, and even three, to a bed in crowded boarding houses. They were given four looms to operate instead of one. The working day grew longer, beginning at 5:00 A.M. and lasting until after dark. In 1836, the workers took action. **A strike** shut down the mills of Lowell. More than 1500 workers refused to return to work until their demands for better working conditions were met.

▼ New England factory workers head home at the end of the day. What ages and types of people are represented in this painting?

13. Factory-made goods that were low in price and easy to get began to change the way Americans lived. Even something as small as a nail brought changes. After 1830, cheap nails cut by machine could be bought in any town. Carpenters began nailing pieces of 2 × 4 lumber together to make the framework of a house. They no longer had to use a chisel and peg to break heavy timbers, over a foot thick. Houses were built more cheaply than ever before and more people had the money to buy them.

14. Factory products also made life in the home easier. By the 1850s, there were carpets on the floors and machine-made furniture in most rooms. In the kitchen, the wood-burning stove took the place of the huge fireplace of colonial times. Gone was the 60-pound iron kettle that had caused many back injuries and burns. In its place were light tin pots. Another product welcomed by American homemakers was the sewing machine, invented in 1846 by Elias Howe.

15. Many other factory products made life easier for Americans in the 1850s. There were boots and raincoats made with **vulcanized** (VUL-kuh-nyzed) rubber. Charles Goodyear had discovered how to vulcanize, or strengthen, rubber in 1839. There were also sausage stuffers, egg beaters, and factory-made clothes.

Spotlight on Sources

16. There was a dark side to the progress of industry. Anthony Trollope, a novelist from Britain, had this to say about Pittsburgh and its iron factories in the 1860s.

> Even the filth and wondrous [great] blackness of the place are picturesque [colorful] when looked down upon from above. The tops of the churches are visible, and some of the larger buildings may be partially traced through the thick, brown, settled smoke. But the city itself is buried in a dense [thick] cloud.
>
> —*North America,* Anthony Trollope

▶ Pollution was one problem caused by the rise of industry. What were some others?

▲ The promise of work in the mills brought many farm workers into town. This picture shows the mills of Lowell as they looked in the 1830s.

Outlook

17. In the early 1800s, improvements in transportation and in the way goods were made helped industries grow. By 1860, machines had changed the way most Americans did their jobs and lived their lives. But even bigger changes were soon to follow. Once new sources of power such as the steam engine were unlocked, new inventions and improvements on older machines followed rapidly. Americans greeted each new invention with excitement. What problems might some of these inventions have caused in the years to follow? How are these problems similar to those created by new inventions today?

439

CHAPTER REVIEW

VOCABULARY REVIEW

► Match the words in the following list with the definitions below.

1. vulcanized
2. interchangeable parts
3. strike
4. mechanical reaper

a. The power of flowing or falling water used to run machines

b. A machine for cutting grain

c. A refusal by workers to return to work until their demands are met

d. Parts so much alike that one can be used in place of another

e. Having been strengthened with a special treatment

SKILL BUILDER: READING A GRAPH

► The graph below shows the total miles of railroad track in use in the United States from 1835 to 1860. Look at the graph, then answer the questions on a separate sheet of paper.

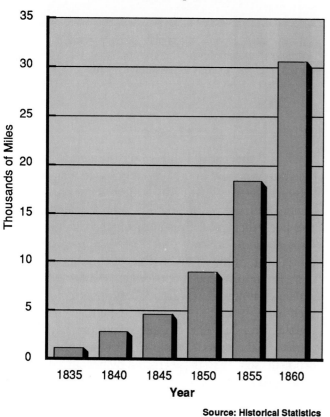

Railroad Mileage, 1835-1860

Source: Historical Statistics

1. During which years were the most miles of track put down?

2. About how many thousands of miles of track were put down between 1850 and 1855?

3. Compare the amount of track that existed in 1840 with the amount that existed 20 years later.

4. Make a generalization about the growth of railroads based on figures in this graph.

SKILL BUILDER: CRITICAL THINKING AND COMPREHENSION

I. Sequencing

▶ Which came first? Look at the pairs of events below. Decide which event in each pair came first. Then fill in the years of the two events on another sheet of paper. Use the text for help.

1. _____ Eli Whitney introduces "interchangeable parts."
   _____ Factory-made nails are used to build houses.

2. _____ A steamboat can travel from New Orleans, Louisiana, to Louisville, Kentucky, in five days.
   _____ The *Clermont* appears on the Hudson.

3. _____ The number of miles of railroad track are laid down in the United States reaches 3,000.
   _____ A horse wins a race against *Tom Thumb*.

4. _____ Lowell opens a mill beside builds a mill on Merrimack River in Massachusetts.
   _____ Workers in Lowell go on strike.

II. Classifying

▶ Make two columns on a separate sheet of paper. Label them as follows: "Transportation and Communication" and "Industry." Classify the following terms by writing them in the correct column.

Tom Thumb   *Clermont*   telegraph   Lowell Workers

division of labor   locomotives   canals   newspaper

III. Drawing Conclusions

▶ Reread paragraph 14. Draw a conclusion about how the products described in this paragraph would have changed the work of the American homemaker.

USING PRIMARY SOURCES

▶ Reread the Spotlight on Sources section, paragraph 16. What are some problems that people living in Pittsburgh might have had because of the "dense cloud" described?

ENRICHMENT

1. Find illustrations of an early cotton gin, a reaper, a thresher, or another farm machine. Chose one of the machines. Draw "before and after" pictures showing how this machine changed farm work. Arrange the pictures on a poster. Add a title to the poster.

2. Imagine that you are working at one of the mills in Lowell. Write a poem that expresses your feelings about life as a mill worker.

3. Write a report that answers these questions about the area where you live. What are the most important industries here? When did they become important? What caused their growth? Before these industries appeared, how did most people make a living?

CHAPTER 2

An Industrial Nation

> OBJECTIVE: How did the United States become an industrialized nation?

1. It weighed 700 tons (630 metric tons). Through 23 miles (36.8 km) of shafts and 40 miles (64 km) of belts, it powered 13 acres (5.2 hectares) of machines. Yet its movements were smooth and quiet. This was the giant steam engine shown at the 1876 Centennial Exhibition in Philadelphia. Americans who saw the huge engine were sure that industry had made a great leap ahead since the Civil War. Much of the credit for the quick rise of industry belonged to steam engines, especially those on rails.

Railroads In what ways did railroads help the nation's economy grow?

2. During the last 30 years of the 1800s, a railroad building boom swept the nation. After the Transcontinental Railroad was completed in 1869, four more rail lines linking East and West were built. By 1900, the United States had more than six times as many track miles as it had in 1860. During the railroad building boom, railway **tycoons** (ty-KOONZ), or powerful business leaders, began buying up local lines and putting them together. By 1873, Cornelius Vanderbilt's New York Central Railroad could run its trains all the way from New York to Chicago. The cost of shipping goods between the two cities was cut in half. As the big railroad companies connected their lines, a rail network across the country was created. When factory

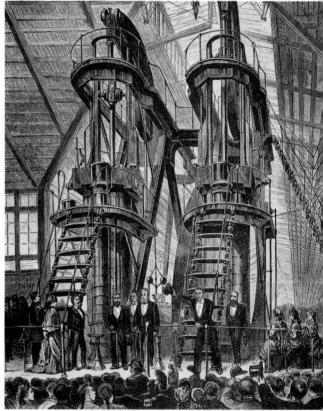

▲ President Ulysses S. Grant and the Brazilian Emperor Dom Pedro II had the honor of starting the giant engine at the opening of the Centennial Exhibition in 1876.

owners saw that their goods could reach customers anywhere in the country, what do you think they did?

3. The railroads helped industries grow by opening up a nationwide market for goods. Now a factory owner in New York could sell

In Chapter 2 you will apply these critical thinking skills to the historical process:

 Recognizing Cause and Effect: Recognizing the action or event that makes something happen; identifying the result of an action or event.

> **Predicting:** Telling what you believe will happen on the basis of clues and facts.

goods almost anywhere in the United States. In addition, the railroads bought large amounts of products and raw materials. For every mile of track, 2,500 wooden ties were needed. Wire factories supplied tons of wire for telegraph lines along the tracks. Most important of all was the steel needed for rails and engines.

Inventions   What new industries and new sources of energy developed in America?

4. Steel making became a major industry after the Civil War. Before the war, iron was the main industrial metal. But iron rails wore out quickly and machine parts made from iron sometimes broke. Steel, which was made of iron and carbon, was stronger than iron, but it was very expensive to make. In the 1850s, a British inventor named Henry Bessemer (BES-uh-mer) found a way to make steel cheaply. Bessemer blew hot air into melting iron, burning away the unwanted materials. Bessemer's method used less coal and took much less time than earlier methods of steel making. After the Civil War, the Bessemer process was widely used in the United States.

5. While steel making raced ahead, another series of inventions put electrical power within reach of many more people. Cheap electric power was made possible by the **turbine** (TUR-byne), the **dynamo** (DY-nuh-moh), and the electric motor. A turbine is a machine that has a wheel with curved blades. The wheel is made to turn by flowing water or by steam. A dynamo is a machine that produces electricity. When a turbine is attached to a dynamo, large amounts of electricity can be produced. In 1894, turbines and dynamos were set up at Niagara Falls, N.Y. Within a few years, electricity was flowing to factories many miles away. Americans were delighted by the many uses of electricity. In 1879, Thomas Edison perfected the electric light. During the next ten years, electric elevators and streetcars were introduced.

6. Another new source of power, the gasoline engine, led to the automobile. In the early 1890s, two Americans, Frank and Charles Dur-

yea, put a gasoline engine on a buggy frame and called it a "motor wagon." Soon, other inventors were making "horseless carriages," "petrocars," and "motorigs." When orders for these cars started coming in, the automobile industry was born.

People in History

7. Jan Matzeliger   While new inventions were improving many industries, shoes were still being made mostly by hand. After the war, a number of shoemaking machines were invented. One of the inventors who brought the shoe industry into the machine age was Jan Matzeliger (MAT-zuh-lig-er). Matzeliger was an African American working in a Lynn, Massachusetts, shoe factory. After years of work, he completed a shoe-lasting machine in 1882. This invention shaped and fastened the leather over the sole of a shoe. The young inventor did not have enough money to set up a factory to make his machines. Because of this, he sold his **patent** (PAT-ent) to a shoe machinery company. A patent is the legal right to produce and sell an invention. Matzeliger received only a small share of the profits from his valuable machine.

New Methods in Industry   How did large companies change the way people worked?

8. Factory workers faced important changes in their jobs. Before the Civil War, most workers labored in small shops. Their employers were usually skilled craftspeople who worked side by side with them and knew them by name. In a large factory, the owner of the company was not able to know all the employees. Supervisors were hired to direct the employees. Since work was now divided into simple tasks, there was less talk about how work should be done. Instead workers were told how much, and how fast, work should be done.

9. Employers found new ways to increase the amount of work their employees could do. In 1913 Henry Ford set up a moving **assembly** (uh-SEM-blee) **line** at his automobile fac-

Background: Bessemer's discovery was duplicated by William Kelly, an American working independently in the United States.

443

Linking Geography and History

★ ★ ★

The Geography of Iron and Steel Five basic ingredients are needed for successful steel manufacturing. They are (1) a market for steel; (2) iron ore; (3) coke, a fuel made from coal that helps turn iron into steel; (4) limestone, which helps remove impurities from molten iron; and (5) water for cooling.

Rapid industrialization of the northeastern United States after the Civil War provided a large market for steel. The strong metal was needed to make the machinery, tools, farm equipment, railroads, and transportation equipment needed for an industrializing nation.

Four of the ingredients for making steel were plentiful in the Northern United States, but were unevenly distributed. Iron ore was plentiful along the shores of Lake Superior. Coke from coal was abundant in the Appalachian Mountains. The coal fields were about 1,000 miles (1,600 km) downstream from the iron ore mines along Lake Superior. Limestone is found in Michigan along the shores of Lake Huron. Water, too, is unusually abundant in the region of the five Great Lakes.

The map below shows movement along the Great Lakes of the coal and iron ore used in making steel. All-water routes, like those across the Great Lakes, nearly always moved cargoes more cheaply than road or rail routes. At first, waterfalls and narrow channels between the main lakes slowed lake transportation. To correct these problems, canals were cut around waterfalls at Sault Ste. Marie and Niagara. In addition, the Detroit and St. Clair rivers were deepened. When iron ore movements from Lake Superior began in 1889, about 25 million tons (22.5 million mt) of cargo moved across the lakes. By 1916, lake traffic had increased five-fold to more than 125 million tons (112.5 million mt).

Now study the map below to find answers to these questions.

1. What early steel centers are located on or close to the Appalachian coal field?

2. What early steel centers developed on or close to the Lake Superior iron ore deposits?

3. How did movement of coal and iron ore on the Great Lakes affect the development of lakeshore cities?

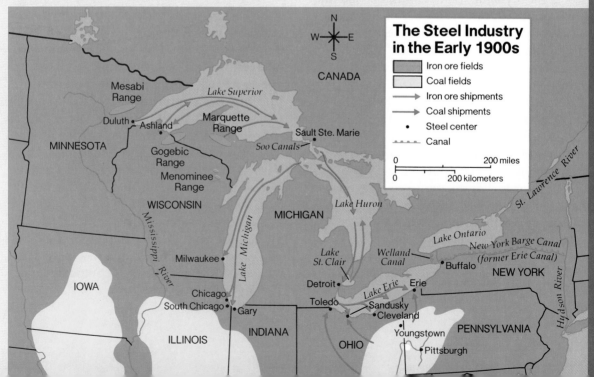

The Steel Industry in the Early 1900s

- Iron ore fields
- Coal fields
- → Iron ore shipments
- → Coal shipments
- • Steel center
- ‥‥‥ Canal

tory in Highland Park, Michigan. Machines and workers were arranged in a line. The cars were put together while being moved along from one worker to the next. Each worker added a few parts as the car passed. By 1914, the time needed to finish a Ford "Model T" had been cut from twelve and a half hours to 93 minutes. Ford's Highland Park factory became an example of **mass production,** the process of making goods quickly and cheaply.

🦅 Spotlight on Sources

10. When cars first appeared on American roads, factories put out handbooks to help new owners care for their cars. This passage is from the 1905 Oldsmobile Owner's Manual:

> Don't take anybody's word for it that your tanks have plenty of gasoline and water and your oil cup plenty of oil. They may be guessing.
>
> Don't do anything to your motor without good reason or without knowing what you are doing. . . .
>
> Don't make "improvements" without writing the factory. We know all about those improvements and can advise you.
> —from *The American Heritage History of the Automobile in America*, Stephen W. Sears

▶ What advice might still be needed for car owners today?

A Strong Economy   Why did the United States become the world's leading industrial nation?

11. By 1900, the United States led the world in industry. There were many reasons for the nation's success. First, the railroads joined factory owners with a huge market across the country. Second, a flood of inventions increased the amount of goods factories could make. Third, American factory owners saw the value of machines more quickly than European factory owners did. Fourth, large numbers of people from Europe began to arrive in the 1840s. These immigrants provided American

INVENTIONS IN THE GROWTH OF INDUSTRY		
Year	Inventor	Invention
1857	Elisha Otis	Elevator
1868	Christopher Sholes	Typewriter
1876	Alexander Graham Bell	Telephone
1877	Thomas Edison	Phonograph
1895	Guglielmo Marconi	Radio
1903	Wright Brothers	First successful airplane

▲ What developments made it easier for inventors and manufacturers to create and produce new products in the late 1800s?

---

industries with a large pool of workers who did not ask for high wages. Another reason for industry's rapid growth was the rich supply of natural resources in the United States.

12. American business people also were helped by their government. There were no federal taxes on profits or on personal income. State taxes were very low. Both federal and state government followed a **laissez faire** (LESS-say FAIR) policy toward business. "Laissez faire" is a French term meaning, "Let them do as they please." This meant that the government did not put controls on how business owners ran their companies.

Outlook

21. Railroads, new inventions, immigrant workers, and a friendly government all helped the United States become a world leader in industry. But there was also something about Americans themselves that played a part. Americans were willing to take chances with their money because they saw their country as a land of opportunity. If a person failed, there was always something else to try. Are Americans ◀ today still willing to take chances?

Activity: Ask members of the class to research the early history of the automobile in America. Some might prepare drawings of people and automobiles in interesting situations. Others should find, and read to the class, descriptions of car travel by pioneer drivers and passengers.

CHAPTER REVIEW

VOCABULARY REVIEW

▶ Fill in the blanks in the following sentences with words from the list below.

1. A(n) _____ is an arrangement of machines and workers in which a product is put together while being moved from one worker to the next.

2. A(n) _____ is a wealthy business leader.

3. The term _____ means a policy of allowing business freedom from government interference.

4. A(n) _____ is a machine in which a wheel with curved blades is made to turn by flowing water or steam.

5. The _____ is a machine that generates electricity.

6. A(n) _____ is the legal right to produce and sell an invention.

7. The process of manufacturing goods quickly and at low cost is _____ .

a. tycoon

b. turbine

c. assembly line

d. patent

e. dynamo

f. laissez faire

g. mass production

h. locomotive

SKILL BUILDER: INTERPRETING A PHOTOGRAPH

▶ Study the photograph. Answer the questions on a separate sheet of paper.

1. What happened before this photograph was taken? What tells you that the driver of the car was prepared for this to happen?

2. What do you see that would tell you that an automobile ride in those days might be uncomfortable?

3. What might the man in the carriage be thinking as his carriage passes the car?

SKILL BUILDER: CRITICAL THINKING AND COMPREHENSION

I. Classifying

▶ The list below is made up of names of people you read about in Chapter 2. Classify each person according to whether he was a tycoon or an inventor. Number your paper from 1 to 5. Put a *T* next to the number if the person was a tycoon. Write an *I* if he was an inventor.

Jan Matzeliger   Henry Ford   Frank and Charles Duryea

Cornelius Vanderbilt   Henry Bessemer

II. Predicting

▶ Write each of the facts listed below on a sheet of paper. Make a prediction about each fact.

1. **Fact:** One mile of railroad track needed 2500 wooden ties.
   Predict: What will happen to the trees?

2. **Fact:** The government had a policy of "let them do as they please."
   Predict: What will big business do?

3. **Fact:** Henry Bessemer developed a way to make steel more cheaply.
   Predict: Will factories use more steel or less steel than before?

III. Point of View

▶ Read the statements below. Which ones would more likely have been made by a factory owner? Which ones would more likely have been made by a factory worker? Write your answers on a separate sheet of paper.

1. My job has become very boring as a result of mass production.

2. I'm glad to see that the immigrants are willing to work for low wages.

3. The new factory we are planning should be opened closer to the coal mines.

4. I intend to vote for Candidate X. He is in favor of limiting the number of hours per week an employee can be required to work.

USING PRIMARY SOURCES

▶ Reread the Spotlight on Sources selection, paragraph 10. Why might a farmer in the late 1800s have been tempted to make "improvements" on his automobile?

ENRICHMENT

1. Look through an illustrated history of American industry. Choose an invention or newly developed machine, such as the Bessemer converter. Draw a picture of the machine in operation and explain to the class how it worked.

2. Read a biography of Thomas Edison, Alexander Graham Bell, or some other inventor. Tell the class what you thought was interesting about the person you chose.

CHAPTER 3

The Rise of Big Business

OBJECTIVE: What was the role of big business in America's new industrial economy?

1. "The host's eldest brother wore a costume of Louis XVI. His wife appeared as 'The Electric Light,' in white satin, trimmed with diamonds, and her head one blaze of diamonds." In 1890, a writer gave this account of a costume party in New York City. A few Americans were able to become very wealthy as a result of the growth of industry in the late 1800s. They built fancy homes and threw huge parties for each other. Some Americans admired these "captains of industry" for their energy and daring. To others, however, the wealthy business leaders were "robber barons" who gained their riches in ▶ unfair ways. Which groups of people might have been the most bothered by the growth of big business in the United States?

▲ The Newport, Rhode Island home of the Vanderbilt family faces the Atlantic Ocean. How did the Vanderbilts build their wealth?

Business Tycoons   How did business leaders gain control of important industries?

2. As companies grew, new types of businesses were needed. Large sums of money were needed to buy land, buildings, and machinery. The need to raise this money was the chief reason for changes in how industries were set up. Most of the companies built by the tycoons, or leaders, of industry were organized as **corporations** (kor-poh-RAY-shunz). The managers of a corporation raise money by offering shares of stock for sale. A person who buys stock in the corporation becomes a **stockholder**, or partial owner of the company. Railroad corporations were the first big businesses in the United States.

3. Andrew Carnegie (KAHR-nuh-gee), who had worked for the Pennsylvania Railroad, built an empire in the steel industry. In 1872,

In Chapter 3 you will apply these critical thinking skills to the historical process:

○ **Generalizing:** Making a statement that links several facts.

▥ **Understanding Points of View:** Recognizing why people have different attitudes about the same thing.

near Pittsburgh, Carnegie built the largest steel plant in the country. He was the first American steel maker to use Bessemer's new way of making steel on a large scale. Carnegie's company soon was making more steel than any other company in the United States. As other steel makers copied his methods, steel production rose sharply. In order to sell all the steel they were producing, steel makers had to **compete** (kum-PEET) for customers. To compete is to go after the same thing as other people. Everyone began cutting prices. The falling prices, however, lowered profits. To keep his profits as high as possible, Carnegie set out to cut the costs of making steel.

4. To lower the cost of his raw materials, Carnegie stopped buying iron ore from other companies. Instead, he bought iron mines of his own, near the western end of Lake Superior. To bring the ore to Pittsburgh, he bought some lake ships and built his own railroad. Carnegie also bought other steel companies. By 1899 Carnegie was making more steel than Great Britain.

5. If Andrew Carnegie was the steel king, John D. Rockefeller was the emperor of oil. In 1859, when Rockefeller was 20 years old, the nation's first oil well was drilled in western Pennsylvania. A process for **refining** (ree-FY-ning) crude oil had been invented a few years earlier. To refine oil is to remove unwanted material mixed in with the pure oil. Most crude oil was refined into kerosene, a fuel for lamps. During the 1860s, Rockefeller began buying oil refineries in the Cleveland area. By 1870, he had built a huge corporation, the Standard Oil Company of Ohio. Rockefeller faced the same need to cut prices that Carnegie did. To end price wars among oil refiners, he bought other refineries. If an owner refused to sell the refinery, Rockefeller would cut the price of his kerosene until the other company was ruined. Then he would raise his price again.

6. Like Carnegie, Rockefeller made his company larger by controlling every step in making the product. His docks, tanker ships, and pipelines brought crude oil to his refineries. Rock-

efeller was refining 90 percent of the nation's oil by 1880. During the next ten years he gained a near **monopoly** (muh-NOP-oh-lee), or complete control, over the oil industry.

7. In 1882 Rockefeller introduced a new, even more powerful, form of business, the **trust.** A trust is a group of corporations whose stock is held by a single team of managers. Rockefeller's new business, the Standard Oil Trust, set an example for other business leaders. The "sugar trust," the "lead trust," and many other trusts were started. As smaller companies were eaten up by the trusts, Americans began to fear the growing power of big business. It was time, many felt, for the government to step in.

Regulation   How did the government respond to the rise of big business?

8. The first big businesses to attract the government's attention were the railroads. The railroads had angered people by charging unequal freight rates. Railroads gave **refunds** to their best customers, the big companies. A refund is money given back to a customer after payment has been made. State governments passed laws against unequal rates. But the Supreme Court ruled that such laws were unconstitutional. The railroads carried goods across state lines. Only the federal government, said the Court, could control **interstate commerce,** or trade across state borders.

9. In 1887, Congress set up the Interstate Commerce Commission (ICC) to regulate the railroads. The ICC could gather facts about a railroad and take it to court for charging unjust rates. However, the courts usually ruled in favor of the railroads. In its early years, the ICC had very little power. But it set an important example. In the future, the federal government would set up commissions of experts to regulate many different industries.

10. Rather than regulate the trusts, the government tried to break them up. In 1890, Congress passed the Sherman Antitrust Act. The act outlawed any business group that sought to control "trade or commerce among

Background: Born in Scotland, Carnegie settled in Pennsylvania with his family at the age of 13. While working 14-hour shifts in a textile mill, he took night classes in bookkeeping. At age 18 he began working for the Pennsylvania Railroad, where he learned how to manage a corporation and how to invest. By the age of 30 he was a rich man.

449

the several states." The Antitrust Act had little effect on big business in the 1890s. Rockefeller made the Standard Oil Trust into a single, large corporation and continued to grow. The act was also weakened by the Supreme Court. The court had a "laissez faire," or "Let them do as they please" view about businesses.

Spotlight on Sources

11. Small businesses were harmed in the age of big business, and no group had bigger problems than did African American business people. Banks refused to lend them money, and white customers often would not buy from them. Yet there were success stories. In 1900 Dr. A. J. Love, of Chattanooga, Tennessee, traveled to Boston for the first convention of the National Negro Business League. Here is part of Love's report to the meeting's 400 delegates.

> . . . (W)e are in the iron manufacturing business ourselves. We have two foundries there, owned, operated, controlled and worked . . . by colored [African American] men. . . . (T)hey have succeeded in the manufacture of stoves and cooking utensils and skillets, and grates for furnaces . . . and right there in Chattanooga they have a great demand for that work. . . . I feel that they are doing a work which the race, if they knew about it, might be proud of.
> —from *The Black American: A Documentary History*, by Leslie H. Fishel and Benjamin Quarles

What inventions or other new developments in the 1800s might have made it easier for Dr. Love's business to succeed?

Boom and Bust Why did Americans face both good times and economic hardship in the late 1800s?

12. During the rise of big business, the economy had highs and lows that frightened many Americans. For a few years the economy would race wildly ahead. Business people would borrow money from banks and rush to invest it

wherever they smelled a profit. Railroads were built beside other railroads in a battle for freight customers. Factory owners made more goods than they could sell. Then the news would go out that the railroads and factory owners were not making a profit. Loans could not be paid back. Bankers would be afraid to make loans, and the economy would come crashing down. Up–down zigzags had been part of the American economy since colonial times. In the years after the Civil War, however, the ups grew higher and the downs lower.

13. In 1893 a **depression** (dee-PRESH-un), or serious economic downturn, hit the country. By 1895, more than 150 railroads had gone out of business, and nearly 500 banks had closed their doors. Factories fell silent and millions were out of work. In police stations and government buildings across the land, halls and stairways were filled with homeless people. By 1897, the economy had recovered and was growing again. However, Americans did not forget the "Panic of 1893" and the suffering it had brought.

New Ways to Sell How did business people sell large amounts of low-priced goods?

14. Despite hardships caused by the boom-and-bust economy, Americans had much to be thankful for. They could buy a wide variety of factory goods, and prices were falling. Before the Civil War, most Americans had done their buying at a general store. People asked for what they wanted and the storekeeper took it down from a shelf or scooped it out of a barrel. In the cities there were stores that sold only one product, such as hats or men's clothing. Prices were often set by bargaining, or discussion about the cost, between the shop owner and the customer.

15. As factory goods began to flood the nation, business people found new ways to sell goods. In 1862, A. T. Stewart opened an eight-story department store in New York City. Goods were put out on low counters where people could see and handle them. Prices were low because Stewart bought in large amounts, straight from the factory. R. H. Macy in New York, John Wanamaker in Philadelphia, and Marshall Field in Chicago followed Stewart's example and opened department stores.

People in History

16. Margaret Getchell One of the reasons for the early success of the Macy department store in New York was R. H. Macy's cousin Margaret Getchell. In 1860, when Getchell was 19, she was hired as the store's bookkeeper. R. H. Macy noticed his cousin's ability and allowed her to make changes in the department store.

17. Getchell had a talent for spotting new fashions and coming up with ideas to sell more goods. As people in the city began taking day trips to the country, she set up a department to sell picnic supplies. At her suggestion, departments for jewelry, housewares, gifts, clocks, and sterling silver were set up. She put a soda fountain in the center of the store to draw in thirsty shoppers. As his business grew, R. H. Macy often needed to make buying trips to Europe. He wanted someone he could count on to run Macy's while he was away. At the age of 25, Margaret Getchell became the first woman to manage a department store.

18. In 1872, Montgomery Ward, a Midwestern business man, opened the first mail-order house in Chicago. This made it possible for farmers and people living in small towns to shop by mail. A few years later, Richard W. Sears, who had been a railroad station agent, started another mail-order business in Chicago. The mail-order houses sent out catalogs that offered clothing, household goods, and tools at low prices. All the shoppers had to do was send in their order and wait for the goods to arrive.

19. To increase sales, business people began to **advertise** more. To advertise is to make something known by announcing it in a public way, for example, in a newspaper. The department store owners had to sell many goods to make a profit because their prices were low. Store owners soon learned that newspaper ad-

▲ This cartoon is called "The Bosses of the Senate." Who did the artist think had control over lawmaking—the senators or the people in charge of the trusts?

vertisements brought in customers. Manufacturers, too, saw the value of advertising. They began to develop **trademarks**. A trademark is a picture, a symbol, or a word that stands for a certain product. These trademarks, and brand names like Burpee Seeds, helped Americans remember the manufacturers' products. Advertising slogans, like an automobile company's "Ask the man who owns one," were soon known to every American.

Outlook

20. Between 1865 and 1900, big business took charge of the nation's industries. Americans found a wide variety of low-priced goods in department stores and mail-order catalogs. But the growing power of big business and the boom-and-bust economy caused many Americans to worry. When one group gains control of too many businesses, what might happen?

451

CHAPTER REVIEW

VOCABULARY REVIEW

▶ Match the word or words on the left with their correct meaning on the right.

1. corporation(s)

2. trust(s)

3. depression(s)

4. stockholder(s)

5. refining

6. compete

7. trademark

8. refund

9. advertise

10. interstate commerce

11. monopoly

a. to go after, or strive for, the same thing as other people

b. a company owned by stockholders

c. money given back to a customer after payment has been made

d. a lower price offered to certain customers

e. persons who buy stock in a corporation

f. a combination of companies whose stock is held by a group of managers

g. a process of removing unwanted matter

h. a severe economic downturn

i. trade across state borders

j. complete control over an industry

k. a picture, word, or symbol that stands for a certain product

l. to make something known in a public way

SKILL BUILDER: MAKING A TIME LINE

▶ Use the events and dates below to make a time line on a separate sheet of paper. Draw the time line from 1835–1900. Make each ten-year period one inch long.

1890   Sherman Antitrust Act is passed

1887   Congress sets up the Interstate Commerce Commission

1894   Turbines are in use at Niagara Falls

1879   Edison invents the electric light

1846   Elias Howe invents the sewing machine

1850   Bessemer process is invented

1859   First oil well is drilled in America

1882   Matzeliger invents the shoe-lasting machine

1899   Carnegie is making more steel than Great Britain

1900   First convention of the National Negro Business League takes place

SKILL BUILDER: CRITICAL THINKING AND COMPREHENSION

I. Generalizing

▶ Imagine that you are working for Western Union in the 1850s. Your job is to send the shortest messages possible. Reduce each set of sentences to one by generalizing.

1. Make a generalization about what has happened from the following sentences.
   a. Railroads are bankrupt.
   b. Banks have closed.
   c. Factories have closed.

2. Make a generalization from the following sentences about the department store.
   a. Goods were placed on low counters where customers could handle them.
   b. One store sold a wide variety of goods.
   c. Items for sale were priced reasonably.

II. Fact *versus* Opinion

▶ Read each statement below. Decide whether it is a fact or opinion. Write your answer next to the numbers 1 through 4 on a sheet of paper.

1. Andrew Carnegie became very wealthy from his steel business.

2. Department stores were more fun to shop in than the smaller general stores.

3. People could get into the cities faster by trolley than by horse and carriage.

4. It is better to work for a corporation than for a company owned by only one person.

III. Cause and Effect

▶ Read the pairs of facts given below. Decide which fact in each pair is a cause, and which is an effect. Write your answer on a separate sheet of paper.

1. **a.** Rockefeller cut the price of his kerosene.
   b. Rockefeller's rivals were put out of business.

2. **a.** Carnegie was able to cut the cost of producing steel.
   b. Carnegie bought iron mines and a fleet of ships to transport the iron to the steel plant.

USING PRIMARY SOURCES

▶ Reread the Spotlight on Sources passage, paragraph 11. What qualities do you think that Dr. Love had that helped his business to succeed?

ENRICHMENT

1. Work with two or three other classmates to find out more about the depression of 1893–1896. Present your findings to the class in the form of interviews with persons who participated in events such as the Pullman Strike or the march of Coxey's Army.

2. Think of a food product such as a new cereal or a sandwich spread. Design a trademark or symbol and make up a brand name for the product. Then design an advertisement that combines a picture of the product, its trademark, and its brand name.

CHAPTER 4

Immigrants Bring New Ways of Life to America

OBJECTIVE: How did millions of immigrants help build the United States?

1. "I have a very great wish to go to America. I want to leave my native country because we are six children and we have very little land. . . . I am a healthy boy of 24 years old. I do not fear any work." The young man from Poland who wrote this letter was ready to take his chances in a new land. He and others like him, from thousands of villages around the globe, helped make America the great mixture of peoples it is today. Between 1820 and 1860, nearly five million immigrants came to the United States. During the next 50 years, another 23 million arrived.

Immigration Grows What new groups of people came to America seeking a better life?

2. In the last years of the 1800s, a large group of people came to the United States from southern and eastern Europe. Until the 1890s, most of the immigrants had come from northern and western Europe. They mainly included the English, Germans, Irish, and Scandinavians. During the mid-1880s, however, large numbers of Eastern and Southern European Jews, Poles, and Italians, as well as Czechs, Slovaks, Hungarians, and Greeks began to arrive. These Europeans saw the United States as the great hope for their future.

3. Like earlier European immigrants, most of the newcomers were peasants. These people

▲ Immigrants from Europe in the late 1800s went first to Ellis Island, a receiving center in the New York harbor.

could no longer support themselves on the worn-out farms of their countries. They saw little hope for the future in their native villages. Moving to America seemed to be the only answer. Millions packed their few belongings and set sail for the new land of opportunity across the ocean.

In Chapter 4 you will apply these critical thinking skills to the historical process:

▌ **Comparing and Contrasting:** Recognizing similarities and differences.

◯ **Generalizing:** Making a statement that links several facts.

4. To the Jewish people of Eastern Europe, America offered freedom. In Russia and Poland, where most of them came from, Jews were forced to live in certain parts of the country. In the cities, they had to live in segregated communities called **ghettoes** (GET-ohz). They were not permitted to own land. Beginning in the 1880s, a number of bloody massacres against Jewish communities, called **pogroms** (poh-GRAHMZ), took place. It was no wonder that thousands of Jews looked to America as a land where they could escape this persecution.

Arriving in America
Where did immigrants live and how did they earn a living?

5. Most of the immigrants from Eastern and Southern Europe settled in the industrial cities of the East and Midwest. They most often settled in New York City, Boston, Chicago, and Cleveland. They did not travel to the Great Plains and become farmers because, by 1890, the price of farmland was rising. In the cities, they crowded into immigrant ghettos or neighborhoods made up of people from one group or country. Many lived in slum **tenements** (TEN-uh-ments), or buildings divided into tiny apartments. Why do you think most immigrants at first chose to live with other people from the same country?

6. Needing work badly, the immigrants did the nation's dirtiest and most dangerous jobs. Italians replaced the Irish as the main source of labor in the building industry. Poles, Czechs, and Hungarians worked long hours at low pay in coal mines, meat slaughterhouses, and steel mills. In New York City, many East European Jews found work in clothing factories. Many more brought factory work back to their tenement homes. In 1907, a magazine reported, "In unaired rooms, mothers and fathers sew by day and by night. . . . And the children are called in from play to . . . drudge [work hard] beside
▶ their elders. . . ." Why do you think many immigrant children had to work like adults?

7. In New York City's clothing factories, immigrant workers worked 13 hours a day, often seven days a week. Their income was usually five or six dollars a week. While these European immigrants were grateful to have jobs, they knew that they were being treated unfairly. The workers, many of them women, soon organized **labor unions.** Labor unions are groups of workers who band together to improve working conditions.

People in History

8. Rose Schneiderman One of the garment workers' heroes was Rose Schneiderman (SHNY-dur-man), a spellbinding speaker with bright red hair. She stood only 4 feet 6 inches (1.37 meters) tall. Born a Jew in Russian Poland, Schneiderman came to America in 1891 as a child of nine. After working in a department store, she found a job sewing cap linings. In 1903, when she was 21, Schneiderman helped to form the Cap Makers Union.

9. Rose Schneiderman spent her life helping the people she called her "sister workers." She went on to become a union leader. She walked **picket lines** and collected money and food for strikers. Picket lines are made up of workers on strike who march, often with signs, outside a business as a form of protest. Schneiderman also fought against child labor and taught immigrant workers their legal rights. Immigrants like Rose Schneiderman were able to stand up for their rights in America.

10. On the West Coast, immigrants continued to arrive from Asia. The Chinese still did much of the most dangerous work in the mines and on the railroads. In the 1880s, Japanese farmers began to replace Chinese workers in Hawaii's pineapple and sugar cane fields. Many Japanese saved enough money to travel to California and become successful farmers there.

Immigrants Face Hostility
How did native-born Americans respond to the newcomers?

11. Some native-born Americans greeted the new immigrants with anger or distrust. During the 1840s and 1850s, many Americans had

THE ITALIANS

Italian immigrants arrived in America with many memories of their homeland. They thought of their beautiful peninsula surrounded by the blue Mediterranean. They remembered its pleasant climate, olive trees, rocky hilltops, and grapes ripening in the sun. But other memories were less happy. In the 1880s and 1890s, falling prices for crops and cloth destroyed southern Italy's economy. There were famines and peasant revolts. Starving in their tiny stone huts, southern Italy's peasants began to sing a new song: "Today, landlord you will plow your own field. Because we are leaving for America."

During the late 1800s, most of the immigrants from Italy were young men. With money earned in America they hoped to return to Italy, marry, and start a family. Or, they planned to bring their families to America as soon as they could. Dragging battered suitcases, they arrived in New York Harbor without money and often without friends. They were likely to be met by the **padrone** (puh-DROH-nay), or labor boss. The padrone could speak enough English to make deals with business people. He was paid to bring workers to the job site, feed them, and give them their pay. The padrone gave the workers as little as possible. Padrones sent work crews of young Italians to dig ditches, unload ships, and mix concrete. Italian women also had to take whatever jobs they could find. Many joined the East European Jews in the clothing factories.

Immigrants from Italy formed their own Italian-speaking neighborhoods in New York, Boston, Philadelphia, and many other cities. At first, living conditions in the nation's "Little Italies" were hard. As many as 12 people lived in three-room apartments in dark and airless tenement buildings. Life in the tenements was unhealthy. Diseases spread quickly in the crowded spaces, and many immigrants fell sick and died. Even so, the Italians worked hard to improve their lives. Pushcart peddlers opened grocery stores and restaurants. Families found better apartments, with flush toilets, bathtubs, and windows that let in the sun. "Pasta e fagioli," a mixture of pasta and beans, was less often eaten.

When their parents began to earn better pay, the children were able to spend less time working and more time in public school. Some of these children grew up to be leaders in business, politics, and many other fields. Others became famous for what they did in the arts and in sports.

▼ This Italian family has just arrived in New York in 1910. Why might they have decided to come to the United States? What experiences lie ahead for them?

Now answer the following questions.

1. In what ways were the experiences of Italian immigrants like those of Irish immigrants? In what ways were they different?

2. What did the padrone do to help the newcomers? How might he be in a position to trick the immigrants?

3. Why was education important to the newcomers?

worried about German and Irish immigrants. Neither of these groups, some people said, could ever be "real" Americans. The Germans were not trusted because they formed their own German-speaking communities. Other Americans blamed the Irish for the bad state of the city slums. The Irish also were disliked because they were the first large Catholic group to arrive in a mostly Protestant country. In some eastern cities, Irish and German immigrants were attacked by mobs.

12. There was an even greater uprising against immigrants during the 1880s and 1890s. This time the "new" immigrants from Eastern and Southern Europe, and from Asia, were the targets. In 1891, 11 Italian prisoners were dragged from a New Orleans jail and killed. Six years later, near Hazleton, Pennsylvania, 21 unarmed Polish and Hungarian strikers were shot to death by sheriffs' deputies. Chinese immigrants were attacked by mobs and driven out of mining towns throughout the West.

13. There were many reasons for the growing anger toward the immigrants. First, immigrants worked for low wages. They were often brought in to replace workers on strike. This angered workers who were trying to organize unions and get better pay. Second, the languages and habits of the newcomers seemed strange to most Americans and made them feel uncomfortable. Third, during the 1880s and 1890s, many Americans were deeply troubled. Big-city slums were spreading and crime seemed out of control. The boom-and-bust economy gave jobs and then took them away. Striking workers were fighting the police. The country seemed to be falling apart and no one could figure out why. Many Americans looked for a **scapegoat** (SKAYP-goht), or someone to blame. Why were the newcomers from other nations an easy target for that blame?

Spotlight on Sources

14. Children of immigrant parents began to feel more like Americans after they started pub-lic school. They learned to speak English in class and met children from other neighborhoods. Sometimes however, this caused trouble at home. One 16-year-old boy whose parents had come from Poland wrote:

> I don't like to bring my American friends around. They were born here and so were their parents. My mother speaks "English" to them, and they make fun of her. . . . My father won't allow us to play ball on the lot. He says it's a waste of time. . . . He was raised in Poland. . . . My parents . . . make many sacrifices [give up a lot] to keep up their traditions [customs], but they don't mean anything much in my life. . . . That's just why I don't like to stay home. I don't want to hurt my parents and I can't follow their advice. . . .
>
> —from *Looking for America*, Stanley I. Kutler

What is this boy's attitude to his parents' Polish traditions? What would you do if you were in his situation?

Outlook

15. In the years following the Civil War, the largest number of immigrants ever came to the United States. They came with the same high hopes for freedom and opportunity as had the colonists before them. After 1890, many immigrants came from Eastern and Southern Europe. The newcomers provided the labor needed for the nation's growing industries. They were sometimes treated unfairly by native-born Americans. But they worked hard, began to succeed, and soon became an important part of the American work force. In time, many of the cultural traditions they brought with them were enjoyed and adopted by all Americans. For most immigrants, the struggle for a better life took place in the nation's growing cities, where opportunities were greater. The new Americans had to struggle hard for equal opportunities and better working and living conditions. In spite of this, most Europeans and Asian immigrants were glad that they had come to America. Why do you think this was so?

CHAPTER REVIEW

VOCABULARY REVIEW

▶ Fill in each blank with the word that best completes each idea.

ghetto(es)   tenements(s)   labor union(s)   pogrom(s)

padrone(s)   picket line(s)   scapegoat(s)

In the late 1800s, many Europeans came to America to start a new life. Jewish people from Eastern Europe came to escape injustices such as being forced to live in ___1___ and enduring cruel ___2___ . Italians coming into New York harbor were often met by a ___3___ who helped them get work. The new Americans did not always find life easy in the United States. They were treated as ___4___ instead of being welcomed into communities. They often had to live in crowded ___5___ . Working conditions were hard, but the immigrants joined with other Americans in forming ___6___ to fight for workers' rights. After many hours on ___7___ , the union leaders won better conditions for factory workers in many parts of the United States.

SKILL BUILDER: READING A MAP

▶ If large numbers are used in maps and charts, the figures are often shown in the thousands. To arrive at the actual number, you need to add three zeros at the end. In the map below, the numbers of immigrants from each country are given in thousands. Look carefully at the map, then answer the questions on a separate sheet of paper.

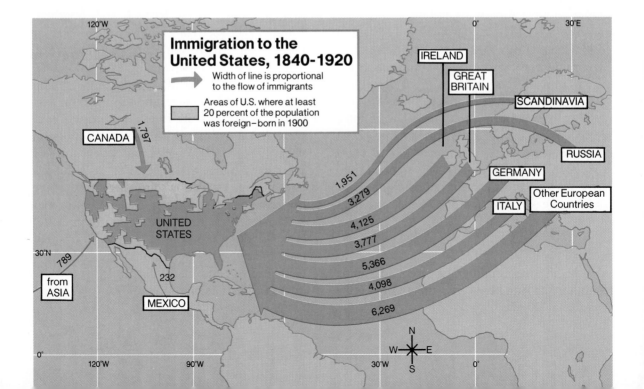

Immigration to the United States, 1840-1920

→ Width of line is proportional to the flow of immigrants

▢ Areas of U.S. where at least 20 percent of the population was foreign-born in 1900

CANADA — 1,797

UNITED STATES

from ASIA — 789

MEXICO — 232

IRELAND
GREAT BRITAIN
SCANDINAVIA
RUSSIA
GERMANY
ITALY
Other European Countries

1,951
3,279
4,125
3,777
5,366
4,098
6,269

Which area of Europe had the fewest immigrants to the United States in the period of time shown on the map?

2. Which country in Europe had the most immigrants to the United States in the period of time shown on the map?

3. Make a generalization about the numbers of immigrants from Mexico and Canada.

4. Make a generalization that compares the number of immigrants from Ireland with the number from Italy.

SKILL BUILDER: CRITICAL THINKING AND COMPREHENSION

I. Compare and Contrast

1. Imagine that you are an Italian peasant who has come to America in the late 1800s. Write one or two sentences that contrast your life before coming to America with your life after coming to America.

2. Reread the "Spotlight on Sources" section, paragraph 14. Make a list of attitudes or habits of the parents that seem to trouble the son. For each item on your list, add a contrasting item that represents a more "American" way of looking at things.

II. Generalizing

▶ Write a sentence that makes a generalization about each of the following topics.

1. why immigrants came to America

2. the types of jobs immigrants held

3. a typical immigrant home in the late 1880s

III. Main Idea

▶ Reread paragraph 5. Then choose the statement that best expresses the main idea of that paragraph.

a. Farmland was expensive in the 1890s.
b. Immigrants usually settled in the cities.
c. Tenements were buildings divided into small apartments.

USING PRIMARY SOURCES

▶ Reread the "Spotlight on Sources" feature, paragraph 14. How do you think this teenager will feel about his parents 10 years later?

ENRICHMENT

1. Imagine that you are an immigrant arriving in New York Harbor during the 1890s. Write a letter describing what you were expecting to find and your first impressions of America.

2. Find out about the history of your own community. What immigrant groups settled there in the late 1800s? Are these groups still in your community today, or have they been replaced by others?

CHAPTER 5

The Growth of Cities

OBJECTIVE: How did America become a nation of cities?

1. "The city has become a serious menace [threat] to our civilization," warned Reverend Josiah Strong in 1885. By "our civilization," Strong meant the kind of small-town American life he had known as a boy. In 1860, when Strong was 13, less than one-fifth of all Americans were city dwellers. In 1885, a third were. By the time Strong reached the age of 63, in 1910, nearly half of the population lived in cities. Strong wrote several books attacking slums and other big-city problems. Most Americans shared his concerns. At the same time, many enjoyed the advantages of city life.

Factories and Cities How did industry help cities grow?

2. Urbanization (ur-ben-uh-ZAY-shun), or the growth and development of cities, took place rapidly in the United States. Between 1860 and 1910 the number of cities of more than 100,000 went from nine to 50. The greatest growth took place in the nation's largest cities. Chicago, a prairie village in the 1830s, had half a million people by 1880. Its population doubled during the next ten years, and doubled again by 1910. By this time, New York was one of the world's largest cities, with almost five million people.

3. Industry played a key part in the urbanization of the United States. Before the Civil

▲ Traffic jams were common in large cities during the 1800s. This picture shows Broadway, in New York City, in 1875. What traffic controls are in a city today that are not seen here?

War, thousands of Americans from the country came to the cities to work in mills and slaughterhouses. Others found jobs in factories making textiles, iron, furniture, and many other products. After the Civil War, industry grew even more quickly. Some cities were known

In Chapter 5 you will apply these critical thinking skills to the historical process:

▶ **Drawing Conclusions:** Making a statement that explains the facts and evidence.

Sequencing: Putting a series of events in the correct time order.

for certain products made there. Pittsburgh, Pennsylvania, and Birmingham, Alabama, became known as steel-making centers. Holyoke, Massachusetts, was known for paper making. Schenectady, New York, was known for its electrical goods. The largest cities had a wider mix of industries. Factory jobs were a powerful magnet, pulling millions of people away from America's farms and Europe's villages.

Waterways and Cities What geographical features and natural resources influenced the growth of cities?

4. Throughout the growth of America, its largest cities were usually located on major waterways. The first settlements were often founded near sheltered harbors and riverbanks. Some of these settlements grew into cities after they became centers for trading and shipping goods. The leading cities of the 1700s, Philadelphia, New York, Boston, Baltimore, and Charleston, were all seaports. Between 1800 and 1850, many inland river towns grew into cities. The main river cities were Pittsburgh, Cincinnati, Louisville, St. Louis, Memphis, and New Orleans. Detroit and Chicago were important shipping centers on the Great Lakes. San Francisco Bay provided a sheltered harbor for the West Coast's leading city.

5. Some of the nation's cities grew because they were located near important mineral resources such as coal, iron, or gold. Steel makers came to Pittsburgh because the coal they needed to make steel was close by. Cleveland, Ohio, located near oil fields, was a major oil refining center. Many of the West's cities began as mining towns. Denver, Colorado, and Reno, Nevada, are examples. Even the West's leading seaport, San Francisco, owed its early growth to the mining boom.

Living Conditions in the Cities What problems did city families face?

6. By the late 1800s, the nation's largest cities were facing major problems. Dozens,

sometimes hundreds, of families were arriving every day seeking places to live. Slum landlords took advantage of the need for housing. They packed people into tiny, unheated apartments in five- or six-story tenement buildings. Often an apartment had only one cold-water faucet. The tenement buildings were built close together. This cut off air and light. By 1900, tenements on New York's Manhattan Island housed about 1,585,000 people.

7. City governments had to build miles of streets, pipe fresh water in, drain sewage out, and haul away garbage. None of these services kept up with population growth. In the 1880s, three-fourths of Chicago's streets were still unpaved. Alleyways were clogged with mounds of garbage. In most large cities, dirty water caused **epidemics** (eh-puh-DEM-iks), or outbreaks of disease that killed thousands.

8. During the late 1800s, city and state governments worked to make city life safer. **Reservoirs** (REZ-ur-vwahrzs) for collecting fresh drinking water were built. The reservoirs were connected to cities by **aqueducts** (AK-wuh-dukts). These human-made channels or pipes carried fresh water over great distances. Plants to clean, or purify, water were also built. By 1910, one city dweller in four was drinking filtered water. City boards of health were given tax money to hire more inspectors. Under the inspectors' watchful eyes, garbage collection and sewage disposal improved.

City Governments What did city governments do to improve life for people living in cities?

9. In 1901, New York City passed a Tenement Law that became a model for other cities. The law set fire safety standards for apartment buildings. It also stated that every family apartment must have a separate bathroom. While tenement laws brought some improvements, they failed to stop big-city slums from spreading. Poor immigrant families crowding into the cities took whatever living space they could find.

10. As cities grew, **corruption** (kuh-RUP-shun), or dishonesty, in city government grew

Background: The germ theory was accepted in Europe by the 1860s. Americans, however, believed that "sewer gas" or poisons leaking from decaying garbage caused disease. These beliefs led to improved garbage collection and sewage disposal, but the need for water purification was not recognized until city boards of health accepted the germ theory.

as well. Growing cities needed electric power lines and streetcars. Private companies competed for the right to provide these services. City officials often chose the company that paid the biggest **bribe**. A bribe is payment given to someone in order to cause him or her to act in a certain way. The officials belonged to political groups called "machines." Each political machine had a "boss," who rewarded loyal supporters with government jobs. One reason that machine politicians won city elections was that they worked to get the support of the immigrants. Politicians provided free coal, road-building jobs, and other favors to immigrants in exchange for votes. The immigrants were grateful to the bosses. No one else seemed to care about their problems.

People in History

11. Jane Addams One American who did care about the people in the slums was Jane Addams. Addams grew up in Illinois and grad-

uated from college there. In the 1880s, Addams traveled to England and learned about **settlement houses** there. Settlement houses offered advice, training, and recreation to people in poor neighborhoods. In 1889 Addams and her friend Ellen Gates Starr opened their own settlement house for immigrants in the Chicago slums. It was called Hull House. The two women started with a kindergarten program for the small children in the neighborhood. Before long, they had added a day nursery to provide child care for working mothers. Hull House also had clubs for older women, classes in music and art, a gym, and an employment service. When people in other cities heard about Hull House, they began their own settlement house programs. Where are programs like those of ◄ Hull House found today?

12. Throughout her life, Jane Addams worked to aid the poor and bring about world peace. She did this by speaking out against child labor. She also helped immigrant workers form unions. Addams also was president of the

MAP SKILL BUILDER: Learn from the map about the largest cities in the United States in the 1900s.
1. What cities had over one million people?   **2.** What cities had 300,000 to one million people?

The Largest U.S. Cities in 1900

■ More than 1 million inhabitants
● 300,000 - 1 million inhabitants
• 150,000 - 300,000 inhabitants

Cities labeled in red type were among the 24 largest cities of 1850

0   600 miles
0   800 kilometers

Women's International League for Peace and Freedom, a group that worked to outlaw war. She published several books about life at Hull House and about the need for world peace. In 1931, Jane Addams was awarded the Nobel Peace Prize for her efforts to bring about world peace.

Benefits of City Life   In what ways did city living make people's lives better?

13. While city life was not pleasant for the poor, it did improve for middle-class families. Builders built new apartment houses away from the slums. Apartments for the middle class had hot and cold running water, central heating, electric elevators, gas stoves, and iceboxes. The new apartment buildings had doormen, elevator operators, and a cleaning and repair crew. Families found much to enjoy when they went "downtown" to visit department stores and attend plays, concerts, and operas.

14. New kinds of transportation made travel within cities faster. The electric **trolley car** was introduced in Richmond, Virginia, in 1888. The trolley car was a streetcar that ran on tracks. An electric wire ran above the tracks. This wire fed electricity to the car through its trolley, a pole that reached up to the wire. Before long, trolley cars began to replace the horse and buggy in most cities. It was cheaper and faster to hop onto a streetcar than to hire a horse and buggy. In 1897, Boston opened the first subway system in the United States. A subway is an underground electric railroad.

15. Electric trolley lines also helped the growth of **suburbs**, or communities that grew up on the outskirts of cities. Many people who worked in the crowded cities longed for the quiet of the countryside. Suburbs had appeared before the Civil War, but few people lived in them. Travel by horse and carriage from suburban homes to city jobs was slow. By the 1890s, electric trolley lines had been built in Chicago, Boston, and New York City. These lines ran from the center of the city out toward the country. Suburbs began to grow rapidly. In

these "streetcar suburbs," most of the buildings were single-family homes or apartments. Far less than half of all city dwellers could afford even the cheapest suburban homes. But, to many in the slums, a house in the suburbs was a dream worth working for.

Spotlight on Sources

16. Newspapers played an important role in providing information about city life. Here is part of an article from the Chicago *Sunday Times*.

> Chicago, for its size, is more given to suburbs than any other city in the world. . . . The number of suburbs of all sorts . . . is nearly a hundred, and they [have a total] population of 50,000 or more. . . . Real estate offices are crowded daily with eager purchasers [buyers], and everybody . . . is kept busy from morning till night . . . answering questions regarding [about] railroad facilities, the water supply, educational advantages. . . . Each . . . morning the real estate dealer comes down to his office, contemplates [studies] the hungry crowd of would-be purchasers . . . and, after taking off his coat, the first thing he does is to turn to the head man and whisper, "John, add another $10 a foot."
> —Chicago *Sunday Times*, May 4, 1873

What effect might this article have on someone who was thinking about buying a house site in the suburbs?

Outlook

17. As the United States became an industrial nation, American cities grew rapidly. Many Americans were able to enjoy the pleasures that city life had. But slums and other big-city problems caused widespread concern. Looking ahead to the next century, reformers began to work to improve life in the cities. Which problem do you think they attacked first?

Activity: Ask a group of students to read about vaudeville or some other form of theater entertainment available to city dwellers around the turn of the century. Students able to read music should find songs from the period and put on a performance. Other students can report on the careers of vaudeville performers.

463

CHAPTER REVIEW

VOCABULARY REVIEW

▶ Match the following words with the definitions at the right.

1. urbanization

2. epidemic

3. reservoir

4. aqueduct

5. settlement house

6. bribe

7. trolley car

8. corruption

9. suburbs

a. a place for collecting water

b. a place that offered advice, training, and recreation to people in poor neighborhoods

c. the growth and development of cities

d. an outbreak of disease

e. dishonesty

f. a human-made channel or pipe for carrying water

g. an electric streetcar that runs on tracks

h. payment given to someone to cause him or her to act in a certain way

i. communities found on the outskirts of cities

j. a way to make things quicker and cheaper

SKILL BUILDER: USING A TIME LINE

▶ Look at the time line below. Then answer the questions on a sheet of paper.

Less than 20% of Americans live in cities 1860

About 33% of Americans live in cities 1885

Jane Addams opens Hull House in Chicago, 1889

Nearly 50% of Americans live in cities 1900

1860 — 1870 — 1880 — 1890 — 1900 — 1910

Electric trolley car is introduced in Richmond, Virginia 1888

Boston opens the first subway in the United States 1897

New York City passes Tenement Law 1901

1. How long after the electric trolley car was introduced did the first subway open?

2. When Jane Addams opened Hull House, about what percentage of Americans were living in cities?

3. When New York City passed the Tenement Law, about what percentage of Americans were living in cities?

4. Why might a Tenement Law have been needed in New York City by 1901?

SKILL BUILDER: CRITICAL THINKING AND COMPREHENSION

I. Classifying

▶ Copy the list of cities given below on a sheet of paper. Classify each city by where it is located. If it is on a sea coast, label it *S*. If it is on a river, label it *R*. If it is on a lake, label it *L*. Reread paragraph 4 if you need help.

1. Pittsburgh	4. Detroit	7. Baltimore
2. Philadelphia	5. Charleston	8. Boston
3. San Francisco	6. Cincinnati	9. Chicago

II. Sequencing

▶ Copy these events onto a piece of paper. Put numbers in front of each event to show the order in which they happened.

a. The electric trolley car was introduced.

b. Jane Addams opened Hull House.

c. Several cities had electric trolley lines.

d. One in four city dwellers was drinking filtered water.

e. The New York Tenement Law was passed.

f. The first subway began to operate in Boston.

III. Drawing Conclusions

▶ Read the paragraph below. Then decide which conclusion makes the most sense. Copy the conclusion onto a piece of paper.

The immigrants often were crowded into small apartments with no heat or hot water. Sometimes there was only one water faucet per apartment. Outside, garbage piled up in the alleys. In spite of these conditions, immigrants still kept coming to America.

Conclusions:

1. City governments did nothing for the immigrants.

2. Immigrants would have been better off if they had stayed in Europe.

3. Immigrants experienced hardships in America, but these hardships were not as bad as those they had left behind in Europe.

USING PRIMARY SOURCES

▶ Reread the "Spotlight on Sources" on page 463. Compare the questions that the real estate agents were asked with the questions an agent might be asked today.

ENRICHMENT

1. Both baseball and football became popular in America during the late 1800s. Look up the history of these sports in encyclopedias or other reference books. Work with other class members to prepare a report on one of the sports for the class. Include drawings of uniforms and information about how the rules of the sport have changed.

2. Read a biography of Jane Addams, Lillian Wald, Jacob Riis, or another American who helped people in poor neighborhoods. Give a report on the book to the class.

UNIT REVIEW

SUMMARY

The late 1800s brought many changes to the United States. Factory owners found that with improved machinery and transportation, they could produce greater quantities of goods. With a network of railroads that reached across America, these goods could reach more customers. Industrialists such as Andrew Carnegie and John D. Rockefeller were able to build huge fortunes from industry. These giants often put their rivals out of business, but the government did little to stop them.

Large numbers of immigrants came to America from southern and eastern Europe during this time. These people were seeking relief from famine and poverty. They were willing to work hard and did not ask for high wages. The lives of all Americans were enriched by the variety of customs and ways of life that these newcomers brought. As immigrants and other workers poured into the cities to live, their populations grew rapidly. At first, cities were not able to keep up with the need for housing and public services. In time, however, life became both healthier and safer for city dwellers.

SKILL BUILDER: READING A MAP

▶ Look carefully at the map and map key. Answer the questions on a separate sheet of paper.

1. Where are most of the coal fields located in North America?

2. Which southern state has a large iron ore deposit?

3. Around what bodies of water are iron ore deposits found?

4. Where in Canada are the largest iron ore deposits located? Would iron from these fields probably have been used for making steel in the United States in 1900? Why or why not?

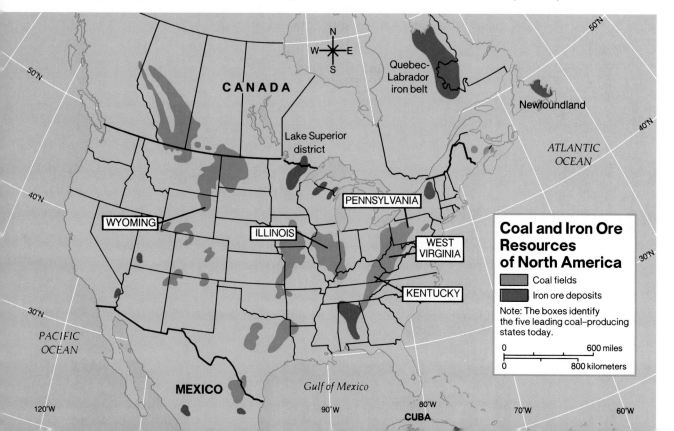

Coal and Iron Ore Resources of North America

- Coal fields
- Iron ore deposits

Note: The boxes identify the five leading coal-producing states today.

0   600 miles
0   800 kilometers

SKILL BUILDER: CRITICAL THINKING AND COMPREHENSION

I. Point of View

▶ The following statements are points of view that might have been held by people mentioned in Unit 10. Write the numbers of the statements (1–5) on a sheet of paper. Next to each letter, write the name of the person who might have held that point of view. Choose from this list of names: Jane Addams, Thomas Edison, John D. Rockefeller, Henry Ford, Samuel Morse. A name may be used more than once.

1. There is nothing wrong with giant trusts.

2. America is profiting from the work of immigrants, but no one is doing much to help them.

3. It does not really matter if smaller businesses are put out of operation because of the growth of corporations.

4. Using a moving assembly line in our factory would be a good way to cut production costs.

5. If we offered training and cultural events for immigrants, they would have an easier time adjusting to America.

II. Predicting

▶ Read each group of sentences below. Then write the statement that is the best prediction on a separate sheet of paper.

1. The most successful store in our town has used newspaper ads to bring in more customers. Everyone seems to be going there now. I need to bring more customers to my store.
   a. My store will close.
   b. I will place an ad for my store in the newspaper.
   c. I will install an elevator in my store.

2. A peasant in Italy is having a hard time feeding his family. He receives a letter from his cousin, who has moved to New York. The letter describes life in the city and the job the cousin's factory job. "Life in America is not easy," he writes, "but none of us is starving."
   a. The peasant moves his family to Rome.
   b. The peasant goes to America, gets a job, and later sends for his family.
   c. The peasant begins his own factory in Italy.

ENRICHMENT

1. Work in groups to find out more about some of the inventions listed in the chart on page 445. Do research to find out how the inventions were developed and how they were first used. Share what you learned with the class. Your presentation could include: (1) drawings of the inventions, (2) who used the invention, (3) improvements made, (4) how each invention was first received.

2. Many new types of buildings were erected during the late 1800s. These included tenement houses, the first skyscrapers, libraries, schools, and luxurious homes. Find pictures of buildings built during these years. Make a model of one, or draw a picture of it.

UNIT 11

REFORM MOVEMENTS

Chapter

UNIT OVERVIEW   Unit 11 will help you understand how Americans tried to achieve a better society through reforms in government and through private programs.

UNIT SKILLS OBJECTIVES   In Unit 11, three critical thinking skills are emphasized:

Classifying: Organizing facts into categories based on what they have in common.

Drawing Conclusions: Making a statement that explains the facts and evidence.

Summarizing: Giving the main idea of a group of paragraphs in a brief form.

You will also use two important social studies skills:
Understanding Economics   Making a Time Line

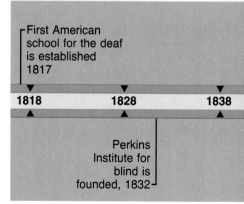

First American school for the deaf is established 1817

| 1818 | 1828 | 1838 |

Perkins Institute for blind is founded, 1832

ESL/LEP Strategy: Have students select a person from their countries of origin or those of their family members who helped reform the country. After students have completed the unit, ask them to compare that person's contributions to those of a person mentioned in the unit.

▲ By the 1890s, women were finding work outside the home in new industries like the telephone companies.

┌Seneca Falls
convention for
women's rights
1848

┌Morrill Land
Grant Act is
passed
1862

American Federation┐
of Labor is formed;
Haymarket riot
1886

Panama-U.S.┐
agreement on
canal, 1903

Progressive movement flourishes
1890s–1920s
Eighteenth Amendment,┐
Prohibition, 1919

| 1848 | 1858 | 1868 | 1878 | 1888 | 1898 | 1908 | 1918 |

Farmers
establish the
Grange
1867┘

Populist Party wins more
than one million votes;
Homestead Strike
occurs, 1892┘

Upton Sinclair's
The Jungle is
published
1906┘

Twentieth
Amendment
gives women
the vote, 1920┘

Points of View

During the late 1800s, America was rapidly growing and changing. Millions of immigrants from European nations were arriving in America each year. American cities were growing so fast they had great trouble meeting people's needs for housing and jobs. The nation's farmers were protesting the low prices they often received for their crops. Giant corporations were in control of many industries and fixed the prices of many products and services. American workers were forming labor unions to fight for higher pay and better working conditions. Women and African Americans were still struggling for equality in American society.

All this unrest and rapid change caused many problems in American society. Americans were not sure how to deal with these problems. Many

▲ Jane Addams was one of the many individuals who took responsibility for helping the poor. She opened her settlement house in Chicago in 1889 to help poor people and their children.

WILLIAM GRAHAM SUMNER'S VIEW

❝A [person] who has studied . . . any social question for [long] enough to be [confused] by its difficulties will [probably] propose some form of legislation [law] about it. . . . [I believe] the last thing to do is to legislate [pass a law]. . . .

It is not possible to experiment with a society and just drop the experiment whenever we choose. The experiment enters into the life of the society and never can be got out again. . . . Therefore . . . the doctrine [belief] of noninterference [not taking any action] is the highest wisdom.❞

Essays of William Graham Sumner, Albert G. Keller and Maurice R. Davie, eds.

How To Deal with America's Problems

Americans were confident that by hard work and careful planning, people could solve society's problems. Other Americans strongly believed that trying to improve society would only make things worse.

William Graham Sumner was a professor at Yale University. As you will read in the first section below, Sumner believed that society's problems were too difficult for people to be able to solve. He was especially against new laws to try to improve society.

President Theodore Roosevelt, on the other hand, had a strong belief that many things that were wrong in American society could be reformed. In the second selection below, he explains that he is certain that people can work together to change their lives.

A PRESIDENT'S VIEW

"We recognize . . . the evils [problems] of today. The remedies [cures] are . . . partly to be obtained [achieved] by laws, and in greater part to be obtained by individual . . . effort. . . . These remedies include a religious and moral teaching which shall increase the spirit of human brotherhood; an educational system which shall train men [people] for every form of useful service. . . . a division of the profits of industry as shall tend to encourage intelligent and thrifty tool-users [workers] to become tool-owners [business owners]; and a government so strong, just, wise, and democratic that . . . it may do its full share in promoting these ends [achieving these things]."

The Outlook, Theodore Roosevelt.

▲ President Theodore Roosevelt believed government should play a part in reforming society. Here he is attacking the trusts with his "big stick."

Using Primary Sources

1. Why did Sumner believe it was dangerous to try to make great changes in American society?

2. What did Roosevelt believe were the best cures for the problems of American society?

3. Which person's ideas about reforming society do you agree with? Explain the reasons for your answer.

471

CHAPTER 1

Unions Help Workers

OBJECTIVE: How did unions try to improve the lives of American workers?

1. Picture yourself in a steel mill in the late 1800s. The temperature is nearly 130 degrees. You have been working since 6 A.M. It is now nearly 6 P.M., and every muscle in your body aches with pain and exhaustion. You earn fourteen cents an hour. It's not enough to feed your family, so your wife and two children work in the textile mill down the road. Suddenly you slip on the wet floor and fall on your arm. You groan in pain and pray that the arm is not broken. If it is, you must somehow manage to go to work tomorrow—or you will lose your job. Your neighbor lost his job when he fell and broke his leg last year. The company paid him nothing during the months it took him to get back on his feet again. Now the workers in the plant are talking about getting together to force the company to raise wages and improve working conditions. At first, you were afraid of such talk. But now, with this injury, what is there to lose?

▲ Unions helped improve dangerous factory conditions and insisted injured workers be paid while they were away from the job.

Early Labor Unions How did labor unions start and what were the early ones like?

2. Almost from the time factories were first set up in the United States, workers united to improve their working conditions. The first **labor unions** were organized in the 1800s. A labor union is an organization that workers form to improve conditions in the places where they work. In some cities, workers formed small local unions. Each union consisted of skilled workers in a certain trade, such as shoe-making or carpentry. A union of skilled workers in a certain trade is called a **craft union**. At this time, why were unions made up of only skilled workers? The first unions tried to get members

472

In Chapter 1 you will apply these critical thinking skills to the historical process:

▲ **Identifying Fact *versus* Opinion:** Specifying whether information can be proved or whether it expresses feelings or beliefs.

➥ **Recognizing Cause and Effect:** Recognizing the action or event that makes something happen; identifying the result of an action or event.

and employers to agree on certain wages. If employers refused, a union's workers might go on **strike**. In a strike workers refuse to continue to work until their demands are met. Employers argued that strikes were illegal because they slowed or even stopped free trade. Usually, the ▶ courts agreed. For what other reasons might employers oppose labor unions?

The First National Unions What became of the first national labor unions?

3. Around the time of the Civil War, American workers created several national unions. The labor movement was expanding at this time, mainly because the growth of American industry created more wage earners. Like early local labor groups, the first national unions were craft unions. This meant that they kept out most immigrants, African Americans, and women, because these groups worked mainly at unskilled jobs. In the late 1860s, many national unions and several local unions joined to form the National Labor Union. It was a **federation** (fed-uh-RAY-shuhn), meaning that it was made up of organizations that remained independent.

4. The early national labor movement had only limited success. By 1808, it did persuade Congress to reduce the work day for federal employees to eight hours. But its approach was not very practical. For instance, the National Labor Union did not believe in the strike, one of the chief tools of organized labor. Also, many leaders of the movement were more interested in long-range reforms of society than in gaining immediate benefits for workers.

The Knights of Labor What gains did this organization make for labor?

5. An unusual kind of union, the Knights of Labor, gained many members in the 1870s. The Knights of Labor at first met in secret to keep employers from finding out which workers were members. One of the Knights' strongest leaders, Terence Powderly, believed that if secrecy was ended the union would attract more members.

He was right. By 1886, after the policy of secrecy was ended, the Knights of Labor claimed more than 700,000 members. Why did ◀ secrecy work against the growth of the union?

6. The Knights of Labor advanced the cause of labor on several fronts. The union was open to unskilled as well as skilled workers. It thus included many immigrants, African Americans, and women—an unusual practice in the late 1800s. The Knights were also able to get the federal government to set up a Department of Labor. Even though many of its leaders like Powderly were against strikes, the union did strike, with great success. At one point, the Knights were able to force a powerful railroad to restore wage cuts. The Knights also managed to get the mighty Missouri Pacific railway to **recognize** (rek-uhg-NYZ) the union. To recognize a union means that an employer agrees that the union represents and speaks for its workers. These gains made it easier for unions to enter into **collective bargaining** (kuh-LEK-tiv BAHR-guh-ning) with owners. Collective bargaining occurs when owners and workers agree to sit down and discuss wages and working conditions. Among the aims the Knights continued to fight for were an eight-hour workday, equal pay for men and women, and an end to child labor.

7. Despite their achievements, the Knights of Labor soon lost members and influence. Like the earlier National Labor Union, the Knights also wanted to bring about changes in America that had nothing to do with labor. One of these was turning the ownership of railroads over to the government. Ideas such as these often proved unpopular and took attention from the union's central message.

The Haymarket Riot and the Homestead Strike How did violence affect the unions in their effort to help workers?

8. In 1886 an incident during a strike in Chicago seriously weakened the union movement. The strike was against the McCormick Harvester Company. During the strike workers

Background: Summarize for students some of the other terminology associated with the American labor movement. Terms might include sweatshop, mediation, arbitration, contract, closed shop, and open shop. Along with the strike and picketing, workers' weapons included the boycott. Employers made use of the blacklist, lockout, and yellow-dog contract.

473

▲ The Haymarket Riot took place in Chicago on May 4, 1886. What event during the strike has the artist chosen to emphasize? Why?

decided to hold a protest meeting near Chicago's Haymarket Square. After some speeches, the police tried to break up what had been a peaceful meeting. Suddenly, someone—no one ever learned who—threw a bomb that exploded near the line of police. Seven police officers died and more than 60 others were injured. The police fired into the crowd. Panic broke out. Four strikers were killed and several were wounded. But the greatest injury was to unions everywhere. Even though the source of the bomb was unclear, newspapers played up the union's role in the tragedy. As people began to view unions as dangerous, membership in the Knights of Labor and other unions fell sharply.

9. The Homestead strike was another bloody strike that had bitter results. In 1892 the Carnegie Steel Company in Homestead, near Pittsburgh, Pennsylvania, announced pay cuts. The angered workers went on strike. The owners replied by shutting down the plant and hiring 300 guards so that new workers could be hired. As the guards approached the plant in riverboats, townspeople and strikers met them.

Both sides were armed. Violence broke out, with seven guards and nine strikers killed. Hundreds were injured. Troops were sent in to restore order. Once again the reputation of unions had suffered.

Spotlight on Sources

10. A year after the Homestead strike, Pittsburgh journalist Arthur Burgoyne published an account of the episode. Here is his description of the tragic events:

As the barges [of guards] drew nearer to Homestead, the noise on the shore grew louder and louder and soon the sharp crack of rifles rang out, giving a foretaste of what was in store for the unwelcome visitors. . . . On the beach were several hundred men and women—for mothers, wives and sisters had joined in the mad rush to the landing-place—some of them half dressed, some carrying loaded guns, some with stones or clubs in their hands. . . . Suddenly a shot was fired—whether from the barges or from the shore has always been a mystery. . . . A score of [many] . . . rifles were discharged into the crowd on the bank with deadly effect. Several of the workmen were seen to fall. The first blood had been shed and now the one thought of the men of Homestead was *vengeance* [revenge], merciless and complete, on the strangers who had come to shoot them down.

—from *The Homestead Strike of 1892*, by Arthur G. Burgoyne

▶ Could violence at Homestead have been avoided? How?

The American Federation of Labor   Why did the AFL have more success than earlier labor unions?

11. The American Federation of Labor, or AFL, was founded in 1886 and succeeded where many other unions had failed. Like the National Labor Union, it was made up of many individual craft unions. But AFL leaders believed in using strikes to win their goals. They did not aim for long-range social or political reform. Instead, the federation worked on gaining higher wages, shorter hours, and safety in the workplace for its members. Every year the AFL gained new members. By 1900 the AFL claimed a membership of one million. The federation continued to grow, reaching a peak of four million members in 1920.

People in History

12. Samuel Gompers   The AFL was led for almost 40 years by Samuel Gompers. Born in London to Dutch Jewish parents, he began his working career as a cigarmaker in New York City in 1863. It was Gompers who led the AFL to stress what he called "pure and simple unionism," rather than try to remake society. Gompers believed that effective unions made good citizens because they taught people to stand up for their rights. "Wherever trades unions have organized and are most firmly

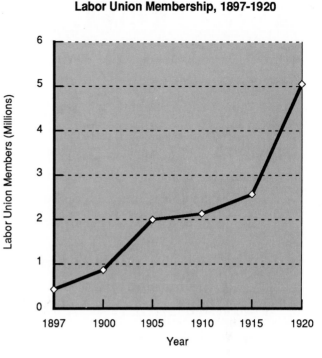

Labor Union Membership, 1897-1920

Source: Historical Statistics

▲ How many workers were union members in 1920? In what year was union membership the lowest? What was the general trend in union membership between 1897 and 1920?

organized," he said, "there are the rights of the people most respected." Why would Gompers's ◀ message appeal to average wage earners?

Outlook

13. Workers began organizing labor unions at about the time goods began to be produced in factories. The right of workers to organize unions that protected them and their interests was one of the freedoms of American society. Early local and national unions helped workers to make some gains. In the late 1800s, union demands for better pay and working conditions sometimes led to violence. With the founding and growth of the AFL, the American labor movement steadily expanded. It won gains for workers such as better pay and working conditions. Labor unions are still active today in protecting the rights of American workers.

Ask: Ask students to compare workers and unions in America with those in other nations. Can workers strike in communist countries? Why do unions have more power in democratic nations?

475

CHAPTER REVIEW

VOCABULARY REVIEW

▶ Select one of the words in the following list to complete each of the sentences below.

labor union   federation   strike   recognize

craft union   wages   collective bargaining

1. A _____ is limited to skilled workers in a certain trade.

2. A refusal to work until certain demands are met is a _____ .

3. A _____ is an organization formed by workers—skilled or unskilled—to improve working conditions.

4. A labor organization consisting of a number of independent unions is a _____ .

5. _____ refers to discussions about wages and working conditions between owners and workers.

6. When owners _____ a union, they accept it as representing the workers.

SKILL BUILDER: INTERPRETING A CARTOON

▶ Study the 1887 cartoon below. Then answer the questions that follow.

1. How does the cartoon show the monopoly capitalists?
2. How does the cartoon show the working class?
3. Whom does the cartoon blame for greed and the problems of America?
4. What political view does the cartoonist have about the capitalist and the working class?

SKILL BUILDER: CRITICAL THINKING AND COMPREHENSION

I. Fact *versus* Opinion

▶ Decide whether each of the following statements is a fact or an opinion. On a separate sheet of paper, write each statement and label it *F* for fact or *O* for opinion.

1. When labor union supporters and police met in the late 1800s there was sometimes violence.

2. If workers were paid better, protests would have always been peaceful.

3. Labor unions are always violent.

4. At first, unions had to meet in secret.

II. Cause and Effect

▶ On a separate sheet of paper, write the causes and match them with their effects.

Causes

1. The early labor movement did not believe in strikes and also wanted changes in society.

2. The Knights of Labor ended secret meetings.

3. Newspapers played up the role of unions in the Haymarket tragedy.

4. Carnegie Steel announced pay cuts.

Effects

a. The union attracted many new members and by 1886, claimed more than 700,000 members.

b. The first unions had limited success.

c. Angered workers went out on strike.

d. People began to view unions as dangerous.

III. Generalizing

▶ On a separate sheet of paper, write a generalization from each set of facts.

1. a. In the late 1800s, working conditions in factories were bad.
   b. Factory wages were low.
   c. Workers who were injured on the job might be fired.

2. a. The American Federation of Labor used strikes to win its goals.
   b. The AFL did not get involved in political reform.
   c. The AFL tried to get higher wages for its members.

USING PRIMARY SOURCES

▶ Reread the Spotlight on Sources, on pages 474 and 475. Do you think this account of the Homestead Strike is fair? Why or why not? Name one thing in the account to which the steel company managers would object. Name one thing to which the strikers would object.

ENRICHMENT

1. Use an almanac or other reference book to find out how many American workers belong to unions today. What percentage of the total working population do they form?

2. Look through one or more issues of a newspaper to find an article that deals with unions. Which union is involved? What do its members want?

CHAPTER 2

Farmers Face Hard Times

OBJECTIVE: How did farmers of the late 1800s try to solve their problems? This picture was drawn in 1873.

▲ How does the picture of farm life above contrast with the mood of the words to the song in paragraph 1?

1. "I take my pen in hand to let you know that we are starving to death." This is what a Kansas farm wife of the 1880s wrote as she watched her family's crops dry up because of lack of rain. The years after the Civil War were hard for farmers. Some of their troubles came from natural disasters, such as seasons without rain or a grasshopper plague. Other troubles came from human policies and decisions. Many farmers on the Great Plains gave up and moved back East. They painted "In God We Trusted: In Kansas We Busted" on their wagons. But even if a farm family's crops did well, they still had a tough time. The price they got for those crops kept dropping, while the cost of supplies and of shipping crops to the cities kept rising. A song popular with farmers in the 1890s expressed their bitterness:

> Oh, the farmer is the man,
> The farmer is the man,
> Lives on credit [loans] till the fall;
> And his pants are wearing thin,
>
> His condition, it's a sin,
> He's forgot that he's the man who feeds them all.

Hard times had fallen on America's farmers, and despair and discontent would bring serious changes.

Farmers How did the farmers' situation change in the late 1800s?

2. One change for farmers was a big increase in crop production. For instance, in 1866 farmers grew about 730 million bushels (25.6 million kiloliters) of corn. In 1900 they produced

In Chapter 2 you will apply these critical thinking skills to the historical process:

Understanding Points of View: Recognizing that people may have different attitudes about the same thing.

Classifying: Organizing facts into categories based on what they have in common.

2½ billion bushels (87.5 million kiloliters)—over three times as much. There were two main reasons for such increases. First, there were more farms and thus more land being farmed. As you have read, Americans settled many parts of the West after the Civil War. Second, the use of farm machinery kept increasing. Mechanical reapers and threshers were becoming more and more common. Farmers could grow and harvest much more by using machinery. What disadvantages might farm machinery have?

3. Another change for farmers was a big drop in prices. Take wheat, for example. In 1866 a bushel sold for over $2.00. In 1900 it brought only 62 cents. Cotton, worth almost 10 cents a pound in the 1870s, fell to less than 5 cents a pound 20 years later. The decrease in prices was a result of overproduction. With so many products flooding the market, the value of goods dropped. In a sense, you could say that farmers were a victim of their own success. Nevertheless, the price drops brought many farmers to the edge of financial ruin. One farm woman wrote to her aunt, "No one can depend on farming for a living in this country."

Farmers and the Railroads   Why were railroads important to farmers?

4. In the late 1800s, railroads were very important for farmers, especially those who did not live near rivers. Trains carried goods to farmers and transported their crops to market. In many areas of the West, farmers actually bought their land from the railroads. The railroads had received **land grants**—big areas of land given by the government—and sold what they did not need. Many people praised the railroads. One said, "There is nothing which so rapidly pushes forward the car of progress and civilization as the railroad locomotive."

5. As time went on, however, farmers began to blame the railroads for many of their hardships. For one thing, farmers found railroad **rates**—the amounts charged for transporting goods—too high. Another problem was that railroads did not treat all shippers equally. For

example, rates in the West were sometimes three times higher than rates in the East. Big companies received **rebates**, or refunds, so that they paid less than small shippers, such as farmers. In most areas, there was only one railroad. It had a **monopoly** (muh-NAHP-uh-lee) on transportation—that is, no competition. What could farmers do if they objected to a railroad's rates?

The Grange   In what ways did the Grange try to help farmers?

6. An organization known as the Patrons of Husbandry, or the National Grange, was founded in the 1860s to help farmers. By 1875, the Grange had some 300,000 members in roughly 20,000 local lodges. The aims of the Grange were to give information to its members and provide social contacts for them. Farmers led lonely lives in this era before cars, trucks, telephones, and television. As its strength grew, the Grange began to focus on economic matters. Many Grangers banded together to sell their goods to **cooperatives** (koh-AHP-uh-ruh-tivz), or organizations that the members owned. Such cooperation among Grangers often lowered their costs. The Grange also tried to get state governments to regulate railroads so that they would not charge such high rates. Some laws were passed, but they did not help much because they were not enforced. Why do you think the laws were not enforced?

Spotlight on Sources

7. This is an account of a Grange meeting in the 1870s. The Grange had several ranks, or degrees, that its members could earn.

> The Patrons of Grange 435 met Saturday night to confer [give] the fourth degree upon a new member. The lady members had prepared a fine table filled with the many blessings bestowed upon [given to] us by Our Heavenly Father. It was our harvest feast and we appreciated it very much. After the table was cleared, Sister Hupp read an essay upon Butter Making,

The Growth of Chicago Cities grow in two ways. One is the increase in the number of purposes, or functions, they serve. The other is the increase in their population and in the size of the areas they serve. Between 1850 and 1900, Chicago's functions increased so that by the end of that period it was the leading transportation, trade, and industrial city for lands west of the Appalachians. In turn, these varied functions provided jobs for thousands of newcomers, many of them immigrants from Europe. The new settlers boosted Chicago's population from 30,000 in 1850 to over 2 million in 1900.

Chicago's first function was as a lake port. Port activities began in the 1840s as steamboat traffic expanded on the Great Lakes. By the 1850s, about 400 lake vessels went in and out of Chicago each year. Chicago's port became an unloading point for settlers bound for western farms. It also became the chief shipping port for the grains and livestock the farms produced.

Later, Chicago prospered as a great railroad center. The railroads had to pass around the lower end of Lake Michigan as they went westward. Most railroad builders found it profitable to take their railroads through nearby Chicago to take advantage of this major trading center. In all, ten main line railroads and 11 branch lines went through Chicago.

The railroads enlarged Chicago's trading area and made the city a great commercial center. Farmers from rich farmlands throughout the Midwest sent their grains, hogs, and livestock by rail to Chicago's markets and stockyards. The farmers also looked to Chicago to meet all their banking, insurance, equipment, and other needs.

Manufacturing functions followed, and Chicago became the largest manufacturing city west of the Appalachians. Steel mills turned out steel for factories making items such as farm machinery and railroad cars. After refrigeration was developed in the 1870s, huge meat-packing plants grew up around the stockyards. Still other factories turned milk from surrounding farms into butter, cheese, and ice cream.

Study the map of Chicago in about 1900 below. Use the map to answer the following questions.

1. What city functions were probably carried out in Chicago's central business district?

2. What city functions were found near the stockyards?

3. Why are there so many railroads on the map?

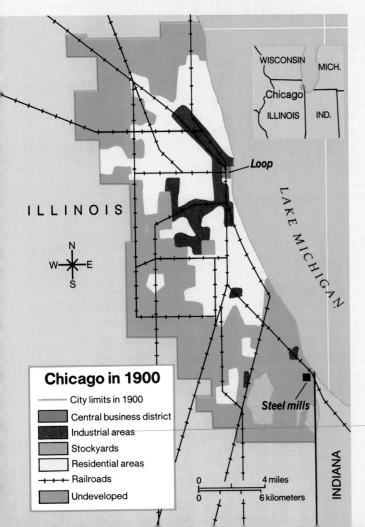

Chicago in 1900

— City limits in 1900
▪ Central business district
▪ Industrial areas
▪ Stockyards
▪ Residential areas
+++ Railroads
▪ Undeveloped

0   4 miles
0   6 kilometers

and a speech was made by a brother from Hazel Wood Grange. . . . The question for the next debate will be "Can anything be made by feeding, to hogs, corn worth fifty cents per bushel, when hogs sell for five cents per pound?"

—from *Prairie Farmer*, 1874

▶ What "blessings" is the writer referring to? Why do you think a woman rather than a man read an essay on butter making?

The Populist Party   Why did the Populist party rise and decline?

8. Farmers, still troubled by hard times, helped form the **Populist party** in the 1890s. This political party wanted the government to own the railroads and telegraph lines. It also wanted a national income tax and an eight-hour day for workers, neither of which existed at this time.

9. However, by 1900 the Populist party had lost most of its support. The Populists first gained acceptance because many people—farmers, laborers, minorities—believed that the Populists spoke their language. The Populists tried to gain power and influence for those who had least. At their peak, in 1892, Populists ran a presidential candidate who received more than one million votes. Nearly 1,500 Populists won in local and state elections. One reason for the Populists' decline was the presidential election of 1896. The candidate backed by the Populists, William Jennings Bryan, lost. Another reason was that prices for farm crops were beginning to rise. Thus, farmers had fewer complaints than earlier. Even though the Populist party died out, its influence continued into the early 1900s.

People in History

10. Mary Elizabeth Lease   One of the best-known Populists was Mary Elizabeth Lease. Born in Ridgeway, Pennsylvania, in 1853, she later moved to Kansas and took up the farmers' cause as a public speaker. A tall woman with sharp features, she had a deep

▲ Mary E. Lease was a busy Populist campaigner. In one campaign she made over 150 speeches.

voice that carried well—a big help in the days before loudspeakers. She was best known for her advice to farmers to "raise less corn and more hell." Lease's outspoken ways soon got her into trouble. After quarreling with the Populist governor of Kansas, she moved back East, where she lived quietly the rest of her life.

Outlook

11. Farmers, who suffered from hard times after the Civil War, tried to improve their situation through the Grange and the Populist party. Although neither of these organizations succeeded, they did show farmers' strength in the late 1800s. The influence of farmers was never again so powerful, for people were leaving farms for cities. At the time of the Civil War, farm people made up nearly two-thirds of the total population. By 1920 they formed less than one-third of it. What do you think caused this ◀ decline?

Activity: If possible, invite a local farmer to class. Help students develop a list of questions to ask, such as the size of the farm, the products grown, and the problems of present-day farming.

481

CHAPTER REVIEW

VOCABULARY REVIEW

▶ Match the words in the following list with the definitions below.

1. land grants
2. rates
3. rebates
4. monopoly
5. populist party
6. cooperatives

a. amounts charged for services

b. refunds

c. complete control over a product or service

d. big areas given by the government

e. organizations that members owned

f. a political group that wanted the government to own the railroads and telegraphs

g. a group that speaks the same language

SKILL BUILDER: COMPLETING A TABLE

▶ Farmers experienced many changes in their economic situation. Copy the table below on another sheet of paper. Then complete it by describing how each factor given helped or hurt the farmer. If the factor both helped and hurt the farmer, fill in both columns.

Factor	Helped the Farmer	Hurt the Farmer
cooperatives		
railroad monopoly		
high production		
railroad land grants		

SKILL BUILDER: CRITICAL THINKING AND COMPREHENSION

I. Point of View

▶ Think about each statement below. Then write the statement and the name of the person who might have said it on a sheet of paper.

1. If you want to go broke, do what I do.

2. We can charge more for our services in the West than in the East, so let's do it.

3. We're trying to get the government to regulate the railroads.

4. Prices of wheat are so low that I can hardly make a living.

5. Farmers can help themselves by joining our cooperative.

6. A national income tax is fairer for working people than other kinds of taxes.

7. The railroads are not fair to us.

II. Classifying

▶ Classify the beliefs or descriptions below under the correct heading. Write them on a sheet of paper. Some may go under both headings, or under neither.

Populist Party   **The Grange**

1. had ranks for members

2. mostly farmers

3. wanted national income tax

4. wanted eight-hour work day for workers

5. provided social contacts

6. wanted government to own the railroads

7. organized cooperatives

8. wanted government to control railroads rates

9. wanted government to own the telegraph system

III. Sequencing

▶ On a sheet of paper put the following events in the order in which they occurred.

a. The Populist presidential candidate loses.

b. The Grange is founded.

c. Farmers make up less than one-third of the population.

d. Courts restore power to the railroads.

e. The Populist party is formed.

USING PRIMARY SOURCES

▶ Reread the Spotlight on Sources on pages 479 and 481. What kinds of activity went on at this Grange meeting? If you were a farmer in the 1870s, why would you or would you not want to belong to the Grange? Base your answer on what went on at this meeting.

ENRICHMENT

1. Use an almanac or other reference book to find out how many people live on farms in the United States today. What percentage of the total population do they form?

2. Draw an illustration of the Grange meeting described on pages 479 and 481.

3. Write a report that answers these questions about your state: How many farms are there? Where are most farms located? What are the main products of these farms?

4. Farmers in the late 1800s were affected by the amount of money available. Research the following terms and tell how they affected the farmers: inflation, deflation, mortgage rates, land values, crop values.

CHAPTER 3

Women Fight for Equal Rights

OBJECTIVE: How did women work to gain equality in American society?

1. The year was 1840, the place, London, England. People had come from many parts of the world to attend an important antislavery meeting. Among the delegates were two American abolitionists, Lucretia Mott and Elizabeth Cady Stanton. They had made the long transatlantic trip to speak out against the evils of slavery. But could they take part in the meeting? No, said the organizers. Could they even sit openly among the spectators? They were told no again. Mott and Stanton were forced to take seats in the balcony and were told to sit quietly. This was an era when almost everyone believed that women should not play any active role in society. Mott and Stanton disagreed. They returned home determined to make some changes.

The Seneca Falls Meeting Why was the Seneca Falls meeting important?

2. As far as women were concerned, there was plenty for Mott and Stanton to change. Since the beginning of American history, women had only limited rights. Although they were citizens, they were second-class citizens compared to men. They could not vote. Most colleges and jobs were closed to them. If they were married, they could not own property, control whatever money they might earn, or bring cases to court. If they were divorced, they

▲ An 1894 cartoon predicts the success of the women's rights movement. Do you think the cartoonist took the struggle for women's rights seriously? Why or why not?

rarely received the right to keep their children. In their daily lives, women were expected to spend their time on home, children, and church.

3. After Mott and Stanton returned from London in 1840, they began organizing the women's rights movement. This was a move-

In Chapter 3 you will apply these critical thinking skills to the historical process:
▲ **Summarizing:** Giving the main idea of a group of paragraphs in a brief form.
◤ **Making Judgments:** Stating a personal opinion based on historical facts.

ment to gain women equal rights with men. Believers in this cause are known today as **feminists** (FEM-uh-nists). Feminists have always included men as well as women. Among the early women's rights leaders were famous abolitionists, such as Frederick Douglass and William Lloyd Garrison. Why would abolitionists be interested in women's rights? As the Abolition Movement raised questions about the status and rights of individuals, women began to look at their own position and to speak out.

4. In 1848 Mott, Stanton, and others held a women's rights convention at Seneca Falls, New York. Stanton lived in Seneca Falls with her husband and their seven children. Women—and some men—traveled many miles by horse and wagon to meet at this small town. Sojourner Truth, a well-known abolitionist, took part in this meeting. There the delegates approved a "Declaration of Sentiments" based on the American Declaration of Independence. They resolved that women should no longer be "satisfied with their present position." The Seneca Falls meeting was important for two reasons. First, it was the first women's rights convention. Second, the declaration that was put out by the convention summed up women's many complaints in one program for action.

Spotlight on Sources

5. The Seneca Falls Declaration, like the Declaration of Independence, first attacked the treatment of women that made the document necessary. Whereas the colonists blamed the British, the feminists at Seneca Falls blamed men. Then, also like the Declaration of Independence, the Seneca Falls Declaration listed specific complaints. The feminists listed many "injuries" that man had done to woman in trying to establish "an absolute tyranny [dictatorship] over her." Here are some of them:

He has never permitted her to exercise her inalienable [not able to be taken away] right to the elective franchise [the vote]. . . . He has taken from her all right in property, even to the wages she earns. . . .

He has monopolized [completely controlled] the profitable employments. . . . He has denied her the facilities for obtaining a thorough education. . . . He has endeavored [tried], in every way that he could, to destroy her confidence in her own powers, to lessen her self-respect and to make her willing to lead a dependent and abject [lowly] life.

—from *History of Woman Suffrage*, ed. by Elizabeth C. Stanton et al.

If you were a woman in 1848, which of the injustices listed here would bother you the most? ◄

Achievements and Changes How did women's opportunities increase in the late 1800s?

6. Although the women's rights movement made few gains at first, many individual women were able to achieve success. Even before the Seneca Falls meeting, educator Mary Lyon had established Mount Holyoke, the first women's college in the United States. Several women writers gained wide audiences. They included Louisa May Alcott, who wrote *Little Women*, and Harriet Beecher Stowe, author of *Uncle Tom's Cabin*. Against all odds, a few women were able to succeed in fields usually closed to them. For instance, many people were against Elizabeth Blackwell's effort to become the first American woman physician. Maria Mitchell, an astronomer, was the first woman, and the only one for 100 years, to be elected to the American Academy of Arts and Sciences.

7. More important than such individual successes were changes that affected thousands of women. One change was education. Beginning in the 1860s, several new state universities accepted both women and men. These were called **coeducational** schools. In 1870, only about 20 percent of college students were women. By 1910, this figure had doubled. Another change concerned jobs. More and more women were working outside the home. For instance, there were four times as many women in the industrial work force in 1910 as there had been in 1870. However,

Background: Only one woman present at the Seneca Falls convention was still alive when the Nineteenth Amendment was adopted. She was Charlotte Woodward, who had ridden to Seneca Falls as a 15-year-old farm girl, watched the proceedings from a back row, and signed her name to the Seneca Falls Declaration.

485

women who worked the same long hours as men were paid less than men. Why might working outside the home make women more interested in gaining equality with men?

8. By 1900 women had gained many rights that had been denied them in the 1840s. In the majority of states, they could now control their own property, keep their earnings, and bring suits against others in court. In some states, divorced women had equal rights with men to care for their children. But, in most states, they still lacked what feminists thought of one of the most important rights of all—the right to vote.

The Struggle for the Vote How and why did women finally win the right to vote?

9. After the Civil War, the right to vote, or **suffrage** (SUF-ruhj), became the main goal for most feminists. As a result of the adoption of the Fifteenth Amendment, African American men had gained the right to vote, at least in

theory. Now it seemed to be women's turn. Opponents of women's suffrage, which included many women, argued that politics would corrupt women's "gentler nature." **Suffragists**—those who wanted women's suffrage—held that it was exactly this "gentler nature" that would clean up politics. Suffrage opponents believed giving women the right to vote would break up families and disturb society. Suffragists argued that just the opposite would occur since the votes of women would improve society. Can you think of other arguments for, or against, woman suffrage?

10. After decades of effort, women finally won the right to vote. In the late 1800s, suffragists began to make real progress. The two main suffrage organizations, long separate, joined together. The suffrage crusade came under the direction of a strong new leader, Carrie Chapman Catt. The Progressive movement, which will be discussed later, gained followers for many reforms, including women's rights. By

MAP SKILL BUILDER: The map below is a thematic or special purpose map. Thematic maps show special distribution of information. **1.** What type of information does this map show? **2.** Where did women win voting rights in 1900–1919?

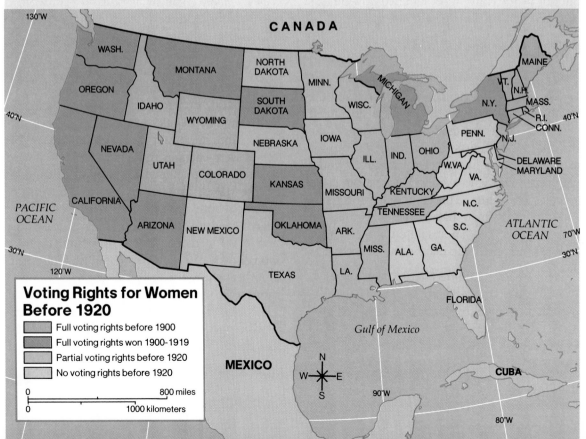

Voting Rights for Women Before 1920

- Full voting rights before 1900
- Full voting rights won 1900-1919
- Partial voting rights before 1920
- No voting rights before 1920

▲ Elizabeth Cady Stanton speaks to the convention at Seneca Falls, New York, on June 20, 1848. What other struggle for equality was going on at the same time?

the early 1900s, many states began to give women the right to vote in some elections.

11. Perhaps most important in the drive for women's suffrage was World War I. American women played a vital role in this great war. Partly to recognize women for their role in the war, a new amendment was added to the Constitution. This was the Nineteenth Amendment, passed in 1920. At long last it gave American women the right to vote.

People in History

12. Susan B. Anthony The best known of all Americans who worked for women's rights, especially suffrage, was Susan B. Anthony. As a young woman in the 1840s, she tried teaching, but hated earning less than men doing the same work. When she met Elizabeth Cady Stanton in the early 1850s, the two formed a lifelong partnership. They worked closely together to fight for equality for women. Anthony was a brilliant organizer, while Stanton was an extremely able speaker and writer. Anthony's ability to organize caused one woman to compare

her to Napoleon, the French military leader. For the next 50 years Anthony worked tirelessly for women's rights. She edited a women's rights weekly journal. In 1872, she voted in the presidential election, and was arrested for doing so. She was fined $100 but never paid the fine. Though mocked at first, she later won worldwide respect. She died in 1906, before American women won the vote. Her final message —"Failure is impossible!"—inspired those who carried on her work.

Outlook

13. It was a long road from Seneca Falls to the adoption of the Nineteenth Amendment, which gave women the vote. Along the way, many women gained individual success. Events in the wider world—better educational opportunities, experience in the world of work, and wartime contributions—had a greater effect on the women's rights movement. But women still had a hard and long struggle ahead of them. What are some of the rights at the present time ◀ that women still have not achieved?

Ask: Do women today have rights equal to those of men? Should they? Why or why not? Class members may want to discuss whether they think men and women have special roles in society that each sex is better able to perform.

CHAPTER REVIEW

VOCABULARY REVIEW

▶ Write the following sentences on a sheet of paper. Then fill in the blanks with the words that best define the words in heavy type.

1. **Feminists** believe that women should _____ .
   a. restrict their interests to the home.
   b. have rights equal to those of men.
   c. stay out of politics.
   d. emphasize feminine qualities.

2. A **coeducational** institution _____ .
   a. is limited to men.
   b. is limited to women.
   c. admits both men and women.
   d. admits an equal number of men and women.

3. African-American men gained **suffrage** _____ .
   a. before the Civil War.
   b. during the Civil War.
   c. after the Civil War.
   d. in 1920.

4. **Suffragists** wanted to win the vote for _____ .
   a. women.
   b. blacks.
   c. women's rights leaders.
   d. Americans under 18.

SKILL BUILDER: READING A TIME LINE

▶ Use the time line below to answer these questions on a sheet of paper.

Antislavery meeting in London, England 1840	*Uncle Tom's Cabin* published 1852	Fifteenth Amendment gives African Americans the right to vote 1870	Two main suffrage organizations join to form the National American Women Suffrage Association 1890	Nineteenth Amendment passed 1920
1840	**1860**	**1880**	**1900**	**1920**
	Seneca Falls Convention 1848	Anthony arrested for voting 1872	Oregon becomes the fifth state to adopt women's suffrage 1910	U.S. enters WWI 1917

1. In what year was the book by the famous abolitionist, Harriet Beecher Stowe, published?

2. What year did Mott and Stanton's efforts finally gain women the right to vote?

3. What major event for the women's movement occurred in 1848?

4. How many years after African Americans were able to vote did women earn this right?

5. Which preceeding event may have influenced Anthony to vote although it was against the law? What kind of statement was she attempting to make?

USING PRIMARY SOURCES

▶ Reread the Spotlight on Sources on page 485. What does the source say about women's right to keep the money they earned? Do you agree that this was an injury?

SKILL BUILDER: CRITICAL THINKING AND COMPREHENSION

▶ I. Drawing Conclusions

▶ Read the facts about women's suffrage below. Then select the one conclusion that best fits the facts.

Facts

1. At the beginning of the women's movement, women were expected to devote most of their time to home, family, and church.

2. Two years after the end of World War I, women earned the right to vote.

Possible Conclusions

a. During World War I, people valued home, family, and church less so women could spend more time working.

b. During World War I, women filled many jobs previously held only by men, showing they were capable of equal responsibility.

c. Participation in war is necessary to achieve equal rights.

▲ II. Summarizing

▶ Nothing in a newspaper summarizes an article better than a headline. Write headlines for each of the following events in the history of women's rights. Make each headline five words or less.

1. The Nineteenth Amendment is ratified, guaranteeing women the right to vote.

2. The Seneca Falls convention is held in 1848.

3. A woman, Elizabeth Blackwell, graduates from medical school and becomes the first American woman physician.

▬ III. Making Judgments

▶ Make judgments about the *fairness* or *unfairness* of these events. Write the event and your decision on a sheet of paper.

1. Two women abolitionists had to sit in the balcony at a meeting so that no one could see them.

2. Women were not allowed to own property in 1840.

3. Women traveled to Seneca Falls to organize the women's rights movement.

ENRICHMENT

1. Suffragists used to stage big parades to win support for their cause. Design a poster that a suffragist might carry in such a parade.

2. Use an almanac or other reference book to find out how many women are in the work force today. What percentage of the total working population do they form?

3. Read a biography of another leader in the women's rights movement and report on it to class. Some possibilities: Lucy Stone, Charlotte Perkins Gilman, Anna Howard Shaw, and Carrie Chapman Catt.

CHAPTER 4

Americans Improve Their Lives

OBJECTIVE: How did Americans of the 1800s benefit from other changes in society?

1. She couldn't believe her eyes. Four people were caged in a dark, foul-smelling basement cell. When she asked what their crime was, she was told they were not criminals—they were insane. When she asked why they had no heat on this freezing March day, she was told the insane can't feel cold. The woman's name was Dorothea Dix, and after that experience she vowed she would struggle for better care for the mentally ill. By 1841—the year of this visit—America had made many improvements in its way of life. It had much farther to go, however, in the treatment of the mentally ill, the blind, the deaf, and others. Dorothea Dix was just one of many reformers of the 1800s who fought to bring the promise of America to all its people.

Education   In what ways did American education improve in the 1800s?

2. In the early 1800s, ordinary Americans had few chances for a good education. Children from well-to-do families went to private schools, where their parents paid fees. But there were few public schools—free schools supported by taxes. Those public schools that did exist, mostly in New England, were often not very good. In the average public school, an untrained teacher might have as many as 80 pupils crammed into a single room. There were

▲ Reformer Dorothea Dix was shocked at the cruel way the mentally ill were treated. She did much to have laws passed that improved their care.

no chalkboards and few books. Pupils might learn the basic "three R's"—reading, 'riting, and 'rithmetic—but little else. Most of them attended school only one or two months a year.

3. A pioneer in improving education was Horace Mann. Beginning in the 1830s, he ran public schools in Massachusetts. Mann got the

In Chapter 4 you will apply these critical thinking skills to the historical process:

❯ **Predicting:** Telling what you believe will happen on the basis of clues and facts.

Recognizing Cause and Effect: Recognizing the action or event that makes something happen; identifying the result of an action or event.

state legislature to increase funds for the public school system so that buildings and equipment could be improved and so that teachers could be paid more. The school year was lengthened to six months, and children had to attend school. Many high schools and teacher training schools were founded. The Massachusetts example was followed by other states.

Spotlight on Sources

4. Horace Mann's ideas were spread to other states through the yearly reports he wrote for Massachusetts. Here, in a report from the 1840s, Mann links education with the future of American democracy:

> If we do not prepare children to become good citizens—if we do not develop their capacities [abilities], if we do not enrich their minds with knowledge, imbue [fill] their hearts with the love of truth and duty, and a reverence [respect] for all things sacred and holy, then our republic must go down to destruction, as others have gone before it, and mankind must sweep through another vast [huge] cycle of sin and suffering, before the dawn of a better era can arise upon the world. It is for our government, and for that public opinion which, in a republic, governs the government to choose between the alternatives [choices] of weal [well-being] or woe [sadness].
>
> —from *Freedom's Ferment,* ed. by Alice Felt Tyler

▶ What does Mann say are the qualities of a good citizens? What does Mann say would be the result of not educating children?

5. In the later 1800s, public education improved further. At the time of the Civil War, the average person attended school for only four years. About 20 percent of the people were **illiterate** (il-LIT-uh-ruht)—that is, they could not read or write. There were two main improvements in the late 1800s. One was an increase in the number of public high schools. In 1860 there were only about 300 in the whole

▲ By the 1860s, most schoolteachers were women. Many were poorly trained and had to teach several grades in the same crowded classroom.

country. By 1900 there were 6,000. This meant that the average student could go to school for more years and learn more.

6. The second improvement in education was an increase in the number of colleges and universities. Colleges and universities make up what are called schools of higher education. The Morrill Land Grant Act was passed during the Civil War. The act gave money for states to set up their own systems of higher education. Many Midwestern universities were founded under this act. Between the 1870s and 1900, the number of college students tripled. What are some of the disadvantages of being poorly educated in today's world?

Medicine What progress did Americans make in the field of medicine?

7. Care for the mentally ill was one of the first improvements in American medicine. In

Background: The Morrill Land Grant Act of 1862 provided that every state was to receive 30,000 acres of land for each senator and representative to which it was entitled in Congress. This land was to serve as an endowment for the state university. For this reason, universities founded under this act are often call land-grant schools.

491

the early 1800s, many mentally ill people were chained in jails because no one knew what else to do with them. Dorothea Dix, a New Englander, began visiting the insane and reporting on her findings to the Massachusetts legislature. A man had to read her speeches in the legislature because women were not supposed to speak in public. As a result of her activities, Massachusetts, and other states as well, soon began building special care-giving places for the mentally ill called **asylums** (uh-SY-luhms).

8. Another improvement in medical care involved the use of **anesthetics** (an-uhs-THET-iks). Anesthetics are chemicals, like ether, that deaden feeling or cause a sleeplike state. Before the use of anesthetics, as you can imagine, surgery was very painful. In the 1840s a Boston dentist named William Morton began using ether when he pulled teeth. Soon dentists and doctors all over the country were using ether to deaden the pain during surgery.

9. Hospital care did not begin to improve much until the late 1800s. This was mainly because, until the 1860s, people did not know

that germs caused disease. What dangers do you think existed in hospitals before they knew about germs? Then hospitals began using **antiseptics** (an-tuh-SEP-tiks)—substances that kill germs. Hospitals also began to train nurses as professionals. In 1873, Boston, Massachusetts, New Haven, Connecticut, and New York City became the first cities to open nursing schools.

Prisons How did Americans try to reform prisons?

10. Some American reformers of the 1820s succeeded in beginning to make badly needed improvements in the prison system. They believed that prisons should be places not just for punishment but also for **rehabilitation** (ree-huh-bil-uh-TAY-shuhn). To rehabilitate means to restore. One way prison officials tried to rehabilitate prisoners was to keep them locked up alone in cells to study the Bible and repent their sins. In another type of rehabilitation, prisoners were taught a trade and given work in prison shops.

▼ This New York City prison was typical of prisons in the United States in the mid 1800s. The only purpose of prisons, it was thought, was to punish criminals. Little effort was made to educate them or help them to live worthwhile lives after they had served their sentences.

Ask: Nineteenth century reforms tended to isolate certain groups—notably the mentally ill and the handicapped —from society. Today the trend is toward "mainstreaming." After introducing these concepts, ask students to discuss the advantages and disadvantages of each approach.

492

Background: Braille type for the blind was invented by a blind Frenchman, Louis Braille. The blind were further aided by the invention of the Braille typewriter by an American, Frank Hall, in the 1890s.

11. Prison reform had very little success. It did not slow crime. Nor did it rehabilitate many prisoners. Communities became discouraged and cut funds. Then, of course, even less could be done. By the time of the Civil War, most prisons were simply overcrowded warehouses for ▶ wrong-doers. Why might people be unwilling to spend tax money on prisoner rehabilitation?

The Handicapped How was life changed for handicapped Americans?

12. Handicapped (HAN-di-kapt) people are those who have physical or mental problems that make it difficult for them to lead full lives. Until the 1800s, the handicapped were looked ▶ down upon and often made fun of. Why do you think people acted this way toward the handicapped? Rarely did anyone try to help them overcome their handicaps. Among the first handicapped Americans to receive special help were the deaf. The pioneer in this field was Thomas Gallaudet. In France he learned **signing**, the system of communicating by hand signals. In 1817 he opened the first American school for the deaf. Within 35 years, 14 other states had set up similar schools.

People in History

13. Thomas Gallaudet Most of Thomas Gallaudet's life was dedicated to helping the deaf. He first became interested in their cause when he met a little girl, Alice Cogswell, who was deaf and did not speak. Alice's father helped to pay for a trip abroad for Gallaudet so that he could study methods of teaching the deaf in Europe. After several months in Paris, he returned to open his school in Hartford in 1817. Although at first it had only seven pupils, its numbers grew. One of its later students, Sophia Fowler, married Gallaudet. After he retired from the school, he became active in improving the training of teachers.

14. The blind also had a supporter. He was Samuel Gridley Howe of Massachusetts. In 1831, Howe was offered the job of running a

▲ Gallaudet's work made it possible for deaf people all over the United States to become well educated. This 1880 picture shows a class of deaf children in New York.

school for the blind. He spent several days blind-folded so that he could better understand their problems. This school, the Perkins Institute, opened in Boston in 1832. It was soon a model for other schools for the blind throughout the country. Howe lived up to his motto—"Obstacles are things to be overcome." He believed in the blind and offered them every possible means to realize their ability to learn.

Outlook

15. Americans, who have always had a strong belief in progress, tried to improve many aspects of their society in the 1800s. They were most successful in the field of education, and least so in prison reform. In medicine and help for the handicapped, they made important beginnings that laid the foundation for further changes in the 1900s. What recent advances in ◀ medicine have you benefited from?

Activity: The English novelist Charles Dickens visited the Pekins Institute in 1842 and was very impressed by what he saw. Read, or have a student read, from his account, published in his book *American Notes,* Chapter III, "Boston."

CHAPTER REVIEW

VOCABULARY REVIEW

▶ Match the words in the following list with the definitions below.

1. illiterate
2. asylums
3. anesthetics
4. antiseptics
5. rehabilitate
6. signing
7. handicapped

a. method of communication for the deaf
b. substances that prevent people from feeling pain
c. unable to read or write
d. places that provided special care for the mentally ill
e. restore people to useful lives
f. substances that kill germs
g. people with physical or mental disabilities

SKILL BUILDER: MAKING A TIME LINE

▶ On a separate sheet of paper, copy the time line below. Write on the time line the following events, including the dates.

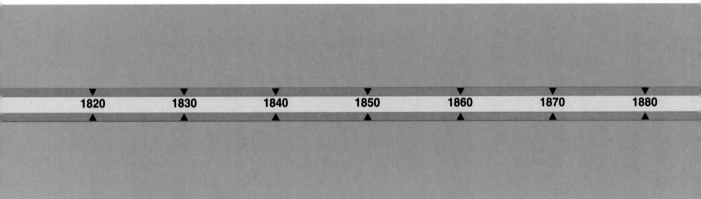

| 1820 | 1830 | 1840 | 1850 | 1860 | 1870 | 1880 |

The first nursing schools are opened in three American cities.

Thomas Gallaudet opens his school in Hartford.

Samuel Gridley Howe is offered the job of running a school for the blind.

Perkins Institute opens in Boston.

In this decade, people now know that germs caused diseases.

In this decade, prison reforms begin.

SKILL BUILDER: CRITICAL THINKING AND COMPREHENSION

❯ I. Predicting

▶ Predict what will happen. On a separate sheet of paper, write your predictions.

1. If the United States government cuts a large part of the budget for public education.

2. If more money was spent on prison reform.

3. If no special schools for the blind and deaf were started in the United States.

◯ II. Generalizing

1. Read paragraph 10. On a sheet of paper, write why you think the following generalization is either a good or a poor generalization about the paragraph.

Prisons improved greatly during the 1820s.

2. Read paragraph 5. Write two titles for the paragraph and tell why you think each one would be a good title for the paragraph.

➡ III. Cause and Effect

▶ On a separate sheet of paper, write the effects of the following.

1. Anesthetics started to be used in medical care.
Effect: _____

2. Prison reform was not successful.
Effect: _____

3. Money was given to states to set up their own systems of higher education.
Effect: _____

USING PRIMARY SOURCES

▶ Reread the Spotlight on Sources, page 491. Why does Mann believe education is important? Do you think American democracy today depends on public education? Why or why not?

ENRICHMENT

1. Write a brief paragraph about a problem of today that you think needs attention. What is the problem? Why is it important? What do you think should be done about it?

2. The first person to link germs to disease was a French scientist, Louis Pasteur. Read a biography of him in an encyclopedia and report on it to class.

3. Use your telephone book or other reference work to see what care your community offers for the handicapped. If you live in a big city, you may want to concentrate on a single group, such as the blind.

CHAPTER 5

The Progressive Movement

OBJECTIVE: How did the Progressive movement change American society?

1. American cities and fields in the early 1900s were full with over 2 million children at work. Children as young as seven or eight picked crops for twelve hours at a time. Girls and boys worked in dark and dirty factories for long hours. Some worked at night in mills, with cold water thrown in their faces to keep them from falling asleep. These children earned only pennies a day and were often homeless. One foreign visitor called the newsboys and bootblacks "the weakest spot in America's fine front of national well-being." Many Americans, too, were shocked by child labor that robbed children of schooling, of health—indeed, of childhood itself.

The Progressives   What was the Progressive movement?

2. The **Progressive** (pruh-GRES-iv) **movement**, or Progressivism, grew out of earlier reform movements. You have read about wage earners, farmers, and other groups that tried to improve conditions for themselves and society at large. The Progressives had many similar goals. In fact, many Progressives had been Grangers or Populists, and among them were suffragists as well. But the Progressives, from the late 1890s to about 1920, wanted to make society as a whole work better.

3. One of the key ways that Progressives

▲ Ida Tarbell was one of the best known of the journalists who were called muckrakers. They exposed the greed and corruption of large corporations and city governments.

tried to pressure government to address citizens' needs was through writing. Writers wrote about many Progressive causes in newspapers, magazines, and books. The wrongs they addressed included child labor, slums, corrupt politics, unfair business practices, and discrimination

496

In Chapter 5 you will apply these critical thinking skills to the historical process:

📁 **Classifying:** Organizing facts into categories based on what they have in common.

▌ **Comparing and Contrasting:** Recognizing similarities and differences.

(dis-krim-uh-NAY-shuhn) against women and immigrants. To discriminate is to treat someone differently because of his or her beliefs or physical traits. Critics called such reporters **muckrakers** because they dug up "dirt" about conditions in the United States. The muckrakers' reports often led to new laws aimed at correcting wrongs. In what ways does the tradition of the muckrakers continue today?

Spotlight on Sources

4. *McClure's Magazine* was well known for its muckraking articles. In 1903 its publisher, Samuel S. McClure, wrote a now-famous editorial urging his readers not to rely on others to correct wrongs.

> The public is the people. We forget that we all are the people; that while each of us in his group can shove off on the rest the bill of today, the debt is only postponed [put off]; the rest are passing it on back to us. We have to pay in the end, every one of us. And in the end the sum total of the debt will be our liberty.
> —from *McClure's Magazine*, January 1903

What does McClure mean, if we do not pay "the bill of today," the price will be our liberty?

People in History

5. Ida Tarbell   One of the most important muckrakers was Ida Tarbell. She grew up in a part of Pennsylvania that produced oil. Even as an adult, she could not forget that her father had been ruined by a large oil company. Her father had owned one of the smaller oil companies. So, when *McClure's Magazine* asked her to write a story about the biggest oil company, she jumped at the chance. In 1906, her story appeared. It exposed Standard Oil Company's practices of price fixing, limiting production to drive prices up, and crushing the competition. Tarbell's articles resulted in a huge outcry against big business. In response, laws that regulated monopolies were passed.

THE PRESIDENTS' CORNER

The popular "Teddy Bear" toy was named after **Theodore Roosevelt**, America's President from 1901 to 1909. He was like this furry, feisty stuffed animal in looks and personality. A truly popular hero because of his adventures as a cowboy-rancher, Roosevelt enjoyed what he called "the strenuous life." Teddy Roosevelt was also known as a tough leader and reformer. As President, he acted to limit the power of big business. He supported programs to protect food and drugs and our national forests and parks. He strengthened the U.S. Navy, built the Panama Canal, and limited the role of European powers in Latin America. He also was awarded the Nobel Peace Prize for working to end the Russo-Japanese War.

Reforms in Cities and States   How did the Progressive movement affect cities and states?

6. Several Progressive reforms were aimed at improving life in American cities. Some cities set fair wages for their employees and adopted **civil service** systems. This meant that they hired workers through tests rather than by choosing political favorites. Still other cities cleaned up slums and built parks and playgrounds. Cities also tried new forms of government that resulted in less corruption.

7. Many states also made changes in government during the Progressive era. Several adopted the **initiative** (i-NISH-ee-uh-tiv), **referendum** (ref-uh-REN-duhm), and **recall** (REE-kawl). The initiative says that a state legislature must think about passing a law if enough voters sign a petition asking for it. The referendum says that certain bills before the legislature must be submitted to the people for a vote. The recall says that citizens can vote an

Ask: Samuel M. ("Golden Rule") Jones, a Progressive mayor in Toledo, Ohio, changed the "Keep Off the Grass" signs in city parks to read "Citizens, Protect Your Property." Ask students why they think he did this. How do the two signs differ in meaning?

497

America's People

THE JAPANESE

One of the interests of the Progressives was the unfair treatment of immigrants. In many ways, the history of the Japanese in the United States is a study of prejudice and intolerance. In the 1880s, California farmers looked to Japan as a new source of cheap labor. In response, thousands of Japanese flocked to the United States. In 1880, only 150 Japanese lived in California. By 1910, the number had climbed to 90,000. United States law said these immigrants, called Issei, could never become citizens. However, their children who were born in the United States, or Nisei, were citizens.

Japanese immigrants quickly began to buy or rent farmland of their own. Entire families worked long, tough hours in the desert sun. Other Japanese immigrants branched out into the fishing and canning industries. The Japanese grew successful as they became producers as well as suppliers and distributors of many different goods.

As Japanese prospered, white Californians felt economically threatened and often attacked them. In 1906, San Francisco required Japanese students to attend segregated schools. Then, in 1907 under the so-called "Gentlemen's Agreement," Japan agreed not to give passports to workers headed for California. Still not satisfied, the California legislature in 1913 made it illegal for non-citizens to own land. In 1924, Congress ended all immigration from Japan.

Much of the anger that Americans felt about Japan's surprise attack on Pearl Harbor in 1941 was directed at Japanese Americans. Over 110,000 Japanese Americans, two-thirds of them American citizens, were forced to go to detention camps after the attack. These camps consisted of poorly-built barracks with no indoor plumbing or central heating. Most of the internees had to give up or sell their possessions at a loss. Beginning in the 1970s,

▲ Despite the bitter experience of their internment during World War II, Japanese Americans today are proud of their loyalty to the United States.

Japanese Americans worked for Congress to review this injustice. Finally, in the late 1980s, Congress apologized to Japanese Americans for the government's treatment. Congress approved cash payments for the surviving victims and for Japanese American communities.

Now answer the following questions.

1. Why did Americans limit immigration in the late 1800s and early 1900s? Do you think immigration should have limits?

2. Why do you think it was important to Japanese Americans to have Congress recognize the injustice of their wartime internment? Do you think their requests were reasonable?

elected official out of office. Another change was **worker's compensation** (kom-puhn-SAY-shuhn), which provided for payment to employees for job-related injuries.

Progressive Gains   What Progressive measures did the federal government adopt under Roosevelt?

8. Theodore Roosevelt was the first Progressive President. He supported reforms in business, public health, and the new area of **conservation** (kon-ser-VAY-shun). Conservation is the protecting of our natural resources, especially our forests. The government limited the huge power of large businesses. One new law denied railroad rebates and controlled railroad rates. Roosevelt, an outdoorsman and hiker, was the first **environmentalist** (en-vy-ruhn-MEN-tuh-list) President. An environmentalist tries to solve problems such as water and air pollution. Roosevelt got the government to set aside thousands of acres of land as forest re-
▶ serves. Why do you think Roosevelt thought that saving land was important?

9. Public health received attention mainly through muckraking. Upton Sinclair published a vivid novel, called *The Jungle,* in 1906. It described the horrors of the meatpacking industry in Chicago. Thousands of Americans were sickened to read about workers injured by butcher knives. They read about sausages that contained moldy bread and dead rats. The result was a meat inspection act that gave the government power to enforce cleanliness standards in meatpacking plants. Another bill, the Pure Food and Drug Act, said that foods and drugs
▶ must have labels listing their contents. How would laws like these protect the public?

President Wilson   In what ways did President Wilson further Progressivism?

10. Woodrow Wilson, President from 1913 to 1921, was a Democrat and a Progressive. During Wilson's presidency, the government took steps to control banking, limit child labor,

and provide worker's compensation for federal employees. Most important were four amendments to the Constitution. The Sixteenth Amendment, ratified in 1913, allowed for a federal income tax. With the Seventeenth Amendment, senators for the first time were to be elected directly by voters—rather than by state legislatures. The Eighteenth Amendment prohibited alcoholic drinks. This step, called **Prohibition** (pro-hi-BI-shuhn), had long been a goal of reformers. The law took effect in 1920 but was repealed in 1933. What did the Nineteenth Amendment do?

Progressives and African Americans   What was the Progressives' attitude toward African Americans' problems?

11. A major social question that the Progressives did not deal with was discrimination against African Americans. However, in 1909, after a bloody race riot in Springfield, Illinois, a few white Progressives joined with leading African Americans. Among these leaders were W.E.B. Du Bois, Ida Wells-Barnett, and Mary Church Terrell. Together they formed the National Association for the Advancement of Colored People (NAACP). Under Du Bois's leadership, the NAACP was active in trying to stop lynching and in fighting for voting rights. Du Bois believed strongly in the idea of **Pan-Africanism,** meaning that people of African descent should join together to overcome common problems. The NAACP used knowledge of the law to fight prejudice.

Outlook

12. Progressivism, a nationwide reform movement, gained many successes. It made American government more democratic and improved the everyday lives of Americans. The Progressive movement came to an end when the United States became involved in World War I in 1917. If Progressivism were alive today, what ◀ conditions do you think Progressives would try to improve?

CHAPTER REVIEW

VOCABULARY REVIEW

▶ Number a separate sheet of paper 1 to 8. Complete each of the numbered sentences by writing the correct word next to the number.

1. Through the _____ , citizens petition the legislature to consider a bill.

2. _____ provides payment to an employee injured on the job.

3. _____ made the manufacture and sale of alcoholic drinks illegal.

4. An _____ attempts to solve problems such as water and air pollution.

5. In a _____ , citizens vote on a bill being considered by the legislature.

6. Competitive exams are used to hire workers in a _____ system.

7. A government concerned with _____ may set aside land as a forest reserve.

8. People who wanted to make society as a whole work better were part of the _____ .

9. Citizens can vote an elected official out of office with a _____ .

10. Many of the ills of American society were exposed by the _____ .

11. _____ is the idea that all people of African descent should unite to solve common problems.

a. civil service	**e.** referendum	**i.** environmentalist
b. recall	**f.** worker's compensation	**j.** Progressive movement
c. Pan-Africanism	**g.** conservation	**k.** muckrakers
d. initiative	**h.** Prohibition	**l.** legislature

SKILL BUILDER: COMPLETING A TABLE

▶ The table on the preceding page describes important legislation that was passed during the Progressive Era. Copy the table on another sheet of paper, and then fill in the missing information. In some cases, you may need to use an encyclopedia.

Year	Legislation	Short Description
1890	Sherman Antitrust Act	
1906	Pure Food and Drug Act	
	16th Amendment	
1919	17th Amendment	
1913	Federal Reserve Act	
1914	Clayton Antitrust Act	
	18th Amendment	
	19th Amendment	

500

SKILL BUILDER: CRITICAL THINKING AND COMPREHENSION

I. Classifying

▶ Compile a list of all the names mentioned in Chapter 5. Classify them into groups according to their name, accomplishments or goals as reformers.

II. Sequencing

▶ Write the following events in the order in which they occurred.

a. *The Jungle* is published.

b. Federal income tax established.

c. Ida Tarbell's article on the Standard Oil Company is published.

d. Prohibition repealed.

e. Women are given the vote.

f. The NAACP is founded.

g. Immigration from Japan is ended.

h. System of government control of banking is set up.

III. Comparing and Contrasting

▶ List the differences and similarities between Theodore Roosevelt and Woodrow Wilson as Progressives.

USING PRIMARY SOURCES

▶ Reread the Spotlight on Sources on page 497. In what ways is McClure's editorial just as true today as when it was written? Write at least two ways.

ENRICHMENT

1. Imagine that you are a muckraking reporter on a local newspaper. What subject would you want to write about? Make a list of the steps you would take to research your topic.

2. Find out what kind of government your city or community has, and who represents the area in which your school is located. Call or write this representative to obtain information on how your local government works.

3. Choose a topic that interested the Progressives. Write a letter to an imaginary newspaper on the topic. Suggest reforms in your letter to correct the problem. Possible topics: government corruption, big business, unsafe housing or working conditions, segregation, child labor.

4. Find out about muckrakers in an encyclopedia. Choose one to do further research on. Write a report on this person, including his or her background and the subject of investigation.

UNIT REVIEW

SUMMARY

Americans of the 1800s and early 1900s wanted to reform society. The need for change came from growing divisions between the "haves" and "have-nots," which threatened to shake the roots of democracy. The reformers saw their responsibility as bettering the lives of people and defending democratic principles.

These reformers struggled for changes on several fronts. One front involved labor unions and farm organizations. Both the Grange movement and the later Populists fought against what they saw as injustices by big business and government against common people. Labor unions struggled to get the eight-hour day and an end to child labor accepted. We accept these rules without question today. Another goal, equal pay

for men and women, is not yet as widely accepted.

On the political front, women's rights began to take center stage. The women's suffrage movement struggled for the right to vote. It would take many years, until 1920, when voting rights for women would be guaranteed in the Nineteenth Amendment to the Constitution.

An earlier group of reformers wanted better treatment of prisoners, the mentally ill, and the handicapped. Others brought about better schools and better government.

A later group of reformers, the Progressives, brought about improvements in the daily lives of Americans. Americans continue to struggle for change. What kinds of changes are Americans seeking today?

SKILL BUILDER: READING A MAP

▶ Study the map below. Then answer the questions on the next page.

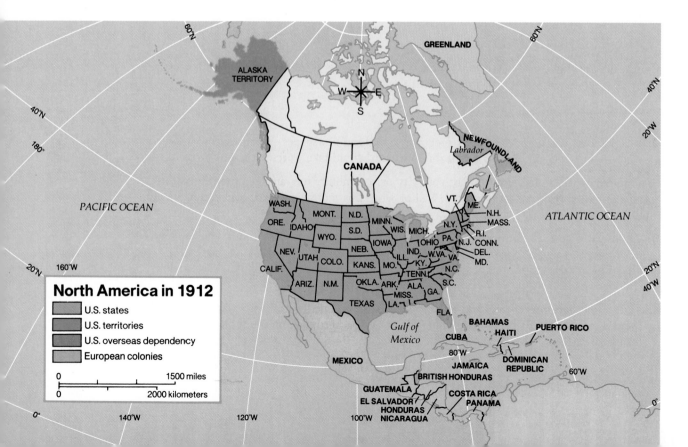

North America in 1912

- U.S. states
- U.S. territories
- U.S. overseas dependency
- European colonies

0 — 1500 miles
0 — 2000 kilometers

1. Name the European colonies on the North American continent.

2. Which United States overseas dependency is shown on the map?

3. Which European colony is closest to the United States mainland?

4. Which American territory shown on the map later became a state?

5. Which states border on Canada? On Mexico?

SKILL BUILDER: CRITICAL THINKING AND COMPREHENSION

I. Generalizing

▶ Find the sentences from the unit that support the following two generalizations. On a separate sheet of paper, write the number and the supporting sentences.

1. Farmers and factory workers led to the Populist and labor union movements.

2. Women's rights leaders worked for more than 70 years to gain suffrage for women.

II. Comparing and Contrasting

1. Write a paragraph comparing and contrasting life in rural and urban America in the late 1800s and early 1900s.

2. On a separate sheet of paper, make a chart about issues that Progressives were involved in during the late 1800s and early 1900s. On your chart, compare and contrast attitudes and actions between then and today.

III. Making Judgments

▶ Using your ability to make judgments, answer the following questions.

1. Do you think unions properly represented their members in the 1870s to 1890s? Why or why not?

2. In your judgment, which of the events below most affected the labor union movement? Why?
   a. Homestead strike of 1892
   b. Haymarket riot of 1886
   c. Formation of the Knights of Labor
   d. Formation of the American Federation of Labor

ENRICHMENT

1. Suppose you are a movie producer who wants to make a movie about the nineteenth and early twentieth centuries. Write a proposal to a movie studio. Explain what you want to put into your documentary and what you want to focus on.

2. Create an 1890s poster, brochure, or booklet explaining why someone should join a union, vote Populist, or work in the suffrage campaign.

UNIT 12

THE UNITED STATES AS A WORLD LEADER

Chapter

UNIT OVERVIEW   Unit 12 will help you understand the steps the United States took to become a major force in world affairs.

UNIT SKILLS OBJECTIVES   In Unit 12, two critical thinking skills are emphasized:

Understanding Points of View: Recognizing why people have different attitudes about the same thing.

Comparing and Contrasting: Recognizing similarities and differences.

You will also use two important social studies skills:

Reading a Map   Using a Timeline

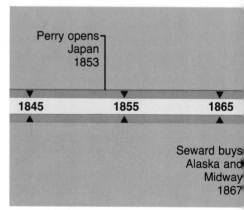

Perry opens Japan 1853

| 1845 | 1855 | 1865 |

Seward buys Alaska and Midway 1867

ESL/LEP Strategy: Explain that many of the vocabulary words in this unit are words about war and peace that students may hear on the nightly news even today. List those words on the chalkboard, discuss their meanings, and have students apply them to current or recent events.

▲ On November 11, 1918, the Germans signed the Armistice, ending the Great War. People in Paris and all over the world celebrated.

Hay proposes Open Door Policy 1899	Boxer Rebellion; Hawaii becomes a U.S. territory 1900		Meuse-Argonne offensive; Armistice signed 1918	Good Neighbor Policy is pledged 1933

1875	1885	1895	1905	1915	1925	1935	1945

Spanish-American War; U.S. gains Puerto Rico, the Philippines, Guam 1898

Panama Canal opens; World War I begins 1914

United States enters World War I 1917

Lusitania is sunk, 1915

Points of View

By the mid-1800s, the United States had expanded its borders "from sea to shining sea." It had achieved its "Manifest Destiny." Surely it did not need to expand any further—or did it? Americans could see that the industrial nations of Europe were continuing to expand their territories. Nations like Britain and France wanted to create markets for trade, to spread their ideas and culture, and to prevent their rivals from doing the same. They were claiming vast areas in Asia and Africa, just as they had earlier in the Americas. They were taking

▲ The eagle represents the United States. Many people who supported imperialistic policies saw the nation as helping weaker countries.

THE CASE FOR AMERICAN EXPANSION

❝American factories are making more than the American people can use. American soil is producing more than they can consume. Fate has written our policy for us: the trade of the world must and shall be ours. . . . We will establish trading-posts throughout the world as distributing points for American products. We will cover the oceans with our merchant marine [trading ships]. Great colonies, . . . flying our flag and trading with us, will grow about our posts of trade. . . . American law, American order, American civilization, and the American flag will plant themselves on shores hitherto [before now] bloody and benighted [backward]. . . .❞

—*The Shaping of America*, Richard O. Curry et al

American Expansion: For and Against

control of the government of the people there and creating new colonies. Should the United States do the same thing? Should the United States develop new markets and export democracy at the same time?

The two selections that follow present different answers to these questions. In the first, which was written in 1889, an American senator, Albert Beveridge of Indiana, tells why the United States must expand. In the second, written in 1899, Carl Schurz, another political leader, argues against expansion.

THE CASE AGAINST AMERICAN EXPANSION

66 We hold that the policy known as imperialism [gaining overseas lands] is hostile to liberty and tends toward militarism [a policy of aggressive military preparedness], an evil from which it has been our glory to be free. We regret that it has become necessary in the land of Washington and Lincoln to reaffirm [state positively again] that all men, of whatever race or color, are entitled to life, liberty, and the pursuit of happiness. We maintain that governments derive their just powers from the consent of the governed. We insist that the subjugation of any people [forcibly taking over rule of them] is "criminal aggression" and open disloyalty to the distinctive principles of our government. . . . 99

—"THE POLICY OF IMPERIALISM, LIBERTY TRACTS NUMBER FOUR," Carl Schurz

▲ In this anti-expansion cartoon, Uncle Sam orders Emilio Aguinaldo, fighter for Filipino independence, to come out from behind the tree and surrender.

Using Primary Sources

1. What reasons does Beveridge give in favor of American expansion? What groups of people in the United States might agree with Beveridge?

2. Why does Schurz think American expansion is wrong? Who might agree with his point of view?

507

CHAPTER 1

The Spanish-American War

OBJECTIVE: Why did the United States fight a war with Spain, and what were the results of the war?

1. In 1896, an American newspaper reporter cabled his paper from Cuba: "Blood on the roadsides, blood in the fields, blood on the doorsteps, blood, blood, blood. Is there no nation wise enough, brave enough, and strong enough to restore peace in this blood-smitten land?" Two years later, the United States would answer the reporter's plea. Cuban rebels had been fighting to rid their island of Spanish rule. "Cuba Libre!"—"Free Cuba!"— was their battle cry. In April 1898, Congress declared war on Spain. American forces began to sweep the Spanish from Cuba and from other Spanish colonies as well. A new period of American history began—a time that centered on ex-

▶ pansion overseas instead of at home. What changes in the United States do you predict will happen as the country begins to look beyond the North American continent to expand its control?

▲ Two African American troops of cavalry fought at San Juan Hill. Their horses, which cavalry normally ride, were left in America by mistake.

Revolt in Cuba What caused Cubans to rise up against Spanish rule?

2. Cuba was one of Spain's last colonies in the Americas. By the 1820s, most of Spain's colonies in Latin America were independent. Cuba and Puerto Rico were the only ones that were not. Spain ruled Cuba with an iron hand. Spanish-born officials ran the Cuban government, and many of them were corrupt. Cubans were heavily taxed. Most of the money was sent back to Spain so Cubans received no help from

their taxes. As a result, most Cubans were poor and miserable.

3. Cubans had tried to free their country, but without success. In 1868, a band of rebels declared Cuba's independence and began a war against the Spanish. It was a **guerrilla** (guh-RIL-uh) war. In a guerrilla war, rebels go into hiding. They attack the enemy with surprise raids and then disappear. For ten years, this war dragged on. Finally it ended without victory,

In Chapter 1 you will apply these critical thinking skills to the historical process:
▲ **Summarizing:** Giving the main idea of a group of paragraphs.

➡ **Recognizing Cause and Effect:** Matching the action or event that makes something happen to what happens as a result.

and its Cuban leaders went into **exile** (EX-yl). That is, they were forced to leave their country. In 1895, Cuban rebels again rose up, touching off the bloody struggle that the American journalist in the chapter introduction reported to his paper.

People in History

4. José Martí Perhaps the most devoted fighter for Cuban independence was José Martí (mahr-TEE). Born in 1853, in Havana, Cuba's capital, he began to believe in revolution while still a boy. When he was 16, he was sent to prison for six months at hard labor for his revolutionary activities. Then he was sent to
▶ exile in Spain. Why might he have been punished so harshly?

5. During the next 25 years, Martí kept working for Cuban freedom. As an exile, he visited Europe and other parts of Latin America. From 1881 to 1895, he lived in New York City. He soon became famous as a writer and journalist. His works fueled the fires of Cuban independence. When, in 1895, Cuban rebels rose once again, Martí raced back to join the fight. Just one month later, he was killed in battle.

🦅 Spotlight on Sources

6. Martí's ringing words lived on, giving strength and purpose to the Cuban rebels who still fought on.

> Let us rise up for the true republic, those of us who, with our passion for right and our habit of hard work, will know how to preserve [save] it. Let us rise up to give graves to the heroes whose spirits roam [wander] the world, alone and ashamed. . . . And let us place around the star of our new flag this formula of love triumphant [successful]: "With all, for the good of all."
> —from *Our America*, by José Martí

▶ What does Martí suggest as the motto for a free Cuba? What kind of country does Martí hope Cuba will become?

War with Spain Why did America go to war with Spain, and where was the war fought?

7. American sympathy built up for the Cuban rebels. In 1896, Spain sent General Valeriano Weyler to put down the rebellion. He put about 200,000 civilian Cubans in concentration camps, where disease and hunger were widespread. Many died. American newspapers competed with one another to report terrible stories of deaths caused by "Butcher Weyler." They also reported that the war was destroying American investments in Cuba, such as sugar plantations and refineries. This use of shocking and sometimes untrue reporting is called **yellow journalism.**

8. Whipped up by yellow journalism, many Americans wanted to enter the war on the side of the Cubans. Americans thought that with their help, the Cubans could at last be free. In helping the Cubans against Spain, the United States could take its rightful place as a leader in world affairs. However, President William McKinley urged the nation to stay neutral.

9. In 1898, American **neutrality** (noo-TRAL-uh-tee), or refusal to take sides, came to an abrupt end. In January, President McKinley sent a U.S. naval battleship, the *Maine*, into Havana harbor. It was there supposedly to protect American lives and property in Cuba. On the night of February 15, the *Maine* blew up, killing 260 of its crew. No one really knows what caused the explosion, but the American press quickly blamed Spain. Why, do you suppose, did "Remember the *Maine*!" become a rallying cry across America? In April, Congress declared war on Spain.

10. For Americans, the fighting began not in Cuba but in the far-off Pacific. Weeks earlier, Assistant Secretary of the Navy Theodore Roosevelt had thought war with Spain was coming. He ordered a U.S. naval squadron under Commodore George Dewey to sail to the Spanish-controlled Philippine Islands. Just days after war began, Dewey conquered the Philippines and seized the harbor of its capital, the city of Manila.

11. The United States sent troops to join the fight in Cuba. In June 1898, 17,000 American soldiers landed at the port of Daiquirí (dy-kee-REE), in eastern Cuba. Though these men were eager to fight, they had little training and military equipment. Their uniforms were heavy, better for winter than for a tropical summer. Many of them grew ill with yellow fever and malaria, and there were few medical supplies. In fact, more American soldiers died of yellow fever and other tropical diseases than from Spanish bullets.

12. On July 1, American and Cuban troops stormed San Juan Hill, a Spanish stronghold protecting the important bay at Santiago (sahn-ti-AH-goh). One leader of this charge was Theodore Roosevelt. As soon as war began, Roosevelt had quit his navy post and formed his own regiment. Made up mainly of cowboys and college boys, his men called themselves the "Rough Riders." The Rough Riders included Hispanic soldiers, among them Captain Maximiliano Lima. Another unit to charge the hill that day was the Tenth Cavalry, made up entirely of African American troops. After two days of hand-to-hand fighting, the Americans won the hill.

13. The Spanish-American War ended only ten weeks after it had begun. Once American troops aimed their artillery at Santiago Bay, the Spanish fleet anchored there tried to escape. The U.S. Navy destroyed Spain's ships in four hours' time. Santiago surrendered on July 17. A few days later, American troops landed on Puerto Rico and met no Spanish forces. Spain asked for peace, and the fighting stopped.

14. Cuba, now independent of Spain, would not become free for another four years. Although Spanish troops left Cuba, American troops did not. Thinking that the Cubans were not yet ready to run their country, an American military government was set up. It worked to restore order, rebuild war-torn towns and villages, and set up hospitals and schools. American troops did not leave until 1902, when Cuba officially became a republic. Are there any circumstances in which one nation has the right to rule another nation? Explain.

▼ On April 31, Dewey opened fire on the Spanish fleet in Manila. After five passes, all the Spanish ships were destroyed. Not one American was killed, and Dewey's fleet was undamaged.

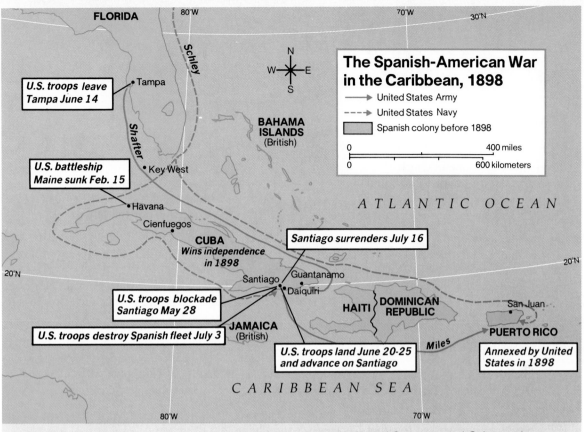

The Spanish-American War in the Caribbean, 1898

→ United States Army

---→ United States Navy

Spanish colony before 1898

0 400 miles

0 600 kilometers

FLORIDA

U.S. troops leave Tampa June 14

Tampa

Schley

Shafter

BAHAMA ISLANDS (British)

U.S. battleship Maine sunk Feb. 15

Key West

ATLANTIC OCEAN

Havana

Cienfuegos

CUBA
Wins independence in 1898

Santiago surrenders July 16

Santiago

Guantanamo

Daiquiri

U.S. troops blockade Santiago May 28

HAITI

DOMINICAN REPUBLIC

San Juan

JAMAICA (British)

U.S. troops destroy Spanish fleet July 3

U.S. troops land June 20-25 and advance on Santiago

Miles

PUERTO RICO

Annexed by United States in 1898

CARIBBEAN SEA

MAP SKILL BUILDER: A map can help you understand why the United States wanted Cuba to win independence from Spain. **1.** How far is Cuba from the United States? **2.** Which sea lanes could Spain control from Cuba?

The United States Wins an Empire   How did the United States govern the lands won from Spain?

15. The peace treaty ending the Spanish-American War started the United States as a new world power. Spain gave Puerto Rico and the Pacific island of Guam to the United States. It also gave up the Philippine Islands in return for an American payment of $20 million.

16. Puerto Rico was placed under American rule. Until 1900, Puerto Rico had an American military government. Then it was ruled by a United States-appointed governor and a house of delegates elected by Puerto Ricans. In 1917, Puerto Ricans became citizens and gained the right to elect both houses of their legislature.

17. Questions about how to deal with the Philippines caused bitter debates in the United States. Many Filipinos did not want American rule. Like the Cubans, they wanted an independent republic. Many Americans agreed. They argued that the United States had no right to force its rule on another people. Other Americans argued that it was the United States' duty and right to rule an American empire. Who do you think was right? Why?

18. The American empire builders won the debate, and the Philippines did not become independent for many years. However, before American government could take hold, Filipino troops battled American troops for nearly three years. In 1902, the Filipinos were defeated and were given a government like Puerto Rico's.

Outlook

19. The United States fought the Spanish-American War for a variety of reasons. Americans understood Cuba's wish to throw off foreign rule, and they wanted to protect American investments in Cuba. However, Americans also had dreams of an expanding empire.

511

CHAPTER REVIEW

VOCABULARY REVIEW

▶ Choose the answer that completes the sentence most accurately.

1. A guerilla war is one in which
   a. soldiers fight in tight formations.
   b. only foreign soldiers fight.
   c. rebels attack with surprise and sabotage.

2. An exile is
   a. someone forced to leave his or her country.
   b. a war veteran.
   c. someone who had just won office.

3. Neutrality is taking
   a. the side of the underdog.
   b. the side of the favorite.
   c. neither one side nor the other.

4. Yellow journalism is
   a. exaggerated, sensational reporting of news events.
   b. articles about cowardly actions in battle.
   c. information printed about such diseases as malaria and yellow fever.

SKILL BUILDER: READING A MAP

▶ The map below shows the location of the Philippines and the events in the Philippines that led to the end of Spanish rule there. Study the map carefully, then answer the questions that follow.

1. Which two groups worked together to take over the Philippines from Spain?

2. On what day did the United States Navy destroy the Spanish fleet?

3. About how many islands make up the Philippines?

4. Why do you think first Spain and then the United States wanted to control the Philippine Islands? Why do you think the United States keeps military bases in the Philippines today?

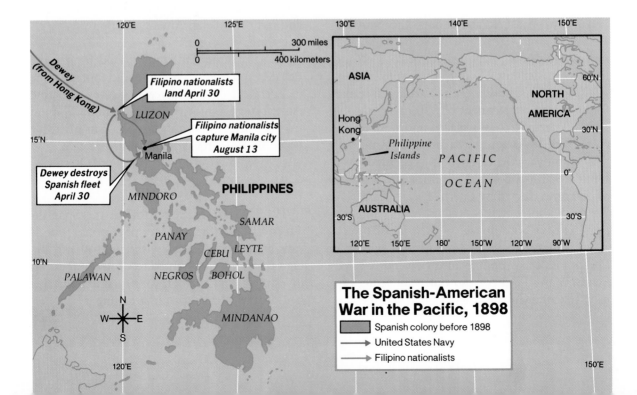

SKILL BUILDER: CRITICAL THINKING AND COMPREHENSION

▲ I. Summarizing

▶ On a separate piece of paper, write summaries about the following historical events.

1. How did Cuba free itself from Spain?

2. How did the United States build an empire outside of North America?

➪ II. Cause and Effect

▶ Review the chapter, and then decide the causes or effects in the following sequences. On a separate piece of paper, write the missing cause or effect.

1. Cause: The battleship *Maine* blew up in Havana harbor.
Cause: American newspapers blamed Spain.
Effect: _____

2. Cause: Spain ceded Puerto Rico and Guam to the United States.
Cause: United States received the Philippines for $20 million dollars.
Effect: _____

III. Point of View

▶ Below is a list of people. After them are statements that the individuals might have made. Read the statements. Decide who might have said each one. Write your answer on a separate sheet of paper.

Cubans   Filipinos   Spaniards   Americans   Puerto Ricans

1. In order to put down rebellions, we must imprison thousands of rebels. Some will die. That is to be expected.

2. We have gained broader powers of self-government, but we would like more. Perhaps we can become a state.

3. We did not want to exchange Spanish rule for American rule so we rebelled.

4. Let us rebel, throw out the Spanish masters, and form our own republic in the Caribbean.

5. We must form an empire to protect and expand our trade and markets for our goods.

USING PRIMARY SOURCES

In paragraph 6, to whom is José Martí referring when he writes about "the heroes whose spirits roam the world, alone and ashamed. . . . "? Why does he want to give them graves?

ENRICHMENT

1. Read what it was like to be a soldier in the Spanish-American War in a book about that war. Then write a letter to a friend describing the hardships you face.

2. Make a poster that urges young men to join the "Rough Riders" or the Tenth Cavalry. Let your poster tell what a recruit will be fighting for and why he should join.

CHAPTER 2

Relations with Latin America

OBJECTIVE: What were the relations between the United States and the nations of Latin America?

1. First, over 50 holes were drilled into the solid rock. Next, 22 tons of dynamite were carefully placed into the openings. Then it happened. The whole charge blew up in a huge roar. Too much dynamite made the explosion too powerful. When the dust settled, 23 workers on the Panama Canal were dead. Explosions were just one of the horrors the canal workers had to face. There were mudslides that buried men and trains. A hot, steamy climate destroyed workers' health. Mosquitoes carried yellow fever and malaria. Many died, but the work did not stop until the canal was completed.

The Panama Canal Why did Latin American nations worry when the United States built the Panama Canal?

2. Now that the United States had an empire in the Pacific Ocean, it wanted to build a **canal** to link the Pacific with the Atlantic Ocean. Such an artificial waterway could be cut across Panama, in Central America. The canal would make the voyage from ocean to ocean thousands of miles shorter for trading and naval ships.

3. In 1901, President Theodore Roosevelt set plans for the canal in motion. Panama was a part of the Republic of Colombia. The United States offered Colombia's government $10 million for rights to the land. Colombia refused.

▲ Workers on the Panama Canal dig out the side of a mountain. What importance did the canal have for the United States Navy?

4. While Colombia hoped to get better terms by refusing, people in Panama did not want to lose the canal. Panamanian leaders decided to break away from Colombia and create a separate nation. President Roosevelt was eager to support them. When Panamanians staged an uprising against Colombia, an Amer-

In Chapter 2 you will apply these critical thinking skills to the historical process:
○ **Generalizing:** Making a statement that links several facts.
◤ **Comparing and Contrasting:** Recognizing similarities and differences.

ican warship kept Colombian ships from landing troops to put down the revolt. The United States then recognized Panama as an independent country.

5. The United States and Panama quickly signed a canal treaty. For permanent rights to a canal zone 10 miles (16 kilometers) wide, the United States paid Panama $10 million. The United States also agreed to pay rent of $250,000 a year. In 1914, the Panama Canal opened to sea traffic. In 1921, the United States paid $425 million to Colombia to make up for ▶ the loss of Panama. If you had been a Colombian, how would you have reacted to the treatment your country received?

People in History

6. George Washington Goethals Only a great engineer could have directed the building

MAP SKILL BUILDER: Use the map grid below to locate places along the Panama Canal.
1. What parts of the canal are in map box B1?
2. What parts of the canal are in map box D3?

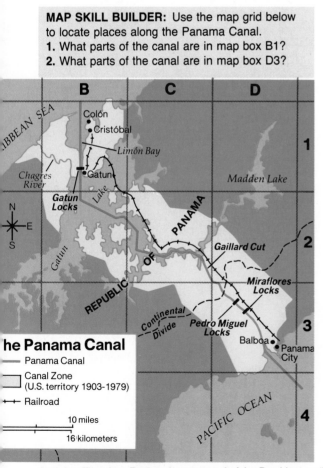

he Panama Canal
— Panama Canal
☐ Canal Zone (U.S. territory 1903–1979)
+—+ Railroad
10 miles
16 kilometers

of the Panama Canal. The United States found such a man in George Washington Goethals. Goethals was an 1880 graduate of the United States Military Academy at West Point, New York. Goethals made his career in the United States Army Corps of Engineers, building dams, harbors, and canals on American inland waterways. In building the Panama Canal, he directed the work of thousands of men and hundreds of huge steam shovels. The workers struggled ten years to make their way through the jungle, cutting gorges and building canal locks in 120-degree heat.

The Roosevelt Corollary Why did the United States act as a "police force" in Latin America?

7. Beginning with the Monroe Doctrine in 1823, the United States tried to keep European nations from interfering in Latin American affairs. By 1900, European nations had lent large sums of money to Latin America. Nations like Venezuela and the Dominican Republic had trouble paying their debts. The Europeans threatened to use force to make them pay.

8. In 1904, President Roosevelt added the Roosevelt Corollary to the Monroe Doctrine. This **corollary** (KOR-uh-leh-ree), or additional point, stated that the United States would exercise "international police power" in Latin America. The American government would settle differences between Europe and Latin America. For example, American officials would collect taxes to pay the foreign debts of the Dominican Republic. Latin Americans resented the United States acting as "policeman." Why do you suppose they objected?

Dollar Diplomacy Why did efforts to protect American investors cause problems?

9. Roosevelt's successor, President William Howard Taft, encouraged American banks and businesses to invest in Latin America. Taft hoped that such investments would help the United States influence Latin America in a peaceful way. This investment policy came to be

Activity: Theodore Roosevelt was as colorful a President as the United States has had, and he was a popular subject for cartoonists. Have volunteers go through books about "TR" and make copies of cartoons of him that appear in them. Arrange the cartoons in a bulletin board display.

515

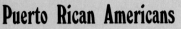

Puerto Rican Americans

After the Spanish-American War, the United States took control of Spain's former colony, Puerto Rico. In 1952 Puerto Rico became a commonwealth of the United States. As a commonwealth, all the people living in Puerto Rico are free to move to and from the American mainland. They do not pay federal taxes, but the people of Puerto Rico cannot vote in federal elections.

Puerto Ricans trace their roots to the native Taino Indians of the Caribbean islands. After Columbus's arrival, Puerto Rico was under Spanish rule for 400 years. Africans were brought as slaves to Puerto Rico and other Caribbean islands. As a result, influences of Spanish culture joined with African and Taino Indian cultures to make up the distinct Puerto Rican character. Today, while many Puerto Ricans still speak Spanish as their native tongue, many younger Puerto Ricans speak English as their primary language.

Since World War II more than 2 million, or almost one half of all Puerto Ricans, live in the Northeast and Midwest of the mainland United States. Puerto Ricans make up about 12 percent of Hispanic Americans.

Most Puerto Ricans came to the mainland United States to escape the poverty of their island. Some became migrant workers who did seasonal work on tobacco and other farms. Others went to work in factories, hotels, and the garment industry in large cities.

Many Puerto Ricans arrived with few job skills and little education. They faced discrimination in jobs and housing. In 1974, Puerto Ricans led the effort to broaden the Voting Rights Act of 1965 so that Spanish-speaking Americans and other "language minorities" did not have to know English to be able to vote. Today, many Puerto Rican Americans become business people, teachers, doctors lawyers, and political leaders.

1. How are Puerto Ricans a people of mixed cultures and languages?

2. What common struggles do Puerto Ricans share with other minorities?

▼ After World War II, as many as 1500 Puerto Ricans a month came to New York City, a favorite location for a new home.

▶ called **dollar diplomacy**. Why do you think the policy was given this name?

10. Unfortunately, dollar diplomacy increased tensions between Latin America and the United States. Americans wanted their investments protected. In 1906, the United States sent troops to Cuba and set up a military government. In 1910, American marines were sent to crush a revolt in Nicaragua, and soon American troops were also occupying Haiti.

11. Civil war in Mexico led to further American involvement in Latin America. The Mexican Revolution began in 1910. Taft's successor, President Woodrow Wilson, twice sent troops into Mexico after Americans had been threatened. The Mexicans protested these actions, and resentment against Americans deepened.

The "Good Neighbor" Policy   How did relations with Latin America improve?

12. When Franklin Delano Roosevelt was inaugurated as President in 1933, he pledged to "dedicate this nation to the policy of the good neighbor." He wanted the United States to be a neighbor who "respects himself and because he does, respects the rights of others."

13. Roosevelt took steps to become Latin America's good neighbor. He removed American troops from Nicaragua and Haiti. He pledged not to send troops into Latin America again. In addition, he made trade agreements with Latin America that would benefit both nations there and the United States.

🦅 Spotlight on Sources

14. Here is how Roosevelt explained his Good Neighbor policy.

> The American republics to the south of us have been ready always to cooperate with the United States on a basis of equality and mutual [shared] respect. But . . . there was among them resentment [displeasure] and fear, because certain administrations in Washington had slighted their national pride and sovereign [independent] rights. Throughout the Americas the spirit of the

▲ Roosevelt, standing second from the right, speaks to a group of Latin Americans. In spite of efforts to promote friendlier relations with Latin America, hard feelings towards the United States remained.

> good neighbor is a practical and living fact. The twenty-one American republics are not only living together in friendship and in peace. They are united in the determination so to remain.
>
> —from *Peace and War: United States Foreign Policy, 1931–1941*

Why do you think Roosevelt changed American ◀ policy toward Latin America?

Outlook

15. The United States strained relations with Latin America when it used its military and economic power to protect American interests. Over time, Latin American countries and the United States worked out ways to deal with one another more as partners. However, the past policies of the United States left some bad feelings among its neighbors.

Activity: Discuss why Latin American nations still resent the United States.

CHAPTER REVIEW

VOCABULARY REVIEW

▶ Choose the answer that completes the sentence most accurately. Write your answer on a separate sheet of paper.

1. A canal is
   a. a resort hotel in Panama.
   b. the upper floor of a warehouse.
   c. an artificial waterway.

2. A corollary is
   a. a heart attack.
   b. a further explanation.
   c. a disease spread by mosquitoes.

3. Dollar diplomacy is
   a. judging a person on factors such as race, wealth, or nationality.
   b. a policy of American investment in Latin America.
   c. a court of law.

SKILL BUILDER: MAKING AN OUTLINE

▶ Complete this outline of the events that went before the opening of the Panama Canal. Write the outline on a separate sheet of paper.

  I. President Roosevelt made plans for the canal.
    A. _____
    B. _____

 II. _____
    A. Roosevelt supported them.
    B. _____

III. The United States recognized Panama as a state.
    A. The two countries made a treaty.
        1. _____
        2. _____
    B. _____

SKILL BUILDER: CRITICAL THINKING AND COMPREHENSION

 I. Generalization

▶ On a separate piece of paper, list three facts that support each generalization listed below.

1. American treatment of her Latin American neighbors was not always fair.

2. Puerto Rican immigrants to the United States faced difficulties.

II. Compare and Contrast

▶ Complete the chart comparing and contrasting how the United States acted in Panama and in Mexico. Then, write a brief concluding paragraph stating whether you think American actions in the two countries had more similarities or more differences.

Countries	Similarities	Differences
Panama	1. United States armed forces involved	1. encouraged rebellion
	2.	2.
	3.	3.
Mexico	1. United States armed forces involved	1. tried to stay out
	2.	2.
	3.	3.

III. Point of View

▶ Write a post card to a friend telling about building the Panama Canal from the point of view of George Washington Goethals. Then write another post card on the same subject from the point of view of a person who was working on the canal.

USING PRIMARY SOURCES

▶ Reread Spotlight on Sources on page 517. Then answer these questions. How to you think Latin American countries reacted to Roosevelt's Good Neighbor policy? Why do you think they reacted in that way?

ENRICHMENT

1. In a book about the Panama Canal, read what it was like to work on its construction. Write four journal entries in which you describe the jobs you do and the conditions under which you work. You might review the first paragraph of this chapter for ideas.

2. Set up a debate. Your topic will be "Resolved: the United States acted properly in becoming an 'international policeman'." Prepare for the debate by listing arguments for and against the United States acting as it did.

CHAPTER 3

Opening the Pacific

OBJECTIVE: How did the United States become a power in the Pacific region?

1. The ship's name was *Empress of China*. It had traveled halfway around the world, and now the ship was sailing into New York harbor filled with tea and beautiful silk cloth. The year was 1785. It was the first American ship to make the long trip to China and back. Besides silk and tea, the vessel carried all sorts of Asian treasures. These included hand-painted plates and cups, ivory carvings, fine wooden furniture, fans made of tortoise shell and silver, combs, carpets, and statues. All had such beauty and style that the cargo brought enormous profits, and American consumers wanted more. The voyage encouraged other traders to follow. The United States had discovered the Far East, and America's China trade was born. The United States was beginning to learn the importance of the Pacific region.

Perry in Japan How did the United States Navy open Japan to American trade?

2. The success of the China trade made American merchants eager to open trade with Japan too. Japan, however, had closed itself off from other countries because it did not trust foreigners. It allowed only one trading ship a year—a Dutch ship—to make a brief stop in the harbor of Nagasaki. Any shipwrecked sailors unlucky enough to wash up on Japanese shores were badly treated.

3. In 1852, President Millard Fillmore sent an expedition to open Japan to trade. On July 8, 1853, any Japanese looking out over Tokyo Bay

▲ Commodore Perry's arrival in Japan marked the opening of Japan to the world. This is how a Japanese artist of the time viewed the event.

saw something new and frightening—"four black dragons." Four black warships, their smokestacks puffing smoke, had appeared. Cannon jutted from their sides. It was the U.S. naval fleet of Commodore Matthew C. Perry. He carried a letter from the President demanding trade and kind treatment for shipwrecked sailors. A year later, the Japanese reluctantly accepted the American demands. Why do you suppose they agreed to American wishes?

In Chapter 3, you will apply these critical thinking skills to the historical process:

➡ **Recognizing Cause and Effect:** Matching the action or event that makes something happen to what happens as a result.

❯ **Predicting:** Guessing what will happen on the basis of clues and facts

4. American interest in the Pacific was renewed when the United States bought Alaska. In 1867, Secretary of State William Seward learned that Russia was willing to sell Alaska for $7.2 million. Many people laughed at him for wanting to buy it because they thought it was worthless. "Seward's Folly," they called it. But the jeering stopped when gold was discovered there 30 years later.

The Open Door Policy   How did America try to keep China from being taken over by other nations?

5. Toward the end of the 1800s, the United States began to find its trade with China threatened. Other imperialist nations like Britain, France, Germany, Russia, and Japan competed with America for trade in China. These nations were carving China up into **spheres** (SFEERZ) **of influence**. Each "sphere" was a section of China where only one foreign nation could trade. That country also affected politics in its area. No other nations was allowed to conduct business there.

6. In 1899, Secretary of State John Hay presented the Open Door Policy. He asked the other nations to "open the door" in China to equal trading rights for all. Halfheartedly, the ▶ other nations agreed. For what reasons might the other nations have been reluctant to do this?

7. Many Chinese resented the power over their country that spheres of influence gave to foreigners and rebelled. In 1900, a secret society called the Righteous Order of Fists, nicknamed the Boxers, attacked foreigners all over China. About 300 foreigners were killed. The aim of this Boxer Rebellion was to drive all foreigners out of China. The foreign nations involved, including the United States, sent in an international army and crushed the rebellion within two months.

8. Now some of the imperialist powers saw their chance to take control of more land in China. However, the United States, with British support, came to China's aid. Secretary of State Hay broadened the Open Door policy. He said that the United States was now going to help China preserve its rights over its own territory.

Hawaii   What events led the United States to take control of Hawaii?

9. America had long been interested in Hawaii as a port and a market for goods and ideas. Ships bound for the Far East or engaged in whaling stopped there for food and water. In 1820, Protestant missionaries came to Hawaii from New England to convert the Hawaiians to Christianity. Their descendants founded huge sugar plantations and other successful businesses there.

10. By the 1890s, these Americans were a powerful influence in Hawaii. They controlled about two-thirds of Hawaii's land. They had succeeded in forcing the Hawaiian king, Kalakaua, to accept a constitution that reduced his governing power while increasing theirs.

11. In 1891, Queen Liliuokalani (lee-lee-oo-oh-kah-LAH-nee) tried to regain Hawaiian ruling power. She had come to the throne after her brother Kalakaua's death. Wanting to preserve their own power, the Americans in Hawaii forced her off the throne in 1893. Then they asked the United States to annex Hawaii. Many Americans were angry about the overthrow of the Hawaiian queen. Nevertheless, in 1898, Congress voted for annexation, and in 1900, Hawaii became a territory of the United States. What was unusual about the way the United ◀ States obtained Hawaii?

People in History

12. Queen Liliuokalani   Born in 1838 in Honolulu, Liliuokalani was a strong-willed Hawaiian patriot. She was well educated by American missionaries who had come to the islands. She was married to John O. Dominis, the American governor of Oahu, who died the year she succeeded her brother King Kalakaua to the throne. An accomplished musician, she wrote the popular Hawaiian song "Aloha Oe."

Ask: Remind the students that 60 years after gold was discovered, vast oil fields were found in Alaska. Ask students "What would you say to someone who ridiculed Seward's purchase of Alaska?"

521

Linking Geography and History

★ ★ ★

The United States and the Pacific Ocean

Captain Alfred Thayer Mahan was a 19th century naval officer. From his study of history, Mahan concluded that national greatness depended on control of the world's oceans.

Mahan's views were popular in the United States at that time. Americans saw how Europeans had used seapower to build large overseas colonial empires. Feelings ran high that the strength of the United States depended on control of the Pacific Ocean.

The map below shows where American expansion occurred in the Pacific in the late 1800s. Many islands and borderlands were involved. Control of mid-ocean islands was highly important because sailing ships took four weeks or more to cross the Pacific Ocean. The islands were useful stopover points where ships could refuel and take on fresh food and water. In 1867, the United States annexed Midway Island. In 1878, it annexed Pago Pago in Samoa. In 1887, Pearl Harbor in Hawaii was made an American coaling station. It soon became an American naval base. Formal annexation of all the Hawaiian Islands followed in 1898.

Expansionist goals led to the purchase of Alaska from Russian in 1867. Some Americans saw the Alaska purchase as a step to taking what was left of British North America.

American interests on the Asian side of the Pacific focused on China, Japan, and the Philippines. Japan and China had luxuries— especially silk, tea, and porcelain called "china"—that wealthy Americans wanted. Yankee clipper ships had begun trading with China in the 1840s. Trade with Japan was opened by force in 1853. The Philippines were ceded to the United States by Spain in 1898.

Now use the map to answer these questions.

1. Why was the Panama Canal important to American control of the Pacific?

2. Why are the Hawaiian Islands important to American control of the Pacific?

3. Why is Alaska important to American control of the Pacific?

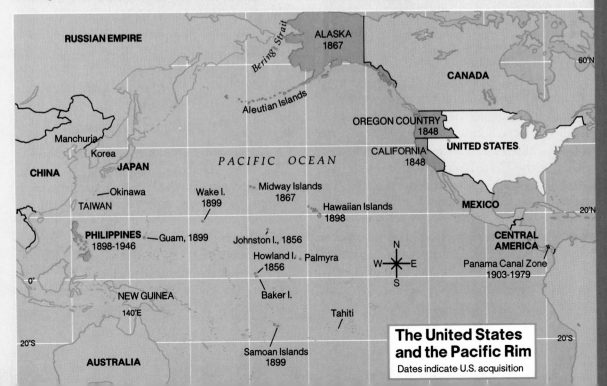

The United States and the Pacific Rim

Dates indicate U.S. acquisition

13. As queen, she disregarded the constitution forced on the Hawaiian Islands by Americans in an attempt to reestablish the power of the monarchy. For this she was overthrown. In 1895 she made another attempt to regain the throne, but she was unsuccessful. Afterwards she lived in the United States and then in Honolulu, where she died on November 11, 1917.

14. Her overthrow made Liliuokalani feel bitter toward the United States. She even sued its government for a half million dollars for the losses she claimed it had cost her.

Spotlight on Sources

15. Here is how Liliuokalani stated her bitterness at Hawaii's fate.

> We had allowed [the American settlers] to give us a constitution and control the offices of government. Not without protest, indeed, for this usurpation [taking of power] was unrighteous and caused us much humiliation and distress. But we did not resist it by force. It had not entered our hearts to believe that these friends and allies from the United States . . . would ever go so far as to overthrow our form of government, seize our nation by the throat, and turn it over to an alien [foreign] power.
>
> —from *Hawaii's Story by Hawaii's Queen*, by Liliuokalani

▶ How do you think the American rebels justified their takeover of an independent nation? Do you think they were right? Explain.

▲ Queen Liliuokalani fought to keep Hawaii independent, but she was defeated by a group of American businessmen living in Hawaii.

in 1898. A year later, Wake Island and part of Samoa joined them. These islands were like a series of American-owned stepping stones across the Pacific Ocean.

Outlook

17. In the late 1800s, expansion was the desire of many Americans. They wanted more land, profitable trade, and influence as a world power. The Pacific and its lands offered all of these. The United States took control of Pacific lands as the nation became an imperialistic power. What kinds of problems can occur because of the competition among rival imperialist powers? How is this situation similar to what is happening in the world today? ◀

Other Pacific Islands Why did the United States take control of other Pacific islands?

16. American ships sailing the Pacific needed **naval bases** on islands along the way for ships to refuel, repair, and restock fresh water and food. Secretary of State Seward began gathering such bases by buying Midway Island in the central Pacific in 1867. As you have seen, the Philippines and Guam came under American control

Activity: Have students role play a confrontation between Queen Liliuokalani and the Americans who want to dethrone her. Have a student act as a lawyer representing the queen. Make each side present arguments for their positions.

523

CHAPTER REVIEW

VOCABULARY REVIEW

▶ Choose the answer that most accurately completes the sentence.

1. A sphere of influence is
a. a continent that has only one country.
b. an area where only one nation can trade.
c. a European body of laws.

2. A naval base is
a. a harbor where ships can resupply and refuel.
b. a port where no trade is allowed.
c. a factory.

SKILL BUILDER: INTERPRETING A TIME LINE

▶ On a separate sheet of paper, copy the time line below. Write on the time line the following events, including the dates.

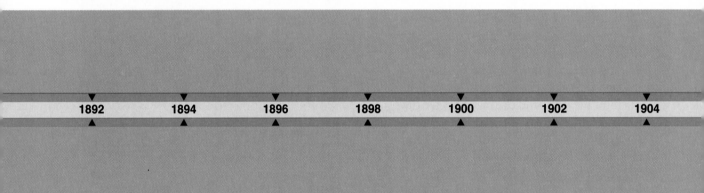

| 1892 | 1894 | 1896 | 1898 | 1900 | 1902 | 1904 |

1. Secretary of State John Hay created the Open Door Policy.

2. The Boxer Rebellion occurred in China.

3. Queen Liliuokalani forced off the Hawaiian throne.

4. Hawaii became a territory of the United States.

5. Guam came under American control.

SKILL BUILDER: CRITICAL THINKING AND COMPREHENSION

I. Fact *versus* Opinion

▶ Decide whether each statement is a fact or an opinion. Write the number of each statement on a separate piece of paper. Label each statement **F** for fact or **O** for opinion.

1. Japan had closed itself to foreigners before 1853.

2. Queen Liliuokalani was embittered toward the United States.

3. Trading with Japan was not a good idea.

STUDY HINT For a quick review of a chapter, go through the chapter and read the first sentence of each paragraph. These topic sentences give the main idea of each paragraph. Added together, they make up a skeleton of the chapter's main ideas.

4. Secretary of State William Seward was smart because he wanted to buy Alaska.

5. The "Open Door" policy was the best thing for China.

6. By the 1890s, Americans were very powerful in Hawaii.

II. Cause and Effect

▶ Write each of the statements below on a separate sheet of paper. Fill in the missing cause or effect.

1. Cause: The United States needed naval bases on islands in the Pacific.
Effect: _______

2. Cause: The Chinese resented other countries carving up their country into "spheres of influence."
Effect: _______

3. Cause: _______
Effect: Queen Liliuokalani sued the United States government for a half million dollars.

III. Classifying

▶ The United States treated each of the three countries discussed in the chapter differently. Write the names of the three countries at the top of a column as shown below. Then fill in the chart with at least three examples of how America treated each country.

	Japan	China	Hawaii
1.			
2.			
3.			

USING PRIMARY SOURCES

▶ Reread the excerpt written by Queen Liliuokalani. What kind of a person do you think she was? What characteristics to you find that show that she was a good ruler?

ENRICHMENT

1. In an encyclopedia or in a history book, read more about Commodore Perry's arrival in Japan. Pretend that you are a writer for a Japanese newspaper of the time and write a news story reporting his arrival and Japanese reaction to it.

2. Divide into five groups, each representing one of the following: Britain, France, Germany, Russia, and Japan. In an encyclopedia or in a history book about China, find where your sphere of influence was in China and what trade goods you specialized in. Group by group, present your findings to the class, and locate your sphere on a wall map.

CHAPTER 4

World War I

OBJECTIVE: Why did the nations of Europe go to war, and how did Americans try to stay neutral?

1. On the night of August 3, 1914, the British statesman Edward Grey stared moodily out of the windows of the Foreign Office in London. "The lamps are going out all over Europe," he whispered sadly. "We shall not see them lit again in our lifetime." What had brought Grey to such a grim prediction? It was war, a war that was taking in most nations of Europe and soon would involve other parts of the world. The Great War, they called it at first. Later it would be called World War I. Whatever its name, it was the worst war the world had yet seen, and it was a war the United States could not avoid.

World War I Begins What were the causes of World War I, and what nations fought in this war?

2. A feeling of nationalism within the nations of Europe was creating strong competition among them. Britain, France, Germany, Austria-Hungary, Russia, Italy were among the strongest competitors for foreign colonies and military power. As they tried to outdo one another, they also grew fearful and suspicious of one another. They began to build up their armies and navies.

3. Fear and suspicion caused the European nations to form alliances. In an **alliance** (uh-LY-uhns), one nation promises to help another if it is attacked. Britain, France, and Russia formed one alliance, called the **Triple Entente**

▲ In one battle of World War I, allied soldiers hid in trees to fire machine guns. Machine guns were faster and more accurate than earlier weapons.

(ahn-TAHNT). Germany, Austria-Hungary, and Italy formed another, called the **Triple Alliance.**

4. Europe grew tense under the system of alliances. It was like a powder keg that a small spark could explode. An assassin's bullet provided the spark. On June 28, 1914, Archduke Franz Ferdinand, heir to the Austria-Hungary throne, was slain. The murder took place in Sarajevo, Bosnia (in present-day Yugoslavia),

In Chapter 4, you will apply these critical thinking skills to the historical process:
Making Judgments: Stating a personal opinion based on historical facts.
Sequencing: Putting a series of events in the correct time order.

ruled by Austria-Hungary. The killer was a young student from Serbia who thought Bosnia should be part of his nation.

5. The archduke's death set Europe's alliances against each other. The events that followed were like falling dominoes. Austria-Hungary threatened Serbia with war. Serbia's friend, Russia, prepared to defend Serbia against Austria-Hungary. In response, Austria-Hungary's ally, Germany, declared war on Russia and France and invaded Belgium. Britain then declared war on Germany. What made these events almost sure to happen?

6. By August 1914, Germany and Austria-Hungary, now called the **Central Powers**, stood against Britain, France, and Russia, now called the **Allies**. Italy also joined the Allies in 1915, rejecting its former allies' offensive action in Serbia. A brutal war had begun. Before it was over, it would involve 33 nations across the world. Only a handful of nations were able to remain neutral.

The Allies against the Central Powers   Why was neither side able to win a quick victory in the war?

7. Both sides expected the war to be brief, but it lasted more than four long and deadly years. The Central Powers had to wage war on two fronts in Europe. On the western front, Germany hoped to defeat France by quickly marching through neutral Belgium and fighting toward Paris. British and French forces were able to stop them about 20 miles (32 km) outside Paris. On the eastern front, Germans and Austrians battled the Russians, but neither side made much headway.

8. By late 1914, each side had fought the other to a standstill. On the western front, both sides built lines of trenches stretching for 600 miles (960 km) across northern France. Soldiers lived in the deep trenches, leaving them only to attack the enemy. Little ground was won or lost, but hundreds of thousands of troops were killed. Both sides were slowly bleeding to death, and there was no end in sight.

America Seeks Neutrality   Why did America try to stay out of World War I?

9. For nearly three years, America tried to remain neutral. Long ago, both George Washington and Thomas Jefferson had warned Americans to stay out of Europe's troubles. The current American President, Woodrow Wilson, echoed these warnings.

10. Americans also were divided about whom they wanted to win the war. Many favored the Allies, recalling the cultural heritage the United States shared with Britain and France's role in helping it win independence. Others, especially those of German ancestry, favored the Central Powers.

▼ Archduke Franz Ferdinand and his wife were riding in an open car when they were attacked and killed by Gavrilo Princip, a young Serbian nationalist.

Activity: Several major new weapons were first used in World War I—gas, the tank, the submarine, the machine gun, and the airplane. Have three groups of volunteers each research these weapons' early development and their use in the war and present their findings to the class.

▲ On May 7, 1915, the *Lusitania* was sunk by a German submarine off the coast of Ireland. The ship sank very quickly, so that there was no time to load many of the lifeboats. As a result, 1,198 people died.

People in History

11. William Jennings Bryan One American who wanted to keep the United States neutral was William Jennings Bryan, the secretary of state. A gifted speaker, Bryan had been called "the Boy Orator of the Plains." Three times he ran for the Presidency, and three times he was defeated. As war raged in Europe, Bryan pleaded with Americans to stay out of it. Americans should never "get down and wallow in the mire of human blood," he cried. But his country was moving toward entry into the war. Powerless to stop it, he resigned as secretary of state.

America Enters the War What caused America to join the war on the side of the Allies?

12. Early in the war, the British set up a blockade of Germany. Britain placed ships near German ports to prevent boats from entering or leaving. Through this blockade, Britain hoped to cut off needed supplies from Germany.

13. In 1915, Germany responded to the British blockade by using submarines to block-ade British and French ports. In May of that year, without warning, a German submarine sent one torpedo into the British liner *Lusitania* and sent it to the bottom of the sea. More than a thousand people, including 128 Americans, lost their lives. President Wilson sent a strong protest to the German government. The Germans finally promised not to sink passenger ships without first warning them. How might ◄ Germany's actions lead to a change in American neutrality?

14. Early in 1917, three events occurred that ended American neutrality. First, Germany broke its promise and said it would start unrestricted submarine warfare again. Second, Wilson learned that Germany was trying to get Mexico to attack the United States. Germany promised to help Mexico win back Texas and other states. Third, a revolution in Russia toppled the undemocratic rule of the **tsar** (ZAHR), or emperor, and took the country out of the war. A Russia without a tsar was more acceptable to Wilson. However, France and Great Britain were in great danger because now Germany could focus on the western front. Wilson sadly read the reports of German submarines sinking American ships. He decided that the United States finally had to join the Allies.

Spotlight on Sources

15. On April 1, 1917, Wilson addressed Congress, his voice husky with emotion.

> The present German submarine warfare against commerce [trading ships] is a warfare against mankind. . . . Neutrality is no longer [possible] or desirable where the peace of the world is involved. . . . The world must be made safe for democracy. There are, it may be, many months of fiery trial and sacrifice ahead of us. . . . We shall fight for the things which we have always carried nearest our hearts—for democracy, for the right of those who submit to

▼ In this famous recruiting poster, Uncle Sam seems to be ordering the viewer to join the army. How effective do you think this kind of advertisement would have been?

THE PRESIDENTS' CORNER

Historians think of **Woodrow Wilson**, President from 1913 to 1921, as one of the most successful Presidents of the United States. Before he became President, Wilson was a scholar, teacher, university president, and governor of New Jersey. After he became President in 1913, Wilson's programs helped the United States become a great industrial nation.

At the end of World War I, Wilson met with the Allied leaders at Versailles to plan the peace treaty. He wanted to form a League of Nations, an organization to keep world peace. This League of Nations was Wilson's greatest dream. On December 10, 1920, Wilson was awarded the Nobel Peace Prize for his efforts in seeking a lasting and fair peace agreement.

> authority [obey the law] to have a voice in their own governments, for the rights and liberties of small nations, . . . [to] make the world itself at last free.
> —from *The Congressional Record*

What did Wilson say was the purpose for ◄ fighting the war? Do you think that Wilson's goals were realistic?

Outlook

16. Fierce competition pushed European nations into a system of alliances, and the alliances pushed them into a dreadful war. Separated from European shores by 3,000 miles (4,800 km) of the Atlantic Ocean, America tried to keep itself out of the battle there. The desire for freedom over that very sea finally drew the United States into it. However, the United States would never again be able to remain uninvolved in world affairs. Why might America be a deciding factor in World War I?

CHAPTER REVIEW

VOCABULARY REVIEW

▶ Fill in the blank with the words below that correctly complete the sentence.

alliance	tsar	Central Powers	Triple Alliance
neutral	Allies	Triple Entente	

1. An _____ is an agreement among nations to come to one another's aid.

2. The _____ became the Allies and consisted of France, Britain, and Russia.

3. The _____ was formed by Germany, Austria-Hungary, and Italy.

4. The emperor of Russia was the _____ .

5. By August 1914, Germany and Austria-Hungary became known as the _____ .

6. In 1915, Italy joined the _____ .

SKILL BUILDER: READING A MAP

▶ Compare the two maps below for political change, then answer these questions.

1. What countries gained territory after World War I?

2. What new countries were created after World War I?

3. What countries lost territory after World War I? How can you account for these losses?

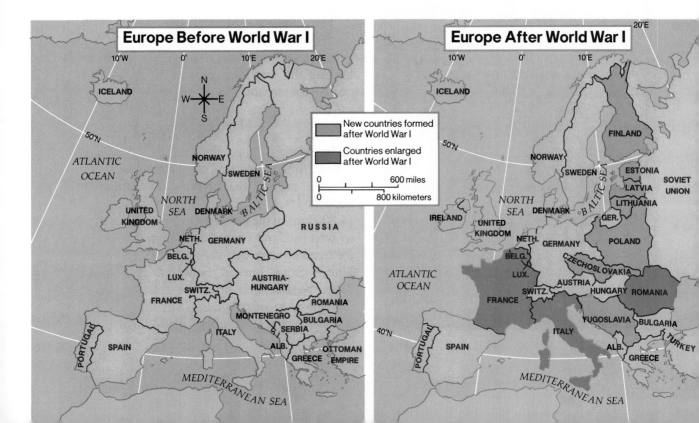

I. Sequencing

Copy these events on a separate sheet of paper. Put numbers in front of these events in the order they happened

a. Archduke Franz Ferdinand is killed by an assassin.
b. The United Staes enters the war on the side of the Allies.
c. Austria-Hungary threatens Serbia with war.
d. Italy joins the Allies
e. France and Britain declare war on Germany.
f. Germany declares war on Russia.
g. Russia defends Serbia.

II. Comparing and Contrasting

▶ Compare World War I with the War of 1812. You can review the War of 1812 in Chapter 6 of Unit 6. Complete this chart to show the similarities and differences. Then use the chart to answer these questions: Are the two wars more similar than different or more different than similar? Why do you think so?

	War of 1812	World War I
Allies		
Where Fought		
Methods of Fighting		
Who Won		
Outcomes of the War		

III. Making Judgments

▶ To make a good judgment, you should base your ideas on facts and evidence. Make a judgment about whether the United States should or should not have entered World War I. On a separate sheet of paper, write your judgment, and support it with at least three reasons that are based on facts.

USING PRIMARY SOURCES

▶ Reread the Spotlight on Sources on page 529. Why do you think President Wilson's statement, "The world must be made safe for democracy," became so well known it almost was a battle cry?

ENRICHMENT

1. Three major monarchies of Europe fell as a result of World War I—Russia, Austria-Hungary, and Germany. In a group choose one of these and do research on its ruler. Then write a television script on your subject, giving important facts about his life and telling what finally happened to him.
2. In books about World War I, look for pictures and descriptions of important battles. Use this information to create a model or a diagram of the stages of the battle.

531

CHAPTER 5

America Goes to War

> OBJECTIVE: How did the United States help the Allies win World War I and join in planning the peace?

1. President Wilson had warned Americans that "fiery trial and sacrifice" awaited them in war. That is just what awaited 600 American soldiers under the command of Major Charles W. Whittlesey. On October 2, 1918, during a bitter battle in France, they found themselves completely surrounded by German forces. For five days, they fought desperately, as food, water, and ammunition ran out. When the Germans called for their surrender, they refused. Finally, on October 8, American relief troops were able to reach them. Fewer than 200 of this "Lost Battalion" limped out alive. The Lost Battalion was a symbol of the trial and sacrifice that all Americans were undergoing, at home and in battle, during the Great War.

Americans on the Home Front In what ways did the American people support the war effort?

2. Two huge tasks, raising troops and gathering supplies, faced the American people as the country entered World War I. First, they had to raise a fighting force of millions of men. Second, they had to produce the food, uniforms, and weapons to equip this force and to resupply the Allies in Europe.

3. A first step was to increase food production. Farmers planted "from fence to fence." They plowed up more land for farming than

▲ These women are operating punch presses in an electrical equipment factory. Many women did such work during World War I.

ever before. All citizens were urged to conserve food. Colorful posters encouraged them not to eat wheat on Mondays or meat on Tuesdays. "Wheatless Mondays" and "Meatless Tuesdays" would save food that could be shipped overseas, they were told. Some people planted "victory gardens" to grow their own food.

In Chapter 5, you will apply these critical thinking skills to the historical process:
▶ **Drawing Conclusions:** Making a statement that explains the facts and evidence.

▲ **Summarizing:** Giving the main idea of a group of paragraphs in a brief form.

4. A second step was to retool industry to produce war materials and find people to run the machines. Factories that had made coats now began to make uniforms. Car makers made tanks and military trucks instead. As men left their jobs to go into military service, women replaced them. Women took over on the production lines in factories. They also replaced men as police officers, mechanics, trolley conductors, and even barbers. African and Hispanic Americans also found new job opportunities during the war. However, for all three groups, the wartime opportunities were short-lived. Once the war ended, they were forced to return to their earlier positions.

5. Americans had to support the war with money, too. They paid higher taxes to pay for war production, but still more money was needed. The government sold Liberty Bonds as a way to borrow money for the war. A **bond** is an interest-earning certificate that promises to pay the owner a certain amount of money when due. The government used **propaganda** (prah-puh-GAN-duh) to encourage Americans to buy Liberty Bonds. Propaganda is the effort to persuade people to take on certain ideas or attitudes. Posters were one form of propaganda. Huge rallies at which movie stars urged people to buy bonds were another. This propaganda was so successful that more than half the nation bought Liberty Bonds.

Americans Fight in Europe How did American forces turn the war in favor of the Allies?

6. Fresh troops and new arms were just what the Allies needed for success. When the United States declared war, its army numbered only 200,000. Through volunteers and a military **draft**, or picking individuals for service, this number would reach four million within a year. General John J. Pershing was named commander of the American Expeditionary Force, or AEF. The first American troops reached France in the summer of 1917. At first, they fought with British and French troops along the

MAP SKILL BUILDER: Learn from the map about the division of Europe in World War I. **1.** What countries were the Allied powers? **2.** What countries were the Central Powers?

western front. However, Pershing wanted the Americans to fight as a single force. He demanded that they have their own area of the ▶ front to defend. Why would Pershing, the commander of the American forces, want this?

People in History

7. General John J. Pershing The commander of American forces in World War I, General John J. Pershing, played a role in many events in American history. His first combat came in the Indian wars in the American West. In 1898, he led the charge of African American troops up San Juan Hill in Cuba. He fought the Filipino rebels following the Spanish-American War. And he led one of the American military expeditions into Mexico during the civil war there.

8. As commander of the American Expeditionary Force, Pershing believed that American forces were repaying the French for their help in the American Revolution. With this in mind, he visited the grave of the Marquis de Lafayette. A news reporter described what happened then: "Pershing stepped up to it [the grave] and saluted in his best manner and then said in a loud voice, 'Lafayette, we are here.' "

9. By spring of 1918, two million American troops had arrived in France. Among them were many African Americans and Hispanics. The Americans were just in time. The Germans were massing a new drive toward Paris. In May, General Pershing led American troops in the capture of Cantigny (kahn-teen-YEE). In June, Americans helped the Allies win the battles of Chateau-Thierry (sha-TOH tee-ay-REE) and Belleau (bel-LOH) Wood. In July, American forces helped push German forces back in the Second Battle of the Marne. This victory marked the turning point in the war.

10. Now the Allies went on the attack. In September, Pershing led American troops in attack, capturing San Mihiel (sahn mi-YEL). Next, American forces triumphed in the Meuse-Argonne (MOOZ ar-GUN) attack. By October, the Germans were in full retreat.

11. Germany knew the tide of war had changed and asked for peace. The Germans asked the Allies for an **armistice** (AHR-mis-tis), an agreement to stop fighting. On November 11, 1918, in a railroad car in a forest in France, the Allies and the Central Powers signed the armistice. At 11:00 A.M. on the 11th day of the 11th month, the guns finally fell silent all across Europe. After four long years, the Great War was over at last.

The Treaty of Versailles What was President Wilson's role in planning the peace treaty, and what were its terms?

12. In December 1918, President Wilson arrived in Europe to help draw up the peace treaty. Crowds cheered him everywhere he went. He looked forward to presenting his plan for peace to the other Allied leaders at Versailles (vair-SY). The leaders were called the "Big Four." They included Wilson, Georges Clemenceau of France, David Lloyd George of Britain, and Vittorio Orlando of Italy.

13. At the heart of Wilson's plan for peace were his **Fourteen Points**. These were ways he hoped to ensure peace in the future. They included an end to secret agreements among nations, freedom of the seas for all, and free trade. The Fourteen Points also asked for a reduction of weapons and for the right of all nationalities to govern themselves. The last point called for forming an organization of nations where nations could settle their problems. It was to be called the League of Nations. Wilson also wanted defeated Germany to be treated fairly.

14. Although the Treaty of Versailles did include some of Wilson's ideas, it treated Germany harshly. It took land away from Germany, and it required Germany to pay huge **reparations** (rep-uh-RAY-shuhnz) to the Allies. Reparations are payments for damage done in wartime. What effects might these payments have ◀ on Germany? Although Wilson was not fully satisfied with the Treaty of Versailles, he asked the United States Senate to approve it. After all,

Activity: Discuss the term "morale" with the class, the keeping up of spirits and dedication in time of war. Have students find examples in their texts of how Americans kept up their morale during World War I.

534

▲ African American soldiers, with bayonets (long knives) attached to their rifles, fought in the trenches of northern France during World War I.

the treaty did include the League of Nations. Wilson believed that the League could correct any problems that the treaty created.

🦅 Spotlight on Sources

15. Here is how Wilson explained the need for a League of Nations:

> The League of Nations . . . [is] the only possible guarantee against war. . . . Is it an absolute guarantee? No; there is no absolute guarantee against human passion; but even if it were only ten percent of a guarantee, would not you rather have ten percent guarantee against war than none? . . . I can predict with absolute certainty that within another generation there will be another world war if the nations of the world do not concert [arrange] a method by which to prevent it.
>
> —from *The Public Papers of Woodrow Wilson*, Ray S. Baker and William E. Dodd, eds.

What does Wilson expect from the League of ◄ Nations? What does he believe will happen if the League is not approved?

The League of Nations How did America's failure to join the League return the nation to isolationism?

16. The Senate did not share Wilson's belief in the League of Nations. At least 14 senators opposed the League in any form. They did not want the United States to join in any international organization. Another large group feared that joining the League would lessen America's independence. Wilson took his case in favor of the League to the people. He crossed the country, making speech after speech in city after city. However, in September 1919, he suffered a stroke and had to return to Washington, ill and broken.

17. In November 1919, the Senate rejected the Treaty of Versailles. The United States would not join the League of Nations. Most Americans were ready to return to America's traditional **isolationism** (eye-soh-LAY-shun-izm), the belief that the country should keep itself apart from other nations and from international alliances. Do you think that the Sen- ◄ ate's decision to reject the League of Nations was a wise decision?

Outlook

18. The United States proved the deciding factor in turning the war in the Allies' favor. Americans were able to form a great army and send it across the ocean. They also were able to fulfill the agricultural and industrial needs of a powerful war effort. However, Americans were less willing to join other countries in trying to keep the peace. They rejected the League of Nations, even though it was an idea that had come from their own President. Instead, they pinned their hopes on isolationism to keep them out of war in the future. As the nation returned to ◄ peace, how possible do you think it would be to remain isolationist in the modern world?

535

CHAPTER REVIEW

VOCABULARY REVIEW

▶ Write each of the following words on a piece of paper, and write the definition for each world. Then use each word in a sentence of your own.

1. propaganda

2. armistice

3. reparations

4. isolationism

5. bond

6. Fourteen Points

SKILL BUILDER: USING A TIME LINE

▶ Use the time line below to answer the questions that follow. Write your answers on a separate sheet of paper.

Federal Reserve System established 1913	Archduke Ferdinand assassinated 1914	Lusitania sunk by German submarine 1915		Americans enter World War I 1917			Woodrow Wilson wins Nobel Peace Prize 1920
1913	**1914**	**1915**	**1916**	**1917**	**1918**	**1919**	**1920**
				November 11 Armistice ends World War I 1918		United States Senate refuses to join the League of Nations 1919	

1. How many years after the sinking of the *Lusitania* did the United States enter the war?

2. How many years had World War I been going one before America joined the fight?

3. In what year did Woodrow Wilson receive the Nobel Peace Prize?

4. How long were Americans involved in World War I?

SKILL BUILDER: CRITICAL THINKING AND COMPREHENSION

⇨ I. Cause and Effect

▶ On a separate sheet of paper, write the causes and effects for each pair given below. If there is more than one answer, include all the causes or all the effects.

1. **Cause:** _____
   Effect: The Senate rejected the Treaty of Versailles.

2. **Cause:** _____
   Effect: Americans bought Liberty Bonds to support the war.

536

3. **Cause:** Men left their jobs to go into military service.
   Effect: _____

4. **Cause:** President Wilson wanted to ensure peace in the future.
   Effect: _____

II. Classifying

▶ Classify each of the following items or actions according to whether it involved supporting the war effort or creating a peace treaty. Write your classifications on a separate sheet of paper. Label each group.

buying Liberty Bonds

producing uniforms and tanks

ending secret agreements among nations

conserving food

forming a League of Nations

making the seas free for all

paying reparations

getting millions of men into the military

III. Drawing Conclusions

▶ On a separate sheet of paper, write the conclusion you believe is correct for the facts below.

1. **Facts:** American troops captured Cantigny.
   American troops took the offensive and capture San Mihiel.
   By October, 1918, the Germans were in full retreat.
   Conclusion: _____

2. **Facts:** Fourteen Senators did not want the United States to join any international group.
   Some feared the League of Nations would lessen America's independence.
   Americans wanted to return to isolationism.
   Conclusion: _____

USING PRIMARY SOURCES

▶ Woodrow Wilson was correct in his prediction that there would be another world war. Do you think he was also correct in stating that the League of Nations would prevent such a war? Explain your reasoning.

ENRICHMENT

1. Read about the life of American soldiers (or "doughboys," as they were called) in books about World War I, like the Time-Life series. Imagine that you are a "doughboy," and use what you learn to write a letter to your family back home describing your experiences as a soldier in France.

2. Use the encyclopedia or books on the history of World War I to research one of the following World War I battles: the First Battle of the Marne, Cantigny, Chateau-Thierry, Belleau Wood, the Second Battle of the Marne, San Mihiel, Meuse-Argonne. Form a group with two or three students who have researched other battles. Write a radio newscast about the progress of the war from the information you found. Add vivid details or create striking quotations to make your radio program seem real.

UNIT REVIEW

SUMMARY

As the nineteenth century drew to a close, the United States took the first steps toward becoming a leader in world affairs. By opening trade with Japan and insuring access to China with the Open Door policy, the United States became important in world trade. After its victory in the Spanish-American War, the United States gained the new possessions of the Philippines, Puerto Rico, and Guam. The nation also increased its territories by adding Alaska, Hawaii, and the Virgin Islands.

Relations with the nations of Latin America were a problem. Latin Americans were worried by America's forceful behavior as the Panama Canal was built. The Roosevelt Corollary and Dollar Diplomacy added to Latin America's growing resentment. Not until President Franklin D. Roosevelt proposed the Good Neighbor Policy did relations improve.

When the nations of Europe were drawn into World War I, the United States tried to remain neutral. However, Americans found themselves pulled into the fighting. After the war, the country tried to return to isolationism. But the United States would never again be able to remain separate from world politics.

SKILL BUILDER: READING A MAP

▶ Study the map below. It shows which side the countries of the world took in World War I. Notice that some countries countries were neutral, or not involved in the war.

1. What color represents the Allies and their supporters?

2. Give three supporters of the Central Powers in Africa.

3. What neutral country is the closest to the United States?

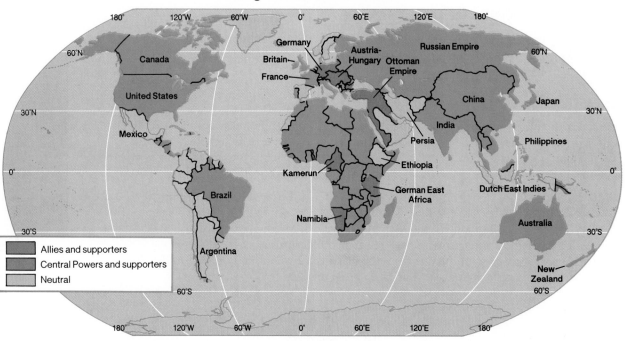

Taking Sides in World War I

SKILL BUILDER: CRITICAL THINKING AND COMPREHENSION

I. Point of View

▶ Below is a list of people. After them are statements that the individuals might have made. Decide who might have said each one. Write your answer on a separate sheet of paper.

A Filipino   A Cuban   A Panamanian

A Hawaiian   A Puerto Rican   An American

1. Although we are imprisoned and even executed, we will throw off the chains of our Spanish masters with or without the help of the Americans.

2. Let us have broader powers of self-government and become citizens of the United States. Perhaps, in time, our island can become a state itself.

3. We must control the trade in the world and spread our laws, culture, and democracy.

4. We do not want to exchange Spanish rule for American rule. We will rebel against the United States if we do not gain independence.

5. If Colombia will not sell the land to the United States, let us create a separate nation and grant rights to build the canal to our northern neighbor ourselves.

6. We allowed Americans into our land. We let them control our government. We allowed them to participate in our economy. We let their missionaries teach us about their religion. Now, they overthrow our government and remove our rightful ruler.

II. Comparing and Contrasting

▶ Study the following events. Decide how they are similar and how they are different. Then write one short paragraph comparing and contrasting the events in #1. Write another short paragraph pointing out the similarities and differences in the second situation.

1. Compare and contrast American trade involvement in China and Japan. Consider how Americans began trading in the countries. What did they do to protect their businesses? What were American relations with Japan and China?

2. Compare and contrast American involvement in the Spanish-American War and World War I. What were the types of warfare involved? What were the results?

ENRICHMENT

1. In a group with three or four other students, review the important people you studied in Unit 12. Have each group member choose an individual and research that person in books or encyclopedias. Then, write a play in which these historical people "meet" at a political gathering. Have them discuss how they feel about how the United States behaved as it became a world power. If there is time, perform your play for the class.

2. Write a letter to the editor of a newspaper expressing your opinion about American's imperialistic behavior. Support your ideas with facts from the unit that prove your point.

UNIT 13

PEACE, DEPRESSION, AND ANOTHER WAR

Chapter

UNIT OVERVIEW   Unit 13 will help you understand how America was changing in the 1920s, how the Great Depression affected Americans, and what the causes and results of World War II were.

UNIT SKILLS OBJECTIVES   In Unit 13, three critical thinking skills are emphasized:

○ **Generalizing:** Making a statement that links several facts.
◜ **Comparing and Contrasting:** Recognizing similarities and differences.
❯ **Predicting:** Telling what you believe will happen on the basis of clues and facts.

You will also use two important social studies skills:
Reading a Map   Interpreting a Photograph

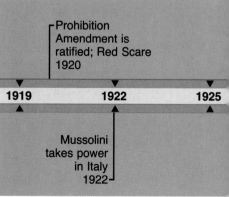

Prohibition Amendment is ratified; Red Scare 1920

| 1919 | 1922 | 1925 |

Mussolini takes power in Italy 1922

540   ESL/LEP Strategy: Divide students into four teams representing the Roaring 20s, the Great Depression, World War II, Peace. Have each team find the vocabulary terms related to the subject in the text and discuss the possible meanings. Students should then check their definitions in the Glossary or in a dictionary.

▲ During the Great Depression people desperate for work tried to find jobs through employment agencies.

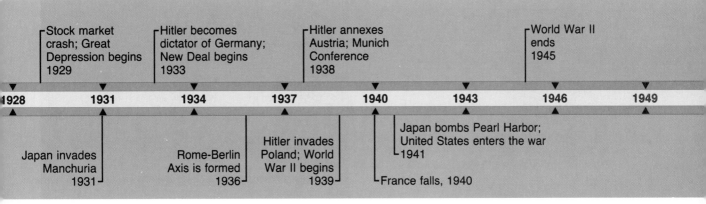

Stock market crash; Great Depression begins 1929

Hitler becomes dictator of Germany; New Deal begins 1933

Hitler annexes Austria; Munich Conference 1938

World War II ends 1945

1928   1931   1934   1937   1940   1943   1946   1949

Japan invades Manchuria 1931

Rome-Berlin Axis is formed 1936

Hitler invades Poland; World War II begins 1939

Japan bombs Pearl Harbor; United States enters the war 1941

France falls, 1940

Points of View

Should the government take an active role to help the poor and underprivileged? Or is government involvement in the economy a danger to liberty and freedom? Those questions were hotly debated in the 1920s and 1930s, especially after the nation was plunged into a deep economic depression. The selections that follow show how two American Presidents differed on the issue

Thawing Out the System
—Page in the Louisville "Courier-Journal."

▲ To what does this cartoon compare the economy during President Hoover's administration? What does the President seem to be doing to correct the situation?

HERBERT HOOVER'S "RUGGED INDIVIDUALISM"

❝ During the war [World War I] we necessarily turned to the Government to solve every difficult economic problem. . . . However justified in time of war, if continued in peace time, it would destroy not only our American system but with it our progress and freedom as well. . . . I should like to state to you the effect that this projection [control] of government in business would have upon our system of self-government and our economic system. That effect would reach to the daily life of every man and woman. It would impair [hurt] the very basis of liberty and freedom. . . .

Even if governmental conduct of business could give us more efficiency instead of less efficiency, the fundamental objection to it would remain unaltered [unchanged]. . . . It would . . . increase . . . abuse and corruption. It would stifle [choke] initiative and invention. It would undermine the development of leadership. It would cramp and cripple the mental and spiritual energies of our people. It would extinguish [put out] equality and opportunity. It would dry up the spirit of liberty and progress. ❞

Government and the Economy

of what role of government should play in the nation's economy. The first selection expresses the views of Herbert C. Hoover, which he stated before the Great Depression began. The second selection gives the views of Franklin D. Roosevelt, which he set forth in his first Inaugural Address in 1933.

FRANKLIN D. ROOSEVELT ON GOVERNMENT RESPONSIBILITY

❝Our greatest primary task is to put people to work. This is no unsolvable problem if we face it wisely and courageously.

It can be accomplished in part by direct recruiting by the government itself, treating the task as we would treat the emergency of a war, but at the same time, through this employment, accomplishing greatly needed projects to stimulate the use of our natural resources. . . .

The task can be helped by definite efforts to raise the values of agricultural products. . . . It can be helped by national planning for and supervision of all forms of transportation and of communications and other utilities which had a definitely public character. . . .

[T]here must be a strict supervision of all banking and credits and investments; there must be an end to speculation with other people's money, and there must be provision for an adequate but sound currency.❞

▲ President Franklin D. Roosevelt's ideas about how to deal with the Great Depression were very different from President Hoover's. How does this cartoon show Roosevelt's plan?

Using Primary Sources

1. Which speaker supported the idea that the best government is the one that governs the least? Why did he support that view?

2. If Roosevelt were President today, do you think he would support laws to protect the environment? Why or why not?

543

CHAPTER 1

America in the 1920s

OBJECTIVE: What were the goals and concerns of Americans in the 1920s?

1. On May 21, 1927, newspapers throughout the world announced an amazing achievement. Headlines told the story: "Lindy Does It—to Paris in 33½ hours." Lindy was Charles A. Lindbergh, a 25-year-old American aviator. He had flown a tiny airplane through fog, rain, and sleet nonstop across the Atlantic from Long Island, New York, to Paris, France. In Paris, thousands of people had waited anxiously at the airport to witness the arrival of the "Lone Eagle." Lindbergh was the first person to make the nonstop flight across the 3,600 miles (5,800 km) of ocean. In Washington, D.C., he was given the Congressional Medal of Honor. In New York, he was honored with a ticker tape parade. Lindbergh became an instant star.

2. The Lindbergh craze was one of many wild excitements of the 1920s. The age has been called the "Roaring Twenties" because of the boom in business and the excitement of popular fads. Crossword puzzles and flagpole sitting were among the many fads of the 20s. Behind the frantic search for enjoyment, major changes were taking place in American life.

▲ Charles Lindbergh is shown here standing in front of the tiny plane that carried him, all alone, on the first non-stop flight to Paris.

Return to Normalcy   What economic forces shaped America in the 1920s?

3. After World War I, Americans longed for what President Warren Harding called a "return to normalcy." To Americans, this meant the "good old days" before the war years. But new forces were taking Americans along a different path. By the 1920s, more Americans lived in cities than in rural areas. No longer were most people farmers. Instead most Americans worked in business and industry. After the war, business boomed. President Calvin Coolidge summed up

In Chapter 1, you will apply these critical thinking skills to the historical process:
○ **Generalizing:** Making a statement that links several facts.
▌ **Comparing and Contrasting:** Recognizing similarities and differences.

the 1920s when he declared, "The chief business of America is business."

4. During the Coolidge years, 1923 to 1929, business prospered. Many Americans earned more money than ever before. Factories increased their output to meet a growing demand for consumer goods, such as radios, washing machines, and refrigerators. The greatest boom occurred in the auto industry. In the early 1900s, only the rich could afford cars. Enter Henry Ford, the genius who invented the Model T, a lower-priced automobile. Aside from inventing the Model T, Ford introduced the assembly line. As you learned in Unit 10, the assembly line made it possible to produce cars much faster and more cheaply.

5. The boom in auto sales gave a boost to other industries. Cars needed steel, paint, tires, and gasoline. The country needed better roads so new highways were built. Gas stations and restaurants appeared along the new roads. The housing industry boomed as people moved out of crowded cities into suburbs.

People in History

6. Henry Ford Once Americans could buy cars, their daily life completely changed almost overnight. Henry Ford developed a car that was cheap and efficient. His cars also were sturdy enough to survive on the rough dirt roads of the early 1900s. Ford had little formal schooling, but he was fascinated with machines and mechanical inventions. In 1903, he set up the Ford Motor Company and was soon mass-producing the Model T Ford. Americans bought millions of his cars. No longer were Americans isolated in rural towns and villages. In their Model T's, farmers drove to the city, and city dwellers rode out into the country.

Life in the "Jazz Age" How did life change for many Americans in the 1920s?

7. New products such as cars changed the way of life for many Americans. Cars gave people the freedom to visit other parts of the

▲ As soon as Americans could afford to buy cars, driving became a favorite pastime. This photo was taken on a typical Sunday afternoon in St. Louis, Missouri, in the early 1900s.

country more easily than ever before. Radios and the movies brought further changes. They offered new forms of entertainment. Millions of Americans tuned in each night to their favorite radio programs. They heard news within hours after it happened. They could listen to broadcasts of the World Series and college football games. The movies created new heroes and heroines. Hollywood grew from a village into the movie capital of the world. Names of stars such as Charlie Chaplin, Clara Bow, and Rudolph Valentino were as familiar as Presidents Harding, Coolidge, and Hoover.

8. The 1920s are sometimes called the jazz age because this new, energetic kind of music reflected the spirit of the times. Jazz began

Background: Calvin Coolidge greatly admired business. "The man who builds a factory," Coolidge once said, "builds a temple . . . the man who works there worships there." Ask students to agree or disagree with Coolidge's view of business.

545

among African American musicians in New Orleans. In the 1920s, jazz swept the country and the world. Musicians such as Louis Armstrong won lasting fame for their contributions to jazz. They helped to fuel the **Harlem Renaissance** (HAHR-luhm REN-uh-sahns)**,** or rebirth of African American culture. In the 1920s, African American writers and artists flocked to Harlem in New York City. They produced novels, poems, and works of art that reflected the African experience in America.

Spotlight on Sources

9. One of the best-known authors of the Harlem Renaissance was Langston Hughes. Although Hughes published many books, plays, and other works, he had a hard time making a living as a writer. In poems such as "I, Too, Sing America," he dealt with the feelings of African Americans.

I, Too, Sing America

I, too, sing America.
I am the darker brother.
They send me to eat in the kitchen
When company comes,
But I laugh,
And eat well,
And grow strong.
Tomorrow,
I'll be at the table
When company comes.
Nobody'll dare
Say to me,
"Eat in the kitchen,"
Then.
Besides,
They'll see how beautiful I am
And be ashamed—
I, too, am America
                    —*Selected Poems*, Langston Hughes

▶ Whose "darker brother" is the poet? Why does he think "they" will be ashamed?

10. Thousands of African Americans of the 1920s were attracted to a movement started by Marcus Garvey. Garvey's ideas offered hope for a brighter future. Garvey, a Jamaican by birth, urged African Americans to rely on themselves rather on whites to improve their lives. A magnetic speaker, he told African Americans to be proud of their race and themselves as human beings. Because African Americans could not expect their lives to improve in the United States, he advised them to go "back to Africa." Garvey's movement fell apart when it was discovered that he had used his organization's money dishonestly. However, the sense of pride he brought to African Americans has survived to this day.

11. The changes of the 1920s also affected women's lives. The Nineteenth Amendment to the Constitution was ratified in 1920. Now, for

▼ Here a type of 1920s young woman known as a flapper is dancing to an exciting new kind of music known as jazz. Flappers were young women whose free behavior often shocked their elders.

Activity: Have students read a poem from the 1920s and use jazz music to accompany their reading.

the first time, women had the right to vote in national elections. New products made women's lives easier. Factories turned out low-priced, ready-made clothes so women did not have to spend their time sewing. The spread of electricity brought refrigerators, vacuum cleaners, and electric irons. These appliances made housework much easier. Women enjoyed new freedom. They "bobbed," or cut short, their hair and wore shorter skirts. Why would such behavior have been considered shocking before the war?

Behind the Prosperity   What groups did not share in the prosperity of the 1920s?

12. Not everyone in the 1920s shared in the pleasure and prosperity of the times. These years had their share of serious problems. Many factory workers and miners earned so little money that they could barely provide their families with the basics of life. Farmers produced more food than they could sell. As a result, prices for farm products remained low, leaving many farmers deeply in debt. Why did farm prices fall with increased production? Farm workers such as Mexican Americans in the Southwest earned low wages and so could not afford the new consumer goods.

13. The 1920s were also a time of lawlessness and crime. The Eighteenth Amendment, better known as the **Prohibition Amendment**, was adopted in 1919. It prohibited, or outlawed, the manufacture and sale of liquor in the United States. Millions of Americans broke the law, however. People known as **bootleggers** supplied liquor to fill the demand. Gangsters organized the illegal liquor trade and fought one another for control of cities. They **bribed** the police and public officials to allow them to operate. To bribe is to pay for an illegal favor. A sense of contempt for the law spread in the nation. In the end, Prohibition, which had been seen as a "noble experiment" failed, and the amendment was repealed in 1933.

14. The 1920s also saw renewed racist feeling against African Americans. During and after

World War I, many African Americans moved from rural areas in the South to cities in the North. They found work in the factories. However, race riots broke out as whites objected to the hiring of black workers. The Ku Klux Klan, which had terrorized blacks in the South during Reconstruction, gained new strength. It spread from the South to the largely Protestant white Midwest and West. The new Klan preached hatred of blacks, Catholics, Jews, and immigrants. Klan members attacked and terrorized individuals in an effort to drive them out their homes and jobs.

15. Feelings against foreign-born Americans also erupted in the 1920s. Millions of factory workers were immigrants who had come to the United States since the 1900s. When the workers went on strike for better pay, many native-born Americans feared a communist revolution. In 1919 and 1920, the United States was swept up in the **Red Scare.** Attorney General A. Mitchell Palmer had thousands of people arrested and jailed on the grounds that they were "reds." Reds were radicals who wanted to overthrow the government.

16. The Red Scare soon faded, but demands for limits on immigration increased. During the 1920s, Congress passed immigration laws that included a **quota** (KWO-tuh) **system.** Under this system, only a certain number of people would be allowed to enter the United States from each country. The quota system greatly limited the number of immigrants coming from Eastern Europe, China, and Japan. Was the United States right in limiting immigration?

Outlook

17. In 1928, Herbert Hoover, an able, energetic, self-made millionaire, won the office of President. As he took office, Hoover spoke confidently. "Ours is a land rich in resources . . . blessed with comfort and opportunity," he declared. "I have no fear for the future of our country." Like many Americans, Hoover expected the prosperity of the 1920s to continue. Was Hoover correct in predicting a rosy future for the United States? ◄

Ask: The quota system was set up to favor immigrants from western and northern Europe. Why did many Americans want to encourage immigration from those areas and limit it from other parts of Europe?

CHAPTER REVIEW

VOCABULARY REVIEW

▶ Write each of the following sentences on a sheet of paper. Then fill in the blank with the word that best completes each sentence.

bribed   Harlem Renaissance   bootleggers

Prohibition Amendment   Red Scare   quota system

1. During the _____ many Americans feared that workers might lead a communist revolution.

2. To limit immigration, Congress set up a _____ .

3. The _____ was intended to end the manufacture and sale of alcohol in the United States.

4. During the _____ , African Americans celebrated their cultural heritage.

5. People who smuggled illegal liquor were called _____ .

6. Gangsters _____ public officials so that they could continue illegal activities.

SKILL BUILDER: READING A MAP

▶ The map below is about an important part of African American history. Answer the questions that follow to test your skill at reading a map.

1. What do the vertical bars on the map show?

2. Which three cities had the largest African American populations from 1910 to 1920?

3. Which three cities had the largest increase in African American populations from 1910 to 1920?

4. Why is this part of African American history called the "Great Migration"?

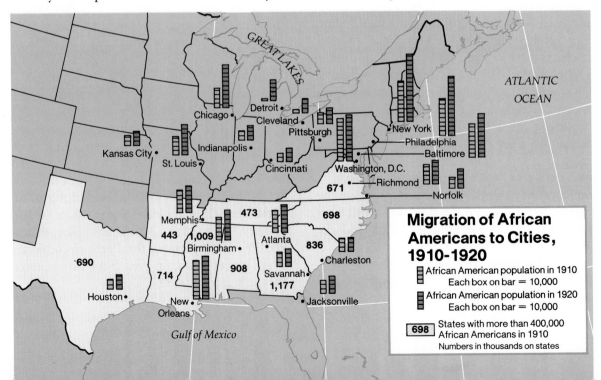

Migration of African Americans to Cities, 1910-1920

- African American population in 1910
  Each box on bar = 10,000
- African American population in 1920
  Each box on bar = 10,000

698 States with more than 400,000 African Americans in 1910

Numbers in thousands on states

Make a chart with two columns. Label one column "Changes" and the other "Effect on Daily Life." Then complete the chart by listing the major changes of the 1920s and explaining how each change affected people's lives.

SKILL BUILDER: CRITICAL THINKING AND COMPREHENSION

I. Generalizing

▶ Find sentences in the chapter that support the following generalizations. Write them on a sheet of paper.

1. The automobile had a great effect on the lives of Americans.

2. Some people did not share in the prosperity of the 1920s.

3. African Americans of the 1920s had a popular leader.

II. Comparing and Contrasting

▶ Copy the table below on a sheet of paper. Then complete each contrast by filling in the blanks with information from the chapter.

	Before World War I	After World War I
1. Women's hairstyles	long hair	short "bobbed" hair
2. Where many African Americans lived		
3. Heroes and heroines		
4. Where most Americans lived		
5. Roads in the United States		
6. Women's right to vote		

USING PRIMARY SOURCES

▶ Reread the Spotlight on Sources on page 546. What does the poem tell you about the feelings of African Americans?

ENRICHMENT

1. A famous trial took place in the 1920s involving two foreign-born workers, Sacco and Vanzetti. They were accused of having committed a murder during a holdup. Find out about the Sacco and Vanzetti trial. Then prepare a debate on whether or not the accused received a fair trial.

2. Prepare a brief illustrated report on the dances of the 1920s.

3. Investigate the career of Marcus Garvey as a leader of African Americans in the 1920s. Find out why so many people were attracted to his movement. Learn how other African American leaders felt about Garvey and his message.

4. Use encyclopedias or other reference books to find out more about Lindbergh's flight. Sketch or build a model of his plane and give a brief presentation to the class, explaining the risks involved in his flight.

CHAPTER 2

The Great Depression and the New Deal

> **OBJECTIVE:** What did the government do to help Americans during the hard times of the 1930s?

1. "Anyone not only can be rich but ought to be rich." These encouraging words came from John J. Raskob, a top General Motors executive. In the spring and summer of 1929 thousands of Americans bought shares of company stocks. Doctors, factory workers, homemakers by the thousands put all or part of their savings into stocks. Week after week, they saw stock prices reach new highs. Stories spread about poor widows who made fortunes from the stock market or plumbers buying huge estates with their new wealth.

2. Then on Tuesday, October 29, 1929, prices crashed, and the life savings of many people were wiped out in hours. Black Tuesday, as the day was later called, marked the end of the Roaring Twenties. It brought in a period of hard times known as the **Great Depression.** A depression is a time when production and sales of goods decline and many people are unemployed. The Great Depression was the worst economic crisis in the nation's history. Many other countries of the world also had serious depressions at this time.

▲ In the Great Depression, many people had so little money that they had to depend on breadlines like this as their main source of food.

The Great Depression What were the causes of the Great Depression?

3. The production of goods that people could not afford to buy was a major cause of the Great Depression. As you have read, many workers and farmers did not share in the prosperity of the 1920s. They did not have the money to buy the goods factories were producing. Factories cut back on production and laid off workers. Workers without jobs were not able to buy goods so the demand fell further.

In Chapter 2, you will apply these critical thinking skills to the historical process:

Classifying: Organizing facts into categories based on what they have in common.

Predicting: Telling what you will believe will happen on the basis of clues and facts.

4. The failure of many banks helped deepen the depression. Thousands of banks had made loans to people who could not repay them after the stock market crash. When banks closed, customers lost their life savings. Furthermore, banks stopped making loans to businesses. At the same time, many businesses went bankrupt.

Hard Times   What hardships did Americans face during the 1930s?

5. By 1932, almost one in every four workers was unemployed. Millions of jobless people could not pay their rent or mortgages. Many were **evicted** or put out of their homes. Many families lived in shanties made of cardboard boxes. The unemployed workers lined up for hours in the hope of getting work. Breadlines formed in almost every city. People hunted through garbage for scraps to feed hungry children.

 Spotlight on Sources

6. At first, government and business leaders assured Americans that the hard times would soon end. Instead, conditions grew worse. Popular songs, like "Brother, Can You Spare a Dime?" showed how helpless Americans felt.

Once I built a railroad,
Made it run,
Made it race against time.
Once I built a railroad; now it's done.
Brother, can you spare a dime?

And so I followed the mob—
When there was earth to plough or guns to bear
I was always there—right on the job.
They used to tell me I was building a dream
With peace and glory ahead—
Why should I be standing in line
Just waiting for bread?
        —Copyright 1932 by Harms, Inc.

▶ What were the three accomplishments of the person in the song?

The New Deal   How did the government respond to the Great Depression?

7. In the election of 1932, Americans turned to a new leader, Franklin Delano Roosevelt. During the campaign, Roosevelt promised Americans a "**New Deal**." On taking office, Roosevelt moved swiftly. Between March and June 1933, many New Deal laws were passed. First came a law to end the banking crisis. The new law regulated banks so that people's money would be protected. Other laws set up programs to hire the jobless. The federal government helped state and local agencies employ people for **public works programs**. The programs included building roads, post offices, and schools. Some New Deal laws were written to help farmers by paying them to raise fewer crops. Why did the President want farmers to ◀ cut back on their production of crops? Other laws set up guidelines for industry that would

▼ One New Deal program was the Civilian Conservation Corps (CCC). In the CCC young men built bridges, planted trees, and worked on flood control.

Background: Children remembered the Great Depression as a time when they did not have enough to eat, had no heat or electricity at home, and hid whenever the bill collectors came around.

The Dust Bowl   In the 1930s, in Midwestern cities like St. Louis, Missouri, and Chicago, Illinois, great clouds hid the sun for days at a time. The clouds consisted of dust that had been blown by strong winds from hundreds of miles away in a region of the Great Plains that came to be called the Dust Bowl. The dust was really bare soil that had been picked up by the winds because there were no plants to hold the soil in place.

The Dust Bowl lies in an area that receives varying amounts of rainfall. Most of the region receives an average of less than the 20 inches (51 cm) of rain a year that are needed to grow a variety of crops. Most Dust Bowl land receives an average of only 15 inches (38 cm) of rain. Only a crop like wheat can be grown with this amount of rainfall.

Aside from the changing average amount of rainfall, Dust Bowl farmers never know how much rain will fall in any given year. The map below shows how the location of the 20-inch (51-cm) line of rainfall changes in wet and dry years. When this line moves west there is plenty of rain, and Dust Bowl farmers prosper. When the 20-inch (51 cm) rainfall line moves east, Dust Bowl farms are too dry, and farmers there get only small crops or no crops at all.

Before 1900, the plains were used for cattle grazing. The natural vegetation of short grasses had roots deep enough to survive the dry years, and the deep-rooted grasses protected the soil from blowing away. Then, beginning in the 1900s, new farm machinery made it possible for one farmer to plant and harvest hundreds of acres. The flat plains looked like an ideal place to farm with the new machines, despite the varying amounts of rainfall.

The prosperous 1920s coincided with a series of wet years, and plains farmers made a great deal of money. They expanded their farms to land normally too dry for growing wheat. Then two unfavorable developments hit the farmers. Wheat prices dropped sharply in the Great Depression of the 1930s. At the same time, a long period of drought also set in. As a result, the wheat dried up in the fields, and the dust storms began. Many prairie farmers went bankrupt. Others moved away. Those who remained had to learn to adjust to the risk of drought and how to protect the soil.

Now use the map to answer these questions.

1. What states were most affected by the Dust Bowl of the 1930s?

2. What is the importance of the 20-inch (51 cm) rainfall line?

3. Explain why you think farming was good for the Dust Bowl region. Why was it bad?

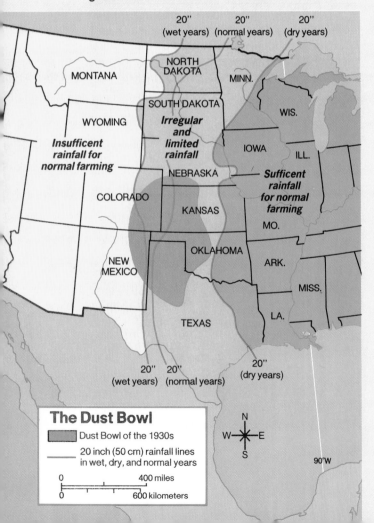

The Dust Bowl

Dust Bowl of the 1930s

20 inch (50 cm) rainfall lines in wet, dry, and normal years

0   400 miles
0   600 kilometers

protect jobs and ensure safe working conditions. Still other laws regulated the stock market to prevent another crash.

8. One of the most daring New Deal programs was the **Tennessee Valley Authority,** or TVA. The TVA brought new life to an entire large region of the country, the extremely poor Tennessee Valley. Under the TVA, dams were built to produce electricity and control floods. Forests were planted to protect the soil, and farmers were taught new methods of producing crops. The TVA built fertilizer factories. The Tennessee River was made into an important waterway.

Effects of the New Deal   How did the New Deal change American society?

9. New Deal laws helped working people and the elderly. Laws were passed that helped labor unions bargain for better working conditions and wages. Congress passed the Social Security Act. This law set up **pensions** (PEN-shuhnz), or retirement income, for people who stopped working at age 65. The law also provided unemployment benefits for people who had lost their jobs.

10. Under the New Deal, the government took a much larger role in the lives of ordinary Americans. Not everyone agreed that this was right. Critics of the New Deal warned that the government was becoming too powerful. The government, they said, should not interfere in the economy. Nevertheless, many Americans came to expect the government would help solve economic and social problems.

People in History

11. Eleanor Roosevelt   During the 1930s, Eleanor Roosevelt, the President's wife, worked tirelessly. She traveled to areas hard hit by the depression. She helped out in soup kitchens and offered hope that the New Deal would bring better times. Eleanor Roosevelt served as the "eyes and ears" of her husband, the President. But she did much more. She promoted laws to

▲ Eleanor Roosevelt addressing a meeting as noted educator Mary McLeod Bethune listens.

provide job training for young Americans. She spoke against racial prejudice. She prodded the government to improve education, housing, and medical care. Eleanor Roosevelt was both admired and criticized. Supporters praised her efforts to help the needy. Critics claimed the First Lady should stay out of politics. But all agreed that she was the most active First Lady America had ever had.

Outlook

12. The Great Depression left generations of Americans with grim memories of years of struggle. Minority groups such as African Americans suffered more than whites. They were laid off first and were often refused public works jobs. The Great Depression dragged on throughout the 1930s. In the end, it was not the New Deal that ended the hard times but World War II. Why do you think a war might lead the country out of a deep depression?

553

CHAPTER REVIEW

VOCABULARY REVIEW

▶ Each of the following statements uses one of the vocabulary words from this chapter. Decide whether the statement is true or false. If a statement is false, rewrite it to make it true.

1. The Tennessee Valley Authority was set up to end the Dust Bowl.

2. The stock market crash helped trigger the Great Depression.

3. The main purpose of public works programs was to improve the appearance of cities.

4. The New Deal was President Hoover's program to limit the power of the government.

5. During the Great Depression, many people were evicted because they could not pay their rent.

6. Older people collect pensions once they retire from their jobs.

SKILL BUILDER: INTERPRETING A PHOTOGRAPH

▶ Look at the photograph below. Then answer the questions that follow on a separate sheet of paper.

1. From what you have read in the chapter, in what part of the United States do you think the people in the photograph live?

2. In this picture, a father and his sons make their way home through a blinding dust storm. What does this photograph show about the effects of the weather?

3. What kind of work do you think these people did? Why do you think so?

SKILL BUILDER: CRITICAL THINKING AND COMPREHENSION

I. Classifying

▶ Copy the two headings below on a separate sheet of paper. Then write each of the statements 1–6 under the correct heading.

Heading 1: Causes of the Great Depression

Heading 2: Things That Happened During the Great Depression

Statements to Classify:

1. Factories laid off workers since people were not buying goods.

2. Stock prices went down.

3. Banks stopped making loans.

4. The government built schools and post offices.

5. The Social Security Act was passed.

6. Many people were evicted because they couldn't pay the rent.

II. Predicting

▶ Read each of the statements below. Then write your predictions on a sheet of paper.

1. The time is the Great Depression. You have just lost your job and you have no money to feed your family. What might you do to help your family?

2. It is March 1933. You have just been inaugurated President. Predict which of the nation's problems you would take action on immediately.

3. You own a farm in the Dust Bowl. Predict what you would do to improve your life.

USING PRIMARY SOURCES

▶ Reread "Brother, Can You Spare a Dime?" on page 551. Explain how the song expresses the feeling of many people in the Great Depression.

ENRICHMENT

1. During the Great Depression, many people wrote to President or Mrs. Roosevelt describing their troubles and asking for help. Imagine you are a man, woman, or child living in a particular region of the United States during the depression. Write a letter to the President about the troubles you face.

2. During the depression, many Americans escaped from the hardships of daily life by going to the movies. Find out which movies were popular during the depression. Then make a poster advertising one of the movies of the 1930s.

3. Look in books about the depression and find two or three pictures that you think capture the spirit of the times. Show the pictures to the class and explain why you chose them.

CHAPTER 3

World War II Begins

OBJECTIVE: Why was the world plunged into war again in 1939?

1. "So many people are worried that the dignity of our country will be imperiled [endangered] by inviting Royalty to a . . . hot dog picnic." So wrote Eleanor Roosevelt, the President's wife, in June 1939. This was two weeks before King George VI and Queen Elizabeth of Great Britain were to come to the United States. It would be the first time a reigning British monarch would visit the country. The First Lady need not have worried. The hot dog picnic was a huge success. The royal couple apparently enjoyed the American specialty, judging from the news photographs.

2. As the royal couple prepared to leave the United States, the President bade them farewell. "Good luck to you," he said. "All the luck in the world!" The British monarch would need "All the luck in the world." Within months of the royal visit, Europe would again be plunged into a devastating world war. Why? The answer lies in part with the ruthless dictators who had risen to power in Europe and Asia.

▲ Thousands of British people were made homeless by German bombing raids in 1940. Here a London family stands amid the furnishings they were able to rescue from the wreckage of their home.

The Rise of Dictators How did dictators come to power in Europe?

3. Because many European nations suffered from serious political and economic problems after World War I, dictators were able to rise to power. In Italy, an ambitious leader, Benito Mussolini, seized power in 1922. With the aid of his followers in the **Fascist Party**, Mussolini established a dictatorship. Many Italians supported Mussolini because he promised to restore order at home and build an empire abroad. Mussolini pursued his goal of empire by invading the African nation of Ethiopia in 1935. A

In Chapter 3, you will apply these critical thinking skills to the historical process:
▲ **Recognizing Main Idea:** Identifying the most important idea in a paragraph.

Recognizing Cause and Effect: Recognizing the action or event that makes something happen; identifying the result of an action or event.

few years later, Mussolini seized Albania in Eastern Europe.

4. Economic and political troubles helped another dictator, Adolf Hitler, to gain power in Germany. In the 1920s, Germany suffered from severe inflation. Prices skyrocketed, and money became worthless. Hitler organized the Nationalist Socialist, or **Nazi**, party. Hitler blamed the Jews for Germany's defeat in World War I and for its postwar economic problems. When the Great Depression struck Germany, many people turned to Hitler. They believed that only he could solve the nation's problems. In 1933, Hitler became dictator of Germany. He silenced critics, ended freedom of the press, and built up Germany's military forces. Hitler made Germany into a **totalitarian state.** In a totalitarian state, a single political party controls the government and strictly regulates the lives of the people. Later, the Nazis forced Jews and anyone who opposed them into concentration camps where they were tortured and murdered.

5. In the Soviet Union, another dictator, Joseph Stalin, held power in the 1930s. Like Germany under Hitler, the Soviet Union under Stalin was a totalitarian state. Stalin feared Hitler's ambitions to expand German territory. During the 1930s, therefore, he tried to strengthen the nation's armed forces.

Japan Expands in Asia Why did Japan seize lands in Asia?

6. The Great Depression brought disaster to Japan. The Japanese economy depended on world trade, but the depression slowed this trade to a trickle. In the resulting crisis, a group of military leaders seized power. They plotted to conquer all of Asia and gain control of raw materials that their tiny island nation needed. In 1931, Japan began its **aggression** by invading Manchuria in northeastern China. Aggression is any warlike act by one country against another without just cause. By 1937, Japanese forces occupied much of China's territory.

7. The United States responded to Japanese actions by condemning its aggression. President Roosevelt warned that such acts threatened the

▼ In 1939, Nazi soldiers rounded up the Jews of Warsaw, Poland, where thousands died. They were sent to concentration camps.

Background: Mussolini was known as Il Duce, or the leader. He established strict control of the economy and strengthened the military. He banned opposition political parties and taught total obedience to the state. "Mussolini is always right."

peace of the world. However, most Americans wanted to avoid war at any cost. They supported the policy of **isolationism** (eye-soh-LAY-shun-izm). That is, they believed the United States should stay out of world affairs.

The Road to War   What events led to the outbreak of World War II?

8. While Japan was seizing lands in Asia, Mussolini and Hitler were creating their own empires. As you have read, Mussolini invaded Ethiopia in 1935. Hitler rearmed Germany although the Treaty of Versailles had forbidden it. In 1936 Hitler and Mussolini formed a military alliance known as the **Rome–Berlin Axis**. (Later, Japan joined the Axis powers.) In 1938, Hitler annexed Austria and then claimed part of Czechoslovakia.

9. Leaders in Britain and France followed a policy of **appeasement**. Appeasement is a policy of giving in to aggressor nations in order to keep the peace. The Europeans remembered the horrors of World War I and wanted to avoid another bloody conflict. They condemned Axis aggression but took no other action. At the **Munich Conference** in 1938, Britain and France agreed to Hitler's demand for part of Czechoslovakia. In exchange, Hitler promised not to take any more territory. Ignoring his promise, however, Hitler soon seized the rest of Czechoslovakia. His next goal was Poland. Alarmed, Britain and France agreed to stand by Poland. Why did the policy of appeasement not work in stopping Axis aggression? ◄

10. By the summer of 1939, the threat of war hung over Europe. In August, Hitler signed a treaty with Stalin. Although the two dictators despised each other, they agreed not to attack each other. The treaty allowed Hitler to invade Poland without having to fight the Soviets. Then, without warning, on September 1, 1939, German forces poured into Poland and overwhelmed it. Two days later, Britain and France declared war on Germany. World War II was now under way. How were Britain's and ◄ France's actions different from the way they had dealt with Hitler in 1938?

▼ Adolf Hitler, the German dictator, enjoyed the support of most of the German people in his bid to conquer all of Europe. This goal led to the start of World War II in 1939.

World War II What successes did the Axis powers have in the early years of the war?

11. World War II quickly spread around the globe. The major Axis powers were Germany, Italy, and Japan. The Allies included Britain, France, China, and later the Soviet Union and the United States. In Asia, Japan continued its conquests, seizing most of China and Southeast Asia. In Europe, many nations fell to the German **blitzkrieg** (BLITS-kreeg), or lightning war. Using airplanes, tanks, and heavy guns, Nazi forces crushed Denmark, Norway, Holland, and Belgium. France fell to the German onslaught in June 1940.

12. Hitler then planned to invade Great Britain. The German air force began a series of brutal air raids on British military bases and cities. This was the first step in Hitler's plan for the German armies to sweep across the English Channel. In this **Battle of Britain**, German bombs rained down day after day. Winston Churchill, the new British prime minister, gave the British people the courage to withstand the attacks. With stirring words, he declared, "We shall defend our island, whatever the cost may be. We shall fight on the beaches. We shall fight on the landing grounds. We shall fight on the fields and in the streets. We shall fight in the hills. We shall never surrender."

People in History

13. Edward R. Murrow "This . . . is London," the familiar American voice crackled over the airwaves. Each night through the autumn of 1940, Americans tuned their radios to hear Edward R. Murrow report on the German bombing of London during the Battle of Britain. Murrow's eyewitness accounts of a city under siege helped Americans understand the horrors of war. Night after night, Murrow reported from rooftops as air raid sirens wailed and bombs thundered in the background. Murrow described the bombs falling and told of the courage of bomb squads that removed unexploded bombs before the next batch was

dropped. He reported, too, how Londoners went out to work each day in the midst of smashed homes and blocks of buildings destroyed by explosions.

Spotlight on Sources

14. Early in 1941, President Franklin D. Roosevelt outlined his goals for the postwar world in his famous "Four Freedoms" speech.

> In the future days, . . . we look forward to a world founded upon four essential [necessary] human freedoms. The first is freedom of speech and expression—everywhere in the world. The second is freedom of every person to worship God in his own way—everywhere in the world. The third is freedom from want—which . . . will secure to every nation a healthy peacetime life for its inhabitants [people]—everywhere in the world. The fourth is freedom from fear—which . . . means a worldwide reduction of armaments [weapons of war] . . . [so] that no nation will be in a position to commit an act of physical aggression [attack] against any neighbor—anywhere in the world.
> —Four Freedoms Speech, January 6, 1941

What would be the effect on world peace if ◄ these goals were adopted in peace treaties?

Outlook

15. By 1941, the outlook was grim for those who believed in democratic freedoms. Brutal dictators in Germany, Italy, and Japan had pounded their neighbors into defeat. With the resources of the countries they had seized, the Axis powers seemed unbeatable. But the Allies kept fighting. Before year's end, two powerful nations would join the Allies in the fighting. In June 1941, Hitler invaded the Soviet Union. The invasion would prove more costly than he could have imagined. In December 1941, the United States would be swept into the fighting. Why do you think the United States became ◄ involved in World War II?

Ask: Have students organize a debate around this topic: Appeasement was a major cause of World War II.

CHAPTER REVIEW

VOCABULARY REVIEW

▶ Match each name or term in Column 1 with the correct definition in Column 2.

1. Fascist party
2. Nazi party
3. totalitarian state
4. aggression
5. isolationism
6. Rome–Berlin Axis
7. appeasement
8. Munich Conference
9. blitzkrieg
10. Battle of Britain

a. bombing of Britain by German planes

b. policy of staying out of world affairs

c. Mussolini's political party

d. any warlike act by one country against another without just cause

e. giving in to an aggressor to keep peace

f. Hitler's political party

g. military alliance between Hitler and Mussolini

h. a country in which one political party controls the government and the lives of the people

i. to build an empire

j. meeting at which Britain and France gave in to Hitler's demand for part of Czechoslovakia

k. lightning war fought by Germans

SKILL BUILDER: MAKING A TIME LINE

▶ Copy the time line below, which covers a 20-year period, onto a sheet of paper. Then place the following events leading to World War II with their dates on the time line.

Mussolini seizes power

Hitler becomes dictator

Hitler annexes Austria

Japan invades Manchuria

Rome–Berlin Axis formed

Hitler invades Russia

Germany invades Poland

Britain and France declare war on Germany

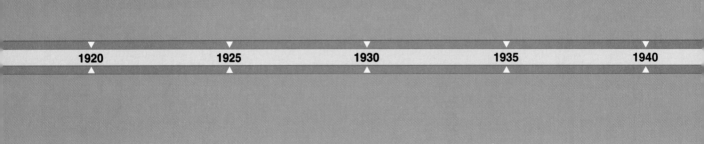

| 1920 | 1925 | 1930 | 1935 | 1940 |

SKILL BUILDER: CRITICAL THINKING AND COMPREHENSION

▲ I. Main Idea

▶ Several main ideas from Chapter 3 are listed below. Write each main idea. Under each main idea write three facts that support the main idea.

1. By 1940, it looked as though the Axis Powers might conquer the world.

2. After World War I, dictators rose to power in several European countries.

3. The policy of appeasement did not stop Hitler's aggression.

❯ II. Predicting

▶ On a separate sheet of paper, predict what might have happened if the following had taken place. Give reasons for your prediction.

1. Great Britain and France refused to allow Hitler to take over Czechoslovakia in 1938.

2. Stalin refused to sign a treaty with Hitler in 1939.

⇨ III. Cause and Effect

▶ On a separate sheet of paper, write the missing cause or effect.

1. **Cause:** _____
   Effect: Britain and France declared war on Germany.

2. **Cause:** The Japanese economy depended on world trade, and the Great Depression had greatly slowed trade.
   Effect: _____

3. **Cause:** Most Americans wanted to avoid war at all cost.
   Effect: _____

USING PRIMARY SOURCES

▶ Reread President Franklin Roosevelt's "Four Freedoms" speech on page 559. What form of government do you think the President wanted for other nations? Why do you think so?

ENRICHMENT

1. Read more about the Battle of Britain. Then imagine you are an American living in Great Britain in 1941. Write at least three postcards to friends back home in the United States about what is happening in Great Britain.

2. Create an illustrated time line for events leading up to the outbreak of World War II.

3. In a small group, research the Munich Conference in order to write a radio play about it. Include dialogue between the British and French leaders and Hitler.

⚭ 4. Role-play a broadcast by Edward R. Murrow. One person should play the part of Murrow and broadcast a short report on the Battle of Britain. Others should play the part of an American family reacting to the broadcast.

CHAPTER 4

The United States in World War II

OBJECTIVE: How did the Allies succeed in defeating the Axis nations?

1. For most Americans, Sunday, December 7, 1941, started as a quiet day. In the afternoon, as usual, many were listening to the weekly broadcast of a symphony concert from New York. But in the middle of the broadcast, an anxious voice broke in with the announcement that Japanese bombers had attacked Pearl Harbor. Most Americans had never heard of Pearl Harbor, Hawaii, an important naval base in the Pacific. Early that morning sailors on board the American warships at anchor in the harbor had been busy with their duties. Suddenly, Japanese planes appeared overhead, catching the American navy wholly unprepared. The planes dropped their bombs with deadly results. They left behind 19 ships burned or sunk and more than 2,400 Americans dead. The bombing of Pearl Harbor immediately brought the United States into World War II.

Arsenal of Democracy Why did the United States help the Allies during the early years of the war?

2. When World War II broke out, President Roosevelt announced that the United States would remain neutral. In 1939, Americans were still recovering from the Great Depression. They had no energy to spare for war. Yet, as Nazi forces swept across Europe in 1940, Roosevelt realized that aiding the Allies would

▲ This statue in Arlington, Virginia, shows U.S. marines raising the American flag on the Pacific island of Iwo Jima in March 1945 after defeating the Japanese there.

be in America's best interest. In what way would this be true? Roosevelt pushed Congress to aid the Allies. "We must become the 'arsenal' of democracy," he declared. An **arsenal** is a place where weapons are made and stored. If Britain fell to the Axis power, he claimed, the

In Chapter 4, you will apply these critical thinking skills to the historical process:

562   ▲ **Summarizing:** Giving the main idea of a group of paragraphs in brief form.   ◼ **Comparing and Contrasting:** Recognizing similarities and differences.

Americas would be "living at the point of a gun—a gun loaded with explosive bullets, economic as well as military." In March 1941, the President signed the **Lend-Lease Act.** This law let the President sell or lend war materials to the Allies. Soon convoys of American ships were ferrying planes, tanks, and guns to Britain.

War Is Declared   Why was the United States forced to declare war in 1941?

3. As Japan continued its advance in Southeast Asia, relations with the United States worsened. The United States stopped selling oil and other goods to Japan while diplomats on both sides tried to ease the growing tension. Yet, even as the talks dragged on, leaders in Japan made the decision to attack the United States. As you read at the beginning of this chapter, that attack came on December 7, 1941.

4. On the day after Pearl Harbor, a solemn, angry President asked Congress to declare war on Japan. December 7, he said, was "a date which will live in infamy [disgrace]". Congress quickly passed a declaration of war. Japan followed up its bombing of Pearl Harbor with attacks on the Philippines, Guam, and other American possessions in the Pacific. As Japanese forces stormed across the Pacific, the outlook for the United States looked desperate.

Americans Mobilize for War   How did Americans help the war effort?

5. With their country now in the war, Americans rallied to the cause. They lent the government money by buying millions of dollars worth of war bonds. The government put the economy on a war footing. Factories changed from making cars and refrigerators to producing tanks and airplanes. Men were drafted or enlisted in the armed services. Women, too, joined the military. Many women took jobs in offices and factories or managed farms, replacing men who had gone to war.

6. Americans of all backgrounds united behind the war effort. Despite discrimination and

THE PRESIDENTS' CORNER

Americans associate **Franklin D. Roosevelt**, who was President from 1933 to 1945, with three outstanding achievements. The first is his courage in coping with the crippling effects of polio. When he was 39 years old, he was stricken with this dread disease. For the rest of his life, he was unable to walk without braces on his legs. His second great achievement was launching the New Deal, which was a series of laws that aimed to lift the United States out of the greatest depression it had ever known. Finally, Roosevelt was also a strong leader of the Allied struggle against the Axis in the World War II. He was the only President to have been elected to that office four times. Not all Americans approved of Roosevelt's policies, but few deny that he was a great political leader.

racial prejudice, Americans of minority groups enlisted in the armed forces in large numbers. Although African Americans were forced into segregated, or all-black, units, they proved their courage under fire. Spanish-speaking Americans and Native Americans also wore their uniforms proudly, fighting heroically for their country.

7. World War II brought tragedy to Japanese Americans. After the bombing of Pearl Harbor, some Americans claimed that Japanese Americans on the West Coast were a danger to the nation. They feared they might spy for the Japanese government. No evidence was ever given to support this claim, but the government acted on this fear. It forced Japanese Americans to sell their property and move to "relocation" camps inland. There they lived in shabby barracks surrounded by barbed wire. Despite this harsh treatment, thousands of Japanese Americans in the armed forces served loyally.

The Drive to Victory   How did the Allies win the war in Europe and in the Pacific?

8. Between 1942 and 1944, the Allies launched attacks in North Africa, Europe, and the Pacific. After regaining control of North Africa, they pushed across the Mediterranean into Sicily and Italy. The Italian dictator Mussolini was overthrown, but the Allies had to battle German forces that controlled much of Italy. In the meantime, German armies had bogged down in their attack on the Soviet Union. The Soviets suffered terribly under German sieges, but in the end they forced the Germans into retreat.

9. On June 6, 1944, Allied forces under General Dwight D. Eisenhower crossed the English Channel to start a drive that would take them to the heart of Germany. On **D-Day**, as it came to be called, 9,000 vessels carried thousands of troops, who stormed ashore along the beaches of Normandy, France. This was the largest amphibious (am-FIB-ee-uhs), or combined land and water operation, in history. The Allied forces met with deadly German resistance, but six weeks later, they broke through German coastal defenses and headed for Paris. They captured the French capital in August 1944. By September, Eisenhower's forces had reached the western border of Germany.

10. The Soviet army, meanwhile, was making a strong push from the east and took Berlin, Hitler's stronghold, in April 1945. When Hitler realized that defeat was certain, he committed suicide in his shelter deep below the streets of Berlin. Why do you think he took this action? ◀ On May 7, 1945, a week after Hitler's death, Germany's military leaders agreed to an unconditional surrender. The next day, the Western world celebrated V-E Day, Victory in Europe Day. After more than five years and eight months, the war in Europe was over.

11. In the Pacific, the Allies gained ground slowly. The United States adopted an **island-hopping** plan. That is, they set out to retake some islands held by the Japanese and bypass

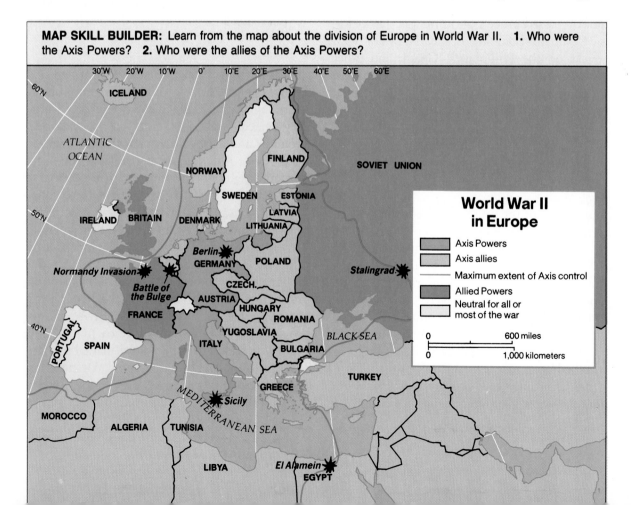

MAP SKILL BUILDER: Learn from the map about the division of Europe in World War II.   **1.** Who were the Axis Powers?   **2.** Who were the allies of the Axis Powers?

World War II in Europe

- Axis Powers
- Axis allies
- Maximum extent of Axis control
- Allied Powers
- Neutral for all or most of the war

0 — 600 miles
0 — 1,000 kilometers

others. They planned to use the captured islands as stepping stones toward the Philippines, which the Japanese had captured in 1942. Once they freed the Philippines, the Allies planned to attack Japan itself. By early 1945, American bombers were attacking Japanese cities in preparation for an invasion.

People in History

12. Bob Hope   For American soldiers, or GIs, as they were called, thousands of miles from home, nothing was more welcome than the visits of entertainers from back home. The most popular of these entertainers was the British-born comedian Bob Hope. War-weary troops laughed and cheered as Hope brought his quick wit and humor to bases around the world. For a few minutes, GIs could forget the horrors of battle and laugh at Hope's jokes. With a troupe of dancers and singers, Hope covered hundreds of thousands of miles flying to Africa, to Britain, to Sicily, to the Pacific, wherever troops were stationed. With endless energy, he gave several shows a day at one base before catching a plane to the next one. Hope claimed that he never tired of entertaining the troops. "I love it," he explained. "I don't consider it work." President Kennedy later called Hope "America's most prized ambassador of goodwill throughout the world."

Spotlight on Sources

13. During World War II, reporter Ernie Pyle lived in the front lines with American troops in North Africa and Italy. He died on the front lines in the Pacific. In this report, Pyle pays tribute to American soldiers who were fighting in North Africa.

I love the infantry because they are the underdogs. They are the mud-rain-frost-and-wind boys. They have no comforts, and they even learn to live without the necessities. And in the end they are the guys that wars can't be won without. . . .
On their shoulders and backs they carry

heavy steel tripods, machine gun barrels, leaden boxes of ammunition. Their feet seem to sink into the ground from the overload they are bearing. . . . In their eyes as they pass is not hatred, not excitement, not despair, not the tonic of their victory. There is just the simple expression of being there as if they had been doing that forever, and nothing else.

—from *Voices from America's Past*, volume 3, ed. by Richard B. Morris and James Woodruff

What does Pyle admire about the infantry?   ◀

14. In April 1945, President Franklin D. Roosevelt died suddenly and was succeeded by Harry S. Truman. The new President faced a difficult decision. The United States had developed a deadly new weapon, the atomic bomb. Truman's advisers argued that the bomb would end the war quickly and save American lives in the battle for Japan. Truman called on the Japanese to surrender or face destruction. They did not reply. On August 6, 1945, an American bomber dropped an atomic bomb on Hiroshima, Japan, killing about 100,000 people. Three days later, a second bomb was dropped on Nagasaki. On August 14, the Japanese surrendered. This day is known as V-J Day, the day of victory over Japan.

Outlook

15. When World War II ended, both the victors and the losers were exhausted. For six years, the nations of the world had pounded each other into ruins. Only the United States had escaped the destructive air war that left cities in rubble. What hope did the future hold? In August 1941, even before the United States had entered the war, President Roosevelt met with the British prime minister, Winston Churchill. The two signed the **Atlantic Charter**, a statement outlining goals for the postwar world. In it, they agreed to seek no territorial gains, to "respect the right of all peoples to choose the form of government under which they will live," and to set up a "permanent system of general security." Were those goals ◀ met after the war?

Background: In 1948, President Truman ended segregation in the armed services.

565

CHAPTER REVIEW

VOCABULARY REVIEW

▶ Write each of the following sentences on a sheet of paper. Then fill in the blank with the word that best completes each sentence.

Lend-Lease Act   island hopping   arsenal

D-Day   Atlantic Charter

1. The Allied invasion of France in 1944 is known as _____ .

2. The purpose of the _____ was to outline the goals for the postwar world.

3. Under the _____ , the United States helped the Allies by sending them war supplies.

4. In the Pacific war, the United States began by _____ to gain bases from which to invade the Philippines and Japan.

5. Weapons are made and stored in the _____ .

SKILL BUILDER: INTERPRETING A MAP

▶ Locate on the map the island "stepping stones" used by the Allies to close in on Japan in World War II. Then answer the following questions on a separate sheet of paper.

1. What islands lie between Australia and Japan?

2. What islands lie between Hawaii and Japan?

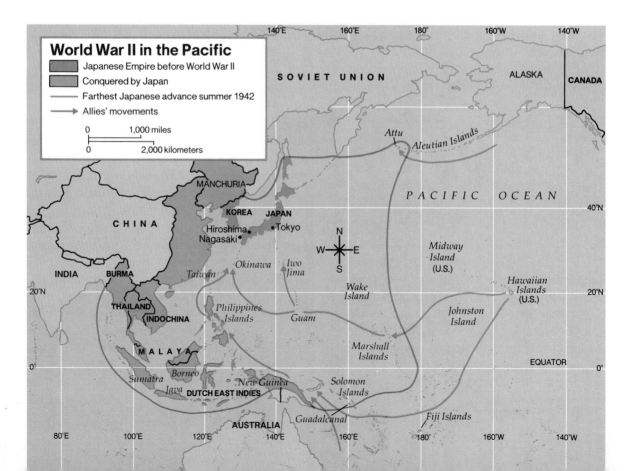

▲ I. Summarizing

▶ Summarize each of the following events on a separate sheet of paper. Write at least two sentences in each of your summaries.

1. The American plan to overcome Japan

2. Bob Hope's contribution to the war effort

3. What happened on the home front during the war

▌ II. Comparing and Contrasting

▶ Answer the following activities on a separate sheet of paper.

1. Compare the actions of President Roosevelt and President Truman during World War II.

2. Contrast the invasion of Normandy Beach with the bombing of Pearl Harbor. In your answer, state who was the aggressor, the mode of attack, and the locations.

3. Contrast the final year of the war in Europe with the attack on Japan.

▶ III. Drawing Conclusions

▶ On a separate sheet of paper, write the conclusion you can draw from each of the following statements.

1. Japan bombed Pearl Harbor and then took the Philippines and Guam in the Pacific.

2. After entering the war, the United States needed war supplies almost overnight and was able to produce them.

3. There was no evidence to show the Japanese Americans were disloyal to the United States, but they were placed in "relocation" camps.

USING PRIMARY SOURCES

▶ Reread the Spotlight on Sources on page 565. How do you think Ernie Pyle came to develop this attitude toward the infantry?

ENRICHMENT

1. Choose a major battle in World War II such as El Alamein, Midway, Coral Sea, Iwo Jima, or the Battle of the Bulge. Then write a brief report telling where and when the battle took place, why it was important, and who won.

2. Interview someone who remembers the day of the attack on Pearl Harbor. Prepare for the interview by reading more about the events surrounding the attack and by making a list of questions to ask your subject.

3. Imagine you are an Allied or Axis commander such as Dwight Eisenhower, George S. Patton, or Erwin Rommel. Give an oral report on "My Most Frustrating Moment in the War."

CHAPTER 5

The World Returns to Peace

OBJECTIVE: What were the immediate results of World War II? Why was the United Nations set up?

1. "Give me ten years," said Adolf Hitler in 1933, "and you will not be able to recognize Germany." Hitler's promise held a horrible truth. By 1939, Hitler had plunged Germany and the world into the most destructive war the world had ever known. By 1945, German cities such as Berlin, Hamburg, and Dresden lay in rubble, and millions of Germans faced starvation. The victims of Axis aggression counted their losses in millions of dead and wounded. Even as the Allies celebrated victory, they faced the huge task of building a peaceful new world.

The Results of World War II What challenges faced the Allies at the end of the war?

2. World War II took an unthinkable toll in lives and property. Over 55 million soldiers and civilians died in the war. Cities in Europe and Asia had been bombed, and roads, bridges, factories, and farms had been destroyed. Millions of people had been taken from their homes in Europe and forced to work in slave labor factories. Many of these persons had no homes to return to. Millions of Germans were left homeless by Allied bombing raids. Economic life was at a standstill and starvation threatened many people in Europe and Asia.

3. With the war at an end, the Allies had to decide what should be done with Germany and

▲ As President Truman looks on, his Secretary of State prepares to sign the United Nations charter in June 1945. Many people hoped the UN would keep world peace after World War II.

Japan. Churchill, Stalin, and Roosevelt had agreed to divide Germany into zones of occupation. Why did the Allied leaders want to ◄ divide Germany? In 1945, therefore, the Russians occupied much of eastern Germany. French, British, and American troops each took

In Chapter 5, you will apply these critical thinking skills to the historical process:
○ **Generalizing:** Making a statement that links several facts.
◢ **Making judgments:** Stating a personal opinion based on historical facts.

over a zone in western Germany. The city of Berlin, Hitler's capital, was also divided into four zones of occupation. American forces occupied Japan. Under the direction of General Douglas MacArthur, the Japanese adopted a democratic constitution. The new constitution stated that Japan was not allowed to maintain a ▶ military force. Why do you think this rule was included in the constitution?

The Holocaust   What was the Holocaust, and how did the Allies punish war criminals?

4. As the Allies conquered Poland and Germany in 1945, they found terrible signs of Hitler's "final solution." It was his policy to kill the Jews of Europe. Today, this policy is called the **Holocaust.** A holocaust is the total destruction of life. During the war, Nazi troops rounded up Jews from occupied Europe. They sent the Jews to death camps in Eastern Europe and Germany. More than 6 million Jews were killed, many of them by being gassed. The Nazis also slaughtered other groups, such as Gypsies

and Poles, as well as the physically and mentally handicapped. After the war, the Allies decided to punish the German and Japanese leaders who had committed these brutal "crimes against humanity." War crimes trials were held in Nuremberg, Germany, and Tokyo, Japan. A number of high-ranking Nazis and Japanese were convicted of war crimes and executed. Others were imprisoned. Why do you think the ◀ Allies felt it was important to put the Axis leaders on trial?

Spotlight on Sources

5. After the war, survivors of the Nazi death camps wandered across Europe, hoping against hope to find their relatives alive. Simon Wiesenthal, who was a concentration camp survivor, gave this report of the search.

> Across Europe a wild tide of frantic survivors was flowing. People were hitchhiking, getting short jeep rides, or hanging on to dilapidated [falling apart] railway coaches without windows or doors. They

▼ The Nazis killed millions of Jews in the gas chambers of concentration or death camps. On the left, are starving survivors found by Allied troops at one camp. On the right, are thousands of wedding rings the Nazis stripped from women's fingers before putting them to death.

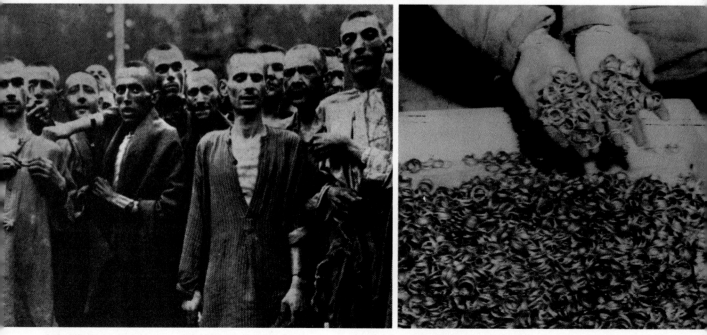

Ask: What was the purpose of the war crimes trials? Do you agree or disagree with critics who charged that the trials were Allied propaganda? Why or why not?

MEXICAN AMERICANS

As peace came to the United States, Americans became aware as never before how many minority groups were part of the nation. Among them were the many Mexican Americans who had come to work in the United States during the war. Numbering about 12.6 million, Mexican Americans now make up the second largest minority group in the country.

Mexican Americans live throughout the United States, but about 70 percent are found in California and Texas. Los Angeles, which is home to about 700,000 Mexican Americans, boasts the largest Mexican American population of any American city. Most Mexican Americans trace their ancestry back to the Maya, Aztec, and other Native Americans.

Mexican Americans became part of the United States in two ways. The ancestors of some present-day Mexican Americans lived in parts of Mexico that were taken over by the United States after the war with Mexico.

▼ These El Paso, Texas, graduating students are among the growing number of Mexican Americans who realize how important education is in improving the lives of their people.

California, Nevada, Utah, New Mexico, Arizona, Texas, and parts of Wyoming and Colorado were once Mexican territories. The people who were living there at the time became Americans.

Many Mexican Americans became American citizens by immigration. The first large wave of Mexican immigration began in 1910, after a revolution in Mexico that caused much violence and hardship in the country. Between 1900 and 1930, more than 600,000 Mexicans settled in the United States. When the Great Depression hit, however, the wave of immigration stopped. In fact, many Americans of Mexican origin were forced to return to Mexico so that they would not compete for jobs with other Americans.

The shortage of workers in the United States in World War II spurred a new wave of immigration from Mexico. During the war years, thousands of Mexican Americans entered the armed forces. Mexico has remained a poor country, so its people continue to stream into the United States in search of a better life.

Like other minority groups, Mexican Americans have faced many problems. Without a knowledge of English, many Mexican Americans have found it difficult to get a good education. As a result, most of them hold low-paying jobs that require little education. Many work as migrant farmers or in factories. Still, the number of Mexican Americans who enter the mainstream of American society is growing. More and more Mexican Americans hold high positions in government. Business people and entertainers of Mexican origin have enjoyed success. At the same time, they continue to be proud of the heritage that their ancestors brought with them from the land south of the border.

Now answer the following questions.

1. In what two ways did Mexican Americans join the population of the United States?

2. Describe the handicaps and achievements of Mexican Americans as a group.

sat in huddled groups on hay carts, and some just walked. . . . Many of them didn't really know where to go. To the place where one had been with his family before the war? To the concentration camp where the family had last been heard of? Families had been torn apart too suddenly to make arrangements for the day when it would be all over. . . .

And yet the survivors continued their pilgrimage [journey] of despair. . . . Someone might tell where to find a wife, a mother, children, a brother—or whether they were dead. Better to know the truth than to know nothing.

—*The Murderers Among Us*,
by Simon Wiesenthal

▶ What were two reasons concentration camp survivors wandered over Europe? What does Wiesenthal mean when he says the survivors continued their "pilgrimage of despair"?

The United Nations   Why was the United Nations set up, and how does it work?

6. In 1945, as the war drew to a close, the Allies drew up a charter for the **United Nations**, an international peacekeeping organization. The UN, as it was soon called, has a General Assembly with delegates from every member nation. Nations can bring disputes and other issues before the Assembly or before the UN's Security Council. The United States, Britain, China, France, and the Soviet Union hold permanent seats on the Security Council. Ten other nations hold the remaining seats in rotation. Since 1945, the UN has been called on to keep the peace in many parts of the world. However, member nations have often disagreed on what course to follow, so the UN's peacekeeping efforts have sometimes had limited success.

7. Besides peacekeeping, members of the UN work together to solve other pressing world problems such as hunger and disease. The UN has a number of special agencies devoted to these issues such as the Food and Agricultural Organization. UN agencies have helped poor nations improve education and medical care. They have provided relief after floods and other natural disasters, and they have worked for human rights.

People in History

8. Ralph Bunche   In 1948, an American diplomat named Ralph Bunche faced a dangerous and difficult task. He took on the job as UN **mediator** (MEE-dee-ay-tor), or peace maker, in Palestine. The previous UN mediator, Count Folke Bernadotte, had been assassinated. For years Arabs and Jews had been battling for power. Bunche knew the job would take all his skills and patience. In the end, he got both sides to agree to an armistice. Later, he won the Nobel Peace Prize for his efforts, becoming the first African American to gain such an honor.

9. Bunche, the grandson of slaves, worked his way through the University of California at Los Angeles, graduating with highest honors. During World War II, he worked for the State Department. At war's end, he joined the UN, and for more than 20 years was a key UN peacekeeper. Through patient negotiations, Bunche helped ease tensions in Cyprus, the Middle East, and Africa.

Outlook

10. Shortly before his death in April 1945, Franklin D. Roosevelt prepared a speech about what the future held. "[If] civilization is to survive," he wrote, "we must cultivate [encourage] the science of human relationships—the ability of all peoples, of all kinds, to live together and work together in the same world, at peace. . . ." Yet as World War II ended, new challenges to the peace arose. In the coming years there would be disagreements between the United States and the Soviet Union, who had once fought a common enemy. Now they would look at each other with distrust. Why do you think such feelings between the West and the Soviet Union arose? Do they continue to exist at the present time?

Ask: Why has the UN had limited success in peacekeeping? Why are the UN achievements in health, education, and disaster relief important?

CHAPTER REVIEW

VOCABULARY REVIEW

▶ Choose the word or term that best completes each of the following statements.

1. The destruction of millions of Jews by the Nazis is called the
 a. Nuremberg trials.
 b. Holocaust.
 c. Great Depression.

2. The peacekeeping organization set up after World War II is the
 a. League of Nations.
 b. Rome–Berlin Axis.
 c. United Nations.

3. A person who helps enemies come to peaceful terms is a
 a. dictator.
 b. survivor.
 c. mediator.

SKILL BUILDER: MAKING A TIME LINE

▶ Copy the following time line. Look up the dates for the events that follow. Then draw a time line of the events on a separate sheet of paper.

1940	1942	1944	1946	1948	1950

World War II begins.

United Nations charter is drawn up.

Ralph Bunche becomes the UN mediator in Palestine.

America enters World War II.

Lend-Lease Act

D-Day

Japan surrenders.

First atomic bomb is dropped.

SKILL BUILDER: CRITICAL THINKING AND COMPREHENSION

I. Generalizing

▶ On a separate sheet of paper, choose the best generalization from each set below for the topic given. Then explain why you feel that generalization is the best one.

1. **Topic:** The United States in World War II
   a. In World War II the United States fought with other countries against the Axis.
   b. American soldiers fought in France in World War II.
   c. America followed an island-hopping policy in the Pacific.

2. **Topic:** The Holocaust
   a. Allied troops were horrified when they saw how the Nazis had treated the Jews.
   b. Over 6 million Jews were killed in German concentration camps.
   c. The Holocaust is the name now given to the German extermination the Jews of Europe.

II. Point of View

▶ Copy each of the following statements on a sheet of paper. Then name the persons from the chapter who made these statements and explain what each statement means.

1. "Give me ten years, and you will not be able to recognize Germany."

2. "If civilization is to survive, we must cultivate the science of human relationships."

III. Making Judgments

▶ Copy the following statements on a sheet of paper. Then state whether or not you agree with each statement, and explain why.

1. Anyone involved with the killing of people in concentration camps should be put to death.

2. An organization like the United Nations will never work because making war is part of human nature.

3. Ralph Bunche deserved the Nobel Peace Prize.

USING PRIMARY SOURCES

▶ Reread the Spotlight on Sources on pages 569 and 571. What does Wiesenthal's account tell you about conditions in Europe after World War II was over?

ENRICHMENT

1. Read more about the charges against the Nazi leaders accused of war crimes. Then write the opening statement the prosecutor at the Nuremberg trials might have made.

2. Create a poster that sums up the destruction of World War II.

3. Give an oral report on what changes American occupation brought to Japan after World War II.

4. Prepare a debate on this question: Can the nations of the world prevent another Holocaust against a group of people?

UNIT REVIEW

SUMMARY

American life was changing rapidly in the 1920s. Automobiles and other new products made life easier in many ways. Behind the prosperity of the 1920s, however, were serious problems, especially for farmers and others who did not benefit from the good times. In October 1929, the stock market crashed and ushered in the Great Depression. For the next ten years, Americans suffered from hard times. Millions of people lost their jobs as banks, businesses, and factories closed or cut back on production.

During the depression, President Roosevelt introduced the New Deal. It included many laws aimed at easing the effects of the depression for workers, farmers, and others. The New Deal, however, greatly increased government's role in the economy.

By the late 1930s, war clouds hung over the international scene. Ambitious dictators in Italy and Germany and military leaders in Japan seized land from neighboring countries. In 1939, World War II broke out after Hitler invaded Poland. At first, the Axis powers in Europe and Asia advanced rapidly. In 1941, the United States entered the war after Japan bombed Pearl Harbor. In time, the Allies turned back the Axis advance and by 1945 forced the Axis powers to surrender.

At war's end, the world counted the staggering losses caused by destructive bombing and years of fighting. The horrors of Nazi death camps were fully revealed, and some Axis leaders were tried for their crimes. To ensure the peace, the United Nations was organized.

SKILL BUILDER: READING A MAP

▶ Study the map below. Then answer the questions that follow on a separate sheet of paper.

1. According to the map, what were the two sides that fought in World War II?

2. Which side conquered the most nations? In what part of the world were most of the conquered nations located?

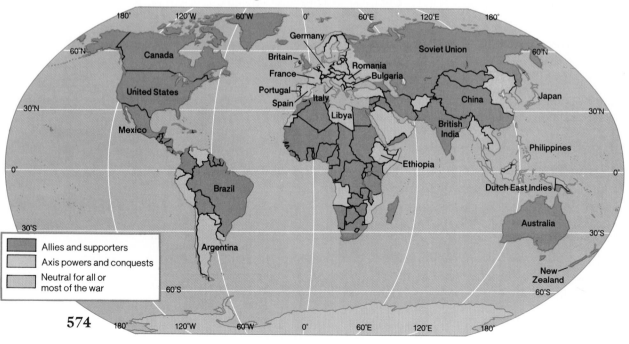

Taking Sides in World War II

Legend:
- Allies and supporters
- Axis powers and conquests
- Neutral for all or most of the war

3. Which European country that fought in the war was not conquered by the Axis?

4. Which Asian countries or lands were conquered by the Axis?

5. Name three European countries that were neutral during the war.

6. On which three continents did the Axis make no conquests?

SKILL BUILDER: CRITICAL THINKING AND COMPREHENSION

▲ I. Main Idea

▶ Read the sentences in each set below. Decide which sentence is the main idea and which sentences are details that support the main idea. Write each set on a sheet of paper, with the main idea first and the details below it.

1. **a.** Most people lived in cities and made a lot of money.
   b. Factories increased their output.
   c. Many people bought cars.
   d. During the Coolidge years, 1923–1929, American business prospered.

2. **a.** Over 55 million people died in World War II.
   b. World War II took a great toll in people and property.
   c. Many cities in Europe were destroyed by bombs.
   d. Large numbers of people had no homes to go back to.

▲ II. Fact *versus* Opinion

▶ Copy each sentence below and state whether it is a fact or an opinion.

1. The world would not be safe today if the United States had not dropped the atomic bomb on Japan.

2. The Germans sank the *Lusitania* in 1915.

3. The United Nations has more members today than when it started.

4. The United Nations is an organization that everyone should admire.

5. The quota system is unfair to the people who would like to move to the United States.

ENRICHMENT

1. Work in groups of three or four students. Each group writes a short radio play in which several different people—a business person, a farmer, a banker, a stockholder, for example—talk about the stock market crash the day after it happened. Read the plays in class and have the students vote on which ones best present the seriousness and shock of the event.

2. Imagine you are General Dwight D. Eisenhower. Write an entry in his diary on the day before D-Day. In the entry, write about his feelings about the coming event, his responsibilities, and prospects for the future of the war.

UNIT 14

THE UNITED STATES BECOMES A SUPERPOWER

Chapter

UNIT OVERVIEW   Unit 14 will help you learn how the United States tried to build lasting peace in the postwar world.

UNIT SKILLS OBJECTIVES   In Unit 14, these critical thinking skills are emphasized:

○ **Generalizing:** Making a statement that links several facts.
▲ **Summarizing:** Giving the main idea of a group of paragraphs.

You will also use two important social studies skills:
   Using an Encyclopedia   Making a Chart

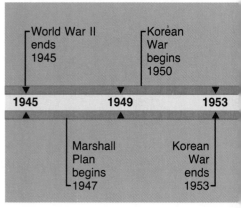

┌World War II ends 1945		┌Korean War begins 1950
1945	**1949**	**1953**
	Marshall Plan begins └1947	Korean War ends 1953┘

       ESL/LEP Strategy: Ask teams of students to preview the unit and select a person from this unit as the subject of a class presentation. Students may write an article, create a visual display, prepare a dialogue, or role play a major contribution.

▲ Achievements in outer space were an important example of the United States' world leadership in the years after World War II.

		Cuban Missile Crisis 1962	Nuclear Test Ban Treaty is signed 1963		OPEC oil embargo against United States; Vietnam War ends 1973		Civil war erupts in Lebanon 1975		U.S. sends soldiers to Grenada 1983	
957	1961	1965	1969	1973	1977	1981	1985

		U.S. starts to send troops to Vietnam 1964		SALT I is signed; U.S. and China reestablish relations 1972		Camp David Accord is signed 1979

Points of View

For many years after the end of World War II, the United States and the Soviet Union were bitter enemies. They engaged in a Cold War, accusing each other of following policies that were intended to harm the other country. Part of this conflict was carried on as a war of words. Here are two examples of

HOW TO CLOSE THE GAP?

▲ This cartoon reflects President Truman's view that the Soviet Union was determined to control Berlin and Eastern Europe.

AN AMERICAN PRESIDENT'S VIEW

❝ Since the close of hostilities [the end of World War II], the Soviet Union and its agents have destroyed the independence and democratic character of a whole series of nations in Eastern and Central Europe. It is this ruthless [tough] course of action, and the clear design [plan] to extend it to the remaining free nations of Europe, that have brought about the critical [serious] situation in Europe today. . . . The Soviet Union and its satellites [followers] were invited to cooperate in the European Recovery Program [Marshall Plan]. They rejected [turned down] the invitation. . . . They see it as a major obstacle [hurdle] to their designs to subjugate [conquer] . . . Europe. I am sure that the determination [wish] of the free countries of Europe to protect themselves will be matched by an equal determination on our part to help them. ❞

Address to Congress, Harry S. Truman

The Cold War of Words

how this war was fought. The first statement below was made to Congress by President Harry S. Truman in March 1948. The second is by Andrei Zhdanov, a high official of the Soviet government in the Soviet newspaper *Pravda* in October 1947.

THE VIEW FROM THE EAST

"Inasmuch as the Soviet Union and the countries of the new democracies [communist countries] become obstacles [blocks] to the realization [carrying out] of the imperialist [dominating] plans of struggle for world control, the United States announced a crusade [holy war] against the Soviet Union. This was supported by threats of a new war on the part of the most extreme imperialist politicians in the United States. . . . The Truman-Marshall plan is only one part of a general plan for the policy of global expansion carried on by the United States in all parts of the world."

PRAVDA, October 8, 1947

▲ This Soviet cartoon portrays President Truman as a postwar Statue of Liberty with an atomic bomb in one hand and a bag of money from the Marshall Plan in the other.

Using Primary Sources

1. Of what does President Truman accuse the Soviet Union?

2. What does Zhdanov say is the real intention of the United States in creating the Marshall Plan?

579

CHAPTER 1

America in the Postwar World

OBJECTIVE: How did America's strong postwar economy help make the United States a great power?

1. It was August 14, 1945, six days after the United States had dropped the second atomic bomb on Japan. At a center for American service men and service women near Naples, Italy, the Andrews Sisters, a popular singing trio, had just finished singing "Don't Sit Under the Apple Tree." The audience saw a man come on the stage and hand a slip of paper to one of the singers. She glanced at the paper and then screamed out, "Japan has surrendered. The war is over." Cheers rang out as hats and shoes were flung into the air. It was V-J Day—Victory over Japan Day. In Japan the emperor announced the news over the radio. In the United States drivers sped around the street honking their horns. Now the country could become "normal" again. People looked forward to the soldiers' return. They wanted to live normal family lives and be able to buy the things they had missed during the war. People realized there would be problems ahead, but for now the future was bright. As one American put it, the United States was in "the number one position in the world."

One Car you can use for Most Everyt...

With its steel body and top, big cargo space, and functional styling, the "Jeep" Station Wagon sets a new pattern for all-around usefulness. It's a smart, comfortable family car—fleet and smooth-riding. And it also serves as a utility vehicle, practical for business and farm hauling. Economical, too, thanks to its low weight, 2-wheel drive and famous "Jeep" Engine with overdrive.

Look to Willys-Overland for cars that really fit your needs—functionally designed for usefulness, engineered for low-cost operation and long life.

Willys-Overland
TOLEDO, OHIO
Makers of America's Most Useful Vehicles

`Jeep`
Station Wago...
WITH STEEL BODY AND TOP

▲ Because new cars were not sold during World War II, many people bought new ones in the years just after the war. In this ad the Jeep, an army car, returns from the war as a station wagon.

The Postwar Boom   How did the change to peacetime industry keep America powerful?

2. As soon as World War II ended, servicemen wanted to come home, and their families were eager to have them. As a result, the **demo-** **bilization** (dee-moh-buh-luh-ZAY-shuhn) of the armed forces took place quickly. Demobilization means the discharging of people from the armed forces. In a few months, most of the 12,000,000 armed service members had returned to civilian life.

In Chapter 1 you will apply these Critical Thinking Skills to the historical process:
○ **Generalizing:** Making a statement that links several facts.

Understanding Points of View: Recognizing why people have different attitudes about the same thing.

3. Many people were afraid that the return of the soldiers would end the prosperity of the wartime years, as it had after World War I. At that time, soldiers had returned to a country that had no jobs for them. The prosperous years of the war had ended in 1920, leaving many people out of work. However, the situation at the end of World War II proved different.

4. In 1945, people were eager to buy things that had not been available during the war. During the war most Americans had earned good salaries. There were few **consumer**, or household, goods to buy. Factories were making ships, planes, tanks, guns, and all the other things that the armed forces needed. Americans had plenty of money, but not much to buy with it. When the war ended, people wanted to use the money to buy the things they had gone without for four years.

5. Manufacturers were eager to provide the goods that people wanted. Factories retooled quickly, so that goods were soon available. A new, postwar **boom** was under way. A boom is a period of prosperity. New cars, in particular, led the list of purchases. Cars were followed by radios, stoves, refrigerators, and other household appliances. Soon a new appliance, the television set, became a best-selling item. As people bought more goods, factories hired more workers. These workers then had the money to buy other consumer products. Returning soldiers found many jobs available. The boom continued and grew.

6. The boom was helped by government programs to aid veterans, or persons who had served in the armed forces. One program paid veterans who wanted to go to college. Many veterans took advantage of this program. Another program helped veterans buy homes at low cost. This program led to the building of many new houses, and so it created yet more jobs. Why do you think the government created these programs for veterans?

7. Farmers, too, shared in the postwar prosperity because there was a great demand for American grain and other farm products. Farmers had had a hard time during the Depression,

often staying in business only with the help of government support. The war saved many farms. Their crops went to feed the troops fighting the war and, often, the troops of wartime allies as well. Now, after the war, many farming regions in other parts of the world were in ruins, and needed the food American farmers could supply. At the same time, improved farming methods made American farms the most productive in the world. At last farmers shared fully in America's prosperity.

8. During the war, Congress had imposed price controls to prevent **inflation** (in-FLAY-shuhn). Inflation is a rapid rise in prices. In 1946, these controls were lifted, and prices jumped upward. Beef, for example, doubled in price, and other products jumped nearly as much. People were earning more, but their money was buying less. However, this condition did not last long. Soon the inflation rate declined, and people could afford to buy what they needed.

The Truman Years What were the main issues during the presidency of Harry S. Truman?

9. When Franklin Roosevelt died in April 1945, Vice-President Harry S. Truman became President. He proposed a set of laws that he called the Fair Deal. These were a continuation of Roosevelt's New Deal policies, many of which had been interrupted by the war.

Spotlight on Sources

10. In September 1945, only a few days after Japan surrendered, President Truman introduced his domestic program in a speech to Congress. He called his program an "economic bill of rights":

> The objectives [goals] of our domestic economy which we seek in our long-range plans were summarized by the late President Franklin D. Roosevelt over a year and a half ago. . . . Let's make the attainment [achieving] of those rights the essence [heart] of . . . American economic life. . . .

Among these are:

The right to a useful and remunerative [well-paying] job in the industries or shops or farms or mines of the Nation.

The right to earn enough to provide adequate [proper] food and clothing and recreation. . . .

The right . . . to a decent home. . . .

The right to adequate protection from the economic fears of old age, sickness, and unemployment.

The right to a good education.

—Harry S. Truman, *Special Message to Congress, September 6, 1945*

▶ How does Truman show his support of Roosevelt's policies? How many of these "rights" have been accomplished today?

11. Truman's program was not popular. The American people were tired of sacrificing. They wanted to relax and enjoy peace and prosperity. They elected a Congress that shared their feelings. Truman called this Congress a "do-nothing Republican Congress" because it refused to pass many of his Fair Deal proposals.

12. Fears about communism were widespread during the time Truman was President. During these years, the Cold War with the Soviet Union was at its height. (You will read about the Cold War in the next chapter.) Within the United States, there was a small Communist party whose members believed in the policies of Stalin and the Soviet Union. This party operated mainly in secret. In this tense atmosphere, worries were expressed about communists within the American government. There were fears that such people were acting as spies for the Soviet Union. In the late 1940s, a few people were arrested and tried for such activities. In 1953, two people were executed for giving atomic secrets to the Soviet Union.

13. Joseph McCarthy, a United States senator from Wisconsin, created controversy by taking advantage of the public's concern about communism. In 1950, McCarthy gave a speech

THE PRESIDENTS' CORNER

Harry S. Truman was President from 1945 to 1953. Once an unsuccessful businessman, Truman started up the political ladder in his native Missouri. People admired Truman for his down-to-earth style, strong personality, and fighting spirit. As President, Truman had to make one of the most difficult decisions ever when he ordered atomic bombs dropped on Japan to end the war. He saw the need to help rebuild many countries wrecked by the war and put forward the Marshall Plan.

People remember the battle Truman fought to be reelected in 1948. All the public-opinion polls predicted that his challenger, Republican Thomas E. Dewey, would win. With tremendous fighting spirit, Truman carried on an exhausting campaign, making more than 350 speeches. In one of the biggest upsets in history, Truman won by a narrow 3 million popular votes.

in which he claimed to have a list of 205 Communist party members. These communists, he said, were working in the United States State Department. No one ever saw this list. However, over the next few years, McCarthy made other similar charges. He named people who, he said, were communists, but he never provided any evidence to back up these charges. Some of the people McCarthy accused lost their jobs or were hurt in other ways, even though they were loyal Americans.

14. Gradually, however, most people decided that McCarthy was a **demagogue** (DEM-uh-gahg) of the worst sort. A demagogue is a person who tries to gain power by stirring up people's emotions and prejudices. In 1954, McCarthy lost much influence after a series of Congressional hearings. His behavior during these hearings, which were shown on television, turned many Americans against him. They could see that McCarthy abused and bullied witnesses and their attorneys. They also realized that McCarthy's accusations did not stand up to close examination. Later that year the Senate **censured** (SEN-shuhrd) him. To censure is to

▶ formally condemn a person. Why do people often refer to McCarthy's activities as a "witch hunt"?

The Postwar World What made the United States so powerful at the end of World War II?

15. The prestige of the United States was at its highest after World War II. The United States army, navy, and air force had played an important part in winning the war. The United States also had provided huge amounts of food, supplies, and military equipment to its allies. Both its allies and its enemies had suffered huge losses from destruction of their cities, factories, and farms. Only the United States and its neighbor Canada came out of the war with their industries and farms operating efficiently.

16. The United States also came out of the war as the world's leader in scientific research. One reason was that its universities and other research organizations had not been damaged in the war. Another reason was that before the war, many European scientists had fled the Nazi or Fascist governments of their homelands and moved to the United States. American science became known for its achievements in many fields, from atomic physics to medicine.

People in History

17. Jonas Salk Because of the work of Jonas Salk, Americans were freed from polio, one of the most frightening diseases that they knew. During World War II, Salk worked on developing a **vaccine** (vak-SEEN) against the flu. A vaccine is a medicine that protects a person from a disease. This experience helped him develop a vaccine against polio. Polio struck without warning, usually in the summer.

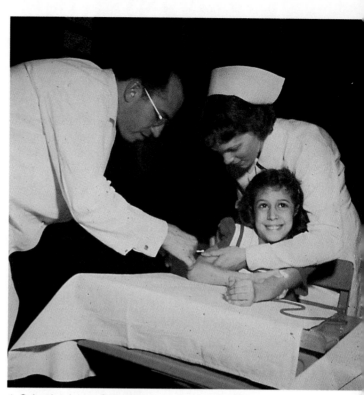

▲ Scientist Jonas Salk discovered a vaccine that saved thousands of children from the dreaded crippling disease of polio.

Most of its victims were children. Some of them died. Many others were left completely or partly paralyzed. Then, in 1953, Salk introduced a vaccine that protected against polio. Ever since, this has been called the Salk vaccine. The next year, the vaccine was given to almost every child in America, and the threat of polio was on the way to being wiped out.

Outlook

18. The end of World War II was an important turning point for Americans. An era of prosperity began that lasted for many years. For many reasons, the United States was now the strongest nation in the world. However, Americans were more concerned with their fears about communism. How do you think the ◀ United States used its new power in the world? Why might other countries have opposed the United States as it tried to use its power?

CHAPTER REVIEW

VOCABULARY REVIEW

▶ Write each of the following sentences on a sheet of paper. Then fill in the blank with the word that best completes each sentence.

consumer	demagogueboom
inflation	boom
vaccine	censure
demobilization	

1. A period of economic prosperity is called a _____ .

2. Rising prices are a sign of _____ .

3. Polio is a disease that can be prevented by the use of a _____ .

4. Articles such as stoves, cars, and televisions are _____ products.

5. Army troops are released from service during _____ .

6. People who believe in a _____ are often stirred by prejudice and emotion.

7. When the Senate condemns a member's action, it is said to _____ him or her.

SKILL BUILDER: USING AN ENCYCLOPEDIA

▶ One of the most useful places to find information about a subject is an encyclopedia. An encyclopedia is a set of books that gives facts about important people, places, and events. Most encyclopedias consist of many volumes. The articles in an encyclopedia are arranged in alphabetical order from the first volume to the last. You can tell which part of the alphabet any one volume covers by looking on the spine of the volume. For example, one volume of one encyclopedia contains all the articles that begin with F. In another encyclopedia, the spine shows the name of the first article and the last article, such as Photography to Pumpkin. The spine of each encyclopedia volume also contains the number of the volume in the set. To help you find where an article is in a volume, there are guide words on each page that tell you what article or articles are found on that page. Each encyclopedia also has one volume that contains the index. You can use the index to find out which volume contains the information you are looking for and the page of that volume where that information is located.

   Use an encyclopedia to find further information on one of the following topics you read about in this chapter. Then, on a separate sheet of paper, write a short report on the topic you chose.

inflation

President Truman

Cold War

polio

Joseph McCarthy

Joseph Stalin

584

SKILL BUILDER: CRITICAL THINKING AND COMPREHENSION

I. Generalizing

▶ On a separate sheet of paper, make a generalization about the following issues.

1. How Americans felt about the end of World War II

2. How the American people felt about Truman's Fair Deal program

3. What Americans were doing after World War II

II. Cause and Effect

▶ Write each of the statements on a separate sheet of paper. Then fill in the missing cause or effect.

1. **Cause:** In a war, many people are hired to produce weapons and to do other wartime jobs.
   Effect: _____

2. **Cause:** _____
   Effect: People bought many consumer products after World War II.

3. **Cause:** Many world farming regions were devastated by the war.
   Effect: _____

III. Point of View

▶ On a separate sheet of paper, write two points of view about the following:

1. Truman's Fair Deal plan

2. The postwar boom

3. Joseph McCarthy

USING PRIMARY SOURCES

▶ Reread the Spotlight on Sources on pages 581 and 582. Why is the right to a good education considered to be part of an "economic bill of rights"?

ENRICHMENT

1. Use an almanac or other reference source to find prices of several food items over a 20-year period. Make a diagram showing how prices increased in this period. Write a paragraph explaining the information on your diagram.

2. Choose a consumer product that existed at the end of World War II. Think of an advertising campaign to sell this product. You may include slogans, posters, or radio and television commercials. Remember, your purpose is to sell more of your product.

3. Find out more about the anti-communism movement in the postwar United States. Prepare a report that discusses who the leaders were, what actions they took, who was affected, and what the result of the movement was.

CHAPTER 2

The Cold War Begins

> OBJECTIVE: What was the Cold War, and how did the United States become the leader of the Western nations?

1. "The sound of the engines is music to our ears," said one citizen of Berlin. Every three minutes, 24 hours a day, another airplane flew over the bombed-out ruins and landed in the city. Thirty minutes later, emptied of its cargo, it was headed west again. The drone of the planes went on throughout the year. It was 1949, and the Soviet Union had cut off all land routes to the American, British, and French zones of West Berlin. The United States and its allies were determined to keep the city alive. They planned to bring badly needed supplies to the 2,500,000 people of West Berlin by airplane: food, clothes, medicine, fuel, even cars and Christmas candy. Incredibly, the airlift was a success. After almost a year, the Soviet Union lifted the blockade. The Berlin airlift was the most vivid sign of a new stage of international relations. The Cold War had begun.

▲ Three years after World War II, the Western powers and the Soviet Union clashed over access to Berlin. The Berlin airlift flew vital supplies to the city for 11 months until the Soviet Union lifted its blockade.

The Communist Threat How did the Soviet Union's efforts to take over Greece and Turkey start the Cold War?

2. At the end of World War II, much of Europe was in ruins. Entire cities had been wiped out in bombing raids. Factories had been destroyed. There wasn't enough coal. People were starving. There were food riots in France and Italy.

3. The end of the war found the Soviet Union occupying Eastern Europe and determined to keep its hold on this region. A few months before the war's end, leaders of the Allied nations had met at Yalta, in the Soviet Union. They agreed that after the war, there

In Chapter 2 you will apply these critical thinking skills to the historical process:

➡️ **Recognizing Cause and Effect:** Recognizing the action or event that makes something happen; identifying the result of an action or event.

🔺 **Identifying Fact *versus* Opinion:** Specifying whether information can be proved or whether it expresses feelings or beliefs.

would be free elections in all the countries that were freed from the Germans. Now it became evident that the Soviet Union would not keep this agreement. First in Poland and then in other countries of Eastern Europe, the Soviet Union set up puppet governments that were loyal to the Soviet Union.

4. The governments that Stalin set up in Eastern Europe took away many of their people's rights. These included the right to disagree with the government, to choose their own leaders, and to leave the country if they wished. In 1946, Winston Churchill said that these countries were being held behind an "iron curtain." What did Churchill mean by the "iron curtain"? Countries under Soviet control, such as Poland, Czechoslovakia, Hungary, Romania, and Bulgaria, came to be called Soviet **satellites** (SAT-uh-lyts) or **Iron Curtain** countries.

5. In 1947, to help Greece and Turkey keep their independence from the Soviet Union, Truman announced the **Truman Doctrine**. The Truman Doctrine was a statement that the United States would help any country that was resisting a communist takeover. Under the Truman Doctrine, the United States sent aid to the Greek and Turkish governments. As a result, both countries survived the communist threat.

6. The Truman Doctrine was the first American move of the **Cold War**. The Cold War was a struggle between the two superpowers, the United States and the Soviet Union, and their allies. The struggle was called a "cold war" because neither side used guns, bombs, or other weapons against each other. Instead of these "hot" weapons, the war was fought with ideas and words.

The Marshall Plan   Why did the United States offer aid to the nations of Europe?

7. Western Europe's recovery from World War II was slow. Two years after the war, most people still were much worse off than they had been before the war. Communist parties promised people a better life, and more and more people were coming to believe them. In Italy

and France, in particular, it seemed that the communists might take over the countries in free elections.

8. To help Europe recover, Truman and his secretary of state, George C. Marshall, proposed the European Recovery Program, or **Marshall Plan**. Under this plan, the United States would lend about $17 billion over a four-year period to the shattered countries of Europe. The aid was offered to every country in Europe, including the Soviet satellites. Why did the United States include the Soviet-controlled countries in its offer? However, the Soviet leaders called the plan a "capitalist plot" and forced the countries under their control to refuse American aid.

▼ The Marshall Plan helped the war-torn countries of Western Europe to rebuild. What does the title of the cartoon tell about the other accomplishments of the Marshall Plan?

PEACE-MONGERING

Activity: Help students create a "Cold War Glossary." Include the vocabulary terms in this chapter and more current expressions like "détente," "SALT Treaty," and "glasnost."

587

Spotlight on Sources

9. Marshall announced the European Recovery Program in a speech in 1947. In his speech, he explained his support for the plan.

> Europe's requirements for the next three or four years are so much greater than her present ability to pay that she must have substantial [large] additional help. . . .
>
> It is logical that the United States should do whatever it is able to assist in the return of normal economic health in the world, without which there can be no political stability [steadiness] or secured [sure] peace. Our policy is directed not against any country or doctrine [set of beliefs] but against hunger, poverty, desperation [hopelessness], and chaos [disorder].
>
> —from *Plain Speaking: An Oral Biography of Harry S. Truman* by Merle Miller

▶ What kinds of aid could the United States offer postwar Europe? Why would it be in the United States' interest to provide such aid?

People in History

10. **George C. Marshall** The first military leader to hold the important posts of secretary of state and secretary of defense was George C. Marshall. Marshall was an officer in the United States army in World War I, and in peacetime he held a number of important army posts. Then in 1939, he became army chief of staff. Marshall held this position as top general in the army throughout World War II. Two years after the war ended, President Truman named him secretary of state. It was in this position that he earned his greatest fame as creator of the European Recovery Program, or Marshall Plan. Winston Churchill called the Marshall Plan "the most unsordid [generous] act in history." Later Marshall was awarded the Nobel Peace Prize for this great contribution to world peace.

11. Spurred by fears of a communist takeover of all Europe, Congress voted money for the Marshall Plan in 1948. Soon, ships loaded with industrial and farming equipment were crossing the Atlantic Ocean to Europe. How ⟹

MAP SKILL BUILDER: This map shows the division of Europe in the Cold War. **1.** What European countries joined NATO? **2.** What countries joined the Warsaw Pact?

The Cold War Divides Europe

- Original NATO member
- Joined NATO after 1950
- Original Warsaw Pact member
- Withdrew from Warsaw Pact in 1968
- Neutral nations
- ■ Chief Soviet ports
- A = Albania
- B = Belgium
- L = Luxembourg
- N = Netherlands

0   400 miles
0   600 kilometers

ATLANTIC OCEAN
ICELAND
FINLAND
Arkhangel'sk
Leningrad
NORWAY
SWEDEN
BALTIC SEA
SOVIET UNION
DENMARK
IRELAND
UNITED KINGDOM
E. GER.
POLAND
N
B
W. GER.
CZECHOSLOVAKIA
Odessa
L
AUSTRIA
HUNGARY
ROMANIA
BLACK SEA
SWITZ.
FRANCE
YUGOSLAVIA
BULGARIA
ITALY
TURKEY
A
GREECE
SPAIN
PORTUGAL
MEDITERRANEAN SEA
60°N
50°N
50°N
40°N
30°W
20°W
10°W
20°E
30°E
N W E S

did the Marshall Plan help the American economy? Within four years, most of the 16 European countries that took part in the Marshall Plan had rebuilt their industries. The United States had saved Europe from starvation and collapse.

Divided Germany   How did the split with the Soviet Union lead to a divided Germany?

12. At the end of World War II, the victorious allies had divided Germany into four zones of occupation. Each zone was to be governed by one of the allies. The four zones were the American, British, French, and Soviet zones. Berlin, the former German capital, also was divided into four such zones. Berlin lay deep within the Soviet zone of Germany. As a result, the Americans, British, and French had to cross areas controlled by the Soviet Union to get to their zones of Berlin.

13. The Western allies and the Soviet Union were supposed to cooperate in the running of Germany, but the Soviet Union often failed to do so. In June 1948, the Western allies decided to act without the Soviets. They introduced policies in their zones to revive the German economy. Stalin reacted quickly. He ordered the Soviet army to close all the roads and railroads to Berlin. Supplies could now reach the Western zones of the city only by airplane. Stalin expected that the Western allies would be forced to leave Berlin.

14. To counter the Soviet blockade of Berlin, the Western allies organized a massive **airlift** of supplies into the city. Every day, army transport planes of the United States, Britain, and France carried 4,500 tons of supplies into West Berlin. After 321 days, Stalin gave up and called off the blockade. West Berlin could once again be supplied by trucks and trains.

15. In 1949, Germany was officially divided into two countries. The Western allies organized a new, freely elected, democratic government in their three zones of occupation. This government, called the Federal Republic of Germany, or West Germany for short, has grown into a powerful, prosperous nation. In the Soviet Zone, German communists under Soviet direction set up a government called the German Democratic Republic, or East Germany. For most people, life in East Germany was hard. Many people left East Germany by going to East Berlin and crossing from there into West Berlin. In 1961 the East German government built the Berlin Wall to stop the flow of people out of East Berlin.

NATO Is Formed   How does the North Atlantic Treaty Organization protect Western Europe?

16. In 1949, the North Atlantic Treaty Organization, or **NATO**, was formed to meet the threat of a Soviet military attack in Europe. Members included the United States, Canada, and most of the non-communist countries of Europe. Under the alliance, each country agreed to help any other member country that was attacked. In the NATO alliance, the United States committed itself to joining wars in Europe. This was an important change in American policy, for the United States had always avoided treaties that might drag it into foreign wars. However, the threat of communism was strong enough to bring about this change in foreign policy. It was clear that the United States needed its allies in the Cold War.

Outlook

17. The Soviet threat to the free countries of Europe led to the Cold War. The Truman Doctrine stated that America's policy was to stop the spread of communism by aiding countries that were threatened by communism. The Marshall Plan helped Europe recover from World War II. The Berlin Airlift preserved the freedom of West Berlin. The NATO alliance promised military help if it were needed. How were these policies different from earlier American foreign policies? How is America's policy toward the Soviet Union different today?

Activity: Explain to students that the countries of Eastern Europe belong to a military alliance called the Warsaw Pact. Have them research the Warsaw Pact. They should find the date it was begun, list its members, and explain the main commitments of the treaty.

589

CHAPTER REVIEW

VOCABULARY REVIEW

▶ Copy these sentences. As you write them, replace the underlined word or words in each sentence with a word or phrase that makes the statement true.

1. The Marshall Plan helped the countries of all of Europe.

2. A Cold War is a war that is fought with guns and bombs.

3. The Truman Doctrine encouraged the spread of communism.

4. In an airlift, large quantities of supplies are carried in hot air balloons.

5. Satellites are nations under the control of each other.

6. The countries of North America and Eastern Europe formed the NATO alliance.

7. People behind the Iron Curtain were allowed to leave whenever they wanted.

SKILL BUILDER: READING A MAP

As a defeated nation in World War II, Germany was divided into four zones after the war. Berlin, the capital, was also divided into four zones.

▶ Study the map below and, on a separate sheet of paper, answer the questions that follow.

1. In which country's zone was Berlin located?

2. To which Eastern European nations did Germany lose territory?

3. Which Allied country had a zone adjoining its own national territory?

4. Which rivers made up East Germany's eastern border?

5. Which zones were larger, the Soviet zone or the combined Allied zones?

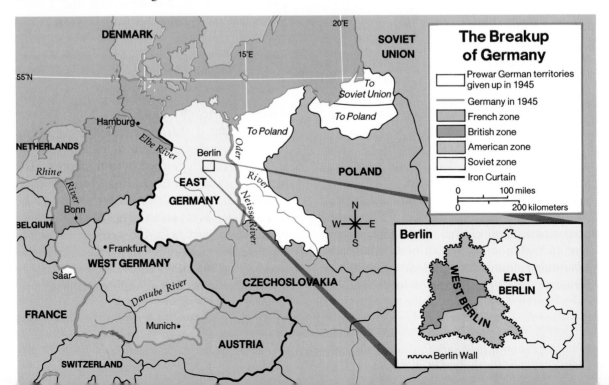

SKILL BUILDER: CRITICAL THINKING AND COMPREHENSION

▲ I. Summarizing

▶ On a separate sheet of paper, write a sentence or two to summarize the following subjects from this chapter.

1. The objective of the Truman Doctrine

2. The objective of the Marshall Plan

3. Why NATO was formed

4. Why the Cold War started

5. The division of Germany

⇨ II. Cause and Effect

▶ Write each of the statements on a sheet of paper. Then fill in the missing cause or effect.

1. **Cause:** The Truman Doctrine sought to contain communism.
   Effect: _____

2. **Cause:** _____
   Effect: The Marshall Plan was proposed to help with Europe's recovery.

3. **Cause:** The Western allies and the Soviet Union did not agree on how Germany was to be run after World War II.
   Effect: _____

▲ III. Fact *versus* Opinion

▶ Decide whether each statement below is a fact or opinion. Write the number of each statement on a separate sheet of paper. Label each statement *F* for fact or *O* for opinion.

1. Communism would have taken over the world if the United States had not opposed it.

2. After 321 days, Stalin gave up the blockade of Berlin.

3. A cold war is better than a "hot war."

4. People are not happy behind the Iron Curtain.

USING PRIMARY SOURCES

▶ Reread the Spotlight on Sources on page 588. Why do you think Marshall emphasized that the Marshall Plan was not directed against any country or set of beliefs?

ENRICHMENT

∞ 1. Work with other students to prepare a debate on the Marshall Plan. Choose teams to support and attack the plan. Have each team prepare arguments. Try to anticipate what the other team's arguments will be. Present your debate to the class. Have the class vote to decide which team won.

CHAPTER 3

United States Involvement in Asian Conflicts

OBJECTIVE: Why did the United States fight wars in Korea and Vietnam against communist armies?

1. Trinh Minh stared at the calm ocean from his family's fishing boat in San Francisco Bay. His thoughts wandered back to when his family escaped from Vietnam. Trinh would never forget the horror of their flight. The war was ending. Many Vietnamese were afraid for their future. With only a few days' supply of food and fresh water, Trinh and his family drifted for weeks in a small boat on the rough South China Sea. Like so many other Vietnamese, they hoped to get to Hong Kong or Macao. From there, they would try to make their way to the United States and start new lives.

The Korean War Why did American forces aid South Korea, and what were the results of the war?

2. Korea, located on the eastern border of China, was a battleground between communist and non-communist forces in the 1950s. Directly west of Japan, Korea had been occupied for many years by Japan before World War II. In 1945, at the end of the war, it was divided at the 38th parallel into two zones of occupation. The northern part was occupied by the Soviet Union and ruled by a communist dictatorship. The south was occupied by the United States and governed by a constitutional government. By 1949, both the Soviet Union and the United

▲ As the communists took over South Vietnam, thousands of people were desperate to flee. The only way out for many was by small boats that sailed into the dangerous open sea.

States had withdrawn most of their troops from Korea.

3. In 1950, North Korean troops invaded South Korea. President Truman appealed to the United Nations to take action against the invasion. The United Nations condemned the inva-

In Chapter 3 you will apply these critical thinking skills to the historical process:
Comparing and Contrasting: Recognizing similarities and differences.
Identifying Points of View: Recognizing why people have different attitudes about the same thing.

sion. Many of its member nations sent troops under Douglas MacArthur's command to fight the North Korean invaders. The United States sent by far the largest number of troops.

4. At first, the war went badly for the South Koreans and their allies, but then a brilliant move by MacArthur shattered the North Korean army. In two months, the United Nations forces not only drove the invaders from South Korea but also took over most of North Korea. At this point, large numbers of Chinese troops came to the aid of the North Koreans. The United Nations forces were pushed southward. ▶ Why did the Chinese come into the war at this point? By the middle of 1951, the war had settled into a **stalemate** along a line very near to where it had begun. A stalemate is a situation in which neither side can win.

People in History

5. Douglas MacArthur In World War II, Douglas MacArthur was commander of allied forces in the Southwest Pacific. His many victories made him a national hero. After the war, he was in charge of the occupation of Japan. There he set up that country's first democratic government. During the Korean War, he was commander of the United Nations forces. MacArthur favored attacking China. Because he asked Congress for support, President Truman dismissed him. MacArthur then retired from the army.

6. In 1953, President Eisenhower kept his campaign promise to end the Korean War. The line separating the armies became the permanent border between North and South Korea. In the years after the war, North Korea became one of the most rigid and strict of the communist countries. Although the government of South Korea ruled with a strong hand, the country became a prosperous, independent nation.

The Vietnam War How did the United States become involved in fighting in Vietnam?

7. Vietnam, a country in Southeast Asia, soon became another place where the struggle

THE PRESIDENTS' CORNER

Dwight D. Eisenhower, who held the office of President from 1953 to 1961, led the United States in an era of economic prosperity at home. However, in the Eisenhower years, bitter fights broke out over school desegregation in the South. In 1957 Eisenhower had to send federal troops to Little Rock, Arkansas, to enforce the 1954 Supreme Court ruling that school segregation was unconstitutional.

The Eisenhower years were also years of the Cold War with the Soviet Union. Eisenhower sent United States forces to many parts of the world to counter communist advances. He brought an end to the Korean War. Eisenhower left office as one of the most popular of American Presidents.

between communist and non-communist forces was fought. Vietnam had been ruled by France until 1954. After the French departed, the country was left, like Korea, with a communist northern part and a non-communist southern part. Then a Vietnamese communist guerrilla army, called the **Viet Cong**, tried to overthrow the South Vietnamese government. In 1961, President Kennedy committed the United States to helping South Vietnam resist communism. After Kennedy's assassination, President Johnson stepped up the American involvement. Johnson was afraid of a **domino effect**. A domino effect means that the fall of one country to communism leads to the fall of many other countries, one after the other, like a row of dominoes.

Spotlight on Sources

8. President Johnson needed the consent of Congress before he could send troops to Vietnam. In 1964, Congress gave its consent with these words:

Background: President Kennedy believed that communist aggression must be met with firmness. His success in the 1962 Cuban Missile Crisis convinced him of this policy. However, he became disillusioned with the South Vietnamese government, and before his death was considering withdrawing American support.

KOREANS AND VIETNAMESE

Koreans and Vietnamese have come to the United States to escape poverty and political and economic upsets in their homelands. The first immigrants from Korea came to the United States after 1903 by way of Hawaii. All men, they came to Hawaii to work on sugar plantations. The few thousand male Koreans in the United States lived here without their families. The reason was that Japan, which then ruled Korea, would not let family members leave. In this way, Japan made sure that money flowed back into their native country. As a result, the small Korean communities were largely "bachelor societies" of young male workers. Anti-Asian prejudice and laws made life for the newcomers even more difficult.

Things began to change in the 1950s. Korean women started to enter the United States as "war brides" of American soldiers who were returning from the Korean War. Also, immigration laws were slowly relaxed. Beginning in 1965, Koreans and other Asians

▼ Korean Americans have become known for the fine food markets they have set up in many cities.

could enter the United States in greater numbers. Korean doctors and nurses came to work in American hospitals. Jobs were available for Korean scientists and technology workers. Many Korean immigrants started businesses in the United States, such as small family-run grocery stores, restaurants, and service businesses. Most of the nearly 1 million Korean Americans live and work in the major American cities such as New York, Los Angeles, and Chicago.

During the last days of the Vietnam War, many South Vietnamese feared a communist takeover of their country. Fleeing to the United States, this first wave of Vietnamese immigrants was made up of mostly professionals and former government officials. Later, after the communists took control of Vietnam, a second wave of immigrants arrived. Many had barely escaped Vietnam with their lives. Often they had to make the difficult and dangerous trip across miles of open sea in small boats. For this reason, these refugees were called "boat people." Most of the people in this group were poor and uneducated. For these Vietnamese Americans, adjusting to life in America has been a hard struggle. To help Vietnamese refugees and immigrants, government programs were created in job training and English. Like the Koreans, the Vietnamese have started their own small, family-run businesses. Using their fishing skills from their home country, Vietnamese Americans have also started fishing businesses in coastal areas. As with other Asian Americans, the Koreans and Vietnamese are working to build a better life in America.

Now answer the following questions.

1. What was unusual about the first wave of Korean immigration?

2. How have the Korean and Vietnam Wars affected immigration to America from these countries?

The United States regards the preservation [saving] of the independence of South Vietnam as vital to its national interests and to world peace. . . .

The United States is prepared to use all measures, including the commitment of armed forces, to assist in the defense of its [Vietnam's] territorial integrity [freedom from invasion] against aggression [attack] or subversion [overthrowing] from any communist country.

—Southeast Asia Congressional Resolution, August 7, 1964

▶ What did Congress mean when it said South Vietnam is vital to our "national interests"?

9. Under President Johnson, there was a steady **escalation** (es-kuh-LAY-shuhn) of the war. Escalation is the causing of something to grow step by step. In January 1968, at the beginning of Tet, the Vietnamese New Year, the Viet Cong launched the **Tet Offensive**. They captured many South Vietnamese cities and took American troops completely by surprise. They were eventually pushed back, but now more and more Americans began to doubt that the Viet Cong could be defeated.

10. At home, many Americans began speaking out against the war. There were parades called "peace marches." Some young men burned their draft registration cards as a sign of protest. In 1970 President Richard Nixon ordered bombing raids on Cambodia, Vietnam's neighbor. This event brought more than 200,000 people to Washington, D.C., in a protest march. In 1971, a newspaper published a secret army study that concluded that the war could not be won. This document was called the Pentagon Papers after the headquarters of the armed forces. It was clear that most Americans no longer supported the war.

11. In 1973, a peace treaty was signed, and American forces withdrew. Two years later South Vietnam was overrun by North Vietnamese troops. Vietnam was now a unified communist country. The Vietnamese War was the longest war in America's history. Over 58,000

Americans lost their lives, and 300,000 were wounded. The cost in money was enormous—over $150 billion.

Watergate How did the Watergate scandal force President Nixon to resign?

12. The Watergate scandal had its origins in a burglary and ended in the resignation of a President. In 1972, Richard Nixon, a Republican, was now running for re-election. In June, four months before the election, several men were caught breaking into the offices of the rival Democratic party. Their purpose was to plant listening devices, or "bugs," in the Democrats' telephones. The burglary and the events that followed are called Watergate after the name of the building where the Democratic offices were located. In November, Nixon easily won the election.

13. However, early in 1973, evidence began to come out suggesting that some of the truth about the Watergate burglary had been hidden. Congress formed a special committee, which held a series of televised hearings. For months the American people watched television, amazed by the illegal actions of people close to Nixon. Finally, evidence came out that Nixon himself had been involved in these illegal acts. Congress began taking steps to impeach Nixon. In August 1974, before an impeachment could take place, Nixon resigned. By resigning, Nixon avoided becoming the second American President to be impeached.

Outlook

14. In the effort to keep communist governments from spreading to new countries, the United States fought two wars in Asia. The Korean War preserved the independence of South Korea. The Vietnam War, on the other hand, was unsuccessful in the long run. Unlike earlier wars that the United States had fought, neither the Korean War nor the Vietnam War was popular. This was true even though both wars were fought to prevent the spread of communism.

CHAPTER REVIEW

VOCABULARY REVIEW

▶ Copy the words in the left-hand column and then, after each word, write the letter of the correct definition from the right-hand column.

1. domino effect
2. escalation
3. Tet Offensive
4. Viet Cong
5. stalemate

a. a major battle of the war in Vietnam

b. the idea that one country's turn to communism leads to the fall of other countries

c. a situation in which neither side can win

d. a communist guerilla army in Vietnam

e. the increasing of a war effort

f. to accuse an official of breaking the law

SKILL BUILDER: READING A MAP

▶ Look at the maps of Korea and Vietnam. Then on a separate sheet of paper, answer the following questions.

1. What natural boundaries separate China and Korea?

2. In Southeast Asia, which countries became communist after 1965?

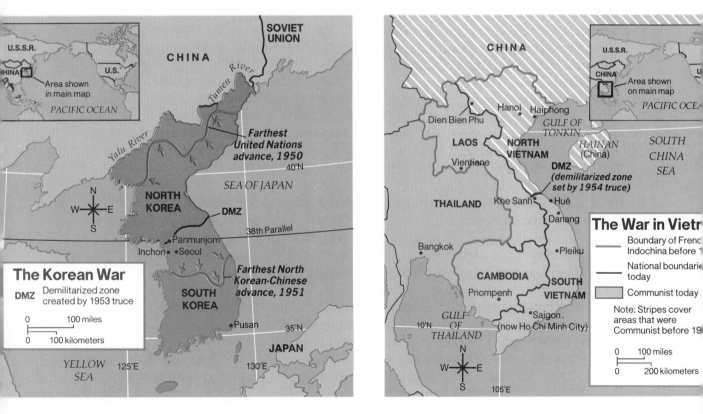

The Korean War

DMZ Demilitarized zone created by 1953 truce

0   100 miles
0   100 kilometers

Farthest United Nations advance, 1950

Farthest North Korean-Chinese advance, 1951

The War in Vietr

Boundary of Frenc Indochina before

National boundari today

Communist today

Note: Stripes cover areas that were Communist before 19

0   100 miles
0   200 kilometers

3. How do you think Hainan could have been important during the Vietnam War?

4. Which city in South Vietnam has changed its name since the end of the Vietnam War?

SKILL BUILDER: CRITICAL THINKING AND COMPREHENSION

I. Comparing and Contrasting

▶ On a separate sheet of paper, compare or contrast the following.

1. **Compare:** how the Vietnam and Korean wars started, who was involved in each war, and how the wars ended.

2. **Contrast:** how Americans felt about the Vietnam War and World War II.

II. Point of View

▶ On a separate sheet of paper, describe two points of view toward the following.

1. United States involvement in the Korean War

2. the escalation of United States involvement in Vietnam

III. Making Judgments

▶ On a separate sheet of paper, defend or attack the judgments made in the following situations.

1. General MacArthur was a very popular general, yet he went over President Truman's head in asking Congress to support his plan. If you were President Truman would you have dismissed him? Explain your answer.

2. Even after many Americans protested the Vietnam War, President Johnson continued the war. Was he right in making this decision? Explain your answer.

3. Did President Nixon make the right judgment in deciding to resign as President, or should he have waited to be impeached so that he could defend himself? Explain your answer.

USING PRIMARY SOURCES

▶ Reread the Spotlight on Sources on page 595. Which country or countries did Congress have in mind when it said it would help defend Vietnam from any communist country?

ENRICHMENT

1. Draw an outline map of the Korean peninsula. Use two colors to show the location of North Korea and South Korea. Mark the 38th parallel. Mark the capital of each country. Locate Inchon, the city where MacArthur attacked the North Koreans from the rear. Explain your map to your classmates.

2. Arrange a debate on this question: "Should the United States have been involved in the war in Vietnam?" Divide into two teams, one in favor of American involvement, the other against it. Use magazines and newspapers in your research as well as textbooks. Present your debate in class and let the class vote for the winning side.

CHAPTER 4

The United States and the Middle East

OBJECTIVE: Why did the United States become involved in events in the Middle East?

1. Ibn Saud, king of Saudi Arabia, placed his hand on the valve and gave it a turn. Oil now began to flow from the underground pipeline into the tanker ship *El Segundo*. It was 1939, and the place was the port of Ras Tanura on the Persian Gulf. This symbolic turning of the valve started the flow of oil which would supply energy worldwide. Ten years earlier, Ibn Saud's country had been one of the world's poorest. Ten years later, it would become one of the most important. The reason was that one fourth of the world's oil reserves lay beneath Ibn Saud's desert kingdom. An area that few outsiders had paid much attention would soon became one of the most critical spots on the map.

Oil and the Middle East Where is the Middle East? Why is it important to the United States?

2. Since shortly after World War II, the **Middle East** has become a major exporter of oil to the United States. The Middle East is the area at the eastern end of the Mediterranean Sea. It is made up of the western part of Asia, from Iran west to the Mediterranean, including the Arabian peninsula. It also includes Egypt and other countries in the northeastern part of Africa. Most countries of the Middle East are ruled by strong leaders or parties and are not democra-

▲ In 1978, President Jimmy Carter, President Anwar Sadat of Egypt, and Israeli Prime Minister Menachem Begin worked out a peace agreement between Egypt and Israeli at Camp David.

cies. See the map on page 600 to locate the countries of the Middle East.

3. Most of the people of the Middle East are Arabs. Most Arabs are **Muslims** (MUZ-luhmz). Muslims follow the Islamic religion, founded by the prophet Muhammad in the

In Chapter 4, you will apply these critical thinking skills to the historical process:
Sequencing: Putting a series of events in the correct time order.
❯ **Predicting:** Telling what you believe will happen on the basis of clues and facts.

seventh century. One Middle Eastern country that is not Arab is Israel. Israel is a Jewish state.

4. There is more oil in the Middle East than in any other part of the world. The United States, Western European nations, and Japan need the oil of the Middle East for their homes, cars, and factories. Oil wells in the United States do not produce all the oil it needs. Therefore, what happens in the Middle East is of great importance to the United States.

5. Israel was formed as an independent, democratic state in 1948, shortly after the end of World War II. In ancient times the area called Palestine, with its ancient capital city of Jerusalem, had been the home of the Jews. However, in the second century A.D. the Romans had driven them from it. Since then, the Jews were scattered in many places in the world.

6. In about 1900, Jewish settlers began to move back into Palestine in order to escape persecution in Eastern Europe. They sought to establish a Jewish homeland. Many Jews who had survived the Holocaust also came to Palestine after World War II. Why would Holocaust survivors come to Israel? The United States supported Israel with money, technical help, and arms from the beginning of its existence as a state. Why would the United States give such support to Israel?

7. Thousands of Arabs, whose ancestors had settled in the Jerusalem area centuries before, were living there. Bitter **hostility** (hahs-TIL-uh-tee) developed between the Israelis and the Arabs. Hostility is a feeling of unfriendliness against an enemy. Both Jews and Arabs claimed the land of Israel as their home. In 1948, a series of wars began. Israel was on one side. Palestinian Arabs and several of the neighboring Arab countries were on the other side. Why would other Arab states join in the fight against Israel? One of the most bitter of the Arab–Israeli wars took place in 1973.

The Oil Crisis   Why did the Arab nations cut off oil supplies to the United States in 1973?

8. In the Arab–Israeli war of 1973, the United States aided Israel by sending arms and supplies. In return, the Arab states refused to ship oil to the United States. The Arab oil countries belonged to the Organization of Petroleum Exporting Countries (OPEC). They succeeded in persuading all other members of OPEC to join in this embargo.

Spotlight on Sources

9. Sheikh Ahmad Zaki Yamani was the oil minister of Saudi Arabia, a main oil producer, during the oil embargo. This is how he later recalled what happened:

> The king [of Saudi Arabia] still wanted to give America a chance to stay out of the fighting. So we agreed to cut back production by just 5 percent per month. A full embargo, we agreed, was something we would implement [put into effect] only if we felt things were absolutely hopeless.
> —*The Kingdom*, by Robert Lacey

What did the Arabs hope to force the United States to do? Did their plan work?

10. As a result of the embargo, there were severe oil shortages in the United States. Long lines formed at gas stations. The price of oil and gasoline soared. A wave of inflation hit the United States. Why would a rise in the price of oil affect the prices of other products? This experience showed how dangerous it was for the United States to depend so heavily on oil from foreign sources.

The Camp David Accords   What was the role of the United States in arranging peace between Israel and Egypt?

11. In 1977, President Anwar Sadat (AHN-wahr suh-DAHT) of Egypt surprised the world by going to Israel to meet with Israeli prime minister Menachem Begin (muh-NAHK-uhm BAY-gin). His objective was to try to improve relations between the two former enemies. President Sadat was the first Arab head of state to visit Israel.

Oil in the Middle East Approximately 25 percent of the world's total oil supply comes from the Middle East. The region produces about 14 million barrels a day.

The map below shows that most Middle East oil fields are near the Persian Gulf. A second group of oil fields is located in Iraq along the Tigris River. Countries on the Mediterranean side of the Middle East have little or no oil. These oil-poor countries are Israel, Lebanon, Jordan, Turkey, and Syria.

Five Persian Gulf countries control the Middle East oil production. The largest oil producer is Saudi Arabia, which accounts for about one-third of all Middle East oil. Iran and Iraq compete for second place. Together Iran and Iraq produce another one-third of Middle East oil. Kuwait and the United Arab Emirates account for most of the remaining one-third.

Most, but not all, Middle East producers belong to OPEC (Organization of Petroleum Exporting Countries). OPEC members work together to limit oil output so that world oil prices remain high. Without OPEC's controls, the Middle East could produce much more oil.

Names of OPEC members are underlined on the map below.

The Persian Gulf is the chief outlet for Middle East oil. Tankers carry most of the oil through the Persian Gulf. Pipelines also get oil to the market. One Saudi Arabian pipeline runs to its Red Sea port off Yenbo, another to Aqaba in Jordan. Iraq's pipelines carry oil to Syria and Turkey.

In 1990, Saddam Hussein, the ruler of Iraq, invaded Kuwait, threatening the oil supply of the United States and European countries. In 1991, when he did not withdraw, members of the United Nations, including the United States, went to war with Iraq.

Now use the map below to answer these questions.

1. Where are most of the Middle East's oil fields and tanker terminals?

2. Which countries have coastlines on the Persian Gulf?

3. Which of the countries on the map are OPEC members?

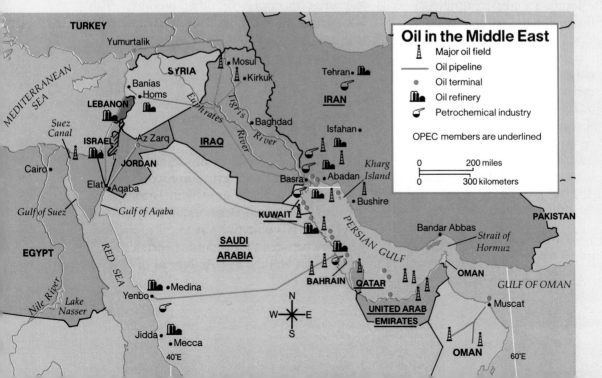

Oil in the Middle East

- Major oil field
- Oil pipeline
- Oil terminal
- Oil refinery
- Petrochemical industry

OPEC members are underlined

0   200 miles
0   300 kilometers

People in History

12. Jimmy Carter The President of the United States, Jimmy Carter, now saw an opportunity to arrange for peace between Israel and Egypt, which had been enemies since 1948. In the past, the United States had aided Israel in its wars with Arab states. However, it had always been interested in bringing peace to this troubled area of the world. In 1978, Carter invited Sadat and Begin to the United States to work out a peace treaty. For 12 days, Carter, Sadat, and Begin met at Camp David, the presidential retreat in Maryland. The result was the Camp David Accords, which provided a framework for a peace treaty between Egypt and Israel. A formal peace treaty was signed the next year. Egypt thus became the first Arab country to recognize Israel.

13. Other Arab nations and Egyptian extremists condemned the peace treaty and Sadat for having signed it. Sadat paid for his bold move with his life three years later. He was killed by his enemies in Egypt. His death dimmed hopes for peace between Israel and its neighbors.

The United States and Iran How did a revolution in Iran affect the United States?

14. Although President Carter scored a triumph in negotiating the Camp David Accords, he was less fortunate in dealing with Iran. Iran is also located in the Middle East. In 1979, an Islamic revolution took place in Iran. The country's ruler, the shah, was overthrown. Iranian revolutionaries hated the United States because it had supported the shah's regime. Later also the United States allowed the exiled shah to come to the United States for medical treatment. In November 1979, a group of young Iranian **radicals** (RAD-uh-kuhlz) seized the American embassy in Tehran, the capital. A radical is a person who believes in policies or views that require extreme change from the existing structure. They made the Americans there **hostages** (HAHS-tuh-jez). A hostage is a person who is being held prisoner until certain demands are

met. The Iranians held 52 of the hostages until the last day of Carter's term of office in 1981. Many Americans voted against Carter in the 1980 election because they believed he had not done enough to free the hostages.

Israel and Lebanon How did fighting in these countries involve the United States?

15. Just north of Israel is the country of Lebanon, which has been another Middle East trouble spot. Beginning in 1975, a civil war raged there between Lebanon's Christian and Muslim people. To complicate matters, thousands of Palestinians who had fled Israel in 1948 were living in Lebanon. Lebanon became the headquarters of the Palestine Liberation Organization (PLO). The PLO waged guerilla war against Israel using Lebanon as its base. In return, Israel launched a massive invasion into Lebanon in 1982 to wipe out the PLO.

16. The United States and other countries tried unsuccessfully to bring peace to Lebanon. Terrorist activity increased despite the presence of peacekeeping forces from the United States, France, and Italy. Then, in April 1983, a terrorist suicide mission bombed the American embassy, killing 50 people. Worse was to come in October, when a truck loaded with explosives drove into the American Marine base. More than 230 Marines were killed. In the United States, an outcry arose against American involvement in Lebanon, and President Ronald Reagan ordered American troops home.

Outlook

17. Many countries depend on the Middle East for their oil. This is one reason why the United States helps to maintain peace in the region. One of its greatest achievements in this respect was working out a peace treaty between Egypt and Israel. But because the United States is a supporter of Israel, many Middle Easterners think of the United States as an enemy. The next time you hear a newscast, be on the alert for word about this troubled region.

Background: The PLO was founded in 1964 in Jordan to consolidate all organizations of Palestinians opposed to Israel. The organization has many internal groups, some of which are rivals. In 1989, its leader, Yasir Arafat, went on record renouncing its aim to destroy Israel, but some PLO members repudiated his statements.

CHAPTER REVIEW

VOCABULARY REVIEW

▶ Write each number and word on a sheet of paper. Then write the letter of the definition next to the word it defines.

1. Middle East
2. Muslims
3. hostility
4. hostage
5. radicals

a. a person who is held prisoner until certain demands are met
b. feeling of unfriendliness against an enemy
c. believers in the religion of Islam
d. persons who believe in policies or views that require extreme change from the existing structure
e. a member of a terrorist organization
f. the region of the world that includes the western part of Asia, from Iran west to the Mediterranean Sea, including the Arabian peninsula

SKILL BUILDER: MAKING AN OUTLINE

▶ On a separate sheet of paper, copy the outline below. Read the topic sentences listed. Choose the correct topic sentence for the supporting sentences in the outline and write it in the blank.

The United States and the Middle East

The United States has had both success and failure in the Middle East.

The Arab–Israeli conflict affects the United States.

I. _____
   A. Arab states oppose Israel and use oil as a political weapon.
   B. OPEC places embargo on United States in 1973.
   C. Oil prices sharply rise in the United States.
II. _____
   A. President Carter works to bring about the Camp David Accords between Egypt and Israel.
   B. Iran revolutionaries hold 52 Americans hostage.

SKILL BUILDER: CRITICAL THINKING AND COMPREHENSION

I. Cause and Effect

▶ On a separate sheet of paper, write the following statements. Then fill in the missing cause or effect.

1. **Cause:** _____
   Effect: An oil embargo by OPEC was placed on the United States.

2. **Cause:** Iranian revolutionaries hated the United States for supporting the shah.
   Effect: _____

3. **Cause:** The PLO waged guerilla war against Israel from Lebanon.

   Effect: _____

II. Sequencing

▶ Copy the following events on a separate sheet of paper. Number the events in the order in which they happened.

a. Israel launches invasion into Lebanon to strike at PLO bases.

b. Civil war erupts in Lebanon between Christian and Muslim people.

c. Iranians seize the United States embassy.

d. State of Israel is formed.

e. Oil embargo is placed on United States during the Arab–Israeli war.

f. Ibn Saud opened the valve to start the flow of oil from Saudi Arabia.

g. President Anwar Sadat meets with Prime Minister Menachem Begin in Israel.

h. A peace treaty is signed between Egypt and Israel.

i. Jewish settlers from Eastern Europe begin to move to Palestine.

III. Predicting

▶ Read each of the statements below. Then on a separate sheet of paper write your predictions and explain why you made them.

1. What might have happened if the United States had not supported the shah of Iran before 1979?

2. What might have happened if President Carter had successfully negotiated the release of hostages in Iran?

USING PRIMARY SOURCES

▶ Reread the Spotlight on Sources on page 599. What does the statement tell you about why the Middle East is important to the United States?

ENRICHMENT

1. Imagine you are an artist during the 1973 oil embargo. You have been asked to make a poster to remind people to save oil and gasoline. Describe or make such a poster. Try to think of a catchy slogan that would help you get your idea across.

2. Find out about all the wars that have been fought between Israel and the Arabs since 1948. Describe each one, mentioning how it began, where it was fought, and who the winner was.

3. In the library, read about developments that have taken place in the Middle East in the last six months. Listen to news broadcasts about the latest events in the Middle East. Take notes to prepare for making an oral report to your class.

CHAPTER 5

America Works for Peace

OBJECTIVE: What steps did the United States take to try to end the Cold War?

1. On October 26, 1962, an American newspaper reporter was having lunch with a Russian diplomat. The reporter had never seen the man look so frightened. "War seems about to break out," the Russian said. "Something must be done to save the situation." The diplomat was not the only one who feared that war might break out. People everywhere were afraid that the world was facing a nuclear war between the Soviet Union and the United States. They feared that a nuclear war would be worse than any war previously fought. There were doubts that anyone could survive such a horrible war. Demonstrators marched in front of the United Nations building in New York City in a plea for peace. College students held peace rallies across the country. All this was taking place because the Soviet Union had placed missiles in Cuba. President John F. Kennedy had responded with a warning: If the Soviets did not remove the missiles, war might break out. To prove he meant business, Kennedy ordered American naval vessels to blockade Cuba. The world held its breath waiting to see what the Soviet Union would do. Rather than risk a nuclear war, the Soviets agreed to remove the missiles from Cuba. The crisis was part of the Cold War between the United States and the Soviet Union. In this chapter, you will read how American and Soviet leaders tried to end the Cold War.

▲ In 1972, President Nixon became the first American President to visit Communist China while in office. What was the purpose of his visit?

The Cuban Missile Crisis How did Soviet missile bases in Cuba almost lead to war?

2. One of the most dangerous events in the Cold War centered on Cuba. Cuba was ruled by a communist government. In October 1962, President Kennedy learned that the Soviet

In Chapter 5 you will apply these critical thinking skills to the historical process:

◢ **Making Judgments:** Stating a personal opinion based on historical facts.

▌ **Comparing and Contrasting:** Recognizing similarities and differences.

Union had sent **guided missiles** to Cuba. Guided missiles are military rockets that are controlled by radio or radar. Kennedy also discovered that the Soviets were building bases there from which to launch the missiles. He was deeply worried by this news because he knew that the missiles would be able to carry nuclear warheads. Cuba was only 90 miles (145 kilometers) south of Florida. Kennedy decided that he must act to remove this grave threat.

3. Some advisors urged Kennedy to destroy the missiles by bombing Cuba. However, Kennedy believed that this might cause a war with the Soviet Union. Instead, he decided to send the United States Navy to blockade Cuba. He also warned the Soviet leader, Nikita Khrushchev (nuh-KEE-tuh KROOSH-chawf), to remove the missiles from Cuba. On October 22, Kennedy made a speech on television telling Americans about the Cuban missile crisis.

4. For the next six days, Americans waited and worried. No one knew what Khrushchev would do. Unless he agreed to remove the missiles, the United States might have to bomb the missile sites. But then a terrible nuclear war ► might take place. Why did Americans and people everywhere fear such a war? Finally, Khrushchev gave in. He agreed to take the Soviet missiles out of Cuba. Kennedy's firm action had forced the Soviet Union to back down. Even so, the Cuban missile crisis showed how dangerous the Cold War had become.

5. After the Cuban Missile Crisis, the United States and the Soviet Union tried to improve relations with each other. Kennedy and Khrushchev set up a **hot line**. A hot line is a special telephone used in times of emergency or crisis. It allows the leaders of the two nations to talk instantly and directly to each other. In this way, they could try to solve dangerous problems before they got out of hand.

Spotlight on Sources

6. Kennedy now made peace his most urgent goal as President. In June 1963, he explained his feelings to a group of college students.

▲ A year before the 1962 Cuban Missile Crisis, President Kennedy and Soviet leader Nikita Khrushchev held a summit meeting in Vienna.

Some say that it is useless to speak of world peace until the leaders of the Soviet Union adopt a more enlightened attitude [become more reasonable]. But we must not see conflict [war] as inevitable [certain to come]. If we cannot now end our differences, at least we can help make the world safe.

—from the Commencement Address at American University in Washington, D.C., President John F. Kennedy, June 10, 1963

Explain whether or not President Kennedy ◄ thought war between the United States and the Soviet Union was inevitable.

Limiting Weapons What arms agreements did the United States make with the Soviet Union to reduce the danger of war?

7. When the United States exploded two atomic bombs over Japan in 1945, the world

605

realized how destructive nuclear weapons could be. Ever since, people have lived with the fear of a nuclear war. To prevent such wars, the nations with nuclear weapons agreed that **arms limitation agreements** should be worked out. Arms limitation agreements are agreements that limit the number of nuclear weapons the nations should be allowed to manufacture.

8. President Kennedy signed a nuclear test-ban treaty with the Soviet Union in 1963. In this treaty, both countries agreed to stop testing nuclear arms above ground. Kennedy hoped this agreement would stop the race to build more and more weapons. However, Kennedy's hopes for peace soon faded. The Soviet Union began a strong build-up of its military forces, and the United States became involved in the war in Vietnam. (You have read about the Vietnam War in Chapter 3.)

9. In 1972, President Nixon worked out another arms limitation agreement with the Soviet Union called the Strategic Arms Limitation Treaty (SALT). SALT limited both countries in the numbers and types of nuclear weapons each country could have.

Détente How did American relations with the Soviet Union and Communist China improve in the 1970s?

10. In the early 1970s, President Richard Nixon took important steps to try to end the Cold War. Nixon believed that the United States and the Soviet Union should work toward a policy of **détente** (day-TAHNT). Détente means relaxation of tensions between nations. Nixon felt that 1972 was the right time to start this policy of better relations. By that time, the Soviet Union and Communist China had become enemies. Large numbers of Soviet soldiers were stationed along the border with China. As a result, both countries wanted to improve their relations with the United States.
▶ Why would they want to do this at this time?

11. In February 1972, Nixon traveled to Communist China. He spent a week in Beijing (bay-jing), the Chinese capital, talking with

THE PRESIDENTS' CORNER

At the age of 43, **John F. Kennedy** became the youngest man ever elected President of the United States. Kennedy was also the first Roman Catholic to hold the office of President. He served from 1961 until his assassination in 1963. While he was President, his leadership and personality came to stand for the spirit of youth and change of the 1960s. Many young people volunteered for the Peace Corps, started by Kennedy to help people in poor countries of the world.

Kennedy proved that even though he was young, he could stand up to the Soviets during the Cuban Missile Crisis. In his administration, preparations to send American astronauts to the moon began. African Americans struggling for civil rights made more gains during the Kennedy Administration than in any earlier administration since the Civil War.

Communist China's leaders. The two countries agreed to trade with each other for the first time in many years. They agreed that Chinese and Americans should be able to travel to each other's lands. They also promised to work for peace and closer relations in the future. Nixon's policy of détente with China was a great success.

12. In May 1972, President Nixon continued his efforts for détente by traveling to the Soviet Union. There he met with Soviet leaders to explore ways of improving relations. Nixon and the Soviet leader, Leonid Brezhnev (LAY-oh-need BREZH-nef), agreed to increase trade between their nations.

People in History

13. Henry Kissinger In working for détente, Nixon received important help from Henry Kissinger (KIS-uhn-juhr). Kissinger had come to the United States as a teenage Jewish refugee from Nazi Germany in 1938. After college, he became a professor at Harvard University. In 1969, Nixon selected him as his special advisor on foreign policy. Kissinger's views helped shape Nixon's views on world affairs. For example, Kissinger thought of the United States and the Soviet Union as **superpowers**. Superpowers are nations so powerful that their actions affect the whole world. Kissinger believed that the superpowers had to find ways to live together and to work for peace. Thus, Kissinger helped Nixon plan détente.

14. President Carter, like Nixon, favored better relations with the Soviet Union. In 1979, Carter and Brezhnev met to sign the SALT II treaty. In this agreement, both countries agreed to limit the number of their long-range missiles. However, the United States Senate did not approve SALT II. Many senators believed the treaty would allow the Soviets to become too powerful. Further, the Soviet invasion of Afghanistan (see paragraph 16) so upset the senators, they had no interest in signing a new treaty with the Soviet Union.

15. Carter's policies on **human rights** also caused trouble with the Soviet Union. Human rights are the basic freedoms that all people should have. These include the right of free speech and the right to move to another country. Carter insisted that all nations must protect their people's human rights. However, in the Soviet Union, the government denied people important human rights. For example, many Jews wanted to leave the Soviet Union, but the government would not let them go. When Carter urged Soviet leaders to allow Jewish citizens to move to Israel or the United States, the Soviets angrily refused. They said Carter must stop interfering in Soviet affairs.

16. Carter's plans for better relations with the Soviet Union were also set back by Soviet actions. The Soviet Union sent weapons advisors to help communist fighters in several African countries. Then, early in 1979, Soviet armies invaded the Asian nation of Afghanistan. Carter protested the invasion by halting grain sales to the Soviet Union. He also withdrew the United States from the 1980 Olympic Games in Moscow. However, Carter was powerless to take stronger action. He left office in 1981 bitterly disappointed that the period of détente seemed to have come to an end.

Outlook

17. The Cold War almost led to a nuclear war during the Cuban Missile Crisis. Then, in the 1970s, Nixon's policy of détente improved America's relations with Communist China and with the Soviet Union. However, Soviet policy hardened once again during Jimmy Carter's presidency. Carter left office with the two nations on very unfriendly terms. To many Americans, it seemed that the Cold War would go on forever. What do you think had caused the ◄ greatest trouble between the two superpowers?

▼ President Jimmy Carter's efforts to improve relations with the Soviet Union were hampered by Soviet actions in Afghanistan and elsewhere.

Ask: Briefly review with the class the foreign policies of Nixon and Carter. Which President's policies do students think were more effective?

CHAPTER REVIEW

VOCABULARY REVIEW

▶ Write each number and word on a sheet of paper. Then write the letter of the definition next to the word it defines.

1. détente
2. human rights
3. superpowers
4. guided missile
5. hot line
6. arms limitation agreements
7. nuclear warheads

a. a rocket controlled by radio or radar
b. agreements about nuclear weapons
c. people's basic freedoms
d. very powerful nations
e. relaxation of relations between countries
f. a special telephone line that can be used by the leaders of two nations

SKILL BUILDER: MAKING A TIME LINE

▶ On a sheet of paper, copy the time line below. Then place the events on the time line.

Soviet Union invades Afghanistan

Nixon visits China and the Soviet Union

Cuban Missile Crisis

Nixon is impeached

Carter and Brezhnev sign the SALT II treaty

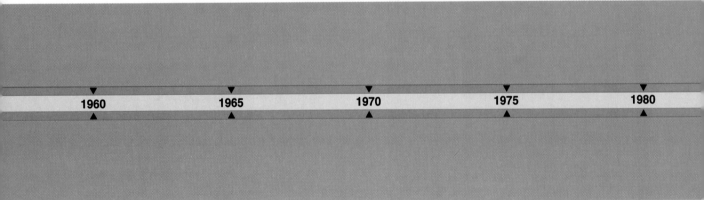

| 1960 | 1965 | 1970 | 1975 | 1980 |

USING PRIMARY SOURCES

▶ Reread the Spotlight on Sources on page 605. Does President Kennedy believe that world peace is possible? Explain your answer. What change has taken place in the Soviet Union regarding its "more enlightened attitude"?

SKILL BUILDER: CRITICAL THINKING AND COMPREHENSION

I. Making Judgments

1. Imagine that you are President of the United States in 1962. You find out that the Soviet Union has sent missiles to Cuba. Make a judgment about which of the actions below you would take. On a separate sheet of paper, give reasons for your judgment.
   a. bomb Cuba
   b. do what Kennedy did
   c. do nothing

2. Now imagine that you are President Carter in 1979. The Soviet Union has just sent troops into Afghanistan. Make a judgment about which of the following actions to take. On a separate sheet of paper, give reasons for your judgment.
   a. send American troops to Afghanistan
   b. do what Carter did
   c. call a meeting of the United Nations to demand that the Soviets leave Afghanistan

II. Drawing Conclusions

1. Imagine you are the President of the United States. A powerful country is giving arms to your close neighbor. Draw a conclusion about what you might do if the neighbor is unfriendly.

2. Now draw a conclusion as to what you might do if the neighbor is friendly.

III. Compare and Contrast

1. Compare the success of Nixon's visit to China with his visit to the Soviet Union.

2. Contrast the success of Nixon's "détente" with the success of Carter's push for human rights.

ENRICHMENT

1. In this chapter, you have read about the Cuban Missile Crisis. Interview someone in your family or a friend who remembers this crisis. Then make believe you are that person and write entries in a diary about how you felt at the time and what happened.

2. When Krushchev was in power in the Soviet Union, he made a speech about the terrible things that Joseph Stalin had done as the Soviets' leader. Find and read that speech through library research, and then write how you think a Soviet person would have felt after hearing about it.

3. In this chapter you have read about two Soviet leaders, Khrushchev and Brezhnev. Read about Soviet leaders who came after Brezhnev, how they were chosen, what their policies were, and what they accomplished. Write a radio play summarizing that period in Soviet history, assign roles to your classmates, and present the play to the class.

4. Work in teams to collect recent newspaper and magazine accounts of Soviet-American relations. Photocopy articles from these sources to bring to class.

UNIT REVIEW

SUMMARY

After World War II, the United States was one of the strongest countries in the world. Many other countries had been ruined by the war. The United States and other Western countries and the Soviet Union competed for control of other countries weakened by the war. Many people were turning to communism, and the Soviet Union gained much influence over the countries of Eastern Europe as well as parts of Asia. The United States and the Soviet Union became embroiled in a Cold War.

The United States fought two wars in Asia to contain communism. The first was the Korean War in the early 1950s, which left Korea divided. In the 1960s, the United States became entangled in the Vietnam War. Thousands of American troops were sent to fight a war the United States did not win. Many Americans protested United States involvement in the Vietnam War, and in 1973 American troops pulled out.

In the 1970s, Presidents Nixon and Carter both began to seek peace with the Soviet Union and to improve relations with Communist China. This was the era of détente.

Many Americans hoped that before long the United States and the Soviet Union would be able to work out their differences. They look forward to the time when the world would be free to tackle problems like the pollution of the environment and feeding its hungry people.

SKILL BUILDER: INTERPRETING A MAP

▶ The map below identifies NATO members and CEMA members. CEMA (Council for Economic and Mutual Assistance), an alliance of communist governments, was formed in 1955. Study the map, then answer the questions.

1. In what part of the world did NATO member countries border directly on CEMA member countries?

2. Which two CEMA countries were closest to the United States?

The Superpowers and Their Allies

NATO members (United States, Belgium, Canada, Denmark, France, West Germany, Greece, Iceland, Italy, Luxembourg, Netherlands, Norway, Portugal, Spain, Turkey, United Kingdom)

CEMA members (Soviet Union, Bulgaria, Cuba, Czechoslovakia, East Germany, Hungary, Mongolia, Poland, Romania, Vietnam)

3. After studying the map, write a paragraph explaining how geography affected the relationship of the United States and the Soviet Union in an age of guided missiles. Include an explanation of why Canada, Greenland, and Cuba were important.

SKILL BUILDER: CRITICAL THINKING AND COMPREHENSION

I. Cause and Effect

▶ Write each statement on a separate sheet of paper. Fill in the missing cause or effect.

1. **Cause:** The United States feared communism and wanted to contain its spread.
   Effect: _____

2. **Cause:** _____
   Effect: America was a very powerful nation after World War II.

3. **Cause:** The United States sent troops to fight on the side of South Vietnam.
   Effect: _____

4. **Cause:** _____
   Effect: The United States began a policy of détente.

II. Making Judgments

▶ On a separate sheet of paper, write a few sentences in which you make a judgment of the actions described below.

1. Senator Joseph McCarthy said that communists were gaining influence in the United States and accused people of being disloyal.

2. President Lyndon B. Johnson believed in the domino effect in Southeast Asia and stepped up United States involvement in South Vietnam.

3. The United States Senate did not approve the SALT II treaties.

ENRICHMENT

1. Many people feel that the Vietnam War changed the way Americans think about their government. Research this period in American history and describe the changes the country was going through.

2. In magazines or books find photographs from the 1950s, 1960s, and 1970s that capture important events in the world and the United States. Xerox these photographs and group them by decade. Then arrange them on a large display board. Write a time line for each decade, giving the important dates and events.

3. By the 1960s, some people began to think of the countries of the world as being in one of three "worlds." The "first world" was the United States and the countries of Western Europe. The "second world" was the U.S.S.R. and the countries of Eastern Europe. And the "third world" was made up of the rest of the world—mostly the developing countries of Asia, Africa, and Latin America. Research which countries belong to each of these "worlds" and explain why they are placed in these "worlds."

UNIT 15

AMERICANS STRENGTHEN THEIR NATION

Chapter

UNIT OVERVIEW   Unit 15 will help you to understand what people did to make the United States a stronger, fairer, and safer nation in the latter half of the twentieth century.

UNIT SKILLS OBJECTIVES   In Unit 15, two critical thinking skills are emphasized:

Making Judgments: Stating a personal opinion based on historical facts.

Comparing and Contrasting: Recognizing similarities and differences.

You will also use two important social studies skills:
Using a Map   Reading Graphs and Charts

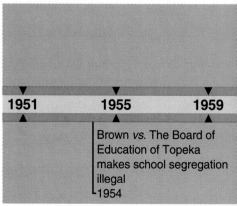

1951	1955	1959

Brown *vs.* The Board of Education of Topeka makes school segregation illegal
1954

ESL/LEP Strategy: Have the students, working in teams, use the letters of the word *opportunities* as the initial letters of words or concepts that make them think about the United States as a land of opportunity. Ask the teams to compare their lists with those of other teams and discuss the lists in class.

▲ Wearing uniforms of George Washington's Continental Army, Americans gather before the Capitol in 1987 to celebrate the first 200 years of the Constitution.

Chavez starts National Farm Workers Association, 1962

The March on Washington takes place, 1963

Clean Air Act passes 1970

Equal Employment Opportunities Act passes, 1972

Gorbachev visits the United States; Exxon Valdez oil spill occurs 1987

Persian Gulf War is fought. Soviet Union collapses 1991

| 963 | 1967 | 1971 | 1975 | 1979 | 1983 | 1987 | 1991 |

The Civil Rights Act is passed 1964

Chavez calls for national boycott of grapes, 1967

Dr. Martin Luther King, Jr., leads a voting rights march in Montgomery, Alabama 1965

Indian Self-Determination Act passes, 1976

All Handicapped Children Act passes, 1975

Los Angeles riots occur 1992

Points of View

Americans can be proud of the many accomplishments they have made in this century. While many problems do face the nation, Americans have shown the willingness to tackle them. Though sometimes change has been slow and hard, reforms have been brought about by dedicated and courageous Americans.

There have been many changes in the recent past. New immigrants from Asia and Latin America have come to the United States seeking opportunity and freedom. Technology has grown in tremendous leaps. Computers, new scientific and medical discoveries, and space travel are all part of the many achievements. But along with these advances, there have been problems both old and new that face our nation.

A VIEW FROM THE WEST COAST

"In the state of California, minorities will soon be the majority. I know in my neighborhood, we already are. I see more and more Asian American artists, teachers, police, business people, and even judges and politicians. Many Asian Americans believe that studying hard and doing well in school will help in getting a good job in science, medicine, or business. I think education is important. We need more teachers and books and better ways for all students to learn. Through education, people will come to appreciate the different heritages and cultures that make up this diverse population, and so learn to work together.

California is a beautiful state. But oil spills along the coast and car exhaust fumes in the cities have caused pollution. We need stronger laws and penalties for people who hurt our environment. After all, everyone must breathe the same air, drink the same water, eat the same foods. We have to protect the environment for the future. I know people have begun to recycle their garbage, conserve energy, and use public transportation. These are things individuals can do to make a difference.

When people come together, things can change. We can do food drives to help poor and homeless people. Through voting we can choose government officials who will work to create jobs, training, and affordable housing. When this happens, people feel there is hope. With these improvements, more people will turn away from drugs and crime and turn to hope and happiness."

San San Wong, aged 14, Los Angeles, California

Using Primary Sources

1. What similar problems do these teenagers see in the United States? Do you agree with them? Why?

2. Both writers suggest similar solutions for racism. Do you agree with their solution? Explain your reasons.

614

Looking to Tomorrow

Americans and people around the world must work harder for world peace. With the power to destroy the planet, no one can afford another world war. At home, America will continue its progress toward justice and equal opportunities for people of all races, nationalities, and beliefs. Problems of drugs, homelessness, poverty, discrimination, pollution, and other must be tackled with determination and boldness. Americans will continue to be active to improve their society.

What problems are most important to Americans today? What is there to look forward to in the future? What do young people think about the future? Here are the opinions of two teenagers—one an Asian American from California, the other an African American from New York.

A VIEW FROM THE EAST COAST

"Poverty, homelessness, and illiteracy are some of our biggest problems. Our government should be going out of its way to provide shelter for all Americans and to give the homeless hope for a better life. Learning centers should be built to provide places where people can learn how to read and write and take classes to earn a high school diploma. Then the homeless and the poor would be able to get jobs and support themselves.

The drug situation is another major problem because it affects everyone. It's most obvious that the laws against drugs and drug smuggling are not being taken seriously or being strictly enforced. Our war against drugs might work better if the government used more tax money on drug programs instead of on new weapons and new space programs. More police officers on the street are needed as well as neighborhood watches to protect the areas in which we live. If local or federal governments would start more rehabilitation centers, addicts might have a chance to "kick the habit."

The most important thing for the future is brotherhood: a unified country no matter what race, creed, or color you may be. This would call for the elimination of racism. I believe racism will stop if ignorant people begin to realize that understanding, not hate, is the answer.

The United States is supposed to be a free democracy in action. But we're not free if we are not united. We, the people, make up the United States of America. If we unite as one, we can have a brighter and better future."

Mona Young, aged 16, Queens, New York

3. Are the problems faced by Americans today better or worse than problems faced by Americans in the past? How do you think George Washington, Thomas Jefferson, Ben Franklin and James Madison would deal with the problems Americans face today?

CHAPTER 1

Equal Rights for African Americans

OBJECTIVE: How have African Americans worked for equal rights?

1. In 1951, third-grader Linda Brown had to walk half a mile to the bus stop and then ride two miles on the bus. Linda could not go to the nearby school with the white children because it was against the state law for her to do so. Kansas and 20 other mostly southern states had laws that said African Americans and whites had to attend separate schools. Linda's father and other African American parents thought that these laws were unfair. With help from the National Association for the Advancement of Colored People (NAACP), they sued the school board of Topeka.

Segregation and Civil Rights What forms of segregation did the civil rights movement fight against?

2. In 1947, Jackie Robinson made an important step towards equality for all African Americans. He became the first African American to break the color barrier in major league baseball, ▶ playing for the Brooklyn Dodgers. Why is Jackie Robinson's achievement important in the struggle for civil rights? Nevertheless, when the Dodgers played in Southern cities, Robinson had to follow the segregation laws. For example, he could not eat in restaurants or room in hotels with his white teammates.

3. In the South, certain practices limited African Americans from improving their lives.

▲ Linda Brown's lawsuit against the Topeka Board of Education gave the civil rights movement one of its first and greatest victories.

Even into the 1950s, Southern states continued to keep African Americans from voting. White Southerners did this through poll taxes, grandfather clauses, literacy tests, and threats of violence. Even in other parts of the United States, few African Americans were elected to government positions.

In Chapter 1 you will apply these critical thinking skills to the historical process:

➡ **Recognizing Cause and Effect:** Recognizing the action or event that makes something happen; identifying the result of an action or event.

▲ **Identifying Fact *versus* Opinion:** Specifying whether information can be proved or whether it expresses feelings or beliefs.

4. By the early 1950s, most African Americans realized that progress toward equality had been painfully slow. On December 1, 1955, an incident took place in Montgomery, Alabama, that led to what came to be called the **civil rights movement**. The goal of the civil rights movement was to overturn practices that denied African Americans and other minorities their civil rights.

5. The incident, which led to a major boycott, involved an African American woman named Rosa Parks. Parks was a seamstress from Montgomery who, on that day, refused to give up her city bus seat to a white man. She chose to face arrest rather than give in to this Jim Crow tradition one more time. Her decision inspired a boycott of the city's buses. About 17,000 African Americans were led by a 27-year-old minister named Martin Luther King. These boycotters refused to ride the city buses until they could sit where they pleased. King and his followers used a strategy called **nonviolent,** or passive, **resistance.** King had learned about passive resistance from the Hindu leader Mahatma Gandhi. People who used passive resistance drew attention to unjust laws by refusing to obey them. They also accepted the risk of being arrested for breaking the law. The Montgomery bus boycott and other similar boycotts of places such as restaurants and theaters were effective. In 1956, the Supreme Court ruled that segregated seating on buses was unconstitutional.

6. For many African Americans, religion and community churches had always been centers of community life. Therefore, African Americans turned to their ministers for leadership during the civil rights movement. Many ministers were involved in the Southern Christian Leadership Conference (SCLC), which Dr. King formed during the Montgomery bus boycott.

7. In the 1960s, the civil rights movement gathered strength. Young people formed the Congress of Racial Equality (CORE). Under the leadership of James Farmer, its members, both African American and white, traveled through the South on **freedom rides** to end

▲ The Montgomery, Alabama, protest movement, which Rosa Parks began, soon came under the leadership of a young minister, Martin Luther King, Jr.

segregation on interstate buses. Members of another group, the Student Nonviolent Coordinating Committee (SNCC), fought segregation laws by holding **sit-ins** and registering citizens to vote. During a sit-in, African Americans sat at all-white lunch counters and refused to leave. Often they were carried out by the police. Dr. King held marches to end segregation in Birmingham, Alabama, that attracted national attention through the television. Viewers were shocked to see women, children, and students attacked by the police and their dogs. As a result, Americans of all backgrounds spoke out for civil rights.

8. Getting African Americans to vote was one of Dr. King's most important goals, but there was resistance. In 1964, while trying to enroll African American voters, three civil rights workers, two whites and one black, who were members of SNCC, were murdered in Mississippi. In 1965 King led a peaceful voting rights march from Selma to Montgomery, Alabama. The march attracted national attention when local police and state troopers tried to stop it with cattle prods and arrests.

People in History

9. Martin Luther King, Jr. Born and raised in Atlanta, Georgia, Martin Luther King, Jr., became a minister in 1954 when he was 26. Ten years later, he received the Nobel Peace prize for his nonviolent civil rights crusade. From 1955 to 1965, King led many demonstrations all over the United States. Under his leadership the civil rights movement made important advances toward equal rights.

10. Probably the high point of King's activity came in the summer of 1963. King, along with African American union leader A. Philip Randolph, organized the March on Washington. The purpose of the march was to protest racial injustice and celebrate the hundredth anniversary of the Emancipation Proclamation. More than 200,000 Americans attended. Millions more watched on television as King, from the steps of the Lincoln Memorial, poured forth the words, "I have a dream that one day this nation will rise up and live out the true meaning of its creed: 'We hold these truths to be self-evident; that all men are created equal.' "

11. Not all African Americans shared King's views. Some groups, such as the Black Muslims and Black Panthers, preached **black separatism** (SEP-uh-ruh-tizm). Black separatism means living in separate communities, apart from white Americans. Black Muslim leaders Elijah Muhammad and Malcolm X and Black Panther leaders Eldridge Cleaver and Huey Newton had different beliefs from King. The Muslims believed in the Islamic religion. The Panthers believed in revolution. Both groups felt that African Americans should fight back and defend themselves when attacked. In the late 1960s, some CORE and SNCC leaders popularized the idea of **Black Power.** Black power meant self-determination for African Americans—the ability and means to make their own economic and political decisions. How was black power similar to the ideas of Marcus Garvey? ◄

12. Many white Americans blamed the Black Power movement for riots in cities such as Los Angeles, Cleveland, Newark, Boston, New York, Detroit, and Washington. The riots occurred between 1964 and 1967. In reality, these riots broke out because the problems of poverty and segregation had not been solved by the civil rights movement. Most African Americans realized that violence and destruction were not going to solve their problems.

Civil Rights and the Federal Government What did the federal government do to aid equality for African Americans?

13. From the 1940s to the 1960s, the Supreme Court was taking action to ban laws that limited the rights of African Americans. In 1946, the Supreme Court ruled that a Virginia law requiring segregation on interstate buses was illegal. In the 1940s, the Supreme Court also ruled that people could not discriminate when it came to the sale of property.

Spotlight on Sources

14. In 1954, the Supreme Court made school segregation illegal. *Brown versus the Board of Education of Topeka* was the lawsuit that Linda Brown's father brought. In his decision, Chief Justice Earl Warren wrote the following:

> Does segregation of children in public school solely on the basis of race, even though the physical facilities [buildings] and other tangible [capable of being touched] factors may be equal, deprive [deny] children of the minority group of equal educational opportunities? We believe that it does. We conclude that in the field of public education, the doctrine of "separate but equal" has no place. Separate educational facilities are inherently [by their very nature] unequal.
> —from *Brown v. the Board of Education of Topeka*

▲ Jesse Jackson first became well known as a civil rights leader in Chicago. He won national attention when he ran for the Democratic nomination for President in 1988.

▶ Why do you think the court felt separate facilities are unequal?

15. The Supreme Court has also had to decide the hotly debated issue of **affirmative action** programs. Affirmative action programs help people who are victims of past injustices. They also help people get jobs in fields where they were discriminated against in the past. In recent years, the Supreme Court has set up guidelines for affirmative action programs.

16. As a result of the civil rights movement of the 1950s and 1960s, Congress passed a series of civil rights acts. The federal government outlawed all barriers to voting rights for African Americans. The Civil Rights Act of 1964 outlawed racial segregation in employment and education. The act also guaranteed African Americans the same rights as whites to use public places. In the Civil Rights Act of 1968, Congress outlawed racial bias in the sale or rent of most of the nation's housing.

The Balance Sheet   What have African Americans gained, and what problems do they still face?

17. Through the civil rights movement, with support from the Supreme Court and Congress, African Americans led the way toward equality for all Americans. When African Americans began to vote in increasing numbers, they gained political power. Major cities, such as Los Angeles and New York, have elected African American mayors. Hundreds of African Americans are members of state legislatures, and many have been members of Congress. In 1984 and 1988, Jesse Jackson was a serious candidate for the presidency. In the late 1980s, Ron Brown became head of the Democratic party. Colin Powell became chairman of the Joint Chiefs of Staff, the nation's top military post.

18. African Americans have also made great progress in education since the early years of the civil rights movement. One third of the African American population has now completed high school, three times as many as in 1960. Ten out of every 100 African Americans have been graduated from college, compared with three out of 100 in 1960. African American leaders agree that education is the most important factor today in aiding young African Americans to succeed in tomorrow's world. This does not mean that discrimination has disappeared. However, through education and active participation among African Americans, the barriers weaken with each passing year.

Outlook

19. In 1983, Martin Luther King's birthday became a national holiday. Each year on January 15, Americans now honor the memory of the man who became a symbol of African Americans' struggle for equal rights. During his lifetime, Congress and the courts swept away segregation laws. However, much remains to be done. If you were an African American leader, ◀ what improvements in the lives of African Americans would you fight for now?

Activity: Listen to the song, "Happy Birthday," by singer Stevie Wonder. How did this song help to make a national holiday for Dr. Martin Luther King, Jr.? Why was the struggle for this holiday important?

CHAPTER REVIEW

VOCABULARY REVIEW

▶ Write each number and term on a separate sheet of paper. Then write the correct definition of the term. (See Glossary, pages 678–688.)

1. black separatism
2. civil rights movement
3. nonviolent resistance
4. freedom rides

5. Black Power
6. affirmative action
7. sit-ins

SKILL BUILDER: READING A MAP

▶ Use the map and graph below to answer these questions.

1. What state has the most African Americans?
2. What region of the United States has the most African Americans?
3. What state has the second largest African American population?
4. Which two states have almost the same numbers of African Americans?
5. How many states have more than 1,000,000 African Americans?

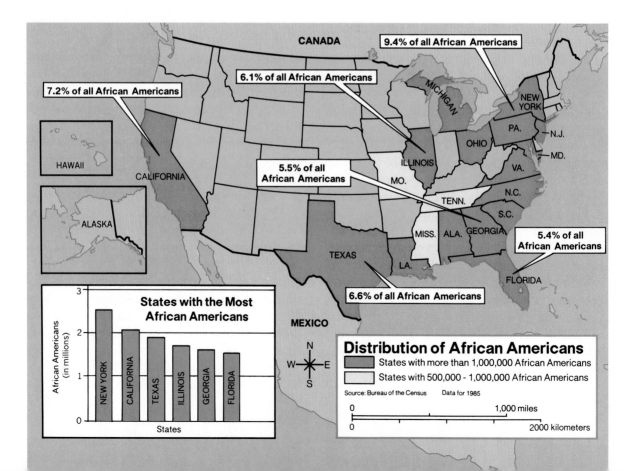

9.4% of all African Americans

6.1% of all African Americans

7.2% of all African Americans

5.5% of all African Americans

5.4% of all African Americans

6.6% of all African Americans

States with the Most African Americans

African Americans (in millions)

NEW YORK · CALIFORNIA · TEXAS · ILLINOIS · GEORGIA · FLORIDA

States

Distribution of African Americans

States with more than 1,000,000 African Americans

States with 500,000 - 1,000,000 African Americans

Source: Bureau of the Census   Data for 1985

0   1,000 miles

0   2000 kilometers

SKILL BUILDER: CRITICAL THINKING AND COMPREHENSION

I. Cause and Effect

▶ On a separate sheet of paper, answer the following questions about cause and effect in the struggle of African Americans for equal rights.

1. Why were few African Americans elected to government positions before 1960?

2. According to the Supreme Court Decision of *Brown vs. Board of Education* in 1954, what was the effect of "separate but equal"?

3. What incident sparked the civil rights movement?

II. Fact *versus* Opinion

▶ Decide whether each of the following statements is a fact or opinion. Write each statement on a separate sheet of paper. Next to each statement, write *F* for fact or *O* for opinion.

1. Affirmative action is unfair to whites.

2. When African Americans began to vote in increasing numbers, they gained political power.

3. Southern states used poll taxes, grandfather clauses, literacy tests, and threats of violence to keep African Americans from voting.

4. Nonviolent civil disobedience is more effective than black separatism or black power.

III. Comparing and Contrasting

▶ On a separate sheet of paper, write a few sentences either comparing or contrasting the following.

1. Contrast the views of Malcolm X and Martin Luther King, Jr.

2. Compare the Civil Rights Act of 1964 and the *Brown vs. Board of Education* of Topeka Supreme Court decision of 1954.

3. Contrast the situation of African Americans before 1960 and today.

USING PRIMARY SOURCES

▶ Reread the Spotlight on Sources on page 619. On a separate sheet of paper, explain why you agree or disagree with the Supreme Court in *Brown v. the Board of Education of Topeka*.

ENRICHMENT

1. Find pictures of different African American political leaders in this century. Write a paragraph about their background and what methods they used in the fight for equality.

2. Jackie Robinson was the first African American to play major-league baseball. Do library research to find out about other African American "firsts." For example, who was the first African American to have his/her own network television show? To sit on the Supreme Court? To run for President?

CHAPTER 2

Equal Opportunities for American Women

OBJECTIVE: What important steps have women made toward equality, and what problems do women still face?

1. The words on the poster read, "Don't Iron While the Strike Is Hot!" Another sign read "Don't Cook Dinner—Starve a Rat." These and thousands of similar signs were carried by women across America on August 26, 1970. They were part of the demonstrations and parades held during the National Women's Strike for Equality. The women who marched that day had goals for themselves and for all women everywhere. The women felt that not enough people were listening to them as they spoke of their ambitions. To get attention for their cause, they took to the streets of towns and cities in every state. They would not be ignored any longer. Many people, both men and women, disagreed with what the women said. However, change was sure to come.

Women's Roles How did women's roles in society change in the 1950s and 1960s?

2. World War II had shown that women were capable factory workers, builders, and managers. After the war, some of the women who had worked at these jobs went back to their homes. Those who remained were often moved into lower-level positions to make room for returning veterans and received few promotions. Some employers even required women to quit their jobs if they married.

▲ In the 1970s, the number of public demonstrations involving issues directly related to women increased sharply.

3. In the 1950s, a greater number of women went to college than ever before. However, almost two thirds of them did not graduate. Most of these women left college to get married, and few of them came back to school later. Women rarely continued beyond college for advanced degrees, such as those required for

In Chapter 2 you will apply these critical thinking skills to the historical process:

➡ **Recognizing Cause and Effect:** Recognizing the action or event that makes something happen; identifying the result of an action or event.

▶ **Drawing Conclusions:** Making a statement that explains the facts and evidence.

lawyers, doctors, or college teachers. In fact, a greater percentage of women graduates earned advanced degrees in the 1920s and 1930s than in the 1950s. In the 1960s and 1970s, however, the picture changed. More women studied for advanced degrees, and some colleges helped women students by offering child-care services.

4. Women's attitudes about their lives and their work began to change. In earlier times, work done at home had filled up a woman's day. Now appliances such as washing machines and dryers made the work faster and more efficient. In addition, many food items such as frozen dinners could now be bought rather than prepared at home. Therefore, women had more time during the day. They also discovered that they had many years to live productively after their children had grown. Many women began to look for other roles for themselves beyond the role of homemaker.

5. Women who followed the role of housewife and mother often found additional activities outside the home. Many worked in their communities, often as volunteers without pay. They set up libraries, worked in hospitals, set up cultural programs, and helped out in schools.

6. Women who worked for pay, however, found that fewer jobs were open to them than to men. They also were less likely to be promoted, and usually they were paid less than men for similar work. The message seemed to be that women belonged in the home and that they should not try to join a "man's world." Women began to feel that they should have chances equal to men's in the workplace.

People in History

7. **Betty Friedan** In the late 1950s, Betty Friedan (free-DAN) was raising a family and writing magazine articles. She had graduated from a women's college in 1942. Fifteen years later she sent a questionnaire to her former classmates, asking about their feelings and experiences since college. The answers she got back raised "strange questions" about women's roles in American life. Friedan spent the next

five years writing a book about those questions. Her book, *The Feminine Mystique*, was published in 1963. In it, Friedan explained that many women were not satisfied with their lives, and she told about the kinds of things they wanted.

8. When they read *The Feminine Mystique*, many women were relieved to know that other women felt as they did. There were some women, however who felt threatened by the book. They felt that it attacked the foundations of family life because it said that many women wanted something more than family life. These different reactions would follow the women's rights movement for many years. Why do some ◄ people still feel threatened by the women's movement?

9. Recall that in 1964 Congress passed a Civil Rights Act. The law prohibited job discrimination on the basis of race. It also prohibited job discrimination on the basis of sex.

▼ Betty Friedan's ideas caused lively debates about the role of women as homemakers, mothers, and participants in the workplace.

Background: After World War II, the traditional nuclear family become the symbol of a free society and its values. The image of a wife and mother at home stood for stability.

623

Thousands of complaints were filed by women in response to this law, but little was done to enforce it. Tired of broken promises, a few women, including Betty Friedan, founded the National Organization for Women, or NOW, in 1966. Its purpose was "to take action to bring women into full participation [taking part in] in the mainstream [center] of society now . . . in truly equal partnership with men." NOW and other organizations worked to have the laws enforced. They also **lobbied** for newer, more effective laws. To lobby is to try to influence lawmaking. Their efforts began to have an effect. In 1971, the Supreme Court ruled that discrimination based on sex was unconstitutional.

🕊 Spotlight on Sources

10. That same year, 1971, the House of Representatives overwhelmingly passed the Equal Rights Amendment to the Constitution, or ERA. The Senate approved it a few months later. The amendment read:

> Equality of rights under the law shall not be denied or **abridged** [reduced or cut back] by the United States or by any state on account of sex.

▶ Should the amendment have said more or is it complete as is? Give your reasons.

11. The amendment was simple and straightforward, but the fight to ratify it was long and complex. To ratify the amendment, 38 states had to approve it within seven years. Later, the seven years were extended to ten. Only a year after being passed by Congress, 30 states had approved the ERA. Then it stalled, mostly because of a Stop ERA movement led by Phyllis Schlafly. Those people who were in favor of ERA focused on how ERA would outlaw the unfair treatment of women. Schlafly, on the other hand, focused on what women might lose under such an amendment. Her examples included child support, alimony, and protection from the military draft. Schlafly's main point, however, was that the ERA might

change family life for the worse. Other people felt that the amendment was unnecessary as long as existing laws were enforced. In the end, the amendment's 1982 deadline for ratification came and went. ERA had been defeated.

12. Despite the loss of ERA, women made progress in other areas. The Equal Employment Opportunities Act was passed in 1972. This law strengthened the rights of women employees in privately owned companies. By the end of the 1980s, women held nearly 40 percent of the jobs as managers and professionals. In television, radio, and newspapers, women achieved key jobs. Women such as Jane Pauley, Barbara Walters, and Connie Chung not only became television newscasters, they also became role models for other women. Even television programs and movies began showing women in roles such as lawyers, doctors, business executives, and police officers.

▼ Charlayne Hunter-Gault, a prominent television journalist, was active in the civil rights movement in the early 1960s.

Background: The ERA amendment was the first to receive a three-year extension of its ratification deadline. The question also arose as to whether a state could rescind, or take back, its ratification.

624

▲ Kathryn Sullivan took her first walk in space during a voyage of the *Challenger* in October, 1984. Today, women astronauts routinely form part of space crews. What special obstacles might women have faced in entering this profession?

13. The 1980s found women breaking down many barriers. Sandra Day O'Connor became the first female member of the Supreme Court. Geraldine Ferraro became the first woman to be nominated by a major political party as its candidate for Vice-President. Sally Ride became the first American woman in space, and Kathryn Sullivan was the first to take a walk in space. Women were making strong gains in such fields as law, politics, and science, where they had been banned at one time. What other careers that once were limited to men are now being entered by women?

14. In spite of progress, not every goal has been reached. The most difficult problem has been the issue of equal pay. The average woman's income is about **64** percent of the average man's income. Other issues include day care for children and **leaves**, or unpaid time off, for the parents of newborn children. Some companies provide day care for their employees' children. However, most parents must struggle to find good care that they can afford.

15. An important barrier to equality is that of attitudes. In 1989, a survey pointed out differences in how men and women view each other and their roles. Old prejudices still affect people's actions in housework and raising children. Many women want their husbands to share these responsibilities at home. They feel that equality will not be achieved until all areas of life are shared and all choices are open.

Outlook

16. In the 1950s and 1960s, women began to hold more jobs outside the home. These jobs, however, were often low-level or volunteer jobs. As women began to speak out for equality, they began to organize. Congress listened and overwhelmingly passed an Equal Rights Amendment, but it was never ratified by the states. Progress has been made and continues as women's share of the job market continues to grow. In what areas do women need to continue to work for equal rights? What are people doing about them now?

Activity: Hold a class discussion on the following questions: What is the difference between protection and discrimination? When a group has been discriminated against, what can be done to overcome the negative impact of that prejudice?

625

CHAPTER REVIEW

VOCABULARY REVIEW

▶ Write the sentences below on a separate sheet of paper. Fill each blank space with one of the vocabulary words.

abridged

lobbied

leaves

focused

1. The ERA would not allow any rights to be _____ because of a person's sex.

2. Some of today's issues for women's rights include day care and _____ .

3. The National Organization of Women _____ for the Equal Rights Amendment.

SKILL BUILDER: READING A GRAPH

▶ Read the graph below and then answer the questions on a separate sheet of paper.

1. About how many women were in the United States labor force in 1950? In 1988?

2. What is the increase in the number of women who entered the labor force from 1950 to 1980? To 1988?

3. In which decade did the largest number of women enter the labor force?

4. How many more men than women were in the labor force in 1950? In 1988?

5. From this graph, what could you say is happening to the labor force in the United States?

6. How do you think the number of men and women in the labor force will compare by the year 2000?

U.S. Labor Force, 1950–1990

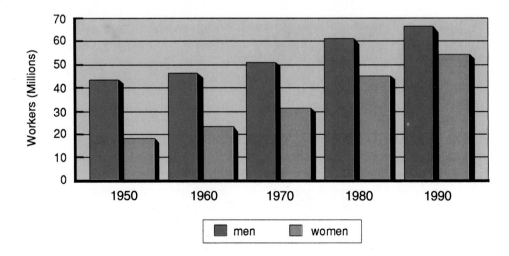

Source: Bureau of Labor Statistics

SKILL BUILDER: CRITICAL THINKING AND COMPREHENSION

I. Cause and Effect

▶ Write the cause or effect of the following events on a separate sheet of paper.

1. After the 1940s, what caused women to look for new roles?

2. What was the effect of World War II on women's job opportunities?

3. What caused the ERA to be defeated?

4. What effect do television programs that show working women who compete successfully with men and speak their mind have on American men and women's attitudes?

II. Compare and Contrast

▶ Compare or contrast the following issues. Write your answers on a separate sheet of paper.

1. **Contrast:** the views of Phyllis Schafly and Betty Friedan.

2. **Contrast:** women's roles in the 1950s and the 1980s.

3. **Compare:** the problems women had gaining equal rights with the problems African Americans had gaining equal rights.

III. Drawing Conclusions

▶ Draw a conclusion from the following groups of facts. Write your conclusions on a separate sheet of paper.

1. **Facts:**
   a. In the 1990s, women still earn, on the average, 64 percent of the average income of men.
   b. Many people still have the attitude that a woman's role is in the home.
   c. Many women have difficulty finding affordable child care.

2. **Facts:**
   a. In the 1980s, Sandra Day O'Connor became the first woman justice on the Supreme Court.
   b. In the 1980s, Sally Ride became the first American woman in space.
   c. In the 1990s, women excel in such fields as law, politics, and science.

USING PRIMARY SOURCES

▶ Reread the Spotlight on Sources on page 624. On a separate sheet of paper, explain why an equal rights amendment to the Constitution is necessary or unnecessary, in your opinion.

ENRICHMENT

1. Set up a debate on the Equal Rights Amendment. Find out what arguments were used by each side in the 1970s. Then develop your own arguments to fit the present day.

2. Write a letter for a time capsule. In it, describe male and female roles as they are today. Then write what you would hope for men and women 100 years from now.

CHAPTER 3

Opportunities for All Americans

OBJECTIVE: How have Hispanic Americans and Native Americans worked for equal rights?

1. In the fall of 1968, many students and teachers at San Francisco State College were demonstrating. Hispanic Americans, Native Americans, Asian Americans, African Americans, and a good number of Anglo–Americans carried banners and signs. The signs read "We Demand **Ethnic Studies!**" Ethnic studies are school and college courses that teach about minority groups and cultures. They wanted to learn about the people of their own groups. After weeks of demonstrating, the protestors got their wish. San Francisco State College became the first American college to start an ethnic studies department. The demonstrations in San Francisco were just one example of the growing importance of minorities.

Hispanic Achievements What progress have Hispanic Americans made in gaining equality in American society?

2. The 1960s and 1970s were a time of great change for Hispanic Americans. One man, César Chávez (SAY-sahr CHAH-vez), a Mexican-American farm worker, had a lot to do with the change. In 1962, Chávez started the **National Farm Workers Association** (NFWA). In 1965, Chávez called for a strike against the grape growers in Delano, California. He wanted better working conditions for the farm

▲ Every year, people from all over the world become United States citizens. What reasons might these people have for seeking a new life here?

laborers, most of whom were Mexican Americans. The strike grew throughout the state. In 1967, Chávez called for a national boycott of grapes. People throughout the country did not buy grapes. This was the first successful national boycott in the history of the United States.

In Chapter 3 you will apply these critical thinking skills to the historical process:

▌ **Comparing and Contrasting:** Recognizing similarities and differences.

◢ **Making Judgments:** Stating a personal opinion based on historical facts.

3. The five-year strike finally ended in victory for the union, which was now known as the United Farm Workers Organizing Committee (UFWOC). The union was recognized by growers. Hispanic Americans saw how powerful they could be when they worked together.

▶ Why might the farm workers' success inspire other groups working for civil rights?

4. Other people became leaders in Hispanic communities. In New Mexico, Reies López Tijerina (tee-heh-REE-nah) created the Alianza Federal de los Pueblos Libres (Federal Alliance of Free Peoples). Tijerina felt that Hispanic Americans should have all the land taken from them by Anglo–Americans more than a century earlier returned. José Angel Gutiérrez (goo-TYEH-rez) of Texas formed a new political party called La Raza Unida. **La raza** means "the race" and includes all Spanish-speaking people in the Western Hemisphere. The party supported everything from community classes to draft counseling during the Vietnam War.

5. Hispanic Americans have worked hard to gain full voting rights. In the 1970s, Hispanic citizens also organized the Southwest Voter Registration Education Project to encourage Hispanics in that region to vote in all elections. Puerto Ricans, too, organized registration drives to encourage voters to go to the polls on election day. Puerto Rican voters became a powerful group of voters in elections in New York and other Northeastern cities.

6. As the number of Hispanic voters grew, Hispanic Americans gained more political power. In this way, they helped elect members of state legislatures, governors, city mayors, and members of Congress. By the mid 1980s, more than 3,000 Hispanic Americans were serving as

▶ government officials. How could these government officials help Hispanic American causes?

People in History

7. Lauro Cavazos Hispanic Americans also served as high officials in the federal government. Lauro Cavazos (kah-VAH-zohs), a Mexican American, was the first Hispanic

American who served in a President's cabinet. He taught at Texas Tech and the Medical College of Virginia. In 1975, Cavazos became Dean of the School of Medicine at Tufts University. Cavazos's outstanding career as a teacher and scholar caused President Reagan to choose him as secretary of education. As secretary of education, he headed the drive to improve public education. Cavazos continued in this important office under President Bush.

Native Americans How did Native Americans fight for equal rights?

8. The same spirit that stirred African Americans and Hispanic Americans to fight for their rights rose up among Native Americans.

Spotlight on Sources

9. In 1961, 500 Native Americans from 67 nations started the Native American movement at a meeting called the **American Indian Chicago Conference.** Native Americans made the following "Declaration of Indian Purpose."

> We believe in the . . . rights of all people to retain [keep] spiritual and cultural values . . . the free exercise [use] of these values is necessary to the normal development of any people. Indians exercised [used] this inherent [basic] right to live their own lives for thousands of years before the white man came and took their lands. . . . but they mean to hold the scraps and parcels [of the land they have left] as earnestly [seriously] as any small nation and ethnic group was ever determined to hold onto their identity and survival.
> —from *The Way: An Anthology of American Literature*, edited by Shirley Hill Watt and Stan Steiner

What basic right were Native Americans determined to take back? ◀

10. Later in the 1960s, more militant Native Americans formed their own organizations. Many of the groups were based on the Black Power model that you read about in Chapter 1

CUBANS

More than 200,000 Cubans came to the United States in the 1960s after communist dictator Fidel Castro seized control of Cuba. Thousands of Cubans escaped by boat and plane. Many of these newcomers were successful business people, teachers, doctors, and lawyers. They refused to allow Castro to take away their freedom. Instead, they left their homes and property to seek new lives in the United States.

Some Cubans were allowed to leave legally. In 1965, Castro let Cubans who wanted to join their relatives in the United States leave. Planes hired by the United States brought 4,000 Cubans to freedom. This was called the **Freedom Airlift.** In 1980, Castro allowed 125,000 Cubans to leave. These **Mariel boat people** were not as welcome as earlier Cubans because some had criminal records. However, most have become productive members of society.

Some Cubans settled in New Jersey, New York, and California, but most settled in

▼ Cuban Americans have used their talents to make important contributions in the fields of fashion, business, and the arts.

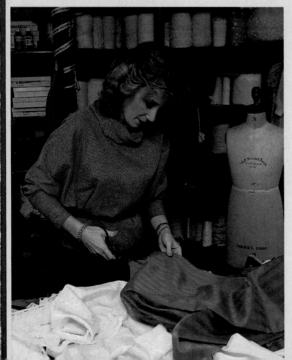

Florida, mainly in Miami. They soon began to take a leading part in the life of that city. Cuban Americans now have become the largest group in southern Florida.

Cubans have succeeded because of hard work and their traditions. Most Cubans had to give up everything to come to the United States. But they were determined to do well. For example, when Carlos Arboleya (ahr-BOH-lay-ah) arrived in the United States, he had only $40. Now he is vice chairman of an important Florida bank. Another reason for their success is the Cuban tradition of helping one another. Newcomers often received help from successful Cubans who were business people or professionals. The newcomers, in turn, would help poorer Cubans who came later. Also, many Cuban women work outside the home to make the family better off financially. Since three generations often live together in Cuban households, traditions, values, and language can be maintained.

Cuban Americans have built a new life in the United States. Cubans have become a powerful political force and have held positions in local, state, and federal government. Many have achieved prominent positions in American business. Other Cuban Americans have become well-known educators, scientists, and artists. Pop singers like Gloria Estafan and painters like Demi have combined Cuban and American culture successfully. Today, Cuban Americans occupy an important place in American life.

Now answer the following questions.

1. Why did Cubans come to the United States in the 1960s?

2. How have Cuban Americans used their political power in Florida?

3. Why do you think Cuban Americans have been able to play so important a part in American life?

Activity: Have students read excerpts from one of the following books and encourage them to share their thoughts and feelings. Dee Brown, *Bury My Heart at Wounded Knee*; Vine Deloria, Jr., *Custer Died for Your Sins*; N. Scott Momaday's Pulitzer Prize-winning *House Made of Dawn*.

of this unit. In 1961, the National Indian Youth Conference was held at Gallup, New Mexico. Native American youths wanted better conditions for their people. They demanded a say in the making of government policy concerning the reservations. Their call for reform in the treatment of Native Americans became known as "Red Power." In 1966, the Alaskan Federation of Natives was formed to protect the land and fishing rights of the Inuit. The most powerful group was the American Indian Movement (AIM). Together, these groups were successful in creating an awareness of the problems of Native Americans among other Americans.

11. In the late 1960s and 1970s, Native American groups turned to direct action to get attention. During the 1960s, Native Americans across the nation staged sit-ins and marches to bring attention to their cause. In 1968, Congress finally granted full civil rights to all Native American peoples in the **Indian Civil Rights Act**. But the effects of the law were minor, and the protest continued. In November 1969, a group of Native Americans took control of a former prison on Alcatraz Island in San Francisco Bay. In 1972, more than 500 Native Americans took over the Bureau of Indian Affairs in Washington, D.C. In February 1973, members of AIM seized the town of Wounded Knee, South Dakota. Wounded Knee was the place of the 1890 massacre of Sioux Indians by federal soldiers. The Native Americans demanded civil rights. They wanted great changes in the way the government ran the reservation. They also insisted the government honor its treaty promises.

12. The protests resulted in some success. The **Indian Self-Determination Act** of 1976 gave Native Americans a voice in the federal housing, schooling, and job training programs on the reservations. Native Americans were also given full responsibility for managing the federal funds for the reservations.

13. More effective than the militant protests, however, were the victories tribes won in court. Native Americans in Maine, Alaska, Wisconsin, New Mexico, and Arizona successfully argued

▲ The march on Wounded Knee brought the needs of Native Americans to the attention of people across the country.

that the United States government had broken its early treaties with Native American peoples. Some Native American groups today are demanding the return of the lands stolen from their ancestors. By 1989, the courts had awarded Native American tribes $81.5 million as repayment for losing their lands.

Outlook

14. In 1986, Americans celebrated the 100th anniversary of the Statue of Liberty. Many paused to think about what it means to be an American. Because so many Americans themselves are the children of immigrants, they cheered the courage, hard work, and sacrifices made by the people fighting for all their rights as citizens. However, while many battles for civil rights have been won, the war is not over. What else needs to be done so that all citizens ◄ are treated equally? What can you do to help?

Activity: Conduct a class debate on the following statement: "The United States should welcome any person who wants to emigrate here."

CHAPTER REVIEW

VOCABULARY REVIEW

▶ On a separate piece of paper, use each of the chapter vocabulary words in an original sentence. Use the Glossary on page 678 to check the definition of each word.

Ethnic studies

American Indian Chicago Conference

Indian Civil Rights Act

Indian Self-Determination Act

La Raza

National Farm Workers Association

Freedom Airlift

Mariel boat people

SKILLBUILDER: READING A MAP

▶ Study the map below. Then answer the questions that follow.

1. What state has the largest Hispanic American population?

2. What is the Hispanic population in Texas?

3. In what section of the United States do most of the Hispanic Americans live? Explain why they live there.

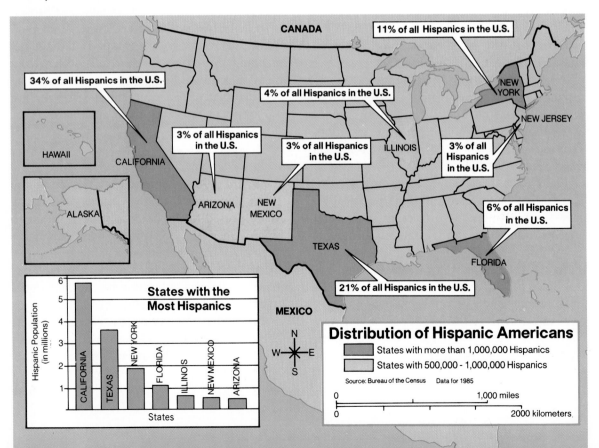

SKILLBUILDER: CRITICAL THINKING AND COMPREHENSION

I. Comparing and Contrasting

▶ Compare the Native American Movement with the efforts of Hispanic Americans to gain their civil rights. What were the methods of each group and what did they achieve?

II. Fact *versus* Opinion

▶ Read the statements below and decide whether each is a statement of fact or opinion. Write the letter of each statement on a separate sheet of paper. Next to each letter, write *F* for fact or *O* for opinion.

   a. César Chávez started the National Farm Workers Association.

   b. The United States should return all lands stolen from Native Americans by white settlers.

   c. Hispanic Americans were the most successful of all groups in the struggle to gain civil rights.

   d. In the mid 1980s, several thousand Hispanic Americans were government officials.

III. Making Judgments

▶ Tell whether you agree or disagree with these statements. On a separate sheet of paper, give the reasons for your judgments.

   a. Cuban immigrants lived together in Miami and other communities because they did not want to become part of American society.

   b. Sit-ins, strikes, and marches are a good way to create change.

USING PRIMARY SOURCES

▶ Reread the Spotlight on Sources on page 629. What did the Native Americans say was the basic right of all peoples? Who took this right away? When they speak of the "continent" they gave up, what do they mean? Write your answers on a separate sheet of paper.

ENRICHMENT

   1. Knowing where your ancestors came from can help you learn more about yourself. Prepare a genealogy (jeen-ee-AHL-uh-jee), or family history, by interviewing family members and tracking down records such as birth certificates. Share your findings with the class.

   2. Write a brief biography of one of these Hispanic Americans, or any other you would like to learn more about: Rodolfo "Corky" Gonzales (activist), Armando Valladares (political prisoner and poet), Felisa Rincón de Gautier (mayor), Rita Moreno (actress), José Feliciano (musician), Gloria Moreno-Wycoff (activist), Linda Ronstadt (singer), Xavier Suarez (mayor).

   3. Research the incidents at Wounded Knee in 1890 and in 1973. Then imagine it is 1973. You are a reporter in South Dakota. Americans are waiting to hear your report about the Native American takeover of the trading post. Prepare a lively radio or TV report to deliver to the class.

CHAPTER 4

A Changing America

OBJECTIVE: What groups of people are changing America today?

1. Every year, the Westinghouse Science Talent Search provides a national competition for high school students. Forty students become finalists. Out of those forty, ten students win college scholarships. In recent years, over half of the 60 scholarship winners have been the children of immigrants. Hong Huynh, 16 years old when he became a finalist in 1988, fled Vietnam with his parents in 1980. They escaped on a crowded boat. Of his parents Huynh said, "They gave up their home, furniture, everything, so I could be here. I don't want to disappoint them." Sheeyun Park, a physics finalist, also expressed appreciation for his parents, who left Korea for New York in 1974. "If I needed books for courses, they gave me the money," he said. "If I wanted sneakers, they said, 'Keep the old pair.'" These two finalists show just one kind of contribution immigrants make to the United States.

▲ Many winners of the Westinghouse Science Contest have gone on to distinguished careers in research, teaching, and industry.

Immigration Today What changes are taking place in the population of the United States?

2. Throughout America's history, waves of immigrants have changed this nation. Until the second half of this century, most immigrants arrived from Europe. In the 1980s more than half of all immigrants were Asians. Many others were from the Western Hemisphere. Now, the Philippines, Korea, Vietnam, and India along with Mexico are the chief sources of immigration. China, the Dominican Republic, and Cuba follow close behind. The flow of people from those countries continues to change America gradually. For example, African Americans are currently the largest minority group, making up 12 per cent of the total population. Hispan-

In Chapter 4 you will apply these critical thinking skills to the historical process:

N **Comparing and Contrasting:** Recognizing similarities and differences.

▲ **Identifying Fact *versus* Opinion:** Specifying whether information can be proven or whether it expresses feelings or beliefs.

ics are the second largest racial minority. They make up 7 per cent of the population. By the end of this century, however, Hispanics are expected to become the largest ethnic minority in the United States.

People in History

3. Maya Lin An American woman with Chinese parents, Maya Lin designed the Vietnam Veterans Memorial while in her early twenties. The memorial, which stands in Washington, D.C., consists of polished, black granite walls. On those walls are inscribed the names of the 58,000 Americans who died in the war. The design began as a contest entry—No. 1,026. After it was chosen the winner, it created much political and artistic controversy. However, most people thought the memorial succeeded. They saw it as a tribute to the dead and to the veterans who came home to a lukewarm welcome.

4. The daughter of immigrants, Lin is proud of her heritage. She calls her artistic vision "distinctly Asian" in its simplicity. Though born in the United States, she did not feel she fitted into American society until college. Since designing the Vietnam Veterans Memorial, Maya Lin has worked as an architect, a stage designer, and a sculptor. Her most recent project was the Civil Rights Memorial in Montgomery, Alabama. Maya Lin had not studied the civil rights movement before taking on this project. She was too young during the 1960s to have participated in the movement. However, Maya Lin used her feelings and intelligence to come up with a design. She carved the names and events of the civil rights era on stone with water flowing over them. "If you don't remember history accurately," she said, "how can you learn?" Her experience proves that you do not necessarily have to take part in an event, or a group's struggle, to understand and appreciate it.

5. In the 1980s, the United States pressed the Soviet Union to ease its **emigration laws** and allow more people to leave Russia. The Soviet Union did not open emigration channels until the late 1980s, when Mikhail Gorbachev brought change to emigration policy. In 1989, the Soviet Union offered to ease its emigration laws even further. If the United States would lift barriers against Soviet exports, the Soviet Union would let more people leave. President Bush pressed the Soviets for more changes. He offered "most favored nation" status in exchange for allowing even more people, especially Jews, to emigrate. The result has been a greater number of Soviet immigrants than ever before. Why would people from the Soviet ◄ Union want to come to the United States?

6. The most recent change in American immigration policy is the Immigration Reform and Control Act of 1986. It allows illegal immigrants who lived in the United States since January 1, 1982, to apply for **amnesty**, or pardon. Migrant workers here illegally can also apply if they lived in America for at least 90 days between May 1, 1985, and May 1, 1986. During 1987 and 1988 two million illegal immigrants applied. If approved, each was given legal permission to remain in the United States and to apply for citizenship after 6½ years. However, there were problems. In New York City, only about 35 percent of all illegal immigrants signed up. To apply for amnesty cost money—$185 for the application fee, $90 for a medical exam—and required an AIDS test. People with the AIDS virus are not allowed to immigrate to the United States.

7. A second problem was that some people could not prove they had lived here long enough. Their employers feared punishment since it is illegal to hire illegal immigrants. Employers must check that their employees are citizens. Employers of illegal aliens can be fined and jailed. Therefore, many employers refused to help employees qualify, although the Immigration and Naturalization Services promised to keep records secret. Now, with the deadline for amnesty passed, illegal immigrants still struggle in this country. Some earn as little as two dollars an hour because of employers who take advantage of their illegal status.

635

Shifting Trends   What other population changes and groups are making a difference in the United States?

8. Though the American family has grown smaller, the number of people over 65 has increased from 8 percent to about 12 percent since 1945. This is partly because of better health care for older people. The **Grey Panthers,** an organization that fights age discrimination, has 100 local chapters and 100,000 members. It proposes an end to **mandatory,** or required, retirement and age segregation in housing. The organization also demands reforms in nursing home care and federal health programs. Laws already exist that protect the rights of older Americans. The Age Discrimination in Employment Act of 1967 keeps employers and potential employers from discriminating against older Americans. In 1980 the airline company Pan Am had to pay $17.2 million to pilots they laid off at age 60.

9. The **handicapped** make up a large portion of the United States population. They are people with a physical or mental disability, such as blindness, deafness, and muscular and nervous disorders. There are 35 million handicapped people in America. Fifteen million of these are of working age, but only one third of them are employed. Six million live on Social Security and disability insurance.

10. The handicapped are actively voicing their right to participate in society. Since the 1970s, ramps for people with wheelchairs have been installed to make buildings accessible to them. They continue to demand more ramps, as well as lift-equipped buses. The Rehabilitation Act of 1973 prohibits unfair treatment of the handicapped. For example, no longer can someone with cerebral palsy be barred from a restaurant. The Education for All Handicapped Children Act of 1975 insists that states give free education to every handicapped child. **Mainstreaming** has become an important trend in the education of the handicapped. In mainstreaming, handicapped students attend regular classrooms and participate in most class activities. There they receive special help to insure their success. "Handicapped for a Day" programs teach about the needs of the handicapped by putting the general public in wheelchairs or blindfolds, for a day-long experience in coping with a disability. Special Olympics is an international program that gives the handicapped the opportunity to compete in athletics.

▼ Many older Americans contribute their time and experience to help others gain valuable skills and education.

Spotlight on Sources

11. Before the Education for All Handicapped Children Act of 1975 was passed, Congress held hearings about the law. At one of the hearings, a witness explained why the education of the handicapped varied from place to place.

Mr. Jeffords [a member of Congress]: There are significant [major] differences between rural areas and urban areas as far as education of the handicapped children, are there not?

Mr. Weintraub [Assistant Executive Director, The Council for Exceptional Children]: I don't think that there is any question of that. I think that there is also a question of leadership. The question of whether a handicapped child gets an education is really left to the vulnerability, or the whim of some local decision makers. So, you can go into communities in Vermont, I can show you some little rural community in Vermont that probably had the most incredible special education program I have ever seen. If you go 15 miles down the road, to a similar community, and there is absolutely nothing. The distinction is that there is a local school superintendent in one community who believes in doing this, and there is another community with a superintendent who does not believe in doing it at all. So I think that it is the kind of *arbitrary* [subject to individual and random decision] . . . decision making that we wish to eliminate.

— *Congressional Record*, 1975

▶ According to the witness, why was a law on educating the handicapped needed?

12. Another trend in education is the growing use of **bilingual education,** wherein students are taught in their native language in schools. They learn basic subjects in their native language and English while studying English as a second language. People who support bilingual education claim that students can learn subjects in their native language while they master English. Opponents say that a bilingual education allows children to avoid learning English. With immigrants from so many different countries now coming to American schools, some schools have difficulty providing teachers who are fluent in all the languages of their students. What is your opinion of bilingual ◀ education?

13. In response to this issue and to other problems concerning language, many states have made English their official language. However, Federal law requires election ballots to be printed in other languages in certain districts. If a large number of people in a district do not speak English well, ballots must be in their **primary language** or first language. Do you ◀ think English should be the official language of the country? Why or why not?

14. Still another trend concerns the question of the declining percentage of people who vote in elections. Despite the fact that a greater number of people than ever before are qualified to vote, a smaller percentage actually vote. The 23rd Amendment, ratified in 1961, gave citizens in Washington, D.C., the right to vote in presidential elections. A decade later, the 26th Amendment lowered the voting age to 18 for both state and national elections. Before 1971, only ten states had allowed people under 21 to vote in the state elections. Yet in the 1970s and 1980s, only about 55 per cent of all qualified voters took part in presidential elections. The United States has the worst voting record of all Western democracies.

Outlook

15. For decades, the United States was known as a "melting pot" where immigrants of different cultures were absorbed into American culture. Today, some people prefer to compare the United States to a salad bowl, where ethnic groups preserve their own cultures while still fitting into the general culture. Besides the varied national backgrounds in the United States, racial minorities, older Americans, and the handicapped add to the challenge of assimilating, or integrating, large groups of Americans into one society. Many Americans now agree that **assimilation** should mean not only requiring a minority to adjust to the majority. It should also mean the majority accepting, understanding, and learning from the minority.

Ask: Why is there incorrect English in the Spotlight on Sources? Explain that in the *Congressional Record* sentences are printed exactly as they were spoken, without corrections. Point out these government records are fascinating as examples of how law is made, especially in their presentations of cases nationwide that call for the specific change.

CHAPTER REVIEW

VOCABULARY REVIEW

▶ Write each of the following words on a separate sheet of paper. Then write the correct definition for each word. Use the glossary in the back of this book to help you.

Grey Panthers   emigration laws   mainstreaming

bilingual education   amnesty   mandatory

assimilation   primary language   handicapped

SKILL BUILDER: INTERPRETING A GRAPH

▶ Study the graph below. On a sheet of paper, answer the following questions.

Americans over 65 Years Old, 1900–2000

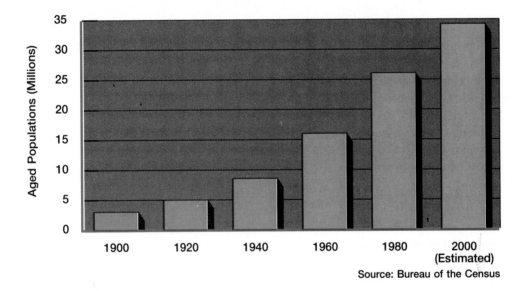

Source: Bureau of the Census

1. In what year did the number of Americans over age 65 reach 5 million?

2. In 1960 the elderly made up approximately how many millions of the total United States population? In 1980?

3. How many elderly, in millions, are there estimated to be in 2000? About how many were there in 1900?

4. In which 20-year period did the number of Americans over the age 65 show the greatest increase?

5. Based on the population trend shown on this graph, what do you predict will happen between 2000 and 2050?

SKILL BUILDER: CRITICAL THINKING AND COMPREHENSION

I. Comparing and Contrasting

▶ Write a short paragraph to answer this question: How are the Grey Panthers similar to groups that fought for African American civil rights? Think about what each group wanted, what methods they used, and how successful they were.

II. Fact *versus* Opinion

▶ Decide whether each of the following statements is a fact or an opinion. Write each statement on a sheet of paper. Next to each statement, write *F* for a fact or *O* for an opinion.

1. Education helps immigrants assimilate into American society.

2. Bilingual education is a poor system because it helps students avoid learning English.

3. It is against the law to hire illegal immigrants.

4. Older people can always do just as good a job as younger people.

5. Only one third of the 15 million disabled of working age are employed.

III. Making Judgments

▶ Using your ability to make a judgment, answer these questions on a separate sheet of paper.

1. Because the United States encouraged the Soviet Union to liberalize its emigration laws, should our country accept all the Soviet citizens who wish to live here?

2. Should people be required to vote, as they are in some other countries?

3. Do you think you have to speak English to be a good American?

USING PRIMARY SOURCES

▶ Reread the Spotlight on Sources on page 637. Then answer these questions.

1. Why does Mr. Weintraub think that the federal government should do something about education for the handicapped?

2. Why do you think government records of Congressional hearings are important?

ENRICHMENT

1. Participate in a class census. Ask each person about the nationality of his or her ancestors. Make a record of each person's birthplace. If a family moved from one region to another, find out the reasons.

2. If you had to emigrate from the United States to another country, which country would you choose? Write your reasons in a paragraph.

3. Franklin D. Roosevelt was a handicapped President. Find a book on President Roosevelt in your local or school library. Write a report of one or two pages on his handicap and the way he handled it.

CHAPTER 5

The United States: A Nation of Cities

OBJECTIVE: What are some problems of American cities and how are cities handling them?

1. Parents held their children's hands as they marched along Detroit's streets. The marchers carried signs that read "Drugs Spell Death" and "Crime Spells Jail." People on the sidewalk clapped loudly and shouted their support. They strongly backed this march protesting drug dealing in their neighborhood. In city after city, people are fighting back against drugs. They know that their city's future and their children's future depend on winning this war.

Housing and the Homeless
How are American cities dealing with serious housing problems?

2. Today, many of the nation's cities have difficulty meeting the housing needs of their citizens. Some people live in poor, unsafe, and overcrowded houses and apartments. Others have no homes at all. Every night about 735,000 people are homeless in America. Almost a quarter of these people hold jobs, and more than a third are families with children.

3. In New York City, as in some other cities, a homeless family often ends up in a shelter. There they can stay until they find housing they can afford. Most shelters are paid for by taxes and run by the government. Churches and community groups also provide food and housing for the homeless. Yet these shelters are often ▶ little better than the streets. How can a nation

▲ The group who organized this march in Detroit was named WE-PROS, or We the People Reclaiming Our Streets. What messages do such marches send to drug dealers?

of such wealth have a homeless problem? What can Americans do to help?

4. To improve housing problems, the Department of Housing and Urban Development (HUD) of the federal government provided money for more than 224,000 **subsidized**

In Chapter 5 you will apply these critical thinking skills to the historical process:
❯ **Predicting:** Telling what you believe will happen on the basis of clues and facts.

▲ **Identifying Fact *versus* Opinion:** Specifying whether information can be proved or whether it expresses feelings or beliefs.

(SUB-suh-dyzd) dwellings in 1981. In a subsidized building, the government pays part of the cost of the rent. However, the government cut back on funds for subsidized housing between 1981 and 1987. In 1987, HUD provided money for only 88,136 dwellings.

5. In some cities, the local government has tried to solve the housing problem by **homesteading**. It offers empty houses and apartment buildings to families at low prices or even for free. In exchange for ownership, families agree to repair the buildings. In this way, thousands of city families have been able to get good housing. Why do you think a family might be interested in homesteading?

Spotlight on Sources

6. In cities throughout the country, tenants of public housing have banded together to force the owners and managers to improve the buildings. Bertha Knox Gilkey, an activist for tenants' rights in St. Louis, Missouri, successfully obtained over $30 million in federal funds for improvements and new buildings in her city. She explained her first success in these words:

> The city voted, the housing authority and the mayor said to tear Cochran [Gardens —a housing project] down. We said, "Over our dead bodies. . . ." I took the gang leaders, second and third offenders, and created renovation [remodeling] crews. Kids that were normally vandalizing [destroying or defacing public or private property], setting these units on fire, were now restoring them. We changed the people before we changed the building. Cochran is clearly a revolution of its own. It was supposed to fail because tenants don't manage; we managed. . . . We [now] control our own destiny, we control how we live, how our children live, the quality of life our children will get. To me that's revolution.

> —from *I Dream a World: Portraits of Black Women Who Changed America*, by Brian Lanker

Why do you think Bertha Knox Gilkey was successful in improving Cochran Gardens?

Education How can schools provide the skills necessary in a changing world?

7. In 1988, the Carnegie Foundation for the Advancement of Teaching reported that recent improvements in education had missed city schools. Fewer than 72 percent of American high school students graduate. Many students who finish high school can only read or write at an eighth grade level. These students are unable to hold jobs in the business world, where good reading and writing skills are required. What can be done to encourage students to finish high school?

8. There are many obstacles to improving education in America's cities. Money in most city school districts is scarce. There are not enough funds in the budget to carry out the programs that could make the schools more effective. Nor are there funds to build new schools in the inner cities, where schools are overcrowded. In fact, many school districts do not have the money needed to repair buildings and replace broken equipment. Because of the low wages, many teachers are leaving the profession. Low salaries make it difficult to attract the best people into teaching. In 1989, President Bush held a conference of governors in Virginia to discuss problems in education. You will read about the conclusions made at the conference in the next chapter. Why do you think the President invited the governors to this conference? What role in education do governors have?

People in History

9. **Eugene Lang** A successful businessman in New York City, Eugene Lang decided to do something to encourage students not to drop out of school. Lang had been invited to speak at the graduation of a sixth-grade class in New York. On the spot, he promised to pay the costs of a college education for every member of the class who completed high school. Later, he

The Los Angeles–Long Beach Metropolitan Area Most of America's cities were founded in the 1700s and 1800s. In those years, cities were fairly small and compact. Their size was limited because most people walked to work or used public transportation. As a result, houses, shops, and factories were built near the waterfronts, railroad terminals, or highways central to a city's economy.

Increased use of automobiles in the 1930s changed the nature of cities. Automobile ownership allowed Americans to live many miles from where they worked. Families began to move away from the older, crowded cities to residential communities called **suburbs**. A suburb is a small community on the outskirts of a large city.

The spread of urban areas increased rapidly in the United States after World War II. Today, more people live in suburbs than in the cities these suburbs surround.

The development of suburbs filled in the open spaces around cities. As suburbs spread, the land area between some urban areas became so built up that the term "metropolitan area" came into use.

The map below shows the built-up area that now surrounds Los Angeles and nearby cities in southern California. The Los Angeles metropolitan area sprawls across 100 square miles (260 sq. km.) and has more than 11 million inhabitants.

Less than three million people live within the city limits of Los Angeles. The remaining 8 million live in suburbs and other cities surrounding Los Angeles. Three of the nearby cities—San Bernardino, Riverside, and Anaheim—have suburbs of their own. Multilane highways further link these cities.

Now use the map to answer these questions.

1. How wide from east to west is the built-up area surrounding Los Angeles?
2. How wide is the built-up area from north to south?
3. In what ways do you think suburbanization benefits people living in the Los Angeles metropolitan area? How does it harm them?

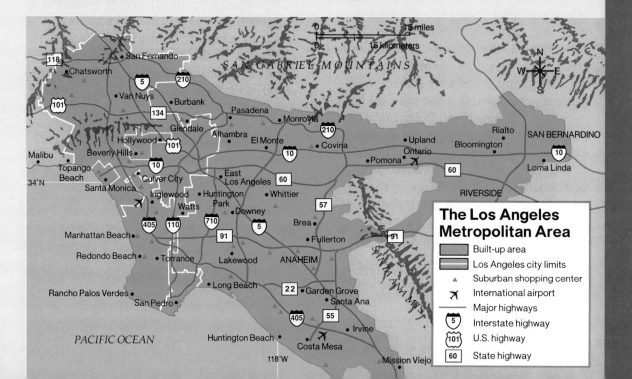

The Los Angeles Metropolitan Area

- Built-up area
- Los Angeles city limits
- ▲ Suburban shopping center
- ✈ International airport
- — Major highways
- Interstate highway
- U.S. highway
- State highway

▶ set up programs to help these students deal with the problems they faced in high school. How do you think Lang's offer might have changed the lives of these students?

10. Business leaders in New York and other cities have followed Lang's example. In addition, business groups in many cities are working with teachers to offer special programs in the schools. For example, some programs teach high school students writing and reading skills needed in business. They also offer students summer jobs in local businesses. In this way, city schools and business people are helping to train the skilled workers cities now need. Also, for adults, the government has literacy programs to help them learn to read and write.

Pollution   What problems does pollution cause for cities?

11. Many American cities, towns and other places suffer from **pollution**. Pollution makes the air, water, or land dirty or unhealthful. Factories send smoke and fumes into the air and often pour their wastes into nearby streams, rivers, and lakes. As a result, the air becomes dangerous to breathe, and the water becomes unfit for drinking, bathing, or fishing. Also, the Americans themselves are responsible for another kind of pollution. People create so much trash and garbage that it is impossible to get rid of all of it. Garbage dumps and land fills have had to close because there is no more room for cities' trash. In 1986–87, a barge filled with New York City garbage took almost a year to get rid of its cargo. No place could be found to take the trash.

12. The trash problem has become so serious that many Americans now realize that they must do something to clean up the environment. Many cities like New York and San Francisco have passed laws that require **recycling**. Recycling means that certain items such as cans, bottles, and newspapers are collected and used again. In 1989, the federal government passed new laws to reduce air pollution. You will read more about this in Chapter 9.

Drugs and Crime   What can cities do to combat crime and drug-related problems?

13. Since the 1980s, drugs and crime have become a serious nationwide problem. America's cities have been hardest hit by this growing problem. Drug dealers sell crack, heroin, and other illegal drugs in many city neighborhoods. Drug users become **addicts**, or people who depend on drugs. To get the money to buy the drugs they need, many addicts turn to crime.

14. In different communities across the country, citizens have joined together to fight the drug war. For example, in Los Angeles, California, Danny Bakewell, head of the Brotherhood Crusade Black United Fund, and 50 men stopped drug selling at a local crack house. In Detroit, Michigan, Rantine McKesson organized a march that let dealers know the neighborhood wanted the dealers out, and it worked. In Providence, Rhode Island, the Elmwood Neighbors for Action use cellular phones to let police know about drug sales that are under way. What else can citizens do to fight drug ◀ activity in the community?

Outlook

15. *Bladerunner*, a motion picture popular in the 1980s, presented a dark and frightening view of cities of the future. In the film, poverty, drugs, and crime control city life. Many filmgoers felt that fate awaited their cities as well. They felt city problems were too overwhelming to be solved. Yet some of the things happening in cities today are giving people hope. Urban renewal, the repair of rundown homes and buildings in cities, is just one sign of improving conditions. Government programs like Head Start give urban children a chance to succeed in school. Private groups and individuals help the homeless and runaways. In New York City, the homeless are helping themselves by publishing and selling a newspaper called "Street News." How do you see cities—as grim and frighten- ◀ ing, or full of life and hope? What must be done to make cities better places in which to live?

CHAPTER REVIEW

VOCABULARY REVIEW

▶ Write each word of the following on a sheet of paper. Then write the correct definition for each word. Use the glossary in the back of this book to help you.

1. addicts

2. homesteading

3. suburbs

4. subsidized

5. pollution

6. recycling

SKILL BUILDER: READING A MAP

▶ The 25 largest cities in the United States are shown on the map below, ranging in size from 486,000 people in Seattle, Washington to 7,263,000 in New York City. Use the map to answer these questions.

1. What region of the United States has most of the largest cities?

2. How many of America's largest cities are along the Pacific Ocean? Which ones?

3. Which of the largest American cities are within 300 miles (480 km) of the Gulf of Mexico?

4. Which of the largest American cities are in the Southwest, from Texas to Arizona?

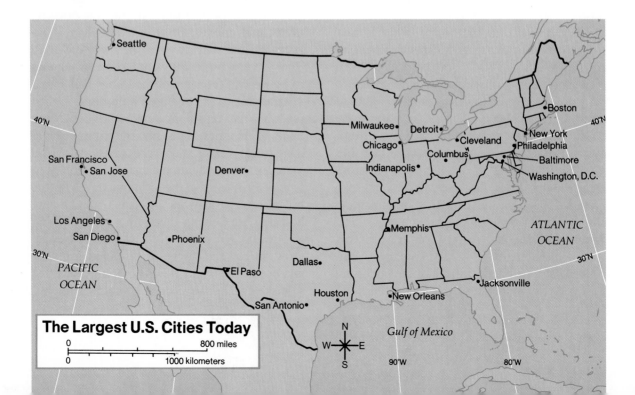

The Largest U.S. Cities Today

SKILL BUILDER: CRITICAL THINKING AND COMPREHENSION

❱ I. Predicting

▶ On a separate sheet of paper, make a prediction about what will happen in American cities.

1. How will cities deal with pollution and traffic problems?

2. If most teenagers drop out of school, what will happen to their lives?

3. If high rents drive out small businesses and cultural organizations, how will city life be affected?

▲ II. Fact *versus* Opinion

▶ Read the statements below. On a separate sheet of paper, write the letter of each statement. Label each statement *F* for fact or *O* for opinion.

1. America's cities will be worse in the next ten years because Americans don't care.

2. Cities have set up drug education programs, but they need more support.

3. Most people would rather live in the country than in the city.

4. Cities are never a good place to raise a family.

◢ III. Making Judgments

▶ Using your ability to make judgments, answer these questions on a sheet of paper.

1. In your town, should more funds be put into building new housing or into improving existing housing? Why?

2. Which tactic is more effective in fighting drugs: the arrest of users and sellers of drugs or a national program of anti-drug prevention and education? Why?

USING PRIMARY SOURCES

▶ Reread the Spotlight on Sources on page 641. Would Gilkey's methods work in your community? Explain why. Why were the gang members willing to repair Cochran Gardens?

ENRICHMENT

1. Cities are often cultural and entertainment centers with museums, theaters, concert halls, restaurants, libraries, galleries. Make a list of your favorite cultural and entertainment places. Find out if they are commercial or supported by public funds.

2. Cities depend on tourism for money. Find out how important tourism is to your city or town. What attracts visitors? Go to your local tourism board and get a list of services provided for tourists. Create an advertisement to get tourists to visit your community.

3. There are many needy people living in cities. Find out about the programs and services in your city that have been set up to help these people. For example, find out where clothes or food can be donated and also about job training programs, neighborhood health clinics, and family counseling services. Make a list of important agencies and how to contact them.

New Leaders for the Nation

1. A visit to Washington, DC, that Bill Clinton made when he was 16 years old was an occasion he would never forget. Along with other high school students, Clinton was taken on a tour of the White House. Then the students assembled on the grounds outside the White House. To Clinton's delight and surprise, the group was greeted by President John F. Kennedy himself. As Clinton later recalled, when he shook the young President's hand and looked into his smiling face, he knew that he had made up his mind about his future career. He would enter public service and one day run for public office. Perhaps he, too, as President, one day would greet young visitors to the White House. This dream became a reality when Clinton was elected President in 1992.

Reagan as President What were President Reagan's policies?

2. When Ronald Reagan became President in 1981, he had very clear ideas about what he wanted to accomplish. He wanted to reduce the role of government in people's lives, lower taxes, cut the federal budget, and increase military spending.

▲ President Bill Clinton, shown here with Hillary Clinton greeting supporters, pledged to stimulate the nation's economy and provide health care for all Americans.

In Chapter 6 you will apply these critical thinking skills to the historical process:

○ **Generalizing:** Making a statement that links several facts.

▶ **Drawing Conclusions:** Making a statement that explains the facts and evidence.

3. President Reagan persuaded Congress to lower income taxes on corporations. He promised not to impose any new taxes. If people paid less in taxes, he reasoned, they would invest more money in businesses. Then businesses would grow and hire more workers.

4. President Reagan also believed that the federal government's **social programs** had grown too large and cost too much money. Social programs include welfare, food stamps, Medicaid, and aid to education, which help lower-income families. President Reagan cut expenditures for such programs drastically.

5. President Reagan also wanted to reduce government control of business and industry. Such **deregulation** would, he declared, "get the government off the backs of the people." Companies had been regulated to protect the public and ensure fair prices. Industry argued that the restrictions increased their costs. Industries such as banking, trucking, and the airlines were deregulated.

6. In Reagan's second term, the federal government's **budget deficit** caused serious problems. When the government spends more money than it takes in, the difference is a budget deficit. Between 1982 and 1988, the deficit averaged a record $180 billion per year, and the federal debt reached $2.6 trillion. The Democrats, who then controlled Congress, proposed cutting the President's large increases in defense spending to balance the budget. President Reagan opposed such cuts and favored deeper cuts in social programs. As a compromise, the President and Congress agreed to the Gramm-Rudman-Hollings Act. This law provided that the budget deficit be cut each year until the budget was balanced.

7. President Reagan had strong ideas about many other issues. He favored amendments to the U.S. Constitution to allow prayers in public schools. He opposed affirmative action plans to give special help to African Americans, Hispanic Americans, and women in the areas of jobs, education, and housing. However, the President was unable to get Congress to accept most of these ideas. As a

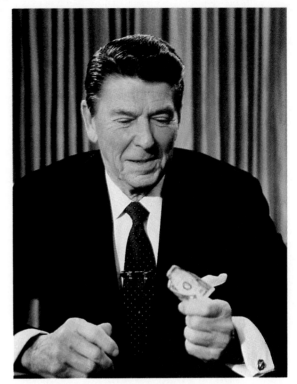

▲ President Reagan went on television frequently to explain his ideas to the American people. Here he dramatizes the dangers of inflation.

result, he believed his best chance of carrying out these programs was to appoint conservative justices to the Supreme Court.

People in History

8. Sandra Day O'Connor One of Reagan's appointees to the Supreme Court was Sandra Day O'Connor, the first woman to become a Supreme Court justice. After graduating from the Stanford University law school, she set up her own law office in Arizona. There she raised her three children and was elected to the state senate. She later became a judge in Arizona's state courts. As a U.S. Supreme Court justice, she generally took conservative positions. But occasionally she favored less conservative views on such matters as affirmative action and a woman's right to an abortion.

Background: One of the major pieces of legislation of the Reagan administration was a new immigration act, which allowed illegal aliens living in the United States to legalize their status and to become citizens.

647

▲ Sandra Day O'Connor, appointed to the Supreme Court in 1981, has won respect as a skilled and dedicated justice.

9. President Reagan ended his term in office in 1989 as one of the most popular Presidents in the nation's history. Even people who did not agree with his policies were charmed by his easy good humor and his relaxed, informal way of presenting complicated issues. He left his successor, Vice-President George Bush, a legacy of enormous good will toward the presidency.

President Bush in Office What were President Bush's main domestic goals and achievements?

10. When President Bush took office, he offered a more moderate program than President Reagan. Like Reagan, Bush promised not to raise taxes and to cut the federal deficit. At the same time, he said he wanted to make the United States "a kinder, gentler nation."

11. One of President Bush's goals was to wage a war on drugs. Drugs, he declared, were the greatest danger the nation faced.

12. In one of his war-on-drugs speeches, President Bush said this:

> Drugs are a real and terribly dangerous threat to our neighborhoods, our friends, and our families. This is a challenge we must face as Americans. The war on drugs will be hard-won, neighborhood by neighborhood, block by block, child by child. Victory over drugs is our cause, and with your help, we are going to win. . . .
> —*The New York Times*, September 6, 1989

13. Bush named a "drug czar" to coordinate the war on drugs. However, he warned that because of the large federal deficit, he would not be able to launch an expensive anti-drug program. Despite some drop in the use of drugs, imports of drugs from other countries continued on a large scale.

14. The deficit also affected administration policies on education and the environment. Bush had said he wished to be known as the education President and the environment President. In 1989, he organized a conference of the nation's governors on education. But he made clear that state and local governments would have to pay for the recommended changes. True to his promise about the environment, in 1990 President Bush signed a tough bill to curb air pollution. However, he did not support environmental measures that would be too costly to American businesses and thus might hurt the entire economy.

15. Another challenge the President faced was the large number of savings and loan banks that had failed and were in danger of seriously damaging the economy. In the 1980s, many of these banks had made loans that had not been repaid. To keep the entire banking industry from breaking down, the Bush administration took over hundreds of the failing banks, at a cost to the taxpayers of billions.

16. In the spring of 1992, an incident took place that rocked the entire nation. Months earlier, an African American named Rodney King had been severely beaten by white Los Angeles police officers for supposedly resisting arrest in a traffic incident. A video recording made by a bystander showed the officers beating and kicking King as he lay on the ground. When the tape was shown on national television, Americans were outraged at such brutality. The officers involved were put on trial. When they were acquitted, a shocked African American community in Los Angeles erupted in violence. Stores were wrecked and looted. Flames and smoke from buildings set afire could be seen for miles around. Stores owned by Korean Americans were attacked. Rodney King himself pleaded for calm, asking, "Can't we all live together?" Most Americans deplored the violence of the protest. But a horrified nation was forced to realize how deeply African Americans felt that they could not always rely on securing justice. The Bush administration then announced that the police officers involved in the beating would be tried for violating King's civil rights.

17. President Bush carried on President Reagan's policy of appointing Supreme Court justices who were conservative in their views. One such appointment was that of Clarence Thomas, an African American, to succeed the retired Thurgood Marshall, a liberal African American justice. Thomas was confirmed by the Senate after a series of bitter hearings that involved charges of sexual harassment.

18. During most of the Reagan years, the economy had been strong. But the picture began to change almost from the beginning of the Bush administration. By 1990, the nation was in the grip of a severe economic **recession,** or sharp downturn in business. Thousands of people were thrown out of work. Matters had not improved by the time of the 1992 election campaign. President Bush lost much support because he downplayed the seriousness of the recession. His Democratic opponent in the election campaign, Governor Bill Clinton of Arkansas, blamed Bush for not taking steps to improve the economy and swept into office as the nation's 42nd President.

Outlook

19. Between 1981 and 1993, under Presidents Reagan and Bush, the United States enjoyed periods both of prosperity and recession. Over the entire period hung the questions of how to pay for the many programs of the federal government and which ones to eliminate or cut back. In foreign policy, on the other hand, the United States could point to many positive achievements.

CHAPTER REVIEW

VOCABULARY REVIEW

▶ Write each of the following sentences on a separate sheet of paper. Then fill in the blank with the word that best completes each sentence.

social programs   deregulation

recession   budget deficit

1. By increasing military spending, President Reagan increased the _____ .

2. Democrats disagreed with President Reagan about cutting _____ to the needy.

3. During a _____ , the nation's economy slows down and workers lose their jobs.

4. The process that frees industries from government regulations is called _____ .

SKILL BUILDER: INTERPRETING A CARTOON

▶ Answer the following questions about the cartoon below. Write your answers on a separate sheet of paper.

1. Who is represented in the picture on the wall behind the teacher?

2. Why is the student praying that these social programs be saved?

3. Why were these programs in danger?

4. What is the connection between the student's prayer and the picture on the wall?

5. What do you think is the cartoonist's point of view in this cartoon?

SKILL BUILDER: CRITICAL THINKING AND COMPREHENSION

I. Generalizing

▶ On a separate sheet of paper, write facts given in the chapter that support the following generalizations.

1. President Reagan had definite ideas about what the role of government in people's lives should be.

2. As a conservative, President Reagan reduced the amount of money spent on social programs.

3. President Bush took steps to carry out his wish to be known as the education and environment President.

II. Drawing Conclusions

▶ On a separate sheet of paper, write the facts given in the chapter to support the following conclusions.

1. The size of the federal deficit helped determine the policies of Presidents Reagan and Bush.

2. The Supreme Court became more conservative under Presidents Reagan and Bush.

3. Fighting drugs became an important issue in the late 1980s.

III. Making Judgments

▶ On a separate sheet of paper, write your judgment about these issues.

1. Should social programs be cut or taxes be raised to cut the budget deficit?

2. If you had been a voter in the 1992 election, would you have joined many other Americans in blaming President Bush for the economic recession of his last years in office?

3. What challenges does any new President, such as Bill Clinton, face?

USING PRIMARY SOURCES

Reread the Spotlight on Sources on page 648. How do you think Americans can win the war on drugs? Write your suggestions on a separate sheet of paper.

ENRICHMENT

1. In his election campaign of 1980, Ronald Reagan asked Americans, "Are you better off now than you were four years ago?" Do research in your library to find out what the answer was for most Americans and why.

2. Many people criticized President Reagan for having favored the rich and big business. Do research to find out how American workers felt about the Reagan administration.

3. Why is victory in the war on drugs so difficult to achieve? What factors in American life might add to the drug problem? What steps do you think you and other students can take to fight the war on drugs?

CHAPTER 7

Dealing with Other Nations

OBJECTIVE: How did the United States deal with revolutionary changes in Communist countries? What new challenges does the United States face in other parts of the world?

1. Soviet communism, warned President Reagan in 1983, is the "focus of evil in the modern world." Five years later, a smiling Ronald Reagan was standing next to Soviet leader Mikhail Gorbachev (GAWR-buh-chawf) in Moscow's Red Square. Gorbachev took a little boy from the arms of his mother and handed him to the President, saying, "Shake hands with grandfather Reagan." In just five years, relations between the United States and the Soviet Union had improved dramatically. By 1990, the Cold War was over. In 1991, the Soviet Union collapsed. Yet, the United States faced challenges from Europe and Japan. The nation also had to deal with problems in southern Africa, the Middle East, and Central America.

▲ President Ronald Reagan and the Soviet leader Mikhail Gorbachev held four summit meetings. Their efforts helped to thaw the Cold War.

The Cold War Ends   How did sweeping changes in the Communist world affect the United States?

In Chapter 7 you will apply these critical thinking skills to the historical process:

▲ **Recognizing Main Idea:** Identifying the most important idea in a paragraph.

▲ **Summarizing:** Giving the main idea of a group of paragraphs in a brief form.

2. During President Reagan's second term, relations between the Soviet Union and the United States improved dramatically. The reason was a huge wave of reform that swept the Communist world. The change began in 1985, when Mikhail Gorbachev became the Soviet leader. Gorbachev began a campaign to permit more freedoms in his country. This policy was called **glasnost** (GLAHS-nohst). As Soviet citizens began to speak more freely, Gorbachev hoped they would support his program of **perestroika** (peh-ruh-STROY-kuh) for reform of the sluggish Soviet economy.

3. Gorbachev also wanted to improve relations with the United States and Western Europe. In 1987, the United States and the Soviet Union signed a treaty to destroy many of their missiles. It was the first time since the nuclear arms race began that the two countries agreed to reduce their stocks of nuclear weapons.

Spotlight on Sources

4. Between 1985 and 1989, Presidents Reagan and Gorbachev held four summit meetings. At first, suspicion on both sides got in the way of efforts to reach agreements. By the third Reagan/Gorbachev meeting, however, the two leaders trusted each other. In December 1987, Reagan welcomed Gorbachev to the United States with these words:

> Like the people of your country, we [Americans] believe our country should be strong, but we desire peace. Have no doubt about that. The longing for peace runs deep here, second only to our fervency [strong desire] for the preservation of liberty. Americans believe people should be able to disagree and still respect one another, still live in peace with one another.

Which do you think is more important, peace or liberty? Explain your answer.

5. During 1989, the Soviet Union's satellite empire in Eastern Europe collapsed. The Communist governments there had almost no

▼ In November 1989, the Berlin Wall was opened. The wall, which had been built by the Communists in 1961 to keep people from leaving East Germany, had been a symbol of the Cold War.

Background: In the 1980s, the United States placed restrictions on imported steel, autos, machine tools, textiles, and sugar. Japan kept high tariffs on rice and a few other products. Non-tariff barriers were a more serious problem. American exporters had difficulty marketing their products through Japan's inefficient distribution system of multiple wholesalers and "Mom and Pop" stores.

public support. In August, the Communist government of Poland fell. By the end of the year, the Communist governments of Hungary, Czechoslovakia, East Germany, Bulgaria, and Romania had fallen. With the exception of the events in Romania, these revolutionary changes took place with virtually no violence.

People in History

6. Lech Walesa. Nobody was more important in the struggle of Eastern Europe against communism than a Polish electrician named Lech Walesa. In 1980, he led a huge strike in which Polish workers won the right to form a trade union free of government control. The next year the Polish Communist government declared that union illegal. Walesa was arrested and held in prison until 1982. Many people in the West admired Walesa for his courage. He was awarded the Nobel Peace Prize in 1984. In 1989, Walesa led the successful effort to bring down Poland's Communist dictatorship. A year later, he was elected president of a democratic Poland.

7. Soviet control of Eastern Europe was the most important cause of the Cold War. The events of 1989 thus helped to end that conflict. In 1990, the United States, the Soviet Union, and more than 30 other nations declared the Cold War over. On December 25, 1991, the Soviet Union officially was abolished. It broke up into 15 independent states. The country that since World War II had challenged the United States for world leadership no longer existed.

Trouble Between Allies How did economic growth in Western Europe and Japan affect the United States during the 1980s and early 1990s?

8. During the 1980s and early 1990s, the United States faced strong economic competi-

tion from other industrialized nations. Foreign-made goods poured into the country. The United States was buying more goods from other countries than it was selling. When a country does this it has a **trade deficit.** As people in the United States bought more and more foreign-made goods, many Americans who made these products lost their jobs.

9. The United States' strongest competitor in trade was Japan. The Japanese rebuilt their country after World War II. By the 1980s, they had become the world's most efficient producer of cars, ships, and many electronic products.

10. The United States also faced strong competition from Western Europe. The twelve nations of the European Community (EC) hoped to create a single market free of tariffs and other barriers against one another's goods by 1993. Although Presidents Reagan and Bush were able to get some barriers against U.S. goods removed, trade tensions between the United States and its European allies continued.

11. One country that many in the United States paid attention to during the 1980s was South Africa. In South Africa, the white minority controlled the country. The majority of the population was black Africans who had few political rights. The races in South Africa were kept separate by a strict system of segregation, called **apartheid.**

12. Beginning in 1985, the U.S. and other governments placed restrictions on trade with South Africa. Economic pressure and the winding down of the Cold War helped bring change in South Africa. The South African government removed many restrictions on black Africans. In 1990, it ended its ban on the African National Congress (ANC), the country's most powerful black organization. It also released Nelson Mandela, the ANC's leader, from prison after 28 years. While South Africa still had a long way to go before there was racial fairness, the process of reform now underway could not be stopped.

Activity: Have the class create a Cold War chronology. Draw a time line for the years 1945 to 1990 on the blackboard and ask students to provide the main Cold War events. Include events like the signing of the Limited Test Ban Treaty of 1963, that reduced tensions as well as events that increased tensions.

▲ President George Bush visited U.S. troops in Saudi Arabia for Thanksgiving 1990. This was shortly before the beginning of Operation Desert Storm, in which U.S. and other UN forces drove the Iraqis from Kuwait.

The Middle East and Desert Storm   How did the end of the Cold War lead to successful efforts to stop aggression in the Middle East?

13. In August 1990, the Middle East nation of Iraq invaded its small, oil-rich neighbor Kuwait. President Bush launched an international effort to force the Iraqis out of Kuwait. When these peaceful efforts to get Iraq to leave Kuwait failed, in early 1991 the armed forces of the United States and several other countries drove the Iraqis from Kuwait.

Central America   What problems did the United States face in Central America?

14. In the early 1980s, leftist rebels were trying to overthrow the government of El Salvador. The rebels were supported by Nicaragua, where the left-wing Sandinista (san-duh-NEES-tuh) Front had won a civil war and taken power in 1979. The Sandinistas received military and economic aid from both the Soviet Union and Cuba.

15. The United States sent military and economic aid to the government of El Salvador. It also provided training, money, and weapons to Nicaraguan rebels, called *contras,* fighting the Sandinistas. Many people in the United States disagreed with this policy. In 1984, Congress banned aid to the contras. Despite the ban by Congress, the Reagan administration secretly aided the contras. The money came from secret arms sales to Iran. Profits from those sales were used to aid the contras in Nicaragua. When these dealings were exposed in 1986, the scandal embarrassed the Reagan administration. Despite U.S. help, the contras failed to defeat the Sandinistas. In 1990, the Sandinistas were forced to hold the first free election since they had come to power. A non-Communist alliance then soundly defeated the Sandinistas.

Outlook

16. The end of the Cold War and the breakup of the Soviet Union created new opportunities for peace in the world. At the same time, the United States faced some serious new problems across the globe. A weakened economy reduced influence with many nations. The United States faced both opportunities and serious challenges in its efforts to make a better world.

CHAPTER REVIEW

VOCABULARY REVIEW

▶ Choose the best definition for the words below. Write your answers on a separate sheet of paper.

1. glasnost
   a. putting a factory or farm under control of the government
   b. effort to bring more freedom to the Soviet Union
   c. breakup of the Soviet Union into 15 republics
   d. arms control agreement between the Soviet Union and the United States

2. trade deficit
   a. a shortage of goods for export
   b. a favorable balance of trade
   c. a failure to import large quantities of goods
   d. an excess of imports over exports

3. apartheid
   a. denying people the right to vote because of their race
   b. easing of tensions between the United States and South Africa
   c. strict system of racial segregation
   d. granting independence to Namibia

SKILL BUILDER: USING AN ENCYCLOPEDIA

▶ Many of the products Americans consume originate in other countries. Some products from Japan and Europe are very common in the United States. Use an encyclopedia to find out from what part of the world the following products or raw materials come. On a separate sheet of paper, write the name of the product or material and where it originates.

1. rubber

2. coffee

3. bauxite used in aluminum

4. cacao beans used in chocolate

5. videocassette recorders

SKILL BUILDER: CRITICAL THINKING AND COMPREHENSION

▲ I. Main Idea

▶ Read each sentence below. On a separate sheet of paper, write the number of each sentence. For each sentence that gives a main idea from the chapter, write *M*. For each sentence that gives a supporting detail, write *D*.

1. The Sandinistas also accepted economic and military aid from the Soviet Union and Cuba.

2. Opponents of funding (to the contras) insisted that Nicaragua was not a threat to the United States.

3. In the 1980s and 1990s, the U.S. faced strong economic competition from other industrial countries.

4. During the 1980s, a wave of reform swept through the Communist world.

5. Relations between the United States and the Soviet Union began to improve in the late 1980s.

6. President Reagan welcomed Mikhail Gorbachev to the United States in December 1987.

▲ II. Summarizing

▶ On a separate sheet of paper, write two or three sentences that summarize the following topics discussed in the chapter.

1. the debate in the United States over U.S. aid to the contras

2. the U.S. trade deficit

3. changes in the Communist world

▍III. Comparing and Contrasting

▶ On a separate sheet of paper, follow the directions to compare or contrast the following:

1. Compare the U.S. role in Central America in the 1980s with the U.S. role in Southeast Asia in the 1960s.

2. Contrast the domestic policies of the Soviet Union in the 1980s with those in the 1940s and 1950s.

3. Compare economic relations between the United States and Europe in the 1980s and 1990s with relations after World War II.

4. Contrast Soviet and U.S. relations in the late 1980s and the late 1950s.

USING PRIMARY SOURCES

▶ Reread the Spotlight on Sources on page 654. Compare this speech with Reagan's warning about the "evil empire" on page 652. How does it show a change in the attitude of the United States toward the Soviet Union? Explain your answer on a separate sheet of paper.

ENRICHMENT

1. From back issues of magazines and newspapers, collect information for a report on the Iran-Contra Scandal. Your report should answer these questions: Who were the people who arranged the arms sales to Iran and secret funding for the contras? What were their goals? How was the operation kept secret from Congress?

2. Research and write a report on the policies of Mikhail Gorbachev while he was in power. In your report, be sure to explain and discuss: Gorbachev's policies of *glasnost* and *perestroika*, opposition to Gorbachev from old-line Communists, why his policies failed, and what happened to the Soviet Union.

3. Read further about recent changes in the former Soviet Union and Eastern Europe. How should the United States respond to these changes? Discuss this question with a group of your classmates. Write down the group's conclusions and present them to the class.

657

CHAPTER 8

Science and Technology Transform America

OBJECTIVE: How have discoveries in science and technology changed life in America?

1. Today, people can listen to music in their homes on small discs the size of a cookie. A person can send a drawing across the world by making a phone call. A meal can be cooked in less than ten minutes in a microwave oven without a splatter of grease. A few years ago, none of these things was possible. Then a revolution took place, not of guns and of swords, but of **microchips**. A microchip is a piece of silicon smaller than a thumbnail that stores data, or information, for a computer. What electronic wonders will the next ten years bring? Experts predict machines that answer to spoken commands, tape decks the size of a loaf of bread, computers so tiny you can slip them into a pocket, and a machine you step through to get a complete physical exam. Every year, new technology changes the way Americans live.

Computers How has the use of computers changed the nature of jobs?

2. During World War II, people began building machines that could solve problems. These machines were called **computers** (kum-PYOO-terz) from the verb *compute*, which means to work out an answer by using math. As new electronic parts were developed, computers became smaller, faster, and cheaper. Large amounts of information could be stored on

▲ The first computer, called the Mark I, was completed in 1944. Today, computers are an accepted and ordinary part of American life. How do computers affect the way you live?

computers. Computers sorted mail, controlled traffic lights, solved math and science problems, and sent rockets into outer space. In their search for drilling sites, oil companies used computers to study geologic data.

3. Computer literacy, the ability to use a computer comfortably, has become a skill im-

In Chapter 8 you will apply these critical thinking skills to the historical process:

❯ **Predicting:** Telling what you believe will happen on the basis of clues and facts.

▲ **Identifying Fact *versus* Opinion:** Specifying whether information can be proved or whether it expresses feelings or beliefs.

portant to success in school. As early as kindergarten, students use computers in school. Not only do computers help students with math but also with science, English, and composition. Personal computers also have uses in the home. For example, they help Americans with their income tax returns, replace typewriters, and provide entertainment with video games. More than 3.3 million American homes now contain personal computers.

4. Automation (aw-toh-MAY-shun) makes it possible for companies to produce more goods in less time with fewer workers. Automation is the use of computer-controlled machines, which need little or no human help. For example, each year 90 billion phone calls are made in the United States. The calls are placed through automated switchboards. To make these calls without automation, the phone companies would need a staff equal to the entire population of American women between the ages of 18 and 30. Banks offer automated tellers that allow people to put in or take out money at their convenience. As the 1980s ended, robots and computerized machines built more and more

▶ automobiles. Where else is automation being used today?

5. The multibillion-dollar computer industry has created many new jobs. Data processors, computer programmers, and systems planners did not exist fifty years ago. Since computers have made many new products and services possible, the number of **white collar jobs** has increased. White-collar workers include manag-

▶ ers, technicians, and sales people. Why is "white collar" used to describe these jobs?

6. Although automation has brought about many good changes in business, some people blame automation for some problems in the work force. High unemployment rates result from introducing automation into factories, they say. These people argue that automated machines take jobs away from people. Others feel that automation has contributed to workers feeling unappreciated and dehumanized, or machinelike. Some feel this has contributed to a decline in the quality of products.

Spotlight on Sources 🦅

7. Studs Terkel, a radio interviewer, talked to workers around the country about their jobs. In his book *Working*, he reported what they said. With so many robots and automated machines as co-workers, many workers felt dehumanized and not recognized as individuals. Here, a worker in a midwestern steel mill says what he dislikes most about the changing work scene in America.

> You can't take pride any more. You remember when a guy could point to a house he built, how many logs he stacked. He built it and he was proud of it. . . . It's hard to take pride in a bridge you're never [going] to cross, in a door you're never [going] to open. You're mass-producing things and you never see the end result. . . . I would like to see on one side of [a building] a foot-wide strip from top to bottom with the name of every bricklayer, the name of every electrician, with all the names. So when a guy walked by, he could take his son and say, "See, that's me over there on the forty-fifth floor. I put the steel beam in." . . . Everybody should have something to point to.
> —from *Working*, by Studs Terkel

How does this worker's job make him feel? Do ❯ other people feel the same way? What can be done to make workers more productive?

Medicine What new medical tools have improved the health and well-being of Americans?

8. Technology is helping doctors identify, prevent, and treat disease. Blood, body fluids, tissue samples, and chemicals can be tested faster and better by computer. Machines in hospitals record heart rates, breathing rates, body temperatures, and blood pressures of patients. Also, doctors can use computers to **simulate** (SIM-yoo-layt), or imitate, the workings of the human body. By using computer simula-

Activity: Have students find out about computer-aided design, CAD for short, computer-aided manufacturing, or CAM, and computer-integrated manufacturing. Have them prepare a report on what each term means, where and how it is used, and what effects they will have on business.

659

tion, for example, doctors can see how certain drugs, foods, or cosmetics will affect the body.

9. Today's doctors can take clearer pictures of the inside of the human body. In the mid-1970s, doctors began using **CAT-scanners** to take pictures of soft body parts, such as the brain. The patient is placed inside the CAT-scanner, which is a large, cylinder-shaped machine. The scanner then moves around the patient, taking many X-rays from different angles. A computer in the CAT-scanner collects and arranges the X-rays to show a single, three-dimensional picture.

10. In the 1980s, hospitals began using **magnetic** (mag-NET-ik) **resonance** (REZ-uh-

▼ The CAT scan is useful in diagnosing diseases such as finding tumors. CAT stands for computerized axial tomography, the name of the method used to produce the three dimensional picture.

nuhns) **imaging**, or MRI, to take pictures of soft body tissues. MRI offers doctors a way to take pictures of the inside of the body without exposing patients to harmful X-rays. The MRI, which was first used on a human being in 1977, uses magnets and sound energy to form pictures. Unlike X-rays, MRI can pass through bone tissue. Doctors most often use MRI to look through the skull for tumors and damaged blood vessels in the brain.

11. New medical tools are making some handicapped people's lives easier. For example, today's artificial arms and legs have tiny computers inside them. The body's nerve endings signal the computer to produce movement in the artificial limb. An **Optacon** (AHP-tuh-kahn) is a hand-held machine that changes letters on a page into raised symbols. Each symbol stands for a letter of the alphabet. By feeling the symbols, a blind person can "read." An **Autocuer** (aw-toh-KYOO-er) is a tiny computer that "hears" words. The Autocuer helps a deaf person read lips by translating spoken words into written words on a screen.

12. With the help of technology, scientists have discovered medicines to treat diseases that were once incurable. Interferon, a drug discovered in the 1980s, cures one form of hepatitis, a liver disease. Other medicines have been discovered that are useful in treating Parkinson's disease, a nerve disease that results in serious trembling and rigid muscles, and in attacking some kinds of cancer.

13. New medical technologies allow doctors to fix the inside of a body without cutting it open. **Optical** (AHP-ti-cuhl) **fibers** (FY-berz) are glass tubes so narrow that they can be threaded through a human blood vessel. A tiny camera in the fiber takes pictures, which are arranged by computer and shown on a screen. A **laser** (light amplification by stimulated emission of radiation) is a tool that makes light stronger, narrower, and hotter. The laser light beam can cut, destroy, or join body tissues. First used in 1973 to stop bleeding ulcers, lasers are now being used to seal wounds, clear blockages, and remove tumors.

▲ Twenty-two year old Nan Davis has been paralyzed for four years. She has just been connected to a computer that will help her use her legs again. Sensors were placed on her hips, knees and ankles to tell the muscle system to move.

People in History

14. Charles H. Townes The inventor of the laser, Charles H. Townes (1915–), and a partner, Arthur L. Schawlow, discovered that a thin, strong, hot beam of light could be produced that would travel in only one direction. Such a light could carry the signals of many different television shows or telephone calls at once. In 1958, Townes and Schawlow announced their concept of the laser, which made light waves stronger. Theodore H. Maiman, another American, built the first laser and put it

into operation in 1960. Lasers function in photocopiers, compact disc players, and in the system that reads price codes in supermarkets. Scientists are also developing lasers to process uranium for nuclear reactors. Telephone companies use fiber-optic systems that carry voices in laser light through strands of glass. In 1964, Townes won the Nobel Prize for physics.

Daily Life How has technology changed the way Americans live?

15. People today are living longer and healthier lives. In 1900, an American could expect to live to be 50 years old. In 1988, the average life expectancy had grown to 75. Technological advances in farming have made better nutrition possible. The ability to transport food long distances has led to a greater variety of produce and meats available the entire year. The motorized farm equipment that replaced animals made the American farmer more productive as well. The average farmer today can feed 77 people for the year. In 1910 a farmer could only supply seven people with food.

16. People have more free time now than ever before. In the 1800s, workers put in 12 to 16 work hours a day, six days a week. The twentieth century introduced the 40 hour work week. People have more leisure time, and technology has improved that too. Video cassette recorders (VCRs) allow people to record television shows and watch them at their convenience. New materials have created better, safer sporting equipment like graphite tennis rackets and inflatable basketball shoes.

Outlook

17. Every year, new technology changes the way Americans live. Usually a new invention is expensive at first, but the price declines as more are produced. What was once only available to the few becomes common throughout the nation. What electronic wonders will the next ten years bring?

Ask: What problems and concerns arise with the growth of computers? What solutions might be proposed to solve the problems? Encourage students to think about such issues individual privacy, dehumanization, medical definitions of life and death, and others that result from technological advances.

661

CHAPTER REVIEW

VOCABULARY REVIEW

▶ Write each of the following words on a sheet of paper. Then write the correct definition for each word. Use the glossary on pages 678–688 to help you.

1. automation
2. simulate
3. computers
4. microchips
5. Optacon
6. laser
7. computer literacy
8. white-collar jobs
9. CAT scanners
10. magnetic resonance imaging
11. Autocuer
12. optical fibers

SKILL BUILDER: READING A GRAPH

▶ The graph below shows the number of robots used in the United States during the 1980s. Study the graph and then answer these questions.

1. How many more robots were in use in 1989 than in 1980?

2. Which year had the greatest increase in the number of robots in use?

3. What generalization can you make about the trend in the use of robots?

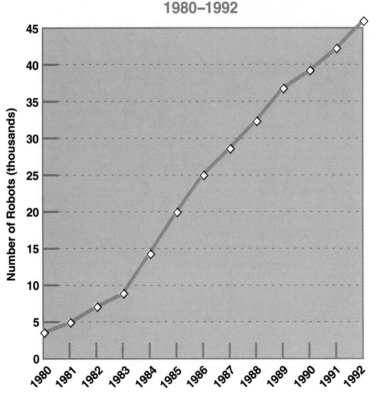

ROBOTS IN USE IN THE UNITED STATES
1980–1992

Source: Robotic Industries Association

SKILL BUILDER: CRITICAL THINKING AND COMPREHENSION

I. Generalizing

▶ Find sentences from the chapter that support the following generalizations.

1. Computers have had a positive effect on society.

2. Computers have had a negative effect on society.

II. Predicting

▶ Scientists and other people have made predictions about what technology will create in the future. What do you predict will develop in these fields? Give reasons for your predictions.

1. computers

2. automation and robotics

3. medicine

4. daily life and leisure time

III. Fact *versus* Opinion

▶ On a sheet of paper, write three statements of fact based on information you have read in this chapter. Then write a statement of opinion about each of the facts. For example:

Fact: Under the Economic Opportunity Act, heads of household who attend training schools are given small allowances.
Opinion: The government should pay these allowances to heads of household.

USING PRIMARY SOURCES

▶ Reread the Spotlight on Sources on page 659. On a separate sheet of paper, discuss why people should be able to take pride in their work.

ENRICHMENT

1. Interview three people about their jobs. Ask them what they like and don't like about their jobs. Discuss how technology has affected their work, if at all. Write down their responses in a report.

2. Participate in a class poll. Read the following list aloud to the class: VCR, television, microwave oven, compact disc player, home computer. Have students raise their hands when their family owns the item mentioned. Write down the results, then figure out what percentage of the class owns each item. If you wish, hold a second poll asking the same questions for five years ago.

3. In a small group, discuss what you think the technological advances of the future will be. Decide how they will affect all aspects of lift—job, home, leisure time, school, sports, entertainment, transportation, health care. Then, decide on a method to present your view of the future. Your group may choose to make a model, write a story, publish a magazine, or present a television program. Include in your presentation the reasons why you predict each new advance and what effects the advance will have on American society and culture.

663

Protecting the Environment

OBJECTIVE: What steps can Americans take to protect the environment?

1. The Arctic National Wildlife Reserve in Alaska contains 1.5 million acres (607,000 hectares) of some of the richest oil deposits in the United States. Only a handful of people, the Gwich'in and Inupiat Indians, live in this wilderness. These two Native American groups disagree over oil development in the park. The Gwich'in argue that it would change the path of caribou herds, their chief source of food. They also fear the changes outsiders would bring. The Inupiat feel that money from oil drilling in the park will improve their standard of living. Like the Gwich'in, many people want to keep the few remaining forests and wilderness areas as they are. Many others, like the Inupiat, want to develop the rich natural resources of these lands.
▶ Where do you stand on this issue?

The Environmental Movement How and when did a nationwide movement to protect the earth and air begin?

2. In 1961, a writer alerted people everywhere to the dangers of **pesticides** (PEST-uh-sydz). Pesticides are the chemicals used to destroy insects and other organisms harmful to plants and food crops. The author was Rachel Carson.

People in History

3. Rachel Carson As a **marine biologist,** Rachel Carson studied underwater plants and

▲ A layer of thick smog often hangs over Los Angeles and other cities. Smog, a kind of air pollution caused by mainly cars, is a major problem in modern cities.

animals. She was also a science writer. As a child, she spent time learning about wildlife in the woods around her Pennsylvania home. At college during the 1920s, she studied zoology and biology. She was one of the first women hired by the Bureau of Fisheries in a non-secretarial position. Carson worked for the Bu-

In Chapter 9 you will apply these critical thinking skills to the historical process:
▶ **Predicting:** Telling what you believe will happen on the basis of clues and facts.

Understanding Points of View: Recognizing why people have different attitudes about the same thing.

reau, which was later renamed the U.S. Fish and Wildlife Service, most of her adult life.

4. She and other scientists became aware that the use of pesticides, especially DDT, was threatening all kinds of life. These pesticides killed not only insects but also some helpful bacteria, algae, and animals. To warn the American people about the dangers she saw, Carson wrote the book called *Silent Spring.*

🦅 Spotlight on Sources

5. In this passage from *Silent Spring*, Carson writes that pesticides are poisoning the earth and the air and are killing off America's wildlife.

> Since the mid-1940s over 200 basic chemicals have been created for use in killing insects, weeds, rodents, and other organisms described in the modern vernacular as "pests"; and they are sold under several thousand different brand names.
>
> These sprays, dusts, and aerosols are now applied almost universally to farms, gardens, forests, and homes—nonselective chemicals that have the power to kill every insect, the "good" and the "bad," to still the song of birds and the leaping of fish in the streams, to coat the leaves with a deadly film, and to linger on in soil—all this though the intended target may be only a few weeds or insects. Can anyone believe it is possible to lay down such a barrage of poisons on the surface of the earth without making it unfit for all life? They should not be called "insecticides," but "biocides."
>
> —from *Silent Spring* by Rachel Carson
> Copyright ©1962 by Rachel Carson.
> Reprinted by Houghton Mifflin Company

▶ What warning does the title *Silent Spring* give about the continued use of pesticides? Why should people care if wildlife is killed?

6. Carson's book launched a nationwide movement to protect the earth and air. President John F. Kennedy formed a special committee to study the effects of pesticides on the environment. On New Year's Day 1970, Presi-

dent Nixon signed into law the National Environmental Policy Act. In April, the first Earth Day was held throughout America. Millions of people demonstrated against the use of pesticides. President Nixon then created the Environmental Protection Agency (EPA) in July. The EPA enforces environmental protection laws. It also regulates the use of pesticides and other poisonous substances in business and industry. The Clean Air Act of 1970 limited the amount of pollutants in car exhaust fumes. Under the Clean Water Act of 1972, the EPA works with state governments to set quality standards for tap water.

Air Pollution How does air pollution damage the environment?

7. Today, the United States is part of a world-wide effort to protect the earth's **ozone** (OH-zohn) **layer.** The ozone layer is a covering of gas that shields the earth from the harmful ultraviolet rays of the sun. Certain chemicals known as **chlorofluorocarbons** (KLOR-oh-FLOO-roh-cahr-buhnz), or CFCs, are used in automobile air conditioning, spray cans, and foam packaging. **Ecologists** (ee-KAHL-uh-jists) have shown that these chemicals eat away at the ozone layer. Ecologists are people who study our natural surroundings. In March 1988, the United States Senate approved an international treaty that promises to reduce the use of CFCs by 50 percent by 1999. The use of CFCs in spray cans is now illegal in the United States. What can American shoppers do to protest the ◀ use of CFCs?

8. Ecologists warn that the buildup of carbon dioxide in the atmosphere could create a **greenhouse effect** and cause serious climate changes. For example, with the warming of the climate, the ocean level could rise and cause the coastline to flood. Also, production of food crops in the Midwest could be reduced by as much as one fourth.

9. In the greenhouse effect, carbon dioxide in the upper atmosphere acts as a blanket, causing a gradual warming of the earth's sur-

Activity: Have groups of students read and study other passages from *Silent Spring*. Have each group present the main ideas in the passage and their reactions to it. Have the entire class discuss the presentations. Encourage students to consider solutions to environmental problems.

665

face. **Industrial emissions** (ee-MISH-uhnz) are a leading cause of the greenhouse effect. They increase the carbon dioxide in the atmosphere by 25 percent. Industrial emissions are the **toxic**, or poisonous, fumes and chemicals from the smokestacks of manufacturing plants. Car exhaust, electric power plants, and **deforestation** (dee-fohr-uh-STAY-shun) also contribute to the greenhouse effect. Deforestation is the cutting down of forests. Trees "breathe" in carbon dioxide and convert it to oxygen. When trees are cut down, more carbon dioxide remains in the atmosphere. One year of deforestation in America alone leaves about a billion tons of carbon dioxide in the air.

▼ Acid rain is a major threat to the forests and wildlife in the United States and neighboring areas in Canada. It has been the cause of conflict between Canada and the United States.

10. Because acid industrial emissions dissolve in water, rainfall often has a heavy acid content. Such rain is called **acid rain.** Acid rain destroys trees, contributing to deforestation problems. Acid rain also causes underwater plants such as algae to overgrow. The overgrown plants use up most of the oxygen in the water. What happens to fish in lakes and streams that have been polluted by acid rain?

America's Waterways What steps are being taken to stop the dumping of toxic waste and other poisons into America's waterways?

11. In the 1960s and 1970s, companies poisoned America's waterways by dumping toxic wastes. Uncaring Americans also poisoned the waters by dumping their garbage and trash. Styrofoam and plastic trash can be especially dangerous. When animals try to eat the plastic or become tangled in it, they may die. However, due to the efforts of the EPA and concerned Americans, America's polluted waters are being cleaned up. State governments and private organizations help drain, clean, and restore lakes. By 1986, 80 percent of America's river mileage was again safe for swimming and fishing. Atlantic salmon have been seen in some of these rivers for the first time since the 1700s.

12. Today, the dumping of toxic wastes into America's waterways is illegal. The EPA heavily fines companies found guilty of this crime. Other laws have been passed making the dumping of sewage illegal. Not all companies pay attention to these laws, however.

13. On March 24, 1989, an oil tanker called the *Exxon Valdez* hit a reef in Alaska's Prince William Sound, causing the worst oil spill in United States history. More than 11 million gallons of crude oil leaked into one of the purest bodies of water in the world. By mid-April, the oil covered 1600 square miles of water and 800 miles of shoreline in one of the world's richest wildlife areas. The glue-like quality of the oil caused many birds to drown. Many otters and other animals froze because the coat of oil destroyed the insulating ability of their fur. The

▲ As a result of the *Exxon Valdez* oil spill, at least 984 sea otters and 34,000 birds—including 139 bald eagles—had died by September 1989. Scientists believe that the real number of animal deaths may be as high as 350,000.

oil cut off the oxygen that fish and underwater plants need to breathe. Thousands of underwater plants and animals died as a result.

14. With 1,400 boats, 85 aircraft, 11,300 people, and six months of hard work, much of the oil was cleaned up. Scientists said the area's wildlife populations would survive. However, the fishing industry in Alaska lost $12 million in profits. The *Exxon Valdez* oil spill was the worst in United States history, but it is not the only one. Other spills have occurred on both coasts. ▶ What should be done to help people who were put out of work by the oil spill?

A New Environmental Policy What policies did President Bush suggest for improving the environment?

15. In June 1989, President Bush announced a plan for reducing air pollution. To reduce **smog,** he tightened standards for automobile exhaust by 40 percent. Smog is an unhealthy mixture of smoke, water vapor, and dust in the air caused by industrial emissions and auto exhaust. In 1990, gas pumps in cities with the worst air were required to have anti-vapor nozzles to capture toxic fumes. To reduce acid rain, coal-burning power plants must slash their sulfur-dioxide emissions in half by the year 2000. Bush also recommended the development of cars that use cleaner-burning fuels than gasoline. Raising taxes on gasoline would also cut down on auto exhaust fumes, but Bush was reluctant to do so. Why do you think he wants ◀ to develop better cars in the future instead of raising gasoline taxes now?

Outlook

16. Environmentalists feel that several steps have been taken that will help improve the environment. However, environmentalists know that there is much more to be done. What ◀ changes do you think must be made? How is America facing the challenge of saving the environment of the nation and the world?

CHAPTER REVIEW

VOCABULARY REVIEW

▶ Write the definition of each vocabulary word listed below.

1. deforestation
2. smog
3. greenhouse effect
4. marine biologist

5. ozone layer
6. ecologists
7. pesticides
8. chlorofluorocarbons

9. acid rain
10. industrial emissions
11. toxic

SKILL BUILDER: READING A CHART

▶ The chart below is a record of how the United States federal government spent its money in 1975, 1985, and 1990. Using the chart, answer these questions on a separate sheet of paper.

1. Which department received the most money in 1990?

2. Which department received the second largest amount of money in 1990?

3. How many more billions of dollars did the Department of Defense receive in 1985 than in 1975?

4. How many more billions of dollars did the Department of Transportation get in 1990 than the Department of Education?

5. Which department got less money in 1990 than it did in 1985?

6. Rank the departments 1 through 13 according to how much money they received in 1990.

FEDERAL BUDGET OUTLAYS, BY DEPARTMENT
(in billions of dollars)

Department	1975	1985	1990
Agricuture	15.6	55.5	46.0
Commerce	1.1	2.1	3.7
Defense	93.1	263.9	289.8
Education	7.6	16.7	25.0
Energy	3.2	10.6	12.0
Health and Human Services	104.2	315.5	438.7
Housing and Urban Development	7.5	28.7	20.2
Interior	2.2	4.8	5.8
Justice	2.1	3.6	6.7
Labor	17.7	23.9	25.3
State	.8	2.6	4.0
Transportation	10.1	25.0	28.6
Treasury	41.3	164.9	255.3

—from *Statistical Abstract of the United States, World Almanac, 1992*

SKILL BUILDERS: CRITICAL THINKING AND COMPREHENSION

❱ I. Predicting

▶ Choose one of the following questions to make a prediction. Write your prediction on a separate sheet of paper.

1. Predict what would happen to your state if the greenhouse effect made the temperature rise ten degrees.

2. The *Exxon Valdez* oil spill was one of America's worst disasters in recent years. Predict what will happen to the Alaskan environment and economy as a result of this disaster.

II. Point of View

▶ Environmentalists and Big Business often have opposing points of view. Choose which group holds each of the following points of view. Write your answer on a separate sheet of paper.

1. Too many regulations and taxes and fines will only hurt by cutting profits and lowering workers wages.

2. Too much progress isn't always a good thing.

3. More government support needs to go into solar energy.

4. Americans want perfect-looking fruit on their table. Pesticides can't be avoided if fruits are to be sold.

III. Making Judgments

1. In your opinion, which problem is more important to solve—homelessness or pollution? Why? Explain your answer on a separate sheet of paper.

2. Make a judgment by deciding whether you agree or disagree with the following statement. Then explain your answer on a separate sheet of paper.

The environment is our greatest natural resource.

USING PRIMARY SOURCES

▶ Reread the Spotlight on Sources on page 665. Then answer this question: Should all pesticides be banned? Is there another solution? Are there other sides to the issue that should be considered? Explain your opinion.

ENRICHMENT

1. Create a poster that in some way encourages environmental protection. Display your poster on the bulletin board.

2. Review the chart on government spending on page 668. If you made the decisions about how the federal government spends its money, to which department would you give the most money? To which department would you give the least money? Explain your answer on a separate sheet of paper.

UNIT REVIEW

SUMMARY

In the second half of the twentieth century, many groups of Americans made progress in gaining their civil rights. African Americans were one of the first groups to realize that they could win power by working together. Under the leadership of people such as Martin Luther King, Jr., African Americans were successful in forcing laws that insured civil rights. Women's groups also organized to demand equal rights. They demonstrated and lobbied to get laws passed that guaranteed women the same opportunities as men. Hispanic Americans and Native Americans also demanded and received their civil rights. Other groups such as the Gray Panthers and handicapped Americans organized to ensure their demands were met.

Americans were also concerned with other issues. Immigration from Eastern Europe, Latin America, and Asia added to the population. However, the number of people who participated in government was smaller. In fact, a smaller percentage of Americans voted than in any other western democracy. Relationships with communist nations became friendlier as many of those countries moved closer to democracy and a free economy. Although there were challenges in cities, the nation, and the environment, Americans worked to solve problems. Resulting laws helped reduce pollution of the air, water, and the soil. Technology not only helped to solve some of these problems, but also improved the quality of American life.

SKILL BUILDER: READING A MAP

▶ Use the map below to answer the following questions:

1. From which countries or regions does the United States import the most goods?

2. What neighbor imports the most goods from the United States?

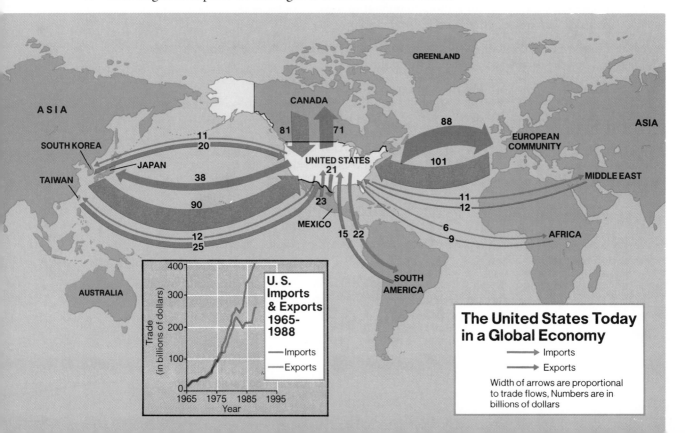

3. What was the trade deficit in 1985? (Hint: The trade deficit is the difference between imports and exports.)

4. Why might a trade deficit be a problem for the United States?

5. What was the one area of the world in which the United States sold more than it bought?

6. Why does the map not show how much trade the United States has with Australia? With Greenland?

SKILL BUILDER: CRITICAL THINKING AND COMPREHENSION

I. Making Judgments

1. In your opinion, which group made the most progress in gaining civil or equal rights in the second half of the twentieth century? Explain the reasons for your choice in a short paragraph.

2. How would you grade the United States government in protecting the environment? Explain your answer in a short paragraph.

II. Comparing and Contrasting

▶ On a sheet of paper, make a chart about how different groups of people worked to insure their rights. The chart should show at least two ways that the groups' methods are similar and two ways they are different. Use the headings below in your chart.

	Similarities	Differences
African Americans		
Women		
Native Americans		
Hispanic Americans		
Older Americans		
Handicapped Americans		

ENRICHMENT

1. With a partner or in a small group, create a newspaper that reports on the latter half of the twentieth century. You should include events and people mentioned in Unit 15. You can include additional articles that you have researched. Illustrate your newspaper with pictures, cartoons, graphs, maps, or charts. Remember to have an editorial page where the reporters can give their opinions about important issues.

2. Choose one important issue in Unit 15 that interests you. Research the issue in the library. You will probably need to read magazines and newspapers for current information. Then present your findings to the class.

ARCTIC OCEAN

80°N

GREENLA

Arctic Circle

66½°N

UNITED
STATES

60°N

CANADA

NORTH

AMERICA

40°N

Chicago Detroit

New York

Washington Philadelphia

ATLANTI

OCEAN

UNITED STATES

Los Angeles

23½°N Tropic of Cancer

MEXICO

CUBA

DOMINICAN
REPUBLIC

20°N

Mexico City

JAMAICA HAITI

HONDURAS

GUATEMALA NICARAGUA

EL SALVADOR

PACIFIC

TRINIDAD AND TOBA

COSTA RICA VENEZUELA GUYANA

SURINAME

PANAMA Bogotá FRENCH GUI

OCEAN

COLOMBIA

0° Equator

ECUADOR

SOUTH

PERU AMERICA

Lima BRAZIL

BOLIVIA

20°S

Río d

PARAGUAY Jane

23½°S Tropic of Capricorn São Paul

CHILE

Buenos

Santiago Aires URUGUAY

ARGENTINA

40°S

60°S

66½°S Antarctic Circle

80°S ANTARCTICA

World Political Map

Africa

B = Burkina Faso
BU = Burundi
L = Lesotho
R = Rwanda
S = Swaziland

Asia

AR = Armenia
AZ = Azerbaijan
B = Bhutan
CY = Cyprus
G = Georgia
I = Israel
J = Jordan
K = Kuwait
LE = Lebanon
TU = Turkmenistan
UAE = United Arab
       Emirates
UZ = Uzbekistan

Europe

A = Austria
AL = Albania
B = Belgium
BE = Belarus
BH = Bosnia & Herzegovina
C = Czechoslovakia
CR = Croatia
E = Estonia
G = Germany
H = Hungary
L = Luxembourg
LA = Latvia
LI = Lithuania
M = Moldova
MA = Macedonia
N = Netherlands
P = Poland
R = Romania
S = Switzerland
SL = Slovenia
Y = Yugoslavia

Note: This map omits countries with fewer
than 500,000 inhabitants.

0	1000	2000	3000 Miles

0	1000	2000	3000 Kilometers

Robinson Projection

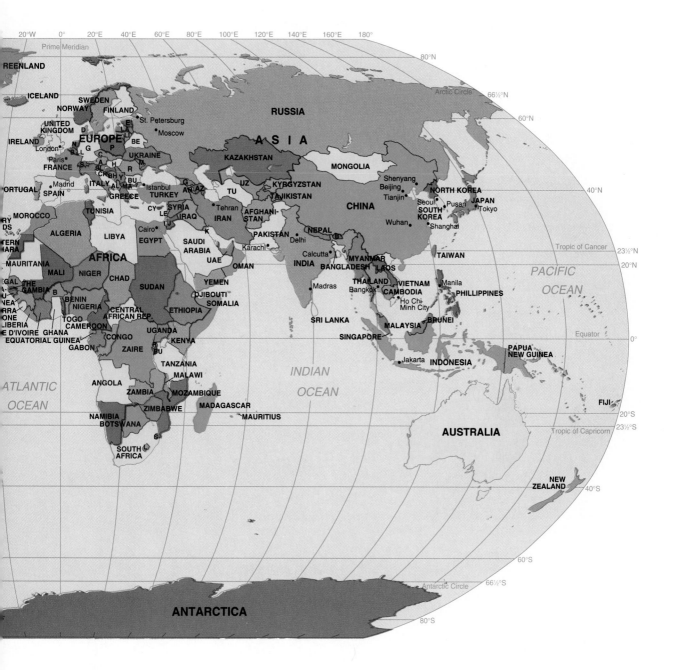

• Vancouver

Regina •

Winnipeg •

WASHINGTON

Olympia ★ • Seattle • Spokane

▲ Mt. Rainier
14,410 ft/4,393 m

Mt. St. Helens
8,364 ft/2,550 m ▲

Portland •

Columbia River

• Helena ★

MONTANA

Missouri River

Yellowstone River

NORTH DAKOTA

★ Bismarck

GREAT PLAINS

★ Salem

CASCADE RANGE

COAST RANGES

OREGON

★ Boise

IDAHO

Snake River

ROCKY MOUNTAINS

WYOMING

BLACK HILLS

SOUTH DAKOTA

★ Pierre

Missouri River

45°N

40°N

Sacramento River

SIERRA NEVADA

Sacramento ★

Carson City ★

Great Salt Lake ★

Salt Lake City •

Cheyenne
★

COLORADO

Denver ★

NEBRASKA

Om

Platte River

Linc

San Francisco •

San Jose •

San Joaquin River

NEVADA

UTAH

Colorado River

ROCKY MOUNTAINS

▲ Mt. Elbert
14,433 ft/4,400 m

▲ Pikes Peak
14,110 ft/4,302 m

Arkansas River

KANSAS

Tope

Wichita •

35°N

125°W

COAST RANGES

▲ Mt. Whitney
14,494 ft/4,419 m

Las Vegas •

Lake Mead

CALIFORNIA

Rio Grande

Santa Fe ★

PL

Tuls

★ Oklahoma C

OKLAHOM

• Los Angeles

Salton Sea

ARIZONA

• Albuquerque

NEW MEXICO

PACIFIC

OCEAN

• San Diego

★ Phoenix

NEW MEXICO

30°N

Gila River

Tucson •

• El Paso

Pecos River

TEXAS

Dalla

Rio Grande

Brazos Riv

Gulf of California

120°W

Austin ★

San Antonio •

Ho

Kauai

22°N

Oahu

HAWAII

ARCTIC   OCEAN

SOVIET UNION

170°W

Honolulu •

Maui

PACIFIC OCEAN

BROOKS RANGE

ALASKA

ARCTIC CIRCLE

20°N

0   100 miles

Mauna Kea
13,796 ft/4,206 m ▲

Hawaii

• Hilo

• Nome

Yukon River

Fairbanks •

0   150 kilometers

160°W   155°W

170°E   180°

170°W

▲ Mt. McKinley
20,320 ft/6,195 m

ALASKA RANGE

CANADA

MEXICO

50°N

Bering Sea

Anchorage •

60°N

Juneau ★

170°E

674

ALEUTIAN ISLANDS

0   300 miles

0   400 kilometers

PACIFIC OCEAN

180°   50°N   170°W   160°W   150°W   140°W

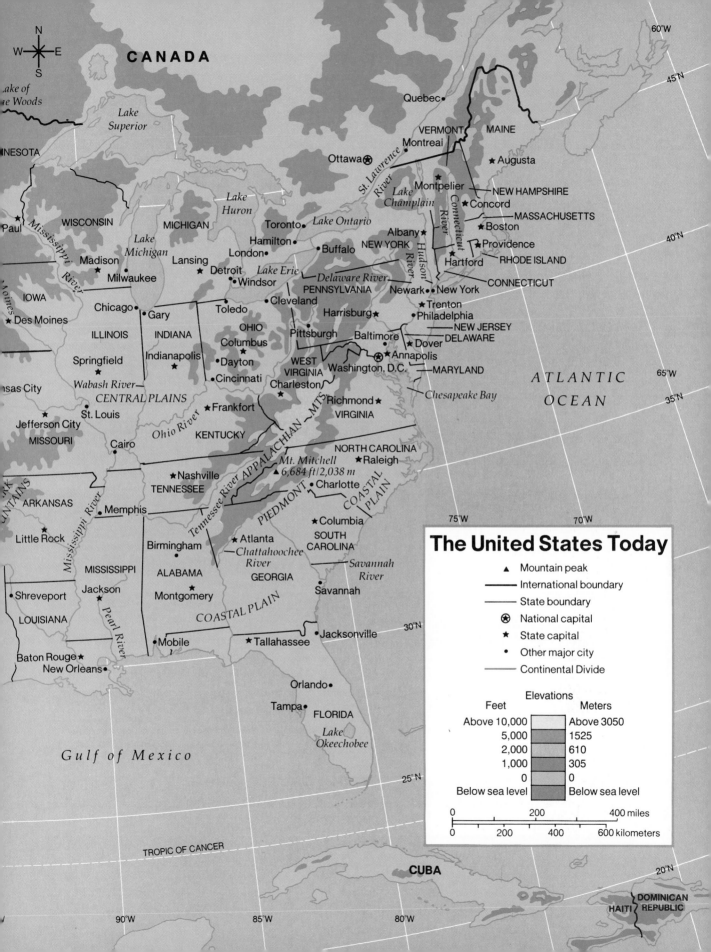

PRESIDENTS OF THE UNITED STATES

President	Term of Office	Political Party	Home State	Other Occupation	Presidential Quotations
1. George Washington	1789–1797	None	VA	Planter	"I hope I shall always possess firmness of virtue enough to maintain the character of an honest man."
2. John Adams	1797–1801	Fed.	MA	Lawyer	"(The 4th of July) ought to be (done) with . . . parades, shows, games, and illuminations from one end of the continent to the other. . . ."
3. Thomas Jefferson	1801–1809	Dem.-Rep.	VA	Lawyer	"The God who gave us life, gave us liberty."
4. James Madison	1809–1817	Dem.-Rep.	VA	Lawyer	"The advise . . . deepest in my convictions is that the Union of the States be cherished and perpetuated."
5. James Monroe	1817–1825	Dem.-Rep.	VA	Lawyer	"A little flattery will support a man through great fatigue."
6. John Quincy Adams	1825–1829	Nat. Rep.	MA	Lawyer	"I am a man of reserved, cold, austere, and forbidding manners."
7. Andrew Jackson	1829–1837	Dem.	TN	Lawyer, Soldier	"I am sworn to uphold the Constitution as Andy Jackson understands it and interprets it."
8. Martin Van Buren	1837–1841	Dem.	NY	Lawyer	(As to the sun rising in the East) "I understand that's the common acceptance, but I never get up till after dawn, I can't really say."
9. William H. Harrison	1841	Whig	OH	Soldier	"Sir, I wish you to understand the principles of the Government. I wish them carried out. I ask nothing more."
10. John Tyler	1841–1845	Whig	VA	Lawyer	"It would not be proper for the president to ride around in a secondhand carriage."
11. James K. Polk	1845–1849	Dem.	TN	Lawyer	"(I must) give my vigilant attention even to the form and details of my subordinates' duties."
12. Zachary Taylor	1849–1850	Whig	LA	Soldier	"My life has been devoted to arms, yet I look upon war . . . , as a national calamity, to be avoided if compatible with national honor."
13. Millard Fillmore	1850–1853	Whig	NY	Lawyer	"They would probably ask: Who's Fillmore? . . . and then my name would I fear, give them an excellent opportunity to makes jokes at my expense."
14. Franklin Pierce	1853–1857	Dem.	NH	Lawyer	Antislavery petitions in his state were not signed by legal voters but by women and children, "who knew not what they did."
15. James Buchanan	1857–1861	Dem.	PA	Lawyer	"I am the last President of the United States."
16. Abraham Lincoln	1861–1865	Rep.	IL	Lawyer	"You can fool all of the people part of the time and part of the people all of the time but you can't fool all of the people all of the time."
17. Andrew Johnson	1865–1869	Rep.	TN	Tailor	"Treason must be made infamous and traitors must be impoverished."
18. Ulysses S. Grant	1869–1877	Rep.	IL	Soldier	"I know only two tunes. One is 'Yankee Doodle' and the other isn't."
19. Rutherford B. Hayes	1877–1881	Rep.	OH	Lawyer	"He who serves his country best serves his party best."

20. James A. Garfield	1881	Rep.	OH	Teacher, Lawyer	[After taking office] "What is there in this place that a man should ever want to get into it?"
21. Chester A. Arthur	1881–1885	Rep.	NY	Lawyer	"If it were not for the reporters I would tell you the truth, because I know you are intimate friends and devoted adherents to the Rep. Party."
22. Grover Cleveland	1885–1889	Dem.	NY	Lawyer	"Public Office is a Public Trust."
23. Benjamin Harrison	1889–1893	Rep.	IN	Lawyer	"I want it understood that I am the grandson of nobody. I believe that every man should stand on his own merits."
24. Grover Cleveland	1893–1897	Dem.	NY	Lawyer	"While the people should patriotically and cheerfully support their government, its functions do not include the support of the people."
25. William B. McKinley	1897–1901	Rep.	OH	Lawyer	"Wars should never be entered upon until every agency of peace has failed. . ."
26. Theodore Roosevelt	1901–1909	Rep.	NY	Rancher, Writer	"Do what you can with what you've got, where you are, but do it."
27. William Howard Taft	1909–1913	Rep.	OH	Lawyer	"I am afraid I am a constant disappointment to my party."
28. Woodrow Wilson	1913–1921	Dem.	NJ	Lawyer, Teacher	"The world must be made safe for democracy."
29. Warren G. Harding	1921–1923	Rep.	OH	Journalist	"America's present need . . . is not nostrums but normalcy."
30. Calvin Coolidge	1923–1929	Rep.	MA	Lawyer	"If you don't say anything, you can't be called on to repeat it."
31. Herbert C. Hoover	1929–1933	Rep.	CA	Engineer	"The crisis (depression) will be over in sixty days."
32. Franklin D. Roosevelt	1933–1945	Dem.	NY	Lawyer	"The only thing we have to fear is fear itself."
33. Harry S. Truman	1945–1953	Dem.	MO	Merchant	"It is much better to go down fighting for what is right than to compromise your principles."
34. Dwight D. Eisenhower	1953–1961	Rep.	NY, PA	Soldier	"Why give a speech, if you don't want the audience to take away a specific message"
35. John F. Kennedy	1961–1963	Dem.	MA	Writer, Teacher	"We stand on the edge of a new frontier, a frontier of unknown opportunities and perils."
36. Lyndon B. Johnson	1963–1969	Dem.	TX	Teacher, Rancher	"This administration here and now declares an unconditional war on poverty."
37. Richard M. Nixon	1969–1974	Rep.	NY, CA	Lawyer	"No words can describe the depth of my regret and pain at the anguish my mistakes over Watergate have caused this nation. . . ."
38. Gerald R. Ford	1974–1977	Rep.	MI	Lawyer	"I'm a Ford, not a Lincoln."
39. Jimmy (James Earl) Carter	1977–1981	Dem.	GA	Farmer	"I have been accused of being an outsider,— I plead guilty."
40. Ronald W. Reagan	1981–1989	Rep.	CA	Actor	"When I was announcing sports I was happy and thought that was all I wanted out of life."
41. George Bush	1989–1993	Rep.	TX	Businessman	"So long as we remember the American idea . . . the state of the Union will remain sound and strong."
42. William (Bill) Clinton	1993–	Dem.	AR	Lawyer	"We can make government work again by making it more aggressive and leaner and more effective at the same time."

GLOSSARY

A

abolish (uh-BAH-lish) To do away with something completely.

abolitionist (ab-uh-LISH-uh-nist) A person in favor of ending slavery.

abridge To cut back or reduce.

acid rain Pollutants that are absorbed into the atmosphere and later returned to the earth in rain.

Adams-Onís Treaty An 1819 agreement between Spain and the United States. The United States received Florida and land in Alabama and Mississippi along the Gulf of Mexico for $5 million.

addict A person who is physically dependent on a drug.

administrator (ad-MIN-uh-stray-tuhr) A person who manages or directs a company or organization.

adobe (uh-DOH-bee) A kind of sun-dried brick, or a house made of these bricks.

advertise (AD-vuhr-tyz) To try to sell something by means of television, radio, newspapers, or other media.

affirmative action (uh-FURM-uh-tiv) Hiring program for the historically disadvantaged to correct past injustices and inequities.

aggression (uh-GRESH-uhn) An attack against another country.

agriculture (AG-ruh-kul-chuhr) The science or art of farming.

airlift Sending food and other supplies to a place entirely by airplane.

Albany Plan of Union A 1754 plan to join the 13 Colonies together under one government.

alliance (uh-LY-uhns) An agreement between nations to help each other.

Allies (AL-lyz) Britain, France, Russia, the United States, and a number of smaller countries in World War I and World War II .

amendment (uh-MEND-muhnt) A change in a constitution or other legal document.

American Antislavery Society An organization that wanted immediate freedom for slaves.

American Indian Chicago Conference A meeting in 1961 of 500 Native Americans from 67 tribes that began the Native American Movement.

American Colonization Society An organization formed in 1817 to send freed African American slaves to Africa.

American System An 1816 plan to encourage American manufacturing, develop roads, and make other internal improvements.

amnesty (AM-nuhs-tee) A pardon given to those who have broken the law.

ancestor (AN-ses-tur) A person from whom one is descended.

anesthetic (an-uhs-THET-ik) A drug that deadens pain.

annex (uh-NEKS) To add a territory to an existing country.

antiseptic (an-tuh-SEP-tik) A chemical that prevents infections by killing or stopping the growth of germs.

appeasement (uh-PEEZ-muhnt) A policy of giving in to an aggressor nation in order to keep the peace.

apprentice (uh-PREN-tis) A person learning a trade, art, or profession.

aqueduct (AK-wuh-dukt) A channel or pipe for carrying water.

archaeologist (ahr-kee-AHL-uh-jist) A scientist who studies ancient ruins and other remains.

armada (ahr-MAH-duh) A large fleet of warships, especially the one sent by Spain against England in 1588.

armistice (AHR-mis-tis) An agreement to stop fighting.

arms limitation agreement An agreement to limit the number of nuclear weapons in a nation's arsenal.

arsenal (AHR-suh-nuhl) A building for making and storing guns and ammunition.

Articles of Confederation (kuhn-fed-uh-RAY-shuhn) The first constitution of the United States, in effect from 1781 to 1789.

artifact (AHR-tuh-fakt) Anything made by human work.

assimilation (uh-sim-uh-LAY-shuhn) Absorption of a minority group into the mainstream of a society.

assembly line (uh-SEM-blee) An arrangement of machines and workers in which a product is manufactured in the course of moving from one worker to the next.

astronomy (uh-STRAH-nuh-mee) The science that studies planets and other heavenly bodies.

asylum (uh-SY-lum) Institution for the mentally ill or other people who need care.

Atlantic Basin The circular area in the Atlantic Ocean formed by the coastlines of North American, South America, and Europe.

Atlantic Charter A statement issued by Winston Churchill and Franklin D. Roosevelt in 1941, outlining the peaceful goals of the Allies after World War II.

atlas (AT-luhs) A book of maps and charts.

audiencia (ow-dee-en-SEE-ah) Spanish word for court.

autocuer (aw-toh-KYOO-uhr) A computer that translates spoken words into written form.

automation (aw-toh-MAY-shuhn) Use of systems of machines to do routine work.

B

Bacon's Rebellion An armed conflict in Virginia in 1676, between backcountry farmers and wealthy landowners on the coastal plain.

backcountry Less-settled areas; frontier.

banish (BAN-ish) To expel, to force to leave.

barrio (BAH-ree-oh) A Spanish-speaking neighborhood.

Battle of Britain The bombing of Great Britain by the German air force in 1940.

Battle of Bunker Hill Battle fought near Boston in 1775 during the American Revolution.

Battle of New Orleans A United States victory in the War of 1812.

bilingual (by-LING-gwuhl) Able to speak two languages.

Bill of Rights The first ten amendments of the United States Constitution, protecting the rights of the individual citizen.

black codes Laws that denied the rights of African Americans in the South during Reconstruction.

black power Self-help through racial pride, solidarity, and economic enterprises; control by African Americans of their lives and their plans for the future.

black separatism (SEP-uh-ruh-tizm) The idea that African Americans should live in separate communities, apart from white Americans.

Bleeding Kansas Kansas before the Civil War, when many people lost their lives in armed attacks between proslavery and antislavery groups.

blight (BLYT) A disease that kills plants.

blitzkrieg (BLITS-kreeg) Attack using airplanes, tanks, and heavy guns; German for "lightning war."

blockade Militarily shutting off a nation's ports from trade.

boom A period of economic prosperity.

boomtown A town that springs up almost overnight.

bootlegger A person who illegally makes, sells, or transports liquor.

boycott (BOY-kaht) To refuse to buy certain goods or to buy from a particular company.

Breadbasket Colonies American colonies where wheat was the chief cash crop.

bribe (BRYB) An illegal payment to someone in order to cause him or her to act in a certain way.

bridging point A narrow spot in a river where the banks are close enough to build a bridge.

budget deficit (BUJ-uht DEF-uh-siht) When a government spends more money than it takes in, the difference between the two amounts.

burgess (BUR-juhs) An elected representative to the colonial Virginia Assembly, a lawmaking body founded in the early 1600s.

C

campaign (kam-PAYN) A series of military operations carried out to gain a particular objective.

caravan (KA-ruh-van) A group of traders or other travelers who travel together for protection or safety.

caravel (KA-ruh-vel) A sailing ship with slanted, triangular sails that allow sailing into the wind.

caribou (KA-ruh-boo) A large deer that roams in herds across frozen regions of North America.

carpetbagger A Northerner who moved to the South after the Civil War.

cartography (kahr-TAHG-ruh-fee) The science of making maps and charts.

cash crop A crop that is grown to be sold.

censure (SEN-shuhr) To formally condemn a person's actions.

census (SEN-sus) An official count of people.

Central Powers Germany, Austria-Hungary, the Ottoman Empire, and Bulgaria in World War I.

charter (CHAHR-tuhr) A document that establishes a company, colony, or other organization.

checks and balances A system under which each branch of government has powers that check the other branches, creating a balance of power.

chlorofluorocarbon (KLOR-oh-FLOO-roh-kar-buhn) A kind of gas used in air-conditioners, refrigerators, aerosol cans, and foam packaging, proved to be harmful to the environment.

circumnavigate (suhr-kuhm-NAV-uh-gayt) To travel completely around the globe.

city manager plan A form of city government in which the city is run by a hired professional manager rather than by an elected official.

civil right A legal right guaranteed to all citizens.

civil rights movement A movement of the 1950s and 1960s to overturn practices that denied their rights to African Americans and other minorities.

civil service (SIV-uhl SUR-vis) A system under which government agencies hire workers through competitive exams instead of hiring political allies.

class A division in society based on social, economic, religious, or racial factors.

coeducational Admitting both males and females.

collective bargaining (kuh-LEK-tiv BAHR-guh-ning) Negotiations between an employer and a union to agree on wages, hours, and working conditions.

Cold War The war fought with words, not with weapons, between the United States and the Soviet Union after World War II.

colony (KAHL-uh-nee) A territory governed by a foreign nation.

commission (kuh-MISH-uhn) A document that makes an appointment official.

commission plan A form of city government under which a city is run by a group of elected officials.

Committee of Correspondence A group of colonists who wrote about what was happening in their colony.

compass A device with a magnetic needle that shows directions.

compete (kuhm-PEET) To go up against or challenge.

computer (kuhm-PYOO-tuhr) An electronic machine that processes, retrieves, and stores data.

computer literacy (LIT-uh-ruh-see) The ability to understand and operate computers.

compromise (KAHM-pruh-myz) A settlement of a quarrel or difference of opinion in which both sides give up something.

confederation (kuhn-fed-uh-RAY-shuhn) A league or alliance of independent units.

confederacy (kuhn-FED-uh-ruh-see) A union of people, groups, or states that join together for a specific purpose

Confederacy The 11 Southern states that seceded from the United States, causing the Civil War.

containment (kun-TAYN-muhnt) A policy to keep communism from spreading.

conquistador (kahn-KEES-tuh-dohr) Spanish word for conqueror.

conservation (kah-suhr-VAY-shuhn) Planned management of natural resources.

consumer goods (kuhn-SOO-muhr) Food, clothing, and household products.

Continental (kahn-tuh-NEN-tuhl) Money printed by the Continental Congress during and after the American Revolution.

Continental Army The army of the United States during the Revolutionary War.

convent (KON-vent) A community of nuns.

convert (kuhn-VERT) To change from one belief, faith, or religion to another.

cooperative (koh-AHP-uh-ruh-tiv) An organization formed to enable its members to buy, sell, or become involved in other economic ventures.

corollary (KAWR-uh-lair-ee) An addition to an existing document or policy.

corporation (kor-puh-RAY-shuhn) A company owned by stockholders.

corruption (kuh-RUP-shuhn) Dishonesty on an organized or official level.

cotton gin A machine invented by Eli Whitney that separates cotton seeds from cotton fibers.

council (KOWN-suhl) A group of people meeting together to plan or decide something; in the colonies, a group of citizens appointed by the king to help the colonial governor of a colony.

coureurs de bois (koo-ROOR duh BWAH) French fur trappers in North America.

cowboy A man who works, usually on horseback, at driving cattle herds on ranches and to market.

cradle A method of filtering gold from sand.

craft union A labor organization of skilled workers in a certain trade.

creditor (KRED-uh-tuhr) A person to whom money is owed.

criollo (kree-OH-yoh) A person born in the Americas whose parents were from Spain.

crop rotation (roh-TAY-shuhn) Method of farming by which a different crop is planted on a piece of land each year.

CT scanner A machine that x-rays a patient from different angles.

culture (KUL-chuhr) A people's way of life, including customs, beliefs, arts, language, and technology.

Cumberland Gap An opening through the Cumberland Mountains between Virginia and Tennessee.

customs officer An official who inspects and collects taxes on imported goods.

D

Daughters of Liberty An organization of colonial women who showed their patriotism by boycotting British goods.

D-Day June 6, 1944, the day of the Allied invasion of France in World War II.

debt (DET) Money owed by one person or organization to another.

debtor (DET-uhr) A person or organization that owes money.

declaration (dek-luh-RAY-shuhn) A formal announcement or statement.

de facto segregation (dee-FAK-toh seg-ruh-GAY-shuhn) Separation of races by custom rather than by law.

deforestation (dee-fawr-uhs-TAY-shuhn) Clearing land of all its trees.

de jure segregation (dee-JOOR-ee) Separation of races by law.

delegate (DEL-uh-guht) A person chosen or elected to act as a representative for an individual or group.

demagogue (DEM-uh-gahg) A leader or politician who appeals to people's emotions and prejudices in order to advance his or her own political power.

demobilization (dee-moh-buh-luh-ZAY-shuhn) After a war, the release of members of a nation's armed forces.

democracy (di-MOK-ruh-see) A government ruled by the people

depression (di-PRESH-uhn) A severe economic downturn

deregulation (dee-reg-yuh-LAY-shuhn) Reduction of government control over business and industry.

desert (DEZ-ert) An arid, barren area of land where rainfall is less than 10 inches (25.4 cm) a year.

détente (day-TAHNT) A period of improved relations between the United States and the Soviet Union; the French word for "relaxation."

dictator (DIK-tay-tuhr) A person who rules with absolute power.

discrimination (dis-krim-uh-NAY-shuhn) Unfair treatment of an individual or group.

dissenter (dis-EN-tuhr) A person who disagrees or holds opinions different from others.

division of labor A system in which each worker is given a part of a manufacturing process.

domesticate (doh-MES-tuh-kayt) To tame animals or plants for human use.

domino effect The theory that if one country falls to communism, others will fall, one after the other, like a row of dominoes.

draft To choose a person for military service.

dropout A student who leaves his or her studies before completion.

dynamo (DY-nuh-moh) A machine that generates electricity.

E

ecologist (ee-KAHL-uh-jist) A person who studies the relation of living things to their environment.

emancipate (i-MAN-suh-payt) To set free from slavery or oppression.

embargo (em-BAHR-goh) A government order preventing certain kinds of trade.

Embargo Act An act of 1807 under which American merchants were forbidden to trade with any foreign nation.

emigration (em-uh-GRAY-shuhn) The act of moving out of a country.

emissions (ee-MISH-uhnz) Chemical fumes from industrial smokestacks and car exhaust.

empire (EM-pyr) A group of countries controlled by a foreign government.

encomienda (en-koh-mee-EN-dah) A system under which Spanish colonists demanded tribute or payment from Native Americans.

enlist To join a nation's armed forces.

enumerated articles (i-NOO-muhr-ay-tuhd) Goods that American colonists were required to sell only to Britain.

environmentalist (en-vy-run-MEN-tuh-list) A person concerned about the quality of the environment.

epidemic (ep-uh-DEM-ik) A sudden and widespread outbreak of disease.

"Era of Good Feelings" The period from 1816 to 1825, when political differences in the United States faded in importance.

Erie Canal A human-made waterway from the Hudson River to Lake Erie.

escalation (es-kuh-LAY-shuhn) An increase in intensity or expansion of a conflict.

estimate (ES-tuh-mayt) To guess or judge; to approximate.

ethnic (ETH-nik) Having to do with nationality or cultural grouping.

ethnic studies The study of history, philosophy, language, literature, and art forms of an ethnic group.

evict (ee-VIKT) To put out of a home or business location.

executive (ek-ZEK-yoo-tiv) A person who directs a large organization.

executive branch The branch of government that carries out and enforces the laws.

exile (EKS-yl) To force a person to leave a country

expedition (eks-puh-DISH-uhn) A journey for the purpose of exploration.

exports (EKS-ports) Goods sent to other countries for trade or sale.

F

fall line A boundary between two regions of different elevation, land surface, and underlying rock.

famine (FAM-in) A severe shortage of food.

fascism (FASH-izm) A system of government based on one-party dictatorship, militarism, nationalism, racism, and intolerance to opposition.

federal government (FED-uh-ruhl) The national government in a union of states.

federation (fed-uh-RAY-shuhn) The joining of groups or states under one governing body.

feminist (FEM-uh-nist) A person who believes in equal rights for women.

forge (FORJ) A furnace used to make ore into iron.

Fourteen Points List of war aims drawn up by President Wilson during World War I.

49th Parallel The boundary line between the United States and Canada west of the Great Lakes.

freedmen Slaves who were set free.

Freedmen's Bureau A government agency created toward the end of the Civil War, responsible for the education and well-being of former slaves.

freedom airlift Transportation by airplane of 4,000 Cubans to the United States in 1965.

freedom rides Bus trips taken by civil rights workers to protest segregation on interstate buses.

French and Indian War A war between France and Britain for control of North America, 1754-1763.

friar (FRY-uhr) A monk in certain Catholic orders.

fugitive (FYOO-juh-tiv) A person who runs away or tries to escape from the law.

Fundamental Orders (fun-duh-MEN-tuhl) A plan of government written in 1639 by Connecticut settlers.

funding Money set aside for a specific purpose.

G

geographer (jee-AHG-ruh-fuhr) A person who studies the surface of the earth and the people who live on it.

ghetto (GET-oh) A neighborhood where people of a particular ethnic background live or are required to live.

girdling (GERD-ling) Removing bark from around the trunk of a tree in order to kill it.

glacier (GLAY-shuhr) A large body of ice moving slowly down a slope or valley.

glasnost (GLAS-nohst) The policies of greater freedom for the Soviet people that were put into effect in the late 1980s; the Russian word for "openness."

glyph (GLIF) A picture symbol used in Mayan writing.

grandfather clause A provision in Southern election laws designed to keep African Americans from voting, according to which no one could vote unless his grandfather had been a voter.

Great Awakening The spirit of religious revival and church reform in the 1730s and 1740s.

Great Depression (dee-PRESH-uhn) A severe economic downturn or business slump in the 1930s, the worst and longest period of high unemployment and low business activity in modern times.

Great Wagon Road A road from Philadelphia to Lancaster, Pennsylvania, then south into the Piedmont region of Virginia and North Carolina.

greenhouse effect The gradual warming of the earth's surface as a result of increased carbon dioxide in the air.

Grey Panthers An organization that fights for the rights of elderly Americans.

guerrilla (guh-RIL-uh) One of a small group of soldiers who make surprise attacks on an enemy.

guerilla war Warfare carried on by surprise attacks on an enemy.

guided missile A rocket whose course toward a target may be changed by radio signals or a built-in target-seeking device.

H

habitant (ah-bee-TAWN) A farmer in New France.

hacendado (ah-sen-DAH-doh) Spanish term for land-owner.

hacienda (ah-see-EN-dah) A large farm in New Spain that grew one or two cash crops.

handicapped (HAN-di-kapt) Having a physical or mental disability, such as blindness or deafness.

Harlem Renaissance (HAHR-luhm REN-uh-sahns) A movement of African American writers and artists in Harlem, New York City, during the 1920s.

head of navigation (nav-uh-GAY-shuhn) On a river, the farthest point inland that ships can reach.

hemisphere (HEM-uh-sfeer) The surface of half of the earth.

Hessian (HESH-uhn) A German soldier hired to fight for the British in the American Revolution.

hogan (HOH-guhn) A one-room house made of poles covered with packed earth and brush used by Native Americans of the Southwest.

Holocaust (HAHL-uh-kost) The organized killing of six million Jews by the Nazis during World War II.

homesteader A person who settled on free land offered by the government under the Homestead Act.

hostage (HAHS-tij) A person being held prisoner until certain demands are met.

hostility (hahs-TIL-uh-tee) Unfriendliness or open acts of warfare.

hotline A special telephone line between the leaders of two countries such as the United States and the Soviet Union.

Huguenot (HYOO-guh-naht) A French Protestant.

human rights Basic freedoms that all people should have.

I

igloo (IG-loo) A round temporary building made of packed snow.

illiterate (ih-LIT-uh-rit) Not able to read or write.

impeach (im-PEECH) To formally accuse a President or other public official of breaking the law.

imperialism (im-PEER-ee-uhl-izm) The extension of a nation's power and influence beyond its borders.

imports Goods that come in from a foreign country.

implied powers Authority beyond the written provisions of the Constitution.

impressment The act of seizing someone for service, especially in a navy.

inaugural address (ih-NAWG-yoo-ruhl uh-DRES) Speech given by a President or other official after taking the oath of office.

income tax A tax based on the amount of money a person earns.

indentured servant (in-DEN-chuhrd) A person who signed a contract to work without pay for a period of years, in return for free passage to the American colonies.

Indian Civil Rights Act A law passed in 1968 granting full civil rights to all Native Americans.

Indian Self-Determination Act of 1976 A law passed in 1976 giving Native Americans a greater voice in the management of reservations.

indigo (IN-di-goh) A plant from which blue dye is made.

Industrial Revolution (in-DUS-tree-uhl rev-uh-LOO-shun) The change that took place in the late 1700s and early 1800s from making goods in small work-shops to making goods with machines in factories.

inferior (in-FEER-ee-uhr) Something or someone that is lower in position, rank, quality, or importance.

inflation (in-FLAY-shun) A rapid rise in prices that lessens the purchasing power of money.

initiative (in-ISH-uh-tiv) The procedure by which citizens may propose laws to a legislature or to the voters.

intendant (in-TEN-dahnt) An official in the French colonies who supervised economic growth and en-forced the laws.

interchangeable (in-ter-CHAYNJ-uh-buhl) Capable of being used in place of something.

intolerable (in-TAHL-uh-ruh-buhl) Impossible to put up with.

Inuit (IN-yoo-wit) The people of the Far North, also called Eskimo.

Iron Curtain The border between the Soviet satellites and the rest of Europe.

irrigation (ir-uh-GAY-shuhn) A system for bringing water to dry land.

island hopping An American World War II strategy of taking some of the Pacific islands held by Japan and bypassing others.

isolationism (y-soh-LAY-shuhn-izm) The policy of not becoming involved in world affairs.

isthmus (IS-muhs) A narrow strip of land that con-nects two larger bodies of land.

J

Jacksonian Democracy (jak-SOH-nee-uhn) The pres-idential policies of Andrew Jackson, giving more Americans a greater voice in government.

jerky (JUR-kee) Buffalo meat or beef cut into strips and dried in the sun.

Jesuit (JEZH-oo-it) A member of the Society of Jesus, a Roman Catholic religious order founded in 1534.

Jim Crow The policy of segregating and discriminating against African Americans.

joint stock company A company owned by investors who have shares that they can buy or sell.

judicial branch (joo-DISH-uhl) The branch of the na-tional government consisting of the Supreme Court and other federal courts.

judicial review The power of the Supreme Court to declare laws unconstitutional.

justice (JUS-tuhs) One of the nine judges who sit on the Supreme Court.

justify (JUS-tuh-fy) To provide a reason or explanation for something.

K

kachina (kuh-CHEE-nuh) A powerful spirit in the Pueblo religion

kayak (KY-ak) A hunting boat built for speed, usually seating one person.

King's Daughters Young French women who went to New France to marry settlers.

kiva (KEE-vuh) A place where Pueblo men held religious ceremonies.

L

labor union (LAY-buhr YOON-yuhn) An organization that represents the workers in bargaining for improved working conditions and other benefits.

laissez-faire (les-ay-FAIR) A policy allowing businesses freedom from government interference.

land company A company that bought large tracts of land and resold them in small parcels.

land grant Land given by the government.

la raza (lah RAH-zah) Spanish for "the race"; all Spanish-speaking people in the Western Hemisphere.

laser (LAY-zuhr) An intense, amplified beam of light.

league (LEEG) An association of persons or groups with a common goal.

leave (LEEV) Permission to be absent from work.

legislative branch (LEJ-is-lay-tiv) The branch of a government that makes laws.

legislature (LEJ-is-lay-chuhr) The lawmaking body of a government.

Lend-Lease Act A law that allowed the President to sell or lend war materials to other countries during World War II.

libel (LY-buhl) A false statement that injures a person's reputation.

Liberty Bond A bond sold by the United States government to pay the costs of World War I.

literacy test (LIT-uh-ruh-see) A test to determine whether a person can read and write; once used in the South to deny the vote to African Americans.

lobby (LAH-bee) To try to influence lawmakers.

long house An Iroquois house, usually housing eight families.

loom A machine for weaving threads into cloth.

Louisiana Territory (loo-wee-zee-AN-uh TER-uh-toh-ree) The land area between the Mississippi River and the Rocky Mountains and from the Gulf of Mexico to Canada, purchased from France in 1803.

loyalist (LOY-uh-list) An American colonist who stayed loyal to Britain during the American Revolution.

M

magnetic resonance imaging (mag-NET-ik REZ-uh-nuhns) A machine that uses magnets and sound in place of x-rays, eliminating exposure to radiation.

mainstreaming Placing handicapped persons in regular classes.

maize (MAYZ) Corn.

mandatory (MAN-duh-toh-ree) Required.

Manifest Destiny (MAN-uh-fest DES-tuh-nee) The idea that the United States had the right to rule all of North America.

manta (MAN-tuh) A kind of blanket woven by Native Americans.

Marbury v. Madison The court case that established the right of the Supreme Court to decide whether laws are unconstitutional.

marine biologist A scientist who studies underwater life.

maser A device that uses the energy of molecules or atoms to make radio waves.

Mariel boat people A group of about 125,000 Cubans who in 1980 were allowed to leave Cuba by boat for the United States.

Marshall Plan The European Recovery Program, a United States program to help rebuild Europe after World War II.

Massachusetts School Law A law that established the first public schools in North America.

massacre (MAS-uh-kuhr) To kill a large number of people.

mass production The manufacture of large quantities of goods, using machinery and division of labor.

Mayflower Compact An agreement among the Pilgrim to create a government.

McCulloch v. Maryland A court case that resulted in expanding the powers of the federal government over the powers of state governments.

mediator (MEE-dee-ay-tuhr) A person who tries to make peace between conflicting groups or nations.

medicine man A person believed by some Native Americans to have magic powers to keep away evil spirits and heal the sick and injured.

megalopolis (meg-uh-LAHP-uh-lis) A heavily populated area including several large cities and their suburbs.

meeting house A place for worship and town meetings in the New England colonies.

mercantilism (MUR-kuhn-teel-iz-uhm) An economic system based on regulating trade.

mesa (MAY-suh) A flat-topped hill with steep sides.

mestizos (mes-TEE-zohs) People of Latin America who are of mixed European and Native American descent.

Mexican Cession (SESH-uhn) The territory that became part of the United States after the Mexican War (1848), including California, Nevada, Utah, Arizona, and parts of New Mexico, Colorado, and Wyoming.

microchip (MY-kroh-chip) A piece of silicon smaller than a thumbnail that stores information in a computer.

Middle East The area at the eastern end of the Mediterranean Sea.

midnight appointment During the President John Adams's adminstration, the last-minute appointment of an official before he left office.

migration (my-GRAY-shuhn) The movement of a large number of people from one country, place, or locality to another.

migratory workers (MY-gruh-taw-ree) Farm workers who move from place to place following the harvests.

militia (muh-LISH-uh) A volunteer, part-time army.

mill A building used for grinding grain into flour or for manufacturing.

mining camp A temporary camp at or near a mine.

Minuteman An American citizen-soldier who was prepared to fight on a minute's warning at the time of the Revolution.

mission (MISH-uhn) A group of people sent to spread a religion; a place where such people operate.

missionary (MISH-uh-nair-ee) A person sent on a mission, especially to teach a religion.

monopoly (muh-NAHP-uh-lee) Control of the market of a particular product or service.

Monroe Doctrine (DOK-truhn) A policy issued by President James Monroe warning European nations against trying to retake their former colonies in Latin America.

Moor (MOOR) One of a group of North African Muslims who at one time ruled much of Spain.

mountain man A fur trapper in the wilderness beyond the Rocky Mountains.

Muslim (MUZ-lim) A follower of Islam.

Munich Conference (MYOO-nik) A conference in 1938 at which Britain and France agreed to Hitler's demand for part of Czechoslovakia.

N

National Farm Workers' Association The first labor union for farm workers, organized in 1965.

nationalism (NASH-uh-nuhl-izm) Devotion to the interests of one's own nation.

nationalist (NASH-uh-nuhl-ist) A person devoted to his or her nation.

nationalize (NASH-uh-nuhl-yz) To remove from private ownership and place under government ownership.

National Road A toll free road built by the federal government from Baltimore to Vandalia, Illinois.

NATO The North Atlantic Treaty Organization, a military alliance of countries in Europe and North America formed to meet the threat of Soviet aggression in Europe.

naval base A harbor where warships can be refueled and repaired.

Navigation Acts (nav-uh-GAY-shuhn) A series of British laws regulating trade between the colonies and Britain.

Nazi (NAH-tsee) A member of Hitler's National Socialist German Workers Party.

neutral (NOO-truhl) Not taking sides in a war or other dispute.

New Deal The programs of President Franklin D. Roosevelt designed to ease the economic crisis of the 1930s.

New France France's possessions in North America.

nomad (NOH-mad) One of a group of people who move from place to place in search of food or grazing land for their animals.

nominating convention A meeting of party delegates to choose their party's candidates for office.

nonviolent resistance Peacefully disobeying a law in order to prove that the law is unjust.

Northwest Ordinance An act of the Continental Congress establishing the method of governing the Northwest Territory.

Northwest Passage A water route, which many explorers looked for but never found, connecting the Atlantic and Pacific Oceans across North America.

Northwest Territory The present-day states of Ohio, Indiana, Illinois, Michigan, and Wisconsin.

O

Old Southwest The present-day states of Kentucky and Tennessee.

optacon (AHP-tuh-kahn) A hand-held machine that changes letters on a page into raised symbols, to aid the blind in reading.

optical fiber (AHP-ti-kuhl FY-buhr) Narrow glass tubing that transmits light.

orders in council British laws forbidding American ships from entering French ports.

ordinance (OR-duh-nuhns) A law.

overseer (OH-vuhr-see-uhr) A supervisor of slaves.

ozone layer (OH-zohn) A layer of gas in the upper atmosphere that shields the earth from the sun's harmful ultraviolet rays.

P

padrone (puh-DROH-nee) A labor boss.

Pan-Africanism (PAN AF-ruh-kuhn-izm) The idea that all people of African descent share a common experience and should join in a worldwide political movement.

Parliament (PAHR-luh-muhnt) The lawmaking body of Great Britain.

patent (PAT-uhnt) The legal right to be the only producer and seller of an invention for a period of years.

patriot (PAY-tree-uht) American who supported the War for Independence.

peace treaty A negotiated agreement between countries ending a war.

pelt The skin of a fur-bearing animal.

peninsula (peh-NIN-syoo-luh) A piece of land nearly surrounded by water.

peninsulares (puh-nin-soo-LAH-rays) People in the Spanish colonies who were born in Spain.

persecution (pur-suh-KYOO-shuhn) The forcing of people to suffer because of their religion, politics, or race.

pesticide (PEST-uh-syd) A chemical used to destroy insects, weeds, or other organisms.

petroglyph (PET-roh-glif) A Native American painting on a cave wall.

Piedmont (PEED-mahnt) The region between the Atlantic coastal plain and the Appalachian Mountains.

picket line A line of workers on strike who march, often with signs, outside a business or institution as a form of protest.

Pilgrim (PIL-gruhm) One of a group of English colonists who founded Plymouth, the first permanent settlement in New England.

plantation (plan-TAY-shuhn) A large farm on which cash crops are grown.

planter A plantation owner.

pogrom (poh-GRAHM) An organized killing of a minority group, especially Jews.

poll tax A tax a voter must pay in order to vote.

pollution (puh-LOO-shuhn) Chemicals and other impurities in the air, water, and elsewhere in the environment.

popular sovereignty (SAHV-uh-ruhn-tee) The policy of allowing settlers to decide whether to allow slavery in a territory

Populist party (PAH-yoo-luhst) A political party, formed in 1891, that represented farming interests.

portage (PAWR-tuhj) The carrying of canoes and supplies overland from one body of water to another.

postwar The period after a war.

potlatch (PAHT-lach) A celebration or festival of Native Americans in the Pacific Northwest.

preamble (PREE-am-buhl) The introduction to a legal document.

prejudice (PREJ-oo-dis) Distortion or bias in a person's thinking and judgment; specifically, the dislike of people because of their race or religion.

presidio (preh-SEED-ee-oh) A Spanish small fort or fortified settlement.

primary language The first language a person learns.

Proclamation of 1763 (prahk-luh-MAY-shuhn) An order by King George III that closed off the lands west of the Appalachian Mountains to American settlers.

Prohibition (pro-huh-BI-shuhn) The constitutional amendment that forebade the manufacture and sale of alcoholic beverages, in effect from 1920 to 1933.

Progressive movement (proh-GRES-iv) A movement for widespread reforms in American government and business.

propaganda (prah-puh-GAN-duh) Communication designed to promote certain ideas and attitudes.

proprietary colony (proh-PRY-uh-tair-ee) A colony given by the British king to another person.

proprietor (proh-PRY-uh-tuhr) A person given a land grant or proprietary colony by the king.

prospector (PRAHS-pek-tuhr) A person who looks for gold or other minerals.

Public Lands Act of 1796 A law that provided for the sale and settlement of Native American lands.

public works program A program to employ people building or repairing roads, bridges, and public buildings.

public utility (yoo-TIL-uh-tee) A company that supplies electricity, gas, or water.

pueblo (PWEB-loh) A group of flat-roofed stone or mud houses built one on top of the other; a Native American village in the Southwest.

Q

Quakers (KWAY-kuhrz) A religious group, also called the Society of Friends.

Quartering Act (KWAWR-tuhr-ing) An act that required American colonists to provide British troops with food and shelter.

quipu (KEE-poo) Bundles of knotted and colored string used by the Inca to keep records and send messages.

quota system (KWOH-tuh) A system limiting the number of immigrants from any particular country.

R

racial segregation (RAY-shuhl seg-ruh-GAY-shuhn) The separating or setting apart of people on the basis of race.

racism (RAY-sizm) The belief that one racial group is better than others.

radical (RAD-uh-kuhl) A person who believes in extreme change from existing ways.

Radical Republican (ree-PUB-li-kuhn) A member of the Republican party who believed that the South should be treated like a conquered nation after the Civil War.

ranchero (rahn-CHAIR-oh) A large ranch where cattle are raised.

rate The amount charged for a unit of service, such as transporting goods.

ratify (RAT-uh-fy) To approve.

real wages Wages measured according to how much can be bought with them at any given time.

reaper (REEP-uhr) A machine for cutting grain.

rebate (REE-bayt) A sum of money refunded or given back.

recall (REE-kawl) The process of voting an elected official out of office.

recession (ree-SESH-uhn) A period of downturn in business activity.

recognize (REK-uhg-nyz) To acknowledge that a union has the right to speak for a group of workers.

Reconstruction (ree-kuhn-STRUK-shuhn) The period from 1865 to 1876 when the Southern states rejoined the Union.

recruit (ree-KROOT) To enlist or bring in new members.

recycling (ree-SYK-ling) Processing glass, metal, paper, and other substances so that they can be used again.

Redcoat A British soldier in the American Revolution, so called because of the color of his uniform.

Red Scare Fear of communism in the United States after World War I.

referendum (ref-uh-REN-duhm) A direct vote of the people on a bill or other issue.

refining (ree-FYN-ing) The process of removing impurities from crude oil.

reform (ree-FORM) A change intended to make something better.

rehabilitation (ree-huh-bil-uh-TAY-shuhn) Restoring or changing behavior of people to make them productive in society.

Removal Act A law that forced Native Americans to leave their homelands and relocate farther west.

reparations (rep-uh-RAY-shuhnz) Payments by a defeated nation for damages or losses suffered during a war.

repeal To formally withdraw or cancel something, such as a law.

Republican A political party founded in 1854 that was committed to stopping the spread of slavery in new territories.

reservation (rez-uhr-VAY-shuhn) Land set aside by the United States government for Native Americans.

reservoir (REZ-uhr-vwahr) A place for collecting water.

retreat To go back or withdraw.

revenue (REV-uh-nyoo) Income.

right of deposit The right to load and unload goods in a foreign port without paying a tax.

right of way The land used by a railroad for its tracks.

Rome-Berlin Axis Alliance of Nazi Germany and Fascist Italy in 1936.

royal colony A colony owned by the king and governed by his personal representative.

Rush-Bagot Agreement An agreement by the United States and Great Britain to limit warships on the Great Lakes.

rustler (RUS-luhr) A person who steals cattle.

S

Sabbath (SAB-uhth) A day of the week set aside for rest and worship.

satellite (SAT-uh-lyt) A country under the control of another country, especially an Eastern European country under Soviet control after World War II.

scalawag (SKAL-uh-wag) A white Southerner who supported Reconstruction in the Southern states.

scapegoat (SKAYP-goht) A person or group that is blamed for someone else's mistakes.

sea dog An English sailor who attacked Spanish ships in the West Indies.

secede (see-SEED) To leave or withdraw from.

segregation (seg-ruh-GAY-shuhn) The policy of keeping a race, ethnic group, or class separate from the rest of society.

seigniory (SAYN-yuh-ree) In New France, a large tract of land owned by one person.

self-sufficient (suh-FISH-uhnt) Producing everything needed; not depending on outside sources.

separate but equal The idea that racial segregation is legal so long as each race is treated equally.

separation of powers The division under the Constitution of government among three branches, each with its own powers.

Separatist (SEP-uh-ruh-tist) A member of a religious group that wanted to withdraw from the Church of England.

settlement house A place that offers education and recreation to poor people.

shaman (SHAH-muhn) A religious leader in some Native American groups.

sharecropper (SHAYR-krah-puhr) A farmer who pays a portion of his or her crop as rent to a landowner.

siege (SEEJ) In war, surrounding an enemy fort or city to prevent food and supplies from reaching the people inside.

signing or **sign language** A system of hand signals deaf people use to communicate.

simulate (SIM-yoo-layt) To imitate.

sit-in A way of protesting racial segregation by sitting at a segregated lunch counter or elsewhere and refusing to move.

slave code A set of laws that regulated the lives of African American slaves.

slave state A state where slavery was legal before the Civil War.

social program A government program intended to help needy people improve their lives.

small farmers In the South before the Civil War, farmers too poor to own slaves.

smog (SMAHG) A mixture of smoke and fog that pollutes the air.

smuggling Transporting goods across a border illegally.

sod A surface layer of soil thick with grass.

sod house A house with a roof covering made from sod.

sphere of influence (SFEER, IN-floo-uhns) A part of one country that is occupied or controlled by another country.

spiritual (SPIR-i-choo-uhl) An African American religious song.

spoils system The practice of the winner of an election giving jobs to loyal campaign workers.

stalemate (STAYL-mayt) A situation in which no competitor can win.

stampede (stam-PEED) A sudden rush of frightened cattle running wild.

staple crop (STAY-puhl) The main crop in a particular region.

states' rights The theory that the power of a state government is or should be greater than that of the federal government.

steles (STEE-leez) Tall stone shafts in front of pyramids or temples in ancient Mexico.

stock A share in a business.

stockholder A person who owns stock in a corporation.

strait (STRAYT) A narrow body of water that joins two larger ones

strict constructionist (kuhn-STRUK-shuhn-ist) A person who believes that the federal government can do only those things that are specifically named in the Constitution.

strike A form of protest in which people refuse to work until their demands are met.

subsidize (SUB-suh-dyz) To give money, often by a government, as support or assistance.

subsistence farming Growing only enough for a farm family's own needs.

suburb (SUB-urb) A small community on the outskirts of a city.

suffrage (SUHF-rij) The right to vote.

Sugar Act A tax imposed by Parliament in 1764 on molasses and sugar imported from the French West Indies.

Sunbelt The Southern and Western states.

superpower A nation so powerful that its actions influence the whole world; refers usually to the United States and the Soviet Union.

surplus Extra; more than needed.

surplus crops Extra crops.

surveying (sur-VAY-ing) Measuring and plotting an area of land.

T

tallow (TAL-oh) Animal fat that is made into soap and candles.

terrace (TER-uhs) A step of earth cut into hillsides to increase the amount of farming land.

tenant farmer (TEN-uhnt) A farmer who pays rent to a landowner for the use of land.

tenement (TEN-uh-muhnt) A rundown, overcrowded apartment building.

Tennessee Valley Authority A government agency that builds dams and reservoirs in the valley of the Tennessee River.

territory (TER-ruh-toh-ree) A part of the United States that is under the direct control of the federal government and is not one of the states.

terrorist (TER-uhr-ist) A person who uses violence and fear of violence to gain some political end.

Tet Offensive A series of attacks by the Viet Cong against United States troops in 1968 during Tet, a Vietnamese holiday.

textile Cloth.

Three-Fifths Compromise A provision in the Constitution that allowed three fifths of the slave population of a state to count in the state's census.

Tidewater Fertile lowlands on the coastal plain.

toleration (tahl-uh-RAY-shun) Respect for the beliefs of others.

totalitarian (toh-tal-uh-TAIR-ee-uhn) Having to do with a government controlled by a single political party and strictly regulating the lives of the people.

total war A conflict in which an army aims to destroy everything the enemy can use to feed and support itself.

totem pole (TOH-tuhm) A pole carved with animal and other symbols.

toxic Poisonous.

trade deficit (DEF-uh-sit) The difference between the value of imports and the value of exports, when the value of the imports is greater.

trade laws Laws that control trade with other countries.

trademark A picture, symbol, or word that stands for a certain product.

Trail of Tears The route taken by Native Americans who were forced to move from their homelands to barren lands west of the Mississippi; many suffered and died along the trail.

traitor (TRAY-tuhr) A person who turns against his or her country.

transcontinental (trans-kahn-tuh-NEN-tuhl) Crossing a continent.

Treaty of Ghent (GENT) The treaty that ended the War of 1812, signed in December 1814.

trench warfare The type of warfare on the western front in World War I in which soldiers attacked from trenches.

triangular trade (try-ANG-gyuh-luhr) In the 1700s, the exchange of rum from New England, slaves from Africa, and sugar from the West Indies.

tributary (TRIB-yoo-tair-ee) A stream or small river that flows into a larger river or body of water.

Triple Alliance An alliance of Germany, Austria-Hungary, and Italy, 1882.

Triple Entente (ahn-TAHNT) An agreement of cooperation among Great Britain, France, and Russia, 1904.

trolley car An electric streetcar that takes its power from overhead wires.

Truman Doctrine Post-World War II policy to assist any country threatened by communist takeover.

tribute (TRIB-yoot) A payment that one nation is forced to make to another.

trust A combination of corporations managed by a single group of people.

turbine (TUR-byn) A kind of engine driven by water, steam, or air.

turnpike A road on which tolls are collected.

tycoon (ty-KOON) A wealthy business leader.

tyrant (TY-ruhnt) A ruler who exercise absolute power in an oppressive or brutal manner.

U

unconstitutional A law or action that is in conflict with the Constitution.

underground railroad A network of homes, churches, barns, cellars, caves, and secret rooms where runaway slaves could hide and rest while escaping north to freedom.

Union The Northern and border states that remained loyal to the United States in the Civil War; also another name for the United States.

United Nations An international peacekeeping organization founded in 1945.

university (yoo-nuh-VUR-suh-tee) An institution of learning on the highest level.

urbanization (ur-buh-ny-ZAY-shuhn) The process by which a country changes from one of farm-dwelling people to one of city-dwelling people.

V

vaccine (vak-SEEN) A substance that protects against a specific disease.

vaquero (vah-KAIR-oh) The Spanish word for cowboy.

vestment (VEST-muhnt) A religious garment.

veteran (VET-uh-ruhn) A person with experience, especially in the military.

veto (VEE-toh) The legal right to reject a new law.

viceroy (VYS-roi) A governor in New Spain.

Viet Cong (VYET-et KONG) The communist South Vietnamese National Liberation Front that fought a guerilla war against the South Vietnam government and American troops.

vulcanize (VUL-kuh-nyz) To make rubber stronger and more elastic.

W

warehouse A place for storing goods or merchandise.

War Hawks A group of Congressmen who favored driving the British from North America in 1810.

waterpower The use of flowing or falling water to run machines.

Western Reserve A section of the Northwest Territory, on Lake Erie, now part of Ohio.

white-collar jobs Jobs that do not require manual labor, such as managers, technicians, and sales people.

wickiup (WIK-ee-up) A hut used by Native Americans of the Southwest made of grass, twigs, and tree branches.

wigwam A domed Algonquin single family home.

Wilderness Road A trail, blazed by Daniel Boone, from the Blue Ridge Mountains of North Carolina through the Cumberland Gap.

workers' compensation (kom-puhn-SAY-shuhn) Payment to employees for job-related injuries.

writ of assistance A legal document that allowed tax collectors to search colonists' homes and businesses for smuggled goods.

Y

yellow journalism (JUR-nuh-liz-uhm) Exaggerated and sometimes untrue reporting of news events.

INDEX

Text credits are given below. Numerals in **boldface** refer to page numbers on which the selections of text appear.

UNIT 1

From *We Talk, You Listen*, p. **5**
By Vine Deloria, Jr. Copyright © 1970 Vine Deloria, Jr. Reprinted with permission of Macmillian Publishing Company.

From *America's Fascinating Indian Heritage*, p. **19**
By Readers Digest Editors. Copyright © 1978 by Readers Digest Association, Inc. Random House.

From *The Incas*, p. **33**
By Garcilaso de la Vega, edited by Alain Gheerbrant, Avon, 1961.

UNIT 2

From *The Travels of Marco Polo, the Venetian*, p. **44**
By Manuel Komroff. Liveright Publishing, 1953.

From *The Five Letters*, pp. **61–62**
By Hernán Cortés, translated by J. Bayard Morris. Routledge & Kegan Paul. Used by permission.

UNIT 3

From *Roger Williams: His Contribution to the American Tradition*, p. **103**
By Perry Miller, Copyright © The Estate of Elizabeth Miller. Atheneum, 1962.

From *Deputyes and Libertyes: The Origins of Representative Government in Colonial America*, p. **111**
By Michael Kammen. Copyright © 1969 by Alfred A. Knopf, Inc. Alfred Knopf, 1972.

From *America : Changing Times to 1877*, volume 1, 2nd ed., p. **115**
Edited by Charles M. Dollar. John Wiley, 1981.

UNIT 4

From *Agricultural History*, 1X (1935), p. **127**
Reprinted by permission of the Agricultural History Society.

UNIT 5

From *The Papers of Benjamin Franklin*, volume 4, p. **176**
Edited by Leonard W. Labaree. Copyright © 1961 Yale University Press.

Reprinted by permission of the publishers from *The Book of Abigail and John: Selected Letters of the Adams Family 1762–1784*, p. **215**
Edited by Lyman H. Butterfield, Cambridge, Mass.: Harvard University Press, Copyright © 1975 by the Massachusetts Historical Society.

UNIT 6

From *The Articles of Confederation*, p. **227**
By Merrill Jensen. University of Wisconsin Press, 1963. Used by permission.

UNIT 7

From *The American Heritage History of the Indian Wars*, p. **309**
By Robert M. Utley & Wilcomb E. Washburn. Copyright © 1977 by American Heritage Publishing Company, Inc. Reprinted with permission.

From *The Writings of Junipero Serra*, volume 1, p. **324**
Edited by Antoine Tibesar. Academy of America Franciscan History, 1955.

From *Coming to America*, p. **337**
By Linda Perrin. Delacorte, 1980.

From *Mollie: Journal of Mollie Dorsey Sanford in Nebraska and Colorado Territories, 1857–1866*, p. **343**
By Mollie D. Sanford. University of Nebraska Press, 1959. (Rights: United Bank of Denver).

UNIT 8

From *Eyewitness: The Negro in American History*, 3rd ed., p. **384**
By William Loren Katz. Copyright © 1974 by David S. Lake Publishers. Renewed by William Loren Katz. Fearon Education, a Division of D.S. Lake, a subsidiary of Globe Book Company.

UNIT 9

From *Living Ideas for America*, pp. **401–402**
Edited by Henry Steele Commager. Harper & Row, 1951. Used by permission.

UNIT 10

From *The American City: A Documentary History*, pp. **434–435, 439**
By Charles N. Glaab © 1963 by The Dorsey Press, Inc. Reprinted by permission of Wadsworth, Inc.

From *Looking for America*, p. **457**
By Stanley Kutler. Copyright © 1980 by Stanley Kutler. W.W. Norton.

UNIT 11

From *The Granger Movement: A Study of Agricultural Organization and Its Political, Economic and Social Manifestations, 1870–1880*, p. **479**
By Solon Justus Buck. Copyright © 1913 by Harvard University.

From *Freedom's Ferment*, p. **490**
By Alice Felt Tyler. University of Minnesota Press, 1944. Used by permission.

The Muckrakers, p. **497**
Excerpted with permission from Arthur and Lila Weinberg, *The Muckrakers* (Simon and Schuster). Copyright © Arthur and Lila Weinberg, renewed 1989 Lila Weinberg.

UNIT 12

From *The Shaping of America*, p. **506**
By Richard O. Curry, Kenyon Cramer and John G. Sproat. Holt, Rinehart and Winston, 1972.

From *Our America*, p. **509**
By José Martí, edited by Philip S. Foner. Monthly Review Press, 1977. Copyright © 1977 by Philip S. Foner. Reprinted by permission of Monthly Review Foundation.

UNIT 13

From *A Documentary History of the United States*, pp. **542–543**
Edited by Richard D. Heffner. New American Library, 1952.

From *Selected Poems*, p. **546**
By Langston Hughes. Alfred Knopf. Copyright © 1926 by Alfred A. Knopf, Inc., and renewed 1954 by Langston Hughes.

From *Brother, Can You Spare a Dime: The Great Depression, 1929–1933*, p. **551**
By Milton Meltzer. Copyright © 1969 New American Library.

From *Voices from America's Past*, volume 3, p. **565**
Edited by Richard B. Morris and James Woodruff. E.P. Dutton, 1963.

From *The Murderers Among Us*, p. **570**
By Simon Wiesenthal. Copyright © Simon Wiesenthal. McGraw-Hill, 1967.

UNIT 14

From *Plain Speaking: An Oral Biography of Harry S. Truman*, p. **588**
By Merle Miller. Copyright © 1973, 1974 by Merle Miller. Reprinted by permission of the Berkley Publishing Group.

Excerpt abridged from *The Kingdom*, p. **599**
Copyright © 1981 by Robert Lacey, reprinted by permission of Harcourt Brace Jovanovich, Inc.

UNIT 15

From *The Way: An Anthology of American Literature*, p. **629**
Edited by Shirley Hill Witt and Stan Steiner. Alfred A. Knopf, 1972.

From *I Dream a World: Portraits of Black Women Who Changed America*, p. **641**
By Brian Lanker. Copyright © 1989 Brian Lanker. Stewart, Tabori and Chang, 1989.

From *The New York Times*, p. **649**
September 6, 1989, p. B6. Copyright © 1989 by The New York Times Company. Reprinted by permission.

From *The New York Times*, p. **654** December 9, 1987, p. 6
Copyright © 1987 by The New York Times Company. Reprinted by permission.

From *Working: People Talk About What They Do All Day and How They Feel About What They Do*, p. **659**
By Studs Terkel. Copyright © 1972, 1974 by Studs Terkel. Reprinted by permission of Pantheon Books, a division of Random House, Inc.

PHOTO CREDITS

pp.xxii Granger; Omni Photo Communication/John Lei; Missouri Historical Society; pp.xxiii Historical Society of Delaware; Granger; Herblock/The Washington Post; Linda Bartlett/Photo Researchers, Copyright 1954 by the New York Times Company, Reprinted by permission.

Unit 1: p.2 The Thomas Gilcrease Institute of American History and Art, Tulsa, Oklahoma; p.3 Cleveland Public Library; p.5 The Plain Dealer, Cleveland, Ohio; p.6 Los Angeles County Museum; p.9 Stock Market/ Harvey Lloyd; p.12 Woodfin Camp/C. Bonington; p.14 The Bernice P. Bishop Museum; p.18 The Granger Collection; p.21 The Philbrook Collection; p.22 The Smithsonian Institute; p.24 The Granger Collection; p.26 The Granger Collection; p.27 James Jerome Hill Library, St. Paul Minnesota; p.30 Photo Researchers; p.32 National Palace, Mexico City/ Bob Schwalkwijk; p.33 The Granger Collection.

Unit 2: pp.38–39 E.T. Archive, London; p.40 The Granger Collection; p.41 National Gallery of Art; p.42 The Stock Market/Luis Villota; p.48 The Granger Collection; pp.52–53 Fred Kabotie/The Philbrook Collection; p.54 The Granger Collection; p.56 The Granger Collection; p.57 The Granger Collection; p.60 Harvard College Library; p.63 The Granger Collection; p.66 The Granger Collection; p.68 The Granger Collection; p.69 David Muench; p.72 M. Timothy O'Keefe/Bruce Coleman; p.74 Viviane Holbrooke/The Stock Market; p.75 Mark Stein; p.78 National Gallery of Art, Wash., D.C.; p.84 Virginia State Library; p.87 The Granger Collection.

Unit 3: p.93 The Granger Collection; p.94 Essex Institute/Mark Sexton; p.95 The Thomas Gilcrease Institute of American History and Art, Tulsa, Oklahoma; p.96 The Granger Collection; p.98 The Granger Collection; p.99 The Granger Collection; p.102 The Granger Collection; p.103 The Granger Collection; p.105 Shelburne Museum, Shelburne, Vt. p.108 The Granger Collection; p.110 The Granger Collection; p.112 Maryland Historical Society; p.115 The Granger Collection.

Unit 4: pp.122–123 Washington Univ. Gallery of Art; p.124 The Granger Collection; p.125 The Granger Collection; p.126 The Granger Collection; p.128 The Granger Collection; p.129 Metropolitan Museum of Art; p.132 Library Company of Philadelphia; p.134 The Granger Collection; p.138 The Granger Collection; p.140 The Granger Collection; p.141 The Granger Collection; p.144 The Granger Collection; p.145 The Granger Collection; p.146 The Granger Collection; p.147 The Granger Collection; p.150 Royal Ontario Museum; p.152 The Granger Collection; p.153 Collection of the Montreal Botanical Garden Library Sarracenia purpurea; (ill. by S. Edwards) Curtis Botanical Magazine, vol. 21, pl. 849, 1985; p.156 Hispanic Society of America; p.158 Laurie. Pratt. Winfrey/ Carousel Research, Inc.; p.159 The Granger Collection; p.162 The Granger Collection; p.165 The Granger Collection.

Unit 5: p.180 Brooklyn Museum; p.182 The Granger Collection; p.183 The Granger Collection; p.186 The Granger Collection; p.188 The Granger Collection; p.189 The Granger Collection; p.192 The Granger Collection; p.195 The Granger Collection; p.198 The Granger Collection; p.200 The Granger Collection; p.201 Library of Congress; p.208 Valley Forge Historical Society; p.214 The Granger Collection; p.216A Florida State Archives; p.216B Brian D. Hunt/Pennsylvania Capitol Building.

Unit 6: p.223 The Granger Collection; p.224 The Carnegie Museum of Art, Pittsburgh, Howard N. Eavenson Americana Collection/Richard Stoner; p.225 Patrick Henry Memorial Foundation, Brookneal, VA; p.232 The Granger Collection; p.235 New York Historical Society; p.228 The Granger Collection; p.229 The Granger Collection; p.238 Harney; p.240 The Granger Collection; p.241 The Granger Collection; p.242 Globe Illustrator; p.245 The Bettmann Archive; p.247 The Stock Market; p.255 Photo Researchers; p.259 Pete Saloutos/The Stock Market; p.274 Chicago Historical Society; p.277 Granger; p.280 Chicago Historical Society; p.282 The Granger Collection; p.283 The Granger Collection; p.285 National Park Service; p.286 US Naval Academy; p.292 Corcoran Gallery of Art, Washington, DC; p.298 The Granger Collection; p.299 The Granger Collection.

Unit 7: p.292 The Granger Collection; p.309 National Gallery of Canada; p.310 The Granger Collection; p.313 The Granger Collection; p.316 Brigham Young University; p.317 Bettmann Archive; p.318 Brigham Young University; p.319 The Granger Collection; p.322 The Granger Collection; p.323 Michel Heron/Santa Barbara Mission, Archive; p.324 American Heritage/California Historical Society; p.325 The Thomas Gilcrease Institute of American History and Art, Tulsa, Oklahoma; p.326 Pan American Union; p.328 The Granger Collection; p.329 San Jacinto Museum; p.334 California Historical Society; p.335 University of California at Berkeley/Bancroft Library; p.336 The Granger Collection; p.340 The Granger Collection; p.343 Nebraska State Historical Society/Solomon D. Butcher Collection; p.344 Culver; p.344 American Museum of Natural History; p.346 The Granger Collection; p.348 Colorado Historical Society.

Unit 8: pp.354–355 The Warner Collection of Gulf States Paper Corporation, Tuscaloosa, Alabama; p.355 The Granger Collection; p.357 The Granger Collection; p.358 The Collection of Jay P. Altmeyer; p.364 Historic New Orleans Collection; p.367 Maryland Historical Society; p.370 Philbrook Art Center; p.372 Library of Congress; p.373 The Granger Collection; p.376 Yale University/Mabel Brady Garvan Collection; p.378 The Granger Collection; p.382 The Granger Collection; p.385 Culver Pics., Inc.; p.388 The Granger Collection.

Unit 9: p.396 Wadsworth Atheneum, Gift of Citizens; p.397 The Granger Collection; p.399 The Granger Collection; p.400 The Granger Collection; p.403 Bettmann Archives; p.406 The Granger Collection; p.418 The Granger Collection; p.421 The Granger Collection; p.414 Witte Museum; p.424 Los Angeles County Museum; p.426 Nebraska State Historical Society/Solomon D. Butcher Collection; p.427 Bettmann Archive; p.428 Mark Stein.

Unit 10: p.436 Bethlehem Steel Corp; p.435 The Granger Collection; p.436 The Granger Collection; p.438 The Granger Collection; p.439 The Granger Collection; p.442 The Granger Collection; p.448 Bruce Coleman; p.451 The Granger Collection; p.454 Culver Pics., Inc.; p.456 The Granger Collection; p.460 The Granger Collection.

Unit 11: p.469 The Granger Collection; p.471 The Granger Collection; p.470 Chicago Historical Society; p.472 Bettmann Archives; p.474 The Granger Collection; p.476 Culver Pics., Inc. p.478 The Granger Collection; p.481 Culver Pics, Inc.; p.484 The Granger Collection; p.487 The Granger Collection; p.490 The Granger Collection; p.491 The Thomas Gilcrease Institute of American History and Art, Tusla, Oklahoma; p.492 The Granger Collection; p.493 The Granger Collection; p.496 Alleghany College, Alleghany, Pa.; p.497 The Granger Collection; p.498 Richard Hutchins/Photo Research.

Unit 12: p.504 The Whitney Museum of American Art; p.505 The Granger Collection; p.507 Culver Pictures, Inc.; p.508 The Granger Collection; p.510 The Granger Collection; p.514 The Granger Collection; p.516 Culver Pics., Inc.; p.517 The Granger Collection; p.520 Peabody Museum, Salem, Mass. p.523 The Granger Collection; p.526 Bettmann Archive; p.527 The Granger Collection; p.528 Culver Pics., Inc.; p.529 The Granger Collection; p.532 Bettmann Archive; p.535 Bettmann Archive.

Unit 13: p.540 The Whitney Museum of American Art; p.542 Culver Pics., Inc.; p.543 The Granger Collection; p.544 Bettmann Archive; p.545 Brown Brothers; p.546 Culver Pics., Inc.; p.550 Bettmann Archive; p.551 Culver Pics., Inc.; p.553 Bettmann Archives; p.554 The Granger Collection; p.556 Bettmann Archives; p.557 Bettmann Archives; p.558 FPG International; p.562 Cameron Davidson/Bruce Coleman; p.564 The Granger Collection; p.568 Wide World; p.569 a) FPG International; p.569 b) Wide World; p.570 Woodfin Camp/Bartlett.

Unit 14: p.576 NASA; p.578 The Granger Collection; p.579 The Granger Collection; p.580 The Granger Collection; p.582 The Granger Collection; p.583 Bettmann Archive; p.586 Bettmann Archive; p.587 The Granger Collection; p.592 Bartlett/Woodfin Camp; p.593 The Granger Collection; p.594 Lee Skoogfors/Woodfin Camp; p.598 The Jimmy Carter Library; p.604 Bettmann Archive; p.605 The Granger Collection; p.606 Henriques/Magnum, inc.; p.607 Magnum, inc.

Unit 15: p.616 US News and World Report; p.616 Mary Kate Denny/ PhotoEdit; p.616 Elaine Wicks/Taurus Photos; p. 616 Wide World; p.616 The New York Times Company. Reprinted by permission; p.617 Bettmann Archives; p.617 Dan Budnick/Woodfin/Camp; p.619 Nashua; p.622 J.P. Laffont/Sygma; p.623 Nancy Ellison/Sygma; p.624 Brian Lanker from his book, "I Dream A World"; p.625 NASA; p.628 Arnie Saks/Sygma; p.630 Paul Conklin/Monkmeyer Press; p.631 Blackstar/ Michel Abramson; p.634 John Bowden/US News and World Report; p.636 Monkmeyer Press; p.640 Charles Tines/The Detroit News; p.646 Cynthia Johnson/Gamma Liaison; p.647 Dirck Halstead/Time; p.648 Blackstar; p.649 Bettmann Archive; p.650 George Fisher/Arkansas Gazette; p.652 EuroSummits/Moscow USSR; p.654 George S. Merillon/Gamma Liaison; p.655 Bettman Archive; p.658 Dick Luria/ Science Source; p.660 Kevin Byron/Bruce Coleman; p.661 J.P. Laffont/Sygma; p.664 Chuck O'Rear/Woodfin Camp; p.666 Tom Mc Hugh/ Photo Researchers, Inc.; p.667 I.L. Atlan/Sygma.